A TEXT BOOK OF

STRUCTURAL ANALYSIS - I

WITH MULTIPLE CHOICE QUESTIONS

FOR
SEMESTER - II
SECOND YEAR DEGREE COURSE IN CIVIL ENGINEERING

According to New Revised Syllabus of University of Pune
w.e.f. Academic Year 2013-14

H. M. SOMAYYA
M. E. (Structures)
Former, Assistant Professor
Applied Mechanics Department
Maharashtra Institute of Technology
Paud Road, PUNE

•

Dr. S. R. PAREKAR
B. E. (Civil), M. E. (Structures), Ph.D.
Professor
Civil Engineering Department,
Sinhgad Academy of Engineering,
Kondhwa (Bk), PUNE.

NIRALI PRAKASHAN

S.E. STRUCTURAL ANALYSIS – I (CIVIL ENGINEERING)

ISBN 978-93-83750-89-4

First Edition : January 2014

© : **Authors**

The text of this publication, or any part thereof, should not be reproduced or transmitted in any form or stored in any computer storage system or device for distribution including photocopy, recording, taping or information retrieval system or reproduced on any disc, tape, perforated media or other information storage device etc., without the written permission of Authors with whom the rights are reserved. Breach of this condition is liable for legal action.

Every effort has been made to avoid errors or omissions in this publication. In spite of this, errors may have crept in. Any mistake, error or discrepancy so noted and shall be brought to our notice shall be taken care of in the next edition. It is notified that neither the publisher nor the authors or seller shall be responsible for any damage or loss of action to any one, of any kind, in any manner, therefrom.

Published By :
NIRALI PRAKASHAN
Abhyudaya Pragati, 1312, Shivaji Nagar,
Off J.M. Road, PUNE – 411005
Tel - (020) 25512336/37/39, Fax - (020) 25511379
Email : niralipune@pragationline.com

Printed By :
Repro India Ltd,
Mumbai.

DISTRIBUTION CENTRES

PUNE

Nirali Prakashan
119, Budhwar Peth, Jogeshwari Mandir Lane
Pune 411002, Maharashtra
Tel : (020) 2445 2044, 66022708, Fax : (020) 2445 1538
Email : bookorder@pragationline.com

Nirali Prakashan
S. No. 28/25, Dhyari,
Near Pari Company, Pune 411041
Tel : (020) 24690204 Fax : (020) 24690316
Email : dhyari@pragationline.com
bookorder@pragationline.com

MUMBAI
Nirali Prakashan
385, S.V.P. Road, Rasdhara Co-op. Hsg. Society Ltd.,
Girgaum, Mumbai 400004, Maharashtra
Tel : (022) 2385 6339 / 2386 9976, Fax : (022) 2386 9976
Email : niralimumbai@pragationline.com

DISTRIBUTION BRANCHES

NAGPUR
Pratibha Book Distributors
Above Maratha Mandir, Shop No. 3, First Floor,
Rani Jhanshi Square, Sitabuldi, Nagpur 440012,
Maharashtra, Tel : (0712) 254 7129

BENGALURU
Pragati Book House
House No. 1, Sanjeevappa Lane, Avenue Road Cross,
Opp. Rice Church, Bengaluru – 560002.
Tel : (080) 64513344, 64513355,
Mob : 9880582331, 9845021552
Email:bharatsavla@yahoo.com

JALGAON
Nirali Prakashan
34, V. V. Golani Market, Navi Peth, Jalgaon 425001,
Maharashtra, Tel : (0257) 222 0395
Mob : 94234 91860

KOLHAPUR
Nirali Prakashan
New Mahadvar Road,
Kedar Plaza, 1st Floor Opp. IDBI Bank
Kolhapur 416 012, Maharashtra. Mob : 9855046155

CHENNAI
Pragati Books
9/1, Montieth Road, Behind Taas Mahal, Egmore,
Chennai 600008 Tamil Nadu, Tel : (044) 6518 3535,
Mob : 94440 01782 / 98450 21552 / 98805 82331, Email : bharatsavla@yahoo.com

RETAIL OUTLETS

PUNE

Pragati Book Centre
157, Budhwar Peth, Opp. Ratan Talkies,
Pune 411002, Maharashtra
Tel : (020) 2445 8887 / 6602 2707, Fax : (020) 2445 8887

Pragati Book Centre
Amber Chamber, 28/A, Budhwar Peth,
Appa Balwant Chowk, Pune : 411002, Maharashtra,
Tel : (020) 20240335 / 66281669
Email : pbcpune@pragationline.com

Pragati Book Centre
676/B, Budhwar Peth, Opp. Jogeshwari Mandir,
Pune 411002, Maharashtra
Tel : (020) 6601 7784 / 6602 0855

PBC Book Sellers & Stationers
152, Budhwar Peth, Pune 411002, Maharashtra
Tel : (020) 2445 2254 / 6609 2463

MUMBAI
Pragati Book Corner
Indira Niwas, 111 - A, Bhavani Shankar Road, Dadar (W), Mumbai 400028, Maharashtra
Tel : (022) 2422 3526 / 6662 5254, Email : pbcmumbai@pragationline.com

PREFACE

The book titled **"Structural Analysis-I"** is written according to the revised syllabus of Pune University. This book serves as a text book for the students of second year degree course in civil engineering.

It consists of thirteen chapters covering all six units of new revised syllabus. We have simplified these complicated units in the simple and smaller chapters. Each topic gives fundamental and simple treatment to the subject with a clear and distinct presentation of theoretical concepts and well graded examples. **Multiple choice questions also have been included in four units.**

We express our sincere thanks to Prof. Wakchaure and Prof. Sable (Amrutvahini, COE, Sangamner), Prof. Awari & Prof. Lad. (AISSPMS COE), Prof. Deulkar (D. Y. Patil COE), Prof. Mrs. Pathak (M.I.T.), Prof. Bhilare, Prof. Sable (R.S. COE).

We will be missing if we don't thank our family and wives Mrs. Chhaya Somayya and Mrs. Smita Parekar whose moral support and wishes have gone a long way in making of this book.

We express our sincere thanks to Shri. Dineshbhai Furia, Jignesh Furia, and M. P. Munde for publishing this book. We are also thankful to Mr. Santosh (D.T.P.), Roshan Khan (Proof Reader), Mr. Ravi (Cover Designing), Mrs. Anjali (Diagrams), Ms. Chaitali and Mrs. Deepa for their kind help.

Suggestions for improvements and constructive criticism of this book are warmly wellcomed and will be incorporated in next edition.

Authors

SYLLABUS

SECTION – I

Unit 1 : Fundamentals of Structure, Slope and Deflection

(a) Types and classification of structures based on structural forms, concept of indeterminacy, static and kinematics degree of indeterminacy. **(02 Hours)**

(b) Slope and deflection and determinate beams by Macaulay's method, concept of moment area method and conjugate beam method and its application. **(04 Hours)**

(c) Strain energy, Castigliano's first theorem, application to determine slope and deflection of determinate beams and frames. **(02 Hours)**

Unit 2 : Analysis of Indeterminate Beams and Frames

(a) Propped cantilever and fixed beams by strain energy method, analysis of continuous beams by three moment theorem (Clapeyron theorem) up to three unknowns. **(04 Hours)**

(b) Castigliano's second theorem, analysis of beams and rectangular portal frames with indeterminacy up to second degrees. **(04 Hours)**

Unit 3 : Analysis of Pin Jointed Plane Trusses

(a) Joint displacement of determinate trusses by Castigliano's first theorem. **(04 Hours)**

(b) Analysis of redundant trusses by Castigliano's second theorm, lack of fit, sinking of support, temperature changes (indeterminacy up to second degrees). **(04 Hours)**

SECTION – II

Unit 4 : Influence Line Diagram

(a) Basic concept, Muller-Braslau's principle, influence line diagram for reaction, shear and moment to simply supported and overhanging beams, applications of influence line diagram to determine reaction, shear and moment in beams. **(04 Hours)**

(b) Influence line diagram for axial force in trusses, application of influence line diagram to determine axial forces in the members of plane determinate trusses under dead load and live load. **(04 Hours)**

Unit 5 : Analysis of Arches

(a) **Three hinged arches :** Concepts, types of arches, analysis of parabolic arch with supports at same and different levels, semicircular arches with support at same level, determination of horizontal thrust, radial shear and normal thrust for parabolic and circular arch. **(04 Hours)**

(b) **Two hinged arches :** Analysis of parabolic and semicircular arches with supports at same level, determination of horizontal thrust, radial shear and normal thrust. **(04 Hours)**

Unit 6 : Plastic Analysis of Structure

(a) True and idealized stress-strain curve for mild steel in tension, stress distribution in elastic, elasto-plastic and plastic stage, concept of plastic hinge and collapse mechanism, statical and kinematical method of analysis, upper, lower bound and uniqueness theorem. **(04 Hours)**

(b) Plastic analysis of determinate and indeterminate beams, single bay single storied portal frame. **(04 Hours)**

CONTENTS

UNIT - I

1. BASIC CONCEPTS OF STRUCTURAL ANALYSIS — 1.1 – 1.28

- 1.1 Structural Systems — 1.1
- 1.2 Types of Skeletal Structures — 1.3
- 1.3 Structural Behaviour — 1.5
- 1.4 Primary Concepts — 1.6

2. SLOPE AND DEFLECTION OF BEAMS — 2.1 – 2.136

- 2.1 Introduction — 2.1
- 2.2 Assumptions — 2.1
- 2.3 Slope, Deflection and Radius of Curvature — 2.1
- 2.4 Methods of Displacement Analysis — 2.3
- 2.5 Macaulay's Method — 2.4
- 2.6 Boundary Conditions — 2.5
- 2.7 Sign Conventions — 2.5
- 2.8 Bending Moment Equations for Macaulay's Method — 2.6
- 2.9 Moment Area Methods – Mohr's Theorems — 2.55
- 2.10 Applications of Moment - Area Method to Cantilever Beams — 2.59
- 2.11 Applications of Moment – Area Method to Simply Supported and Overhanging Beams — 2.73
- 2.12 Conjugate Beam Method — 2.89
- 2.13 Support Conditions — 2.81
- Exercise — 2.125

3. DEFLECTION OF BEAMS AND FRAMES — 3.1 – 3.72

- 3.1 Castigliano's First Theorem of Complementary Energy — 3.1
- Exercise — 3.45
- **Multiple Choice Questions** — 3.56

UNIT - II

4. INDETERMINATE BEAMS — 4.1 – 4.102

- 4.1 Principle of Superposition — 4.1
- 4.2 Clerk – Maxwell's Theorem of Reciprocal Deflection — 4.3
- 4.3 Maxwell – Betle's Law — 4.6

4.4	Fixed Beams	4.7
4.5	Equations for Fixed End Moments	4.7
4.6	The Fixed Beams have Some Advantages as well as Some Disadvantages over the Simply Supported Beams	4.8
4.7	There are Different Types of the Loading on the Fixed Beams Some of the Standard Cases are Noted below	4.9
4.8	Steps to be followed for Analysis of Fixed Beams	4.9
4.9	Different Cases	4.10
4.10	Continuous Beams	4.48
4.11	Clapeyron's Theorem	4.48
4.12	Modified Theorem of Three Moments for Uniformly Distributed Loads	4.50
4.13	Different Types of Continuous Beams	4.51
	Exercise	4.92

5.	**ENERGY METHOD FOR DISPLACEMENT**	**5.1 – 5.62**
5.1	Introduction	5.1
5.2	Castigliano's Second Theorem	5.1
5.3	Frames	5.14
	Exercise	5.32
	Multiple Choice Questions	5.44

UNIT - III

6.	**DEFLECTION OF TRUSSES**	**6.1 – 6.34**
6.1	Introduction	6.1
6.2	Strain Energy	6.1
6.3	The Unit Load Method	6.1
6.4	Castigliano's First Theorem	6.3
	Exercise	6.30

7.	**INDETERMINATE TRUSSES**	**7.1 – 7.68**
7.1	Introduction	7.1
7.2	Force Method for Analysis of Indeterminate Trusses	7.2
7.3	Basic Formulation of Force Method for Trusses	7.4
7.4	Externally Indeterminate Trusses	7.8
7.5	Internally Indeterminate Trusses	7.18
7.6	Indeterminate Trusses with Lack of Fit	7.29

	7.7	Temperature Effects in Indeterminate Trusses	7.35
	7.8	Effects of Yielding of Support in Indeterminate Trusses	7.40
		Multiple Choice Questions	7.55

UNIT - IV

8. INFLUENCE LINES — 8.1 – 8.36

	8.1	Introduction	8.1
	8.2	Influence Lines for Simply Supported Beam	8.1
	8.3	Influence Line Diagram for Shear Force at a given Section of Girder	8.10
	8.4	Influence Line Diagram for the B.M. at a given Section	8.15
	8.5	Simply Supported Beams with Overhang	8.22
		Exercise	8.35

9. INFLUENCE LINE DIAGRAMS FOR PLANE — 9.1 – 9.64

	9.1	Introduction	9.1
	9.2	I.L.D. for Different Methods of N Type Truss	9.1
	9.3	I.L.D. for Deck Type Bridge Truss	9.12
		Exercise	9.51
		Multiple Choice Questions	9.53

10. THREE-HINGED ARCHES — 10.1 – 10.28

	10.1	Introduction	10.1
	10.2	Theoretical Arch or Line of Thrust	10.1
	10.3	Eddy's Theorem for Bending Moment	10.2
	10.4	Three Hinged Arch	10.3
		Exercise	10.28

11. TWO-HINGED ARCHES — 11.1 – 11.34

	11.1	Introduction	11.1
	11.2	Derivation for Horizontal Thrust	11.1
	11.3	Horizontal Thrust for Concentrated Load at Crown	11.2
	11.4	Two-Hinged Parabolic Arch Subjected to any General System of Loads	11.3
	11.5	Two-Hinged Arch Loaded with U.D.L.	11.5
		Exercise	11.34

UNIT - VI

12. PLASTIC THEORY — 12.1 – 12.24

- 12.1 Primary Concepts of Plastic Collapse — 12.1
- 12.2 Assumptions of Plastic Theory — 12.3
- 12.3 Elastic – Plastic Bending — 12.4
- 12.4 Shape Factor and Plastic Section Modulus — 12.8

13. PLASTIC ANALAYSIS — 13.1 – 13.58

- 13.1 Introduction — 13.1
- 13.2 Types of Mechanisms — 13.1
- 13.3 Fundamental Theorems of Plastic Analysis — 13.5
- 13.4 Plastic Analysis of Structures — 13.6
- 13.5 Application of Plastic Analysis to Steel Beams — 13.9
- 13.6 Application of Plastic Analysis to Steel Frames — 13.32
- 13.7 Standard Results of Plastic Analysis — 13.43
- 13.8 Plastic Design of Steel Beams and Frames — 13.45
- Exercise — 13.53

SECTION - I
UNIT I

Chapter 1
BASIC CONCEPTS OF STRUCTURAL ANALYSIS

1.1 STRUCTURAL SYSTEMS

A structure is any construction built in a stable equilibrium configuration of a particular form or shape consisting of

(i)   members or elements

(ii) joints or nodes and

(iii) supports or constraints.

A structure has to resist the external forces or disturbances and transfer them safely to other points, joints and finally to supports of the structure so that there is no rigid body movement. According to the configuration, the structures are idealised as follows :

(i) Discrete System : It consists of one-dimensional elements also called *line elements* which are long in comparison to their cross-sectional dimensions, such as ties, struts, columns, beams, shafts, cables, arches etc. Skeletal structures or framed structures like continuous beams, portal frames, trusses are the examples of the discrete system.

(ii) Continuum System : It consists of two-dimensional or three-dimensional elements.

(a) Surface structures such as plates, slabs, shells etc. consist of two-dimensional plane or curved surface elements. Two dimensions of surface elements are large compared to third dimension i.e. thickness.

(b) Volume structures like walls, deep beams, dams, massive foundations etc. consist of three-dimensional elements. All dimensions of such elements are significant.

(iii) Combined System : Hybrid structures made of line elements and surface or volume elements are considered as combined system. Stiffened plates, bridge decks, beam and slabs of buildings are the examples of hybrid structures.

The different structural systems are outlined in Fig. 1.1.

(1.1)

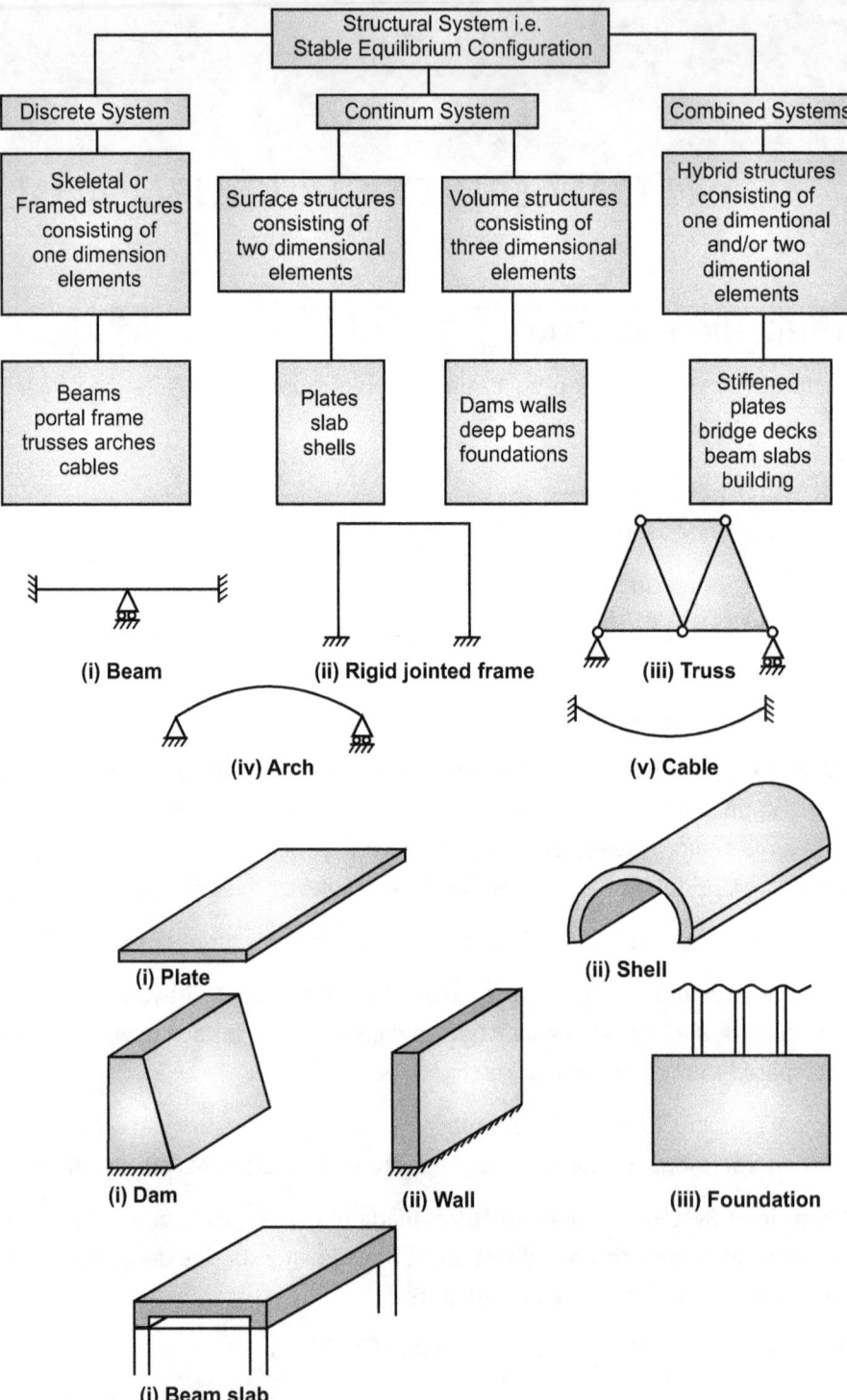

Fig. 1.1 : Structural systems

1.2 TYPES OF SKELETAL STRUCTURES

Skeletal structures are idealised as theoretical models with the assumption of one-dimensional behaviour of members and point specifications of joints. Skeletal structures are also termed as framed structures.

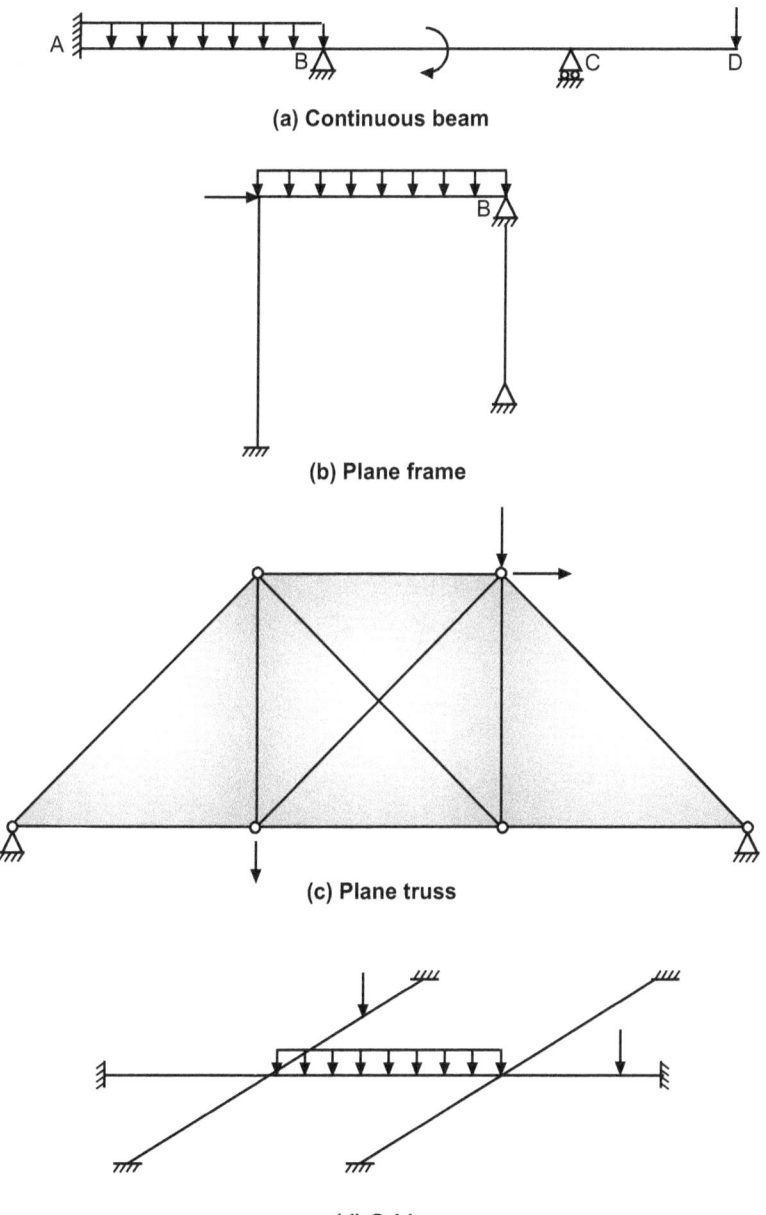

(a) Continuous beam

(b) Plane frame

(c) Plane truss

(d) Grid

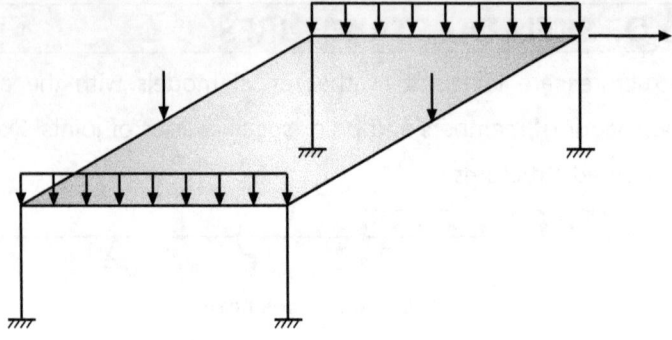

(e) Space frame

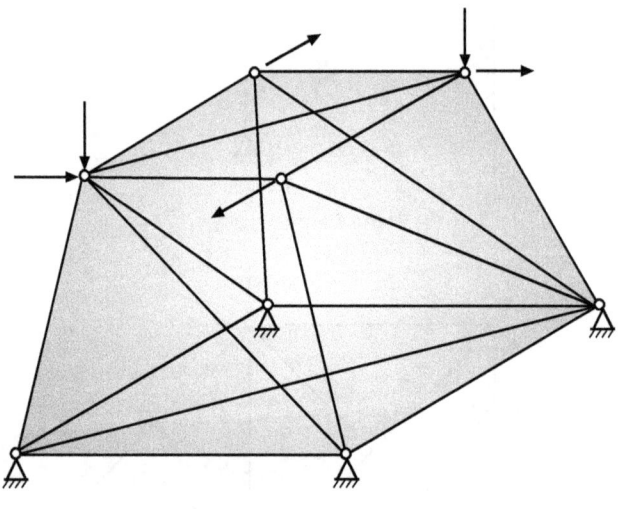

(f) Space truss

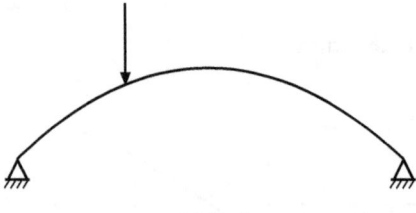

(g) Arch

Fig. 1.2 : Types of skeletal structures

A framed structure is considered as an assembly of prismatic members, joints and supports. Framed structure ≡ Members + Joints + Supports. The basic feature of a framed structure is that the individual members of the structure are treated as one-dimensional or line members. Therefore, framed structures are represented by lined diagrams. A straight member of uniform cross-section is termed as a prismatic member.

The joints of a framed structure are : (i) points of intersection of the prismatic members, (ii) points of supports and (iii) free ends of the members.

The joints may be (i) rigid or (ii) pinned.

The supports of a structure may be (i) fixed, (ii) hinged, (iii) roller. The loads on a structure may be (i) concentrated forces, (ii) distributed loads and (iii) couples applied directly or indirectly.

The types of framed structures are categorised by their geometrical form and by the method of connection of the individual members one to another, as given below.

(i) Continuous beam, shown in Fig. 1.2 (a), consists of members aligned in a common direction and supported at different points by different types of supports.

(ii) Plane rigid jointed frame, shown in Fig. 1.2 (b), is an assembly of members rigidly connected to each other such that any rotation of the joint is common to all members meeting the joint. Such structure is also called as plane frame. All members of the plane frame lie in a single plane and all applied loads act in this plane. The plane frame can carry loads distributed along the lengths of the members as well as at the joints. The members of the frame are subjected to bending moments, shear forces and axial forces.

(iii) Plane truss, shown in Fig. 1.2 (c), is a structure in which the joints are assumed as the frictionless pins so that all members are free to rotate individually at the joint. A structure and all applied loads lie in a single plane. Moreover, the loads are applied at the pin joints only and the members are assumed to carry only an axial force.

(iv) Grid, shown in Fig. 1.2 (d), is a two-dimensional rigid jointed frame but is distinguished from the plane frame by the fact that loads applied to the grid, act normal to the plane of the grid rather than in the plane of the grid.

(v) Rigid jointed space frame, shown in Fig. 1.2 (e), is a structure of unrestricted geometrical form consisting of members, connected by rigid joints and supports in three dimensions. The members are subjected to axial and shearing forces, bending moments and twisting moments due to the application of a general type of loading.

(vi) Space truss, shown in Fig. 1.2 (f), is a ball-jointed space frame of unrestricted geometrical form. The members of the space truss are assumed and carry only axial forces set up by the joint loads only.

Arch, shown in Fig. 1.2 (g), is the special type of skeletal structure consisting of curved line elements. Therefore, arches are considered separately and not included in framed structures.

Analysis of the following structures is only dealt within this text :
(i) Continuous beams, (ii) Plane frames
(iii) Plane trusses (iv) Two hinged arches

1.3 STRUCTURAL BEHAVIOUR

The effects of the external forces or disturbances acting on a structure, can be listed as follows :

(i) Strains and stresses are developed in the material of the structure.
(ii) The deformations of the members occur and the structure deforms.
(iii) All points, except immovable points of supports, are displaced to new positions due to cumulative effects of deformation.
(iv) Internal forces i.e. stress resultants exist at any cross-section of a member of a structure.
(v) Reactions are induced at the supports.

Thus, the behaviour of a structure is stated as if certain forces and/or displacements are imposed upon a structure at some points than at other points the forces and/or displacements are developed in the structure. This is called *response of a structure*. The calculation of these developed forces and displacements is the essential part of structural analysis. Forces and/or displacements are considered as the causes and the effects. Structural behaviour or analysis is interpreted as cause-effect phenomenon.

$$\text{Structural behaviour} \equiv \text{Cause-Effect Phenomenon}.$$

The behaviour of a structure is mathematically modelled by force-displacement equations using the concepts of equilibrium, compatibility, stress-strain laws and superposition.

Depending upon the nature of loading, the structure may respond in the different ways as follows :

(i) It may deform statically in stable elastic manner - static analysis.
(ii) It may yield - Plastic analysis of structure.
(iii) It may vibrate - Dynamic analysis.
(iv) It may buckle - Stability analysis.

The purpose of structural analysis is to predict accurately the response of a given structure to a given loading. This text is mainly concerned with the static behaviour in the elastic range i.e. static analysis of linear elastic structure.

1.4 PRIMARY CONCEPTS

Mechanics is the soul of structural engineering. Mechanics is the study of forces and displacements. It may be mechanics of rigid bodies, mechanics of materials or mechanics of structures. The relationship between forces and displacements is the main theme of structural analysis. Therefore, it is worth to review the important concepts related to mechanics. The information of these concepts will help to pave the way of the subject.

1.4.1 Frame of Reference

The basic quantities involved in structural analysis such as forces and displacements, are specified with respect to cartesian co-ordinate system i.e. rectangular right hand system of mutually perpendicular axes OX, OY and OZ as shown in Fig. 1.3 (a). The plane structures are considered to lie in X - Y plane, in general.

The quantities are considered positive if they are in positive directions of axes of co-ordinate system.

1.4.2 Forces

A force is defined as the action of one body on the other, either through direct contact or otherwise. A force in general, has a tendency to cause a translation and/or a rotation of a body and hence a force means either a translational force or a rotational force i.e. moment, couple. A force is completely specified by the following information :

(i) **Magnitude :** Numerical value of the force with its unit.
(ii) **Direction :**
 (a) Line of action of the force.
 (b) Angle of line of action of the force with respect to the reference axis.
 (c) Sense in which the force acts along the line of action represented by the arrow head.

(iii) Point of application of the force and the plane in which the force acts :

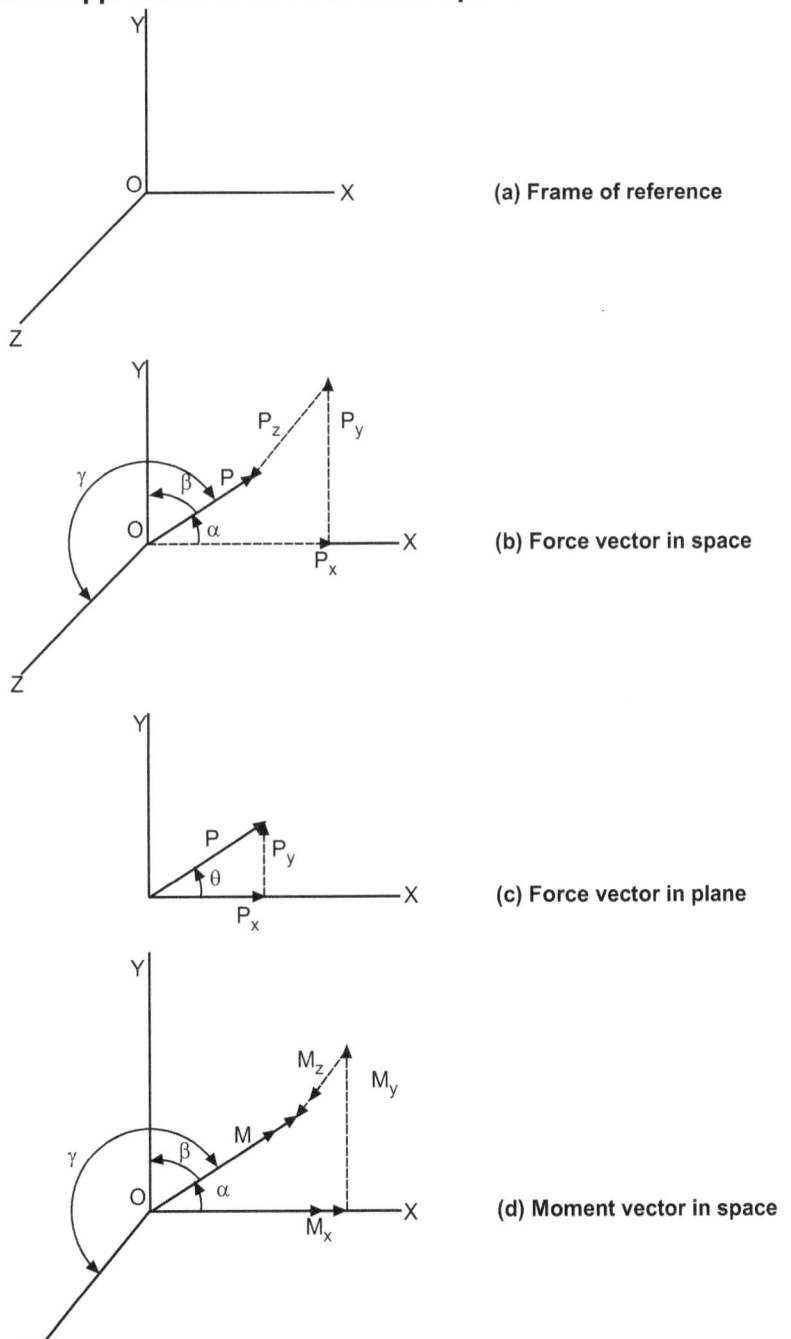

(a) Frame of reference

(b) Force vector in space

(c) Force vector in plane

(d) Moment vector in space

Fig. 1.3 : Reference system

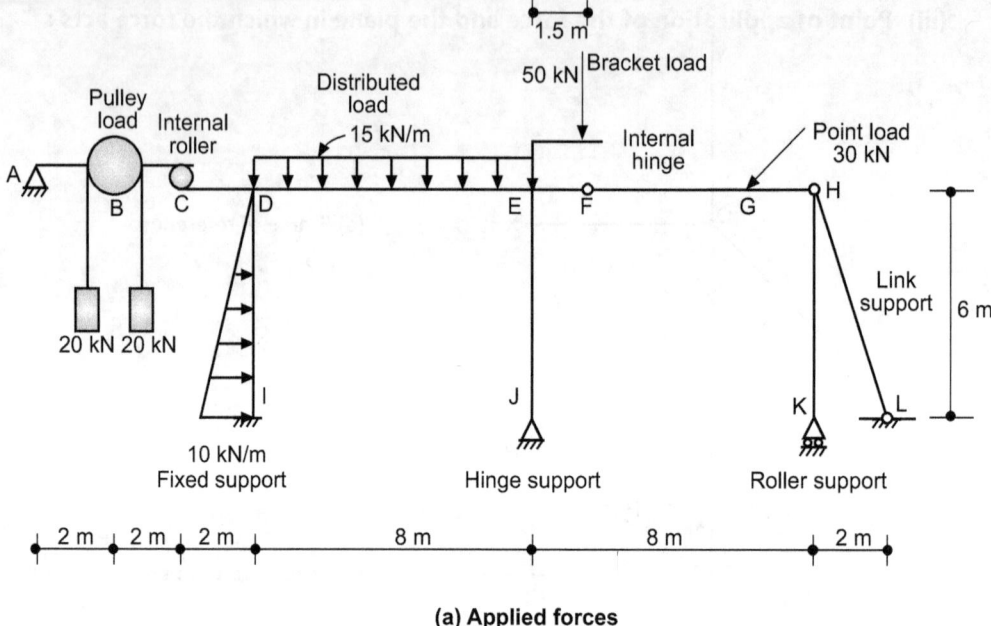

(a) Applied forces

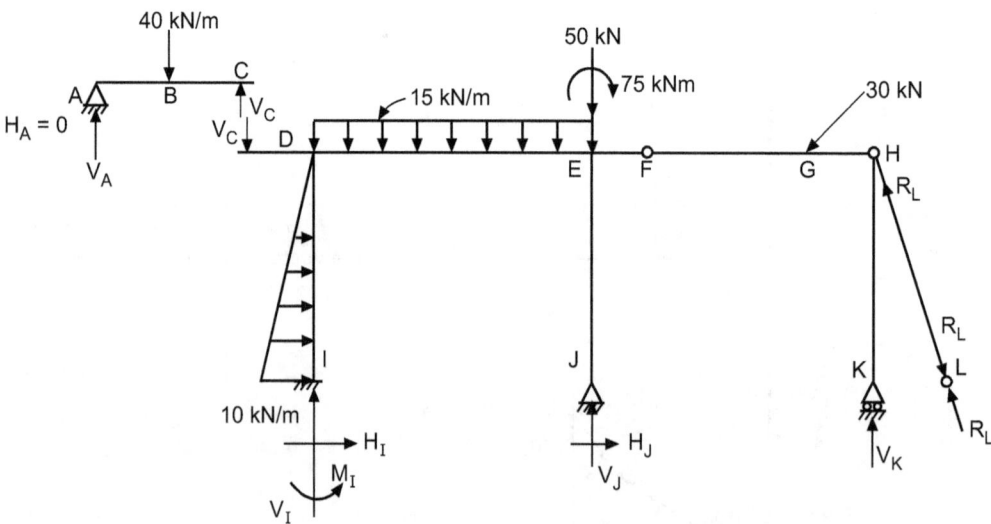

(b) Active and reactive forces

Fig. 1.4 : External forces

A translational force, generally called only force, P, is represented by a vector having magnitude and direction defined by the angles α, β, γ measured with respect to x, y, z axes of the co-ordinate system. A force is also specified by its orthogonal components in three co-ordinate axes directions as $P_x = P \cos \alpha$, $P_y = P \cos \beta$ and $P_z = P \cos \gamma$ as shown in Fig. 1.3 (b).

A force P in plane is generally represented by its components $P_x = P \cos \theta$ and $P_y = P \sin \theta$ as shown in Fig. 1.3 (c).

A rotational force, generally called moment M, is represented by a vector with double headed arrow, having magnitude and direction normal to the plane in which it acts. The direction of the arrow is that of the advancement of the right handed screw turned in the same sense as the moment. A moment is also specified by its components,

$M_x = M \cos \gamma$, $M_y = M \cos \beta$, $M_z = M \cos \gamma$ as shown in Fig. 1.3 (d).

The moment in the plane x - y is represented by $M_z = M$.

For static analysis of structure, all forces are considered as static forces and assumed to be gradually applied.

The forces acting on a structure are classified as follows :

(i) External Forces : The forces acting on a structure as a whole are considered as external forces. Body forces and surface forces are mainly considered as the external forces. They may be applied forces i.e. active forces and reactive forces.

  (a) Applied forces are also called *loads*. The loads may be concentrated load, distributed load and couple or moment acting directly or indirectly through the arrangements like bracket, pulley etc. The applied forces are shown in Fig. 1.4 (a).

  (b) Reactive forces are the actions of supports on a structure. According to the types of supports, the reactive forces may be forces and moments as shown in Fig. 1.4 (b).

(ii) Internal Forces : The stresses are developed to resist the external forces and deformations of a structure. The stress resultant at the cut section of the member of a structure is considered as the internal force. Internal forces can also be interpreted as the actions of a part of structure on the adjacent part of the structure and in this sense the internal forces are also considered as the reaction forces. Thus, the member end forces are the internal forces.

(iii) Load Effects : Load effects at a section of a member of a structure are the algebraic sum of the external forces or algebraic sum of the moments of the external forces acting on one side of the section. The load effects at a section are equal in magnitude but opposite in direction of the internal forces at that section. In this context, at a section, the load effects are actions and internal forces are reactions and may be of the following types in general as shown in Fig. 1.5.

  (a) Axial force, P_x
  (b) Shear forces, P_y and P_z
  (c) Twisting moment, M_x
  (d) Bending moments, M_y and M_z.

Three force components and three moment components i.e. six components may exist at a section as the actions.

Corresponding to these basic structural actions as shown in Fig. 1.5, the structural members are named as :

  (a) Axial member i.e. tie, strut
  (b) Shear member i.e. pin, rivet, bolt
  (c) Bending member i.e. beam
  (d) Twisting member i.e. shaft.

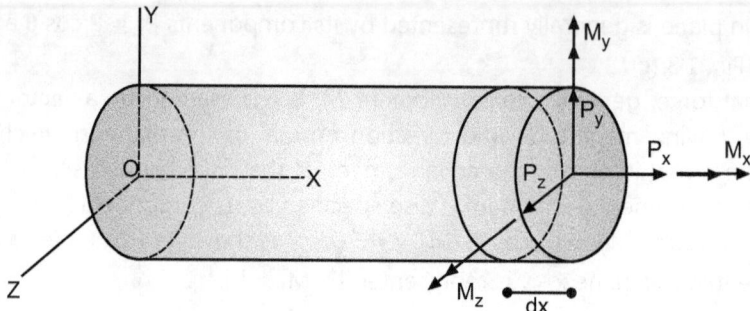

Fig. 1.5 : Basic structural actions

1.4.3 Deformation and Displacement

A structure deforms under the action of forces. The change in the shape is called *deformation*. Corresponding to the structural actions, deformations are basically of the following types, as shown in Fig. 1.6 : (a) Axial deformation, (b) Shearing deformation, (c) Bending or flexural deformation and (d) Twisting deformation. The displacement at a point of the structure is the cumulative effect of the deformations. All points, except immovable points of supports, will be displaced to new positions. The physical and material properties are required to obtain the displacements. The displacements are of two types : (i) translational displacement and (ii) rotational displacement.

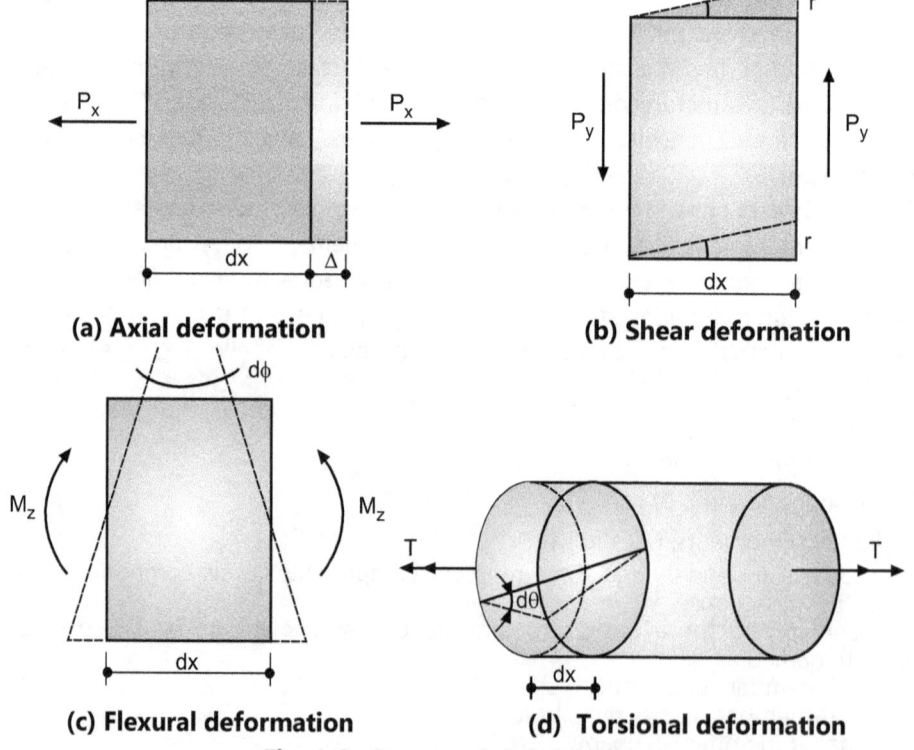

(a) Axial deformation

(b) Shear deformation

(c) Flexural deformation

(d) Torsional deformation

Fig. 1.6 : Structural deformation

A translation, generally called as *displacement*, means the distance moved by a point in the structure. A displacement at a point is represented by a vector having magnitude and direction. A displacement at a point is specified by its three independent components in three co-ordinate axes and denoted by u, v, w. For plane structures, a displacement is represented by two components, u and v only.

A rotation refers to the angle of rotation of the axis of member. The deformed axis of the member is called the *elastic curve*. The rotation at a point is considered as the cumulative effects of curvature. A rotation at a point is represented by the vector having magnitude in radians and direction shown by double headed arrow. A rotation at a point is specified in general by three components θ_x, θ_y and θ_z as rotations about co-ordinate axes. For plane structures in x-y plane, a rotation at a point is specified by only one component $\theta_z = \theta$.

Three translation-components and three rotation-components i.e. six components may exist as displacements at a point of a structure. These six components of the displacement at a point are also referred as the degrees of freedom (DOF).

1.4.4 Correspondence Between Force and Displacement

Force and displacement are corresponding when they are analogous and located at the same point on a structure without regard to the actual cause. This is known as one to one correspondence between force and displacement and stated as :

(i) Translation at a point is corresponding to the concentrated force acting at the same point. The translation is not necessarily caused by the force at that point. The translation must be in the direction (i.e. line of action and sense) of the force.

Fig. 1.7 : Co-ordinate numbering

(ii) Rotation at a point is corresponding to the concentrated moment at the same point. The rotation is not necessarily caused by the moment at that point. The rotation must be in the direction (i.e. line of action and sense) of the moment.

This correspondence is established by the co-ordinate numbering i.e. i, j as shown in Fig. 1.7 where i, j may be particular numbers.

i represents vertical translation at B i.e. Δ_B and vertical force at B i.e. P_B.

j represents rotation at B i.e. θ_B and moment at B i.e. M_B.

This technique of co-ordinate numbering will be of great help to develop the concepts of stiffness and flexibility coefficients in matrix methods.

1.4.5 Equilibrium

A body, that is initially at rest and remains at rest when acted upon by a system of forces, is said to be in a state of static equilibrium. For a body to be in equilibrium, the resultant of the system of forces must be zero. Therefore, the independent equations of equilibrium, in general, are : $\sum F_x = 0$, $\sum F_y = 0$, $\sum F_z = 0$, $\sum M_x = 0$, $\sum M_y = 0$, $\sum M_z = 0$

Three force equilibrium equations and three moment equilibrium equations i.e. six equations are called as *conditions of equilibrium*.

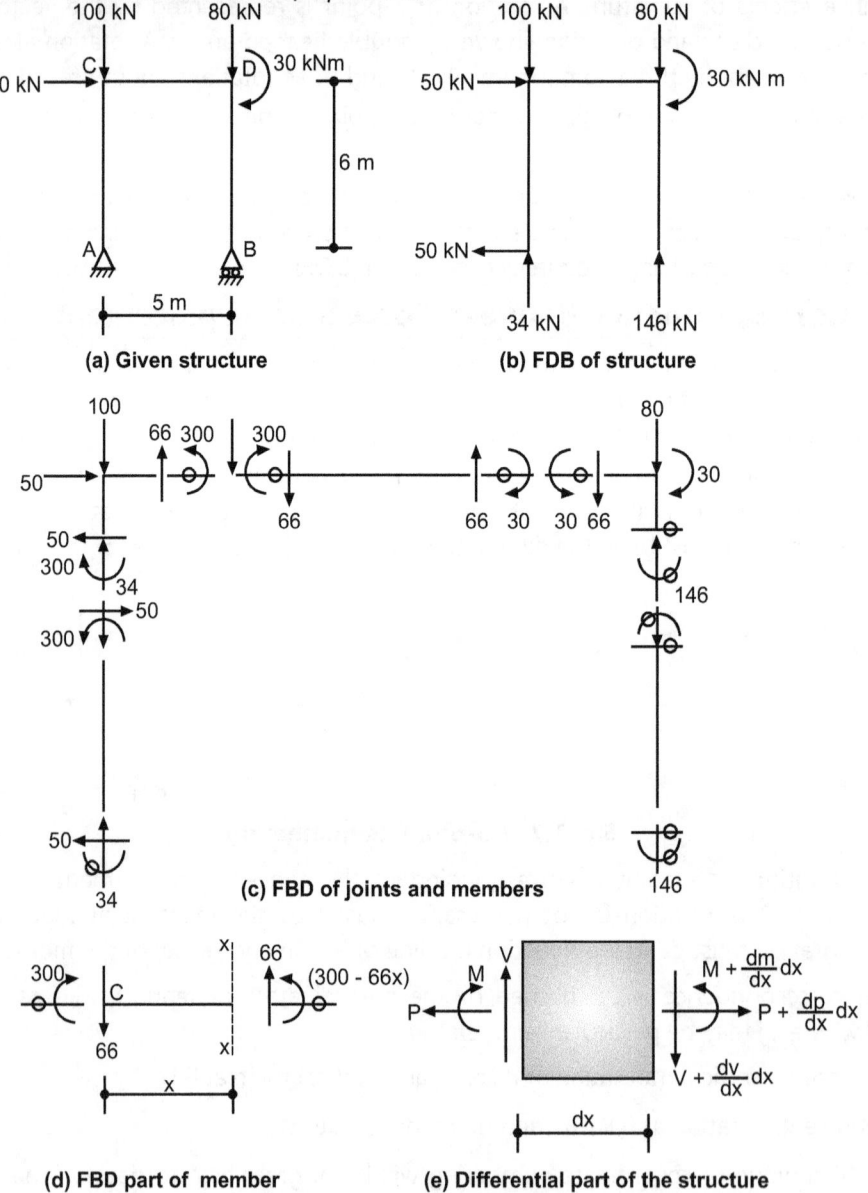

Fig. 1.8 : Free body diagrams

The fundamental concept of a structure is the static equilibrium. A structure as a whole must be in equilibrium under the external forces i.e. applied loads and reactions of the supports. If a structure is in equilibrium, then its part and parcel will be in equilibrium under external and internal forces. It implies that any part of the structure, each member, each joint, any point must be in equilibrium.

For plane structures, the conditions of equilibrium are $\sum F_x = 0$, $\sum F_y = 0$, $\sum M = 0$ i.e. two force equilibrium equations and one moment equilibrium equation. These three equations may be replaced by the independent moment equations, $\sum M_A = 0$, $\sum M_B = 0$ and $\sum M_C = 0$ where A, B, C are the points which do not lie in a straight line.

1.4.6 Free Body Diagram (FBD)

FBD is a diagram showing (i) the body isolated from its surroundings and (ii) all the forces acting on the body. FBD is the effective technique employed extensively in considering the equilibrium of (i) a structure, (ii) a part of the structure, (iii) a member of the structure, (iv) a part of the member, (v) a joint, (vi) a differential part of the member, as shown in Fig. 1.8 (a) to (e).

1.4.7 Compatibility

The displacements of any point of a structure must be compatible with the overall deformation of the whole structure corresponding to the types of joints and types of the supports. The geometrical condition of displacements, consistent with the constraints, is called *compatibility*. This is the physical requirement of a structure for the continuity. The conditions of deformations along with the force conditions are explained subsequently as per types of supports and joints.

1.4.8 Types of Supports

A structure must be constrained by the supports so that there is no rigid body movement of the structure upon the application of any type of loads. The restrictions on rigid body motion of a structure are called the restraints. Such restraints are provided by the supports which connect the structure to stationary body.

The forces exerted by the supports, to prevent the movements, are called the reactions.

The supports may be classified as (i) position restraint, (ii) direction restraint. Accordingly the following types of the supports are commonly used for plane structures to provide the particular restraint.

(i) Roller support, represented in Fig. 1.9 (a), provides (a) the complete restraint against the translation perpendicular to the plane of the support, (b) no restraint to the translation along the plane of the support and (c) no restraint to the rotation.

Therefore, the force condition at a point of roller support specifies that roller support 'A' provides a reactive force which is acting at known point and acts in a known direction of perpendicular to the plane of the support but the magnitude of which is unknown. The sense of the reaction may be either away or to the structure. There cannot be moment as a reaction. Thus, one unknown reaction component is considered at a roller support.

Displacement condition at a point of roller support, in general, is stated as there is the translation along the plane of roller and the rotation i.e. two DOF.

The compatibility condition at a point of roller support is specified by zero translation perpendicular to the plane of support.

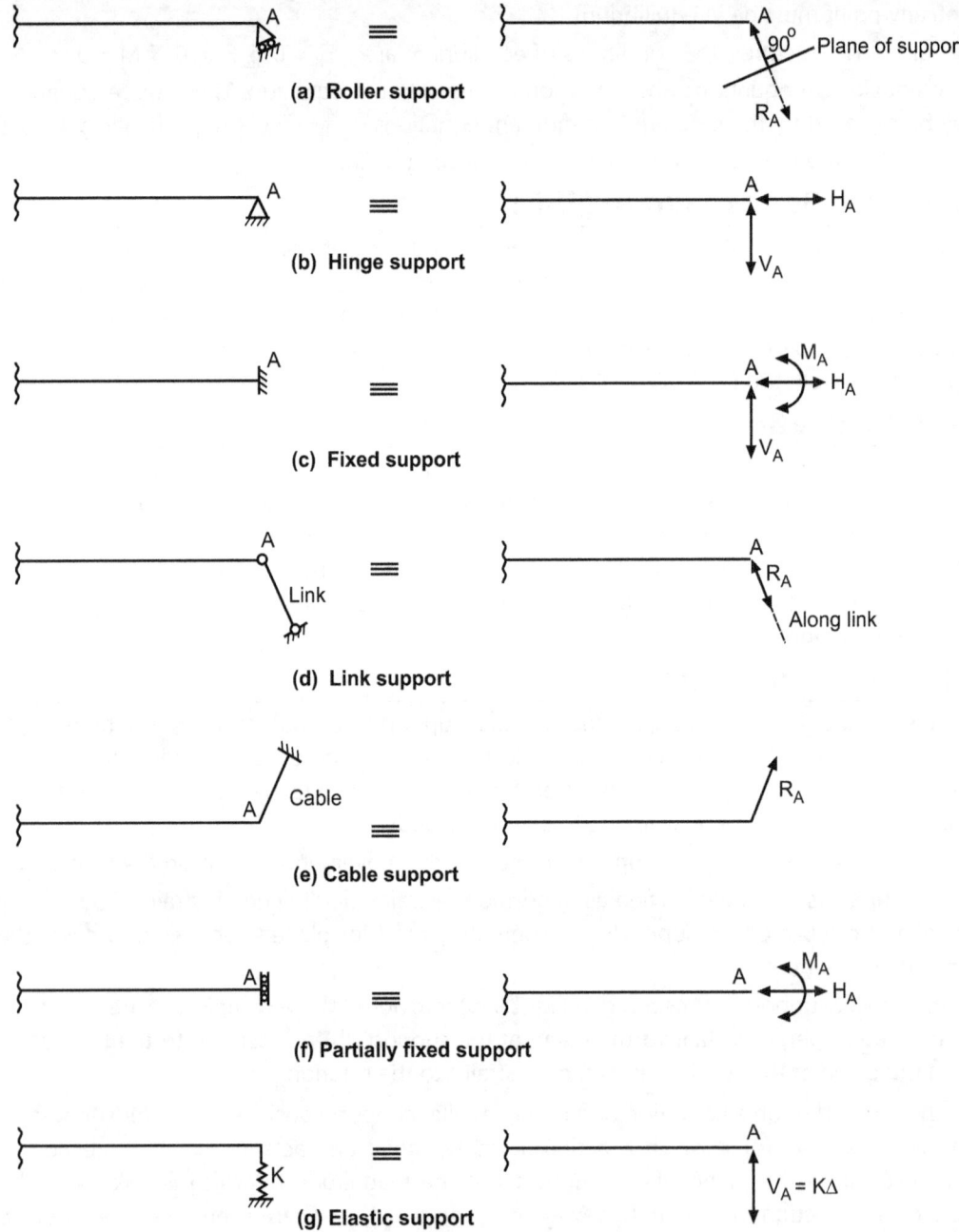

Fig. 1.9 : Types of supports

(ii) Hinge support, shown in Fig. 1.9 (b), provides (a) the full restraint against translation in any direction and (b) no restraint against rotation. Therefore, the force condition at a point of the hinge support is that there is the reaction of known point of application but unknown magnitude and unknown direction i.e. line of action. The same condition is interpreted as two unknown orthogonal components of the reaction in x and y directions. There cannot be a moment as a reaction. Thus, two reaction components are considered at a hinge support.

The displacement condition at a point of hinge support is that translation is zero but the rotation exists i.e. one DOF.

The compatibility condition at a point of hinge support is given by zero translations in x and y directions i.e. u = v = 0.

(iii) Fixed support, shown in Fig. 1.9 (c), provides the complete restraint against translations and rotations. Therefore, the force condition at a point of fixed support is that there is a unknown reactive moment and two unknown force components of the reactions in x and y directions. Thus, three unknown reaction components are considered at a fixed support.

All displacement components at a point of fixed support are zero, thus the dof is zero.

The compatibility condition at fixed support is therefore given by the equations u = 0, v = 0 and θ = 0.

(iv) Link support is analogous to the roller support. It provides the reaction force of known direction along the link, as shown in Fig. 1.9 (d), and known point of application but of unknown magnitude.

(v) Cable support offers only reaction force of tensile nature i.e. tension in the cable as shown in Fig. 1.9 (e).

(vi) Partially fixed support or fixed guide support shown in Fig. 1.9 (f) provides the full restraint against rotation but may not provide complete restraint against translations. One of the component of translations is free and other is restrained.

(vii) Elastic support : According to the elastic property of the support, it provides partial restraint to the corresponding translation or rotation. The reactive force is proportional to the stiffness of the elastic support and therefore reactive force is given by the product of the stiffness and displacement at the point of the support as shown in Fig. 1.9 (g).

1.4.9 Types of Joints

A structure is formed by inter-connection of members. The inter-connections are called as *joints*. The joints are idealised as pinned or rigid. The types of joints play the key role in the behaviour of structures. Analysis of a structure is characterized by the joint displacements.

Following information of types of joints will be very useful for further work :

(i) Pinned Joint : A joint shown in Fig. 1.10 (a) which provides no restraint to rotation is considered as pinned joint. Therefore, the force condition at a point of pinned joint is that it can resist and transfer forces only and it cannot resist moments. A pinned joint is the non-moment resisting joint.

The displacement conditions at a point of pinned joint can be stated as : (a) There may be translations in x and y directions for plane structures. (b) There is relative rotation between the connected members. It means that there are different rotations at ends of the members meeting at the joint; causing discontinuity.

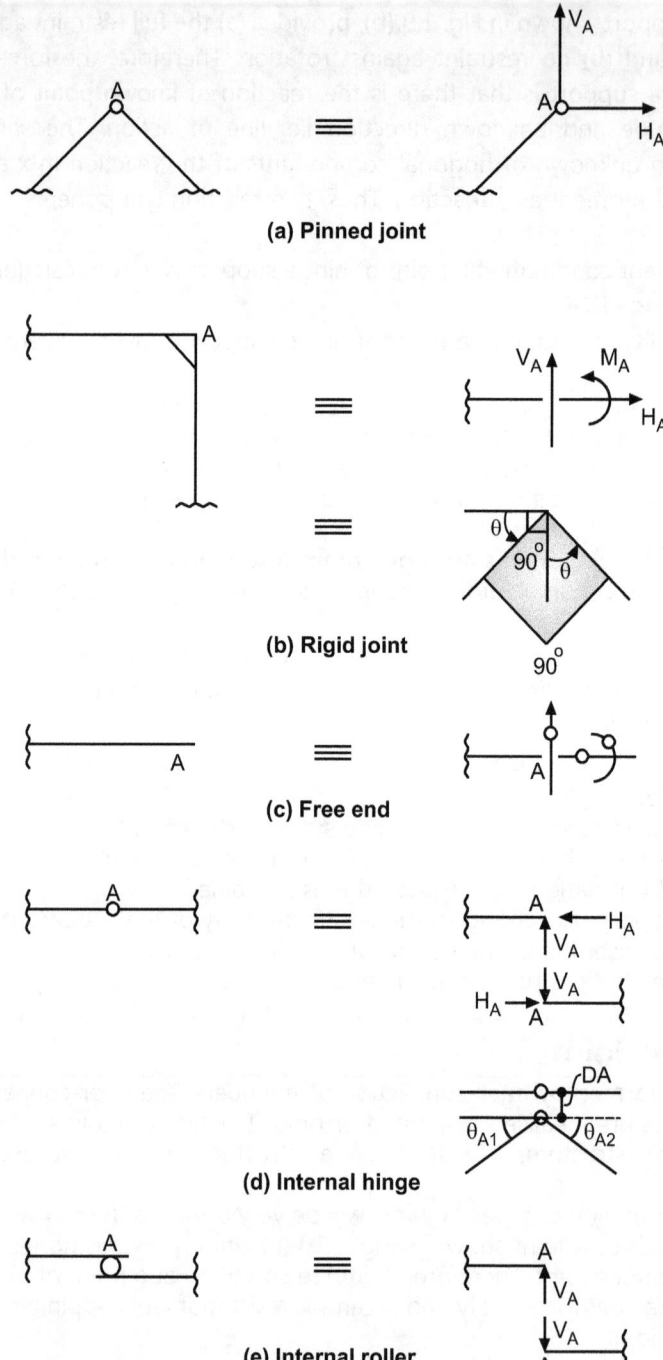

Fig. 1.10 : Types of joints

The compatibility condition at a point of pinned joint is that there is no continuity of deformation.

(ii) Rigid Joint : A joint, shown in Fig. 1.10 (b), which rotates as a whole is called as *rigid joint*. The force condition at a point of rigid joint is that it can resist and transfer forces as well as moments. Therefore, a rigid joint is the moment-resisting joint.

The displacement condition at a point of rigid joint of a plane structure in x - y plane is considered as follows : (a) There may be translations in x and y directions. (b) There is no relative rotation, but a single rotation of joint as a whole maintaining the continuity of a structure.

The compatibility condition at a point of rigid joint is specified as follows :

The rotations at ends of the members meeting at the joint are the same in magnitude and direction. It implies that the angle between the members remains constant even on loading. The number of DOF at a rigid joint is three.

(iii) Free End : Free end of a structure, shown in Fig. 1.10 (c), is also considered as the joint, if necessary. There are no forces and moment at unloaded free end. However, there may be displacements and therefore the number of DOF at free end of a plane structure is three i.e. two translations and one rotation.

(iv) Internal Hinge : If a hinge, as shown in Fig. 1.10 (d), is inserted in a continuous beam or a plane frame, then it is considered as a joint and additional conditions of forces and displacements are to be considered carefully. Displacement conditions are the same that of hinge joint having discontinuity with respect to rotation. Force conditions are stated as follows :

(a) If two members are connecting at a hinge, then one additional equation of equilibrium of zero moment at the point of hinge is taken into account in addition to the conventional equations of equilibrium.

(b) If three members are meeting at a hinge, then two additional equations of equilibrium are considered.

(v) Internal Roller : If a roller, shown in Fig. 1.10 (e), is inserted in a continuous beam or a plane frame to transfer the load from one member to another, then it is considered as joint. Displacement conditions are that there may be two translations and one rotation unlike rigid joint. Force condition specifies that the force along the plane of the roller is zero and moment at the point of roller is also zero. Therefore, two additional equations are available at the point of internal roller, in addition to the conventional equations of equilibrium.

1.4.10 Shear and Bending Moment Diagrams

The relation between load w, shear v and bending moment m, are $\frac{dv}{dx} = w$ and $\frac{dm}{dx} = v$.

Accordingly the load diagrams, shear force diagrams and bending moment diagrams for beams subjected to transverse loads are drawn by using the following principles :

(i) The slope of the shear force diagram at any point is equal to the intensity of the distributed load at that point.

(ii) Sudden changes in the ordinates of the shear diagram occur at points of application of concentrated loads.

(iii) The slope of the bending moment diagram at any point is equal to the ordinate of the shear force diagram at that point.
(iv) At points of concentrated loads, there are sudden changes in the ordinates of the shear force diagram and abrupt changes in the slopes of the bending moment diagram.
(v) It is usually necessary to compute the numerical values of the ordinates of the shear force diagram and bending moment diagrams only at points where the shapes of the diagrams change or points where the maximum or minimum values occur.
(vi) The difference in the ordinates of the shear force diagram between any two points is equal to the total load applied to the beam between these two points.
(vii) The difference in the ordinates of the bending moment diagram between any two points is equal to the area under shear force diagram between these two points.
(viii) The shear force diagram is one degree higher curve than the load diagram.
(ix) The bending moment diagram is one degree higher curve than the shear force diagram.

1.4.11 Stability

Stability of a structure essentially means the stability of its equilibrium configuration. Equilibrium is a kinematic state of body. In the context of stability, three types of equilibrium i.e. (a) stable, (b) unstable and (c) neutral, are considered as shown in Fig. 1.11 (a). In a mathematical sense, stability is interpreted to mean that infinitesimal disturbances will cause only infinitesimal displacements of the structure. Loss of structural stability is termed as structural instability. Although there are different types of instability, the present study of this text is mainly concerned with the stable equilibrium and corresponding stability. Structural stability corresponding to stable state of equilibrium is defined as the ability of structure to remain in position when subjected to any system of forces.

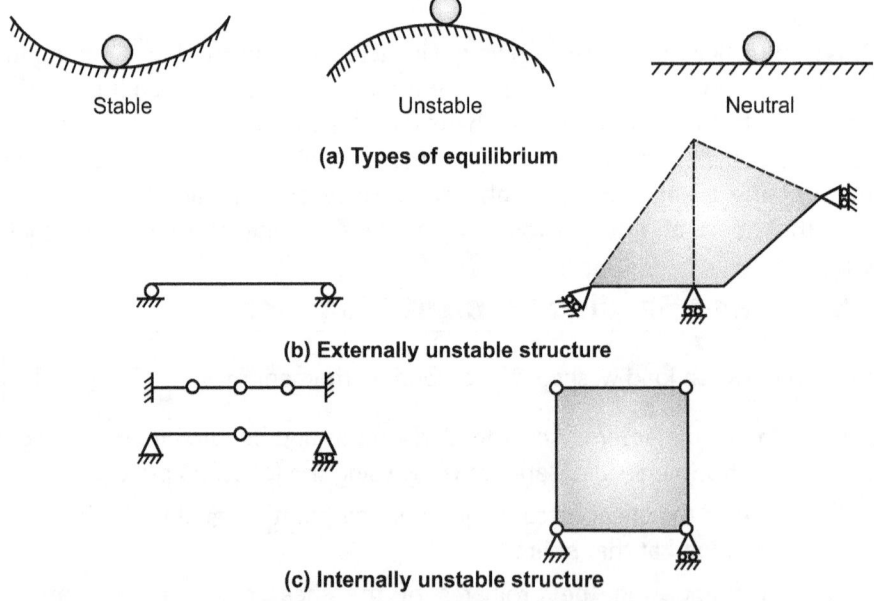

(a) Types of equilibrium

(b) Externally unstable structure

(c) Internally unstable structure

Fig. 1.11 : Stability of structure

(i) External stability is related to the support system of a structure. A structure should be supported adequately so that there is no rigid body motion. A structure is externally stable if the supports are capable of providing the required number of independent reaction components for static equilibrium of the structure. For stability of a plane structure, according to three conditions of equilibrium, the support system should provide non-trivial reaction forces along any two orthogonal axes in the plane of structure and a non-trivial reaction couple about any point in this plane. It means that for stability, the three reactive forces should be (i) non-parallel and (ii) non-concurrent. It may be noted that the structures having support systems shown in Fig. 1.11 (b) are not stable.

(ii) Internal stability depends on the types and arrangements of the joints and members of the structure. The arrangement should be such that the geometry of the structure or part of the structure should not change under any system of forces. A structure is internally stable, if internal forces are developed in the members of a structure as a result of even small deformation i.e. changes in the geometry. This means that a structure should resist the deformation by developing the internal forces. If the changes in the geometry do not cause the internal forces, then it is known as a mechanism and not a structure. The structures, shown in Fig. 1.11 (c), are not stable internally.

Therefore, a structure must be stable externally as well as internally.

1.4.12 Linearity and Elasticity

The deformation of a structure is assumed to be linear (reversible) and elastic. Linearity implies that the magnitudes of the displacements and internal forces of the structure are directly proportional to the magnitude of the external loading. The property of regaining original size and shape of the body after removal of force is known as *elasticity*. It means that the internal forces and displacements are recovered completely on removal of external forces and there should be no permanent deformation of a structure. In this context it is said that a structure behaves like a spring and cause-effect relationship is linear. The assumption that structural behaviour is linear elastic leads to considerable simplification in analysis and is justified in practice since most real structures respond approximately linearly to loads within their working range.

1.4.13 Statically Determinate Structures

If all reactions and internal forces in a structure can be found using the equilibrium conditions alone, then the structure is statically determinate. Statically determinate structures are also named as *determinate structures*. Internal forces in the determinate structure are independent of the physical and material properties of the structure. Displacements of determinate structure can be obtained separately from internal forces by using the concepts of elasticity and compatibility.

1.4.14 Statically Indeterminate Structures

If the reactions and internal forces in a structure cannot be found using the conditions of equilibrium, then the structure is statically indeterminate or hyperstatic or redundant. It is necessary to use directly three concepts of elasticity, equilibrium and compatibility so as to obtain the forces and displacements in the structure.

As the forces and displacements of an indeterminate structure are related to the physical and material properties of the structure, it needs prior knowledge of cross-sectional properties and material properties of the structure.

1.4.15 Static Indeterminacy

The reactive forces and the internal forces of a structure are considered as unknown forces in general. Available equations of equilibrium and unknown forces are compared to decide the static stability, determinacy and indeterminacy.

If the unknown forces are less than that the available equations of equilibrium, then the structure is not stable.

If the unknown forces are equal to the available equations of equilibrium, then the structure is statically determinate and can be analysed by statics only.

If the unknown forces are more than the available equations of equilibrium, then the structure is statically indeterminate and cannot be solved by statics only.

A statically indeterminate structure is said to have a degree of static indeterminacy or degree of redundancy. A degree of static indeterminacy is defined as the number of unknown reaction and internal force components in excess of the number of available equations of static equilibrium. A degree of static indeterminacy is denoted by the symbol (D_{si}) and given by

(D_{si}) = (Number of unknown reaction and internal force components)

– (Available equations of static equilibrium)

The most fundamental approach to determine the degree of static indeterminacy is to remove supports and/or to cut members until the structure has been reduced to a statically determinate and stable structure.

(D_{si}) = The number of restraints removed to reduce the given structure to determinate.

Alternatively the degree of static indeterminacy may be investigated as follows :

The degree of static indeterminacy is considered in the following two parts :

(i) Degree of External Indeterminacy : It is denoted by the symbol $(D_{si})_e$ and it is related to the reaction components of the supports of a structure. $(D_{si})_e$ is defined as the number of unknown reaction components in excess of number of equations of static equilibrium of a structure as a whole. The number of reaction components, denoted by r, depends on the types of supports of a structure. For plane structures, the number of equations of equilibrium is three in general. Therefore, $(D_{si})_e$ is given by the equation

$$(D_{si})_e = r - 3 \qquad \ldots (1.1) \text{ (a)}$$

If r < 3, then it means that the structure is not adequately supported and the structure is not stable. Therefore, r should not be less than three.

If r = 3, then the structure is determinate externally and the reaction components can be obtained by the equations of equilibrium alone.

If r > 3, the structure is statically indeterminate externally and the reaction components can only be obtained by all conditions of structure i.e. equilibrium, compatibility and elasticity.

(ii) Degree of Internal Indeterminacy : It is related to the internal forces i.e. member forces. Member forces depend on the type of structure. After knowing the reaction components of the structure, if member forces can be found using conditions of equilibrium alone, then the structure is said to be internally determinate. If not, the structure is internally indeterminate, and degree of internal indeterminacy denoted by $(D_{si})_i$ needs additional considerations of type of the structure and the number and arrangement of members in the structure, as explained below.

(a) Continuous Beams : The internal forces of a member of a continuous beam are generally axial force, shear force and bending moment i.e. three components of internal forces for a member. Once the reaction components are known, these internal forces can be obtained by statics. Therefore, continuous beams are internally determinate.

i.e. $\qquad (D_{si})_i = 0. \qquad \ldots (1.1) \text{ (b)}$

(b) Plane Frames : A plane frame is statically determinate internally if it has open configuration i.e. no loops. The member forces of a plane frame are specified by the axial force, shear and bending moment i.e. three components of internal forces for a member. An internally indeterminate plane frame may be converted into a statically determinate by making sufficient number of cuts 'C', to have open configuration of the frame. At each cut, three components of internal forces are released. Therefore, the degree of internal indeterminacy is given by the equation

$$(D_{si})_i = 3C \qquad \ldots (1.1) \text{ (c)}$$

(c) Plane Trusses : The internal force in a member of a truss is the axial force in the member i.e. one component. A plane truss is statically determinate internally if the truss has number of members, m, equals to (2j – 3) where j is the number of joints of the truss. If m is less than (2j – 3), then the truss is not stable and if m is greater than (2j – 3), then the truss is internally indeterminate and the degree of internal indeterminacy is given by the equation

$$(D_{si})_i = m - (2j - 3) \qquad \ldots (1.1) \text{ (d)}$$

For the cantilever trusses :

$$(D_{si})_i = m - 2j \qquad \ldots (1.1)\ (e)$$

where j is number of joints except support joints, m is number of members excluding support plane.

(iii) Combined Degree of Static Indeterminacy :

(A) First Approach : The combined degree of static indeterminacy of a structure (D_{si}) is obtained as the sum of $(D_{si})_e$ and $(D_{si})_i$.

i.e. $\qquad (D_{si}) = (D_{si})_e + (D_{si})_i$

Accordingly, for different plane structures, the (D_{si}) may be obtained as follows :

(a) Continuous beams

$$(D_{si}) = (D_{si})_e + (D_{si})_i$$

$$\therefore \quad (D_{si}) = (r - 3) + 0$$

$$\therefore \quad (D_{si}) = (r - 3) \qquad \ldots (1.2)\ (a)$$

(b) Plane frames

$$(D_{si}) = (D_{si})_e + (D_{si})_i \qquad \ldots (1.2)\ (b)$$

$$\therefore \quad (D_{si}) = (r - 3) + 3C$$

(c) Plane trusses

$$(D_{si}) = (D_{si})_e + (D_{si})_i$$

$$\therefore \quad (D_{si}) = (r - 3) + [m - (2j - 3)]$$

$$\therefore \quad (D_{si}) = r - 3 + m - 2j + 3$$

$$\therefore \quad (D_{si}) = (m + r - 2j) \qquad \ldots (1.2)\ (c)$$

Cantilever trusses

$$D_{si} = (m - 2j) \qquad \ldots (1.2)\ (d)$$

(B) Second Approach : The combined degree of static indeterminacy is directly obtained by this general approach from the basic concept of

(D_{si}) = (Number of unknown reaction components and internal forces)

− (Available equations of equilibrium)

Unknown reaction components are counted according to the type of supports of the structure as follows : One reaction component for each roller support, two reaction components for each hinged support, three reaction components for each fixed support. Unknown internal forces are counted according to the type of structure as follows : One internal force component for each member of a truss, three internal force components for each member of a continuous beam or a frame. Available equations of equilibrium are counted according the joint of a type of structure as follows : Two equations for each joint of a truss including support, three equations for each joint of a beam or a frame including support. Additional available equations of equilibrium are counted for the insertion of a hinge in a beam or a frame, as follows :

(number of members meeting at the internal pin -1) equation for each internal pin. The number of additional equations is represented by 'h'.

Additional available equations of equilibrium are counted for the insertion of roller in a continuous beam structure. Two equations for each roller inserted in a beam structure. The number of additional equations is represented by 'ro'.

As per above rules, the criteria of stability and determinacy for the different plane structures can be generalised as follows :

(a) Continuous Beams

If $(3m + r) < (3j + h + ro)$, the continuous beam is unstable.

If $(3m + r) = (3j + h + ro)$, the continuous beam is statically determinate.

If $(3m + r) > (3j + h + ro)$, the continuous beam is statically indeterminate.

$$\therefore \quad (D_{si}) = (3m + r) - (3j + h + ro) \quad \ldots (1.3)\,(a)$$

(b) Plane Frames

If $(3m + r) < (3j + h)$, the frame is unstable

If $(3m + r) = (3j + h)$, the frame is statically determinate

If $(3m + r) > (3j + h)$, the frame is statically indeterminate

$$\therefore \quad (D_{si}) = (3m + r) - (3j + h) \quad \ldots (1.3)\,(b)$$

(c) Plane Trusses

If $(m + r) < (2j)$, the truss is unstable

If $(m + r) = (2j)$, the truss is statically determinate

If $(m + r) > (2j)$, the truss is statically indeterminate

$$\therefore \quad (D_{si}) = (m + r) - (2j) \quad \ldots (1.3)\,(c)$$

In this approach, $(D_{si})_e$ and $(D_{si})_i$ cannot be identified separately. Using this approach, static stability, determinacy and indeterminacy of different structures are investigated as given in Tables 1.1, 1.2 and 1.3.

Table 1.1 : Stability and Indeterminacy of Beams

Sr. No.	Structure	m	r	j	h	ro	(3m+r)	3j+h+ro	D_{si} (3m+r) – (3j+h–ro)	D_{ki}	Remarks
1.		1	2	2	–	–	5	6	–1	2	Unsable
2.		2	3	3	–	–	9	9	0	3	Statically determinate
3.		1	6	2	1	–	9	7	2	3	Indeterminate to second degree
4.		1	6	2	–	2	9	8	1	2	Indeterminate to first degree
5.		2	4	3	–	2	10	11	–1	5	Unstable
6.		2	3	3	–	–	9	9	0*	3	* Rule fails, unstable as three links intersect at the point
7.		2	8	3	–	–	14	9	5	1	Indeterminate to fifth degree
8.		3	6	4	1	–	15	13	2*	6	* Indeterminate to first degree
9.		1	6	2	2	–	9	8	1&	6	* Rule fails. The structure is determinate
10.		1	4	2	1	–	7	7	0*	5	* Rule fails. The structure in unstable.

Table 1.2 : Stability and Indeterminacy of Frames

Sr. No.	Structure	m	r	(3m+r)	j	h	(3j + h)	D_{si} (3m+r) − (3j+h)	D_{ki}	Remarks
1.		2	3	9	3	–	9	0	3	Determinate
2.		2	3	9	9	–	9	0*	3	* Rule fails unstable as reactions are concurrent
3.		3	3	12	4	–	12	0	6	Determinate
4.		5	9	24	6	–	18	6	4	Indeterminate sixth degree
5.		3	6	15	4	–	12	3	3	Indeterminate third degree
6.		3	6	15	4	1	13	2	4	Indeterminate second degree
7.		5	9	24	6	2	20	4	8	Indeterminate fourth degree
8.		3	6	15	4	3	15	0*	–	Rule fails, unstable.

Table 1.3 : Stability and Indeterminacy of Trusses

Sr. No.	Structure	m	r	(m+r)	j	(2j)	D_{si} (m+r) – (2j)	D_{ki}	Remarks
1.		13	3	16	8	16	0	–	*Rule fails, unstable
2.		2	4	6	3	6	0	2	Determinate
3.		5	4	9	4	8	1	4	Indeterminate, first degree
4.		5	4	9	4	8	1	4	Indeterminate, first degree
5.		6	4	10	4	8	2	4	Indeterminate, second degree
6.		5	4	9	4	8	1	4	Indeterminate, first degree

1.4.16 Kinematic Indeterminacy

Any structure, determinate or indeterminate, is said to have a certain degree of freedom. The degree of freedom is also called as degree of *kinematic indeterminacy* of a structure and denoted by (D_{ki}). In structural analysis, the overall behaviour of a structure is characterised by the displacements at the joints of the structure. The degree of kinematic indeterminacy of a structure is defined as the number of non-zero joint displacements of the structure. It may be noted again that the points of supports are also considered as the joints.

As per frame of reference, non-zero displacement components of all joints are counted, taking into account the compatibility conditions according to types of joints and types of supports and types of structures. For a plane structure, the general rules to count the non-zero joint displacements are given below as per the type of structure.

(i) Continuous Beams : At a point of a continuous beam, there are in general three degrees of freedom i.e. two translations in the direction of x and y axes and one rotation about z-axis. The axial deformation of the members of this structure is generally assumed to be neglected, being insignificant. Therefore, the horizontal translation in x-axis i.e. beam axis is not considered and hence the degree of freedom at a point is reduced to two. The points of supports and free ends are taken as the joints. Accordingly, to determine the degree of kinematic indeterminacy, the non-zero displacements are counted as follows :

Two displacement components for each roller support in the inclined plane.

One displacement component for each roller support in the horizontal plane.

One displacement component for each hinge support.

Two displacement components for each free end.

One displacement component for each fixed vertical guides support.

Three displacement components for each insertion of a hinge in a structure.

Two displacement components for each insertion of a roller in a structure.

(ii) Rectangular Plane Frames : At a point of a plane frame also there are three DOF unlike continuous beams. As the axial deformations of the members are generally neglected, the vertical translations at the joints of a rectangular frame are considered as zero and the horizontal translations at the joints at a beam level are assumed to be the same. This is known as sway. The concept of a rigid joint specifies a single rotation at the joint. Therefore, non-zero displacements are counted as per the following rules :

One displacement component for each rigid joint.

One displacement component for each pair of rigid joints at the same level.

Two displacement components for each roller support in the horizontal plane.

One displacement component for each roller support in the vertical plane.

One displacement component for each hinge support.

One displacement component for each fixed vertical guide support.

Three displacement components for each insertion of a hinge in a member.

(iii) Plane Trusses : At a point of plane truss, there are in general two translations along x and y axes. There is no rotation as joints are pinned. Therefore, the counts of non-zero displacements are as follows :

Two displacement components for each joint.

One displacement component for each roller support in horizontal plane, two displacement components for each roller support in inclined plane.

Using above methods, kinematic indeterminacy of different structures is investigated as given in Tables 1.1, 1.2 and 1.3.

Chapter 2
SLOPE AND DEFLECTION OF BEAMS

2.1 INTRODUCTION

Under the action of external loads the beam deflects from its initial position. Exact values of deflections are required in many designs. For example, in buildings, floor beams shall not deflect beyond the specified limit to maintain the sense of security of the occupants. Also study of deflection is necessary to check the dimensional accuracy of various machine elements, under the action of variety of loads.

Basically, beam is subjected to flexure and shear. Both of these actions are responsible for causing deflection. However, deflections due to shear are generally neglected, being smaller in magnitude as compared to that due to bending.

When the cross section of beam is designed to resist bending stresses safely, it is called as design for *strength criterion*. And when the cross section of beam is designed such that deflection is within specified limit, it is called as *stiffness criterion* of design. Practically, design of flexure member is required for strength as well as stiffness criteria.

2.2 ASSUMPTIONS

When line members are subjected to bending without twisting (i.e. the plane of the external forces acting on member must pass through the shear centre of the cross section) their axis does not elongate and their cross sections do not twist. Moreover, because the dimensions of the cross sections of line members are small compared to their length, the following assumptions as to the geometry of their deformed configuration can be made.

(i) Plane sections normal to the axis of a line member prior to the deformation can be considered plane subsequent to deformation, that is the warping of cross section of a line member is assumed negligible.

(ii) Plane sections normal to the axis of a line member before deformation can be considered normal to its deformed axis subsequent to deformation. This implies that, the effect of shearing components of strain on transverse components of translation of cross sections is negligible.

2.3 SLOPE, DEFLECTION AND RADIUS OF CURVATURE

A segment of initially straight beam is shown in a deformed state in Fig. 2.1. The deflected axis of the beam is called *elastic curve*, which bends into an arc of a circle with radius of curvature R as shown in Fig. 2.1. The elastic curve is very flat and its slope at any point is very small.

$$\tan \theta = \frac{dy}{dx}$$

$$\therefore \quad \theta = \frac{dy}{dx} \qquad \ldots (2.1)$$

$$\therefore \quad \frac{d\theta}{dx} = \frac{d^2y}{dx^2} \qquad \ldots (2.2)$$

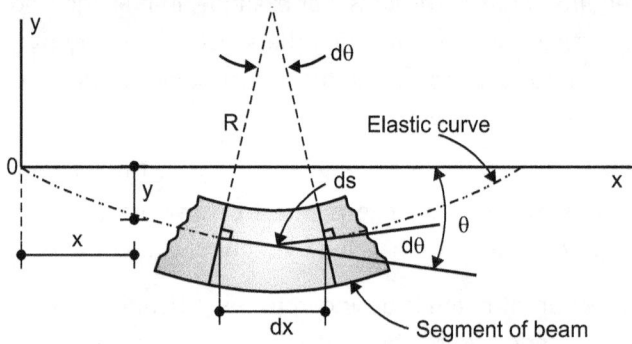

Fig. 2.1

From Fig. 2.1,

$$ds = R\, d\theta \qquad \ldots (2.3)$$

where, R = radius of curvature for arc of length ds

$$\therefore \quad \frac{1}{R} = \frac{d\theta}{ds} \approx \frac{d\theta}{dx} = \frac{d^2y}{dx^2} \qquad \ldots (2.4)$$

In deriving the flexure formula, we have obtained

$$\frac{1}{R} = \frac{M}{EI} \qquad \ldots (2.5)$$

Equating values of $\frac{1}{R}$ from equations (2.4) and (2.5), we get

$$EI \frac{d^2y}{dx^2} = M \qquad \ldots (2.6)$$

Equation (2.6) is known as differential equation of the elastic curve of a beam. The product EI is called *flexural rigidity* of the beam.

The exact value of $\frac{1}{R}$ is given by

$$\frac{1}{R} = \frac{\dfrac{d^2y}{dx^2}}{\left[1 + \left(\dfrac{dy}{dx}\right)^2\right]^{3/2}} \qquad \ldots (2.7)$$

However, $\frac{dy}{dx}$ being very small its square is still smaller compared to unity and hence neglected.

Assuming EI = constant along the length of beam and integrating equation (2.6), we get

$$EI \frac{dy}{dx} = \int M\, dx + C_1 \qquad \ldots (2.8)$$

Equation (2.8) is a slope equation, where M represents the bending moment equation in terms of x and C_1 is the constant of integration to be evaluated knowing the boundary conditions.

Integrating equation (2.8), we get

$$EIy = \int \int M dx + C_1 x + C_2 \qquad \ldots (2.9)$$

Equation (2.9) is a deflection equation, where C_2 is another constant of integration to be evaluated knowing the boundary conditions.

2.4 METHODS OF DISPLACEMENT ANALYSIS

Several methods are available for determining slopes and deflections of beams. Although based on the same principles, they differ in technique and their immediate objective. The three methods that are discussed in detail are :

(i) Macaulay's method
(ii) Moment area method and
(iii) Conjugate beam method.

2.5 MACAULAY'S METHOD

This is a convenient method of displacement analysis particularly when the beam is subjected to different loading conditions. In this method, single bending moment equation is written such that it becomes continuous for the entire length of beam inspite of the discontinuity of loading.

For example, consider a beam AB supported and loaded as shown in Fig. 2.2.

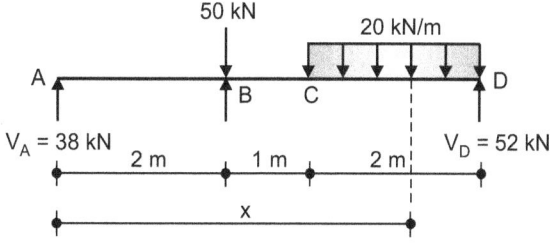

Fig. 2.2

Reactions V_A and V_D are obtained from statics as shown in Fig. 2.2.

Bending moment equations for different zones can be written as under;

$$M_{AB} = 38x$$
$$M_{BC} = 38x - 50(x-2)$$
$$M_{CD} = 38x - 50(x-2) - \frac{20(x-3)^2}{2}$$

It should be noted that bending moment equation of zone CD is valid for zones AB and BC also provided that the terms $(x-2)$ and $(x-3)^2$ are neglected for values of x less than 2 m and 3 m respectively. For the ease of working, the section shall be considered in the last zone and bending moment equation for it shall be written with vertical lines of division as shown

$$EI\frac{d^2y}{dx^2} = M_x = 38x \underbrace{\Big|}_{AB} -50(x-2) \underbrace{\Big|}_{BC} - \frac{20(x-3)^2}{2} \underbrace{}_{CD} \quad \text{... (a)}$$

The above equation is valid for the complete length of beam if we neglect the negative values of terms in brackets.

Thus, equation (a) is the general equation of bending moment for the beam considered.

Integrating equation (a) with respect to x, we get

$$EI \cdot \frac{dy}{dx} = 38\frac{x^2}{2} + C_1 \Big| -\frac{50(x-2)^2}{2} \Big| - \frac{20(x-3)^3}{6}$$

$$= 19x^2 + C_1 \Big| -25(x-2)^2 \Big| -3.33(x-3)^3 \quad \text{... (b)}$$

Equation (b) is general equation of slope for the beam considered. Integrating this equation further with respect to x, we get

$$EI \cdot y = \frac{19x^3}{3} + C_1 x + C_2 \Big| \frac{-25(x-2)^3}{3} \Big| - \frac{3.33(x-3)^4}{4}$$

$$= 6.33x^3 + C_1 x + C_2 \Big| -8.33(x-2)^3 \Big| - 0.83(x-3)^4 \quad \text{... (c)}$$

Equation (c) is general equation of deflection for the beam considered.

In equations (b) and (c) C_1, C_2 are constants of integrations which can be evaluated using boundary conditions. Then substituting different values of x and considering proper terms from equations (b) and (c) slope and deflection at desired sections can be obtained.

Following points must be noted regarding slope and deflection equations :
(i) Constants of integration C_1 and C_2 must be written before the first vertical line of division.
(ii) Terms in the bracket shall be integrated as a whole. For example,

$$\int (x-a)\,dx = \frac{(x-a)^2}{2}$$

2.6 BOUNDARY CONDITIONS

For the solution of beam deflection problems, in addition to the differential equations, boundary conditions must be prescribed. Several types of homogeneous boundary conditions are as shown in Table 2.1.

Table 2.1 : Boundary conditions

Support type	Displacements restrained	Displacements allowed
Fixed	$\cdot x, \cdot y, \cdot z$	NIL
Hinged	$\cdot x, \cdot y$	$\cdot z$
Horizontal Roller	$\cdot y$	$\cdot x, \cdot z$
Horizontal Guide	$\cdot y, \cdot z$	$\cdot x$

Note 1 : Δ_x ; Δ_y indicate translations in x and y directions respectively while θ_z represents rotation @ z-axis.

Note 2 : All the supports are assumed in x-y plane.

2.7 SIGN CONVENTIONS

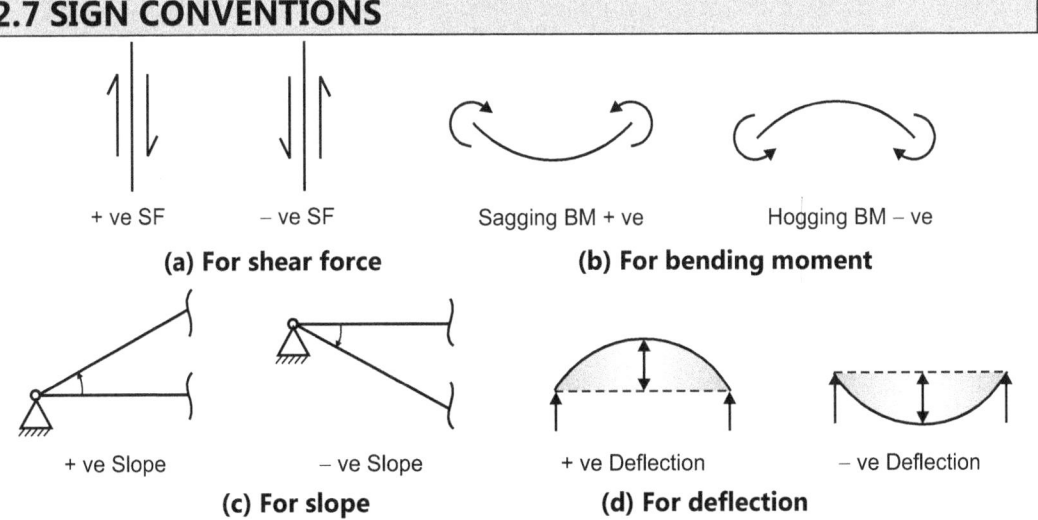

Fig. 2.3 : Sign conventions

2.8 BENDING MOMENT EQUATIONS FOR MACAULAY'S METHOD

Following are some of the variety of loadings that we generally come across for displacement analysis. Bending moment equations are written after each type of loading considering extreme left end of the beam as origin. Few cases of simply supported beams are discussed, while cantilever beams and beams with overhangs can be analysed based on same principles.

Case (i) : Beam with point loads :

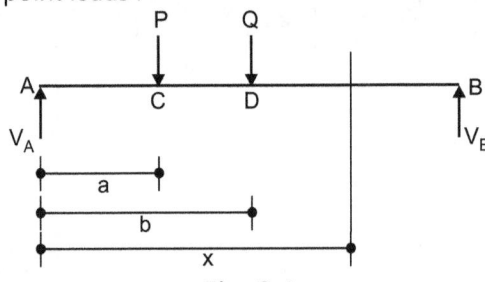

Fig. 2.4

$$EI\frac{d^2y}{dx^2} = V_A(x) \bigg| - P(x-a) \bigg| - Q(x-b)$$

Case (ii) : Beam with partial UDL and point load :

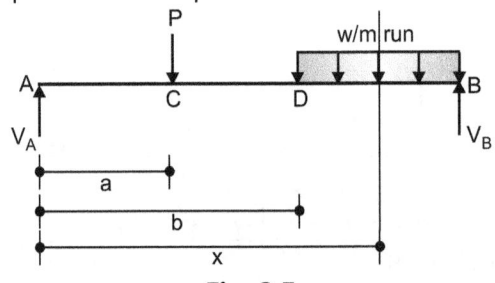

Fig. 2.5

$$EI \cdot \frac{d^2y}{dx^2} = V_A(x) \bigg| - P(x-a) \bigg| - \frac{w}{2}(x-b)^2$$

Case (iii) : Beam with partial UDL and point load :

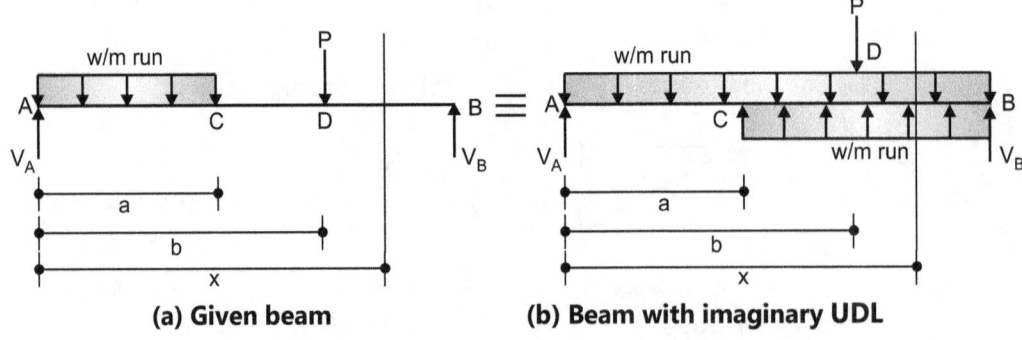

(a) Given beam   (b) Beam with imaginary UDL

Fig. 2.6

In case if partial UDL does not continue upto last zone i.e. DB as shown in Fig. 2.6 (a); an imaginary UDL is required to be considered to maintain the continuity of bending moment equation as shown in Fig. 2.6 (b). Bending moment equation for the above case now can be written as,

$$EI \cdot \frac{d^2y}{dx^2} = V_A(x) - \frac{w}{2}(x)^2 \bigg| + \frac{w}{2}(x-a)^2 \bigg| - P(x-b)$$

Case (iv) : Beam with point load and couple :

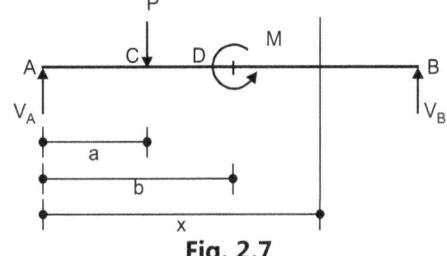

Fig. 2.7

$$EI \cdot \frac{d^2y}{dx^2} = V_A(x) \bigg| - P(x-a) \bigg| - M(x-b)^0$$

SOLVED PROBLEMS

Problem 2.1 : Derive expressions for slope and deflection at free end of cantilever beam carrying point load 'P' at free end.

Solution :

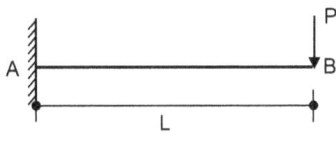

(a) Given beam   (b) FBD of beam

Fig. 2.8

(i) Reactions for equilibrium :
$\Sigma M_A = 0$; $M_A - PL = 0$ ∴ $M_A = PL$ (↺)
$\Sigma F_y = 0$; $V_A - P = 0$ ∴ $V_A = P$ (↑)
$\Sigma F_x = 0$; $H_A = 0$

(ii) Equations of BM; slope and deflection :
Consider section at a distance 'x' from 'A'.

$$EI\left(\frac{d^2y}{dx^2}\right) = P(x) - PL(x)^0 \qquad \ldots (I)$$

$$EI\left(\frac{dy}{dx}\right) = \frac{P}{2}(x)^2 - PL(x) + C_1 \qquad \ldots (II)$$

$$EI(y) = \frac{P}{6}(x)^3 - \frac{PL}{2}(x)^2 + C_1(x) + C_2 \qquad \ldots (III)$$

Note : For simplicity of equations; BM at a distance 'x' from 'A' can be written from RHS as

$$EI \frac{d^2y}{dx^2} = -P(L-x)$$

$$EI \left(\frac{dy}{dx}\right) = \frac{-P}{2}(L-x)^2 + C_1$$

$$EI(y) = \frac{-P}{6}(L-x)^3 + C_1(x) + C_2$$

However, now values of C_1 and C_2 will not be zero as obtained in the present analysis.

(iii) Boundary conditions :

At A i.e. $x = 0$; $\frac{dy}{dx} = 0$ put in equation (II) ∴ $C_1 = 0$

At A i.e. $x = 0$; $y = 0$ put in equation (III) ∴ $C_2 = 0$

Substituting C_1 and C_2, equations (II) and (III) are written as

$$EI\left(\frac{dy}{dx}\right) = \frac{P}{2}(x)^2 - PL(x) \qquad \ldots \text{(II)}$$

$$EI(y) = \frac{P}{6}(x)^3 - \frac{PL}{2}(x)^2 \qquad \ldots \text{(III)}$$

(iv) Slope and deflections :

For slope and deflection at free end put $x = L$ in equations (II) and (III) respectively.

$$EI\left(\frac{dy}{dx}\right)_B = \frac{P}{2}(L)^2 - PL(L) \qquad \therefore \left(\frac{dy}{dx}\right)_B = \frac{-PL^2}{2EI} = \frac{PL^2}{2EI} (\circlearrowleft)$$

$$EI(y)_B = \frac{P}{6}(L)^3 - \frac{PL}{2}(L)^2 \qquad \therefore (y)_B = \frac{-PL^3}{3EI} = \frac{PL^3}{3EI} (\downarrow)$$

Problem 2.2 : Derive the expressions for slope and deflection at free end of cantilever beam carrying UDL throughout the span.

Solution :

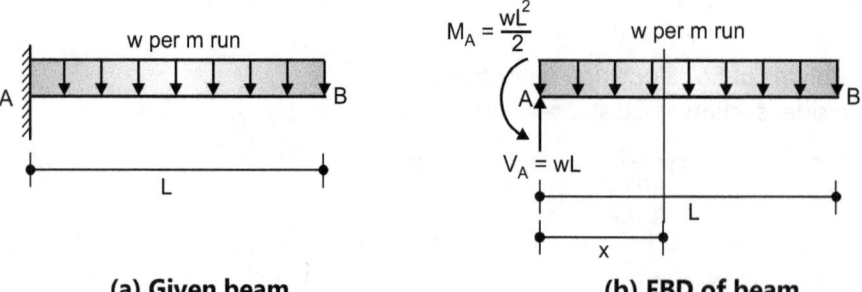

(a) Given beam   (b) FBD of beam

Fig. 2.9

(i) Reactions for equilibrium :

$\Sigma M_A = 0;$ $M_A - \dfrac{wL^2}{2} = 0$ $\therefore M_A = \dfrac{wL^2}{2}\ (\circlearrowleft)$

$\Sigma F_y = 0;$ $V_A - wL = 0$ $\therefore V_A = wL\ (\uparrow)$

$\Sigma F_x = 0;$ $H_A = 0$

(ii) Equations of BM; slope and deflection : Consider a section at a distance 'x' from 'A'.

$$EI\left(\dfrac{d^2y}{dx^2}\right) = wL(x) - \dfrac{wL^2}{2}(x)^0 - \dfrac{wx^2}{2} \qquad \ldots (I)$$

$$EI\left(\dfrac{dy}{dx}\right) = \dfrac{wL}{2}(x)^2 - \dfrac{wL^2}{2}(x) - \dfrac{w(x)^3}{6} + C_1 \qquad \ldots (II)$$

$$EI(y) = \dfrac{wL}{6}(x)^3 - \dfrac{wL^2}{4}(x)^2 - \dfrac{w(x)^4}{24} + C_1(x) + C_2 \qquad \ldots (III)$$

Note : For simplicity of equations; BM at a distance 'x' from 'A' can be written from R.H.S. as

$$EI\left(\dfrac{d^2y}{dx^2}\right) = -\dfrac{w}{2}(L-x)^2$$

$$EI\left(\dfrac{dy}{dx}\right) = -\dfrac{w}{6}(L-x)^3 + C_1$$

$$EI(y) = -\dfrac{w}{24}(L-x)^4 + C_1(x) + C_2$$

However, now values of C_1 and C_2 will not be zero as obtained in present analysis.

(iii) Boundary conditions :

At A i.e. $x = 0$; $\dfrac{dy}{dx} = 0$; put in equation (II) $\therefore$ $C_1 = 0$

At A i.e. $x = 0$; $y = 0$; put in equation (III) $\therefore$ $C_2 = 0$

Substituting values of C_1 and C_2; equations (II) and (III) are written as

$$EI\left(\dfrac{dy}{dx}\right) = \dfrac{wL}{2}(x)^2 - \dfrac{wL^2}{2}(x) - \dfrac{w}{6}(x)^3 \qquad \ldots (II)$$

$$EI(y) = \dfrac{wL}{6}(x)^3 - \dfrac{wL^2}{4}(x)^2 - \dfrac{w}{24}(x)^4 \qquad \ldots (III)$$

(iv) Slope and deflection :

For slope and deflection at free end; put $x = L$ in equations (II) and (III) respectively.

$$EI\left(\dfrac{dy}{dx}\right)_B = \dfrac{wL}{2}(L)^2 - \dfrac{wL^2}{2}(L) - \dfrac{w}{6}(L)^3$$

$\therefore$ $\left(\dfrac{dy}{dx}\right)_B = -\dfrac{wL^3}{6EI} = \dfrac{wL^3}{6EI}\ (\circlearrowleft)$

$$EI(y)_B = \dfrac{wL}{6}(L)^3 - \dfrac{wL^2}{4}(L)^2 - \dfrac{w}{24}(L)^4$$

$(y)_B = \dfrac{-wL^4}{8EI} = \dfrac{wL^4}{8EI}\ (\downarrow)$

Problem 2.3 : Derive expressions for slope and deflections at free end of cantilever beam carrying couple 'M' at free end.

Solution :

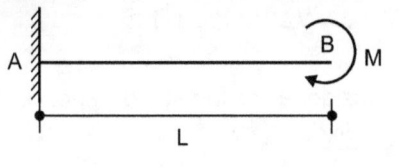
(a) Given beam

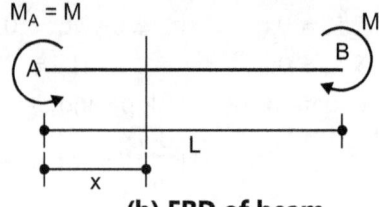
(b) FBD of beam

Fig. 2.10

(i) Reactions for equilibrium. $M_A = M$ (↺)

(ii) Equations of BM ; slope and deflection.

$$EI \left(\frac{d^2y}{dx^2}\right) = -M(x)^0 \quad \ldots (I)$$

$$EI \left(\frac{dy}{dx}\right) = -M(x) + C_1 \quad \ldots (II)$$

$$EI(y) = \frac{-M(x)^2}{2} + C_1(x) + C_2 \quad \ldots (III)$$

(iii) Boundary conditions.

At $x = 0$; $\frac{dy}{dx}$ and $y = 0$ ∴ $C_1 = C_2 = 0$

(iv) Slope and deflections.

Substituting $x = L$ in equations (II) and (III)

$$\left(\frac{dy}{dx}\right)_B = \frac{ML}{EI} \; (↺)$$

$$(y)_B = \frac{ML^2}{2EI} \; (\downarrow)$$

Problem 2.4 : Derive expression for slope and deflection at free end of cantilever shown in Fig. 2.11 (a).

Solution :

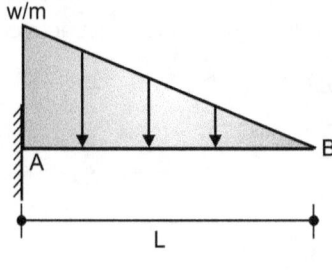
(a) Given beam

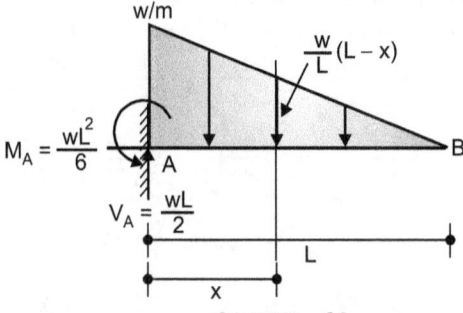
(b) FBD of beam

Fig. 2.11

(i) Reactions for equilibrium :

$\sum M_A = 0;$ $M_A - \frac{1}{2}(w \times L) \times \frac{1}{3}(L) = 0$ $\therefore$ $M_A = \frac{wL^2}{6}$ (↺)

$\sum F_y = 0;$ $V_A - \frac{1}{2}(w \times L) = 0$ $\therefore$ $V_A = \frac{wL}{2}$ (↑)

$\sum F_x = 0;$ $H_A = 0$

(ii) Equations of BM; slope and deflection :

Considering a section at a distance 'x' from 'A', intensity of load at this section $= \frac{w}{L}(L - x)$.

Note : BM equation is written from RHS for simplicity.

$$EI \left(\frac{d^2y}{dx^2}\right) = -\frac{1}{2}(L-x)\left[\frac{w}{L}(L-x)\right]\frac{(L-x)}{3}$$

$$= -\frac{w}{6L}[L-x]^3 \qquad \ldots (I)$$

$$EI \left(\frac{dy}{dx}\right) = \frac{-w}{24L}(L-x)^4 + C_1 \qquad \ldots (II)$$

$$EI (y) = \frac{-w}{120L}(L-x)^5 + C_1(x) + C_2 \qquad \ldots (III)$$

(iii) Boundary conditions :

At A i.e. $x = 0$; $\frac{dy}{dx} = 0$; put in equation (II)

$\therefore$ $C_1 = -\frac{wL^3}{24}$

At A i.e. $x = L$; $y = 0$ put in equation (III)

$\therefore$ $C_2 = \frac{wL^4}{120}$

Substituting values of C_1 and C_2, equations (II) and (III) are written as

$$EI \left(\frac{dy}{dx}\right) = -\frac{w}{24L}(L-x)^4 - \frac{wL^3}{24} \qquad \ldots (II)$$

$$EI (y) = -\frac{w}{120L}(L-x)^5 - \frac{wL^3}{24}(x) + \frac{wL^4}{120} \qquad \ldots (III)$$

(iv) Slope and deflections :

For slope and deflection at free end, put $x = L$ in equations (II) and (III) respectively.

$$EI \left(\frac{dy}{dx}\right)_B = \frac{-wL^3}{24}$$

$\therefore$ $\left(\frac{dy}{dx}\right)_B = \frac{wL^3}{24 EI}$ (↻)

$$EI\,(y)_B = \frac{-wL^3}{24}(L) + \frac{wL^4}{120}$$

$$\therefore \quad (y)_B = \frac{-wL^4}{30\,EI} = \frac{wL^4}{30\,EI}\,(\downarrow)$$

Special case : Find slope and deflection at free end of cantilever shown in Fig. 2.12.

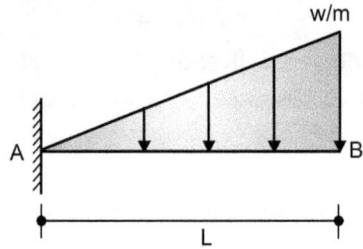

Fig. 2.12 : Given beam

Using principle of superposition.

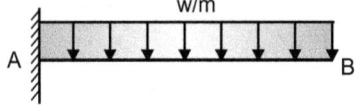

Fig. 2.13 : Beam with UDL **Fig. 2.14 : Beam with UVL**

$$\left(\frac{dy}{dx}\right)_B = -\frac{wL^3}{6\,EI} \qquad \left(\frac{dy}{dx}\right)_B = \frac{wL^3}{24\,EI}$$

$$(y)_B = -\frac{wL^4}{8\,EI} \qquad (y)_B = \frac{wL^4}{30\,EI}$$

$$\therefore \quad \text{For the given beam ;} \left(\frac{dy}{dx}\right)_B = \frac{-wL^3}{6\,EI} + \frac{wL^3}{24\,EI}$$

$$= \frac{-wL^3}{8\,EI} = \frac{wL^3}{8\,EI}\,(\circlearrowright)$$

$$(y)_B = \frac{-wL^4}{8\,EI} + \frac{wL^4}{30\,EI} = -\frac{11}{120}\frac{wL^4}{EI} = \frac{11}{120}\frac{wL^4}{EI}\,(\downarrow)$$

Special tricks for cantilever beam :

(i)

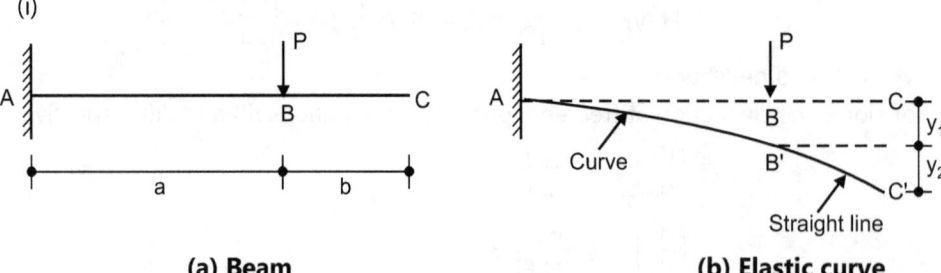

(a) Beam (b) Elastic curve

Fig. 2.15

Slope at B = $\dfrac{-Pa^2}{2EI}$

Deflection at B = $\dfrac{-Pa^3}{3EI}$

Slope at C = Slope at B = $\dfrac{-Pa^2}{2EI}$

Deflection at C = $y_1 + y_2$ = deflection at B + slope at B × L (BC)

$= \dfrac{-Pa^3}{3EI} - \dfrac{Pa^2}{2EI}(b)$

$= \dfrac{-P}{EI}\left(\dfrac{a^3}{3} + \dfrac{a^2 b}{2}\right)$

$= \dfrac{-Pa^2}{EI}\left(\dfrac{a}{3} + \dfrac{b}{2}\right)$

(ii)

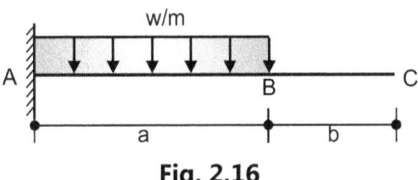

Fig. 2.16

∴ Slope at B = Slope at C = $-\dfrac{wa^3}{6EI}$

Deflection at B = $-\dfrac{wa^4}{8EI}$

Deflection at C = $-\dfrac{wa^4}{8EI} - \dfrac{wa^3}{6EI}(b)$

$= -\dfrac{wa^3}{EI}\left(\dfrac{a}{8} + \dfrac{b}{6}\right)$

(iii)

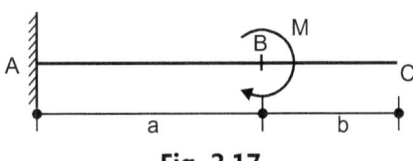

Fig. 2.17

Slope at B = Slope at C = $-\dfrac{Ma}{EI}$

Deflection at B = $-\dfrac{Ma^2}{2EI}$

Deflection at C $= -\dfrac{Ma^2}{2\,EI} - \dfrac{Ma}{EI}\,(b)$

$= -\dfrac{Ma}{EI}\left(\dfrac{a}{2} + b\right)$

Problem 2.5 : Find slope and deflection at 'C' for cantilever beam shown in Fig. 2.18.

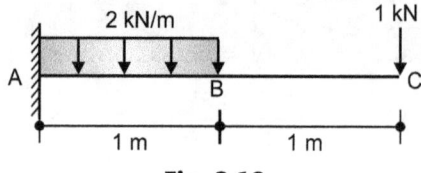

Fig. 2.18

Solution : Using principle of superposition and standard results.

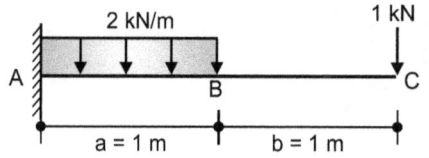

Fig. 2.19 : Beam with UDL   Fig. 2.20 : Beam with point load

$\left(\dfrac{dy}{dx}\right)_C = \dfrac{-wa^3}{6\,EI} = \dfrac{-2\,(1)^3}{6\,EI}$ $\left(\dfrac{dy}{dx}\right)_C = \dfrac{-PL^2}{2\,EI} = \dfrac{-1\,(2)^2}{2\,EI}$

$= \dfrac{-1}{3\,EI}$ $= \dfrac{-2}{EI}$

$(\because a + b = L = 2m)$

$(y)_C = \dfrac{-wa^3}{EI}\left(\dfrac{a}{8} + \dfrac{b}{6}\right)$ $(y)_C = \dfrac{-PL^3}{3\,EI} = \dfrac{-1 \times 2^3}{3\,EI}$

$= \dfrac{-2 \times 1^3}{EI}\left(\dfrac{1}{8} + \dfrac{1}{6}\right)$ $= \dfrac{-2.67}{EI}$

$= \dfrac{-0.583}{EI}$

∴   Slope at C $= \dfrac{-1}{EI}\left(\dfrac{1}{3} + 2\right) = \dfrac{-2.33}{EI} = \dfrac{2.33}{EI}\,(\circlearrowright)$

Deflection at C $= \dfrac{-1}{EI}(0.583 + 2.67)$

$= \dfrac{-3.25}{EI} = \dfrac{3.25}{EI}\,(\downarrow)$

Problem 2.6 : For the cantilever beam shown in Fig. 2.21, find the magnitude of couple 'M', so that deflection at free end is zero.

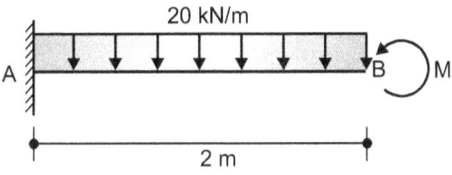

Fig. 2.21

Solution : Using principle of superposition and standard results,

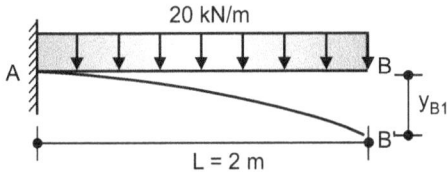

Fig. 2.22 : Beam with UDL

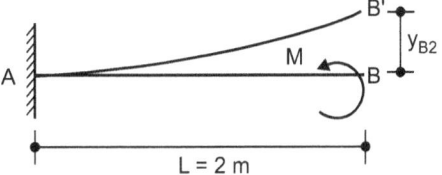

Fig. 2.23 : Beam with couple

$$y_{B_1} = \frac{-wL^4}{8\,EI} = \frac{-20\,(2)^4}{8\,EI}$$

$$= \frac{-40}{EI}$$

$$y_{B_2} = \frac{ML^2}{2\,EI} = \frac{M\,(2)^2}{2\,EI} = \frac{2M}{EI}$$

For deflection at free end, $y_B = 0$

$$y_{B_1} + y_{B_2} = \frac{-40}{EI} + \frac{2M}{EI} = 0$$

∴ $M = 20$ kN.m

Problem 2.7 : Find slope and deflection at free end of cantilever beam shown in Fig. 2.24 (a). If cross section of beam is 100 mm wide and 200 mm deep. Assume E = 11 GPa.

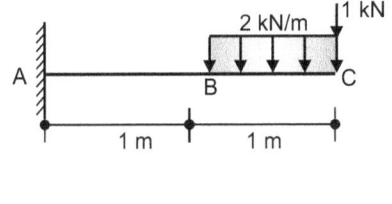

(a) Given beam

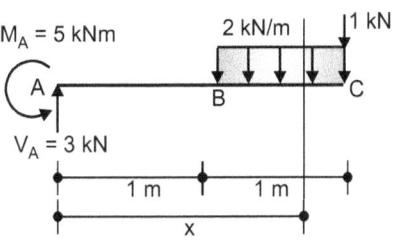

(b) FBD of beam

Fig. 2.24

Data : As shown in Fig. 2.24.
Required : Slope and deflection at C.
Concept : Consider 'A' as origin and section at a distance 'x' from A for BM equation.
Solution : (i) Reactions for equilibrium.

$\Sigma M_A = 0$; $M_A - 2 \times 1 \times 1.5 - 1 \times 2 = 0$ $\therefore M_A = 5$ kNm (↻)

$\Sigma F_y = 0$; $V_A - 2 \times 1 - 1 = 0$ $\therefore V_A = 3$ kN (↑)

$\Sigma F_x = 0$; $H_A = 0$

(ii) Equations of BM ; slope and deflection :

$$EI\left(\frac{d^2y}{dx^2}\right) = 3x - 5(x)^0 \Big| \frac{-2(x-1)^2}{2} \quad \ldots (I)$$

$$\underset{\text{AB}}{\longleftrightarrow}$$
$$\underset{\text{BC}}{\longleftrightarrow}$$

$$EI\left(\frac{dy}{dx}\right) = 1.5 x^2 - 5(x) + C_1 \Big| - 0.33(x-1)^3 \quad \ldots (II)$$

$$EI(y) = 0.5 x^3 - 2.5(x)^2 + C_1(x) + C_2 \Big| - 0.0825(x-1)^4 \quad \ldots (III)$$

(iii) Boundary conditions :

At A i.e. x = 0 ; $\frac{dy}{dx} = 0$ and y = 0

Substituting in equations (II) and (III)

$\therefore \quad C_1 = C_2 = 0$

$\therefore$ Equations (II) and (III) are written as ;

$$EI\left(\frac{dy}{dx}\right) = 1.5(x)^2 - 5(x) \Big| - 0.33(x-1)^3 \quad \ldots (II)$$

$$EI(y) = 0.5(x)^3 - 2.5(x)^2 \Big| - 0.0825(x-1)^4 \quad \ldots (III)$$

(iv) Slope and deflections :

For slope and deflection at free end, put x = 2 m in equations (II) and (III) respectively.

$$EI\left(\frac{dy}{dx}\right)_C = 1.5(2)^2 - 5(2) - 0.33(2-1)^3$$

$$\left(\frac{dy}{dx}\right)_C = \frac{-4.33}{EI}$$

$$EI(y)_C = 0.5(2)^3 - 2.5(2)^2 - 0.0825(2-1)^4$$

$$(y)_C = \frac{-6.0825}{EI}$$

$$I = \frac{bD^3}{12} = \frac{100 \times 200^3}{12} = 66.67 \times 10^6 \text{ mm}^4$$

$$E = 11 \text{ GPa}$$

$$\therefore \quad EI = 11 \times 66.67 \times 10^6 \text{ kNmm}^2$$

$$= 733.33 \text{ kNm}^2$$

$$\therefore \quad \left(\frac{dy}{dx}\right)_C = \frac{-4.33}{733.33} = 2.9 \times 10^{-3} \text{ rad } (\circlearrowright)$$

$$(y)_C = \frac{-6.0825}{733.33} \times 10^3 = 8.29 \text{ mm } (\downarrow)$$

Problem 2.8 : Find slope and deflections at 'C' and 'D' of cantilever beam shown in Fig. 2.25 (a) in terms of EI.

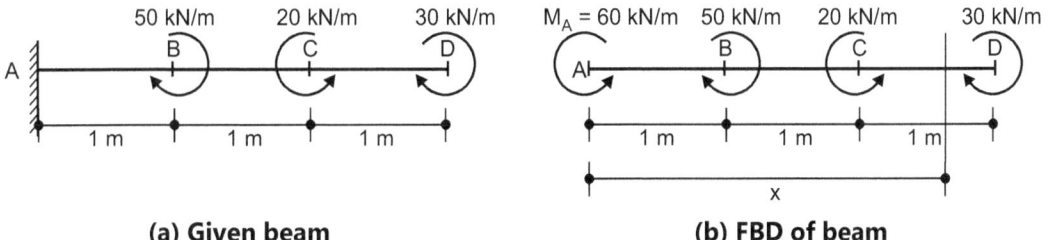

(a) Given beam **(b) FBD of beam**

Fig. 2.25

Data : As shown in Fig. 2.25
Required : Slope and deflection at free end ds and C.
Concept : Consider 'A' as origin and section at a distance 'x' from 'A' in zone CD for BM equation.
Solution : (i) Reactions for equilibrium :

$\Sigma M_A = 0$; $\quad M_A - 50 + 20 - 30 = 0 \quad \therefore \quad M_A = 60 \text{ kNm } (\uparrow)$
$\Sigma F_y = 0$; $\quad V_A = 0$
$\Sigma F_x = 0$; $\quad H_A = 0$

(ii) Equations of BM; slope and deflection :

$$EI\left(\frac{d^2y}{dx^2}\right) = -60(x)^0 \,\big|\, +50(x-1)^0 \,\big|\, -20(x-2)^0 \quad \ldots \text{(I)}$$

$$\underset{\text{AB}}{\longleftrightarrow} \quad \underset{\text{BC}}{\longleftrightarrow} \quad \underset{\text{CD}}{\longleftrightarrow}$$

$$EI\left(\frac{dy}{dx}\right) = -60(x) + C_1 \,\big|\, +50(x-1) \,\big|\, -20(x-2) \quad \ldots \text{(II)}$$

$$EI(y) = -30(x)^2 + C_1(x) + C_2 \,\big|\, +15(x-1)^2 \,\big|\, -10(x-2)^2 \quad \ldots \text{(III)}$$

(iii) Boundary conditions :

At A i.e. $x = 0$; $\frac{dy}{dx} = 0$ and $y = 0$, put in equations (II) and (III).

We get ; $C_1 = C_2 = 0$ ∴ equations (II) and (III) are written as

$$EI\left(\frac{dy}{dx}\right) = -60(x) \mid +50(x-1) \mid -20(x-2) \qquad \ldots (II)$$

$$EI(y) = -30(x)^2 \mid +25(x-1)^2 \mid -10(x-2)^2 \qquad \ldots (III)$$

(iv) Slope and deflections :

For slope and deflection at C; put $x = 2$ m in equations (II) and (III) respectively.

$$EI\left(\frac{dy}{dx}\right)_C = -60(2) + 50(2-1) \quad \therefore \quad \left(\frac{dy}{dx}\right)_C = \frac{-70}{EI} = \frac{70}{EI}\ (\circlearrowright)$$

$$EI(y)_C = -30(2)^2 + 25(2-1)^2 \quad \therefore \quad (y)_C = \frac{-95}{EI} = \frac{95}{EI}\ (\downarrow)$$

For slope and deflection at D ; put $x = 3$ m in equations (II) and (III) respectively.

$$EI\left(\frac{dy}{dx}\right)_D = -60(3) + 50(3-1) - 20(3-2)$$

∴ $$\left(\frac{dy}{dx}\right)_D = \frac{-100}{EI} = \frac{100}{EI}\ (\circlearrowright)$$

$$EI(y)_D = -30(3)^2 + 15(3-1)^2 - 10(3-2)^2$$

∴ $$(y)_D = \frac{-180}{EI} = \frac{180}{EI}\ (\downarrow)$$

Problem 2.9 : Derive the expression for slope at supports, deflection under the load and maximum deflection for the beam shown in Fig. 2.26.

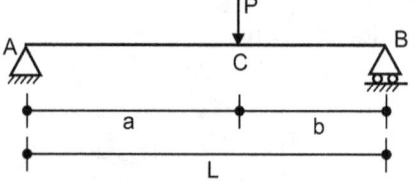

Fig. 2.26 : Given beam

Data   : As shown in Fig. 2.26.
Required : Slopes at supports ; deflection under load and maximum deflection.
Concept : (i) Consider 'A' as origin and section at a distance 'x' from 'A' in zone CB for BM equation.

(ii) At a section of maximum deflection, slope is zero hence to locate the section of maximum deflection; slope equation for the assumed zone is equated to zero. The zone of maximum deflection shall be decided by inspection. As in the present case assuming a > b; maximum deflection will occur in zone AC.

Solution : (i) Reactions for equilibrium :

$\sum M_A = 0$; $\quad V_B \times L - P \times a = 0 \quad \therefore V_B = \dfrac{Pa}{L}(\uparrow)$

$\sum F_y = 0$; $\quad V_A + V_B - P = 0 \quad \therefore V_A = P - \dfrac{Pa}{L} = \dfrac{Pb}{L}(\uparrow)$

$\sum F_x = 0$; $\quad H_A = 0$

FBD of beam is as shown in Fig. 2.27.

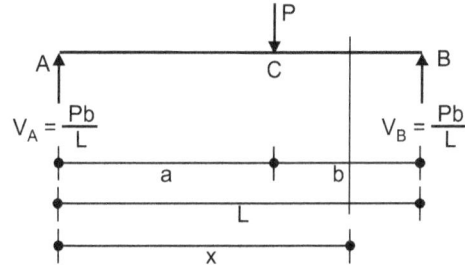

Fig. 2.27 : FBD of beam

(ii) Equations for BM; slope and deflection :

$$EI\left(\dfrac{d^2y}{dx^2}\right) = \dfrac{Pb}{L}(x) \left| - P(x-a) \right. \quad \ldots (I)$$

$\qquad\qquad\qquad\qquad |\!\leftarrow\! AC \!\rightarrow\!|$
$\qquad\qquad\qquad|\!\leftarrow\!\qquad CB \qquad\!\rightarrow\!|$

$$EI\left(\dfrac{dy}{dx}\right) = \dfrac{Pb}{2L}(x)^2 + C_1 \left| \dfrac{-P(x-a)^2}{2} \right. \quad \ldots (II)$$

$$EI(y) = \dfrac{Pb}{6L}(x)^3 + C_1(x) + C_2 \left| \dfrac{-P(x-a)^3}{6} \right. \quad \ldots (III)$$

(iii) Boundary conditions :

At 'A' i.e. $x = 0$; $y = 0$ put in equation (III) $\quad \therefore C_2 = 0$

At 'B' i.e. $x = L$; $y = 0$ put in equation (III)

$$0 = \dfrac{Pb}{6L}(L)^3 + C_1(L) + C_2 - \dfrac{P}{6}(L-a)^3$$

$\therefore \qquad 0 = \dfrac{Pb}{6}(L)^2 - L\, C_1 - \dfrac{Pb^3}{6}$

$\therefore \qquad C_1 = \dfrac{-Pb}{6L}(L^2 - b^2)$

Substituting values of C_1 and C_2, equations, (II) and (III) are written as ;

$$EI\left(\dfrac{dy}{dx}\right) = \dfrac{Pb}{2L}(x)^2 - \dfrac{Pb}{6L}(L^2 - b^2) \left| - \dfrac{P}{2}(x-a)^2 \right. \quad \ldots (II)$$

$$EI(y) = \dfrac{Pb}{6L}(x)^3 - \dfrac{Pb}{6L}(L^2 - b^2)(x) \left| - \dfrac{P}{6}(x-a)^3 \right. \quad \ldots (III)$$

(iv) Slope and deflections :

For slopes at A and B; put $x = 0$ and $x = L$ in equation (II) respectively.

$$EI \left(\frac{dy}{dx}\right)_A = -\frac{Pb(L^2 - b^2)}{6L}$$

$$\therefore \left(\frac{dy}{dx}\right)_A = \frac{Pb}{6EIL}(L^2 - b^2) \; (\circlearrowright) \qquad \ldots (E_1)$$

$$\therefore EI \left(\frac{dy}{dx}\right)_B = \frac{Pb}{2L}(L)^2 - \frac{Pb}{6L}(L^2 - b^2) - \frac{P}{2}(L-a)^2$$

$$= \frac{Pb}{2}(L) - \frac{Pb}{6L}(L^2 - b^2) - \frac{P}{2}(b)^2$$

$$= \frac{Pb}{6L}[2L^2 + b^2 - 3Lb]$$

$$= \frac{P(L-a)}{6L}[2L^2 - L^2 - 2La + a^2 - 3L^2 + 3La] \qquad (\because b = L - a)$$

$$= \frac{P(L-a)}{6L}[La + a^2]$$

$$= \frac{Pa}{6L}[L^2 - a^2]$$

$$\therefore \left(\frac{dy}{dx}\right)_B = \frac{P \cdot a}{6EIL}(L^2 - a^2) \; (\circlearrowright) \qquad \ldots (E_2)$$

For deflection under load; put $x = a$ in equation (III)

$$EI(y)_C = \frac{Pb}{6L}(a)^3 - \frac{Pb}{6L}(L^2 - b^2) a$$

$$= -\frac{Pab}{6L}(L^2 - b^2 - a^2)$$

$$= -\frac{Pab}{6L}[a^2 + b^2 + 2ab - b^2 - a^2] \qquad (\because a + b = L)$$

$$= -\frac{Pa^2 b^2}{3L}$$

$$\therefore y_C = \frac{Pa^2 b^2}{3EIL} (\downarrow) \qquad \ldots (E_3)$$

For maximum deflection; equating slope equation for zone 'AC' to zero.

$$0 = \frac{Pb}{2L}(x)^2 - \frac{Pb}{6L}(L^2 - b^2)$$

$$\therefore x^2 = \frac{L^2 - b^2}{3}$$

$$\therefore x = \sqrt{\frac{L^2 - b^2}{3}} \qquad \ldots (E_4)$$

Put in equation (III)

$$EI(y)_{max} = \frac{Pb}{6L}\left[\sqrt{\frac{L^2-b^2}{3}}\right]^2 - \frac{Pb}{6L}(L^2-b^2)\left[\sqrt{\frac{L^2-b^2}{3}}\right]$$

$$= \frac{-Pb}{6L}(L^2-b^2)^{3/2}\left[\frac{1}{\sqrt{3}} - \frac{1}{3^{3/2}}\right]$$

$$= \frac{-Pb}{6L}(L^2-b^2)^{3/2}\left(\frac{2\sqrt{3}}{9}\right)$$

$$= \frac{-Pb(L^2-b^2)^{3/2}}{9\sqrt{3}\cdot L}$$

$$\therefore \quad y_{max} = \frac{Pb(L^2-b^2)^{3/2}}{9\sqrt{3}\,EIL}(\downarrow) \qquad \ldots (E_5)$$

Special case 1 : For simply supported beam carrying point load 'P' at centre, find slope at supports and maximum deflection.

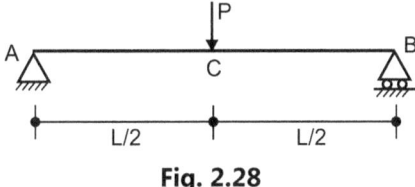

Fig. 2.28

For slope at supports using equations (E_1) and (E_2) and substituting $a = b = \dfrac{L}{2}$

By symmetry,

$$-\left(\frac{dy}{dx}\right)_A = \left(\frac{dy}{dx}\right)_B = \frac{PL^2}{16\,EI} \qquad \ldots (E_6)$$

Also, maximum deflection occurs at centre i.e.; under point load. Using equation (E_3) and substituting $a = b = \dfrac{L}{2}$

$$y_{max} = \frac{PL^3}{48\,EI}(\downarrow) \qquad \ldots (E_7)$$

Special case 2 : For the beam shown in Fig. 2.29 (a), find 'a' in terms of 'L' such that central deflection is same as that of deflection at free ends.

$$\text{Deflection at centre} = \frac{PL^3}{48\,EI} \qquad \ldots (I)$$

Deflection at ends A/E = Slope at support × Length of overhang

$$= \frac{PL^2}{16\,EI}(a) \qquad \ldots (II)$$

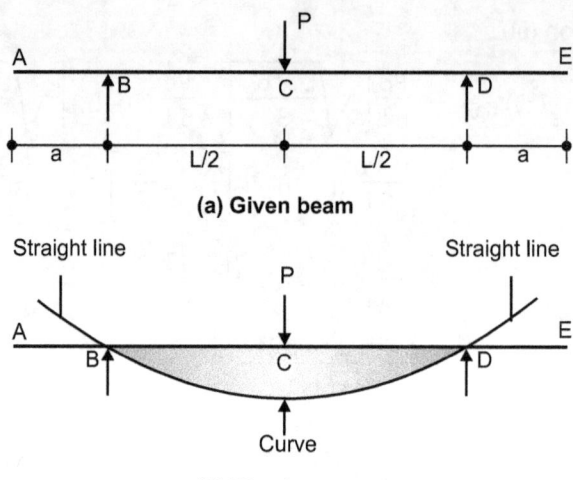

Fig. 2.29

Equating equations (I) and (II),

$$\frac{PL^3}{48\,EI} = \frac{PL^2}{16\,EI}(a)$$

$$a = \frac{L}{3}$$

Thus, for $a = \frac{L}{3}$, deflection at ends = midspan deflection.

Problem 2.10 : Derive the expressions for slope at supports and maximum deflection for the simply supported beam carrying UDL throughout the span.

Solution :

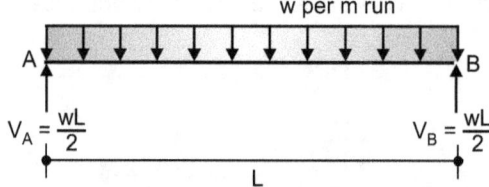

Fig. 2.30 : FBD of beam

Let;   w = Intensity of UDL

             L = Span of the beam

(i) Reactions for equilibrium :

$$V_A = V_B = \frac{wL}{2}\,(\uparrow) \qquad (\because \text{symmetry})$$

(ii) Equations of BM; slope and deflection :

$$EI\left(\frac{d^2y}{dx^2}\right) = \frac{wL}{2}(x) - \frac{w(x)^2}{2} \quad \ldots (I)$$

$$EI\left(\frac{dy}{dx}\right) = \frac{wL}{4}(x)^2 - \frac{w}{6}(x)^3 + C_1 \quad \ldots (II)$$

$$EI(y) = \frac{wL}{12}(x)^3 - \frac{w}{24}(x)^4 + C_1(x) + C_2 \quad \ldots (III)$$

(iii) Boundary conditions :
At A i.e. $x = 0$; $y = 0$ put in equation (III) $\therefore C_2 = 0$
At B i.e. $x = L$; $y = 0$ put in equation (III)

$$0 = \frac{wL}{12}(L)^3 - \frac{w(L)^4}{24} + C_1(L)$$

$$\therefore \quad C_1 = -\frac{wL^3}{24}$$

Substituting values of C_1 and C_2, equations (II) and (III) are written as

$$EI\left(\frac{dy}{dx}\right) = \frac{wL}{4}(x)^2 - \frac{w}{6}(x)^3 - \frac{wL^3}{24} \quad \ldots (II)$$

$$EI(y) = \frac{wL}{12}(x)^3 - \frac{w}{24}(x)^4 - \frac{wL^3}{24}(x) \quad \ldots (II)$$

(iv) Slope and deflections :
For slope at support A put $x = 0$ in equation (II).

$$EI\left(\frac{dy}{dx}\right)_A = -\frac{wL^3}{24} \quad \therefore \left(\frac{dy}{dx}\right)_A = \frac{wL^3}{24\,EI}\ (\circlearrowright)$$

$$\left(\frac{dy}{dx}\right)_B = \frac{wL^3}{24\,EI}\ (\circlearrowleft)$$

Maximum deflection will occur at midspan due to symmetry ; put $x = \frac{L}{2}$ in equation (III).

$$EI(y)_{max} = \frac{wL}{12}\left(\frac{L}{2}\right)^3 - \frac{w}{24}\left(\frac{L}{2}\right)^4 - \frac{wL^3}{24}\left(\frac{L}{2}\right)$$

$$\therefore \quad y_{max} = -\frac{5}{384} \cdot \frac{wL^4}{EI}$$

Problem 2.11 : Derive the expressions for slope at supports and deflection at point of application of couple for the beam shown in Fig. 2.31.

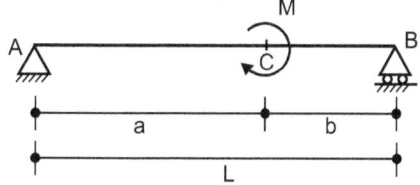

Fig. 2.31 : Given beam

Data : As shown in Fig. 2.31.

Required : Slope at supports and deflection at 'C'.

Concept : Consider 'A' as origin and section at a distance 'x' from 'A' in zone CB for BM equation.

Solution : (i) Reactions for equilibrium.

$\sum M_A = 0;$ $\quad V_B \times L - M = 0$ $\quad \therefore \quad V_B = \dfrac{M}{L} (\uparrow)$

$\sum F_y = 0;$ $\quad V_A + V_B = 0$ $\quad \therefore \quad V_A = \dfrac{M}{L} (\downarrow)$

FBD of beam is as shown in Fig. 2.32.

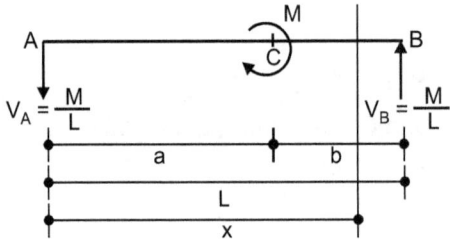

Fig. 2.32 : FBD of beam

(ii) Equation of BM; slope and deflection :

$$EI\left(\dfrac{d^2y}{dx^2}\right) = -\dfrac{M}{L}(x) + M(x-a)^0 \qquad \ldots (I)$$

$$\underbrace{}_{AC}$$
$$\underbrace{}_{CB}$$

$$EI\left(\dfrac{dy}{dx}\right) = -\dfrac{M}{2L}(x)^2 + C_1 \bigg| + M(x-a) \qquad \ldots (II)$$

$$EI(y) = -\dfrac{M}{6L}(x)^3 + C_1(x) + C_2 \bigg| + \dfrac{M}{2}(x-a)^2 \qquad \ldots (III)$$

(iii) Boundary conditions :

At A i.e. $x = 0; y = 0$ put in equation (III) $\therefore C_2 = 0$

At B i.e. $x = L; y = 0$ put in equation (III)

$$0 = -\dfrac{M}{6L}(L)^3 + L \cdot C_1 + \dfrac{M}{2}(L-a)^2$$

$\therefore \qquad C_1 = -\dfrac{M}{6L}(2L^2 - 6La + 3a^2)$

Substituting values of C_1 and C_2, equations (II) and (III) can be written as

$$EI\left(\frac{dy}{dx}\right) = -\frac{M}{2L}(x)^2 - \frac{M}{6L}(2L^2 - 6La + 3a^2) \Bigg| + M(x-a) \qquad \ldots \text{(II)}$$

$$EI(y) = -\frac{M}{6L}(x)^3 - \frac{M}{6L}(2L^2 - 6La + 3a^2)x \Bigg| + \frac{M}{2}(x-a)^2 \qquad \ldots \text{(III)}$$

(iv) Slope and deflections :

For slope at 'A' put $x = 0$ in equation (II).

$$EI\left(\frac{dy}{dx}\right)_A = -\frac{M}{2L}(0) - \frac{M}{6L}(2L^2 - 6La + 3a^2)$$

$$\therefore \left(\frac{dy}{dx}\right)_A = -\frac{M}{6\,EIL}(2L^2 - 6La + 3a^2) \qquad \ldots (E_1)$$

For slope at 'B' put $x = L$ in equation (II).

$$EI\left(\frac{dy}{dx}\right)_B = -\frac{M}{2L}(L)^2 - \frac{M}{6L}(2L^2 - 6La + 3a^2) + M(L-a)$$

$$= -\frac{M}{6L}(3L^2 + 2L^2 - 6La + 3a^2 - 6L^2 + 6La)$$

$$= -\frac{M}{6L}(3a^2 - L^2)$$

$$\therefore \left(\frac{dy}{dx}\right)_B = -\frac{M}{6\,EIL}(3a^2 - L^2) \qquad \ldots (E_2)$$

For deflection at C; put $x = a$ in equation (III).

$$EI(y_C) = -\frac{M}{6L}(a)^3 - \frac{M}{6L}(2L^2 - 6La + 3a^2)a$$

$$= -\frac{Ma}{6L}[a^2 + 2L^2 - 6La + 3a^2]$$

$$= -\frac{Ma}{3L}(L-a)(L-2a)$$

$$\therefore y_C = -\frac{Ma}{3\,EIL}(L-a)(L-2a) \qquad \ldots (E_3)$$

Special case : Find slope at supports and deflection at point of application of couple for simply supported beam carrying couple 'M' at centre.

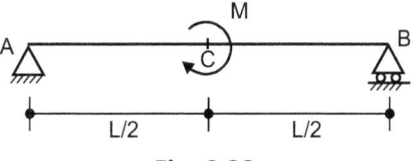

Fig. 2.33

For slope ; put $a = \dfrac{L}{2}$ in equation (E_1) or (E_2).

$$\left(\dfrac{dy}{dx}\right)_A = \left(\dfrac{dy}{dx}\right)_B = \dfrac{ML}{24\,EI}\,(\circlearrowleft)$$

For deflection, put $a = \dfrac{L}{2}$ in equation (E_3)

$$(y)_C = 0$$

Problem 2.12 : Find slope at supports, central and maximum deflection for the beam shown in Fig. 2.34 (a).

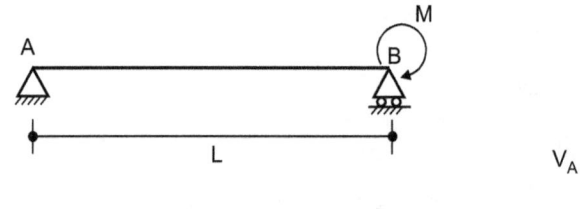

(a) Given beam (b) FBD of beam

Fig. 2.34

Data : As shown in Fig. 2.34 (a).
Required : Slope at supports and maximum deflection.
Concept : Consider 'A' as origin and a section at a distance 'x' from 'A' for BM equation.
Solution : (i) Reactions for equilibrium :

$\Sigma M_A = 0;$ $V_B \times L - M = 0$ $\therefore$ $V_B = \dfrac{M}{L}\,(\uparrow)$

$\Sigma F_y = 0;$ $V_A + V_B = 0$ $\therefore$ $V_A = \dfrac{M}{L}\,(\downarrow)$

$\Sigma F_x = 0;$ $H_A = 0$

FBD of beam is as shown in Fig. 2.34 (b).

(ii) Equations of BM; slope and deflection :

$$EI\left(\dfrac{d^2y}{dx^2}\right) = -\dfrac{M}{L}(x) \qquad \ldots (I)$$

$$EI\left(\dfrac{dy}{dx}\right) = -\dfrac{M}{2L}(x)^2 + C_1 \qquad \ldots (II)$$

$$EI\,(y) = -\dfrac{M}{6L}(x)^3 + C_1 x + C_2 \qquad \ldots (III)$$

(iii) Boundary conditions :
At A ; x = 0 ; y = 0 put in equation (III) $\therefore$ $C_2 = 0$
At B ; x = L ; y = 0 put in equation (III)

$$0 = -\frac{M}{6L}(L)^3 + L \cdot C_1$$

$$\therefore \quad C_1 = \frac{ML}{6}$$

Substituting values of C_1 and C_2, equations (II) and (III) can be written as

$$EI\left(\frac{dy}{dx}\right) = -\frac{M}{2L}(x)^2 + \frac{ML}{6} \qquad \ldots \text{(II)}$$

$$EI(y) = -\frac{M}{6L}(x)^3 + \frac{ML}{6}(x) \qquad \ldots \text{(III)}$$

(iv) Slope and deflections :

For slope at A; put $x = 0$ in equation (II).

$$EI\left(\frac{dy}{dx}\right)_A = \frac{ML}{6} \quad \therefore \left(\frac{dy}{dx}\right)_A = \frac{ML}{6EI} \, (\circlearrowleft)$$

For slope at B ; put $x = L$ in equation (II).

$$EI\left(\frac{dy}{dx}\right)_B = -\frac{M}{2L}(L)^2 + \frac{ML}{6}$$

$$\therefore \quad \left(\frac{dy}{dx}\right)_B = -\frac{ML}{3EI} = \frac{ML}{3EI} \, (\circlearrowleft)$$

For deflection at centre, put $x = \frac{L}{2}$ in equation (III).

$$EI(y)_{centre} = -\frac{M}{6L}\left(\frac{L}{2}\right)^3 + \frac{ML}{6}\left(\frac{L}{2}\right)$$

$$= -\frac{ML^2}{48} + \frac{ML^2}{12}$$

$$\therefore \quad y_{centre} = \frac{ML^2}{16EI} \, (\uparrow)$$

For maximum deflection equating slope equation to zero.

$$0 = -\frac{M}{2L}(x)^2 + \frac{ML}{6}$$

$$\therefore \quad x = \left(\sqrt{\frac{1}{3}}\right)L$$

Put in equation (III).

$$EI(y)_{max} = -\frac{M}{6L}\left(\sqrt{\frac{1}{3}}L\right)^3 + \frac{ML}{6}\left(\sqrt{\frac{1}{3}} \cdot L\right)$$

$$= (-0.032 + 0.0962)\,ML^2$$

$$= 0.0642\,ML^2$$

$$\therefore \quad y_{max} = 0.0642\,\frac{ML^2}{EI} \, (\uparrow)$$

Special case : Find slope at supports for the beam loaded as shown in Fig. 2.35.

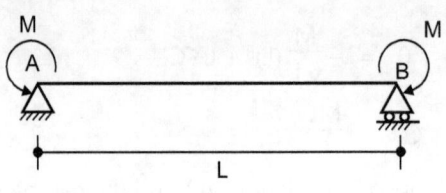

Fig. 2.35

Using principle of superposition.

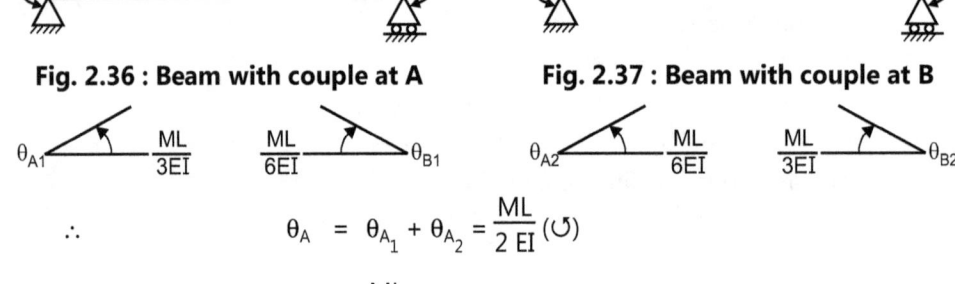

Fig. 2.36 : Beam with couple at A   Fig. 2.37 : Beam with couple at B

$\theta_{A_1} \quad \dfrac{ML}{3EI} \quad \dfrac{ML}{6EI} \quad \theta_{B_1}$ $\theta_{A_2} \quad \dfrac{ML}{6EI} \quad \dfrac{ML}{3EI} \quad \theta_{B_2}$

$$\therefore \quad \theta_A = \theta_{A_1} + \theta_{A_2} = \dfrac{ML}{2EI} \ (\circlearrowleft)$$

Similarly $\quad \theta_B = \dfrac{ML}{2EI} \ (\circlearrowleft)$

Note : Maximum deflection for this case occurs at centre and is given by $\dfrac{ML^2}{8EI} (\uparrow)$.

Problem 2.13 : Find slope at supports and deflection at centre for the beam shown in Fig. 2.38.

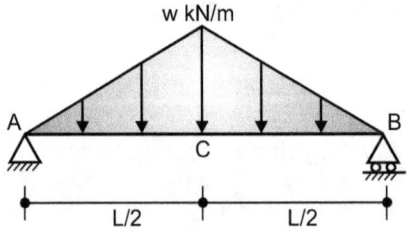

Fig. 2.38 : Given beam

Data   : As shown in Fig. 2.38.
Required : Slope at supports and deflection at centre.
Concept : By considering section at a distance 'x' from 'A' in zone 'CB', BM equation will be complicated. Hence, consider section in zone AC and make use of symmetry.
Solution : (i) Reactions for equilibrium.

$$V_A = V_B = \dfrac{wL}{4} (\uparrow)$$

FBD of beam is as shown in Fig. 2.39.

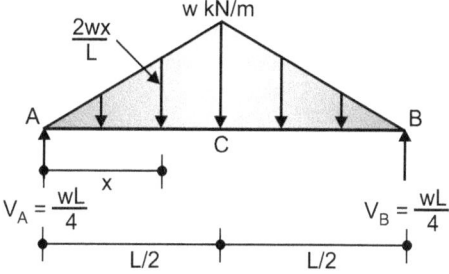

Fig. 2.39 : FBD of beam

(ii) Equation of BM; slope and deflection :

Intensity of load at a distance 'x' from 'A' = $\dfrac{2wx}{L}$

$\therefore \quad EI\left(\dfrac{d^2y}{dx^2}\right) = \dfrac{wL}{4}(x) - \dfrac{1}{2}(x)\dfrac{2wx}{L}\left(\dfrac{x}{3}\right)$ $\left(\because 0 \leq x \leq \dfrac{L}{2}\right)$

$= \dfrac{wL}{4}(x) - \dfrac{wx^3}{3L}$ ... (I)

$\overset{\longmapsto}{AC}$

$EI\left(\dfrac{dy}{dx}\right) = \dfrac{wL}{8}(x)^2 - \dfrac{w}{12L}(x)^4 + C_1$ ... (II)

$EI(y) = \dfrac{wL}{24}(x)^3 - \dfrac{w}{60L}(x)^5 + C_1(x) + C_2$ ... (III)

(iii) Boundary conditions :

At A i.e. $x = 0$; $y = 0$ put in equation (II) $\therefore C_2 = 0$

Due to symmetry, maximum deflection occurs at centre.

$\therefore$ At C i.e. $x = \dfrac{L}{2}$; $\dfrac{dy}{dx} = 0$ put in equation (II)

$0 = \dfrac{wL}{8}\left(\dfrac{L}{2}\right)^2 - \dfrac{w}{12L}\left(\dfrac{L}{2}\right)^4 + C_1$

$C_1 = \dfrac{-5}{192}wL^3$

Note : Condition of $x = L$; $y = 0$ cannot be employed because BM equation is applicable only for zone AC.

Substituting values of C_1 and C_2, equations (II) and (III) are written as

$EI\left(\dfrac{dy}{dx}\right) = \dfrac{wL}{8}(x)^2 - \dfrac{w}{12L}(x)^4 - \dfrac{5}{192}wL^3$ ... (II)

$EI(y) = \dfrac{wL}{24}(x)^3 - \dfrac{w}{60L}(x)^5 - \dfrac{5}{192}wL^3(x)$ ... (III)

(iv) Slope and deflections :

For slope at A ; put x = 0 in equation (II).

$$EI \left(\frac{dy}{dx}\right)_A = -\frac{5}{192} wL^3 \quad \therefore \quad \left(\frac{dy}{dx}\right)_A = \frac{5}{192} \frac{wL^3}{EI} \; (\circlearrowright)$$

By symmetry, $\left(\dfrac{dy}{dx}\right)_B = \dfrac{5 wL^3}{192 EI}$ $(\circlearrowleft)$

For deflection at 'C' ; put $x = \dfrac{L}{2}$ in equation (III).

$$EI (y)_C = \frac{wL}{24}\left(\frac{L}{2}\right)^3 - \frac{w}{60L}\left(\frac{L}{2}\right)^5 - \frac{5}{192} wL^3 \left(\frac{L}{2}\right)$$

$$\therefore \quad y_C = -\frac{wL^4}{120\, EI}$$

$$y_C = \frac{wL^4}{120\, EI} \; (\downarrow)$$

$$= y_{max}$$

Problem 2.14 : For the beam shown in Fig. 2.40, find slope at A, B, and C. Also find deflection at C; at centre of A, B and maximum deflection between A and B.

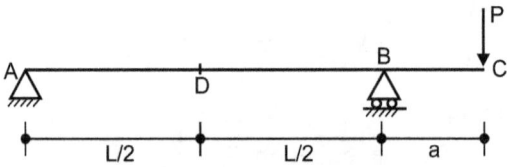

Fig. 2.40 : Given beam

Data : As shown in Fig. 2.40.

Required : Slope at A, B, C and deflection at D, C and maximum deflection between AB.

Concept : For slope and deflection at C ; we shall work from first principles. Slope at A, B; maximum deflection between AB and deflection at 'D' can be obtained by using standard results as illustrated.

Solution : (i) Reactions for equilibrium.

$\sum M_A = 0;$ $V_B \times L - P(L + a) = 0$ $\therefore$ $V_B = \dfrac{P}{L}(L + a) \; (\uparrow)$

$\sum F_y = 0;$ $V_A + V_B - P = 0$ $\therefore$ $V_A = \dfrac{Pa}{L} \; (\downarrow)$

$\sum F_x = 0;$ $H_A = 0$

FBD of beam is as shown in Fig. 2.41.

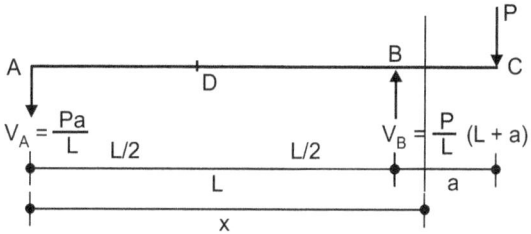

Fig. 2.41 : FBD of beam

(ii) Equation of BM; slope and deflection :

$$EI\left(\frac{d^2y}{dx^2}\right) = \underbrace{-\frac{Pa}{L}(x)}_{AB} \Big| \underbrace{+\frac{P}{L}(L+a)(x-L)}_{BC} \qquad ...(I)$$

$$EI\left(\frac{dy}{dx}\right) = -\frac{Pa}{2L}(x)^2 + C_1 \Big| + \frac{P(L+a)}{2L}(x-L)^2 \qquad ...(II)$$

$$EI(y) = -\frac{Pa}{6L}(x)^3 + C_1(x) + C_2 \Big| + \frac{P(L+a)}{6L}(x-L)^3 \qquad ...(III)$$

(iii) Boundary conditions :

At A i.e. $x = 0$; $y = 0$ put in equation (III) $\therefore C_2 = 0$

At B i.e. $x = L$; $y = 0$ put in equation (III)

$$0 = -\frac{Pa}{6L}(L)^3 + C_1(L) + \frac{P(L+a)}{6L}(L-L)^3$$

$$\therefore \quad C_1 = \frac{PaL}{6}$$

Substituting values of C_1 and C_2; equations (II) and (III) are written as

$$EI\left(\frac{dy}{dx}\right) = -\frac{Pa}{2L}(x)^2 + \frac{PaL}{6} \Big| + \frac{P}{2L}(L+a)(x-L)^2 \qquad ...(II)$$

$$EI(y) = -\frac{Pa}{6L}(x)^3 + \frac{PaL}{6}(x) \Big| + \frac{P}{6L}(L+a)(x-L)^3 \qquad ...(III)$$

(iv) Slope and deflection at 'C' :

Put $x = (L + a)$ in equations (II) and (III) respectively.

$$EI\left(\frac{dy}{dx}\right)_C = -\frac{Pa}{2L}(L+a)^2 + \frac{PaL}{6} + \frac{P}{2L}(L+a)(L+a-L)^2$$

$$\therefore \left(\frac{dy}{dx}\right)_C = -\frac{Pa}{6\,EI}(2L+3a) = \frac{Pa}{6\,EI}(2L+3a)\ (\circlearrowright)$$

$$EI\,(y)_C = -\frac{Pa}{6L}(L+a)^3 + \frac{PaL}{6}(L+a) + \frac{P}{6L}(L+a)(L+a-L)^3$$

$$y_C = -\frac{Pa^2}{3\,EI}(L+a) = \frac{Pa^2}{3\,EI}(L+a)\ (\downarrow)$$

(v) Use of standard results :

Load at C is transferred to B as force couple system as shown in Fig. 2.42.

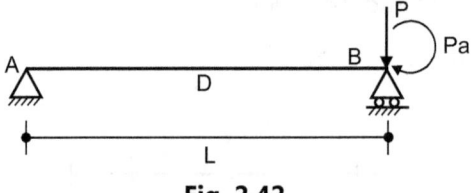

Fig. 2.42

Load P acting at B does not produce any slope or deflection for the beam. Hence, beam can be considered to have only couple at 'B' of magnitude M = Pa.

∴ Using equations derived for simply supported beam with couple acting at end of the beam,

$$\left(\frac{dy}{dx}\right)_A = \frac{ML}{6\,EI} = \frac{PaL}{6\,EI}\ (\circlearrowright)$$

$$\left(\frac{dy}{dx}\right)_B = \frac{ML}{3\,EI} = \frac{PaL}{3\,EI}\ (\circlearrowright)$$

$$y_D = \frac{ML^2}{16\,EI} = \frac{PaL^2}{16\,EI}\ (\uparrow)$$

Maximum deflection between AB occurs at $\left(\sqrt{\frac{1}{3}}\right)L$ from A and its magnitude is y_{max}.

$$= 0.0642\,\frac{ML^2}{EI}$$

$$= 0.0642\,\frac{PaL^2}{EI}\ (\uparrow)$$

Problem 2.15 : Find the magnitude of 'W' for the beam shown in Fig. 2.43 such that deflection at free end A of the beam is zero.

Data   : As shown in Fig. 2.43.

Required : Magnitude of W for deflection at 'A' to be zero.

Concept : Principle of superposition.

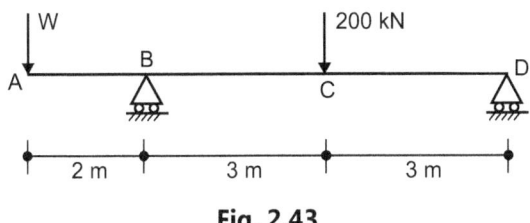

Fig. 2.43

Solution :

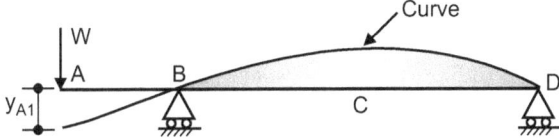

Fig. 2.44 : Elastic curve due to W

$$y_{A_1} = \frac{Wa^2}{3EI}(L + a)$$

$$= \frac{W(2)^2}{3EI}(6 + 2) = \frac{10.67}{EI}W \; (\downarrow)$$

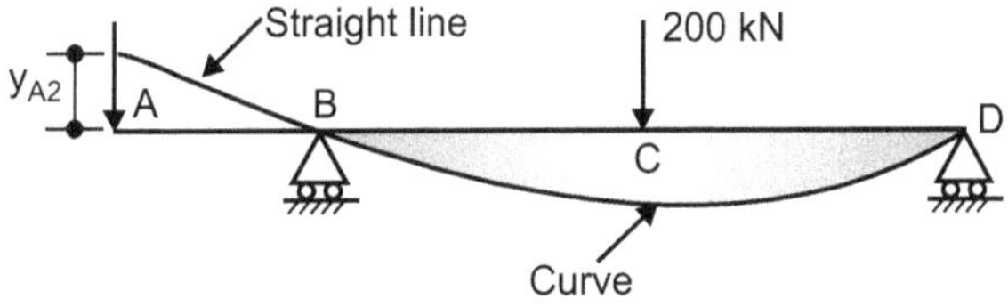

Fig. 2.45 : Elastic curve due to 200 kN load

$$y_{A_2} = \text{slope at } B \times l \, (AB)$$

$$= \frac{PL^2}{16 EI} \times l \, (AB)$$

$$= \frac{200 \times 6^2}{16 EI} \times 2$$

$$= \frac{900}{EI} \; (\uparrow)$$

For $y_A = 0$;

$$y_{A_1} = y_{A_2}$$

$$\frac{10.67 \, W}{EI} = \frac{900}{EI}$$

∴ $W = 84.375$ kN

Problem 2.16 : For the beam shown in Fig. 2.46, find slope at each support, deflection at centre and free end of the beam.

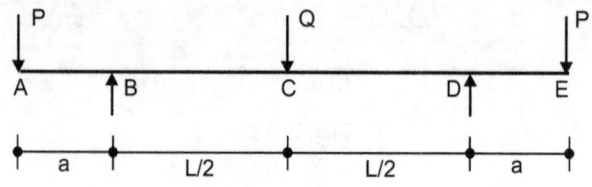

Fig. 2.46 : Given beam

Data : As shown in Fig. 2.46.

Required : Slope at B, C and deflections at A, C.

Concept : Use of standard results and principle of superposition.

Solution : (i) Analysis for load 'Q' :

$$\text{Slope at B/D} = \frac{QL^2}{16\ EI}$$

$$\text{Deflection at centre} = \frac{QL^3}{48\ EI}\ (\downarrow)$$

$$\text{Deflection at A/E} = \frac{QL^2}{16\ EI}\ (a)\ (\uparrow)$$

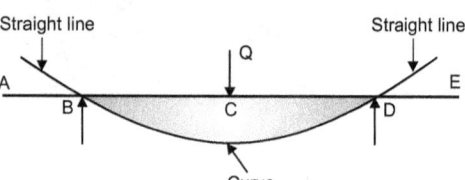

Fig. 2.47 : Elastic curve due to load 'Q'

($\because$ Slope at supports × length a)

(ii) Analysis for load 'P' :

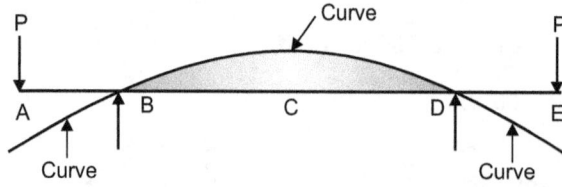

Fig. 2.48 : Elastic curve due to load 'P'

By considering two couples each at B and D, Couple = M = Pa.

$$\text{Slope at B/D} = \frac{PaL}{2\ EI}$$

$$\left(\because \frac{ML}{2\ EI}\right)$$

$$\text{Deflection at centre} = \frac{PaL^2}{8\ EI}\ (\uparrow)$$

$$\left(\because \text{Central deflection} = \frac{ML^2}{8\ EI}\ ;\ M = Pa\right)$$

Deflection at A/E = deflection due to slope at B/D
+ deflection due to cantilever action.

$$= \frac{PaL}{2\ EI} \times (a) + \frac{Pa^3}{3\ EI} = \frac{Pa^2}{6\ EI}\ (2a + 3L)\ (\downarrow)$$

(iii) Superposition :

$$\text{Net slope at B/D} = \frac{QL^2}{16\,EI} - \frac{PaL}{2\,EI} = \frac{L}{16\,EI}(QL - 8\,Pa)$$

$$\text{Net deflection at centre} = -\frac{QL^3}{48\,EI} + \frac{PaL^2}{8\,EI} = \frac{L^2}{48\,EI}(6\,Pa - QL)$$

$$\text{Net deflection at free ends} = \frac{QL^2}{16\,EI}(a) - \frac{Pa^2}{6\,EI}(2a + 3L)$$

Problem 2.17 : For the beam shown in Fig. 2.49, find slope at supports; deflection under the load and maximum deflection.

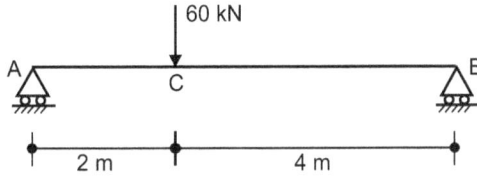

Fig. 2.49 : Given beam

Data   : As shown in Fig. 2.49.
Required : Slope at A; B; deflection at C and maximum deflection.
Concept   : Consider 'A' as origin and section at a distance 'x' from A in zone CB for BM equation.
Solution : (i) Reactions for equilibrium :

$\Sigma M_A = 0;$ $\quad V_B \times 6 - 60 \times 2 = 0$ $\quad \therefore \quad V_B = 20$ kN ($\uparrow$)
$\Sigma F_y = 0;$ $\quad V_A + V_B - 60 = 0$ $\quad \therefore \quad V_A = 40$ kN ($\uparrow$)
$\Sigma F_x = 0;$ $\quad H_A = 0$

FBD of beam is as shown in Fig. 2.50.

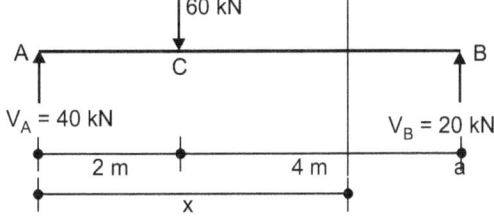

Fig. 2.50 : FBD of beam

(ii) Equations of BM, slope and deflection :

$$EI\left(\frac{d^2y}{dx^2}\right) = \underbrace{40(x)}_{AC} \Big| \underbrace{-60(x-2)}_{CB} \qquad \ldots \text{(I)}$$

$$EI\left(\frac{dy}{dx}\right) = 20(x)^2 + C_1 \,\Big|\, -30(x-2)^2 \qquad \ldots (II)$$

$$EI(y) = \frac{20}{3}(x)^3 + C_1(x) + C_2 \,\Big|\, -10(x-2)^3 \qquad \ldots (III)$$

(iii) Boundary conditions :

At A i.e. $x = 0$; $y = 0$ put in equation (III).

$$0 = 0 + 0 + C_2 \qquad \therefore \; C_2 = 0$$

At B i.e. $x = 6$ m ; $y = 0$ put in equation (III).

$$0 = \frac{20}{3}(6)^3 + C_1(6) + C_2 - 10(6-2)^3 \quad (\because C_2 = 0)$$

$$0 = 1440 + 6C_1 - 640$$

$$\therefore \qquad C_1 = -133.33$$

Substituting values of C_1 and C_2, equations (II) and (III) are written as

$$EI\left(\frac{dy}{dx}\right) = 20(x)^2 - 133.33 \,\Big|\, -30(x-2)^2 \qquad \ldots (II)$$

$$EI(y) = \frac{20}{3}(x)^3 - 133.33(x) \,\Big|\, -10(x-2)^3 \qquad \ldots (III)$$

(iv) Slopes and deflections :

For slope at 'A' put $x = 0$ in equation (II).

$$EI\left(\frac{dy}{dx}\right)_A = 0 - 133.33 \quad \therefore \; \left(\frac{dy}{dx}\right)_A = \frac{-133.33}{EI} = \frac{133.33}{EI} \; (\circlearrowright)$$

For slope at 'B' put $x = 6$ m in equation (II).

$$EI\left(\frac{dy}{dx}\right)_B = 20(6)^2 - 133.33 - 30(6-2)^2$$

$$\therefore \qquad \left(\frac{dy}{dx}\right)_B = \frac{106.67}{EI} = \frac{106.67}{EI} \; (\circlearrowleft)$$

For deflection at 'C' put $x = 2$ m in equation (III).

$$EI(y)_C = \frac{20}{3}(2)^3 - 133.33(2)$$

$$\therefore \qquad y_C = \frac{-213.33}{EI} = \frac{213.33}{EI} \; (\downarrow)$$

For maximum deflection;

let maximum deflection occurs in zone CB i.e. $(2 < x < 6)$

Equating slope equation (II) for zone CB to zero.

$$0 = 20(x)^2 - 133.33 - 30(x-2)^2$$

$$0 = 10x^2 - 120x + 253.33$$

Solving $\qquad x = 2.73$ m Assumption is OK.

Put x = 2.73 m in equation (III) to get maximum deflection.

$$EI\,(y)_{max} = \frac{20}{3}(2.73)^3 - 133.33\,(2.73) - 10\,(2.73-2)^3$$

$$(y)_{max} = \frac{-232.24}{EI} = \frac{232.24}{EI}\,(\downarrow)$$

Problem 2.18 : Find slope at supports ; deflection under loads and maximum deflection for the beam shown in Fig. 2.51. Assume E = 200 GPa ; I = 3 × 10⁸ mm⁴.

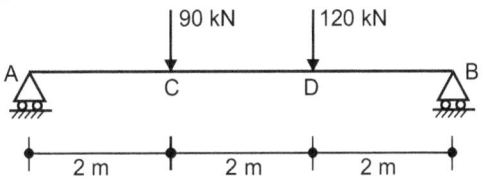

Fig. 2.51 : Given beam

Data : As shown in Fig. 2.51 ;
EI = 200 × 3 × 10⁸ = 6 × 10¹⁰ kN.mm² = 6 × 10⁴ kN.m²

Required : Slopes at A, B; and deflection at C, D and maximum deflection.

Concept : Consider 'A' as origin and section at a distance 'x' from A in zone DB for BM equation.

Solution : (i) Reactions for equilibrium :

$\Sigma M_A = 0;$ $\quad V_B \times 6 - 120 \times 4 - 90 \times 2 = 0 \quad \therefore \quad V_B = 110\text{ kN }(\uparrow)$

$\Sigma F_y = 0;$ $\quad V_A + V_B - 90 - 120 = 0 \quad \therefore \quad V_A = 100\text{ kN }(\uparrow)$

$\Sigma F_x = 0;$ $\quad H_A = 0$

FBD of beam is as shown in Fig. 2.52.

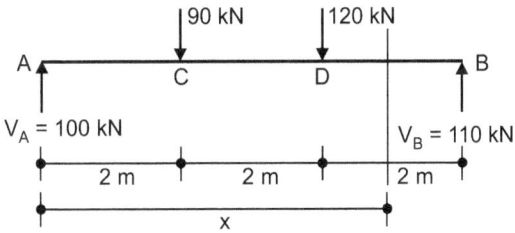

Fig. 2.52 : FBD of beam

(ii) Equations of BM, slope and deflection :

$$EI\left(\frac{d^2y}{dx^2}\right) = 100\,(x)\,\Big|_{AC} - 90\,(x-2)\,\Big|_{CD} - 120\,(x-4)\,\Big|_{DB} \qquad \ldots \text{(I)}$$

$$EI\left(\frac{dy}{dx}\right) = 50(x)^2 + C_1 \Big| -45(x-2)^2 \Big| -60(x-4)^2 \quad \ldots \text{(II)}$$

$$EI(y) = 16.67(x)^3 + C_1(x) + C_2 \Big| -15(x-2)^3 \Big| -20(x-4)^3 \quad \ldots \text{(III)}$$

(iii) Boundary conditions :

At 'A' i.e. $x = 0$; $y = 0$; put in equation (III).
$$C_2 = 0$$

At 'B' i.e. $x = 6$ m ; $y = 0$; put in equation (III).
$$0 = 16.67(6)^3 + C_1(6) + C_2 - 15(6-2)^3 - 20(6-4)^3$$

$$\therefore \quad C_1 = -413.45$$

Substituting values of C_1 and C_2, equations (II) and (III) are written as

$$EI\left(\frac{dy}{dx}\right) = 50(x)^2 - 413.45 \Big| -45(x-2)^2 \Big| -60(x-4)^2 \quad \ldots \text{(II)}$$

$$EI(y) = 16.67(x)^3 - 413.45(x) \Big| -15(x-2)^3 \Big| -20(x-4)^3 \quad \ldots \text{(III)}$$

(iv) Slopes and deflections :

For slope at 'A', put $x = 0$ in equation (II).

$$EI\left(\frac{dy}{dx}\right)_A = -413.45 \quad \therefore \quad \left(\frac{dy}{dx}\right)_A = \frac{413.45}{EI} \;(\circlearrowleft)$$

$$\therefore \quad \left(\frac{dy}{dx}\right)_A = \frac{413.45}{6 \times 10^4} = 6.89 \times 10^{-3} \text{ rad }(\circlearrowleft)$$

For slope at B ; put $x = 6$ m in equation (II).

$$EI\left(\frac{dy}{dx}\right)_B = 50(6)^2 - 413.45 - 45(6-2)^2 - 60(6-4)^2$$

$$\therefore \quad \left(\frac{dy}{dx}\right)_B = \frac{426.55}{EI}$$

$$\therefore \quad \left(\frac{dy}{dx}\right)_B = \frac{426.55}{6 \times 10^4} = 7.11 \times 10^{-3} \text{ rad }(\circlearrowright)$$

For deflection at 'C', put $x = 2$ m in equation (III).

$$EI(y)_C = 16.67(2)^3 - 413.45(2)$$

$$\therefore \quad (y)_C = \frac{-693.54}{EI} = \frac{-693.54}{6 \times 10^4} = -0.01155 \text{ m} = 11.55 \text{ mm }(\downarrow)$$

For deflection at 'D', put $x = 4$ m in equation (III).

$$EI(y)_D = 16.67(4)^3 - 413.45(4) - 15(4-2)^3$$

$$y_D = \frac{-706.92}{EI} = 11.78 \text{ mm }(\downarrow)$$

For maximum deflection ;
let maximum deflection occurs in zone CD i.e. $2 < x < 4$.

∴ Equating slope equation (II) for zone CD to zero.

$$0 = 50(x)^2 - 413.45 - 45(x-2)^2$$
$$0 = 5x^2 + 180x - 593.45$$

∴ $\quad x = 3.04 \text{ m}$ Assumption is OK.

Put $\quad x = 3.04$ m in equation (III)

$$EI(y_{max}) = 16.67(3.04)^3 - 413.45(3.04) - 15(3.04-2)^3$$

∴ $\quad y_{max} = \dfrac{-805.43}{EI}$

$\quad\quad\quad\quad = 13.42 \text{ mm } (\downarrow)$

Problem 2.19 : Find slope at 'B', 'C' and deflection at 'C' and 'D' for the beam shown in Fig. 2.53. Assume E = 200 GPa ; I = 2×10^8 mm^4.

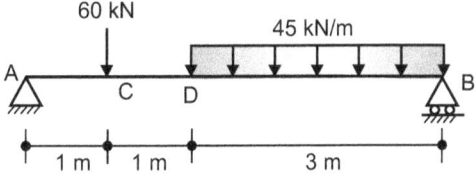

Fig. 2.53 : Given beam

Data : As shown in Fig. 2.53 ; EI = 4×10^4 kN.m^2.

Required : Slope at 'B', 'C' and deflection at 'C' and 'D'.

Concept : Consider 'A' as origin and section at a distance 'x' from 'A' in zone DB for BM equation.

Solution : (i) Reactions for equilibrium :

$\sum M_A = 0;$ $\quad V_B \times 5 - 45 \times 3 \times 3.5 - 60 \times 1 = 0 \quad$ ∴ $\quad V_B = 106.5$ kN (↑)

$\sum F_y = 0;$ $\quad V_A + V_B - 60 - 45 \times 3 = 0 \quad$ ∴ $\quad V_A = 88.5$ kN (↑)

$\sum F_x = 0;$ $\quad H_A = 0$

FBD of beam is as shown in Fig. 2.54.

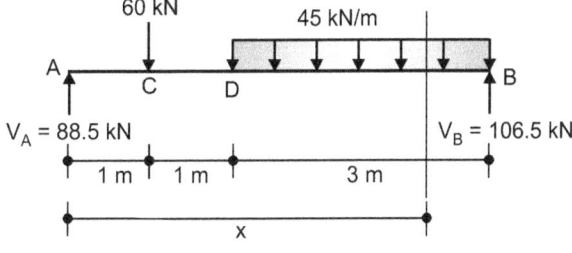

Fig. 2.54 : FBD of beam

(ii) Equations of BM ; slope and deflection.

$$EI\left(\frac{d^2y}{dx^2}\right) = 88.5\,(x) \mid -60\,(x-1) \mid -45\,\frac{(x-2)^2}{2} \quad \ldots (I)$$

```
|———————|
     AC
     |————————————|
          CD
     |————————————————————|
              DB
```

$$EI\left(\frac{dy}{dx}\right) = 44.25\,(x)^2 + C_1 \mid -30\,(x-1)^2 \mid -7.5\,(x-2)^3 \quad \ldots (II)$$

$$EI\,(y) = 14.75\,(x)^3 + C_1\,(x) + C_2 \mid -10\,(x-1)^3 \mid -1.875\,(x-2)^4 \quad \ldots (III)$$

(iii) Boundary conditions :

At A i.e. $x = 0$; $y = 0$ put in equation (III).
$$C_2 = 0$$

At B i.e. $x = 5$ m ; $y = 0$ put in equation (III).
$$0 = 14.75\,(5)^3 + C_1\,(5) - 10\,(5-1)^3 - 1.875\,(5-2)^4$$

$\therefore \quad C_1 = -210.375$

Substituting values of C_1 and C_2, equations (II) and (III) are written as

$$EI\left(\frac{dy}{dx}\right) = 44.25\,(x)^2 - 210.375 \mid -30\,(x-1)^2 \mid -7.5\,(x-2)^3 \quad \ldots (II)$$

$$EI\,(y) = 14.75\,(x)^3 - 210.375\,(x) \mid -10\,(x-1)^3 \mid -1.875\,(x-2)^4 \quad \ldots (III)$$

(iv) Slopes and deflections : For slope at 'B' put $x = 5$ m in equation (II).

$$EI\left(\frac{dy}{dx}\right)_B = 44.25\,(5)^2 - 210.375 - 30\,(5-1)^2 - 7.5\,(5-2)^3$$

$$\therefore \quad \left(\frac{dy}{dx}\right)_B = \frac{213.375}{EI} = 5.33 \times 10^{-3} \text{ rad } (\circlearrowleft)$$

For slope at 'C' put $x = 1$ m in equation (II)

$$EI\left(\frac{dy}{dx}\right)_C = 44.25\,(1)^2 - 210.375$$

$$\left(\frac{dy}{dx}\right)_C = \frac{-166.125}{EI} = 4.153 \times 10^{-3} \text{ rad } (\circlearrowright)$$

For deflection at 'C' put $x = 1$ m in equation (III).

$$EI\,(y)_C = 14.75\,(1)^3 - 210.375\,(1)$$

$$\therefore \quad y_C = \frac{-195.625}{EI} = 4.89 \text{ mm } (\downarrow)$$

For deflection at 'D' put $x = 2$ m in equation (III).

$$EI\,(y)_D = 14.75\,(2)^3 - 210.375\,(2) - 10\,(2-1)^3$$

$$\therefore \quad y_D = \frac{-312.75}{EI} = 7.82 \text{ mm } (\downarrow)$$

Problem 2.20 : For the beam shown in Fig. 2.55, find slope and deflection at 'C' and 'D'. Assume E = 210 GPa and I = 3.6×10^7 mm⁴.

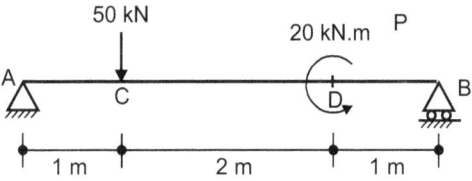

Fig. 2.55 : Given beam

Data : As shown in Fig. 2.55 ; EI = 7560 kN.m².

Required : Slope and deflection at C and D.

Concept : Consider 'A' as origin and section at a distance 'x' from 'A' in zone DB for BM equation.

Solution : (i) Reactions for equilibrium :

$\Sigma M_A = 0$; $V_B \times 4 + 20 - 50 \times 1 = 0$ ∴ $V_B = 7.5$ kN (↑)

$\Sigma F_y = 0$; $V_A + V_B = 50$ ∴ $V_A = 42.5$ kN (↑)

$\Sigma F_x = 0$; $H_A = 0$

FBD of beam is as shown in Fig. 2.58.

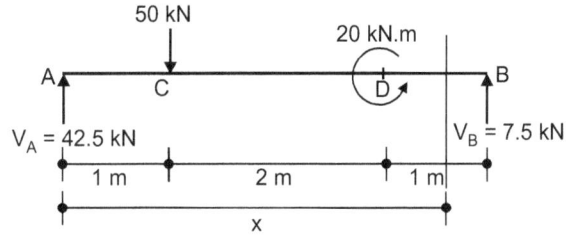

Fig. 2.56 : FBD of beam

(ii) Equations for BM ; slope and deflection :

$$EI \left(\frac{d^2y}{dx^2}\right) = 42.5 \,(x) \,\Big| -50\,(x-1)\,\Big| -20\,(x-3)^0 \qquad \ldots \text{(I)}$$

$$\begin{array}{l} \vdash\!\!-\!\!\dashv \\ \text{AC} \\ \vdash\!\!-\!\!-\!\!-\!\!\dashv \\ \quad\text{CD} \\ \vdash\!\!-\!\!-\!\!-\!\!-\!\!-\!\!\dashv \\ \qquad\text{DB} \end{array}$$

$$EI\left(\frac{dy}{dx}\right) = 21.25\,(x)^2 + C_1 \,\Big| -25\,(x-1)^2 \,\Big| -20\,(x-3) \qquad \ldots \text{(II)}$$

$$EI\,(y) = 7.08\,(x)^3 + C_1 x + C_2 \,\Big| -8.33\,(x-1)^3 \,\Big| -10\,(x-3)^2 \qquad \ldots \text{(III)}$$

(iii) Boundary conditions :

At 'A' i.e. x = 0; y = 0 put in equation (III) ∴ $C_2 = 0$

At 'B' i.e. $x = 4$ m; $y = 0$ put in equation (III).

$$0 = 7.08 (4)^3 + 4 C_1 - 8.33 (4-1)^3 - 10 (4-3)^2$$

$$\therefore \quad C_1 = -54.55$$

Substituting values of C_1 and C_2, equations (II) and (III) are written as

$$EI\left(\frac{dy}{dx}\right) = 21.25 (x)^2 - 54.55 \mid -25 (x-1)^2 \mid -20 (x-3) \quad \ldots \text{(II)}$$

$$EI (y) = 7.08 (x)^3 - 54.55 x \mid -8.33 (x-1)^3 \mid -10 (x-3)^2 \quad \ldots \text{(III)}$$

(iv) Slopes and deflections :

For slope and deflection at 'C' put $x = 1$ m in equations (II) and (III) respectively.

$$EI\left(\frac{dy}{dx}\right)_C = 21.25 (1)^2 - 54.55$$

$$\therefore \quad \left(\frac{dy}{dx}\right)_C = \frac{-33.3}{EI} = 4.4 \times 10^{-3} \text{ rad } (\circlearrowright)$$

$$EI (y)_C = 7.08 (1)^3 - 54.55 \; (\uparrow)$$

$$y_C = \frac{-47.47}{EI} = 6.28 \text{ mm } (\downarrow)$$

For slope and deflection at D ; put $x = 3$ m in equations (II) and (III) respectively.

$$EI\left(\frac{dy}{dx}\right)_D = 21.25 (3)^2 - 54.55 - 25 (3-1)^2$$

$$\left(\frac{dy}{dx}\right)_D = \frac{36.7}{EI} = 4.85 \times 10^{-3} \text{ rad } (\circlearrowleft)$$

$$EI (y)_D = 7.08 (3)^3 - 54.55 (3) - 8.33 (3-1)^3$$

$$y_D = \frac{-39.13}{EI} = 5.18 \text{ mm } (\downarrow)$$

Problem 2.21 : Find slope at C and deflection at 'C' and 'D' for the beam shown in Fig. 2.57. Assume $EI = 32.5 \times 10^3$ kN.m².

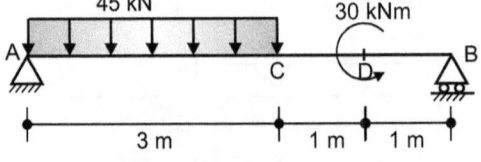

Fig. 2.57 : Given beam

Data : As shown in Fig. 2.57 ; $EI = 32.5 \times 10^3$ kN.m².

Required : Slope at 'C' and deflection at 'C' and 'D'.

Concept : Consider 'A' as origin and section at a distance 'x' from 'A' in zone 'DB' for BM equation.

Solution : (i) Reactions for equilibrium :

$\sum M_A = 0;$ $\quad V_B \times 5 + 30 - 45 \times \dfrac{3^2}{2} = 0$ $\quad \therefore V_B = 34.5 \text{ kN} (\uparrow)$

$\sum F_y = 0;$ $\quad V_A + V_B - 45 \times 3 = 0$ $\quad \therefore V_A = 100.5 \text{ kN} (\uparrow)$

$\sum F_x = 0;$ $\quad H_A = 0$

FBD of beam is as shown in Fig. 2.58.

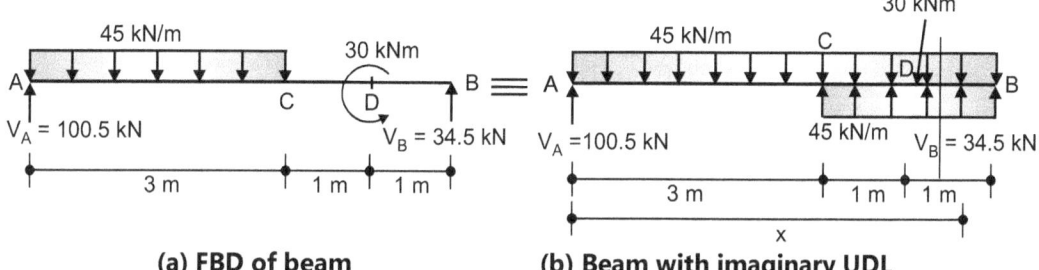

(a) FBD of beam **(b) Beam with imaginary UDL**

Fig. 2.58

(ii) Equations of BM ; slope and deflection :

$$EI \left(\dfrac{d^2y}{dx^2}\right) = 42.5\,(x) \,\Big|\, - 50\,(x-1) \,\Big|\, - 20\,(x-3)^0 \quad \ldots (I)$$

AC
CD
DB

$$EI \left(\dfrac{dy}{dx}\right) = 50.25\,(x)^2 - 7.5\,(x)^3 + C_1 \,\Big|\, + 7.5\,(x-3)^3 \,\Big|\, - 30\,(x-4) \quad \ldots (II)$$

$$EI\,(y) = 16.75\,(x)^3 - 1.875\,(x)^4 + C_1\,(x) + C_2 \,\Big|\, + 1.875\,(x-3)^4 \,\Big|\, - 15\,(x-4)^2 \quad \ldots (III)$$

(iii) Boundary conditions :

At 'A' i.e. $x = 0$; $y = 0$ put in equation (III) $\therefore C_2 = 0$

At 'B' i.e. $x = 5$ m ; $y = 0$ put in equation (III).

$0 = 16.75\,(5)^3 - 1.875\,(5)^4 + 5\,C_1 + 1.875\,(5-3)^4 - 15\,(5-4)^2$

$\therefore \quad C_1 = -187.375$

Substituting values of C_1 and C_2, equations (II) and (III) are written as

$$EI \left(\dfrac{dy}{dx}\right) = 50.25\,(x)^2 - 75\,(x)^3 - 187.375 \,\Big|\, + 7.5\,(x-3)^3 \,\Big|\, - 30\,(x-4) \quad \ldots (II)$$

$$EI\,(y) = 16.75\,(x)^3 - 1.875\,(x)^4 - 187.375\,(x) \,\Big|\, + 1.875\,(x-3)^4 \,\Big|\, - 15\,(x-4)^2 \quad \ldots (III)$$

(iv) Slopes and deflections :

For slope and deflection at 'C' put $x = 3$ m i.e. equations (II) and (III) respectively.

$$EI \left(\dfrac{dy}{dx}\right)_C = 50.25\,(3)^2 - 7.5\,(3)^3 - 187.375$$

$$\therefore \quad \left(\frac{dy}{dx}\right)_C = \frac{62.375}{EI} = 1.91 \times 10^{-3} \text{ rad } (\circlearrowleft)$$

$$EI\,(y)_C = 16.75\,(3)^3 - 1.875\,(3)^4 - 187.375\,(3)$$

$$\therefore \quad y_C = \frac{-261.75}{EI} = 8.05 \text{ mm } (\downarrow)$$

For deflection at 'D' put x = 4 m in equation (III).

$$EI\,(y)_D = 16.75\,(4)^3 - 1.875\,(4)^4 - 187.375\,(4) + 1.875\,(4-3)^4$$

$$\therefore \quad y_D = \frac{-155.625}{EI} = 4.79 \text{ mm } (\downarrow)$$

Problem 2.22 : Find slope and deflections at 'C' and 'D' for the beam shown in Fig. 2.59 (a) in terms of EI.

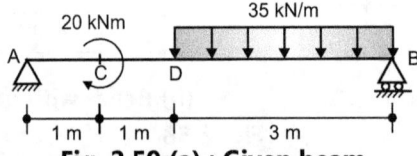

Fig. 2.59 (a) : Given beam

Data   : As shown in Fig. 2.59 (a).
Required   : Slope and deflections at 'C' and 'D'.
Concept   : Consider 'A' as origin and section at a distance 'x' from 'A' in zone 'DB' for BM equation.
Solution   : (i) Reactions for equilibrium :

$\Sigma M_A = 0;$ $\quad V_B \times 5 - 35 \times 3 \times 3.5 - 20 = 0 \quad \therefore \quad V_B = 77.5 \text{ kN } (\uparrow)$
$\Sigma F_y = 0;$ $\quad V_A + V_B - 35 \times 3 = 0 \quad \therefore \quad V_A = 27.5 \text{ kN } (\uparrow)$
$\Sigma F_x = 0;$ $\quad H_A = 0$

FBD of beam is as shown in Fig. 2.59 (b).

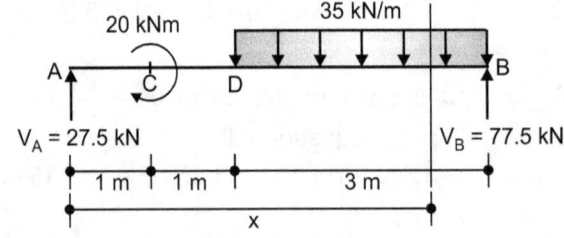

Fig. 2.59 (b) : FBD of beam

(ii) Equations for BM ; slope and deflection :

$$EI\left(\frac{d^2y}{dx^2}\right) = 100.5\,(x) - 45\,\frac{(x)^2}{2}\bigg| + 45\,\frac{(x-3)^2}{2}\bigg| - 30\,(x-4)^0 \quad \ldots \text{(I)}$$

AC
CD
DB

$$EI\left(\frac{dy}{dx}\right) = 13.75\,(x)^2 + C_1\Big| + 20\,(x-1)\Big| - 5.83\,(x-2)^3 \qquad \ldots \text{(II)}$$

$$EI\,(y) = 4.58\,(x)^3 + C_1(x) + C_2\Big| + 10\,(x-1)^2\Big| - 1.46\,(x-2)^4 \qquad \ldots \text{(III)}$$

(iii) Boundary conditions :

At 'A' i.e. $x = 0$; $y = 0$ put in equation (III) $\therefore C_2 = 0$

At 'B' i.e. $x = 5$ m; $y = 0$ put in equation (III).

$$0 = 4.58\,(5)^3 + 5\,C_1 + 10\,(5-1)^2 - 1.46\,(5-2)^4$$

$\therefore \qquad C_1 = -122.85$

Substituting values of C_1 and C_2 in equations (II) and (III),

$$EI\left(\frac{dy}{dx}\right) = 13.75\,(x)^2 - 122.85\Big| + 20\,(x-1)\Big| - 5.83\,(x-2)^3 \qquad \ldots \text{(II)}$$

$$EI\,(y) = 4.58\,(x)^3 - 122.85\Big| + 10\,(x-1)^2\Big| - 1.46\,(x-2)^4 \qquad \ldots \text{(III)}$$

(iv) Slopes and deflections :

For slope and deflection at 'C' put $x = 1$ m in equations (II) and (III) respectively.

$$EI\left(\frac{dy}{dx}\right)_C = 13.75\,(1)^2 - 122.85 \quad \therefore \quad \left(\frac{dy}{dx}\right)_C = \frac{109.1}{EI}\,(\circlearrowleft)$$

$$EI\,(y_C) = 4.58\,(1)^3 - 122.85\,(1) \quad \therefore \quad y_C = \frac{118.27}{EI}\,(\downarrow)$$

For slope and deflection at 'D' put $x = 2$ m in equations (II) and (III) respectively.

$$EI\left(\frac{dy}{dx}\right)_D = 13.75\,(2)^2 - 122.85 + 20\,(2-1) \quad \therefore \quad \left(\frac{dy}{dx}\right)_D = \frac{47.85}{EI}\,(\circlearrowleft)$$

$$EI\,(y_D) = 4.58\,(2)^3 - 122.85\,(2) + 10\,(2-1)^2 \quad \therefore \quad y_D = \frac{199.06}{EI}\,(\downarrow)$$

Problem 2.23 : For the beam shown in Fig. 2.60, derive equation of elastic curve and find deflection at centre in terms of EI.

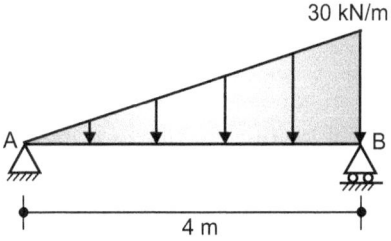

Fig. 2.60 : Given beam

Data : As shown in Fig. 2.60.
Required : Equation of elastic curve ; deflection at centre.
Concept : Equation of elastic curve is nothing but the deflection equation.

Solution : (i) Reactions for equilibrium :

$\Sigma M_A = 0$; $V_B \times 4 - \left(\dfrac{1}{2} \times 30 \times 4\right) \dfrac{2}{3} \times 4 = 0$ $\therefore$ $V_B = 40$ kN ($\uparrow$)

$\Sigma F_y = 0$; $V_A + V_B - \dfrac{1}{2} \times 30 \times 4 = 0$ $\therefore$ $V_A = 20$ kN ($\uparrow$)

$\Sigma F_x = 0$; $H_A = 0$

FBD of beam is as shown in Fig. 2.61.

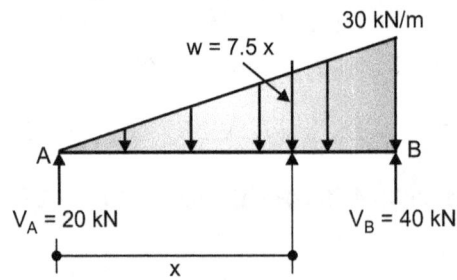

Fig. 2.61 : FBD of beam

(ii) Equations of BM ; slope and deflection :

Considering section at a distance 'x' from 'A'.

Intensity of load at 'x' from 'A' = $W = \dfrac{30}{4} x = 7.5 x$

$\therefore$ $EI \left(\dfrac{d^2y}{dx^2}\right) = 20x - \dfrac{1}{2}(x \times 7.5x) \dfrac{x}{3}$

$EI \left(\dfrac{d^2y}{dx^2}\right) = 20x - 1.25 x^3$ ... (I)

|— AB —|

$EI \left(\dfrac{dy}{dx}\right) = 10 (x)^2 - 0.3125 (x)^4 + C_1$ ... (II)

$EI (y) = 3.33 (x)^3 - 0.0625 (x)^5 + C_1 x + C_2$ ... (III)

(iii) Boundary conditions :

At A i.e. x = 0 ; y = 0 put in equation (III) $\therefore C_2 = 0$

At B i.e. x = 4 m ; y = 0 put in equation (III).

$0 = 3.33 (4)^3 - 0.0625 (4)^5 + 4 C_1$

$\therefore$ $C_1 = -37.28$

Substituting values of C_1 and C_2, equations (II) and (III) are written as ;

$EI \left(\dfrac{dy}{dx}\right) = 10 (x)^2 - 0.3125 (x)^4 - 37.28$ ... (II)

$EI (y) = 3.33 (x)^3 - 0.0625 (x)^5 - 37.28 x$ ... (III)

Equation (III) is the required equation of elastic curve.

(iv) Deflection at centre (y_C):

Put $x = 2$ m in equation (III).
$$EI\,(y_C) = 3.33\,(2)^3 - 0.0625\,(2)^5 - 37.28 \times 2$$
$$\therefore \quad y_C = \frac{50}{EI}\,(\downarrow)$$

Problem 2.24: Find slope and deflections at 'D' and 'E' for the beam shown in Fig. 2.62. Assume $E = 200$ GPa and $I = 6.2 \times 10^7$ mm^4.

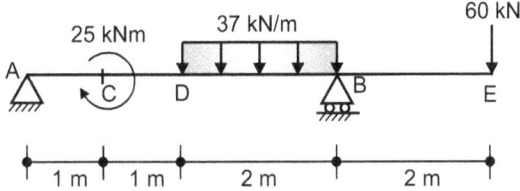

Fig. 2.62 : Given beam

Data : As shown in Fig. 2.62; $EI = 12.4 \times 10^3$ kN.m^2.

Required : Slope and deflections at 'D' and 'E'.

Concept : Consider 'A' as origin and section at a distance 'x' from 'A' in zone BE from BM equation. Imaginary UDL is required to be considered in zone BE.

Solution : (i) Reactions for equilibrium.

$\Sigma M_A = 0;$ $V_B \times 4 - 37 \times 2 \times 3 - 60 \times 6 - 25 = 0$ $\therefore$ $V_B = 151.75$ kN ($\uparrow$)

$\Sigma F_y = 0;$ $V_A + V_B - 37 \times 2 - 60 = 0$ $\therefore$ $V_A = -17.75$ kN

$\Sigma F_x = 0;$ $H_A = 0$ $= 17.75$ kN ($\downarrow$)

FBD of beam is as shown in Fig. 2.63.

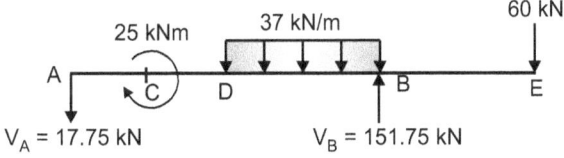

(a) FBD of beam

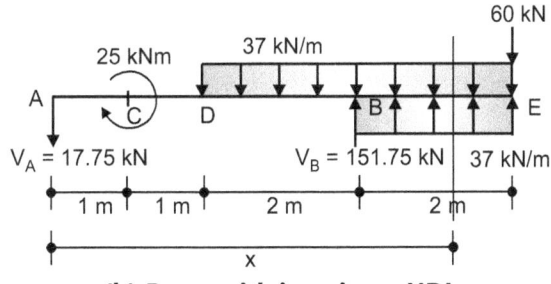

(b) Beam with imaginary UDL

Fig. 2.63

(ii) Equations of BM; slope and deflection :

$$EI\frac{d^2y}{dx^2} = -17.75(x)\Big| + 25(x-1)^0\Big| - 37\frac{(x-2)^2}{2}\Big| + 151.75(x-4) + \frac{37(x-4)^2}{2} \quad \text{...(I)}$$

```
|——————|  AC
    |——————|  CD
    |————————————|  DB
|————————————————————————|  BE
```

$$EI\frac{dy}{dx} = -8.87(x)^2 + C_1\Big| + 25(x-1)\Big| - 6.17(x-2)^3\Big| + 75.875(x-4)^2 + 6.17(x-4)^3 \quad \text{...(II)}$$

$$EI(y) = -2.96(x)^3 + C_1(x) + C_2\Big| + 12.5(x-1)^2\Big| - 1.54(x-2)^4\Big| + 25.29(x-4)^3 + 1.54(x-4)^4 \quad \text{...(III)}$$

(iii) Boundary conditions :

At A i.e. $x = 0$; $y = 0$ put in equation (III) ∴ $C_2 = 0$

At B i.e. $x = 4$ m; $y = 0$ put in equation (III).

$$0 = -2.96(4)^3 + 4C_1 + 12.5(4-1)^2 - 1.54(4-2)^4$$

∴ $C_1 = 25.4$

Substituting values of C_1 and C_2, equations (II) and (III) can be written as

$$EI\left(\frac{dy}{dx}\right) = -8.875(x)^2 + 25.4\Big| + 25(x-1)\Big| - 6.17(x-2)\Big| + 75.875(x-4)^2 + 6.17(x-4)^3 \quad \text{...(II)}$$

$$EI(y) = 2.96(x)^3 + 25.4(x)\Big| + 12.5(x-1)^2\Big| - 1.54(x-2)^4\Big| + 25.29(x-4)^3 + 1.54(x-4)^4 \quad \text{...(III)}$$

(iv) Slopes and deflections :

For slope and deflection at 'D' put $x = 2$ m in equations (II) and (III) respectively.

$$EI\left(\frac{dy}{dx}\right)_D = -8.875(2)^2 + 25.4 + 25(2-1)$$

∴ $\left(\frac{dy}{dx}\right)_D = \frac{14.9}{EI} = 1.2 \times 10^{-3}$ rad (↻)

$$EI(y_D) = -2.96(2)^3 + 25.4(2) + 12.5(2-1)^2$$

∴ $y_D = \frac{39.62}{EI} = 3.19$ mm (↑)

For slope and deflection at 'E' put $x = 6$ m in equations (II) and (III) respectively.

$$EI\left(\frac{dy}{dx}\right)_E = -8.875(6)^2 + 25.4 + 25(6-1) - 6.17(6-2)^3 + 75.875(6-4)^2 + 6.17(6-4)^3$$

$$\left(\frac{dy}{dx}\right)_E = \frac{-211.12}{EI} = 17.03 \times 10^3 \text{ rad } (\circlearrowleft)$$

$$EI\,(y)_E = -2.96\,(6)^3 + 25.4\,(6) + 12.5\,(6-1)^2 - 1.54\,(6-2)^4 +$$
$$25.29\,(6-4)^3 + 1.54\,(6-4)^4$$

$$\therefore \quad y_E = \frac{-341.74}{EI} = 27.56 \text{ mm } (\downarrow)$$

Problem 2.25 : Find deflections at 'C' and 'D' for the beam, shown in Fig. 2.64. Assume $EI = 8.4 \times 10^3$ kN.m².

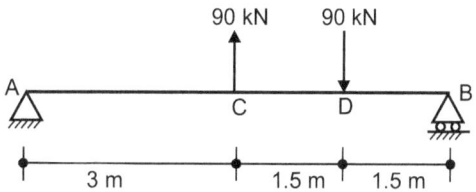

Fig. 2.64 : Given beam

Data : As shown in Fig. 2.64 ; $EI = 8.4 \times 10^3$ kN.m².

Required : Deflections at 'C' and 'D'.

Concept : Consider 'A' as origin and section at a distance 'x' from 'A' in zone DB for BM equation.

Solution : (i) Reactions for equilibrium :

$\Sigma M_A = 0$; $V_B \times 6 - 90 \times 4.5 + 90 \times 3 = 0$ $\therefore$ $V_B = 22.5$ kN ($\uparrow$)

$\Sigma F_y = 0$; $V_A + V_B = 0$ $\therefore$ $V_A = 22.5$ kN ($\downarrow$)

$\Sigma F_x = 0$; $H_A = 0$

FBD of beam is as shown in Fig. 2.65.

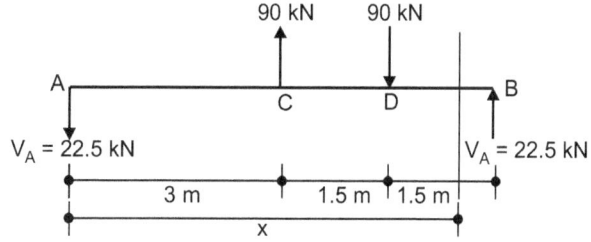

Fig. 2.65 : FBD of beam

(ii) Equations of BM; slope and deflection.

$$EI\left(\frac{d^2y}{dx^2}\right) = -22.5\,(x)\,\Big|+90\,(x-3)\Big|-90\,(x-4.5) \qquad \ldots (I)$$

AC

CD

DB

$$EI\left(\frac{dy}{dx}\right) = -11.25\,(x)^2 + C_1 \big| + 45\,(x-3)^2 \big| - 45\,(x-4.5)^2 \qquad \ldots \text{(II)}$$

$$EI\,(y) = -3.75\,(x)^3 + C_1\,(x) + C_2 \big| + 15\,(x-3)^3 \big| - 15\,(x-4.5)^3 \qquad \ldots \text{(III)}$$

(iii) Boundary conditions :

At A i.e. $x = 0$; $y = 0$ put in equation (III) $\therefore C_2 = 0$

At B i.e. $x = 6$ m ; $y = 0$ put in equation (III).

$$0 = -3.75\,(6)^3 + C_1\,(6) + 15\,(6-3)^3 - 15\,(6-4.5)^3$$

$\therefore \quad C_1 = 75.94$

Substituting values of C_1 and C_2, equation (III) is written as

$$EI\,(y) = -3.75\,(x)^3 + 75.94\,(x) \big| + 15\,(x-3)^3 \big| - 15\,(x-4.5)^3 \qquad \ldots \text{(III)}$$

(iv) Deflections at 'C' and 'D' :

For deflection at 'C' put $x = 3$ m in equation (III).

$$EI\,(y)_C = -3.75\,(3)^3 + 75.94\,(3)$$

$\therefore \quad y_C = \dfrac{126.57}{EI} = 15.07$ mm ($\uparrow$)

For deflection at 'D', put $x = 4.5$ m in equation (III).

$$EI\,(y)_D = -3.75\,(4.5)^3 + 75.94\,(4.5) + 15\,(4.5-3)^3$$

$\therefore \quad y_D = \dfrac{50.64}{EI} = 6.03$ mm ($\uparrow$)

Problem 2.26 : For the beam shown in Fig. 2.66, find position and magnitude of maximum deflection. Assume $E = 210$ GPa ; $I = 8 \times 10^7$ mm^4.

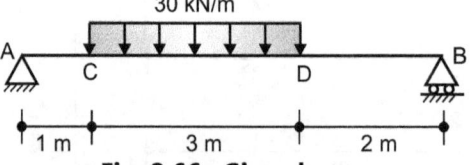

Fig. 2.66 : Given beam

Data : As shown in Fig. 2.66 ; $EI = 16.8 \times 10^3$ kN.m^2.

Required : Position and magnitude of maximum deflection.

Concept : (i) Consider 'A' as origin and section at a distance 'x' from 'A' in zone DB for BM equation.

          (ii) Imaginary UDL is required in zone DB.

Solution : (i) Reactions for equilibrium :

$\Sigma M_A = 0$; $\quad V_B \times 6 - 30 \times 3 \times 2.5 = 0 \quad \therefore \quad V_B = 37.5$ kN ($\uparrow$)

$\Sigma F_y = 0$; $\quad V_A + V_B - 30 \times 3 = 0 \quad \therefore \quad V_A = 52.5$ kN ($\uparrow$)

$\Sigma F_x = 0$; $\quad H_A = 0$

FBD of beam is as shown in Fig. 2.67.

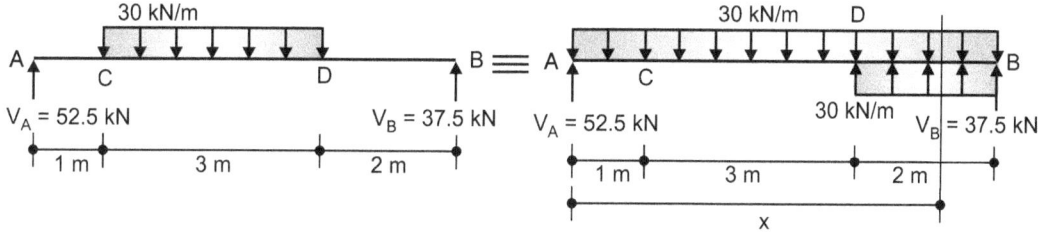

(a) FBD of beam **(b) Beam with imaginary UDL**

Fig. 2.67

(ii) Equations of BM ; slope and deflection :

$$EI\left(\frac{d^2y}{dx^2}\right) = 52.5\,(x) \left| \frac{-30\,(x-1)^2}{2} \right| + \frac{30\,(x-4)^2}{2} \quad \ldots (I)$$

AC
CD
DB

$$EI\left(\frac{dy}{dx}\right) = 26.25\,(x)^2 + C_1 \left| -5\,(x-1)^3 \right| + 5\,(x-4)^3 \quad \ldots (II)$$

$$EI\,(y) = 8.75\,(x)^3 + C_1\,(x) + C_2 \left| -1.25\,(x-1)^4 \right| + 1.25\,(x-4)^4 \quad \ldots (III)$$

(iii) Boundary conditions :

At A i.e. $x = 0$; $y = 0$ put in equation (III) $\therefore C_2 = 0$

At B i.e. $x = 6$ m; $y = 0$ put in equation (III).

$$0 = 8.75\,(6)^3 + C_1\,(6) - 1.25\,(6-1)^4 + 1.25\,(6-4)^4$$

$\therefore \quad C_1 = -188.12$

Substituting values of C_1 and C_2, equations (II) and (III) are written as

$$EI\left(\frac{dy}{dx}\right) = 26.25\,(x)^2 - 188.12 \left| -5\,(x-1)^3 \right| + 5\,(x-4)^3 \quad \ldots (II)$$

$$EI\,(y) = 8.75\,(x)^3 - 188.12\,(x) \left| -1.25\,(x-1)^4 \right| + 1.25\,(x-4)^4 \quad \ldots (III)$$

(iv) Maximum deflection :

Assuming maximum deflection to occur in zone CD. Hence, equating slope equation for CD to zero,

$$0 = 26.25\,(x)^2 - 188.12 - 5\,(x-1)^3$$

Solving by trial and error, $x = 2.916$ m. $\therefore$ Assumption is OK.

For maximum deflection; put $x = 2.916$ m in equation (III).

$$EI\,(y)_{max} = 8.75\,(2.916)^3 - 188.12\,(2.916) - 1.25\,(2.916-1)^4$$

$$\therefore \quad y_{max} = \frac{-348.49}{EI} = 20.74 \text{ mm } (\downarrow)$$

Problem 2.27 : For the beam shown in Fig. 2.68, find the magnitude of 'P' such that deflection at 'C' is 10 mm (↓). Assume EI = 19.2×10^3 kN.m².

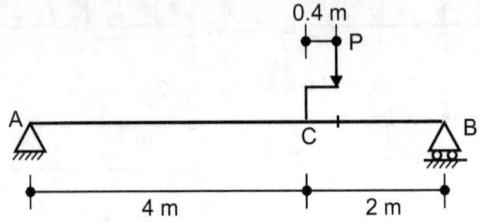

Fig. 2.68 : Given beam

Data : Deflection at 'C' = 10 mm (↓) ; EI = 19.2×10^3 kN.m².

Required : Magnitude of 'P'.

Concept : Force on bracket will be transferred at 'C' as force couple system as shown in Fig. 2.69.

Solution : (i) Reactions for equilibrium :

$\sum M_A = 0$; $V_B \times 6 - 4P - 0.4P = 0$ ∴ $V_B = \dfrac{22}{30} P (\uparrow)$

$\sum F_y = 0$; $V_A + V_B - P = 0$ ∴ $V_A = \dfrac{8}{30} P (\uparrow)$

$\sum F_x = 0$; $H_A = 0$

FBD of beam is as shown in Fig. 2.69.

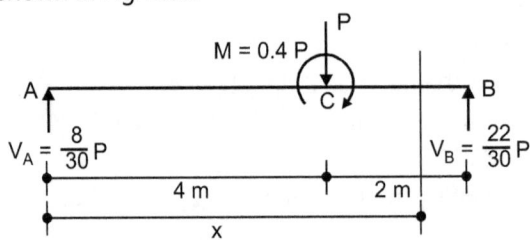

Fig. 2.69 : FBD of beam

(ii) Equations of BM ; slope and deflection.

$$EI \left(\dfrac{d^2y}{dx^2}\right) = \underbrace{\dfrac{8}{30} \cdot P(x)}_{AC} \underbrace{\left| -P(x-4) + 0.4P(x-4)^0 \right.}_{CB} \quad \ldots (I)$$

$$EI \left(\dfrac{dy}{dx}\right) = \dfrac{4}{30} (P)(x)^2 + C_1 \left| \dfrac{-P}{2}(x-4)^2 + 0.4P(x-4) \right. \quad \ldots (II)$$

$$EI(y) = \dfrac{4}{90}(P)(x)^3 + C_1(x) + C_2 \left| \dfrac{-P}{6}(x-4)^3 + 0.2P(x-4)^2 \right. \quad \ldots (III)$$

(iii) Boundary conditions :

At A i.e. $x = 0$; $y = 0$ put in equation (III) $\therefore C_2 = 0$

At B i.e. $x = 6$ m; $y = 0$ put in equation (III).

$$0 = \frac{4}{90}(P)(6)^3 + 6C_1 \left| -\frac{P}{6}(6-4)^3 + 0.2P(6-4)^2 \right.$$

$$\therefore \quad C_1 = -1.51\,P$$

Substituting values of C_1 and C_2, equation (III) can be written as

$$EI(y) = \frac{4}{90}(P)(x)^3 - 1.51\,P(x) \left| \frac{-P}{6}(x-4)^3 + 0.2P(x-4)^2 \right. \quad \ldots \text{(III)}$$

(iv) Magnitude of "P" :

At 'C' i.e. $x = 4$ m; $y_C = 10$ mm ($\neg$) given;

$$\therefore \quad y_C = \frac{-10}{10^3}\,m = -0.01\,m$$

Substituting;

$$-19.2 \times 10^3 \times 0.01 = \frac{4}{90}(P)(4)^3 - 1.51(P)(4)$$

$$\therefore \quad P = 60\,kN$$

Problem 2.28 : Determine central deflection and slope at supports for the beam shown in Fig. 2.70.

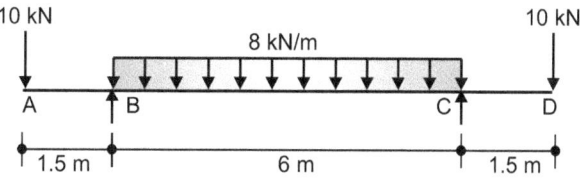

Fig. 2.70

Data : As shown in Fig. 2.70.

Required : Slope at supports and deflection at centre.

Concept : Due to symmetry, maximum deflection in zone BC will occur at centre, hence this condition will be used to evaluate constant of integration and only half the part of beam will be considered for analysis.

Solution : (i) Reactions for equilibrium :

$$V_B = V_C = \frac{1}{2}(\text{Total load}) = \frac{1}{2}[2 \times 10 + 8 \times 6] = 34\,kN\;(\uparrow)$$

FBD of beam is as shown in Fig. 2.71.

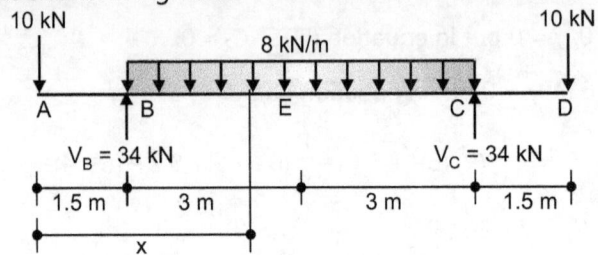

Fig. 2.71 : FBD of beam

(ii) Equations of BM ; slope and deflection : For section in zone BE ($0 \leq x \leq 4.5$ m)

$$EI\left(\frac{d^2y}{dx^2}\right) = \underbrace{-10x}_{AB} \underbrace{\Big| + 34(x-1.5) - \frac{8(x-1.5)^2}{2}}_{BE} \quad \ldots (I)$$

$$EI\left(\frac{dy}{dx}\right) = -5x^2 + C_1 \Big| + 17(x-1.5)^2 - 1.33(x-1.5)^3 \quad \ldots (II)$$

$$EI(y) = -1.67x^3 + C_1(x) + C_2 \Big| + 5.67(x-1.5)^3 - 0.33(x-1.5)^4 \quad \ldots (III)$$

(iii) Boundary conditions :

At E i.e. $x = 4.5$ m; $\frac{dy}{dx} = 0$; put in equation (II).

$$0 = -5(4.5)^2 + C_1 + 17(4.5-1.5)^2 - 1.33(4.5-1.5)^3$$

∴ $\quad C_1 = -15.84$

At B i.e. $x = 1.5$ m ; $y = 0$ put in equation (III).

$$0 = -1.67(1.5)^3 + (-15.84)(1.5) + C_2$$

∴ $\quad C_2 = +29.4$

Substituting values of C_1 and C_2, equations (II) and (III) are written as;

$$EI\left(\frac{dy}{dx}\right) = -5(x)^2 - 15.84 \Big| + 17(x-1.5)^2 - 1.33(x-1.5)^3 \quad \ldots (II)$$

$$EI(y) = -1.67(x)^3 - 15.84(x) + 29.4 \Big| + 5.67(x-1.5)^3 - 0.33(x-1.5)^4 \quad \ldots (III)$$

(iv) Slope and deflections.

For slope at supports, put $x = 1.5$ m in equation (II).

$$EI\left(\frac{dy}{dx}\right)_B = -5(1.5)^2 - 15.84$$

∴ $\quad \left(\frac{dy}{dx}\right)_B = \frac{-27.09}{EI} = \left(\frac{dy}{dx}\right)_C$

For deflection at centre, put $x = 4.5$ m in equation (III).

$$EI(y)_E = -1.67(4.5)^3 - 15.84(4.5) + 29.4 + 5.67(4.5-1.5)^3 - 0.33(4.5-1.5)^4$$

∴ $\quad (y)_E = \frac{-67.69}{EI}$

2.9 MOMENT AREA METHODS – MOHR'S THEOREMS

The moment area method provides convenient means of determining slopes and deflections in beams. The method is especially suitable when it is desired to find the slope or deflection at a given point of the beam instead of the complete equation of the deflection curve. Depending on geometry of elastic curve, the moment area method emphasizes the physical significance of slope and deflection. We first discuss the two basic theorems of the method.

Consider a simply supported beam shown in Fig. 2.72 (a). The elastic curve and $\frac{M}{EI}$ diagram is also shown in Fig. 2.81 (b) and Fig. 2.72 (c) respectively. Consider portion AB of the elastic curve of the beam. The tangents to the curve at two cross sections C and D of the beam at a distance ds apart, will intersect at angle dθ which is the change in slope from C to D.

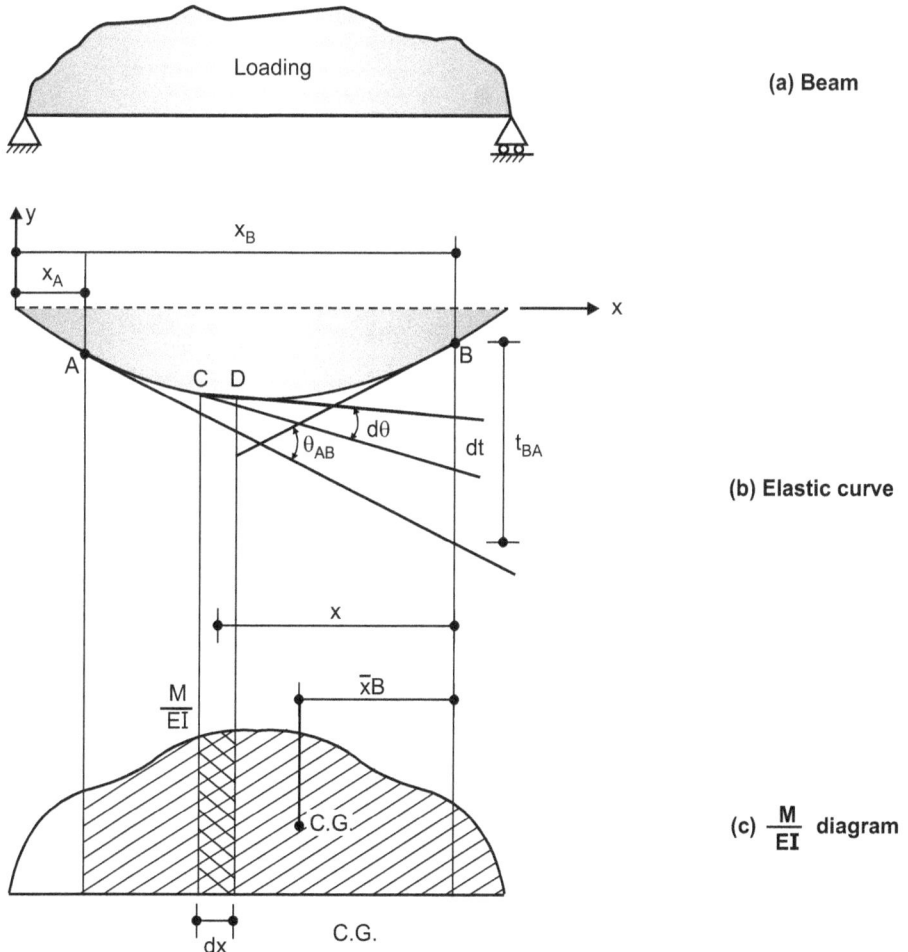

(a) Beam

(b) Elastic curve

(c) $\frac{M}{EI}$ diagram

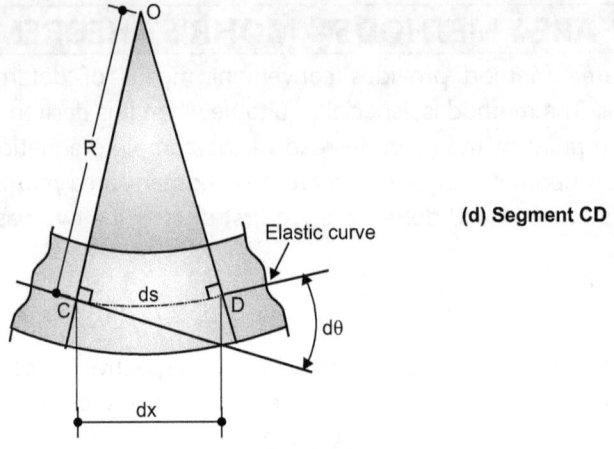

(d) Segment CD

Fig. 2.72

From flexural formula, we have

$$\frac{1}{R} = \frac{M}{EI}$$

Since $ds = R \cdot d\theta$

$$\frac{1}{R} = \frac{M}{EI} = \frac{d\theta}{ds} \quad \therefore d\theta = \frac{M}{EI} \cdot ds$$

Assuming the length ds to be equal to its projection dx,

$$d\theta = \frac{M}{EI} \cdot dx \qquad \ldots (2.10)$$

From Fig. 2.72 (d), it is clear that tangents drawn to elastic curve at C and D are separated by the same angle $d\theta$ by which sections OC and OD rotate relative to each other. Hence, change in slope between tangents drawn to the elastic curve at any two points A and B will be equal to the sum of such small angles.

$$\theta_{AB} = \int_{\theta_A}^{\theta_B} d\theta = \frac{1}{EI} \int_{x_A}^{x_B} M \cdot dx \qquad \ldots (2.11)$$

Thus, we obtain the following theorem.

First Moment - Area Theorem : The angle between the tangents drawn at two points A and B of an elastic curve is equal to the area of the $\frac{M}{EI}$ diagram between A and B.

From Fig. 2.72 (b), it can also be noted that, the distance from B on the elastic curve (measured perpendicular to the original position of the beam) that will intersect a tangent drawn to this curve at any other point A is the sum of intercepts dt created by tangents to the curve at adjacent points. Each of these intercepts may be considered as the arc of a circle of radius x subtended by angle $d\theta$.

$$dt = x \cdot d\theta$$

$$t_{BA} = \int dt = \int x \cdot d\theta$$

From equation (2.10), substituting for $d\theta$,

$$t_{BA} = \frac{1}{EI} \int_{x_A}^{x_B} x \cdot (M \cdot dx) \qquad \ldots (2.12)$$

Second Moment-Area Theorem : The displacement of any point B on elastic curve relative to a tangent drawn to the elastic curve at any other point A, in a direction perpendicular to the original position of beam, is equal to the moment of area of $\frac{M}{EI}$ diagram between A and B taken about B.

Thus, $\qquad t_{BA} = (Area)_{BA} \cdot \bar{x}_B \qquad \ldots (2.13)$

Thus, in Fig. 2.73,

and $\qquad \left. \begin{array}{l} t_{AB} = (Area)_{AB} \cdot \bar{x}_A \\ t_{BA} = (Area)_{BA} \cdot \bar{x}_B \end{array} \right\} \qquad \ldots (2.14)$

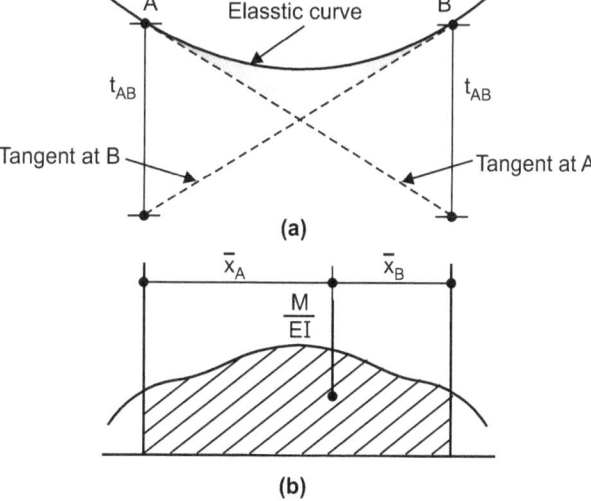

Fig. 2.73

2.9.1 Sign Conventions

For slope and deflection

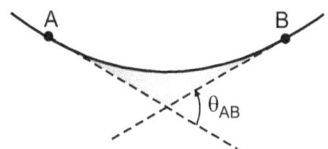
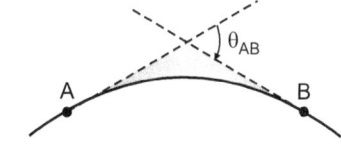

(a) Positive change of slope; θ_{AB} is anticlockwise from left tangent

(b) Negative change of slope; θ_{AB} is clockwise from left tangent

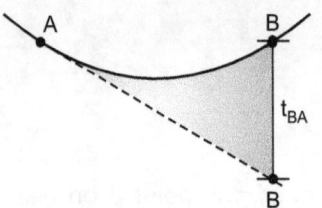
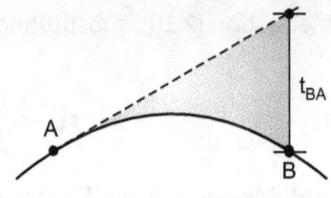

(c) Positive displacement; B is located above tangent at A

(d) Negative displacement; B is located below tangent at A

Fig. 2.74

Fig. 2.74 (a) and (b) show that; positive value of change in slope θ_{AB} between points A and B on elastic curve means that the angle measured from left tangent (at A) to right tangent (at B) is anticlockwise and vice versa.

Fig. 2.74 (c) and (d) show that; displacement at any point is positive if the point lies above the tangent drawn at reference point from which the displacement is measured; and negative if the point lies below tangent drawn at reference point.

Moment area method thus involves computing area of $\frac{M}{EI}$ diagram between the two points of interest; and also to find moment of area of $\frac{M}{EI}$ diagram between two points about any of the point. A method of doing this from calculus is to integrate the two expressions $\int \frac{M}{EI} dx$ and $\int \left(\frac{M}{EI}\right) \cdot x \cdot dx$ between proper limits; where bending moment M is expressed in terms of x. For replacing integration by simple numerical calculations, $\frac{M}{EI}$ diagram is divided into parts whose areas and centroids are known. Geometric properties of such several figures are shown in Table 2.2.

Table 2.2

Sr. No.	Diagram	Degree of curve	Area	$\bar{x}$
1.	rectangle, base b, height h	zero	bh	$\frac{b}{2}$
2.	right triangle, base b, height h	one	$\frac{1}{2}bh$	$\frac{b}{3}$

No.	Shape	Degree	Area	$\bar{x}$
3.	(b, h with $\bar{x}$)	two	$\dfrac{1}{3}bh$	$\dfrac{b}{4}$
4.	(b, h with $\bar{x}$)	three	$\dfrac{1}{4}bh$	$\dfrac{b}{5}$
5.	(b, h with $\bar{x}$)	two	$\dfrac{2}{3}bh$	$\dfrac{3}{8}b$
6.	(a, b, h, L with $\bar{x}$)	one	$\dfrac{1}{2} \cdot Lh$	$\dfrac{L+b}{3}$

2.10 APPLICATION OF MOMENT-AREA METHOD TO CANTILEVER BEAMS

Consider cantilever beam AB of constant flexural rigidity (EI) throughout and let it is required to find slope and deflection at C.

Fig. 2.75 (b) shows $\dfrac{M}{EI}$ diagram and Fig. 2.75 (c) shows elastic curve.

Slope at C = θ = Angle between tangents drawn at A and C' since the tangent drawn at A to elastic curve is horizontal.

∴ By first theorem of moment area,

$$\theta = \text{Area (PQST)}$$

Due to hogging bending moment above area will be negative which indicates that angle measured from tangent drawn at A to tangent drawn at C' is clockwise and θ is treated negative i.e. (↻).

Also deflection at C = y_C = Displacement of C' with respect to tangent drawn at A = t_{CA}.

= Moment of area of $\frac{M}{EI}$ diagram between A and C' about C'.

∴ By second theorem of moment area, y_C = Area (PQST) $\bar{x}$.

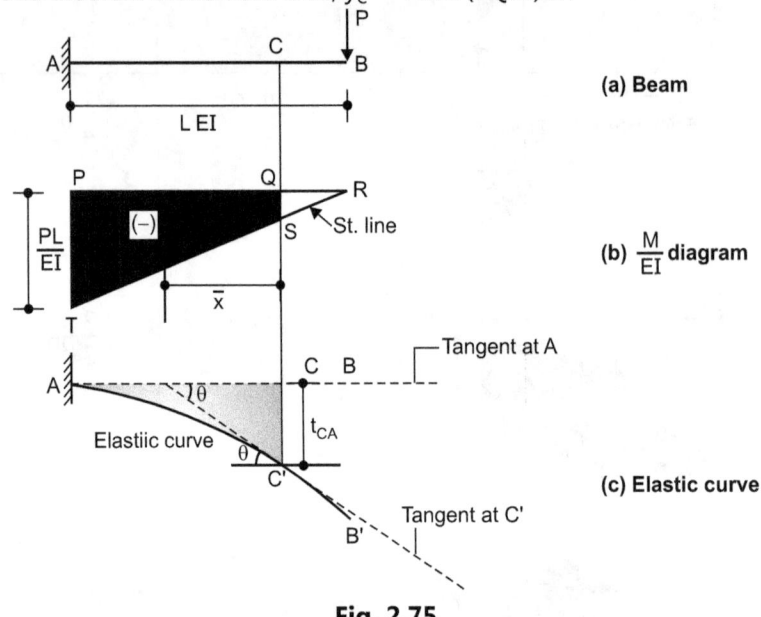

Fig. 2.75

Due to hogging bending moment, the moment of above area will also be negative which indicates that C' is located below the tangent drawn at reference point. A. In this case, t_{CA} directly gives the value of deflection at C since the tangent drawn at A to elastic curve is horizontal. The above deflection is treated negative i.e. (↓). Thus, for finding slope and deflection at any point on cantilever beam, moment area method is very simple to apply. Application of method to cantilever beams is illustrated in the following examples.

SOLVED EXAMPLES

Problem 2.29 : Determine slope and deflection at free end of cantilever. Take W = 10 kN; L = 5 m; I = 6.5 × 10^7 mm^4; E = 2 × 10^5 MPa. Use moment area method. Assume uniform flexural rigidity. [Refer Fig. 2.76 (a)].

Solution :

(i) $\theta_B = \theta_A + \Delta\theta_{AB}$

where; $\Delta\theta_{AB}$ = Change of slope from A to B

= Angle between tangents drawn at A and B.

= Area of $\frac{M}{EI}$ diagram between A and B

= $\frac{1}{2}\left[\frac{-50 \text{ kN.m}}{EI}\right] \times 5 = -\frac{125 \text{ kN.m}^2}{EI}$

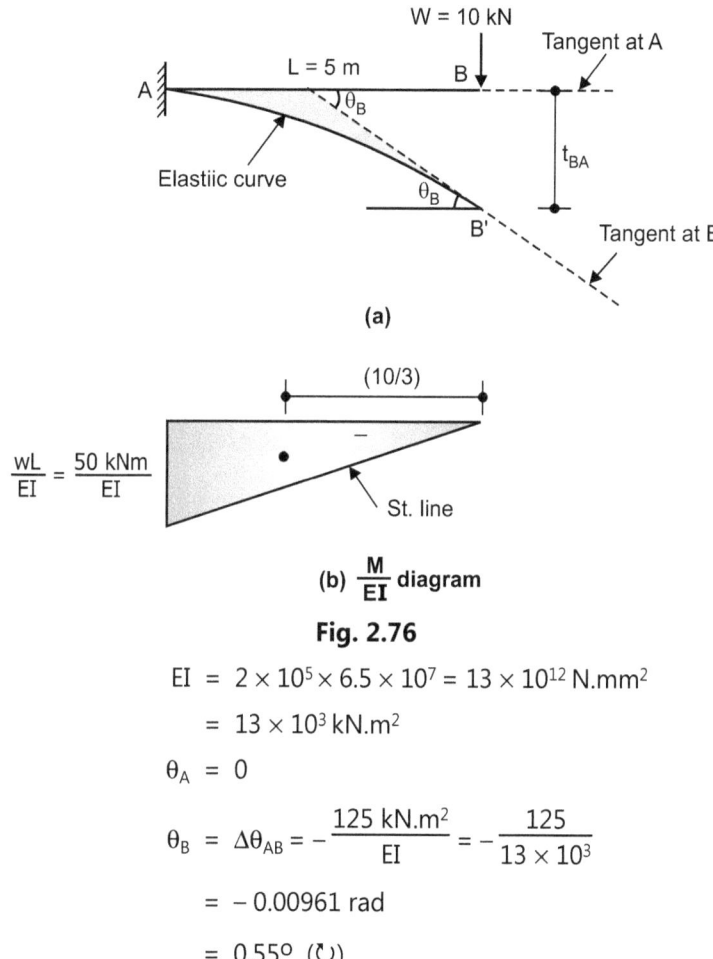

Fig. 2.76

$EI = 2 \times 10^5 \times 6.5 \times 10^7 = 13 \times 10^{12}$ N.mm²

$= 13 \times 10^3$ kN.m²

Also $\theta_A = 0$

∴ $\theta_B = \Delta\theta_{AB} = -\dfrac{125 \text{ kN.m}^2}{EI} = -\dfrac{125}{13 \times 10^3}$

$= -0.00961$ rad

$= 0.55°$ (↻)

(−ve sign indicates that angle made by tangent drawn at A with tangent drawn at B' is clockwise.)

(ii) Displacement of B' with respect to tangent drawn at A = t_{BA}

∴ t_{BA} = Moment of area of $\dfrac{M}{EI}$ diagram between A and B' about B'.

∴ $t_{BA} = y_B = \left[\dfrac{1}{2} \times \dfrac{-50 \text{ kN.m}}{EI}\right] \times 5 \times \dfrac{2}{3}$ (5)

$= -\dfrac{416.67 \text{ kN.m}^3}{EI}$

$= -\dfrac{416.67 \times 10^3}{13 \times 10^3} = 32.051$ mm (↓)

(− ve sign indicates that, B' is below tangent drawn at A)

Problem 2.30 : Find slope and deflections at B and C for cantilever shown in Fig. 2.77 (a); using moment area method. Take $E = 2 \times 10^5$ MPa, $I = 4 \times 10^7$ mm^4, l (AB) = 2 m, l (BC) = 1 m.

Solution :

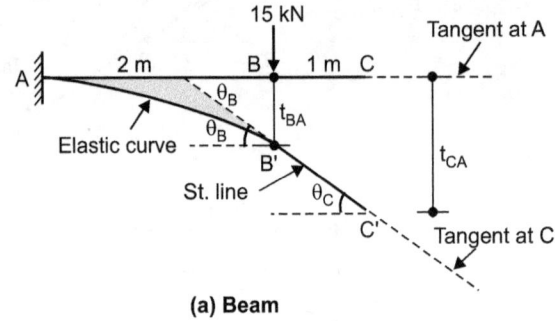

(a) Beam

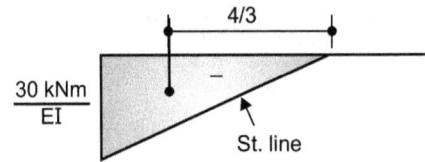

(b) $\dfrac{M}{EI}$ diagram

Fig. 2.77

(i) θ_B = Angle between tangent drawn at A and B' as tangent at A is horizontal

= Area of $\dfrac{M}{EI}$ diagram between A and B'

$= \left[\dfrac{1}{2} \times (-30) \dfrac{\text{kN.m}}{EI} \right] \times 2 = \dfrac{-30 \text{ kN.m}^2}{EI}$

$EI = 2 \times 10^5 \times 4 \times 10^7 = 8 \times 10^{12}$ Nmm^2

$= 8 \times 10^3$ kN.m^2

$\theta_B = \dfrac{-30 \text{ kN.m}^2}{EI} = \dfrac{-30}{8 \times 10^3}$

$= -0.00375$ rad

$= 0.214°$ (↻)

$\theta_C = \theta_B = 0.214°$ (↻)

$y_B = t_{BA}$

= Displacement of B' with respect to tangent drawn at A

= Moment of area of $\dfrac{M}{EI}$ diagram between A and B' about B'

$$= \left[\frac{-30 \text{ kN.m}^2}{EI}\right] \times \frac{4}{3}$$

$$= -\frac{40 \text{ kN.m}^3}{EI} = -\frac{40 \times 10^3}{8 \times 10^3} = 5 \text{ mm } (\downarrow)$$

$y_C = t_{CA}$

= Displacement of C' with respect to tangent drawn at A

= Moment of area of $\frac{M}{EI}$ diagram between A and C' about C'

$$= \left[-\frac{30 \text{ kN.m}^2}{EI}\right]\left(1 + \frac{4}{3}\right)$$

$$= -\frac{70 \text{ kN.m}^3}{EI} = -\frac{70 \times 10^3}{8 \times 10^3}$$

$$= 8.75 \text{ mm } (\downarrow)$$

Problem 2.31 : Using moment area method, derive expression for slope and deflection at free end of cantilever of uniform section carrying uniformly distributed load of intensity 'w' per unit run, throughout the span.

Solution : [Refer Fig. 2.78 (a)]

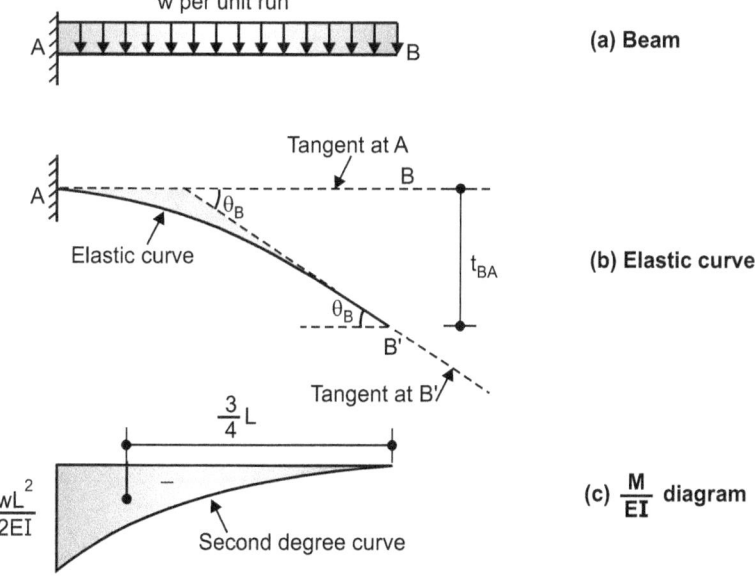

Fig. 2.78

θ_B = Angle between tangents drawn at A and B'; as tangent at A is horizontal

= Area of $\dfrac{M}{EI}$ diagram between A and B'

$= -\left(\dfrac{1}{3} \times L \times \dfrac{wL^2}{2\,EI}\right) = \dfrac{wL^3}{6\,EI}$ (↺)

$y_B = t_{BA}$ = Displacement of B' with respect to tangent drawn at A

= Moment of area of $\dfrac{M}{EI}$ diagram between A and B' about B'

$= -\left(\dfrac{wL^3}{6\,EI}\right)\dfrac{3}{4}(L) = \dfrac{wL^4}{8\,EI}$ (↓)

Problem 2.32 : For the cantilever beam shown in Fig. 2.79 (a), find slope and deflection at free end using moment area method. Take EI = Constant.

Solution :

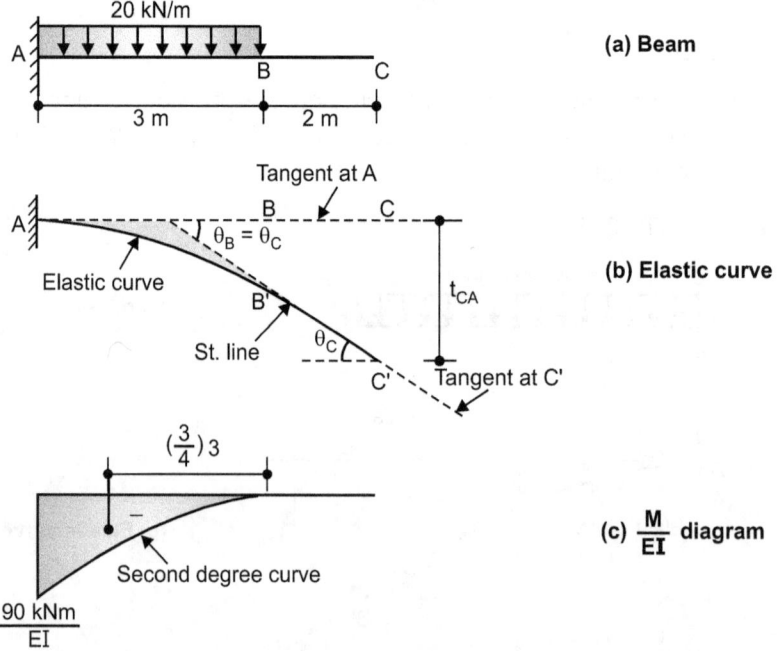

Fig. 2.79

Slope at free end = θ_C = Angle between tangents drawn at A and C' as tangent at A is horizontal.

= Area of $\dfrac{M}{EI}$ diagram between A and C'

$= -\left[\dfrac{1}{3} \times 90\,\dfrac{kN.m}{EI} \times 3\right] = 90\ kN.m^2/EI$ (↺)

$y_C = t_{CA}$ = Displacement of C' with respect to tangent drawn at A

= Moment of area of $\dfrac{M}{EI}$ diagram between A and C' about C'

$$y_C = -\left[\dfrac{90 \text{ kN.m}^2}{EI}\right]\left(2 + \dfrac{3}{4}(3)\right)$$

$$= \dfrac{382.5 \text{ kN.m}^3}{EI} \ (\downarrow)$$

Problem 2.33 : Determine slope and deflection at free end and at point C, 2 m from fixed end A for the cantilever beam shown in Fig. 2.80 (a), using moment area method,

Take $E = 2 \times 10^5$ MPa; $I = 5 \times 10^8$ mm^4.

Solution :

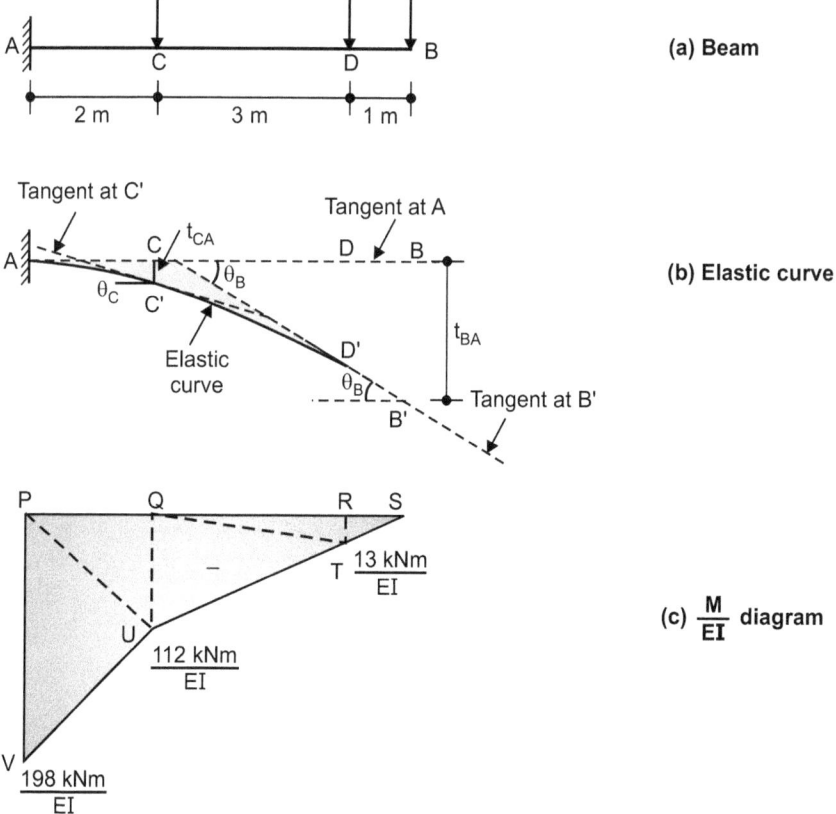

Fig. 2.80

Table 2.3

Area	Distances of C.G. from C' (m)	Distances of C.G. from B' (m)	Moment of area @ C'	Moment of area @ B'
Δ PUV $= -\dfrac{1}{2} \times \dfrac{198 \text{ kN.m}}{EI} \times 2$ $= -198 \text{ kN.m}^2/EI$	$\left(\dfrac{2}{3}\right) 2 = \dfrac{4}{3}$	$4 + \dfrac{4}{3} = \dfrac{16}{3}$	$-264 \dfrac{\text{kN.m}^3}{EI}$	$-1056 \dfrac{\text{kN.m}^3}{EI}$
Δ PQU $= -\dfrac{1}{2} \times 2 \times \dfrac{112 \text{ kN.m}}{EI}$ $= -112 \text{ kN.m}^2/EI$	$\left(\dfrac{1}{3}\right) 2 = \dfrac{2}{3}$	$4 + \dfrac{2}{3} = \dfrac{14}{3}$	$-74.67 \dfrac{\text{kN.m}^3}{EI}$	$-522.67 \dfrac{\text{kN.m}^3}{EI}$
Δ QTU $= -\dfrac{1}{2} \times 3 \times \dfrac{112 \text{ kN.m}}{EI}$ $= -168 \text{ kN.m}^2/EI$	–	$1 + \dfrac{2}{3}(3) = 3$	–	$-504 \dfrac{\text{kN.m}^3}{EI}$
Δ QTR $= -\dfrac{1}{2} \times 3 \times \dfrac{13 \text{ kN.m}}{EI}$ $= -19.5 \text{ kN.m}^2/EI$	–	$1 + \dfrac{1}{3}(3) = 2$	–	$-39 \text{ kN.m}^3/EI$
Δ RST $= -\dfrac{1}{2} \times 1 \times \dfrac{13 \text{ kN.m}}{EI}$ $= -6.5 \text{ kN.m}^2/EI$	–	$\dfrac{2}{3}$	–	$-4.33 \dfrac{\text{kN.m}^3}{EI}$
Total			$-338.67 \dfrac{\text{kN.m}^3}{EI}$	$-2126 \dfrac{\text{kN.m}^3}{EI}$

(i) Slope and deflection at C :

θ_C = Angle between tangents drawn to elastic curve at A and C' as tangent at A is horizontal

= Area of $\dfrac{M}{EI}$ diagram between A and C'

$= -(198 + 112) \text{ kN.m}^2/EI = -\dfrac{310 \text{ kN.m}^2}{EI}$

$EI = 2 \times 10^5 \times 5 \times 10^8 \text{ Nmm}^2$
$= 10 \times 10^{13} \text{ Nmm}^2 = 10 \times 10^4 \text{ kN.m}^2$

∴ $\theta_C = -\dfrac{310}{10 \times 10^4} = -0.0031 \text{ rad} = 0.177° \;(\circlearrowleft)$

Deflection at C = $y_C = t_{CA}$

= Displacement of C' with respect to tangent drawn at A

= Moment of area of $\frac{M}{EI}$ diagram between A and C' about C'

$= -\dfrac{338.67 \text{ kN.m}^3}{EI}$

$= -\dfrac{338.67 \times 10^3}{10 \times 10^4}$

= 3.3867 mm (↓)

(ii) Slope and deflection at B :

θ_B = Angle between tangents drawn to elastic curve at A and B' as tangent at A is horizontal.

= Area of $\frac{M}{EI}$ diagram between A and B'

= − (198 + 112 + 168 + 19.5 + 6.5) kN.m²/EI

$= -\dfrac{504 \text{ kN.m}^2}{EI}$

$= -\dfrac{504}{10 \times 10^4}$

= − 0.00504 rad

= 0.288° (↺)

Deflection at B = $y_B = t_{BA}$

= Displacement of B' with respect to tangent drawn at A

= Moment of area of $\frac{M}{EI}$ diagram between A and B' about B'

$= -\dfrac{2126 \text{ kN.m}^3}{EI}$

$= -\dfrac{2126 \times 10^3}{10 \times 10^4}$

= 21.26 mm (↓)

Problem 2.34 : Determine slope and deflection at free end and at C for cantilever shown in Fig. 2.81 (a), using moment area method.

Take $E = 2 \times 10^5$ MPa ; $I = 5 \times 10^8$ mm⁴.

Solution : $EI = 2 \times 10^5 \times 5 \times 10^8$

$= 10 \times 10^{13}$ Nmm²

$= 10 \times 10^4$ kN.m²

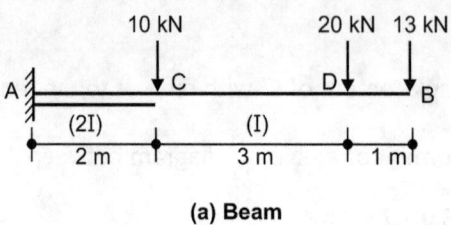

(a) Beam

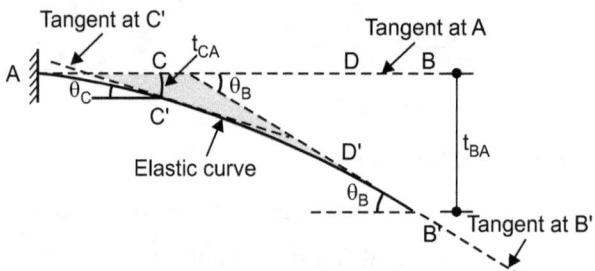

(b) Elastic curve

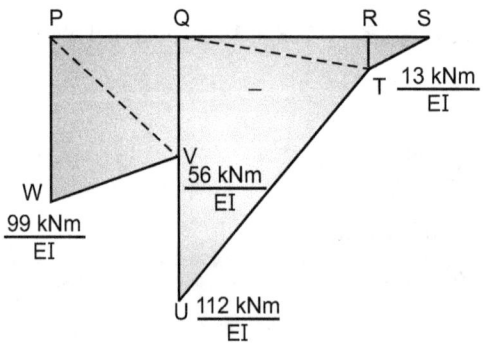

(c) $\dfrac{M}{EI}$ diagram

Fig. 2.81

Table 2.4

Area	Distances of C.G. from C' (m)	Distances of C.G. from B' (m)	Moment of area @ C'	Moment of area @ B'
Δ PVW $= -\dfrac{1}{2} \times 2 \times \dfrac{99 \text{ kN.m}}{EI}$ $= -99 \dfrac{\text{kN.m}^2}{EI}$	$\dfrac{2}{3}(2) = \dfrac{4}{3}$	$4 + \dfrac{4}{3} = \dfrac{16}{3}$	$-132 \dfrac{\text{kN.m}^3}{EI}$	$-528 \dfrac{\text{kN.m}^3}{EI}$

... Contd.

Δ PQV $= -\frac{1}{2} \times 2 \times 56 \frac{kN.m}{EI}$ $= -56 \frac{kN.m^2}{EI}$	$\frac{1}{3}(2) = \frac{2}{3}$	$4 + \frac{2}{3} = \frac{14}{3}$	$-37.33 \frac{kN.m^3}{EI}$	$-261.33 \frac{kN.m^3}{EI}$
Δ QUT $= -\frac{1}{2} \times 3 \times 112 \frac{kN.m}{EI}$ $= -168 \ kN.m^2/EI$	—	$1 + \frac{2}{3}(3) = 3$	—	$-\frac{504 \ kN.m^3}{EI}$
Δ QRT $= -\frac{1}{2} \times 3 \times 13 \frac{kN.m}{EI}$ $= -19.5 \ kN.m^2/EI$	—	$1 + \frac{1}{3}(3) = 2$	—	$-\frac{39 \ kN.m^3}{EI}$
Δ RST $= -\frac{1}{2} \times 1 \times \frac{13 \ kN.m}{EI}$ $= -6.5 \frac{kN.m^2}{EI}$	—	$\frac{2}{3}(1) = \frac{2}{3}$	—	$-\frac{4.33 \ kN.m^3}{EI}$
		Total	$-\frac{169.33 \ kN.m^3}{EI}$	$-\frac{1336.67 \ kN.m^3}{EI}$

(i) θ_C = Angle between tangents drawn at A and C' as tangent drawn at A is horizontal

= Area of $\frac{M}{EI}$ diagram between A and C'

$= -(99 + 56) \frac{kN.m^2}{EI} = -\frac{155 \ kN.m^2}{EI} = -\frac{155}{10 \times 10^4} = 0.00155$ rad (↻)

$= 0.088°$ (↻)

$y_C = t_{CA}$

= Displacement of C' with respect to tangent drawn at A

= Moment of area of $\frac{M}{EI}$ diagram between A and C' about C'

$= -\frac{169.33 \ kN.m^3}{EI} = -\frac{169.33 \ (10)^3}{10 \times 10^4} = 1.693$ mm (↓)

(ii) θ_B = Angle between tangents drawn at A and B' as tangent drawn at A is horizontal

= Area of $\frac{M}{EI}$ diagram between A and B'

$$= -[99 + 56 + 168 + 19.5 + 6.5] \text{ kN.m}^2/EI$$
$$= -349 \text{ kN.m}^2/EI$$
$$= -\frac{349}{10 \times 10^4} = 3.49 \times 10^{-3} \text{ rad } (\circlearrowleft) = 0.199° (\circlearrowleft)$$

$y_B = t_{BA}$
= Displacement of B' with respect to tangent drawn at A
= Moment of area of $\frac{M}{EI}$ diagram between A and B' about B'
$$= -\frac{1336.67 \text{ kN.m}^3}{EI} = -\frac{1336.67 \times (10)^3}{10 \times 10^4} = 13.36 \text{ mm } (\downarrow)$$

Problem 2.35 : Determine slope and deflection at free end of cantilever shown in Fig. 2.82 (a), using moment area method. Take E = 2×10^5 MPa; I = 8×10^8 mm^4.

Solution :

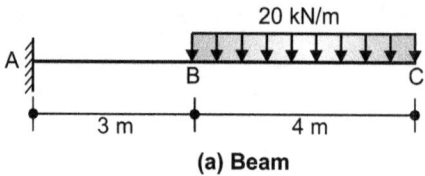

(a) Beam

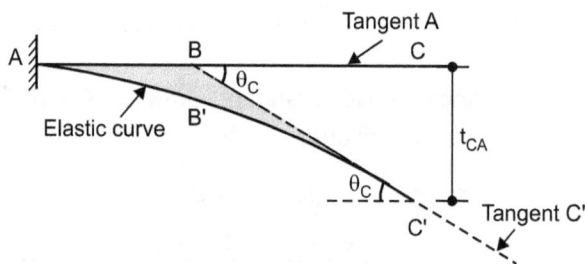

(b) Elastic curve

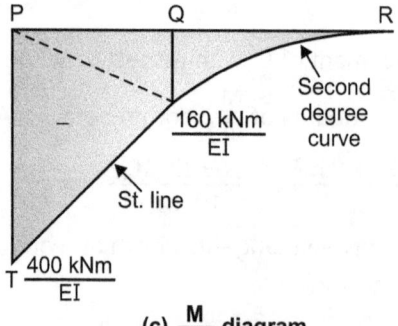

(c) $\frac{M}{EI}$ diagram

Fig. 2.82

Table 2.5

Area	Distances of C.G. from C' (m)	Moment of area @ C'
$\Delta \text{ PST} = -\dfrac{1}{2} \times 3 \times \dfrac{400 \text{ kN.m}}{EI}$ $= \dfrac{-600 \text{ kN.m}^2}{EI}$	$4 + \dfrac{2}{3}(3) = 6$	$\dfrac{-3600 \text{ kN.m}^3}{EI}$
$\Delta \text{ PQS} = -\dfrac{1}{2} \times \dfrac{160 \text{ kN.m}}{EI} \times 3$ $= \dfrac{-240 \text{ kN.m}^2}{EI}$	$4 + \dfrac{1}{3}(3) = 5$	$\dfrac{-1200 \text{ kN.m}^3}{EI}$
$\Delta \text{ QRS} = -\dfrac{1}{3} \times 4 \times \dfrac{160 \text{ kN.m}}{EI}$ $= \dfrac{-213.33 \text{ kN.m}^2}{EI}$	$\dfrac{3}{4}(4) = 3$	$\dfrac{-640 \text{ kN.m}^3}{EI}$
	Total	$\dfrac{-5440 \text{ kN.m}^3}{EI}$

$$EI = 2 \times 10^5 \times 8 \times 10^8$$
$$= 16 \times 10^{13} \text{ N-mm}^2$$
$$= 16 \times 10^4 \text{ kN.m}^2$$

θ_C = Angle between tangents drawn at A and C' as tangent drawn to elastic curve at A is horizontal

$\quad$ = Area of $\dfrac{M}{EI}$ diagram between A and C'

$\quad = -(600 + 240 + 213.33) \text{ kN.m}^2/EI$

$\quad = -1053.33 \text{ kN.m}^2/EI$

$\quad = -\dfrac{1053.33}{16 \times 10^4} = -0.00658 \text{ rad}$

$\quad = 0.377° \; (\circlearrowleft)$

$y_C = t_{CA}$

$\quad$ = Displacement of C' with respect to tangent drawn at A

$\quad$ = Moment of area of $\dfrac{M}{EI}$ diagram between A and C' about C'

$\quad = -\dfrac{5440 \text{ kN.m}^3}{EI} = -\dfrac{5440 \times 10^3}{16 \times 10^4}$

$\quad = 34 \text{ mm } (\downarrow)$

Problem 2.36 : Find slope and deflection at C for cantilever beam of uniform section shown in Fig. 2.83 (a) using moment area method. Take $E = 2 \times 10^5$ MPa, $I = 5 \times 10^8$ mm^4.

Solution :

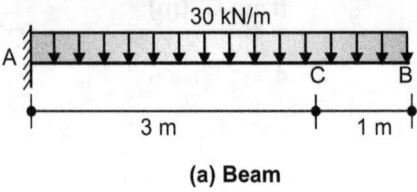

(a) Beam

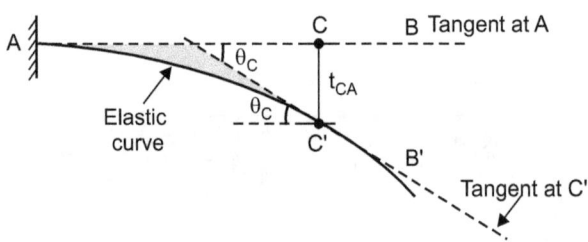

(b) Elastic curve

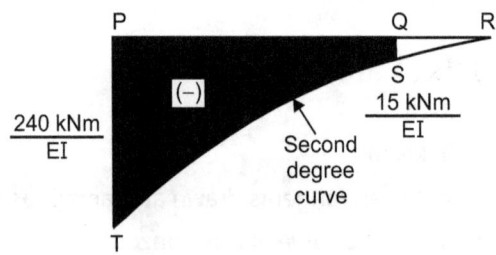

(c) $\dfrac{M}{EI}$ diagram

Fig. 2.83

$EI = 2 \times 10^5 \times 5 \times 10^8 = 10 \times 10^{13}$ N.mm^2
$ = 10 \times 10^4$ kN.m^2

θ_C = Angle between tangents drawn at A and C' as tangent drawn at A is horizontal

 = Area of $\dfrac{M}{EI}$ diagram between A and C' = Area PQST

Let, a_1 = Area PRT

$ = -\dfrac{1}{3} \times 4 \times 240 \;\dfrac{\text{kN.m}}{EI} = \dfrac{-320 \text{ kN.m}^2}{EI}$

a_2 = Area QRS

$ = -\dfrac{1}{3} \times 1 \times \dfrac{15 \text{ kN.m}}{EI} = -\dfrac{5 \text{ kN.m}^2}{EI}$

∴ Area PQST $= -(320-5)\dfrac{kN.m^2}{EI} = -315$ kN.m²/EI

∴ $\theta_C = -\dfrac{315}{10 \times 10^4} = -0.00315$ rad $= 0.180°$ (↻)

Let x_1 and x_2 be distances of centre of gravity of area 1 and 2 from R.

$$x_1 = \dfrac{3}{4}(4) = 3 \text{ m}, \quad x_2 = \dfrac{3}{4}(1) = \dfrac{3}{4} \text{ m}$$

∴ $\bar{x}$ = Distance of centre of gravity of area PQST from R

$$= \dfrac{a_1 x_1 - a_2 x_2}{a_1 - a_2}$$

$$\bar{x} = \dfrac{320 \times 3 - 5 \times \dfrac{3}{4}}{315} = 3.0357 \text{ m}$$

∴ Distance of C.G. of area PQST from Q $= (3.0357 - 1) = 2.0357$ m

$y_C = t_{CA}$

= Displacement of C' with respect to tangent drawn at A

= Moment of area of $\dfrac{M}{EI}$ diagram between A and C' about C'

$= -(315 \times 2.0357)$ kN.m³/EI $= -641.25 \dfrac{kN.m^3}{EI}$

$= -\dfrac{641.25 \times 10^3}{10 \times 10^4} = 6.4125$ mm (↓)

2.11 APPLICATION OF MOMENT-AREA METHOD TO SIMPLY SUPPORTED AND OVERHANGING BEAMS

Consider a simply supported beam AB as shown in Fig. 2.84 (a). Assuming the beam has constant flexural rigidity and let, it be required to find slope at supports A and B and deflection under load point.

$$\theta_A = \dfrac{t_{BA}}{L}$$

and $\theta_B = \dfrac{t_{AB}}{L}$

where, t_{BA} = Displacement of B with respect to tangent drawn at A and
t_{AB} = Displacement of A with respect to tangent drawn at B

Here, t_{AB} and t_{BA} will be positive due to sagging bending moments; indicating that A and B are located above the tangents drawn at B and A respectively. By second theorem of moment area;

$$t_{AB} = \text{Area (PQR) } \bar{x}_A \text{ and}$$

$$t_{BA} = \text{Area (PQR) } \bar{x}_B$$

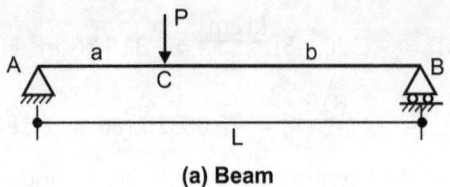

(a) Beam

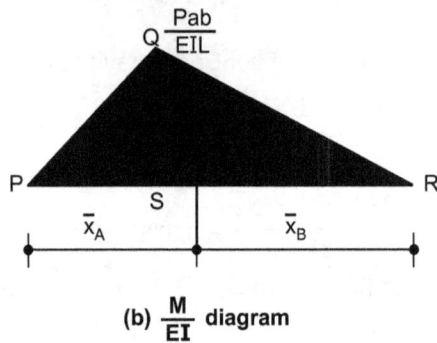

(b) $\dfrac{M}{EI}$ diagram

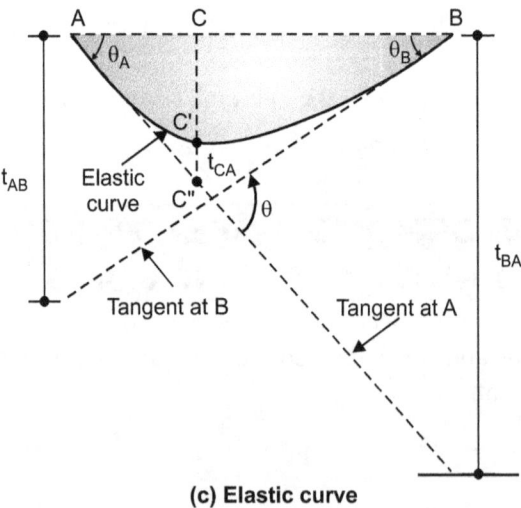

(c) Elastic curve

Fig. 2.84

From Fig. 2.84 (c).

Deflection under load = y_C = CC′ = CC″ − C′C″

where   CC″ = $(\theta_A) \cdot a$ and C′C″ = t_{CA}

        = Displacement of C′ with respect to tangent drawn at A to elastic curve.

        = Moment of area of $\dfrac{M}{EI}$ diagram between A and C′ about C′

        = Area (PQS) × Distance of C.G. of area (PQS) from S i.e. (C′)

Here, t_{CA} will be positive indicating that C' is above tangent at A. Note that, slope and deflection at various points of simply supported beam cannot be determined directly as in case of cantilevers. Application of moment-area method to determine slope and deflection at various points of simply supported and overhanging beams is illustrated in the following examples.

SOLVED PROBLEMS

Problem 2.37 : Using moment-area method, find deflection at centre and slope at supports for simply supported beam of uniform section carrying concentrated load P at centre. [Refer Fig. 2.85 (a)].

Solution :

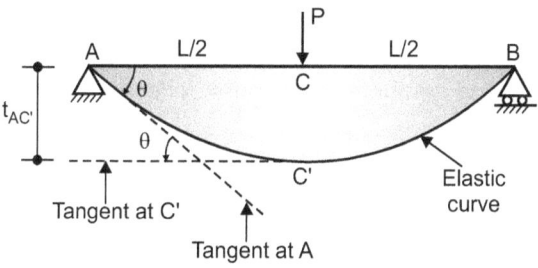

(a) Beam and Elastic curve

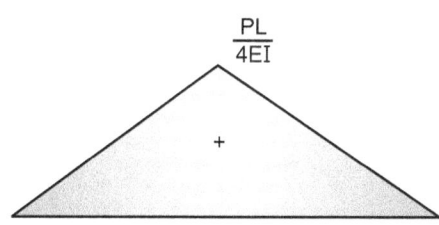

(b) $\dfrac{M}{EI}$ diagram

Fig. 2.85

Due to symmetry; maximum deflection occurs at centre and tangent drawn to elastic curve at centre is horizontal.

∴ Angle between tangents drawn at A and C'

$$= \theta = \text{Slope at A} = \text{Area of } \frac{M}{EI} \text{ diagram between A and C'}$$

$$= \frac{1}{2}\left(\frac{L}{2}\right) \times \frac{PL}{4\,EI} = \frac{PL^2}{16\,EI} \;(\circlearrowleft)$$

+ve sign indicates that angle made by tangent drawn at A with tangent drawn at C' is anticlockwise.

By symmetry, slope at B = θ = $\dfrac{PL^2}{16\,EI}$ $(\circlearrowright)$

Displacement of A with respect to tangent drawn at C' = t_{AC}

= Moment of area of $\frac{M}{EI}$ diagram between A and C' about A

∴ $t_{AC'} = \left[\frac{1}{2}\left(\frac{L}{2}\right)\frac{PL}{4EI}\right]\frac{2}{3}\left(\frac{L}{2}\right)$

$= \frac{PL^3}{48 EI}$

Point A is above the tangent at C', hence $t_{AC'}$ is + ve.

$$y_C = y_{max} = t_{AC'} = \frac{PL^3}{48 EI} (\downarrow)$$

Problem 2.38 : For simply supported beam shown in Fig. 2.86 (a), find slope and deflection at centre of beam. Use moment-area method and assume uniform flexural rigidity. Also find position and amount of maximum deflection.

Solution :

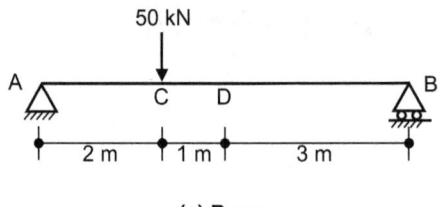

(a) Beam

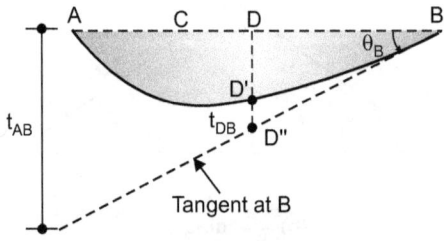

(b) Elastic curve

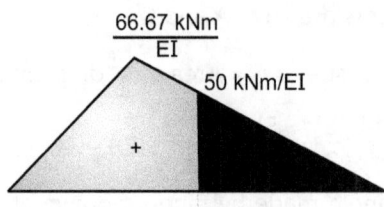

(c) $\frac{M}{EI}$ diagram

Fig. 2.86

(i) From elastic curve :

$$y_D = \text{Deflection at centre} = DD' = DD'' - D'D''$$

where, $\quad DD'' = (\theta_B) \times 3$ and

$\quad D'D'' = $ Displacement of D' with respect to tangent drawn at B $= t_{D'B}$

$\quad\quad\quad = $ Moment of area of $\dfrac{M}{EI}$ diagram between D' and B about D'

To find DD'', $\quad DD'' = (\theta_B) \times 3$

where, $\quad \theta_B = \dfrac{t_{AB}}{6}$

$\quad t_{AB} = $ Displacement of A with respect to tangent drawn at B

$\quad\quad\quad = $ Moment of area of $\dfrac{M}{EI}$ diagram between A and B about A

$$= \left[\dfrac{1}{2} \times 6 \times 66.67 \dfrac{kN.m}{EI}\right] \times \left(\dfrac{6+2}{3}\right)$$

$$= \dfrac{533.33 \text{ kN.m}^3}{EI}$$

∴ $\quad \theta_B = \dfrac{t_{AB}}{6} = \dfrac{533.33 \text{ kN.m}^3}{6 \quad EI} = \dfrac{88.88 \text{ kN.m}^2}{EI}$

∴ $\quad DD'' = \left(\dfrac{88.88 \text{ kN.m}^2}{EI}\right) \times 3 = 266.67 \dfrac{\text{kN.m}^3}{EI}$

To find $\quad D'D'' = t_{D'B}$

$$= \dfrac{1}{2} \times \dfrac{50 \text{ kN.m}}{EI} \times (3) \times \dfrac{1}{3} \times (3) = \dfrac{75 \text{ kN.m}^3}{EI}$$

∴ $\quad y_D = DD'' - D'D'' = (266.67 - 75) \text{ kN.m}^3/EI$

$$y_D = \dfrac{191.67 \text{ kN.m}^3}{EI} \; (\downarrow)$$

The positive sign of t_{AB} and $t_{D'B}$ indicates that, points A and D' are above the tangent at B.

(ii) To find slope at centre (θ_D) :

We have, $\quad \theta_B = \theta_D + \Delta \theta_{DB}$

where, $\quad \Delta \theta_{DB} = $ Change of slope from D to B

$\quad\quad\quad = $ Angle between the tangents drawn at D and B to elastic curve

$\quad\quad\quad = $ Area of $\dfrac{M}{EI}$ diagram between D and B

$$= \frac{1}{2} \times 3 \times 50 \frac{kN.m}{EI} = \frac{75 \; kN.m^2}{EI}$$

$$\therefore \quad \theta_D = \theta_B - \Delta\theta_{DB} = (88.88 - 75)\frac{kN.m^2}{EI} = \frac{13.88 \; kN.m^2}{EI} \text{ radians } (\circlearrowleft)$$

(iii) To locate point of maximum deflection :

Tangent drawn to elastic curve at a point where maximum deflection occurs will be horizontal i.e. slope will be zero at that point. Let the point be at a distance 'x' from B. [As l (CB) > l (AC)]

$$\therefore \quad \theta_x = 0$$
$$\theta_B = \theta_x + \Delta\theta_{xB}$$
$$\therefore \quad \theta_B = \Delta\theta_{xB}$$

where, $\Delta\theta_{xB}$ = Change of slope between x and B

$$= \text{Area of } \frac{M}{EI} \text{ diagram between x and B}$$

$$= \frac{1}{2}(x) \frac{66.67 \; kN.m}{EI} \left(\frac{x}{4}\right) = \frac{66.67}{8}(x^2)\frac{kN.m^2}{EI}$$

$$\therefore \quad \theta_B = \theta_{xB}$$

$$88.88 \frac{kN.m^2}{EI} = \frac{66.67}{8}(x^2)\frac{kN.m^2}{EI}$$

$$\therefore \quad x = 3.265 \text{ m from B}$$

$\therefore$ Maximum deflection at 3.265 m from B

$$= y_{max} = xx' = xx'' - x'x'' \qquad \text{[Refer Fig. 2.87]}$$

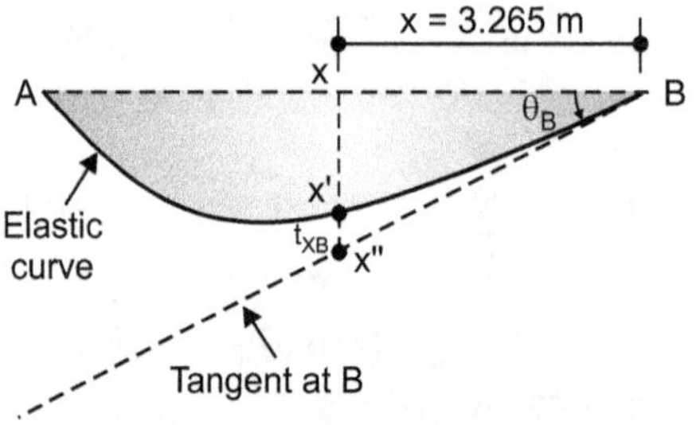

Fig. 2.87

$$xx'' = (\theta_B) \times 3.265 = 88.88 \frac{kN.m^2}{EI} \times 3.265$$

$$= 290.22 \frac{kN.m^3}{EI}$$

$x'x''$ = Displacement of x' with respect to tangent drawn at B = t_{xB}

$$= \text{Moment of area of } \frac{M}{EI} \text{ diagram between x and B about x}$$

$$= \frac{1}{2}(3.265)(66.67)\frac{kN.m}{EI} \times \left(\frac{3.265}{4}\right) \times \frac{3.265}{3}$$

$x' x'' = 96.68 \text{ kN.m}^3/EI$

$y_{max} = xx'' - x' x'' = (290.22 - 96.68) \text{ kN.m}^3/EI$

$y_{max} = 193.54 \dfrac{\text{kN.m}^3}{EI} (\downarrow)$

Problem 2.39 : Determine the central deflection and slope at supports for simply supported beam shown in Fig. 2.88 (a). Take $E = 2.1 \times 10^5$ MPa and $I = 3 \times 10^7$ mm^4.

Solution :

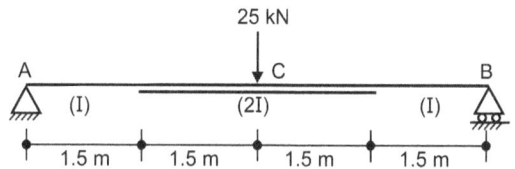

(a) Beam

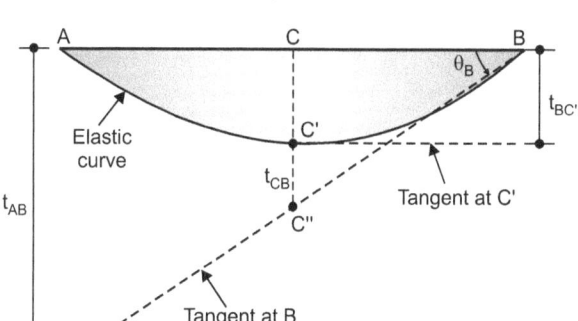

(b) Elastic curve

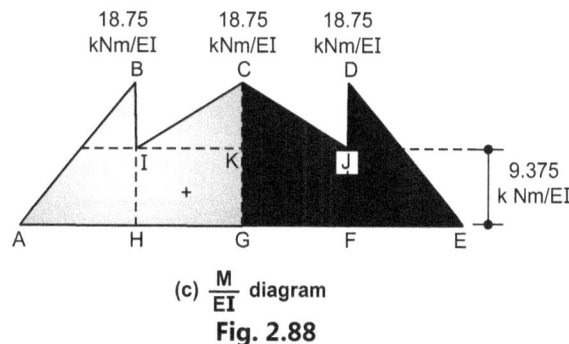

(c) $\dfrac{M}{EI}$ diagram

Fig. 2.88

(i) To find slope at supports :

t_{AB} = Displacement of A with respect to tangent drawn at B

= Moment of area of $\dfrac{M}{EI}$ diagram between A and B about A

Table 2.6

Area	Distances of C.G. from A (m)	Moment of area @ A
$ABH = \frac{1}{2} \times 1.5 \times \frac{18.75 \text{ kN.m}}{EI}$ $= \frac{14.0625 \text{ kN.m}^2}{EI}$	$\frac{2}{3}(1.5)$	$\frac{14.0625 \text{ kN.m}^3}{EI}$
$ICJ = \frac{1}{2} \times 3 \times \frac{9.375 \text{ kN.m}}{EI}$ $= \frac{14.0625 \text{ kN.m}^2}{EI}$	3	$\frac{42.1875 \text{ kN.m}^3}{EI}$
$IJHF = 3 \times \frac{9.375 \text{ kN.m}}{EI}$ $= 28.125 \frac{\text{kN.m}^2}{EI}$	3	$\frac{84.375 \text{ kN.m}^3}{EI}$
$DFE = \frac{1}{2} \times 1.5 \times \frac{18.75 \text{ kN.m}}{EI}$ $= \frac{14.0625 \text{ kN.m}^2}{EI}$	$4.5 + \frac{1}{3}(1.5) = 5$	$\frac{70.3125 \text{ kN.m}^3}{EI}$
	Total	$210.9375 \text{ kN.m}^3/EI$

$\therefore \quad t_{AB} = 210.9375 \text{ kN.m}^3/EI$

$\therefore \quad \theta_B = \frac{t_{AB}}{6} = \frac{210.9375 \text{ kN.m}^3/EI}{6} = 35.156 \frac{\text{kN.m}^2}{EI}$

$EI = 2.1 \times 10^5 \times 3 \times 10^7 \text{ Nmm}^2$
$= 6.3 \times 10^{12} \text{ N.mm}^2$
$= 6.3 \times 10^3 \text{ kN.m}^2$

$\therefore \quad \theta_B = \frac{35.156}{6.3 \times 10^3} = 0.00558 \text{ rad} = 0.319° \text{ (↻)}$

Due to symmetry,

$\theta_A = \theta_B = 0.319° \text{ (↻)}$

(ii) To find central deflection : Due to symmetry, central deflection is the maximum deflection, hence tangent drawn to elastic curve at C will be horizontal.

$\therefore \quad y_C = t_{BC'}$
$= $ Displacement of B with respect to tangent drawn at C'
$= $ Moment of area of $\frac{M}{EI}$ diagram between B and C about B

Table 2.7

Area	Distances of C.G. from B (m)	Moment of area @ B
$CKJ = \frac{1}{2} \times \frac{9.375 \text{ kN.m}}{EI} \times 1.5$ $= \frac{7.03125 \text{ kN.m}^2}{EI}$	$1.5 + \frac{2}{3} \times 1.5 = 2.5$	$\frac{17.578 \text{ kN.m}^3}{EI}$
$KJGF = 9.375 \frac{\text{kN.m}}{EI} \times 1.5$ $= 14.0625 \frac{\text{kN.m}^2}{EI}$	$1.5 + \frac{1.5}{2} = 2.25$	$\frac{31.64 \text{ kN.m}^3}{EI}$
$DFE = \frac{1}{2} \times 1.5 \times 18.75 \frac{\text{kN.m}}{EI}$ $= 14.0625 \frac{\text{kN.m}^2}{EI}$	$2/3 \ (1.5) = 1$	$14.0625 \text{ kN.m}^3/EI$
	Total	$63.2806 \text{ kN.m}^3/EI$

$\therefore \quad y_{max} = 63.2806 \dfrac{\text{kN.m}^3}{EI} = \dfrac{63.2806 \times 10^3}{6.3 \times 10^3} = 10.04 \text{ mm} (\downarrow)$

Problem 2.40 : Find slope at A, B and C and central deflection for a beam shown in Fig. 2.89 (a).

Solution :

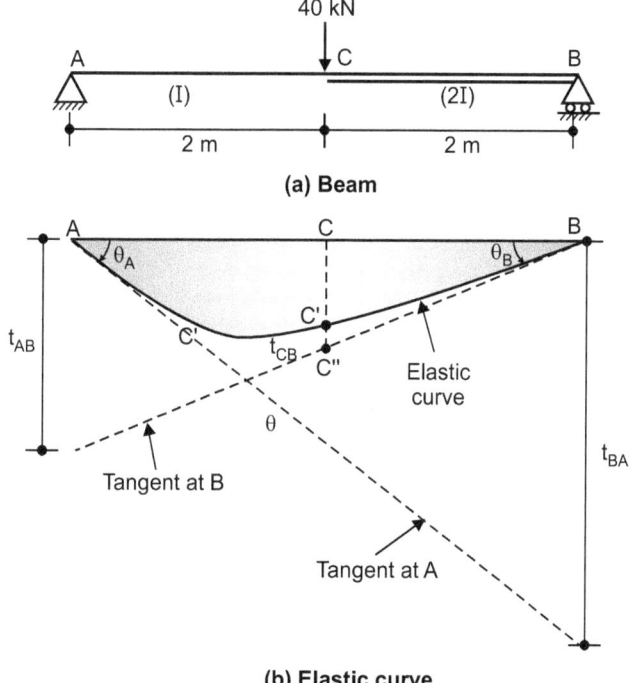

(a) Beam

(b) Elastic curve

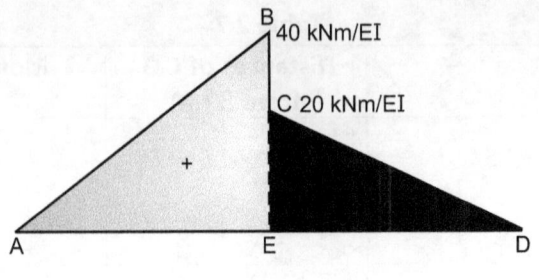

(c) $\frac{M}{EI}$ diagram

Fig. 2.89

(i) To find slope at A and B :

Table 2.8

Area	Distances of C.G. from A (m)	Distances of C.G. from B (m)	Moment of area @ A	Moment of area @ B
ABE $= \frac{1}{2} \times 2 \times \frac{40 \text{ kN.m}}{EI}$ $= 40 \text{ kN.m}^2/EI$	$\frac{2}{3}(2) = \frac{4}{3}$	$2 + \frac{2}{3} = 2.67$	$\frac{53.33 \text{ kN.m}^3}{EI}$	$\frac{106.8 \text{ kN.m}^3}{EI}$
CDE $= -\frac{1}{2} \times 2 \times \frac{20 \text{ kN.m}}{EI}$ $= 20 \text{ kN.m}^2/EI$	$2 + \frac{2}{3} = 2.67$	$\frac{2}{3}(2) = \frac{4}{3}$	$\frac{53.4 \text{ kN.m}^3}{EI}$	$\frac{26.67 \text{ kN.m}^3}{EI}$
		Total	$\frac{106.73 \text{ kN.m}^3}{EI}$	$\frac{133.47 \text{ kN.m}^3}{EI}$

∴ $t_{AB} = 106.73 \dfrac{\text{kN.m}^3}{EI}$

  $t_{BA} = 133.47 \dfrac{\text{kN.m}^3}{EI}$

∴ $\theta_B = \dfrac{t_{AB}}{4} = \dfrac{106.73}{4} \dfrac{\text{kN.m}^2}{EI}$

  $= \dfrac{26.68 \text{ kN.m}^2}{EI}$ (↻)

  $\theta_A = \dfrac{t_{BA}}{4} = \dfrac{133.47}{4} \dfrac{\text{kN.m}^2}{EI}$

  $= \dfrac{33.36 \text{ kN.m}^2}{EI}$ (↻)

(ii) To find slope at C :

$$\theta_B = \theta_C + \Delta\theta_{CB}$$

where, $\Delta\theta_{CB}$ = Change of slope from C to B

= Angle between tangents drawn at C and B to elastic curve

= Area of $\frac{M}{EI}$ diagram between C and B

$$= \frac{1}{2} \times 2 \times 20 \text{ kN.m}/EI$$

$$= 20 \text{ kN.m}^2/EI$$

∴ $\theta_C = \theta_B - \Delta\theta_{CB}$

$$= (26.68 - 20) \frac{\text{kN.m}^2}{EI}$$

$$= 6.68 \frac{\text{kN.m}^2}{EI} \ (\circlearrowleft)$$

(iii) To find deflection at C :

$$y_C = CC' = CC'' - C'C''$$

where, $CC'' = (\theta_B) \times 2$

$$= 26.68 \frac{\text{kN.m}^2}{EI} \times 2 = 53.36 \frac{\text{kN.m}^3}{EI}$$

$C'C'' = t_{CB}$

= Displacement of C with respect to tangent drawn at B.

= Moment of area of $\frac{M}{EI}$ diagram between C and B about C

$$= \left[\frac{1}{2} \times 2 \times 20 \frac{\text{kN.m}}{EI}\right] \left(\frac{2}{3}\right)$$

$$= 13.33 \frac{\text{kN.m}^3}{EI}$$

∴ $y_C = CC'' - C'C''$

$$= (53.36 - 13.33) \text{ kN.m}^3/EI$$

$$= 40.03 \frac{\text{kN.m}^3}{EI}$$

∴ $y_C = 40.03 \frac{\text{kN.m}^3}{EI} \ (\downarrow)$

Problem 2.41 : Find slope at supports and deflection at D for a simply supported beam of uniform section shown in Fig. 2.90 (a); using moment area method. Take E = 2 × 10⁵ MPa; I = 3 × 10⁸ mm⁴.

Solution : Analysis of given beam;

$$V_B \times 6 = 20 \times 3 \times \frac{3}{2} + 60 \times 4 \Rightarrow V_B = 55 \text{ kN } (\uparrow)$$

$$V_A + V_B = 20 \times 3 + 60 \Rightarrow V_A = 65 \text{ kN } (\uparrow)$$

$$\therefore \quad M_C = 65 \times 3 - 20 \times 3 \times \frac{3}{2} = 105 \text{ kN.m (sagging)}$$

$$M_D = 55 \times 2 = 110 \text{ kN.m (sagging)}$$

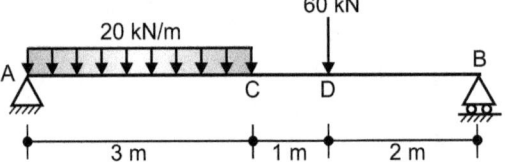

(a) Beam

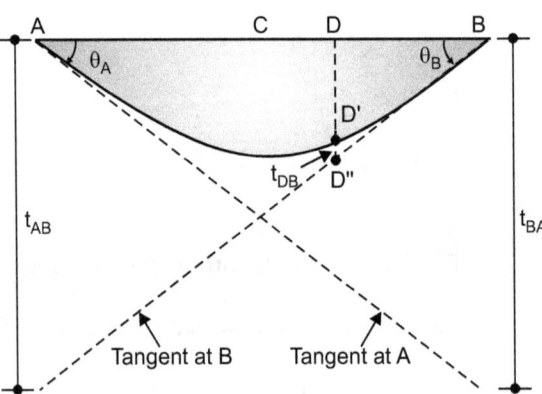

(b) Elastic curve

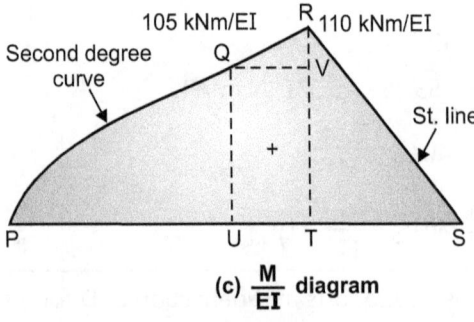

(c) $\frac{M}{EI}$ diagram

Fig. 2.90

Table 2.9

Area	Distances of C.G. from A (m)	Distances of C.G. from B (m)	Moment of area about A	Moment of area about B
PQU $= \frac{2}{3}(3) \frac{105 \text{ kN.m}}{EI}$ $= \frac{210 \text{ kN.m}^2}{EI}$	$\frac{5}{8}(3) = \frac{15}{8}$	$3 + \frac{3}{8}(3) = \frac{33}{8}$	$\frac{393.75 \text{ kN.m}^3}{EI}$	$\frac{866.25 \text{ kN.m}^3}{EI}$
QVUT $= 1 \times \frac{105 \text{ kN.m}}{EI}$ $= \frac{105 \text{ kN.m}^3}{EI}$	3.5	2.5	$\frac{367.5 \text{ kN.m}^3}{EI}$	$\frac{262.5 \text{ kN.m}^3}{EI}$
QVR $= \frac{1}{2} \times 1 \times \frac{5 \text{ kN.m}}{EI}$ $= 2.5 \frac{\text{kN.m}^2}{EI}$	$3 + \frac{2}{3}(1) = \frac{11}{3}$	$2 + \frac{1}{3}(1) = \frac{7}{3}$	$\frac{9.167 \text{ kN.m}^3}{EI}$	$\frac{5.833 \text{ kN.m}^3}{EI}$
RST $= \frac{1}{2} \times 2 \times \frac{110 \text{ kN.m}}{EI}$ $= 110 \frac{\text{kN.m}^2}{EI}$	$4 + \frac{1}{3}(2)$ $= \frac{14}{3}$	$\frac{2}{3}(2) = \frac{4}{3}$	$\frac{513.33 \text{ kN.m}^3}{EI}$	$\frac{146.67 \text{ kN.m}^3}{EI}$
		Total	$\frac{1283.74 \text{ kN.m}^3}{EI}$	$\frac{1281.25 \text{ kN.m}^3}{EI}$

$EI = 2 \times 10^5 \times 3 \times 10^8 = 6 \times 10^{13} \text{ N.mm}^2 = 6 \times 10^4 \text{ kN.m}^2$

(i) Slope at $A = \theta_A = \dfrac{t_{BA}}{6}$

where, t_{BA} = Displacement of B with respect to tangent drawn at A

= Moment of area of $\dfrac{M}{EI}$ diagram between A and B about B

∴ $t_{BA} = 1281.25 \dfrac{\text{kN.m}^3}{EI}$ $\quad \begin{bmatrix} \text{+ve sign indicates that B} \\ \text{is above the tangent drawn at A} \end{bmatrix}$

∴ $\theta_A = \dfrac{1281.25}{6} \dfrac{\text{kN.m}^2}{EI}$

$= 213.54 \dfrac{\text{kN.m}^2}{EI} = \dfrac{213.54}{6 \times 10^4} = 0.00356 \text{ rad} = 0.203° \text{ (↺)}$

(ii) Slope at B = $\theta_B = \dfrac{t_{AB}}{6}$

where, t_{AB} = Displacement of A with respect to tangent drawn at B

= Moment of area of $\dfrac{M}{EI}$ diagram between A and B about A

= $\dfrac{1283.74 \text{ kN.m}^3}{EI}$ $\begin{bmatrix} \text{+ve sign indicates that A} \\ \text{is above the tangent drawn at B} \end{bmatrix}$

∴ $\theta_B = \dfrac{1283.74 \text{ kN.m}^2}{6 \quad EI} = \dfrac{213.95 \text{ kN.m}^2}{EI}$

= $\dfrac{213.95}{6 \times 10^4}$ = 0.00356 rad = 0.204° (↻)

(iii) Deflection at D = y_D = DD' = DD" – D'D"

where, DD" = $(\theta_B) 2 = \dfrac{213.95 \text{ kN.m}^2}{EI}(2) = \dfrac{427.9 \text{ kN.m}^3}{EI}$

D'D" = Displacement of D' with respect to tangent drawn at B

= t_{DB}

= Moment of area of $\dfrac{M}{EI}$ diagram between D' and B about D'

= $\left(\dfrac{110 \text{ kN.m}^2}{EI}\right)\left(\dfrac{1}{3}(2)\right) = \dfrac{73.33 \text{ kN.m}^3}{EI}$

∴ y_D = DD' = (427.9 – 73.33) kN.m³/EI

= 354.567 $\dfrac{\text{kN.m}^3}{EI} = \dfrac{354.567 \times 10^3}{6 \times 10^4}$

= 5.909 mm (↓)

(**Note**: Above problem may also be solved by using principle of superposition.)

Problem 2.42: Find slope at supports and deflections at C and D for a simply supported beam of uniform section shown in Fig. 2.91 (a); using moment area method.

Take E = 2×10^5 MPa, I = 4×10^7 mm⁴.

Solution: In this example as loading involves concentrated load and couple, nature of elastic curve cannot be judged quickly. Hence, $\dfrac{M}{EI}$ diagrams for concentrated load and couple are first drawn and by principle of superposition, final $\dfrac{M}{EI}$ diagram is drawn. [Fig. 2.91 (e)]. $\dfrac{M}{EI}$ diagram shows that complete beam is subjected to sagging moment, hence corresponding elastic curve is drawn as shown in Fig. 2.91 (b).

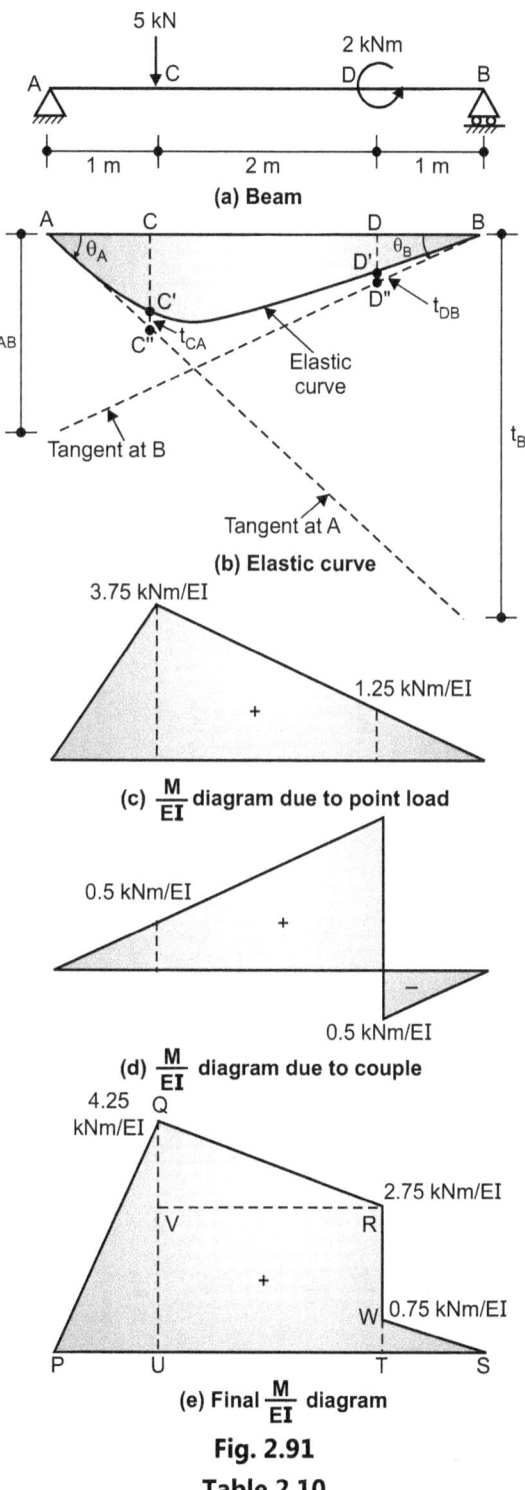

Fig. 2.91

Table 2.10

Area	Distances of C.G. from A (m)	Distances of C.G. from B (m)	Moment of area @ A	Moment of area @ B
Δ PQU $= \dfrac{1}{2} \times 1 \times \dfrac{4.25 \text{ kN.m}}{EI}$ $= \dfrac{2.125 \text{ kN.m}^2}{EI}$	$\left(\dfrac{2}{3}\right)(1) = \dfrac{2}{3}$	$3 + \dfrac{1}{3}(1) = \dfrac{10}{3}$	$1.416 \dfrac{\text{kN.m}^3}{EI}$	$7.083 \dfrac{\text{kN.m}^3}{EI}$
Δ QVR $= \dfrac{1}{2} \times \dfrac{1.5 \text{ kN.m}}{EI} \times 2$ $= \dfrac{1.5 \text{ kN.m}^2}{EI}$	$1 + \dfrac{1}{3}(2) = \dfrac{5}{3}$	$1 + \dfrac{2}{3}(2) = \dfrac{7}{3}$	$\dfrac{2.5 \text{ kN.m}^3}{EI}$	$\dfrac{3.5 \text{ kN.m}^3}{EI}$
☐ VRTU $= \dfrac{2.75 \text{ kN.m}}{EI} \times 2$ $= \dfrac{5.5 \text{ kN.m}^2}{EI}$	2	2	$\dfrac{11 \text{ kN.m}^3}{EI}$	$\dfrac{11 \text{ kN.m}^3}{EI}$
Δ WST $= \dfrac{1}{2} \times 1 \times \dfrac{0.75 \text{ kN.m}}{EI}$ $= \dfrac{0.375 \text{ kN.m}^2}{EI}$	$3 + \dfrac{1}{3}(1) = \dfrac{10}{3}$	$\dfrac{2}{3}(1) = \dfrac{2}{3}$	$\dfrac{1.25 \text{ kN.m}^3}{EI}$	$\dfrac{0.25 \text{ kN.m}^3}{EI}$
		Total	$\dfrac{16.166 \text{ kN.m}^3}{EI}$	$\dfrac{21.833 \text{ kN.m}^3}{EI}$

$$EI = 2 \times 10^5 \times 4 \times 10^7 = 8 \times 10^{12} \text{ N.mm}^2$$
$$= 8 \times 10^3 \text{ kN.m}^2$$

(i) Slope at $A = \theta_A = \dfrac{t_{BA}}{4}$

where, t_{BA} = Displacement of B with respect to tangent drawn at A

= Moment of area of $\dfrac{M}{EI}$ diagram between A and B about B

$= \dfrac{21.833 \text{ kN.m}^3}{EI}$ $\begin{bmatrix}\text{+ve sign indicates that B is} \\ \text{above the tangent drawn at A}\end{bmatrix}$

$\therefore \quad \theta_A = \dfrac{21.833}{4} \dfrac{\text{kN.m}^2}{EI} = 5.45825 \dfrac{\text{kN.m}^2}{EI}$

$\therefore \quad = \dfrac{5.45825}{8 \times 10^3} \text{ rad} = 0.000682 \text{ rad} = 0.039° \text{ (↺)}$

(ii) Slope at B = θ_B = $\dfrac{t_{AB}}{4}$

where, t_{AB} = Displacement of A with respect to tangent drawn at B

= Moment of $\dfrac{M}{EI}$ diagram between A and B about A

= $\dfrac{16.166 \text{ kN.m}^3}{EI}$ $\quad$ [+ve sign indicates that A is above the tangent drawn at B]

∴ $\theta_B = \dfrac{16.166 \text{ kN.m}^2}{4} = 4.0415 \dfrac{\text{kN.m}^2}{EI} = \dfrac{4.0415}{8 \times 10^3}$ rad

= 0.00050 rad = 0.0289° (↻)

(iii) Deflection at C = y_C = CC' = CC" − C'C"

where, CC" = (θ_A) 1 = $5.45825 \dfrac{\text{kN.m}^3}{EI}$

C'C" = t_{CA} = Displacement of C' with respect to tangent drawn at A

= Moment of area of $\dfrac{M}{EI}$ diagram between A and C' about C'

= $\left(\dfrac{2.125 \text{ kN.m}^2}{EI}\right)\left(\dfrac{1}{3}\right) = 0.7083 \dfrac{\text{kNm}^3}{EI}$ [C' is above tangent at A]

∴ y_C = CC' = $(5.45825 - 0.7083) \dfrac{\text{kN.m}^3}{EI} = 4.7499 \dfrac{\text{kN.m}^3}{EI}$

∴ $y_C = \dfrac{4.7499 \times 10^3}{8 \times 10^3} = 0.593$ mm (↓)

(iv) Deflection at D = y_D = DD' = DD" − D'D"

where, DD" = (θ_B) 1 = $4.0415 \dfrac{\text{kN.m}^3}{EI}$

D'D" = t_{DB} = Displacement of D' with respect to tangent drawn at B

= Moment of area of $\dfrac{M}{EI}$ diagram between D' and B about D'

= $\left(\dfrac{0.375 \text{ kN.m}^2}{EI}\right)\left(\dfrac{1}{3}\right) = \dfrac{0.125 \text{ kN.m}^3}{EI}$

(+ve sign indicates that D' is above the tangent drawn at B)

∴ y_D = (4.0415 − 0.125) kN.m³/EI = $3.9165 \dfrac{\text{kN.m}^3}{EI} = \dfrac{3.9165 \times 10^3}{8 \times 10^3}$

= **0.489 mm (↓)**

2.12 CONJUGATE BEAM METHOD

The conjugate beam method is another alternate method for finding slopes and deflections in beams. Successive differentiation of the deflection equation gives the following relations :

$\quad$ E.I. (y) = Deflection $\quad\quad$ ... (a)

$$E.I.\left(\frac{dy}{dx}\right) = \text{Slope} \quad \ldots \text{(b)} \quad \ldots (2.14)$$

$$E.I.\left(\frac{d^2y}{dx^2}\right) = \text{Moment} = M \quad \ldots \text{(c)}$$

$$E.I.\left(\frac{d^3y}{dx^3}\right) = \text{Shear} = V = \frac{dM}{dx} \quad \ldots \text{(d)}$$

$$E.I.\left(\frac{d^4y}{dx^4}\right) = \text{Rate of loading} = \frac{dV}{dx} = \frac{d^2M}{dx^2} \quad \ldots \text{(e)}$$

The validity of these relationships depend on the sign convention used for various quantities. The co-ordinate systems that satisfy these relationships are : y upward and x to the right are positive. Shear and bending moment sign convention is the same as explained earlier. Load is positive when it acts upwards and negative when it acts downwards.

Consider the cantilever beam as shown in Fig. 2.92 (a). Assume that beam has uniform flexural rigidity. Fig. 2.92 (b) shows $\frac{M}{EI}$ diagram for the beam. Consider fictitious beam as shown in Fig. 2.92 (c) wherein free end of real beam is changed to fixed end and fixed end of real beam is changed to free end. Let, fictitious beam be loaded with load diagram corresponding to $\frac{M}{EI}$ diagram for real beam.

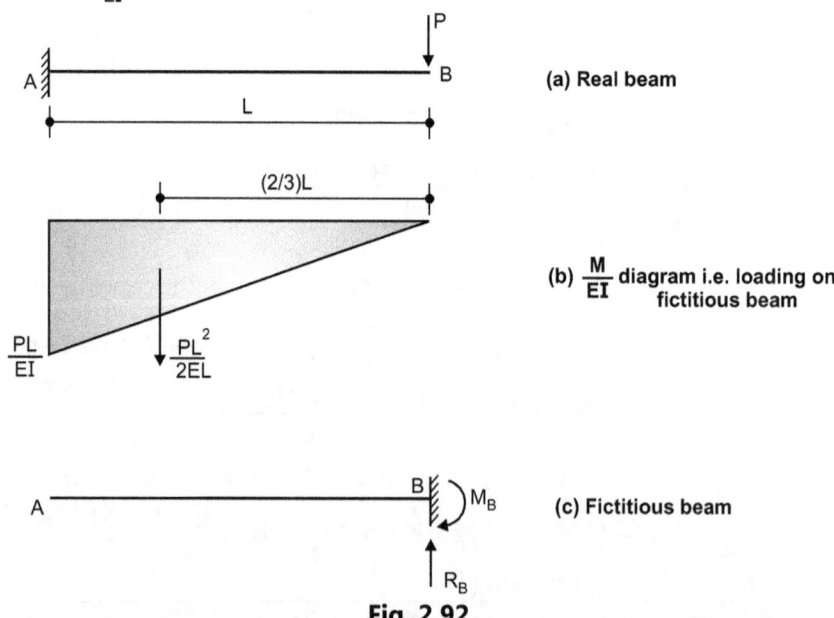

Fig. 2.92

Due to hogging bending moment, negative sign is shown for $\frac{M}{EI}$ diagram. Thus due to this negative sign, when $\frac{M}{EI}$ diagram is treated as load diagram for fictitious beam, it implies downward load. To maintain static equilibrium of fictitious beam; reaction components at B can be found out as,

$\sum F_y = 0$; $R_B = \dfrac{PL^2}{2\,EI}\,(\uparrow)$

$\sum M_B = 0$; $M_B = \dfrac{PL^2}{2\,EI}\left(\dfrac{2}{3}L\right) = \dfrac{PL^3}{3\,EI}\,(\circlearrowleft)$

Shear force at B for fictitious beam = $V_B = \dfrac{-PL^2}{2\,EI}$

(Upward force on R.H.S. of cross section means negative shear.)

Bending moment at B for fictitious beam = $M_B = \dfrac{PL^3}{3\,EI}$ (Hogging)

$$M_B = \dfrac{-PL^3}{3\,EI}$$

(–ve sign is due to hogging bending moment)

Little consideration will show that shear force at B for fictitious beam is nothing but slope at B for real beam.

i.e. $\theta_B = V_B = \dfrac{-PL^2}{2\,EI}$

$\therefore$ $\theta_B = \dfrac{PL^2}{2\,EI}\,(\circlearrowleft)$ (due to negative shear, slope is clockwise)

Also bending moment at B for fictitious beam is equal to deflection at B for real beam.

$\therefore$ $y_B = M_B = -\dfrac{PL^3}{3\,EI}$

$\therefore$ $y_B = \dfrac{PL^3}{3\,EI}\,(\downarrow)$

(due to negative sign for moment, deflection is in negative y direction i.e. downwards).

The fictitious beam thus created is known as *conjugate beam*. We may now define the conjugate beam as follows :

Definition : A conjugate beam is a fictitious beam, which has the same length as the real beam, but is supported in such a manner that when it is loaded with $\dfrac{M}{EI}$ diagram of the real beam, the shear and bending moment at a section in the conjugate beam gives the slope and deflection (in sign and value) for the corresponding section of the real beam.

2.13 SUPPORT CONDITIONS

To apply conjugate beam method correctly, the supports of the conjugate beam shall be so changed that correct slopes and deflections are obtained for real beam. These support conditions are discussed below :

(1) At the fixed end of real beam, slope and deflection both are zero. Shear force and bending moment must be zero for conjugate beam at corresponding section which is possible only if fixed end of real beam is made free end for conjugate beam.

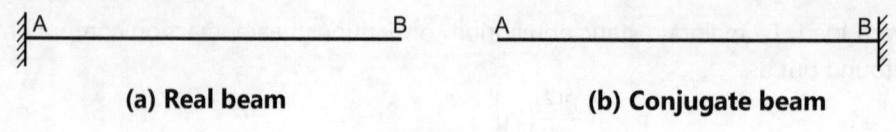

(a) Real beam　　　　　　　　(b) Conjugate beam

Fig. 2.93

At the free end of the real beam, there exist slope and deflection both. In a corresponding conjugate beam, at this end, there should be shear force and bending moment both. This requirement is satisfied only by fixed support.

Thus, fixed end of real beam becomes free end of conjugate beam and free end of real beam becomes fixed end for conjugate beam. [Refer Fig. 2.94].

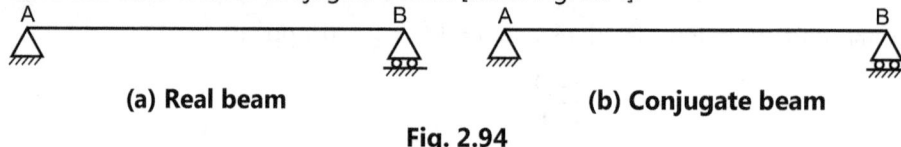

(a) Real beam　　　　　　　　(b) Conjugate beam

Fig. 2.94

(2) At hinge or roller end of the real beam, slope is present but deflection is zero. Therefore, in a corresponding conjugate beam at this end there must be shear force but no moment; which is satisfied by hinge or roller support.

Thus, hinge or roller end of real beam remains as hinge or roller end in corresponding conjugate beam. [Refer Fig. 2.95].

(3) At interior roller support, there is continuity of slope i.e. $\theta_{BA} = \theta_{BC}$. Also there is no deflection at interior roller support. Thus in a corresponding conjugate beam, there must be a support which gives shear force but no bending moment which is obtained by internal hinge which gives equal and opposite shear force on two sides but no moment.

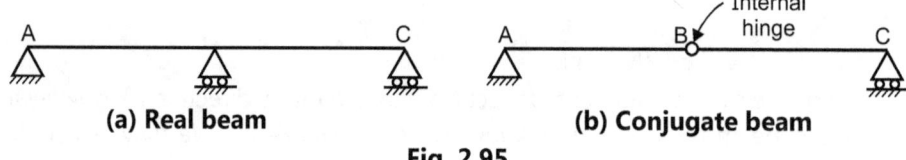

(a) Real beam　　　　　　　　(b) Conjugate beam

Fig. 2.95

Thus, interior support in real beam becomes an internal hinge in a conjugate beam [Refer Fig. 2.96].

(4)

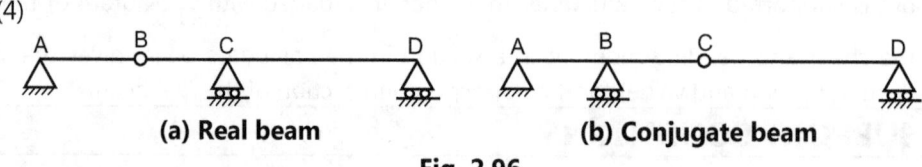

(a) Real beam　　　　　　　　(b) Conjugate beam

Fig. 2.96

At the unsupported internal hinge of a real beam there exist slope and deflection both. Thus, a simple support would be required in a corresponding conjugate beam.

Thus, an unsupported internal hinge in a real becomes interior roller support in a conjugate beam. [Refer Fig. 2.10696

The foregoing conjugate beam support conditions are to be carefully applied while using the method.

It is very important to note that conjugate beam is always statically determinate even though the real beam is indeterminate. Conjugate beam may sometimes appear to be unstable, however, the loading would be so balanced as to give zero reactions if any support is there. For a real fixed beam, conjugate beam is supportless. It should be remembered that conjugate beam is an imaginary beam.

Conjugate beam method is illustrated in the following examples. Following points shall be noted regarding sign convention.

1. Sagging bending moment for real beam gives positive $\frac{M}{EI}$ diagram and hogging bending moment for real beam gives negative $\frac{M}{EI}$ diagram.

2. Positive $\frac{M}{EI}$ diagram means upward loading for conjugate beam and negative $\frac{M}{EI}$ diagram means downward loading for conjugate beam.

3. Positive shear for conjugate beam means anticlockwise rotation of tangent drawn to elastic curve with respect to original position at corresponding point in a real beam and vice versa.

4. Positive bending moment for conjugate beam means upward deflection of a corresponding point in a real beam and vice versa.

SOLVED PROBLEMS

Problem 2.43 : Using the conjugate beam method, calculate the slope and deflection at B. Take $E = 2.1 \times 10^5$ MPa and $I = 117.7 \times 10^6$ mm^4. [Refer Fig. 2.97 (a)].

Solution :

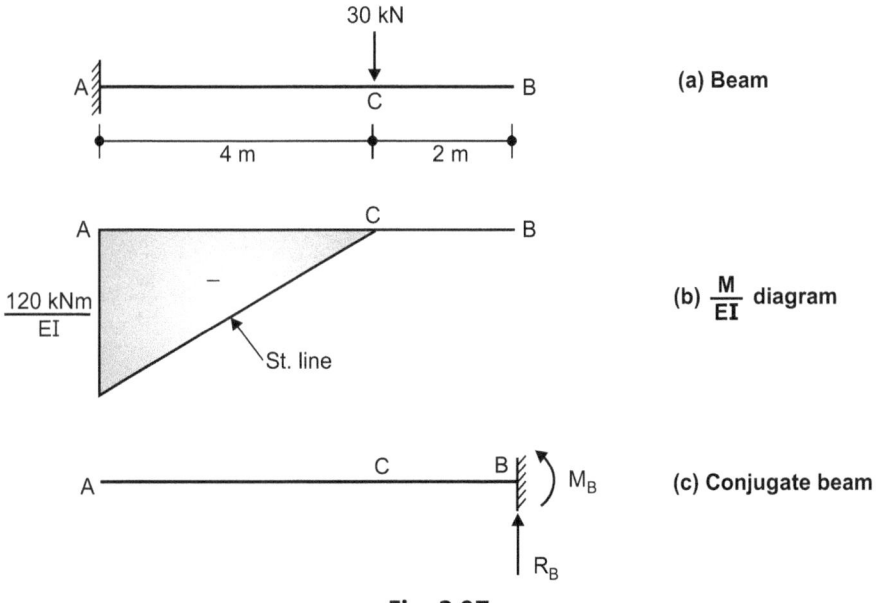

Fig. 2.97

Analysis of conjugate beam :

$\Sigma F_y = 0$ gives Reaction at B = $R_B = \frac{1}{2} \times 4 \times \frac{120}{EI}$

$$R_B = \frac{240}{EI} \text{ kN.m}^2 \text{ (↑)}$$

$\Sigma M_B = 0;$ Moment at B = $\left[\frac{1}{2} \times 4 \times \frac{120}{EI}\right] \times \left[2 + \frac{2}{3} \times 4\right]$

$$M_B = \frac{1120}{EI} \text{ kN.m}^3 \text{ (↶)}$$

Slopes : Slope at B = Shear at B = $V_B = -\frac{240 \text{ kN.m}^2}{EI}$

$\therefore \quad \theta_B = \frac{240 \times 10^3 \times (10^3)^2}{2.1 \times 10^5 \times 117.7 \times 10^6} = 0.009709 \text{ rad (↶)} = 0.556° \text{ (↶)}$

y_B = Deflection at B = B.M. at B

$$M_B = \frac{1120 \text{ kN.m}^3}{EI} \text{ (Hogging)}$$

$\therefore \quad y_B = -\frac{1120 \times 10^3 \times (10^3)^3}{2.1 \times 10^5 \times 117.7 \times 10^6}$ $\begin{pmatrix}\text{–ve sign due to} \\ \text{hogging moment}\end{pmatrix}$

$\quad = 45.312 \text{ mm (↓)}$

Problem 2.44 : For the cantilever beam shown below compute the deflection and slope at free end. Take E = 2.1×10^5 MPa; I = 300×10^6 mm⁴. Use conjugate beam method. [Refer Fig. 2.98 (a)].

Solution :

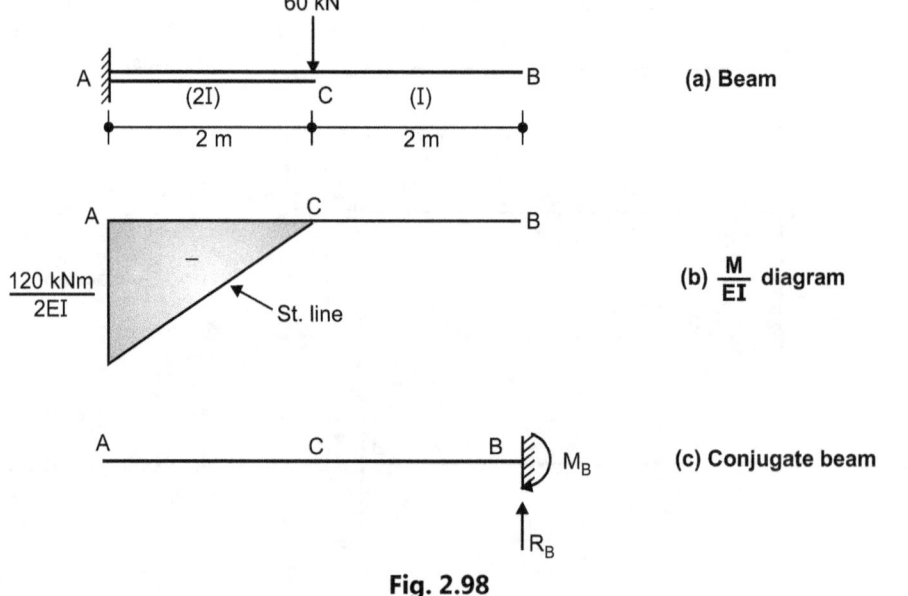

(a) Beam

(b) $\frac{M}{EI}$ diagram

(c) Conjugate beam

Fig. 2.98

Analysis of conjugate beam :

$\Sigma F_y = 0$;   Vertical reaction at B $= \frac{1}{2} \times 2 \times \left[\frac{120}{2\,EI}\right]$

$$R_B = \frac{60}{EI} \text{ kN.m}^2 \; (\uparrow)$$

$\Sigma M_B = 0$;   Moment at B $= M_B = \left[\frac{1}{2} \times 2 \times \frac{120}{2\,EI}\right] \times \left(2 + \frac{2}{3} \times 2\right) = \frac{200}{E} \text{ kN.m}^3 \; (\circlearrowleft)$

Shear force at B $= V_B = -\dfrac{60}{EI} \text{ kN.m}^2$

Bending moment at B $= M_B = \dfrac{200}{EI} \text{ kN.m}^3$ (Hogging)

$\therefore$ Slope at B $= \theta_B = V_B$

$$= \frac{-60 \times 10^3 \times (10^3)^2}{2.1 \times 10^5 \times 300 \times 10^6}$$

$$= 0.00095 \text{ rad}$$

$$= 0.0545° \; (\circlearrowleft)$$

Deflection at B $= y_B = \dfrac{-200 \text{ kN.m}^3}{EI}$

$$= \frac{-200 \times (10^3)(10^3)^3}{2.1 \times 10^5 \times 300 \times 10^6} = 3.174 \text{ mm} \; (\downarrow)$$

Problem 2.45 : Find slope and deflection at free end of cantilever shown below by conjugate beam method. Take $E = 2 \times 10^5$ MPa and $I = 15650$ cm^4. [Refer Fig. 2.99 (a)].

Solution :

Analysis of conjugate beam :

To find R_C :

$\Sigma F_y = 0$; $R_C = \left[\dfrac{1}{2} \times 1 \times 30\right] + \left[\dfrac{1}{2} \times 40 \times 2\right]$

$$= \frac{55 \text{ kN.m}^2}{EI} \; (\uparrow)$$

$\Sigma M_C = 0$; $M_C = \left(\dfrac{1}{2} \times 1 \times 30\right) \times \left(1 + \dfrac{2}{3} \times 1\right)$

$$+ \left(\frac{1}{2} \times 40 \times 2\right) \times \left(\frac{2}{3} \times 2\right)$$

$$= \frac{78.33}{EI} \text{ kN.m}^3 \; (\circlearrowleft)$$

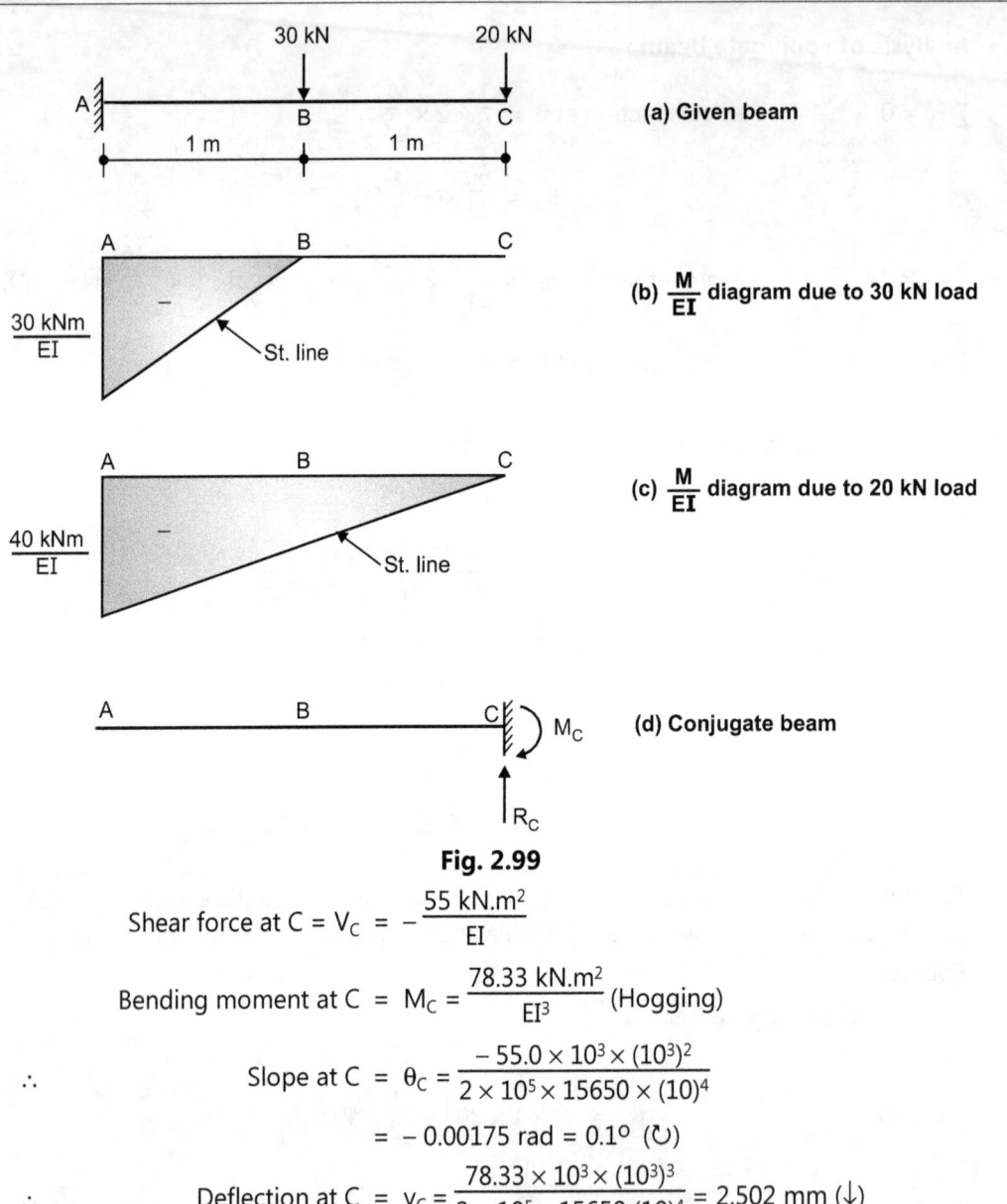

Fig. 2.99

$$\text{Shear force at C} = V_C = -\frac{55 \text{ kN.m}^2}{EI}$$

$$\text{Bending moment at C} = M_C = \frac{78.33 \text{ kN.m}^2}{EI^3} \text{ (Hogging)}$$

∴ $$\text{Slope at C} = \theta_C = \frac{-55.0 \times 10^3 \times (10^3)^2}{2 \times 10^5 \times 15650 \times (10)^4}$$

$$= -0.00175 \text{ rad} = 0.1° \text{ (↻)}$$

∴ $$\text{Deflection at C} = y_C = \frac{78.33 \times 10^3 \times (10^3)^3}{2 \times 10^5 \times 15650 (10)^4} = 2.502 \text{ mm (↓)}$$

Problem 2.46 : Using conjugate beam method, compute slope and deflection at free end of cantilever shown in Fig. 2.100 (a). Take E = 2.1 × 10⁵ MPa; I = 117.7 × 10⁸ mm⁴.

Solution :

Analysis of conjugate beam :

$\Sigma F_y = 0$;

$$R_D - \left(\frac{1}{2} \times 400 \times 3 + \frac{1}{2} \times 160 \times 3 + \frac{1}{3} \times 4 \times 160\right) \frac{\text{kN.m}^2}{EI} = 0$$

$$\therefore \quad R_D = (600 + 240 + 213.33)\frac{kN.m^2}{EI}$$

$$R_D = (1053.33)\frac{kN.m^2}{EI} \ (\uparrow)$$

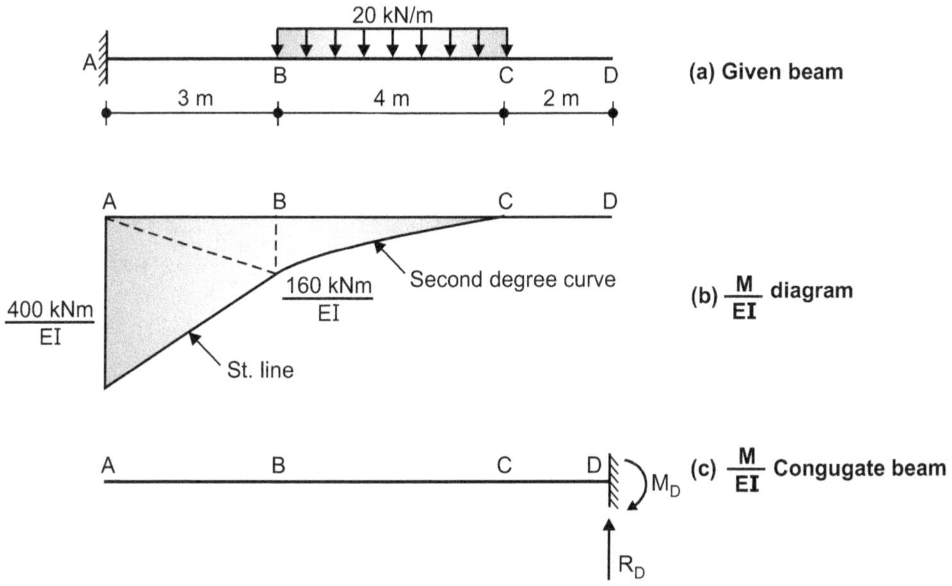

Fig. 2.100

(a) Given beam

(b) $\frac{M}{EI}$ diagram

(c) $\frac{M}{EI}$ Congugate beam

$$\sum M_D = 0; \ -M_D + \left[600\left(2 + 4 + \frac{2}{3}\times 3\right) + 240\left(2 + 4 + \frac{1}{3}\times 3\right) + (213.33)\left(2 + \frac{3}{4}\times 4\right)\right]\frac{kN.m^3}{EI} = 0$$

$$\therefore \quad M_D = 7546.67 \frac{kN.m^3}{EI} \ (\circlearrowleft)$$

$$\text{Shear force at D} = V_D = -\frac{1053.33}{EI} kN.m^2$$

$$\text{Bending moment at D} = M_D = \frac{7546.67}{EI} kN.m^2 \ (\text{Hogging})$$

$$\text{Slope at D} = \theta_D = -\frac{1053.33 \ kN.m^2}{EI} = -\frac{1053.33 \times (10^3)(10^3)^2}{2.1 \times 10^5 \times 117.7 \times 10^8}$$

$$= 0.000426 \ \text{rad} \ (\circlearrowleft) = 0.024° \ (\circlearrowleft)$$

$$\text{Deflection at D} = y_D = -\frac{7546.67 \ kN.m^3}{EI}$$

$$= -\frac{7546.67 \times (10)^3 (10^3)^3}{2.1 \times 10^5 \times 117.7 \times 10^8} = 3.05 \ \text{mm} \ (\downarrow)$$

Problem 2.47 : Find slope and deflection at points B and C for cantilever shown below by conjugate beam method. Take $E = 2 \times 10^5$ MPa and $I = 5 \times 10^8$ mm^4. [Refer Fig. 2.101 (a)].
Solution :

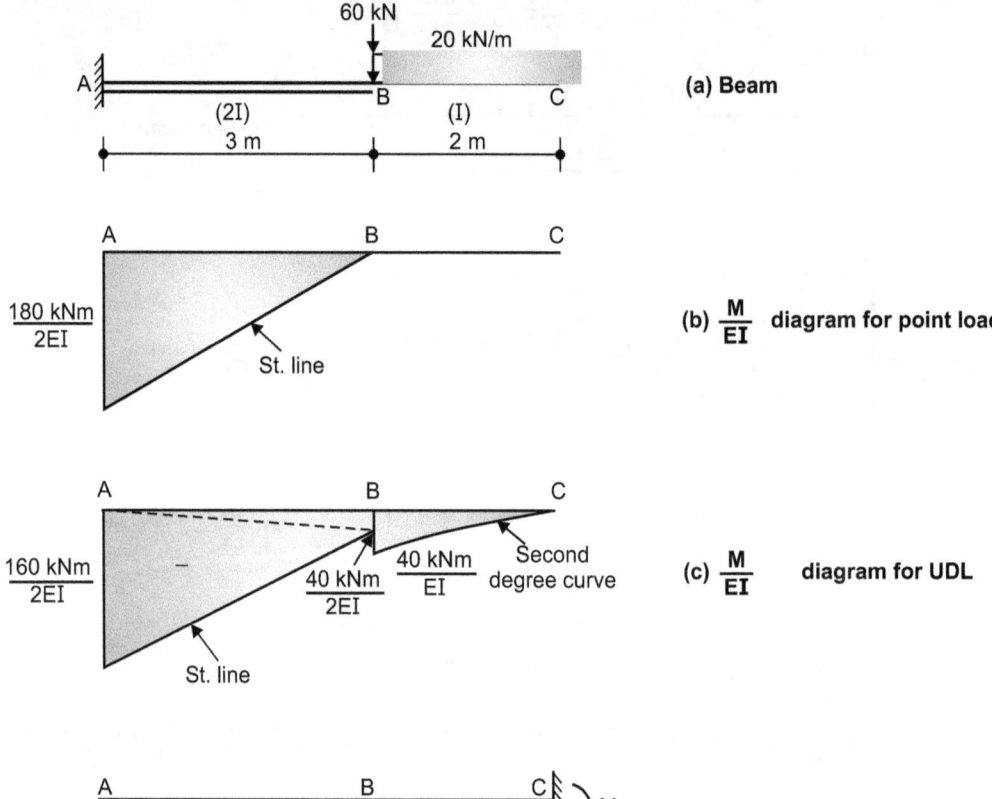

Fig. 2.101

Analysis of conjugate beam :

$\Sigma F_y = 0$;

$$R_C - \left[\frac{1}{2} \times \frac{180}{2} \times 3 + \frac{1}{2} \times \frac{160}{2} \times 3 + \frac{1}{2} \times \frac{40}{2} \times 3 + \frac{1}{3} \times 40 \times 2\right] \frac{kN.m^2}{EI} = 0$$

$$R_C = [135 + 120 + 30 + 26.67] \frac{kN.m^2}{EI} = \frac{311.67 \; kN.m^2}{EI} \; (\uparrow)$$

$\Sigma M_C = 0$;

$$-M_C + \left[135 \times \left(2 + \frac{2}{3} \times 3\right) + 120 \times \left(2 + \frac{2}{3} \times 3\right) + 30 \times \left(2 + \frac{1}{3} \times 3\right) + 26.67 \times \left(\frac{3}{4} \times 2\right)\right] \frac{kN.m^3}{EI} = 0$$

$\therefore \quad M_C = \dfrac{1150 \; kN.m^3}{EI} \; (\circlearrowleft)$

Shear force and bending moment for conjugate beam :

$$V_B = -(135 + 120 + 30)\frac{kN.m^2}{EI}$$

$$= -\frac{285 \text{ kN.m}^2}{EI}$$

$$V_C = -\frac{311.67 \text{ kN.m}^2}{EI}$$

$$M_B = -\left[135 \times \left(\frac{2}{3} \times 3\right) + 120 \times \left(\frac{2}{3} \times 3\right) + 30 \left(\frac{1}{3} \times 3\right)\right]$$

$$= \frac{540 \text{ kN.m}^3}{EI} \text{ (Hogging)}$$

$$M_C = \frac{1150 \text{ kN.m}^3}{EI} \text{ (Hogging)}$$

Slope and deflections :

$$\theta_B = -\frac{285 \text{ kN.m}^2}{EI} = -\frac{285 \times 10^3 \times (10^3)^2}{2 \times 10^5 \times 5 \times 10^8}$$

$$= 0.00285 \text{ rad} = 0.163° \text{ (↻)}$$

$$\theta_C = -\frac{311.67 \text{ kN.m}^2}{EI} = -\frac{311.67 \times 10^3 \times (10^3)^2}{2 \times 10^5 \times 5 \times 10^8}$$

$$= 0.003116 \text{ rad}$$

$$= 0.1785° \text{ (↻)}$$

$$y_B = -\frac{540 \text{ kN.m}^3}{EI} = -\frac{540 \times 10^3 \times (10^3)^3}{2 \times 10^5 \times 5 \times 10^8}$$

$$= 5.4 \text{ mm (↓)}$$

$$y_C = -\frac{1150 \text{ kN.m}^3}{EI} = \frac{-1150 \times 10^3 \times (10^3)^3}{2 \times 10^5 \times 5 \times 10^8}$$

$$= 11.5 \text{ mm (↓)}$$

Problem 2.48 : Determine the deflection and slope at free end of cantilever beam shown in Fig. 2.102 (a).

Solution : Analysis of conjugate beam :

$$\Sigma F_y = 0 \Rightarrow R_C + 2 \times \frac{2 \text{ kN.m}}{EI} - \frac{1}{2} \times 4 \times \frac{1 \text{ kN.m}}{EI} = 0; \text{ i.e. } R_C = -\frac{2 \text{ kN.m}^2}{EI}$$

$$\therefore \qquad R_C = \frac{2 \text{ kN.m}^2}{EI} \text{ (↓)}$$

$$\Sigma M_C = 0 \Rightarrow -M_C - 2 \times 2 \frac{kN.m}{EI} \times (2 + 1) + \frac{1}{2} \times \frac{1 \text{ kN.m}}{EI} \times 4 \times \left(\frac{2}{3} \times 4\right)$$

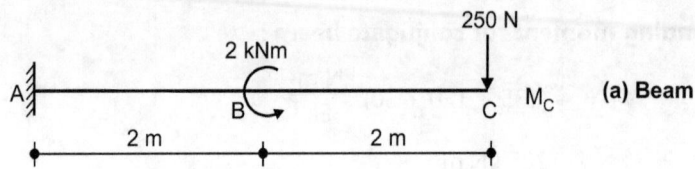

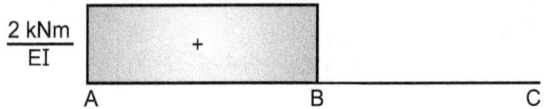

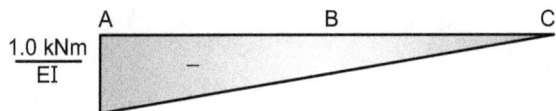

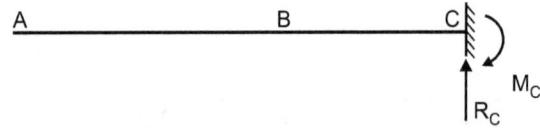

Fig. 2.102

$$\therefore \quad M_C = (-12 + 5.33)\frac{kN.m^3}{EI}$$

$$\therefore \quad M_C = -6.67\frac{kN.m^3}{EI}$$

$$= 6.67\frac{kN.m^3}{EI} \; (\circlearrowleft)$$

Assumed directions of reaction components at C for conjugate beam are wrong.

$$\text{Shear force at C} = V_C = \frac{2 \; kN.m^2}{EI}$$

$$\text{Bending moment at C} = M_C = \frac{6.67 \; kN.m^3}{EI} \; \text{(sagging)}$$

$$\therefore \quad \text{Slope at C} = \theta_C = \frac{2 \; kN.m^2}{EI} \; (\circlearrowleft)$$

$$\text{Deflection at C} = y_C = \frac{6.67 \; kN.m^3}{EI} \; \text{(Upwards)}$$

Problem 2.49 : Find θ_B, θ_C, y_B and y_C for cantilever beam shown in Fig. 2.103 (a). Take $E = 2 \times 10^5$ MPa; $I = 5 \times 10^8$ mm^4.

Solution :

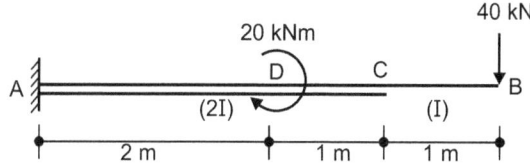

(a) Beam

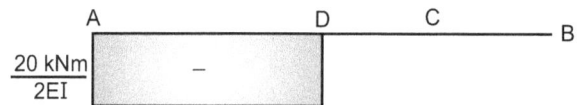

(b) $\dfrac{M}{EI}$ diagram due to couple

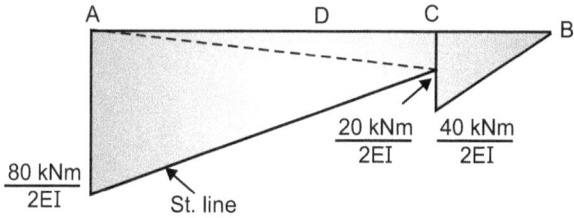

(c) $\dfrac{M}{EI}$ diagram due to point load

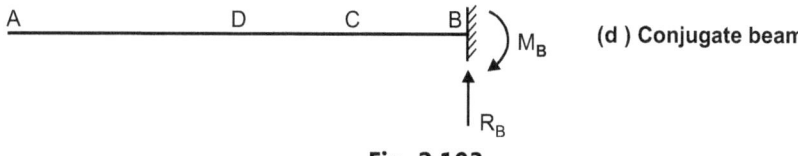

(d) Conjugate beam

Fig. 2.103

Analysis of conjugate beam :

$$\Sigma F_y = 0 \Rightarrow R_B - 2 \times \dfrac{20 \text{ kN.m}}{2 \text{ EI}} - \dfrac{1}{2} \times \dfrac{80 \text{ kN.m}}{EI} \times 3 - \dfrac{1}{2} \times \dfrac{20 \text{ kN.m}}{EI} \times 3 - \dfrac{1}{2} \dfrac{40 \text{ kN.m}}{EI} \times 1 = 0$$

$$\therefore \quad R_B = \dfrac{20 \text{ kN.m}^2}{EI} + \dfrac{120 \text{ kN.m}^2}{EI} + \dfrac{30 \text{ kN.m}^2}{EI} + \dfrac{20 \text{ kN.m}^2}{EI}$$

$$= \dfrac{190 \text{ kN.m}^2}{EI} (\uparrow)$$

$$\Sigma M_B = 0 \Rightarrow -M_B + \dfrac{20 \text{ kN.m}^2}{EI}(2+1) + \dfrac{120 \text{ kN.m}^2}{EI}\left(1 + \dfrac{2}{3} \times 3\right) + \dfrac{30 \text{ kN.m}^2}{EI}\left(1 + \dfrac{1}{3} \times 3\right)$$

$$+ \dfrac{20 \text{ kN.m}^2}{EI}\left(\dfrac{2}{3} \times 1\right) = 0$$

$$\therefore \quad M_B = \frac{60 \text{ kN.m}^3}{EI} + \frac{360 \text{ kN.m}^3}{EI} + \frac{60 \text{ kN.m}^3}{EI} + \frac{40}{3} \frac{\text{kN.m}^3}{EI}$$

$$= \frac{493.33 \text{ kN.m}^3}{EI} \; (\circlearrowleft)$$

Shear force and bending moments for conjugate beam :

Shear at B = V_B.

$$\therefore \quad V_B = -\frac{190 \text{ kN.m}^2}{EI}$$

Shear at C = V_C.

$$\therefore \quad V_C = -\left[\frac{20 \text{ kN.m}^2}{EI} + \frac{120 \text{ kN.m}^2}{EI} + \frac{30 \text{ kN.m}^2}{EI}\right]$$

$$= -\frac{170 \text{ kN.m}^2}{EI}$$

Bending moment at B = $M_B = \dfrac{493.33 \text{ kN.m}^3}{EI}$ (Hogging)

Bending moment at C = M_C

$$M_C = -\left[\frac{20 \text{ kN.m}^2}{EI}(1+1) + \frac{120 \text{ kN.m}^2}{EI}\left(\frac{2}{3} \times 3\right) + \frac{30 \text{ kN.m}^2}{EI}\left(\frac{1}{3} \times 3\right)\right]$$

$$= -[40 + 240 + 30]\frac{\text{kN.m}^3}{EI} = -\frac{310 \text{ kN.m}^3}{EI}$$

$$M_C = \frac{310 \text{ kN.m}^3}{EI} \text{ (Hogging)}$$

Slope and deflections :

$$\theta_B = -\frac{190 \text{ kN.m}^2}{EI}$$

$$= -\frac{190 \times 10^3 \times (10^3)^2}{2 \times 10^5 \times 5 \times 10^8} = -0.0019 \text{ rad} = 0.108° \; (\circlearrowleft)$$

$$\theta_C = -\frac{170 \text{ kN.m}^2}{EI} = -\frac{170 \times 10^3 \times (10^3)^2}{2 \times 10^5 \times 5 \times 10^8}$$

$$= -0.0017 \text{ rad} = 0.097° \; (\circlearrowleft)$$

$$y_B = -\frac{493.33 \text{ kN.m}^3}{EI} = -\frac{493.33 \times 10^3 \times (10^3)^3}{2 \times 10^5 \times 5 \times 10^8}$$

$$= 4.93 \text{ mm} \; (\downarrow)$$

$$y_C = -\frac{310 \text{ kN.m}^3}{EI}$$

$$= -\frac{310 \times 10^3 \times (10^3)^3}{2 \times 10^5 \times 5 \times 10^8} = 3.10 \text{ mm} \; (\downarrow)$$

Problem 2.50 : Find slope at supports and deflection at centre for simply supported beam of span 'L' and carrying UDL of intensity 'w' per unit run throughout. Assume uniform flexural rigidity. [Refer Fig. 2.104 (a)]. Use conjugate beam method.

Solution :

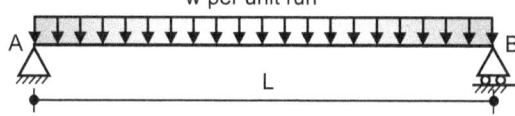
(a) Beam

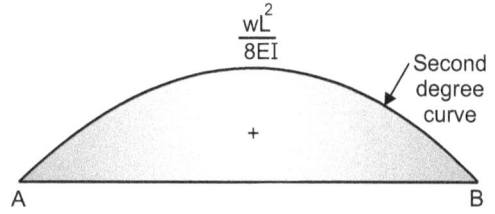
(b) $\frac{M}{EI}$ diagram

(c) Conjugate beam

Fig. 2.104

Analysis of conjugate beam :

By symmetry,
$$R_A = R_B = \frac{1}{2}\left[\frac{2}{3} \times L \times \frac{wL^2}{8\,EI}\right]$$
$$= \frac{wL^3}{24\,EI} \, (\downarrow)$$

Shear force and bending moment for conjugate beam :
$$V_A = -\frac{wL^3}{24\,EI}$$
$$V_B = \frac{wL^3}{24\,EI}$$

Maximum bending moment will occur at centre.
$$M_{max} = -\frac{wL^3}{24\,EI}\left(\frac{L}{2}\right) + \frac{wL^3}{24\,EI} \cdot \left(\frac{3}{8} \times \frac{L}{2}\right)$$
$$= -\frac{wL^4}{48\,EI} + \frac{3\,wL^4}{384\,EI} = -\frac{5}{384} \cdot \left(\frac{wL^4}{EI}\right)$$
$$= \frac{5}{384} \cdot \frac{wL^4}{EI} \text{ (Hogging)}$$

Slope and deflections : $\theta_A = V_A = -\dfrac{wL^3}{24\,EI} = \dfrac{wL^3}{24\,EI}\,(\circlearrowright)$

$\theta_B = V_B = \dfrac{wL^3}{24\,EI}\,(\circlearrowleft)$

$y_{max} = M_{max} = \dfrac{5}{384} \cdot \dfrac{wL^4}{EI}\,(\downarrow)$

Problem 2.51 : For a simply supported beam shown in Fig. 2.105 (a), find slope at supports and deflection at the point of application of couple. Also find maximum deflection. Take EI = 40,000 kN.m². Use conjugate beam method.

Solution :

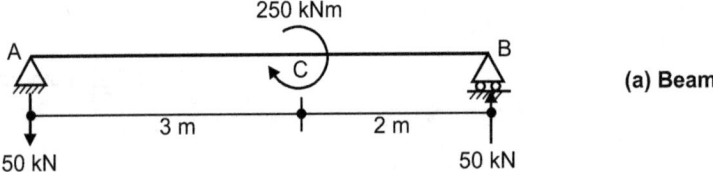
(a) Beam

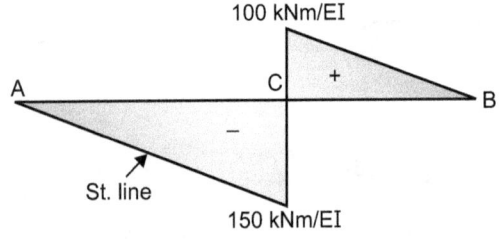
(b) $\dfrac{M}{EI}$ diagram

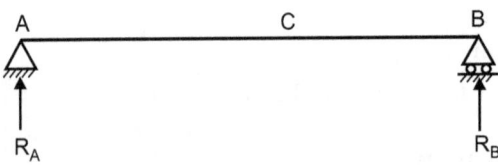
(c) Conjugate beam

Fig. 2.105

Analysis of conjugate beam :

$R_B \times (5) + \dfrac{1}{2} \times (2) \times \dfrac{100 \text{ kN.m}}{EI}\left[3 + \dfrac{1}{2}(2)\right] - \dfrac{1}{2}(3)\dfrac{150 \text{ kN.m}}{EI}\left(\dfrac{2}{3} \times 3\right) = 0$

$\therefore \quad R_B = \left[\dfrac{450 - 366.67}{5}\right]\dfrac{kN.m^2}{EI}$

$= 16.67 \text{ kN.m}^2/EI\,(\uparrow)$

SLOPE AND DEFLECTION OF BEAMS

$$\Sigma F_y = 0 \;;\; R_A + R_B + \frac{1}{2} \times \frac{100 \text{ kN.m}}{EI} \times 2 - \frac{1}{2} \times \frac{3 \times 150 \text{ kN.m}}{EI} = 0$$

$$R_A = \frac{108.33 \text{ kN.m}^2}{EI} = \frac{108.33 \text{ kN.m}^2}{EI} (\uparrow)$$

Shear force and bending moment for conjugate beam :

$$V_A = \frac{108.33 \text{ kN.m}^2}{EI}$$

$$V_B = \frac{-16.67 \text{ kN.m}^2}{EI}$$

$$M_C = \frac{108.33 \text{ kN.m}^2}{EI} \times (3) - \frac{1}{2} \times (3) \times \frac{150 \text{ kN.m}}{EI} \times \left(\frac{1}{3}(3)\right)$$

$$= \frac{100 \text{ kN.m}^3}{EI} \text{ (Sagging)}$$

To locate the point of maximum bending moment. As AC > CB, a point of zero shear force occurs in span AC. Consider a section at a distance 'x' from A.

$$V_x = 108.33 \frac{\text{kN.m}^2}{EI} - \frac{1}{2}(x) \times \frac{150 \text{ kN.m}}{EI}\left(\frac{x}{3}\right) = 0$$

$$\therefore \quad \frac{150 x^2}{6} = 108.33$$

$$\therefore \quad x = 2.082 \text{ m from A}$$

Maximum bending moment = M_{max}

$$= 108.33 \frac{\text{kN.m}^2}{EI}(2.082) - \frac{1}{2}\frac{(2.082)^2}{3} \times \frac{150 \text{ kN.m}}{EI}\left(\frac{2.082}{3}\right)$$

$$= \frac{150.39 \text{ kN.m}^3}{EI} \text{ (Sagging)}$$

Slope and deflections : $\theta_A = V_A = \frac{108.33}{40000} = 0.0027$ rad $= 0.155°$ (↻)

$$\theta_B = V_B = \frac{16.67}{40000}$$

$$= 0.00041 \text{ rad} = 0.0238° \;(\circlearrowleft) \text{ (Note the direction)}$$

$$y_C = M_C = \frac{100}{40000} \times 10^3$$

$$= 2.5 \text{ mm } (\uparrow)$$

$$y_{max} = \frac{150.39 \times 10^3}{40000}$$

$$= 3.759 \text{ mm } (\uparrow)$$

Problem 2.52 : Compute the slope at supports and midspan deflection for beam shown in Fig. 2.106 (a). Take $E = 2 \times 10^5$ MPa and $I = 3 \times 10^7$ mm^4. Use conjugate beam method.

Solution :

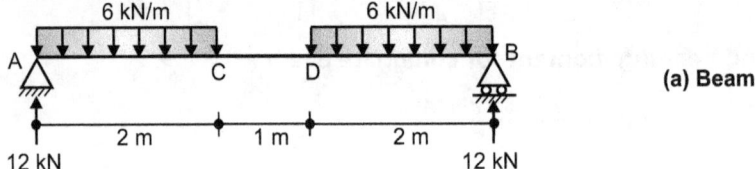
(a) Beam

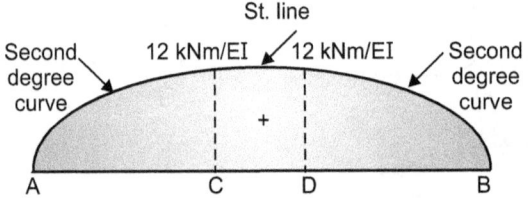
(b) $\dfrac{M}{EI}$ diagram

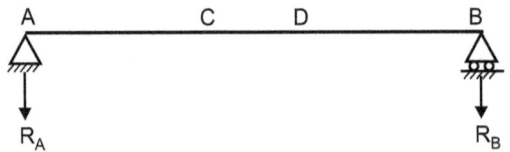
(c) Conjugate beam

Fig. 2.106

Analysis of conjugate beam :

By symmetry, $\quad R_A = R_B = \dfrac{\text{Total load}}{2}$

$$= \dfrac{\left(\dfrac{2}{3} \times 2 \times 12\right) \times 2 + 12 \times 1}{2} = \dfrac{22 \text{ kN.m}^2}{EI} \;(\downarrow)$$

Shear force and bending moment for conjugate beam :

$$V_A = -\dfrac{22 \text{ kN.m}^2}{EI}$$

$$V_B = +\dfrac{22 \text{ kN.m}^2}{EI}$$

By symmetry, maximum bending moment occurs at centre.

$$M_{max} = -\dfrac{22 \text{ kN.m}^2}{EI}(2.5) + \left(\dfrac{2}{3} \times 2 \times \dfrac{12 \text{ kN.m}}{EI}\right)\left(0.5 + \dfrac{3}{8}(2)\right)$$

$$+ \dfrac{12 \text{ kN.m}}{EI}(0.5)\left(\dfrac{0.5}{2}\right)$$

$$= -\dfrac{33.5 \text{ kN.m}^3}{EI}$$

Slope and deflections : $\theta_A = V_A = -\dfrac{22 \text{ kN.m}^2}{EI}$

$$= \dfrac{22 \times (10)^3 \times (10^3)^2}{2 \times 10^5 \times 3 \times 10^7}$$

$$= 0.0036 \text{ rad} = 0.210° \text{ (↻)}$$

$$\theta_B = V_B = \dfrac{22 \text{ kN.m}^2}{EI} = 0.0036 \text{ rad}$$

$$= 0.210° \text{ (↺)}$$

Maximum deflection at centre

$$= y_{max} = M_{max}$$

$$= -\dfrac{33.5 \times (10^3)(10^3)^3}{2 \times 10^5 \times 3 \times 10^7}$$

$$= 5.583 \text{ mm } (\downarrow)$$

Problem 2.53 : For a simply supported beam shown in Fig. 2.107 (a), find slope at supports and deflection at centre using conjugate beam method.

Solution :

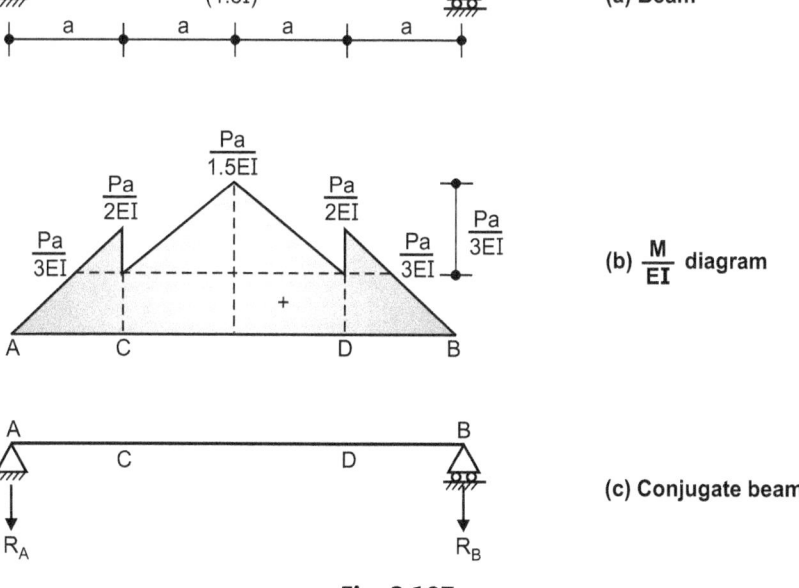

Fig. 2.107

Analysis of conjugate beam :

By symmetry,

$$R_A = R_B = \frac{1}{2} \times a \times \frac{Pa}{2EI} + \frac{Pa}{3EI} \times a + \frac{1}{2}(a)\frac{Pa}{3EI}$$

$$= \frac{Pa^2}{4EI} + \frac{Pa^2}{3EI} + \frac{Pa^2}{6EI} = \frac{9}{12}\frac{Pa^2}{EI} = \frac{9}{12}\frac{Pa^2}{EI} (\downarrow)$$

Shear force and bending moment for conjugate beam :

$$V_A = -\frac{9}{12}\frac{Pa^2}{EI}$$

$$V_B = \frac{9}{12}\frac{Pa^2}{EI}$$

By symmetry, maximum B.M. will occur at centre.

$$M_{max} = -\frac{9}{12}\frac{Pa^2}{EI}(2a) + \frac{Pa^2}{4EI}\left(a + \frac{a}{3}\right) + \frac{Pa^2}{3EI}\left(\frac{a}{2}\right) + \frac{Pa^2}{6EI}\left(\frac{a}{3}\right)$$

$$= -\frac{9}{6}\left(\frac{Pa^3}{EI}\right) + \frac{Pa^3}{4EI} + \frac{Pa^3}{12EI} + \frac{Pa^3}{6EI} + \frac{Pa^3}{18EI}$$

$$= -\frac{34}{36}\left(\frac{Pa^3}{EI}\right)$$

$$= \frac{17}{18}\frac{Pa^3}{EI} \text{ (Hogging)}$$

Slope and deflections :

$$\theta_A = V_A = -\frac{9}{12}\frac{Pa^2}{EI} = \frac{9}{12}\frac{Pa^2}{EI} (\circlearrowleft)$$

$$\theta_B = V_B = \frac{9}{12}\frac{Pa^2}{EI} = \frac{9}{12}\frac{Pa^2}{EI} (\circlearrowright)$$

$$y_{max} = M_{max} = -\left(\frac{17}{18}\right)\frac{Pa^3}{EI} = \frac{17}{18}\frac{Pa^3}{EI} (\downarrow)$$

Problem 2.54 : Using conjugate beam method, determine slope at supports and deflection at centre for the simply supported beam shown in Fig. 2.108 (a). Take $E = 2.1 \times 10^5$ MPa; $I = 250 \times 10^6$ mm^4.

Solution :

Analysis of conjugate beam :

By symmetry, $$R_A = R_B = \frac{1}{2}(4)\left(\frac{200 \text{ kN.m}}{EI}\right) + (2)\left(\frac{100 \text{ kN.m}}{EI}\right) + \frac{1}{2} \times (2) \times \frac{20 \text{ kN.m}}{EI}$$

$$= \frac{620 \text{ kN.m}^2}{EI} (\downarrow)$$

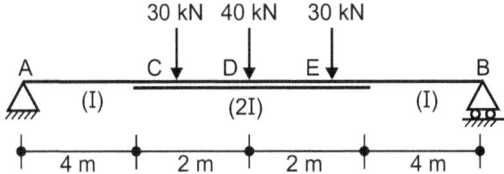

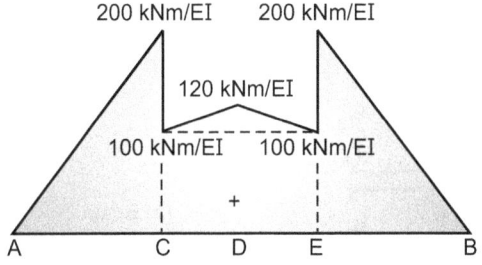

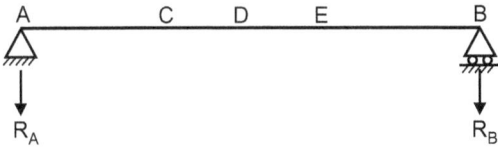

Fig. 2.108

Shear force and bending moment for conjugate beam :

$$V_A = \frac{-620 \text{ kN.m}^2}{EI}$$

$$V_B = \frac{620 \text{ kN.m}^2}{EI}$$

Maximum B.M. will occur at centre.

$$M_{max} = \frac{-620 \text{ kN.m}^2}{EI}(6) + \frac{1}{2}(4)\frac{200 \text{ kN.m}}{EI}\left(2 + \frac{1}{3} \times 4\right)$$

$$+ 2 \times \frac{100 \text{ kN.m}}{EI}\left(\frac{2}{2}\right) + \frac{1}{2} \times 2 \times \frac{20 \text{ kN.m}}{EI}\left(\frac{1}{3} \times 2\right)$$

$$= \frac{-2174 \text{ kN.m}^3}{EI}$$

$$= \frac{2174 \text{ kN.m}^3}{EI} \text{ (Hogging)}$$

Slope and deflections :

$$\theta_A = V_A = -\frac{620 \text{ kN.m}^2}{EI} = -\frac{620 \times 10^3 \times (10^3)^2}{2.1 \times 10^5 \times 250 \times 10^6}$$

$$= -0.0118 \text{ rad}$$

$$= 0.677° \text{ (↻)}$$

$\theta_B = 0.677° \; (\circlearrowright)$

$y_{max} = M_{max} = -\dfrac{2174 \text{ kN.m}^3}{EI} = \dfrac{-2174 \times 10^3 \times (10^3)^3}{2.1 \times 10^5 \times 250 \times 10^6}$

$= 41.4 \text{ mm} \; (\downarrow)$

Problem 2.55 : For a simply supported beam shown in Fig. 2.109 (a), calculate slope and deflections at A, B, C and D. Take $E = 2 \times 10^5$ MPa; $I = 2 \times 10^6$ cm^4. Use conjugate beam method.

Solution :

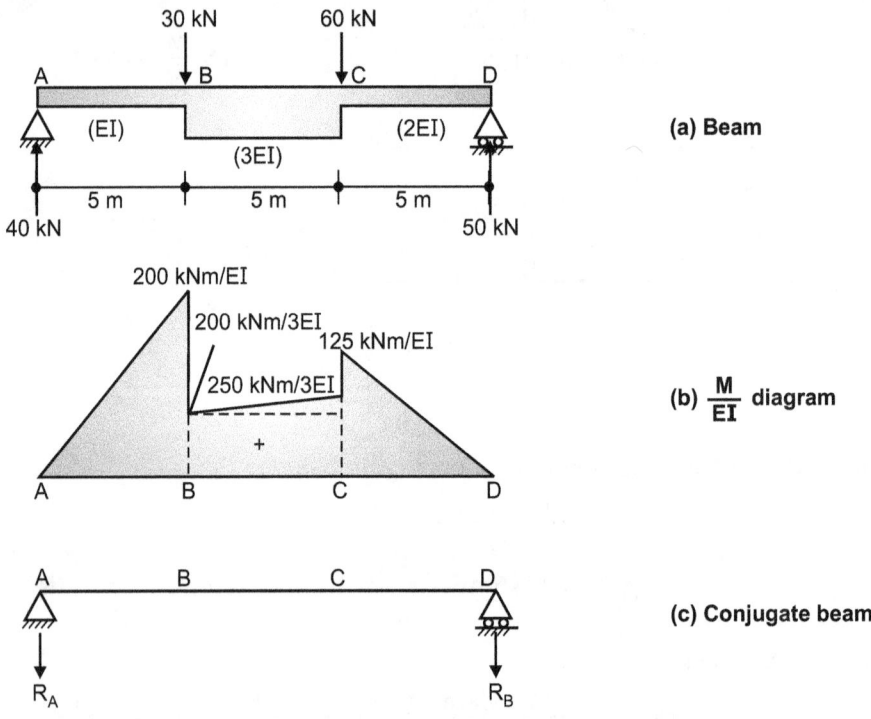

Fig. 2.109

Analysis of given beam :

$\sum M_A = 0; \quad V_D \times 15 - 60 \times 10 - 30 \times 5 = 0$

$\therefore \quad V_D = 50 \text{ kN} \; (\uparrow)$

$\sum F_y = 0; \quad V_A + V_D = 90$

$\therefore \quad V_A = 90 - 50 = 40 \text{ kN} \; (\uparrow)$

$M_B = 40 \times 5 = 200 \text{ kN.m (Sagging)}$

$M_C = 50 \times 5 = 250 \text{ kN.m (Sagging)}$

$\dfrac{M}{EI}$ diagram is as shown in Fig. 2.109.

Analysis of conjugate beam :

Table 2.11

Load component	Magnitude of load	Distance from A (m)	Moment @ A
Load on AB $\frac{1}{2}(5)\frac{200 \text{ kN.m}}{EI}$	$\frac{500 \text{ kN.m}^2}{EI}$	$\frac{2}{3}(5) = \frac{10}{3}$	$\frac{5000 \text{ kN.m}^3}{3 \text{ EI}}$
Load on BC $\left(\frac{200 \text{ kN.m}}{3 \text{ EI}}\right)5$ $\frac{1}{2}\left(\frac{50 \text{ kN.m}}{3 \text{ EI}}\right)5$	$\frac{1000 \text{ kN.m}^2}{3 \text{ EI}}$ $\frac{125 \text{ kN.m}^2}{3 \text{ EI}}$	$5 + \frac{5}{2} = 7.5$ $5 + \frac{2}{3}(5) = 8.33$	$\frac{7500 \text{ kN.m}^3}{3 \text{ EI}}$ $\frac{347.22 \text{ kN.m}^3}{EI}$
Load on CD $\frac{1}{2}\left(\frac{125 \text{ kN.m}}{EI}\right)5$	$312.5 \frac{\text{kN.m}^2}{EI}$	$10 + \frac{5}{3} = 11.67$	$\frac{3645.8 \text{ kN.m}^3}{EI}$
Total :	$1187.5 \frac{\text{kN.m}^2}{EI}$		$8159.68 \frac{\text{kN.m}^3}{EI}$

To find reactions :

$\sum M_A = 0;\quad R_D \times 15 = 8159.68 \Rightarrow R_D = \dfrac{543.97 \text{ kN.m}^2}{EI}\ (\downarrow)$

$\sum F_y = 0;\qquad R_A + R_D = \dfrac{1187.5 \text{ kN.m}^2}{EI}$

$\therefore \qquad R_A = (1187.5 - 543.97)\dfrac{\text{kN.m}^2}{EI} = \dfrac{643.53 \text{ kN.m}^2}{EI}\ (\downarrow)$

Shear force and bending moments :

$V_A = \dfrac{-643.53 \text{ kN.m}^2}{EI}$

$V_B = (-643.53 + 500)\dfrac{\text{kN.m}^2}{EI} = \dfrac{-143.53 \text{ kN.m}^2}{EI}$

$V_C = \left(-643.53 + 500 + \dfrac{1000}{3} + \dfrac{125}{3}\right)\dfrac{\text{kN.m}^2}{EI}$

$\quad = \dfrac{231.47 \text{ kN.m}^2}{EI}$

$V_D = (231.47 + 312.5)\dfrac{\text{kN.m}^2}{EI}$

$\quad = \dfrac{543.97 \text{ kN.m}^2}{EI} = R_D \qquad\qquad\qquad\qquad\qquad\text{(O.K.)}$

$M_A = 0 = M_D$

$M_B = \left(-\dfrac{643.53 \text{ kN.m}^2}{EI}\right) 5 + \left(\dfrac{500 \text{ kN.m}^2}{EI}\right)\left(\dfrac{5}{3}\right)$

$= -\dfrac{2384.32 \text{ kN.m}^3}{EI} = \dfrac{2384.32 \text{ kN.m}^3}{EI}$ (Hogging)

$M_C = \left(-\dfrac{543.97 \text{ kN.m}^2}{EI}\right) 5 + \left(\dfrac{312.5 \text{ kN.m}^2}{EI}\right)\left(\dfrac{5}{3}\right)$

$= -\dfrac{2199 \text{ kN.m}^3}{EI} = \dfrac{2199 \text{ kN.m}^3}{EI}$ (Hogging)

Slope and deflections :

$EI = 2 \times 10^5 \times 2 \times 10^6 \times (10)^4 \text{ N.mm}^2$

$= 4 \times 10^{15} \text{ N.mm}^2$

$= 4 \times 10^6 \text{ kN.m}^2$

$\theta_A = V_A = -\dfrac{643.53}{4 \times 10^6} = -0.00016 \text{ rad} = 0.0092° \text{ (}\circlearrowright\text{)}$

$\theta_B = V_B = -\dfrac{143.53}{4 \times 10^6} = 0.0000358 \text{ rad} = 0.00205° \text{ (}\circlearrowright\text{)}$

$\theta_C = V_C = \dfrac{231.47}{4 \times 10^6} = 0.0000578 \text{ rad} = 0.0033° \text{ (}\circlearrowleft\text{)}$

$\theta_D = V_D = \dfrac{543.97}{4 \times 10^6} = 0.000136 \text{ rad} = 0.0077° \text{ (}\circlearrowleft\text{)}$

$y_A = y_D = 0$

$y_B = M_B = -\dfrac{2384.32}{4 \times 10^6}(10)^3 = 0.596 \text{ mm} (\downarrow)$

$y_C = M_C = \dfrac{-2199 \times (10)^3}{4 \times 10^6} = 0.549 \text{ mm} (\downarrow)$

Problem 2.56 : Find slope and deflections at A, B, C and D for a beam shown in Fig. 2.110 (a) using conjugate beam method. Take $E = 2 \times 10^5$ MPa; $I = 3 \times 10^8$ mm^4.

Solution : Analysis of given beam :

$\sum M_A = 0$; $V_B \times 6 = 20 \times 3 \times \dfrac{3}{2} + 60 \times 4$ $\therefore$ $V_B = 55$ kN ($\uparrow$)

$\sum F_y = 0$; $V_A + V_B = 20 \times 3 + 60$ $\therefore$ $V_A = 65$ kN ($\uparrow$)

Bending moments, $M_A = M_B = 0$

$M_C = 65 \times 3 - 20 \times 3 \times \dfrac{3}{2} = 105$ kN.m (Sagging)

$M_D = 55 \times 2 = 110$ kN.m (Sagging)

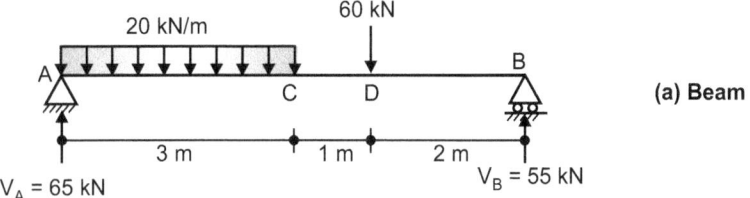

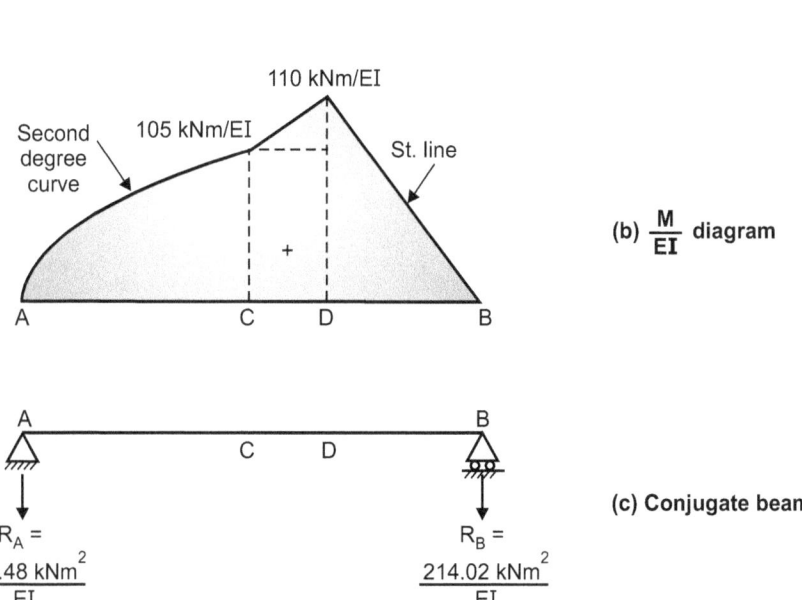

Fig. 2.110

Analysis of conjugate beam :

Table 2.12

Load component	Magnitude of load	Distance from A (m)	Moment about A
Load on AC $\frac{2}{3} \times 3 \times \frac{105 \text{ kN.m}}{EI}$	$\frac{210 \text{ kN.m}^2}{EI}$	$\frac{5}{8}(3) = \frac{15}{8}$	$\frac{393.75 \text{ kN.m}^3}{EI}$
Load on CD $1 \times 105 \frac{\text{kN.m}}{EI}$ $\frac{1}{2} \times 1 \times \frac{5 \text{ kN.m}}{EI}$	$\frac{105 \text{ kN.m}^2}{EI}$ $\frac{2.5 \text{ kN.m}^2}{EI}$	3.5 $3 + \frac{2}{3}(1) = 3.67$	$\frac{367.5 \text{ kN.m}^3}{EI}$ $\frac{9.175 \text{ kN.m}^3}{EI}$
Load on DB $\frac{1}{2} \times 2 \times \frac{110 \text{ kN.m}}{EI}$	$\frac{110 \text{ kN.m}^2}{EI}$	$4 + \frac{1}{3}(2) = 4.67$	$\frac{513.7 \text{ kN.m}^3}{EI}$
Total :	$427.5 \frac{\text{kN.m}^2}{EI}$		$1284.125 \frac{\text{kN.m}^3}{EI}$

To find reactions :

$\Sigma M_A = 0;$ $\qquad R_B \times 6 = 1284.125 \dfrac{kN.m^3}{EI}$

$\therefore \qquad R_B = \dfrac{214.02 \; kN.m^2}{EI}$

$\Sigma F_y = 0;$ $\qquad R_A + R_B = 427.5 \dfrac{kN.m^2}{EI}$

$\therefore \qquad R_A = \dfrac{213.48 \; kN.m^2}{EI}$

Bending moments :

$$M_C = \left(-213.48 \dfrac{kN.m^2}{EI}\right) 3 + \left(\dfrac{210 \; kN.m^2}{EI}\right) \dfrac{3}{8} \cdot (3)$$

$$= -404.19 \dfrac{kN.m^3}{EI} = 404.19 \dfrac{kN.m^3}{EI} \; \text{(Hogging)}$$

$$M_D = \left(-\dfrac{214.02 \; kN.m^2}{EI}\right)(2) + \left(\dfrac{110 \; kN.m^2}{EI}\right)\left(\dfrac{1}{3}(2)\right)$$

$$= -354.7 \dfrac{kN.m^3}{EI} = 354.7 \dfrac{kN.m^3}{EI} \; \text{(Hogging)}$$

$$EI = 2 \times 10^5 \times 3 \times 10^8 \; N.mm^2$$
$$= 6 \times 10^{13} \; N.mm^2 = 6 \times 10^4 \; kN.m^2$$

Slope and deflections :

$$\theta_A = V_A = -213.48 \dfrac{kN.m^2}{EI} = -\dfrac{213.48}{6 \times 10^4} = -0.0035 \; rad$$
$$= 0.203° \; (\circlearrowright)$$

$$\theta_B = V_B = \dfrac{214.02 \; kN.m^2}{EI} = \dfrac{214.02}{6 \times 10^4}$$
$$= 0.003567 \; rad = 0.204° \; (\circlearrowleft)$$

$$\theta_C = (-213.48 + 210) \dfrac{kN.m^2}{EI}$$
$$= -\dfrac{3.48 \; kN.m^2}{EI} = -\dfrac{3.48}{6 \times 10^4} = -0.000058 \; rad$$
$$= 0.0033° \; (\circlearrowright)$$

$$\theta_D = V_D = (214.02 - 110) \dfrac{kN.m^2}{EI}$$
$$= \dfrac{104.02 \; kN.m^2}{EI} = \dfrac{104.02}{6 \times 10^4} = 0.0017 \; rad$$
$$= 0.099° \; (\circlearrowleft)$$

$$y_C = M_C = -\frac{404.19 \text{ kN.m}^3}{EI} = -\frac{404.19}{6 \times 10^4} \times (10^3) = 6.73 \text{ mm} (\downarrow)$$

$$y_D = M_D = -\frac{354.7 \text{ kN.m}^3}{EI}$$

$$= -\frac{354.7}{6 \times 10^4}(10^3)$$

$$= 5.91 \text{ mm} (\downarrow)$$

$$y_A = y_D = 0$$

Problem 2.57 : Find the slope and deflections at A, B, C and D for a simply supported beam shown in Fig. 2.111 (a). Take E = 2×10^5 MPa, I = 4×10^7 mm⁴. Use conjugate beam method.

Solution :

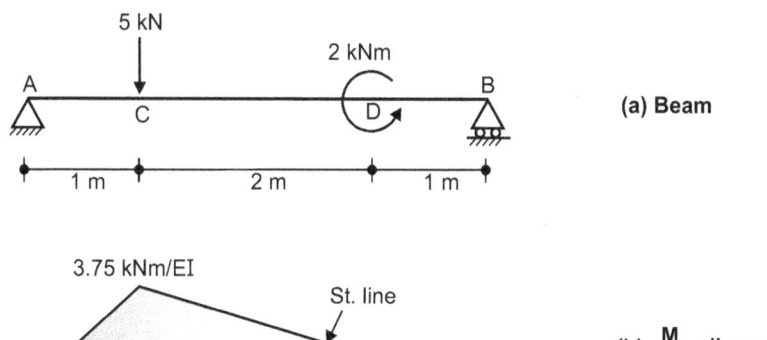

(a) Beam

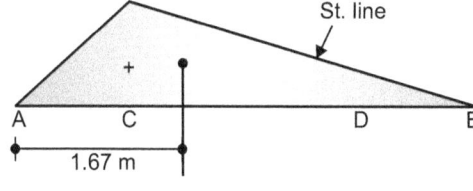

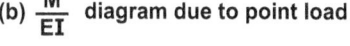

(b) $\frac{M}{EI}$ diagram due to point load

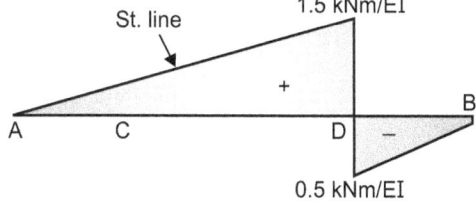

(c) $\frac{M}{EI}$ diagram due to couple

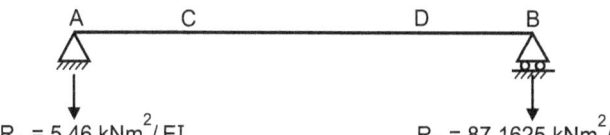

(d) Conjugate beam

Fig. 2.111

Analysis of conjugate beam :

Table 2.13

Load component	Magnitude of load	Distance from A (m)	Moment about A
Load due to point load $\frac{1}{2} \times 4 \times 3.75 \frac{kN.m}{EI}$	$\frac{7.5\ kN.m^2}{EI}$ (↑)	$\frac{4+1}{3} = 1.67$	$\frac{12.5\ kN.m^3}{EI}$ (↻)
Load due to couple $\frac{1}{2} \times 3 \times \frac{1.5\ kN.m}{EI}$	$\frac{2.25\ kN.m^2}{EI}$ (↑)	$\frac{2}{3} \times 3 = 2$	$\frac{4.5\ kN.m^3}{EI}$ (↻)
$\frac{1}{2} \times 1 \times \frac{0.5\ kN.m}{EI}$	$\frac{0.25\ kN.m^2}{EI}$ (↓)	$3 + \frac{1}{3} = 3.33$	$\frac{0.833\ kN.m^3}{EI}$ (↻)
Total :	$9.5 \frac{kN.m^2}{EI}$ (↑)		$16.167 \frac{kN.m^3}{EI}$ (↻)

To find reactions :

$\sum M_A = 0$; $\qquad R_B \times 4 = 16.167 \frac{kN.m^3}{EI} \Rightarrow R_B = \frac{4.04}{EI} kN.m^2$ (↓)

$\sum F_y = 0$; $\qquad R_A + R_B = 9.5 \frac{kN.m^2}{EI} \Rightarrow R_A = 5.46 \frac{kN.m^2}{EI}$ (↓)

Shear force and bending moments for conjugate beam :

$$V_A = -\frac{5.46\ kN.m^2}{EI}$$

$$V_B = \frac{4.04\ kN.m^2}{EI}$$

$$V_C = \left[-5.46 + \frac{1}{2} \times 1 \times 3.75 + \frac{1}{2} \times 1 \times \left(\frac{1.5}{3} \times 1\right)\right] \frac{kN.m^2}{EI}$$

$$= -3.355 \frac{kN.m^2}{EI}$$

$$V_D = \left[4.04 + 0.25 - \frac{1}{2} \times 1 \times 3.75 \left(\frac{1}{3}\right)\right] \frac{kN.m^2}{EI} = \frac{3.665\ kN.m^2}{EI}$$

$M_A = M_B = 0$

$$M_C = -5.46 \frac{kN.m^2}{EI} \times (1) + \frac{1}{2} \times 1 \times \frac{3.75\ kN.m}{EI} \times \left(\frac{1}{3}\right)$$

$$+ \frac{1}{2} \times 1 \times 1.5 \frac{kN.m}{EI} \left(\frac{1}{3}\right)\left(\frac{1}{3}\right)$$

$$= -5.46 \frac{kN.m^3}{EI} + \frac{0.625\ kN.m^3}{EI} + \frac{0.0833\ kN.m^3}{EI}$$

$$= -4.75 \frac{kN.m^3}{EI}$$

$$M_D = -4.04 \frac{kN.m^2}{EI}(1) - \frac{0.25 \, kN.m^2}{EI} \times \left(\frac{1}{3}\right) + \frac{1}{2} \times 1 \times 3.75 \frac{kN.m}{EI}\left(\frac{1}{3}\right)\left(\frac{1}{3}\right)$$

$$= -3.916 \frac{kN.m^3}{EI}$$

Slope and deflections :

$$EI = 2 \times 10^5 \times 4 \times 10^7 = 8 \times 10^{12} \, N.mm^2$$
$$= 8 \times 10^3 \, kN.m^2$$

$$\theta_A = V_A = -\frac{5.46}{8 \times 10^3}$$
$$= -0.00068 \, rad = 0.039° \, (\circlearrowright)$$

$$\theta_B = V_B = \frac{4.04}{8 \times 10^3}$$
$$= 0.000505 \, rad = 0.0289° \, (\circlearrowleft)$$

$$\theta_C = V_C = -\frac{3.355}{8 \times 10^3}$$
$$= -0.000419 \, rad = 0.024° \, (\circlearrowright)$$

$$\theta_D = V_D = \frac{3.665}{8 \times 10^3}$$
$$= 0.000458 \, rad = 0.026° \, (\circlearrowleft)$$

$$y_A = y_B = 0$$

$$\Delta_C = M_C = -\frac{4.75 \, kN.m^3}{EI} = -\frac{4.75 \times 10^3}{8 \times 10^3} = 0.594 \, mm \, (\downarrow)$$

$$y_D = M_D = -\frac{3.916 \, kN.m^3}{EI} = -\frac{3.916 \times 10^3}{8 \times 10^3}$$
$$= 0.489 \, mm \, (\downarrow)$$

Problem 2.58 : Find out θ_C, θ_D, y_C and y_D for the beam shown in Fig. 2.112 (a). Take $E = 2 \times 10^5$ MPa; $I = 3 \times 10^8$ mm^4. Use conjugate beam method.

Solution :

Analysis of conjugate beam :

$\Sigma M_B = 0$; (L.H.S.)

$$R_A \times 6 + \frac{40 \, kN.m}{2 \times EI} \times 6 \, (3.33) + \frac{1}{2}\left(\frac{66.67 \, kN.m}{EI}\right) \times 6 \, (2.67) - \frac{1}{2}\left(\frac{180 \, kN.m}{EI}\right) \times 6 \times \frac{1}{3}(6) = 0$$

$$(R_A) \times 6 + \frac{400 \, kN.m^3}{EI} + \frac{533.33 \, kN.m^3}{EI} - \frac{1080 \, kN.m^3}{EI} = 0$$

$$\therefore \qquad R_A = \frac{24.44 \, kN.m^2}{EI} \, (\uparrow)$$

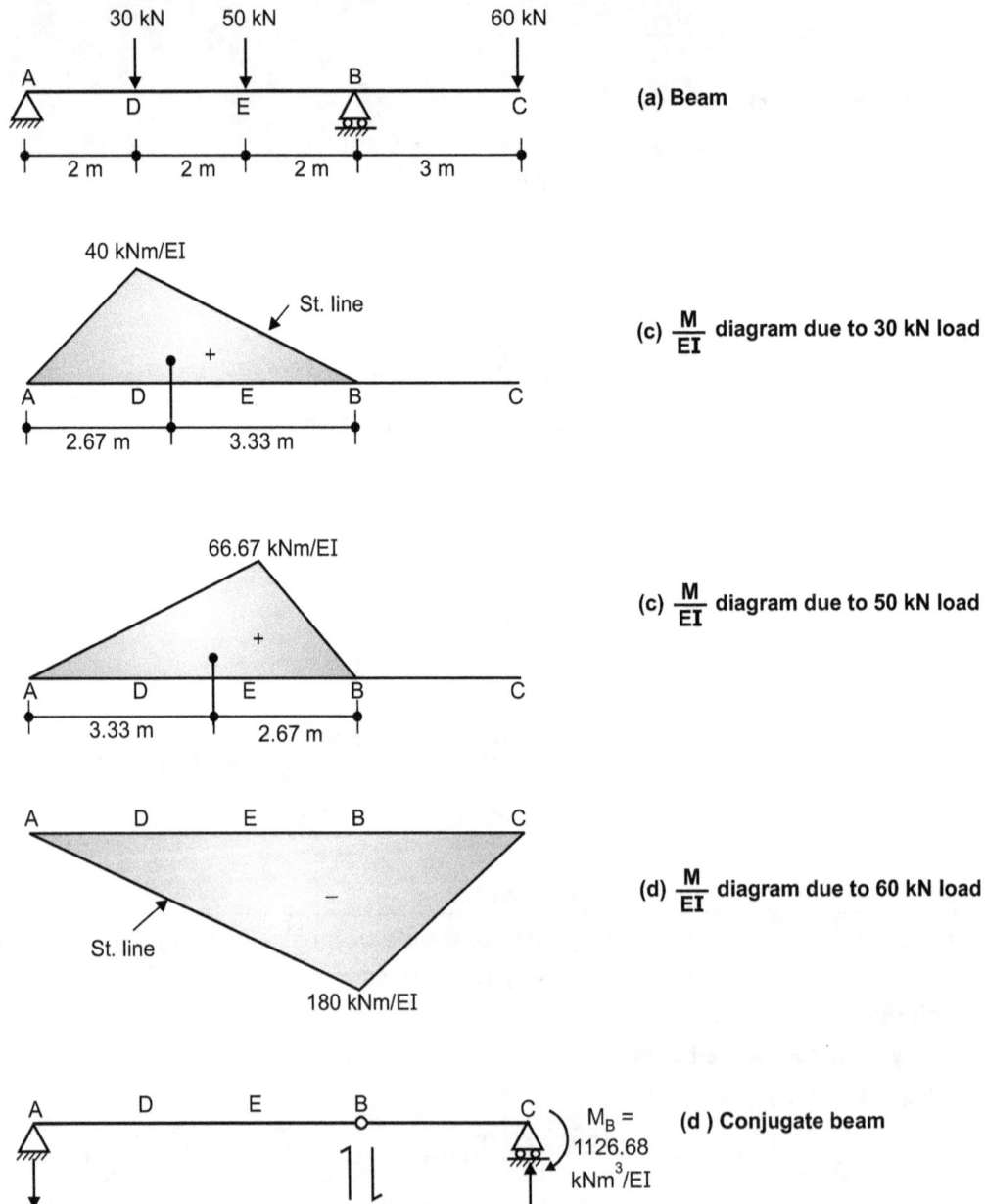

Fig. 2.112

$$\Sigma F_y = 0 \, ; \, R_A + R_B + \frac{40 \text{ kN.m}}{2 \text{ EI}} \times 6 + \frac{66.67 \text{ kN.m}}{2 \text{ EI}} \times 6 - \frac{180 \text{ kN.m}}{2 \text{ EI}} \times 6 = 0$$

$$\frac{24.44 \text{ kN.m}^2}{\text{EI}} + R_B + \frac{120 \text{ kN.m}^2}{\text{EI}} + \frac{200 \text{ kN.m}^2}{\text{EI}} - \frac{540 \text{ kN.m}^2}{\text{EI}} = 0$$

$$\therefore \quad R_B = 195.56 \frac{\text{kN.m}^2}{\text{EI}} \, (\uparrow)$$

$$R_C - 195.56 \frac{\text{kN.m}^2}{\text{EI}} - \frac{1}{2} \times \frac{180 \text{ kN.m}}{\text{EI}} \times 3 = 0$$

$$\therefore \quad R_C = 465.56 \frac{\text{kN.m}^2}{\text{EI}} \, (\uparrow)$$

$$M_C = 195.56 \frac{\text{kN.m}}{\text{EI}} \times 3 + \frac{1}{2} \times \frac{180 \text{ kN.m}}{\text{EI}} \times 3 \times \left(\frac{2}{3} \times 3\right)$$

$$= 1126.68 \frac{\text{kN.m}^2}{\text{EI}} \, (\circlearrowleft)$$

Shear force and bending moments for conjugate beam:

$$V_C = -\frac{465.56 \text{ kN.m}^2}{\text{EI}}$$

$$V_D = 24.44 \frac{\text{kN.m}^2}{\text{EI}} + \frac{1}{2} \times 2 \times 40 \frac{\text{kN.m}}{\text{EI}} + \frac{1}{2} \times \frac{66.67 \text{ kN.m}}{2 \text{ EI}} \times 2$$

$$- \frac{1}{2} \times \frac{180 \text{ kN.m}}{3 \text{ EI}} \times 2$$

$$= 37.77 \frac{\text{kN.m}^2}{\text{EI}}$$

$$M_C = \frac{1126.68 \text{ kN.m}^3}{\text{EI}} \text{ (Hogging)}$$

$$M_D = 24.44 \frac{\text{kN.m}^2}{\text{EI}} \times 2 + \frac{40 \text{ kN.m}^2}{\text{EI}} \left(\frac{2}{3}\right) + \frac{66.67 \text{ kN.m}^2}{2 \text{ EI}} \left(\frac{2}{3}\right)$$

$$- \frac{180}{3} \frac{\text{kN.m}^2}{\text{EI}} \left(\frac{2}{3}\right)$$

$$= (48.88 + 26.67 + 22.22 - 40) \frac{\text{kN.m}^3}{\text{EI}}$$

$$= 57.77 \frac{\text{kN.m}^3}{\text{EI}} \text{ (Sagging)}$$

Slope and deflections:
$$\text{EI} = 2 \times 10^5 \times 3 \times 10^8$$
$$= 6 \times 10^{13} \text{ N.mm}^2$$
$$= 6 \times 10^4 \text{ kN.m}^2$$

$$\theta_C = V_C = -\frac{465.56 \text{ kN.m}^2}{\text{EI}} = -\frac{465.56}{6 \times 10^4} = 0.00775 \text{ rad}$$

$$\therefore \quad \theta_C = 0.445° \, (\circlearrowleft)$$

$$\theta_D = V_D = \frac{37.77 \text{ kN.m}^2}{EI} = \frac{37.77}{6 \times 10^4}$$

$$= 0.00063 \text{ rad} = 0.036° \; (\circlearrowleft)$$

$$y_C = M_C = -\frac{1126.68 \text{ kN.m}^3}{EI} = -\frac{1126.68 \times 10^3}{6 \times 10^4}$$

$$y_C = 18.778 \text{ mm} \; (\downarrow)$$

$$y_D = M_D = \frac{57.77 \text{ kN.m}^3}{EI} = \frac{57.77 \times 10^3}{6 \times 10^4}$$

$$= 0.962 \text{ mm} \; (\uparrow)$$

Problem 2.59 : Determine vertical deflection and slope at B for a beam shown in Fig. 2.113 (a). Use conjugate beam method. Take E = 2 × 10^5 MPa; I = 180 × 10^6 mm^4.

Solution :

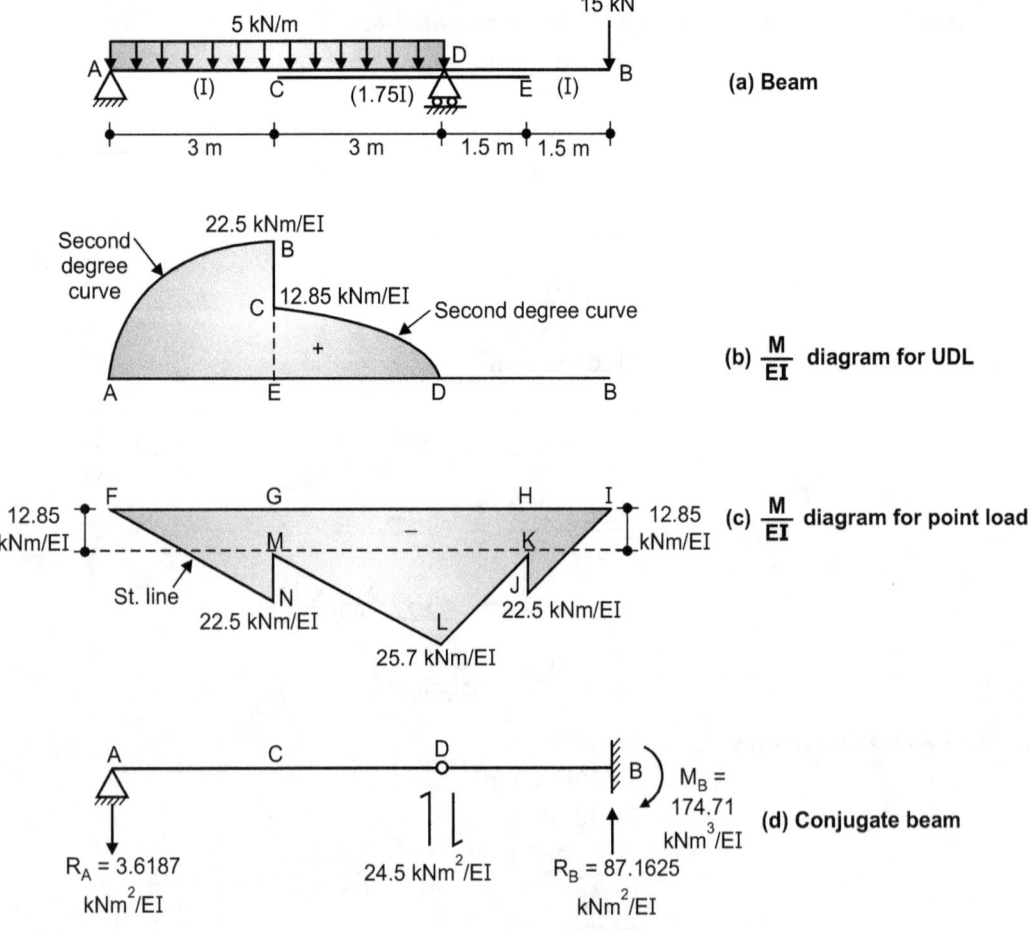

Fig. 2.113

Table 2.14

Component of load	Load magnitude
ABE $= \dfrac{2}{3}(3) \, 22.5 \, \dfrac{kN.m}{EI}$	$45 \, \dfrac{kN.m^2}{EI} \, (\uparrow)$
BED $= \dfrac{2}{3}(3) \, 12.85 \, \dfrac{kN.m}{EI}$	$25.7 \, \dfrac{kN.m^2}{EI} \, (\uparrow)$
FGN $= \dfrac{1}{2}(3) \, 22.5 \, \dfrac{kN.m}{EI}$	$33.75 \, \dfrac{kN.m^2}{EI} \, (\downarrow)$
GHMK $= 12.85 \, \dfrac{kN.m}{EI} \, (4.5)$	$57.825 \, \dfrac{kN.m^2}{EI} \, (\downarrow)$
MKL $= \dfrac{1}{2} \times 4.5 \times \dfrac{12.85 \, kN.m}{EI}$	$28.9125 \, \dfrac{kN.m^2}{EI} \, (\downarrow)$
HIJ $= \dfrac{1}{2} \times (3) \times \dfrac{22.5 \, kN.m}{EI}$	$33.75 \, \dfrac{kN.m^2}{EI} \, (\downarrow)$

Analysis of conjugate beam :

$\Sigma M_D = 0$; (L.H.S.)

$$R_A \times 6 + \dfrac{45 \, kN.m^2}{EI}\left(3 + \dfrac{3}{8}(3)\right) + 25.7 \, \dfrac{kN.m^2}{EI}\left(\dfrac{5}{8}(3)\right)$$

$$- \dfrac{33.75 \, kN.m^2}{EI}\left(3 + \dfrac{1}{3}(3)\right) - \dfrac{57.825 \times 3}{4.5} \, \dfrac{kN.m^2}{EI}\left(\dfrac{3}{2}\right)$$

$$- \dfrac{1}{2} \times \dfrac{12.85 \, kN.m}{EI} \times (3) \times \left(\dfrac{1}{3}\right) 3 = 0$$

$\therefore \quad R_A \times 6 + 185.625 \, \dfrac{kN.m^3}{EI} + 48.1875 \, \dfrac{kN.m^3}{EI} - \dfrac{135 \, kN.m^3}{EI} - 57.825 \, \dfrac{kN.m^3}{EI}$

$$- 19.275 \, \dfrac{kN.m^3}{EI} = 0$$

$\therefore \qquad R_A = -3.6187 \, \dfrac{kN.m^2}{EI} = 3.6187 \, \dfrac{kN.m^2}{EI} \, (\downarrow)$

$\Sigma F_y = 0$; (Part AD)

$$\left(-3.6187 + 45 + 25.7 - 33.75 - \dfrac{57.825 \times 3}{4.5} - 19.275 + R_D\right) \dfrac{kN.m^2}{EI} = 0$$

$$R_D = 24.5 \, \dfrac{kN.m^2}{EI} \, (\uparrow)$$

$\Sigma F_y = 0$; (Part DB)

$$-24.5 \, \dfrac{kN.m^2}{EI} - 12.85 \, \dfrac{kN.m}{EI} \times 1.5 - \dfrac{1}{2} \times 1.5 \times 12.85 \, \dfrac{kN.m}{EI} - 33.75 \, \dfrac{kN.m^2}{EI} + R_B = 0$$

$\therefore \qquad R_B = 87.1625 \, \dfrac{kN.m^2}{EI} \, (\uparrow)$

$\Sigma M_B = 0$;

$$M_B - \left(\frac{24.5 \text{ kN.m}^2}{EI}\right) 3 - 19.275 \frac{\text{kN.m}^2}{EI} \left(1.5 + \frac{1.5}{2}\right)$$

$$- 9.6375 \frac{\text{kN.m}^2}{EI} \left(1.5 + \frac{2}{3}(1.5)\right) - 33.75 \frac{\text{kN.m}^2}{EI} \left(\frac{2}{3}(1.5)\right) = 0$$

$$\therefore \quad M_B = (-73.5 - 43.368 - 24.093 - 33.75) \frac{\text{kN.m}^3}{EI}$$

$$= -174.71 \frac{\text{kN.m}^3}{EI} = \frac{174.71 \text{ kN.m}^3}{EI} \text{ (↺)}$$

$$\therefore \quad \theta_B = V_B = -\frac{87.1625 \text{ kN.m}^2}{EI}$$

$$= -\frac{87.1625 \times 10^3 \times (10^3)^2}{2 \times 10^5 \times 180 \times 10^6} = -0.00242 \text{ rad}$$

$$= 0.138° \text{ (↺)}$$

$$y_B = M_B = -\frac{174.71 \text{ kN.m}^3}{EI} = \frac{-174.71 \times (10^3)(10^3)^3}{2 \times 10^5 \times 180 \times 10^6}$$

$$= 4.85 \text{ mm (↓)}$$

Problem 2.60 : Using conjugate beam method, find the slope and deflection at the free end of a cantilever of span 3 m carrying a load of 75 kN/m over the entire length. Refer Fig. 2.114 (a). Take E = 200 GPa, I = 10^8 mm^4.

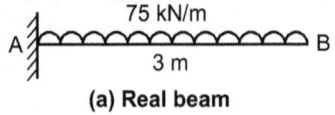

(a) Real beam

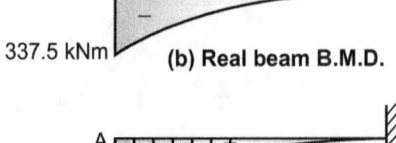

(b) Real beam B.M.D.

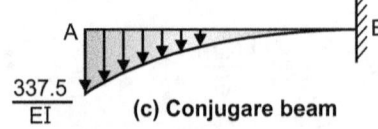

(c) Conjugare beam

Fig. 2.114

Solution : (i) $\quad EI = 200 \times 10^8 \times 10^{-6} = 2 \times 10^4 \text{ kNm}^2$

(ii) $\quad$ Slope at B $= SF_B = -\frac{1}{3} \times \frac{337.5}{EI} \times 3 = \frac{-337.5}{EI} = 0.0168 \text{ rad (↺)}$

(iii) Deflection at B = $BM_B = -\left\{\frac{1}{3} \times \frac{337.5}{EI} \times 3\right\} \frac{3}{4} \times 3$

= -0.0379 m = 37.9 mm (↓)

Problem 2.61 : A beam 8 m long is simply supported at its ends and carries concentrated loads of 20 kN each at points 2 m, from the ends. Calculate by moment-area method, the maximum slope and deflection under each load. EI = 50,000 kN/m³.

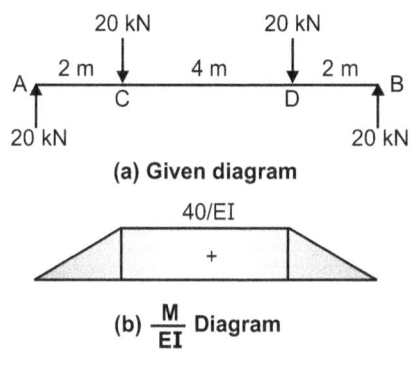

(a) Given diagram

(b) $\frac{M}{EI}$ Diagram

Fig. 2.115

Solution : (i) $\frac{M}{EI}$ diagram.

(ii) Due to symmetry,

$$t_{AB} = t_{BA} = (A)_{AB} \cdot \bar{x}_A = (A)_{AB} \cdot \bar{x}_B$$

$$= \left\{40 \times \frac{(4+8)}{2}\right\} \frac{4}{EI} = \frac{960}{EI}$$

$$\theta_A = \theta_B = \frac{t_{AB}}{8} = \frac{120}{EI} = 0.0024 \text{ rad}$$

(iii) $CC'' = 2\theta_A = \frac{240}{EI}$

$C'C'' = t_{CA} = (A)_{CA} \cdot \bar{x}_C$

= $(1/2 \times 2 \times 40) \, 2/3EI = 26.67/EI$

Deflection at C = $CC'' - C'C''$

= $(240 - 26.67)/EI$

= 4.26 mm (↓)   (∵ $y_C = y_D$)

Problem 2.62 : Determine the ratio P/Q, that will make the deflection at C equal to zero.

Solution :

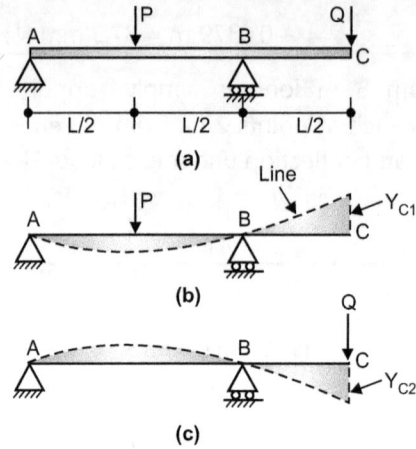

Fig. 2.116

$$y_{C1} + y_{C2} = 0$$

$$\left[\frac{dy}{dx}\right]_B \times 1 \, (BC) - Qa^2 \frac{(2+a)}{3EI} = 0$$

$$\left(\frac{PL^2}{16EI}\right)\frac{L}{2} = Q\left[\frac{L}{2}\right]^2 \frac{(1.5L)}{3EI}$$

∴ $P/Q = 4$

Problem 2.63 : Find the maximum deflection for the beam shown in Fig. 2.117 (a) by conjugate beam method.

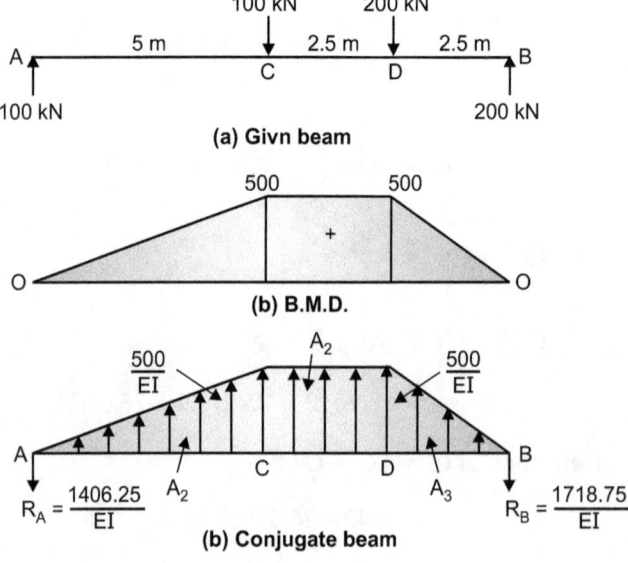

Fig. 2.117

Solution : (i) Analysis of given beam : BMD and conjugate beam is as shown in Fig. 2.117.

(ii) Analysis of conjugate beam :

$A_1 = 1250/EI$, $A_2 = 1250/EI$, $A_3 = 625/EI$.

$\sum M_A = - R_B (10) + (625/EI)(8.33) + (1250/EI)(6.25) + (1250/EI)(3.33) = 0$

∴ $R_B = 1718.75/EI$

∴ $R_A = 1406.25/EI$

For maximum deflection (BM), SF for conjugate beam = 0.

∴ $SF_{(x)}$ (zone CD) $= (-1406.25/EI) + (1250/EI) + (500/EI)(x-5) = 0$

∴ $x = 5.3125$ m from A

∴ Maximum deflection $= BM_{(5.3125)}$

$= \{-1406.25 \times 5.3125 + 1250 \times 1.979 + 500 \times (0.31)^2/2\} \, 1/EI$

$= -4973/EI$

$= 20.72$ mm ($\downarrow$)

EXERCISE

1. A 2 m long cantilever made of steel tube 150 mm external diameter and 10 mm thickness is loaded as shown in Fig. 2.118. Determine the maximum deflection. Assume E = 200 GPa. (13.98 mm ($\downarrow$))

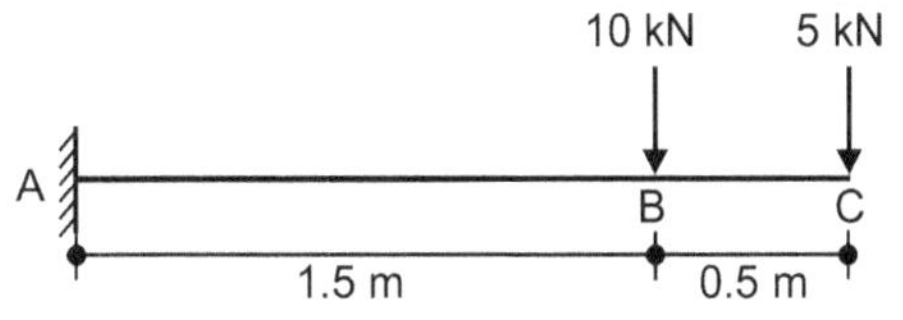

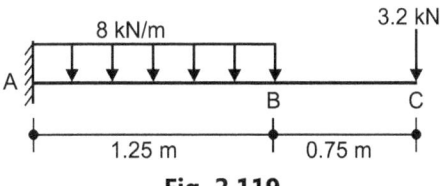

Fig. 2.118

2. A 2 m long cantilever is of rectangular section 100 mm wide and 200 mm deep. It is loaded as shown in Fig. 2.119. Find deflection at free end assuming E = 10 GPa.

(19.39 mm ($\downarrow$))

Fig. 2.119

3. A horizontal cantilever of uniform section and span 'L' is loaded as shown in Fig. 2.120. Find the deflection at free end. $\left(\dfrac{26.76}{EI}(\uparrow)\right)$

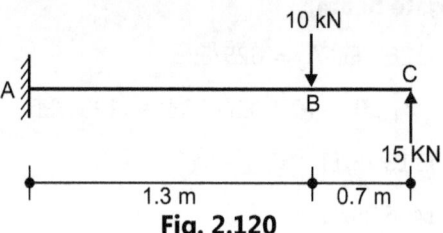

Fig. 2.120

4. A cantilever of uniform section is loaded as shown in Fig. 2.121. Find the deflection at B. If the cantilever is propped at B, find the reaction at prop assuming there is no deflection at B. $\left(y_B = \dfrac{33.75}{EI}(\downarrow);\ V_B = 30\text{ kN}(\uparrow)\right)$

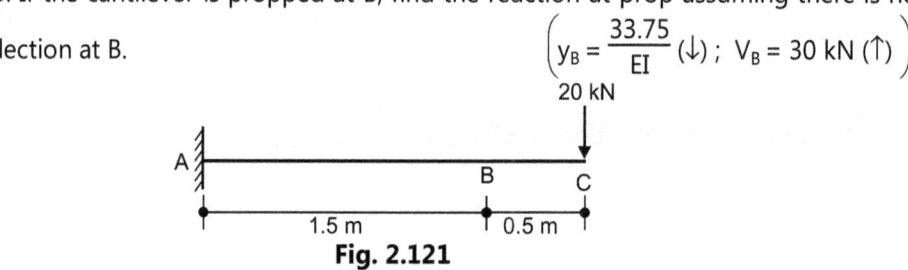

Fig. 2.121

5. A vertical post AB of constant flexural rigidity 4000 kNm² is fixed at the base A and subjected to a horizontal load of 20 kN at C as shown in Fig. 2.122. Determine the necessary force in horizontal tie at B such that the deflection at B is limited to 20 mm to the left. (5.13 kN)

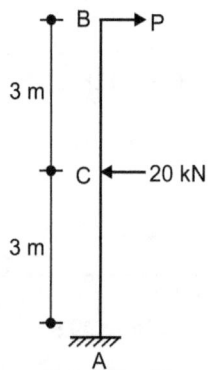

Fig. 2.122

6. Two equal steel beams are built in at one end and connected by a steel rod as shown in Fig. 2.123. Show that the pull in the rod is

$$P = \dfrac{5\,WL^3}{32\left(\dfrac{6\,aI}{\pi d^2} + L^3\right)}$$

where;   d = diameter of the rod and
                I = M.I. of each beam

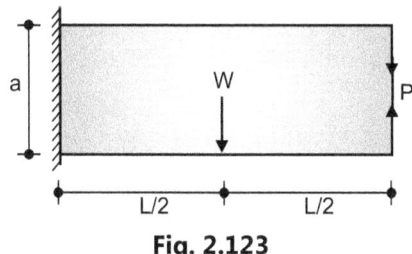

Fig. 2.123

7. For the beam shown in Fig. 2.124, show that the deflection under load is $\dfrac{W}{3.2\,EI}$.

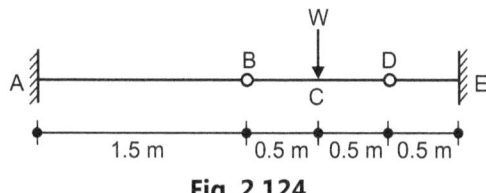

Fig. 2.124

8. A timber beam carries a UDL of 10 kN/m over a span of 6 m. The ends of the beam are simply supported. Determine the section of the beam if the central deflection is limited to 15 mm and the maximum bending stress to 10 MPa. Take E = 12 GPa.

(b = 154 mm, d = 417 mm)

9. The beam is supported and loaded as shown in Fig. 2.125. Find (i) the deflection under the load, (ii) the position and amount of maximum deflection.

Assume E = 200 GPa and I = 50 × 10⁶ mm⁴

(y_C = 6 mm (↓); y_{max} = 6.53 mm (↓) at 2.45 m from A)

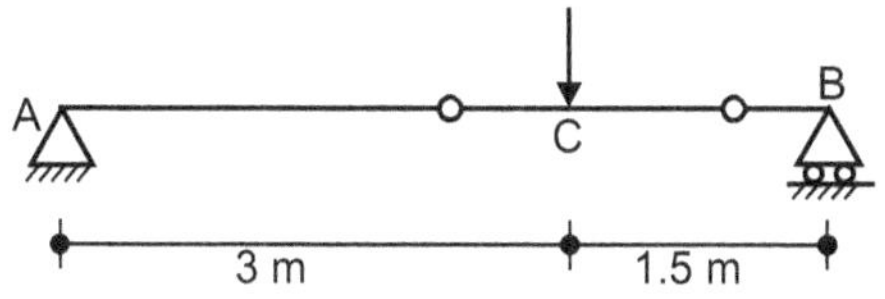

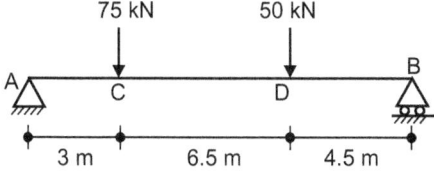

Fig. 2.125

10. The beam is supported and loaded as shown in Fig. 2.126. Find (i) the deflection under loads, (ii) the maximum deflection. Assume E = 200 GPa, I = 70 × 10⁸ mm⁴.

(y_C = 2.34 mm (↓) ; y_D = 2.98 mm (↓) ; y_{max} = 3.54 mm (↓) at 6.87 m from A)

Fig. 2.126

11. The beam is supported and loaded as shown in Fig. 2.127. Determine the position and amount of maximum deflection. $EI = 1.39 \times 10^{11}$ kNmm².

(y_{max} = 6.82 mm (↓) at 4.97 m from A)

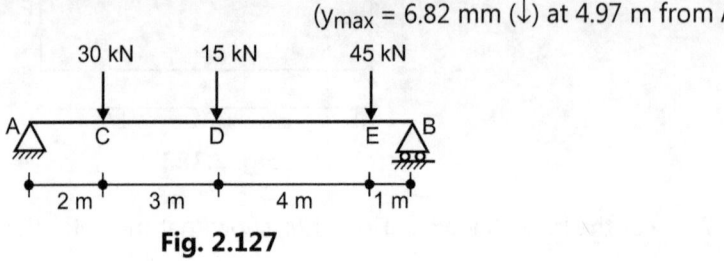

Fig. 2.127

12. The beam is supported and loaded as shown in Fig. 2.128. Find deflection at C.

$$\left(y_C = \frac{3.75}{EI} (\downarrow)\right)$$

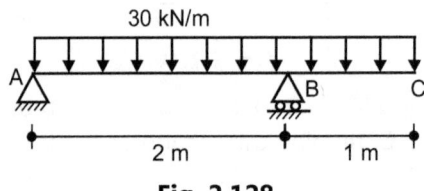

Fig. 2.128

13. The beam is supported and loaded as shown in Fig. 2.129. Assuming E = 200 GPa, I = 40 × 10⁶ mm⁴, find (i) the deflection at C; (ii) the maximum deflection, and (iii) slope at end A.

(y_C = 8.74 mm (↓); y_{max} = 8.75 mm (↓) at 1.958 m from A; θ_A = 0.417° (↺))

Fig. 2.129

14. The beam is supported and loaded as shown in Fig. 2.130. Calculate slope and deflection at point C.

$$\left(\theta_C = \frac{12.67}{EI} (\circlearrowleft) ; y_C = \frac{20.85}{EI} (\downarrow)\right)$$

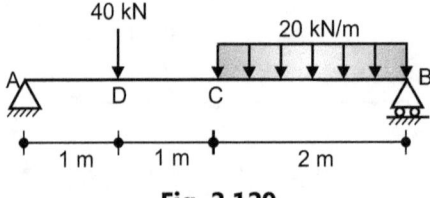

Fig. 2.130

15. A beam of constant section, symmetric about neutral axis is simply supported over a span of 8 m. The beam has to carry a concentrated load of 40 kN at the midspan and a UDL of 15 kN/m over the entire span. If the central deflection is limited to $\frac{1^{th}}{480}$ of the span and the maximum fibre stresses due to bending are not to exceed 118 MPa, determine the required depth of the beam and moment of inertia.

    (d = 435 mm; I_{xx} = 3.686 × 10^8 mm^4)

16. The beam is supported and loaded as shown in Fig. 2.131. Determine the deflections at C and D and maximum deflection assuming EI = 3 × 10^{10} $kNmm^2$.

    (y_C = 12.09 mm (↓); y_D = 13.81 mm (↓); y_{max} = 16.19 mm (↓) at 3.55 m from A)

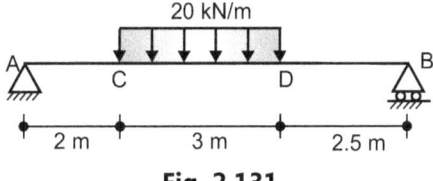

Fig. 2.131

17. Find slope and deflection at C and E for the beam supported and loaded as shown in Fig. 2.132. Assume E = 200 GPa, I = 2 × 10^7 mm^4.

    (θ_C = 0.0047° (↻); y_C = 12.5 mm (↓); θ_E = 0.568° (↻); y_E = 9.916 mm (↑))

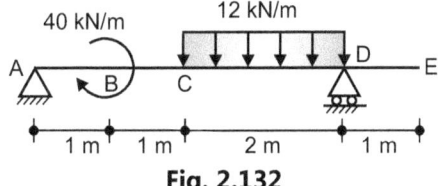

Fig. 2.132

18. A simply supported beam AB of length 'L' just touches a spring of midspan in unloaded condition. Find the stiffness k of the spring that will make the forces on the supports and on the spring equal for a uniformly distributed load. Assume EI = constant.

    (54.857 EI/L^3)

19. The beam is supported and loaded as shown in Fig. 2.133. Determine (i) the deflection at C and (ii) the maximum deflection between A and B. Assume EI = 2700 kNm^2.

    (y_C = 10.08 mm (↓); y_{max} in zone AB = 11.4 mm (↓) at 2.46 m from A)

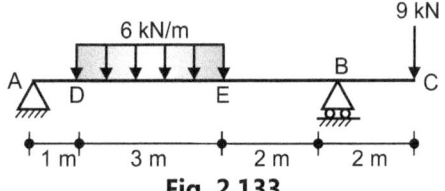

Fig. 2.133

20. Determine slope and deflection at free end of cantilever shown in Fig. 2.134. Assume uniform flexural rigidity. Take E = 2 × 10⁵ MPa; I = 8.5 × 10⁷ mm⁴.

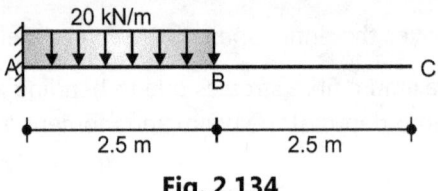

Fig. 2.134

[θ_C = 0.175° ($\circlearrowleft$), y_C = 13.40 mm ($\downarrow$)]

21. Find slope and deflection at free end of cantilever shown in Fig. 2.135. Assume uniform flexural rigidity. Take E = 2 × 10⁵ MPa; I = 2.5 × 10⁸ mm⁴.

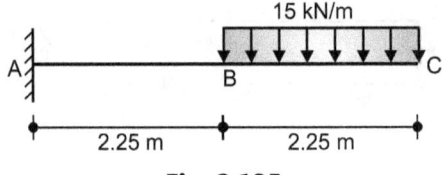

Fig. 2.135

[θ_C = 0.228° ($\circlearrowleft$), y_C = 13.13 mm ($\downarrow$)]

22. Find midspan and maximum deflection for cantilever beam of uniform section shown in Fig. 2.136. Take EI = 7560 kNm².

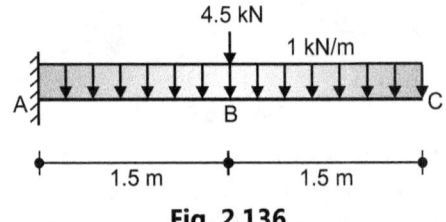

Fig. 2.136

[y_B = 11.44 mm ($\downarrow$), y_{max} = 30.1 mm ($\downarrow$)]

23. Find θ_B; θ_C; y_B; y_C for the cantilever beam shown in Fig. 2.137. Take E = 2 × 10⁵ MPa. I = 5 × 10⁸ mm⁴.

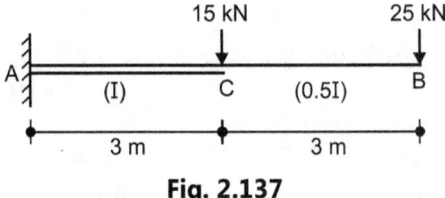

Fig. 2.137

[θ_B = 0.36° ($\circlearrowleft$); θ_C = 0.23° ($\circlearrowleft$); y_B = 23.63 mm ($\downarrow$); y_C = 6.98 mm ($\downarrow$)]

24. Find θ_B; θ_C; y_B; y_C for the cantilever beam shown in Fig. 2.138. Take $E = 2 \times 10^5$ MPa. $I = 5 \times 10^8$ mm⁴.

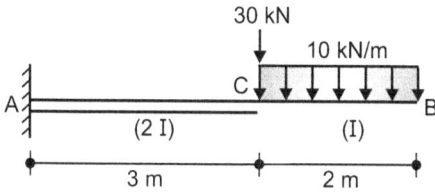

Fig. 2.138

[$\theta_B = 0.09°$ (↻); $\theta_C = 0.08°$ (↻) $y_B = 5.75$ mm (↓); $y_C = 2.7$ mm (↓)]

25. Find slope and deflection at free end of aluminium cantilever shown in Fig. 2.139. Take $E = 70{,}000$ MPa, $I_1 = 2 \times 10^6$ mm⁴, $I_2 = 0.4 \times 10^6$ mm⁴.

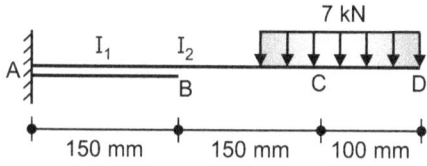

Fig. 2.139

$\left[\theta_D = 0.2575°\ (\circlearrowleft)\ ;\ y_D = 1.124 \text{ mm } (\downarrow)\right]$

26. A cantilever beam shown in Fig. 2.140 has a uniform rectangular cross section having $d = 2b$. Find the values of b, d if maximum deflection is not to exceed 15 mm.

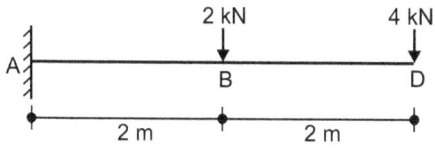

Fig. 2.140

[b = 217.5 mm; d = 435 mm]

27. Find the deflection at free end of cantilever shown in Fig. 2.141.
Take $E = 2 \times 10^7$ MPa, $I = 4 \times 10^6$ mm⁴.

[$y_C = 8.33$ mm (↑)]

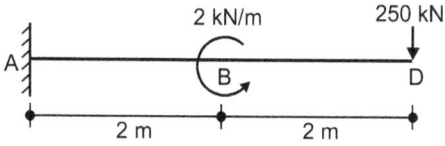

Fig. 2.141

28. Find the deflection at free end of cantilever shown in Fig. 2.142.

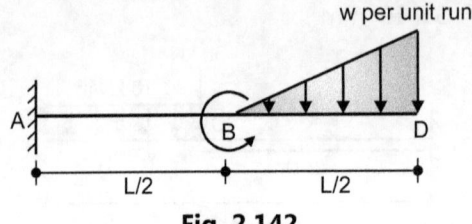

Fig. 2.142

$$\left[y = \frac{121}{1920} \left(\frac{wL^4}{EI} \right) \right]$$

29. Find θ_B; θ_C; y_B and y_C for the cantilever beam shown in Fig. 2.143.
    Take E = 2×10^5 MPa; I = 6×10^8 mm^4.

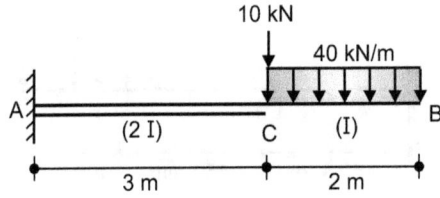

Fig. 2.143

[θ_B = 0.179° (↶); θ_C = 0.153° (↶); y_B = 10.916 mm (↓); y_C = 4.875 mm (↓)]

30. Find θ_B; θ_C; y_B and y_C for the cantilever beam shown in Fig. 2.144.
    Take E = 2×10^5 MPa, I = 5×10^8 mm^4.

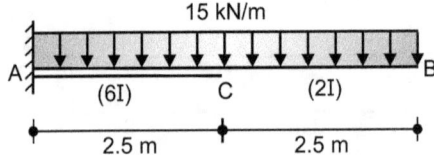

Fig. 2.144

[θ_B = 0.065° (↶); θ_C = 0.045° (↶); y_B = 4.4725 mm (↓); y_C = 1.435 mm (↓)]

31. Find θ_B; θ_C; y_B and y_C for the cantilever beam shown in Fig. 2.145.
    Take E = 2×10^5 MPa; I = 5×10^8 mm^4.

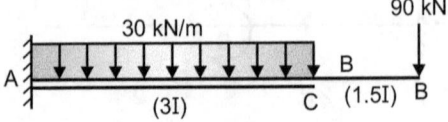

Fig. 2.145

[θ_B = 0.4° (↶); θ_C = 0.34° (↶), y_B = 27.73 (↓); y_C = 14.4 mm (↓)]

32. A beam of constant cross section 10 m long is simply supported at its ends and loaded with two concentrated loads of 6 kN each at a distance 3 m from either supports. Find the ratio of deflection at mid span to that under any one of the load.

(1.22)

33. A simply supported beam of uniform section and span L is loaded with two equal loads w at point L/4 from each end. Show that the central deflection is $\dfrac{11}{384}\left[\dfrac{wL^3}{EI}\right]$.

34. A simply supported beam of uniform section has a span L and carries two equal loads w each at a distance L/3 from either ends. Show that the central deflection is $\dfrac{23}{648}\left[\dfrac{WL^3}{EI}\right]$.

35. Find the maximum deflection for simply supported beam shown in Fig. 2.146. Assume uniform flexural rigidity.

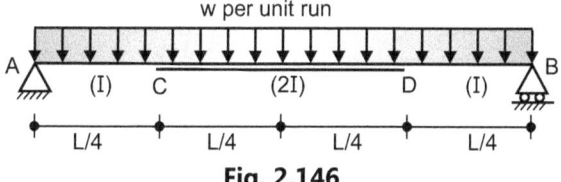

Fig. 2.146

$\left[\dfrac{93}{12288}\left(\dfrac{wL^4}{EI}\right)\right]$.

36. Find θ_C and y_C from simply supported beam shown in Fig. 2.147. Take $E = 2 \times 10^5$ MPa; $I = 6 \times 10^8$ mm^4.

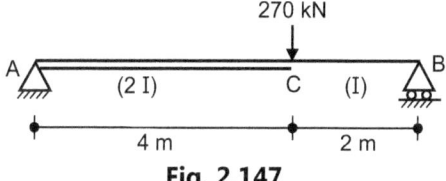

Fig. 2.147

[$\theta_C = 0.0225°$ (↻); $y_C = 3.2025$ mm (↓)]

37. Find θ_A; θ_C; θ_D; y_C and y_D and maximum deflection for the beam shown in Fig. 2.148. Take $E = 2 \times 10^5$ MPa; $I = 3 \times 10^8$ mm^4.

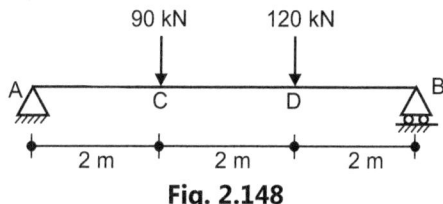

Fig. 2.148

[$\theta_A = 0.3945°$ (↻); $\theta_C = 0.204°$ (↻); $\theta_D = 0.198°$ (↻); $y_C = 11.55$ mm (↓); $y_D = 11.775$ mm (↓); $y_{max} = 13.425$ mm (↓) at 3.04 m from A]

38. Find θ_C and y_C for the beam shown in Fig. 2.149 using $E = 2 \times 10^5$ MPa; $I = 4 \times 10^8$ mm⁴. Assume uniform flexural rigidity throughout.

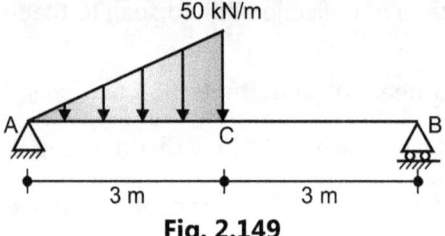

Fig. 2.149

$[\theta_C = 0.01° \ (\circlearrowleft); \ y_C = 3.375 \text{ mm} \ (\downarrow)]$

39. Find θ_A; θ_B; y_C and y_D for the beam shown in Fig. 2.150. Take $E = 2 \times 10^5$ MPa; $I = 4.5 \times 10^8$ mm⁴.

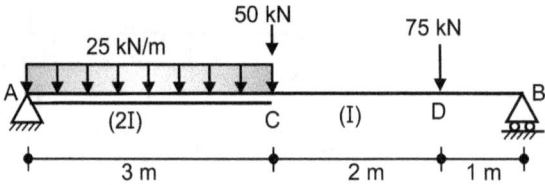

Fig. 2.150

$[\theta_A = 0.13° \ (\circlearrowleft); \ \theta_B = 0.175° \ (\circlearrowleft); \ y_C = 5 \text{ mm} \ (\downarrow); \ y_D = 2.875 \text{ mm} \ (\downarrow)]$

40. Determine the maximum deflection of the beam carrying uniformly distributed load over the middle portion as shown in Fig. 2.151.

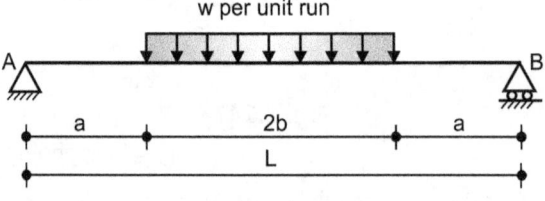

Fig. 2.151

$$\left[y_{max} = \frac{wb}{24 \ EI} (L^3 - 2Lb^2 + b^3) \right]$$

41. A beam of uniform section and length L is simply supported at its ends and carries a symmetrical triangular loading having intensity varying from zero at each end to w at centre. Find the slope at each end and the deflection at centre.

$$\left[\theta = \frac{5}{192} \frac{wL^3}{EI}, \ y = \frac{wL^4}{120 \ EI} (\downarrow) \right]$$

42. A beam 6 m long is subjected to couples as shown in Fig. 2.152. Find the deflections at the points of application of couple. Take E = 2 × 10⁵ MPa; I = 3 × 10⁷ mm⁴.

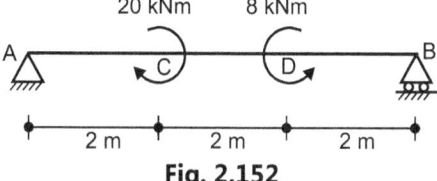

Fig. 2.152

[y_C = 4.44 mm (↓); y_D = 4.88 mm (↓)]

43. Find deflection at D for a beam shown in Fig. 2.153. Take E = 2.1 × 10⁵ MPa and I = 3.7 × 10⁸ mm⁴.

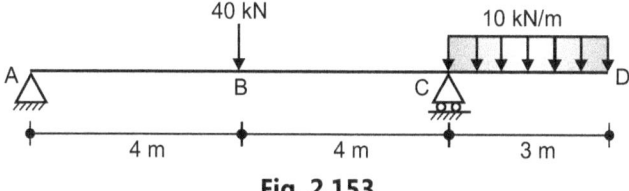

Fig. 2.153

[0.242 mm (↑)]

44. A uniform beam is supported and loaded as shown in Fig. 2.154. Find deflections under the loads and slopes at the supports. Take E = 2 × 10⁵ MPa; I = 6 × 10⁸ mm⁴.

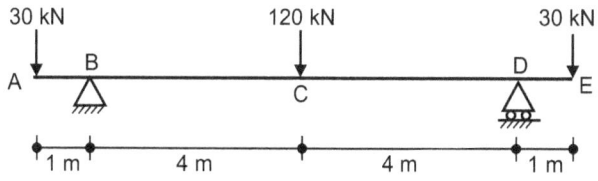

Fig. 2.154

[y_C = 8.67 mm (↓); y_A = y_E = 2.916 mm (↑); θ_B = θ_D = 0.171°]

45. Find out θ_C; θ_D; y_C and y_D for the beam shown in Fig. 2.156. Take E = 2 × 10⁵ MPa; I = 4.5 × 10⁸ mm⁴.

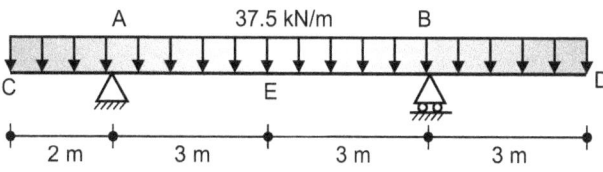

Fig. 2.155

[θ_C = 0.024° (↺), θ_D = 0.155° (↺), y_C = 0.416 mm (↓), y_D = 6.712 (↓)]

46. Determine the deflection at C for a beam shown in Fig. 2.156. Assume uniform flexural rigidity throughout.

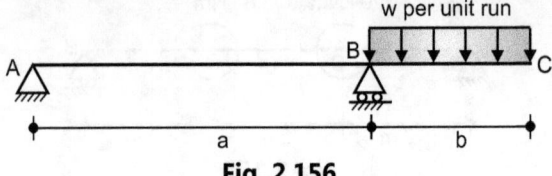

Fig. 2.156

$$\left[y_C = \frac{wb^3}{24\ EI} (4a + 3b) \right]$$

47. Find deflection at C for a beam shown in Fig. 2.157.

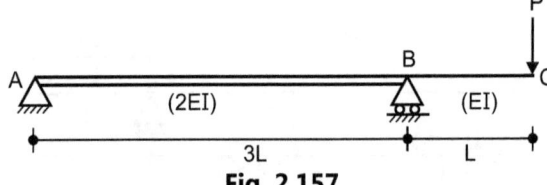

Fig. 2.157

$$\left[y_C = \frac{5\ PL^3}{16\ EI} (\downarrow) \right]$$

❏❏❏

Chapter 3
DEFLECTION OF BEAMS AND FRAMES

3.1 CASTIGLIANO'S FIRST THEOREM OF COMPLEMENTARY ENERGY

Consider a structure in equilibrium under a set of applied loads $P_1, P_2, P_3 \ldots P_k, \ldots P_n$. The material of the structure may be linear or non-linear elastic. Let the load at point k alone be increased by dP_k.

The increase in the complementary energy can be written as

$$dC = \frac{\partial C}{\partial P_k} dP_k \qquad \ldots (3.1)$$

As a result of this increased dP_k, the deflection of various points in the structure will increase.

Fig. 3.1 shows the load deflection graph for any other point j where load P_j is acting. The portion AB shows the effect as the initial loads are applied (portion AB can be non-linear also). When dP_k is added, the value of the load P_j remains constant but deflection increases by dy_j giving rise to the horizontal part BC of the graph. Thus, the value of complementary energy (area above the graph) does not change. External work will be done however, and this is equal to the area BCDE. As a result of the increased dP_k, there will not be any increase in complementary energy at any of the points except point k, where the increase can be written as

$$dC = y_k \, dP_k \qquad \ldots (3.2)$$

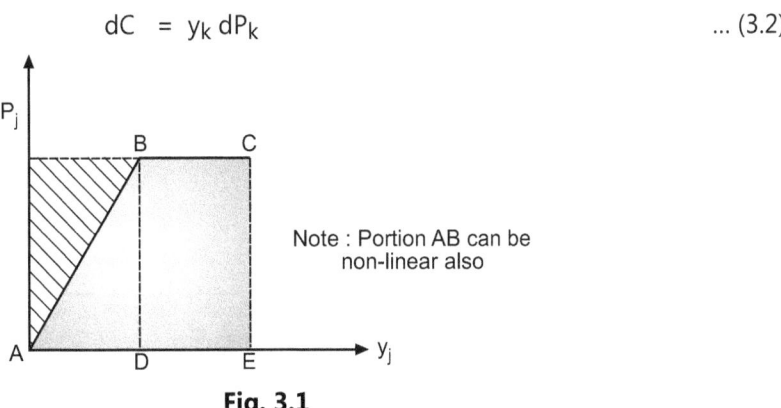

Note: Portion AB can be non-linear also

Fig. 3.1

From equations (3.1) and (3.2),

$$\frac{\partial C}{\partial P_k} dP_k = y_k \, dP_k$$

$$\therefore \quad \frac{\partial C}{\partial P_k} = y_k \qquad \ldots (3.3)$$

If the material of the structure is linear elastic, then complementary energy is equal to the strain energy.

$$\therefore \quad \text{We can write } \frac{\partial U}{\partial P_k} = y_k \qquad \ldots (3.4)$$

This is the first theorem of Castigliano. It can be stated as "*The displacement of the point of application of any load, along the line of action of the load, equals the partial differential coefficient of the total complementary energy (or in particular case of linear elastic material, the total strain energy) with respect to that load*".

Normally, we deal with the materials which are linearly elastic and thus usually we say that the partial differential coefficient of the *total strain energy* with respect to the applied load, gives the corresponding displacement at the point of application of the load. Thus, if the applied loading is a couple M, then the corresponding displacement means the rotation θ in the direction of the couple will be given by,

$$\theta = \frac{\partial U}{\partial M}$$

When displacement at a point, where load is not acting, is required then a fictitious load is applied at the point in the direction of desired displacement and total strain energy is worked out in terms of the given loading and the fictitious load. The partial differential coefficient of the strain energy equation is taken and then the fictitious load is put equal to zero.

SOLVED PROBLEMS

Problem 3.1 : A cantilever beam AB having span 'l' is fixed at end A and carries a point load 'w' at the free end. Find deflection at the free end and at mid span.

Solution : (a) Deflection at free end :

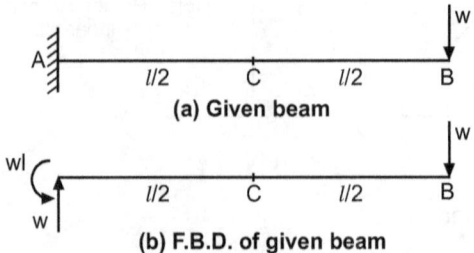

Fig. 3.2

Region	Moment	∂M/∂w	Limit
BA	– wx	(–x)	0 to l

According to Castigliano's first theorem,

$$\delta_B = \frac{\partial U}{\partial w} = \frac{1}{EI}\int_0^l (-wx)(-x)\,dx$$

$$= \frac{1}{EI}\left[\frac{wx^3}{3}\right]_0^l = \frac{wl^3}{3\,EI}$$

(b) Deflection at mid span :

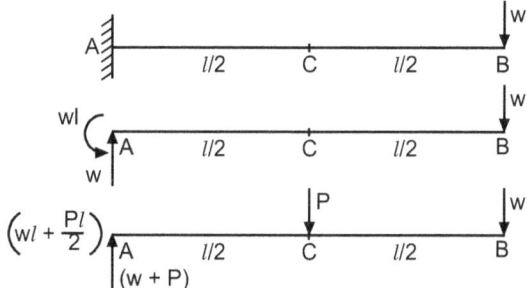

Fig. 3.3

Region	Moment	$\partial M/\partial P$	Limit
BC	$-wx$	0	0 to $l/2$
CA	$-w\left(x+\dfrac{l}{2}\right) - Px$	$-x$	0 to $l/2$

According to Castigliano's first theorem,

$$\delta_C = \frac{\partial U}{\partial P}$$

$$= \frac{1}{EI}\int_0^{l/2}(-wx)(0)\,dx + \frac{1}{EI}\int_0^{l/2}\left[-w\left(x+\frac{l}{2}\right)-Px\right](-x)\,dx$$

As P is fictitious load $\therefore$ put P = 0

$$\delta_C = \frac{1}{EI}\int_0^{l/2} -w\left(x+\frac{l}{2}\right)(-x)\,dx = \frac{1}{EI}\int_0^{l/2} wx^2\,dx + \int_0^{l/2} wx\frac{l}{2}\,dx$$

$$= \frac{1}{EI}\left[\frac{wx^3}{3}\right]_0^{l/2} + \frac{wl}{2}\left[\frac{x^2}{2}\right]_0^{l/2}$$

$$= \frac{wl^3}{24\,EI} + \frac{wl^3}{16\,EI}$$

$$\delta_C = \frac{5\,wl^3}{48\,EI}$$

Problem 3.2 : Determine the deflection and slope at the free end for the beam shown in Fig. 3.4 (a).

Solution :

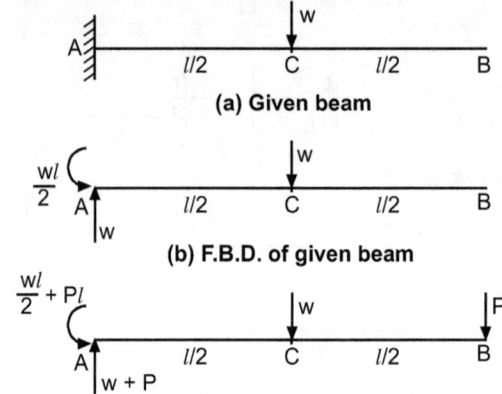

(a) Given beam

(b) F.B.D. of given beam

(c) Beam with fictitious load

Fig. 3.4

Region	Moment	∂M/∂P	Limit
BC	$-Px$	$-x$	0 to $l/2$
CA	$-P\left(x + \dfrac{l}{2}\right) - wx$	$-\left(x + \dfrac{l}{2}\right)$	0 to $l/2$

According to first theorem of Castigliano,

$$\delta_C = \frac{\partial U}{\partial P}$$

$$= \frac{1}{EI}\int_0^{l/2}(-Px)(-x)\,dx + \frac{1}{EI}\int_0^{l/2}[-P(x+l/2) - wx]\cdot -(x+l/2)\,dx$$

As P is fictitious load ∴ put P = 0.

$$\delta_C = \frac{1}{EI}\int_0^{l/2} -wx\left[-\left(x+\frac{l}{2}\right)\right]dx$$

$$= \frac{1}{EI}\int_0^{l/2} wx^2\,dx + \frac{1}{EI}\int_0^{l/2} wx\cdot\frac{l}{2}\,dx$$

$$= \frac{1}{EI}\left[\frac{wx^3}{3}\right]_0^{l/2} + \frac{1}{EI}\left[\frac{wl\,x^2}{2\cdot 2}\right]_0^{l/2}$$

$$= \frac{wl^3}{24\,EI} + \frac{wl^3}{16\,EI}$$

$$\delta_C = \frac{5\,wl^3}{48\,EI}$$

Slope at free end :

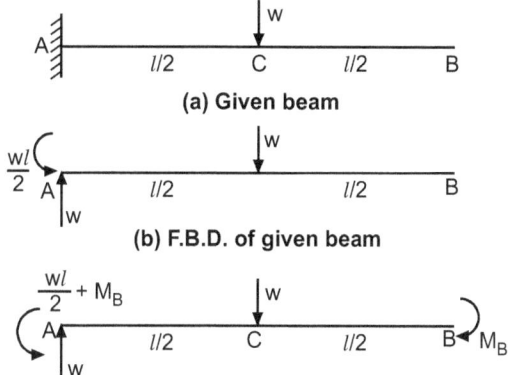

(a) Given beam

(b) F.B.D. of given beam

(c) Beam with fictitious moment

Fig. 3.5

Region	Moment	$\partial M/\partial M_B$	Limit
BC	$-M_B$	-1	0 to $l/2$
CA	$-M_B - wx$	-1	0 to $l/2$

According to Castigliano's first theorem,

$$\theta_B = \frac{\partial U}{\partial M_B} = \frac{1}{EI}\int_0^{l/2} (-M_B)(-1)\,dx + \frac{1}{EI}\int_0^{l/2} (-M_B - wx)(-1)\,dx$$

As M_B is fictitious load $\therefore$ put $M_B = 0$

$$\theta_B = \frac{1}{EI}\int_0^{l/2}(wx)\cdot 1\,dx = \left[\frac{wx^2}{2\,EI}\right]_0^{l/2} = \frac{wl^2}{8\,EI}$$

$\therefore$ Slope at free end is $\dfrac{wl^2}{8EI}$.

Problem 3.3 : Determine the deflection and slope under the concentrated load for the beam AB shown in Fig. 3.6 (a).

Solution : (a) Deflection under concentrated load :

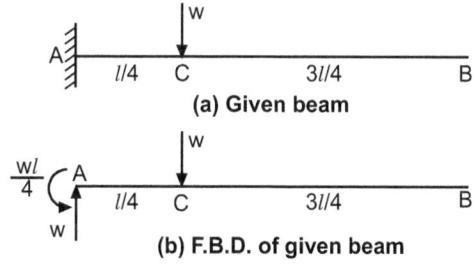

(a) Given beam

(b) F.B.D. of given beam

Fig. 3.6

$\sum F_x = 0$

∴ $R_{Ax} = 0$

$\sum F_y = 0$

∴ $R_{Ay} = w$

$M_A = w \cdot \dfrac{l}{4}$

Region	Moment	∂M/∂w	Limit
BC	0	0	0 to 3l/4
CA	– wx	– x	0 to l/4

According to first theorem of Castigliano,

$$\delta_C = \dfrac{\partial U}{\partial w}$$

$$\delta_C = \dfrac{1}{EI} \int_0^{3l/4} 0 + \dfrac{1}{EI} \int_0^{l/4} (-wx)(-x)\,dx$$

$$= \dfrac{1}{EI} \int_0^{l/4} wx^2\,dx = \left[\dfrac{wx^3}{3\,EI} \right]_0^{l/4}$$

$$= \dfrac{wl^3}{192\,EI}$$

(b)

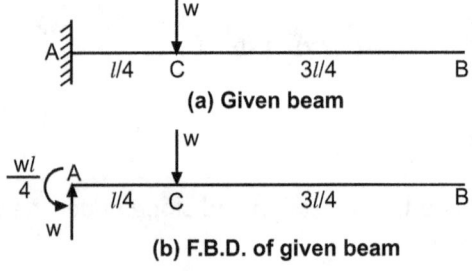

(a) Given beam

(b) F.B.D. of given beam

(c) Beam with fictitious moment

Fig. 3.7

Region	Moment	∂M/∂M_C	Limit
BC	0	0	0 to 3l/4
CA	(– wx – M_C)	– 1	0 to l/4

According to Castigliano's first theorem,

$$\theta_C = \frac{1}{EI} \int M \cdot \frac{\partial M}{\partial M_C} dx$$

$$= \frac{1}{EI} \int_0^{3l/4} 0 + \frac{1}{EI} \int_0^{l/4} (-wx - M_C)(-1) dx$$

As M_C is fictitious moment, so put $M_C = 0$

$$\therefore \quad \theta_C = \frac{1}{EI} \int_0^{l/4} (wx) \cdot dx$$

$$= \frac{1}{EI} \left(w \cdot \frac{x^2}{2} \right)$$

$$= \frac{wl^2}{32\,EI}$$

$$\therefore \quad \text{Slope at } C = \frac{wl^2}{32\,EI}$$

Problem 3.4 : A cantilever AB of span 'l' fixed at end A carries UDL of 'w' kN/m over whole span. Find deflection at free end and at the mid span.

Solution : (a) Deflection at free end :

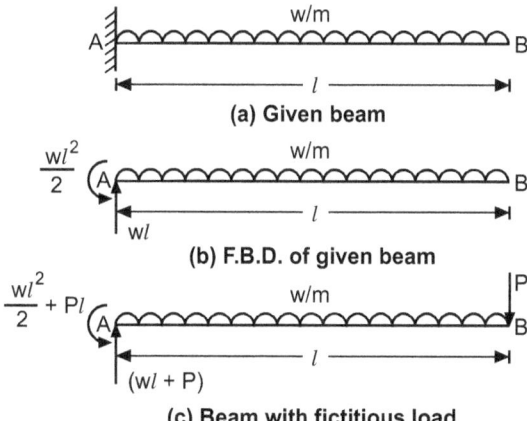

Fig. 3.8

Region	Moment	$\partial M/\partial P$	Limit
BA	$\left(-\dfrac{wx^2}{2} - Px\right)$	$(-x)$	0 to l

According to Castigliano's first theorem,

$$\delta_B = \frac{\partial U}{\partial P}$$

$$\delta_B = \frac{1}{EI} \int_0^l \left(\frac{-wx^2}{2} - Px \right)(-x)\, dx$$

As P is fictitious load $\therefore$ put $P = 0$

$$\delta_B = \frac{1}{EI} \int_0^l \frac{wx^3}{2}\, dx = \left[\frac{wx^4}{8\, EI} \right]_0^l$$

$$= \frac{wl^4}{8\, EI}$$

(b) Deflection at mid span :

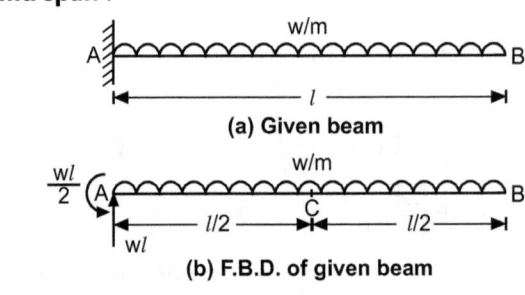

Fig. 3.9

Region	Moment	$\partial M/\partial P$	Limit
BC	$-\dfrac{wx^2}{2}$	0	0 to $l/2$
CA	$\left[-\dfrac{wl}{2}\left(x + \dfrac{l}{4} \right) - Px - \dfrac{wx^2}{2} \right]$	$-x$	0 to $l/2$

According to Castigliano's first theorem,

$$\delta_C = \frac{\partial U}{\partial P}$$

$$= \frac{1}{EI} \int_0^{l/2} 0 + \frac{1}{EI} \int_0^{l/2} \left[-\frac{wl}{2}\left(x + \frac{l}{4} \right) - Px - \frac{wx^2}{2} \right](-x)\, dx$$

As P is fictitious load $\therefore$ put $P = 0$.

$$\delta_C = \frac{1}{EI} \int_0^{l/2} \left[\frac{wl}{2}\left(x^2 + x\frac{l}{4} \right) + \frac{wx^3}{2} \right] dx$$

$$= \int_0^{l/2} wx^2 \frac{l}{2} dx + \int_0^{l/2} \frac{wl^2}{8} x \cdot dx + \int_0^{l/2} \frac{w}{2} \frac{x^4}{4} dx$$

$$= \frac{wl}{2}\left[\frac{x^3}{3}\right]_0^{l/2} + \frac{wl^2}{8}\left[\frac{x^2}{2}\right]_0^{l/2} + w\left[\frac{wl^4}{128}\right] = \frac{wl^4}{48\ EI} + \frac{wl^4}{64\ EI} + \frac{wl^4}{128\ EI}$$

$$\delta_C = \left[\frac{17\ wl^4}{384\ EI}\right]$$

Problem 3.5 : Find the deflection at free end for the beam as shown in Fig. 3.10 (a).

Solution :

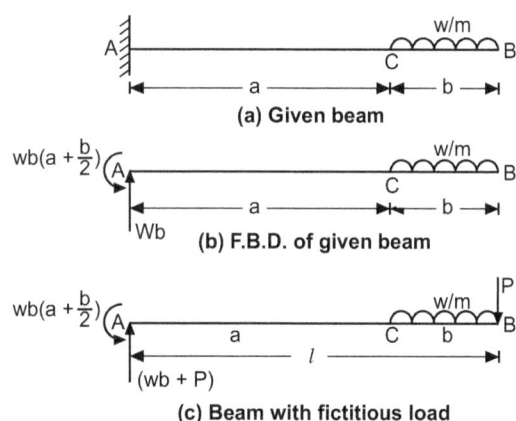

Fig. 3.10

Region	Moment	∂M/∂P	Limit
BC	$-\dfrac{wx^2}{2} - Px$	$-x$	0 to b
CA	$-wb\left(x + \dfrac{b}{2}\right) - P(x+b)$	$-(x+b)$	0 to a

According to Castigliano's first theorem,

$$\delta_B = \frac{\partial U}{\partial P} = \frac{1}{EI}\int_0^b \left(-\frac{wx^2}{2} - Px\right)(-x)\ dx$$

$$+ \frac{1}{EI}\int_0^a \left[-wb\left(x + \frac{b}{2}\right) - P(x+b)\right][-(x+b)]\ dx$$

As P is fictitious load ∴ put P = 0.

$$\therefore \quad \delta_B = \frac{1}{EI}\int_0^b \frac{wx^3}{2} dx + \frac{1}{EI}\int_0^a \left[wb\left(x + \frac{b}{2}\right)(x+b)\right] dx$$

$$= \frac{1}{EI}\int_0^b \frac{wx^3}{2} dx + \frac{1}{EI}\int_0^a wb\left(x^2 + \frac{3}{2}xb + \frac{b^2}{2}\right) dx$$

$$= \left[\frac{wx^4}{8\,EI}\right]_0^b + \left[\frac{wb}{EI}\left(\frac{x^3}{3} + \frac{3}{2}\frac{bx^2}{2} + \frac{b^2}{2}x\right)\right]_0^a$$

$$= \frac{wb^4}{8\,EI} + \left[\frac{wb}{EI}\left(\frac{a^3}{3} + \frac{3}{4}ba^2 + \frac{b^2}{2}a\right)\right]$$

$$= \frac{wb^4}{8\,EI} + \frac{wb}{EI}\left(\frac{a^3}{3} + ab\left(\frac{3}{4}a + \frac{b}{2}\right)\right)$$

$$= \frac{wb^4}{8\,EI} + \frac{wb}{EI}\left(\frac{a^3}{3} + ab\left(\frac{3a+2b}{4}\right)\right)$$

$$\therefore \quad \delta_B = \frac{wb^4}{8EI} + \frac{wb}{EI}\left[\frac{a^3}{3} + ab\left(\frac{2l+a}{4}\right)\right]$$

Problem 3.6 : Find the slope and deflection at free end for the beam shown in Fig. 3.11 (a).

Solution :

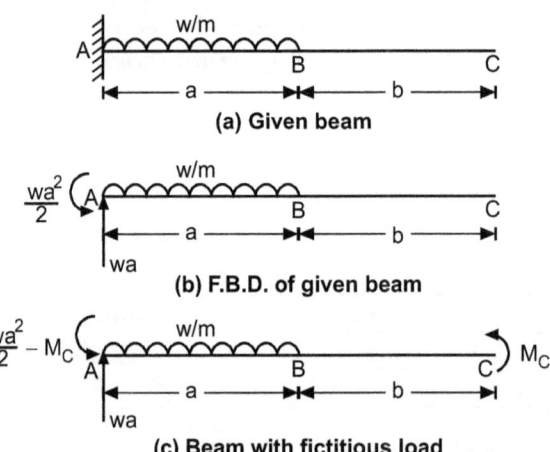

(a) Given beam

(b) F.B.D. of given beam

(c) Beam with fictitious load

Fig. 3.11

Region	Moment	∂M/∂M_C	Limit
CB	M_C	1	0 to b
BA	$M_C - \dfrac{wx^2}{2}$	1	0 to a

According to Castigliano's first theorem,

$$\theta_C = \frac{1}{EI}\int_0^b M_C \cdot 1 \cdot dx + \frac{1}{EI}\int_0^a \left(M_C - \frac{wx^2}{2}\right) 1 \cdot dx$$

As M_C is fictitious moment $\therefore M_C = 0$

$$\therefore \quad \theta_C = \frac{1}{EI}\int_0^a -\frac{wx^2}{2}\,dx = \left[-\frac{wx^3}{6\,EI}\right]_0^a = -\frac{wa^3}{6\,EI}$$

For deflection at C :

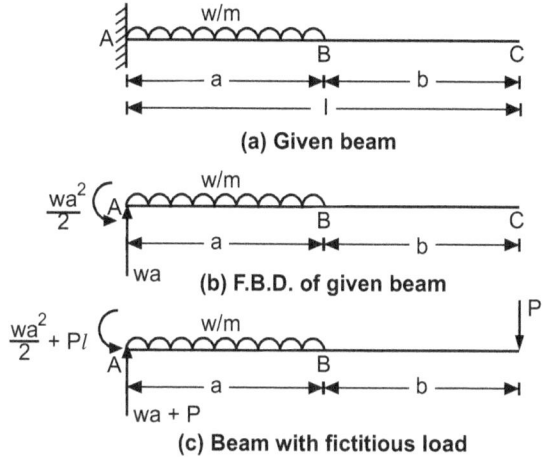

Fig. 3.12

Region	Moment	∂M/∂P	Limit
CB	− Px	(− x)	0 to b
BA	− P (x + b) − $\dfrac{wx^2}{2}$	− (x + b)	0 to a

According to Castigliano's first theorem,

$$\delta_C = \frac{\partial U}{\partial P}$$

$$= \int_0^b (-Px)(-x)\, dx + \int_0^a \left[-P(x+b) - \frac{wx^2}{2} \right] [-(x+b)]\, dx$$

As P is fictitious load ∴ put P = 0.

∴
$$\delta_C = \int_0^a \frac{wx^2}{2}(x+b)\, dx$$

$$= \int_0^a \frac{wx^3}{2}\, dx + \int_0^a \frac{wx^2}{2} \cdot b \cdot dx$$

$$= \left[\frac{wx^4}{8\,EI}\right]_0^a + \left[\frac{wbx^3}{6}\right]_0^a = \frac{wa^4}{8\,EI} + \frac{wa^3 b}{6\,EI} = \frac{wa^3}{24\,EI}(3a + 4b)$$

$$\delta_C = \frac{wa^3}{24\,EI}(3l + b) = \frac{wa^3(3l + b)}{24\,EI}$$

Problem 3.7 : Find the deflection at free end and at 'a' from free end for the beam as shown in Fig. 3.13 (a).

Solution : (a) Deflection at free end :

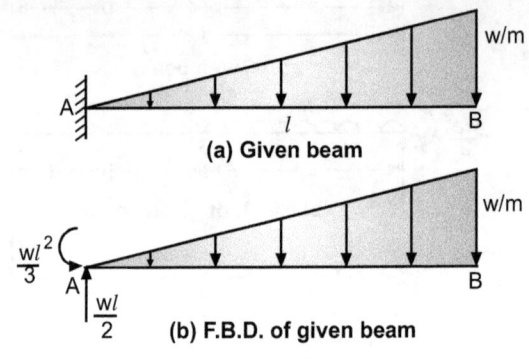

(a) Given beam

(b) F.B.D. of given beam

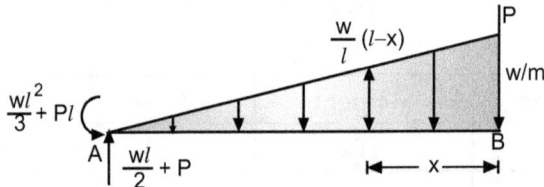

(c) Beam with fictitious load at free end

Fig. 3.13

Region	Moment	∂M/∂P	Limit
BA	$-\left(w + \dfrac{w}{l}(l-x)\right)\dfrac{x}{2}$ $\times \left(\dfrac{2w + \dfrac{w}{l}(l-x)}{w + \dfrac{w}{l}(l-x)}\right) \times \dfrac{x}{3} - Px$	$-x$	0 to l

According to Castigliano's first theorem,

$$\delta_B = \frac{\partial U}{\partial P}$$

$$\delta_B = \frac{1}{EI} \int_0^l \left[\frac{-\left(w + \frac{w}{l}(l-x)\right)}{2} \times \frac{\left(2w + \frac{w}{l}(l-x)\right)}{\left(w + \frac{w}{l}(l-x)\right)} \times \frac{x^2}{3} - Px \right] (-x)\, dx$$

As P is fictitious load ∴ put P = 0.

∴ $$\delta_B = \frac{1}{EI} \int_0^l \left[2w + \frac{w}{l}(l-x) \right] \frac{x^3}{6}\, dx$$

$$= \frac{1}{EI}\left[\frac{2wx^4}{24} + \frac{wx^4}{24} - \frac{w}{l}\frac{x^5}{30}\right]_0^l$$

$$= \frac{1}{EI}\left[\frac{2wl^4}{24} + \frac{wl^4}{24} - \frac{wl^4}{30}\right] = \frac{15wl^4 - 4wl^4}{120\ EI} = \frac{11\ wl^4}{120\ EI}$$

(b) Deflection at 'a' from free end :

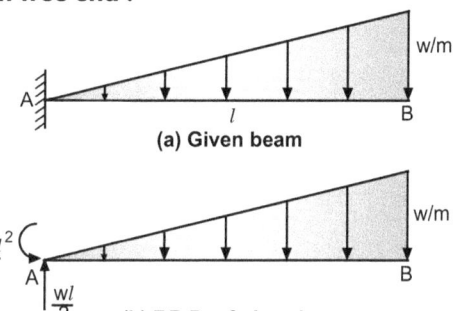

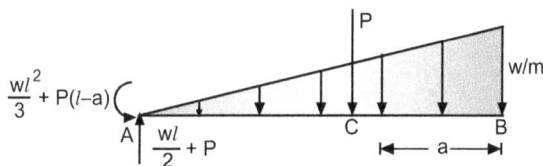

(c) Beam with fictitious load at 'a'

Fig. 3.14

Region	Moment	∂M/∂P	Limit
BC	$-\left(w + \frac{w}{l}(l-a)\right) \times \left(\frac{2w + \frac{w}{l}(l-a)}{w + \frac{w}{l}(l-a)}\right) \cdot \frac{x}{3}$	0	0 to a
CA	$-\left(w + \frac{w}{l}(l-x)\right) \times \left(\frac{2w + \frac{w}{l}(l-x)}{w + \frac{w}{l}(l-x)}\right) \cdot \frac{x}{3} - P(x-a)$	$-(x-a)$	a to l

$$\delta_B = \frac{1}{EI}\int_0^a \left(\frac{-w + \frac{w}{l}(l-a)}{2}\right) \times \left(\frac{2w + \frac{w}{l}(l-a)}{w + \frac{w}{l}(l-a)}\right)\frac{x}{3} \cdot 0 \cdot dx$$

$$+ \frac{1}{EI}\int_a^l \left[\left(\frac{-\left(w + \frac{w}{l}(l-x)\right)}{2}\right) \times \left(\frac{2w + \frac{w}{l}(l-x)}{w + \frac{w}{l}(l-x)}\right) \cdot \frac{x}{3} - P(x-a)\right]$$

As P is fictitious load ∴ put P = 0.

$$\therefore \quad \delta_B = \frac{1}{EI} \int_a^l \left(2w + \frac{w}{l}(l-x)\right) \frac{x^2}{6}(x-a)\,dx$$

$$= \frac{1}{EI} \int_a^l \frac{2wx^3}{6}\,dx - \frac{1}{EI} \int_a^l \frac{2wx^2a}{6} + \frac{1}{EI} \int_a^l \frac{wl\,x^3}{l\,6}\,dx$$

$$- \frac{1}{EI} \int_a^l \frac{w}{l} \cdot l \cdot \frac{x^2}{6} a\,dx - \frac{1}{EI} \int_a^l \frac{w\,x^4}{l\,6}\,dx + \frac{1}{EI} \int_a^l \frac{wa\,x^3}{l\,6}\,dx$$

$$= \frac{2w}{24\,EI}[x^4]_a^l - \frac{2wa}{EI \times 18}(x^3)_a^l + \frac{wl}{24\,EIl}(x^4)_a^l$$

$$- \frac{wa}{18\,EI}(x^3) - \frac{w}{30\,EIl}(x^5)_a^l + \frac{wa}{24\,EI}(x^4)_a^l$$

$$= \frac{2w(l^4-a^4)}{24\,EI} - \frac{wa}{9\,EI}(l^3-a^3) + \frac{w(l^4-a^4)}{24\,EI}$$

$$- \frac{wa(l^3-a^3)}{18\,EI} - \frac{w(l^5-a^5)}{30\,EIl} + \frac{wa}{24\,EIl}(l^4-a^4)$$

$$= \frac{w(l^4-a^4)}{24\,EI}\left(3+\frac{a}{l}\right) - \frac{wa(l^3-a^3)}{6\,EI} - \frac{w(l^5-a^5)}{30\,EIl}$$

Problem 3.8 : Find the slope and deflection at free end of cantilever beam carrying couple at free end.

Solution : (a) Slope at free end :

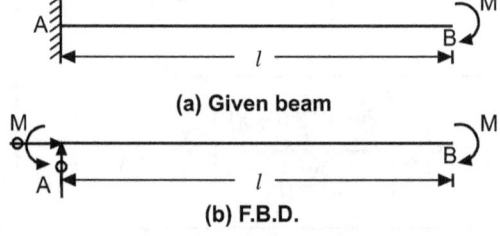

Fig. 3.15

Region	Moment	∂M/∂P	Limit
BA	− M	− 1	0 to l

According to Castigliano's first theorem,

$$\theta_B = \frac{\partial U}{\partial M}$$

$$= \int_0^l (-M)(-1) \cdot \frac{dx}{EI} = \frac{1}{EI} M(x)_0^l = \frac{Ml}{EI}$$

(b) Deflection at free end :

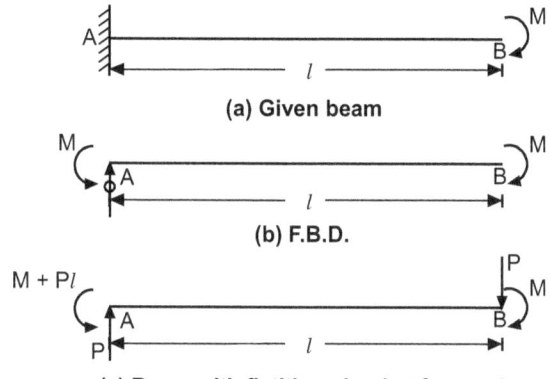

Fig. 3.16

Region	Moment	∂M/∂P	Limit
BA	− M − Px	− x	0 to l

According to Castigliano's theorem,

$$\delta_B = \frac{\partial U}{\partial P} = \int_0^l (-M - Px)(-x)\, dx$$

As load is fictitious load ∴ put P = 0

$$\delta_B = \int_0^l Mx \frac{dx}{EI} = \frac{M}{EI}\left(\frac{x^2}{2}\right)_0^l = \frac{Ml^2}{2EI}$$

Problem 3.9 : A cantilever beam ABCD, span 2.6 m, is loaded as shown in Fig. 3.17 (a). Find the vertical deflection at free end. E = 200 GPa, I = 10^4 cm^4.

Solution :

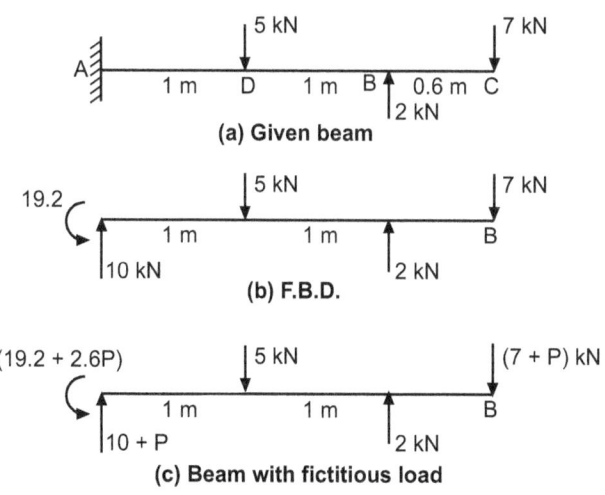

Fig. 3.17

Region	Moment	∂M/∂P	Limit
CB	$-(7 + P)x$	$-x$	0 to 0.6
BD	$-(7 + P)(x + 0.6) + 2x$	$-(x + 0.6)$	0 to 1
AD	$(10 + P)x - (19.2 + 2.6P)$	$(x - 2.6)$	0 to 1

According to Castigliano's first theorem,

$$\delta_C = \frac{\partial U}{\partial P}$$

$$= \int_0^{0.6} -(7+P)x(-x)\,dx + \int_0^1 [-(7+P)(x+0.6) + 2x][-(x+0.6)]\,dx$$

$$+ \int_0^1 [(10+P)x - (19.2 + 2.6P)](x - 2.6)\,dx$$

As P is fictitious load ∴ put P = 0.

$$\delta_D = \frac{1}{EI}\int_0^{0.6} 7x^2\,dx + \frac{1}{EI}\int_0^1 7(x^2 + 1.2x + 0.36)\,dx - \frac{1}{EI}\int_0^1 2(x^2 + 0.6x)\,dx$$

$$+ \int_0^1 10(x^2 - 2.6x)\,dx - \int_0^1 19.2(x - 2.6)\,dx$$

$$= [0.504 + 9.053 - 1.27 - 9.67 + 40.32]\frac{1}{EI}$$

$$= \frac{38.94}{200 \times 10^6 \times 10^4 \times 10^{-8}} = 1.95 \times 10^{-3}\,m$$

$$\delta_D = 1.95\,mm$$

Problem 3.10 : Find the deflection at free end for the beam as shown in Fig. 3.18 (a).

Solution :

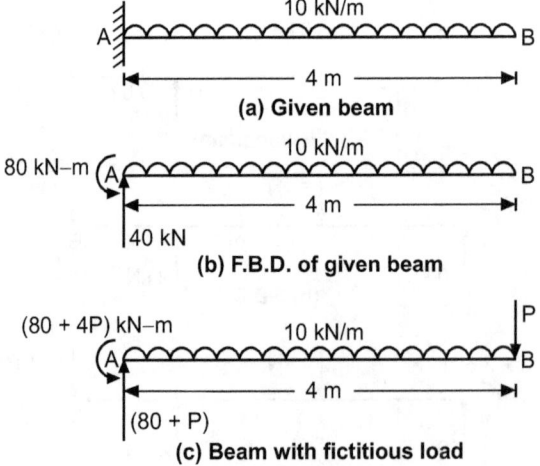

(a) Given beam

(b) F.B.D. of given beam

(c) Beam with fictitious load

Fig. 3.18

Region	Moment	∂M/∂P	Limit
BA	$\left(-\dfrac{10x^2}{2} - Px\right)$	$(-x)$	0 to 4

According to Castigliano's first theorem,

$$\delta_B = \frac{\partial U}{\partial P} = \frac{1}{EI}\int_0^4 \left(-\frac{10x^2}{2} - Px\right)(-x)\, dx$$

As P is fictitious load ∴ put P = 0.

$$\therefore \quad \delta_B = \frac{1}{EI}\int_0^4 5x^3\, dx$$

$$= \frac{1}{EI}\left[\frac{5x^4}{4}\right]_0^4$$

$$= \frac{320}{EI}$$

Problem 3.11 : Find the slope and deflection at free end for the beam as shown in Fig. 3.19 (a).

Solution : (a) Slope at free end :

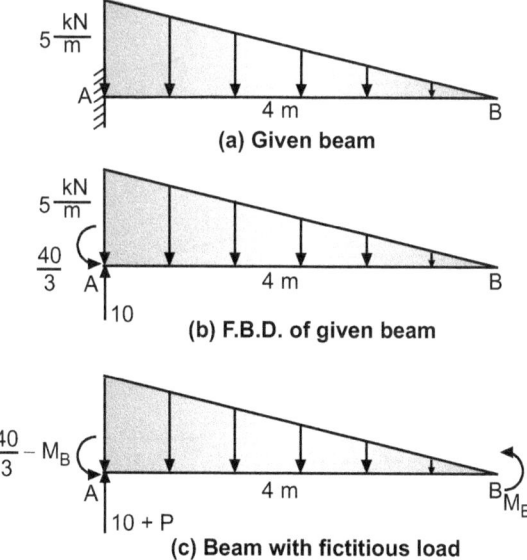

Fig. 3.19

Region	Moment	∂M/∂M_B	Limit
BA	$\left(+M_B - \dfrac{1}{2}\dfrac{wx}{l}\cdot x \cdot \dfrac{x}{3}\right)$	1	0 to 4

According to Castigliano's first theorem,

$$\delta_B = \frac{\partial U}{\partial P}$$

$$= \frac{1}{EI} \int_0^4 \left(M_B - \frac{wx^3}{6l} \right) 1 \cdot dx$$

As M_B is fictitious load ∴ put $M_B = 0$

∴ $$\delta_B = \frac{1}{EI} \int_0^4 -\frac{wx^3}{6l} dx$$

$$= -\frac{w}{6l\,EI}\left(\frac{x^4}{4}\right)_0^4 = -\frac{wl^3}{24\,EI} = -\frac{5 \times 4^3}{24\,EI} = -\frac{13.33}{EI}$$

(b) Deflection at free end :

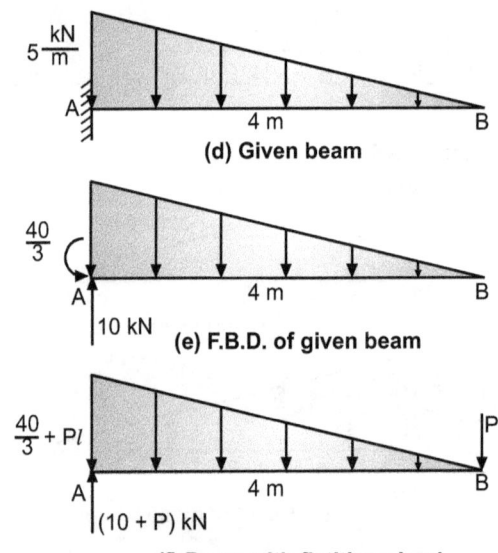

Fig. 3.19

Region	Moment	∂M/∂P	Limit
BA	$\left(-\frac{wx^2}{2l} \times \frac{x}{3} - Px\right)$	$(-x)$	0 to 4

According to Castigliano's first theorem,

$$\delta_B = \frac{\partial U}{\partial P}$$

$$= \frac{1}{EI} \int_0^4 \left(-\frac{wx^3}{6l} - Px\right)(-x)\, dx$$

$$= \frac{1}{EI} \int_0^4 \frac{wx^4}{6l} dx$$

$$= \left[\frac{wl^5}{30EIl}\right]_0^4 = \left[\frac{5 \times 4^4}{30EI}\right]$$

$$\delta_B = \frac{42.67}{EI}$$

Problem 3.12 : A simply supported beam AB of span l carries a central point load "w". Find deflection at the centre i.e. under the load.

Solution : Here the deflection is desired under the load. Hence, fictitious load need not be applied.

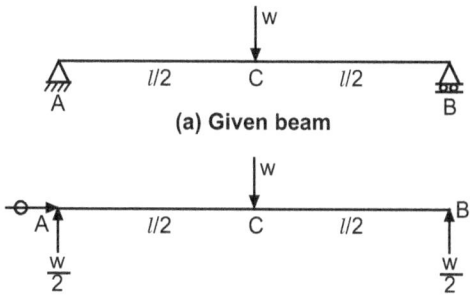

Fig. 3.20

Region	Moment	∂M/∂w	Limit
AC	$\frac{w}{2} x$	$\frac{x}{2}$	0 to $l/2$
BC	$\frac{w}{2} x$	$\frac{x}{2}$	0 to $l/2$

Partial derivative of this moment with respect to the load w is given by

$$\frac{\partial M}{\partial w} = \frac{x}{2}$$

∴ Deflection at C $= \dfrac{\partial U}{\partial w}$

But total strain energy $= U = \int_0^l \dfrac{M^2 dx}{2EI}$

∴ $\delta_C = \dfrac{\partial U}{\partial w} = \int_0^l \dfrac{M}{EI} \times \dfrac{\partial M}{\partial w} dx$

$= 2 \int_0^{l/2} \dfrac{M}{EI} \dfrac{\partial M}{\partial w} dx$

$$= \frac{2}{EI} \int_0^{l/2} \left(\frac{w}{2}x\right)\left(\frac{x}{2}\right) dx$$

$$= \frac{2}{EI} \int_0^{l/2} \left(\frac{w}{4}x^2\right) dx$$

$$= \frac{2}{EI} \times \frac{w}{4}\left[\frac{x^3}{3}\right]_0^{l/2} = \frac{w}{6\,EI}\left[\frac{l^3}{8}\right]$$

$$\delta_C = \frac{wl^3}{48\,EI}. \text{ This is the deflection at the centre.}$$

Problem 3.13 : A simply supported beam AB of span 'l'. A concentrated load is acting at C as shown in Fig. 3.21 (a). Calculate the deflection under the load and at mid span.

Solution : (a) Deflection under the load :

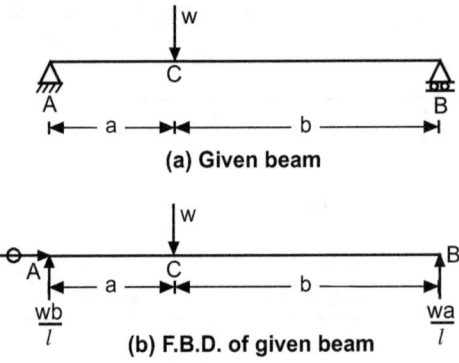

(a) Given beam

(b) F.B.D. of given beam

Fig. 3.21

Region	Moment	∂M/∂w	Limit
AC	$\left(\dfrac{wb}{l}\right)x$	$\left(\dfrac{b}{l}x\right)$	0 to a
BC	$\left(\dfrac{wa}{l}\right)x$	$\left(\dfrac{a}{l}\right)x$	0 to b

According to Castigliano's first theorem,

$$\delta_C = \frac{\partial U}{\partial w}$$

$$= \frac{1}{EI}\int_0^a \left(\frac{wb}{l}x\right)\left(\frac{b}{l}\right)x\,dx + \frac{1}{EI}\int_0^b \frac{wa}{l}x \cdot \frac{a}{l}x\,dx$$

$$= \frac{wb^2}{EI\,l^2}\int_0^a x^2\,dx + \frac{wa^2}{EI\,l^2}\int_0^b x^2\,dx$$

$$= \frac{wb^2}{EIl^2}\left[\frac{x^3}{3}\right]_0^a + \frac{wa^2}{EIl^2}\left[\frac{x^3}{3}\right]_0^b$$

$$= \frac{wa^3b^2}{3\,EIl^2} + \frac{wa^2b^3}{3\,EIl^2} = \frac{wa^2b^2}{3\,EIl^2}(a+b) = \frac{wa^2b^2}{3\,EIl}$$

(b) Deflection at mid span :

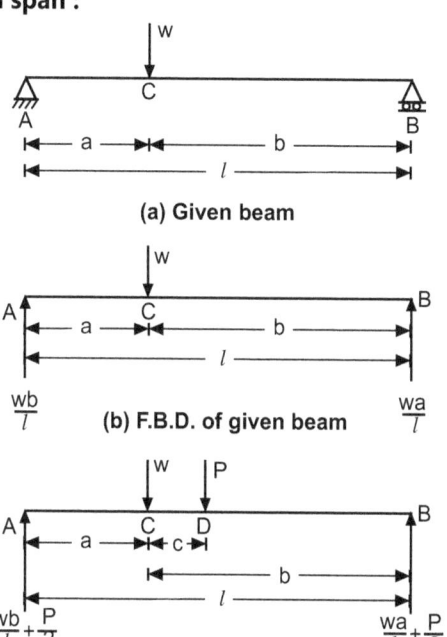

(a) Given beam

(b) F.B.D. of given beam

(c) Beam with fictitious load

Fig. 3.22

Region	Moment	∂M/∂P	Limit
AC	$\left(\frac{wb}{l}+\frac{P}{2}\right)x$	$x/2$	0 to a
BD	$\left(\frac{wa}{l}+\frac{P}{2}\right)x$	$x/2$	0 to (b – c)
CD	$\left(\frac{wb}{l}+\frac{P}{2}\right)(x+a) - wx$	$\frac{1}{2}(x+a)$	0 to c

According to Castigliano's first theorem,

$$\delta_D = \frac{\partial U}{\partial P} = \frac{1}{EI}\int_0^a \left(\frac{wb}{l}+\frac{P}{2}\right)x\cdot\frac{x}{2}dx + \frac{1}{EI}\int_0^{(b-c)}\left(\frac{wa}{l}+\frac{P}{2}\right)x\cdot\frac{x}{2}dx$$

$$+ \frac{1}{EI}\int_0^c \left(\frac{wb}{l}+\frac{P}{2}\right)(x+a)\frac{(x+a)}{2}dx$$

As P is fictitious load ∴ put P = 0.

$$\delta_D = \frac{1}{EI}\int_0^a \frac{wb\,x^2}{l}\cdot\frac{x^2}{2}\,dx + \frac{1}{EI}\int_0^{(b-c)} \frac{wa}{l}\cdot\frac{x^2}{2}\,dx$$

$$+ \frac{1}{EI}\int_0^c \frac{wb}{2l}(x^2 + 2ax + a^2)\,dx$$

$$\delta_D = \frac{wb}{EIl}\left[\frac{x^3}{6}\right]_0^a + \frac{wa}{EIl}\left[\frac{x^3}{6}\right]_0^{(b-c)} + \frac{wb}{2\,lEI}\left[\frac{x^3}{3} + \frac{2ax^2}{2} + a^2x\right]_0^c$$

$$= \frac{wa^3 b}{6\,lEI} + \frac{wa}{6\,EIl}[(b-c)]^3 + \frac{wb}{2\,EIl}\left[\frac{c^3}{3} + ac^2 + a^2c\right]$$

Problem 3.14 : A simply supported beam AB of span "l" carries a UDL of "w" kN/m over the whole span. Find :

(a) Deflection at the centre.

(b) Deflection at quarter span.

Solution :

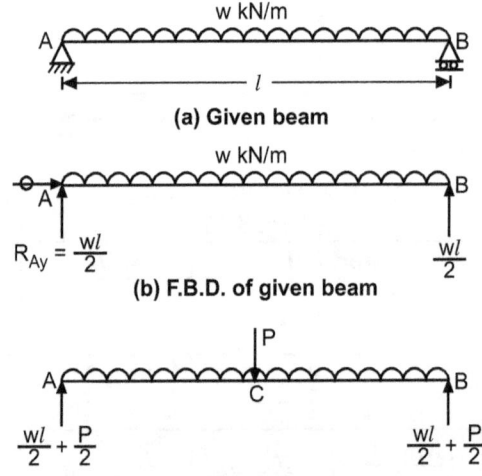

Fig. 3.23

(a) **Deflection at the centre :** Here the deflection is desired at the centre. But at this point there is no concentrated load. Hence, let us assume a fictitious load "P" at the centre.

The reactions R_A and R_B are found out.

$$R_A = \left(\frac{wl}{2} + \frac{P}{2}\right),\quad R_B = \left(\frac{wl}{2} + \frac{P}{2}\right)$$

Region	Moment	∂M/∂P	Limit
AD	$\left(\dfrac{wl}{2}+\dfrac{P}{2}\right)x - \dfrac{wx^2}{2}$	$\dfrac{x}{2}$	0 to $\dfrac{l}{2}$
BD	$\left(\dfrac{wl}{2}+\dfrac{P}{2}\right)x - \dfrac{wx^2}{2}$	$\dfrac{x}{2}$	0 to $\dfrac{l}{2}$

Deflection at C $= \dfrac{\partial U}{\partial P} = \int_0^l \dfrac{M}{EI}\dfrac{\partial M}{\partial P}dx$

$\delta_C = \dfrac{2}{EI}\int_0^{l/2}\left(\dfrac{wlx}{2}-\dfrac{wx^2}{2}\right)\left(\dfrac{x}{2}\right)dx$ (as P = 0)

$= \dfrac{2}{EI}\int_0^{l/2}\left(\dfrac{wlx^2}{4}-\dfrac{wx^3}{4}\right)dx = \dfrac{2}{EI}\left[\dfrac{wl}{4}\dfrac{x^3}{3}-\dfrac{w}{4}\dfrac{x^4}{4}\right]_0^{l/2}$

$= \dfrac{2}{EI}\left[\dfrac{wl}{12}\left(\dfrac{l^3}{8}\right)-\dfrac{w}{16}\left(\dfrac{l^4}{16}\right)\right]$

$= \dfrac{2}{EI}\left[\dfrac{wl^4}{96}-\dfrac{wl^4}{256}\right]$

$\delta_C = \dfrac{5\,wl^4}{384\,EI}$

This is the deflection at centre.

(b) Deflection at quarter span :

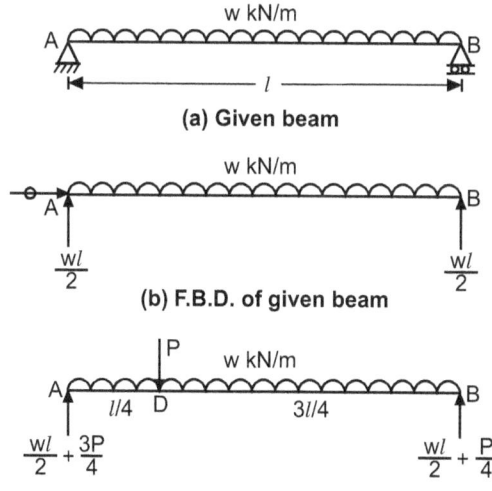

(a) Given beam

(b) F.B.D. of given beam

(c) Beam with fictitious load at centre

Fig. 3.24

Let a fictitious load be applied at the quarter span and reactions are found out.

$$R_A = \left(\frac{wl}{2} + \frac{3P}{4}\right), \quad R_B = \left(\frac{wl}{2} + \frac{1}{4}P\right)$$

Region	Moment	∂M/∂P	Limit
AD	$\left(\frac{wl}{2} + \frac{3P}{4}\right)x - \frac{wx^2}{2}$	$\left(\frac{3}{4}x\right)$	0 to $\frac{l}{4}$
BD	$\left(\frac{wl}{2} + \frac{P}{4}\right)x - \frac{wx^2}{2}$	$\left(\frac{x}{4}\right)$	0 to $\frac{3l}{4}$

Region AD :

$$\delta_{d_1} = \frac{l}{EI}\int M \cdot \frac{\partial M}{\partial P} dx \quad \ldots \text{put } P = 0$$

$$\delta_{d_1} = \frac{l}{EI}\int_0^{l/4} \left(\frac{wlx}{2} - \frac{wx^2}{2}\right)\left(\frac{3}{4}x\right) dx$$

$$= \frac{l}{EI}\int_0^{l/4} \left(\frac{3}{8}wlx^2 - \frac{3}{8}wx^3\right) dx = \frac{l}{EI}\left[\frac{3wl}{8}\frac{x^3}{3} - \frac{3w}{8}\frac{x^4}{4}\right]_0^{l/4}$$

$$= \frac{l}{EI}\left[\frac{wl}{8}\left(\frac{l^3}{64}\right) - \frac{3w}{32}\left(\frac{l^4}{256}\right)\right]$$

$$= \frac{l}{EI}\left[\frac{wl^4}{512} - \frac{3wl^4}{8192}\right]$$

$$= \frac{wl^4}{EI}\left[\frac{16 - 3}{8192}\right]$$

$$= \frac{13\,wl^4}{8192\,EI}$$

Region BD :

$$\delta_{d_2} = \frac{l}{EI}\int M \frac{\partial M}{\partial P} dx \quad \ldots \text{put } P = 0$$

$$= \frac{l}{EI}\int_0^{3l/4} \left(\frac{wlx}{2} - \frac{wx^2}{2}\right)\left(\frac{x}{4}\right) dx = \frac{l}{EI}\int_0^{3l/4} \left(\frac{wlx^2}{8} - \frac{wx^3}{8}\right) dx$$

$$= \frac{l}{EI}\left[\frac{wl}{8}\frac{x^3}{3} - \frac{w}{8}\frac{x^4}{4}\right]_0^{3l/4}$$

$$= \frac{l}{EI}\left[\frac{wl}{24}\left(\frac{27\,l^3}{64}\right) - \frac{w}{32}\left(\frac{81\,l^4}{256}\right)\right]$$

$$= \frac{l}{EI}\left[\frac{27\,wl^4}{1536} - \frac{81\,wl^4}{8192}\right] = \frac{wl^4}{EI}\left[\frac{144 - 81}{8192}\right]$$

$$= \frac{63\,wl^4}{8192\,EI}$$

∴ Final deflection at $d = \delta_{d_1} + \delta_{d_2}$

$$\delta_d = \left[\frac{13\,wl^4}{8192\,EI} + \frac{63\,wl^4}{8192\,EI}\right]$$

∴ $$\delta_d = \frac{76}{8192}\frac{wl^4}{EI}$$

Problem 3.15 : Find the deflection at the centre of the beam shown in Fig. 3.25 (a).

Solution : (a) Slope at mid span :

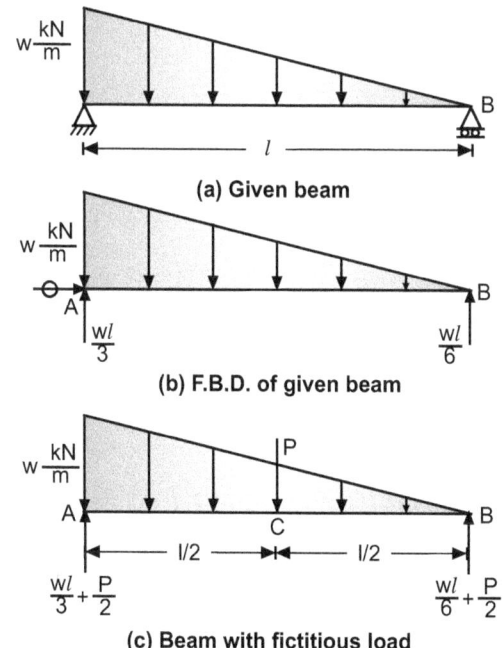

Fig. 3.25

Region	Moment	∂M/∂P	Limit
BC	$\left[\left(\frac{wl}{6} + \frac{P}{2}\right)x - \frac{1}{2}\frac{w}{l}\cdot x \cdot x \cdot \frac{x}{3}\right]$	$x/2$	0 to $\frac{l}{2}$
CA	$\left(\frac{wl}{6} + \frac{P}{2}\right)x - \frac{1}{2}\frac{w}{l}\cdot x \cdot x \cdot \frac{x}{3} - P\left(x - \frac{l}{2}\right)$	$\left(\frac{x}{2} - x + \frac{l}{2}\right) = \frac{1}{2}(l - x)$	$\frac{l}{2}$ to l

According to Castigliano's first theorem,

$$\delta_C = \frac{\partial U}{\partial P} = \frac{1}{EI} \int_0^{l/2} \left[\left(\frac{wl}{6} + \frac{P}{2}\right) x - \frac{wx^3}{6l} \right] \frac{x}{2} \cdot dx$$

$$+ \frac{1}{EI} \int_{l/2}^{l} \left[\left(\frac{wl}{6} + \frac{P}{2}\right) x - \frac{wx^3}{6l} - P\left(x - \frac{l}{2}\right) \right] \frac{1}{2}(l-x) \, dx$$

As P is fictitious load $\therefore$ Put P = 0

$\therefore$
$$\delta_C = \frac{1}{EI} \int_0^{l/2} \frac{wl}{12} x^2 \, dx - \frac{1}{EI} \int_0^{l/2} \frac{wx^4}{12l} \, dx + \int_{l/2}^{l} \frac{wl^2}{12} x \, dx - \int_{l/2}^{l} \frac{wx^3}{12} \, dx$$

$$- \frac{1}{EI} \int_{l/2}^{l} \frac{wl}{12} x^2 \, dx + \frac{1}{EI} \int_{l/2}^{l} \frac{x^4}{12l} \, dx$$

$\therefore$
$$\delta_C = \frac{wl}{12\, EI} \left[\frac{x^3}{3}\right]_0^{l/2} - \frac{w(x^5)_0^{l/2}}{60\, EIl} + \frac{wl^2}{24\, EI} [x^2]_{l/2}^{l}$$

$$- \frac{w}{48\, EI} (x^4)_{l/2}^{l} - \frac{wl}{12\, EI} \left[\frac{x^3}{3}\right]_{l/2}^{l} + \frac{wl}{60\, EIl} (x^5)_{l/2}^{l}$$

$$= \frac{wl}{12\, EI} \left(\frac{l^3}{24}\right) - \frac{wl^4}{60 \times 32\, EI} + \frac{wl^2}{24\, EI} \left[l^2 - \frac{l^2}{4}\right]$$

$$- \frac{w}{48\, EI} \left(l^4 - \frac{l^4}{16}\right) - \frac{wl}{36\, EI} \left(l^3 - \frac{l^3}{8}\right) + \frac{w}{60\, EIl} \left(l^5 - \frac{l}{32}\right)$$

$$= \frac{wl^4}{12 \times 24\, EI} - \frac{wl^4}{60 \times 32\, EI} + \frac{wl^2}{24\, EI} \left(\frac{3l^2}{4}\right)$$

$$- \frac{wl^4 \times 15}{48 \times 16\, EI} - \frac{wl}{36\, EI} \left(\frac{7l^3}{8}\right) + \frac{w}{60\, EIl} \left(\frac{31l^5}{32}\right)$$

$$= \frac{wl^4}{48\, EI} \left[\frac{1}{6} - \frac{1}{40} + \frac{3}{2} - \frac{15}{16} - \frac{7}{6} + \frac{31}{40}\right] = \frac{0.3125\, wl^4}{48\, EI}$$

Problem 3.16 : A simply supported beam of span 8 m carries a point load of 5 kN at a distance of 2 m from the right hand support. Find the deflection at the centre and under the load. Take EI = 30 × 10³ kN-m².

Solution :

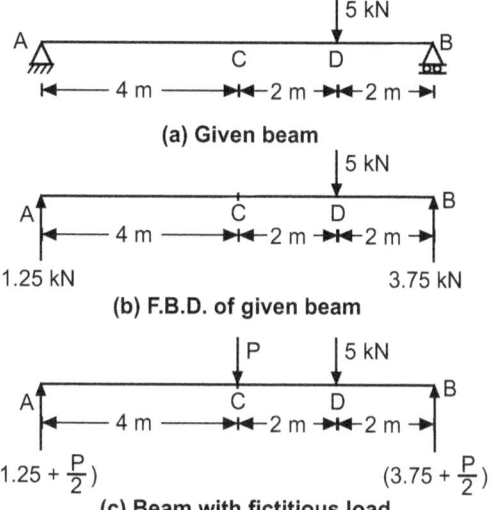

Fig. 3.26

Region	Moment	∂M/∂P	Limit
AC	$\left(1.25 + \dfrac{P}{2}\right)x$	$x/2$	0 to 4
CD	$\left(1.25 + \dfrac{P}{2}\right)(x+4) - Px$	$\left(\dfrac{x}{2} + 2 - x\right) = \left(2 - \dfrac{x}{2}\right)$	0 to 2
BD	$\left(3.75 + \dfrac{P}{2}\right)x$	$\dfrac{x}{2}$	0 to 2

According to Castigliano's first theorem,

$$\delta_C = \frac{\partial U}{\partial P}$$

$$= \frac{1}{EI}\int_0^4 \left(1.25 + \frac{P}{2}\right)x \cdot \frac{x}{2} \cdot dx$$

$$+ \frac{1}{EI}\int_0^2 \left[\left(1.25 + \frac{P}{2}\right)(x+4) - Px\right]\left(2 - \frac{x}{2}\right) dx$$

$$+ \frac{1}{EI}\int_0^2 \left(3.75 + \frac{P}{2}\right)x \cdot \frac{x}{2} dx$$

As P is fictitious load ∴ put P = 0.

$$\delta_C = \frac{1}{EI}\int_0^4 \frac{1.25}{2}x^2\, dx + \frac{1}{EI}\int_0^2 1.25(x+4)\left(2 - \frac{x}{2}\right)dx + \frac{1}{EI}\int_0^2 3.75 \cdot \frac{x^2}{2}\, dx$$

$$= \frac{1.25}{2EI}\left[\frac{x^3}{3}\right]_0^4 + \frac{1.25}{2EI}\left[16x - \frac{x^3}{3}\right]_0^2 + \frac{3.75}{6EI}[x^3]_0^2$$

$$= \frac{13.33}{EI} + \frac{18.33}{EI} + \frac{5}{EI} = \frac{36.66}{EI}$$

$$\therefore \quad \delta_C = \frac{36.66}{30000} = 1.22 \times 10^{-3} \text{ m} = 1.22 \text{ m}$$

Problem 3.17 : A simply supported beam AB of span 8 m carries UDL of 20 kN/m over the right hand half of the beam. Using Castigliano's first theorem calculate the deflection at mid-span. Take EI = 32000 kN-m².

Solution :

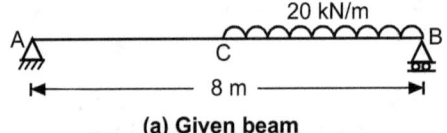
(a) Given beam

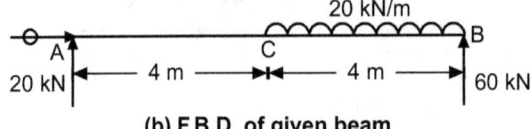
(b) F.B.D. of given beam

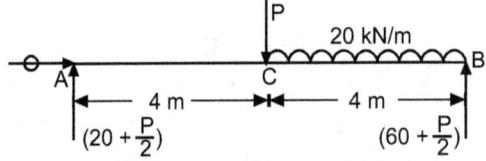
(c) Beam with fictitious load at mid-span

Fig. 3.27

Region	Moment	∂M/∂P	Limit
AC	$\left(20 + \frac{P}{2}\right)x$	x/2	0 to 4
BC	$\left(60 + \frac{P}{2}\right)x - \frac{20x^2}{2}$	x/2	0 to 4

According to Castigliano's first theorem,

$$\delta_C = \frac{\partial U}{\partial P} = \frac{1}{EI}\int_0^4 \left(20 + \frac{P}{2}\right)x \cdot \frac{x}{2} dx + \frac{1}{EI}\int_0^4 \left[\left(60 + \frac{P}{2}\right)x - 10x^2\right]\frac{x}{2} dx$$

As P is fictitious load ∴ put P = 0.

$$\therefore \quad \delta_C = \frac{1}{EI}\int_0^4 10x^2 dx + \frac{1}{EI}\int_0^4 (30x^2 - 5x^3) dx$$

$$= \frac{10}{EI}\left(\frac{x^3}{3}\right)_0^4 + \frac{30}{EI}\left(\frac{x^3}{3}\right)_0^4 - \frac{5}{EI}\left(\frac{x^4}{4}\right)_0^4$$

$$= \frac{533.33}{EI} = \frac{533.33}{32000} = 0.0167 \text{ m} = 16.7 \text{ mm}$$

Problem 3.18 : Using Castigliano's theorem, determine the vertical deflection at quarter span for a simply supported beam of span 4 m and subjected to uniformly distributed load of intensity 20 kN/m. Take EI = 7440 kN-m².

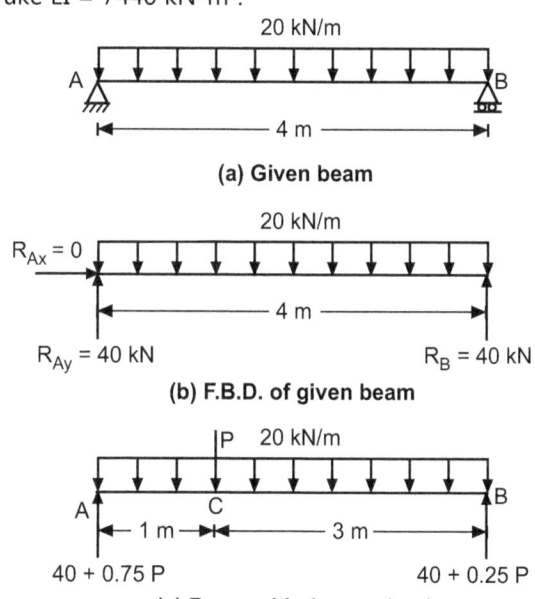

Fig. 3.28

Solution : For deflection at C, apply fictitious load at 'C'.

Applying $\Sigma F_x = 0$

$R_{Ax} = 0$

$\Sigma F_y = 0$

Moment @ B = 0

∴ $R_{Ay} + R_B - 20 \times 4 - P = 0$

∴ $R_{Ay} \times 4 - 20 \times 4 \times 2 - P \times 3 = 0$

∴ $R_{Ay} = (40 + 0.75 P)$

$R_B = (40 + 0.25 P)$

Region	Moment	∂M/∂P	Limit
AC	$(40 + 0.75 P) x - \frac{20x^2}{2}$	$(0.75 x)$	0 to 1
BC	$(40 + 0.25 P) x - \frac{20x^2}{2}$	$(0.25 x)$	0 to 3

According to Castigliano's first theorem,

$$\delta_C = \int M \frac{\partial M}{\partial P} \cdot dx$$

$$\therefore \quad \delta_C = \frac{\delta U}{\partial P} = \frac{1}{EI} \int_0^1 [(40 + 0.75 P) x - 10x^2] (0.75 x) \, dx$$

$$+ \frac{1}{EI} \int_0^3 [(40 + 0.25 P) x - 10x^2] (0.25 x) \, dx$$

As P is fictitious load $\therefore$ put $P = 0$.

$$\therefore \quad \delta_C = \frac{1}{EI} \int_0^1 (40x - 10x^2)(0.75x) \, dx + \frac{1}{EI} \int_0^3 (40x - 10x^2)(0.25x) \, dx$$

$$= \frac{1}{EI} (8.125 + 39.375) = \frac{47.5}{EI} = \frac{47.5}{7440} = 6.384 \times 10^{-3} \, m$$

$$= 6.384 \, mm$$

Problem 3.19 : Find the deflection at mid span for the beam shown in Fig. 3.29 (a).

Solution :

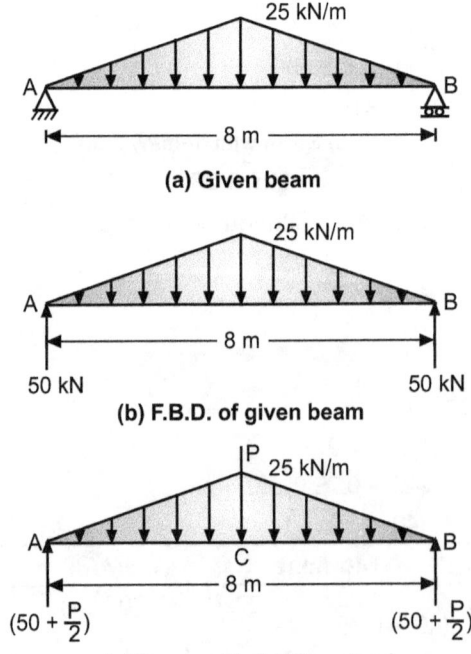

(a) Given beam

(b) F.B.D. of given beam

(c) Beam with fictitious load

Fig. 3.29

Region	Moment	∂M/∂P	Limit
AC	$\left(50 + \dfrac{P}{2}\right)x - \dfrac{25}{24}x^3$	$x/2$	0 to 4
BC	$\left(50 + \dfrac{P}{2}\right)x - \dfrac{25}{24}x^3$	$x/2$	0 to 4

According to Castigliano's first theorem,

$$\delta_C = \frac{\partial U}{\partial P}$$

$$= \frac{1}{EI}\int_0^4 \left[\left(50+\frac{P}{2}\right)x - \frac{25}{24}x^3\right]\frac{x}{2}\,dx + \frac{1}{EI}\int_0^4 \left[\left(50+\frac{P}{2}\right)x - \frac{25}{24}x^3\right]\frac{x}{2}\,dx$$

As P is fictitious load ∴ put P = 0.

$$\delta_C = \frac{2}{EI}\int_0^4 \left(50x - \frac{25}{24}x^3\right)\cdot\frac{x}{2}\,dx = \frac{2}{EI}\left[\frac{50x^3}{6} - \frac{25}{48}\frac{x^5}{5}\right]_0^4$$

$$= \frac{853.33}{EI}$$

Problem 3.20 : Find the deflection at the centre of the beam as shown in Fig. 3.30 (a).

Solution :

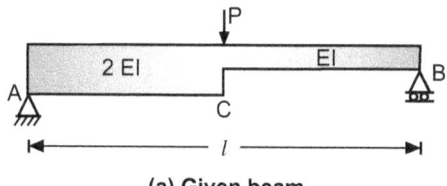

(a) Given beam

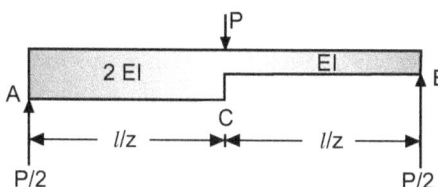

(b) F.B.D. of given beam

Fig. 3.30

Region	EI	Moment	∂M/∂P	Limit
AC	2EI	$\dfrac{P}{2}x$	$\dfrac{x}{2}$	0 to $l/2$
BC	EI	$\dfrac{P}{2}x$	$\dfrac{x}{2}$	0 to $l/2$

According to Castigliano's first theorem,

$$\delta_c = \frac{\partial U}{\partial P} = \frac{1}{2EI}\int_0^{l/2} \frac{P}{2}x \cdot \frac{x}{2}\,dx + \frac{1}{EI}\int_0^{l/2} \frac{P}{2}x \cdot \frac{x}{2}\,dx$$

$$= \frac{1}{2EI}\left[\frac{P}{4}\left(\frac{x^3}{3}\right)\right]_0^{l/2} + \frac{1}{EI}\left[\frac{P}{4}\left(\frac{x^3}{3}\right)\right]_0^{l/2} = \frac{1}{2EI}\left[\frac{Pl^3}{96}\right] + \frac{1}{EI}\left[\frac{Pl^3}{96}\right] = \frac{3Pl^3}{2 \times 96\,EI} = \frac{Pl^3}{64\,EI}$$

Problem 3.21 : A simply supported beam of span 9 m carries two point loads, each 50 kN at 3 m from each support. Using Castigliano's first theorem find deflection at mid-span. EI = 25 × 10³ kN-m². **(May 97)**

Solution :

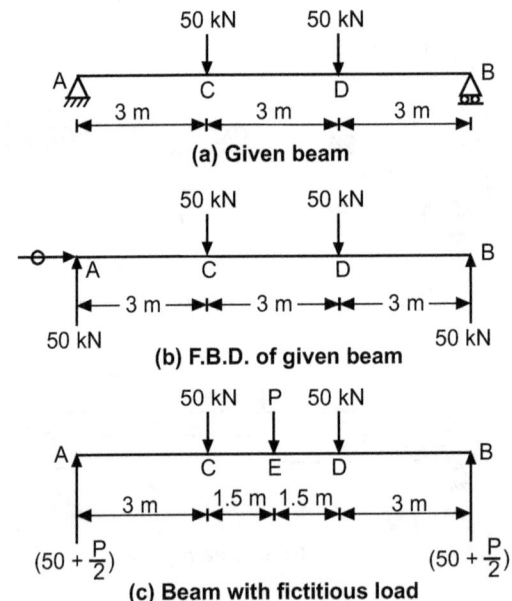

Fig. 3.31 : Beam with fictitious load

Region	Moment	∂M/∂P	Limit
AC	$\left(50 + \dfrac{P}{2}\right)x$	$x/2$	0 to 3
CE	$\left(50 + \dfrac{P}{2}\right)(x+3) - 50x$	$\left(\dfrac{x+3}{2}\right)$	0 to 1.5
BD	$\left(50 + \dfrac{P}{2}\right)x$	$x/2$	0 to 3
DE	$\left(50 + \dfrac{P}{2}\right)(x+3) - 50x$	$\left(\dfrac{x+3}{2}\right)$	0 to 1.5

According to Castigliano's first theorem,

$$\delta_E = \frac{\partial U}{\partial P} = \int_0^3 \left(50 + \frac{P}{2}\right)x \cdot \frac{x\,dx}{2\,EI} + \int_0^{1.5}\left[\left(50 + \frac{P}{2}\right)(x+3) - 50x\right]\left(\frac{x+3}{2}\right)\frac{dx}{EI}$$

$$+ \int_0^3 \left(50 + \frac{P}{2}\right)x \cdot \frac{x}{2EI} + \int_0^{1.5}\left[\left(50 + \frac{P}{2}\right)(x+3) - 50x\right]\left(\frac{x+3}{2}\right)\frac{dx}{EI}$$

As P is fictitious load ∴ put P = 0.

$$\delta_E = 2\left[\int_0^3 25x^2\frac{dx}{EI} + \int_0^{1.5}(50x + 150 - 50x)\frac{x+3}{2}\frac{dx}{EI}\right]$$

$$= \frac{2}{EI}\left[25\frac{x^3}{3}\right]_0^3 + \frac{2}{EI}\left[75\frac{x^2}{2} + 225x\right]_0^{1.5} = \frac{450}{EI} + \frac{843.75}{EI} = \frac{1293.75}{EI}$$

∴ $\delta_E = \dfrac{1293.75}{25000} = 0.0518$ m = 51.8 mm

Problem 3.22 : Using Castigliano's first theorem, find the deflection for the beam shown in Fig. 3.32 (a) at 'C'. Take EI = constant. **(May 2001)**

Solution :

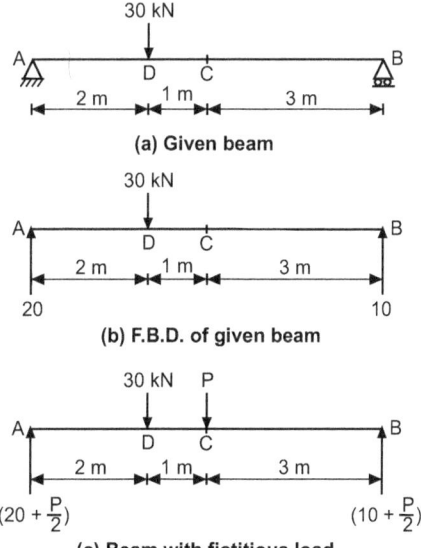

Fig. 3.32

Region	Moment	∂M/∂P	Limit
AD	$\left(20 + \dfrac{P}{2}\right)x$	$x/2$	0 to 2
BC	$\left(10 + \dfrac{P}{2}\right)x$	$x/2$	0 to 3
DC	$\left(20 + \dfrac{P}{2}\right)(x+2) - 30x$	$\left(\dfrac{x+2}{2}\right)$	0 to 1

According to Castigliano's first theorem,

$$\delta_C = \frac{\partial U}{\partial P} = \int_0^2 \left(20 + \frac{P}{2}\right)\frac{x^2}{2}\frac{dx}{EI} + \int_0^3 \left(10 + \frac{P}{2}\right)\frac{x^2}{2}\frac{dx}{EI}$$

$$+ \int_0^1 \left[\left(20 + \frac{P}{2}\right)(x+2) - 30x\right]\left(\frac{x+2}{2}\right)\frac{dx}{EI}$$

As P is fictitious load ∴ put P = 0.

$$\therefore \quad \delta_C = \int_0^2 10x^2 \frac{dx}{EI} + \int_0^3 5x^2 \frac{dx}{EI} + \int_0^1 (40 - 10x)\frac{(x+2)}{2}\frac{dx}{EI}$$

$$= 10\left(\frac{x^3}{3\,EI}\right)_0^2 + 5\left(\frac{x^3}{3\,EI}\right)_0^3 + \left[20\frac{x^2}{2\,EI}\right]_0^1 + 40\left[\frac{x}{EI}\right]_0^1$$

$$- \left[5\frac{x^3}{3\,EI}\right]_0^1 - 10\left[\frac{x^2}{2\,EI}\right]_0^1 = \frac{115}{EI}$$

$$\therefore \quad \delta_C = \frac{115}{EI}$$

Problem 3.23 : Determine the deflection at the centre of the span for the simply supported beam with overhang as shown in Fig. 3.33 (a).

AB = I, BC = 2 I, CD = I. (Dec. 2002)

Solution :

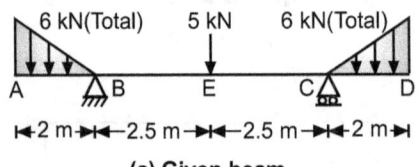

(a) Given beam

(b) F.B.D. of given beam

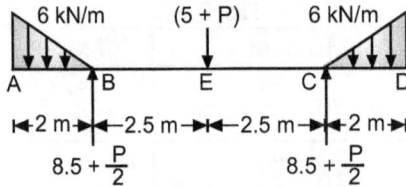

(c) Beam with fictitious load

Fig. 3.33

Region	EI	Moment	∂M/∂P	Limit
AB	EI	$-\left(6 + \frac{6}{2}(2-x)\right) \times x \times \left[\frac{2 \times 6 + \frac{6}{2}(2-x)}{6 + \frac{6}{2}(2-x)}\right]\frac{x}{3}$	0	0 to 2
BE	2EI	$-6 \times \left(\frac{4}{3} + x\right) + \left(8.5 + \frac{P}{2}\right)x$	$\frac{x}{2}$	0 to 2.5

According to Castigliano's first theorem,

$$\delta_E = \frac{\partial U}{\partial P} = 2 \int_0^{2.5} \left[-6\left(\frac{4}{3} + x\right) + \left(8.5 + \frac{P}{2}\right)x\right] \frac{x}{2} \frac{dx}{2\,EI}$$

As P is fictitious load ∴ put P = 0

$$\delta_E = 2 \int_0^{2.5} \left[-6\left(\frac{4}{3} + x\right) + 8.5x\right] \frac{x}{2} \frac{dx}{EI} = 2 \int_0^{2.5} [-8 - 6x + 8.5x] \frac{x}{2 \times 2} \frac{dx}{EI}$$

$$\delta_C = \int_0^{2.5} (2.5x - 8) \frac{x}{2 \times 2} \frac{dx}{EI} = \left[\frac{2.5x^3}{12\,EI} - \frac{4x^2}{4\,EI}\right]_0^{2.5}$$

∴ $\delta_C = \dfrac{-2.99}{EI}$

Problem 3.24 : A vertical load P is applied to the rigid cantilever as shown in Fig. 3.34 (a). Determine the vertical and horizontal deflection at the point 'C'.
Solution : (a) Vertical deflection at 'C' :

Fig. 3.34

Region	Moment	∂M/∂P	Limit
CB	$-Px$	$-x$	0 to $l/2$
BA	$-Pl/2$	$-l/2$	0 to l

According to Castigliano's first theorem,

$$\delta_c = \frac{\partial U}{\partial P}$$

$$= \frac{1}{EI}\int_0^{l/2}(-Px)(-x)\,dx + \frac{1}{EI}\int_0^{l}\left(-\frac{Pl}{2}\right)\left(-\frac{l}{2}\right)dx$$

$$= \frac{1}{EI}\left[\frac{Px^3}{3}\right]_0^{l/2} + \frac{1}{EI}\left[\frac{Pl^2}{4}x\right]_0^{l}$$

$$= \frac{Pl^3}{24\,EI} + \frac{Pl^3}{4\,EI} = \frac{7\,Pl^3}{24\,EI}$$

(b) Horizontal deflection at 'C' :

Region	Moment	∂M/∂w	Limit
CB	$-Px$	0	0 to $l/2$
AB	$-\frac{Pl}{2} - wl + wx$	$(x-l)$	0 to l

According to Castigliano's first theorem,

$$\delta_h = \frac{\partial U}{\partial W} = \frac{1}{EI}\int_0^{l/2}(-Px)(0)\,dx + \frac{1}{EI}\int_0^{l}\left[\left(-\frac{Pl}{2}-wl\right)+wx\right]dx\,(x-l)$$

$$= \frac{1}{EI}\int_0^{l}\left[\left(-\frac{Pl}{2}-wl\right)+wx\right](x-l)\,dx$$

As w is fictitious load ∴ put w = 0

∴ $$\delta_h = \int_0^{l}-\frac{Pl}{2EI}(x-l)\,dx$$

∴ $$= -\frac{Pl}{2EI}\left[\frac{x^2}{2}-lx\right]_0^{l} = -\frac{Pl}{2EI}\left[\frac{l^2}{2}-l^2\right] = \frac{Pl^2}{4EI}$$

Problem 3.25 : A continuous member ABCD is bent in one plane as shown in Fig. 3.35 (a). The member is rigidly fixed at A and carries a vertical load of 20 kN at free end D. Find vertical deflection at the free end.

Take EI = 30×10^3 kN-m²

Solution : Vertical deflection at free end :

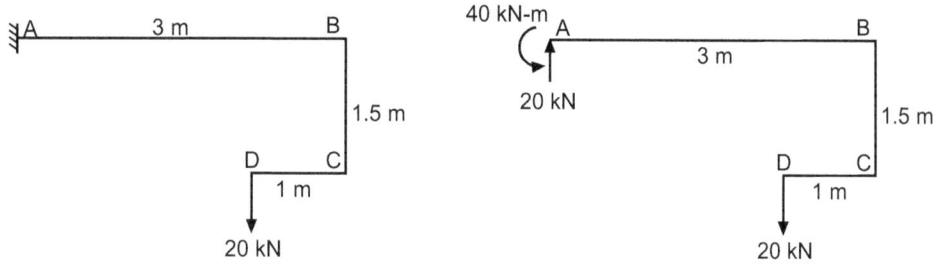

(a) Given frame (b) F.B.D. of given frame

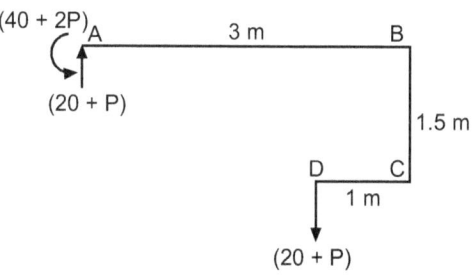

(c) Frame with fictitious load

Fig. 3.35

Region	Moment	∂M/∂P	Limit
DC	$(20 + P) x$	x	0 to 1
CB	$(20 + P)$	1	0 to 1.5
BA	$-(20 + P) x + (20 + P)$	$(-x + 1)$	0 to 3

$$\int_0^1 (20 + P) x \cdot x \, dx + \int_0^{1.5} (20 + P) \, dx + \int_0^3 -[(20 + P) x + (20 + P)](1 - x) \, dx$$

As P is fictitious load ∴ put P = 0.

$$\delta_D = \int_0^1 \frac{20x^2}{EI} + \int_0^{1.5} \frac{20 \, dx}{EI} + \int_0^3 20(1-x)^2 \frac{dx}{EI}$$

$$= \frac{20}{EI}\left[\frac{x^3}{3}\right]_0^1 + \frac{20}{EI}[x]_0^{1.5} + \frac{20}{EI}\left[x - \frac{2x^2}{2} + \frac{x^3}{3}\right]_0^3$$

$$= \frac{20}{3EI} + \frac{30}{EI} + \frac{60}{EI} = \frac{96.66}{EI}$$

$$\delta_D = \frac{96.66}{30 \times 10^3} = 3.22 \times 10^{-3} \text{ m}$$

∴ $\delta_D = 3.22$ mm

Problem 3.26 : A portal frame ABCD is hinged at A and has roller support at D. The frame carries loading as shown in Fig. 3.36 (a). Find horizontal deflection at roller support D. Take $EI = 35 \times 10^3$ kN-m^2.

Solution :

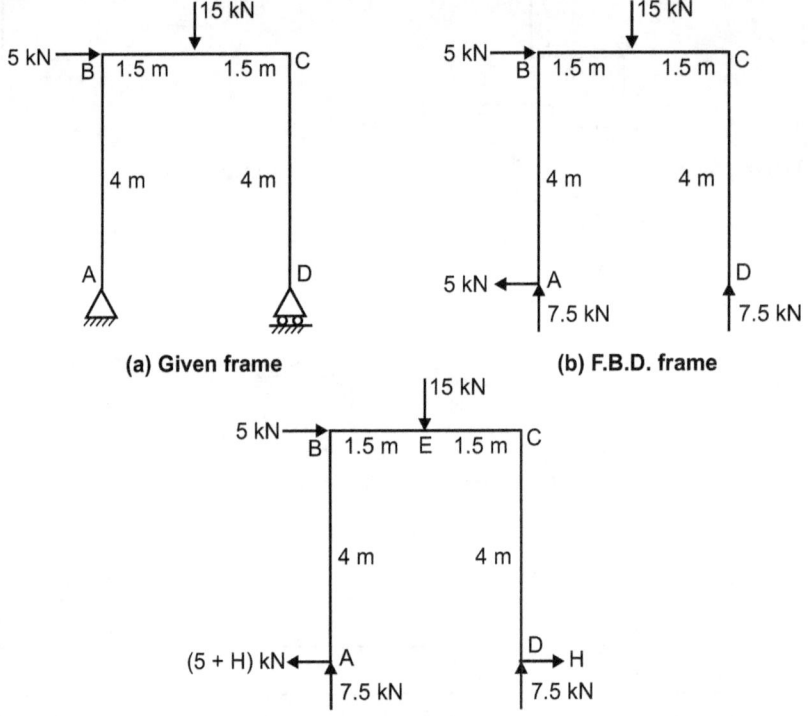

(a) Given frame (b) F.B.D. frame

(c) Frame with fictitious load

Fig. 3.36

Region	Moment	∂M/∂H	Limit
DC	H·x	x	0 to 4
CE	(4H + 7.5x)	4	0 to 1.5
EB	[4H + 7.5 (x + 1.5) − 15x]	4	0 to 1.5
AB	(5 + H) x	x	0 to 4

According to Castigliano's first theorem,

$$\delta_D = \frac{\partial U}{\partial H} = \int_0^4 \frac{Hx \cdot x\, dx}{EI} + \int_0^{1.5} \frac{(4H + 7.5x)}{EI} 4\, dx$$

$$+ \int_0^{1.5} \frac{[4H + 7.5(x+1.5) - 15x]\, 4\, dx}{EI} + \int_0^4 (5+H)\, x \cdot x\, \frac{dx}{EI}$$

As H is fictitious load ∴ put H = 0

∴ $\delta_D = \int_0^{1.5} \frac{30x}{EI} dx + \int_0^{1.5} [30(x+1.5) - 60x] \frac{dx}{EI} + \int_0^{4} \frac{5x^2 \, dx}{EI}$

$= \frac{30}{EI} \left(\frac{x^2}{2}\right)_0^{1.5} + \frac{30}{EI} \left(\frac{x^2}{2} + 1.5x\right)_0^{1.5} - \frac{60}{EI} \left(\frac{x^2}{2}\right)_0^{1.5} + \frac{5}{EI} \left[\frac{x^3}{3}\right]_0^4$

$= \frac{33.75}{EI} + \frac{101.25}{EI} - \frac{67.5}{EI} + \frac{106.67}{EI}$

$= \frac{174.17}{EI}$

$= \frac{174.17}{35 \times 10^3}$

$\delta_D = 4.98 \times 10^{-3}$ m

∴ $\delta_D = 4.98$ mm

Problem 3.27 : For the bent shown in Fig. 3.37 (a), find the vertical and horizontal deflection at free end. Take EI = 80 kN-m².

Solution : (a) Vertical deflection at free end :

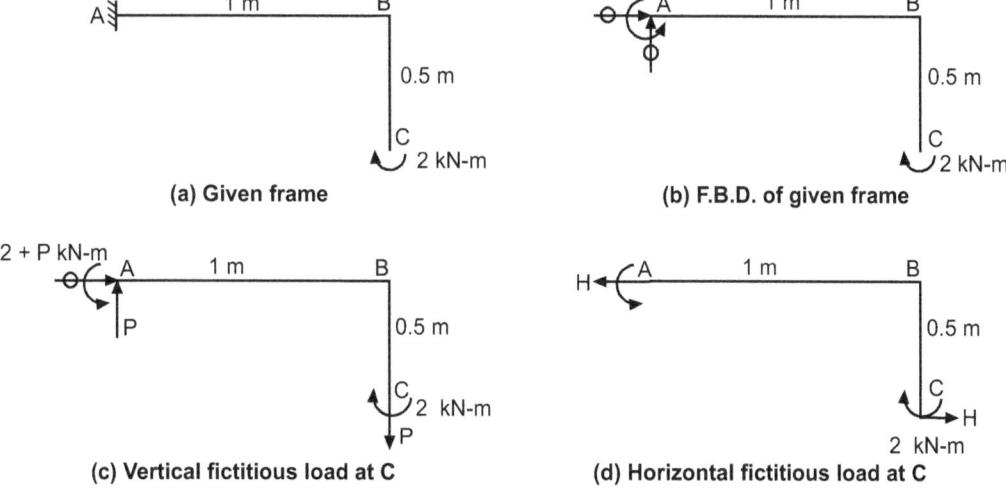

Fig. 3.37

Region	Moment	∂M/∂P	Limit
CB	−2	0	0 to 0.5
AB	−(2 + P) + Px	(x − 1)	0 to 1

According to Castigliano's first theorem,

$$\delta_C = \frac{\partial U}{\partial P}$$

$$= \int_0^1 (Px - 2 - P)(x - 1)\frac{dx}{EI}$$

As P is fictitious load ∴ put P = 0.

∴ $$\delta_V = \int_0^1 -2(x-1)\frac{dx}{EI}$$

$$= -2\left[\frac{x^2}{2} - x\right]_0^1 = \frac{1}{EI} = \frac{1}{80} = 0.0125 \text{ m}$$

∴ $\delta_V = 12.5$ mm

(b) Horizontal deflection at free end :

Region	Moment	∂M/∂H	Limit
CB	(Hx – 2)	x	0 to 0.5
AB	– (2 – 0.5 H)	0.5	0 to 1

According to Castigliano's first theorem,

$$\delta_H = \int_0^{0.5} (Hx - 2) \times \frac{dx}{EI} + \int_0^1 (0.5H - 2)\, 0.5\, \frac{dx}{EI}$$

As H is fictitious load ∴ put P = 0.

$$\delta_H = \int_0^{0.5} -2x\frac{dx}{EI} + \int_0^1 -\frac{dx}{EI} = -\frac{2}{EI}\left[\frac{x^2}{2}\right]_0^{0.5} - \frac{1}{EI}[x]_0^1$$

$$= -\frac{0.25}{EI} - \frac{1}{EI} = -\frac{1.25}{EI}$$

∴ $$\delta_H = -\frac{1.25}{80} = -0.0156 \text{ m}$$

∴ $\delta_H = -15.625$ mm $= 15.625$ mm (←)

Problem 3.28 : Determine the horizontal, vertical and rotational displacements at A in the rigid jointed frame shown in Fig. 3.38 (a). EI is same for all the members.

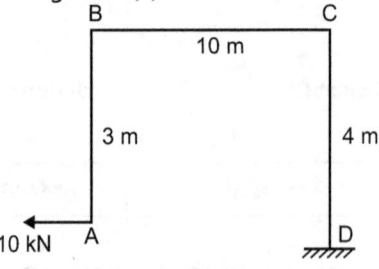

Fig. 3.38 (a)

Solution : Applying dummy loads H_a and V_a along horizontal and vertical directions and M_a is the dummy moment applied at joint A as shown in Fig. 3.38 (b).

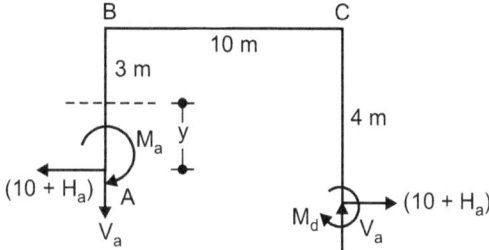

Fig. 3.38 (b)

$\sum M @ D = 0.$

$\therefore \quad -(10 + H_a) \times 1 - V_a \times 10 + M_a + M_d = 0$

$\therefore \qquad M_d = (10 + H_a) + 10 V_a - M_a$

Region	M	$\dfrac{\partial M}{\partial H_a}$	$\dfrac{\partial M}{\partial V_a}$	$\dfrac{\partial M}{\partial M_a}$	Limit of integration
AB	$(10 + H_a) y + M_a$	y	0	1	0 to 3
BC	$(10 + H_a) 3 + M_a - V_a x$	3	$-x$	1	0 to 10
DC	$-M_d + (10 + H_a) \cdot y$ $= -(10 + H_a) - 10 V_a + M_a + (10 + H_a) y$ $= (10 + H_a)(y - 1) - 10 V_a + M_a$	$(y - 1)$	-10	1	0 to 4

$$\delta_H = \int_0^l \dfrac{M}{EI} \cdot \dfrac{\partial M}{\partial H} dx$$

Span AB : $\dfrac{1}{EI} \int_0^3 [(10 + H_a) y + M_a] y\, dy$

Put $H_a = M_a = 0$ as dummy loads.

$\therefore \qquad \dfrac{1}{EI} \int_0^3 [10 y^2]\, dy = 10 \left[\dfrac{y^3}{3}\right]_0^3 = \dfrac{90}{EI}$ ... (1)

Span BC :

$\dfrac{1}{EI} \int_0^{10} [(10 + H_a) 3 + M_a - V_a x]\, 3\, dx$

Put $H_a = M_a = V_a = 0$

$\therefore \qquad \dfrac{1}{EI} \int_0^{10} (30)\, 3\, dx = 90 [x]_0^{10} = \dfrac{900}{EI}$ ... (2)

Span DC :

$$\frac{1}{EI}\int_0^4 [H_a(y+1) + 10(y+1) + 10V_a - M_a](y+1)\,dy$$

Put $H_a = M_a = V_a = 0$

$$\therefore \frac{1}{EI}\int_0^4 10(y+1)^2\,dy = \frac{10}{EI}\int_0^4 (y^2+2y+1)\,dy = \frac{10}{EI}\left[\frac{y^3}{3} + \frac{2y^2}{2} + y\right]_0^4 = \frac{413.33}{EI} \quad \ldots (3)$$

$$\therefore \delta_H = \frac{30 + 900 + 413.33}{EI} = \frac{1403.33}{EI}$$

Now, $\quad \delta_V = \int_0^l \frac{M}{EI} \cdot \frac{\partial M}{\partial V_a}\,dx$

Span AB :

$$\int_0^3 \frac{(10 + H_a)y + M_a \times 0}{EI} = 0 \quad \ldots (4)$$

Span BC :

$$\frac{1}{EI}\int_0^{10} [(10 + H_a)3 + M_a - V_a x](-x)\,dx$$

Put $H_a = M_a = V_a = 0$

$$\therefore \frac{1}{EI}\int_0^{10} (-30x)\,dx = -\frac{30}{EI}\left[\frac{x^2}{2}\right]_0^{10} = -\frac{1500}{EI} \quad \ldots (5)$$

Span DC :

$$\frac{1}{EI}\int_0^4 [H_a(y+1) + 10(y+1) + 10V_a - M_a]\,10\,dy$$

Put $M_a = H_a = V_a = 0$

$$\frac{1}{EI}\int_0^4 100(y+1)\,dy = \frac{100}{EI}\int_0^4 (y+1)\,dy$$

$$= \frac{100}{EI}\left[\frac{y^2}{2} + y\right]_0^4 = \frac{1200}{EI} \quad \ldots (6)$$

$$\therefore \quad \delta_V = \text{Eq. (4)} + \text{Eq. (5)} + \text{Eq. (6)}$$

$$= 0 - \frac{1500}{EI} + \frac{1200}{EI} = \frac{-300}{EI}$$

$$\theta_A = \int \frac{M}{EI} \cdot \frac{\partial M}{\partial M_a} dx$$

Span AB :

$$\frac{1}{EI} \int_0^3 [(10 + H_a) y + M_a] \, 1 \, dy$$

Put $H_a = M_a = 0$

$$\therefore \quad \frac{1}{EI} \int_0^3 (10y) \, dy = \frac{10}{EI} \left[\frac{y^2}{2}\right]_0^3 = \frac{450}{EI} \qquad \ldots (7)$$

Span BC :

$$\frac{1}{EI} \int_0^{10} [(10 + H_a) 3 + M_a - V_a x] \, 1 \, dx$$

$$\therefore \quad \frac{1}{EI} \int_0^{10} 30 \, dx = \frac{30}{EI} [x]_0^{10} = \frac{300}{EI} \qquad \ldots (8)$$

Span CD :

$$\frac{1}{EI} \int_0^4 [H_a (y - 1) + 10 (y - 1) - 10 V_a + M_a] \, 1 \, dy$$

$$= \frac{1}{EI} \int_0^4 (10y - 10) \, dy = \frac{1}{EI} \left[\frac{10y^2}{2} - 10y\right]_0^4 = \frac{40}{EI} \qquad \ldots (9)$$

$$\therefore \quad \theta_A = \text{Eq. (7)} + \text{Eq. (8)} + \text{Eq. (9)}$$

$$= \frac{450}{EI} + \frac{300}{EI} + \frac{40}{EI} = \frac{790}{EI}$$

$\therefore$ Horizontal displacement at $A = \dfrac{1403.33}{EI}$

Vertical displacement at $A = -\dfrac{300}{EI}$

and Rotational displacement at $A = \dfrac{790}{EI}$

Problem 3.29 : Using Castigliano's theorem, find the vertical and horizontal deflection at A for the lamp post loaded and supported as shown in Fig. 3.39 (a). Assume uniform flexural rigidity.

Solution :

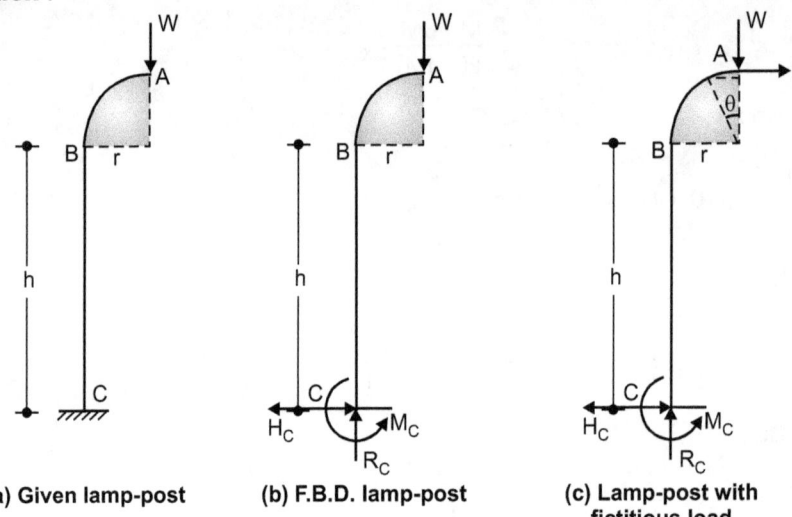

(a) Given lamp-post (b) F.B.D. lamp-post (c) Lamp-post with fictitious load

Fig. 3.39 : Lamp post

$$R_C = W, \; H_C = P, \; M_C = w \cdot r + P(h + r)$$

Region	Moment	$\partial M/\partial W$	$\partial M/\partial P$	Limit
AB	$-w \cdot r \sin\theta - Pr(1 - \cos\theta)$	$-r \sin\theta$	$-r(1 - \cos\theta)$	$0 - \pi/2$
CB	$H_C \cdot x - [wr + P(h + r)]$ $= Px - wr - P(h + r)$	$-r$	$[x - (h + r)]$	$0 - h$

$$\delta_h = \int M \cdot \frac{\partial M}{\partial W} \cdot \frac{dx}{EI}$$

$$\delta_h = \int_0^{\pi/2} [-wr\sin\theta - Pr(1 - \cos\theta)](-r\sin\theta) \cdot \frac{rd\theta}{EI}$$

$$+ \int_0^h [Px - wr - P(h + r)](-r) \cdot \frac{dx}{EI}$$

As P is fictitious load, put P = 0.

$$\delta_h = \int_0^{\pi/2} wr^3 \sin^2\theta \, \frac{d\theta}{EI} + \int_0^h wr^2 \frac{dx}{EI}$$

$$= \frac{wr^3}{2EI}\left(\theta - \frac{\sin 2\theta}{2}\right)_0^{\pi/2} + \frac{wr^2}{EI}(x)_0^h$$

$$= \frac{wr^3}{2EI}\left(\frac{\pi}{2} - 0\right) + \frac{wr^2 h}{EI} = \frac{wr^2}{EI}\left(\frac{\pi r}{4} + h\right)$$

EXERCISE

Solve following examples by Macaulay's method.

1. A 2 m long cantilever made of steel tube 150 mm external diameter and 10 mm thickness is loaded as shown in Fig. 3.40. Determine the maximum deflection. Assume E = 200 GPa.   (13.98 mm ($\downarrow$))

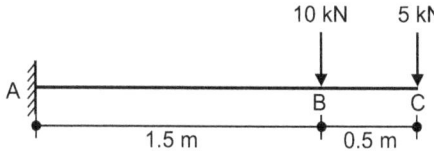

Fig. 3.40

2. A 2 m long cantilever is of rectangular section 100 mm wide and 200 mm deep. It is loaded as shown in Fig. 3.41. Find deflection at free end assuming E = 10 GPa.   (19.39 mm ($\downarrow$))

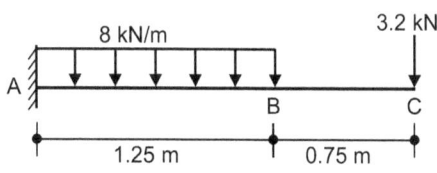

Fig. 3.41

3. A horizontal cantilever of uniform section and span 'L' is loaded as shown in Fig. 3.42. Find the deflection at free end. $\left(\dfrac{26.76}{EI} (\downarrow)\right)$

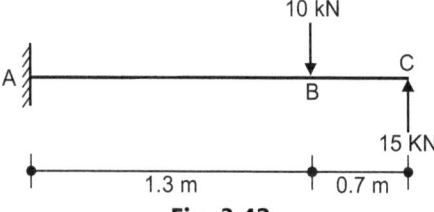

Fig. 3.42

4. A cantilever of uniform section is loaded as shown in Fig. 3.43. Find the deflection at B. If the cantilever is propped at B, find the reaction at prop assuming there is no deflection at B. $\left(y_B = \dfrac{33.75}{EI} (\downarrow) ;\ V_B = 30\ kN\ (\uparrow)\right)$

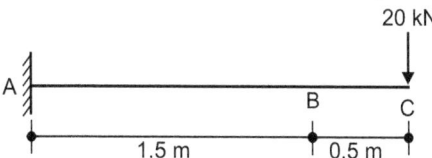

Fig. 3.43

5. A vertical post AB of constant flexural rigidity 4000 kNm² is fixed at the base A and subjected to a horizontal load of 20 kN at C as shown in Fig. 3.44. Determine the necessary force in horizontal tie at B such that the deflection at B is limited to 20 mm to the left.   (5.13 kN)

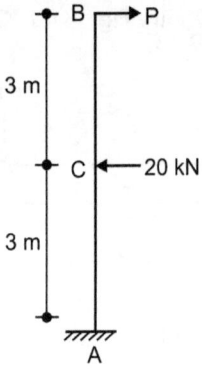

Fig. 3.44

6. Two equal steel beams are built in at one end and connected by a steel rod as shown in Fig. 3.45. Show that the pull in the rod is

$$P = \frac{5wL^3}{32\left(\frac{6aI}{\pi d^2} + L^3\right)}$$

where   d = diameter of the rod

and   I = M.I. of each beam

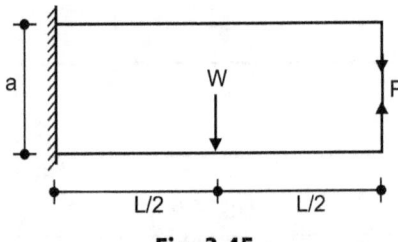

Fig. 3.45

7. For the beam shown in Fig. 3.46, show that the deflection under load is $\dfrac{W}{3.2\,EI}$.

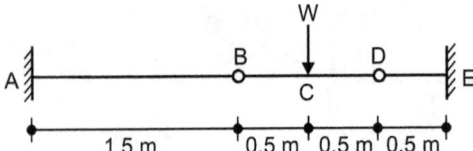

Fig. 3.46

8. A timber beam carries a UDL of 10 kN/m over a span of 6 m. The ends of the beam are simply supported. Determine the section of the beam if the central deflection is limited to 15 mm and the maximum bending stress to 10 MPa. Take E = 12 GPa.

(b = 154 mm, d = 417 mm)

9. The beam is supported and loaded as shown in Fig. 3.47. Find (i) the deflection under the load, (ii) the position and the amount of maximum deflection. Assume E = 200 GPa and I = 50 × 10⁶ mm⁴

(y_C = 6 mm (↓); y_{max} = 6.53 mm (↓) at 2.45 m from A)

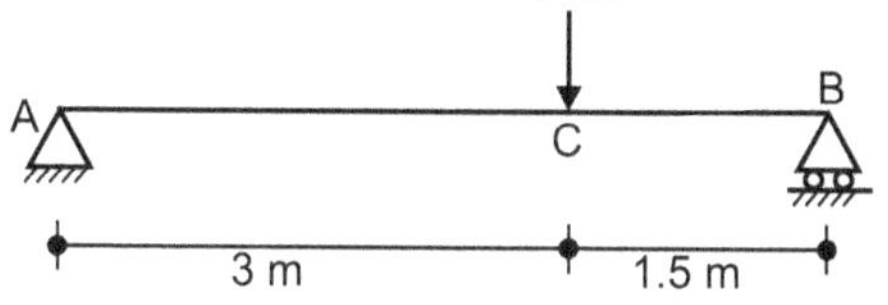

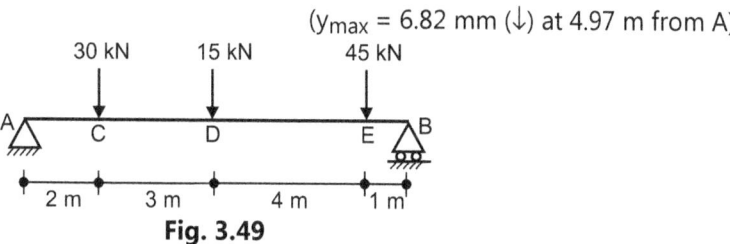

Fig. 3.47

10. The beam is supported and loaded as shown in Fig. 3.48. Find (i) the deflection under loads, (ii) the maximum deflection. Assume E = 200 GPa, I = 70 × 10⁸ mm⁴.

(y_C = 2.34 mm (↓); y_D = 2.98 mm (↓); y_{max} = 3.54 mm (↓) at 6.87 m from A)

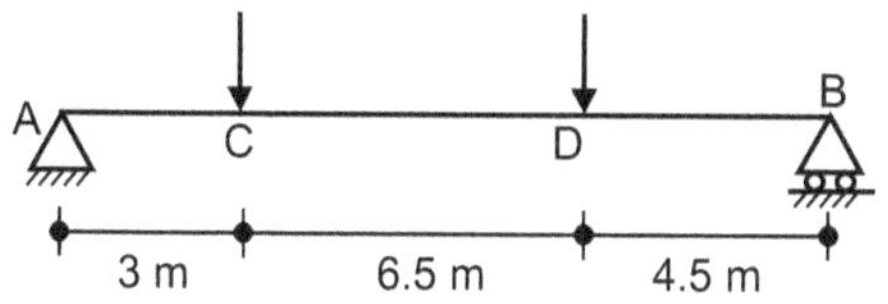

Fig. 3.48

11. The beam is supported and loaded as shown in Fig. 3.49. Determine the position and amount of maximum deflection. EI = 1.39 × 10¹¹ kNmm².

(y_{max} = 6.82 mm (↓) at 4.97 m from A)

Fig. 3.49

12. The beam is supported and loaded as shown in Fig. 3.50. Find deflection at C.

$$\left(y_C = \frac{3.75}{EI} (\downarrow) \right)$$

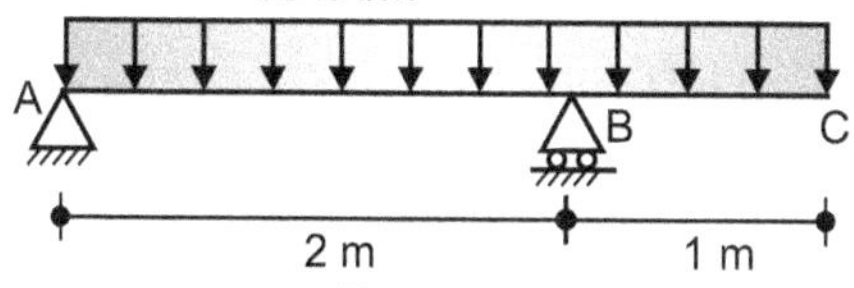

Fig. 3.50

13. The beam is supported and loaded as shown in Fig. 3.51. Assuming E = 200 GPa, I = 40 × 10⁶ mm⁴, find (i) the deflection at C; (ii) the maximum deflection, and (iii) slope at end A.

    (y_C = 8.74 mm (↓); y_{max} = 8.75 mm (↓) at 1.958 m from A; θ_A = 0.417° (↻))

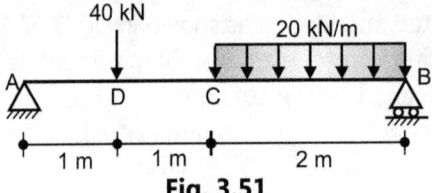

    Fig. 3.51

14. The beam is supported and loaded as shown in Fig. 3.52. Calculate slope and deflection at point C.

    $\left(\theta_C = \dfrac{12.67}{EI} (↻);\ y_C = \dfrac{20.85}{EI} (↓)\right)$

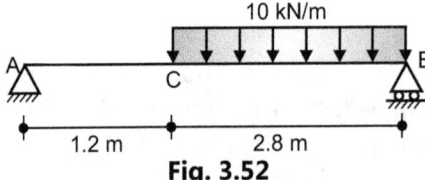

    Fig. 3.52

15. A beam of constant section, symmetric about neutral axis is simply supported over a span of 8 m. The beam has to carry a concentrated load of 40 kN at the midspan and a UDL of 15 kN/m over the entire span. If the central deflection is limited to $\dfrac{1^{th}}{480}$ of the span and the maximum fibre stresses due to bending are not to exceed 118 MPa, determine the required depth of the beam and moment of inertia.

    (d = 435 mm; I_{xx} = 3.686 × 10⁸ mm⁴)

16. The beam is supported and loaded as shown in Fig. 3.53. Determine the deflections at C and D and maximum deflection, assuming EI = 3 × 10¹⁰ kNmm².

    (y_C = 12.09 mm (↓); y_D = 13.81 mm (↓); y_{max} = 16.22 mm (↓) at 3.7 m from A)

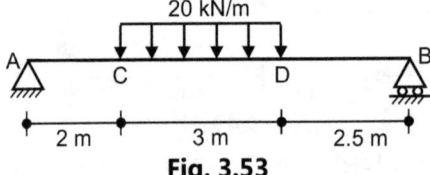

    Fig. 3.53

17. Find slope and deflections at C and E for the beam supported and loaded as shown in Fig. 3.54. Assume E = 200 GPa, I = 2 × 10⁷ mm⁴.

    (θ_C = 0.0047° (↻); y_C = 12.5 mm (↓); θ_E = 0.568° (↻); y_E = 9.916 mm (↑))

    Fig. 3.54

18. A simply supported beam AB of length 'L' just touches a spring of midspan in unloaded condition. Find the stiffness k of the spring that will make the forces on the supports and on the spring equal for a uniformly distributed load. Assume EI = constant.

(54.857 EI/L³)

19. The beam is supported and loaded as shown in Fig. 3.55. Determine (i) the deflection at C and (ii) the maximum deflection between A and B. Assume EI = 2700 kNm².

(y_C = 10.08 mm (↓); y_{max} in zone AB = 11.4 mm (↓) at 2.46 m from A)

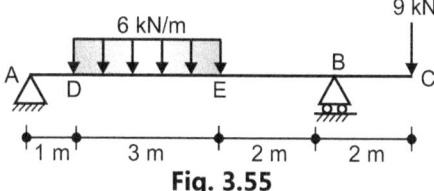

Fig. 3.55

20. Determine slope and deflection at free end of a cantilever shown in Fig. 3.56. Assume uniform flexural rigidity. Take E = 2 × 10⁵ MPa; I = 8.5 × 10⁷ mm⁴.

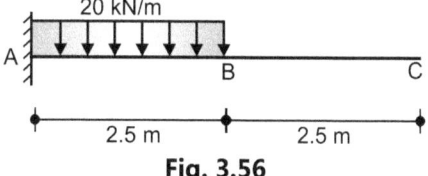

Fig. 3.56

[θ_C = 0.175° (↻), y_C = 13.40 mm (↓)]

21. Find slope and deflection at free end of a cantilever shown in Fig. 3.57. Assume uniform flexural rigidity. Take E = 2 × 10⁵ MPa; I = 2.5 × 10⁸ mm⁴.

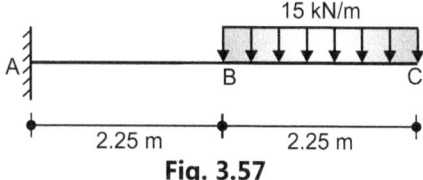

Fig. 3.57

[θ_C = 0.228° (↻), y_C = 13.13 mm (↓)]

22. Find midspan and maximum deflection for cantilever beam of uniform section shown in Fig. 3.58. Take EI = 7560 kNm².

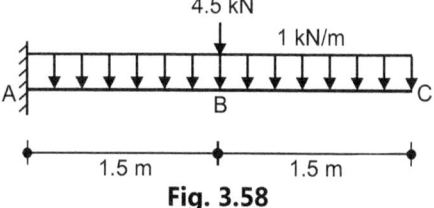

Fig. 3.58

[y_B = 11.44 mm (↓), y_{max} = 30.1 mm (↓)]

23. Find $\theta_B, \theta_C, y_B, y_C$ for the cantilever beam shown in Fig. 3.59. Take $E = 2 \times 10^5$ MPa, $I = 5 \times 10^8$ mm^4.

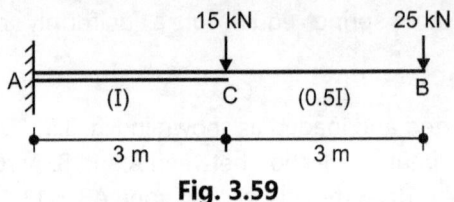

Fig. 3.59

[$\theta_B = 0.36°$ (↻); $\theta_C = 0.23°$ (↻); $y_B = 23.63$ mm (↓); $y_C = 6.98$ mm (↓)]

24. Find $\theta_B, \theta_C, y_B, y_C$ for the cantilever beam shown in Fig. 3.60. Take $E = 2 \times 10^5$ MPa, $I = 5 \times 10^8$ mm^4.

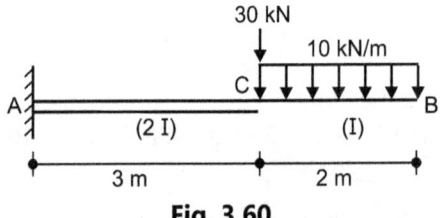

Fig. 3.60

[$\theta_B = 0.09°$ (↻); $\theta_C = 0.08°$ (↻)

$y_B = 5.75$ mm (↓); $y_C = 2.7$ mm (↓)]

25. Find slope and deflection at free end of aluminium cantilever shown in Fig. 3.61. Take $E = 70,000$ MPa, $I_1 = 2 \times 10^6$ mm^4, $I_2 = 0.4 \times 10^6$ mm^4.

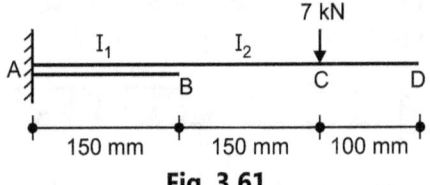

Fig. 3.61

[$\theta_D = 0.2575°$ (↻); $y_D = 1.124$ mm (↓)]

26. A cantilever beam shown in Fig. 3.62 has a uniform rectangular cross section having $d = 2b$. Find the values of b, d if maximum deflection is not to exceed 15 mm.

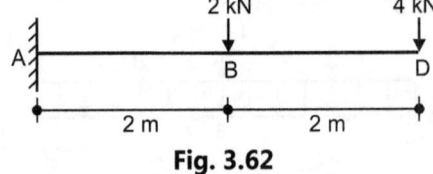

Fig. 3.62

[b = 217.5 mm; d = 435 mm]

27. Find the deflection at free end of a cantilever shown in Fig. 3.63.

Take $E = 2 \times 10^5$ MPa, $I = 4 \times 10^6$ mm^4. [$y_C = 8.33$ mm (↑)]

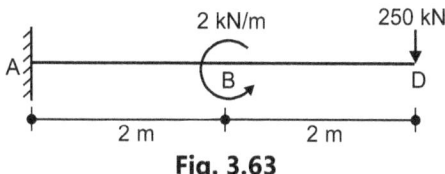

Fig. 3.63

28. Find the deflection at free end of a cantilever shown in Fig. 3.64.

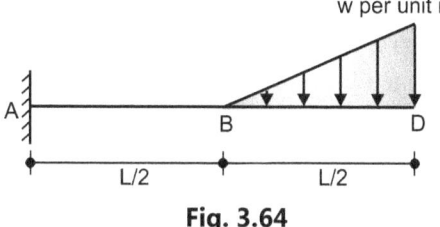

Fig. 3.64

$$\left[y = \frac{121}{1920}\left(\frac{wL^4}{EI}\right) \right]$$

29. Find θ_B, θ_C, y_B and y_C for the cantilever beam shown in Fig. 3.65.
    Take $E = 2 \times 10^5$ MPa, $I = 6 \times 10^8$ mm^4.

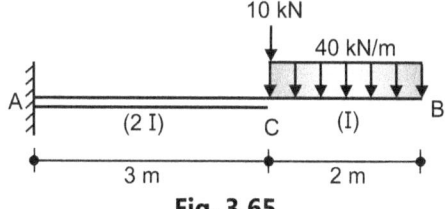

Fig. 3.65

[$\theta_B = 0.179°$ (↻), $\theta_C = 0.153°$ (↻); $y_B = 10.916$ mm (↓); $y_C = 4.875$ mm (↓)]

30. Find θ_B, θ_C, y_B and y_C for the cantilever beam shown in Fig. 3.66.
    Take $E = 2 \times 10^5$ MPa, $I = 5 \times 10^8$ mm^4.

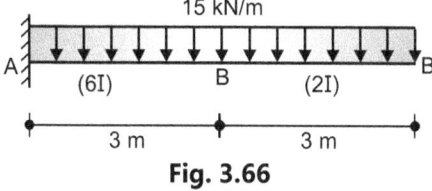

Fig. 3.66

[$\theta_B = 0.065°$ (↻), $\theta_C = 0.045°$ (↻); $y_B = 4.4725$ mm (↓); $y_C = 1.435$ mm (↓)]

31. Find θ_B, θ_C, y_B and y_C for the cantilever beam shown in Fig. 3.67.
    Take $E = 2 \times 10^5$ MPa, $I = 5 \times 10^8$ mm^4.

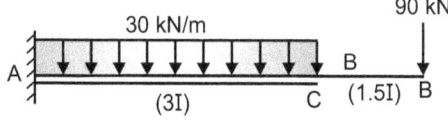

Fig. 3.67

[$\theta_B = 0.4°$ (↻); $\theta_C = 0.34°$ (↻), $y_B = 27.73$ (↓); $y_C = 14.4$ mm (↓)]

32. A beam of constant cross section 10 m long is simply supported at its ends and loaded with two concentrated loads of 6 kN each at a distance 3 m from either supports. Find the ratio of deflection at mid span to that under any one of the load.

(1.22)

33. A simply supported beam of uniform section and span L is loaded with two equal loads w at point L/4 from each end. Show that the central deflection is $\dfrac{11}{384}\left[\dfrac{wL^3}{EI}\right]$.

34. A simply supported beam of uniform section has a span L and carries two equal loads w each at a distance L/3 from either ends. Show that the central deflection is $\dfrac{23}{648}\left[\dfrac{wL^3}{EI}\right]$.

35. Find the maximum deflection for simply supported beam shown in Fig. 3.68. Assume uniform flexural rigidity.

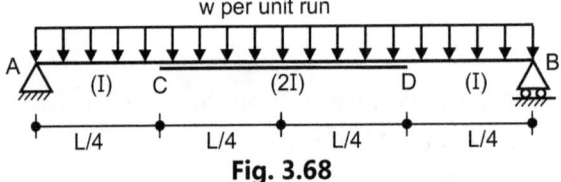

Fig. 3.68

$\left[\dfrac{93}{12288}\left(\dfrac{wL^4}{EI}\right)\right]$.

36. Find θ_C and y_C from simply supported beam shown in Fig. 3.69. Take $E = 2 \times 10^5$ MPa; $I = 6 \times 10^8$ mm^4.

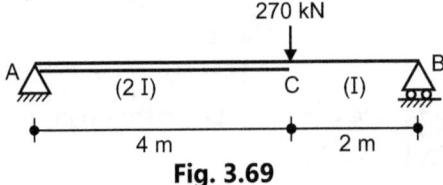

Fig. 3.69

[$\theta_C = 0.0225°$ (↻); $y_C = 3.2025$ mm (↓)]

37. Find θ_A, θ_C, θ_D, y_C and y_D and maximum deflection for the beam shown in Fig. 3.70. Take $E = 2 \times 10^5$ MPa, $I = 3 \times 10^8$ mm^4.

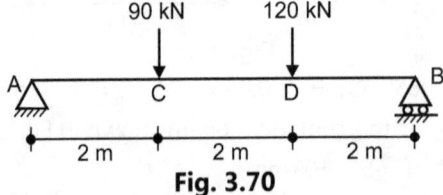

Fig. 3.70

[$\theta_A = 0.3945°$ (↻); $\theta_C = 0.204°$ (↻); $\theta_D = 0.198°$ (↺); $y_C = 11.55$ mm (↓); $y_D = 11.775$ mm (↓); $y_{max} = 13.425$ mm (↓) at 3.04 m from A]

38. Find θ_C and y_C for a beam shown in Fig. 3.71 using $E = 2 \times 10^5$ MPa, $I = 4 \times 10^8$ mm^4. Assume uniform flexural rigidity throughout.

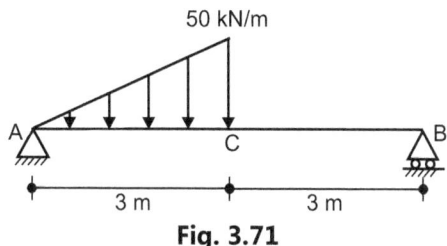
Fig. 3.71

$[\theta_C = 0.01° (\circlearrowleft); y_C = 3.375 \text{ mm} (\downarrow)]$

39. Find θ_A, θ_B, y_C and y_D for the beam shown in Fig. 3.72. Take $E = 2 \times 10^5$ MPa, $I = 4.5 \times 10^8$ mm⁴.

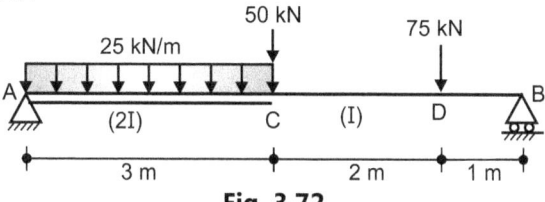
Fig. 3.72

$[\theta_A = 0.13° (\circlearrowleft); \theta_B = 0.175° (\circlearrowleft); y_C = 5 \text{ mm} (\downarrow); y_D = 2.875 \text{ mm} (\downarrow)]$

40. Determine the maximum deflection of the beam carrying uniformly distributed load over the middle portion as shown in Fig. 3.73.

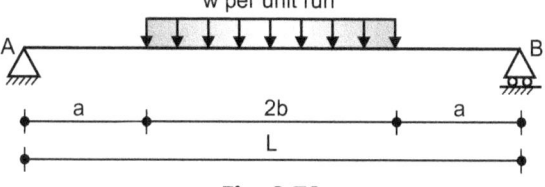
Fig. 3.73

$$y_{max} = \frac{wb}{24 EI}(L^3 - 2Lb^2 + b^3)$$

41. A beam of uniform section and length L is simply supported at its ends and carries a symmetrical triangular loading having intensity varying from zero at each end to w at centre. Find the slope at each end and the deflection at centre.

$$\theta = \frac{5}{192}\frac{wL^3}{EI}, \quad y = \frac{wL^4}{120 EI} (\downarrow)$$

42. A beam 6 m long is subjected to couples as shown in Fig. 3.74. Find the deflections at the points of application of couple. Take $E = 2 \times 10^5$ MPa, $I = 3 \times 10^7$ mm⁴.

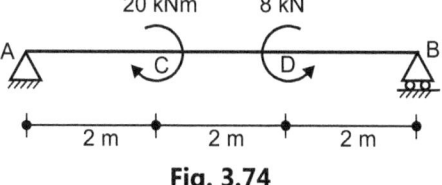
Fig. 3.74

$[y_C = 4.44 \text{ mm} (\downarrow); y_D = 4.88 \text{ mm} (\downarrow)]$

43. Find deflection at D for a beam shown in Fig. 3.75. Take $E = 2.1 \times 10^5$ MPa and $I = 3.7 \times 10^8$ mm^4.

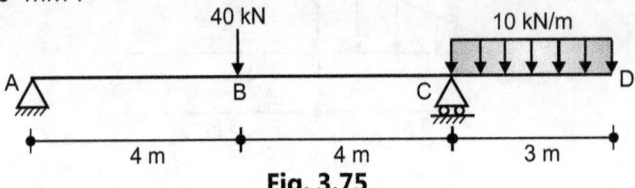

Fig. 3.75

[0.242 mm (↑)]

44. A uniform beam is supported and loaded as shown in Fig. 3.76. Find deflections under the loads and slopes at the supports. Take $E = 2 \times 10^5$ MPa, $I = 6 \times 10^8$ mm^4.

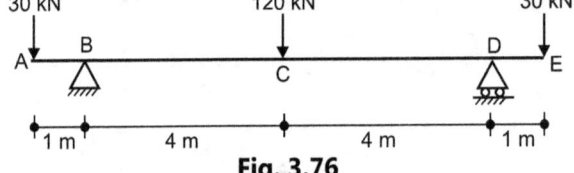

Fig. 3.76

[y_C = 8.67 mm (↓); y_A = y_E = 2.916 mm (↑); θ_B = θ_D = 0.171°]

45. Find out θ_C, θ_D, y_C and y_D for the beam shown in Fig. 3.77. Take $E = 2 \times 10^5$ MPa, $I = 4.5 \times 10^8$ mm^4.

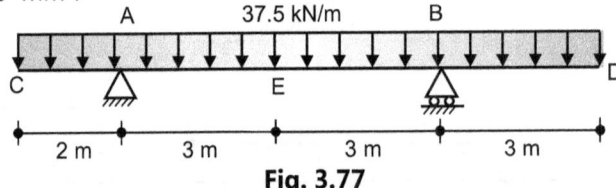

Fig. 3.77

[θ_C = 0.024° (↺), θ_D = 0.155° (↻), y_C = 0.416 mm (↓), y_D = 6.712 (↓)]

46. Determine the deflection at C for a beam shown in Fig. 3.78. Assume uniform flexural rigidity throughout.

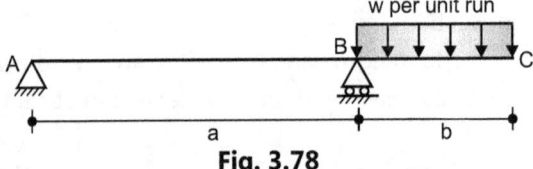

Fig. 3.78

$$\left[y_C = \frac{wb^3}{24\,EI}(4a + 3b) \right]$$

47. Find deflection at C for the beam shown in Fig. 3.79.

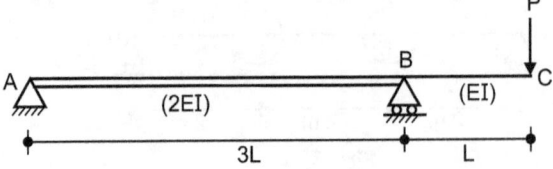

Fig. 3.79

$$\left[y_C = \frac{5\,PL^3}{16\,EI}(\downarrow) \right]$$

48. Find the moments at A, B and C and draw the B.M.D. for the frame shown in Fig. 3.80 by using strain energy method.

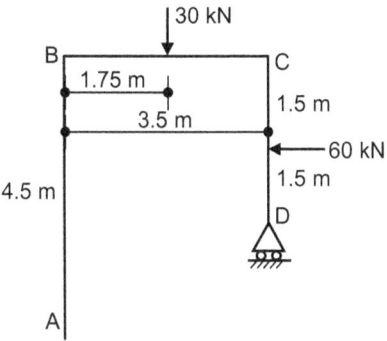

Fig. 3.80

49. Using strain energy method, draw the B.M.D. for the frame shown in Fig. 3.81.

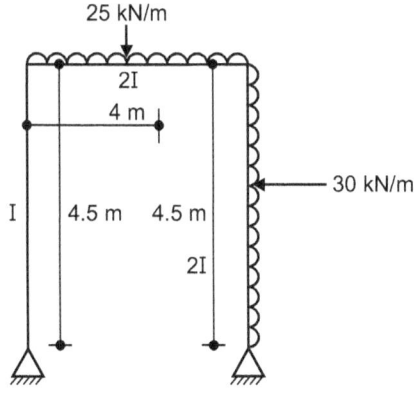

Fig. 3.81

50. Draw the B.M.D. for frame ABC as shown in Fig. 3.82 by using strain energy method.

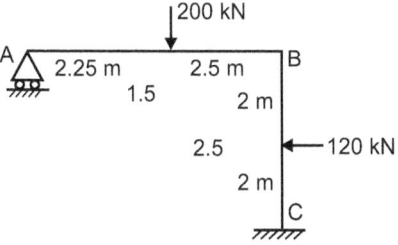

Fig. 3.82

51. Draw B.M.D. for the frame ABCD using strain energy method.

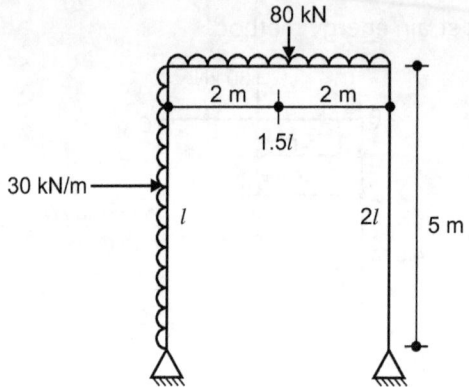

Fig. 3.83

52. Find the moments at joints and draw B.M.D. using strain energy method.

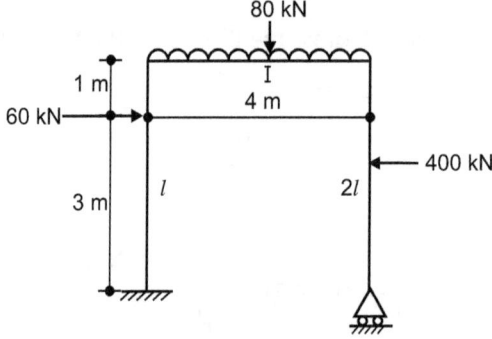

Fig. 3.84

MULTIPLE CHOICE QUESTIONS

1. A cantilever beam AB has a span 5 m. A concentrated load of 50 kN is acting at cantilever end B. Slope at B is
   (a) 125/EI (b) 25/EI (c) 12.5/EI (d) 225/EI

2. A cantilever beam AB has a span 5 m. A concentrated load of 50 kN is acting at cantilever end B. Deflection at B is
   (a) 225.25/EI (b) 256.32/EI (c) 312.15/EI (d) 416.16/EI

3. A cantilever beam AB has a span 5 m. A concentrated load of 50 kN is acting at cantilever end B. Slope at centre is
   (a) 125.25/EI (b) 93.75/EI (c) 112.5/EI (d) 83.25/EI

4. A cantilever beam AB has a span 5 m. A concentrated load of 50 kN is acting at cantilever end B. Deflection at centre B is
   (a) 220.2/EI (b) 112.6/EI (c) 130.2/EI (d) 316.16/EI

5. A cantilever beam CD has a span 5 m. A uniformly distributed load of intensity 40 kN/m is acting throughout the span. Slope at D is
   (a) 21.33/EI   (b) 35.23/EI   (c) 12.5/EI   (d) 26.67/EI
6. A cantilever beam CD has a span 5 m. A uniformly distributed load of intensity 40 kN/m is acting throughout the span. Deflection at D is
   (a) 22/EI   (b) 35/EI   (c) 40/EI   (d) 56/EI
7. A cantilever beam CD has a span 6 m. A uniformly distributed load of intensity 24 kN/m is acting throughout the span. Deflection at 2 m from left end is
   (a) 188/EI   (b) 988/EI   (c) 288/EI   (d) 688/EI
8. A cantilever beam CD has a span 5 m. A uniformly distributed load of intensity 35 kN/m is acting throughout the span. Slope at 3 m form left end is
   (a) 682.5/EI   (b) 512.6/EI   (c) 570.2/EI   (d) 316.6/EI
9. A cantilever beam AB has a span 4 m. A uniformly distributed load of intensity 25 kN/m is acting on 2 m form left end. Slope at 3 m form left end is
   (a) 33.33/EI   (b) 51.63/EI   (c) 47.21/EI   (d) 36.6/EI
10. A cantilever beam AB has a span 5 m. A uniformly distributed load of intensity 20 kN/m is acting on 3 m from left end. Slope at 3 m form left end is
    (a) 312.5/EI   (b) 503.6/EI   (c) 212.5/EI   (d) 416.6/EI
11. A cantilever beam of span L is loaded with a concentrated load W at free end. Deflection at free end is
    (a) $WL^3/3\ EI$ (b) $WL^2/3\ EI$ (c) $WL^3/48\ EI$ (d) $5\ WL^3/48\ EI$
12. A cantilever beam of span L is loaded with a concentrated load W at free end. Deflection at centre of span is
    (a) $WL^3/3\ EI$ (b) $WL^2/3\ EI$ (c) $WL^3/48\ EI$ (d) $5\ WL^3/48\ EI$
13. A cantilever beam of span L is loaded with a concentrated load W at centre of span. Deflection at free end is
    (a) $WL^3/3\ EI$ (b) $WL^2/3\ EI$ (c) $WL^3/48\ EI$ (d) $5WL^3/48\ EI$
14. A cantilever beam of span L and concentrated load W is acting at L/4 from fixed end. Deflection under concentrated load is
    (a) $WL^3/3\ EI$ (b) $WL^3/32\ EI$ (c) $WL^3/48\ EI$ (d) $WL^3/192\ EI$
15. A cantilever beam of span L is loaded with a concentrated load W at free end. Slope at free end is
    (a) $WL^2/3\ EI$ (b) $WL^2/2\ EI$ (c) $WL^2/48\ EI$ (d) $WL^2/192\ EI$
16. A cantilever beam of span L is loaded with a concentrated load W at free end. Slope at centre of span is
    (a) $5\ WL^2/3\ EI$ (b) $3\ WL^2/2\ EI$ (c) $WL^2/48\ EI$ (d) $5\ WL^2/48\ EI$

17. A cantilever beam of span L is loaded with a U.D.L. W throughout the span. Slope at free end is
    (a) $WL^3/6\ EI$
    (b) $WL^3/3\ EI$
    (c) $WL^3/8\ EI$
    (d) $5\ WL^3/4\ EI$

18. A cantilever beam of span L is loaded with a UDL w throughout the span. Deflection at free end is
    (a) $WL^4/3\ EI$
    (b) $3\ WL^4/8\ EI$
    (c) $WL^4/8\ EI$
    (d) $WL^4/9\ EI$

19. A cantilever beam of span 2 m having width 100 mm and depth 200 mm. A U.D.L. of 5 kN/m is loaded on half span. Deflection at free end is
    (a) 0.24 mm
    (b) 0.12 mm
    (c) 0.36 mm
    (d) 0.5 mm

20. A cantilever beam of span 2 m having width 100 mm and depth 200 mm. A U.D.L. of 5 kN/m is loaded on half span. Slope at free end is
    (a) 0.0042 rad
    (b) 0.00042 rad
    (c) 0.42 rad
    (d) 0.042 rad

21. A simply supported beam is of span L. A concentrated load is W is acting at centre. Slope at centre is
    (a) $WL^2/1.5\ EI$
    (b) zero
    (c) $WL^2/48\ EI$
    (d) $WL^2/16\ EI$

22. A simply supported beam is of span L. A concentrated load W is acting at centre. Slope at supports is
    (a) $WL^2/15\ EI$
    (b) zero
    (c) $WL^2/16\ EI$
    (d) $WL^2/24\ EI$

23. A simply supported beam is of span L. A concentrated load P is acting at centre. Deflection at centre is
    (a) $PL^2/3\ EI$
    (b) $PL^2/32\ EI$
    (c) $PL^3/48\ EI$
    (d) $PL^3/192\ EI$

24. A simply supported beam is of span L. A uniformly distributed load is W is acting throughout the span. Deflection at centre is
    (a) $WL^4/384\ EI$
    (b) $3\ WL^4/384\ EI$
    (c) $5\ WL^4/348\ EI$
    (d) $WL^4/192\ EI$

25. A simply supported beam of span L is loaded with a load P at a distance a from left end. Slope at left support is
    (a) $Wb\ (L^2 - b^2)/(6\ EIL)$
    (b) $Wb\ (L^2 - b^2)/(2\ EIL)$
    (c) $Wb\ (L^2 - b^2)/(3\ EIL)$
    (d) $2Wb\ (L^2 - b^2)/(3\ EIL)$

26. A simply supported beam of span L is loaded with a load P at a distance a from left end. Slope at right support is
    (a) $Wa\ (L^2 - a^2)/(6\ EIL)$
    (b) $Wa\ (L^2 - a^2)/(2\ EIL)$
    (c) $Wa\ (L^2 - a^2)/(3\ EIL)$
    (d) $2\ Wa\ (L^2 - a^2)/(3\ EIL)$

27. A simply supported beam of span L is loaded with a load P at a distance a from left end. Maximum deflection is
    (a) $Wa\ (L^2 - a^2)^{3/2}/(15.6\ EIL)$
    (b) $5\ Wa\ (L^2 - a^2)^{3/2}/(15.6\ EIL)$
    (c) $5\ Wa\ (L^2 - a^2)^{3/2}/(6\ EIL)$
    (d) $Wa\ (L^2 - a^2)^{3/2}/(9\ EIL)$

28. The beam is simply supported as shown in Fig. 1. The slope at point C is (Take EI = 12 × 10⁴ kNm²)

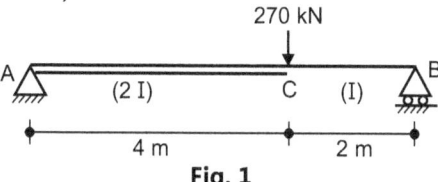

Fig. 1

(a) 0.010   (b) 0.023°   (c) 0.032   (d) 0.04

29. The beam is simply supported as shown in Fig. 2. The deflection at point C is (Take EI = 12 × 10⁴ kNm²)

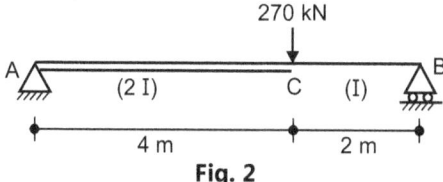

Fig. 2

(a) 4.1 mm   (b) 1.2 mm   (c) 2.1 mm   (d) 3.2 mm

30. The beam is supported and loaded as shown in Fig. 3. The deflection at point C is (Take EI = 6 × 10³ kNm²)

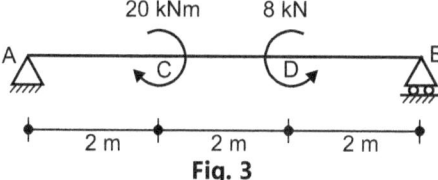

Fig. 3

(a) 3.33 mm   (b) 1.11 mm   (c) 4.44 mm   (d) 2.22 mm

31. The beam is supported and loaded as shown in Fig. 4. The deflection at point D is (Take EI = 6 × 10³ kNm²)

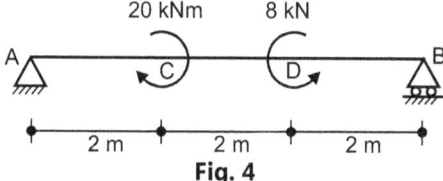

Fig. 4

(a) 4.88 mm   (b) 2.44 mm   (c) 4.22 mm   (d) 3.12 mm

32. The beam is supported and loaded as shown in Fig. 5. The deflection at D is (Take EI = 2.1 × 10⁵ MPa, I = 3.7 × 10⁸ mm⁴)

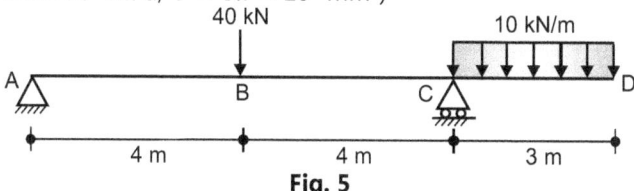

Fig. 5

(a) 0.24 mm   (b) 0.12 mm   (c) 0.36 mm   (d) 0.48 mm

33. The beam is supported and loaded as shown in Fig. 6. The slope at C is
    (Take EI = 9×10^4 kNm^2)

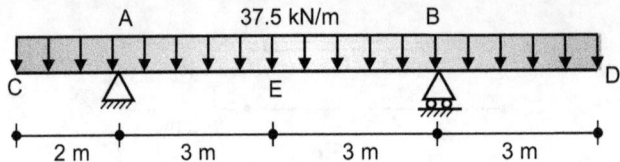

Fig. 6

   (a) 0.012°   (b) 0.024°   (c) 0.036°   (d) 0.048°

34. The beam is supported and loaded as shown in Fig. 7. The slope at D is
    (Take EI = 9×10^4 kNm^2)

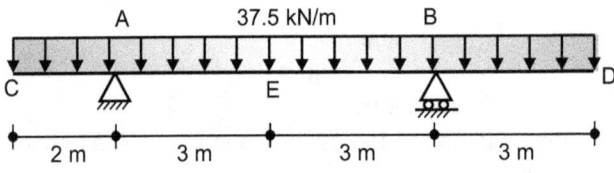

Fig. 7

   (a) 0.21°   (b) 0.06°   (c) 0.26°   (d) 0.16°

35. The beam is supported and loaded as shown in Fig. 8. The deflection at C is
    (Take EI = 9×10^4 kNm^2)

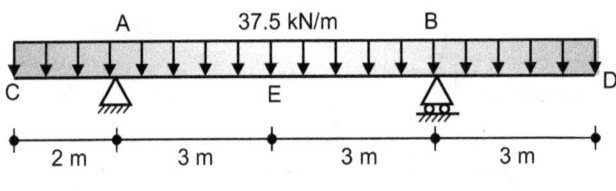

Fig. 8

   (a) 0.42 mm   (b) 0.12 mm   (c) 0.24 mm   (d) 0.30 mm

36. The beam is supported and loaded as shown in Fig. 9. The deflection at D is
    (Take E = 2×10^5 Mpa, I = 4.5×10^8 mm^4)

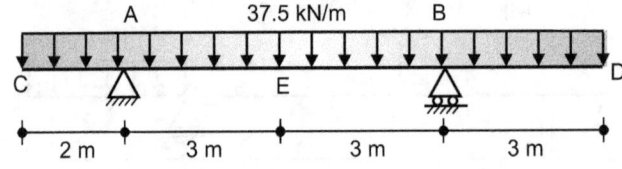

Fig. 9

   (a) 1.22 mm   (b) 4.65 mm   (c) 6.71 mm   (d) 3.21 mm

37. The beam is supported and loaded as shown in Fig. 10. The deflection at C is

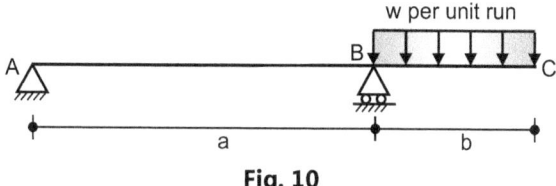
Fig. 10

(a) $\dfrac{Wb^3(4a+3b)}{24\,EI}$ (b) $\dfrac{Wa^2b(4a+3b)}{24\,EI}$

(c) $\dfrac{Wab^2(4a+3b)}{24\,EI}$ (d) $\dfrac{Wab(4a+3b)}{24\,EI}$

38. The beam is supported and loaded as shown in Fig. 11. The deflection at C is

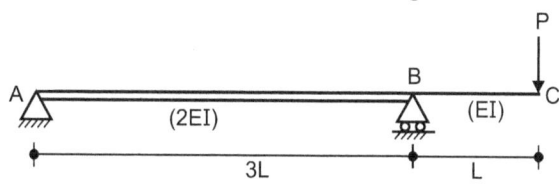
Fig. 11

(a) $\dfrac{3Pl^3}{48\,EI}$ (b) $\dfrac{Pl^3}{48\,EI}$ (c) $\dfrac{5Pl^3}{32\,EI}$ (d) $\dfrac{5Pl^3}{16\,EI}$

39. A 2 m long cantilever made of steel tube 150 mm external diameter and 10 mm thickness is loaded as shown in Fig. 12. The maximum deflection is
(Take E = 2006 GPa)

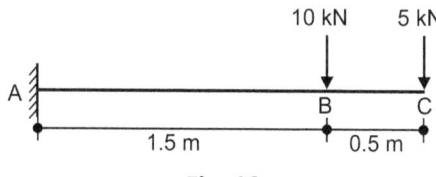
Fig. 12

(a) 11 mm (b) 14 mm (c) 3 mm (d) 0.2 mm

40. A 2 m long cantilever is of rectangular section 100 mm wide and 200 mm deep, EI of section is 10 GPa. The deflection at free end is

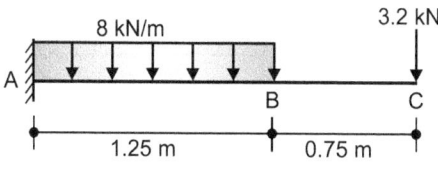
Fig. 13

(a) 19.4 mm (b) 22.3 mm (c) 2.87 mm (d) 8.79 mm

41. A cantilever beam is loaded as shown in Fig. 14. The deflection at free end is

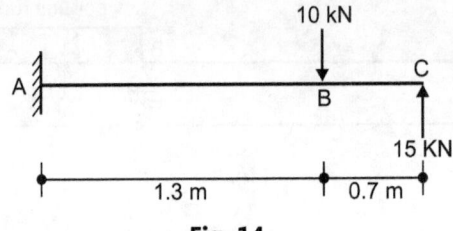

Fig. 14.

(a) 31.9 mm (b) 10.6 mm (c) 26.8 mm (d) 14.0 mm

42. The beam is supported and loaded as shown in Fig. 15. The deflection under 75 kN is (Take E = 200 Gpa, I = 70 × 10^8 mm^4)

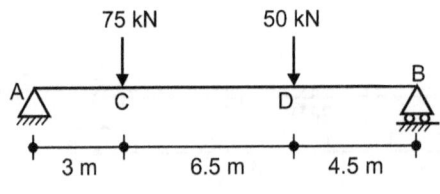

Fig. 15

(a) 2.34 mm (b) 1.34 mm (c) 1.84 mm (d) 0.68 mm

43. The beam is supported and loaded as shown in Fig. 16. The deflection under 50 kN is (Take EI = 14 × 10^5 kNm^2)

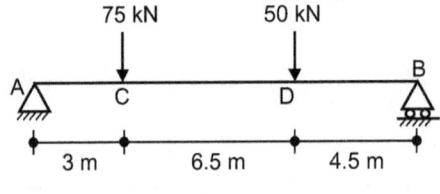

Fig. 16

(a) 0.5 mm (b) 1.5 mm (c) 2.0 mm (d) 3.0 mm

44. The beam is loaded and supported as shown in Fig. 17. Maximum deflection occurs at 6.9 m from A. The value of maximum deflection is

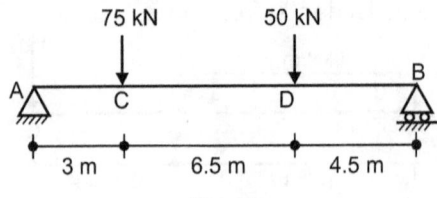

Fig. 17

(a) 6.9 mm (b) 2.6 mm (c) 5.3 mm (d) 3.8 mm

45. The beam is loaded and supported as shown in Fig. 18. The maximum deflection occurs at .... from A.

 (Take EI = 8000 kNm^2)

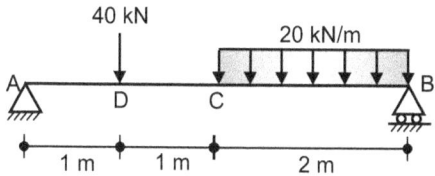

Fig. 18

(a) 1.2 m (b) 2.0 m (c) 3.5 m (d) 2.8 m

46. The cantilever beam is supported and loaded as shown in Fig. 19. The deflection at B is (Take EI = 12 × 10^4 kNm^2)

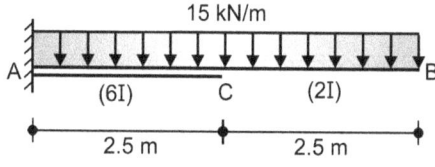

Fig. 19

(a) 3.47 mm (b) 1.47 mm (c) 4.47 mm (d) 2.47 mm

47. The cantilever beam is supported and loaded as shown in Fig. 20. The deflection at C is (Take EI = 12 × 10^4 kNm^2)

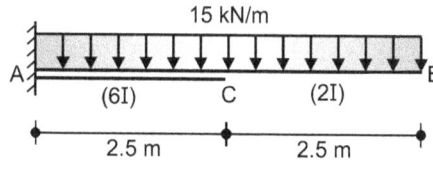

Fig. 20

(a) 4.44 mm (b) 3.44 mm (c) 2.44 mm (d) 1.44 mm

48. The cantilever beam is supported and loaded as shown in Fig. 21. The slope at B is (Take EI = 10 × 10^4 kNm^2)

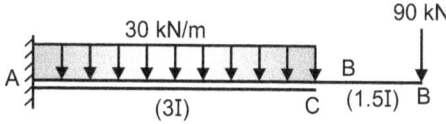

Fig. 21

(a) 0.4° (b) 0.2° (c) 0.1° (d) 0.6°

49. The cantilever beam is supported and loaded as shown in Fig. 22. The slope at C is (Take EI = 10×10^4 kNm^2)

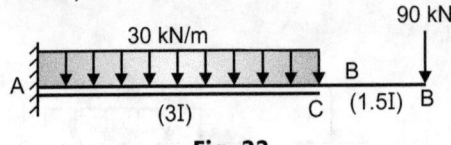

Fig. 22

(a) 0.24° (b) 0.34° (c) 0.14° (d) 0.29°

50. The cantilever beam is supported and loaded as shown in Fig. 23. The deflection at B is (Take EI = 10×10^4 kNm^2)

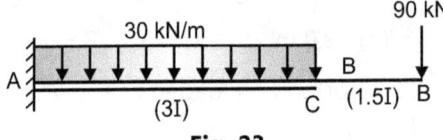

Fig. 23

(a) 15.67 mm (b) 11.22 mm (c) 27.73 mm (d) 16.33 mm

51. The cantilever beam is supported and loaded as shown in Fig. 24. The deflection at C is (Take EI = 10×10^4 kNm^2)

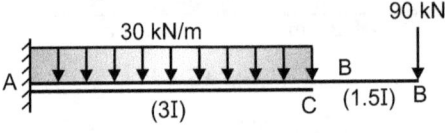

Fig. 24

(a) 1.45 mm (b) 3.25 mm (c) 5.5 mm (d) 14.4 mm

52. The cantilever beam is supported and loaded as shown in Fig. 25. The deflection at B is (Take EI = 10×10^4 kNm^2)

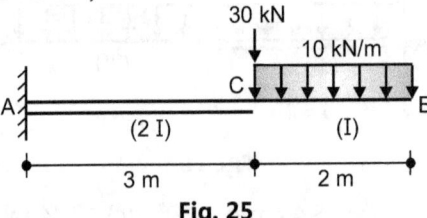

Fig. 25

(a) 5 mm (b) 4.15 mm (c) 5.75 mm (d) 3.25 mm

53. The cantilever beam is supported and loaded as shown in Fig. 26. The deflection at C is (Take EI = 10×10^4 kNm^2)

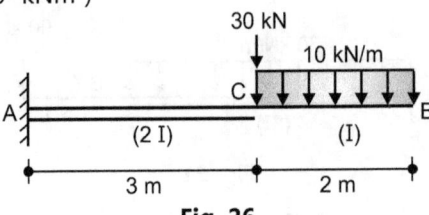

Fig. 26

(a) 1.2 mm (b) 2.14 mm (c) 3.24 mm (d) 2.7 mm

54. The cantilever beam is supported and loaded as shown in Fig. 27. The slope at B is (Take EI = 12 × 10⁴ kNm²)

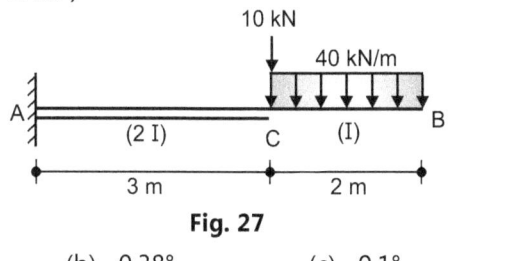

Fig. 27

(a) 0.18° (b) 0.38° (c) 0.1° (d) 0.24°

55. The cantilever beam is supported and loaded as shown in Fig. 28. The slope at C is (Take EI = 12 × 10⁴ kNm²)

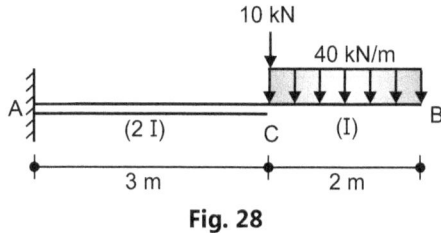

Fig. 28

(a) 0.05° (b) 0.15° (c) 0.45° (d) 0.3°

56. The cantilever beam is supported and loaded as shown in Fig. 29. The deflection at B is (Take EI = 12 × 10⁴ kNm²)

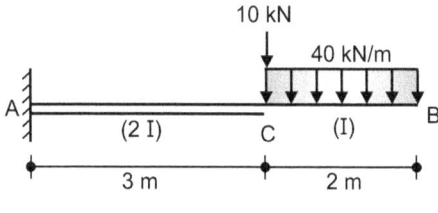

Fig. 29

(a) 2.4 mm (b) 4.9 mm (c) 10.9 mm (d) 15.3 mm

57. The cantilever beam is supported and loaded as shown in Fig. 30. The deflection at C is (Take EI = 12 × 10⁴ kNm²)

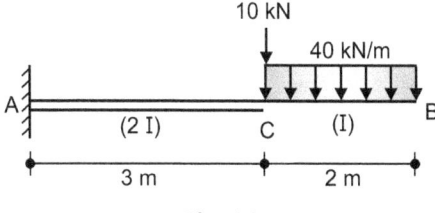

Fig. 30

(a) 6.88 mm (b) 1.88 mm (c) 2.88 mm (d) 4.88 mm

58. The cantilever beam is supported and loaded as shown in Fig. 31. The slope at B is (Take EI = 12×10^4 kNm²)

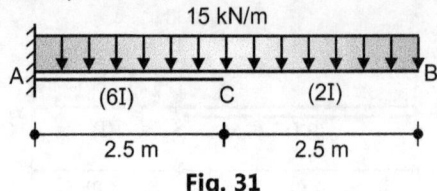

Fig. 31

(a) 0.065° (b) 0.65° (c) 0.25° (d) 0.015°

59. The cantilever beam is supported and loaded as shown in Fig. 32. The slope at C is (Take EI = 12×10^4 kNm²)

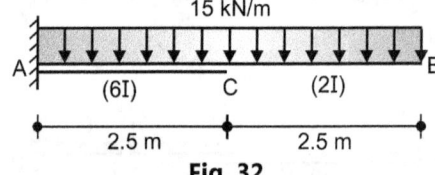

Fig. 32

(a) 0.06° (b) 0.045° (c) 0.015° (d) 0.03°

60. The cantilever beam is supported and loaded as shown in Fig. 33. The deflection at C is (Take EI = 8×10^4 kNm²)

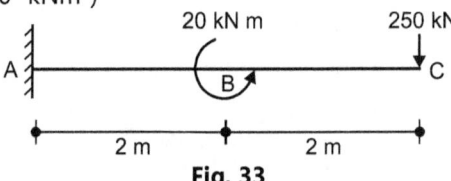

Fig. 33

(a) 8.33 mm (b) 4.33 mm (c) 1.33 mm (d) 6.33 mm

61. The cantilever beam is supported and loaded as shown in Fig. 34. The deflection at free end is

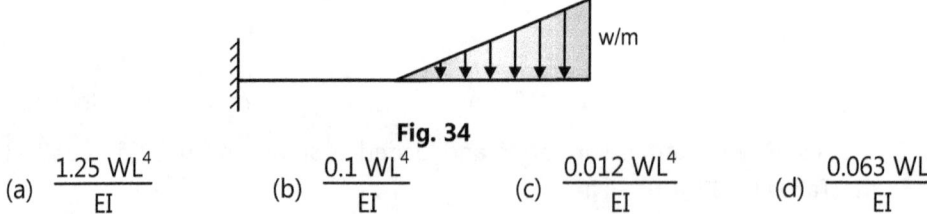

Fig. 34

(a) $\dfrac{1.25\, WL^4}{EI}$ (b) $\dfrac{0.1\, WL^4}{EI}$ (c) $\dfrac{0.012\, WL^4}{EI}$ (d) $\dfrac{0.063\, WL^4}{EI}$

62. The cantilever beam is supported and loaded as shown in Fig. 35. The deflection at C (Take EI = 17×10^3 kN m²)

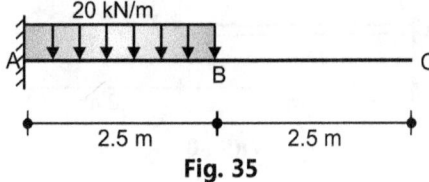

Fig. 35

(a) 11.12 mm (b) 13.40 mm (c) 21.42 mm (d) 16.45 mm

63. The cantilever beam is supported and loaded as shown in Fig. 36. The slope at C is

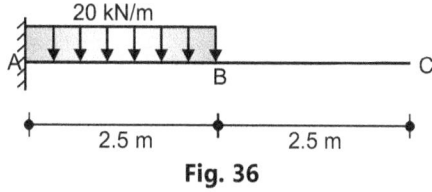

Fig. 36

(a) 0.18°   (b) 0.1°   (c) 0.15°   (d) 0.25°

64. The cantilever beam is supported and loaded as shown in Fig. 37. The slope at C is (Take EI = 5×10^4 kNm^2)

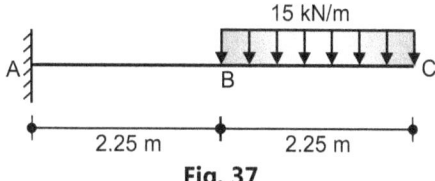

Fig. 37

(a) 0.18°   (b) 0.23°   (c) 0.11°   (d) 0.15°

65. The cantilever beam is supported and loaded as shown in Fig. 38. The deflection at C is (Take EI = 5×10^4 kNm^2)

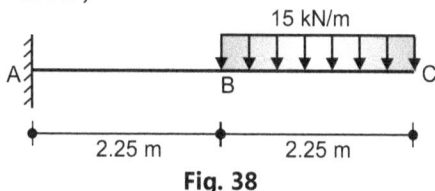

Fig. 38

(a) 9.90 mm   (b) 10.10 mm   (c) 11.11 mm   (d) 13.13 mm

66. The cantilever beam is supported and loaded as shown in Fig. 39. The deflection at D is (Take E = 70000 Mpa, $I_1 = 2 \times 10^6$ mm^4, $I_2 = 0.4 \times 10^6$ mm^4)

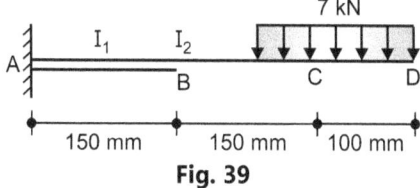

Fig. 39

(a) 0.06°   (b) 0.20°   (c) 0.16°   (d) 0.36°

67. The cantilever beam is supported and loaded as shown in Fig. 40. The slope at D is (Take E = 70000 Mpa, $I_1 = 2 \times 10^6$ mm^4, $I_2 = 0.4 \times 10^6$ mm^4)

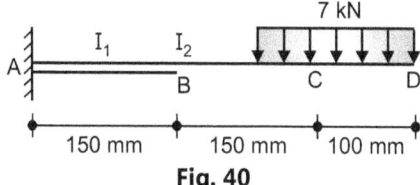

Fig. 40

(a) 0.56 mm   (b) 0.36 mm   (c) 0.82 mm   (d) 1.12 mm

68. The cantilever beam is supported and loaded as shown in Fig. 41. The slope at B is (Take EI = 10×10^4 kNm²)

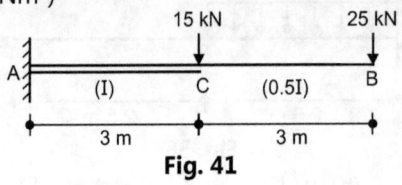

Fig. 41

(a) 0.36°   (b) 0.12°   (c) 0.42°   (d) 0.22°

69. The cantilever beam is supported and loaded as shown in Fig. 42. The slope at C is (Take EI = 10×10^4 kNm²)

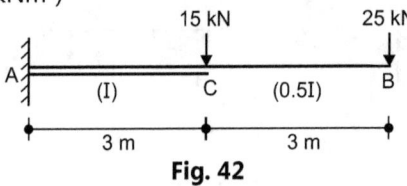

Fig. 42

(a) 0.03°   (b) 0.23°   (c) 0.13°   (d) 0.33°

70. The cantilever beam is supported and loaded as shown in Fig. 43. The deflection at yB is (Take EI = 10×10^4 kNm²)

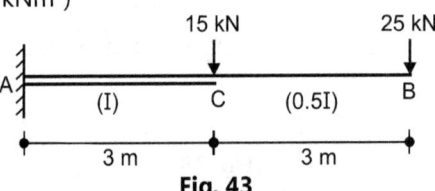

Fig. 43

(a) 15.35 mm   (b) 11.16 mm   (c) 23.63 mm   (d) 9.67 mm

71. The cantilever beam is supported and loaded as shown in Fig. 44. The deflection at C is (Take EI = 10×10^4 kNm²)

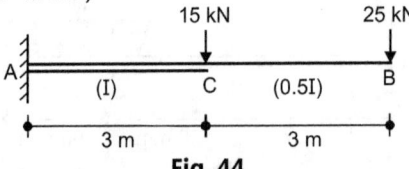

Fig. 44

(a) 5 mm   (b) 2 mm   (c) 4 mm   (d) 7 mm

72. The cantilever beam is supported and loaded as shown in Fig. 45. The slope at B is (Take EI = 10×10^4 kNm²)

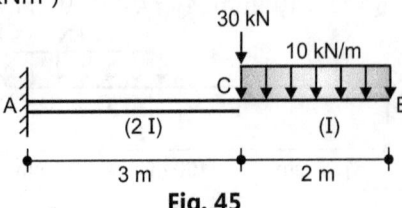

Fig. 45

(a) 0.09°   (b) 0.19°   (c) 0.29°   (d) 0.14°

73. The cantilever beam is supported and loaded as shown in Fig. 46. The slope at C is (Take EI = 10×10^4 kNm²)

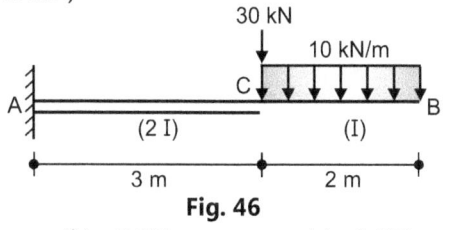

Fig. 46

(a) 0.18° (b) 0.08° (c) 0.13° (d) 0.21°

74. The beam is supported and loaded as shown in Fig. 47. The deflection at C is (Take EI = 3×10^{10} kN mm²)

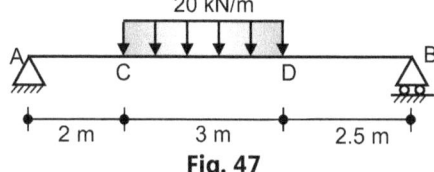

Fig. 47

(a) 12.09 mm (b) 11.13 mm (c) 9.63 mm (d) 4.65 mm

75. The beam is supported and loaded as shown in Fig. 48. The deflection at D is (Take EI = 3×10^{10} kN mm²)

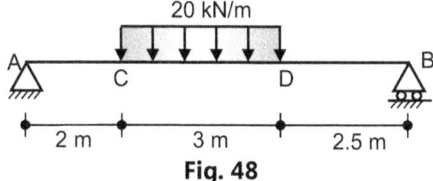

Fig. 48

(a) 19.62 mm (b) 13.81 mm (c) 9.61 mm (d) 4.58 mm

76. The beam is supported and loaded as shown in Fig. 49. The slope at C is (Take EI = 4×10^3 kNm²)

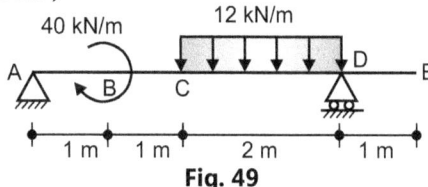

Fig. 49

(a) 0.0017° (b) 0.017° (c) 0.047° (d) 0.0047°

77. The beam is supported and loaded as shown in Fig. 50. The slope at E is (Take EI = 4×10^3 kNm²)

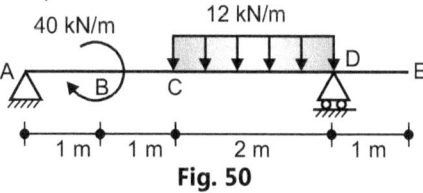

Fig. 50

(a) 0.47° (b) 0.57° (c) 0.27° (d) 0.37°

78. The beam supported and loaded as shown in Fig. 51. The deflection at C is
    (Take EI = 4×10^3 kNm^2)

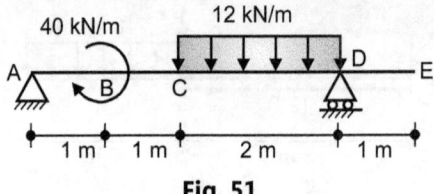

Fig. 51

(a) 12.5 mm (b) 14 mm (c) 16.5 mm (d) 18 mm

79. The beam supported and loaded as shown in Fig. 52. The deflection at E is
    (Take EI = 4×10^3 kNm^2)

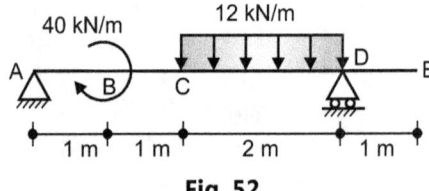

Fig. 52

(a) 8.12 mm (b) 6.72 mm (c) 3.52 mm (d) 9.92 mm

80. The beam supported and loaded as shown in Fig. 53. The deflection at C is
    (Take EI = 2700 kNm^2)

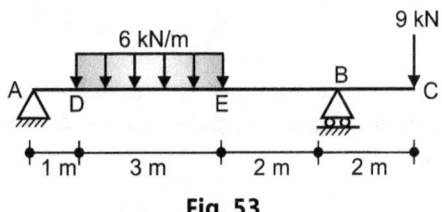

Fig. 53

(a) 2 mm (b) 10 mm (c) 8 mm (d) 7 mm

81. The beam is supported and loaded as shown in Fig. 54. The deflection under the load is
    (Take E = 200 GPa and I = 50×10^6 mm^4)

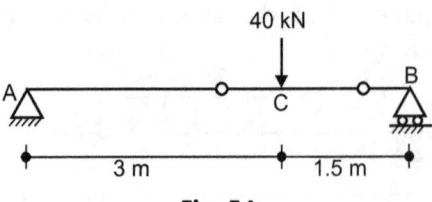

Fig. 54

(a) 6 mm (b) 12 mm (c) 3 mm (d) 4 mm

82. The beam is supported and loaded as shown in Fig. 55. The position of maximum deflection is at .... from A. (Take E = 200 GPa, I = 50 × 10⁶ mm⁴)

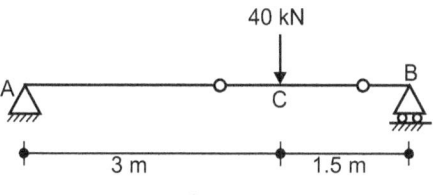

Fig. 55

(a) 3.2 m (b) 2.96 m (c) 2.45 m (d) 4.2 m

83. The beam is supported and loaded as shown in Fig. 56. The deflection under 15 kN is ....

(Take EI = 1.39 × 10¹¹ kN mm²)

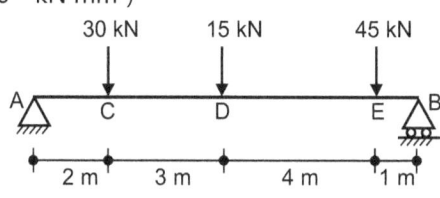

Fig. 56

(a) 9.6 mm (b) 6.8 mm (c) 7.8 mm (d) 3.4 mm

84. The beam is supported and loaded as shown in Fig. 57. The deflection at C is

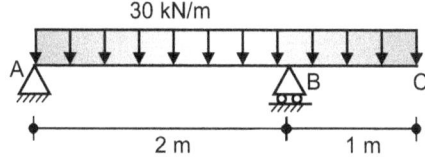

Fig. 57

(a) $\dfrac{1.75}{EI}$ (b) $\dfrac{3.2}{EI}$ (c) $\dfrac{1.25}{EI}$ (d) $\dfrac{3.75}{EI}$

85. The beam is supported and loaded as shown in Fig. 58. The deflection at C is (Take EI = 8000 kNm²)

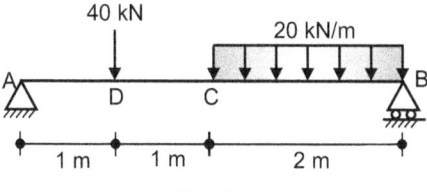

Fig. 58

(a) 8.75 mm (b) 2.75 mm (c) 4.85 mm (d) 6.25 mm

86. The beam is supported and loaded as shown in Fig. 59. The slope at end A is (Take EI = 8000 kNm²)

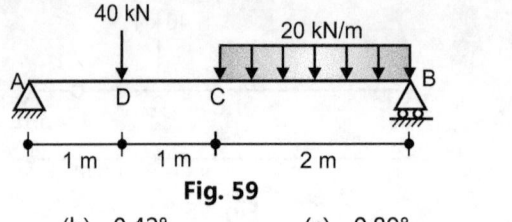
Fig. 59

(a) 0.12° (b) 0.42° (c) 0.89° (d) 1.2°

87. The beam is supported and loaded as shown in Fig. 60. The deflection at C is

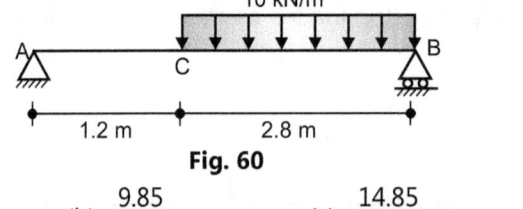
Fig. 60

(a) $\dfrac{20.85}{EI}$ (b) $\dfrac{9.85}{EI}$ (c) $\dfrac{14.85}{EI}$ (d) $\dfrac{18.75}{EI}$

88. The beam is supported and loaded as shown in Fig. 61. The slope at C is

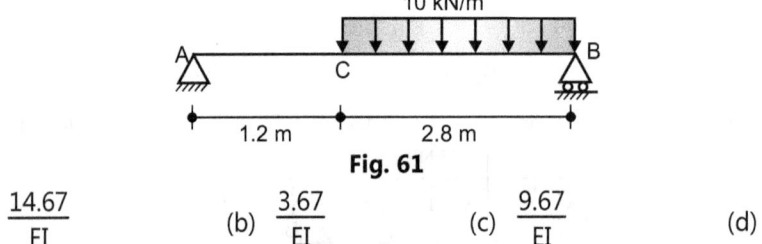
Fig. 61

(a) $\dfrac{14.67}{EI}$ (b) $\dfrac{3.67}{EI}$ (c) $\dfrac{9.67}{EI}$ (d) $\dfrac{12.67}{EI}$

ANSWERS

1. (a)	2. (d)	3. (b)	4. (c)	5. (d)	6. (c)	7. (d)	8. (a)
9. (a)	10. (c)	11. (a)	12. (d)	13. (d)	14. (d)	15. (b)	16. (b)
17. (a)	18. (c)	19. (c)	20. (a)	21. (b)	22. (c)	23. (c)	24. (c)
25. (a)	26. (a)	27. (b)	28. (b)	29. (d)	30. (c)	31. (a)	32. (a)
33. (b)	34. (d)	35. (a)	36. (c)	37. (a)	48. (d)	39. (b)	40. (a)
41. (c)	42. (a)	43. (d)	44. (a)	45. (b)	46. (c)	37. (d)	48. (a)
49. (b)	50. (c)	51. (d)	52. (c)	53. (d)	54. (a)	55. (b)	56. (c)
57. (d)	58. (a)	59. (b)	60. (a)	61. (d)	62. (b)	63. (a)	64. (b)
65. (d)	66. (b)	67. (d)	68. (a)	69. (b)	70. (c)	71. (d)	72. (a)
73. (b)	74. (a)	75. (b)	76. (d)	77. (b)	78. (a)	79. (d)	80. (b)
81. (a)	82. (c)	83. (b)	84. (d)	85. (a)	86. (b)	87. (a)	88. (d)

UNIT II

Chapter 4

INDETERMINATE BEAMS

4.1 PRINCIPLE OF SUPERPOSITION

This principle states that, for a linear elastic system in which changes in geometry are small, the effect m due to a cause M can be added to the effect n due to a cause N, provided that the effect varies linearly as the cause. Thus, the result will be same as the effect (m + n) due to a cause (M + N).

The effect may be shear force, bending moment or deflection at a section. The principle of superposition can sometimes be used to good effect when shear force and bending moment diagrams are required. In every case it would be perfectly possible to draw individual bending moment diagrams for each load applied separately to a beam, and then finally sum up the respective ordinates of the diagrams to get the total effect when all the loads are applied simultaneously.

For example, consider a simply supported beam loaded as shown in Fig. 4.1.

To calculate the reactions at the supports, we can calculate the support reactions due to individual loads and then add up the individual reactions to obtain the final support reaction. To draw the shear force diagram, the diagrams for individual loads are first drawn and the respective ordinates of these individual shear force diagrams are added algebraically to get the ordinates of final shear force diagram. On the similar lines the bending moment diagram for simple loading cases can be obtained by using the principle of superposition.

It is to be noted that, the principle of superposition is not applicable for calculating the total strain energy, since the cause and effect relationship is not linear. In this case, the cause may be axial force P or bending moment M etc. and the effect under consideration is the total strain energy U, stored in a member. We have for axially loaded member,

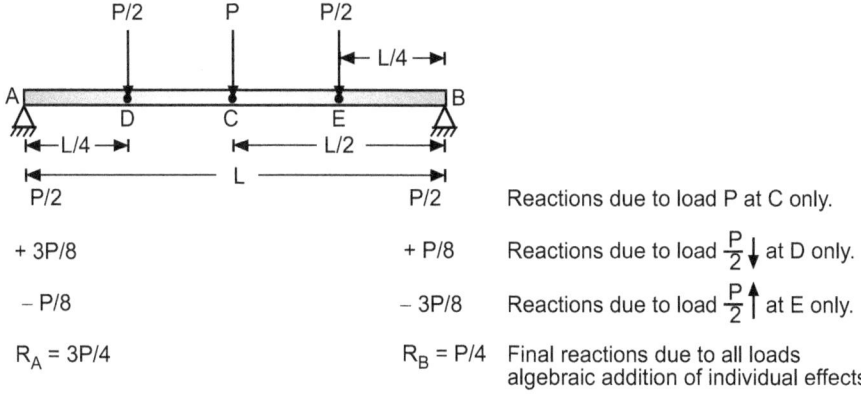

P/2	P/2	Reactions due to load P at C only.
+ 3P/8	+ P/8	Reactions due to load $\frac{P}{2}\downarrow$ at D only.
− P/8	− 3P/8	Reactions due to load $\frac{P}{2}\uparrow$ at E only.
R_A = 3P/4	R_B = P/4	Final reactions due to all loads algebraic addition of individual effects.

(4.1)

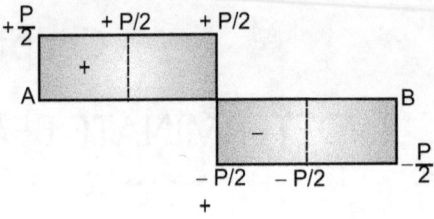
(a) S.F.D. due to load P ↓ at C only.

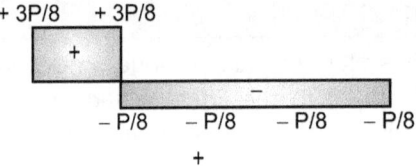
(b) S.F.D. due to load P/2 ↓ at D only

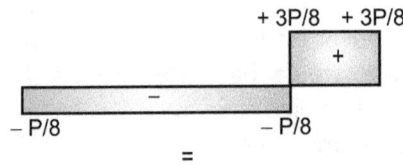
(c) S.F.D. due to load P/2 ↑ at E only

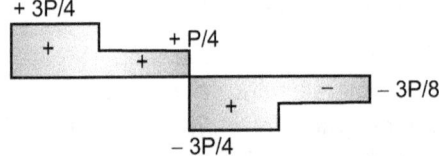
(d) Final S.F.D. obtained by adding the individual effects.

Fig. 4.1

$$U = \frac{P^2 l}{2AE} \text{ for gradually applied load}$$

Consider a member of uniform section with area A and length l subjected to gradually applied load 2P. Let the corresponding deformation be $2\delta l$.

The strain energy stored, U = External work done

$$= \frac{0 + 2P}{2} \times 2\delta l$$

∴ $\quad U = 2P\,\delta l$

Now first apply load P only. The corresponding deformation will be $\frac{1}{2} \times 2\delta l = \delta l$.

∴ Strain energy stored due to load P only will be,

$$U_1 = \text{External work done} = \frac{1}{2} P \delta l$$

The another load P acting separately will also give the same strain energy stored.

Thus, $\quad U_2 = U_1 = \frac{1}{2} P \delta l$

Now according to principle of superposition, the total strain energy stored,

$$U = U_1 + U_2$$
$$= \frac{1}{2}P\delta l + \frac{1}{2}P\delta l$$
$$= P\delta l$$

which is not the same as that obtained when both loads (i.e. P + P = 2P) acting at a time.

4.2 CLERK-MAXWELL'S THEOREM OF RECIPROCAL DEFLECTION

The theorem states that for a linear elastic system, the displacement at point i due to unit load applied at point j is equal to the displacement at point j due to unit load applied at point i. It is to be noted that when the displacement is measured as i, it is in the same direction as the unit load applied at i.

Let us consider a simply supported beam AB. Let W be the gradually applied unit vertical load acting at point j and the corresponding *vertical* deflections at points i and j be δ_i and δ_j respectively.

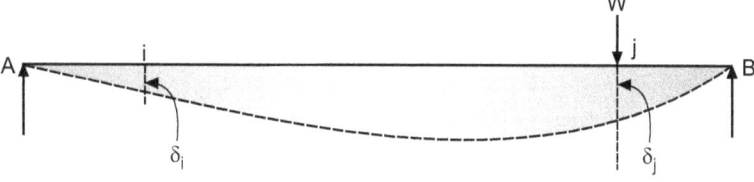

Fig. 4.2

The work done by W at this stage = $\frac{1}{2} W \delta_j$

While this load W acting at j, let us apply another load of same magnitude W at i. Let the deflections at i and j due to load W acting at i only be defined as Δ_i and Δ_j respectively as shown in Fig. 4.3.

Now, consider the work done by load W at i with load W originally acting at j as stage second = $\frac{1}{2} W \Delta_i + W \Delta_j$.

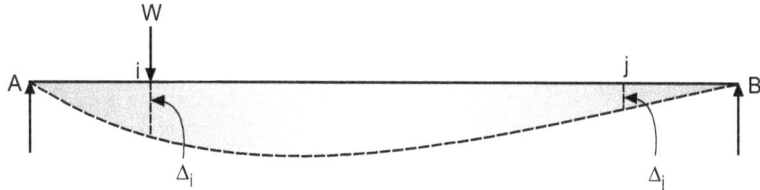

Fig. 4.3

Thus, the total work done = Stage one + Stage two

$$= \frac{1}{2} W \delta j + \frac{1}{2} W \Delta_i W \Delta_j \qquad \ldots (4.1)$$

Now, let us reverse the order in which the loads W are applied. Thus, stage one will be the load W acting at i first.

At stage one the work done on beam = $\frac{1}{2} W \Delta_i$.

Now stage two will be additional load W acting at j.

At this stage two work done = $\frac{1}{2} W \delta_j + W \delta_i$.

∴ The total work done = $\frac{1}{2} W \Delta_i + \frac{1}{2} W \delta_j + W \delta_i$ ... (4.2)

Since, the total work done is independent of the order in which the loads are applied, equations (4.1) and (4.2) are the same.

∴ $\frac{1}{2} W \delta_j + \frac{1}{2} W \Delta_i + W \Delta_j = \frac{1}{2} W \Delta_i + \frac{1}{2} W \delta_j + W \delta_i$

∴ $W \Delta_j = W \delta_i$

∴ $\Delta_j = \delta_i$ ... (4.3)

Thus, vertical deflection at j due to vertical load W at i is equal to vertical deflection at i due to the same vertical load W at j.

Alternatively the proof of Clerk-Maxwell's reciprocal theorem of deflections can be given by considering a cantilever beam of span l, subjected to a load W acting at free end.

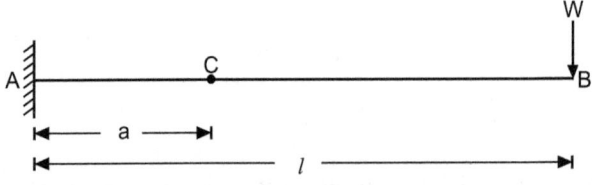

Fig. 4.4

The vertical deflection at a distance 'a' from A i.e. at point C, can be found from usual double integration method as follows :

With origin at A, $M_x = -Wl + Wx$

$= -W(l-x)$

∴ $EI \dfrac{d^2y}{dx^2} = -M_x = +W(l-x)$

Integrating with respect to x,

$EI \dfrac{dy}{dx} = +W\left(lx - \dfrac{x^2}{2}\right) + C_1$

For x = 0, we have $\dfrac{dy}{dx} = 0$ ∴ $C_1 = 0$

∴ $EI \dfrac{dy}{dx} = +W\left(lx - \dfrac{x^2}{2}\right)$ ... Slope equation

Integrating with respect to x,

$$EI\,y = +W\left(l\frac{x^2}{2} - \frac{x^3}{6}\right) + C_2$$

For x = 0, we have y = 0 ∴ $C_2 = 0$

∴ $$EI\,y = W\left(l\frac{x^2}{2} - \frac{x^3}{6}\right) \qquad \text{... Deflection equation}$$

∴ Deflection at C for x = a is

$$y_C = \frac{W}{EI}\left(l\cdot\frac{a^2}{2} - \frac{a^3}{6}\right)$$

$$= \frac{Wa^2}{2\,EI}\left(l - \frac{a}{3}\right) \qquad \text{... (4.4)}$$

Now with the same vertical load W acting at C, vertical deflection at free end B can be found using standard results as follows :

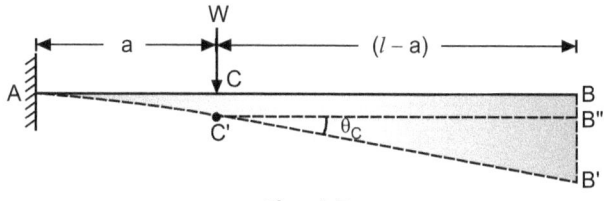

Fig. 4.5

$$y_B = CC' + B''B'$$

$$= \frac{Wa^3}{3\,EI} + \theta_C\,(l-a) = \frac{Wa^3}{3\,EI} + \frac{Wa^2}{2\,EI}(l-a)$$

$$y_B = \frac{Wa^2}{2\,EI}\left(\frac{2}{3}a + l - a\right) = \frac{Wa^2}{2\,EI}\left(l - \frac{a}{3}\right) \qquad \text{... (4.5)}$$

From equations (4.4) and (4.5), $y_C = y_B$.

For simple structure subjected to only one force, the deflection of the loaded point can be found by directly equating the external work done by the force to the strain energy stored in the structure.

Consider the well known case of a cantilever beam of length 'l' subjected to concentrated load P at free end.

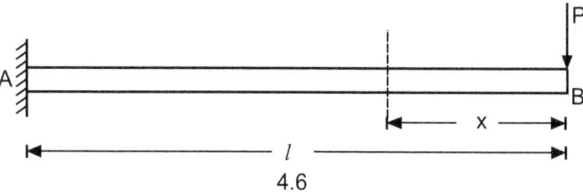

Fig. 4.6

For gradually applied load P, the external work done by the load $= \frac{1}{2} P y_B$, where y_B is vertical (i.e. in the direction of applied load) deflection at loaded point B.

Now, for two-dimensional structure like the beam in question, neglecting the strain energy due to shear, the total strain energy stored in the beam will be due to bending only.

$$U = \int_B^A \frac{M_x^2 \, dx}{2 EI}$$

$$= \int_0^l \frac{(-Px)^2 \, dx}{2 EI}$$

$$= \frac{P^2}{2 EI} \left[\frac{x^3}{3} \right]_0^l$$

$$= \frac{P^2 l^3}{6 EI}$$

Equating the external work done to the total strain energy,

$$\frac{1}{2} P y_B = \frac{P^2 l^3}{6 EI}$$

$$\therefore \quad y_B = \frac{P l^3}{3 EI}$$

4.3 MAXWELL-BETTE'S LAW

In a linearly elastic structure, the virtual work done by a system of forces w_1, w_2, w_3 ... during the distortion caused by a system of forces P_1, P_2, P_3, ... is equal to the virtual W.D. by a system of forces P_1, P_2, P_3 ... during the distortion caused by system of forces w_1, w_2, w_3, ...

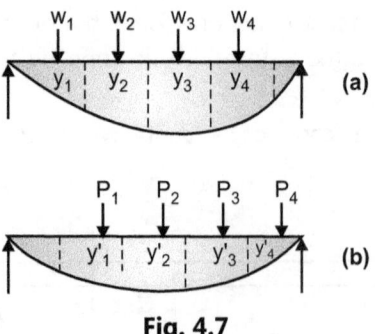

Fig. 4.7

∴ According to Bette's law,

$$w_1 y_1' + w_2 y_2' + w_3 y_3' + w_4 y_4' = P_1 y_1 + P_2 y_2 + P_3 y_3 + P_4 y_4$$

4.4 FIXED BEAMS

Fixed beam is a beam with ends as fixed ends. Fixed end is the end at which rotation is restrained. As rotation is restrained, some moment is developed at the ends.

4.5 EQUATIONS FOR FIXED END MOMENTS

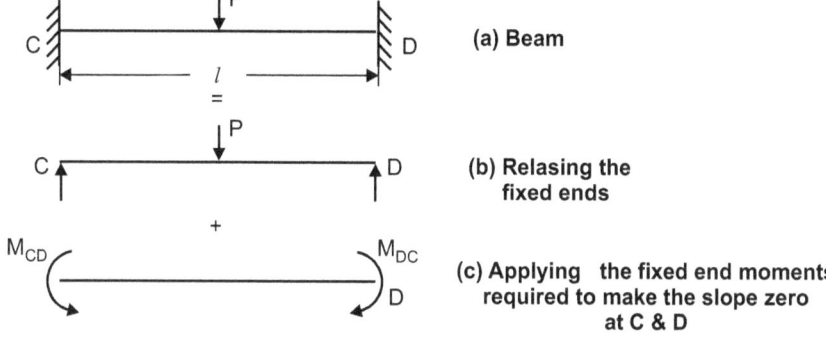

(a) Beam

(b) Relasing the fixed ends

(c) Applying the fixed end moments required to make the slope zero at C & D

Fig. 4.8

$$\therefore \quad EI\frac{d^2y}{dx^2} = \text{Beam moment} - \text{Fixed moment}$$

$$EI\frac{d^2y}{dx^2} = M_{x_1} - M_{x_2} \rightarrow \text{Moment equation}$$

Integrating the above equation from 0 to l,

$$EI\left[\frac{dy}{dx}\right]_0^l = \int_0^l M_{x_1}\,dx - \int_0^l M_{x_2}\,dx$$

At $x = 0$ and at $x = l$, $\frac{dy}{dx} = 0$.

$$\int_0^l M_{x_1}\,dx = \text{Area under the free B.M. diagram} = a_{fr}$$

$$\int_0^l M_{x_2}\,dx = \text{Area under the fixed B.M. diagram} = a_{fi}$$

$$\therefore \quad 0 = a_{fr} - a_{fi}$$
$$\therefore \quad a_{fr} = a_{fi} \qquad \ldots (4.6)$$

| Area of free B.M. diagram = Area of fixed B.M. diagram |

$$EI\frac{d^2y}{dx^2} = M_{x_1} - M_{x_2}$$

Multiplying by x,

$$EI\,x\frac{d^2y}{dx^2} = M_{x_1}x - M_{x_2}x$$

Integrating from 0 to l,

$$EI \int_0^l x \frac{d^2y}{dx^2} = \int_0^l M_{x_1} \cdot x \, dx - \int_0^l M_{x_2} \cdot x \, dx$$

$$EI \left[x \frac{dy}{dx} - y \right]_0^l = \int_0^l M_{x_1} \cdot x \, dx - \int_0^l M_{x_2} \cdot x \, dx$$

At $x = 0$, $\frac{dy}{dx} = 0$, $y = 0$.

At $x = l$, $\frac{dy}{dx} = 0$, $y = 0$

$$\int_0^l M_{x_1} \cdot x \, dx = a_{fr} \times x_{fr}$$

a_{fr} – Area of free B.M.D. and x_{fr} – C.G. of free B.M.D.

$$\int_0^l M_{x_2} \cdot x \, dx = a_{fi} \times x_{fi}$$

a_{fi} – Area of fixed B.M.D. and x_{fi} – C.G. of fixed BMD

∴ $\quad a_{fr} \times x_{fr} = a_{fi} \cdot x_{fi}$

But from equation (4.6), $\quad a_{fr} = a_{fi}$

∴ $\quad x_{fr} = x_{fi}$

∴ $\boxed{\text{C.G. of free B.M.D. = C.G. of fixed B.M.D.}}$

4.6 THE FIXED BEAMS HAVE SOME ADVANTAGES AS WELL AS SOME DISADVANTAGES OVER THE SIMPLY SUPPORTED BEAMS

4.6.1 Advantages

1. As the net B.M. at a section is the algebraic sum of free B.M. and fixed B.M., therefore the B.M. is reduced at the mid span as compared to the simply supported beams. Due to reduction of B.M., section reduces.
2. The deflection is less as compared to the simply supported beams, so this is more strong and stiff.

4.6.2 Disadvantages

1. It is very difficult to achieve full fixity to the supports and calculations are considering the full fixity.
2. Due to dynamic loading, the fixity may be disturbed and due to disturbance of fixity, moments are created on both the ends.
3. As no allowance for temperature changes due to fixity, temperature stresses are developed in the respective members.

4.7 THERE ARE DIFFERENT TYPES OF THE LOADING ON THE FIXED BEAMS SOME OF THE STANDARD CASES ARE NOTED BELOW

1. Fixed beams with central concentrated load.
2. Fixed beams with eccentric load.
3. Fixed beams with U.D.L. on total span.
4. Fixed beams with U.D.L. on some portion.
5. Fixed beams with U.V.L. on whole span.
6. Fixed beams with U.V.L. on some portion.
7. Fixed beams with eccentric couple.
8. Fixed beams with central couple.
9. Fixed beams with ends at the different levels.

4.8 STEPS TO BE FOLLOWED FOR ANALYSIS OF FIXED BEAMS

1. Find the reaction components by considering the given fixed beam as simply supported.

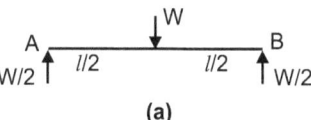

(a)

2. Draw the B.M. diagram for the simply supported beams. (i.e. free bending moment diagram).

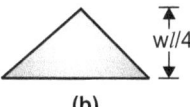

(b)

3. Assume the moments at fixed supports as M_A and M_B.

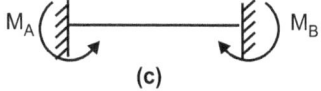

(c)

4. Draw B.M. diagram for fixed end moments M_A and M_B. [If the beam is loaded symmetrically then $M_A = M_B$. If loading on left side of mid-point is greater, then $M_A > M_B$ or if loading on right side of mid-point is greater than left side, then $M_B > M_A$.] B.M. diagrams for above cases are as shown in Fig. 4.9 (d), (e) and (f).

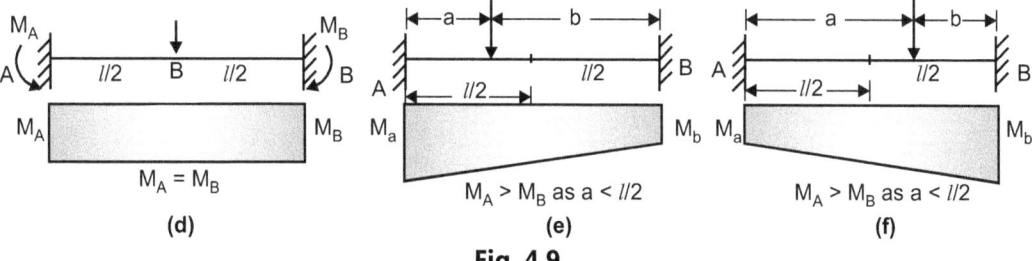

Fig. 4.9

5. Equate the areas of free B.M.D. and fixed B.M.D. We get one equation in terms of M_A and M_B.

6. Equate C.G. of free B.M.D. and fixed B.M.D. We get second equation in terms of M_A and M_B.
7. Solving these two equations, we can easily obtain the values of M_A and M_B.
8. Draw B.M.D. by superposition of the B.M.D. due to fixed end moments on free B.M.D.
9. Draw B.M.D. on tension side.

4.9 DIFFERENT CASES

Case I : Fixed beam carrying a point load at mid span :

Due to symmetry with the centre of the span, $M_A = M_B$.

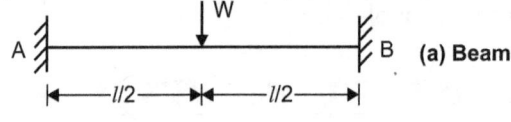

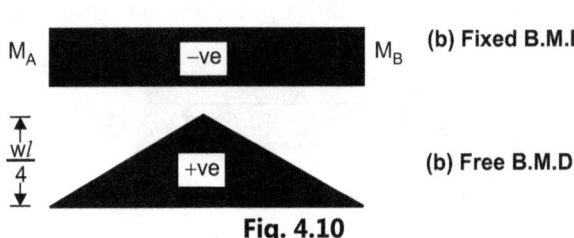

Fig. 4.10

Equating areas of free and fixed B.M. diagrams,

$$a = a'$$

$$\therefore \quad M_A \cdot l = M_B \cdot l = \frac{1}{2} \times \frac{Wl}{4} \times l$$

$$\therefore \quad M_A = M_B = \frac{Wl}{8} \text{ (hogging)}$$

To find deflection :

$$M_x = \text{Moment at any point x from A}$$

$$M_x = EI \frac{d^2y}{dx^2} = \frac{Wx}{2} - \frac{Wl}{8}$$

Integrating,

$$EI \frac{dy}{dx} = \frac{W}{2} \frac{x^2}{2} - \frac{Wl}{8} x + C_1 \qquad \ldots (4.7)$$

$$EI y = \frac{W}{2} \frac{x^3}{6} - \frac{Wl}{8} \frac{x^2}{2} + C_1 x + C_2 \qquad \ldots (4.8)$$

At $x = 0$, $\frac{dy}{dx} = 0$ $\quad \therefore C_1 = 0 \quad$ At $x = 0$, $\frac{dy}{dx} = 0$, $y = 0$ $\therefore C_2 = 0$

$$\therefore \quad EI y = \frac{W}{2} \frac{x^3}{6} - \frac{Wl}{16} x^2$$

Deflection is maximum at slope is zero $\therefore y = l/2$

$\therefore$ At $x = \frac{l}{2}$, $y = y_c \quad EI y_c = \frac{W}{12} \left(\frac{l}{2}\right)^3 - \frac{Wl}{16} \left(\frac{l}{2}\right)^2$

$$EI\, y_C = \frac{Wl^3}{96} - \frac{Wl^3}{64}$$

$$EI\, y_C = \frac{-Wl^3}{192}$$

$$y_C = -\frac{Wl^3}{192\, EI}$$

y_C for simply supported beams :

$$y_{CS} = -\frac{Wl^3}{48\, EI}$$

∴ Deflection for simply supported beams is four times that of fixed beams

Note : As fixed beams with central concentrated loads have both fixed end moments equal, so unknowns are two but value of both unknowns is same (i.e. fixed end moments). By using only first equation i.e. equating the areas of free B.M.D. and fixed B.M.D., we are easily getting the fixed end moments.

But in case of eccentric loading we have two unknowns, so both equations (i.e. equating areas of free and fixed B.M.D. and equating C.G. of both diagrams) are to be used.

SOLVED PROBLEMS

Problem 4.1 : A fixed beam of 2 m span is carrying a point load of 50 kN at its mid point. Find the fixed end moment and deflection of beam at its mid point.

$$EI = 1 \times 10^{14}\ N/mm^2$$

Solution : $M_A = +M_B$

(As beam is symmetrical with the centre)

Area of fixed B.M.D. = Area of free B.M.D.

(Area of rectangle $a_1\ a_2\ a_3\ a_4$) = (Area of Δ $a_1'\ a_2'\ a_3'$)

∴ $2M_A = +2M_B = +\dfrac{1}{2} \times 25 \times 2$

∴ $M_A = +M_B = +12.5$ (Hogging)

∴ $M_A = +12.5$ kN-m and $M_B = 12.5$ kN-m

$M_A = M_B = 12.5$ kN-m (Hogging)

$$\left(\text{By formula : } M_A = -M_B = -\frac{Wl}{8} = -\frac{50 \times 2}{8} = -12.5\ \text{kN-m} \right)$$

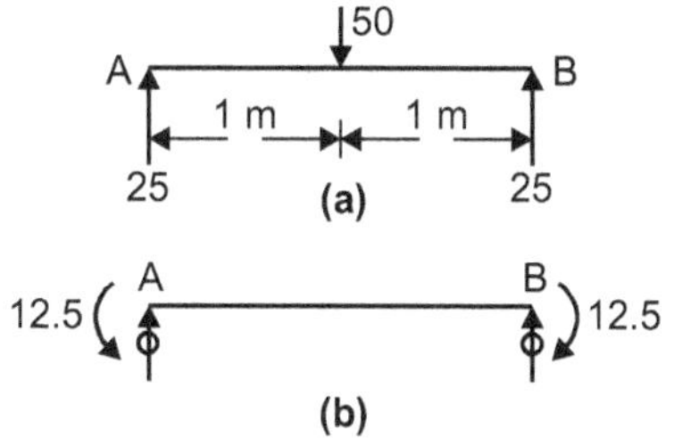

Fig. 4.11

Deflection : (Using Macaulay's Method)

$$EI \frac{d^2y}{dx^2} = 25x - 12.5$$

Integrating,

$$EI \frac{dy}{dx} = \frac{25x^2}{2} - 12.5x + C_1$$

At $x = 0$, $y = 0$ ∴ $C_1 = 0$

$$EI\, y = \frac{25x^3}{6} - \frac{12.5x^2}{2} + C_1 x + C_2$$

At $x = 0$, $y = 0$, ∴ $C_2 = 0$

∴ $$EI\, y = \frac{25x^3}{6} - \frac{12.5x^2}{2}$$

y_c = Maximum deflection is at the centre of span

∴ $x = 1$ m

∴ $$EI\, y_c = \frac{25 \times 1^3}{6} - \frac{12.5 \times 1^2}{2}$$

$EI\, y_c = -2.08$

$EI = 1 \times 10^{14}$ N/mm² $= 10^5$ kN-m²

∴ $y_c = -\dfrac{2.08}{10^5} = -0.000021$ m $= -0.0021$ cm

(– sign indicates that deflection is downward)

By formula, $y_c = -\dfrac{Wl^3}{192\, EI} = -\dfrac{50 \times 2^3}{192 \times 10^5} = -0.000021$ m = **0.0021 cm**

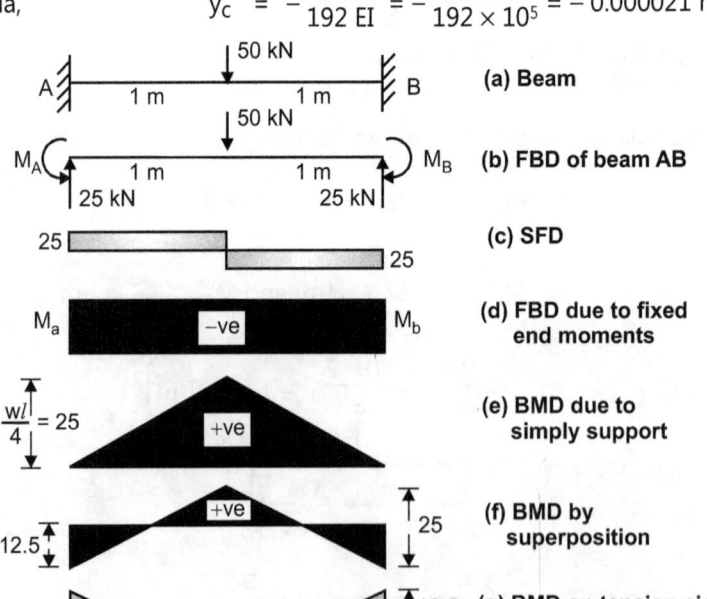

(a) Beam
(b) FBD of beam AB
(c) SFD
(d) FBD due to fixed end moments
(e) BMD due to simply support
(f) BMD by superposition
(g) BMD on tension side

Fig. 4.12

Problem 4.2 : A beam AB is loaded with a central load of 250 kN. Span of beam AB is 11 m. Find the fixed end moments, from first principles.

Solution : Equating areas of free and fixed B.M. diagrams,

$$a = a'$$

$$\therefore \quad M_a \times 11 = \frac{1}{2} \times 687.5 \times 11$$

$$\therefore \quad M_a = 343.75 \text{ kN-m} \quad \text{(hogging)}$$

$$M_b = 343.75 \text{ kN-m} \quad \text{(hogging)}$$

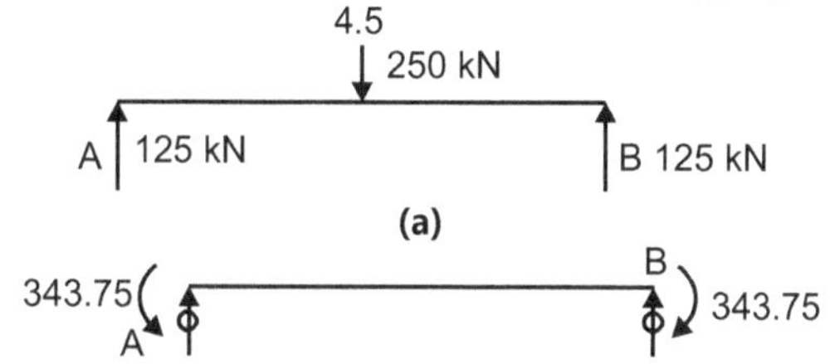

∴ Reaction at B = 125 + 0 = 125 kN
Reaction at C = 125 − 0 = 125 kN

Fig. 4.13

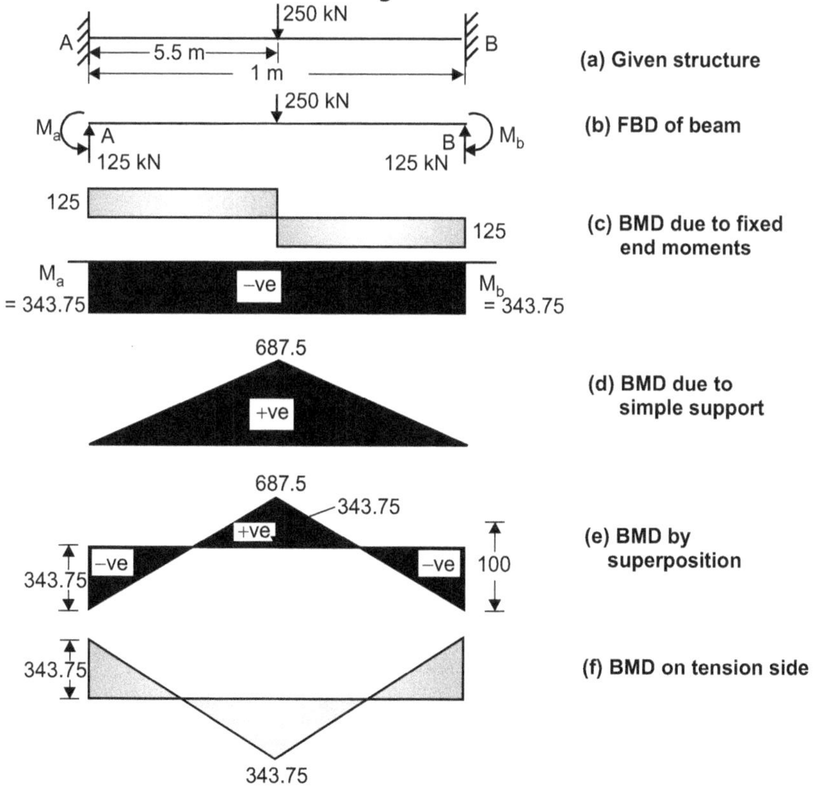

(a) Given structure
(b) FBD of beam
(c) BMD due to fixed end moments
(d) BMD due to simple support
(e) BMD by superposition
(f) BMD on tension side

Fig. 4.14

Case II : Fixed beam carrying a concentrated load eccentrically placed on the span :

Area of the F.E.M. diagram (A) = Area of free B.M. diagram.

$$\left(\frac{M_a + M_b}{2}\right)l = \frac{1}{2}\frac{Wab}{l} \times l$$

$$x = x' \qquad \text{from A.}$$

$$\frac{(M_a + 2M_b)}{(M_a + M_b)}\frac{l}{3} = \frac{(l+a)}{3}$$

$$(M_a + M_b) = \frac{Wab}{l} \qquad \qquad \text{... (1)}$$

$$\frac{l}{3}[(M_a + 2M_b)] = \frac{Wab}{l} \times \left(\frac{l+a}{3}\right) \qquad \text{... (2)}$$

Solving equations (1) and (2),

$$\frac{l}{3}[(M_a + M_b) + (M_b)] = \frac{Wab}{l} \times \left(\frac{l+a}{3}\right)$$

$$\frac{l}{3}(M_b) = \frac{Wab}{l}\left(\frac{l+a}{3}\right) - \frac{Wab}{l} \times \frac{l}{3}$$

$$M_b \cdot \frac{l}{3} = \frac{Wab}{3l}(l + a - l)$$

$$\therefore \qquad M_b = \frac{Wa^2b}{l^2} \qquad \text{(hogging)}$$

Putting in equation (1), $\quad M_a = \dfrac{Wab^2}{l^2} \qquad$ (hogging)

Reactions :– (a) Due to external loads

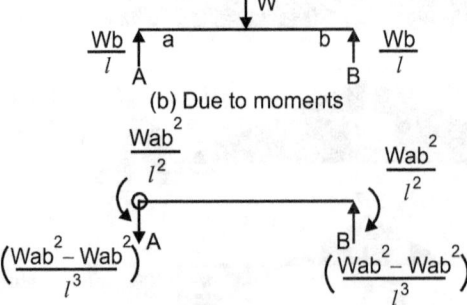

Fig. 4.15

$$\therefore \quad \text{Reaction at A} = \left[\left(\frac{Wb}{l}\right) - \left(\frac{Wa^2b - Wab^2}{l^3}\right)\right]$$

$$\text{Reaction at B} = \left[\frac{Wa}{l} + \left(\frac{Wa^2b - Wab^2}{l^3}\right)\right]$$

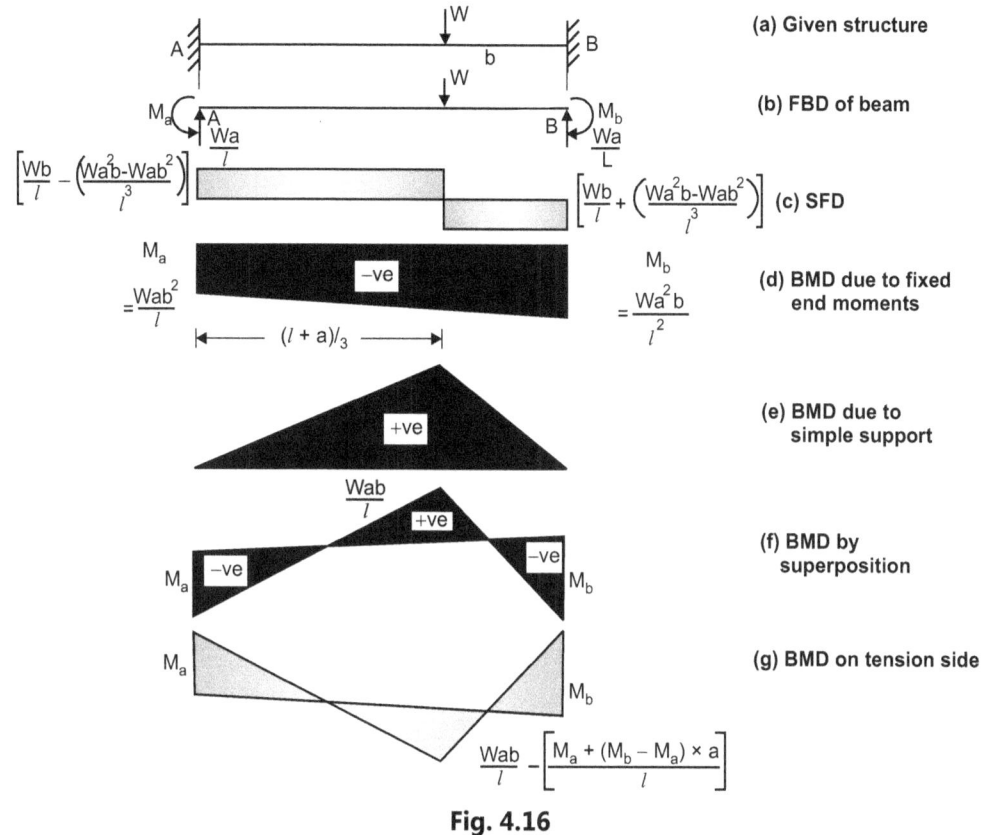

Fig. 4.16

Problem 4.3 : A fixed beam AB of span 6 m, carries a load of 90 kN from the support A at 2 m. Find the fixed end moments.

Solution : As beam is not symmetrically loaded, $M_A \neq M_B$

Equating the areas, $A = A'$

$$\left(\frac{M_A + M_B}{2}\right) l = \frac{1}{2} \frac{Wab}{l} \times l$$

$$\frac{6}{2}(M_A + M_B) = \frac{1}{2} \times 120 \times 6$$

$$(M_A + M_B) = 120$$

Equating C.G.S. of both areas,

$$x = x'$$

$$\therefore \quad \left(\frac{M_A + 2M_B}{M_A + M_B}\right) \frac{l}{3} = \left(\frac{l+a}{3}\right)$$

$$\left(\frac{M_A + 2M_B}{120}\right) \times \frac{6}{3} = \left(\frac{6+2}{3}\right)$$

$$M_A + 2M_B = 160$$

but $M_A + M_B = 120$

$\therefore$ $(M_A + M_B) + M_B = 160$

$\therefore$ $M_B = 40$ kN-m (↻) (hogging)

$M_A = 80$ kN-m (↺) (hogging)

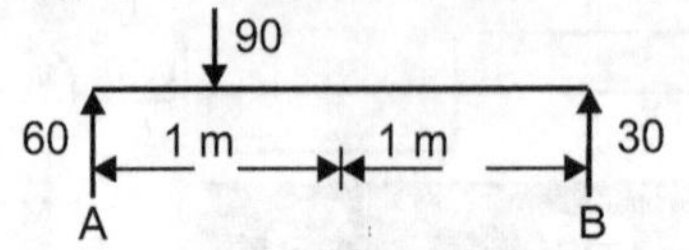
90
60
30
1 m
1 m
A
B

(a) Due to moment

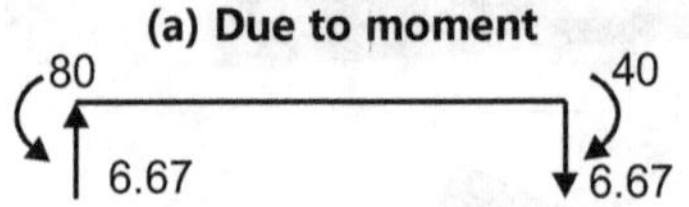
80
40
6.67
6.67

$\therefore$ Reaction at A = 60 + 6.67 = 66.67 kN

Reaction at B = 30 – 6.67 = 23.33 kN

Fig. 4.17

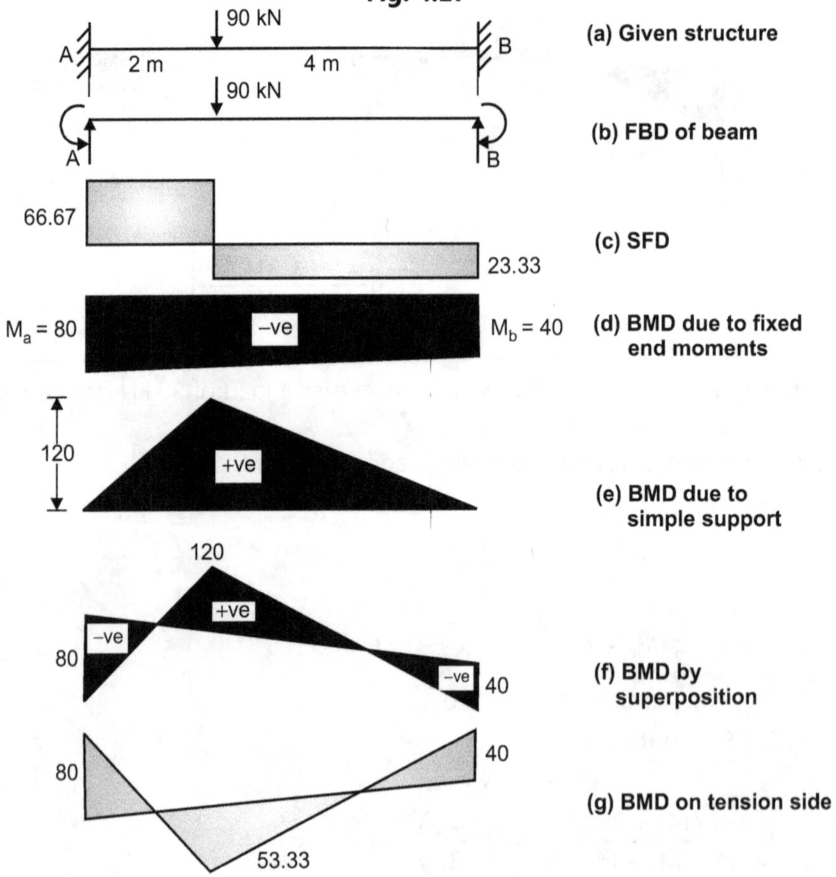
90 kN
A
B
2 m
4 m
(a) Given structure
90 kN
A
B
(b) FBD of beam
66.67
23.33
(c) SFD
M_a = 80
–ve
M_b = 40
(d) BMD due to fixed end moments
120
+ve
(e) BMD due to simple support
120
+ve
–ve
80
–ve
40
(f) BMD by superposition
80
40
53.33
(g) BMD on tension side

Fig. 4.18

By formula,

$$M_A = \frac{Wab^2}{l^2} = \frac{90 \times 2 \times 4^2}{6^2} = 80 \text{ kN-m (hogging)}$$

$$M_B = \frac{Wa^2b}{l^2} = 90 \times \frac{2 \times 2 \times 4}{36} = 40 \text{ kN-m} \quad \text{(hogging)}$$

Problem 4.4 : A built-up beam of span 6 m carries a concentrated load of 60 kN at 1.2 m and 120 kN at 4.5 m from A. Determine the fixed end moments.

Solution : Equating areas of free and fixed B.M.D.,

$$a = a'$$

$$\left(\frac{M_A + M_B}{2}\right) l = \text{Area of free B.M.D.}$$

$$\left(\frac{M_A + M_B}{2}\right) 6 = \frac{1}{2} \times 93.6 \times 1.2 + \left(\frac{153 + 93.6}{2}\right) \times 3.3 + \frac{1}{2} \times 153 \times 1.5$$

$$(M_A + M_B) = \frac{577.8}{3} = 192.6 \quad \ldots \text{(A)}$$

$$x = x'$$

(i.e. equating C.G. of both areas)

$$\therefore \left(\frac{M_A + 2M_B}{M_A + M_B}\right)\frac{l}{3} = \text{C.G. of total free B.M.D.}$$

$$\bar{X} = \frac{M_A + 2M_B}{192.6} \times \frac{6}{3} = \frac{(M_A + 2M_B)}{96.3} \text{ (from A)} \quad \ldots \text{(B)}$$

C.G. of free B.M.D. (from A)

$$\bar{X} = \left[\frac{1}{2} \times 93.6 \times 1.2 \times \frac{2}{3} \times 1.2 + \left(\frac{93.6 + 153}{2}\right) \times 3.3 \right.$$

$$\left. \times \frac{\left[1.2 + \left(\frac{93.6 + 2 \times 153}{93.6 + 153}\right)\frac{3.3}{3}\right] + \frac{1}{2} \times 153 \times 1.5 \times \left(4.5 + \frac{1}{3} \times 1.5\right)}{577.8}\right]$$

$$\bar{X} = 3.171$$

Substituting in (B),

$$\therefore M_A + 2M_B = 96.3 \times 3.171$$

$$(M_A + M_B) + M_B = 96.3 \times 3.171$$

$$\therefore M_B = 112.77 \text{ kN-m} \quad \text{(hogging)}$$

$$M_A = 79.83 \text{ kN-m} \quad \text{(hogging)}$$

By formula :

$$M_A = \frac{Wa_1 b_1^2}{l^2} + \frac{Wa_2 b_2^2}{l^2}$$

$$= \frac{60 \times 1.2 \times (4.8)^2}{36} + \frac{120 \times 4.5 \times (1.5)^2}{36}$$

$$= 79.83 \text{ kN-m} \quad \text{(hogging)}$$

$$M_B = \frac{Wa_1^2 b_1}{l^2} + \frac{Wa_2^2 b_2}{l^2}$$

$$= \frac{60 \times (1.2)^2 \times 4.8}{36} + \frac{120 \times (4.5)^2 \times 1.5}{36}$$

$$= 112.77 \text{ kN-m} \quad \text{(hogging)}$$

Reactions : (a) Due to external loads

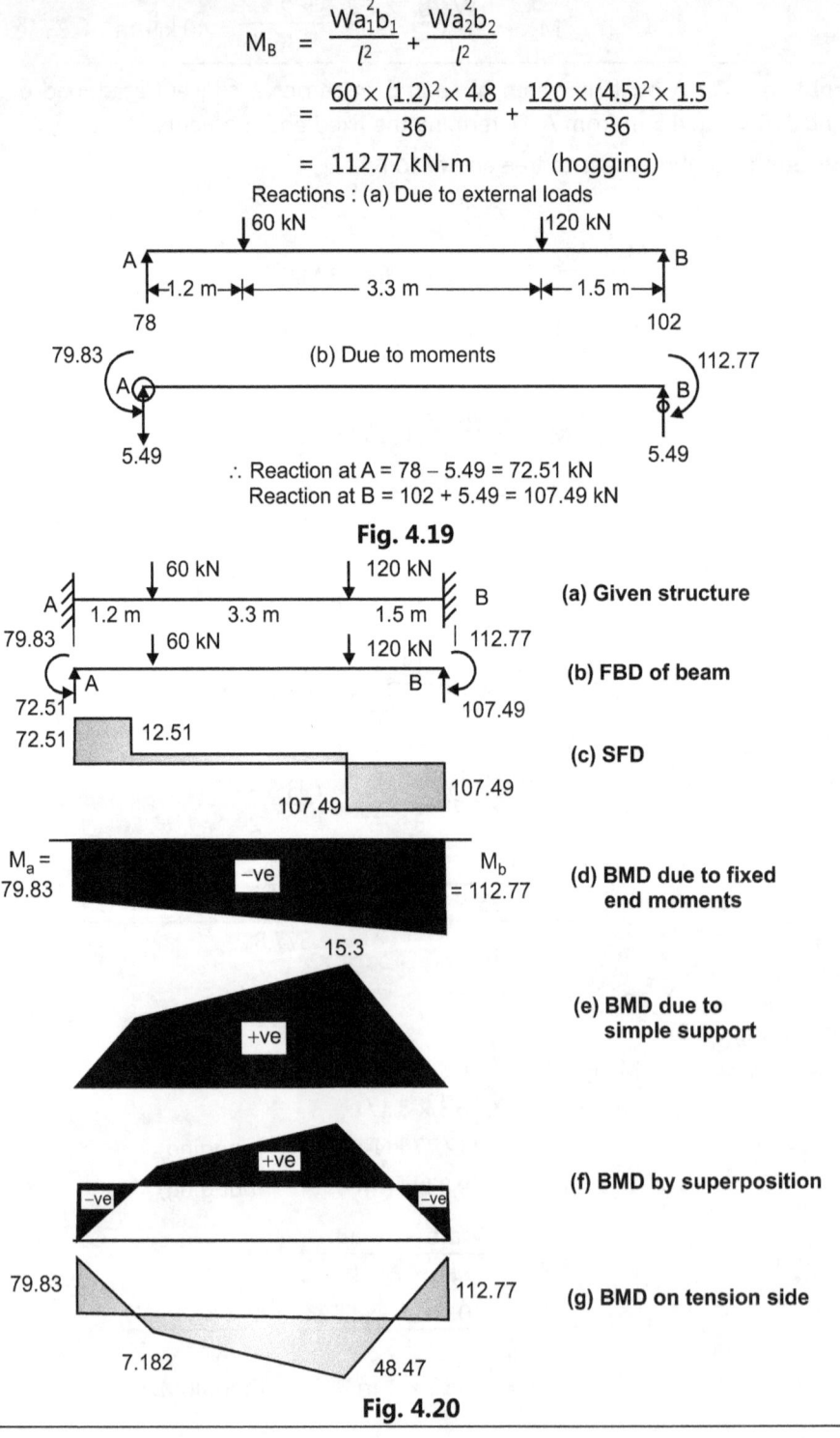

∴ Reaction at A = 78 − 5.49 = 72.51 kN
Reaction at B = 102 + 5.49 = 107.49 kN

Fig. 4.19

Fig. 4.20

Problem 4.5 : A built-up beam of span 12 m loaded with concentrated loads of 90 kN each at 4 m from both the supports and one at the centre of the span. Find the fixed end moment by first principle and check it by the standard formulae.

Solution : As beam is symmetrical with the centre of the span, therefore, both the fixed end moments are equal.

i.e. $M_b = M_c$

So considering only one equation i.e. equating areas of free B.M.D. and fixed B.M.D. we get the fixed end moments

$$a = a'$$

$$a = \text{Area of free B.M.D.}$$

$$= \frac{1}{2} \times 540 \times 4 + 2 \times \left(\frac{540 + 630}{2}\right) \times 2 + \frac{1}{2} \times 540 \times 4$$

or
$$a = 2 \times \left[\frac{1}{2} \times 540 \times 4 + \left(\frac{540 + 630}{2}\right) \times 2\right]$$

$$= 4500 \text{ kN-m}^2$$

$$a' = \text{Area of fixed B.M.D.}$$

$$= M_b \, l = M_c \, l = 12 M_b = 12 M_c$$

∴ $\quad 12 M_b = 4500 \quad \therefore \quad M_b = 375 \text{ kN-m}$

∴ $\quad M_b = M_c = 375 \text{ kN-m} \quad \text{(hogging)}$

By formula :

$$M_b = \frac{Wab^2}{l^2} = \left[\frac{90 \times 4 \times 8^2}{12^2} + \frac{90 \times 6 \times 6^2}{12^2} + \frac{90 \times 8 \times 4^2}{12^2}\right]$$

$$= 375 \text{ kN-m} \quad \text{(hogging)}$$

$$M_c = \left[\frac{90 \times 8 \times 4^2}{12^2} + \frac{90 \times 6^2 \times 6}{12^2} + \frac{90 \times 8^2 \times 4}{12^2}\right]$$

$$= 375 \text{ kN-m} \quad \text{(hogging)}$$

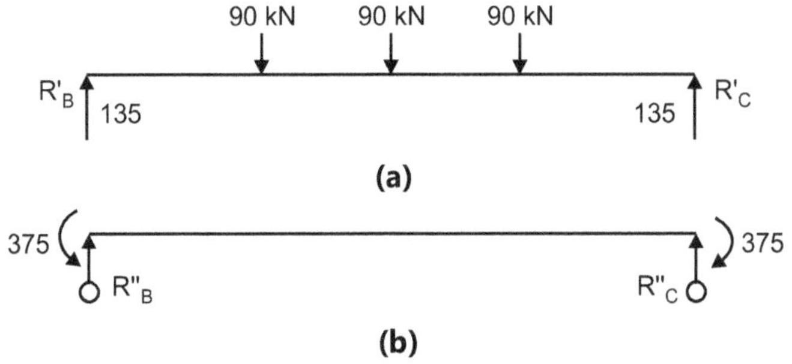

(a)

(b)

∴ Reaction at B = 135 + 0 = 135 kN

Reaction at C = 135 + 0 = 135 kN

Fig. 4.21

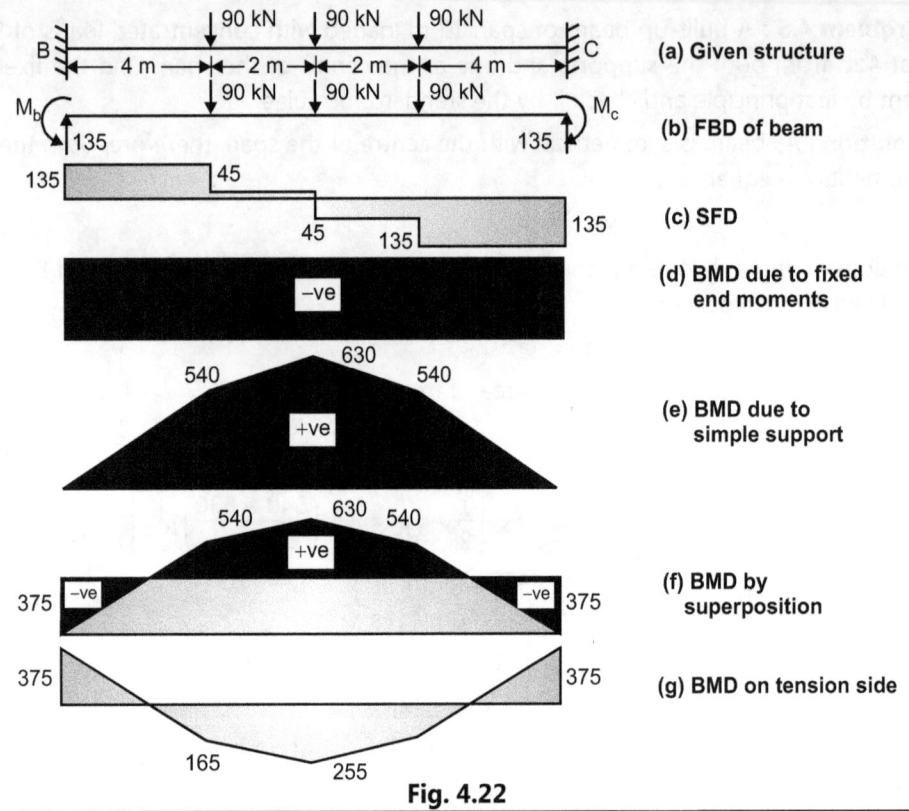

Fig. 4.22

Case III : Fixed beam carrying U.D.L. :

As beam is symmetrical with the centre of the span, $M_C = M_D$
Equating areas of fixed B.M.D. and free B.M.D.,

$$(M_C \cdot l) = (M_D \cdot l) = \frac{2}{3} \times \frac{Wl^2}{8} \times l \quad \therefore M_C = M_D = \frac{Wl^2}{12}$$

$$M_C = \frac{Wl^2}{12} \; (\circlearrowleft) \qquad \text{(hogging)}$$

$$M_D = \frac{Wl^2}{12} \; (\circlearrowright) \qquad \text{(hogging)}$$

Reactions :– (a) Due to external loads :–

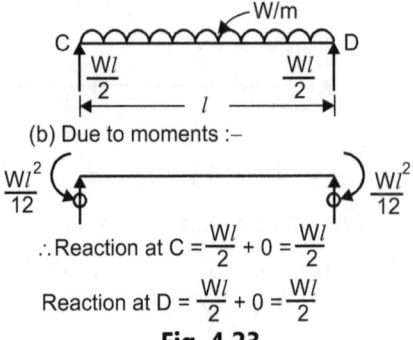

(b) Due to moments :–

$$\therefore \text{Reaction at } C = \frac{Wl}{2} + 0 = \frac{Wl}{2}$$

$$\text{Reaction at } D = \frac{Wl}{2} + 0 = \frac{Wl}{2}$$

Fig. 4.23

Deflection :

$$EI\frac{d^2y}{dx^2} = \frac{Wl}{2}x - \frac{Wl^2}{12} - \frac{Wx^2}{2}$$

Integrating,

$$EI\frac{dy}{dx} = \frac{Wl}{2}\frac{x^2}{2} - \frac{Wl^2}{12}x - \frac{Wx^3}{6} + C_1$$

At $x = 0$, $\frac{dy}{dx} = 0$ $\therefore C_1 = 0$

$$EI\, y = \frac{Wl}{2}\frac{x^3}{6} - \frac{Wl^2}{12}\frac{x^2}{2} - \frac{Wx^4}{24} + C_1 x + C_2$$

At $x = 0$, $y = 0$ $\therefore C_2 = 0$ $\quad EI\, y = \frac{Wl}{12}x^3 - \frac{Wl^2}{24}x^2 - \frac{Wx^4}{24}$

Maximum deflection occurs at the centre, $\therefore x = \frac{l}{2}$

$$EI\, y = \frac{Wl^4}{96} - \frac{Wl^4}{96} - \frac{Wl^4}{384} = \frac{-Wl^4}{384}$$

$$y_c = \frac{-Wl^4}{384\, EI}$$

Deflection in simply supported beams loaded with U.D.L. $= \frac{5}{384} Wl^4$. Thus, the deflection in simply supported beams is five times that of fixed beams.

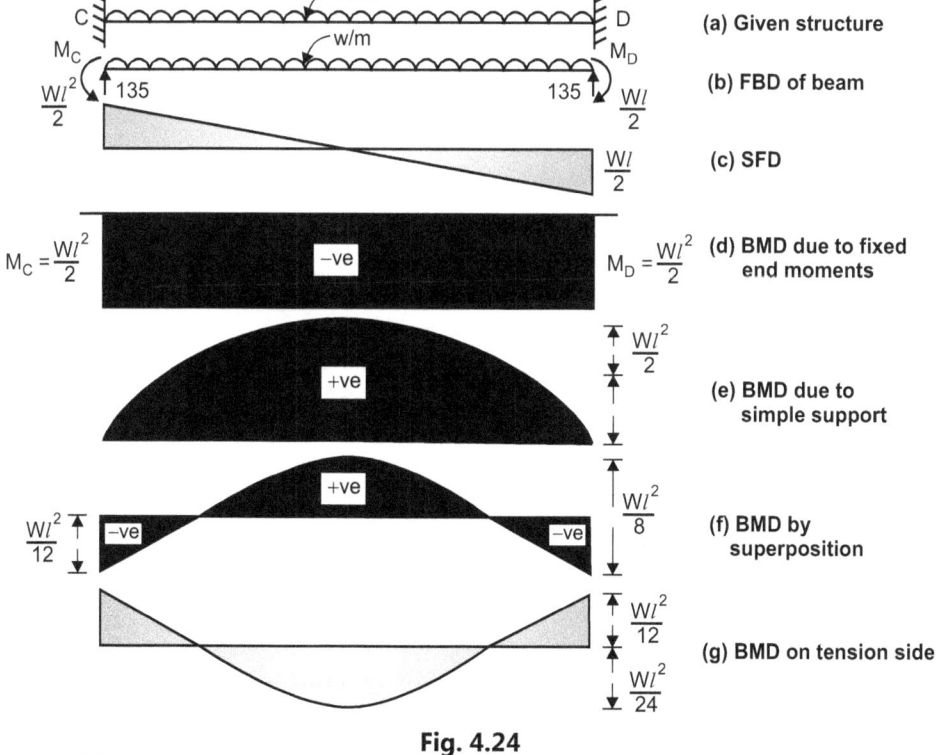

Fig. 4.24

Problem 4.6 : A built-up beam AB, having span 4.5 m is carrying a U.D.L. of 15 kN/m. Find the fixing end moments.

Solution : Equating areas of free and fixed bending moment diagrams,

$$a = a'$$
$$M_A = + M_B$$
$$M_A \times 4.5 = \frac{2}{3} \times 37.97 \times 4.5$$

∴
$$M_A = 25.3125 \text{ kN-m } (\circlearrowleft) \quad \text{(hogging)}$$
$$M_B = 25.3125 \text{ kN-m } (\circlearrowright) \quad \text{(hogging)}$$

Deflection :
$$EI \frac{d^2y}{dx^2} = \frac{Wl}{2} x - \frac{Wl^2}{12} - \frac{Wx^2}{2}$$

∴
$$EI \frac{d^2y}{dx^2} = 33.75x - 25.31 - 7.5x^2$$

Integrating,
$$EI \frac{dy}{dx} = \frac{33.75x^2}{2} - 25.31x - \frac{7.5x^3}{3} + C_1$$

At $x = 0$, $\frac{dy}{dx} = 0$, ∴ $C_1 = 0$

$$EI y = \frac{33.75}{2} \frac{x^3}{3} - \frac{25.31x^2}{2} - \frac{7.5x^4}{12} + C_1 x + C_2$$

At $x = 0$, $y = 0$, ∴ $C_2 = 0$

$$EIy = 5.625x^3 - 12.65x^2 - 0.625x^4$$

At $x = 2.25$ m; $EI y_C = -16.01$

Reactions :– (a) Due to external loads :–

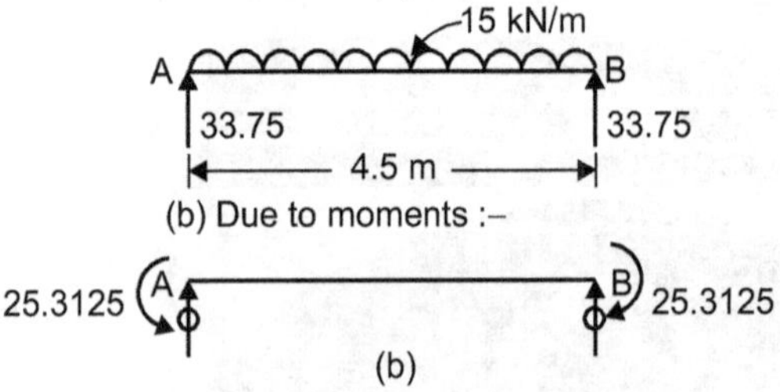

∴ Reaction at A = 33.75 + 0 = 33.75
Reaction at B = 33.75 + 0 = 33.75

Fig. 4.25

∴
$$y_C = -\frac{16.01}{EI}$$

By formula :
$$M_A = \frac{Wl^2}{12} = \frac{15 \times (4.5)^2}{12} = 25.3125 \text{ kN-m}$$

$$y_C = \frac{Wl^4}{384 \, EI} = \frac{15 \times (4.5)^4}{384 \, EI} = \frac{16.01}{EI}$$

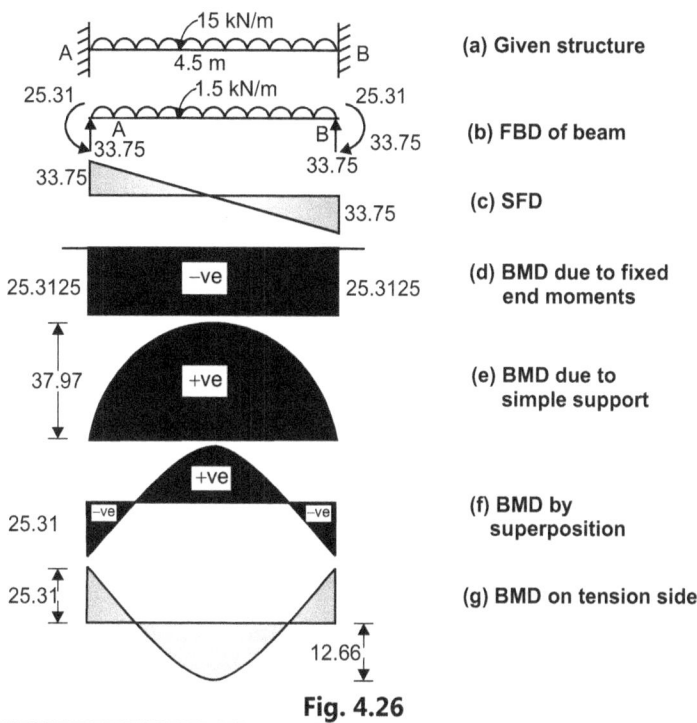

Fig. 4.26

Problem 4.7 : A beam CD of span 16 m and loaded with U.D.L. of 28 kN/m over whole of the span. Find the fixed end moments with first principle and check it by standard formulae.

Solution : Equating areas of free and fixed B.M.D.,

$$a = a'$$

$$a = \text{area of free B.M.D.} = \frac{2}{3} \times 896 \times 16$$

$$a' = \text{Area of fixed B.M.D.} = 16 M_C = 16 M_D$$

$$\therefore \quad 16 M_C = \frac{2}{3} \times 896 \times 16$$

$$\therefore \quad M_C = 597.33 \text{ kN-m} \quad \text{hogging}$$

$$M_D = 597.33 \text{ kN-m}$$

By formula : $M_C = M_D = \dfrac{Wl^2}{12} = \dfrac{28 \times 16^2}{12} = 597.33$ kN-m

$$\therefore \quad M_C = 597.33 \text{ kN-m} \quad \text{(hogging)}$$

$$M_D = 597.33 \text{ kN-m}$$

Reactions : (a) Due to external loads :

```
         28 kN/m
     C ∿∿∿∿∿∿∿∿∿∿ D
     ↑                ↑
   224 kN          224 kN
```

(a)

(b) Due to moments:

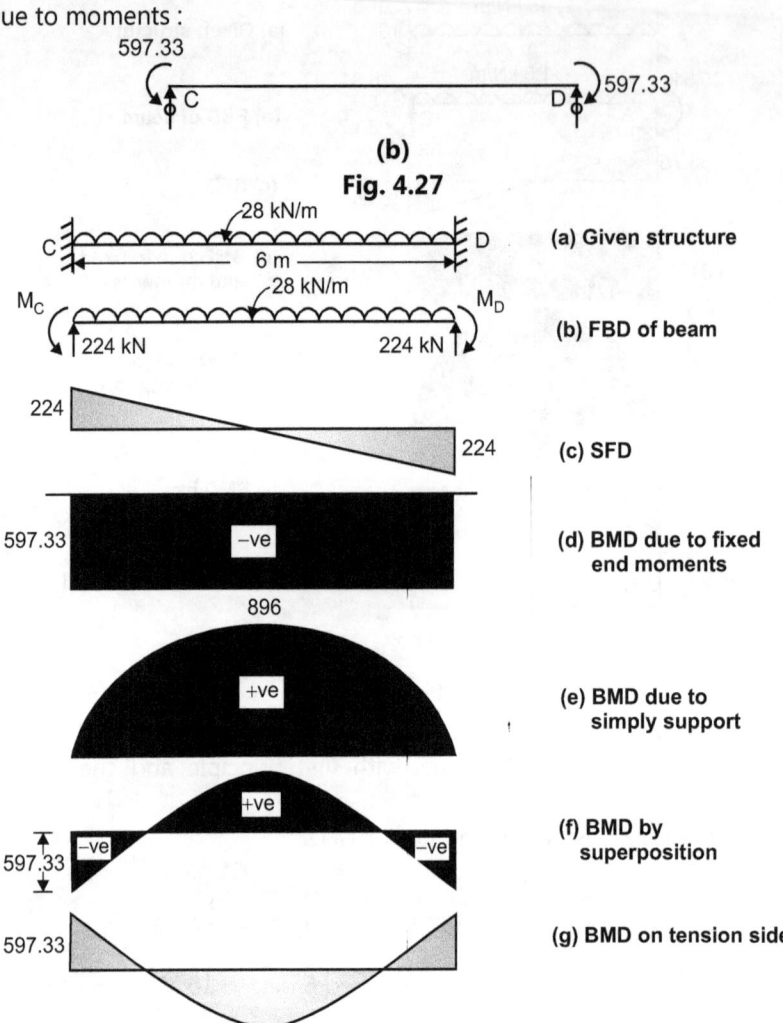

Fig. 4.27

Fig. 4.28

Case IV : Fixed beam carrying a U.D.L. for a given distance from one end :

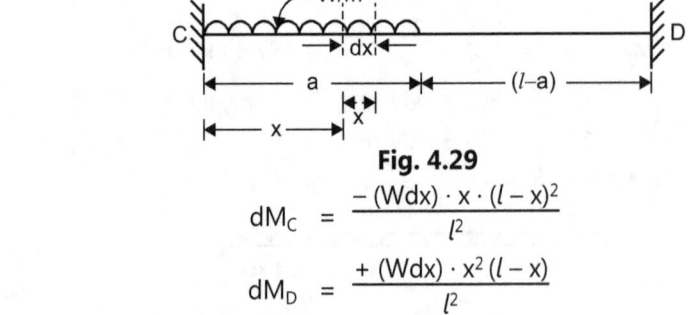

Fig. 4.29

$$\therefore \quad dM_C = \frac{-(Wdx) \cdot x \cdot (l-x)^2}{l^2}$$

$$\therefore \quad dM_D = \frac{+(Wdx) \cdot x^2 (l-x)}{l^2}$$

∴ Total fixing moment at C,

$$M_C = \int_0^a dM_C = -\int_0^a \frac{(Wdx)\, x \cdot (l-x)^2}{l^2}$$

$$= -\frac{W}{l^2}\int_0^a x(l-x)^2 \cdot dx = -\frac{W}{l^2}\int_0^a (xl^2 - 2lx^2 + x^3)\, dx$$

$$= -\frac{W}{l^2}\left[\frac{x^2 l^2}{2} - \frac{2l x^3}{3} + \frac{x^4}{4}\right]_0^a = -\frac{W}{l^2}\left[\frac{l^2 a^2}{2} - \frac{2l a^3}{3} + \frac{a^4}{4}\right]$$

$$= -\frac{W}{12l^2} a^2 [6l^2 - 8l a + 3a^2]$$

Similarly moment at D:

$$M_D = \int_0^a \frac{(Wdx)\, x^2 (l-x)}{l^2} = \frac{W}{l^2}\int_0^a (x^2 l - x^3)\, dx$$

$$= \frac{W}{l^2}\left[\frac{x^3 l}{3} - \frac{x^4}{4}\right]_0^a = \frac{Wa^3}{12l^2}[4l - 3a]$$

When U.D.L. covers the whole span then $a = l$.

∴ $$M_A = -\frac{Wa^2}{12l^2}[6l^2 - 8la + 3a^2]$$

Put $a = l$.

∴ $$M_A = -\frac{Wl^2}{12l^2}[6l^2 - 8l^2 + 3l^2] = -\frac{Wl^2}{12} = -\frac{Wl^2}{12} \text{ (hogging)}$$

(Same as discussed for U.D.L. on whole span.)

$$M_B = \frac{Wa^3}{12l^2}[4l - 3a]$$

Put $a = l$.

∴ $$M_B = \frac{Wl^3}{12l^2}[l] = \frac{Wl^2}{12}$$

[As discussed for U.D.L. on whole span.]

Problem 4.8: A fixed beam of span 8 m carries U.D.L. of 45 kN/m over half the span. Find the fixed end moments and support reactions.

Solution: Free B.M.D. calculations:

$$V_D = \frac{45 \times 4 \times 6}{8} = 135 \text{ kN}$$

$$V_C = \frac{45 \times 4 \times 2}{8} = 45 \text{ kN}$$

∴ $$M_E = V_C \times 4 = 45 \times 4 = 180 \text{ kN-m}$$

Equating areas of fixed and free B.M.D.,

$$a' = a$$

$$a' = \left(\frac{M_C + M_D}{2}\right) \times l = (M_C + M_D)\frac{8}{2} = 4(M_C + M_D)$$

$$a = -\left[\int_0^4 \left(135x - \frac{45x^2}{2}\right)dx + \frac{1}{2} \times 180 \times 4\right]$$

$$= +\left[\left[\frac{135x^2}{2} - \frac{45x^3}{6}\right]_0^4 + 360\right] = +960$$

∴ $M_C + M_D = +240$

Similarly, $\bar{x}' = \bar{x}$

$$\bar{x}' = \left(\frac{M_C + 2M_D}{M_A + M_B}\right)\frac{l}{3} \quad \text{from C}$$

$$= \frac{(M_C + 2M_D)}{+240} \times \frac{8}{3} = \left(\frac{M_C + 2M_D}{+90}\right)$$

$$a\bar{x} = \int_0^4 \left(135x^2 - \frac{45x^3}{2}\right)dx + \frac{1}{2} \times 180 \times 4 \times 5.33$$

$$= \left[\frac{135x^3}{3} - \frac{45x^4}{8}\right]_0^4 + 1920 = 3360$$

∴ $\bar{x} = 3.5$ m from D

and $\bar{x} = 8 - 3.5 = 4.5$ from C

∴ $\bar{x}' = \bar{x}$

$$\frac{M_C + 2M_D}{+90} = 4.5$$

∴ $(M_C + M_D) + M_D = +315$

∴ $M_C = 75$ kN-m (↻) (hogging)

$M_D = 165$ kN-m (↻) (hogging)

Reactions : (a) Due to external loads :

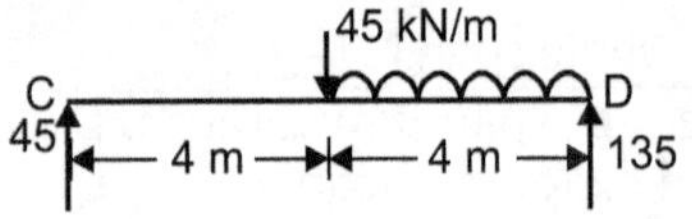

```
        45 kN/m
   C  ~~~~~~~~ D
  45|← 4 m →|← 4 m →|135
```
(a)

(b) Due to moments :

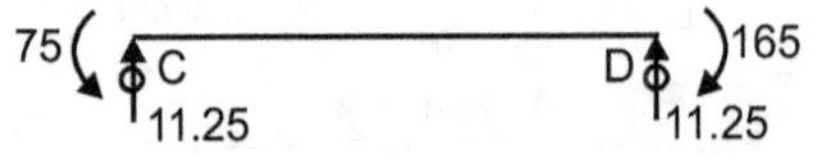

```
  75 ⟲ C          D ⟳ 165
       ↑11.25    ↑11.25
```
(b)

∴ Reaction at C = 35 + 11.25 = 46.25 kN

Reaction D = 45 − 11.24 = 33.75 kN

Fig. 4.30

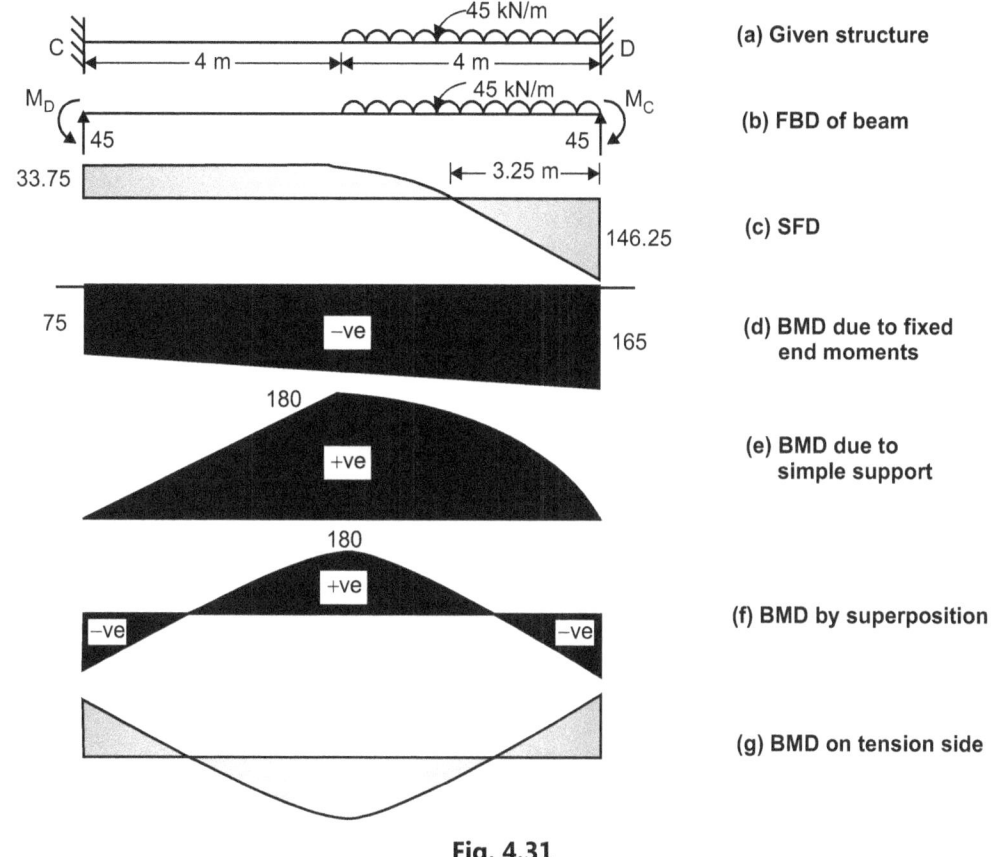

Fig. 4.31

Problem 4.9 : A fixed beam CD of span 10 m carries U.D.L. of 80 kN/m over one third span from A. Find fixed end moments.

Solution : Equating the areas of free and fixed B.M.D.,

$$a' = a$$

$$a' = \frac{(M_C + M_D)}{2} \times l = (M_C + M_D)\, 5$$

$$a = \text{Area of parabola + Area of triangle}$$

$$= a_1 b_1 c_1 + b_1 c_1 d_1$$

$$a = \int_0^{3.33} \left(R_C x - \frac{Wx^2}{2}\right) dx + \frac{1}{2} \times 295.85 \times 6.67$$

$$= \int_0^{3.33} \left(222.04x - \frac{80x^2}{2}\right) dx + 986.66$$

$$= \left[\frac{222.04x^2}{2} - \frac{80x^3}{6}\right]_0^{3.33} + 986.66$$

$$= 738.74 + 986.66 = 1725.4$$

$$(M_C + M_D) = 345.08$$

$$x' = x$$

$$x' = \frac{(M_C + 2M_D)}{(M_C + M_D)} \times \frac{l}{3} \quad \text{from C}$$

$$= \frac{(M_C + 2M_D)}{345.08} \times \frac{10}{3} = \frac{(M_C + 2M_D)}{103.52}$$

$$a\bar{x} = \int_0^{3.33} \left(222.04x^2 - \frac{80x^3}{2}\right) dx + 986.66 \times 5.55$$

$$a\bar{x} = \left[\frac{222.04x^3}{3} - \frac{80x^4}{8}\right]_0^{3.33} + 5475.96$$

$$= 1503.38 + 5475.96$$

$$= 6979.34$$

$$\therefore \quad \bar{x} = 4.05 \text{ m from C}$$

$$\therefore \quad \frac{M_C + 2M_D}{103.52} = 4.05$$

$$\therefore \quad M_C + 2M_D = 419.26$$

$$(M_C + M_D) + M_D = 419.26$$

$$M_D = 74.18 \text{ kN-m} \ (\circlearrowleft) \quad \text{(hogging)}$$

$$M_C = 270.9 \text{ kN-m} \ (\circlearrowleft) \quad \text{(hogging)}$$

Reactions : (a) Due to external loads :

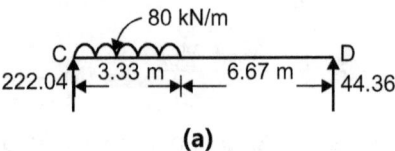

(a)

(b) Due to moments :

(b)

$$\therefore \text{ Reaction at C} = 222.04 + 19.67 = 241.71 \text{ kN}$$

$$\text{Reaction at D} = 44.36 = 19.67 = 24.69 \text{ kN}$$

Fig. 4.32

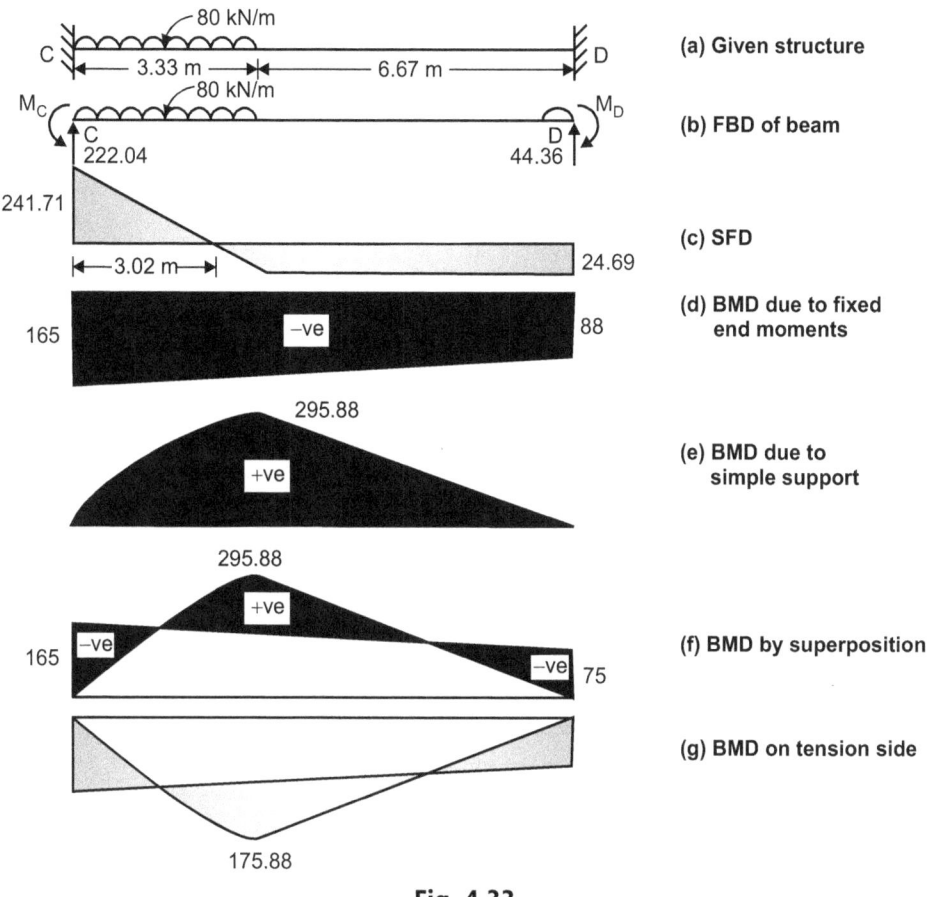

Fig. 4.33

Problem 4.10 : A fixed beam AB is fixed at A and B. The span of the beam is 10 m. It is loaded with U.D.L. of 15 kN/m from 3 m from left support upto 4 m from right support. Find the fixed end moments. Draw S.F.D. and B.M.D.

Solution : Consider a part dx of U.D.L.

Therefore, concentrated load of 15 dx is acting at x from support A. So we can apply the formula for the eccentric concentrated load as follows :

$$\therefore \quad M_a = \int_3^6 \frac{15\, dx \times x \times (l-x)^2}{L^2}$$

$$= \frac{15}{L^2} \int_3^6 x\,(l^2 - 2lx + x^2)\, dx$$

$$= \frac{15}{L^2} \int_3^6 (xl^2 - 2lx^2 + x^3)\, dx$$

$$= \frac{15}{L^2}\left[\frac{x^2 l^2}{2} - \frac{2lx^3}{3} + \frac{x^4}{4}\right]_3^6$$

$$= \frac{15}{10^2}\left[\frac{10^2}{2}(6^2 - 3^2) - \frac{2l}{3}(6^3 - 3^3) + \frac{1}{4}(6^4 - 3^4)\right]$$

$$= \frac{15}{100}\left[1350 - 1260 + \frac{1215}{4}\right]$$

$$= 59.06 \text{ kN-m} \quad \text{(hogging)}$$

$$M_b = \int_3^6 \frac{15 \cdot dx}{L^2} \cdot x^2 (l - x)$$

$$= \frac{15}{100} \int_3^6 (x^2 l - x^3)\, dx = \frac{15}{100}\left[\frac{x^3 l}{3} - \frac{x^4}{4}\right]_3^6$$

$$= \frac{15}{100}\left[\frac{10}{3}(6^3 - 3^3) - \frac{1}{4}(6^4 - 3^4)\right] = \frac{15}{100}[630 - 303.75]$$

$$= 48.94 \text{ kN-m} \quad \text{(hogging)}$$

Reactions: (a) Due to external loads:

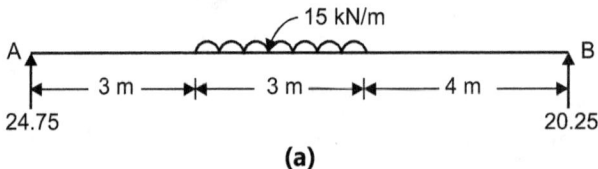

(a)

(b) Due to moments

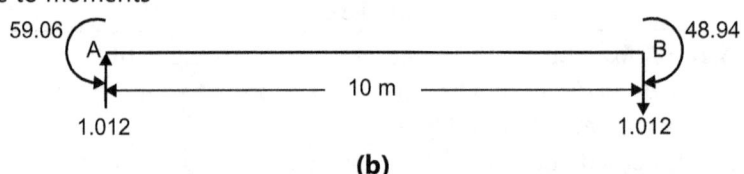

(b)

∴ Reaction at A = 24.75 + 1.012 = 25.762 kN

Reaction at B = 20.25 − 1.012 = 19.24 kN

Fig. 4.34

S.F. at X = $R_A - Wx$

For maximum B.M., S.F. is zero

0 = 25.762 − 15x

∴ x = 1.72 m

∴ S.F. is zero at x = 3.0 + 1.72 = 4.72 m from A

∴ B.M. is maximum at 4.72 m from A.

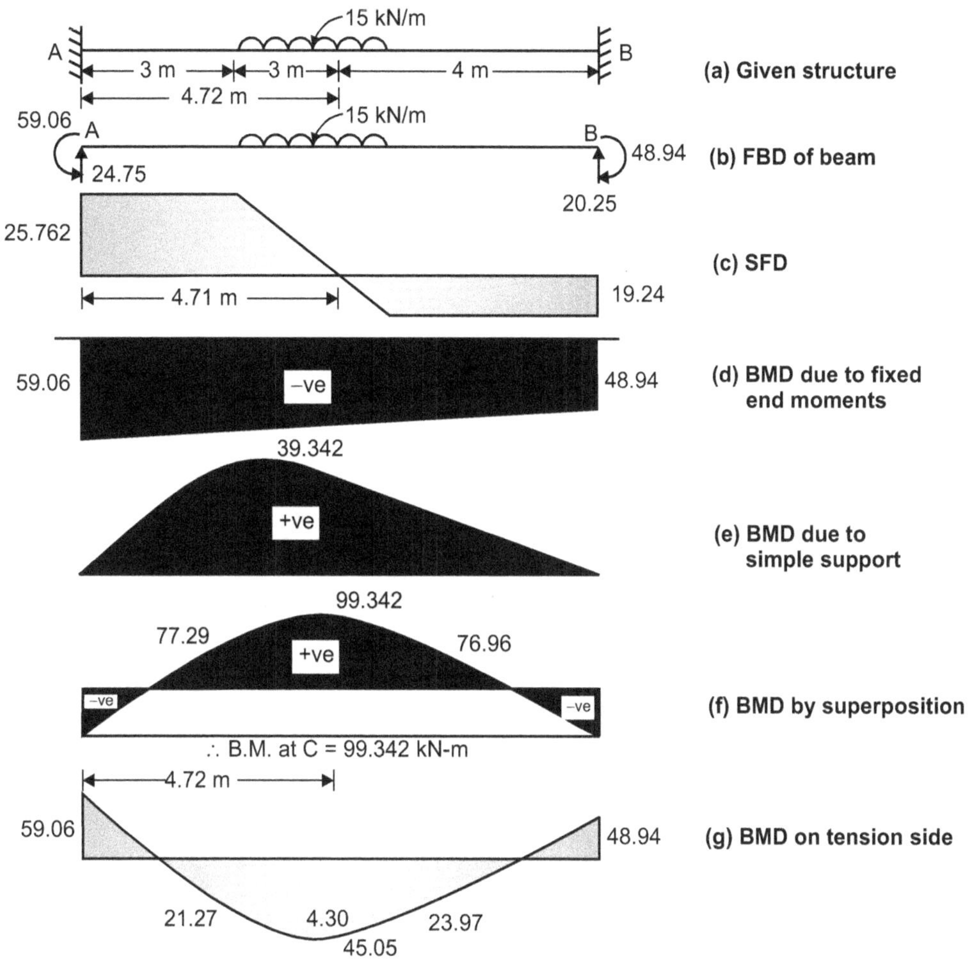

Fig. 4.35

∴ Maximum B.M. at C = 99.342 kN-m

Case V : Fixed beam carrying a triangular load whose intensity varies from zero at one end and W per unit run at the other end :

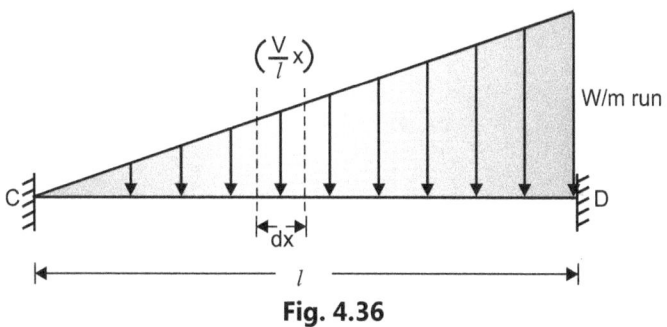

Fig. 4.36

Intensity of loading at $X = \left(\dfrac{W}{l}\right) x$.

Total load on $dx = \left(\dfrac{W}{l}\right) x \, dx$.

$\therefore \quad dM_C = \dfrac{\left(\dfrac{W}{l}\right) x \, dx \cdot x (l-x)^2}{l^2}$

$\left(M_C = \dfrac{Wab^2}{l^2} \text{ and } M_D = \dfrac{Wa^2 b}{l^2}\right)$

$dM_D = \dfrac{\left(\dfrac{W}{l}\right) x \, dx \cdot x^2 (l-x)}{l^2}$

$\therefore \quad M_C = $ Total moment at C

$= \displaystyle\int_0^l \dfrac{W}{l} \cdot \dfrac{x^2 (l-x)^2}{l^2} dx = \dfrac{W}{l^3} \int_0^l x^2 (l-x)^2 \, dx$

$= \dfrac{W}{l^3} \displaystyle\int_0^l x^2 (l^2 - 2lx + x^2) \, dx = \dfrac{W}{l^3} \int_0^l [x^2 l^2 - 2lx^3 + x^4] \, dx$

$= \dfrac{W}{l^3} \left[\dfrac{x^3}{3} l^2 - \dfrac{2l x^4}{4} + \dfrac{x^5}{5}\right]_0^l$

$= \dfrac{W l^5}{l^3} \left[\dfrac{1}{3} - \dfrac{1}{2} + \dfrac{1}{5}\right] = \dfrac{W l^2}{30} (1) = \dfrac{W l^2}{30}$

$M_D = \displaystyle\int_0^l \dfrac{W x^3 (l-x)}{l^3} dx$

$= \dfrac{W}{l^3} \displaystyle\int_0^l [(x^3 l - x^4)] \, dx$

$= \dfrac{W}{l^3} \left[\dfrac{x^4 l}{4} - \dfrac{x^5}{5}\right]_0^l$

$= \dfrac{W l^5}{l^3} \left[\dfrac{1}{4} - \dfrac{1}{5}\right] = \dfrac{W l^2}{20}$

Problem 4.11 : Fixed beam carrying a gradually varying load from zero at one end to W at other end. Find fixed end moments.

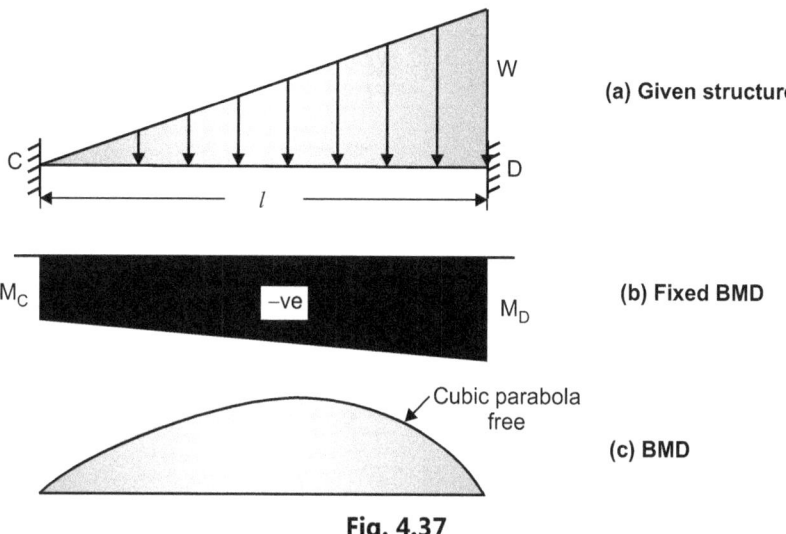

Fig. 4.37

Solution : Equating areas of free B.M. diagram and fixed B.M. diagram,

$$a = a'$$

$$a' = \left(\frac{M_C + M_D}{2}\right) l = (M_C + M_D)\frac{l}{2}$$

$$a = \int_0^l \left(R_C x - \frac{1}{2} \cdot \frac{W}{l} \cdot x \cdot x \times \frac{x}{3}\right) dx$$

$$R_C = \frac{1}{2} \times \frac{W \times l \times \frac{l}{3}}{l} = \frac{Wl}{6}$$

$$\therefore \quad a = \int_0^l \left(\frac{Wl}{6} x - \frac{Wx^3}{6l}\right) dx$$

$$= \left[\frac{Wl}{6}\frac{x^2}{2} - \frac{Wx^4}{24l}\right]_0^l = \left[\frac{Wl^3}{12} - \frac{Wl^3}{24}\right] = \frac{Wl^3}{24}$$

$$\therefore \quad (M_C + M_D) \cdot \frac{l}{2} = \frac{Wl^3}{24}$$

$$(M_C + M_D) = \frac{Wl^2}{12}$$

$$x' = x$$

$$x' = \frac{(M_C + 2M_D)}{(M_C + M_D)} \cdot \frac{l}{3}$$

$$a\bar{x} = \int_0^l \left(R_C x^2 - \frac{Wx^4}{6l}\right)dx = \int_0^l \left(\frac{Wl}{6}x^2 - \frac{Wx^4}{6l}\right)dx$$

$$= \left[Wl\frac{x^3}{18} - \frac{Wx^5}{30l}\right]_0^l = W\left[\frac{l^4}{18} - \frac{l^4}{30}\right] = W\left[\frac{5l^4 - 3l^4}{90}\right] = \frac{Wl^4}{45}$$

$$\therefore \quad \bar{x} = \frac{\frac{Wl^4}{45}}{\frac{Wl^3}{24}} = \frac{24}{45}l \text{ from A}$$

$$\therefore \quad \frac{(M_C + 2M_D)}{(M_C + M_D)}\frac{l}{3} = \frac{24}{45}l$$

$$(M_C + 2M_D) = \frac{Wl^2}{12} \times \frac{24}{15} = \frac{2Wl^2}{15}$$

$$(M_C + M_D) + M_D = \frac{2Wl^2}{15}$$

$$M_D = \frac{2Wl^2}{15} - \frac{Wl^2}{12}$$

$$= \frac{24 - 15}{(15 \times 12)}Wl^2 = \frac{Wl^2}{20} \quad \text{(hogging)}$$

$$M_C + M_D = \frac{Wl^2}{12}$$

$$\therefore \quad M_C = \frac{Wl^2}{12} - \frac{Wl^2}{20}$$

$$= \frac{(5-3)Wl^2}{60} = \frac{Wl^2}{30} \quad \text{(hogging)}$$

Problem 4.12 : A beam CD is fixed at both ends having span 8 m. Intensity of loading is varying from zero at one end to 30 kN/m at the other end. Find the fixed end moments.

Solution :

$a' = a$ Taking moments about D

$$R_C = \frac{\frac{1}{2} \times 30 \times 8 \times \frac{8}{3}}{8} = 40 \text{ kN}$$

$\therefore \quad R_D = 80 \text{ kN}$

$$a' = \left(\frac{M_C + M_D}{2}\right) \times 8 = 4(M_C + M_D)$$

$$a = \int_0^8 \left(40x - \frac{1}{2} \times \frac{30}{8} \times x \times x \times \frac{x}{3}\right)dx = \left[\frac{40x^2}{2} - \frac{5}{8}\frac{x^4}{4}\right]_0^8 = 640$$

∴ $(M_C + M_D) \, 4 = 640$

∴ $(M_C + M_D) = 160$

Now, $x' = x$

$$x' = \frac{(M_C + 2M_D)}{(M_C + M_D)} \frac{l}{3} = \frac{(M_C + 2M_D)}{160} \times \frac{8}{3} = \frac{(M_C + 2M_D)}{60}$$

$$a\bar{x} = \int_0^8 \left(R_C x^2 - \frac{Wx^4}{6l}\right) dx$$

$$a\bar{x} = \int_0^8 \left(40x^2 - \frac{30}{6 \times 8} x^4\right) dx$$

$$= \left[\frac{40x^3}{3} - \frac{5}{8}\frac{x^5}{5}\right]_0^8 = 2730.67$$

$\bar{x} = 4.2667$ from A

∴ $\dfrac{(M_C + 2M_D)}{60} = 4.2667$

$(M_C + M_D) + M_D = 256$

∴ $M_D = 96$ kN-m (↶) (hogging)

$M_C = M_D = 160$ ∴ $M_C = 64$ kN-m (↶) (hogging)

By formula : $M_C = \dfrac{Wl^2}{30} = \dfrac{30 \times 64}{30} = 64$ kN-m (↶) (hogging)

$M_D = \dfrac{Wl^2}{20} = \dfrac{30 \times 64}{20} = 96$ kN-m (↶) (hogging)

Reaction : (a) Due to external loads :

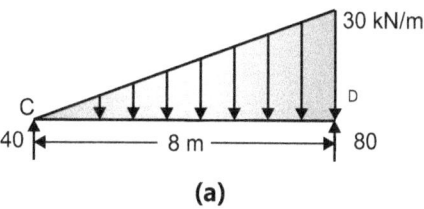

(a)

(b) Due to moments :

∴ Reaction at C = 40 − 4 = 36 kN

Reaction at D = 80 + 4 = 84 kN

Fig. 4.38

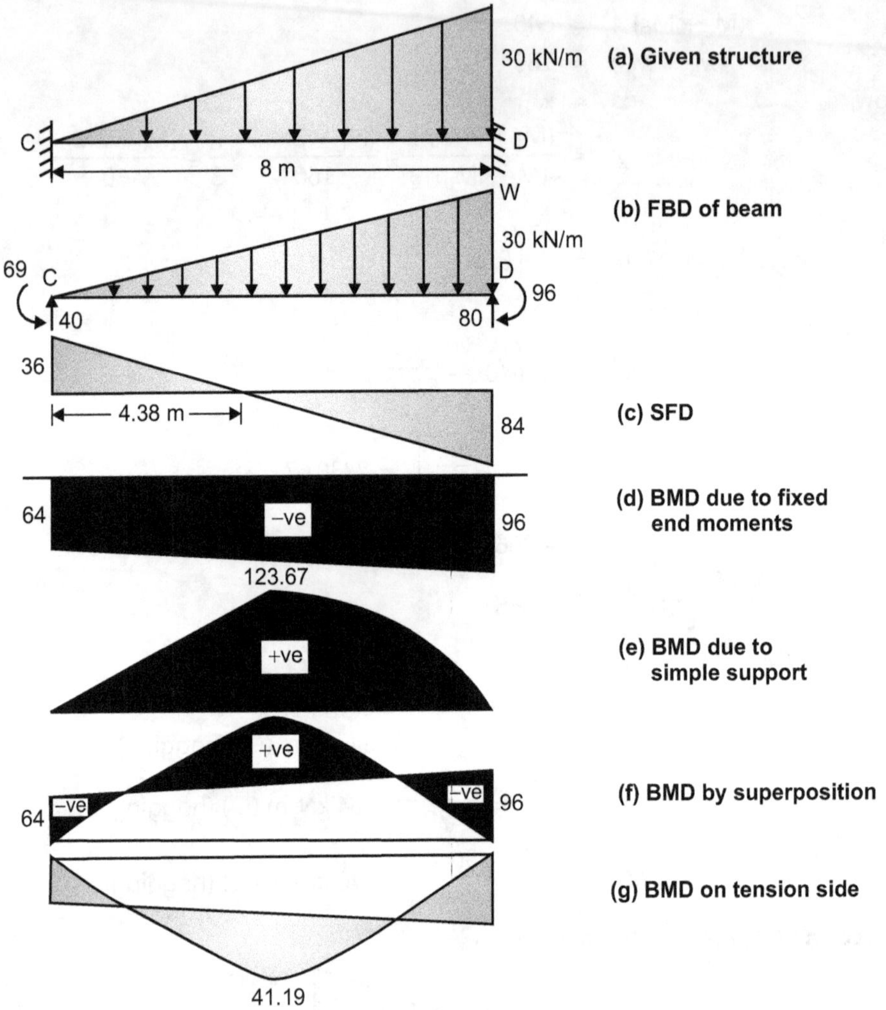

Fig. 4.39

Case VI : Fixed beam carrying a triangular load for a given distance from one end :

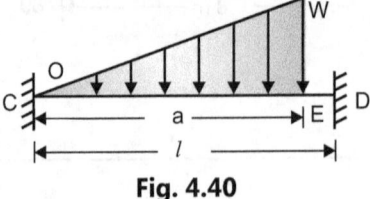

Fig. 4.40

Intensity of loading at x is given by

$$= \frac{W}{a} x$$

Load acting on an element dx $= \frac{W}{a} x\, dx.$

$$\therefore \quad dM_C = \left(\frac{W}{a}x\right)\frac{dx \cdot x \cdot (l-x)^2}{l^2}$$

$$\left(M_C = \frac{Wab^2}{l^2}, \quad M_D = \frac{Wa^2b}{l^2}\right)$$

$$dM_D = \frac{\left(\frac{W}{a}x\right)dx \cdot x^2(l-x)}{l^2}$$

$$M_C = \int_0^a \left(\frac{W}{a}x\right)\frac{dx \cdot x(l-x)^2}{l^2} = \frac{W}{al^2}\int_0^a [x^2 l^2 - 2lx^3 + x^4]\,dx$$

$$= \frac{W}{al^2}\left[\frac{x^3 l^2}{3} - \frac{2lx^4}{4} + \frac{x^5}{5}\right]_0^a = \frac{Wa^3}{al^2}\left[\frac{l^2}{3} - \frac{la}{2} + \frac{a^2}{5}\right]$$

$$= \frac{Wa^2}{30l^2}[10l^2 - 15al + 6a^2]$$

$$M_D = \int_0^a \frac{W}{a}\frac{x^3}{l^2}(l-x)\,dx = \frac{W}{al^2}\int_0^a [x^3 l - x^4]\,dx$$

$$= \frac{W}{al^2}\left[\frac{x^4 l}{4} - \frac{x^5}{5}\right]_0^a = \frac{Wa^3}{20l^2}[5l - 4a]$$

Problem 4.13 : Fixed beam CD carrying U.V.L. zero at one end and 40 kN at the centre. Span of beam CD is 7 m. Find the fixed end moments.

Solution :

$$a' = a$$

$$R_C = \frac{1}{2} \times \frac{40 \times 3.5 \times \left(\frac{3.5}{3} + 3.5\right)}{7} = 46.67 \text{ kN}$$

$$R_D = 23.33 \text{ kN}$$

$$a' = \frac{(M_C + M_D)}{2} \times 7 = 3.5\,(M_C + M_D)$$

$$a = \int_0^{3.5} \left(46.67x - \frac{1}{2} \times \frac{40}{3.5} \times x \times x \times \frac{x}{3}\right)dx + \frac{1}{2} \times 81.67 \times 3.5$$

$$= \left[\frac{46.67 x^2}{2} - \frac{1.9 x^4}{4}\right]_0^{3.5} + 142.92$$

$$= 214.39 + 142.92 = 357.31$$

$$\therefore \quad (M_C + M_D) = 102.1$$

Now, $\quad x' = \bar{x}$

$$x' = \frac{(M_C + 2M_D)}{(M_C + M_D)} \frac{l}{3} = \frac{(M_C + 2M_D)}{102.1} \times \frac{7}{3} = \frac{(M_C + 2M_D)}{43.75}$$

$$a\bar{x} = \int_0^{3.5} (46.75x^2 - 1.9x^4)\, dx + 142.92 \times \left(\frac{3.5}{3} + 3.5\right)$$

$$= \left[\frac{46.75x^3}{3} - \frac{1.9x^5}{5}\right]_0^{3.5} + 666.96 = 1135.51$$

∴ $\quad \bar{x} = 3.17$
∴ $\quad (M_C + 2M_D) = 3.17 \times 43.75$
$\quad (M_C + M_D) + M_D = 138.687$
∴ $\quad M_D = 36.600$ kN-m
$\quad M_C + M_D = 102.1$
∴ $\quad M_C = 65.500$ kN-m

Reaction : (a) Due to external loads :

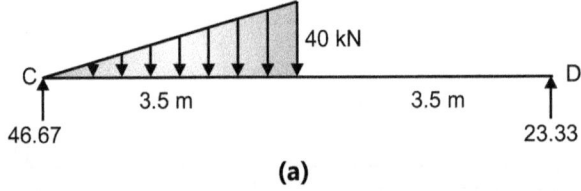

(a)

(b) Due to moments :

```
       C                                              36.6
  ⤴ ↑                                             D ⤵
65.5  4.13                                   4.13
```

(b)

∴ Reaction at C = 46.67 + 4.13 = 50.8 kN
Reaction at D = 23.33 – 4.13 = 19.2 kN

Fig. 4.41

By formula :

$$M_C = \frac{Wa^2}{30l^2}(10l^2 - 15al + 6a^2)$$

$$= \frac{40 \times (3.5)^2}{30 \times 7^2}[10 \times 7^2 - 15 \times 3.5 \times 7 + 6 \times (3.5)^2]$$

$$= 65.33 \text{ kN-m}$$

$$M_D = \frac{Wa^3}{20l^2}(5l - 4a)$$

$$= \frac{40 \times (3.5)^3}{20 \times 7^2}(5 \times 7 - 4 \times 3.5) = 36.75 \text{ kN-m}$$

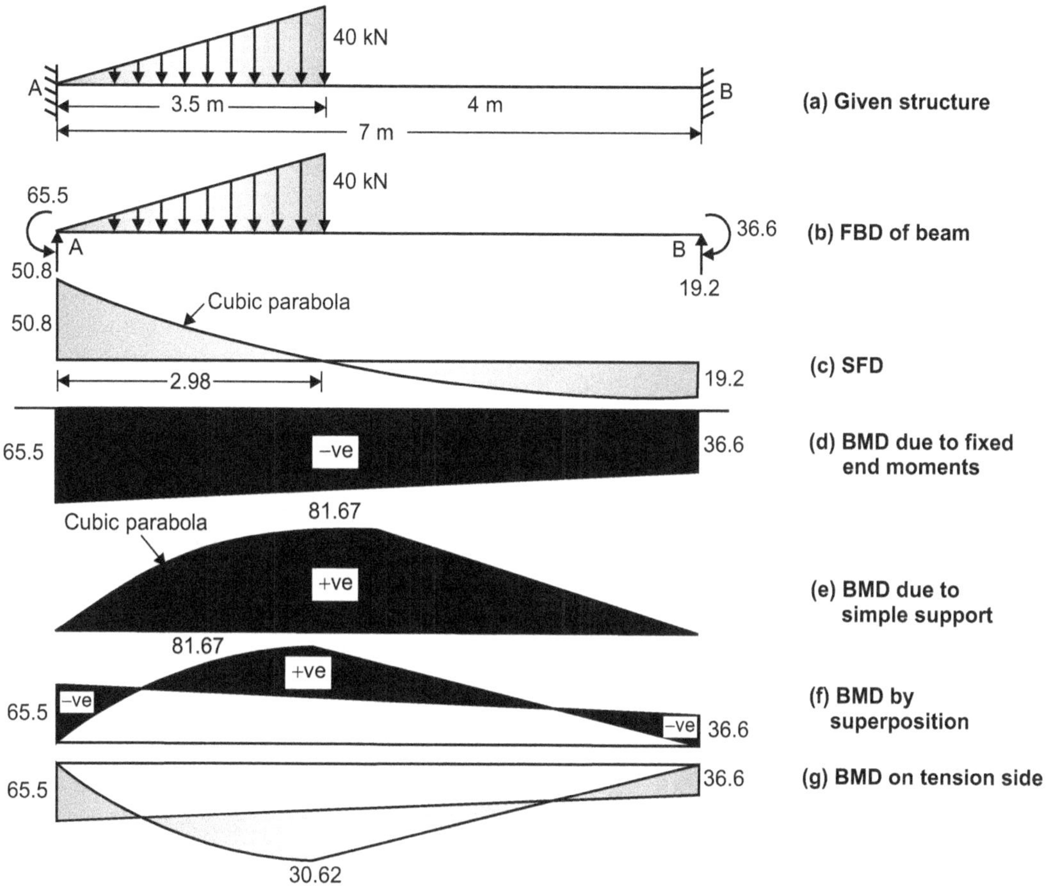

40 kN
A
B
3.5 m
4 m
7 m
(a) Given structure
65.5
40 kN
36.6
(b) FBD of beam
A
B
50.8
19.2
Cubic parabola
50.8
2.98
19.2
(c) SFD
65.5
–ve
36.6
(d) BMD due to fixed end moments
Cubic parabola
81.67
+ve
(e) BMD due to simple support
81.67
+ve
–ve
65.5
–ve
36.6
(f) BMD by superposition
65.5
36.6
(g) BMD on tension side
30.62

Fig. 4.42

Problem 4.14 : A built-up beam AB of span 8 m is carrying U.V.L. with intensity 5 kN/m on support A and 12 kN/m at the other end. Find the support moments using standard formulae. **(P.U. Dec. 99)**

Solution :

12 kN/m
5 kN/m
A
B

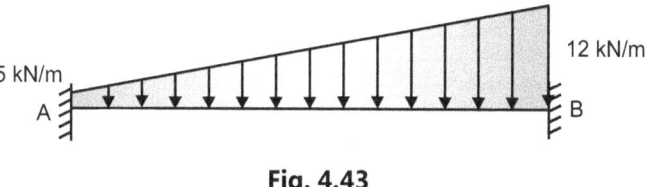

Fig. 4.43

Convert the U.V.L. into two loads :

1. U.D.L. : Intensity 5 kN/m over whole span. (W_1 = 5 kN/m)
2. U.V.L. : Intensity zero at A and 7 kN/m at the other end i.e. B. (W_2 = 7 kN/m)

∴ M_a = Moment due to U.D.L. + Moment due to U.V.L.

$$= \frac{W_1 l^2}{12} + \frac{W_2 l^2}{20} = \frac{5 \times 8^2}{12} + \frac{7 \times 8^2}{30}$$

$$= 26.67 + 14.93$$

$$= 41.60 \text{ kN-m (hogging)}$$

M_b = Moment due to U.D.L. + Moment due to U.V.L.

$$= \frac{W_1 l^2}{12} + \frac{W_2 l^2}{20}$$

$$= \frac{5 \times 8^2}{12} + \frac{7 \times 8^2}{20}$$

$$= 26.67 + 22.4 \qquad \text{(hogging)}$$

$$= 49.07 \text{ kN-m}$$

Note : Fixed beam subjected to couple M_o applied eccentrically on the span :

(Macaulay's Method)

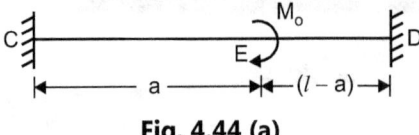

Fig. 4.44 (a)

Consider a beam CD having span l. Moment M_o is applied at point E, which is at a distance 'a' from C as shown in Fig. 4.44 (a).

It may be considered that couple consists of two equal loads W spaced at a distance δa as shown in Fig. 4.44 (b) :

Fig. 4.44 (b)

∴ $$M_C = -\frac{W \cdot a \cdot (l-a)^2}{l^2} + \frac{W(a+\delta a)[(l-a)-\delta a]^2}{l^2}$$

Ignoring δa^2 from the above equation,

$$M_C = -\frac{Wa(l-a)^2}{l^2} + \frac{W}{l^2}[a(l-a)^2 - 2a(l-a)\delta a + \delta a(l-a)^2]$$

$$= -\frac{Wa(l-a)^2}{l^2} + \frac{W}{l^2}[a(l-a)^2 + \delta a(l-a)(l-3a)]$$

$$= \frac{W\delta a}{l^2}(l-a)(l-3a)$$

But $\qquad W\delta a = M_o$

∴ $\quad M_C = \dfrac{M_o}{l^2}(l-a)(l-3a)$

Similarly, $\quad M_D = \dfrac{M_o}{l^2}a(2l-3a)$

Problem 4.15 : A fixed beam AB of span 7 m is subjected to a couple of 40 kN-m at 3 m from A. Find the fixed end moments.

Solution :

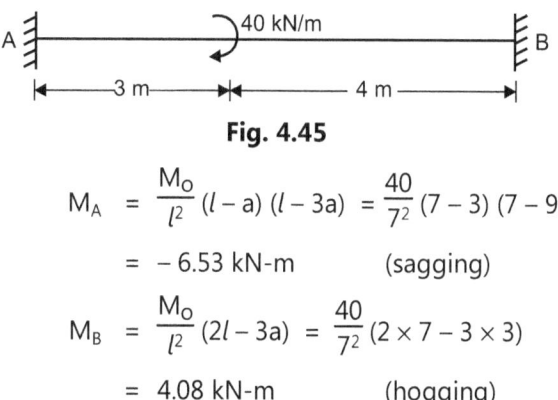

Fig. 4.45

$$M_A = \dfrac{M_o}{l^2}(l-a)(l-3a) = \dfrac{40}{7^2}(7-3)(7-9)$$

$$= -6.53 \text{ kN-m} \quad \text{(sagging)}$$

$$M_B = \dfrac{M_o}{l^2}(2l-3a) = \dfrac{40}{7^2}(2\times 7 - 3\times 3)$$

$$= 4.08 \text{ kN-m} \quad \text{(hogging)}$$

Case VII : Fixed beam carrying moment at a section :

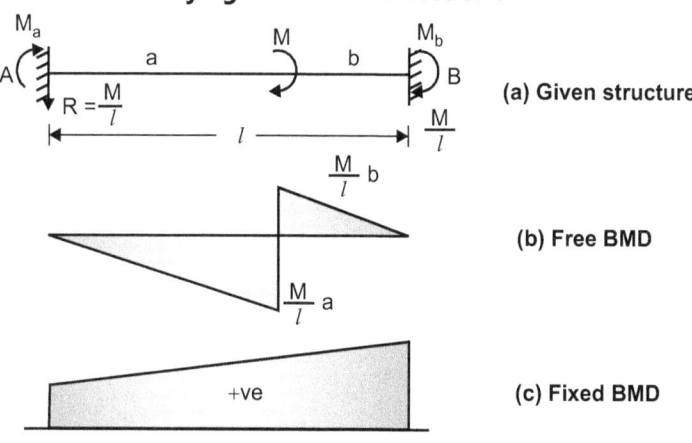

(a) Given structure

(b) Free BMD

(c) Fixed BMD

Fig. 4.46

Equating areas of free and fixed B.M.D.,

$$a = a'$$

$$\left(\dfrac{M_a + M_b}{2}\right)l = -\dfrac{1}{2}\dfrac{M}{l}\times a \times a + \dfrac{1}{2}\dfrac{M}{l}\times b \times b$$

$$(M_a + M_b) = -\dfrac{M}{l^2}[a^2-b^2] = -\dfrac{M}{l}[a-b] \qquad (\because l = a+b)$$

$$a\bar{x} = a'\bar{x}'$$

$$\therefore \left(\frac{M_a + M_b}{2}\right) l \left[\frac{M_a + 2M_b}{M_a + M_b}\right] \cdot \frac{l}{3} = \left[-\frac{M}{2l}\left(a^2 \times \frac{2}{3}a\right) + \frac{M}{2l}\left(b^2 + \left(a + \frac{b}{3}\right)\right)\right]$$

$$\therefore (M_a + 2M_b) = \frac{3M}{l^3}\left[-\frac{2a^3}{3} + \frac{b^2(3a+b)}{3}\right]$$

$$(M_a + 2M_b) = \frac{M}{l^3}[-2a^3 + 3ab^2 + b^3]$$

$$\begin{aligned}-2a^3 + 3ab^2 + b^3 &= -2a^3 + 2ab^2 + ab^2 + b^3 \\ &= 2a(-a^2 + b^2) + b^2(a+b) \\ &= (a+b)[-2a(a-b) + b^2]\end{aligned}$$

$$\therefore (M_a + 2M_b) = \frac{M}{l^3}[(a+b)[-2a(a-b) + b^2]]$$

But
$$M_a + M_b = -\frac{M}{l^2}(a^2 - b^2)$$

$$\therefore M_b = \frac{M}{l^3}\left[(a+b) - [2a(a-b) + b^2] + \frac{M}{l^2}(a^2 - b^2)\right]$$

$$M_b = \frac{M}{l^2}[-2a^2 + 2ab + b^2] + \frac{M}{l^2}(a^2 - b^2)$$

$$(a+b) = l$$

$$\therefore M_b = \frac{M}{l^2}[-2a^2 + 2ab + b^2 + a^2 - b^2]$$

$$= \frac{M}{l^2}[-a^2 + 2ab] = \frac{M_a}{l^2}(-a + 2b)$$

$$\therefore M_b = \frac{M_a}{l^2}(2b - a) = \frac{M_a}{l}\left(\frac{3b}{l} - 1\right)$$

$$M_a + M_b = -\frac{M}{l^2}(a^2 - b^2) = -\frac{M}{l}(a-b)$$

$$\therefore M_a = -\frac{M}{l^2}(a^2 - b^2) - \frac{M_a}{l^2}(2b - a) = -\frac{M}{l^2}(a^2 - b^2 + 2ab - a^2)$$

$$M_a = -\frac{M}{l^2}(2ab - b^2) = -\frac{M_b}{l}\left(\frac{3a}{l} - 1\right)$$

(− sign shows that M_a is sagging).

Case VIII : Fixed beam with central couple :

• **Particular case :**
If moment is acting at the centre as shown below, then

$$a = \frac{l}{2} \text{ and } b = \frac{l}{2}$$

$$M_a = -\frac{M}{l^2}(2ab - b^2)$$

$$= -\frac{M}{l^2}\left(2 \times \frac{l^2}{4} - \frac{l^2}{4}\right) = -\frac{M}{4} = -\frac{M}{4} \text{ (sagging)}$$

$$M_b = \frac{M_a}{l^2}(2b - a)$$

$$= \frac{M}{l^2} \times \frac{l}{2}\left(2 \times \frac{l}{2} - \frac{l}{2}\right)$$

$$= \frac{M}{4} \text{ (hogging)}$$

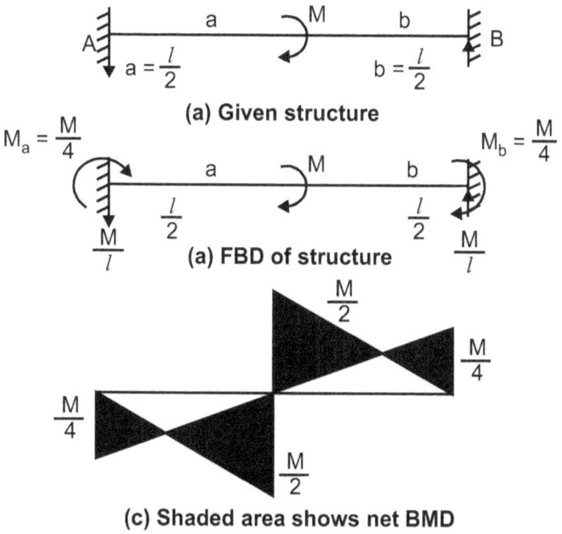
A
a
M
b
B
a = l/2
b = l/2
(a) Given structure
Ma = M/4
Mb = M/4
a
M
b
l/2
l/2
M/l
M/l
(a) FBD of structure
M/2
M/4
M/4
M/2
(c) Shaded area shows net BMD

Fig. 4.47

Problem 4.16 : Consider a built-up beam AB of 15 m. Two couples of values of 20 kN-m and 30 kN-m are acting at 5 m and 7.5 m respectively from support A. Find the fixed end moments.

Solution :

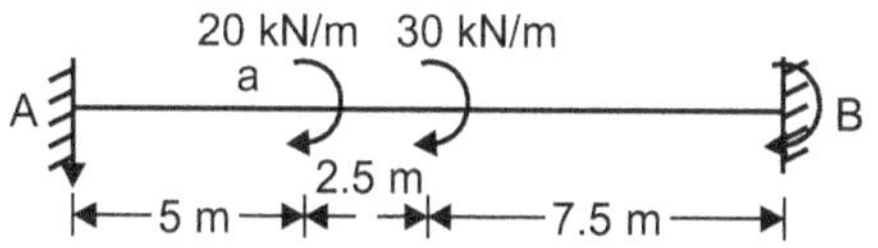
20 kN/m 30 kN/m
a
A
B
2.5 m
5 m
7.5 m

Fig. 4.48

M_a = Moment due to eccentric couple + Moment due to central couple

$$= \frac{M_b}{l}\left(\frac{3a}{l} - 1\right) + \frac{M_2}{4}$$

$$= \frac{20 \times 10}{15}\left(\frac{3 \times 5}{10} - 1\right) + \frac{30}{4} = 6.67 + 7.5$$

$$= 14.17 \text{ kN-m} \qquad \text{(sagging)}$$

$$M_b = \text{Moment due to eccentric couple + Moment due to central couple}$$

$$= \frac{M_1 a}{l}\left(\frac{3b}{l} - 1\right) + \frac{M_2}{4}$$

$$= \frac{20 \times 5}{15}\left(\frac{3 \times 10}{10} - 1\right) + \frac{30}{4} = 13.33 + 7.5$$

$$= 20.83 \text{ kN-m (hogging)}$$

Case IX : Fixed beams with ends at different level : (Effect of sinking of support) :

Let CD be a beam of which C is at higher level than D by δ. Let M_C and M_D be fixed end moments with equal magnitude and opposite sign. Let V be the reaction at each support.

Fig. 4.49

Since rate of loading is zero,

$$\therefore \quad EI\frac{d^4y}{dx^4} = 0$$

Integrating above equation,

$$\therefore \quad EI\frac{d^3y}{dx^3} = C_1$$

At $x = 0$, $\quad$ S.F. $= \dfrac{d^3y}{dx^3} = -V$

$$\therefore \quad C_1 = -V$$

$$EI\frac{d^2y}{dx^2} = -Vx + C_2$$

At $x = 0$, B.M. $= -M_C$

$$\therefore \quad C_2 = -M_C$$

$$EI\frac{dy}{dx} = -\frac{Vx^2}{2} + C_2 x + C_3$$

At $x = 0$, $\dfrac{dy}{dx} = 0$, $\therefore C_3 = 0$

$$EI\, y = -\frac{Vx^3}{6} + \frac{C_2 x^2}{2} + C_3 x + C_4$$

At $x = 0$, $y = 0$ $\therefore C_4 = 0$

$$\therefore \quad EI\, y = -\frac{Vx^3}{6} + \frac{M_C x^2}{2}$$

At $x = l$, $y = -\delta$. $\quad$ (below C)

$$-EI\,\delta = -\frac{Vl^3}{6} + \frac{M_C l^2}{2} \qquad \ldots (4.11)$$

At $x = l$, $\dfrac{dy}{dx} = 0$.

$$\therefore \quad EI\dfrac{dy}{dx} = -\dfrac{Vx^2}{2} + M_C x$$

$$\therefore \quad 0 = -\dfrac{Vl^2}{2} + M_C l$$

$$\therefore \quad M_C = \dfrac{Vl}{2} \quad \text{and} \quad V = \left(\dfrac{2M_C}{l}\right)$$

$$\therefore \quad EI\, y = -\dfrac{Vx^3}{6} + \dfrac{M_C x^2}{2}$$

At $x = l$, $y = -\delta$

$$\therefore \quad -EI\, \delta = \dfrac{-Vl^3}{6} + \dfrac{Vl}{4} \times l^2$$

$$\therefore \quad -EI\, \delta = \dfrac{Vl^3}{12}$$

$$\therefore \quad V = -\dfrac{12 EI\, \delta}{l^3}$$

$$V = \dfrac{2M_C}{l}$$

$$\therefore \quad M_C = -\dfrac{6EI\delta}{l^2}$$

B.M. at any distance at x from C :

$$-M = EI\dfrac{d^2y}{dx^2} = Vx - M_C = \dfrac{2M_C}{l}x - M_C$$

At $x = l$, $M = +M_D$

$$\therefore \quad -M_D = +2M_C - M_C = +M_C$$
$$\therefore \quad M_D = -M_C$$
$$\therefore \quad -M_D = -\dfrac{6EI\delta}{l^2}$$
$$\therefore \quad M_D = \dfrac{6EI\delta}{l^2}$$

Problem 4.17 : A beam CD is of span 6 m. The support D sinks by 1.2 cm. Determine the fixing end moments at C and D. I = 9870 cm^4, E = 2 × 10^5 N/mm^2.

Solution :

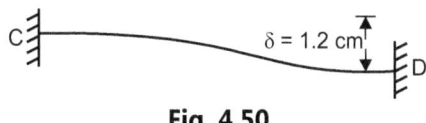

Fig. 4.50

Using the reaction,

$$M_C = -\dfrac{6EI\delta}{l^2}$$

$$= -\frac{6 \times 2 \times 10^5 \times 9870 \times 10^4 \times 12}{(6000)^2}$$

$$= -39.48 \times 10^6 \text{ N-mm}$$

$$= -39.48 \text{ kN-m} \quad \text{(hogging)}$$

$$M_D = \frac{6EI\delta}{l^2} = 39.48 \times 10^6 \text{ N-mm}$$

$$= 39.48 \text{ kN-m} \quad \text{(sagging)}$$

Problem 4.18 : Draw B.M.D. and S.F.D. for a fixed beam AB as in Fig. 4.52 (a).

(P.U. Nov./Dec. 2000)

Solution :

$$a = a'$$

$$\therefore \int_0^4 \left(36.25x - \frac{10x^2}{2}\right) dx + \left(\frac{65 + 57.5}{2}\right) \times 2 + \frac{1}{2} \times 57.5 \times 2 = \left(\frac{M_a + M_b}{2}\right) \times 8$$

$$\left[\frac{36.25x^2}{2} - \frac{10x^3}{6}\right]_0^4 + 122.5 + 57.5 = 4(M_a + M_b)$$

$$M_a + M_b = 90.83$$

$$\bar{x} = \bar{x}'$$

Moment of area @ a :

$$a\bar{x} = \int_0^4 (36.25x - 5x^2) x \, dx + 122.5 \times 4.98 + 57.5 \times 6.67$$

$$= \left[\frac{36.25x^3}{3} - \frac{5x^4}{4}\right]_0^4 + 993.575$$

$$\therefore \quad a\bar{x} = 453.33 + 993.575$$

$$= 1446.91$$

$$\therefore \quad \bar{x} = \frac{1446.91}{363.32} = 3.982$$

$$\bar{x}' = \frac{M_a + 2M_b}{(M_a + M_b)} \times \frac{l}{3} = \frac{M_a + 2M_b}{90.83} \times \frac{8}{3} = \frac{(M_a + 2M_b)}{34.06}$$

Now, $\bar{x} = \bar{x}'$

$$\therefore \quad 3.982 = \left(\frac{M_a + 2M_b}{34.06}\right)$$

$$\therefore \quad M_b = 44.8 \text{ kN-m}$$

and $M_a = 46.03 \text{ kN-m}$

Reaction : (a) Due to external loads :

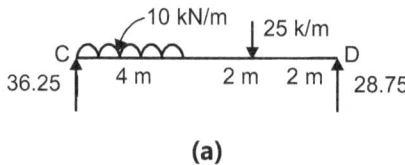

(a)

(b) Due to moments :

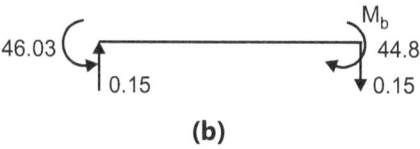

(b)

∴ Reaction at R_A = 36.25 + 0.15 = 36.4 kN

Reaction at R_B = 28.75 – 0.15 = 28.60 kN

Fig. 4.51

(a) Given structure

(b) FBD of beam

(c) SFD

(d) BMD due to fixed end moments

(e) BMD due to simple support

(f) BMD by superposition

(g) BMD on tension side

Fig. 4.52

4.10 CONTINUOUS BEAMS

A continuous beam is an indeterminate structure and it is supported on more than two supports. Clapeyron's theorem is applied to only indeterminate structure. This theorem is derived by taking into account the bending moment at three consecutive supports in a continuous beam so called as *theorem of three moments*.

In a continuous beam, the spans will deflect in downward direction in intermediate part and upward at each support. All the intermediate supports carry the moments and if the end supports are fixed, then moment is developed at the end supports and if the end supports are simply supported, then the moments at end supports are zero.

This theorem is applied to two spans considering the released structure with moments at supports as redundant reactions. Net B.M. diagram is obtained if we superimpose the free B.M. diagram on the fixed B.M.D.

4.11 CLAPEYRON'S THEOREM

A beam is said to be continuous when it is supported by more than two supports. In a continuous beam, every span will deflect downwards in intermediate part and upward at each support. The intermediate supports subjected to some moment and end supports are subjected to moments if the supports are fixed supports and no moments if supports are simply supported.

Net B.M. diagram is occured if we superimpose free B.M. diagram on the fixed B.M. diagram.

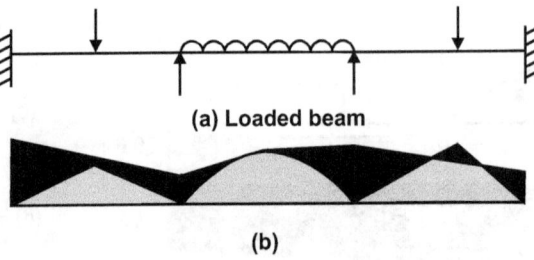

(a) Loaded beam

(b)

Fig. 4.53

Clapeyron's theorem of three moments : It states that if a beam is continuous beam and it has n supports (end supports are fixed) then to find the moments at n supports, we require minimum n equations and that can be obtained from the consecutive spans of the continuous beam.

4.11.1 Proof

Let CD and DE are any two consecutive spans of a continuous beam CDE. This beam is subjected to external loading. Let the support moments are M_C, M_D and M_E. Then according to Clapeyron's theorem, $M_C l_1 + 2M_D (l_1 + l_2) + M_E l_2 = \dfrac{6a_1 x_1}{l_1} + \dfrac{6a_2 x_2}{l_2}$

where,
- a_1 = Area of free B.M. diagram of span CD
- a_2 = Area of free B.M. diagram of span DE
- x_1 = C.G. of free B.M. diagram from support C
- x_2 = C.G. of free B.M. diagram from support E

l_1 = Span of CD
l_2 = Span of DE
I_1 & I_2 = M.I. of CD and DE respectively

Consider span CD :
Let at a distance x from C,

$$\text{Net B.M.} = M_x - M_x'$$

where, M_x = Free B.M. from C

M_x' = Fixed B.M. from C

$$\therefore \quad EI_1 \frac{d^2y}{dx^2} = M_x - M_x'$$

Multiplying above equation by x, we get

$$EI_1 \frac{d^2y}{dx^2} x = (M_x - M_x') x$$

Integrating the above equation,

$$\int_0^{l_1} EI_1 \frac{d^2y}{dx^2} x \, dx = \int_0^{l_1} (M_x - M_x') x \, dx$$

$$EI_1 \left[x \frac{dy}{dx} - y \right] = \int_0^{l_1} M_x \cdot x \, dx - \int_0^{l_1} M_x' \, dx$$

But
(i) At x = 0, y = 0.

(ii) At x = l_1, y = 0 and $\frac{dy}{dx}$ = i_{dc} (Slope at D for CD)

(iii) $\int_0^{l_1} M_x \cdot x \, dx = a_1 x_1$ = Moment of free B.M. diagram on CD @ C.

(iv) $\int_0^{l_1} M_x' \cdot x \, dx = a_1' x_1'$ = Moment of fixed B.M. diagram on CD @ C

$$\therefore \quad EI_1 l_1 i_{dc} = a_1 x_1 - a_1' x_1'$$

a_1' = Area of fixed B.M. diagram on CD = $\left(\frac{M_C + M_D}{2}\right) \times l_1$

x_1' = C.G. of the area from C = $\left(\frac{M_C + 2M_d}{M_C + M_d}\right) \frac{l_1}{3}$

$$\therefore \quad a_1' x_1' = (M_C + 2M_d) \frac{l_1^2}{6}$$

$$\therefore \quad EI_1 \, l_1 \, i_{dc} = a_1 x_1 - (M_c + 2M_d)\frac{l_1^2}{6}$$

$$\therefore \quad \frac{6 \, EI_1 \, l_1 \, i_{dc}}{l_1} = \frac{6a_1 x_1}{l_1} - \frac{(M_c + 2M_d) \, l_1^2}{l_1}$$

$$\therefore \quad 6Ei_{dc} = \frac{6a_1 x_1}{I_1 \, l_1} - (M_c + 2M_d)\frac{l_1}{I_1}$$

Considering span DE, we get the equation as

$$6 \, EI_2 \, i_{de} = \frac{6a_2 x_2}{l_2} - (M_e + 2M_d) \, l_2$$

$$\therefore \quad 6Ei_{de} = \frac{6a_2 x_2}{I_2 \, l_2} - \frac{(M_e + 2M_d) \, l_2}{I_2}$$

$$i_{de} = \text{Slope for span DE at D}$$

But $\quad i_{dc} = -i_{de}$

$\therefore \quad i_{dc} + i_{de} = 0$

$\therefore \quad 6E \, i_{dc} + 6E \, i_{de} = 0$

$$\therefore \quad 0 = \frac{6a_1 x_1}{I_1 l_1} + \frac{6a_2 x_2}{I_2 l_2} - \frac{(M_c + 2M_d) \, l_1}{I_1} - \frac{(M_e + 2M_d) \, l_2}{I_2}$$

$$\therefore \quad \frac{M_c \, l_1}{I_1} + 2M_d \left(\frac{l_1}{I_1} + \frac{l_2}{I_2}\right) + M_e \frac{l_2}{I_2} = \frac{6a_1 x_1}{I_1 \, l_1} + \frac{6a_2 x_2}{I_2 \, l_2}$$

If ABC is a continuous beam then

$$\therefore \quad M_a \left(\frac{l_1}{I_1}\right) + 2M_b \left(\frac{l_1}{I_1} + \frac{l_2}{I_2}\right) + M_c \left(\frac{l_2}{I_2}\right) = \frac{6a_1 \bar{x}_1}{I_1 \, l_1} + \frac{6a_2 \bar{x}_2}{I_2 \, l_2}$$

$$M_a \, l_1 + 2M_b \, (l_1 + l_2) + M_c \, l_2 = \frac{6a_1 \bar{x}_1}{l_1} + \frac{6a_2 \bar{x}_2}{l_2} \quad \text{(EI is constant)}$$

$\bar{x}_1$ and $\bar{x}_2$ are centroids of free B.M. diagram from A and C respectively.

This relation is known as Clapeyron's theorem of three moments.

4.12 MODIFIED THEOREM OF THREE MOMENTS FOR UNIFORMLY DISTRIBUTED LOADS

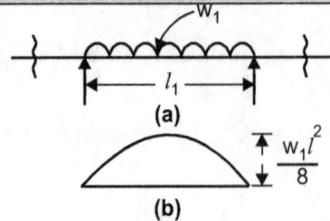

Fig. 4.54

Area of free B.M. diagram $= \dfrac{2}{3} \times \dfrac{W_1 l_1^2}{8} \times l_1 = \dfrac{W_1 l_1^3}{12}$ and $\bar{x}_1 = \dfrac{l_1}{2}$

$\therefore \quad a_1 \bar{x}_1 = \dfrac{W_1 l_1^3}{12} \times \dfrac{l_1}{2} = \dfrac{W_1 l_1^4}{24}$

$\therefore \quad \dfrac{6 a_1 \bar{x}_1}{l_1} = \dfrac{6 \times W_1 l_1^4}{24 \times l_1} = \dfrac{W_1 l_1^3}{4}$

∴ If both spans are loaded with U.D.L. having intensities W_1 and W_2 then theorem of three moments is modified as below.

$$M_A l_1 + 2 M_b (l_1 + l_2) + M_C l_2 = \dfrac{W_1 l_1^3}{4} + \dfrac{W_2 l_2^3}{4}.$$

If one span loaded with U.D.L. of intensity W_1 and other with concentrated or U.V.L. then modified form is as below :

$$M_A l_1 + 2 M_b (l_1 + l_2) + M_C l_2 = \dfrac{W_1 l_1^3}{4} + \dfrac{6 a_2 \bar{x}_2}{l_2}$$

4.13 DIFFERENT TYPES OF CONTINUOUS BEAMS

Types of beams are related with end supports. They are classified as under :
1. Both end supports are simple supports.
2. One end support as simple support and other one is fixed support.
3. Both supports are fixed supports.
4. One end support is simple support and other end is overhang.
5. One end support is fixed support and other end is overhang.
6. Beams with sinking of support.

Procedure for Clapeyron's theorem or theorem of three moments :
1. Assume imaginary spans if the ends of the beam are fixed ends. (If left side end is fixed, then assume imaginary span on left side and if right side end is fixed, then assume imaginary span on right side).

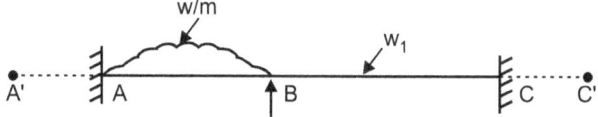

Fig. 4.55 (a)

2. Draw the B.M. diagram by considering each span as simply supported (i.e. free B.M. diagram for each span.)

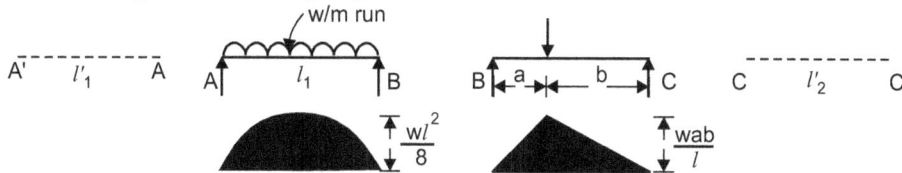

Fig. 4.55 (b)

3. Find the values of areas of free B.M.D. and their C.G.S. from the end supports.

4. Calculate the values of $\dfrac{6a\bar{x}}{l}$ for each span.

$$\left[\text{If beam is loaded with U.D.L., we have modified form as } \dfrac{6a\bar{x}}{l} = \dfrac{Wl^3}{4}\right]$$

5. Apply the theorem of three moments from each continuous spans

$$M_a'\left(\dfrac{l_1}{I_1}\right) + 2M_a\left(\dfrac{l_1}{I_1} + \dfrac{l_2}{I_2}\right) + M_c\left(\dfrac{l_2}{I_2}\right) = \dfrac{6a_1\bar{x_1}}{I_1 l_1} + \dfrac{6a_2\bar{x_2}}{I_2 l_2} \quad \text{(EI is not constant)}$$

6. Perform the equations for the total structure.
7. Solving the above equations, we can easily get the moments at ends (if end supports are fixed) and on continuous supports.
8. Draw the free B.M.D. and superimposed fixed B.M.D. on free B.M.D.
9. Draw B.M.D. on tension side.

4.13.1 Case I : Both End Supports are Simple Supports

In this type of beam, end moments are zero and only moments on intermediate supports are unknown. Thus, in this case the number of equations required are equal to the number of intermediate supports.

SOLVED PROBLEMS

Problem 4.19 : A beam ABC is simply supported at A and C and is continuous over B. It is loaded with U.D.L. Intensity of load on AB is 60 kN/m having span 4 m and on BC 100 kN/m having span 6 m. Find moment at B and draw S.F.D. and B.M.D.

Solution : Applying theorem of three moments, (EI is constant)

$$M_a l_1 + 2M_b (l_1 + l_2) + M_c l_3 = \dfrac{6a_1 \bar{x_1}}{l_1} + \dfrac{6a_2 \bar{x_2}}{l_2}$$

As beam is loaded with U.D.L. only therefore applying modified theorem,

$$\therefore \quad M_a l_1 + 2M_b (l_1 + l_2) + M_c l_3 = \dfrac{W_1 l_1^3}{4} + \dfrac{W_2 l_2^3}{4}.$$

As ends A and C are simply supported,

$$\therefore \qquad M_a = M_c = 0$$

l_1 = 4 m, l_2 = 6 m, W_1 = 60 kN/m, W_2 = 100 kN/m.

$$\therefore \qquad 2M_b (l_1 + l_2) = \dfrac{W_1 l_1^3}{4} + \dfrac{W_2 l_2^3}{4}$$

$$2M_b (4 + 6) = \dfrac{60 \times 4^3}{4} + \dfrac{100 \times 6^3}{4}$$

$$\therefore \qquad M_b = 318 \text{ kN-m}$$

Reactions : (a) Due to external loads :

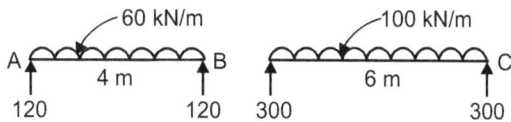

Fig. 4.56 (a)

(b) Due to moments :

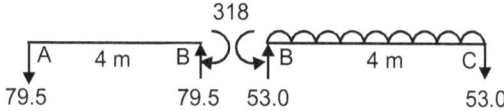

Fig. 4.56 (b)

Reaction at A = 120 − 79.50 = 40.50 kN

Reaction at B = 120 + 300 + 79.50 + 53.0 = 552.50 kN

Reaction at C = 300 − 53.0 = 247.0 kN

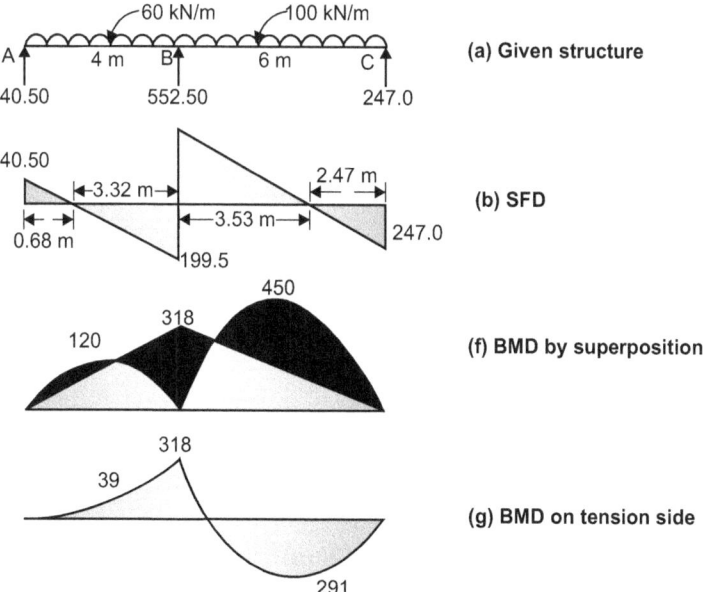

Fig. 4.57

Problem 4.20 : Analyse the continuous beam shown in Fig. 4.58 (a)

Solution :

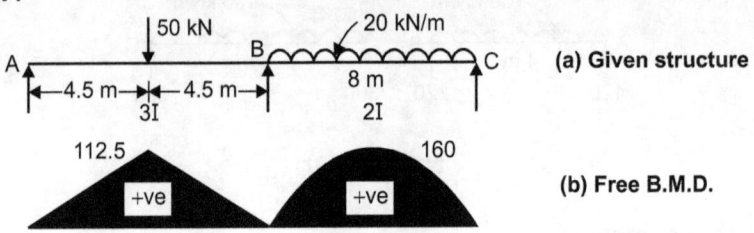

(a) Given structure

(b) Free B.M.D.

Fig. 4.58

AB : $\quad \dfrac{6a_1 \bar{x}_1}{I_1 l_1} = \dfrac{6 \times \frac{1}{2} \times 112.5 \times 9 \times 4.5}{3I \times 9} = \dfrac{506.25}{I}$

BC : $\quad \dfrac{6a_2 \bar{x}_2}{I_2 l_2} = \dfrac{W_1 l_1^3}{I_2 l_2} = \dfrac{20 \times 8^3}{4 \times 2I} = \dfrac{1280}{I}$

Applying theorem of three moments :

$$M_a \dfrac{l_1}{I_1} + 2M_b \left(\dfrac{l_1}{I_1} + \dfrac{l_2}{I_2}\right) + M_c \left(\dfrac{l_2}{I_2}\right) = \dfrac{6a_1 \bar{x}_1}{I_1 l_1} + \dfrac{6a_2 \bar{x}_2}{I_2 l_2}$$

As A and C are simply supported,

∴ $\quad M_A = M_C = 0$

∴ $\quad 2M_b \left(\dfrac{9}{3I} + \dfrac{8}{2I}\right) = \dfrac{506.25}{I} + \dfrac{1280}{I}$

$\dfrac{14 M_b}{I} = \dfrac{1786.25}{I} \quad ∴ \ M_b = 127.59 \text{ kN-m}$

Reactions :

(a) Due to external loads :

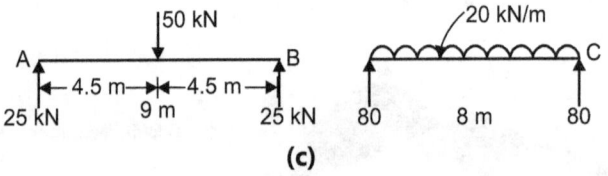

(c)

(b) Due to moments :

```
                127.59
         A        )B(              C
         ↓14.18  14.18↑  ↓15.95  15.95↓
```

Fig. 4.58 (d)

Reaction at A = 25 − 14.18 = 10.82 kN

Reaction at B = 25 + 14.18 + 80 + 15.95 = 135.13 kN

Reaction at C = 80 − 15.95 = 64.05 kN

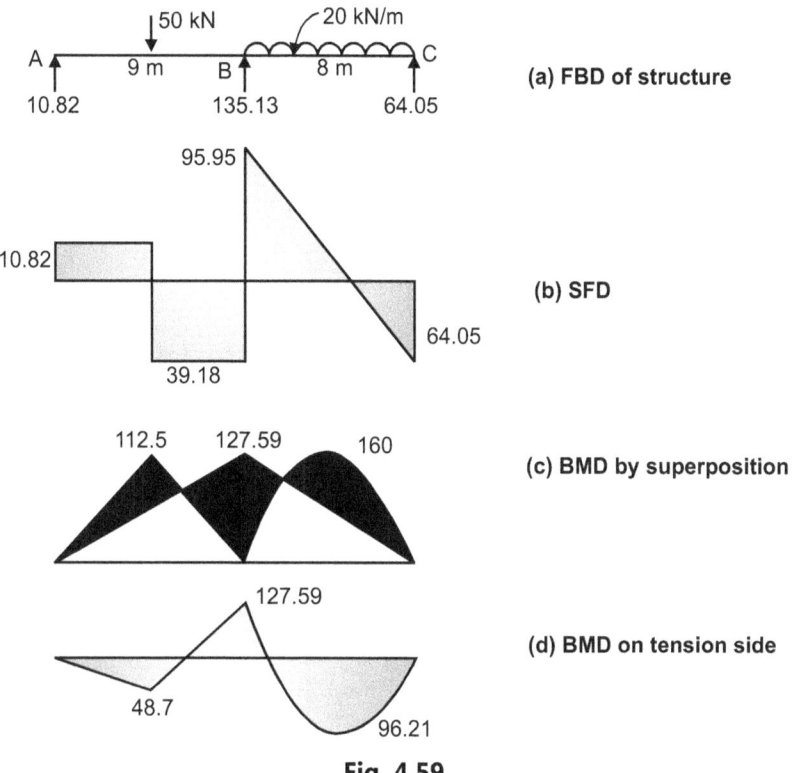

Fig. 4.59

Problem 4.21 : A continuous beam ABCD is simply supported over three spans, such that AB = 8 m, BC = 12 m and CD = 5 m. It carries UDL of 4 kN/m in span AB, 3 kN/m in span BC and 6 kN/m in span CD. Find the support moments over supports B and C. (I is same). Draw S.F.D. and B.M.D.

Solution : Theorem of three moments : (EI is constant)

$$M_A l_1 + 2M_B (l_1 + l_2) + M_C l_2 = \frac{6a_1 \bar{x}_1}{l_1} + \frac{6a_2 \bar{x}_2}{l_2}$$

But for U.D.L.,

$$\frac{6a_1 \bar{x}_1}{l_1} = \frac{W_1 l_1^3}{4}$$

∴ $$M_A l_1 + 2M_B (l_1 + l_2) + M_C l_2 = \frac{W_1 l_1^3}{4} + \frac{W_2 l_2^3}{4}$$

Consider span ABC :

As A is simple support, ∴ $M_A = 0$.

$l_1 = 8$ m, $l_2 = 12$ m, $w_1 = 4$ kN/m, $w_2 = 3$ kN/m

$$\therefore \quad 0 \times 8 + 2 M_B (8 + 12) + M_C \times 12 = \frac{4 \times 8^3}{4} + \frac{3 \times 12^3}{4}$$

$$\therefore \quad 40 M_B + 12 M_C = 512 + 1296 = 1808$$

$$3.33 M_B + M_C = 150.67$$

$$M_C = 150.67 - 3.33 M_B \quad \ldots (1)$$

Consider span BCD :

As D is simply supported, $\therefore M_D = 0$

$l_2 = 12$ m, $l_3 = 5$ m, $W_2 = 3$ kN/m, $W_3 = 6$ kN/m

$$\therefore \quad M_B l_2 + 2 M_C (l_2 + l_3) + M_D l_3 = \frac{W_2 l_2^3}{4} + \frac{W_3 l_3^3}{4}$$

$$12 M_B + 34 M_C + 5 \times 0 = \frac{3 \times 12^3}{4} + \frac{6 \times 5^3}{4} = 1483.5$$

$$0.35 M_B + M_C = 43.63 \quad \ldots (2)$$

From equations (1) and (2),

$$0.35 M_B + 150.67 - 3.33 M_B = 43.63$$

$$M_B = 35.9 \text{ kN-m}$$

Put value of M_B in equation (2).

$$\therefore \quad M_C = 150.67 - 3.33 M_B = 150.67 - 3.33 \times 35.9$$

$$= 31.06 \text{ kN-m}$$

Reactions : (a) Due to external loads :

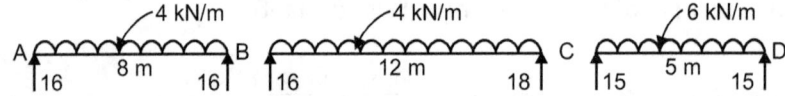

(b) Due to moments :

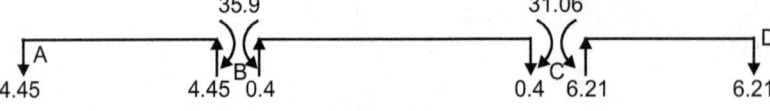

Fig. 4.60

Reaction at R_A = 16 − 4.45 = 11.55 kN

Reaction at R_B = 16 + 18 + 4.45 + 0.4 = 38.85 kN

Reaction at R_C = 18 + 15 + 6.21 − 0.4 = 39.61 kN

Reaction at R_D = 15 − 6.21 = 8.79 kN

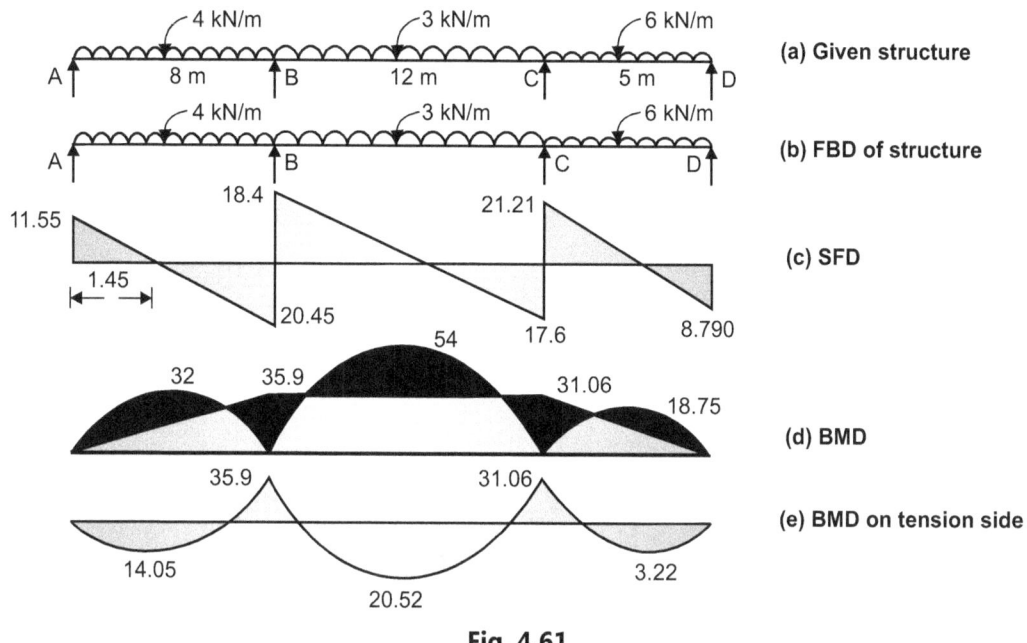

Fig. 4.61

Problem 4.22 : A continuous beam ABCD is simply supported over three spans of 6 m, 5 m and 4 m respectively. The beams are carrying point loads of 90 kN and 80 kN at 2 m and 8 m from support A and U.D.L. of 30 kN/m over span CD. Find moments and reactions at support.

Solution :

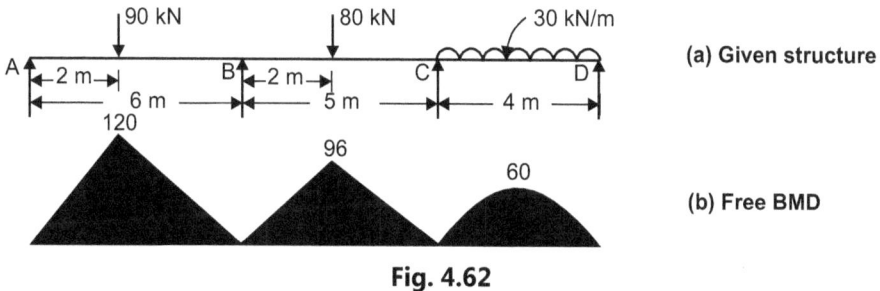

Fig. 4.62

Theorem of three moments :

$$M_a l_1 + 2M_b (l_1 + l_2) + M_c l_2 = \frac{6a_1 \bar{x}_1}{l_1} + \frac{6a_2 \bar{x}_2}{l_2}$$

For span ABC :

$M_A = 0$ as simply supported.

$l_1 = 6$ m, $l_2 = 5$ m, $a = 2$ m, $\bar{x}_1 = \left(\frac{l_1 + a}{3}\right)$, $b = 3$ m, $\bar{x}_2 = \left(\frac{l_2 + b}{3}\right)$. (from C)

$$\frac{6a_1 \bar{x}_1}{l_1} = 6 \times \frac{1}{2} \times \frac{120 \times 6}{6} \times \left(\frac{6+2}{3}\right)$$

$$= 960$$

$$\frac{6a_2 \bar{x}_2}{l_2} = 6 \times \frac{1}{2} \times \frac{96 \times 5}{5} \times \left(\frac{5+3}{3}\right) \text{ (from C)}$$

$$= 768$$

$$\therefore \quad 2M_B(6+5) + M_C \times 5 = 960 + 768$$

$$4.4 M_B + M_C = 345.6$$

$$M_C = 345.6 - 4.4 M_B \qquad \ldots (1)$$

For span BCD :

$$M_B l_2 + 2M_C(l_2 + l_3) + M_D l_3 = \frac{6a_2 \bar{x}_2}{l_2} + \frac{W_3 l_3^3}{4}$$

$$M_D = 0, \; l_2 = 5 \text{ m}, \; l_3 = 4 \text{ m}, \; W_3 = 30 \text{ kN/m}$$

$$\frac{6a_2 \bar{x}_2}{l_2} = 6 \times \frac{1}{2} \times \frac{96}{5} \times 5 \times \left(\frac{5+2}{3}\right) \text{ (from B)}$$

$$\frac{W_3 l_3^3}{4} = \frac{30 \times 4^3}{4} = 480$$

$$\therefore \quad M_B \times 5 + 2M_C(5+4) = 672 + 480$$

$$\therefore \quad 0.28 M_B + M_C = 64$$

Putting M_C from equation (1),

$$0.28 M_B + 345.6 - 4.4 M_B = 64.00$$

$$\therefore \quad M_B = 68.35 \text{ kN-m}$$

Putting in equation (1),

$$\therefore \quad M_C = 345.6 - 4.4 M_B = 345.6 - 4.4 \times 68.35$$

$$= 44.86 \text{ kN-m}$$

Reactions : Span AB :

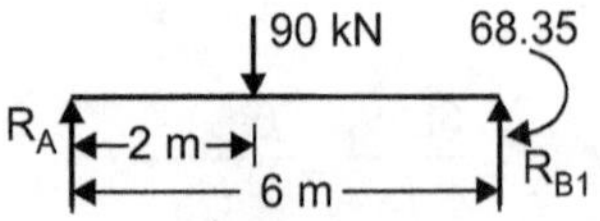

Fig. 4.63 (a)

$$\therefore \quad R_A = \frac{90 \times 4 - 68.35}{6} = 48.6 \text{ kN } (\uparrow)$$

$$R_{B_1} = \frac{90 \times 2 + 68.35}{6} = 41.4 \text{ kN } (\uparrow)$$

Span BC :

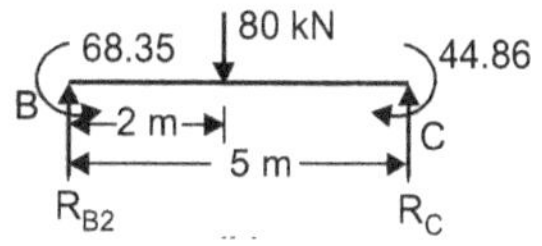

Fig. 4.63 (b)

$$R_{B_2} = \frac{80 \times 3 + 68.35 - 44.86}{5} = 52.7 \text{ kN } (\uparrow)$$

$$R_{C_2} = \frac{80 \times 2 + 44.86 - 68.35}{5} = 27.30 \text{ kN } (\uparrow)$$

Span CD :

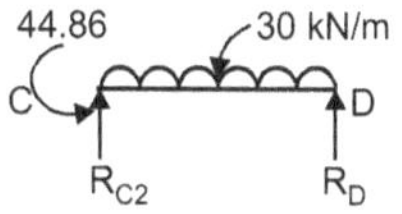

Fig. 4.63 (c)

$$R_{C_2} = \frac{30 \times 4 \times 2 + 44.86}{4} = 71.22 \text{ kN } (\uparrow)$$

$$R_D = \frac{30 \times 4 \times 2 - 44.86}{4} = 48.79 \text{ kN } (\uparrow)$$

∴ **Reactions :**

Reaction at A = $R_A = R_{A_1}$ = 48.6 kN (↑)

Reaction at B = $R_B = R_{B_1} + R_{B_2}$ = 41.4 + 52.7 = 94.1 kN (↑)

Reaction at C = $R_C = R_{C_1} + R_{C_2}$ = 27.30 + 71.22 = 98.52 kN (↑)

Reaction at D = R_D = 48.79 kN

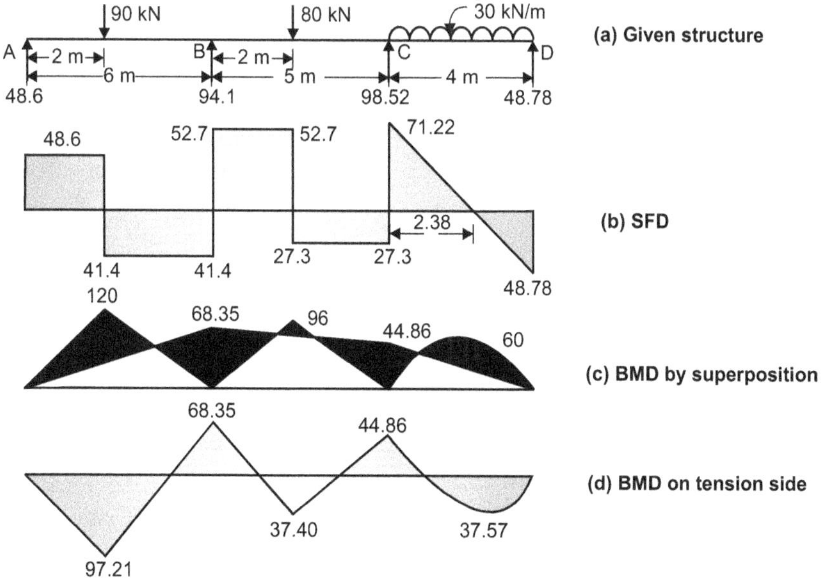

Fig. 4.64

4.13.2 Case II : One End Simple Support and Other End as Fixed Support

In this case, the moment on the simple support is zero. Total number of unknowns are intermediate support plus one. Plus one is due to moment at fixed end. But if we apply the theorem of three moments to continuous beam with above support conditions, we are getting number of equations equal to number of intermediate supports.

To get one additional equation consider the imaginary span on left of support if left support is fixed and on right side of support if right support is fixed support as shown below. All the data values for imaginary span are considered as zero.

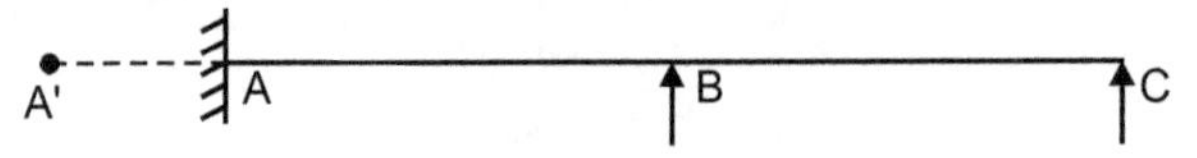

(a) A'A - Imaginary span

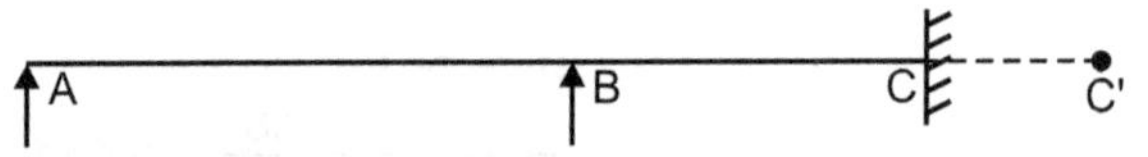

(b) CC' - Imaginary span

Fig. 4.65

Due to consideration of this imaginary span, we get one equation by applying theorem of three moments. Thus, the number of equations available equals the number of unknowns. Thus, this imaginary span makes the analysis of structure.

SOLVED PROBLEMS

Problem 4.23 : A continuous beam ABCD is fixed at A and simply supported at D and continuous over B and C. Loading system is as shown in Fig. 4.66 (a). Draw S.F.D. and B.M.D.

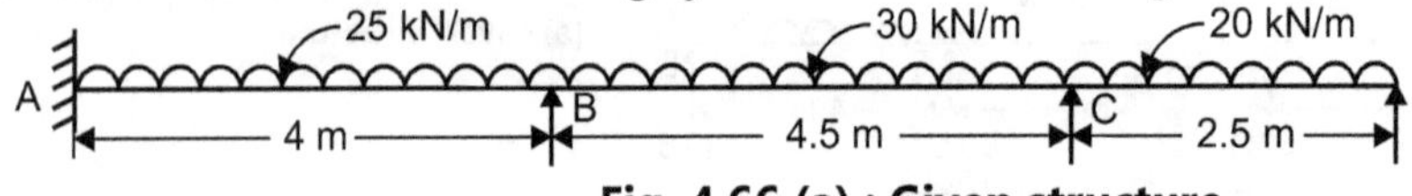

Fig. 4.66 (a) : Given structure

Solution : Applying theorem of three moments to the continuous beam ABCD,

AB : $\quad \dfrac{6a_1 \bar{x}_1}{l_1} = \dfrac{W_1 l_1^3}{4} = \dfrac{25 \times (4)^3}{4} = 400$

BC : $\quad \dfrac{6a_2 \bar{x}_2}{l_2} = \dfrac{W_2 l_2^3}{4} = \dfrac{30 \times (4.5)^3}{4} = 683.44$

CD : $\quad \dfrac{6a_3 \bar{x}_3}{l_3} = \dfrac{W_3 l_3^3}{4} = \dfrac{20 \times (2.5)^3}{4} = 78.125$

As end A is fixed end, therefore consider imaginary span on left side of A as A'A as shown in Fig. 4.66 (b).

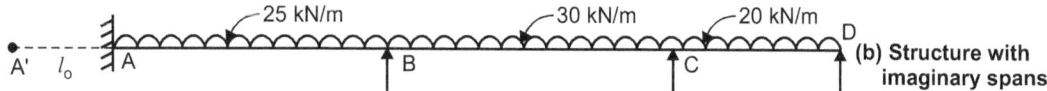

Fig. 4.66 (b) : Structure with imaginary spans

Span A'AB : $M_a' l_0 + 2M_a (l_0 + l_1) + M_b (l_1) = \dfrac{6a_1 \bar{x_1}}{l_1} + \dfrac{6a_2 \bar{x_2}}{l_2}$

Putting all the data values for imaginary span as zero,

∴ $\quad 2M_a (4) + 4 M_b = 400$

∴ $\quad 8M_a + 4 M_b = 400$ ... (1)

Span ABC :

$$M_a l_1 + 2M_b (l_1 + l_2) + M_c l_2 = \dfrac{6a_1 \bar{x_1}}{l_1} + \dfrac{6a_2 \bar{x_2}}{l_2}$$

$4M_a + 2M_b (4 + 4.5) + 4.5 M_c = 400 + 683.44$

$4M_a + 17 M_b + 4.5 M_c = 1083.44$ ... (2)

Span BCD :

$M_D = 0$ as end D is simply supported end.

$$M_b l_2 + 2M_c (l_2 + l_3) + M_D l_3 = \dfrac{6a_2 \bar{x_2}}{l_2} + \dfrac{6a_3 \bar{x_3}}{l_3}$$

$4.5 M_b + 2M_c (4.5 + 2.5) = 683.44 + 78.125$

$4.5 M_b + 14 M_c = 761.565$ ... (3)

Solving equations (1), (2) and (3) we get

$\quad M_b = 47.11$ kN-m

$\quad M_c = 39.25$ kN-m

$\quad M_a = 26.28$ kN-m

Reactions : (a) Due to external loads :

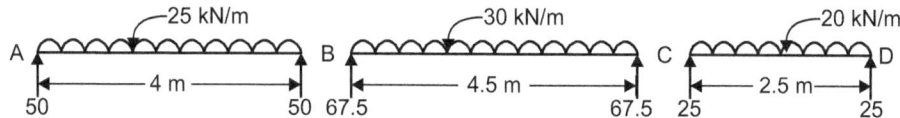

(b) Reactions due to moments :

Fig. 4.67

Reaction at A = 50 − 5.2 = 44.8 kN

Reaction at B = 50 + 67.5 + 5.2 + 1.75 = 124.45 kN

Reaction at C = 67.5 + 25 − 1.75 + 15.7 = 106.45 kN

Reaction at D = 25 − 15.7 = 9.3 kN

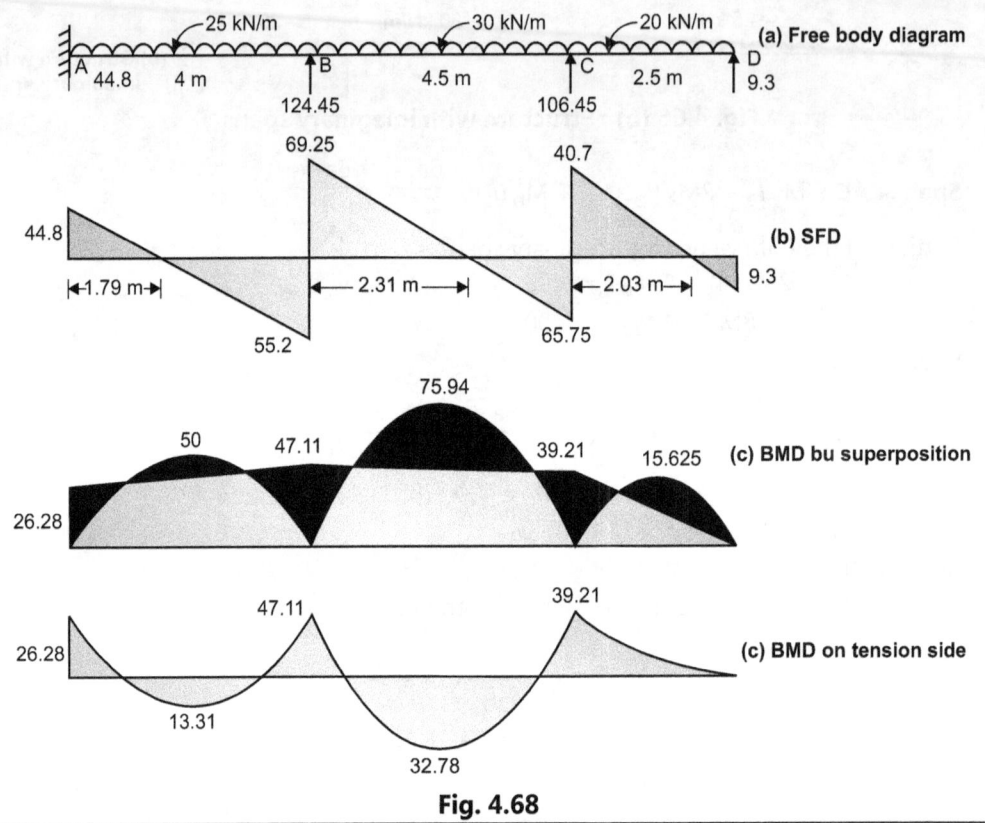

Fig. 4.68

Problem 4.24 : The support A of continuous beam is fixed while supports B and C are kept on rollers. AB = BC = 12 m. It carries U.D.L. of 30 kN/m over AB and a concentrated load of 240 kN over BC at 4 m from support B. Find the support moments and support reactions. Draw S.F.D. and B.M.D.

Solution : As support A is fixed support, therefore, consider an imaginary span A'A on left of A.

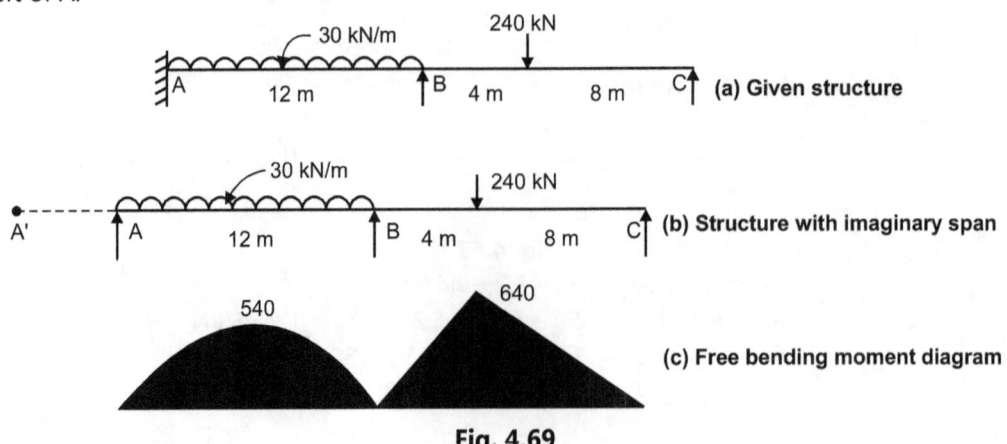

Fig. 4.69

A'A :

$$\frac{6a_1' x_1'}{l_1'} = 0 \quad \text{(Imaginary span)}$$

AB :

$$\frac{6a_1 \bar{x}_1}{l_1} = \frac{W_1 l_1^3}{4} = \frac{30 \times 12^3}{4} = 12960$$

BC :

$$\frac{6a_2 \bar{x}_2}{l_2} = 6 \times \frac{1}{2} \times \frac{640 \times 12}{12} \times \left(\frac{12 + 8}{3}\right) = 12800$$

Applying theorem of three moments :

Span A'AB :

$$M_a' l_1' + 2M_a (l_1' + l_1) + M_b l_1 = \frac{6a_1' x_1'}{l_1'} + \frac{6a_2 \bar{x}_1}{l_1}$$

$$24M_a + 12M_b = 12960 \quad \quad \ldots (1)$$

Span ABC :

$$M_a l_1 + 2M_b (l_1 + l_2) + M_c l_2 = \frac{6a_1 \bar{x}_1}{l_1} + \frac{6a_2 \bar{x}_2}{l_2}$$

$$12M_a + 48M_b + 12M_c = 12960 + 12800$$

As support C is simply supported, $\therefore M_c = 0$.

$$12M_a + 48M_b = 25760 \quad \quad \ldots (2)$$

Solving equations (1) and (2),

$$M_b = 459.05 \text{ kN-m}$$
$$M_a = 310.48 \text{ kN-m}$$

Reactions : (a) Due to external loads :

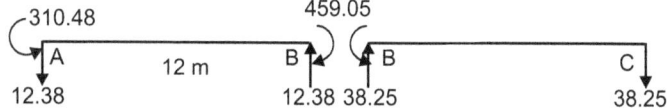

(b) Due to moments :

Fig. 4.70

Reaction at A = 180 − 12.38 = 167.62 kN

Reaction at B = 180 + 160 + 12.38 + 38.25 = 390.63 kN

Reaction at C = 80 − 38.25 = 41.75 kN

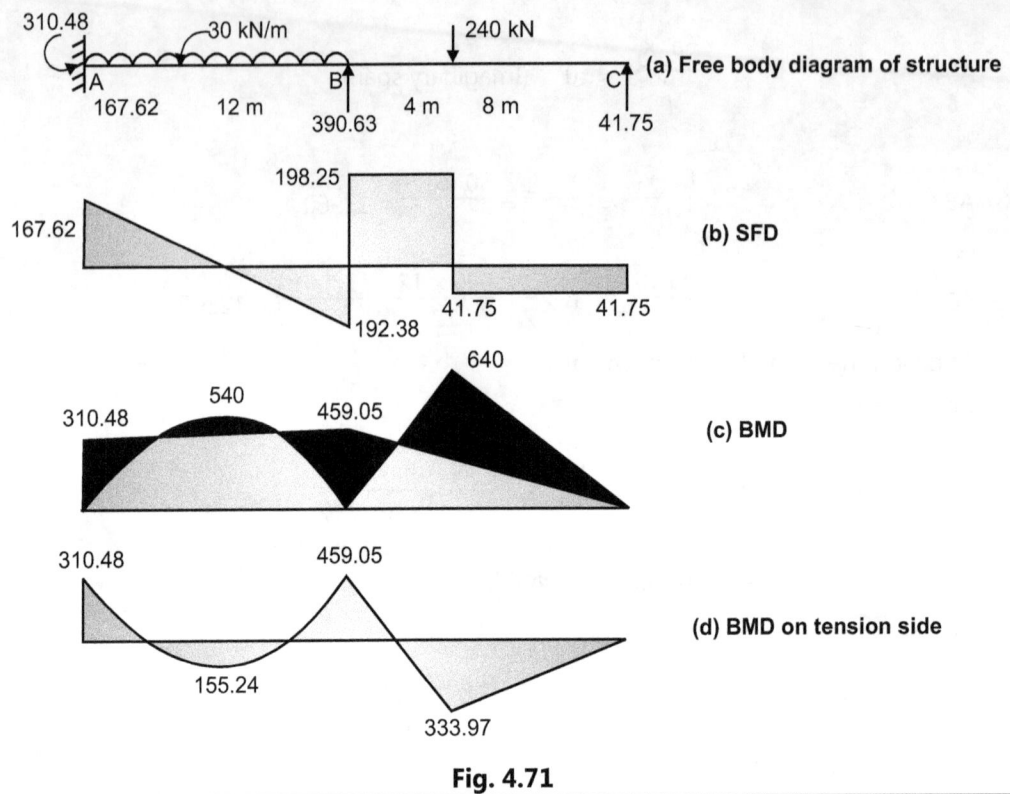

Fig. 4.71

Problem 4.25 : A continuous beam ABCD is fixed at D and roller supports at A, B and C. The length and the loading system is as shown in Fig. 4.72 (a). Draw B.M.D.

Solution :

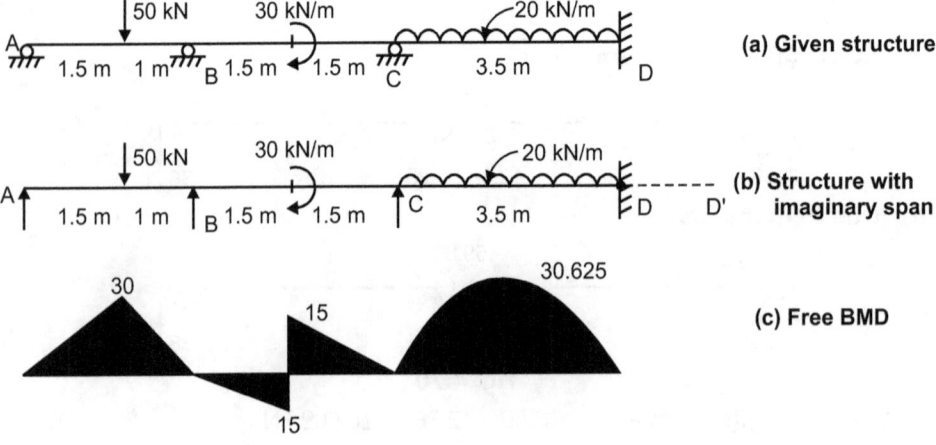

Fig. 4.72

As D is fixed end, therefore, we have to consider imaginary span DD'.

$$AB = \frac{6a_1 \bar{x}_1}{l_1} = \frac{6}{2.5} \times \frac{1}{2} \times 30 \times 2.5 \times \left(\frac{2.5 + 1.5}{3}\right) = 120$$

$$BC = \frac{6a_2 \bar{x}_2}{l_2} = \frac{6}{3}\left[-\frac{1}{2} \times 15 \times 1.5 \times 2 + \frac{1}{2} \times 15 \times 1.5 \times 1\right] = -22.5$$

$$CD = \frac{6a_3 \bar{x}_3}{l_3} = \frac{W_1 l_1^3}{4} = \frac{20 \times (3.5)^3}{4} = 214.375$$

DD' = 0. Imaginary span

Applying theorem of three moments to different spans :

$$M_a l_1 + 2M_b(l_1 + l_2) + M_c l_2 = \frac{6a_1 \bar{x}_1}{l_1} + \frac{6a_2 \bar{x}_2}{l_2}$$

As A is simply supported, ∴ $M_A = 0$

$2M_b(2.5 + 3) + 3M_c = 120 - 22.5$

∴ $\quad 11M_b + 3M_c = 97.50 \qquad \ldots (1)$

Span BCD :

$$M_b l_2 + 2M_c(l_2 + l_3) + M_D l_3 = \frac{6a_2 \bar{x}_2}{l_2} + \frac{6a_3 \bar{x}_3}{l_3}$$

$3M_b + 2M_c(3 + 3.5) + 3.5 M_D = -22.5 + 214.375$

$3M_b + 13 M_c + 3.5 M_D = 191.875 \qquad \ldots (2)$

Span CDD' :

$$M_c l_3 + 2M_D(l_3 + l_3') + M_D l_3' = \frac{6a_3 \bar{x}_3}{l_3} + \frac{6a_3' \bar{x}_3'}{l_3'}$$

$3.5 M_c + 7 M_D = 214.375 \qquad \ldots (3)$

Solving equations (1), (2) and (3),

$M_c = 5.57$ kN-m

$M_b = 7.34$ kN-m

$M_d = 27.84$ kN-m

Reactions : (a) Due to external loads :

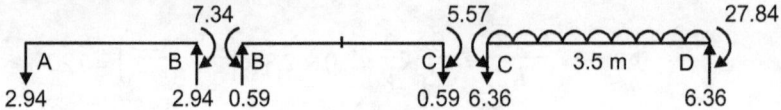

(b) Due to moments :

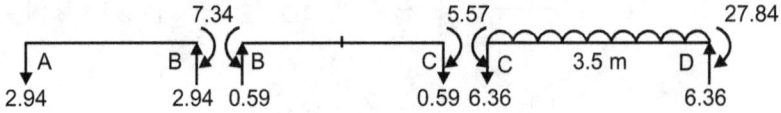

Fig. 4.73

Reaction at A = 20 – 2.94 = 17.06 kN
Reaction at B = 30 – 10 + 2.94 + 0.59 = 23.53 kN
Reaction at C = 10 + 35 – 0.59 – 6.36 = 38.05 kN
Reaction at D = 35 + 6.36 = 41.36 kN

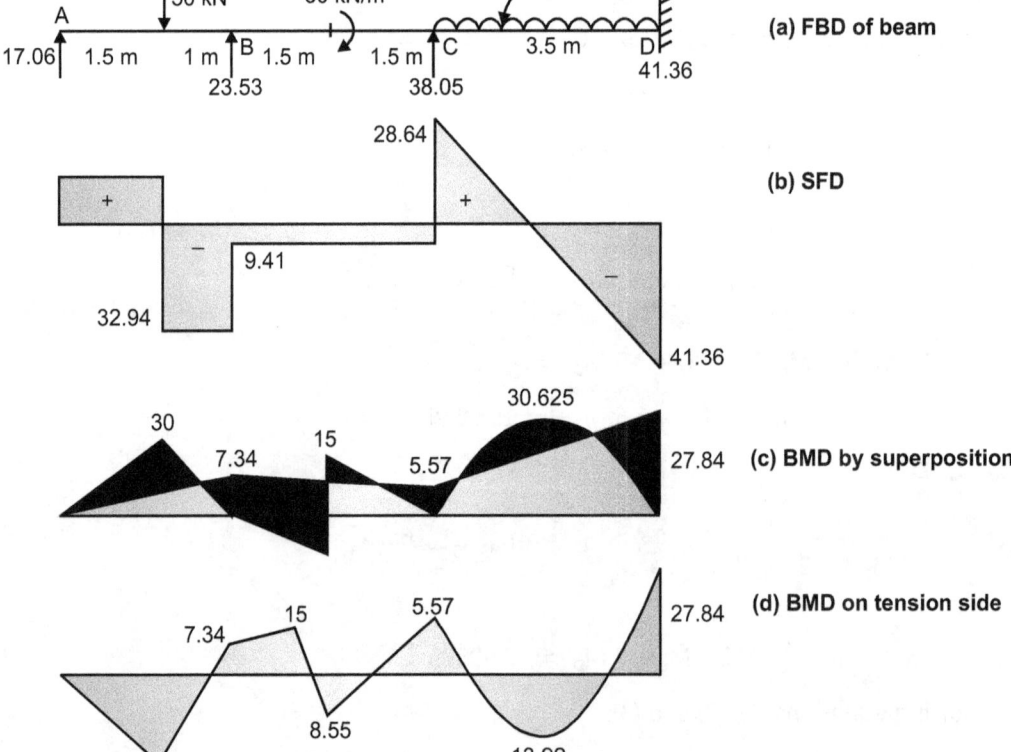

Fig. 4.74

4.13.3 Case III : Both the Ends of the Continuous Beam are Fixed Supports

By applying theorem of three moments for the continuous beams, we are getting number of equations equal to the intermediate supports. As both ends are fixed ends, so we require minimum two more equations for analysis of the beam. These two equations can be obtained by considering imaginary span on both the supports. The imaginary span is on left of left support and on right side of right support as shown in Fig. 4.75 below.

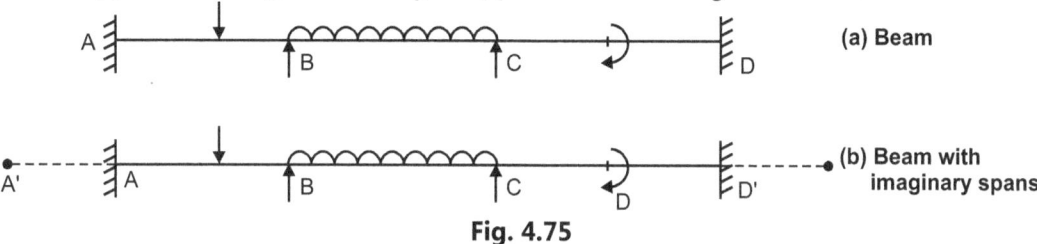

Fig. 4.75

A'A and DD' are the imaginary spans. Considering these imaginary spans, the beam ABCD can be easily analysed.

Problem 4.26 : A continuous beam ABC is fixed at A and C. It is continuous over support B. Span AB carries U.D.L. of 50 kN/m and BC carries U.D.L. of 40 kN/m. AB = 5 m and BC = 6 m. Draw S.F.D. and B.M.D.

Solution :

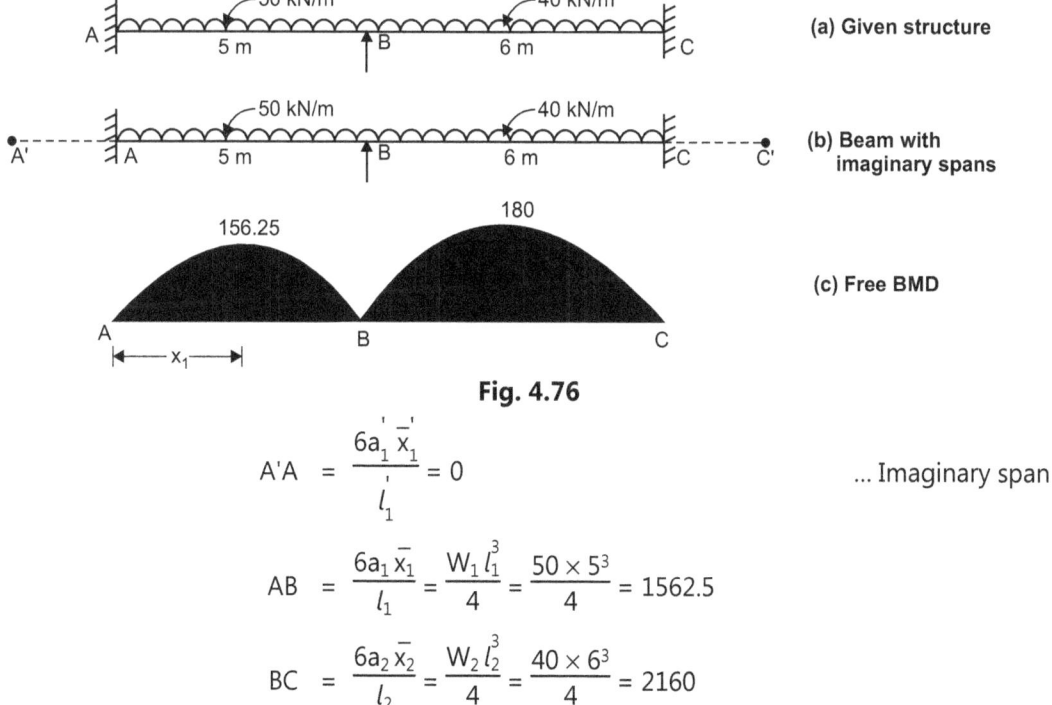

Fig. 4.76

$$A'A = \frac{6a_1' \bar{x}_1'}{l_1'} = 0 \qquad \text{... Imaginary span}$$

$$AB = \frac{6a_1 \bar{x}_1}{l_1} = \frac{W_1 l_1^3}{4} = \frac{50 \times 5^3}{4} = 1562.5$$

$$BC = \frac{6a_2 \bar{x}_2}{l_2} = \frac{W_2 l_2^3}{4} = \frac{40 \times 6^3}{4} = 2160$$

$$CC' = \frac{6a_2' \bar{x}_2'}{l_2'} = 0 \qquad \text{... Imaginary span}$$

Applying theorem of three moments to different spans :

Span A'AB : $\qquad M_a' = 0$

$$M_a' l_1' + 2 M_a (l_1' + l_1) + M_b l_1 = \frac{6a_1' \bar{x}_1'}{l_1'} + \frac{6a_1 \bar{x}_1}{l_1}$$

$$10 M_a + 5 M_b = 1562.5 \qquad \text{... (1)}$$

Span ABC :

$$M_a l_1 + 2 M_b (l_1 + l_2) + M_c l_2 = \frac{6a_1 \bar{x}_1}{l_1} + \frac{6a_2 \bar{x}_2}{l_2}$$

$$5M_a + 2M_b (5 + 6) + 6M_c = 1562.5 + 2160$$

$$5 M_a + 22 M_b + 6 M_c = 3722.5 \qquad \text{... (2)}$$

Span BCC' :

$$M_b l_2 + 2 M_c (l_2 + l_2') + M_c' l_2' = \frac{6a_2 \bar{x}_2}{l_2} + \frac{6a_2' \bar{x}_2'}{l_2'}$$

$$6 M_b + 12 M_c = 2160 \qquad \text{... (3)}$$

Solving equations (1), (2) and (3),

$$M_a = 99.85 \text{ kN-m}$$
$$M_b = 112.8 \text{ kN-m}$$
$$M_c = 123.6 \text{ kN-m}$$

Reactions : (a) Due to external loads :

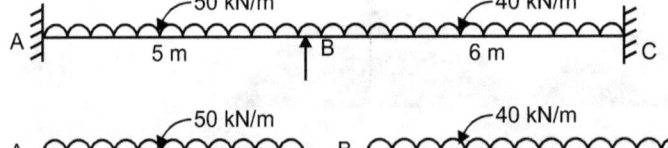

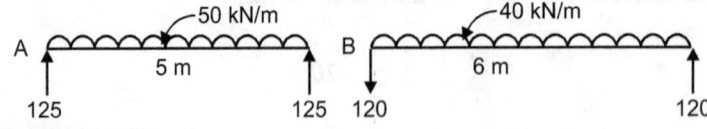

(b) Due to moments :

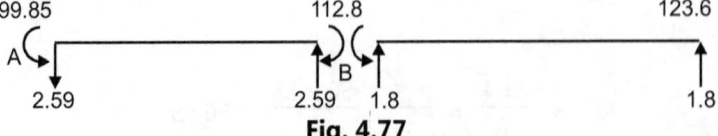

Fig. 4.77

Reaction at A = 125 − 2.59 = 122.41 kN
Reaction at B = 125 + 120 + 2.59 − 1.8 = 245.79 kN
Reaction at C = 120 + 1.8 = 121.8 kN

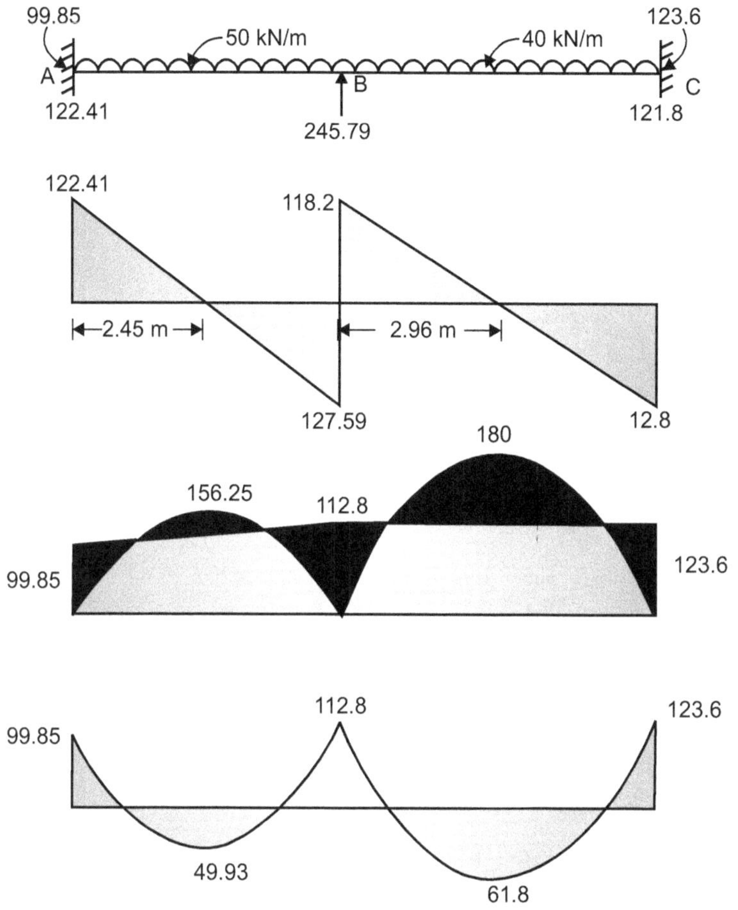

S. E. CIVIL : STRUCTURAL ANALYSIS - I 4.69 INDETERMINATE BEAMS

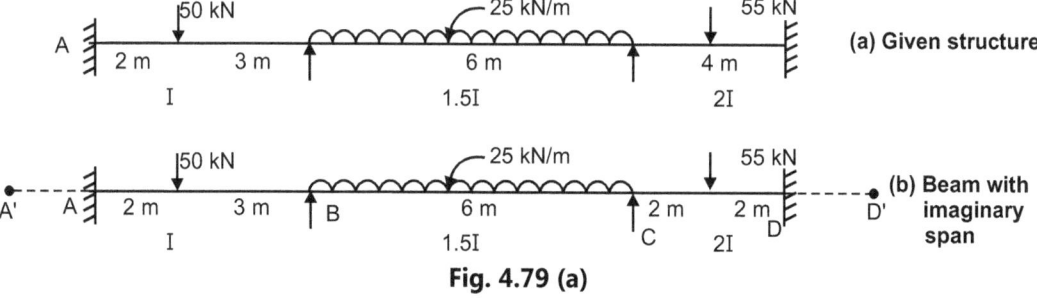

Fig. 4.78

Problem 4.27 : Analyse the continuous beam ABCD with ends A and D as fixed. AB = 5 m, BC = 6 m, CD = 4 m. Span AB is carrying a concentrated load of 40 kN at 2 m from A, BC carries U.D.L. of 25 kN/m and CD carries a concentrated load of 55 kN at 1 m from D.

$$I_{AB} = I, \quad I_{BC} = 1.5\, I, \quad I_{CD} = 2\, I$$

Solution : As both ends are fixed ends, so we have to consider imaginary span on left of A and right of D as below.

Fig. 4.79 (a)

A'A and DD' are the imaginary spans.

Applying theorem of three moments to different spans :

Span A'AB :

$$M_a'\left(\frac{l_1'}{I_1'}\right) + 2 M_a\left(\frac{l_1'}{I_1'} + \frac{l_1}{I_1}\right) + M_b\left(\frac{l_1}{I_1}\right) = \frac{6a_1' \bar{x}_1'}{I_1' l_1'} + \frac{6a_1 \bar{x}_1}{I_1 l_1}$$

Fig. 4.79 (b)

(c) Free BMD

AB : ($\bar{x}_1$ from A) $\quad \dfrac{6a_1 \bar{x}_1}{I_1 l_1} = \dfrac{6}{I} \times \dfrac{1}{2} \times \dfrac{60 \times 5}{5} \times \dfrac{(5+2)}{3} = \dfrac{420}{I}$

AB : ($\bar{x}_1$ from B) $\quad \dfrac{6a_1 \bar{x}_1}{I_1 l_1} = \dfrac{6}{I} \times \dfrac{1}{2} \times \dfrac{60 \times 5}{5} \times \left(\dfrac{5+3}{8}\right) = \dfrac{480}{I}$

BC : $\quad \dfrac{6a_2 \bar{x}_2}{I_2 l_2} = \dfrac{W_2 l_2^3}{4 I_2} = \dfrac{25 \times 6^3}{4 \times 1.5 I} = \dfrac{900}{I}$

CD : $\quad \dfrac{6a_3 \bar{x}_3}{I_3 l_3} = \dfrac{6}{2I} \times \dfrac{1}{2} \times \dfrac{55 \times 4 \times 2}{4} = \dfrac{165}{I}$

As A'A and D'D are imaginary spans,

$\therefore \quad \dfrac{6a_1' \bar{x}_1'}{I_1' l_1'} = \dfrac{6a_3' \bar{x}_3'}{I_3' l_3'} = 0$

$$M_a' = M_d' = 0$$

$$2 M_a\left(\dfrac{5}{I}\right) + M_b\left(\dfrac{5}{I}\right) = \dfrac{480}{I}$$

$$2 M_a + M_b = 96 \qquad \ldots (1)$$

Span ABC :

$$M_a\left(\dfrac{l_1}{I_1}\right) + 2 M_b\left(\dfrac{l_1}{I_1} + \dfrac{l_2}{I_2}\right) + M_c\left(\dfrac{l_2}{I_2}\right) = \dfrac{6a_1 \bar{x}_1}{I_1 l_1} + \dfrac{6a_2 \bar{x}_2}{I_2 l_2}$$

$$M_a\left(\dfrac{5}{I}\right) + 2 M_b\left(\dfrac{5}{I} + \dfrac{6}{1.5 I}\right) + M_c\left(\dfrac{6}{1.5 I}\right) = \dfrac{420}{I} + \dfrac{900}{I}$$

$$5 M_a + 18 M_b + 4 M_c = 1320 \qquad \ldots (2)$$

Span BCD :

$$M_b\left(\frac{l_2}{I_2}\right) + 2M_c\left(\frac{l_2}{I_2} + \frac{l_3}{I_3}\right) + M_D\left(\frac{l_3}{I_3}\right) = \frac{6a_2\bar{x}_2}{I_2 l_2} + \frac{6a_3\bar{x}_3}{I_3 l_3}$$

$$M_b\left(\frac{6}{1.5I}\right) + 2M_c\left(\frac{6}{1.5I} + \frac{4}{2I}\right) + M_d\left(\frac{4}{2I}\right) = \frac{900}{I} + \frac{165}{I}$$

$$\frac{4M_b}{I} + \frac{12M_c}{I} + \frac{2M_d}{I} = \frac{1065}{I}$$

$$4M_b + 12M_c + 2M_d = 1065 \qquad \ldots (3)$$

Span CDD' :

$$M_c\left(\frac{l_3}{I_3}\right) + 2M_d\left(\frac{l_3}{I_3} + \frac{l_3'}{I_3'}\right) + M_d'\left(\frac{l_3'}{I_3'}\right) = \frac{6a_3\bar{x}_3}{I_3 l_3} + \frac{6a_3'\bar{x}_3'}{l_3'}$$

$$M_c\left(\frac{4}{2I}\right) + 2M_d\left(\frac{4}{2I}\right) = \frac{165}{I}$$

$$2M_c + 4M_d = 165 \qquad \ldots (4)$$

$$M_a = 22.27 \text{ kN-m}$$
$$M_b = 51.45 \text{ kN-m}$$
$$M_c = 70.67 \text{ kN-m}$$
$$M_d = 5.95 \text{ kN-m}$$

Reactions :

(a) **Due to external loads :**

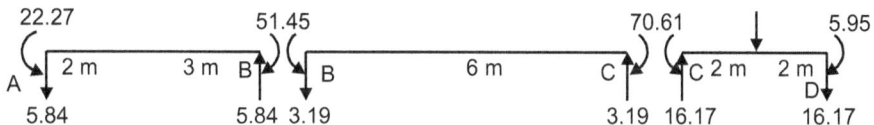

(b) **Due to moments :**

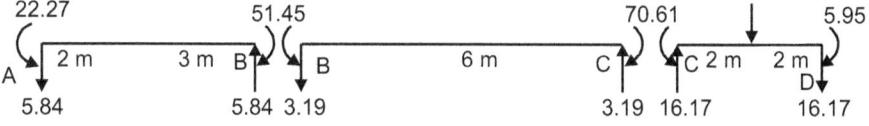

Fig. 4.80

Reaction at A = 30 − 5.84 = 24.16 kN
Reaction at B = 20 + 75 + 5.84 − 3.19 = 97.65 kN
Reaction at C = 75 + 27.5 + 3.19 + 16.17 = 121.86 kN
Reaction at D = 27.5 − 16.17 = 11.33 kN

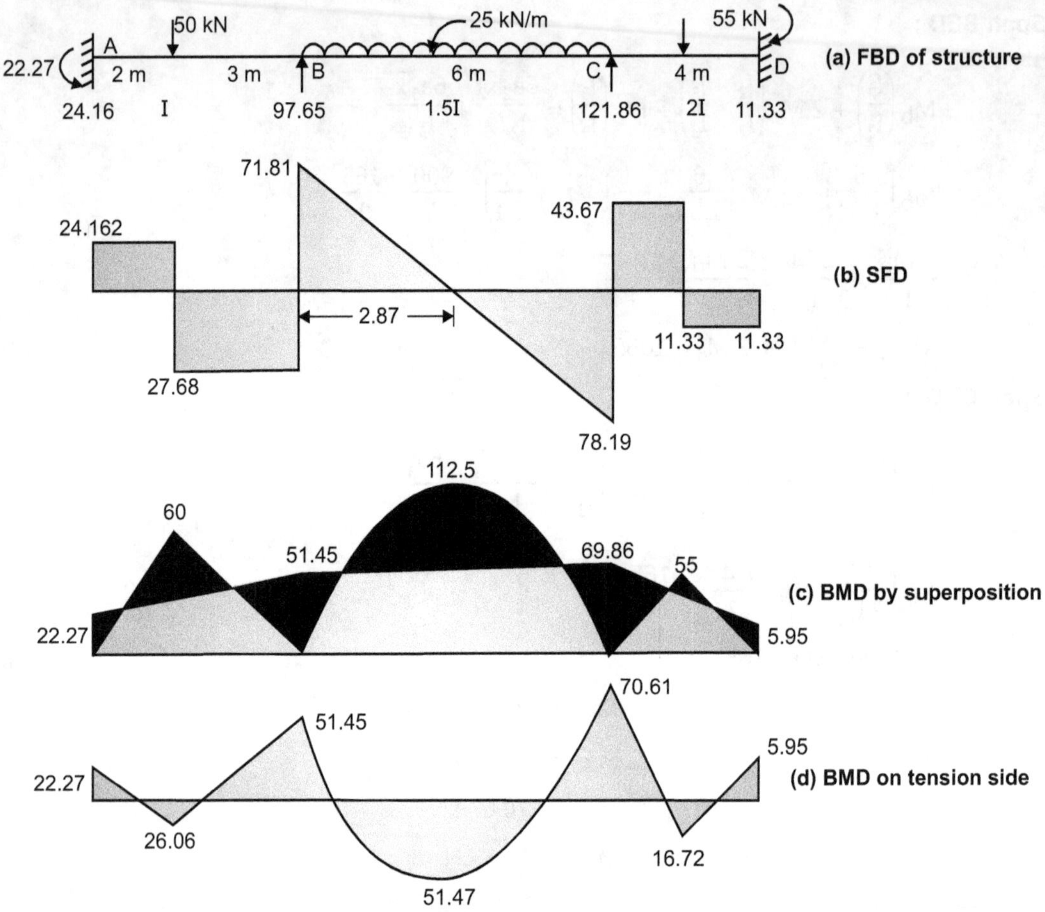

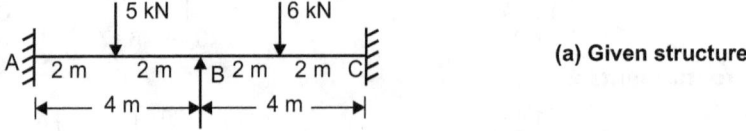

Fig. 4.81

Problem 4.28 : Find the fixed end moment by three moment theorem for the beam ABC in Fig. 4.82 (a).

(a) Given structure

Fig. 4.82 : Given structure

Solution : Three moment theorem :

$$M_a \, l_1 + 2 M_b (l_1 + l_2) + M_c \, l_2 = \frac{6 a_1 \bar{x}_1}{l_1} + \frac{6 a_2 \bar{x}_2}{l_2}$$

Applying theorem to different spans :

Assume imaginary beam span on left of A and right of 'C'.

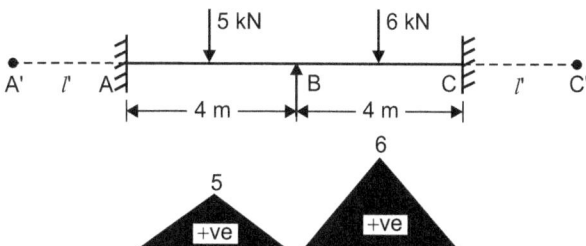

(a) Beam with imaginary span

(b) Free B.M.D.

Fig. 4.83

For A'AB :

$$M_A' l' + 2 M_A (l' + l_1) + M_B l_1 = \frac{6a_1' \bar{x}'}{l'} + \frac{6a_1 \bar{x}_1}{l_1}$$

$l' = M_A' = a_1' = \bar{x}' = 0$

$\therefore \quad 2 M_A l_1 + M_B l_1 = \dfrac{6 \times 10 \times 2}{4} = 30$

$\quad 2 M_A + M_B = 7.5$ ... (1)

For BCC' : (as $l_1' = a' = x' = M_C' = 0$)

$\therefore \quad M_b \cdot l_2 + 2 M_c l_2 = \dfrac{6a_2 \bar{x}_2}{l_2}$

$\quad M_b + 2 M_c = \dfrac{6 \times 12 \times 2}{4} = \dfrac{36}{4} = 9$ ... (2)

For span ABC :

$\quad M_a l_1 + 2 M_b (l_1 + l_2) + M_c l_2 = \dfrac{6a_1 \bar{x}_1}{l_1} + \dfrac{6a_2 \bar{x}_2}{l_2}$

$\quad M_a + 4 M_b + M_c = (30 + 36)/4 = 16.5$ ... (3)

$\therefore \quad 2 M_a + M_b = 7.5$

$\quad M_b + 2 M_c = 9.0$

$\quad M_a + 4 M_b + M_c = 16.5$

$\quad M_b = 9 - 2 M_c$

$\quad 2 M_a - 2 M_c = -1.5$ ... (4)

$\quad M_a + 36 - 8 M_c + M_c = 16.5$

$\quad M_a - 7 M_c = -19.5$ ... (5)

Solving equations (1), (2) and (5),

$\quad M_a = 2.375$ kN-m

$\quad M_b = 2.75$ kN-m

$\quad M_c = 3.125$ kN-m

Reactions :

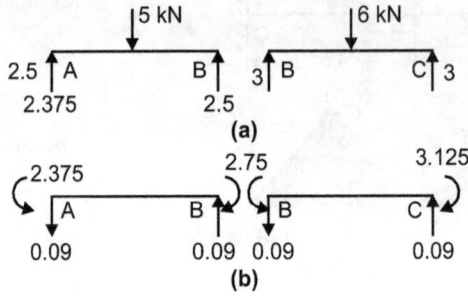

Fig. 4.84

Reaction at A = 2.5 − 0.09 = 2.41 kN
Reaction at B = 2.5 + 3 + 0.09 − 0.09 = 5.5 kN
Reaction at C = 3 + 0.09 = 3.09 kN

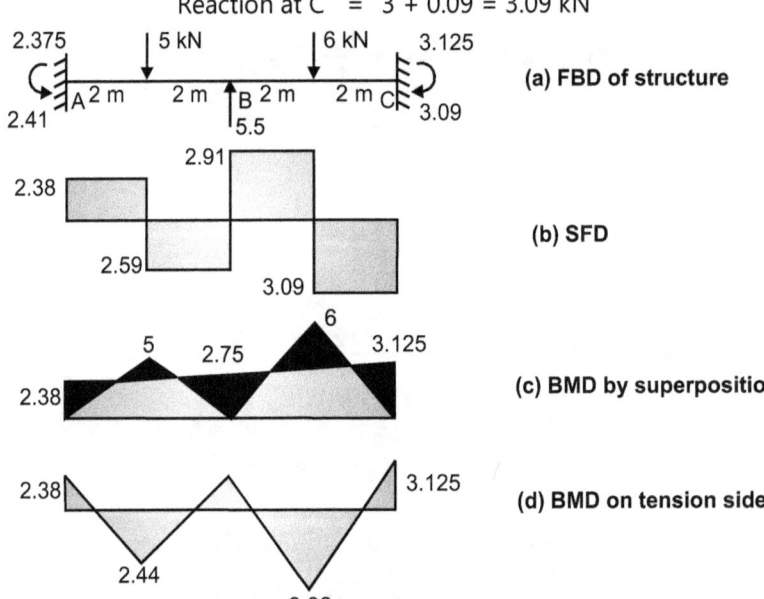

Fig. 4.85

4.13.4 Case IV : One End Support is Simple Support and Other End is Overhang

In this moment on the simple support, support is zero and on overhang side moment at last end support is also known. Therefore, the number of unknowns are equal to the number of intermediate supports. Equations available by applying theorem of three moments also equal to number of intermediate supports. So by application of theorem of three moments, the continuous beam can be easily analysed.

Problem 4.29 : Analyse the continuous beam as shown in Fig. 4.86 (a). Draw B.M.D.
Solution :

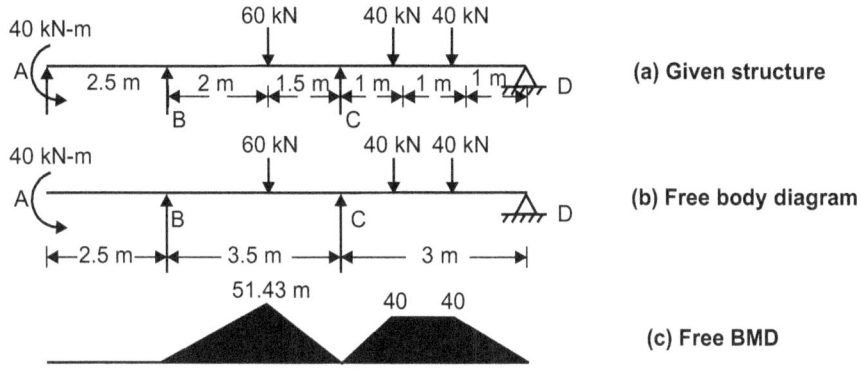

Fig. 4.86

BC : $\quad \dfrac{6a_1 \bar{x}_1}{I_1 l_1} = \dfrac{6}{2I} \times \dfrac{1}{2} \times \dfrac{51.43 \times 3.5}{3.5} \times \dfrac{(3.5 + 2)}{3} = \dfrac{141.43}{I}$

CD : $\quad \dfrac{6a_2 \bar{x}_2}{I_2 l_2} = \dfrac{6}{I} \times \dfrac{(1 + 3)}{2} \times \dfrac{40 \times 1.5}{3} = \dfrac{240}{I}$

Applying theorem of three moments to different spans :
Span BCD :

$$M_b \left(\dfrac{l_1}{I_1}\right) + 2 M_c \left(\dfrac{l_1}{I_1} + \dfrac{l_2}{I_2}\right) + M_D \left(\dfrac{l_2}{I_2}\right) = \dfrac{6a_1 \bar{x}_1}{I_1 l_1} + \dfrac{6a_2 \bar{x}_2}{I_2 l_2}$$

As D is simply supported, $\quad \therefore M_D = 0$
$\quad M_b = + 40$ kN-m (Hogging)

$+ 40 \left(\dfrac{3.5}{2}\right) + 2 M_c \left(\dfrac{3.5}{2} + \dfrac{3}{I}\right) = \dfrac{141.43}{I} + \dfrac{240}{I}$

$\therefore \quad M_c = 23.96$ kN-m

Reactions : (a) Due to external loads :

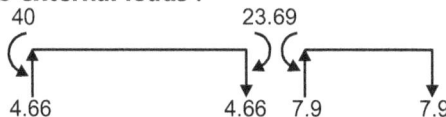

(b) Due to moments :

Fig. 4.87

Reaction at B = 25.71 + 4.66 = 30.37 kN
Reaction at C = 34.29 + 40 − 4.66 + 7.9 = 77.53 kN
Reaction at D = 40 − 7.9 = 32.1 kN

Problem 4.30 : A continuous beam ABCDE as shown in Fig. 4.88 (a) has simple rigid supports at A, B, C and D. DE is overhang of 2 m. It carries point load of 18 kN at 1 m from A on AB and 18 kN load at centre of span BC. CE portion 8 m long supports U.D.L. of 4 kN/m. Evaluate support moment and reactions. Plot S.F.D. and B.M.D. for the beam. Beam has concentrated section.

Solution : Applying theorem of three moments to different spans :

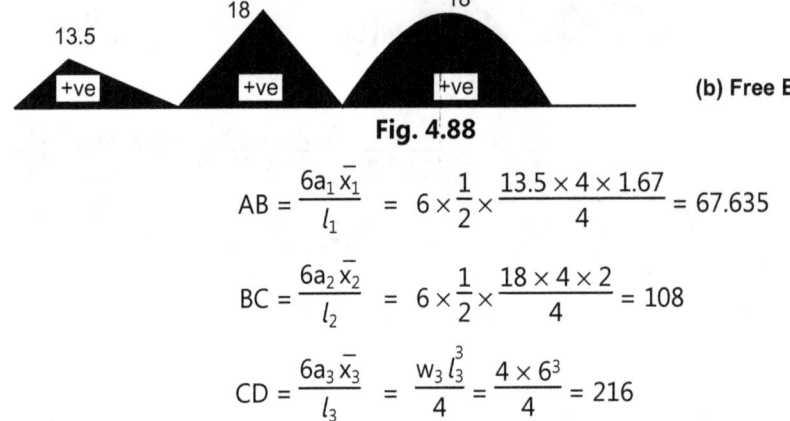

Fig. 4.88

$$AB = \frac{6a_1 \bar{x}_1}{l_1} = 6 \times \frac{1}{2} \times \frac{13.5 \times 4 \times 1.67}{4} = 67.635$$

$$BC = \frac{6a_2 \bar{x}_2}{l_2} = 6 \times \frac{1}{2} \times \frac{18 \times 4 \times 2}{4} = 108$$

$$CD = \frac{6a_3 \bar{x}_3}{l_3} = \frac{w_3 l_3^3}{4} = \frac{4 \times 6^3}{4} = 216$$

Span ABC :

As A is simply supported, $\therefore M_a = 0$.

$$\therefore \quad M_a l_1 + 2 M_b (l_1 + l_2) + M_c l_2 = \frac{6a_1 \bar{x}_1}{l_1} + \frac{6a_2 \bar{x}_2}{l_2}$$

$$2 M_b (4 + 4) + 4 M_c = 67.635 + 108$$

$$4 M_b + M_c = 43.91 \quad \ldots (1)$$

Span BCD :

As DE is overhang,

$\therefore \quad M_D = 8$ kN-m (hogging)

$$M_b l_2 + 2 M_c (l_2 + l_3) + M_D l_3 = \frac{6a_2 \bar{x}_2}{l_2} + \frac{6a_3 \bar{x}_3}{l_3}$$

$$4 M_b + 20 M_c + 48 = 108 + 216$$

$$\therefore \quad 4 M_b + 20 M_c = 276 \quad \ldots (2)$$

Solving equations (1) and (2),

$$M_c = 12.22 \text{ kN-m}$$

$$M_b = 7.92 \text{ kN-m}$$

Reactions : (a) Due to external loads :

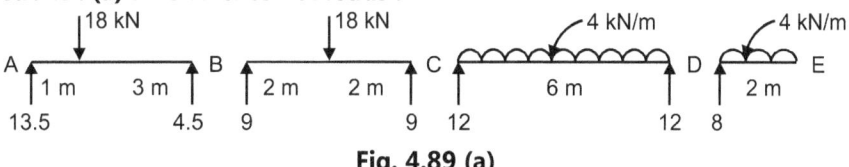

Fig. 4.89 (a)

(b) Due to moments :

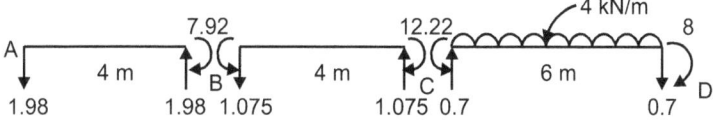

Fig. 4.89 (b)

Reaction at A = 13.5 − 1.98 = 11.52 kN
Reaction at B = 4.5 + 9 + 1.98 − 1.075 = 14.41 kN
Reaction at C = 9 + 12 + 1.075 + 0.7 = 22.78 kN
Reaction at D = 12 + 8 − 0.7 = 19.3 kN

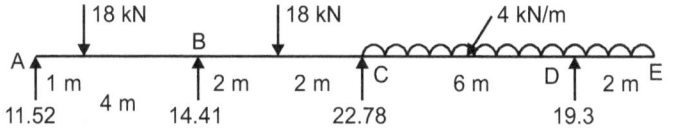

(a) **FBD of structure**

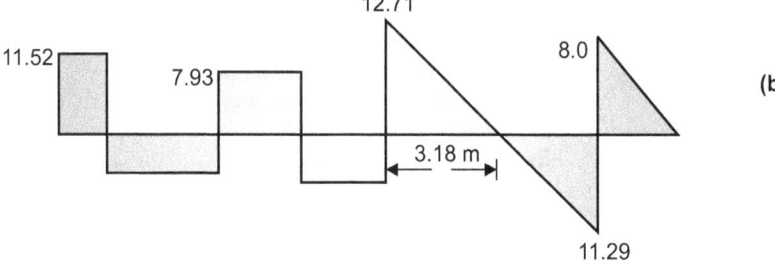

(b) **SFD**

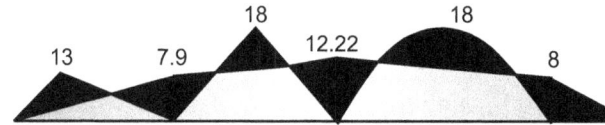

(c) **BMD by superposition**

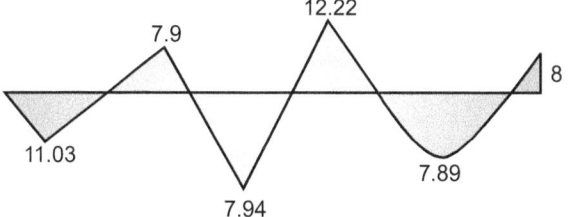

(d) **BMD on tension side**

Fig. 4.90

4.13.5 Case V : One End is Fixed Support and Other End is Overhang

We are getting number of equations equal to the number of intermediate supports by application of theorem of three moments. But as one end is fixed end, so we require one more equation to analyse the beam.

Thus, considering imaginary span on left side, if support on left side is fixed support and on right side if right side support is fixed as shown below.

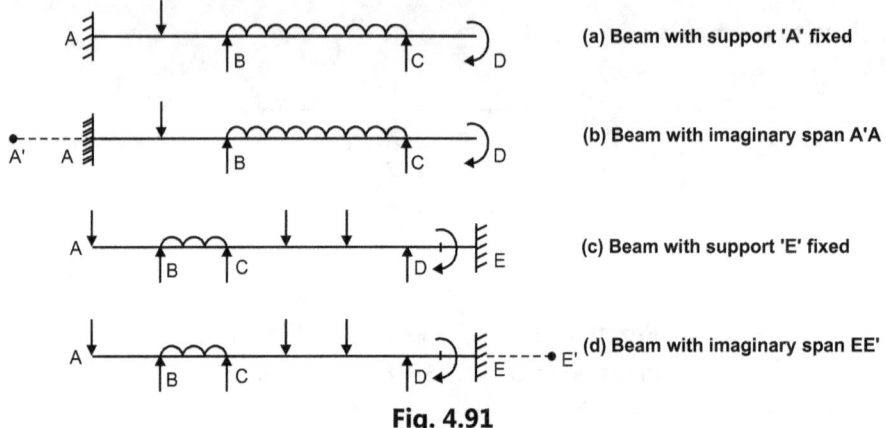

Fig. 4.91

By considering these imaginary spans, we can easily find out the support moment for the beams with one end fixed and other end is overhang.

Problem 4.31 : A continuous beam ABCD is fixed at D and overhang for AB. The beam is as shown in Fig. 4.92 (a). Draw the S.F.D. and B.M.D.

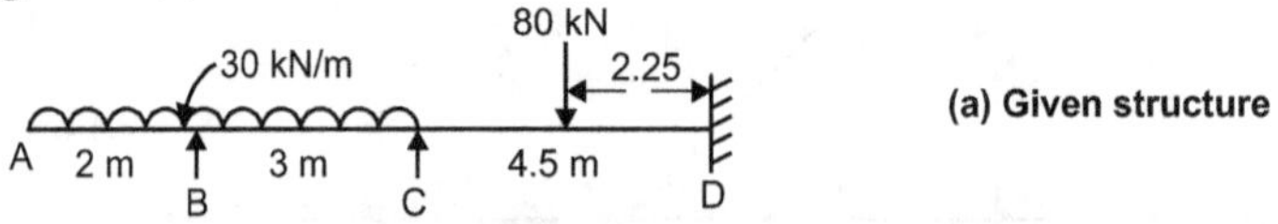

(a) Given structure

Fig. 4.92 (a)

Solution : As beam is fixed at D, therefore, we have to assume the imaginary span on right of D as DD'.

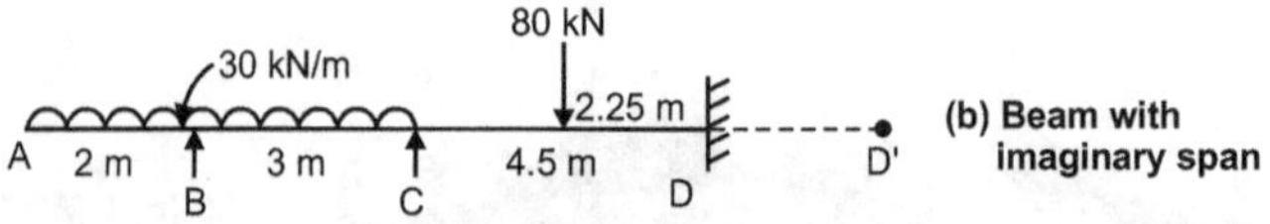

(b) Beam with imaginary span

Fig. 4.92 (b)

Applying theorem of three moments to different spans :
Span BCD : As AB is overhang, $\therefore M_B = 60$ kN-m (hogging)

$$\therefore \quad M_b\, l_1 + 2\, M_c\, (l_1 + l_2) + M_D\, l_2 = \frac{6 a_1 \bar{x}_1}{l_1} + \frac{6 a_2 \bar{x}_2}{l_2}$$

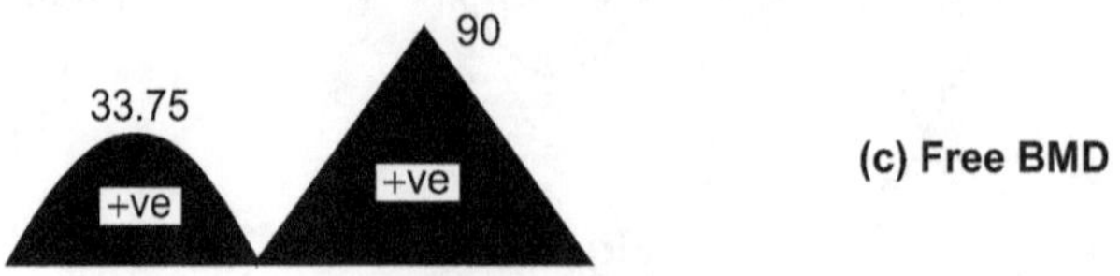

(c) Free BMD

Fig. 4.92 (c)

$$BC = \frac{6a_1 \bar{x}_1}{l_1} = \frac{W_1 l_1^3}{4} = \frac{30 \times 3^3}{4} = 202.5$$

$$CD = \frac{6a_2 \bar{x}_2}{l_2} = \frac{6}{4.5} \times \frac{1}{2} \times 90 \times 4.5 \times 2.25 = 607.5$$

DD' = 0 As imaginary span.

$\therefore \quad 60 \times 3 + 2 M_C (3 + 4.5) + 4.5 M_D = 202.5 + 607.5$

$\quad\quad\quad 15 M_C + 4.5 M_D = 630$ ... (1)

Span CDD' : $M_C l_2 + 2 M_D (l_2 + l_2') + M_D' l_2' = \frac{6a_2 \bar{x}_2}{l_2} + \frac{6a_2' \bar{x}_2'}{l_2'}$

$\quad\quad\quad 4.5 M_C + 9 M_D = 607.5$ ... (2)

Solving equations (1) and (2),

$$M_D = 54.7 \text{ kN-m}, \quad M_C = 25.6 \text{ kN-m}$$

Reactions : (a) Due to external loads :

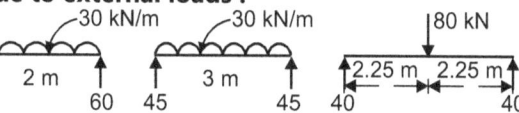

(b) Due to moments :

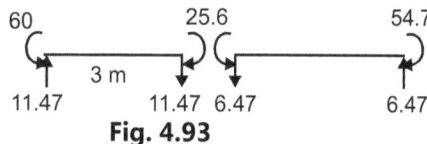

Fig. 4.93

$\therefore \quad$ Reaction at B $= R_B = 60 + 45 + 11.47 = 116.47$ kN

$\quad\quad$ Reaction at C $= R_C = 45 + 40 - 11.47 - 6.47 = 67.06$ kN

$\quad\quad$ Reaction at D $= R_D = 40 + 6.47 = 46.47$ kN

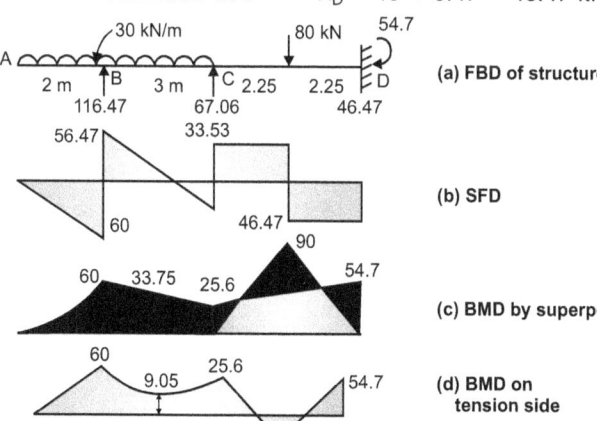

Fig. 4.94

Problem 4.32 : A continuous beam ABCD 20 m long is supported at A and C and CD is the cantilever portion. AB is loaded with U.D.L. of 20 kN/m having span 6.5 m and BC is loaded with a point load at 9 m from A. Span BC = 5 m. A point load is acting at D having value 50 kN. Span CD is 2 m. Find the support moments and draw S.F.D., B.M.D.

Solution :

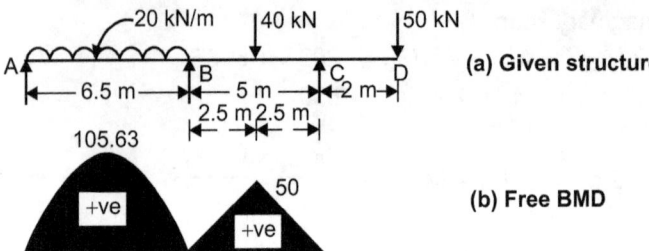

Fig. 4.95

Applying theorem of three moments to different spans :

Span ABC :

As end A is simply supported $\therefore M_a = 0$.

As CD is overhang $\therefore M_c = +100$ kN-m (hogging)

$$\therefore \quad M_a l_1 + 2 M_b (l_1 + l_2) + M_c l_2 = \frac{6a_1 \bar{x}_1}{l_1} + \frac{6a_2 \bar{x}_2}{l_2}$$

$$\frac{6a_1 \bar{x}_1}{l_1} = \frac{W_1 l_1^3}{4} = \frac{20 \times (6.5)^3}{4} = 1373.125$$

$$\frac{6a_2 \bar{x}_2}{l_2} = \frac{6}{5} \times \frac{1}{2} \times 50 \times 5 \times 2.5 = 375$$

$\therefore \quad 23 M_b = 1373.125 + 375 - 500 = 1248.125$

$M_b = 54.26$ kN-m

Reactions : (a) Due to external loads :

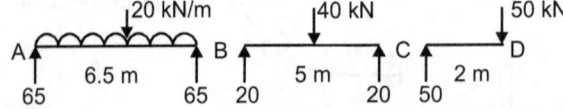

(b) Due to moments :

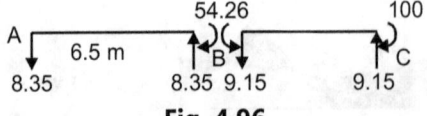

Fig. 4.96

$\therefore$ Reaction at A = 65 − 8.35 = 56.65 kN

Reaction at B = 65 + 20 + 8.35 − 9.15 = 84.2 kN

Reaction at C = 20 + 50 + 9.15 = 79.15 kN

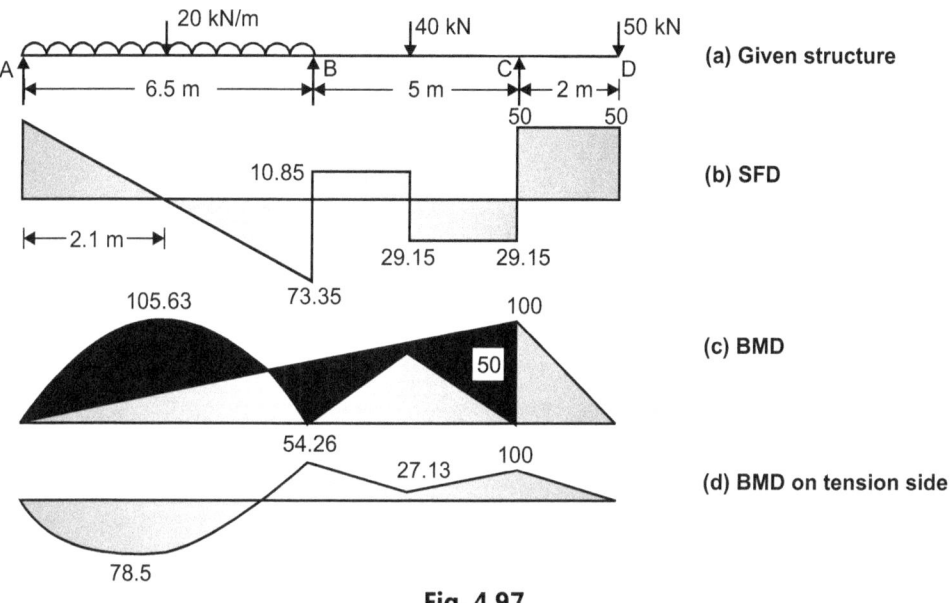

Fig. 4.97

Problem 4.33 : A continuous beam ABC is fixed at A and simply supported at B and C such that AB = BC = 8 m. AB carries a point load of 50 kN at its centre. A clockwise couple of 200 kN-m is acting at the centre of BC. $I_{AB} = 2I$, $I_{BC} = 3I$, E is same. Determine the support moments and draw B.M. diagram.

Solution :

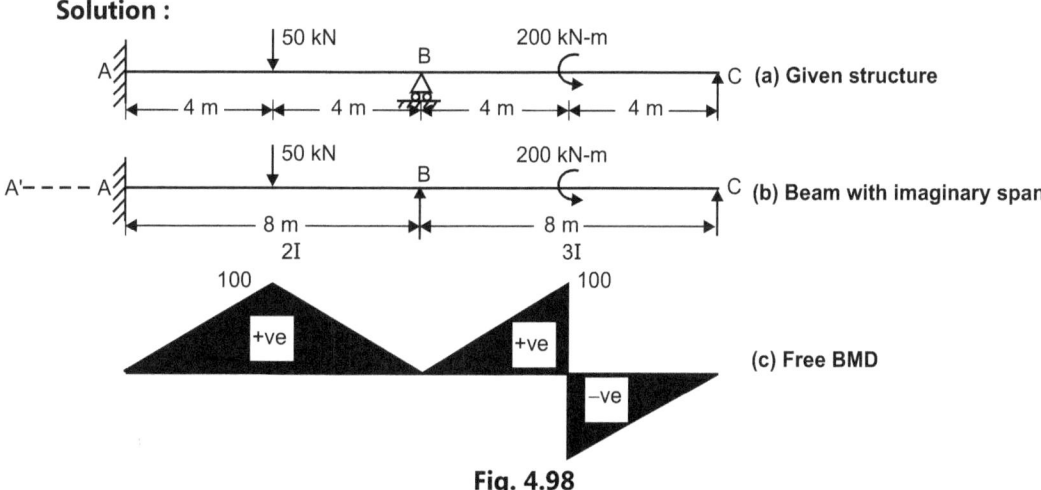

Fig. 4.98

As end A is fixed end, so we have to consider span A'A as shown in Fig. 4.98 (b).
Applying theorem of three moments :

Span A'AB :

$$M_a \frac{l_1'}{I_1'} + 2M_a \left(\frac{l_1'}{I_1'} + \frac{l_1}{I_1} \right) + M_b \frac{l_1}{I_1} = \frac{6a_1' \bar{x}_1'}{I_1' l_1'} + \frac{6a_1 \bar{x}_1}{I_1 l_1}$$

$$\frac{6a_1\bar{x}_1}{I_1 l_1} = \frac{6}{8} \times \frac{1}{2} \times \frac{100 \times 8 \times 4}{2I} = \frac{600}{I}$$

$$\frac{6a_2\bar{x}_2}{I_2 l_2} = \frac{6}{8 \times 3I}\left[\left(\frac{1}{2} \times 100 \times 4 \times 5.33 - \frac{1}{2} \times 100 \times 4 \times 2.67\right)\right]$$

$$= \frac{133}{I}$$

$$2M_a\left(\frac{8}{2I}\right) + M_b\left(\frac{8}{2I}\right) = \frac{600}{I}$$

$$8M_a + 4M_b = 600$$
$$2M_a + M_b = 150$$
$$4M_a + 2M_b = 300 \qquad \ldots (1)$$

Span ABC :

$$M_a\left(\frac{l_1}{I_1}\right) + 2M_b\left(\frac{l_1}{I_1} + \frac{l_2}{I_2}\right) + M_c\left(\frac{l_2}{I_2}\right) = \frac{6a_1\bar{x}_1}{I_1 l_1} + \frac{6a_2\bar{x}_2}{I_2 l_2}$$

$$4M_a + 2M_b\left(\frac{8}{2I} + \frac{8}{3I}\right) + M_c\left(\frac{8}{3I}\right) = \frac{600}{I} + \frac{133}{I}$$

$$4M_a + 13.33M_b + 2.67M_c = 733$$

As C is simply supported, $\therefore \quad M_c = 0$

$$4M_a = 300 - 2M_b$$
$$11.33 M_b = 433 \quad \therefore \quad M_b = 38.22 \text{ kN-m}$$
$$M_a = 55.89 \text{ kN-m}$$

Reactions :

(a) Due to external loads :

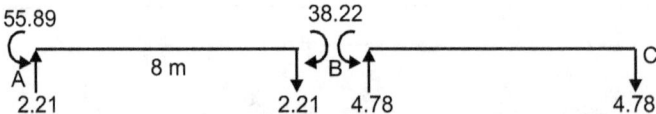

(b) Due to moments :

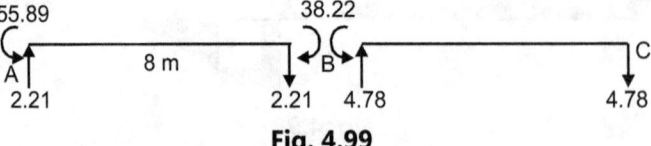

Fig. 4.99

Reaction at A = 25 + 2.21 = 27.21 kN

Reaction at B = 25 + 25 − 2.21 + 4.78 = 52.57 kN

Reaction at C = − 25 − 4.78 = − 29.78 kN

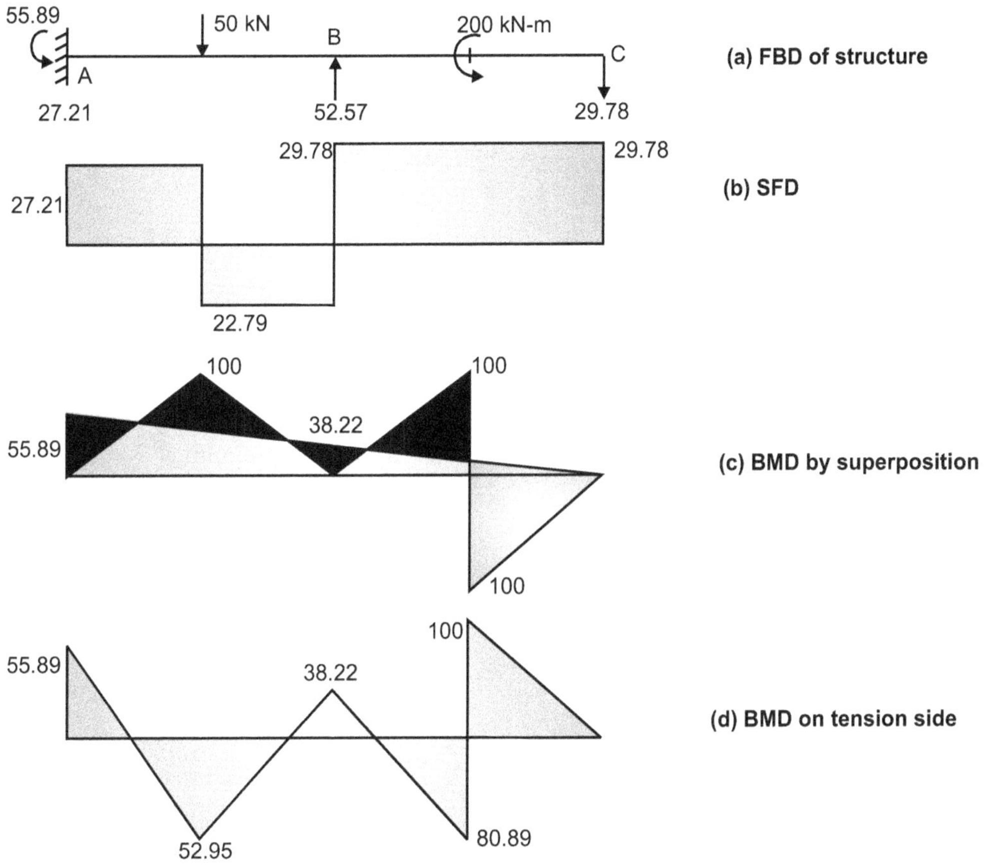

Fig. 4.100

4.13.6 Case VI : Continuous Beam with Supports at Different Level

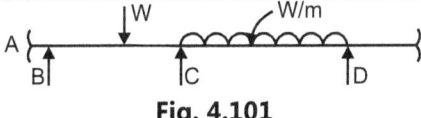

Fig. 4.101

Consider a continuous beam on supports B, C, D. C is below B by δ and below D by δ'.

$$EI\frac{d^2y}{dx^2} = M_x - M_x' \quad \ldots \text{Moment equation}$$

Multiplying above equation by x,

$$\therefore \quad x \cdot EI\frac{d^2y}{dx^2} = M_x \cdot x - M_x' \cdot x$$

For span BC,

$$EI\left[x\frac{dy}{dx} - y\right]_0^{l_1} = \int_0^{l_1} M_x \cdot x\, dx - \int_0^{l_1} M_x' \cdot x\, dx$$

At $x = l_1$, $y = -\delta$ (at point C)

$$\therefore \quad EI[l_1 i_{cb} + \delta] = \int_0^{l_1} M_x \cdot x \, dx - \int_0^{l_1} M'_x \cdot x \, dx$$

$$\int_0^{l_1} M_x \cdot x \, dx = \text{Moment of free } \frac{M}{EI} \text{ diagram @ B} = a_1 \bar{x}_1$$

where, a_1 = Area of free B.M.D.

$\bar{x}_1$ = C.G. of free B.M.D. from B

$$\int_0^{l_1} M'_x \cdot x \, dx = \text{Moment of fixed } \frac{M}{EI} \text{ diagram @ B}$$

$$= a'_1 \bar{x}'_1 = (M_b + 2M_c) \frac{l_1^2}{6}$$

where, a'_1 = Area of fixed B.M.D.

$\bar{x}'_1$ = C.G. of fixed B.M.D. from B.

$$\therefore \quad EI(l_1 i_{cb} + \delta) = a_1 \bar{x}_1 - (M_b + 2M_c) \frac{l_1^2}{6}$$

$$\therefore \quad 6EI \, l_1 i_{cb} = 6a_1 \bar{x}_1 - (M_b + 2M_c) l_1^2 - 6EI\left(\frac{\delta}{l_1}\right)$$

$$\therefore \quad 6EI \, i_{cb} = \frac{6a_1 \bar{x}_1}{l_1} - (M_b + 2M_c) l_1 - 6EI\left(\frac{\delta}{l_1}\right) \quad \ldots (1)$$

Similarly for span CD,

$$6EI \, i_{cd} = \frac{6a_2 \bar{x}_2}{l_2} - (M_d + 2M_c) l_2 - 6EI\left(\frac{\delta'}{l_2}\right) \quad \ldots (2)$$

Adding equations (1) and (2),

$$6EI(i_{cb} + i_{cd}) = \frac{6a_1 \bar{x}_1}{l_1} + \frac{6a_2 \bar{x}_2}{l_2} - (M_b l_1 + 2M_c (l_1 + l_2) + M_d l_2)$$

$$- 6EI\left(\frac{\delta}{l_1} + \frac{\delta'}{l_2}\right)$$

$i_{cb} + i_{cd} = 0$

$$\therefore \quad 0 = \frac{6a_1 \bar{x}_1}{l_1} + \frac{6a_2 \bar{x}_2}{l_2} - [M_b l_1 + 2M_c (l_1 + l_2) + M_d l_2] - 6EI\left(\frac{\delta}{l_1} + \frac{\delta'}{l_2}\right)$$

$$\therefore \quad M_b l_1 + 2M_c (l_1 + l_2) + M_d l_2 = \frac{6a_1 \bar{x}_1}{l_1} + \frac{6a_2 \bar{x}_2}{l_2} - 6EI\left(\frac{\delta}{l_1} + \frac{\delta'}{l_2}\right)$$

Problem 4.34 : A continuous beam ABCD is fixed at A and simply supported on B, C, D. Span AB = 4 m, span BC = 4 m and span CD = 6 m. Span AB is loaded with U.D.L. of 30 kN/m, span BC carries a concentrated load of 60 kN and span CD with a central load of 50 kN. Support C sinks by 1 cm. If E = 21000 kN-m², find fixed end moments. Draw S.F.D. and B.M.D.

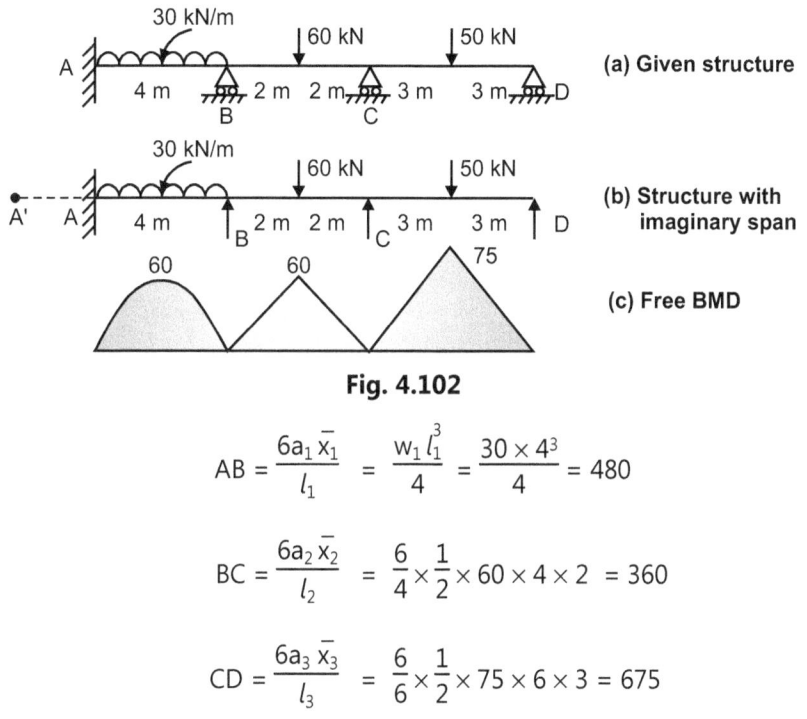

Fig. 4.102

$$AB = \frac{6a_1 \bar{x}_1}{l_1} = \frac{w_1 l_1^3}{4} = \frac{30 \times 4^3}{4} = 480$$

$$BC = \frac{6a_2 \bar{x}_2}{l_2} = \frac{6}{4} \times \frac{1}{2} \times 60 \times 4 \times 2 = 360$$

$$CD = \frac{6a_3 \bar{x}_3}{l_3} = \frac{6}{6} \times \frac{1}{2} \times 75 \times 6 \times 3 = 675$$

Applying theorem of three moments :

As A is fixed end, therefore we have to consider imaginary span A'A as above.

Span A'AB :

$$M_a' l_1' + 2 M_a (l_1' + l_1) + M_b (l_1) = \frac{6a_1' \bar{x}_1'}{l_1'} + \frac{6a_1 \bar{x}_1}{l_1}$$

$$8 M_a + 4 M_b = 480$$

$$2 M_a + M_b = 120 \qquad \ldots (1)$$

Span ABC :

$$M_a l_1 + 2 M_b (l_1 + l_2) + M_c l_2 = \frac{6a_1 \bar{x}_1}{l_1} + \frac{6a_2 \bar{x}_2}{l_2} - (6\,EI) \left[\frac{\delta_A}{l} + \frac{\delta_C}{l} \right]$$

$\delta_A = 0$, $\delta_C = -10$ mm, $6\,EI = 6 \times 210 \times 100$, $l = 4$ m

∴ $\quad 4 M_a + 16 M_b + 4 M_c = 480 + 360 - 6 \times 21000 \left[\dfrac{-10}{4000}\right]$

$\qquad\qquad\qquad\qquad\qquad = 480 + 360 + 315$

$\qquad\qquad M_a + 4 M_b + M_c = 288.75$

∴ $\qquad\qquad M_a + 4 M_b + M_c = 288.75 \qquad\qquad\qquad$ ... (2)

Span BCD :

$$4 M_b + 2 M_c (4 + 6) + 6 M_D = \dfrac{6 a_2 \bar{x}_2}{l_2} + \dfrac{6 a_3 \bar{x}_3}{l_3} - 6 EI \left(\dfrac{\delta_B}{l_{BC}} + \dfrac{\delta_D}{l_{CD}}\right)$$

$\delta_B = 10$ mm, $\delta_D = 10$ mm

As D is simply supported, ∴ $M_D = 0$

∴ $\qquad 4 M_b + 20 M_c + 0 = 360 + 675 - 6 \times 21 \times 10^3 \left(\dfrac{10}{4000} + \dfrac{10}{6000}\right)$

$\qquad\qquad\qquad\qquad\qquad = 360 + 675 - 525 = 510$

$\qquad\qquad\qquad M_b + 5 M_c = 127.5 \qquad\qquad\qquad$ ... (3)

Solving equations (1), (2) and (3),

$\qquad\qquad\qquad M_a = 29.2$ kN-m

$\qquad\qquad\qquad M_b = 61.6$ kN-m

$\qquad\qquad\qquad M_c = 13.2$ kN-m

Reactions : (a) **Due to external loads :**

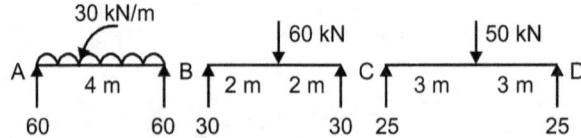

(b) **Due to moments :**

```
             61.6              13.2        │50 kN
   29.2     ⤹)(⤸             ⤹)(⤸         │         D
A │    4 m  ↑↑  2 m    2 m  ↑↑   3 m   3 m ↓
  ↓         B                C
 8.1       8.1 12.1        12.1  2.2        2.2
```

Fig. 4.103

Reaction at A = 60 – 8.1 = 51.9 kN

Reaction at B = 60 + 30 + 8.1 + 12.1 = 110.2 kN

Reaction at C = 30 + 25 – 12.1 + 2.2 = 45.1 kN

Reaction at D = 25 – 2.2 = 22.8 kN

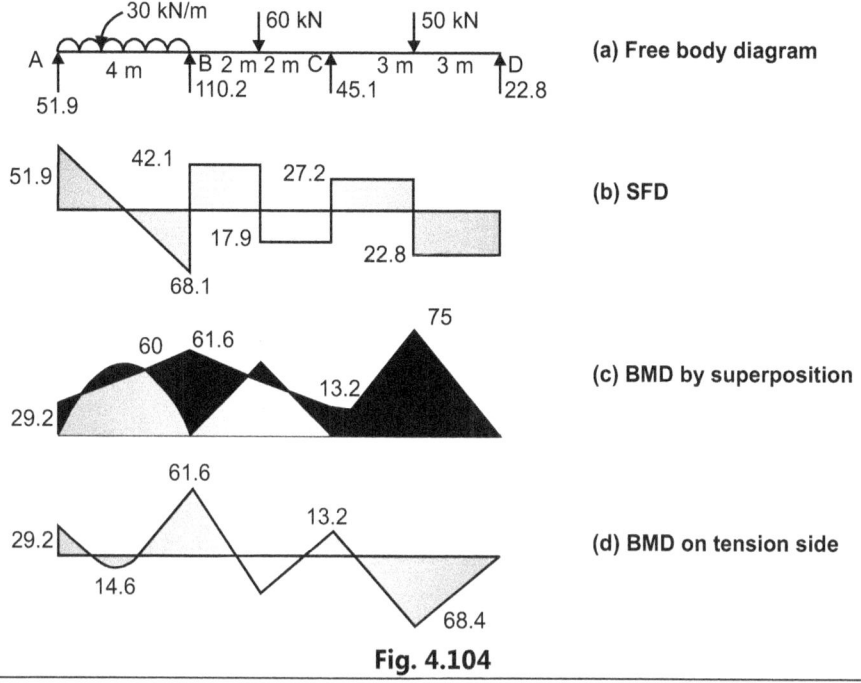

Fig. 4.104

Problem 4.35 : Draw the S.F.D. and B.M.D. for the girder shown in Fig. 4.105 (a) below. Support B sinks by 2.5 mm. $I = 3500 \text{ cm}^4$, $E = 2 \times 10^5 \text{ N/mm}^2$.

Solution : As beam is fixed at A and D, so we have to consider imaginary spans on both sides of beam.

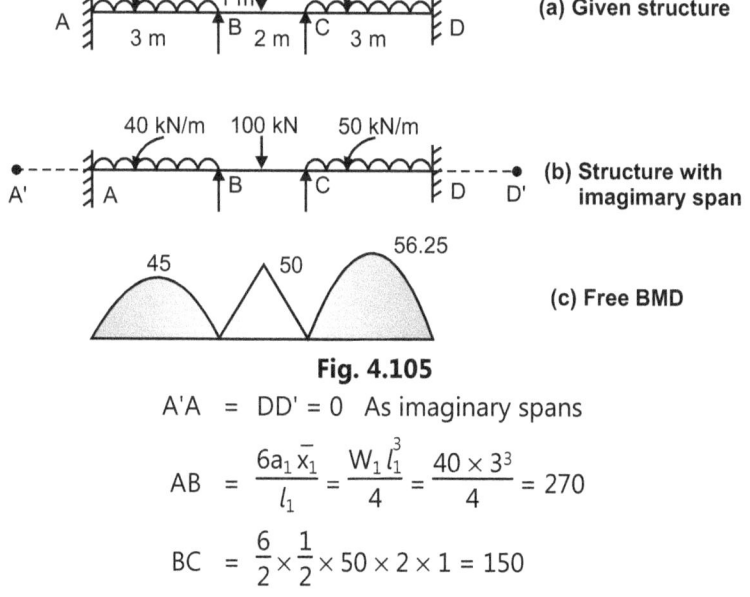

Fig. 4.105

$$A'A = DD' = 0 \quad \text{As imaginary spans}$$

$$AB = \frac{6a_1\bar{x}_1}{l_1} = \frac{W_1 l_1^3}{4} = \frac{40 \times 3^3}{4} = 270$$

$$BC = \frac{6}{2} \times \frac{1}{2} \times 50 \times 2 \times 1 = 150$$

$$CD = \frac{6a_3 \bar{x}_3}{l_3} = \frac{W_3 l_3^3}{4} = \frac{50 \times 3^3}{4} = 337.5$$

$$EI = 3.5 \times 10^7 \times 2 \times 10^5 = 7 \times 10^{12} \text{ N-mm}^2 = 7 \times 10^3 \text{ kN-m}^2$$

Applying theorem of three moments to different spans :

Span A'AB :

$$M_a' l_1' + 2 M_a (l_1' + l_1) + M_b l_1 = \frac{6a_1 \bar{x}_1}{l_1} - 6 EI \left(\frac{\delta_A'}{l_{AA}'} + \frac{\delta_C}{l_{AB}} \right)$$

$$= 270 - 6 \times 7 \times 10^3 \left(\frac{-2.5}{3000} \right)$$

$$6 M_a + 3 M_b = 305 \qquad \ldots (1)$$

Span ABC :

$$M_a l_1 + 2 M_b (l_1 + l_2) + M_c l_2 = \frac{6a_1 \bar{x}_1}{l_1} + \frac{6a_2 \bar{x}_2}{l_2} - 6 EI \left(\frac{\delta_A}{l_{AB}} + \frac{\delta_C}{l_{BC}} \right)$$

$$\delta_A = \delta_C = 2.5 \text{ mm}$$

$$\therefore \quad 3 M_a + 10 M_b + 2 M_c = 270 + 150 - 6 \times 7 \times 10^3 \left(\frac{2.5}{3000} + \frac{2.5}{2000} \right)$$

$$= 270 + 150 - 87.5$$

$$3 M_a + 10 M_b + 2 M_c = 332.5 \qquad \ldots (2)$$

Span BCD :

$$\delta_B = -2.5 \text{ mm}$$

$$M_b l_2 + 2 M_c (l_2 + l_3) + M_d l_3 = \frac{6a_2 \bar{x}_2}{l_2} + \frac{6a_3 \bar{x}_3}{l_3} - 6 EI \left(\frac{\delta_B}{l_{BC}} + \frac{\delta_D}{l_{CD}} \right)$$

$$2 M_b + 10 M_c + 3 M_d = 150 + 337.5 + 52.5$$

$$2 M_b + 10 M_c + 3 M_d = 540 \qquad \ldots (3)$$

Span CDD' :

$$\delta_C = \delta_D' = 0$$

$$\therefore \quad M_c l_3 + 2 M_D (l_3 + l_3') + M_d' l_3' = \frac{6a_3 \bar{x}_3}{l_3}$$

$$3 M_c + 6 M_d = 337.5 \qquad \ldots (4)$$

Solving equations (1), (2), (3) and (4),

$$M_a = 45.06 \text{ kN-m}$$
$$M_b = 11.53 \text{ kN-m}$$
$$M_c = 40.96 \text{ kN-m}$$
$$M_d = 35.76 \text{ kN-m}$$

Reactions : (a) Due to external loads :

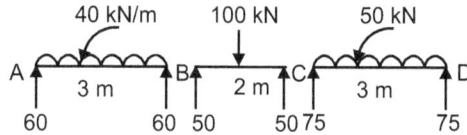

(b) Due to moments :

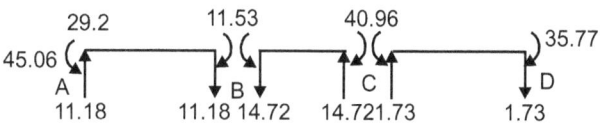

Fig. 4.106

$$\text{Reaction at A} = 60 + 11.18 = 71.18 \text{ kN}$$

$$\text{Reaction at B} = 60 + 50 - 11.18 - 14.72 = 84.1 \text{ kN}$$

$$\text{Reaction at C} = 50 + 75 + 14.72 + 1.73 = 141.45 \text{ kN}$$

$$\text{Reaction at D} = 75 - 1.73 = 73.27 \text{ kN}$$

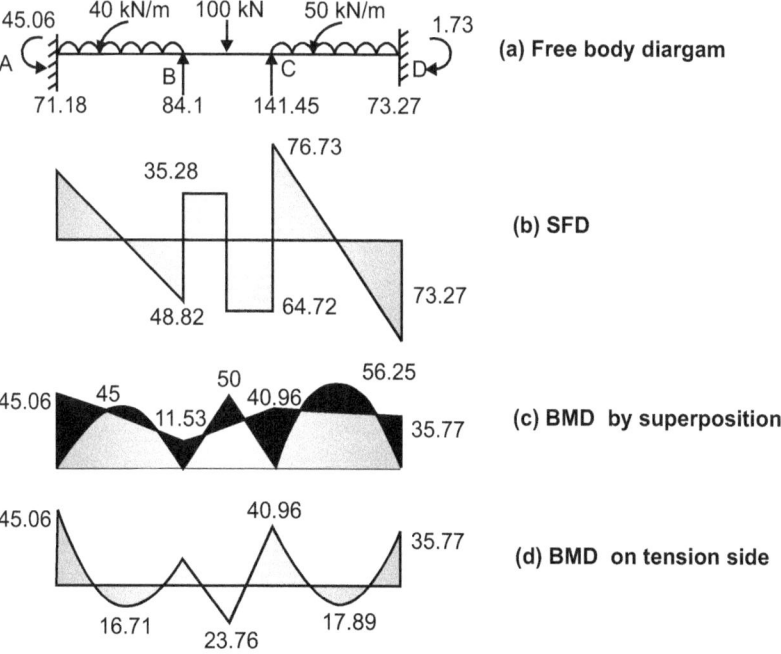

(a) Free body diargam

(b) SFD

(c) BMD by superposition

(d) BMD on tension side

Fig. 4.107

Problem 4.36 : For the continuous beam supported and loaded as shown in Fig. 4.108 (a), determine the support moments by theorem of three moments. **(Dec. 2000)**

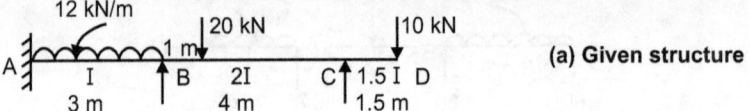
(a) Given structure

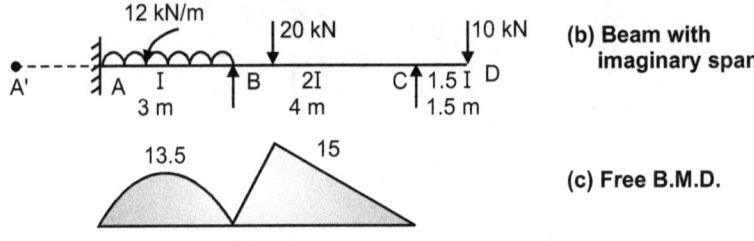
(b) Beam with imaginary span

(c) Free B.M.D.

Fig. 4.108

Solution :

For AB :
$$\frac{6a_1 \bar{x}_1}{I_1 l_1} = \frac{W_1 l_1^3}{4 I_1} = \frac{12 \times 3^3}{4 I} = \frac{81}{I}$$

For BC :
$$\frac{6a_2 \bar{x}_2}{I_2 l_2} = \frac{6}{2I} \times \frac{1}{2} \times \frac{15 \times 4 \times 2.33}{4} = \frac{52.425}{I}$$

Applying theorem of three moments :

$$M_a \left(\frac{l_1}{I_1}\right) + 2 M_b \left(\frac{l_1}{I_1} + \frac{l_2}{I_2}\right) + M_c \left(\frac{l_2}{I_2}\right) = \frac{6a_1 \bar{x}_1}{I_1 l_1} + \frac{6a_2 \bar{x}_2}{I_2 l_2} \quad \text{(General equation)}$$

As end A is fixed end, so consider imaginary span on left of A as shown in Fig. 4.108.

$$M_a' \left(\frac{l_1'}{I_1'}\right) + 2M_a \left(\frac{l_1'}{I_1'} + \frac{l_1}{I_1}\right) + M_b \left(\frac{l_1}{I_1}\right) = \frac{6a_1' \bar{x}_1'}{I_1' l_1'} + \frac{6a_1 \bar{x}_1}{I_1 l_1}$$

As span A'A is imaginary span,

$$\therefore \quad 2 M_a \left(\frac{3}{I}\right) + M_b \left(\frac{3}{I}\right) = \frac{81}{I}$$

$$2 M_a + M_b = 27 \quad \ldots (1)$$

Span ABC :

$$M_a \left(\frac{l_1}{I_1}\right) + 2 M_b \left(\frac{l_1}{I_1} + \frac{l_2}{I_2}\right) + M_c \left(\frac{l_2}{I_2}\right) = \frac{6a_1 \bar{x}_1}{I_1 l_1} + \frac{6a_2 \bar{x}_2}{I_2 l_2}$$

$$M_a \left(\frac{3}{I}\right) + 2 M_b \left(\frac{3}{I} + \frac{4}{2I}\right) + M_c \left(\frac{4}{2I}\right) = \frac{81}{I} + \frac{52.425}{I}$$

$$3 M_a + 10 M_b + 2 M_c = 133.43$$

But as CD is cantilever,

∴ M_c = 15 kN-m

∴ $3 M_a + 10 M_b$ = 133.43 − 30 = 103.43   ... (2)

Solving equations (1) and (2),

∴ M_a = 9.8 kN-m

M_b = 7.4 kN-m

Reactions :

(a) Due to external loads :

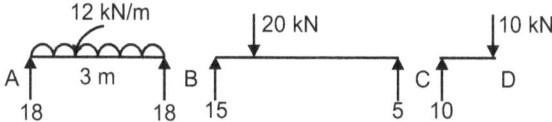

(b) Due to moments :

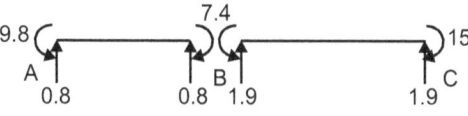

Fig. 4.109

Reaction at A = 18 + 0.8 = 18.8 kN
Reaction at B = 18 + 15 − 0.8 + 1.9 = 34.1 kN
Reaction at C = 5 + 10 − 1.9 = 13.1 kN

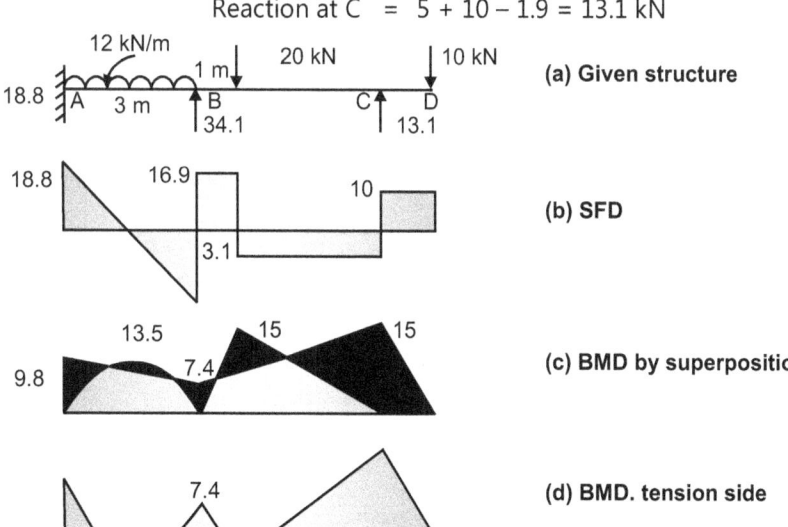

Fig. 4.110

EXERCISE

Find the reactions at the supports and draw S.F. and B.M. diagrams for examples 1 to 14. Consider the flexural rigidity as constant, unless and otherwise specified.

1.

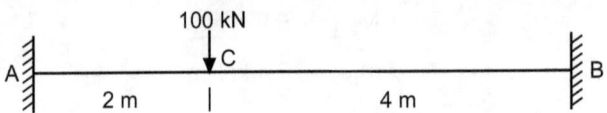

Fig. 4.111

[**Ans.** $M_A = -88.89$ kNm, $M_B = -44.44$ kNm, $V_A = 74.08$ kN (↑), $V_B = 25.92$ kN (↑)]

2.

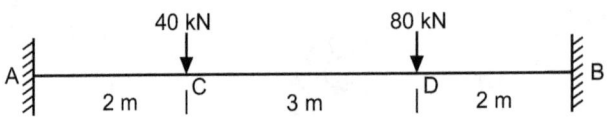

Fig. 4.112

[**Ans.** $M_A = -73.47$ kNm, $M_B = -97.96$ kN.m, $V_A = 47.93$ kN (↑), $V_B = 72.07$ kN (↑)]

3.

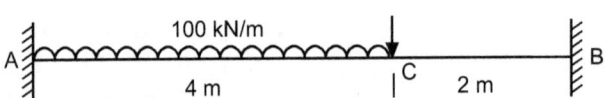

Fig. 4.113

[**Ans.** $M_A = -266.66$ kNm, $M_B = -177.78$ kNm, $V_A = 281.48$ kN (↑), $V_B = 118.52$ kN (↑)]

4.

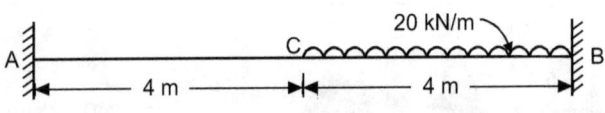

Fig. 4.114

[**Ans.** $M_A = -120$ kNm, $M_B = -40$ kNm, $V_A = 30$ kN (↑), $V_B = 50$ kN (↑)]

5.

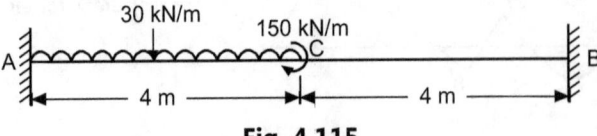

Fig. 4.115

[**Ans.** $M_A = -72.50$ kNm, $M_B = -87.50$ kNm, $V_A = 69.38$ kN (↑), $V_B = 50.62$ kN (↑)]

6.

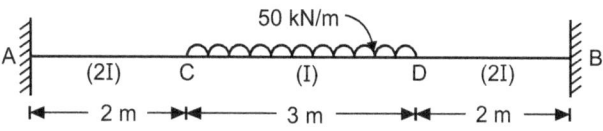

Fig. 4.116

[**Ans.** $M_A = M_B = -142.50$ kNm, $V_A = V_B = 75.83$ kN (↑)]

7.

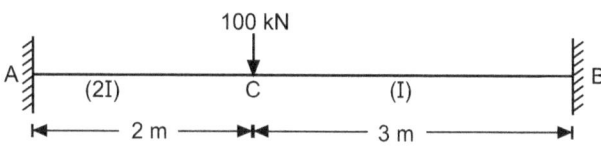

Fig. 4.117

[**Ans.** $M_A = -87.68$ kNm, $M_B = -39.54$ kNm, $V_A = 69.63$ A (↑), $V_B = 30.37$ kN (↑)]

8.

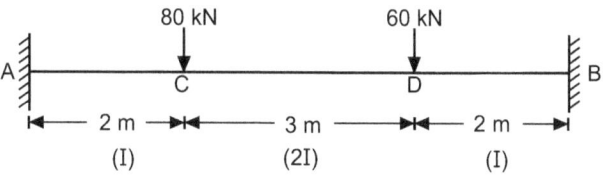

Fig. 4.118

[**Ans.** $M_A = -98.68$ kNm, $M_B = -79.49$ kNm, $V_A = 77.03$ kN (↑), $V_B = 62.97$ kN (↑)]

9.

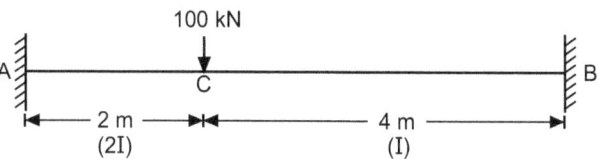

Fig. 4.119

[**Ans.** $M_A = -107.80$ kNm, $M_B = -35.23$ kNm,

$V_A = -78.76$ kN (↑), $V_B = 21.24$ kN (↑)]

10.

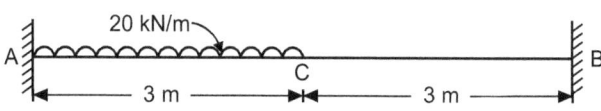

Fig. 4.120

[**Ans.** $M_A = 41.25$ kNm, $M_B = -19.75$ kN, $V_A = 48.75$ kN (↑), $V_B = 11.25$ kN (↑)]

11.

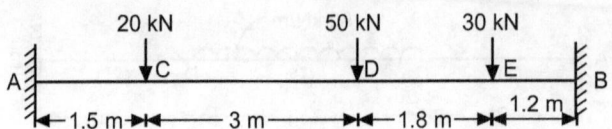

Fig. 4.121

[**Ans.** $M_A = -60.04$ kNm, $M_B = -84.20$ kNm, $V_A = 37.58$ kN (↑), $V_B = 62.42$ kN (↑)]

12.

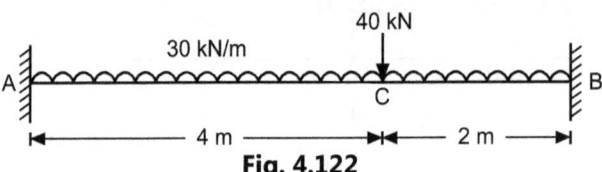

Fig. 4.122

[**Ans.** $M_A = -107.78$ kNm, $M_B = -125.56$ kNm, $V_A = 100.37$ kN (↑), $V_B = 119.63$ kN (↑)]

13.

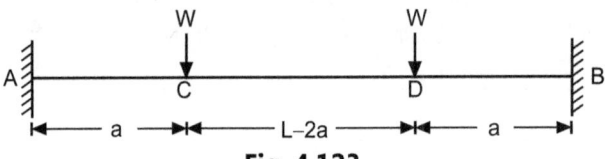

Fig. 4.123

[**Ans.** $M_A = M_B = -Wa\left(\dfrac{L-a}{L}\right)$, $V_A = V_B = W$ (↑)]

14.

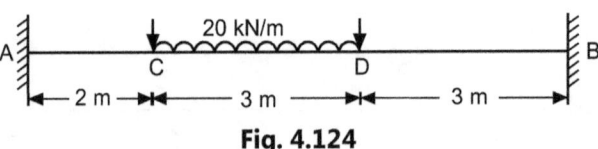

Fig. 4.124

[**Ans.** $M_A = -62.58$ kNm, $M_B = -49.92$ kNm, $V_A = 33.75$ kN (↑), $V_B = 26.25$ kN (↑)]

15. A fixed beam of span L carries two concentrated loads, placed symmetrically at a distance 'a' from each support. Show that the bending moment at the centre of the span is $+\dfrac{Wa^2}{L}$. Locate the points of contraflexure from each support.

$$\left[\text{Ans. } \left(\dfrac{L-a}{2L-a}\right) \cdot a\right]$$

16. A beam fixed at both ends has a span of 9 m. It carries two concentrated loads W_1 and W_2 at 3.0 m from each support. If the fixed end moment at left hand support is 0.75 times that at right hand support, show that $W_2 = 2.5\, W_1$.

17. A fixed beam AB of span 6.0 m carries a concentrated downward load of 60 kN at 2 m from left hand support A and a concentrated upward load of 20 kN at 2 m from right hand support B. Obtain the values of the support moments and the central moment. Also find vertical reactions at both supports.
   [**Ans.** $M_A = -44.44$ kN, $M_B = -8.89$ kNm, $M_{central} = +13.99$ kNm, $V_A = 39.26$ kN (↑), $V_B = 0.74$ kN (↑)]

18. A fixed beam of span L carries a point load W at $\frac{L}{4}$ from the left support, show that the bending moment at the mid span is $+\frac{WL}{32}$.

19. A uniform beam of span 8 m is fixed at both ends. It carries a concentrated load of 20 kN at 2 m from the left support A, and a U.D.L. of 10 kN/m from the centre of the span to the right support B. Find the fixed end moments.
   [**Ans.** $M = -39.15$ kNm, $M_B = -44.15$ kNm]

20. A non-prismatic beam of span L with both ends fixed is subjected to a concentrated load W at the mid point. The beam has a M.I. of 2I for the central half portion and I for the remaining portion. Find the fixed end moments and end support reactions.
   [**Ans.** $M_A = M_B = -\frac{5}{48} WL$, $R_A = R_B = \frac{W}{2}$ (↑)]

21. A non-prismatic beam of span L has both ends fixed. It has a M.I. of I for the central $\frac{L}{2}$ portion and 2I for the remaining portion. It carries a U.D.L. of W/metre run over the entire span. Show that the fixed end moments are $-\frac{3}{32} WL^2$ and the moment at the mid span is $+\frac{WL^2}{32}$.

22. A fixed beam AB of span 5 m is subjected to a clockwise couple of 400 kNm applied at C, 3 m from A. Assuming constant flexural rigidity find the end moments and the reactions at the supports.
   [**Ans.** $M_A = 128$ kNm clockwise, $M_B = 48$ kNm clockwise, $R_A = 115.2$ kN (↑), $R_B = 115.2$ kN (↓)]

23. A beam of span L is fixed at both ends. A couple μ is applied to the beam at the centre of the span. Prove that the fixing couples at each support is $\frac{\mu}{4}$.

24. For the fixed beam shown in Fig. 4.125, find the end moments.

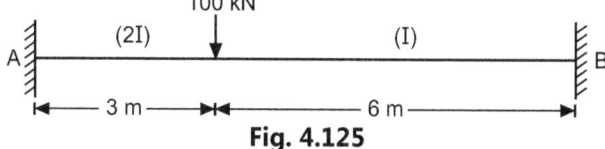

Fig. 4.125

[**Ans.** $M_A = -161.67$ kNm, $M_B = -52.83$ kNm]

25. A built-in beam of span 6 m carries a U.D.L. of 20 kN/m over the entire span. The support A sinks by 8 mm. Find the fixed end moments and support reactions.

    Take E = 210 GPa and $I_{xx} = 10^7$ m^4.

    [**Ans.** $M_A = -57.2$ kNm, $M_B = -62.8$ kNm, $R_A = 59.07$ (↑), $R_B = 60.93$ kN (↑)]

26. A built-up beam AB of span 4 m carries a U.D.L. of 25 kN/m over the entire span. The support B sinks by 10 mm. Find the support moments and support reaction if E = 200 GPa and I = 8 × 10^6 mm^4.

    [**Ans.** $M_A = -39.33$ kNm, $M_B = -27.33$ kNm, $R_A = 53.00$ kN (↑), $R_B = 47$ kN (↑)]

    Find the support moments and support reactions for the continuous beam in the examples 27 to 47 below. Draw SF and BM diagrams.

27.

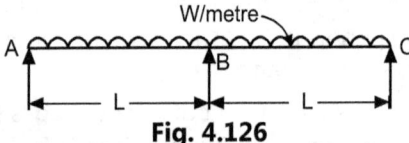

Fig. 4.126

[**Ans.** $M_A = M_C = 0$, $M_B = -\dfrac{WL^2}{8}$, $R_A = R_C = \dfrac{3}{8}WL$ (↑), $R_B = \dfrac{5}{4}WL$ (↑)]

28.

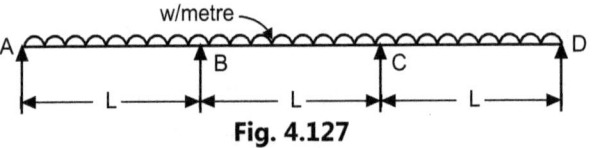

Fig. 4.127

[**Ans.** $M_A = M_D = 0$; $M_B = M_C = -\dfrac{wL^2}{10}$, $R_A = R_D = \dfrac{2}{5}WL$ (↑), $R_B = R_C = \dfrac{11}{10}wL$ (↑)]

29.

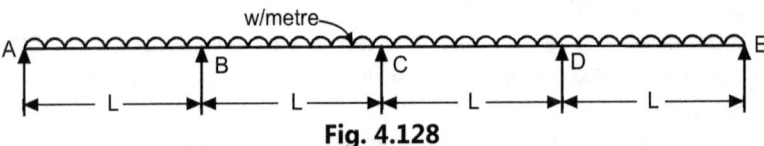

Fig. 4.128

[**Ans.** $M_A = M_E = 0$, $M_B = M_D = -\dfrac{3}{28}WL^2$, $M_C = -\dfrac{WL^2}{14}$, $R_A = R_E = \dfrac{11}{28}WL$ (↑),

$R_B = R_D = \dfrac{8}{7}WL$ (↑), $R_C = \dfrac{13}{14}WL$ (↑)]

30.

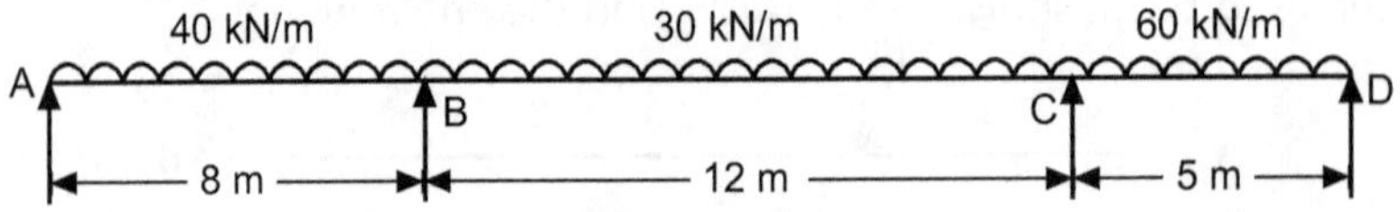

Fig. 4.129

[**Ans.** $M_A = M_D = 0$, $M_B = -359$ kN.m, $M_C = -309.6$ kNm, $R_A = 115.1$ kN (↑); $R_B = 389.0$ kN (↑), $R_C = 387.9$ kN (↑), $R_D = 88.0$ kN (↑)]

31.

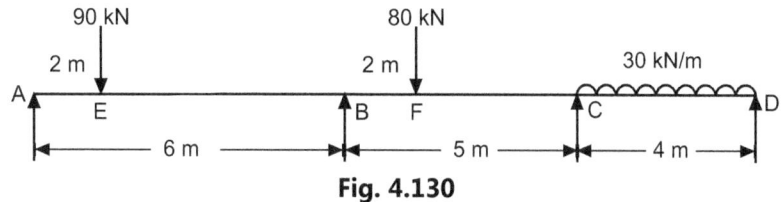

Fig. 4.130

[**Ans.** $M_A = M_D = 0$, $M_B = -68.4$ kN.m, $M_C = -44.8$ kNm, $R_A = 48.6$ kN ($\uparrow$), $R_B = 94.1$ kN ($\uparrow$), $R_C = 98.5$ kN ($\uparrow$), $R_D = 48.8$ kN ($\uparrow$)]

32.

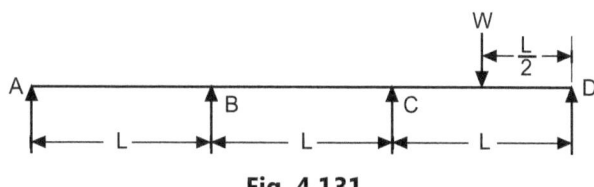

Fig. 4.131

[**Ans.** $M_A = M_D = 0$, $M_B = +\dfrac{WL}{40}$, $M_C = -\dfrac{WL}{10}$, $R_A = \dfrac{W}{40}$ ($\uparrow$),

$R_B = \dfrac{3}{20} W$ ($\downarrow$), $R_C = \dfrac{29}{40} W$ ($\uparrow$), $R_D = \dfrac{2}{5} W$ ($\uparrow$)]

33. In example 31, the support B sinks by 10 mm below A and C.

Take $I_{xx} = 1.316 \times 10^8$ mm^4 and $E = 200$ GPa.

[**Ans.** $M_A = M_D = 0$, $M_B = -36$ kNm, $M_C = -71.5$ kNm, $R_A = 54$ kN ($\uparrow$), $R_B = 76.9$ kN ($\uparrow$), $R_C = 116.975$ kN ($\uparrow$), $R_D = 42.125$ kN ($\uparrow$)]

34. In example 31, the end A is fixed while D is simple.

[**Ans.** $M_A = -77.0$ kNm, $M_B = -45.9$ kNm, $M_C = -51.10$ kNm; $M_D = 0$, $R_A = 65.18$ kN ($\uparrow$), $R_B = 71.78$ kN ($\uparrow$), $R_C = 105.815$ kN ($\uparrow$), $R_D = 47.225$ kN ($\uparrow$)]

35.

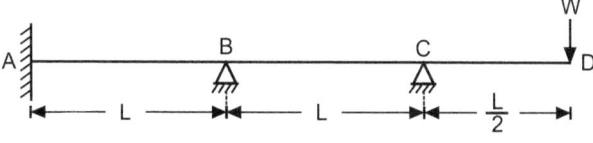

Fig. 4.132

[**Ans.** $M_A = -\dfrac{WL}{14}$, $M_B = +\dfrac{WL}{7}$, $M_C = \dfrac{WL}{2}$, $R_A = \dfrac{3}{14} W$ ($\uparrow$),

$R_B = \dfrac{6}{7} W$ ($\downarrow$), $R_C = \dfrac{23}{14} W$ ($\uparrow$)]

36.

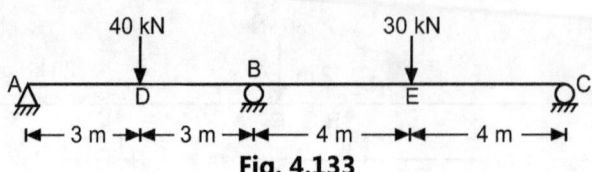

Fig. 4.133

[**Ans.** $M_A = 0$, $M_B = -45$ kNm, $M_C = 0$; $V_A = 12.5$ kN (↑), $V_B = 48.125$ kN (↑), $V_C = 9.375$ kN (↑)]

37.

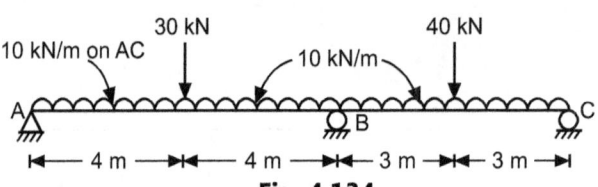

Fig. 4.134

[**Ans.** $M_A = M_C = 0$, $M_B = -110$ kNm, $V_A = 41.25$ kN (↑), $V_B = 137.085$ kN (↑), $V_C = 31.665$ kN (↑)]

38.

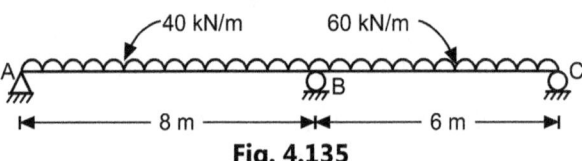

Fig. 4.135

[**Ans.** $M_A = M_C = 0$, $M_B = -298.50$ kN.m, $V_A = 122.68$ kN (↑), $V_B = 427.06$ kN (↑), $V_C = 130.26$ kN (↑)]

39.

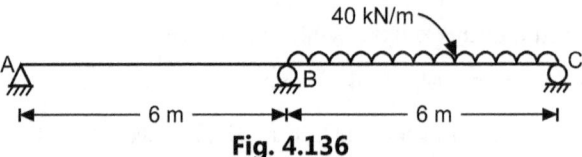

Fig. 4.136

[**Ans.** $M_A = M_C = 0$, $M_B = -90$ kN.m; $V_A = 15$ kN (↓), $V_B = 150$ kN (↑), $V_C = 105.00$ kN (↑)]

40.

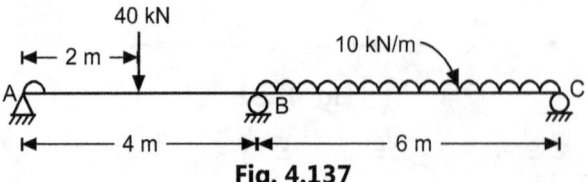

Fig. 4.137

[**Ans.** $M_A = M_C = 0$, $M_B = -39$ kNm, $V_A = 10.25$ kN (↑), $V_B = 66.25$ kN (↑), $V_C = 23.50$ kN (↑)]

41.

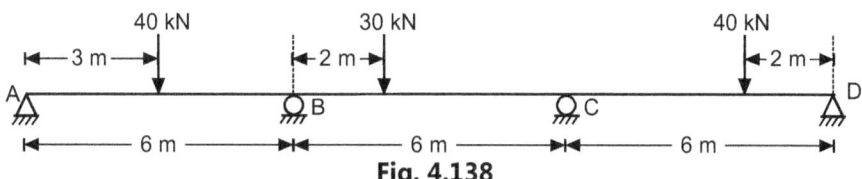

Fig. 4.138

[**Ans.** $M_A = M_D = 0$; $M_B = -33.50$ kN.m, $M_C = -22.75$ kN.m, $V_A = 14.35$ kN (↑), $V_B = 47.5$ kN (↑), $V_C = 25.25$ kN (↑), $V_D = 22.90$ kN (↑)]

42.

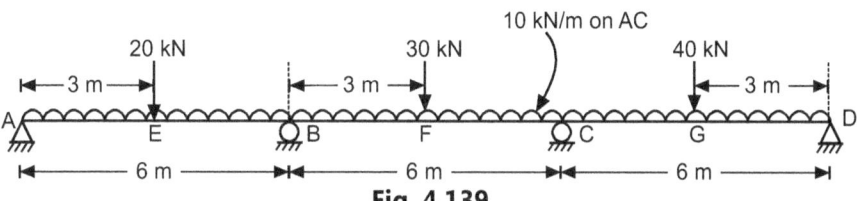

Fig. 4.139

[**Ans.** $M_A = M_D = 0$, $M_B = -60.9$ kN.m, $M_C = -46.8$ kN.m, $V_A = 29.85$ kN (↑), $V_B = 97.50$ kN (↑), $V_C = 70.45$ kN (↑), $V_D = 12.2$ kN (↑)]

43.

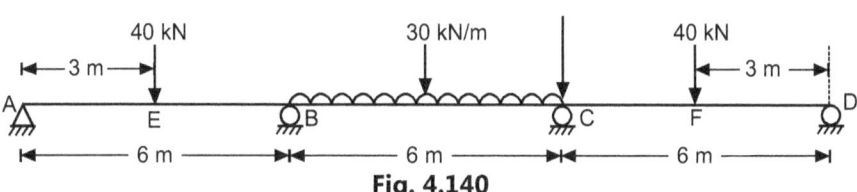

Fig. 4.140

[**Ans.** $M_A = M_D = 0$, $M_B = M_C = -72$ kN.m, $V_A = V_D = 8$ kN (↑), $V_B = V_C = 122$ kN (↑)]

44.

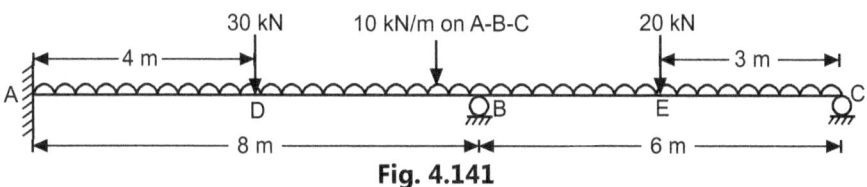

Fig. 4.141

[**Ans.** $M_A = -86$ kN.m, $M_B = -78$ kN.m, $M_C = 0$, $V_A = 56$ kN (↑), $V_B = 107$ kN (↑), $V_C = 27$ kN (↑)]

45.

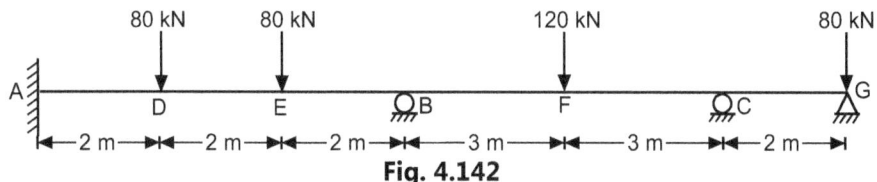

Fig. 4.142

[**Ans.** $M_A = -121.36$ kN.m, $M_B = -77.2$ kN.m, $M_C = -160$ kN.m; $V_A = 87.36$ kN (↑), $V_B = 118.84$ kN (↑), $V_C = 153.8$ kN (↑)]

46.

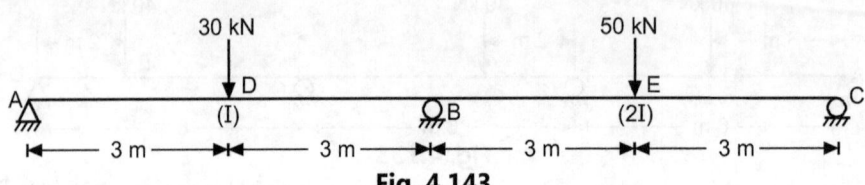

Fig. 4.143

[**Ans.** $M_A = M_C = 0$, $M_B = -41.25$ kN.m; $V_A = 8.125$ kN (↑), $V_B = 53.75$ kN (↑), $V_C = 18.125$ kN (↑)]

47.

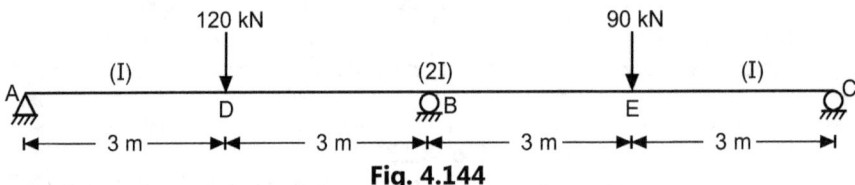

Fig. 4.144

[**Ans.** $M_A = M_C = 0$, $M_B = -140.04$ kNm, $V_A = 36.675$ kN (↑), $V_B = 151.665$ kN (↑), $V_C = 21.66$ kN (↑)]

48. A continuous beam ABCD is shown in Fig. 4.145. If the support B sinks by 2.50 mm below the level of other supports, find the support moments and support reactions. Take the constant value of flexural rigidity equal to 30,000 kN.m².

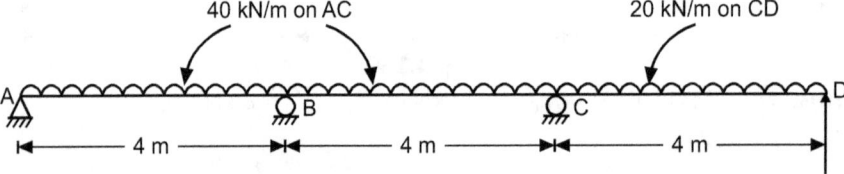

Fig. 4.145

[**Ans.** $M_A = M_D = 0$, $M_B = -49.7$ kNm, $M_C = -64.9$ kNm; $V_A = 67.575$ kN (↑), $V_B = 168.625$ kN (↑), $V_C = 140.025$ kN (↑), $V_D = 23.775$ kN (↑)]

49. A continuous beam ABC as shown in Fig. 4.146 carries a U.D.L. of 50 kN/m over ABC. The support B sinks by 5 mm below A and C. The flexural rigidity is constant and is equal to 66400 kNm². Find the bending moments at A, B and C and the reactions at these supports.

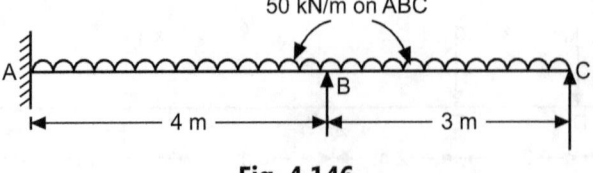

Fig. 4.146

[**Ans.** $M_A = -190.3$ kN.m, $M_B = -56.1$ kN.m, $M_C = 0$, $V_A = 133.55$ kN (↑), $V_B = 155.475$ kN (↑), $V_C = 60.975$ kN (↑)]

50. The support A of a continuous beam is fixed while supports B and C are kept on the rollers. AB = BC = 12 m. It carries a U.D.L. of 30 kN/m over AB and a concentrated load of 240 kN over BC at 4.0 m from the support B. As a result of loading, the support B sinks by 30 mm. Take E = 200 GPa and the constant value of $I_{xx} = 2 \times 10^9$ mm^4. Calculate the support moments and support reactions and draw S.F. and B.M. diagrams.

    [**Ans.** $M_A = -739$ kN.m, $M_B = -102$ kNm, $M_C = 0$, $V_A = 233.08$ kN (↑), $V_B = 295.42$ kN (↑), $V_C = 71.50$ kN (↑)]

51. A fixed beam ABCD is fixed at supports A and D and is simply supported at B and C as shown in Fig. 4.147. It carries a U.D.L. of 10 kN/m over AB, a central load of 100 kN on the span BC and a central load of 50 kN on the span CD. During the loading, the support B sinks by 10 mm. $I_{AB} = I_{CD} = 3 \times 10^8$ mm^4 and $I_{BC} = 2 I_{AB}$. Take E = 200 GPa. Find the support moments and support reactions. Draw S.F. and B.M. diagrams.

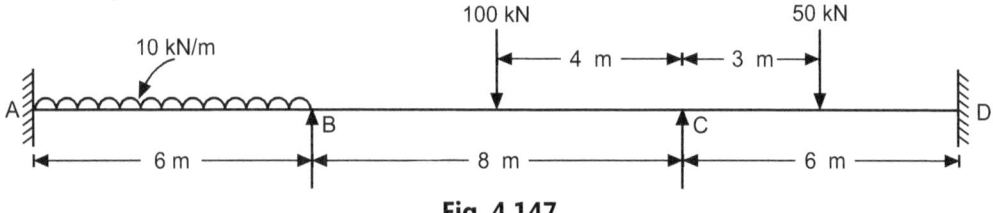

Fig. 4.147

    [**Ans.** $M = -57.4$ kN.m, $M_B = -25.7$ kN.m, $M_C = -92.0$ kNm, $M_D = -20.7$ kN.m, $V_A = 35.28$ kN (↑), $V_B = 66.43$ kN (↑), $V_C = 95.17$ kN (↑), $V_D = 13.12$ kN (↑)]

52. Find the support moments and support reactions and draw S.F.D. and B.M.D. for continuous beam ABCD shown in Fig. 4.148 if the interior support B sinks by 10 mm. Consider I_{xx} of the section = 1.32×10^8 mm^4 and E = 200 GPa.

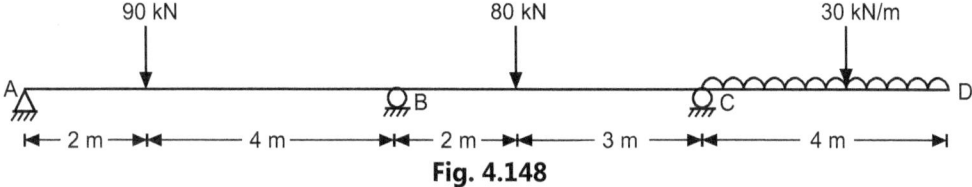

Fig. 4.148

    [**Ans.** $M_A = M_D = 0$, $M_B = -35.87$ kNm, $M_C = -71.56$ kN.m, $V_A = 54$ kN (↑), $V_B = 76.9$ kN (↑), $V_C = 117$ kN (↑), $V_D = 42.1$ kN (↑)]

53. ABCD is a horizontal beam of uniform cross-section and length 12 m. It is freely supported at ends A and D and at two intermediate supports B and C distant 3 m from each end. The supports A and D are rigid but those at B and C sink 3 mm per kN of the load. The beam carries a U.D.L. of 10 kN/m over the entire length AD. The flexural rigidity is constant and is equal to 26500 kN.m^2. Evaluate support moments and support reactions.

    [**Ans.** $M_A = M_D = 0$, $M_B = M_C = +85.03$ kN.m, $V_A = V_D = 76.6$ kN (↑), $V_B = V_C = 16.656$ kN (↑)]

54. A continuous beam ABCD has three equal spans of 6 m each. It is loaded as shown in Fig. 4.149. Supports A, B, C and D sink by 20 mm, 40 mm, 50 mm and 14 mm respectively. If the constant flexural rigidity is equal to 60000 kN/m², determine the support moments and support reactions. Draw S.F.D. and B.M.D.

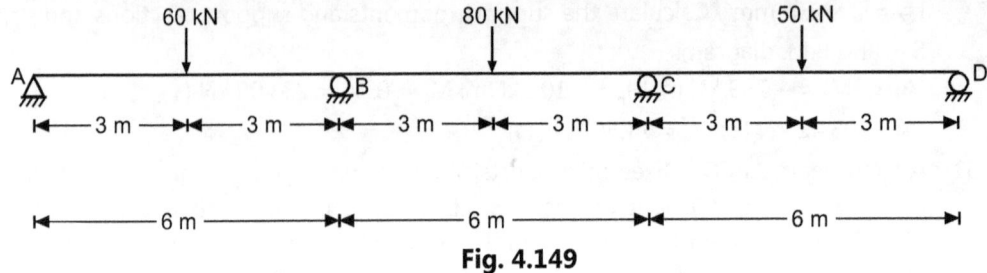

Fig. 4.149

[**Ans.** $M_A = M_D = 0$, $M_B = -68.5$ kN.m, $M_C = +59$ kN.m, $V_A = 18.58$ kN (↑),

$V_B = 102.67$ kN (↑), $V_C = 33.92$ kN (↑), $V_D = 34.83$ kN (↑)]

55. For the continuous beam shown in Fig. 4.150, find the support moments and support reactions. Also draw S.F.D. and B.M.D.

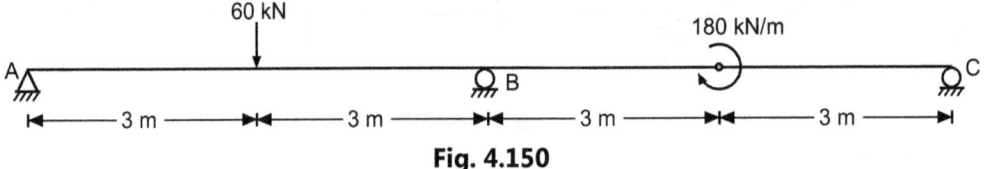

Fig. 4.150

[**Ans.** $M_A = M_C = 0$, $M_B = -22.50$ kNm, $V_A = V_C = 26.25$ kN (↑), $V_B = 7.5$ kN (↑)]

56. In the above example 55, find the support moments and reactions if the applied couple is 180 kN.m anticlockwise instead of clockwise as is given.

[**Ans.** $M_A = M_C = 0$, $M_B = -45$ kN.m, $V_A = 22.5$ kN (↑), $V_B = 75$ kN (↑),

$V_C = 37.5$ kN (↓)]

57. Solve example 55 if $I_{AB} = 2I$ and $I_{BC} = 3I$.

[**Ans.** $M_A = M_C = 0$, $M_B = -31.50$ kN.m, $V_A = V_C = 24.75$ kN (↑),

$V_B = 10.50$ kN (↑)]

Chapter 5
ENERGY METHOD FOR DISPLACEMENT

5.1 INTRODUCTION

The structures which cannot be analysed by the equations of equilibrium, these structures are known as *indeterminate structures*. To analyse these structures, we have to apply compatibility equations. These structures may be analysed by Castigliano's second theorem or principle of least work.

5.2 CASTIGLIANO'S SECOND THEOREM

In any linearly elastic structure, there are number of values for that redundant reaction which satisfy the condition. But exact value of the redundant reaction is the value due to which the energy stored is minimum.

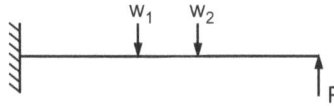

Fig. 5.1

Therefore actual value of P is partial differentiation of the total strain energy with respect to and the value should be minimum i.e.

$$\frac{\partial s}{\partial P} = 0$$

where s = Total strain energy stored

SOLVED PROBLEMS

Problem 5.1 : Analyse the beam shown in Fig. 5.2.
Solution :

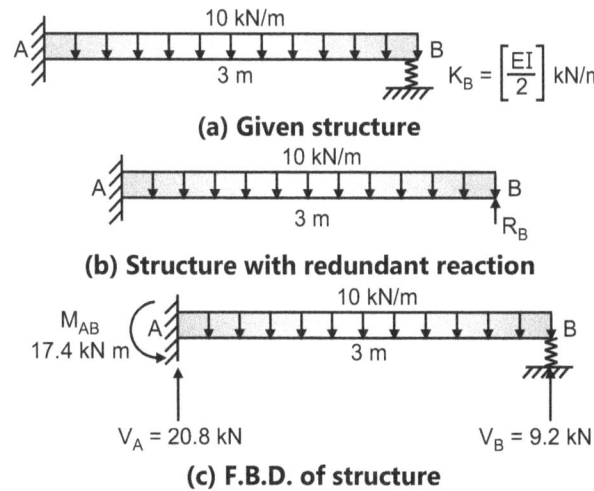

(a) Given structure

(b) Structure with redundant reaction

(c) F.B.D. of structure

(5.1)

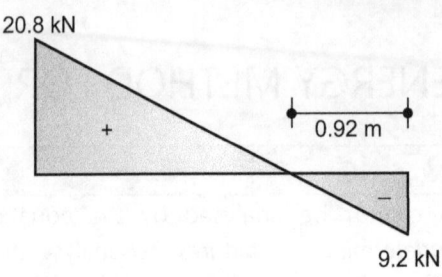

(d) SFD

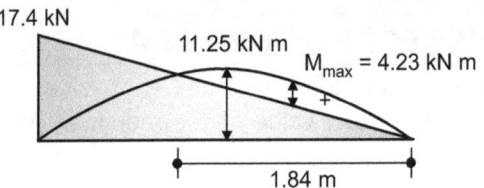

(e) BMD by superposition

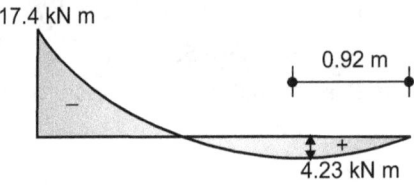

(f) BMD on tension side

Fig. 5.2

$$\int M \frac{\partial M}{\partial R_B} = E_1 I \, \delta_B$$

Member	Origin	Limit	Moment	$\frac{\partial M}{\partial R_B}$
BA	B	0 – 3	$R_B x - \dfrac{10x^2}{2}$	x

$$\delta_B = \frac{R_B}{K_B} = -\frac{R_B}{EI} \cdot 2$$

∴ $$EI \, \delta_B = -\frac{2 R_B \times EI}{EI} = -2R_B$$

$$\int_0^3 (R_B x - 5x^2) \, x \cdot dx = -2R_B$$

$$\int_0^3 R_B \, x^2 \, dx - 5 \int_0^3 x^3 \, dx = -2R_B$$

$$9R_B - 101.25 = -2R_B$$

∴ $\quad 11 R_B = 101.25$

∴ $\quad R_B = 9.20 \text{ kN } (\uparrow)$

∴ $\quad R_A = 20.8 \text{ kN } (\uparrow)$

$\quad M_A = 17.4 \text{ kN-m } (\circlearrowleft)$

Problem 5.2 : Analyse the beam as shown in Fig. 5.3 (a).

Solution : $\quad \Sigma F_y = 0$

$$R_A + R_B + R_C - 10 \times 6 - 30 = 0$$

∴ $\quad R_A = 90 - R_B - R_C$

$\Sigma M @ A = 0$

$$-M_A + 10 \times 6 \times 3 - R_B \times 6 + 30 \times 8 - R_C \times 12 = 0$$

$$M_A = 180 + 240 - 6R_B - 12R_C$$

$$= 420 - 6R_B - 12R_C$$

Member	Origin	Limit	Moment	$\dfrac{\partial M}{\partial R_B}$	$\dfrac{\partial M}{\partial R_C}$
CD	C	0 – 4	$R_C \cdot x$	0	x
DB	D	0 – 2	$R_C (x + 4) - 30x$	0	(x + 4)
BA	B	0 – 6	$R_C (x + 6) - 30 (x + 2) + R_B x - 5x^2$	x	(x + 6)

$$\int M \cdot \frac{\partial M}{\partial R_B} dx = 0$$

$$\int_0^6 [R_C (x + 6) - 30 (x + 2) + R_B x - 5x^2] (x) \, dx$$

$$= \int_0^6 R_C (x^2 + 6x) \, dx - 30 \int_0^6 (x^2 + 2x) + R_B \int_0^6 x^2 \, dx - 5 \int x^3 \, dx$$

$$0 = 180 R_C - 3240 + 72 R_B - 1620$$

$$R_B + 2.5 R_C = 67.5 \qquad \ldots (1)$$

$$\int M \frac{\partial M}{\partial R_C} = 0$$

$$\int_0^4 R_C \cdot x \cdot x \, dx = \int_0^4 R_C x^2 \, dx$$

$$= R_C \left[\frac{x^3}{3}\right]_0^4 = 21.33 R_C \qquad \ldots (A)$$

$$\int_0^2 [R_C(x+4) - 30(x+2)](x+4)\,dx$$

$$= \int_0^2 R_C(x^2 + 8x + 16)\,dx - \int_0^2 30x(x+4)\,dx$$

$$= R_C\left(\frac{x^3}{3} + \frac{8x^2}{2} + 16x\right)_0^2 - 30\left(\frac{x^3}{3} + \frac{4x^2}{2}\right)_0^2$$

$$= 50.67\,R_C - 320 \quad\quad \ldots (B)$$

$$\int_0^6 [R_C(x+6) - 30(x+2) + R_B x - 5x^2](x+6)\,dx$$

$$= R_C \int_0^6 (x^2 + 12x + 36)\,dx - 30\int_0^6 (x^2 + 8x + 12)\,dx$$

$$+ R_B \int_0^6 (x^2 + 6x)\,dx - 5\int_0^6 (x^3 + 6x^2)\,dx$$

$$= R_C\left(\frac{x^3}{3} + \frac{12x^2}{2} + 36x\right)_0^6 - 30\left(\frac{x^3}{3} + \frac{8x^2}{2} + 12x\right)_0^6$$

$$+ R_B\left(\frac{x^3}{3} + \frac{6x^2}{2}\right)_0^6 - 5\left(\frac{x^4}{4} + \frac{6x^3}{3}\right)_0^6$$

$$= 504\,R_C - 8640 + 180\,R_B - 3780 \quad\quad \ldots (C)$$

Adding equations (A), (B) and (C),

$$576\,R_C + 180\,R_B = 12740$$

$$3.2\,R_C + R_B = 70.78 \quad\quad \ldots (2)$$

Solving equations (1) and (2),

$$R_C = 4.69 \text{ kN}$$
$$R_B = 55.77 \text{ kN}$$
$$R_A = 29.54 \text{ kN}$$
$$M_A = 29.1 \text{ kN-m}$$

(a) Given structure

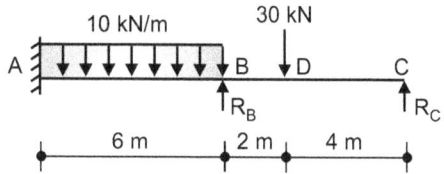

(b) Beam with redundant reactions

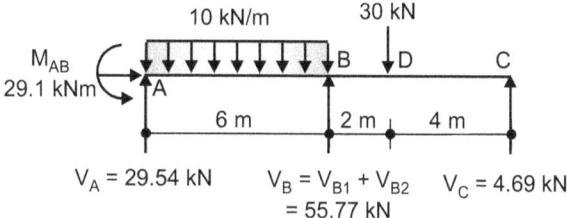

(c) FBD of structure

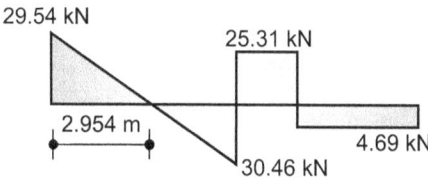

(d) SFD

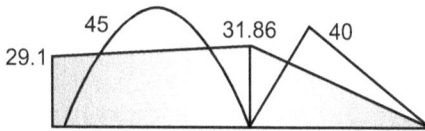

(e) BMD by superposition

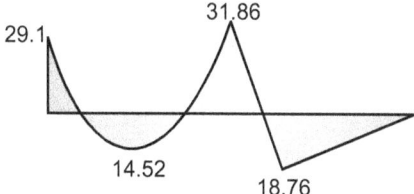

(f) BMD on tension side

(g) Elastic curve
Fig. 5.3

Problem 5.3 : In problem 5.2 if support B sinks by 25 mm and EI = 3800 kN-m², analyse the beam.

Solution : $\int M \dfrac{\partial M}{\partial R_B} = EI\delta_B$

From equation (1) of problem 5.2,

$180 R_C + 72 R_B - 4860 = -3800 \times 25 \times 10^{-3}$

$180 R_C + 72 R_B = 4765$

∴ $2.5 R_C + R_B = 66.18$ ... (1)

Equation (2) remains same as problem 5.2.

∴ $3.2 R_C + R_B = 70.78$ ... (2)

Solving equations (1) and (2),

∴ $R_C = 6.57$ kN
$R_B = 49.76$ kN
$R_A = 33.67$ kN
$M_A = 42.61$ kN-m

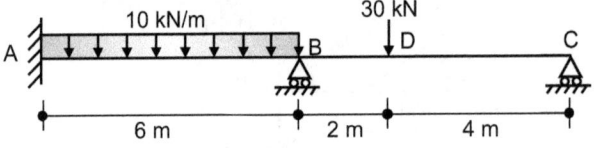

(a) Given structure

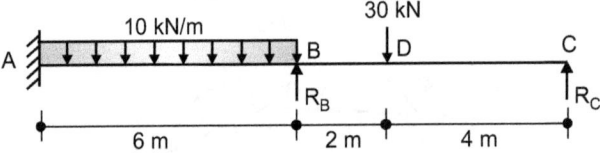

(b) Beam with redundant reactions

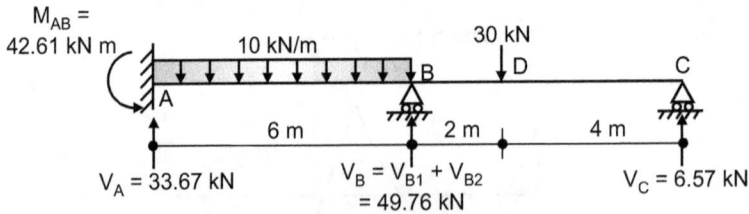

(c) FBD of structure

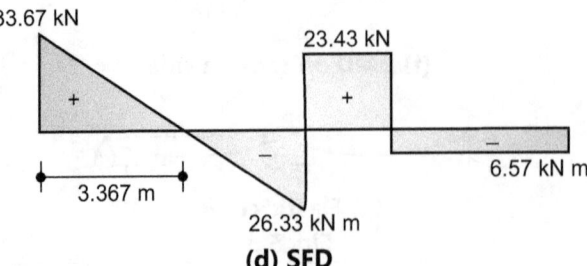

(d) SFD

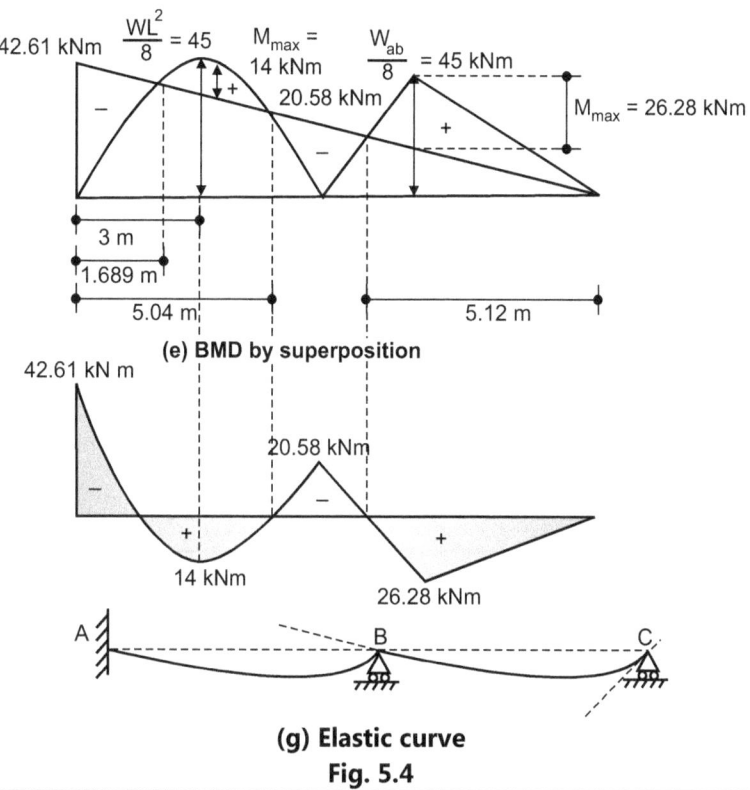

(g) Elastic curve
Fig. 5.4

Problem 5.4 : Analyse the beam shown in Fig. 5.5 (a).
Solution :

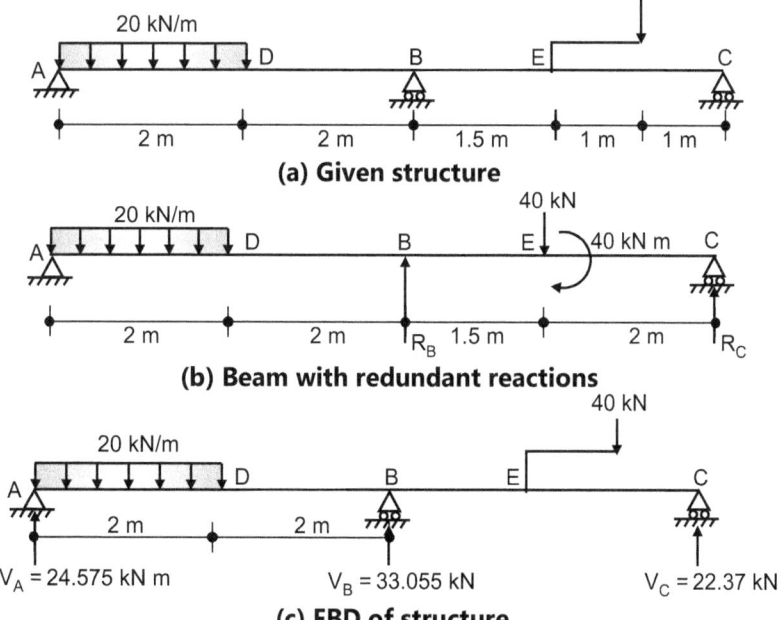

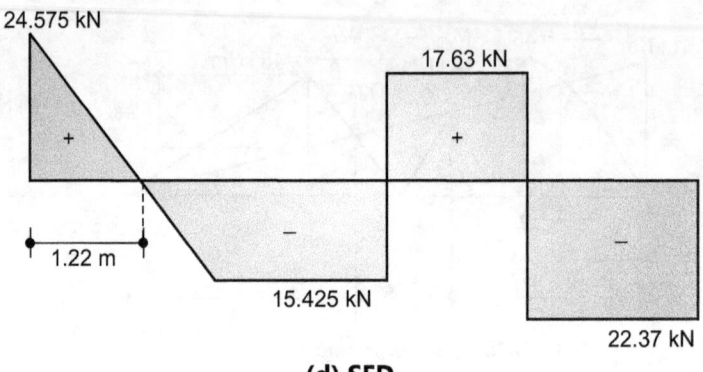

(d) SFD

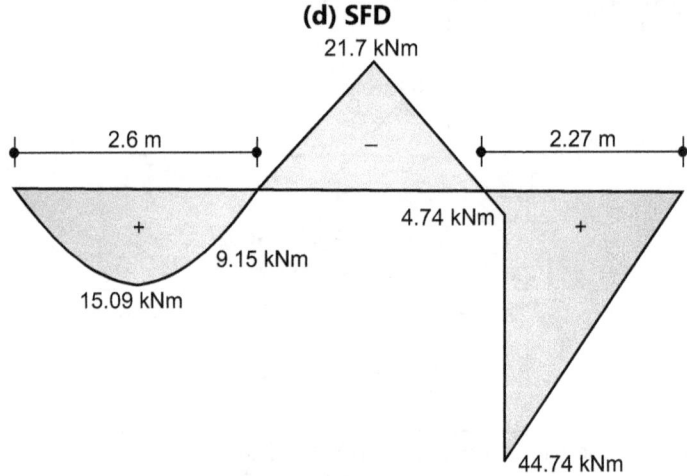

(e) BMD on tension side

Fig. 5.5

$$-R_B \times 4 - R_C \times 7.5 + 20 \times 2 + 40 \times 5.5 + 40 = 0$$
$$R_B = 75 - 1.875\,R_C$$
$$R_A + R_B + R_C = 80$$
$$\therefore R_A = 5 + 0.875\,R_C$$

Member	Origin	Limit	Moment	$\dfrac{\partial M}{\partial R_C}$
AD	A	0 – 2	$(5 + 0.875\,R_C)\,x - \dfrac{20x^2}{2}$	$0.875\,x$
DB	D	0 – 2	$(5 + 0.875\,R_C)(x + 2) - 20 \times 2\,(x + 1)$	$0.875\,(x + 2)$
CE	C	0 – 2	$R_C \cdot x$	x
EB	E	0 – 1.5	$R_C\,(x + 2) - 40x - 40$	$(x + 2)$

$$\int M \dfrac{\partial M}{\partial R_C} = 0$$

Member AD :

$$\int_0^2 [(5 + 0.875\, R_C)\, x - 10x^2]\, 0.875\, x \cdot dx$$

$$= \int_0^2 (4.375\, x^2)\, dx + \int_0^2 0.765\, x^2\, dx - 8.75 \int_0^2 x^3\, dx$$

$$= 11.67 + 2.04\, R_C - 35 \qquad \ldots (A)$$

Member DB :

$$\int_0^2 [(5 + 0.875\, R_C)(x + 2) - 20 \times 2 \times (x + 1)]\, 0.875\, (x + 2)\, dx$$

$$= \int_0^2 4.375\,(x^2 + 4x + 4)\, dx + \int_0^2 0.765\, R_C\,(x^2 + 4x + 4)\, dx$$

$$- 35 \int (x^2 + 3x + 2)\, dx$$

$$= 81.67 + 14.28\, R_C - 443.33 \qquad \ldots (B)$$

Member CE :

$$\int_0^2 R_C \cdot x^2\, dx = 2.67\, R_C \qquad \ldots (C)$$

Member EB : $\displaystyle\int_0^{1.5} [R_C\,(x + 2) - 40x - 40]\,(x + 2)\, dx$

$$= \int_0^{1.5} R_C\,(x^2 + 4x + 4)\, dx - \int_0^{1.5} 40\,(x^2 + 2x)\, dx - \int_0^{1.5} 40\,(x + 2)\, dx$$

$$= 11.625\, R_C - 135 - 165 \qquad \ldots (D)$$

Adding equations (A), (B), (C) and (D),

$$30.615\, R_C - 684.99 = 0$$

$$\therefore \quad R_C = 22.37 \text{ kN}$$
$$R_B = 33.05 \text{ kN}$$
$$R_A = 24.575 \text{ kN}$$

Problem 5.5 : Analyse the beam shown in Fig. 5.6 (a).

Solution :

Member	Origin	Limit	EI	M	$\dfrac{\partial M}{\partial R_C}$	$\dfrac{\partial M}{\partial M_C}$
CB	C	0 - 2	EI	$R_C \cdot x + M_C$	x	1
BD	B	0 - 1	2EI	$R_C\,(x + 2) + M_C$	$(x + 2)$	1
DA	D	0 - 1	2EI	$R_C\,(x + 3) + M_C - 100\, x$	$(x + 3)$	1

$$\int_0^2 \frac{M}{EI} \frac{\partial M}{\partial R_C} \cdot dx = 0$$

Member CB :

$$\frac{1}{EI}\int_0^2 (R_C x + M_C) x \cdot dx = \frac{1}{EI}(2.67 R_C + 2 M_C) \quad \ldots (A)$$

Member BD :

$$\frac{1}{2EI}\int_0^1 [R_C(x+2) + M_C](x+2) \cdot dx = \frac{1}{2EI}\int_0^1 R_C(x^2 + 4x + 4)\,dx + \frac{M_C}{2EI}\int_0^1 (x+2)\,dx$$

$$= \frac{1}{2EI}[6.33 R_C + 2.5 M_C] \quad \ldots (B)$$

Member DA :

$$\frac{1}{2EI}\int_0^1 [R_C(x+3) + M_C - 100x](x+3)\,dx$$

$$= \frac{1}{2EI}\int_0^1 R_C(x^2 + 6x + 9)\,dx + \frac{1}{2EI}\int_0^1 M_C(x+3)\,dx - \frac{100}{2EI}\int_0^1 (x^2 + 3x)\,dx$$

$$\frac{1}{2EI}(12.33 R_C + 3.5 M_C - 183.33) \quad \ldots (C)$$

Adding equations (A), (B) and (C),

$$12 R_C + 5 M_C = 91.67 \quad \ldots (1)$$

$$\int \frac{M}{EI} \cdot \frac{\partial M}{\partial M_C} = 0$$

$$\frac{1}{EI}\int_0^2 (R_C \cdot x + M_C)\,dx = \frac{2R_C + 2M_C}{EI} \quad \ldots (A)$$

$$\frac{1}{2EI}\int_0^1 [R_C(x+2) + M_C]\,dx = \frac{1}{2EI}(2.5 R_C + M_C) \quad \ldots (B)$$

$$\frac{1}{2EI}\int_0^1 [R_C(x+3) + M_C - 100x]\,dx = \frac{1}{2EI}(3.5 R_C + M_C - 50) \quad \ldots (C)$$

Adding equations (A), (B) and (C),

$$5 R_C + 3 M_C = 25 \quad \ldots (2)$$

Solving equations (1) and (2),

$$M_C = -14.395 \text{ kN-m}$$
$$= 14.395 \text{ kN-m } (\circlearrowleft)$$
$$R_C = 13.64 \text{ kN } (\uparrow)$$
$$\therefore \quad R_A = 86.36 \text{ kN}$$
$$M_A = 59.83 \text{ kN-m } (\circlearrowleft)$$

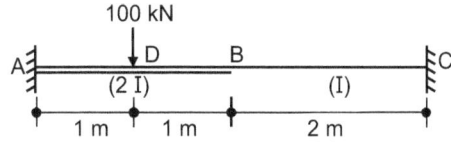

(a) Given structure

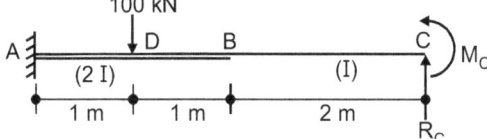

(b) Beam with redundant reactions

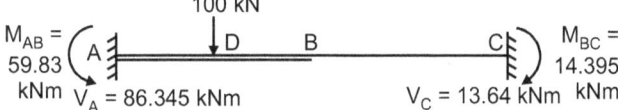

(c) FBD of structure

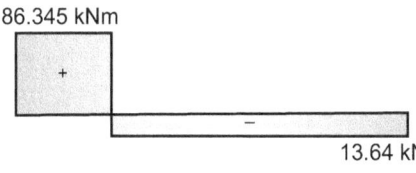

(d) SFD

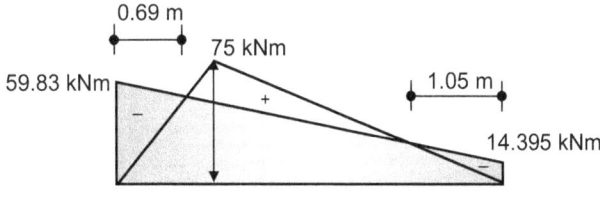

(e) BMD by superposition

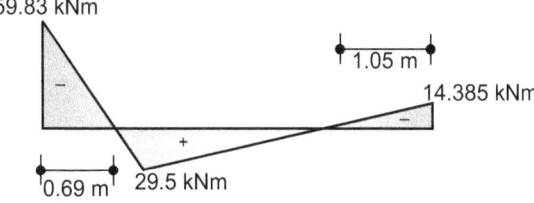

(f) BMD on tension side

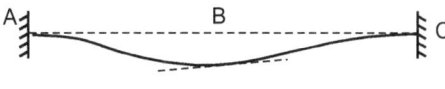

(g) Elastic curve

Fig. 5.6

Problem 5.6 : Analyse the beam shown in Fig. 5.7 (a).

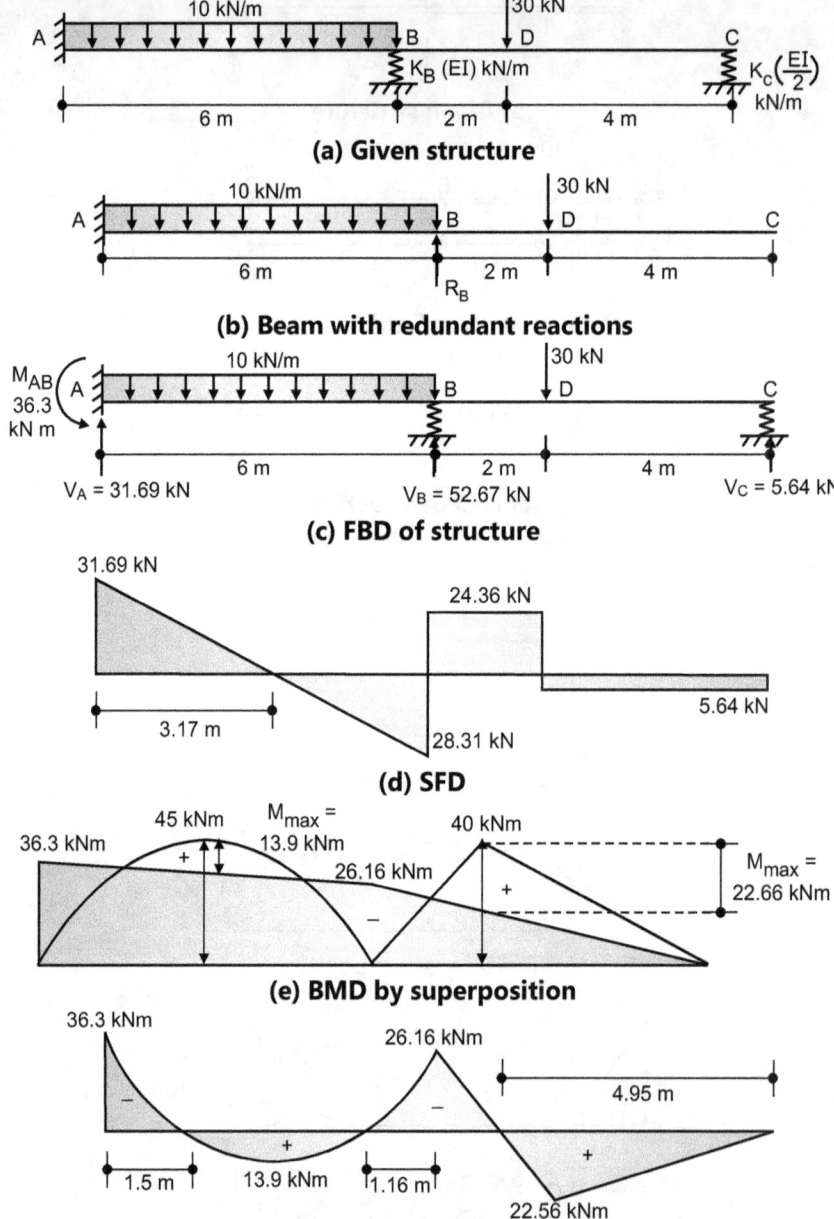

Fig. 5.7

Solution :

$$\Sigma F_y = 0$$

$$R_A + R_B + R_C - 10 \times 6 - 30 = 0$$

$$\therefore \quad R_A = 90 - R_B - R_C$$

$\Sigma M @ A = 0$

$- M_A + 10 \times 6 \times 3 - R_B \times 6 + 30 \times 8 - R_C \times 12 = 0$

$$M_A = 180 + 240 - 6R_B - 12R_C$$
$$= 420 - 6R_B - 12R_C$$

Member	Origin	Limit	Moment	$\dfrac{\partial M}{\partial R_B}$	$\dfrac{\partial M}{\partial R_C}$
CD	C	0 – 4	$R_C \cdot x$	0	x
DB	D	0 – 2	$R_C(x+4) - 30x$	0	$(x+4)$
BA	B	0 – 6	$R_C(x+6) - 30(x+2) + R_B x - 5x^2$	x	$(x+6)$

$$\int M \cdot \dfrac{\partial M}{\partial R_B} dx = EI\delta_B$$

$$\int_0^6 [R_C(x+6) - 30(x+2) + R_B x - 5x^2](x)\, dx$$

$$= \int_0^6 R_C(x^2 + 6x)\, dx - 30 \int_0^6 (x^2 + 2x) + R_B \int_0^6 x^2 dx - 5 \int x^3 dx$$

$$= 180 R_C - 3240 + 72 R_B - 1620$$

$$\delta_B = \dfrac{R_B}{K_B} = \dfrac{R_B}{EI}$$

$\therefore \quad\quad\quad\quad -EI\delta_B = -R_B$

$\therefore \quad 180 R_C - 4860 + 72 R_B = -R_B$

$\therefore \quad\quad 73 R_B + 180 R_C = 4860$

$\therefore \quad\quad R_B + 2.466 R_C = 66.58 \quad\quad\quad\quad\quad\quad …(1)$

$$\int M \dfrac{\partial M}{\partial R_C} = EI\delta_C$$

$$\int_0^4 R_C \cdot x \cdot x \, dx = \int_0^4 R_C x^2 dx = R_C \left[\dfrac{x^3}{3}\right]_0^4 = 21.33 R_C \quad\quad …(A)$$

$$\int_0^2 [R_C(x+4) - 30(x+2)](x+4)\, dx$$

$$= \int_0^2 R_C(x^2 + 8x + 16)\, dx - \int 30(x^2 + 6x + 8)\, dx$$

$$= R_C \left(\dfrac{x^3}{3} + \dfrac{8x^2}{2} + 16x\right)_0^2 - 30\left(\dfrac{x^3}{3} + \dfrac{6x^2}{2} + 8x\right)_0^2$$

$$= 50.67 R_C - 320 \quad\quad\quad\quad\quad\quad …(B)$$

$$\int_0^6 [R_C(x+6) - 30(x+2) + R_B x - 5x^2](x+6)\,dx$$

$$= R_C \int_0^6 (x^2 + 12x + 36)\,dx - 20 \int_0^6 (x^2 + 8x + 12)\,dx$$

$$+ R_B \int_0^6 (x^2 + 6x)\,dx - 5 \int_0^6 (x^3 + 6x^2)\,dx$$

$$= R_C \left(\frac{x^3}{3} + \frac{12x^2}{2} + 36x\right)_0^6 - 30\left(\frac{x^3}{3} + \frac{8x^2}{2} + 12x\right)_0^6$$

$$+ R_B \left(\frac{x^3}{3} + \frac{6x^2}{2}\right)_0^6 - 5\left(\frac{x^4}{4} + \frac{6x^3}{3}\right)_0^6$$

$$= 504\,R_C - 8640 + 180\,R_B - 3780 \qquad \ldots (C)$$

Adding equations (A), (B) and (C),

$$576\,R_C + 180\,R_B = 12740$$

$$\delta_C = \frac{R_C}{K_C} = \frac{R_C}{EI} \times 2$$

$$-EI\,\delta_C = -2R_C$$

$$\therefore 576\,R_C + 180\,R_B - 12740 = -2R_C$$

$$578\,R_C + 180\,R_B = 12740$$

$$3.21\,R_C + R_B = 70.78 \qquad \ldots (2)$$

Solving equations (1) and (2),

$$R_C = 5.64 \text{ kN } (\uparrow)$$
$$R_B = 52.67 \text{ kN } (\uparrow)$$
$$R_A = 31.69 \text{ kN } (\uparrow)$$
$$M_A = 36.3 \text{ kN-m } (\circlearrowleft)$$

5.3 FRAMES

Fig. 5.8 shows the two hinged portal frame ABCD. A and D be the hinge supports. The portal frame is indeterminate structure. The analysis of the portal frame can be done with the help of slope deflection, moment distribution method, strain energy method etc. But in this chapter we are discussing the analysis by strain energy method.

The portal frame ABCD is indeterminate to first degree.

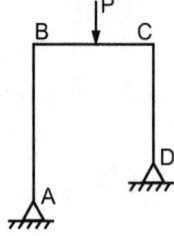

Fig. 5.8

5.3.1 Procedure for Analysis

Assume H_a as the redundant forces. Then all the reactions are found out in terms of H_a. Then using the Castigliano's second theorem, we get the redundant force H_a.

Strain energy :
1. First we have to find the degree of indeterminacy of the structure.
2. Convert the reactions in terms of redundant forces as shown in Fig. 5.9 (b).

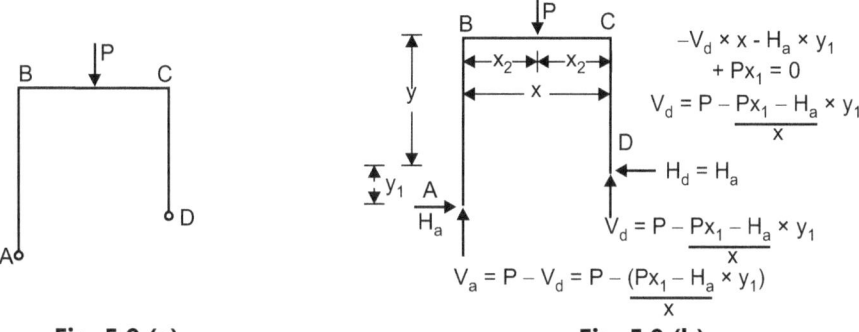

Fig. 5.9 (a) Fig. 5.9 (b)

3. Make the table in the following manner :

Member	Origin	Moment (M)	$\dfrac{\partial M}{\partial H}$	Limit of integration

4. Calculate $\int M \dfrac{\partial M}{\partial H}$ for all members.
5. Use Castigliano's second theorem and generate the equation

$$\int M \dfrac{\partial M}{\partial H} = 0$$

6. After solving above equation, we get the redundant reaction.
7. Find the moments at the joints.

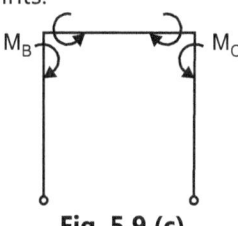

Fig. 5.9 (c)

8. Draw B.M. diagram by superposition.
9. Draw B.M. diagram on tension side.

SOLVED PROBLEMS

Problem 5.7 : Find the moments at B and C for the following portal frame in Fig. 5.10 (a).

Solution : Let H_a and H_d be the horizontal and V_a and V_d be the vertical components of the reactions at A and B.

The portal is statically indeterminate.

∴ Degree of static indeterminacy = R − 3 = 4 − 3 = 1

Consider horizontal reaction as the redundant.

$\Sigma F_x = 0$ ∴ $H_a = H_d = H$.

Taking moment @ A ∴ $H \times 1 + V_d \times 4 - 3 \times 4 \times 2 = 0$

∴ $V_d = \left(\dfrac{24 - H}{4}\right)$, $V_a = \left(\dfrac{24 + H}{4}\right)$

Moment at any section and respective $\dfrac{\partial M}{\partial H}$ values are tabulated as below.

Member	Origin	M	$\dfrac{\partial M}{\partial H}$	Limit of integration
AB	A	$-H \times y$	$-y$	0 − 4
DC	D	$-H \times y$	$-y$	0 − 3
BC	B	$\left[-4H + V_a x - \dfrac{3x^2}{2}\right]$ $= \left[-4H + \left(\dfrac{H + 24}{4}\right)x - \dfrac{3x^2}{2}\right]$	$\left(-4 + \dfrac{x}{4}\right)$	0 − 4

As uniform flexural rigidity is same,

∴ $\Sigma \int M \dfrac{\partial M}{\partial H} ds = 0$

For zone AB : $\displaystyle\int_0^4 H \times y^2 \, dy = \dfrac{Hy^3}{3} = \dfrac{64}{3} H$ ... (1)

For zone DC : $\displaystyle\int_0^3 H \times y^2 \, dy = \dfrac{Hy^3}{3} = 9H$ ... (2)

For zone BC : $\displaystyle\int_0^4 \left[\left[(-4H) + \left(\dfrac{H + 24}{4}\right)x - \dfrac{3x^2}{2}\right]\left(-4 + \dfrac{x}{4}\right)\right] dx$

$= \displaystyle\int_0^4 \left[16H - Hx - 24x + 6x^2 - Hx + \dfrac{Hx^2}{16} + \dfrac{6}{4}x^2 - \dfrac{3}{8}x^3\right] dx$

$= \left[16Hx - \dfrac{Hx^2}{2} - \dfrac{24x^2}{2} + \dfrac{6x^3}{3} - \dfrac{Hx^2}{2} + \dfrac{Hx^3}{48} + \dfrac{6x^3}{12} - \dfrac{3x^4}{32}\right]_0^4$

$= 64H - 8H - 192 + 128 - 8H + \dfrac{4}{3}H + 32 - 24$ ... (3)

Therefore, (1 + 2 + 3) = Total strain energy

$\therefore \quad \dfrac{64}{3}H + 9H + 64H - 8H - 192 + 128 - 8H + \dfrac{4}{3}H + 32 - 24 = 0$

$\therefore \quad 79.67\,H = 56$

$\therefore \quad H = 0.70\text{ kN}$

$\therefore \quad V_d = \left(\dfrac{24 - H}{4}\right) = 5.82\text{ kN}$

$\quad V_a = \left(\dfrac{24 + H}{4}\right) = 6.18\text{ kN}$

$\therefore \quad M_B = H \times 4 = 0.70 \times 4 = 2.81\text{ kN-m} \ (\circlearrowleft)$

$\quad M_C = H \times 3 = 0.70 \times 3 = 2.11\text{ kN-m} \ (\circlearrowleft)$

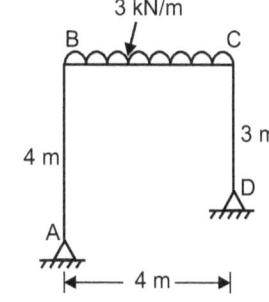

(a) Given structure

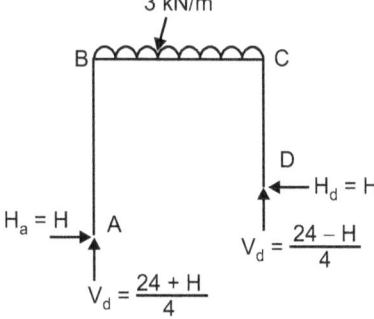

(b) Structure released with redundant force

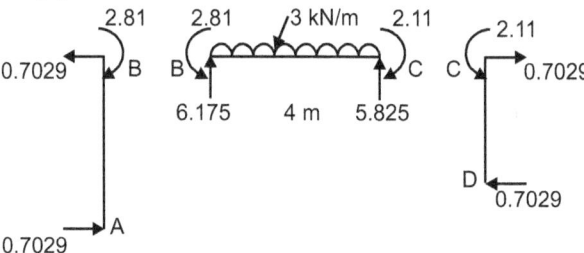

(c) FBD of members

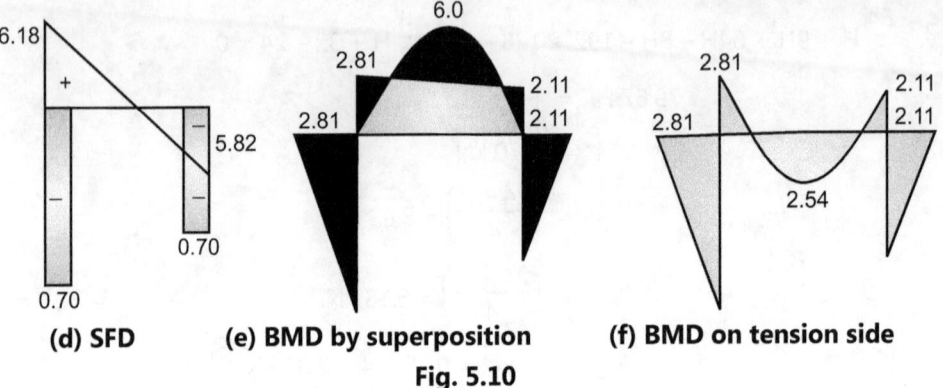

(d) SFD   (e) BMD by superposition   (f) BMD on tension side

Fig. 5.10

Problem 5.8 : Analyse the frame ABCD as shown in Fig. 5.11 (a). Thus, find the B.M. at B and C.

Solution : Let V_a and V_d be the vertical reactions at A and D and H_a and H_d be the horizontal reactions at A and D.

The given frame is statically indeterminate.

∴ Degree of static indeterminacy = R − 3 = 4 − 3 = 1

∴ Consider H_a as the redundant force.

Taking moment @ A i.e. $\Sigma M @ A = 0 = V_d \times 5 - W \times l \times \dfrac{l}{2}$

∴ $\quad V_d \times 5 = 20 \times 5 \times 2.5$ ∴ $V_d = 50$ kN (↑)

$\quad V_a = 50$ kN (↓)

$\quad H_d = 100 - H_a$

Moments at any section and respective $\dfrac{\partial M}{\partial H}$ values are tabulated in the table given below.

Member	Origin	M	$\dfrac{\partial M}{\partial H}$	Limit of integration
AB	A	$H_a \times y - 10y^2$	y	0 – 5
CD	D	$-(100 - H_a)\,y$	y	0 – 5
BC	B	$(5H_a - 250 - 50x)$	5	0 – 5

As uniform flexural rigidity is same for all the members,

∴ $\quad \Sigma \int M \dfrac{\partial M}{\partial H} ds = 0$

$\displaystyle\int_0^5 (H_a \times y - 10y^2)\, y\, dy + \int_0^5 (H_a - 100)\, y^2\, dy + \int_0^5 (5H_a - 250 - 50x)\, 5 \cdot dx = 0$

$$\left[\frac{H_a y^3}{3} - \frac{10y^4}{4}\right]_0^5 + \left[\frac{H_a y^3}{3} - \frac{100y^3}{3}\right]_0^5 + \left[\left(25 H_a x - 1250x - \frac{250x^2}{2}\right)\right]_0^5$$

$$\frac{125 H_a}{3} - \frac{6250}{4} + \frac{125 H_a}{3} - \frac{12500}{3} + 125 H_a - 6250 - \frac{6250}{2} = 0$$

$$\therefore \quad 208.33 H_a = 15104.16$$

$$\therefore \quad H_a = 72.5 \text{ kN}$$

$$\therefore \quad H_d = 100 - 72.5 = 27.5 \text{ kN}$$

$$\text{Moment @ B} = H_a \times 5 - 20 \times 5 \times 2.5 = 72.5 \times 5 - 100 \times 2.5$$

$$= 112.5$$

$$\therefore \quad M_B = 112.5 \text{ (↻)}$$

$$M_C = H_d \times 5 = 27.5 \times 5 = 137.5 \text{ kN-m (↻)}$$

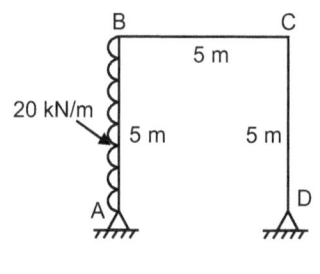

(a) Given structure

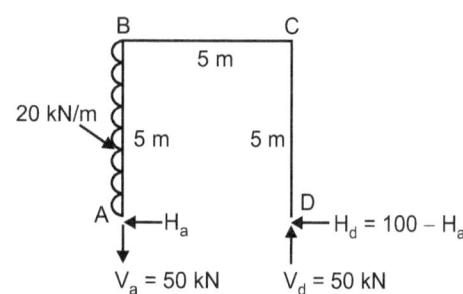

(b) Structure released with redundant force H_a

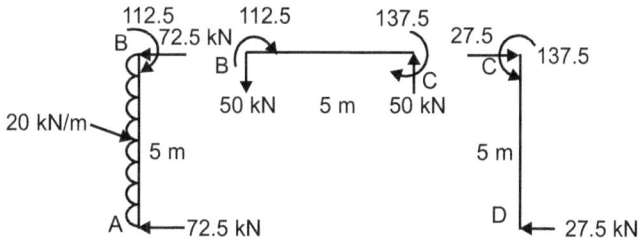

(c) Free body diagram of members

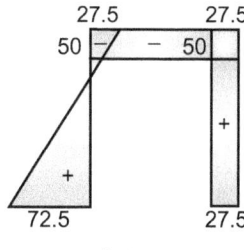

(d) SFD

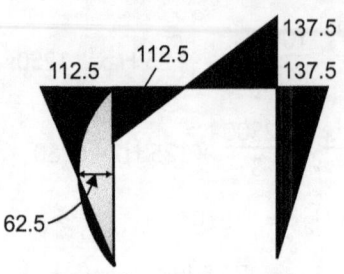

(e) BMD by superposition

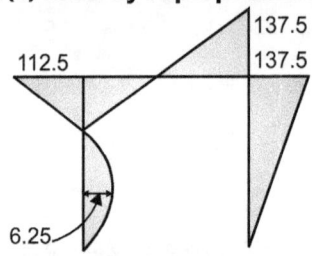

(f) BMD on tension side
Fig. 5.11

Problem 5.9 : Analyse the portal frame ABCD as shown in Fig. 5.12 (a) by strain energy method. Ends A and B are hinged. Draw the B.M. diagram.

Solution : The above frame is statically indeterminate.

Degree of static indeterminacy = R − 3 = 4 − 3 = 1.

∴ Consider H_a as the redundant force.

Applying equilibrium equations,

$\Sigma H = 0$ ∴ $H_a = H_B$

Taking moment @ A = 0 = $V_B \times 3 - 24 \times 1$

$24 \times 1 = V_B \times 3$ ∴ $V_B = 8$ kN

$\Sigma f_y = 0$ ∴ $V_A = 16$ kN

Member	Origin	M	$\dfrac{\partial M}{\partial H}$	Limit of integration
AC	A	$-H_a \times y$	$-y$	0 – 4
BD	B	$-H_a \times y$	$-y$	0 – 4
CE	C	$(-4H_a + 16x)$	-4	0 – 1
DE	D	$(-4H_a + 8x)$	-4	0 – 2

$\int \dfrac{M}{EI} \cdot \dfrac{\partial M}{\partial H} ds = 0.$

∴ Total strain energy stored

$$= \int_0^4 (+H_a \times y) \times y \, dy + \int_0^4 (+H_a y) \times y \times dy$$

$$+ \int_0^1 (-4H_a + 16x)(-4)\,dx + \int_0^2 (-4H_a + 8x)(-4)\,dx$$

$$= \left[+\frac{H_a y^3}{3}\right]_0^4 + \left[+\frac{H_a y^3}{3}\right]_0^4 + \left[16 H_a x - \frac{64x^2}{2}\right]_0^1 + \left[16 H_a x - \frac{32x^2}{2}\right]_0^2$$

$$= +\frac{64}{3}H_a + \frac{64}{3}H_a + 16 H_a - 32 + 32 H_a - 64 = 0$$

$$90.67\, H_a = 96$$
$$H_a = 1.06 \text{ kN}$$
$$M_C = 4.24 \text{ kN-m}$$
$$M_D = 4.24 \text{ kN}$$

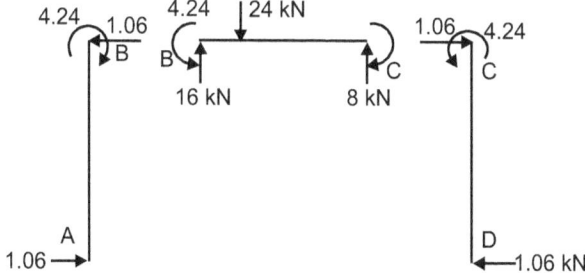

(a) Given structure   (b) Structure released with redundant force H_a

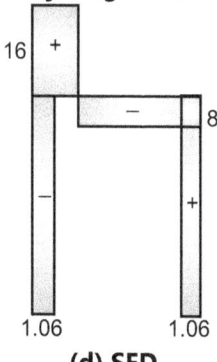

(c) Free body diagram of members

(d) SFD

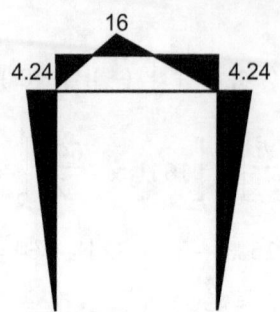

(e) BMD by superposition

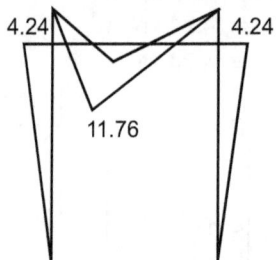

(f) BMD on tension side

Fig. 5.12

Problem 5.10 : Analyse the portal frame shown in Fig. 5.13 (a) if support A yields in rotation 0.0020 radians clockwise and in vertically downward direction by 5 mm. The other support D is fixed. $EI = 4 \times 10^4$ kN-m^2

Solution : In this problem, the external static indeterminacy is $(6 - 3) = 3$. So we require minimum three equations to analyse the frame.

The equations are as follows :

$$\frac{\partial U}{\partial H} = 0 \qquad \text{(As no horizontal deflection)}$$

$$\frac{\partial U}{\partial U} = \delta = 5 \text{ mm}$$

Support A rotates by 0.0020.

Total strain energy stored = $U_{AB} + U_{BC} + U_{DC}$

For equilibrium,

Moment @ D = 0

$-V_a \times 4 + M_a - M_d = 0$

$\therefore \qquad M_d = M_a - 4V_a$

$\Sigma f_x = 0$

$H_a = H_d = H$

$-V_a + V_d = 0$

$\therefore \qquad V_a = V_d$

ENERGY METHOD FOR DISPLACEMENT

Member	Origin	M	$\dfrac{\partial M}{\partial H}$	$\dfrac{\partial U}{\partial V_a}$	Limit of integration
AB	A	$(M_a - H \times x)$	$-x$	0	0 – 4
DC	D	$(-H_d \times x + M_d)$ $= (-H_d + M_d)$ $= (-H_d x + M_a - 4V_a)$ $= (-Hx + M_a - 4V_a)$	$-x$	$-(4)$	0 – 4
BC	B	$(M_a - 4H_d - V_a x)$	-4	$(-x)$	0 – 4

$$\dfrac{\partial U}{\partial H} = \int_0^4 \dfrac{M}{EI} \cdot \dfrac{\partial M}{\partial H} \, dx$$

$$= \int_0^4 \dfrac{(M_a - Hx)}{EI} \cdot -x \cdot dx + \int_0^4 \dfrac{(-Hx + M_a + 4V_a)}{EI} (-x) \, dx$$

$$+ \int_0^4 \dfrac{(M_a - 4H - V_a x)}{EI} (-4) \, dx$$

$$= \int_0^4 \dfrac{(-M_a x + Hx^2)}{EI} \, dx + \int_0^4 \dfrac{(Hx^2 - M_a x + 4V_a x)}{EI} \, dx$$

$$+ \int_0^4 \dfrac{(-4M_a + 16H + 4V_a x)}{EI} \, dx$$

$$= \left[\dfrac{1}{EI} \left[-\dfrac{M_a x^2}{2} + \dfrac{Hx^3}{3} \right]_0^4 + \dfrac{1}{EI} \left[\dfrac{Hx^3}{3} - \dfrac{M_a x^2}{2} + \dfrac{4V_a x^2}{2} \right]_0^4 + \left[\dfrac{-4M_a x + 16Hx + \dfrac{4V_a x^2}{2}}{EI} \right]_0^4 \right]$$

$$-8M_a + \dfrac{64}{3}H + \dfrac{64}{3}H - 8M_a + 32V_a - 16M_a + 64H + 32V_a = 0$$

$$64V_a - 32M_a + 106.67\,H = 0 \qquad \qquad \ldots (1)$$

$$\dfrac{\partial U}{\partial V_a} = \dfrac{5}{1000}$$

Member AB : $\quad \dfrac{\partial U}{\partial V_A} = \int_0^4 \dfrac{(M_a - Hx)}{EI} \times 0 \, dx \qquad$ (As no V_a term)

Member DC :
$$\frac{\partial U}{\partial V_A} = \int_0^4 \frac{(-Hx + M_a - 4V_a)}{EI}(-4)\,dx = \int_0^4 \frac{(4Hx - 4M_a + 16V_a)}{EI}\,dx$$

$$= \frac{1}{EI}\left[\frac{4Hx^2}{2} - 4M_a x + 16V_a x\right]_0^4 = \frac{32H - 16M_a + 64V_a}{EI}$$

Member BC :
$$\frac{\partial U}{\partial V_A} = \int_0^4 \frac{(M_a - 4H - V_a x)}{EI}(-x)\,dx$$

$$= \int_0^4 (-M_a x + 4Hx + V_a x^2)\frac{dx}{EI} = \frac{1}{EI}\left[-\frac{M_a x^2}{2} + \frac{4Hx^2}{2} + \frac{V_a x^3}{3}\right]_0^4$$

$$= \frac{-8M_a + 32H + \frac{64}{3}V_a}{EI}$$

$$\therefore \quad \frac{\partial U}{\partial V_A} = \frac{0 + 32H - 16M_a + 64V_a - 8M_a + 32H + \frac{64}{3}V_a}{EI}$$

$$= \frac{64H - 24M_a + 85.33V_a}{EI} = 0.004 \qquad \ldots (2)$$

$$= 64H - 24M_a + 85.33V_a = 0.004 \times 4 \times 10^4 = 160$$

$$\frac{\partial U}{\partial M_a} = 0.0020$$

Member AB :

$$\int_0^4 (M_a - Hx) \times \frac{1}{EI}\,dx = \frac{1}{EI}\left[M_a x - \frac{Hx^2}{2}\right]_0^4 = \frac{1}{EI}[4M_a - 8H]$$

Member DC :

$$\int_0^4 (-Hx + M_a - 4V_a) \times \frac{1}{EI}\,dx = \frac{1}{EI}\left[-\frac{Hx^2}{2} + M_a x - 4V_a x\right]_0^4 = \frac{1}{EI}[-8H + 4M_a - 16V_a]$$

Member BC :

$$\int_0^4 (M_a - 4H - V_a x) \times \frac{1}{EI}\,dx = \frac{1}{EI}\left[M_a x - 4Hx - \frac{V_a x^2}{2}\right]_0^4 = \frac{1}{EI}[4M_a - 16H - 8V_a]$$

$$\therefore \quad \frac{\partial U}{\partial M_a} = \frac{1}{EI}[4M_a - 8H - 8H + 4M_a - 16V_a + 4M_a - 16H - 8V_a]$$

$$= 12M_a - 32H - 24V_a = 0.0020 \times 4 \times 10^4 = 80 \qquad \ldots (3)$$

Solving equations (1), (2) and (3),

V_a = 6.3 kN
H = 10.0 kN
M_a = 46 kN-m

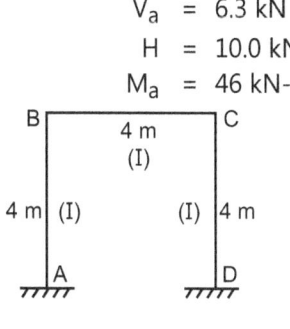

(a) Given structure

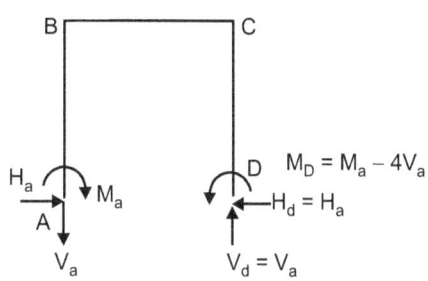

(b) Structure released with redundant force H_a, V_a and M_a

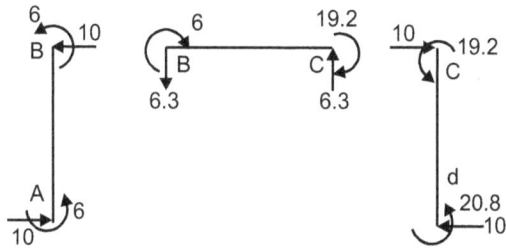

(c) Free body diagram of members

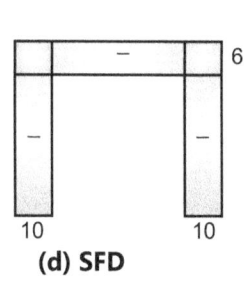

(d) SFD

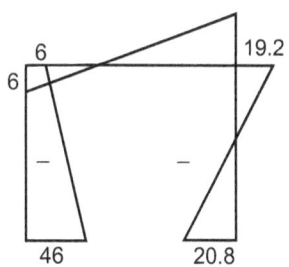

(e) BMD by superposition and BMD on tension side

Fig. 5.13

Problem 5.11 : Analyse the portal frame by strain energy method as in Fig. 5.14 (a).

Solution : As portal frame is statically indeterminate,
Degree of static indeterminacy = R – 3 = 5 – 3 = 2
So we require minimum two equations to analyse the portal frame. Consider V_c and H_c as the redundant reactions.

$\Sigma H_a = 0$ ∴ $\quad H_c + H_a = 50$ kN
$\qquad\qquad\qquad H_a = 50 - H_c$

$\Sigma V = 0$
∴ $\qquad\qquad V_a + V_c = 25 \times 3 = 75$

$\sum M @ A = 0$

$M_a - 4H_c - 3V_c + 25 \times 3 \times 1.5 - 50 \times 2 = 0$

$M_a - 4H_c - 3V_c + 112.5 - 100 = 0$

$\therefore \quad M_a = 4H_c + 3V_c - 212.5$

Total strain energy $= \int \dfrac{M^2 \, ds}{2 \, EI}$

Member	Origin	M	$\dfrac{\partial M}{\partial H_c}$	$\dfrac{\partial M}{\partial V_c}$	Limit of integration
CB	C	$\left(V_c x - \dfrac{25x^2}{2}\right)$	0	$(+ x)$	0 – 3
BE	B	$(3V_c + H_c x - 112.5)$	x	3	0 – 2
EA	E	$(3V_c + H_c (x + 2) - 112.5 - 50x)$	$(x + 2)$	3	0 – 2

Total strain energy $= \int \dfrac{M}{EI} \dfrac{\partial M}{\partial H_c} \cdot dx$

Member CB : $\displaystyle\int_0^3 \left(V_c x - \dfrac{25x^2}{2}\right) \times 0 \times \dfrac{dx}{EI} = 0$ ... (a_1)

Member BE :

$\displaystyle\int_0^2 (3V_c + H_c x - 112.5) \times \dfrac{dx}{EI} = \displaystyle\int_0^2 (3V_c x + H_c x^2 - 112.5x) \dfrac{dx}{EI}$

$= \dfrac{1}{EI}\left[3V_c \dfrac{x^2}{2} + H_c \dfrac{x^3}{3} - 112.5 \dfrac{x^2}{2}\right]_0^2$

$= \dfrac{6V_c + 2.67H_c - 225}{EI}$ ... (a_2)

Member EA :

$\displaystyle\int_0^2 [3V_c + H_c (x + 2) - 112.5 - 50x] \dfrac{(x + 2)}{EI} dx$

$= \displaystyle\int_0^2 [3V_c - 112.5 (x + 2)] \dfrac{dx}{EI} - \displaystyle\int_0^2 50(x^2 + 2x) \dfrac{dx}{EI} + \displaystyle\int_0^2 \left[H_c (x^2 + 4x + 4) \dfrac{dx}{EI}\right]$

$= \dfrac{\left[\left[(3V_c - 112.5)\left(\dfrac{x^2}{2} + 2x\right)\right]_0^2 - \left[50\left(\dfrac{x^3}{3} + \dfrac{2x^2}{2}\right)\right]_0^2 + \left[H_c \left(\dfrac{x^3}{3} + \dfrac{4x^2}{2} + 4x\right)\right]_0^2\right]}{EI}$

$= \dfrac{18V_c - 675 - 333.33 + 18.67H_c}{EI}$ ... (a_3)

Total strain energy $= \int \dfrac{M}{EI}\dfrac{\partial M}{\partial H} dx = 0$

$= (a_1) + (a_2) + (a_3)$
$0 + 6V_C + 2.67H_C - 225 + 18V_C - 675 - 333.33 + 18.67H_C = 0$
$24V_C + 21.34H_C = 1233.33$ ... (1)

Total strain energy $= \int \dfrac{M}{EI}\dfrac{\partial M}{\partial V_C} = 0$

Member CB :

$\int_0^3 \left(V_C x - \dfrac{25x^2}{2}\right)\dfrac{x}{EI} dx = \int_0^3 \left(V_C x^2 - \dfrac{25x^3}{2}\right)\dfrac{dx}{EI} = \dfrac{1}{EI}\left[V_C \dfrac{x^3}{3} - \dfrac{25x^4}{8}\right]_0^3$

$= \dfrac{9V_C - 253.125}{EI}$ ... (b$_1$)

Member BE :

$\int_0^2 (3V_C + H_C x - 112.5) \times 3 \dfrac{dx}{EI} = \int_0^2 (9V_C + 3H_C x - 337.5)\dfrac{dx}{EI}$

$= \dfrac{\left[9V_C x + 3H_C \dfrac{x^2}{2} - 337.5x\right]_0^2}{EI}$

$= \dfrac{[18V_C + 6H_C - 675]}{EI}$ ... (b$_2$)

Member EA : $\int_0^2 (3V_C + H_C (x + 2) - 112.5 - 50x) \times 3 \dfrac{dx}{EI}$

$= \int_0^2 (9V_C + H_C (3x + 6) - 112.5 \times 3 - 150x)\dfrac{dx}{EI}$

$= \dfrac{\left[9V_C x - H_C \left(\dfrac{3x^2}{2} + 6x\right) - 112.5 \times 3x - \dfrac{150x^2}{2}\right]_0^2}{EI}$

$= \dfrac{[18V_C + 18H_C - 675 - 300]}{EI}$

$= \dfrac{(18V_C + 18H_C - 975)}{EI}$ ... (b$_3$)

$\therefore$ Total strain energy $= \int \dfrac{M}{EI}\dfrac{\partial M}{\partial V_a} dx = 0 = (b_1) + (b_2) + (b_3)$

$9V_C - 253.125 + 18V_C + 6H_C - 675 + 18V_C + 18H_C - 975 = 0$

$$45V_C + 24H_C - 1903.125 = 0$$

$$45V_C + 24H_C = 1903.125 \quad \text{... (2)}$$

Solving equations (1) and (2),

$$V_C = 28.67 \text{ kN}$$

$$H_C = 25.55 \text{ kN}$$

$$H_a = 50 - 25.55 = 24.45 \text{ kN}$$

$$V_a = 25 \times 3 - V_C = 75 - 28.67 = 46.33 \text{ kN}$$

$$M_a = 4H_C + 3V_C - 212.5$$

$$= 4 \times 25.55 + 3 \times 28.67 - 212.5 = -24.29 \text{ kN-m}$$

$$\therefore \quad M_a = 24.29 \text{ kN-m } (\circlearrowleft)$$

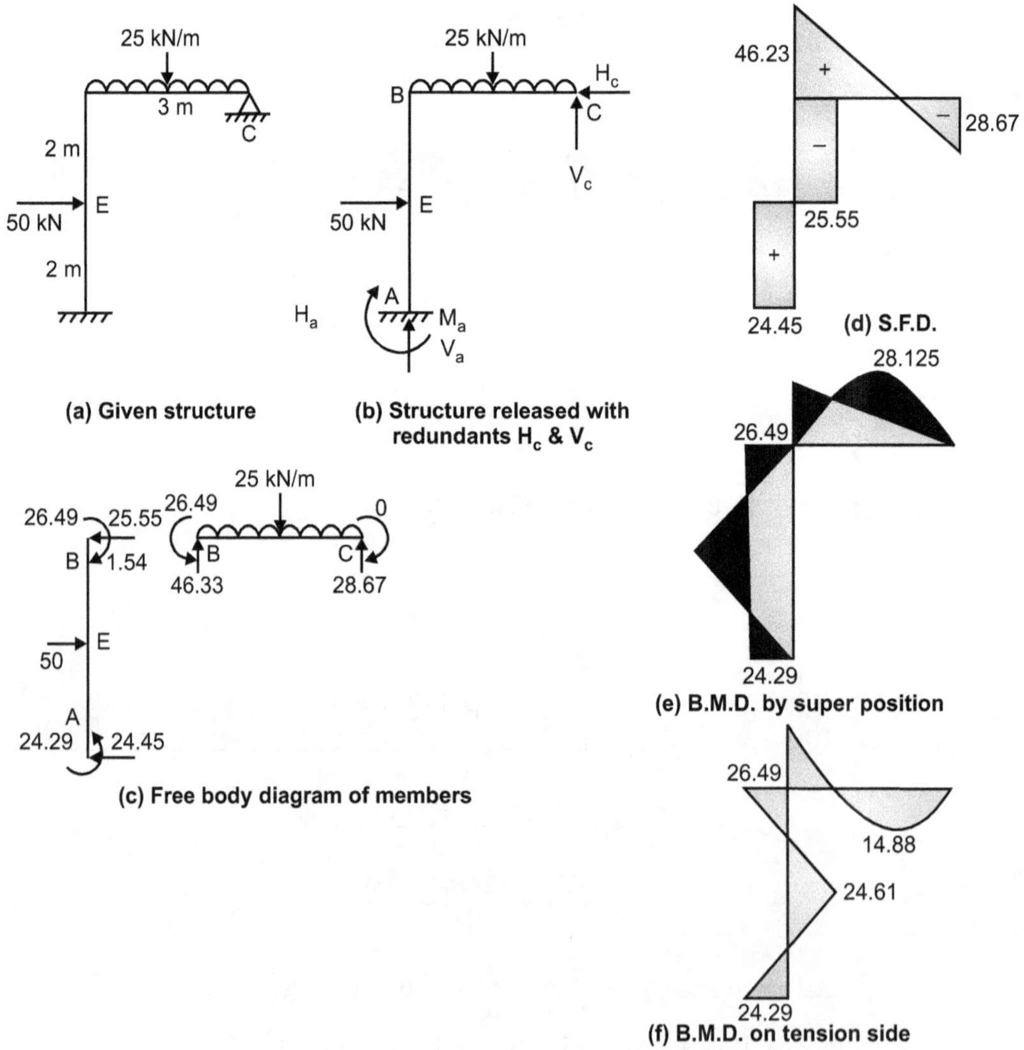
25 kN/m
3 m
2 m
2 m
50 kN
E
C
(a) Given structure
25 kN/m
B
H_c
C
V_c
50 kN
E
A
H_a
M_a
V_a
(b) Structure released with redundants H_c & V_c
46.23
28.67
25.55
24.45
(d) S.F.D.
28.125
26.49
24.29
(e) B.M.D. by super position
25 kN/m
26.49
25.55
26.49
0
B
1.54
B
C
46.33
28.67
E
50
A
24.29
24.45
(c) Free body diagram of members
26.49
14.88
24.61
24.29
(f) B.M.D. on tension side

Fig. 5.14

Problem 5.12 : A portal frame ABCD hinged at both ends is loaded as shown in Fig. 5.15 (a). If $I_{BC} = 2I_{AB} = I_{CD}$, find the reactions at supports and draw the B.M. diagram using strain energy method.

Solution : Let V_a and V_d be the reactions at supports.

$\therefore$ M @ A = 0.

$\therefore \quad V_d \times 4 = 25 \times 2 + 2 \times 5 \times 2.5$
$\quad\quad\quad V_d = 18.75$ kN
$\Sigma f_y = 0 \quad\quad \therefore V_a = 6.25$ kN

Value of horizontal reaction is calculated by Castigliano's theorem, i.e. the partial differentiation w.r.t. horizontal reaction is minimum.

$\therefore \quad \dfrac{\partial w_i}{\partial H_A} = 0$

where, w_i = Total strain energy
H_a = Horizontal reaction at A

Member	M	$\dfrac{\partial M}{\partial H_a}$	Limit of integration
AB	$\left(H_a \times y - \dfrac{2y^2}{2}\right)$	y	0 – 5
BE	$(5H_a - 25 + 6.25x)$	5	0 – 2
CE	$(-(10 - H_a) 5 + 18.75x)$	5	0 – 2
DC	$(-(10 - H_a) \times y)$	y	0 – 5

$\therefore \quad \dfrac{\partial w_i}{\partial H_a} = \int \dfrac{M}{EI} \cdot \dfrac{\partial M}{\partial H} \cdot dy = 0 = \int_0^5 \dfrac{(H_a \times y - y^2) y}{EI} dy + \int_0^5 \dfrac{(5H_a - 25 + 6.25x)}{2 EI} dx$

$+ \int_0^2 \dfrac{(5H_a + 18.75x - 50)}{2 EI} 5 \, dx + \int_0^5 \dfrac{(H_a - 10)}{EI} y^2 \, dy$

$= \left[\left[\dfrac{H_a y^3}{3} - \dfrac{y^4}{4}\right]_0^5\right.$

$+ \dfrac{1}{2}\left[25 H_a x - 125 x + \dfrac{31.25 x^2}{2}\right]_0^2 + \left[25 H_a x + \dfrac{93.75 x^2}{2} - 250 x\right]_0^2$

$\left.+ \left[\dfrac{H_a y^3}{3} - \dfrac{10 y^3}{3}\right]_0^5 \right] / EI$

$0 = \dfrac{125}{3} H_a - \dfrac{625}{4} + \dfrac{1}{2}[50 H_a - 250 + 62.5 + 50 H_a + 187.5 - 500]$

$\quad\quad + \dfrac{125 H_a}{3} - \dfrac{1250}{3}$

$0 = 133.33 H_a - 822.92$
$\therefore \quad H_a = 6.17$ and $H_d = 3.83$
$\therefore \quad M_{BA} = 5.85$ kN-m (↻), $\quad M_{BC} = 5.85$ kN-m (↻)
$\quad\quad M_{CD} = 19.14$ kN-m (↻), $\quad M_{CB} = 19.14$ kN-m (↻)

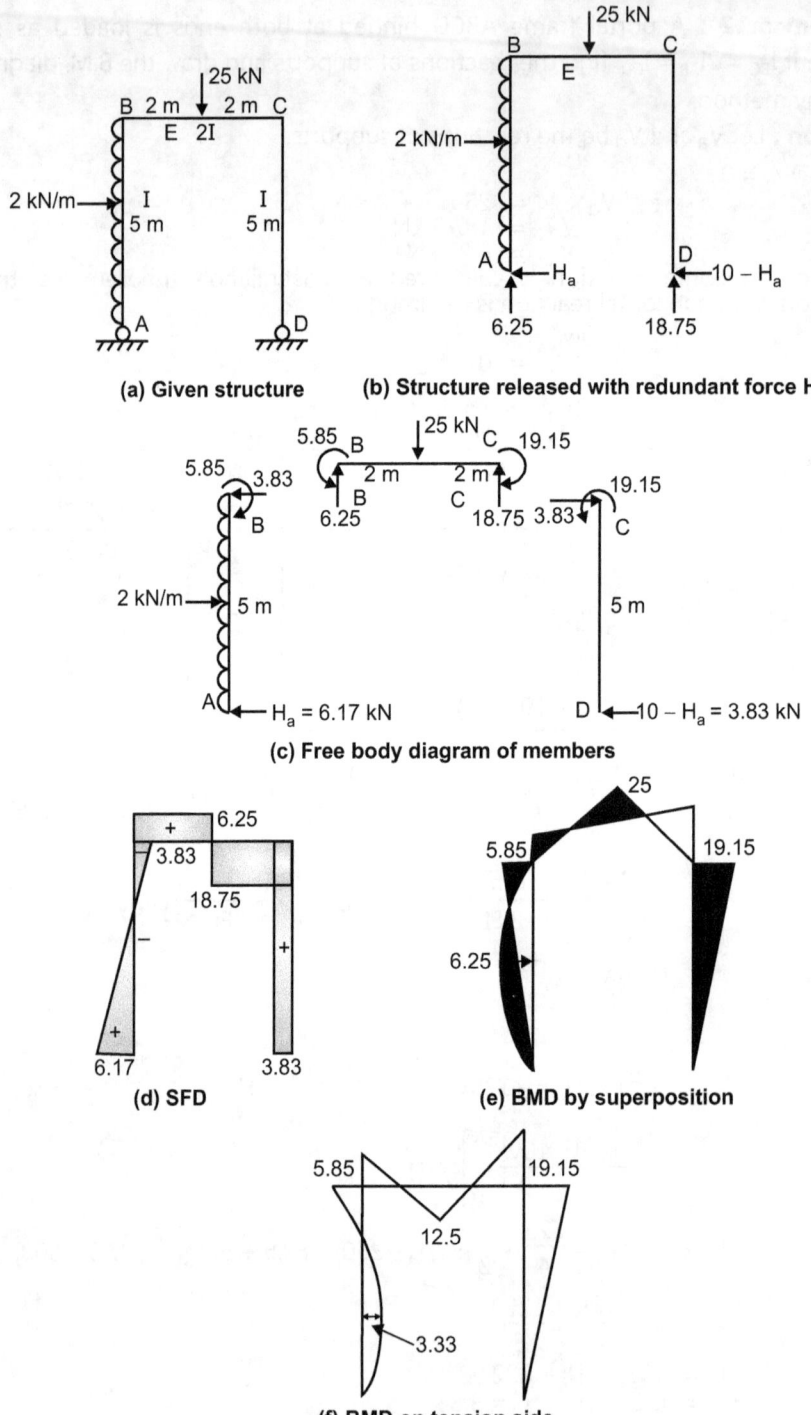

(a) Given structure
(b) Structure released with redundant force H_a
(c) Free body diagram of members
(d) SFD
(e) BMD by superposition
(f) BMD on tension side

Fig. 5.15

Problem 5.13 : Using strain energy method, calculate the support reactions for the compound beam shown in Fig. 5.16 (a) (ii). Assume uniform flexural rigidity.

Solution :

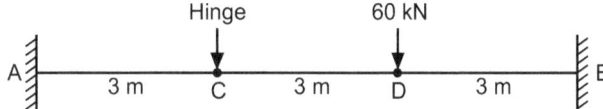

Given beam

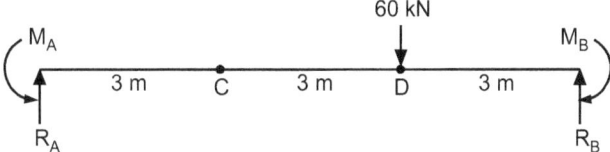

Fig. 5.16

Degree of static indeterminacy = 4 – 3 = 1.
Redundant : R_A. M @ C = 0

∴ $\quad R_A \times 3 - M_A = 0$
∴ $\quad M_A = 3R_A$
$\quad R_B = 60 - R_A$
$\quad M @ C = 0$
$60 \times 3 - R_B \times 6 + M_B = 0$
∴ $\quad M_B = 6R_B - 180 = 6(60 - R_A) - 180 = 180 - 6R_A$

Member	Origin	M	∂M/∂R_A	Limit
AC	A	$R_A x - M_A = R_A x - 3R_A = R_A(x-3)$	$(x-3)$	0 – 3
BD	B	$R_B \cdot x - M_B = (60 - R_A)x - 180 + 6R_A$ $= R_A(6-x) + 60x - 180$	$(6-x)$	0 – 3
CD	C	$R_A(x+3) - M_A = R_A(x+3) - 3R_A$ $= R_A x + 3R_A - 3R_A = R_A x$	x	0 – 3

$$\delta_A = 0 = \int_0^3 R_A(x-3)(x-3)\frac{dx}{EI}$$

$$+ \int_0^3 R_A(6-x)^2 \frac{dx}{EI} + \int_0^3 60x(6-x)\frac{dx}{EI} - \int_0^3 180(6-x)\frac{dx}{EI} + \int_0^3 R_A x^2 \frac{dx}{EI}$$

$\quad 81 R_A = 1350$
∴ $\quad R_A = 16.67$ kN
$\quad R_B = 43.33$ kN
$\quad M_A = 50$ kN-m
$\quad M_B = 80$ kN-m

EXERCISE

Analyse the following beams and frames using energy method. Draw SFD, BMD and elastic curve.

1.

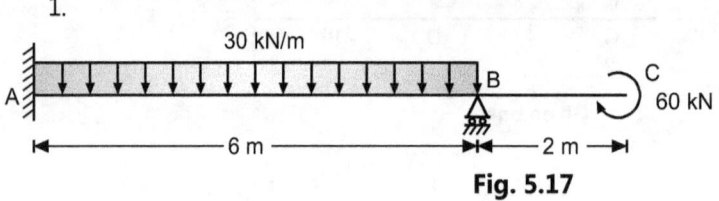

Fig. 5.17

(**Ans.** $M_A = -105$ kN/m, $M_B = -60$ kN/m)

2.

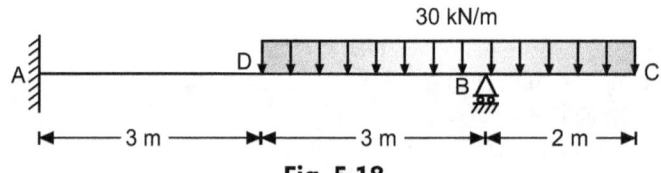

Fig. 5.18

(**Ans.** $M_A = -29.04$ kN/m, $M_B = -60$ kN/m)

3.

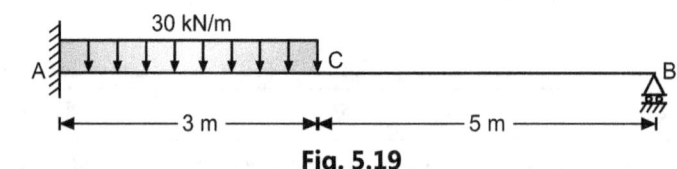

Fig. 5.19

(**Ans.** $M_A = -89.16$ kN/m, $M_B = 0$)

4.

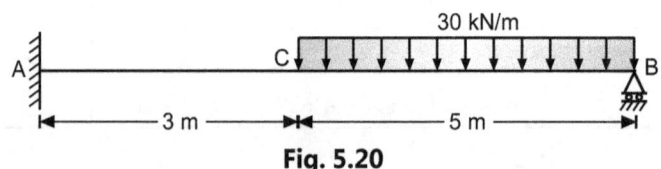

Fig. 5.20

(**Ans.** $M_A = -150.5$ kN/m, $M_B = 0$)

5.

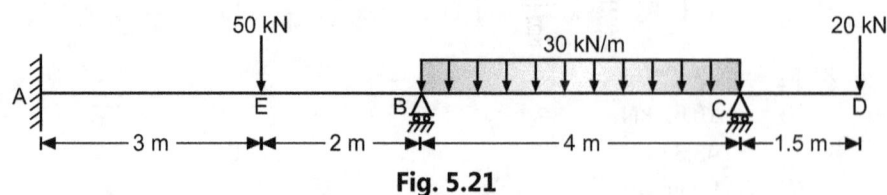

Fig. 5.21

(**Ans.** $M_A = -21.7$ kN/m, $M_B = -40.6$ kN/m, $M_C = -30$ kN/m)

6.

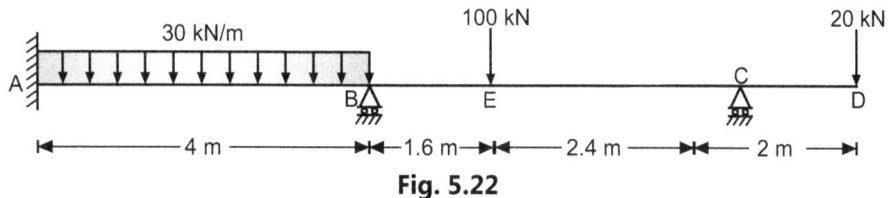

Fig. 5.22

(**Ans.** $M_A = -37.2$ kN/m, $M_B = -49.6$ kN/m, $M_C = -40$ kN/m)

7.

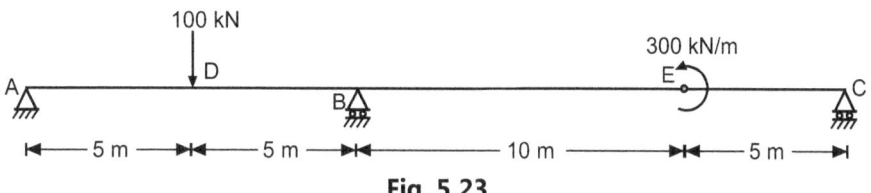

Fig. 5.23

(**Ans.** $M_A = M_C = 0$, $M_B = -135$ kN/m)

8.

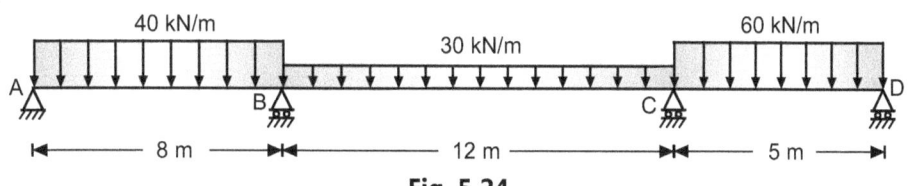

Fig. 5.24

(**Ans.** $M_A = M_D = 0$, $M_B = -359$ kN/m, $M_C = -309.6$ kN/m)

9.

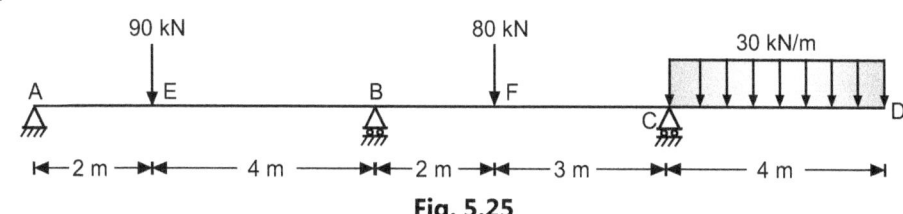

Fig. 5.25

(**Ans.** $M_A = M_D = 0$, $M_B = -68.4$ kN/m, $M_C = -44.8$ kN/m)

10.

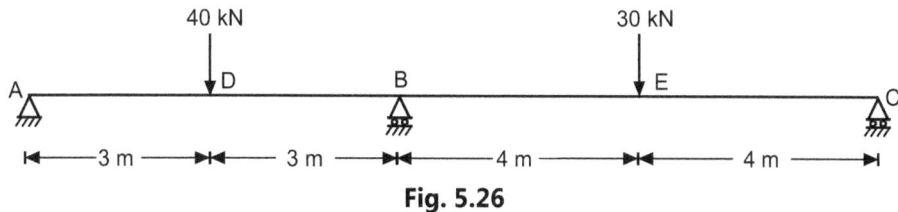

Fig. 5.26

(**Ans.** $M_A = M_C = 0$, $M_B = -45$ kN/m)

11.

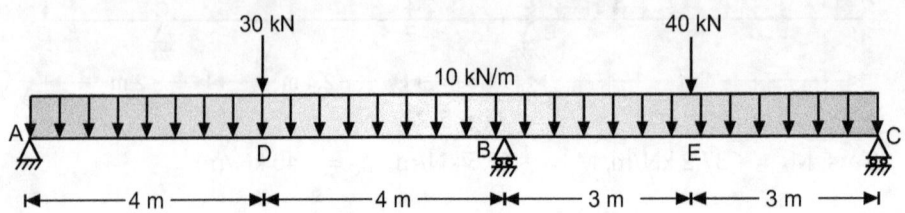

Fig. 5.27

(**Ans.** $M_A = M_C = 0$, $M_B = -110$ kN/m)

12.

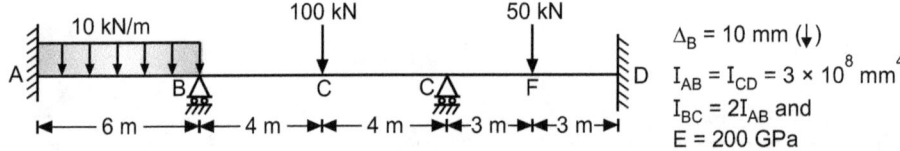

Fig. 5.28

(**Ans.** $M_A = -57.4$ kN/m, $M_B = -25.7$ kN/m, $M_C = -92$ kN/m, $M_D = -20.7$ kN/m)

13.

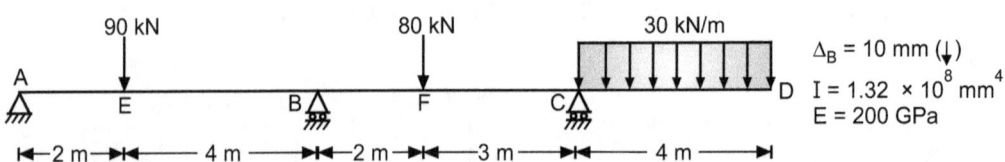

Fig. 5.29

(**Ans.** $M_A = M_D = 0$, $M_B = -35.87$ kN/m, $M_C = -71.56$ kN/m)

14.

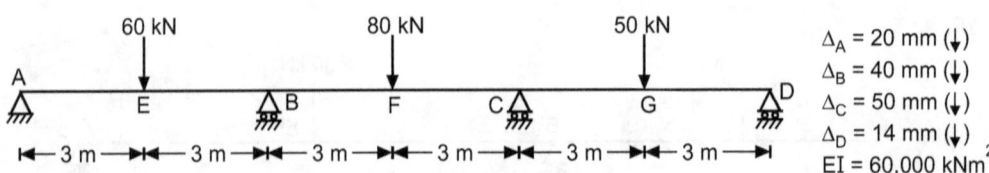

Fig. 5.30

(**Ans.** $M_A = M_D = 0$, $M_B = -68.5$ kN/m, $M_C = 59$ kN/m)

15.

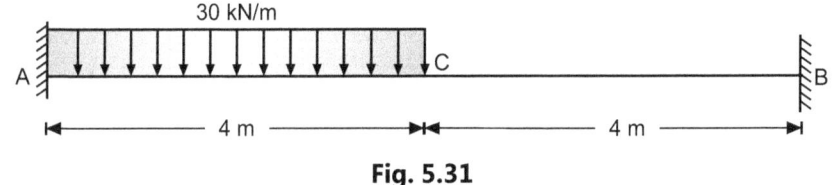

Fig. 5.31

(**Ans.** $M_A = 60$ kN/m, $M_B = -180$ kN/m, $M_C = 0$)

16.

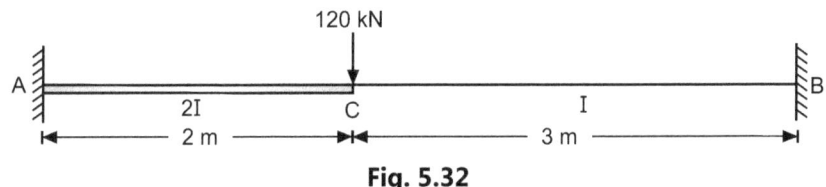

Fig. 5.32

(**Ans.** $M_A = -105.22$ kN/m, $M_B = -47.45$ kN/m)

17.

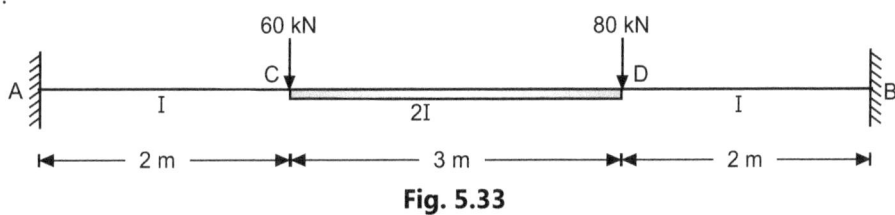

Fig. 5.33

(**Ans.** $M_A = -79.49$ kN/m, $M_B = -98.68$ kN/m)

18.

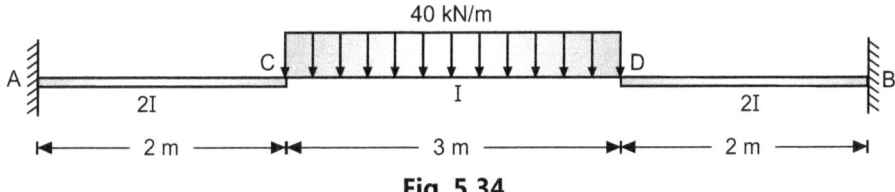

Fig. 5.34

(**Ans.** $M_A = M_B = -114$ kN/m)

19.

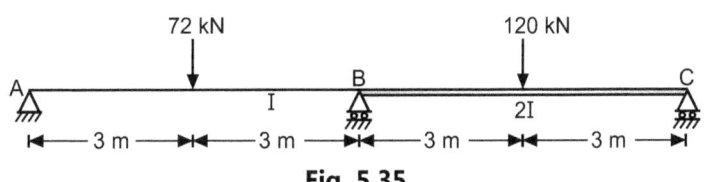

Fig. 5.35

(**Ans.** $M_B = -99$ kN/m)

20.

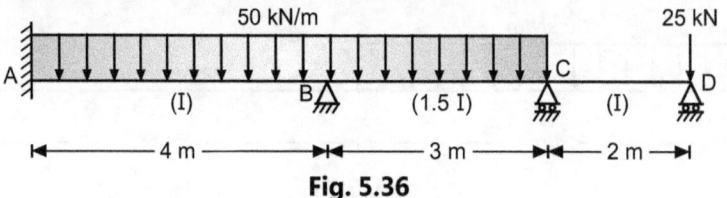

Fig. 5.36

(**Ans.** $M_A = -53.75$ kN/m, $M_B = -52.5$ kN/m, $M_C = -50$ kN/m)

21.

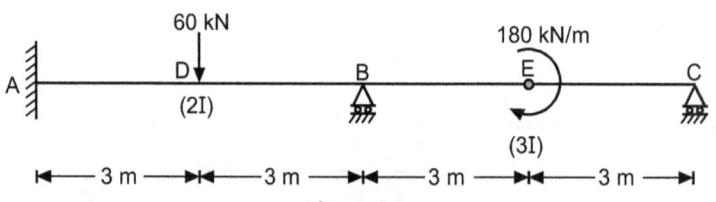

Fig. 5.37

(**Ans.** $M_A = -60.88$ kN/m, $M_B = -13.24$ kN/m, $M_C = 50$ kN/m)

22.

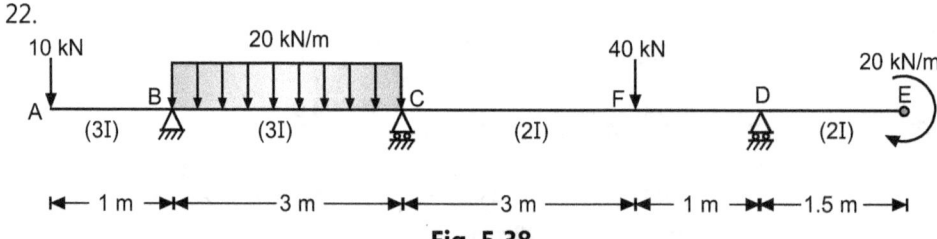

Fig. 5.38

(**Ans.** $M_B = -10$ kN/m, $M_C = -18.33$ kN/m, $M_D = -20$ kN/m)

23.

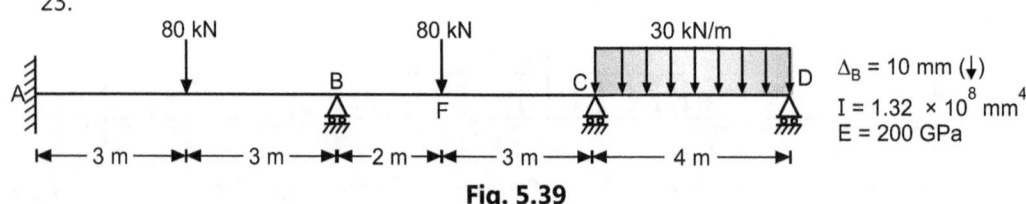

Fig. 5.39

(**Ans.** $M_A = -106.5$ kN/m, $M_B = -10.77$ kN/m, $M_C = -78.56$ kN/m)

24.

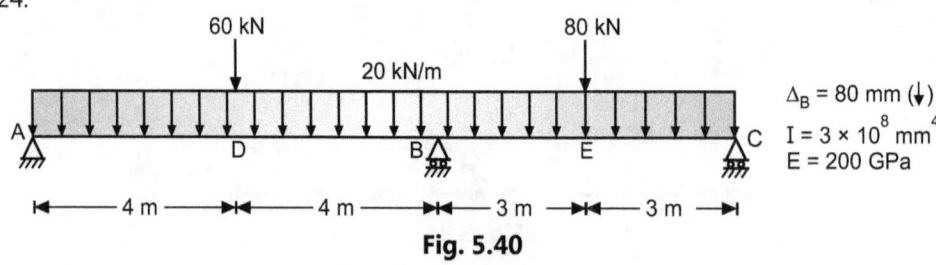

Fig. 5.40

(**Ans.** $M_A = M_C = 0$, $M_B = -80.46$ kN/m)

25.

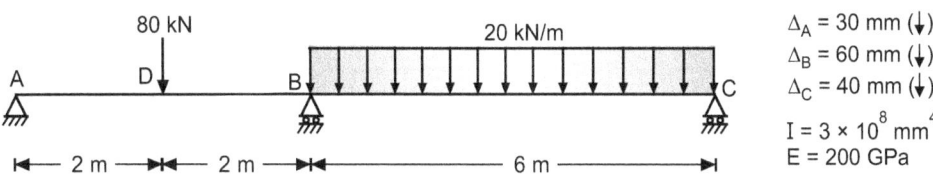

Fig. 5.41

(**Ans.** $M_A = M_C = 0$, $M_B = -42$ kN/m)

26.

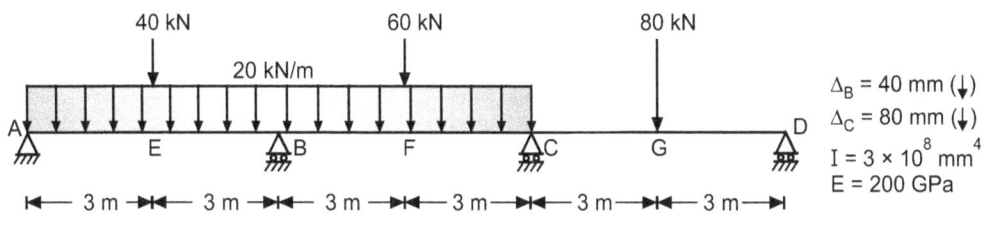

Fig. 5.42

(**Ans.** $M_A = M_D = 0$, $M_B = -203$ kN/m, $M_C = +227$ kN/m)

27.

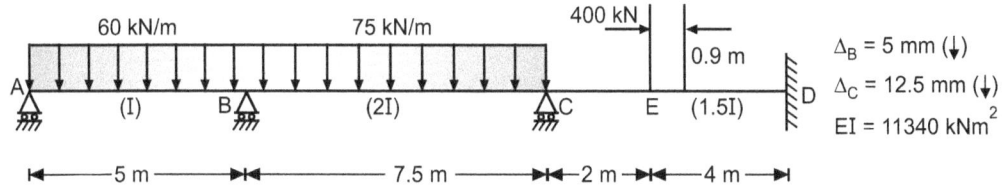

Fig. 5.43

(**Ans.** $M_A = 0$, $M_B = -226.1$ kN/m, $M_C = -191.7$ kN/m, $M_D = -42$ kN/m)

28.

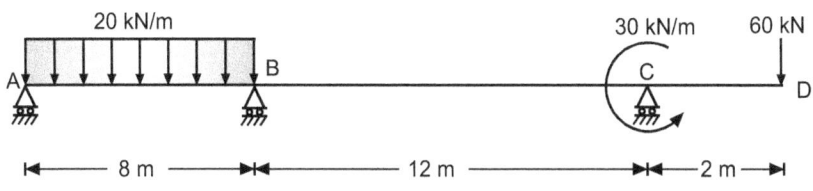

Fig. 5.44

(**Ans.** $M_A = -157$ kN/m, $M_B = -5$ kN/m, $M_{CD} = 120$ kN/m, $M_{CB} = 90$ kN/m)

29.

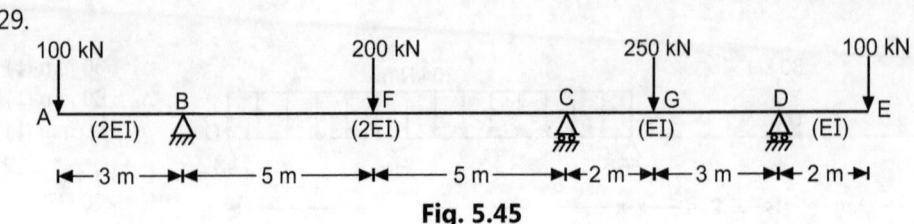

Fig. 5.45

(**Ans.** $M_B = -300$ kN/m, $M_C = -182$ kN/m, $M_D = -200$ kN/m)

30.

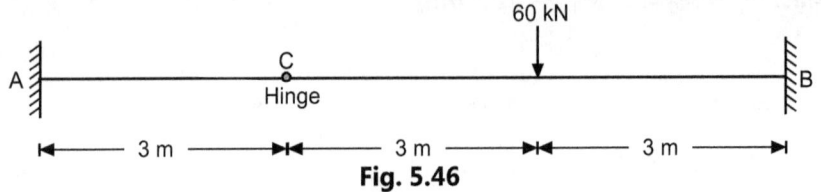

Fig. 5.46

(**Ans.** $M_A = -42.24$ kN/m, $M_B = -78.05$ kN/m)

31.

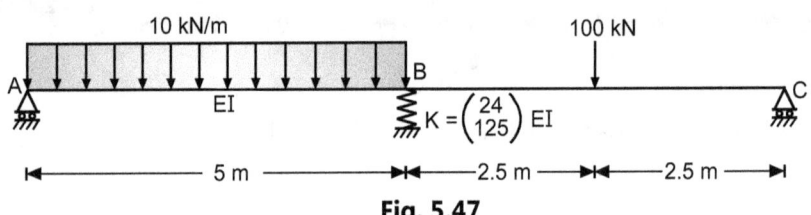

Fig. 5.47

(**Ans.** $M_B = -12.5$ kN/m)

32.

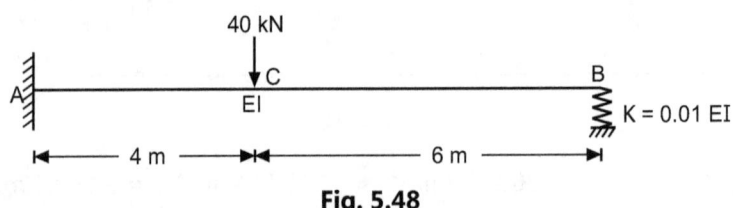

Fig. 5.48

(**Ans.** $M_A = -96$ kN/m)

33.

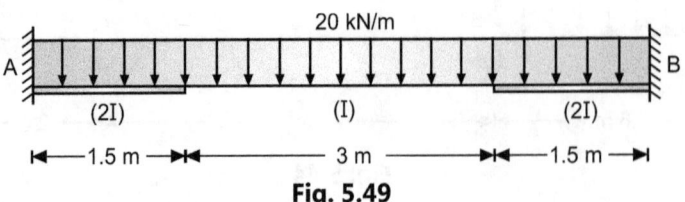

Fig. 5.49

(**Ans.** $M_A = M_B = -67.5$ kN/m)

34.

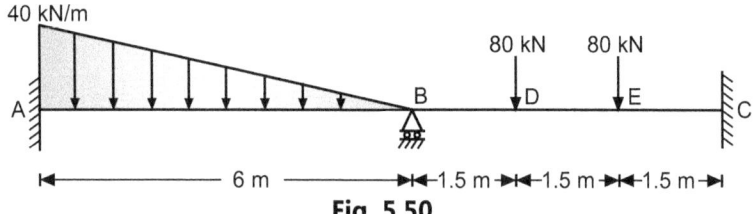

Fig. 5.50

(**Ans.** $M_A = -65.1$ kN/m, $M_B = -61.7$ kN/m, $M_C = -89.2$ kN/m)

35.

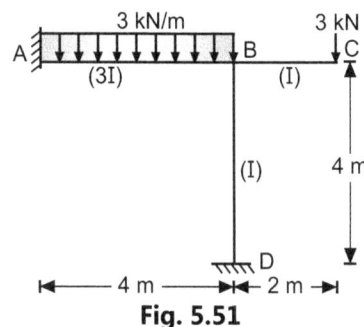

Fig. 5.51

(**Ans.** $M_{AB} = 3.25$ kN/m, $M_{BA} = -5.5$ kN/m, $M_{BD} = -0.5$ kN/m, $M_{DB} = -0.2$ kN/m)

36.

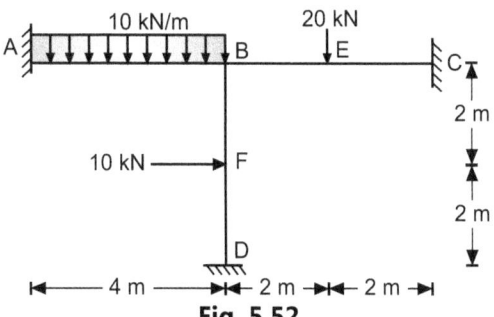

Fig. 5.52

(**Ans.** $M_{BC} = 47.5$ kN/m, $M_{CB} = -8.75$ kN/m, $M_{DB} = 23.75$ kN/m, $M_{BD} = -32.5$ kN.m)

37.

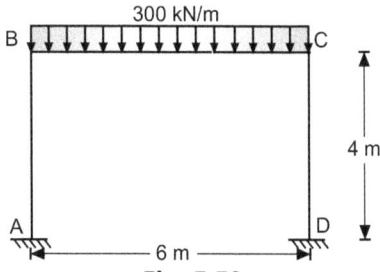

Fig. 5.53

(**Ans.** $M_{AB} = -M_{DC} = -336.9$ kN/m, $M_{BA} = -M_{CD} = -673.8$ kN/m,

$M_{BC} = -M_{CB} = 673.8$ kN/m)

38.

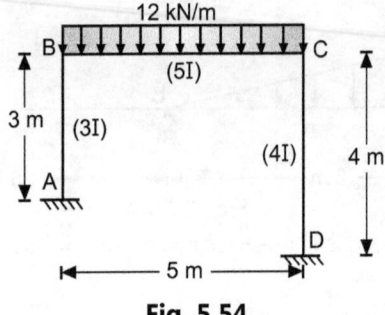

Fig. 5.54

(**Ans.** $M_{AB} = -5.97$ kN/m, $M_{BA} = -15$ kN/m, $M_{BC} = 15$ kN/m, $M_{CB} = -18$ kN/m,

$M_{CD} = 18$ kN/m, $M_{DC} = 9.97$ kN/m)

39.

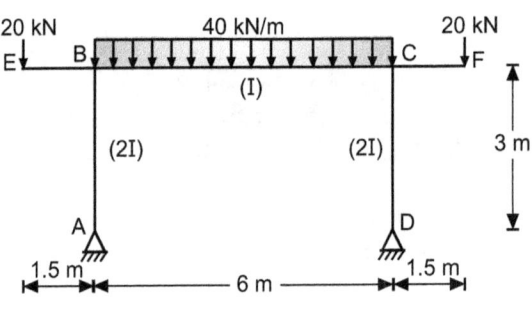

Fig. 5.55

(**Ans.** $M_{AB} = M_{DC} = 0$, $M_{BA} = -M_{CD} = -77$ kN/m, $M_{BE} = -M_{CF} = -30$ kN/m,

$M_{BC} = -M_{CB} = 107$ kN/m)

40.

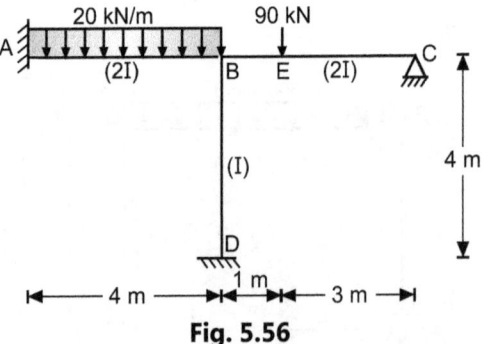

Fig. 5.56

(**Ans.** $M_{AB} = 22$ kN/m, $M_{BA} = -36$ kN/m, $M_{BD} = -4.67$ kN/m,

$M_{BC} = 40.7$ kN/m, $M_{CB} = 0$, $M_{DC} = -2.33$ kN/m)

41.

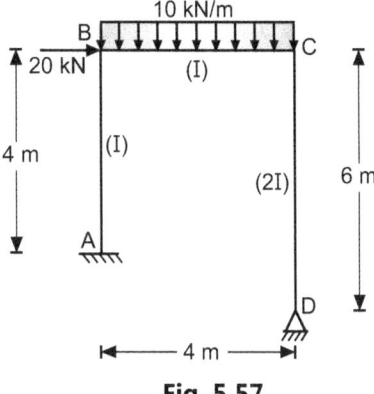

Fig. 5.57

(**Ans.** $M_{AB} = -4.16$ kN/m, $M_{BA} = -8.75$ kN/m, $M_{BC} = 8.75$ kN/m,

$M_{CB} = -8.75$ kN/m, $M_{CD} = 8.75$ kN/m, $M_{DC} = 0$)

42.

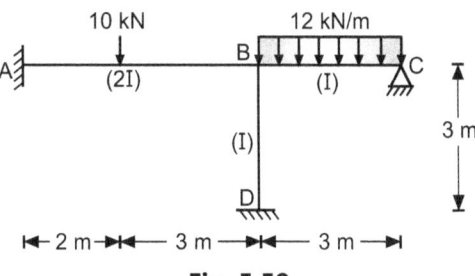

Fig. 5.58

(**Ans.** $M_{AB} = 7.72$ kN/m, $M_{BA} = -3.76$ kN/m, $M_{BC} = 2.9$ kN/m,

$M_{CB} = 0$, $M_{BD} = 0.86$ kN/m, $M_{DB} = 0.48$ kN/m)

43.

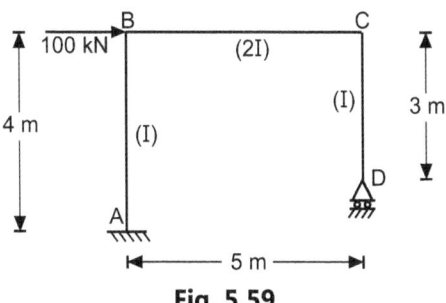

Fig. 5.59

(**Ans.** $M_{AB} = 68.4$ kN/m, $M_{BA} = 47.7$ kN/m, $M_{BC} = -47.7$ kN/m,

$M_{CB} = -43.7$ kN/m, $M_{CD} = 43.7$ kN/m, $M_{DC} = 0$)

44.

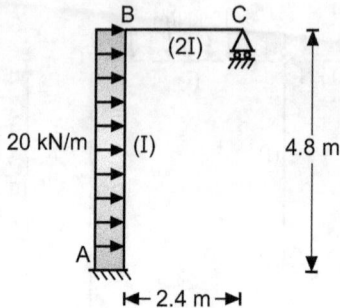

Fig. 5.60

(**Ans.** $M_{AB} = 158.5$, $M_{BA} = -M_{BC} = 70$ kN/m)

45.

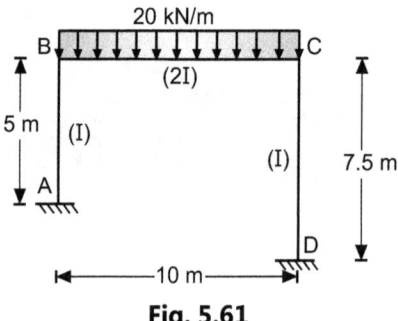

Fig. 5.61

(**Ans.** $M_{AB} = -21$ kN/m, $M_{BA} = -M_{BC} = 91$ kN/m,

$M_{CB} = -M_{CD} = -106$ kN/m, $M_{DC} = 63.5$ kN/m)

46.

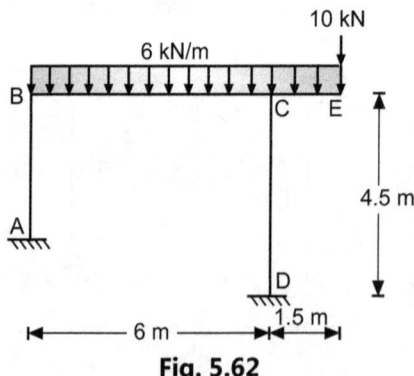

Fig. 5.62

(**Ans.** $M_{AB} = -0.62$ kN/m, $M_{BA} = -M_{BC} = -7.14$ kN/m, $M_{CB} = -24.94$ kN/m,

$M_{CE} = 21.75$ kN/m, $M_{CD} = 3.18$ kN/m, $M_{DC} = 4.54$ kN/m)

47.

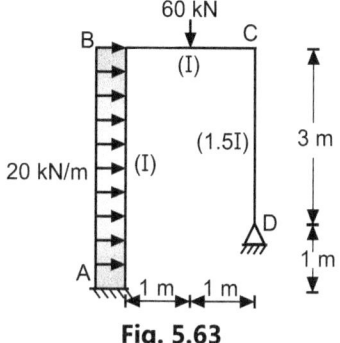

Fig. 5.63

(**Ans.** $M_{AB} = 75.2$ kN/m, $M_{BA} = -M_{BC} = 17.1$ kN/m, $M_{CB} = -M_{CD} = -50$ kN/m, $M_{DC} = 0$)

48.

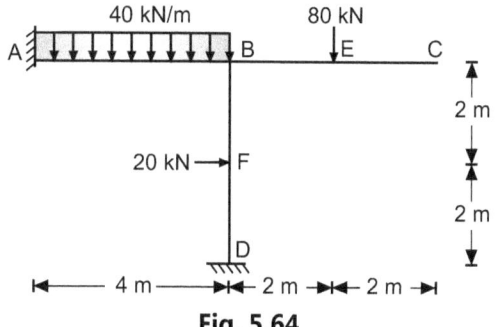

Fig. 5.64

(**Ans.** $M_{AB} = 55.84$ kN/m, $M_{BA} = -48.52$ kN/m, $M_{BC} = 63.66$ kN/m,

$M_{BD} = 15.12$ kN/m, $M_{DB} = 22.44$ kN/m)

49.

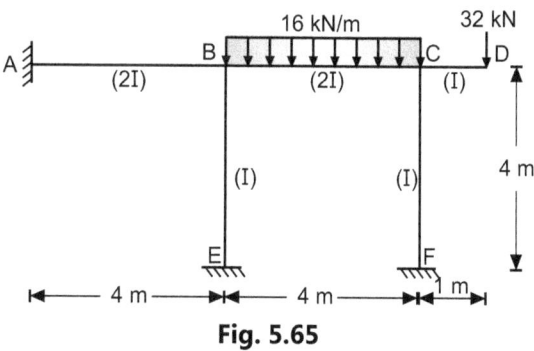

Fig. 5.65

(**Ans.** $M_{AB} = -3.8$ kN/m, $M_{BA} = -7.6$ kN/m, $M_{BC} = 11.43$ kN/m,

$M_{CB} = -29.72$ kN/m, $M_{CD} = 32$ kN/m, $M_{BE} = -3.8$ kN/m,

$M_{EB} = -1.9$ kN/m, $M_{CF} = -2.28$ kN/m, $M_{FC} = -1.14$ kN/m)

50.

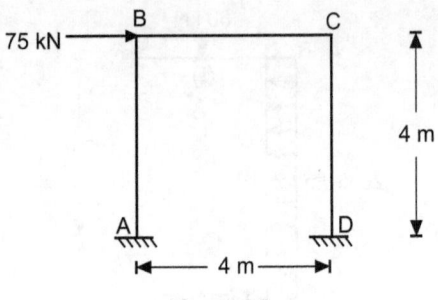

Fig. 5.66

(**Ans.** M_{AB} = 85.71 kN/m, M_{BA} = – M_{BC} = 64.29 kN/m,

M_{CB} = – M_{CD} = – 64.29 kN/m, M_{DC} = 85.71 kN/m)

51.

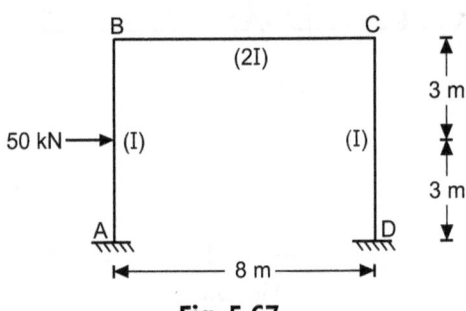

Fig. 5.67

(**Ans.** M_{AB} = – 123.72 kN/m, M_{BA} = –M_{BC} = – 42.575 kN/m,

M_{CB} = – M_{CD} = 58.675 kN/m, M_{DC} = 75.275 kN/m)

MULTIPLE CHOICE QUESTIONS

1. A fixed beam AB of span L is loaded with U.D.L. of intensity 'w' throughout span. Fixed end moment at A is

   (a) $wL^2/12$ (b) $wL^2/8$ (c) $wL/4$ (d) wab^2/L^2

2. A fixed beam AB of span L is loaded with U.D.L. of intensity 'w' throughout span. Fixed end moment at B is

   (a) $wL^2/12$ (b) $wL^2/8$ (c) $wL/4$ (d) Wab^2/L^2

3. A fixed beam AB of span L is loaded with concentrated load W at a distance a from A. Fixed end moment at A is

   (a) $wL^2/8$ (b) $wL^2/12$ (c) Wa^2b/L^2 (d) Wab^2/L^2

4. A fixed beam AB of span is loaded with concentrated load W at a distance a from A. Fixed end moment at B is

   (a) $wL^2/8$ (b) $wL^2/12$ (c) Wa^2b/L^2 (d) Wab^2/L^2

5. A fixed beam AB of span L is loaded with concentrated load W at centre. Fixed end moment at A is

   (a) $wL/12$ (b) $wL/8$ (c) $wL/4$ (d) Wab/L

6. A fixed beam AB of span L is loaded with concentrated load W at centre. Fixed end moment at B is

   (a) $wL/8$ (b) $wL^2/8$ (c) $wL/4$ (d) Wab/L

7. A fixed beam AB of span L subjected to U.D.L. of intensity 'w' over a distance 'a' from left end. Fixed end moment at A is

   (a) $wa^2(4a – 3l)/12l^2$ (b) $wa^3(4l – 3a)/12l^2$
   (c) $wa^2(6l^2 – 8a^2 + 3a)/12l^2$ (d) $wa^2(6l^2 + 3a^2 – 81a)/12l^2$

8. A fixed beam AB of span L is subjected to U.D.L. of intensity 'w' over a distance 'a' from left end. Fixed end moment at B

   (a) $wa^3(4a – 3l)/12l^2$ (b) $wa^3(4l – 3a)/12l^2$
   (c) $wa^2(6l^2 – 8la^2 + 3a)/12l^2$ (d) $wa^2(6l^2 – 3a^2 – 81a)/12l^2$

9. A fixed beam AB of span L is subjected to U.V.L. of zero intensity at left support and intensity 'w' at right support. Fixed end moment at B is

   (a) $wl^2/20$ (b) $wl/20$ (c) $wl^2/30$ (d) $wl^3/30$

10. A fixed bema AB of span L is subjected to U.V.L. of zero intensity at left support and intensity 'w' at right support. Fixed end moment at A is

    (a) $wl^2/20$ (b) $wl/20$ (c) $wl^2/30$ (d) $wl^3/30$

11. A fixed beam AB of span L is subjected to couple M at a distance 'a' from left end. Fixed end moment at B is

    (a) $Ma(l – 3a)/l^2$ (b) $Ma(3l – b)/l^2$
    (c) $Mb(l – 3b)/l^2$ (d) $Ma(3b – l)/l^2$

12. A fixed beam AB of span L is subjected to couple M at a distance 'a' from left end. Fixed end moment at A is

   (a) Mb (l – 3a)/l²
   (b) Ma (3l – b)/l²
   (c) Mb (3a – l)/l²
   (d) Ma (3b – l)/l²

13. A fixed beam AB of span L is subjected to couple M a distance 'a' from left end. Fixed end moment at B is

   (a) M/2   (b) M/4   (c) M/3   (d) 2M/3

14. A fixed beam AB of span L is subjected to couple M at a distance 'a' from left end. Fixed end moment at A is

   (a) M/2   (b) M/4   (c) M/3   (d) 2M/3

15. A fixed beam AB is of span L. Support B is at a lower level of amount 'δ'. Fixed end moment A is

   (a) $6EI\delta/L^2$ (b) $12EI\delta/L^2$ (c) $4EI\delta/L^2$ (d) $4EI\delta/L^2$

16. A fixed beam AB is of span L. Support B is at a lower level of amount 'δ'. Fixed end moment at support B is

   (a) $6EI\delta/L^2$ (b) $12EI\delta/L^2$ (c) $3EI\delta/L^2$ (d) $4EI\delta/L^2$

17. A fixed beam AB of span 7 m carries two concentrated loads 40 kN and 80 kN at 2 m and 5 m from left respectively. Fixed end moment at support A is

   (a) 97.96 kN-m   (b) 40.82 kN-m   (c) 73.47 kN-m   (d) 32.65 kN-m

18. A fixed beam AB of span 7 m carries two concentrated loads 40 kN and 80 kN at 2 m and 5 m from left respectively. Fixed end moment at support B is

   (a) 97.96 kN-m   (b) 40.82 kN-m   (c) 73.47 kN-m   (d) 32.65 kN-m

19. A fixed beam AB of span 6 m carries a couple of 180 kN-m at a distance 4 m from left end. Fixed end moment at support A is

   (a) zero   (b) 45 kN-m   (c) 90 N-m   (d) 60 kN-m

20. A fixed beam AB of span 6 m carries a couple of 180 kN-m at a distance 4 m from left end. Fixed end moment at support B is

   (a) zero   (b) 45 kN-m   (c) 90 N-m   (d) 60 kN-m

21. A fixed beam AB of span 6 m carries a couple of 40 kN-m at centre. Fixed end moment at support A is

   (a) zero   (b) 20 kN-m   (c) 10 kN-m   (d) 40 kN-m

22. A fixed beam AB of span 6 m carries a couple of 40 kN-m at centre. Fixed end moment at support A is

   (a) zero   (b) 20 kN-m   (c) 10 kN-m   (d) 40 kN-m

23. A fixed beam AB of span 5 m carries a concentrated load of 200 kN at 3 m from left support and right end sinks by 10 mm. EI of beam is 6000 kN-m^2. Fixed end moment at B is

   (a) 110 kN-m   (b) 130 kN-m   (c) 82 kN-m   (d) 129.6 kN-m

24. A fixed beam AB of span 5 m carries a concentrated load of 200 kN at 3 m from left support and right end sinks by 10 mm. EI of beam is 6000 kN-m^2. Fixed end moment at A is

   (a) 110 kN-m   (b) 130 kN-m   (c) 82 kN-m   (d) 129.6 kN-m

25. A fixed beam AB of span 8 m carries a uniformly distributed load of intensity 45 kN/m over right half of span. Fixed end moment at A is

   (a) 165 kN-m   (b) 240 kN-m   (c) 210 kN-m   (d) 75 kN-m

26. A fixed beam AB of span 8 m carries a uniformly distributed load of intensity 45 kN/m over right half of span. Fixed end moment at B is

   (a) 165 kN-m   (b) 240 kN-m   (c) 210 kN-m   (d) 75 kN-m

27. A continuous beam ABC is a shown in Fig. 1. The support moment at B is

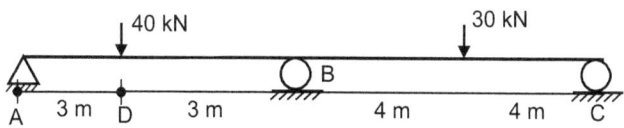

Fig. 1

   (a) 35 kN-m   (b) 45 kN-m   (c) 65 kN-m   (d) 75 kN-m

28. A continuous beam ABC is shown in Fig. 2. The support moment at B is

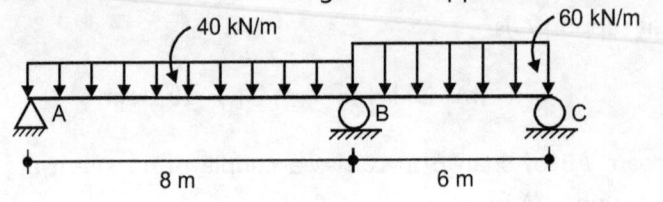

Fig. 2

(a) 158 kN-m   (b) 228 kN-m   (c) 298 kN-m   (d) 128 kN-m

29. A continuous beam ABC is as shown in Fig. 3. The support moment at B is

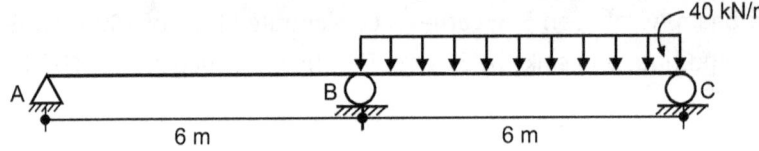

Fig. 3

(a) 90 kN-m   (b) 180 kN-m   (c) 45 kN-m   (d) 135 kN-m

30. A continuous beam ABC is as shown in Fig. 4. The support moment at B is

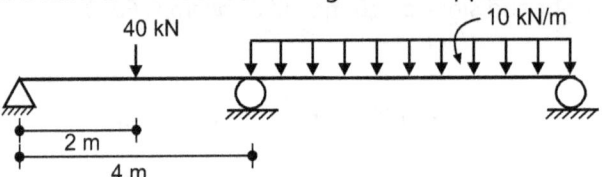

Fig. 4

(a) 93 kN-m   (b) 59 kN-m   (c) 95 kN-m   (d) 39 kN-m

31. A continuous beam ABC is as shown in Fig. 5. The support moment at B is

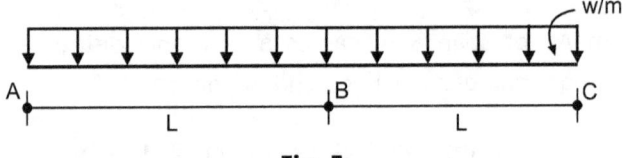

Fig. 5

(a) $wl^2/12$ (b) $wl^2/8$ (c) $wl^2/4$ (d) $wl^2/16$

32. A continuous beam ABCE is as shown in Fig. 6. The support moment at B is

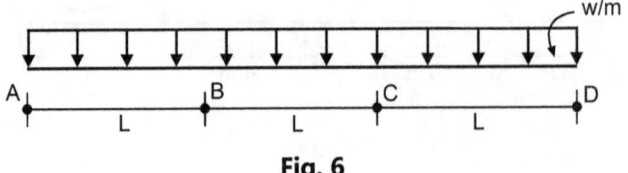

Fig. 6

(a) $wl^2/12$ (b) $wl^2/24$ (c) $wl^2/10$ (d) $wl^2/16$

33. A continuous beam ABCD is as shown in Fig. 7. The support moment at C is

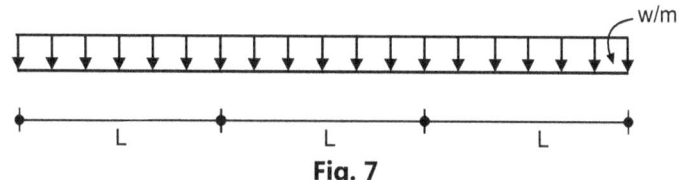

Fig. 7

(a) $wl^2/12$ (b) $wl^2/24$ (c) $wl^2/10$ (d) $wl^2/16$

34. A continuous beam ABCD is shown in Fig. 8. The support moment at is

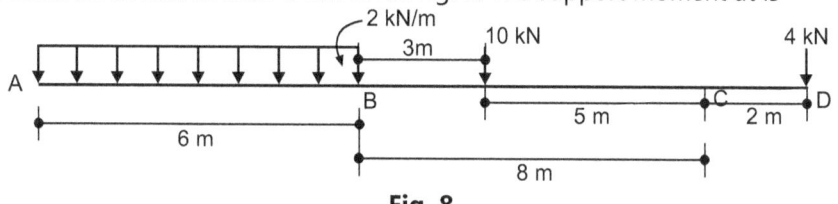

Fig. 8

(a) 10.3 kN-m (b) 19.4 kN-m (c) 5.3 kN-m (d) 25.7 kN-m

35. A continuous beam ABCD is as shown in Fig. 9. If support moment at B is 359 kN-m then the support at C is

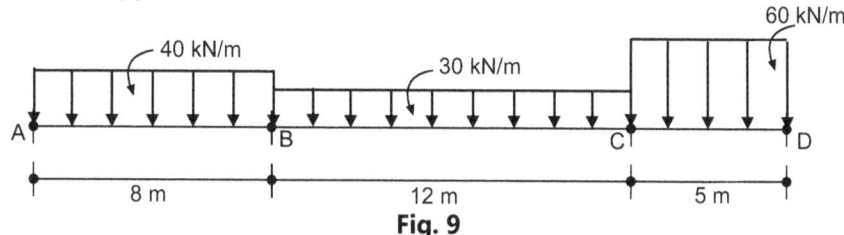

Fig. 9

(a) 393 kN-m (b) 309 kN-m (c) 195 kN-m (d) 239 kN-m

36. A continuous beam ABCD is as shown in Fig. 10. If support moment at C is 44.8 kN-m then the support moment at B is

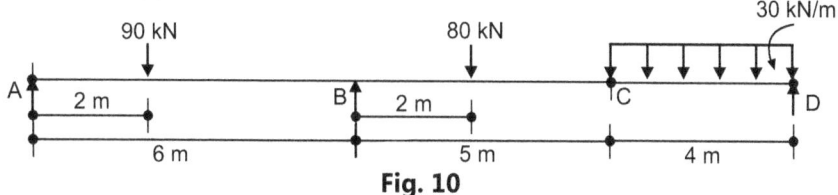

Fig. 10

(a) 68.4 kN-m (b) 59.4 kN-m (c) 95.3 kN-m (d) 39.7 kN-m

37. A continuous beam ABCD is as shown in Fig. 11. If support moment at C is WL/40 then the support moment at B is

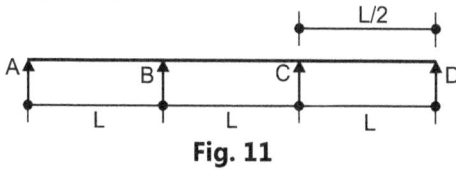

Fig. 11

(a) $Wl/12$ (b) $Wl/25$ (c) $Wl/16$ (d) $Wl/10$

38. A continuous beam ABC is as shown in Fig. 12. The support moment at B is

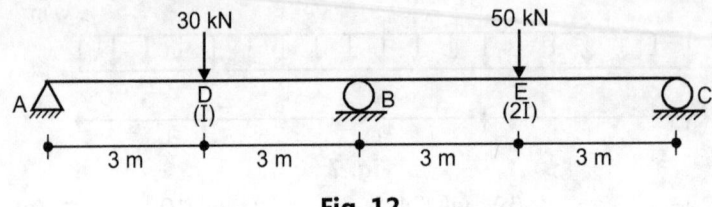

Fig. 12

(a) 38.40 kN-m (b) 41.25 kN-m (c) 69.53 kN-m (d) 39.76 kN-m

39. A continuous beam ABCD is as shown in Fig. 13. The support moment at B is

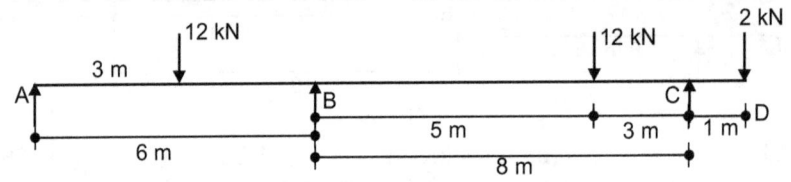

Fig. 13

(a) 19 kN-m (b) 9 kN-m (c) 14 kN-m (d) 23 kN-m

40. A continuous beam ABCD is as shown in Fig. 14. If support moment at B is 40.6 kN-m then the support moment at A is

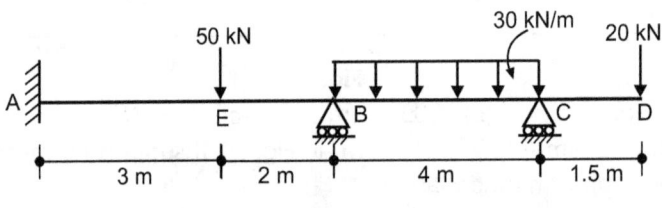

Fig. 14

(a) 21.7 kN-m (b) 35.2 kN-m (c) 19.5 kN-m (d) 42.7 kN-m

41. A continuous beam ABCD is as shown in Fig. 15. If support moment at B is 37.2 kN-m then the support moment at

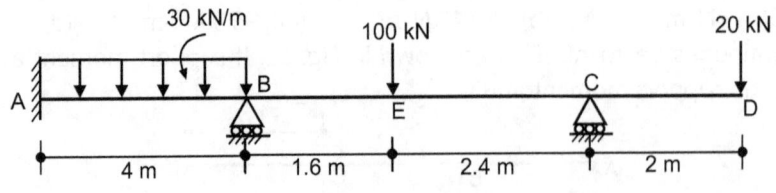

Fig. 15

(a) 28.40 kN-m (b) 41.25 kN-m (c) 49.6 kN-m (d) 59.7 kN-m

42. A continuous beam is as shown in Fig. 16. If the support moment at B is 34.3 kN-m then support moment at A is

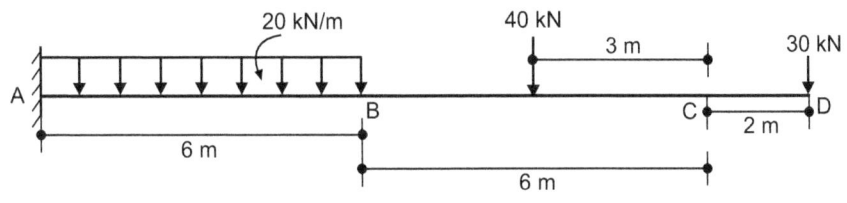

Fig. 16

(a) 83.40 kN-m (b) 51.25 kN-m (c) 93.6 kN-m (d) 72.9 kN-m

43. A continuous beam ABC is as shown in Fig. 17. The support moment at B is

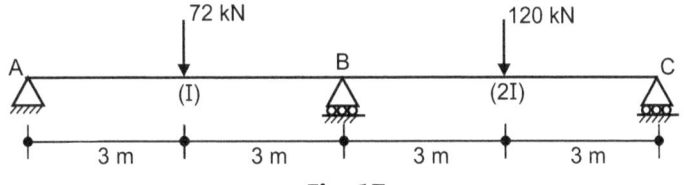

Fig. 17

(a) 28 kN-m (b) 41 kN-m (c) 79 kN-m (d) 99 kN-m

44. A continuous beam ABCD is as shown in Fig. 18. If support moment at B is 13.24 kN-m then the support moment at A is

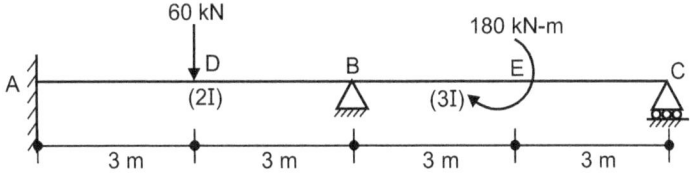

Fig. 18

(a) 23.5 kN-m (b) 60.9 kN-m (c) 59.5 kN-m (d) 49.3 kN-m

45. A beam ABC is supported at A, B and C. AB = 6 m, BC = 5 m. AB carries a U.D.L. of 30 kN/m and BC of 25 kN/m. The support moment at B is

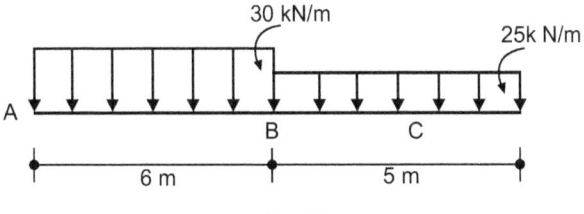

Fig. 19

(a) 109 kN-m (b) 89 kN-m (c) 69 kN-m (d) 129 kN-m

46. A continuous beam ABC is fixed at A and simply supported at B and C. Span AB and BC are 6 m and 4 m respectively. Span AB carries U.D.L. 30 kN/m and BC carries a concentrated load 80 kN at centre. if support moment at A is 18.3 kN-m then support moment at B is

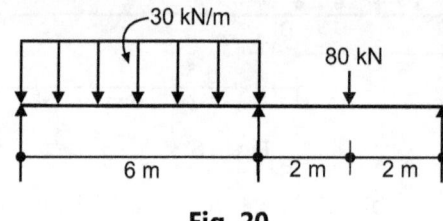

Fig. 20

(a) 22.5 kN-m (b) 60.9 kN-m (c) 48.8 kN-m (d) 56.3 kN-m

47. A continuous beam ABC is as shown in Fig. 21. If the support moment at B is 11.70 kN-m then support moment at C is

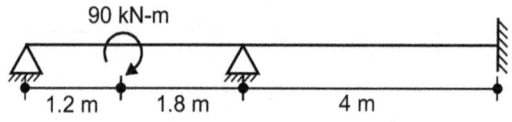

Fig. 21

(a) 13.5 kN-m (b) 10.9 kN-m (c) 11.7 kN-m (d) 5.9 kN-m

48. A continuous beam ABC is as shown in Fig. 22. The support moment at B is

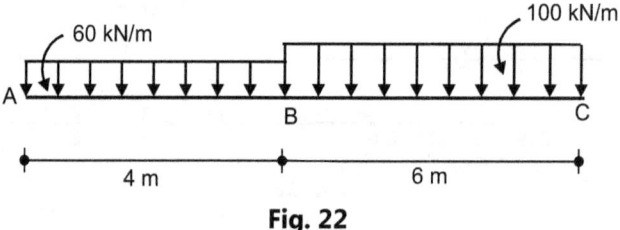

Fig. 22

(a) 318 kN-m (b) 218 kN-m (c) 258 kN-m (d) 158 kN-m

49. A continuous beam ABC is as shown in Fig. 23. If the support moment at B is 11.70 kN-m then support moment at A is

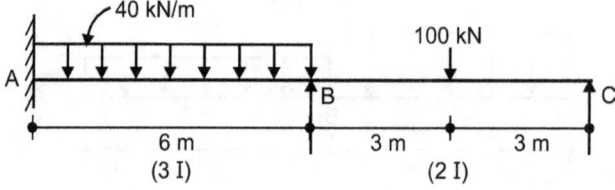

Fig. 23

(a) 98.5 kN-m (b) 208.5 kN-m (c) 122.5 kN-m (d) 128.5 kN-m

50. A continuous beam ABC is as shown in Fig. 24. If support moment at B is 48.8 kN-m then moment at A is

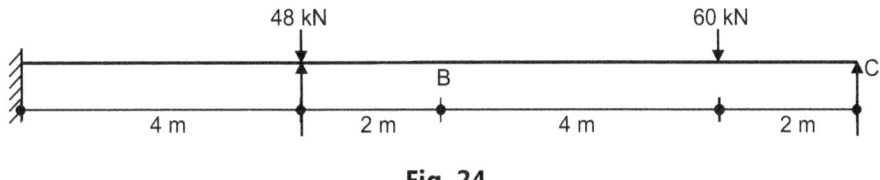

Fig. 24

(a) 15.5 kN-m (b) 18.9 kN-m (c) 21.7 kN-m (d) 18.3 kN-m

51. A continuous beam ABCD is as shown in Fig. 25. If the support moment at C is 47.8 kN-m then support moment at D is

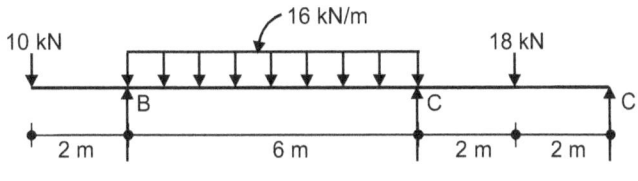

Fig. 25

(a) 35.6 kN-m (b) 19.3 kN-m (c) 44.6 kN-m (d) 25.3 kN-m

52. A continuous beam ABC is as shown in Fig. 26. If support B sinks by 5 mm and EI = 1000 kN-m^2 then support moment at B is

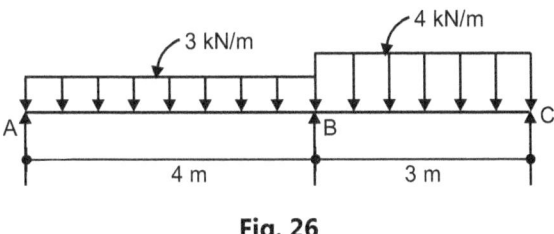

Fig. 26

(a) 11.3 kN-m (b) 4.1 kN-m (c) 21.4 kN-m (d) 15.4 kN-m

53. A continuous beam ABC is as shown in Fig. 27. The support moment at B is

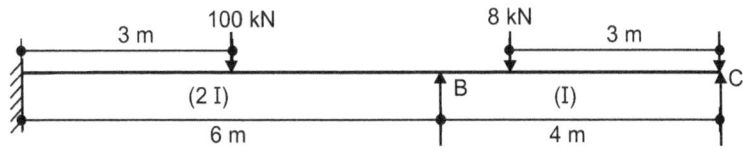

Fig. 27

(a) 78.2 kN-m (b) 48.6 kN-m (c) 93.4 kN-m (d) 51.2 kN-m

54. A continuous beam ABC is as shown in Fig. 28. If support moment at B and at C is 32.3 kN-m and 37.9 kN-m then support beam at A is

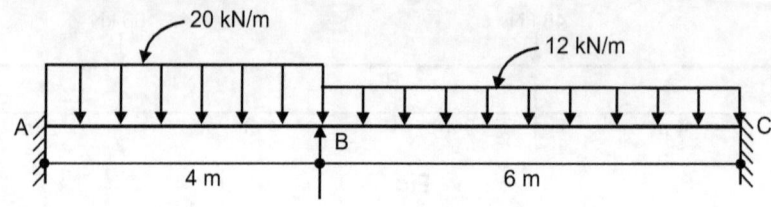

Fig. 28

(a) 58.2 kN-m   (b) 28.6 kN-m   (c) 23.9 kN-m   (d) 41.2 kN-m

55. A continuous beam ABC is as shown in Fig. 29. If support moment at B is 90 kN-m then the support moment at C is

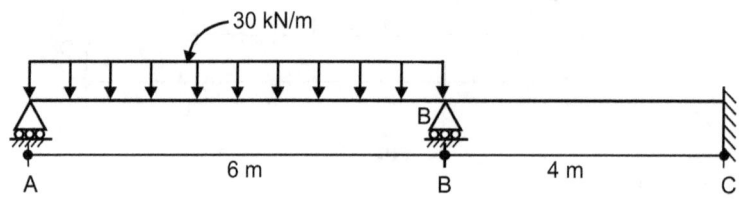

Fig. 29

(a) 90 kN-m   (b) 75 kN-m   (c) 35 kN-m   (d) 45 kN-m

56. A continuous beam ABC is as shown in Fig. 30. The support moment at B is

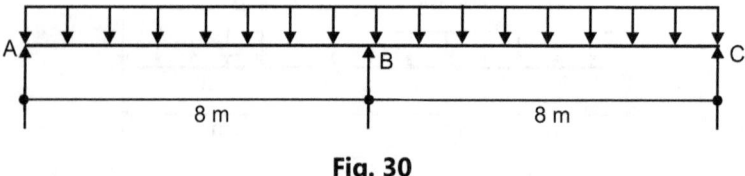

Fig. 30

(a) 640 kN-m   (b) 320 kN-m   (c) 480 kN-m   (d) 240 kN-m

57. A continuous beam ABC is as shown in Fig. 31. The support moment at B is

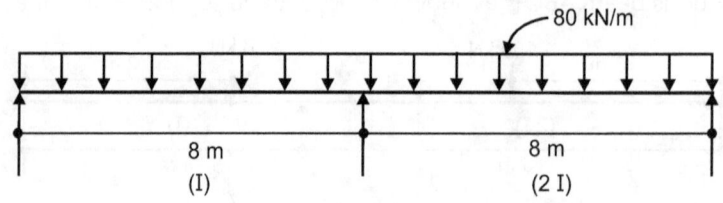

Fig. 31

(a) 640 kN-m   (b) 320 kN-m   (c) 480 kN-m   (d) 240 kN-m

58. A continuous beam ABC is as shown in Fig. 32. If support moment B sinks by 5 mm and EI = 5000 kN-m² then support moment at B is

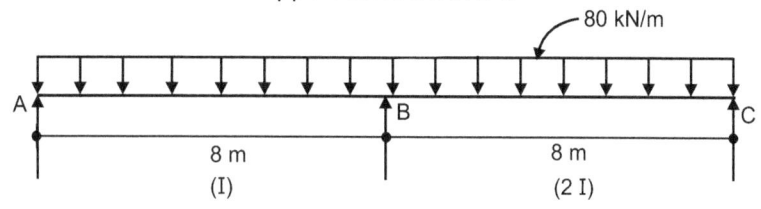

Fig. 32

(a) 610 kN-m (b) 628 kN-m (c) 580 kN-m (d) 640 kN-m

59. A continuous beam ABC is as shown in Fig. 33. If support moment B is 19.63 kN-m then the value of load P is

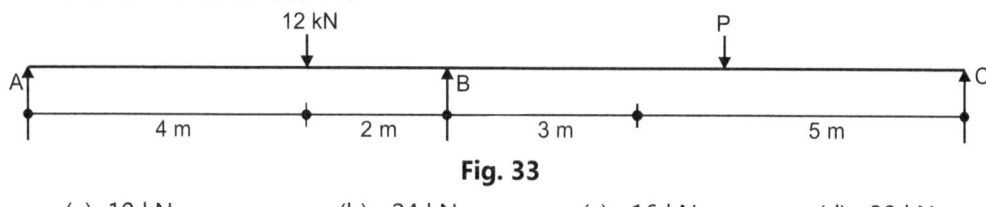

Fig. 33

(a) 10 kN (b) 24 kN (c) 16 kN (d) 30 kN

60. A continuous beam ABC is as shown in Fig. 34. If support moment B is 19.63 kN-m then the value of load P is

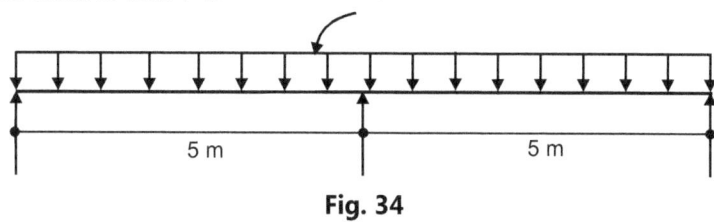

Fig. 34

(a) 74.56 kN-m (b) 93.75 kN-m (c) 53.45 kN-m (c) 88.78 kN-m

61. A beam ABCD is supported at A, B, C and D. Span AB and BC are loaded with U.D.L. 3 kN/m. There is no load on span CD. If the support moment at B is 16.5 kN-m then the support moment at C is

(a) 6.5 kN-m (b) 8.9 kN-m (c) 10.5 kN-m (d) 12.9 kN-m

62. A continuous beam ABC is as shown in Fig. 35. The support moment at B is

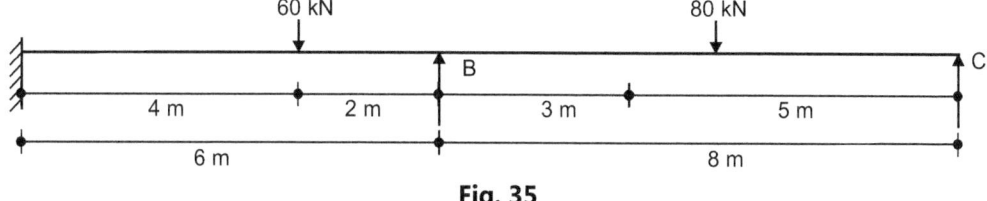

Fig. 35

(a) j56.5 kN-m (b) 68.9 kN-m (c) 80.5 kN-m (d) 98.2 kN-m

63. A continuous beam ABC is as shown in Fig. 36. The support moment at B is

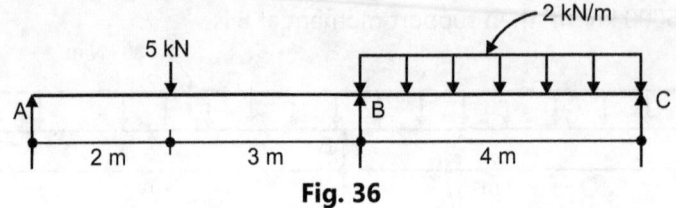

Fig. 36

(a) 4.1 kN-m (b) 2.5 kN-m (c) 5.4 kN-m (d) 8 kN-m

64. A continuous beam ABC is as shown in Fig. 37. If the support moment at B and C are 52.1 kN-m and 67.7 kN-m respectively then the support moment at A is

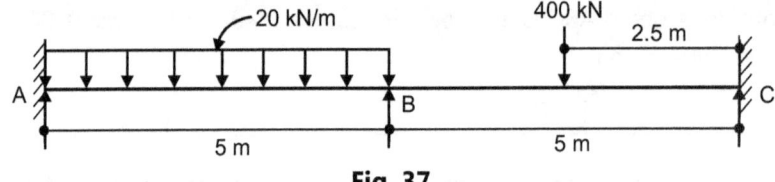

Fig. 37

(a) 29.75 kN-m (b) 36.45 kN-m (c) 43.25 kN-m (d) 51.11 kN-m

65. A continuous beam ABC is as shown in Fig. 38. If the support moment at B is 93.75 kN-m then the support moment at A is

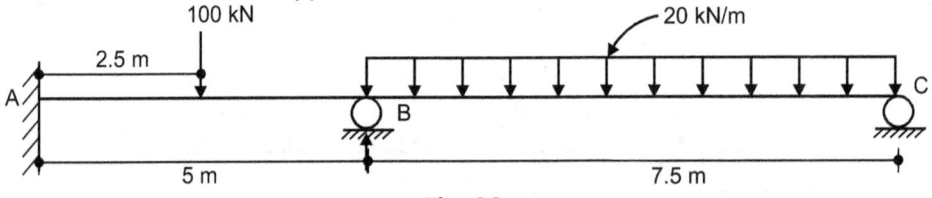

Fig. 38

(a) 26.78 kN-m (b) 39.67 kN-m (c) 46.9 kN-m (d) 33.45 kN-m

66. A propped cantilever is as shown in Fig. 39. The support moment at A is

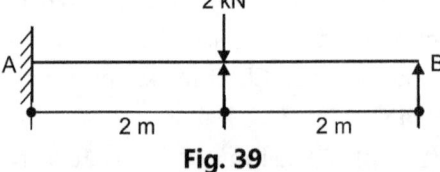

Fig. 39

(a) 6.12 kN-m (b) 3.1 kN-m (c) 4.1 kN-m (d) 1.5 kN-m

67. A propped cantilever is as shown in Fig. 40. The support B sinks by 10 mm and $EI = 200$ kN-m^2. The support moment at A is

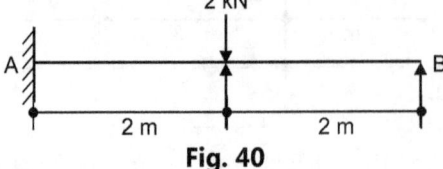

Fig. 40

(a) 2.12 kN-m (b) 1.88 kN-m (c) 3.11 kN-m (d) 4.32 kN-m

68. A propped cantilever is as shown in Fig. 41. The support moment at A is

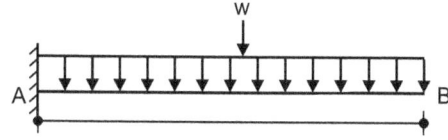

Fig. 41

(a) $wl^2/8$ (b) $wl^2/12$ (c) $wl^2/10$ (d) $wl^2/16$

69. A propped cantilever is as shown in Fig. 42. The support moment at A is

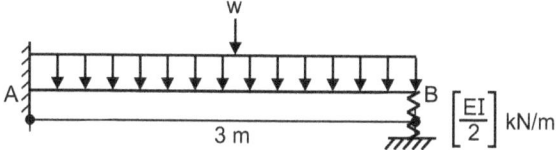

Fig. 42

(a) 3.45 kN-m   (b) 8.93 kN-m   (c) 17.4 kN-m   (d) 11.1 kN-m

70. A propped cantilever is as shown in Fig. 43. The support moment at A is

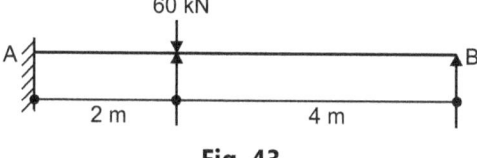

Fig. 43

(a) 56.78 kN-m   (b) 31.67 kN-m   (c) 36.91 kN-m   (d) 66.67 kN-m

71. A continuous beam ABC is as shown in Fig. 44. If the support moment at B is 3.8 kN-m then the support moment at A is

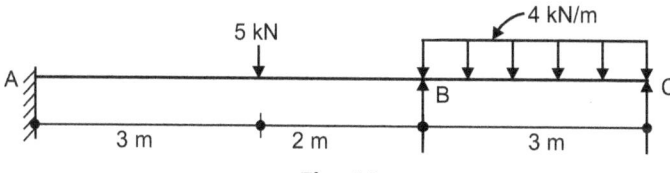

Fig. 44

(a) 5.78 kN-m   (b) 2.3 kN-m   (c) 3.91 kN-m   (d) 6.67 kN-m

72. A continuous beam ABCDE is as shown in Fig. 45. The support moment at B is

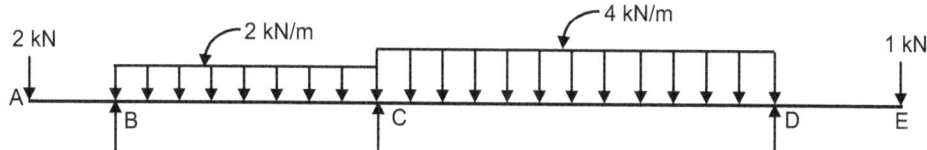

Fig. 45

(a) 11.4 kN-m   (b) 21.3 kN-m   (c) 18.91 kN-m   (d) 26.67 kN-m

73. A continuous beam ABC is as shown in Fig. 46. The support moment at B is

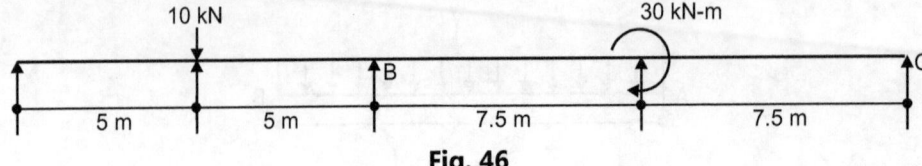

Fig. 46

(a) 10.4 kN-m (b) 14.3 kN-m (c) 5.25 kN-m (d) 19.21 kN-m

74. A continuous beam ABC is as shown in Fig. 47. If the support moment at A is 57.34 kN-m then the support moment at B is

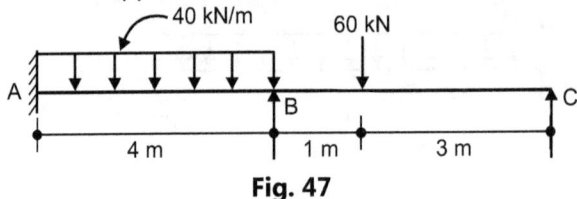

Fig. 47

(a) 19.8 kN-m (b) 34.2 kN-m (c) 25.5 kN-m (d) 45.3 kN-m

75. A continuous beam ABCDEF is as shown in Fig. 48. If the support moment at C is 41.7 kN-m then the support moment at D is

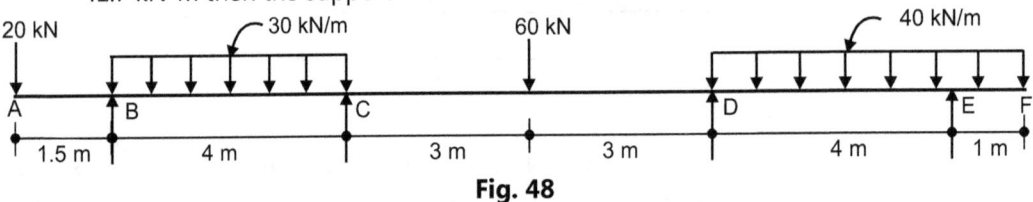

Fig. 48

(a) 39 kN-m (b) 29 kN-m (c) 56 kN-m (d) 67 kN-m

76. A continuous beam ABCDE is as shown in Fig. 49. The support moment at C is

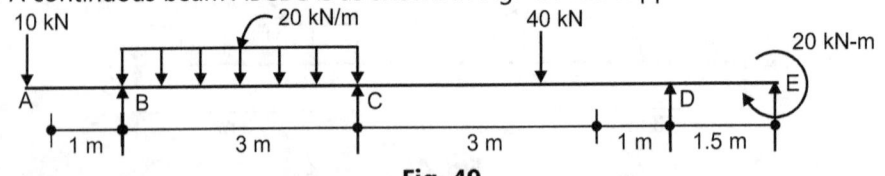

Fig. 49

(a) 11.7 kN-m (b) 24.3 kN-m (c) 35.2 kN-m (d) 41.6 kN-m

77. A continuous beam ABCD is as shown in Fig. 50. If the support moment at B is 35.57 kN-m then the support moment at A is

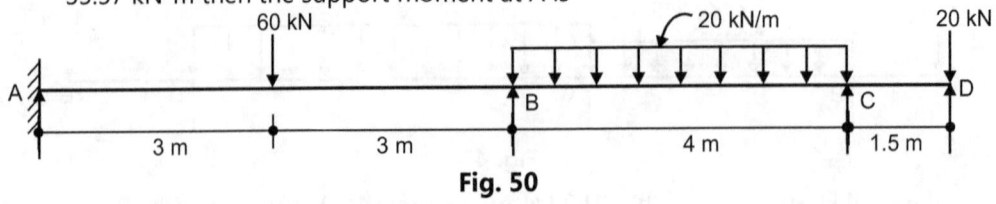

Fig. 50

(a) 29.2 kN-m (b) 31.92 kN-m (c) 28.35 kN-m (d) 49.72 kN-m

78. A continuous beam ABCDE is as shown in Fig. 51. If the support moment at C is 8.5 kN-m then the support moment at B is

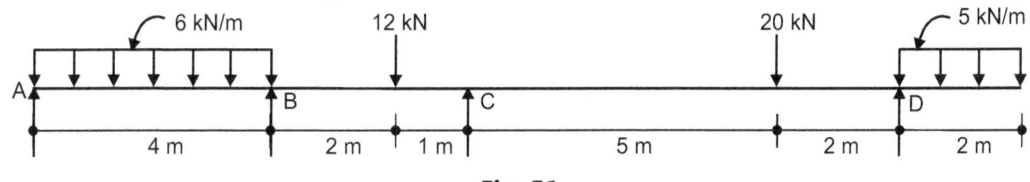

Fig. 51

(a) 16.32 kN-m (b) 11.32 kN-m (c) 7.32 kN-m (d) 25.32 kN-m

79. A continuous beam ABCD is as shown in Fig. 52. If the support moment at B is 6.86 kN-m then the support moment at C is

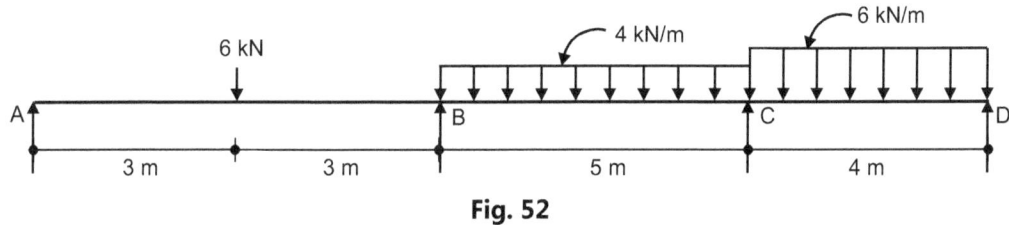

Fig. 52

(a) 10.87 kN-m (b) 14.21 kN-m (c) 21.32 kN-m (d) 32.63 kN-m

80. A continuous beam ABCD is as shown in Fig. 53. Support C sinks by 1 mm and $EI = 21000$ kN-m². If support moment at C is 1.32 kN-m then the support moment at B is

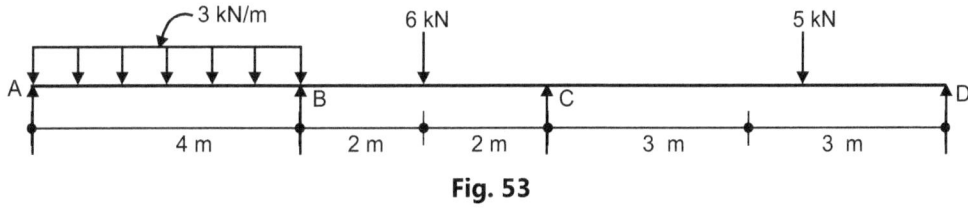

Fig. 53

(a) 7.81 kN-m (b) 6.16 kN-m (c) 5.35 kN-m (d) 8.32 kN-m

81. A continuous beam ABC is as shown in Fig. 54. Support B sinks by 1 mm and $EI = 18000$ kN-m². If support moment at B is 0.57 kN-m then the support moment at A is

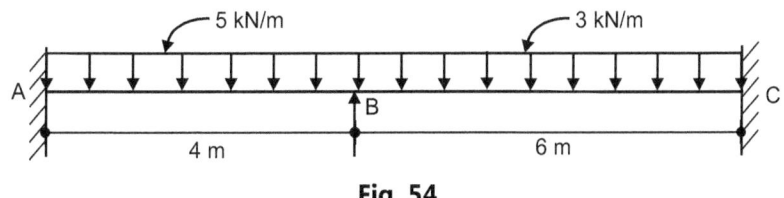

Fig. 54

(a) 19.8 kN-m (b) 31.22 kN-m (c) 13.09 kN-m (d) 25.13 kN-m

82. A continuous beam ABCD is as shown in Fig. 55. If the support moment at C is 5.81 kN-m then the support moment at B is

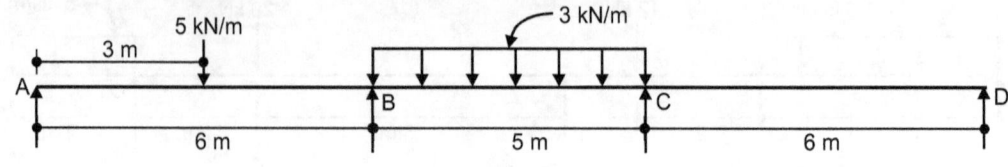

Fig. 55

(a) 8.65 kN-m (b) 5.34 kN-m (c) 6.76 kN-m (d) 8.65 kN-m

83. A continuous beam ABCD is as shown in Fig. 56. If the support moment at B is 28.12 kN-m then the support moment at C is

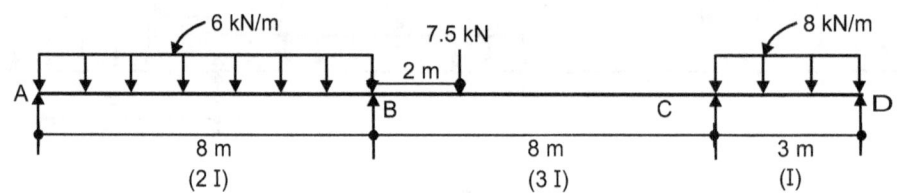

Fig. 56

(a) 16.8 kN-m (b) 22.75 kN-m (c) 25.5 kN-m (d) 45.3 kN-m

84. A continuous beam ABCD is as shown in Fig. 57. If the support moment at A is 6.91 kN-m then the support moment at B is

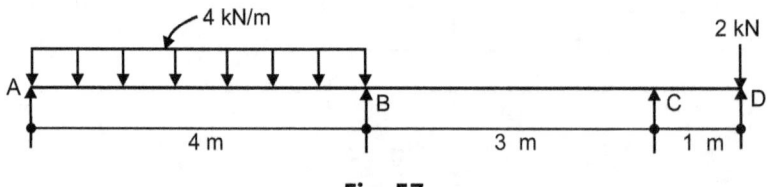

Fig. 57

(a) 1.8 kN-m (b) 3.2 kN-m (c) 2.2 kN-m (d) 4.3 kN-m

85. A continuous beam ABCD is as shown in Fig. 58. If the support moment at B is 3.64 kN-m then the support moment at D is

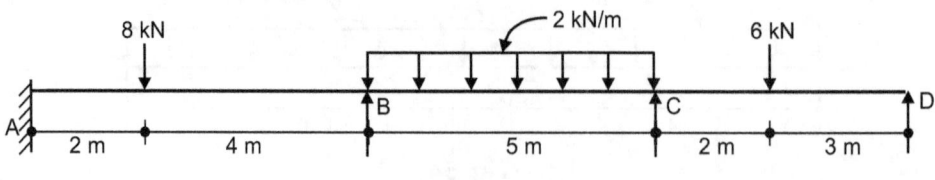

Fig. 58

(a) 5.1 kN-m (b) 4.7 kN-m (c) 5.9 kN-m (d) 4.3 kN-m

86. A continuous beam ABC is as shown in Fig. 59. The support moment at A is 51 kN-m. then the support moment

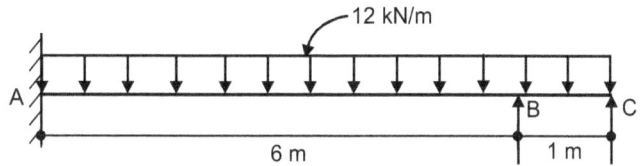

Fig. 59

(a) 12 kN-m (b) 6 kN-m (c) 9 kN-m (d) 8 kN-m

87. A continuous beam ABC is as shown in Fig. 60. The support moment at B is

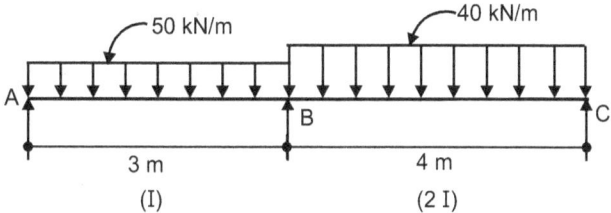

Fig. 60

(a) 23.375 kN-m (b) 40 kN-m (c) 65.75 kN-m (d) 47.125 kN-m

88. A continuous beam ABC is as shown in Fig. 61. The support moment at A is 68.57. Find the support moment at B is

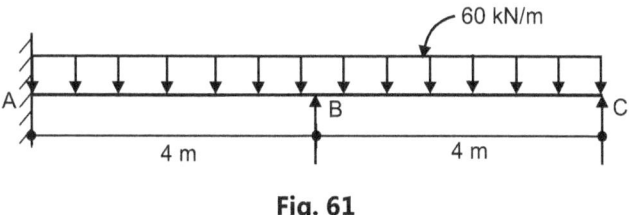

Fig. 61

(a) 0 (b) 102.86 kN-m (c) 68.57 kN-m (d) 34.28 kN-m

89. A continuous beam ABC is as shown in Fig. 62. The support moment at A is 10 kN-m. Then the support moment at B is

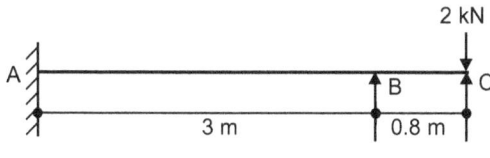

Fig. 62

(a) 10 kN-m (b) 20 kN-m (c) 25 kN-m (d) 40 kN-m

90. The continuous beam ABCD is shown in Fig. 63. The support moment at B is 52.46 kN-m. Then the support moment at C is

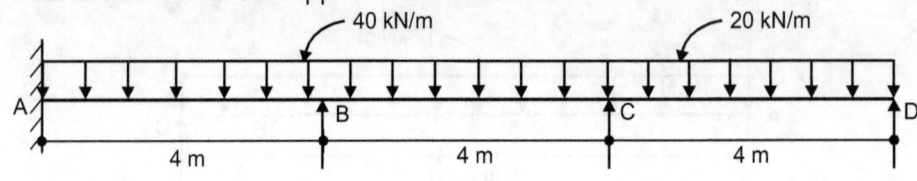

Fig. 63

(a) 53.77 kN-m (b) 53.92 kN-m (c) 13.04 kN-m (d) 20 kN-m

ANSWERS

1. (a)	2. (a)	3. (d)	4. (c)	5. (b)	6. (a)	7. (d)	8. (b)
9. (a)	10. (c)	11. (d)	12. (c)	13. (b)	14. (b)	15. (a)	16. (a)
17. (c)	18. (a)	19. (d)	20. (a)	21. (c)	22. (c)	23. (b)	24. (a)
25. (d)	26. (a)	27. (b)	28. (c)	29. (9)	30. (a)	31. (b)	32. (c)
33. (c)	34. (a)	35. (b)	36. (a)	37. (d)	38. (b)	39. (c)	40. (a)
41. (c)	42. (d)	43. (d)	44. (b)	45. (a)	46. (c)	47. (d)	48. (a)
49. (c)	50. (d)	51. (d)	52. (b)	53. (a)	54. (c)	55. (d)	56. (a)
57. (a)	58. (b)	59. (c)	60. (b)	61. (c)	62. (d)	63. (a)	64. (b)
65. (c)	66. (d)	67. (b)	68. (a)	69. (c)	70. (d)	71. (b)	72. (a)
73. (c)	74. (d)	75. (c)	76. (a)	77. (d)	78. (c)	79. (a)	80. (b)
81. (c)	82. (d)	83. (b)	84. (c)	85. (a)	86. (c)	87. (d)	88. (b)
89. (a)	90. (a)						

UNIT - III

Chapter 6
DEFLECTION OF TRUSSES

6.1 INTRODUCTION

A structure deflects under the action of the load system acting on it. To avoid the ill effects due to the excessive deflection, I.S. has limited the deflection to span/325 or 20 mm, whichever is smaller. While designing a structure, care must be taken to limit the deflection to the above value. It is therefore essential to know the deflection of a structure under the action of given loads. The deflection is determined by using the strain energy methods. In this chapter, we will find the deflection of a truss at a given particular node by using

(i)   Castigliano's first theorem; and

(ii) Unit load method.

6.2 STRAIN ENERGY

As any member of a truss carries an axial force due to the given loads acting on the nodal points, we will derive an expression for the strain energy or resilience of a member carrying an axial force. The change in the length, δL, due to an axial force P is given by $\frac{PL}{AE}$.

As the axial force P is gradually induced, the work done which is also equal to the resilience will be

$$U = \frac{1}{2} P \delta L = \frac{1}{2} P \cdot \frac{PL}{AE}$$

$$= \frac{P^2 L}{2AE} \qquad \ldots (6.1)$$

6.3 THE UNIT LOAD METHOD

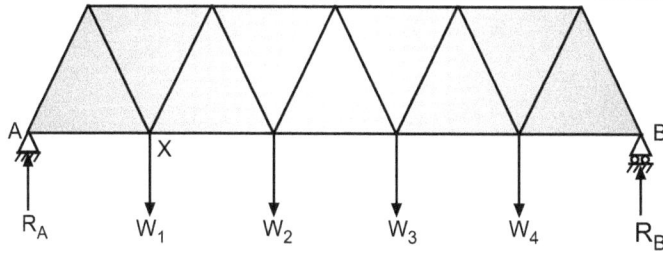

Fig. 6.1

Consider the truss loaded as shown in Fig. 6.1. The load system consists of W_1, W_2, W_3 and W_4 acting at lower nodal points. The deflection of the joint X, where W_1 acts, is required due to the given load system.

Let, $\quad P_1, P_2, P_3 \ldots$ = Axial forces in the members due to given load system

$\quad\quad\quad K_1, K_2, K_3 \ldots$ = Axial forces in the members due to the unit load at the joint X

Let an elementary load δW be gradually applied at X along with W_1 of the load system at X. The axial forces in the members due to δW at X will be $K_1 \delta W$, $K_2 \delta W$, $K_3 \delta W$ etc.

Let δ_V be the vertical deflection of the joint X. As δW is gradually applied, the work done be $\delta W = \frac{1}{2} \delta W \cdot \delta_V$. The axial force in a member say 1 due to the given load system of W_1, W_2, W_3 and W_4 and δW at X will be $(P_1 + K_1 \delta W)$. The elongation of the member 1 due to δW at X will be

$$\delta L_1 = \frac{K_1 \delta W}{A_1 E} L_1$$

The work stored by this member $= \frac{1}{2}(P_1 + K_1 \delta W) \times$ Elongation due to δW

$$= \frac{1}{2}(P_1 + K_1 \delta W) \times \frac{K_1 \delta W}{A_1 E} L_1 = \frac{1}{2} \frac{P_1 K_1 L_1 \delta W}{A_1 E}$$

... neglecting small quantities of the second order.

The total work stored in all the members of the truss

$$= \sum \frac{1}{2} \frac{P_1 K_1 L_1 \delta W}{A_1 E}$$

$$= \sum \frac{1}{2} \frac{p_1 K_1 L_1 \delta W}{E}$$

where $p_1 = \dfrac{P_1}{A_1}$ = Axial stress.

Equating the work supplied by the elementary load δW to the total work stored,

$$\frac{1}{2} \delta W \cdot \delta_V = \left(\sum \frac{1}{2} \frac{p_1 K_1 L_1}{E} \right) \delta W$$

$$\therefore \quad \delta_V = \sum \frac{p_1 K_1 L_1}{E} = \sum K_1 \left(\frac{p_1 L_1}{E} \right)$$

$$= \sum K_1 \delta L_1 \quad\quad \ldots (6.2)$$

Similarly, the expression for horizontal deflection of X is obtained by applying a unit horizontal force at X.

$$\therefore \quad \delta_H = \sum K_1' \delta L_1 \quad\quad \ldots (6.3)$$

K_1 and K_1' may be replaced by $(K_V)_1$ and $(K_H)_1$ for convenience.

6.3.1 Temperature Deflection

δL_1 in equations (6.2) and (6.3) is the change in the length of bar 1 due to the axial stress p_1 induced in it. The change in the length can be due to the rise or fall in the temperature. Then δL_1 will be $L_1 \alpha t$ where α is the coefficient of linear change and t is the change in the temperature. The vertical and horizontal deflections at a joint due to a change of temperature will therefore, be given by,

$$\delta_V = \sum K_1 L_1 \alpha t \qquad \ldots (6.4)$$

and

$$\delta_H = \sum K_1' L_1 \alpha t \qquad \ldots (6.5)$$

6.4 CASTIGLIANO'S FIRST THEOREM

This is another method of finding the deflection of a joint of truss where W_1 acts, the load system consisting of $W_1, W_2, W_3 \ldots$ etc.

6.4.1 Statements

If U represents the total strain energy of a beam or structural frame under a given system of loading $W_1, W_2, W_3 \ldots$ etc. then the partial differential coefficient of U with respect to any one of the loads gives the displacement of that load in its own line of action.

Thus, if $\delta_1, \delta_2, \delta_3$ etc. are the vertical deflections at the joints where the loads W_1, W_2, W_3 etc. respectively act, then

$$\delta_1 = \frac{\partial U}{\partial W_1}, \quad \delta_2 = \frac{\partial U}{\partial W_2}, \quad \delta_3 = \frac{\partial U}{\partial W_3} \text{ etc.}$$

6.4.2 Proof

Consider a truss as shown in Fig. 6.2 loaded at the lower joints. Let P_1, P_2, P_3 etc. be the resulting axial forces in members 1, 2, 3 etc. The strain energy of any member will be $\frac{P^2 L}{2AE}$ ... [equation (6.1)]. The total strain energy, U, of the entire frame will therefore be,

$$U = \frac{1}{2E} \sum \frac{P_1^2 L_1}{A_1}$$

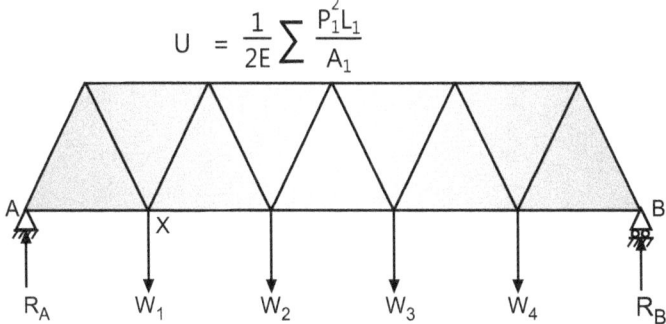

Fig. 6.2 (Repeated)

If we require the deflection of the joint X where W_1 acts, apply a unit load in the direction of W_1. Let K_1, K_2, K_3 etc. be the axial forces in members 1, 2, 3 etc. due to the unit load at X.

The partial differential coefficient of the total strain energy U with respect to W_1 is

$$\frac{\partial U}{\partial W_1} = \frac{1}{2E} \sum \left(2P_1 \frac{\partial P_1}{\partial W_1} \right) \frac{L_1}{A_1}$$

$$\therefore \quad \frac{\partial U}{\partial W_1} = \sum \left(P \frac{\partial P_1}{\partial W_1} \right) \frac{L_1}{A_1 E}$$

But $\frac{\partial P_1}{\partial W_1}$ is the ratio of change in P_1 due to W_1 and is same as K_1 obtained by placing a unit load at the point where W_1 is acting. Therefore,

$$\frac{\partial U}{\partial W_1} = \sum \frac{P_1 K_1 L_1}{A_1 E} = \sum K_1 \delta L_1 = \delta_1 \qquad \ldots (6.6)$$

$$\delta_V (= \delta_1) = \sum K_1 \delta L_1 \text{ already, provided in equation (6.2).}$$

Similarly, $\quad \frac{\partial U}{\partial W_2} = \delta_2$ and $\frac{\partial U}{\partial W_3} = \delta_3$ etc.

SOLVED PROBLEMS

Problem 6.1 : Fig. 6.3 (a) shows a frame hinged at A and supported on roller at B. The various members of the frame are such that under a vertical load of W Newtons at C, the tension members of the frame are subjected to a stress of 100 MPa and the compression members to a stress of 80 MPa. Under the circumstances, find the horizontal movement of the roller end B. Take E = 200 GPa.

(P.U. May 1991)

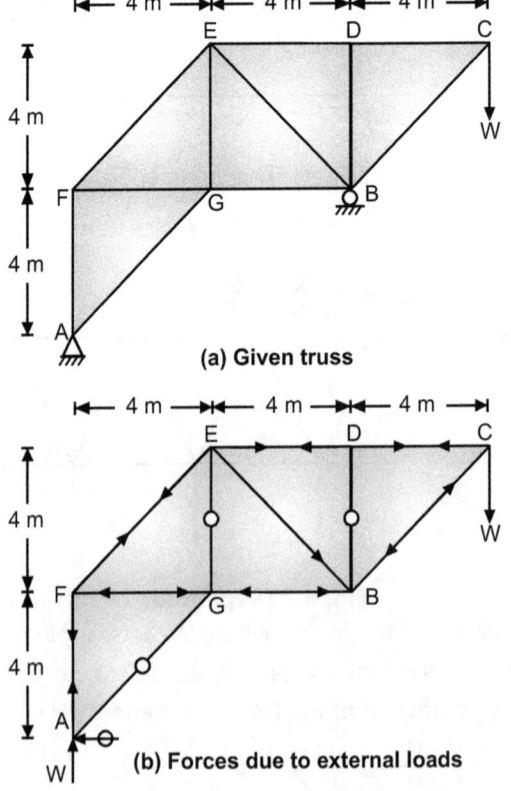

(a) Given truss

(b) Forces due to external loads

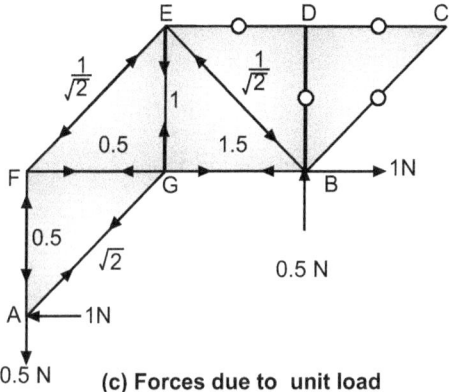

(c) Forces due to unit load

Fig. 6.3

Solution : In Fig. 6.3 (a), the directions of stresses in all members are shown. In Fig. 6.3 (b) a unit horizontal force of 1 N (→) is applied at B. The forces along with their directions in all members are shown in Fig. 6.3 (b). Zero members are found by inspection. These results are tabulated below.

Sr. No.	Member	Stress (σ) MPa	Length (m) – L	K_H (N)	$K_H \sigma L$
1	AG	0	$4\sqrt{2}$	$+\sqrt{2}$	0
2	GB	– 80	4	1.5	– 480
3	BC	– 80	$4\sqrt{2}$	0	0
4	CD	+ 100	4	0	0
5	DE	+ 100	4	0	0
6	EF	+ 100	$4\sqrt{2}$	$-\dfrac{1}{\sqrt{2}}$	– 400
7	FA	+ 100	4	– 0.50	– 200
8	FG	– 80	4	+ 0.50	– 160
9	EG	0	4	+ 1	0
10	EB	– 80	$4\sqrt{2}$	$-\dfrac{1}{\sqrt{2}}$	+ 320
11	BD	0	4	0	0
				$\Sigma K_H \sigma L$	– 920

$$\delta_H = \dfrac{\Sigma K_H \sigma L}{E}$$

$$= \dfrac{-920 \times 1000}{200 \times 10^3 \ (N/mm^2)}$$

$$= -4.6 \text{ mm i.e. } 4.6 \text{ mm } (\leftarrow)$$

Problem 6.2 : A cantilever truss shown in Fig. 6.4 (a) is loaded by a vertical load of 8 kN at the free end. Find the total deflection at the free end in terms of AE which is constant.

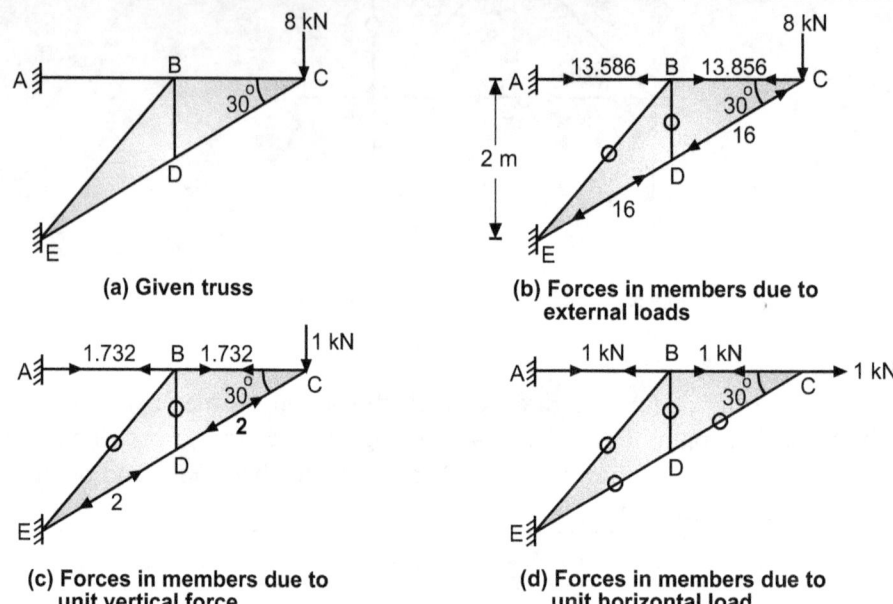

(a) Given truss

(b) Forces in members due to external loads

(c) Forces in members due to unit vertical force

(d) Forces in members due to unit horizontal load

Fig. 6.4

Solution : In Fig. 6.4 (a) and (b), zero members are found by inspection and are marked. Consider Fig. 6.4 (a).

$$F_{CD} = \frac{8}{\sin 30°} = 16 \text{ kN (c)}$$

$$F_{DE} = F_{CD} = 16 \text{ kN (c)}$$

$$F_{CB} = F_{BA} = F_{CD} \cos 30°$$
$$= 16 \times 0.866 = 13.856 \text{ kN (t)}$$

Consider Fig. 6.4 (b). $\quad F_{CB} = F_{BA} = 1 \text{ kN (t)}$

The results are tabulated below :

Sr. No.	Member	Force (kN)	Length (m)	K_V (kN) $= \frac{F}{8}$	K_V PL	K_H (kN)	K_H PL
1	AB	+ 13.856	1.732	1.732	+ 41.568	1.0	24.00
2	BC	+ 13.856	1.732	1.732	+ 41.568	1.0	24.00
3	CD	− 16.00	2.0	− 2.0	+ 64.0	0	0
4	DE	− 16.00	2.0	− 2.0	+ 64.0	0	0
				$\Sigma K_V PL =$	211.136	$\Sigma K_H PL =$	48.00

(Zero members need not be considered).

∴ $\sum K_V PL = +211.136 (\downarrow)$

∴ $\sum K_H PL = 48.00 (\rightarrow)$

Resultant of $\sum K_V PL$ and $\sum K_H PL$ at right angles = 216.523.

If A is in m² and E is in kN/m²,

Resultant deflection of the free end C = $\dfrac{216.523}{AE}$.

Problem 6.3 : Find the horizontal and vertical deflections of joint C of a cantilever truss shown in Fig. 6.5 (a). All members have equal area of 2000 mm². E = 200 GPa.

(P.U. Nov. 1989)

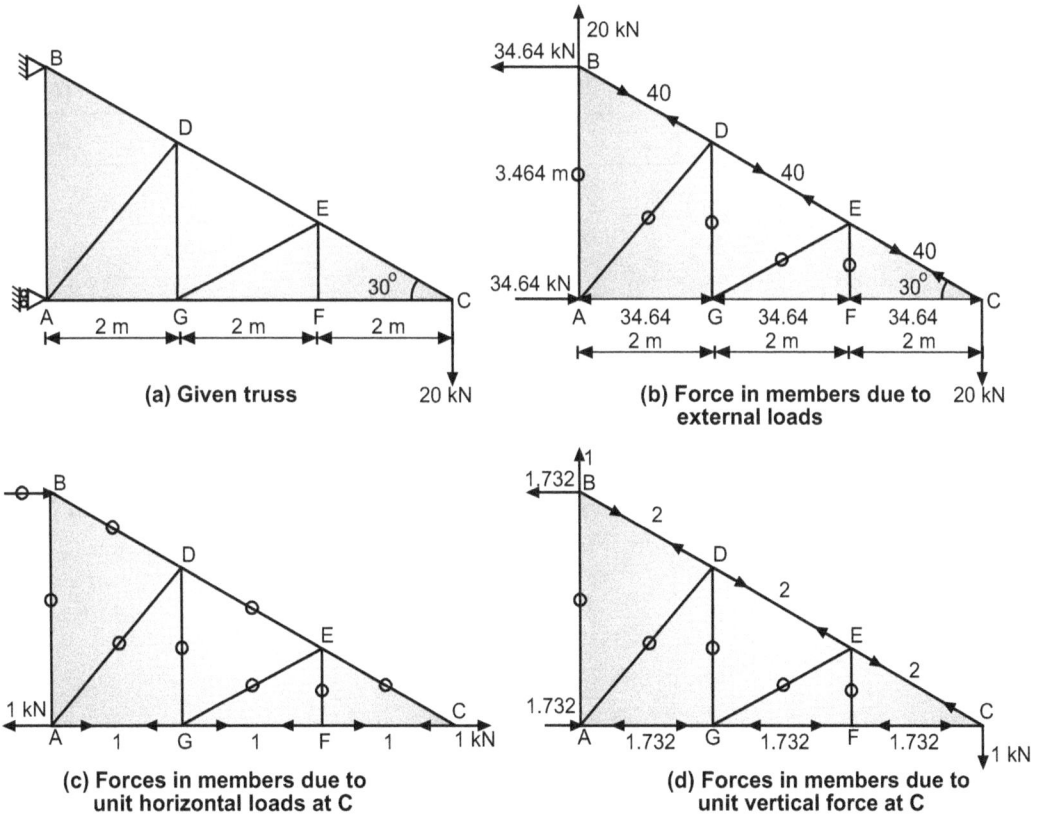

Fig. 6.5

Solution : Lengths of members, direction of axial forces, and zero members are marked in the figures. Consider Fig. 6.5 (b). Solving joint C,

$$F_{CE} = \dfrac{20}{\sin 30°} = 40 \text{ kN (t)} = F_{ED} = F_{DB}$$

$$F_{CF} = F_{CE} \cos 30° = 40 \times 0.866$$
$$= 34.64 \text{ kN} = F_{FG} = F_{GA}$$

These results are tabulated below. Zero members are not considered.

Sr. No.	Member	Force P (kN)	Length L (m)	K_V (kN) $= \dfrac{F}{20}$	K_V PL	K_H (kN)	K_H PL
1	AG	− 34.64	2.00	− 1.732	+ 120	+ 1	− 69.28
2	GF	− 34.64	2.00	− 1.732	+ 120	+ 1	− 69.28
3	FC	− 34.64	2.00	− 1.732	+ 120	+ 1	− 69.28
4	CE	+ 40.00	2.309	+ 2.00	+ 184.72	0	0
5	ED	+ 40.00	2.309	+ 2.00	+ 184.72	0	0
6	DB	+ 40.00	2.309	+ 2.00	+ 184.72	0	0
				$\Sigma K_V PL =$	914.16	$\Sigma K_H PL =$	− 207.8

$$\therefore \quad \delta_C (\downarrow) = \frac{914.16 \times 1000}{AE} = \frac{914.16 \times 1000}{2000 \times 200}$$
$$= 2.2854 \text{ mm}$$

$$\delta_C \text{ (horizontal)} = \frac{-207.84 \times 1000}{2000 \times 200}$$
$$= -0.5196 \text{ mm say} - 0.52 \text{ mm i.e. } 0.52 \text{ mm} (\leftarrow)$$

Note : If P = 20 kN ($\downarrow$)

$$F_{CF} = F_{FG} = F_{GA}$$
$$= 34.64 \text{ kN} = \sqrt{3} \text{ P (c)}$$

and
$$F_{CE} = F_{ED} = F_{DB} = 40 \text{ kN} = 2P \text{ (t)}$$

$$U = \text{Strain energy} = \Sigma \frac{P^2 L}{2AE}$$
$$= \frac{3P^2 \times 2}{2AE} \times 3 + \frac{4P^2 \times 2.309}{2AE} \times 3$$
$$= \frac{9P^2}{AE} + 13.854 \frac{P^2}{AE}$$
$$= 22.854 \frac{P^2}{AE}$$

$$\delta_C (\downarrow) = \frac{\partial U}{\partial P} = 45.708 \frac{P}{AE}$$
$$= \frac{(45.708 \times 1000) \times 20}{2000 \times 200}$$
$$= 2.2854 \text{ mm ... (as before)}$$

Problem 6.4 : In the truss shown in Fig. 6.5 (a), if the members DE, EG and FG only undergo temperature rise of 20°C, find the effect on deflection at C. For steel, coefficient of linear expansion $\alpha = 11 \times 10^{-6}/°C$. **(P.U. Nov. 1989)**

Sol. : We will first calculate the increase in these members due to the rise in temperature.

$$\delta L_{DE} = L_{DE} \alpha t$$
$$= 2309 \times 11 \times 10^{-6} \times 20$$
$$= 0.508 \text{ mm}$$

δL_{EG} need not be calculated as K_V and K_H are zero for EG.

$$\delta L_{FG} = 2000 \times 11 \times 10^{-6} \times 20$$
$$= 0.44 \text{ mm}$$

Now, we will tabulate these results.

Sr. No.	Member	K_V (kN)	K_H (kN)	δL due to temperature rise (mm)	$K_V \delta L$	$K_H \delta L$
1	DE	2	0	+ 0.508	1.016	0
2	FG	− 1.732	+ 1	+ 0.44	− 0.762	+ 0.44
				Σ	0.2539	0.44

$$\delta_V = \frac{\Sigma K_V \delta L}{E} = \frac{0.2539}{200}$$
$$= 0.00127 \text{ mm}$$

$$\delta_H = \frac{\Sigma K_H \delta L}{E} = \frac{0.44}{200}$$
$$= 0.0022 \text{ mm}$$

Thus, δ_C (↓) will increase by 0.00127 mm and becomes (2.2854 + 0.00127) = 2.28667 mm.

δ_H (←) will change in opposite direction by 0.0022 mm and become (− 0.52 + 0.0022) = − 0.5178 (←) mm.

Problem 6.5 : A vertical tower is loaded as shown in Fig. 6.6. The areas of all vertical members are 8×10^{-4} m² and that of all horizontal members are 4×10^{-4} m². The area of all inclined members is 6×10^{-4} m². Calculate the vertical deflection of the point E. Take $E = 2 \times 10^8$ kPa. **(P.U. Nov. 1984)**

Solution : Reactions at hinged and roller end, zero members, directions of axial forces and magnitude of axial forces in terms of P are marked in the figure. Students should do it as an exercise. All vertical and horizontal members are 2 m long and all inclined members are $2\sqrt{2}$ m long. These results are tabulated to find the strain energy stored by the tower.

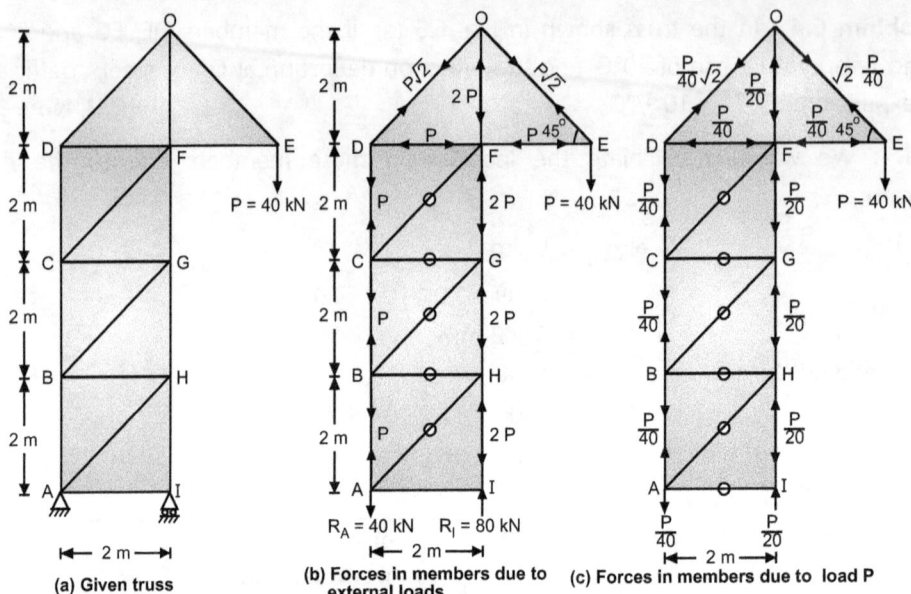

Fig. 6.6

(a) Given truss
(b) Forces in members due to external loads
(c) Forces in members due to load P

Sr. No.	Member	Force P (kN)	Length L (m)	Area (m²)	$\dfrac{P^2 L}{2A}$	K_V
1	AB	+ P	2.00	8 × 10⁻⁴	1250 P²	$+\dfrac{P}{40}$
2	BC	+ P	2.00	8 × 10⁻⁴	1250 P²	$+\dfrac{P}{40}$
3	CD	+ P	2.00	8 × 10⁻⁴	1250 P²	$+\dfrac{P}{40}$
4	IH	− 2P	2.00	8 × 10⁻⁴	5000 P²	$-\dfrac{P}{20}$
5	HG	− 2P	2.00	8 × 10⁻⁴	5000 P²	$-\dfrac{P}{20}$
6	GF	− 2P	2.00	8 × 10⁻⁴	5000 P²	$-\dfrac{P}{20}$
7	FO	− 2P	2.00	8 × 10⁻⁴	5000 P²	$-\dfrac{P}{20}$
8	DF	− P	2.00	4 × 10⁻⁴	2500 P²	$-\dfrac{P}{40}$
9	FE	− P	2.00	4 × 10⁻⁴	2500 P²	$-\dfrac{P}{40}$
10	DO	+ P√2	2√2	6 × 10⁻⁴	4714.05 P²	$+\dfrac{P}{40}\sqrt{2}$
11	EO	+ P√2	2√2	6 × 10⁻⁴	4714.05 P²	$+\dfrac{P}{40}\sqrt{2}$
				$\sum \dfrac{P^2 L}{2A}$	= 38178.05 P²	

$$\therefore \quad U = \frac{38178.10\, P^2}{2 \times 10^8}$$

$$\therefore \quad \delta_E (\downarrow) = \frac{\delta U}{\delta P} = \frac{2 \times 38178.10\, P}{2 \times 10^8}$$

$$= 3.8178 \times 10^{-4} \times 40$$

$$= 15.27 \text{ mm}$$

$$\text{Check} \quad -\sum \frac{K_V\, PL}{AE} = \frac{1}{2 \times 10^8}\left[3\left(\frac{P^2}{40} \times \frac{2}{8 \times 10^{-4}}\right) + 4\left(\frac{P^2}{10} \times \frac{2}{8 \times 10^{-4}}\right) \right.$$

$$\left. + 2\left(\frac{P^2}{40} \times \frac{2}{4 \times 10^{-4}}\right) + 2\left(\frac{P^2}{20} \times \frac{2\sqrt{2}}{6 \times 10^{-4}}\right)\right]$$

$$= \frac{P^2}{2 \times 10^8}[1908.9045]$$

$$= \frac{40 \times 40}{2 \times 10^8} \times 1908.9045 \times 1000 \text{ mm}$$

$$= 15.27 \text{ mm} \qquad \text{... (as before)}$$

Problem 6.6 : A tower is loaded as shown in Fig. 6.7 (a). The C.S. area of all vertical members is 16×10^{-4} m², of all horizontal members is 10×10^{-4} m², and all diagonal members is 12×10^{-4} mm². Calculate the horizontal and vertical deflection of D. Take $E = 2 \times 10^8$ kPa. **(P.U. May 1985)**

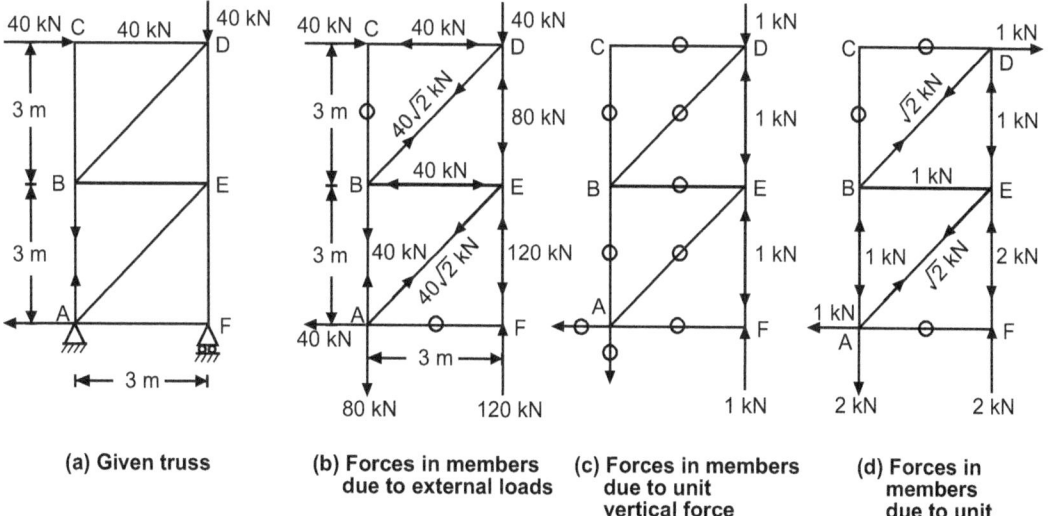

(a) Given truss (b) Forces in members due to external loads (c) Forces in members due to unit vertical force (d) Forces in members due to unit horizontal force

Fig. 6.7

Solution : In Fig. 6.7 (a), zero members are marked after inspection and the axial forces, magnitude and direction, are shown for each member. In Fig. 6.7 (b), a unit load (↓) is applied at D and the axial forces in the members are marked. In Fig. 6.7 (c), a unit horizontal force (→) is applied at D and the axial forces in the members are marked. All these results are tabulated below to find out the vertical and horizontal deflection at D.

Sr. No.	Member	Length L (m)	Area A (m²)	Force P (kN)	K_V (kN)	$\frac{PK_V L}{A}$	K_H (kN)	$\frac{PK_H L}{A}$
1	AB	3.0		40	0	0	1	75000
2	BC	30	16×10^{-4}	0	0	0	0	0
3	FE	3.0		–120	–1	$\frac{360 \times 10^4}{16}$	–2	450000
4	ED	3.0		–80	–1	$\frac{240 \times 10^4}{16}$	–1	150000
5	AF	3.0		0	0	0	0	0
6	BE	3.0	10×10^{-4}	–40	0	0	–1	120000
7	CD	3.0		–40	0	0	0	0
8	AE	$3\sqrt{2}$	12×10^{-4}	$40\sqrt{2}$	0	0	$\sqrt{2}$	282842.71
9	BD	$3\sqrt{2}$	10^{-4}	$40\sqrt{2}$	0	0	$\sqrt{2}$	282842.71
						$\sum \frac{PK_V L}{A} = \frac{600}{16} \times 10^4$		$\sum \frac{PK_H L}{A}$ = 1360685.4

$$\therefore \quad \delta_D (\downarrow) = \frac{\sum PK_V L/A}{E} = \frac{600 \times 10^4}{16 \times 2 \times 10^8} = 1.875 \times 10^{-3} \text{ m}$$
$$= 1.875 \text{ mm}$$

$$\delta_D (\rightarrow) = \frac{\sum \frac{PK_H L}{A}}{E} = \frac{1360685.4}{2 \times 10^8} = 6.803 \times 10^{-3} \text{ m}$$
$$= 6.803 \text{ mm}$$

Problem 6.7 : A framed structure is loaded as shown in Fig. 6.8 (a). Find the vertical deflection of the joint D if
  (a) Area of all horizontal members = 5×10^{-4} m²,
  (b) Area of all vertical members = 10^{-4} m²,
  (c) Area of all inclined members = 5.6×10^{-4} m² and
  (d) E = 2×10^8 kPa.

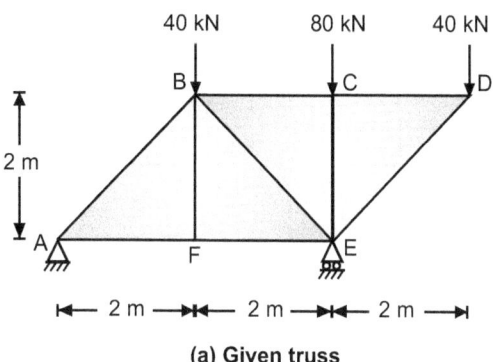

(a) Given truss

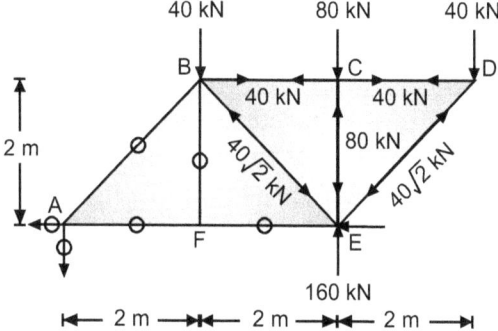

(b) Forces in members due to external loads

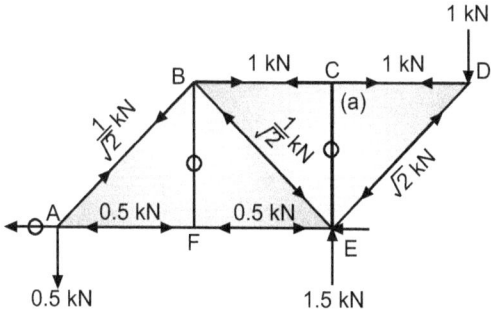

(c) Forces in members due to unit vertical load

Fig. 6.8

Solution : Consider Fig. 6.8 (b). Finding out the reactions and axial forces is left to the students. These values are marked on the figure. Consider Fig. 6.8 (c). A unit load (↓) is applied at the joint D. The axial forces due to the unit load at D are marked on this figure. These calculations are easy and be done mentally. These results are tabulated to find the vertical deflection at the joint D. While tabulating zero members are not considered with respect to Fig. 6.8 (b) and (c).

Sr. No.	Member	Force P (kN)	L (m)	A (m²)	K_V	$K_V \dfrac{PL}{A}$
1	BC	40	2.0	5×10^{-4}	1	16×10^4
2	CD	40	2.0	5×10^{-4}	1	16×10^4
3	EB	$-40\sqrt{2}$	$2\sqrt{2}$	5.6×10^{-4}	$-\dfrac{1}{\sqrt{2}}$	20.20×10^4
4	ED	$40\sqrt{2}$	$2\sqrt{2}$	5.6×10^{-4}	$-\sqrt{2}$	40.41×10^4
					$\sum \dfrac{K_V PL}{A} =$	92.61×10^4

$$\therefore \quad \delta_D (\downarrow) = \dfrac{\sum (K_V PL)/A}{E}$$

$$= \dfrac{92.61 \times 10^4}{2 \times 10^8} = 4.63 \times 10^{-3} \text{ m} = 4.63 \text{ mm}$$

Problem 6.8 : A cantilever truss is loaded as shown in Fig. 6.9 (a). Calculate the vertical deflection of the joint at E. The C.S. areas of members are :

AB : 20×10^{-4} m²,
BC, CD and DE : 10×10^{-4} m²
CE and BF : 10×10^{-4} m²
EF, FG and BE : 12×10^{-4} m²
BG : 16×10^{-4} m²

Take $E = 2 \times 10^8$ kPa

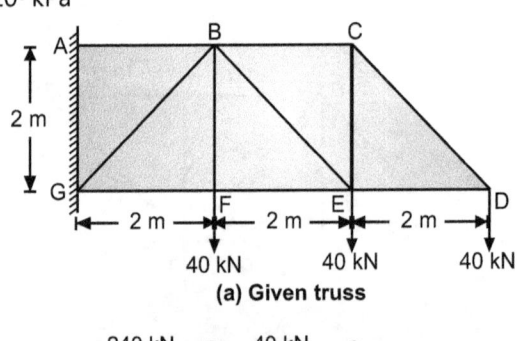

(a) Given truss

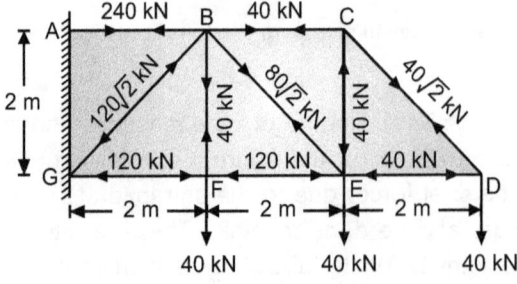

(b) Forces in members due to external loads

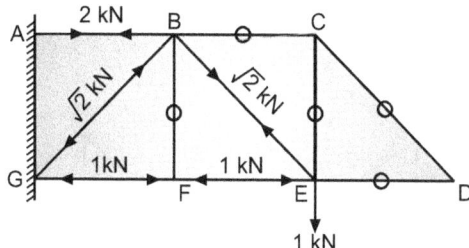

(c) Forces in members due to unit vertical force

Fig. 6.9

Solution : The axial forces in all the members due to given load system are marked in Fig. 6.9 (b). As the vertical deflection of the cantilever at joint E is required a unit force; 1 kN (↓) is applied at E and all the axial forces are marked in Fig. 6.9 (c). The determination of forces in all members is left to the students as it is easy. These results are tabulated to find the required deflection at joint E. Zero members in (b) and (c) are not considered.

Sr. No.	Member	L (m)	A (m²)	P (kN)	K_V (kN)	$K_V \dfrac{PL}{A}$
1	AB	2.0	20×10^{-4}	240	+ 2	48×10^4
2	GF	2.0	12×10^{-4}	– 120	– 1	20×10^4
3	FE	2.0	12×10^{-4}	– 120	– 1	20×10^4
4	BG	$2\sqrt{2}$	16×10^{-4}	$-120\sqrt{2}$	$-\sqrt{2}$	42.426×10^4
5	BE	$2\sqrt{2}$	12×10^{-4}	$80\sqrt{2}$	$+\sqrt{2}$	37.712×10^4
					$\sum K_V \dfrac{PL}{A}$ =	168.138×10^4

$$\delta_E (\downarrow) = \dfrac{\sum \dfrac{K_V PL}{A}}{E} = \dfrac{168.138 \times 10^4}{2 \times 10^8} = 8.407 \times 10^{-3}\,m = 8.407\,mm$$

Problem 6.9 : A truss consisting of two equivalent triangles is loaded as shown in Fig. 6.10 (a). Determine the vertical deflection of the joint C and the horizontal movement of the roller at D. The length of each member is 3 m. The C.S. areas of all ties are 300 mm² each and that of all struts are 600 mm² each. Take E = 200 GPa.　　　　　　　　**(P.U. May 1987)**

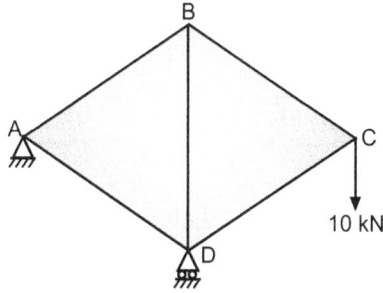

(a) Given truss

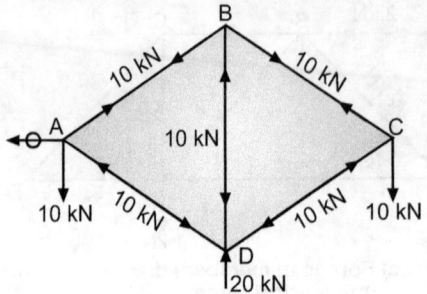

(b) Forces in members due to external loads

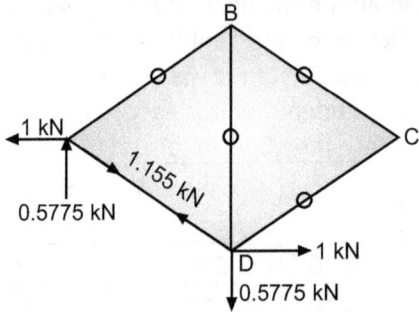

(c) Forces in members due to unit vertical force

Fig. 6.10

Solution : The axial force in each member due to given loading is shown in Fig. 6.10 (b). When we apply a load of 1 kN (↓) at C to determine δ_C (↓), the axial force in each member will be reduced to its $\frac{1}{10}$th of the original value. To determine the horizontal moment at the roller end, we apply 1 kN (→) at D. The axial force in each member due to unit load at D (→) is shown in Fig. 6.10 (c). These results are now tabulated.

Sr. No.	Member	L(m)	A (m²)	P (kN)	K_V	$\frac{PK_VL}{A}$	K_H	$\frac{PK_HL}{A}$
1	AB	3	3 × 10⁻⁴	10	1	10⁵	0	0
2	BC	3	3 × 10⁻⁴	10	1	10⁵	0	0
3	CD	3	6 × 10⁻⁴	−10	−1	5 × 10⁴	0	0
4	DA	3	6 × 10⁻⁴	−10	−1	5 × 10⁴	1.155	−57750
5	BD	3	6 × 10⁻⁴	−10	−1	5 × 10⁴	0	0
					$\sum \frac{PK_VL}{A} = 35 \times 10^4$			

$$\delta_C (\downarrow) = \frac{\frac{PK_VL}{A}}{E} = \frac{35 \times 10^4}{2 \times 10^8 \text{ (kN/m}^2\text{)}} = 1.75 \times 10^{-3} \text{ m} = 1.75 \text{ mm}$$

Alternative method :

If P = 10 kN

U = Strain energy of the structure

$$= \sum \frac{P^2 L}{2AE} = \frac{1}{2E}\left[2(10^4 P^2) + 3\left(10^4 \frac{P^2}{2}\right)\right]$$

$$= \frac{1}{2E}(35000) P^2$$

$$\therefore \quad \delta_C (\downarrow) = \frac{\partial U}{\partial P} = \frac{2 \times 35000 \times P}{2 \times E}$$

$$= \frac{35000 \times 10}{2 \times 10^8} = 1.75 \times 10^{-3} \text{ m}$$

$$= 1.75 \text{ mm} \qquad \text{... (as before)}$$

$$\delta_D (\rightarrow) = \frac{\sum \frac{PK_H L}{A}}{E}$$

$$\delta_{D(H)} = \frac{-57750}{2 \times 10^8} = -2.89 \times 10^{-4} \text{ m}$$

$$= 0.289 \text{ mm} (\leftarrow)$$

Problem 6.10 : A steel truss as shown in Fig. 6.11 (a) is anchored at the end A and is supported on rollers at the end B. All tension members are stressed to 100 MPa while all compression members are stressed to 80 MPa. Find the vertical deflection of the point C. Take E = 200 GPa. **(P.U. Nov. 1987)**

Solution : The forces due to given load system are marked near each member of the truss in Fig. 6.11 (b). In this problem, magnitudes of forces are not required as the stresses are given. In Fig. 6.11 (c), a unit load, 1 kN (↓) is applied at C and all forces are marked near the members. The result is now tabulated. Zero members are not considered.

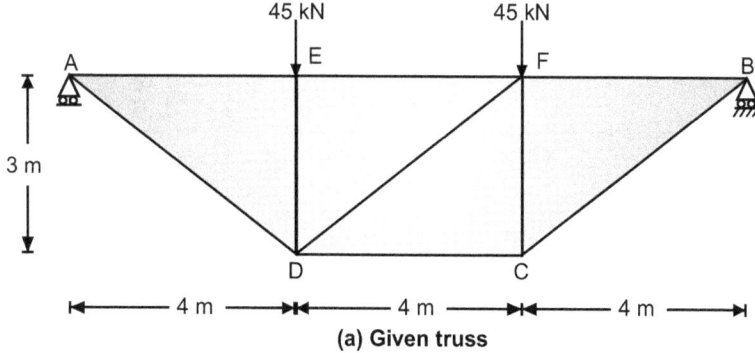

(a) Given truss

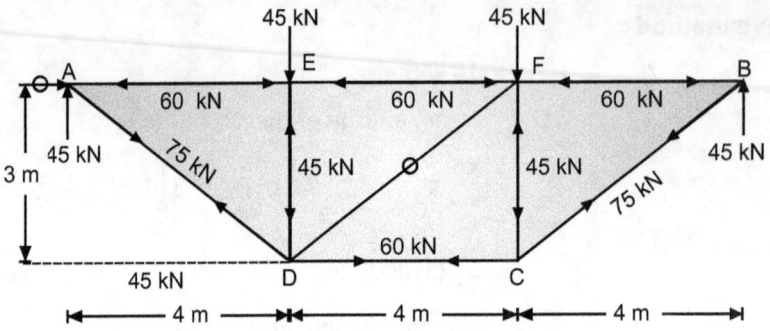

(b) Forces in members due to external loads

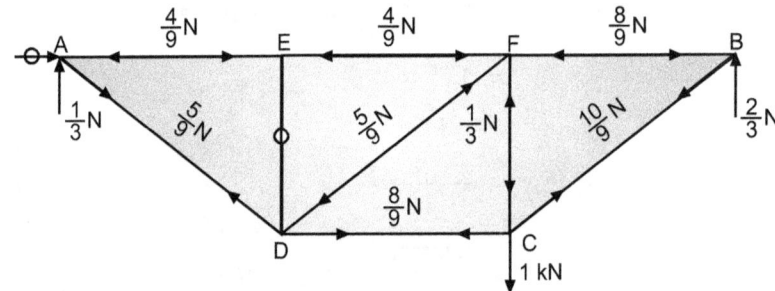

(c) Forces in members due to unit loads

Fig. 6.11

Sr. No.	Member	L (mm)	Stress MPa (σ)	K_V (N)	$K_V \sigma L$
1	AE	4000	− 80	$-\dfrac{4}{9}$	14.22×10^4
2	EF	4000	− 80	$-\dfrac{4}{9}$	14.22×10^4
3	FB	4000	− 80	$-\dfrac{8}{9}$	28.44×10^4
4	CD	4000	100	$\dfrac{8}{9}$	35.56×10^4
5	AD	5000	100	$\dfrac{5}{9}$	27.78×10^4
6	CF	3000	− 80	$\dfrac{1}{3}$	$- 8 \times 10^4$
7	CB	5000	100	$\dfrac{10}{9}$	55.56×10^4
				$\sum K_V \sigma L =$	167.78×10^4

$$\delta_C(\downarrow) = \frac{\Sigma K_V \sigma L}{E}$$

$$= \frac{(167.78 \times 10^4)}{200 \times 10^3} = 8.389 \text{ mm}$$

Problem 6.11 : Determine the vertical and horizontal deflection components of the joint C of the truss shown in Fig. 6.12 (a). E = 200 GPa, A = 10^{-4} m² for all members.

(P.U. May 1988)

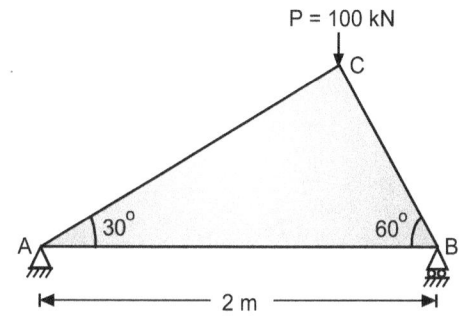

(a) Given truss

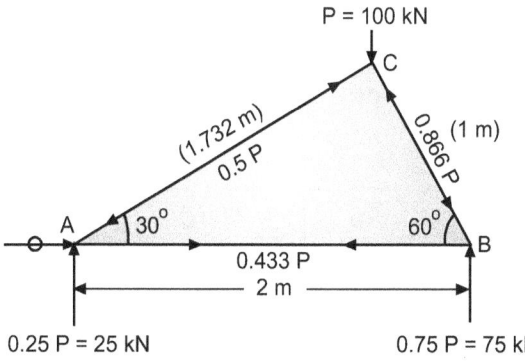

(b) Forces in members due to external loads

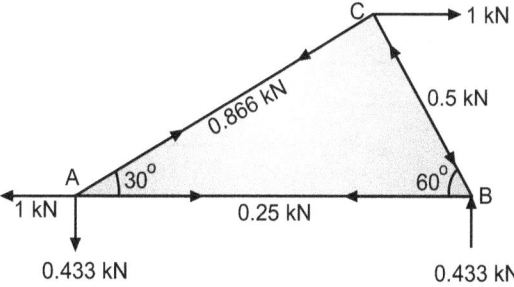

(c) Forces in members due to unit loads

Fig. 6.12

Solution : The forces and lengths are marked in Fig. 6.12 (a). They are tabulated below.

Sr. No.	Member	L (m)	P²	P²L
1	AB	2.0	0.1875 P²	0.375 P²
2	BC	1.0	0.75 P²	0.750 P²
3	CA	1.732	0.25 P²	0.433 P²
				$\sum P^2L = 1.558\ P^2$

$$U = \frac{\sum P^2 L}{2AE}$$

$$= \frac{1.558\ P^2}{2 \times 10^{-4} \times 2 \times 10^8}$$

$\therefore\quad \delta_C (\downarrow) = \dfrac{\partial U}{\partial P}$

$$= \frac{1.558\ P \times 10^4}{2 \times 10^8}$$

$$= \frac{1.558 \times 100 \times 10^4}{2 \times 10^8}$$

$$= 7.79 \times 10^{-3}\ m$$

$$= 7.79\ mm$$

Second method : When a unit force of 1 kN ($\downarrow$) is applied at C, all axial forces i.e. K_V will be $\dfrac{1}{100}$ times the existing forces.

Sr. No.	Member	L (m)	P (kN)	K_V (kN)	K_V PL
1	AB	2.0	0.433 P	$0.433 \dfrac{P}{100}$	$3.75 \times 10^{-3}\ P^2$
2	BC	1.0	– 0.866 P	$-0.866 \dfrac{P}{100}$	$0.75 \times 10^{-2}\ P^2$
3	CA	1.732	– 0.50 P	$-0.5 \dfrac{P}{100}$	$0.433 \times 10^{-2}\ P^2$
					$\sum K_V PL = 1.558 \times 10^{-2}\ P^2$

$\therefore\quad \delta_C (\downarrow) = \dfrac{\sum K_V PL}{AE} = \dfrac{1.558 \times 10^{-2} \times 10^4}{10^{-4} \times 2 \times 10^8}$

$$= 0.779 \times 10^{-2}\ m$$

$$= 7.79\ mm \qquad\qquad \text{... (as before)}$$

Now we will find the horizontal deflection of C. For this purpose, we apply a unit load, 1 kN ($\rightarrow$) at C. The reactions and the forces are marked in Fig. 6.12 (b) and the result is tabulated.

Sr. No.	Member	L (m)	P (kN)	K_H (kN)	K_H PL
1	AB	2.0	+ 43.3	+ 0.25	21.65
2	BC	1.0	– 86.6	– 0.5	43.30
3	CA	1.732	– 50	+ 0.866	– 75.00
					$\Sigma K_H PL = -10.05$

$$\therefore \quad \delta_C (\rightarrow) = \frac{\Sigma K_H PL}{AE}$$

$$= \frac{-10.05 \times 10^4}{2 \times 10^8} = -5.025 \times 10^{-4} \text{ m}$$

$$= 0.5025 \text{ mm} (\leftarrow)$$

Problem 6.12 : Find the vertical deflection of the joint B and the displacement of the roller support D for the truss shown in Fig. 6.13 (a). The area of C.S. of all members is 100 mm² and E = 200 GPa. **(P.U. May 1989)**

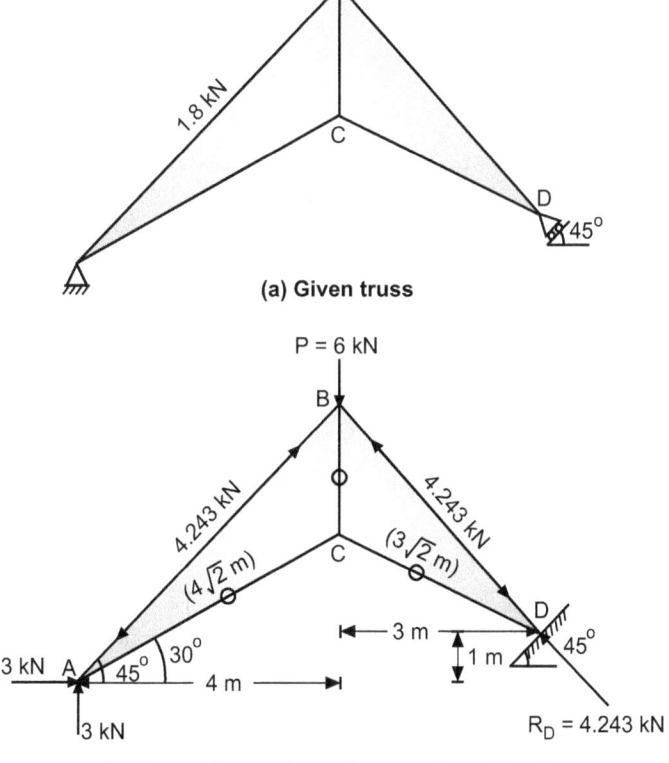

(a) Given truss

(b) Forces in members due to external loads

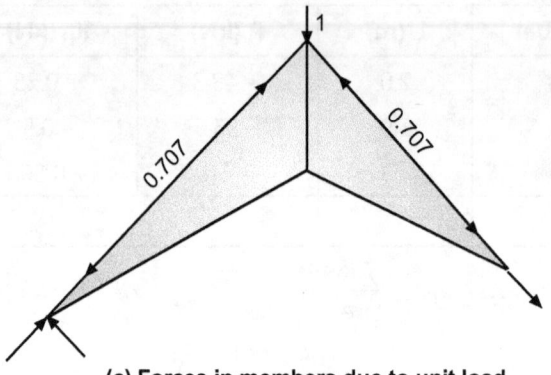

(c) Forces in members due to unit load

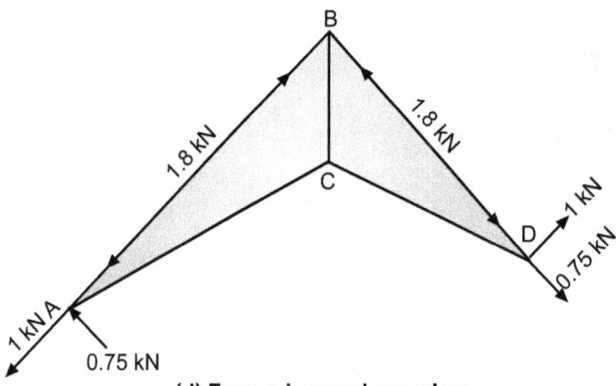

(d) Forces in members when unit load is applied at B

Fig. 6.13

Solution : Taking moments of forces @ A,

$$P \times 4 = R_D 4\sqrt{2}$$

$$\therefore \quad R_D = \frac{P}{\sqrt{2}} = \frac{6}{\sqrt{2}} = 4.243 \text{ kN} = 3\sqrt{2} \text{ kN}$$

The lengths of the members and the axial forces are marked in Fig. 6.13 (b). The results are tabulated below :

Sr. No.	Member	L (m)	P (kN)	K_V	K_V PL
1	AB	$4\sqrt{2}$	$-3\sqrt{2}$	$-\dfrac{1}{\sqrt{2}}$	$12\sqrt{2}$
2	BD	$3\sqrt{2}$	$-3\sqrt{2}$	$-\dfrac{1}{\sqrt{2}}$	$9\sqrt{2}$
					$\Sigma K_V \text{ PL} = 21\sqrt{2}$

S. E. CIVIL : STRUCTURAL ANALYSIS - I   6.23   DEFLECTION OF TRUSSES

$$\therefore \quad \delta_B (\downarrow) = \frac{\Sigma K_V PL}{AE} = \frac{21\sqrt{2}}{10^{-4} \times 2 \times 10^8}$$

$$= 1.48 \times 10^{-3} \text{ m}$$

$$= 1.48 \text{ mm}$$

Alternate method :

$$\Sigma P^2 L = \left(\frac{P}{\sqrt{2}}\right)^2 4\sqrt{2} + \left(\frac{P}{\sqrt{2}}\right)^2 3\sqrt{2}$$

$$= P^2 \times 2\sqrt{2} + P^2 \times 1.5\sqrt{2} = (P^2 \sqrt{2})(3.5)$$

$$U = \frac{\Sigma P^2 L}{2AE} = \frac{\sqrt{2} \times 3.5 \, P^2}{2 \times 10^{-4} \times 2 \times 10^8}$$

$$= 1.2375 \, P^2 \times 10^{-4}$$

$$\delta_B (\downarrow) = \frac{\partial U}{\partial P} = 2P \times 1.2375 \times 10^{-4} = 2 \times 6 \times 1.2375 \times 10^{-4}$$

$$= 1.48 \times 10^{-3} \text{ m}$$

$$= 1.48 \text{ mm} \quad \text{... (as before)}$$

Deflection of the roller end D : It will be along the inclined plane. Apply a unit force of 1 kN along the plane as shown in Fig. 6.13 (c). The axial forces in non-zero members AB and BD due to unit force of 1 kN at D are shown near the members. The result is tabulated below :

Sr. No.	Member	L (m)	P (kN)	K (kN)	KPL
1	AB	$4\sqrt{2}$	$-3\sqrt{2}$	-1.8	43.2
2	BD	$3\sqrt{2}$	$-3\sqrt{2}$	-1.8	32.4
					Σ KPL = 75.6

$$\therefore \quad \delta_D \text{ along the plane } = \frac{\Sigma KPL}{AE} = \frac{75.6}{10^{-4} \times 2 \times 10^8}$$

$$= 37.8 \times 10^{-4} \text{ m}$$

$$= 3.78 \text{ m}$$

Problem 6.13 : For the truss shown in Fig. 6.14 (a) find the vertical deflection of point D. The cross-sectional areas of members are :

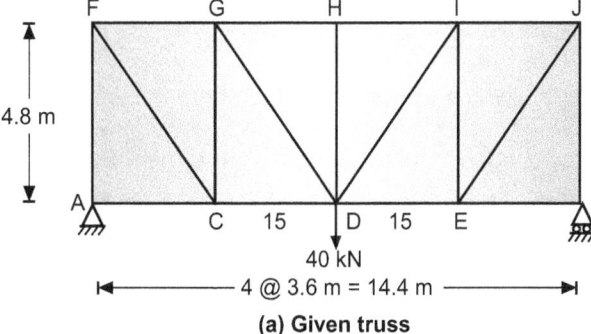

(a) Given truss

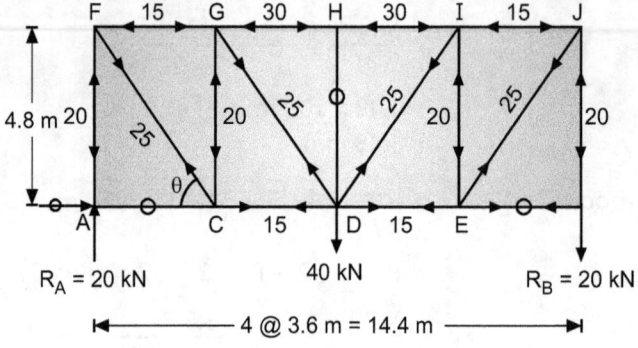

(b) Forces in members due to external loads

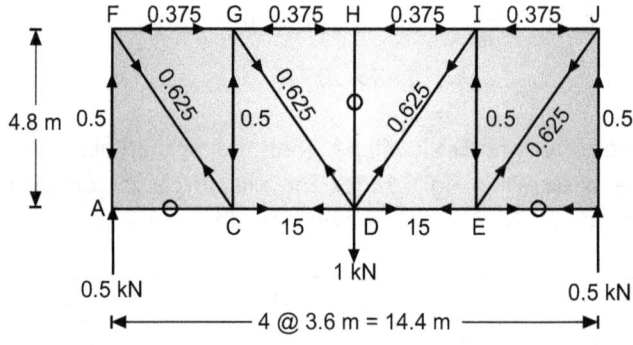

(c) Forces in members due to unit loads

Fig. 6.14

(i) Top chord and vertical members = 1875 mm².

(ii) Lower chord and diagonals = 1250 mm².

Take E = 200 GPa. Calculate the rise in the temperature of upper chords only to have no deflection at D. Take $\alpha = 12 \times 10^{-6}/°C$.

Solution : The angle θ which the diagonal members make with horizontal is $\tan^{-1}\frac{4}{3}$, so that sin θ = 0.8 and cos θ = 0.60. The axial force in the member is written near it. The truss and loading are symmetrical, hence only half the truss may be used to find the required deflection of D. The results are tabulated below. The value of K_V for each member will be $\frac{1}{40}^{th}$ times the value of the axial force. Zero members are not considered in the tabulation.

Sr. No.	Member	L (m)	A (m²)	P (kN)	$K_v = \dfrac{P}{40}$	$\dfrac{PK_vL}{A}$ (kN.m)
1	AF	4.8	18.75 × 10⁻⁴	− 20	− 0.5	25600
2	CG	4.8	"	− 20	− 0.5	25600
3	FG	3.6	"	− 15	− 0.375	10800
4	GH	3.6	"	− 30	− 0.75	43200
5	CD	3.6	12.5 × 10⁻⁴	+ 15	0.375	16200
6	FC	6.0	"	+ 25	0.625	75000
7	GD	6.0	"	+ 25	0.625	75000
					$\sum \dfrac{PK_vL}{A}$	= 271400

$\therefore \quad \delta_D (\downarrow) = \left(\dfrac{\sum PK_vL}{AE}\right) \times 2$

$= \dfrac{271400}{2 \times 10^8} \times 2$

$= 2.714 \times 10^{-3}$ m

$= 2.714$ mm

Problem 6.14 : In the pin-joint plane truss shown in Fig. 6.15 (a), determine the vertical displacement of joint E. The axial flexibility of all members is 0.255 mm/kN. Axial flexibility = L/AE.

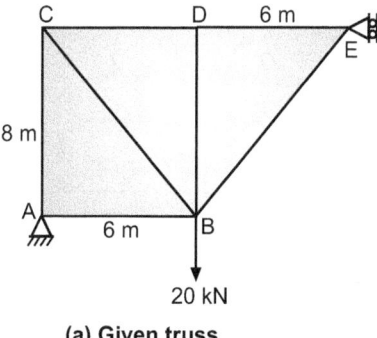

(a) Given truss

Solution : Forces in members :

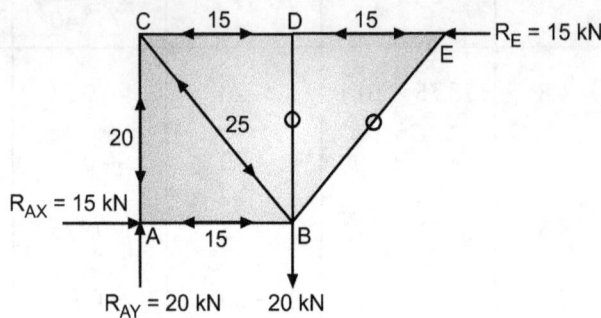

(b) Force in members due to external loads

Applying unit vertical load at point E,

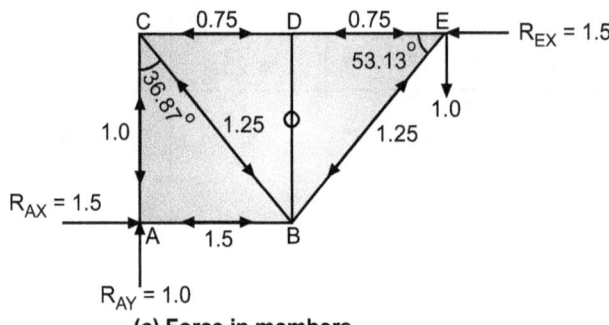

(c) Force in members due to unit load

Fig. 6.15

Member	P	K	PK
AB	15	1.5	22.5
BC	−25	−1.25	31.25
AC	20	1	20
CD	15	0.75	11.25
BD	0	0	0
DE	15	0.75	11.25
BE	0	1.25	0
		Σ PK = 96.25	

$\delta_E = \Sigma(PKL/AE) = 96.25 \times 0.25$ mm = 24.06 mm

$\therefore$ Vertical displacement at E = 24.06 mm

Problem 6.15 : For the truss shown in Fig. 6.16 (a), find the vertical deflection at B.

(May 2001)

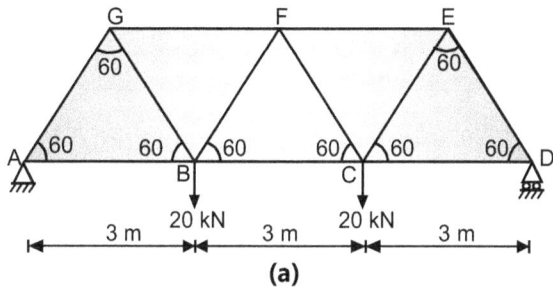

Solution : Sign convention : Tensile (–ve) and compression (+ve).

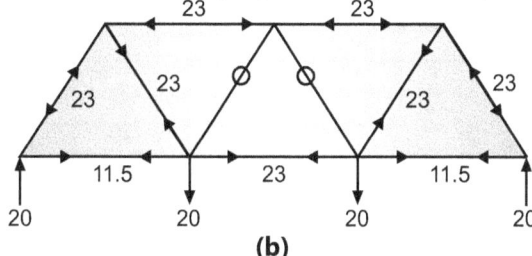

Applying unit load at B,

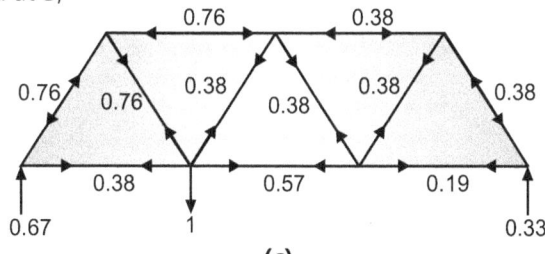

(c)
Fig. 6.16

Member	P	K	PK
AB	–11.5	–0.38	4.37
BC	–23	–0.57	13.11
CD	–11.5	–0.19	2.185
DE	23	0.38	8.74
EF	23	0.38	8.74
FG	23	0.76	17.48
GA	23	0.76	17.48
GB	–23	–0.76	17.48
FB	0	–0.38	0
FC	0	0.38	0
EC	–23	–0.38	8.74
		$\sum$ PK =	98.325

Vertical deflection at B = $\sum \dfrac{PKL}{AE}$

$= \dfrac{98.325 \times 3}{AE} = \dfrac{294.98}{AE}$

Problem 6.16 : The simply supported warren truss shown in Fig. 6.17 has each member of length 4 m. Each member is stressed to 80 MPa, when a vertical load of 100 kN is applied at A. Calculate the deflection at A when a vertical load of 100 kN is applied at B. E = 200 GPa.

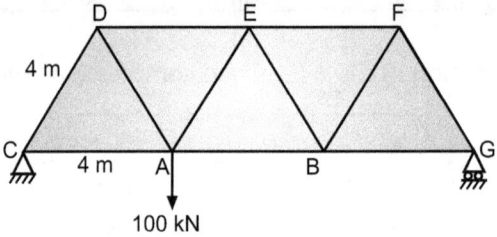

Fig. 6.17 (a) : Given truss

Solution : M @ C = 0.

∴ $100 \times 4 - R_G \times 12 = 0$

$R_G = 33.33$ kN and $R_C = 66.67$ kN

Consider joint G :

$\sum F_y = 0$

$-F_{GF} \sin 60 + 33.33 = 0$

∴ $F_{GF} = 38.49$ kN

∴ $F_{GB} = 19.24$ kN

Joint F :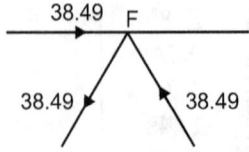

Joint B :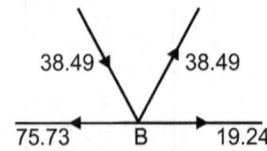

Joint E :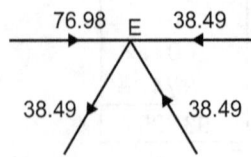

Joint D :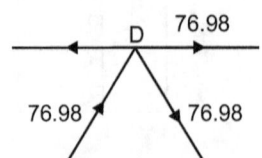

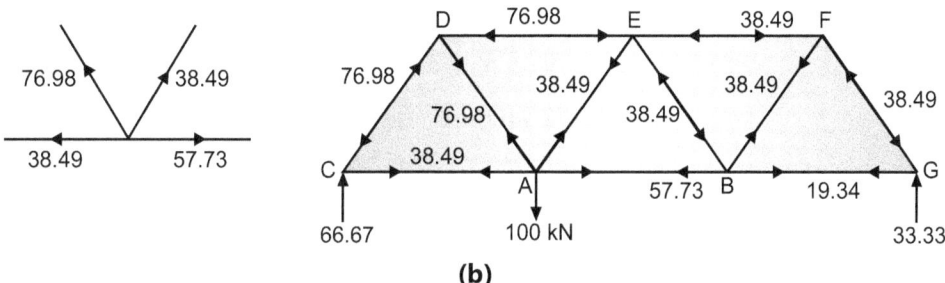

Member	Force due to load at A (kN)	Area	Force due to load at B (kN)	k	Pk/A
CD	76.98	962.25	−38.49	−0.3849	15.39
DE	76.98	962.25	−38.49	−0.3849	15.39
DA	76.98	962.25	38.49	0.3849	15.39
AE	38.49	481.125	−38.49	−0.3849	30.78
AB	57.73	721.625	57.73	0.5773	46.18
BE	38.49	481.125	38.49	0.3849	30.78
BF	38.49	481.125	76.98	0.7698	140.72
BG	19.38	240.562	38.49	0.3849	61.58
FG	38.49	481.125	−76.98	−0.7698	140.72
CA	38.49	481.125	19.24	0.1924	7.69
EF	38.49	481.125	−76.98	−0.7698	140.72
				$\sum \dfrac{Pk}{A}$ = 645.34	

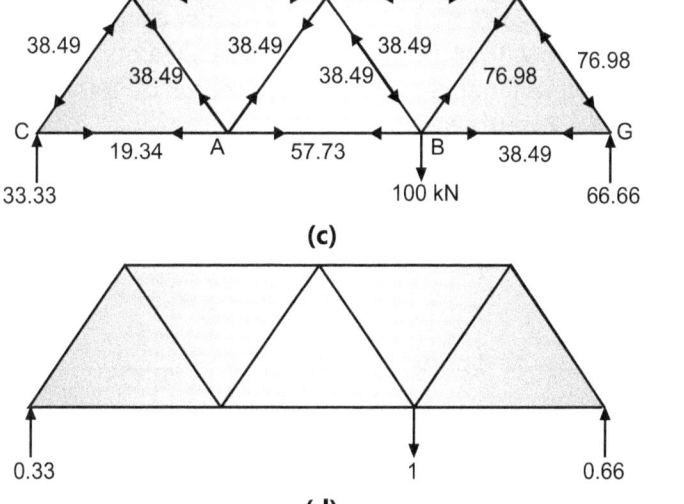

Fig. 6.17

$$\delta_B = \frac{Pkl}{AE} = \frac{645.34 \times 4000}{200 \times 10^3}$$

$$= 12.9 \text{ mm}$$

EXERCISE

1. A jib and crane mechanism is shown in Fig. 6.18. The jib, 7.5 m long has a C.S. area of 1500 mm². The horizontal tie, 6 m long, has a C.S. area of 1000 mm². Calculate the vertical and horizontal deflection of the crane head C for a load 50 kN suspended from it. Take E = 200 GPa.

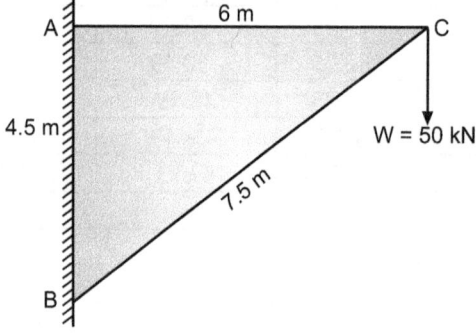

Fig. 6.18

(**Ans.** $\delta C (\downarrow)$ = 6.385 mm, $\delta C (\rightarrow)$ = 2.0 mm)

2. A pratt truss shown in Fig. 6.19 has four bays of 5 m each. The height of the truss is 5 m. It carries a load of 100 kN at each lower joint. All the lower chord members have a C.S. area of 2500 mm² each while all upper chord members have a C.S. area of 4000 mm² each. All verticals have a sectional area of 2000 mm² each and all the diagonals are of 4250 mm² area each. Calculate the central vertical deflection of the joint C. Take E = 2 × 10⁸ kPa.

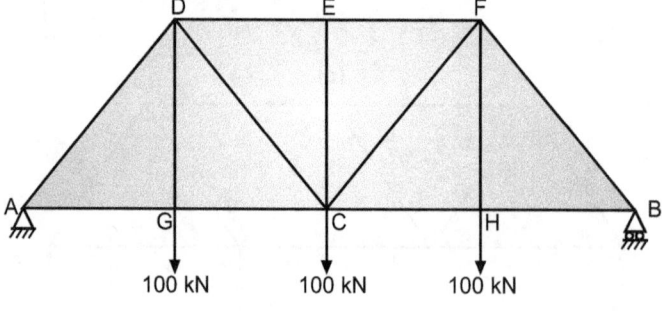

Fig. 6.19

(**Ans.** $\delta_C (\downarrow)$ = 8.835 mm)

3. A truss as shown in Fig. 6.20 carries equal load W at each lower joint. All the compression members are stressed to 80 MPa while all tensile members are stressed to 120 MPa. Each bay is 6 m long and 8 m high. Calculate the central deflection. Take E = 210 GPa.

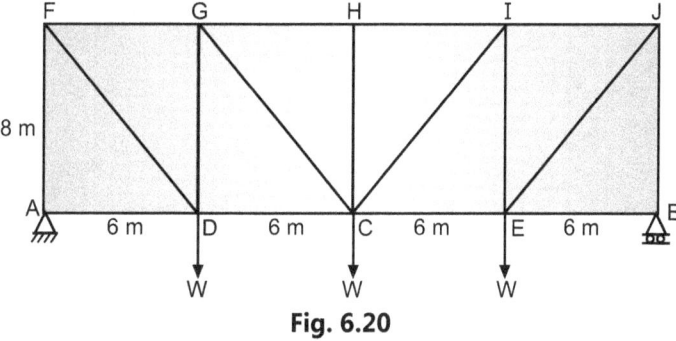

Fig. 6.20

(**Ans.** 28.10 mm)

4. A cantilever truss shown in Fig. 6.21 is so loaded that the compression members are stressed to 100 MPa while the tension members are stressed to 150 MPa. The panels are 2.5 m each and the inclination of the diagonal to the horizontal is 45°. Calculate the vertical and horizontal deflection of the free end D. Take E = 200 GPa.

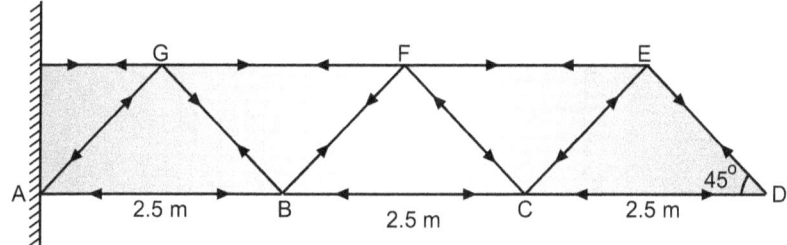

Fig. 6.21

(**Ans.** δ_D ($\downarrow$) = 37.5 mm, δ_D ($\leftarrow$) = 3.75 mm)

5. A warren girder of 12 m span is built up of three equilateral triangles of sides 4 m each as shown in Fig. 6.22. It carries equal loads at the lower joints. The ties and struts are stressed to 96 MPa and 80 MPa respectively. Calculate the vertical deflection under each load. Take E = 210 GPa.

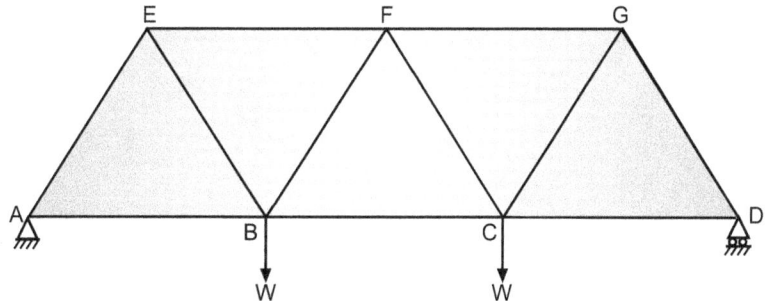

Fig. 6.22

(**Ans.** δ_B = δ_C = 7.74 mm ($\downarrow$))

6. A frame shown in Fig. 6.23 is hinged at A and is supported on rollers at B. It carries a central load of 150 kN. All the members are 1250 mm² in C.S. area. Find the horizontal displacement of the roller end B. Take E = 200 GPa.

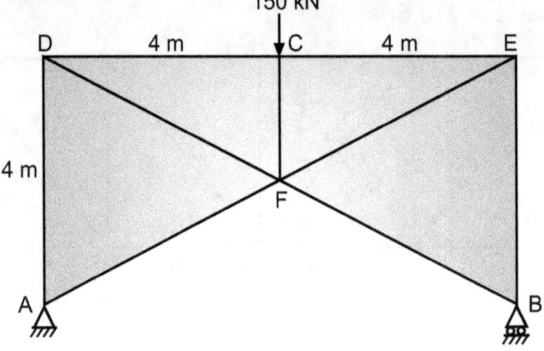

Fig. 6.23

(**Ans.** δ_D = 12.71 mm ($\rightarrow$))

7. A cantilever truss shown in Fig. 6.24 is so loaded at the joints B and C that all struts are stressed to 60 MPa while all ties are stressed to 100 MPa. If the joint E, supporting the horizontal tie ED yields by 3 mm, calculate the vertical deflection of the joint C. Take E = 200 GPa.

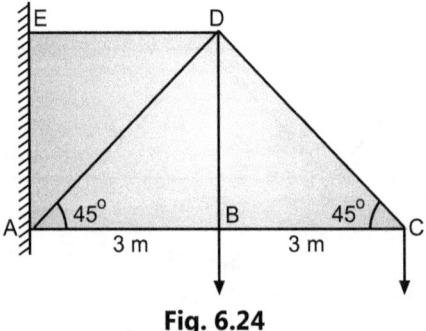

Fig. 6.24

(**Ans.** δ_C = 15.60 mm ($\downarrow$))

8. Determine the vertical and horizontal displacement of the joint C of the frame shown in Fig. 6.25. The C.S. area of AB is 500 mm² and that of AC and BC are 750 mm². E = 200 GPa.

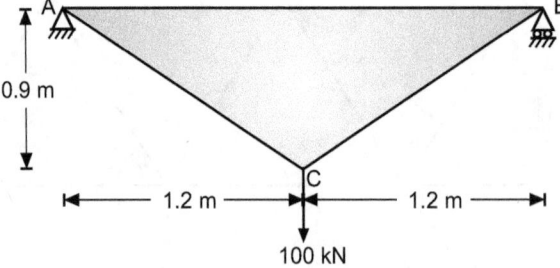

Fig. 6.25   (**Ans.** 2.455 mm, – 0.80 mm)

9. The pin jointed cantilever truss shown in Fig. 6.26 carries loads of 120 kN at D and F. The C.S. area of each member in mm² is marked near it. If E = 200 GPa, find the vertical displacement at D.

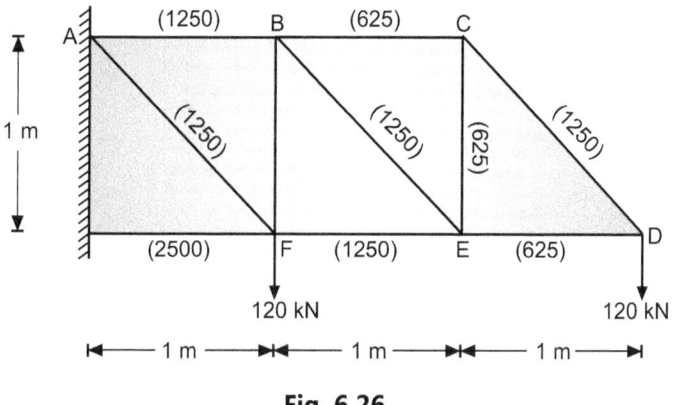

Fig. 6.26

(**Ans.** δ_D = 15.99 mm)

10. A truss as shown in Fig. 6.27 is so designed that under the given loading the ties are stressed to 83.33 MPa and the struts are stressed to 66.67 MPa. Find the vertical deflection of the point C if E = 200 GPa. Find also the lateral deflection of the end B.

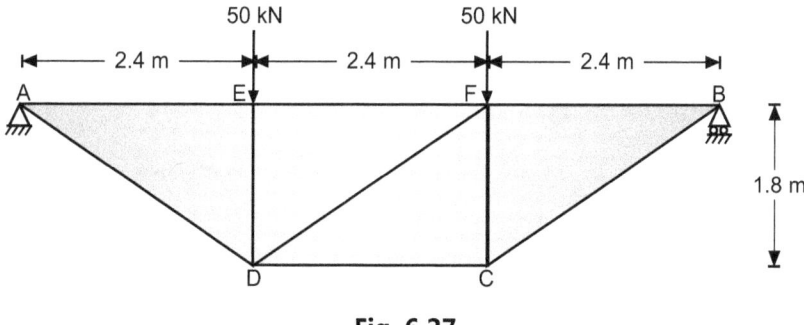

Fig. 6.27

(**Ans.** 4.17 mm, – 2.4 mm)

11. Calculate the deflection of the point C of the deck girder shown in Fig. 6.28, due to loads of 100 kN, each acting on the upper panel points. Figures against the various members represent their cross-sectional areas in mm². Take E = 200 GPa. If there is a uniform rise of temperature in all the members equal to 25°C above the temperature at which the truss was erected, calculate the vertical movements of the point C. Take α = 12 × 10⁻⁶/°C.

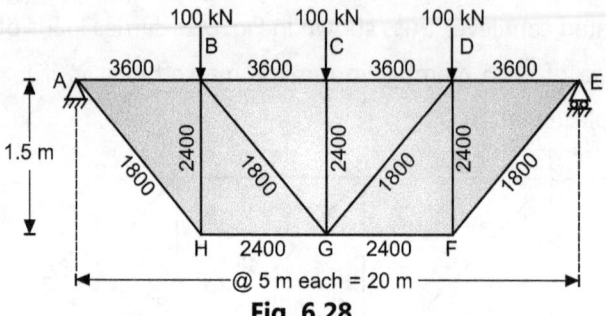

Fig. 6.28

(**Ans.** 15.85, 0.75 mm)

12. Find the horizontal and vertical deflections of the point F of the frame shown in Fig. 6.29. The vertical load at E is such that the tension and compression members are stressed to 100 MPa and 50 MPa respectively. E = 210 GPa.

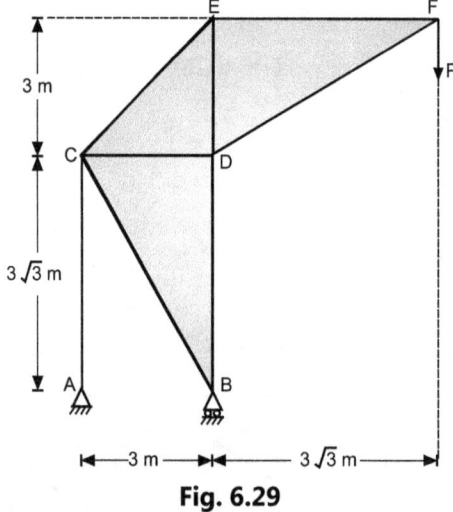

Fig. 6.29

(**Ans.** δ_V = 22.23 mm, δ_H = 14.04 mm)

13. The simply supported Warren truss shown in Fig. 6.30 has each member of length 4 m. Each member is stressed to 80 MPa when a load of 100 kN is applied vertically at A. Calculate the vertical deflection at A when 100 kN load is applied vertically at B. Take E = 200 GPa.

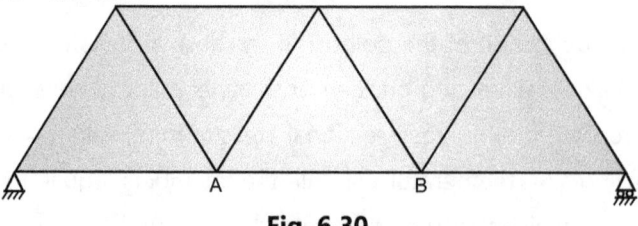

Fig. 6.30

(**Ans.** 6.16 mm)

Chapter 7
INDETERMINATE TRUSSES

7.1 INTRODUCTION

A plane truss is a skeletal structure consisting of number of prismatic members, all lying in one plane and hinged together at their ends in such a manner as to form a rigid i.e. stable configuration.

The analysis of trusses is simplified by considering the truss as ideal with the following assumptions :
1. The members are connected together at their ends by frictionless pin joints though the joints are riveted or welded.
2. Loads and reactions are acting only at joints and in the plane of truss.
3. The centroidal axis of each member is straight and coincides with the line connecting the centres of joints at each end of the member.
4. The members are subjected to only axial forces, though there may be bending moment and shear force as secondary effects.
5. The members remain straight even after the deformation.
6. A member undergoes either elongation or contraction.
7. The displacement of a joint of a truss is specified by the horizontal and vertical translations only.

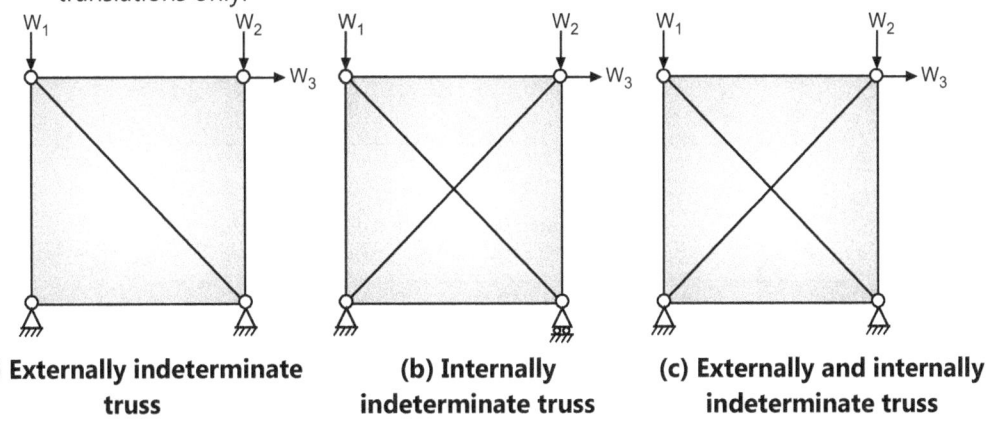

(a) Externally indeterminate truss (b) Internally indeterminate truss (c) Externally and internally indeterminate truss

Fig. 7.1 : Statically indeterminate trusses

The analysis of a truss mainly includes the determination of the axial forces in all members of the truss. Trusses may be statically indeterminate externally and/or internally. If the total number of reaction components is more than three, then the truss will be indeterminate externally as shown in Fig. 7.1 (a) and the degree of external indeterminacy is given by $(r - 3)$ where, r is the number of reaction components. If the total number of members of a truss is more than that required for stable configuration, the truss will be indeterminate internally as shown in Fig. 7.1 (b) and the degree of internal indeterminacy is given by [m – (2j – 3)] for a simply supported truss and [m – 2j] for a cantilever truss, where m is the number of members and j is the number of joints. Fig. 7.1 (c) shows a truss, indeterminate externally as well as internally. Statically indeterminate trusses are analysed by (i) force or flexibility method, (ii) displacement or stiffness method and (iii) energy method.

7.2 FORCE METHOD FOR ANALYSIS OF INDETERMINATE TRUSSES

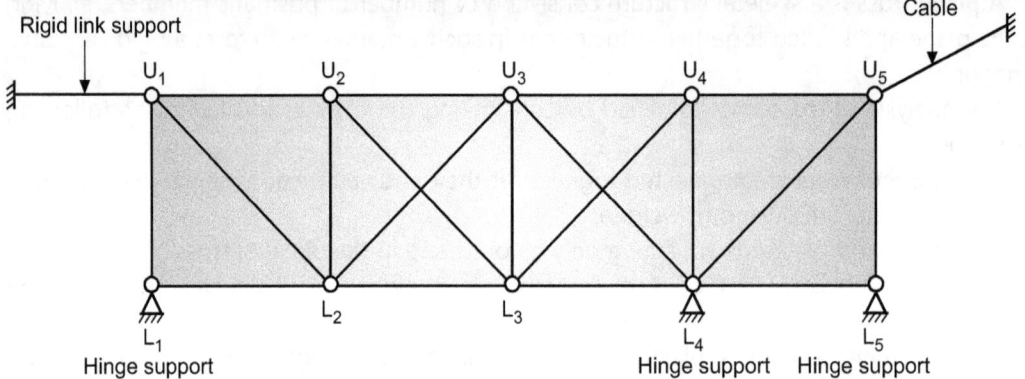

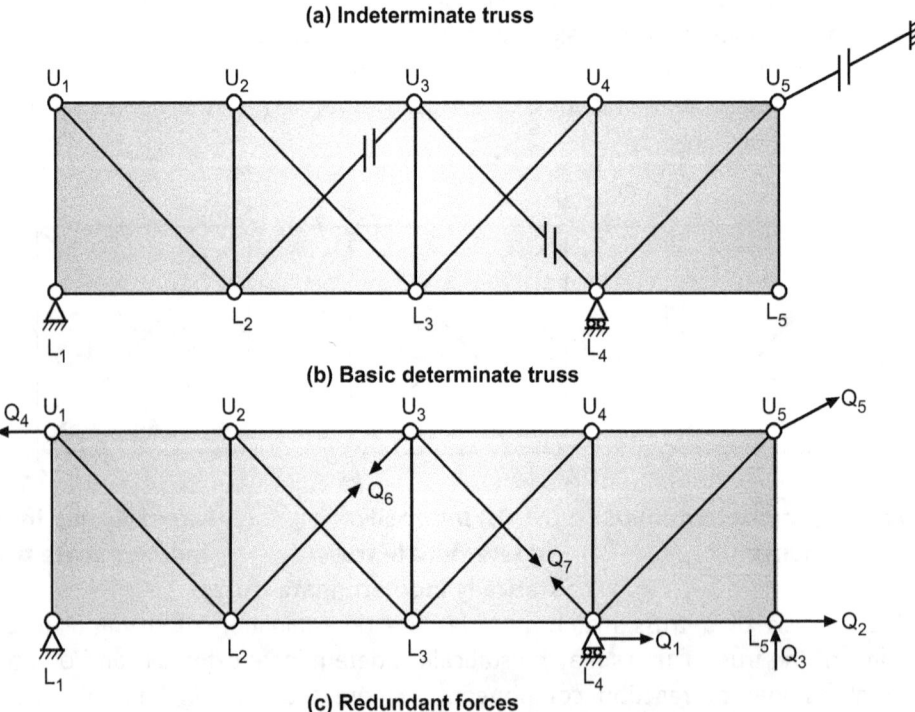

Fig. 7.2 : Released truss and redundant forces

Statically indeterminate trusses are generally analysed by the force method. The degree of kinematic indeterminacy of trusses is normally larger than the degree of static indeterminacy. Moreover, a truss consists of inclined members. Therefore, displacement method is not convenient for the analysis of trusses by hand calculations.

The basic principle of consistent deformation is used to analyse the statically indeterminate trusses by the force method. The main aim of the method is to obtain redundant forces. The method consists of (i) choosing a basic determinate truss on which the applied loads and the redundant forces act and then (ii) applying the conditions of geometry i.e. compatibility requiring that the displacements in the direction of redundant forces must be zero. The redundant force may be the reaction component at the support and/or the axial force in the member. The basic determinate truss, also called *released structure*, is obtained from removing the selected redundants. In doing this, a care must be taken that the released structure must be stable and determinate. This is particularly critical when the truss is internally indeterminate and a member is to be cut or removed to obtain the determinate truss.

The sign convention for axial force in the member of a truss is as follows :

Tensile force is considered as positive and compressive force as negative.

The selection of the redundants, obtaining the basic determinate i.e. released truss and applying the geometrical conditions of deformations are the primary considerations of the force method. This information, in general, is illustrated in Fig. 7.2 (a) and accordingly consolidated in the Table 7.1. The basic determinate truss after removing the redundant is shown in Fig. 7.2 (b) and the redundant forces are shown in Fig. 7.2 (c).

Table 7.1

Sr. No.	Release	Release of the redundant	Redundant force	Geometrical condition of deformation
1.	One component of reaction at hinged support, at L_4.	Hinge support is replaced by the roller support as shown at L_4.	Force perpendicular to the plane of the roller support, Q_1 as shown at L_4.	The translation in the direction of Q_1 at L_4 is zero in the indeterminate truss.
2.	Hinge support at L_5.	Hinge support is removed as shown at L_5.	Two forces perpendicular to each other Q_2 and Q_3 as shown at L_5.	The translations in the direction of Q_2 and Q_3 at L_5 are zero in the indeterminate truss.
3.	Linked support assuming rigid.	The link is removed as shown at U_1.	Force along the link, Q_4 as shown at U_1.	The translation in the direction of the link at U_1 is zero in the indeterminate truss.
4.	Cable support assuming inextensible	The cable is removed as shown at U_5.	The tensile force in the cable Q_5 as shown at U_5.	The translation in the direction of the cable at U_5 is zero in the indeterminate truss.

... Contd.

5.	Member of the truss (a) Member $L_2 - U_3$ (b) Member $U_3 - L_4$	The member is cut with the gap in the member L_2U_3, in the member U_3L_4 at as shown in Fig. 7.2 (b).	Pair of tensile forces along the member. Q_6 forces acting at L_2 and U_3. Q_7 forces acting at U_3 and L_4.	There is no gap i.e. the relative translation along the member is zero in the indeterminate truss as the member is continuous.
6.	Elastic support having flexibility Fes	The elastic support is removed.	The elastic force at the support say Q.	The translation at elastic support is equal to (Fes × Q).

7.3 BASIC FORMULATION OF FORCE METHOD FOR TRUSSES

The superposition equation of the displacements, satisfying the requirement of the compatibility, is the basic equation of the force method as seen previously. This equation is restated in its simplest form of one unknown as

$$D_Q = D_{QL} + F \cdot Q \qquad \ldots (7.1)$$

where,

(i) Q is the unknown redundant force.

(ii) D_Q is the displacement in the given structure corresponding to the selected redundant force Q.

(iii) D_{QL} is the displacement corresponding to the redundant force in the basic determinate or released structure due to the applied loads.

(iv) F is the flexibility i.e. the displacement corresponding and due to unit positive redundant force in the basic determinate structure.

As D_Q is zero for the geometrical condition, the basic equation becomes,

$$0 = D_{QL} + FQ \qquad \ldots (7.2)$$

and therefore, $Q = -\left(\dfrac{D_{QL}}{F}\right)$ gives the required redundant force.

Analysis of indeterminate trusses of one unknown is based on this equation and it consists of the following important phases.

(1) Basic determinate truss :

The selected redundant is removed and the given truss is considered as the equivalent to the superposition of (i) basic determinate truss under given loads and (ii) the basic determinate truss under redundant force 'Q' times unit positive redundant force, as shown in Fig. 7.3.

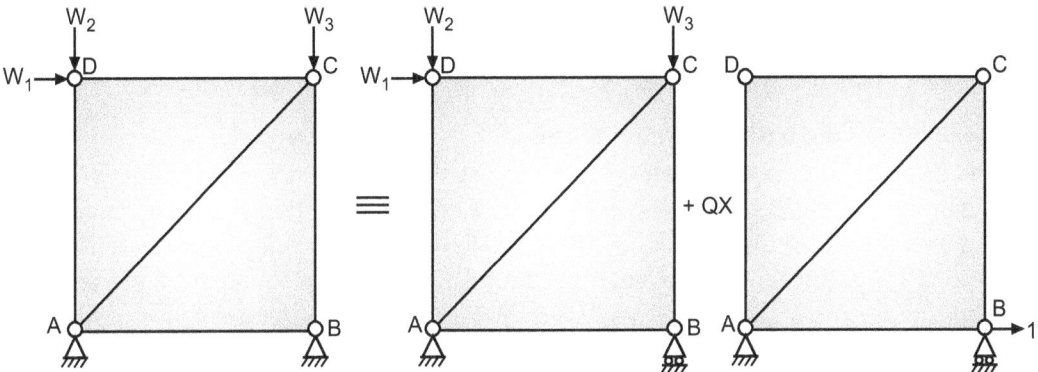

Fig. 7.3 : Superposition technique

(2) P-analysis of basic determinate truss :

Determination of forces in all members of the basic determinate truss due to the applied loads is called as P-analysis. This is the conventional force analysis of a simple determinate truss by laws of statics i.e. method of joints or method of sections. The technique of isolating a single joint with not more than two unknown forces and applying two conditions of static equilibrium, $\Sigma F_x = 0$ and $\Sigma F_y = 0$ for concurrent forces is called the method of joints to obtain the unknown forces. The technique of isolating a portion of a truss by a section and applying the three conditions of equilibrium, $\Sigma F_x = 0$, $\Sigma F_y = 0$ and $\Sigma M = 0$ for a non-concurrent system of forces including certain known applied loads and unknown member forces cut by the section is called the method of sections to obtain the three unknown forces.

(3) K-analysis :

Determination of forces in all the members including redundant members, which are cut, of the basic determinate truss due to only a unit positive force applied at the location and in the direction of the removed redundant is represented as K-analysis. For this also, method of joints or method of sections is used.

(4) Displacement analysis of basic determinate truss :

Using the results of P-analysis and K-analysis, the displacement D_{QL} at the location and in the direction of the redundant force due to applied loads is obtained. According to the unit load method, the displacement D_{QL} is given by the equation

$$D_{QL} = \sum_{\text{All members}} \left(\frac{PKL}{AE}\right) \qquad \ldots (7.3)$$

where P is the force in a member of the basic determinate truss due to applied loads.

K is the force in the member of the basic determinate truss due to a unit positive force corresponding to the unknown redundant force.

L is the length of the member.

A is the area of cross-section of the member.

E is the modulus of elasticity of the material of the member. It may be noted that EA is called axial rigidity of a member and $\frac{L}{EA}$ is termed as the flexibility of a member.

(5) Flexibility of the basic determinate truss :

The displacement of basic determinate truss at the location and in the direction of the redundant due to the unit positive force only applied at the location and in the direction of the redundant is called the flexibility 'F'. Thus, the flexibility F is the displacement (effect) due to the unit force (cause) and obtained by the following similar equation of the unit load method.

$$F = \sum_{\text{All members}} \left(\frac{KKL}{EA}\right) = \sum_{\text{All members}} \left(\frac{K^2L}{EA}\right) \qquad \ldots (7.4)$$

(6) Formulation of the basic equation of the force method :

Applying the condition of consistent deformation that $D_Q = 0$, the unknown redundant force 'Q' is calculated from the equation

$$D_Q = D_{QL} + F \cdot Q$$

$$\therefore \quad 0 = D_{QL} + F \cdot Q$$

$$\therefore \quad Q = -\left(\frac{D_{QL}}{F}\right)$$

$$\therefore \quad Q = -\left(\frac{\sum_{i=1}^{n} \left(\frac{PKL}{EA}\right)_i}{\sum_{i=1}^{n} \left(\frac{K^2L}{EA}\right)_i}\right) \qquad \ldots (7.5)$$

This is the key equation of the analysis of indeterminate trusses by the force method to determine the redundant force. This equation is further modified if the information of E or A or L or EA or $\frac{L}{EA}$ of all members of the truss is same.

Therefore, the basic equation is expressed as

$$Q = -\left(\frac{\sum_{i=1}^{n} \left(\frac{PKL}{EA}\right)_i}{\sum_{i=1}^{n} \left(\frac{K^2L}{EA}\right)_i}\right) \qquad \text{for general case}$$

$$= -\left(\dfrac{\sum_{i=1}^{n}\left(\dfrac{PKL}{A}\right)_i}{\sum_{i=1}^{n}\left(\dfrac{K^2 L}{A}\right)_i}\right) \quad \text{if E is same for all members}$$

$$= -\left(\dfrac{\sum_{i=1}^{n}(PKL)_i}{\sum_{i=1}^{n}(K^2 L)_i}\right) \quad \text{if EA i.e. axial rigidity is same for all members}$$

$$= -\left(\dfrac{\sum_{i=1}^{n}(PK)_i}{\sum_{i=1}^{n}(K^2)_i}\right) \quad \text{if } \dfrac{L}{EA} \text{ i.e. flexibility is same for all members}$$

(7) Forces in the members of a redundant truss :

Using the concept of superposition, the final forces in the members are found from the general equation :

$$P_{fj} = P_i + Q \cdot K_j \qquad \ldots (7.6)$$

The above formulation is processed systematically in the tabular form to analyse the indeterminate trusses. The information of A, L and the results of P-analysis and K-analysis, and their products are presented in the tabular format as shown below :

Sr. No.	Member	Length L	Area A	E	P	K	$\dfrac{PKL}{EA}$	$\dfrac{K^2 L}{EA}$	Q	KQ	$P_f = P + QK$
							Σ =				

This table should include all the members of the truss including redundant members though they are cut. This is to be noted that this is the general format. If the information of E or A is same for all members, the corresponding columns are not necessary. The algebraic sum of the quantities required are directly obtained from this table to find the redundant force and the final forces in all members as shown in the table.

The detailed procedure of the method is illustrated with the examples of trusses for the following cases.

Case I : External indeterminacy.
Case II : Internal indeterminacy.
Case III : Lack of fit or fabrication error.
Case IV : Temperature effects.
Case V : Yielding of supports.

Problems of only one unknown redundant force for each of the above cases are common in practice. Therefore, such examples of trusses with only one unknown are illustrated initially explaining the special features.

7.4 EXTERNALLY INDETERMINATE TRUSSES

Problem 7.1 : Analyse the truss supported and loaded as shown in Fig. 7.4 (a).
Take EA = constant.

Solution : Data :
(i) Truss is supported and loaded as shown in Fig. 7.4 (a).
(ii) EA = constant.

Objects :
(i) Redundant force,
(ii) Forces in all the members of truss and
(iii) Reactions at supports.

Concepts and Equations :
(i) Principle of superposition,
(ii) Analysis of determinate truss,
(iii) Compatibility condition and

(iv) $Q = -\left[\dfrac{\sum\limits_{i=1}^{n} \left(\dfrac{PKL}{EA}\right)_i}{\sum\limits_{i=1}^{n} \left(\dfrac{K^2 L}{EA}\right)_i} \right]$

Procedure :

Step I : Degree of static indeterminacy (D_{si}) :

(a) Degree of external indeterminacy = $(D_{si})_e = r - 3 = 4 - 3 = 1$

(b) Degree of internal indeterminacy = $(D_{si})_i = m - (2j - 3) = 9 - (2 \times 6 - 3) = 0$

Total degree of static indeterminacy = $D_{si} = (D_{si})_e + (D_{si})_i = 1 + 0 = 1$

Step II : Selection of redundant force (Q) :

Let $\quad Q = V_B (\uparrow)$

Step III : Basic determinate truss : Roller support at B is removed and determinate truss is obtained as shown in Fig. 7.4 (b).

Step IV : Superposition : The given indeterminate truss is considered as superposition of (a) basic determinate truss with given loads [Fig. 7.4 (b)] and (b) unknown redundant force Q times the basic determinate truss with unit positive redundant force [Fig. 7.4 (c)].

Step V : P-analysis of basic determinate truss due to applied loads : Considering static equilibrium of truss all the reaction components (R_p) are found out as shown in Fig. 7.4 (b). Also the forces (P) in all the members of truss are found out and shown in Fig. 7.4 (b).

Step VI : K-analysis of basic determinate truss : Unit positive force corresponding to Q is applied as shown in Fig. 7.4 (c). All the reaction components (R_K) and forces (K) in all the members of truss are found out and are shown in Fig. 7.4 (c).

Step VII : Table for numerical computations :

Sr. No.	Member	Length (m)	P (kN)	K	PKL	K^2L	Q (kN)	QK (kN)	$P_f = P + QK$ (kN)
1.	AB	3	47.5	$-1/2$	-71.25	0.75		-26.35	21.15
2.	BC	3	47.5	$-1/2$	-71.25	0.75		-26.35	21.15
3.	CD	3	0	0	0	0		0	0
4.	DE	3	0	0	0	0		0	0
5.	EF	3	-20	0	0	0	52.69	0	-20
6.	FA	3	0	0	0	0		0	0
7.	EB	3	0	-1	0	3		-52.69	-52.69
8.	AE	$3\sqrt{2}$	$-27.5\sqrt{2}$	$1/\sqrt{2}$	$-82.5\sqrt{2}$	$3/\sqrt{2}$		37.25	-1.64
9.	CE	$3\sqrt{2}$	$-47.5\sqrt{2}$	$1/\sqrt{2}$	$-142.5\sqrt{2}$	$3/\sqrt{2}$		37.25	-29.93
				$\Sigma =$	-460.69	8.74			

Step VIII : Calculation of redundant force :

$$Q = -\left[\frac{\sum_{i=1}^{n}\left(\frac{PKL}{EA}\right)_i}{\sum_{i=1}^{n}\left(\frac{K^2L}{EA}\right)_i}\right] = -\left(\frac{\Sigma PKL}{\Sigma K^2L}\right) = -\left(\frac{-460.69}{8.74}\right)$$

$\quad = 52.69$ kN $(\uparrow)$

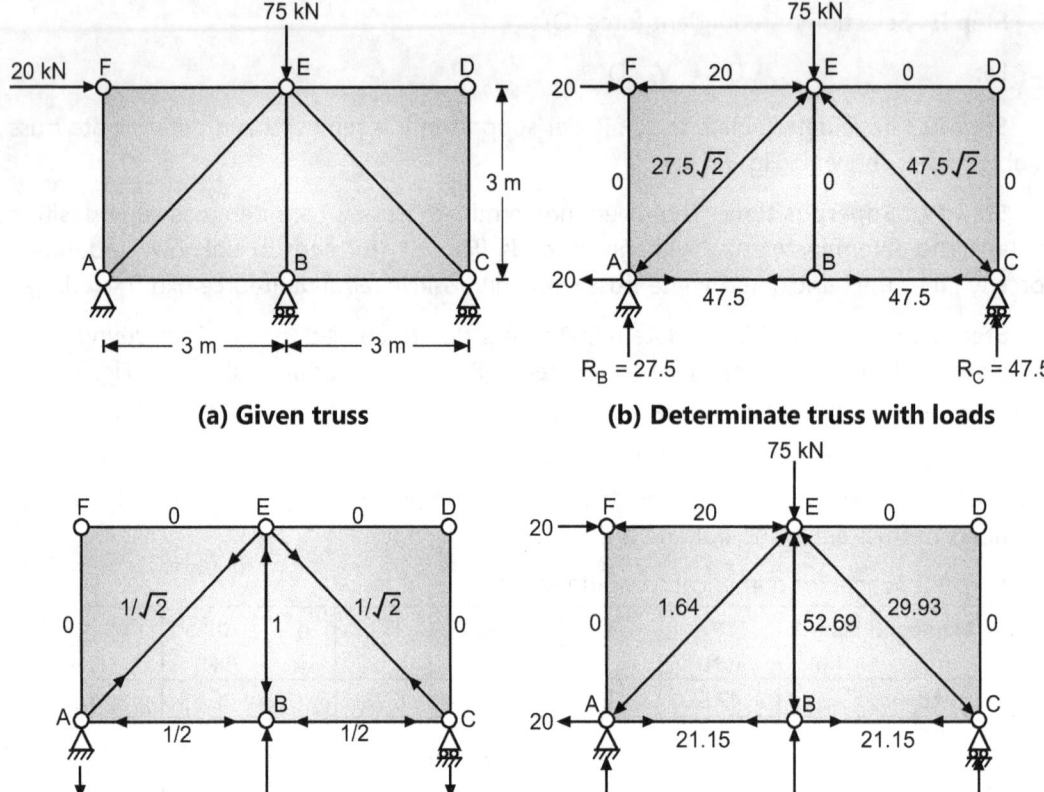

(a) Given truss   (b) Determinate truss with loads

(c) Determinate truss with Q = 1   (d) Final member forces and reactions

Fig. 7.4 : Illustrative Problem 7.1

Step IX : Final forces in all the members of truss (P_f) :

Using the equation :

$$P_f = P + QK$$

final forces in all members of truss are computed and are as tabulated above and shown in Fig. 7.4 (d).

Step X : Final reaction components at supports (R) :

Using the equation, $R = R_p + Q \cdot R_k$

final reaction components at supports are computed and are as shown in Fig. 7.4 (d).

Problem 7.2 : Analyse the truss supported and loaded as shown in Fig. 7.5 (a). Cross-sectional area of each member in cm² is indicated in brackets. Take E = constant.

Solution : Data :

(i) Truss is supported and loaded as shown in Fig. 7.5 (a).

(ii) E = constant.

Objects :

(i) Redundant force, (ii) Forces in all the members of truss and

(iii) Reactions at supports.

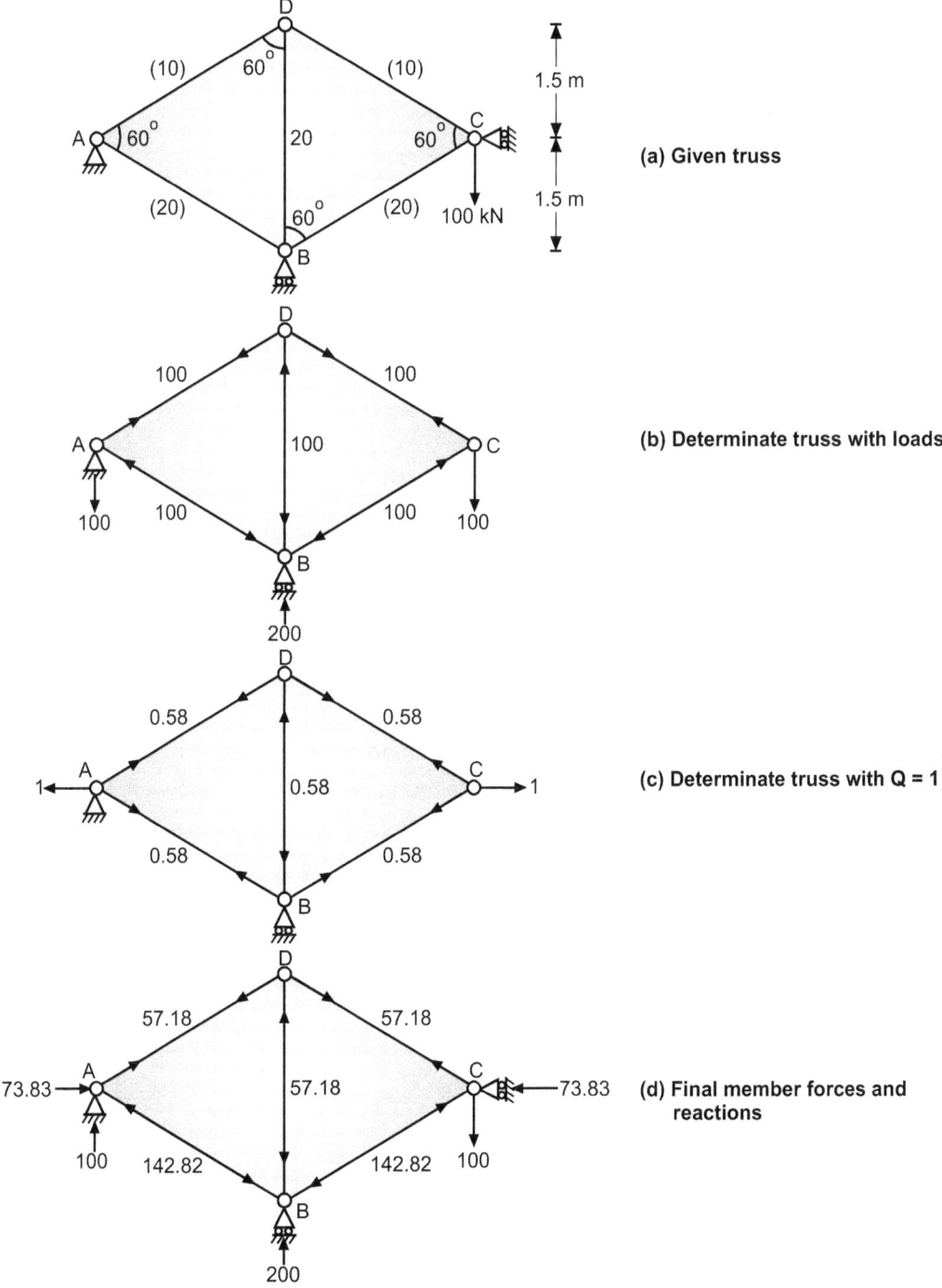

Fig. 7.5 : Illustrative Problem 7.2

Concepts and Equations :
(i) Principle of superposition, (ii) Analysis of determinate truss,
(iii) Compatibility condition and

(iv) $Q = -\left[\dfrac{\sum_{i=1}^{n}\left(\dfrac{PKL}{EA}\right)_i}{\sum_{i=1}^{n}\left(\dfrac{K^2L}{EA}\right)_i} \right]$

Procedure : Step I : Degree of static indeterminacy (D_{si}) :
(a) Degree of external indeterminacy = $(D_{si})_e$ = r − 3 = 4 − 3 = 1
(b) Degree of internal indeterminacy = $(D_{si})_i$ = m − (2j − 3) = 5 − (2 × 4 − 3) = 0
Total degree of static indeterminacy = D_{si} = $(D_{si})_e$ + $(D_{si})_i$ = 1 + 0 = 1

Step II : Selection of redundant force (Q) :
Let, $Q = H_c (\rightarrow)$

Step III : Basic determinate truss :
Roller support at C is removed and determinate truss is obtained as shown in Fig. 7.5 (b).

Step IV : Superposition : The given indeterminate truss is considered as superposition of (a) basic determinate truss with given loads [Fig. 7.5 (b)] and (b) unknown redundant force Q times the basic determinate truss with unit positive redundant force [Fig. 7.5 (c)].

Step V : P-analysis of basic determinate truss due to applied loads : Considering static equilibrium of truss all the reaction components (R_p) are found out as shown in Fig. 7.5 (b). Also the forces (P) in all the members of truss are found out and are as shown in Fig. 7.5 (b).

Step VI : K-analysis of basic determinate truss : Unit positive force corresponding to Q is applied as shown in Fig. 7.5 (c). All the reaction components (R_k) and forces (K) in all the members of truss are found out and are as shown in Fig. 7.5 (c).

Step VII : Table for numerical computations :

Sr. No.	Member	Length (mm)	Area (mm²)	P (kN)	K	$\dfrac{PKL}{A}$	$\dfrac{K^2L}{A}$	Q (kN)	QK (kN)	$P_f = P + QK$ (kN)
1.	AB	3000	2000	− 100	0.58	− 87	0.505		− 42.82	− 142.82
2.	BC	3000	2000	− 100	0.58	− 87	0.505		− 42.82	− 142.82
3.	CD	3000	1000	100	0.58	174	1.01	− 73.83	− 42.82	57.18
4.	DA	3000	1000	100	0.58	174	1.01		− 42.82	57.18
5.	DB	3000	2000	− 100	− 0.58	87	0.505		42.82	− 57.18
						S = 261	3.535			

Step VIII : Calculation of redundant force :

$$Q = -\left[\dfrac{\sum\limits_{i=1}^{n}\left(\dfrac{PKL}{EA}\right)_i}{\sum\limits_{i=1}^{n}\left(\dfrac{K^2L}{EA}\right)_i}\right] = -\left[\dfrac{\sum\left(\dfrac{PKL}{A}\right)}{\sum\left(\dfrac{K^2L}{A}\right)}\right]$$

$$= -\left(\dfrac{261}{3.535}\right) = -73.83 \text{ kN} = 73.83 \text{ kN} (\leftarrow)$$

Step IX : Final forces in all the members of truss (P_f) :

Using the equation :

$$P_f = P + QK$$

final forces in all the members of truss are computed and are as tabulated above and shown in Fig. 7.5 (d).

Step X : Final reaction components at supports (R) :

Using the equation

$$R = R_p + Q \cdot R_k$$

final reaction components at supports are computed and are as shown in Fig. 7.5 (d).

Problem 7.3 : Analyse the truss supported and loaded as shown in Fig. 7.6 (a). Cross-sectional area of each member in cm² is indicated in brackets. Take E = constant.

Solution : Data :
(i) Truss is supported and loaded as shown in Fig. 7.6 (a).
(ii) E = constant

Objects :
(i)   Redundant force,
(ii) Forces in all the members of truss and
(iii) Reactions at supports.

Concepts and Equations :
(i)   Principle of superposition,
(ii) Analysis of determinate truss,
(iii) Compatibility condition and

(iv) $Q = -\left[\dfrac{\sum\limits_{i=1}^{n}\left(\dfrac{PKL}{EA}\right)_i}{\sum\limits_{i=1}^{n}\left(\dfrac{K^2L}{EA}\right)_i}\right]$

Procedure :

Step I : Degree of static indeterminacy (D_{si}) :

(a) Degree of external indeterminacy = $(D_{si})_e = r - 3 = 4 - 3 = 1$

(b) Degree of internal indeterminacy = $(D_{si})_i = m - (2j - 3) = 5 - (2 \times 4 - 3) = 0$

Total degree of static indeterminacy = $D_{si} = (D_{si})_e + (D_{si})_i = 1 + 0 = 1$

Step II : Selection of redundant force (Q) :

Let, $\quad Q = H_B (\rightarrow)$

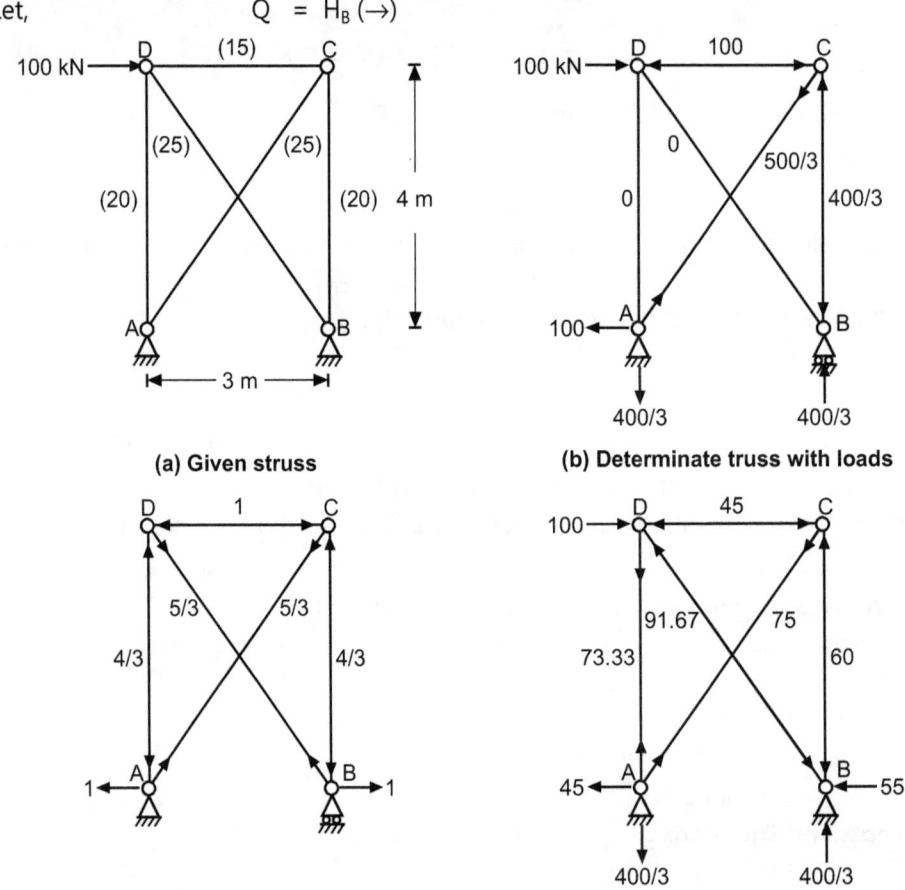

(a) Given struss

(b) Determinate truss with loads

(c) Determinate truss with Q = 1

(d) Final member forces and reactions

Fig. 7.6 : Illustrative Problem 7.3

Step III : Basic determinate truss :

Hinge support at B is replaced by roller support and determinate truss is obtained as shown in Fig. 7.6 (b).

Step IV : Superposition : The given indeterminate truss is considered as superposition of (a) basic determinate truss with given loads [Fig. 7.6 (b)] and (b) unknown redundant force Q times the basic determinate truss with unit positive redundant force [Fig. 7.6 (c)].

Step V : P-analysis of basic determinate truss due to applied loads : Considering static equilibrium of truss all the reaction components (R_p) are found out as shown in Fig. 7.6 (b). Also the forces (P) in all the members of truss are found out and are shown in Fig. 7.6 (b).

Step VI : K-analysis of basic determinate truss : Unit positive force corresponding to Q is applied as shown in Fig. 7.6 (c). All the reaction components (R_K) and forces (K) in all the members of truss are found out and are shown in Fig. 7.6 (c).

Step VII : Table for numerical computation :

Sr. no.	Member	Length (mm)	Area (mm²)	P (kN)	K	$\frac{PKL}{A}$	$\frac{K^2L}{A}$	Q (kN)	QK (kN)	$P_f = P + QK$ (kN)
1.	BC	4000	2000	−400/3	−4/3	355.55	3.55		73.33	−60
2.	CD	3000	1500	−100	−1	200	2.0		55	−45
3.	DA	4000	2000	0	−4/3	0	3.55	−55	73.33	73.33
4.	AC	5000	2500	500/3	5/3	555.55	5.55		−91.67	75
5.	BD	5000	2500	0	5/3	0	5.55		−91.67	−91.67
					Σ =	1111.11	20.2			

Step VIII : Calculation of redundant force :

$$Q = -\left[\frac{\sum_{i=1}^{n}\left(\frac{PKL}{EA}\right)_i}{\sum_{i=1}^{n}\left(\frac{K^2L}{EA}\right)_i}\right] = -\left[\frac{\sum\left(\frac{PKL}{A}\right)}{\sum\left(\frac{K^2L}{A}\right)}\right] = -\left(\frac{1111.11}{20.2}\right)$$

$$= -55 \text{ kN} = 55 \text{ kN} (\leftarrow)$$

Step IX : Final forces in all the members of truss (P_f) :

Using the equation :

$$P_f = P + QK$$

final forces in all the members of truss are computed and are as tabulated above and shown in Fig. 7.6 (d).

Step X : Final reaction components at supports (R) :

Using the equation,

$$R = R_p + Q \cdot R_K$$

final reaction components at supports are computed and are as shown in Fig. 7.6 (d).

Problem 7.4 : Analyse the truss supported and loaded as shown in Fig. 7.7 (a). Cross-sectional area of each member in cm² is indicated in brackets. Take E = constant.

Solution : Data :
(i) Truss is supported and loaded as shown in Fig. 7.7 (a).
(ii) E = constant

Objects :
(i) Redundant force,
(ii) Forces in all the members of truss and
(iii) Reactions at supports.

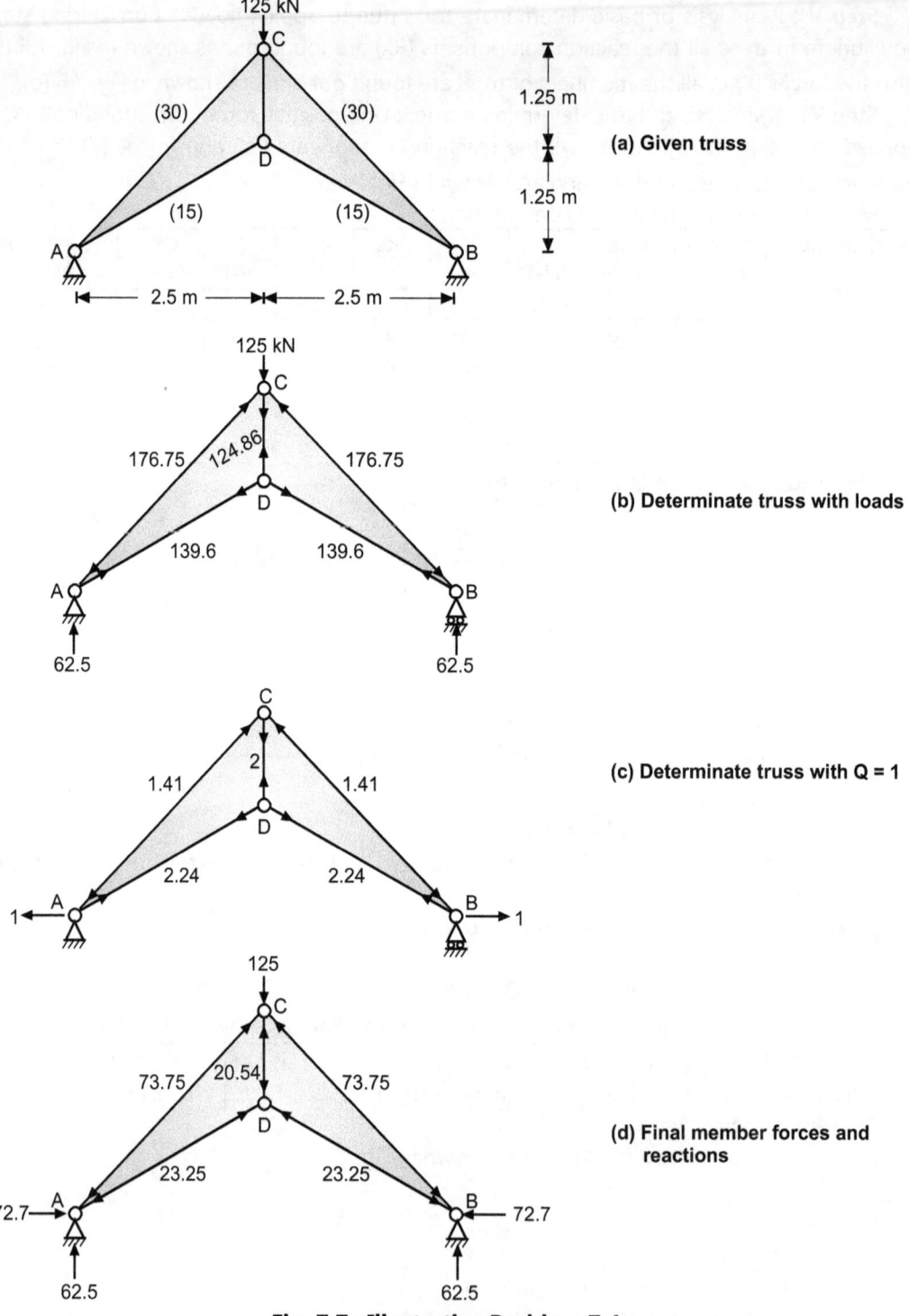

Fig. 7.7 : Illustrative Problem 7.4

Concepts and Equations :

(i) Principle of superposition, (ii) Analysis of determinate truss,

(iii) Compatibility condition and (iv) $Q = -\left[\dfrac{\sum\limits_{i=1}^{n} \left(\dfrac{PKL}{EA}\right)_i}{\sum\limits_{i=1}^{n} \left(\dfrac{K^2L}{EA}\right)_i} \right]$

Procedure :

Step I : Degree of static indeterminacy (D_{si}) :

(a) Degree of external indeterminacy = $(D_{si})_e$ = r − 3 = 4 − 3 = 1
(b) Degree of internal indeterminacy = $(D_{si})_i$ = m − (2j − 3) = 5 − (2 × 4 − 3) = 0
Total degree of static indeterminacy = D_{si} = $(D_{si})_e$ + $(D_{si})_i$ = 1 + 0 = 1

Step II : Selection of redundant force (Q) :
Let,   Q = H_B (→)

Step III : Basic determinate truss : Hinge support at B is replaced by roller support and determinate truss is obtained as shown in Fig. 7.7 (b).

Step IV : Superposition : The given indeterminate truss is considered as superposition of (a) basic determinate truss with given loads [Fig. 7.7 (b)] and (b) unknown redundant force 'Q' times the basic determinate truss with unit positive redundant force. [Fig. 7.7 (c)].

Step V : P-analysis of basic determinate truss due to applied loads : Considering static equilibrium of truss all the reaction components (R_p) are found out as shown in Fig. 7.7 (b). Also the forces (P) in all the members of truss are found out and are shown in Fig. 7.7 (b).

Step VI : K-analysis of basic determinate truss : Unit positive force corresponding to 'Q' is applied as shown in Fig. 7.7 (c). All the reaction components (R_k) and forces (K) in all the members of truss are found out and are shown in Fig. 7.7 (c).

Step VII : Table for numerical computation :

Sr. No.	Mem.	Length (mm)	Area (mm²)	P (kN)	K	$\dfrac{PKL}{A}$	$\dfrac{K^2L}{A}$	Q (kN)	QK (kN)	P_f = P + QK (kN)
1.	AD	2795	1500	139.6	2.24	582.67	9.35		−162.85	−23.25
2.	BD	2795	1500	139.6	2.24	582.67	9.35		−162.85	−23.25
3.	AC	3535	3000	−176.25	−1.41	292.83	2.34	−72.7	102.50	−73.75
4.	BC	3535	3000	−176.25	−1.41	292.83	2.34		102.50	−73.75
5.	CD	1250	1000	124.86	2	312.15	5		−145.4	−20.54
						Σ = 2063.15	28.38			

Step VIII : Calculation of redundant force :

$$Q = -\left[\dfrac{\sum_{i=1}^{n}\left(\dfrac{PKL}{EA}\right)_i}{\sum_{i=1}^{n}\left(\dfrac{K^2L}{EA}\right)_i}\right] = -\left(\dfrac{\sum\dfrac{(PKL)}{A}}{(K^2L/A)}\right) = -\left(\dfrac{1999.5}{28.38}\right)$$

$$= -70.45 \text{ kN} = 70.45 \text{ kN} (\leftarrow)$$

Step IX : Final forces in all the members of truss (P_f) :

Using the equation,

$$P_f = P + QK$$

final forces in all the members of truss are computed and are as tabulated above and shown in Fig. 7.7 (d).

Step X : Final reaction components at supports (R) :

Using the equation, $\quad R = R_p + Q \cdot R_k$

final reaction components at supports are computed and are as shown in Fig. 7.7 (d).

7.5 INTERNALLY INDETERMINATE TRUSSES

Problem 7.5 : Analyse the truss supported and loaded as shown in Fig. 7.8 (a). Cross-sectional area of each member in cm^2 is indicated in brackets. Take E = constant.

Solution : Data :

(i) Truss is supported and loaded as shown in Fig. 7.8 (a).

Objects :

(i) Redundant force, (ii) Forces in all the members of truss and
(iii) Reactions at supports.

Concepts and Equations :

(i) Principle of superposition, (ii) Analysis of determinate truss,
(iii) Compatibility condition and

(iv) $Q = -\left[\dfrac{\sum_{i=1}^{n}\left(\dfrac{PKL}{EA}\right)_i}{\sum_{i=1}^{n}\left(\dfrac{K^2L}{EA}\right)_i}\right]$

Procedure :

Step I : Degree of static indeterminacy (D_{si}) :

(a) Degree of external indeterminacy = $(D_{si})_e = r - 3 = 3 - 3 = 0$
(b) Degree of internal indeterminacy = $(D_{si})_i = m - 2j = 3 - 2 \times 1 = 1$

Total degree of static indeterminacy = $D_{si} = (D_{si})_e + (D_{si})_i = 0 + 1 = 1$

Step II : Selection of redundant force (Q) :

Step III : Basic determinate truss : Member CD is cut and determinate truss is obtained as shown in Fig. 7.8 (b).

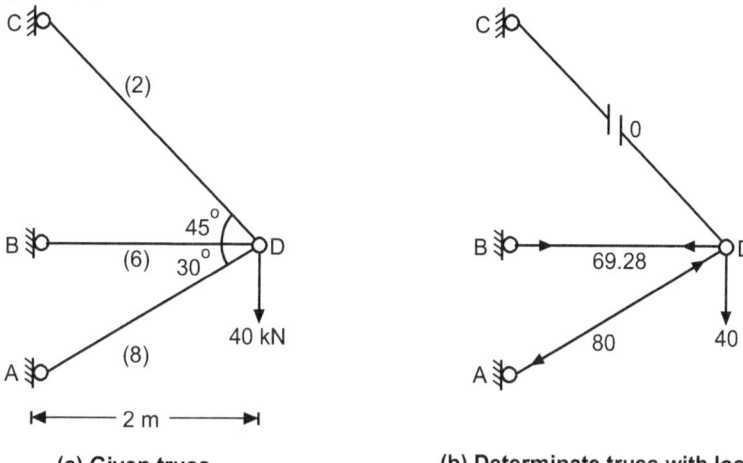

(a) Given truss (b) Determinate truss with loads

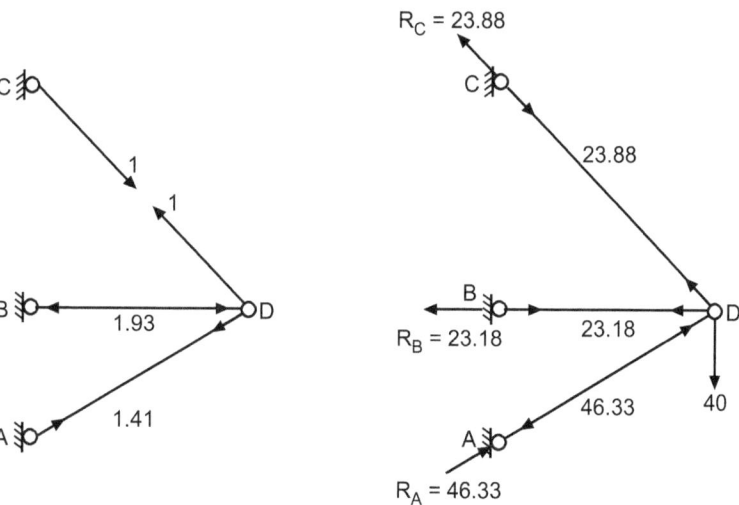

(c) Determinate truss with Q = 1 (d) Final member forces and reactions

Fig. 7.8 : Illustrative Problem 7.5

Step IV : Superposition : The given indeterminate truss is considered as superposition of (a) basic determinate truss with given loads [Fig. 7.8 (b)] and (b) unknown redundant force 'Q' times the basic determinate truss with unit positive redundant force. [Fig. 7.8 (c)].

Step V : P-analysis of basic determinate truss due to applied loads : The forces (P) in all the members of truss are found out and are shown in Fig. 7.8 (b).

Step VI : K-analysis of basic determinate truss : Unit positive force corresponding to 'Q' is applied as shown in Fig. 7.8 (c) forces (K) in all the members of truss are found out and are shown in Fig. 7.8 (c).

Step VII : Table for numerical computations :

Sr. no.	Mem.	Length (mm)	Area (mm²)	P (kN)	K	$\dfrac{PKL}{A}$	$\dfrac{K^2L}{A}$	Q (kN)	QK (kN)	$P_f =$ P + QK (kN)
1.	AD	2310	800	–80	1.41	–325.71	5.74		33.67	–46.33
2.	BD	2000	600	69.28	–1.93	–445.7	12.42	23.88	–46.10	23.18
3.	CD	2828	200	0	1	0	14.14		–23.88	–23.88
						Σ = –771.41	32.3			

Step VIII : Calculation of redundant force :

$$Q = -\left[\dfrac{\sum\limits_{i=1}^{n}\left(\dfrac{PKL}{EA}\right)_i}{\sum\limits_{i=1}^{n}\left(\dfrac{K^2L}{EA}\right)_i}\right] = -\left[\dfrac{\sum\left(\dfrac{PKL}{A}\right)}{\sum\left(\dfrac{K^2L}{A}\right)}\right] = -\left(\dfrac{-771.41}{32.3}\right)$$

= 23.88 kN (Tensile)

Step IX : Final force in all the members of truss (P_f) :

Using the equation,

$$P_f = P + QK$$

final forces in all the members of truss are computed and are as tabulated above and shown in Fig. 7.8 (d).

Step X : Final reaction components at supports (R) :

Using the equation,

$$R = R_p + Q \cdot R_k$$

final reaction components at supports are computed and are as shown in Fig. 7.8 (d).

Problem 7.6 : Analyse the truss supported and loaded as shown in Fig. 7.9 (a). Take EA = constant.

Solution : Data :
(i) Truss is supported and loaded as shown in Fig. 7.9 (a).
(ii) EA = constant

Objects :
(i) Redundant force, (ii) Forces in all the members of truss and
(iii) Reactions at supports.

Concepts and Equations :
(i) Principle of superposition, (ii) Analysis of determinate truss,
(iii) Compatibility condition and

(iv) $Q = -\left[\dfrac{\sum_{i=1}^{n}\left(\dfrac{PKL}{EA}\right)_i}{\sum_{i=1}^{n}\left(\dfrac{K^2L}{EA}\right)_i}\right]$

Procedure :

Step I : Degree of static indeterminacy (D_{si}) :

(a) Degree of external indeterminacy = $(D_{si})_e$ = r − 3 = 3 − 3 = 0

(b) Degree of internal indeterminacy = $(D_{si})_i$ = m − (2j − 3) = 8 − (2 × 5 − 3) = 1

Total degree of static indeterminacy = D_{si} = $(D_{si})_e$ + $(D_{si})_i$ = 0 + 1 = 1

Step II : Selection of redundant force (Q) :

Let,   Q = Force in member BE (Tensile)

Step III : Basic determinate truss :

Member BE is cut and determinate truss is obtained as shown in Fig. 7.9 (b).

Step IV : Superposition : The given indeterminate truss is considered as superposition of (a) basic determinate truss with given loads [Fig. 7.9 (b)] and (b) unknown redundant force 'Q' times the basic determinate truss with unit positive redundant force (Fig. 7.9 (c)).

Step V : P-analysis of basic determinate truss due to applied loads : Considering static equilibrium of truss all the reaction components (R_p) are found out as shown in Fig. 7.9 (b). Also the forces (P) in all the members of truss are found out and are shown in [Fig. 7.9 (b)].

Step VI : K-analysis of basic determinate truss : Unit positive force corresponding to 'Q' is applied as shown in Fig. 7.9 (c).

Forces (K) in all the members of truss are found out and are shown in Fig. 7.9 (c). Reaction components (R_k) are zero for this analysis.

Step VII : Table for numerical computation :

Sr. No.	Member	Length (m)	P (kN)	K	PKL	K^2L	Q (kN)	QK (kN)	P_f = P + QK (kN)
1.	AB	2	25	$-1/\sqrt{2}$	−35.35	1		9.9	34.9
2.	BC	2	25	0	0	0		0	25
3.	CD	$2\sqrt{2}$	$-25\sqrt{2}$	0	0	0		0	$-25\sqrt{2}$
4.	DE	2	−50	$-1/\sqrt{2}$	70.71	1	−14.01	9.9	−40.1
5.	EA	2	0	$-1/\sqrt{2}$	0	1		9.9	9.9
6.	BD	2	0	$-1/\sqrt{2}$	0	1		9.9	9.9
7.	AD	$2\sqrt{2}$	$25\sqrt{2}$	1	100	$2\sqrt{2}$		−14.01	21.35
8.	BE	$2\sqrt{2}$	0	1	0	$2\sqrt{2}$		−14.01	−14.01
				Σ =	135.36	9.66			

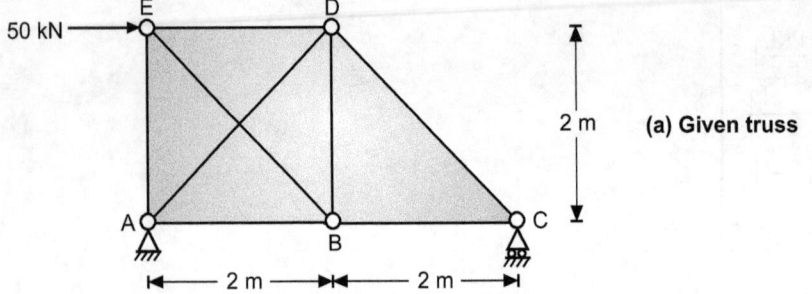

(a) Given truss

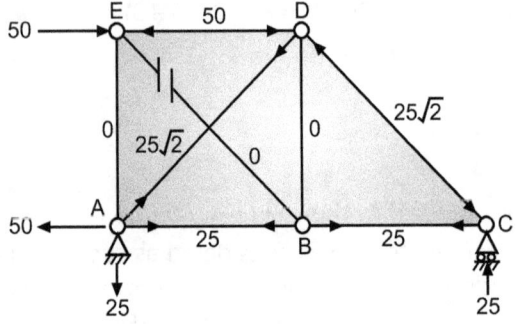

(b) Determinate truss with loads

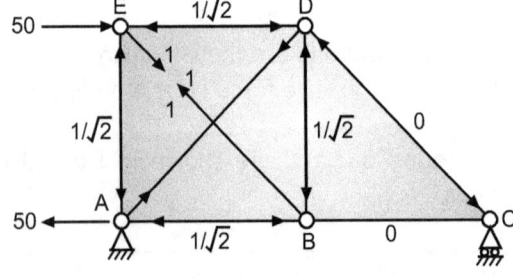

(c) Determinate truss with Q = 1

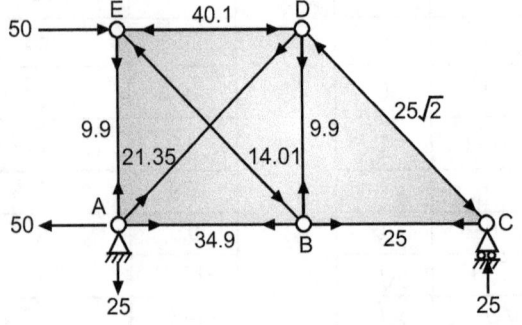

(d) Final member forces and reactions

Fig. 7.9 : Illustrative Problem 7.6

Step VIII : Calculation of redundant force :

$$Q = -\left[\dfrac{\sum_{i=1}^{n}\left(\dfrac{PKL}{EA}\right)_i}{\sum_{i=1}^{n}\left(\dfrac{K^2L}{EA}\right)_i}\right] = -\left(\dfrac{\Sigma(PKL)}{\Sigma(K^2L)}\right) = -\left(\dfrac{135.36}{9.66}\right)$$

$$= -14.01 \text{ kN} = 14.01 \text{ kN (Compressive)}$$

Step IX : Final forces in all the members of truss (P_f) :

Using the equation,

$$P_f = P + QK$$

final forces in all the members of truss are computed and are as tabulated above and shown in Fig. 7.9 (d).

Step X : Final reaction components at supports (R) :

Using the relation,

$$R = R_p + Q \cdot R_k$$

final reaction components at supports are computed and are as shown in Fig. 7.9 (d).

Problem 7.7 : Analyse the truss supported and loaded as shown in Fig. 7.10 (a). Cross-sectional area of each member in cm² is indicated in brackets. Take E = constant.

Solution : Data :
(i) Truss is supported and loaded as shown in Fig. 7.10 (a).
(ii) E = constant

Objects :
(i) Redundant force,
(ii) Forces in all the members of truss and
(iii) Reactions at supports.

Concepts and Equations :
(i) Principle of superposition,
(ii) Analysis of determinate truss,
(iii) Compatibility condition and

(iv) $Q = -\left[\dfrac{\sum_{i=1}^{n}\left(\dfrac{PKL}{EA}\right)_i}{\sum_{i=1}^{n}\left(\dfrac{K^2L}{EA}\right)_i}\right]$

Procedure :

Step I : Degree of static indeterminacy (D_{si}) :

(a) Degree of external indeterminacy = $(D_{si})_e$ = r − 3 = 3 − 3 = 0

(b) Degree of internal indeterminacy = $(D_{si})_i$ = m − (2j − 3) = 6 − (2 × 4 − 3) = 1

Total degree of static indeterminacy = D_{si} = $(D_{si})_e$ + $(D_{si})_i$ = 0 + 1 = 1

Step II : Selection of redundant force (Q) :

Let,   Q = Force in member AB (Tensile)

Step III : Basic determinate truss :

Member AB is cut and determinate truss is obtained as shown in Fig. 7.10 (b).

Step IV : Superposition : The given indeterminate truss is considered as superposition of (a) basic determinate truss with given loads [Fig. 7.10 (b)] and (b) unknown redundant force 'Q' times the basic determinate truss with unit positive redundant force [Fig. 7.10 (c)].

Step V : P-analysis of basic determinate truss due to applied loads : Considering static equilibrium of truss all the reaction components (R_p) are found out as shown in Fig. 7.10 (b). Also the forces (P) in all the members of truss are found out and are shown in Fig. 7.10 (b).

Step VI : K-analysis of basic determinate truss : Unit positive force corresponding to 'Q' is applied as shown in Fig. 7.10 (c).

Forces (K) in all the members of truss are found out and are shown in Fig. 7.10 (c). Reaction components (R_k) are zero for this analysis.

Step VII : Table for numerical computation :

Sr. no.	Mem.	Length (mm)	Area (mm²)	P (kN)	K	$\frac{PKL}{A}$	$\frac{K^2L}{A}$	Q (kN)	QK (kN)	P_f = P + QK (kN)
1.	BC	4000	2000	−400/3	4/3	−355.55	3.55		66.67	−66.67
2.	CD	3000	1500	−100	1	−200	2.0		50	−50
3.	DA	4000	2000	0	4/3	0	3.55	50	66.67	66.67
4.	AC	5000	2500	500/3	−5/3	−555.55	5.55		−83.33	83.33
5.	BD	5000	2500	0	−5/3	0	5.55		−83.33	−83.33
6.	AB	3000	1500	0	1	0	2.0		50	50
						Σ = −1111.11	22.2			

Step VIII : Calculation of redundant force :

$$Q = -\left[\dfrac{\sum_{i=1}^{n}\left(\dfrac{PKL}{EA}\right)_i}{\sum_{i=1}^{n}\left(\dfrac{K^2L}{EA}\right)_i}\right]$$

$$= -\left[\dfrac{\sum\left(\dfrac{PKL}{A}\right)}{\sum\left(\dfrac{K^2L}{A}\right)}\right] = -\left(\dfrac{-1111.11}{22.22}\right) = 50 \text{ kN (Tensile)}$$

Step IX : Final forces in all the members of truss (P_f) :

Using the equation,

$$P_f = P + QK$$

final forces in all the members of truss are computed and are as tabulated above and shown in Fig. 7.10 (d).

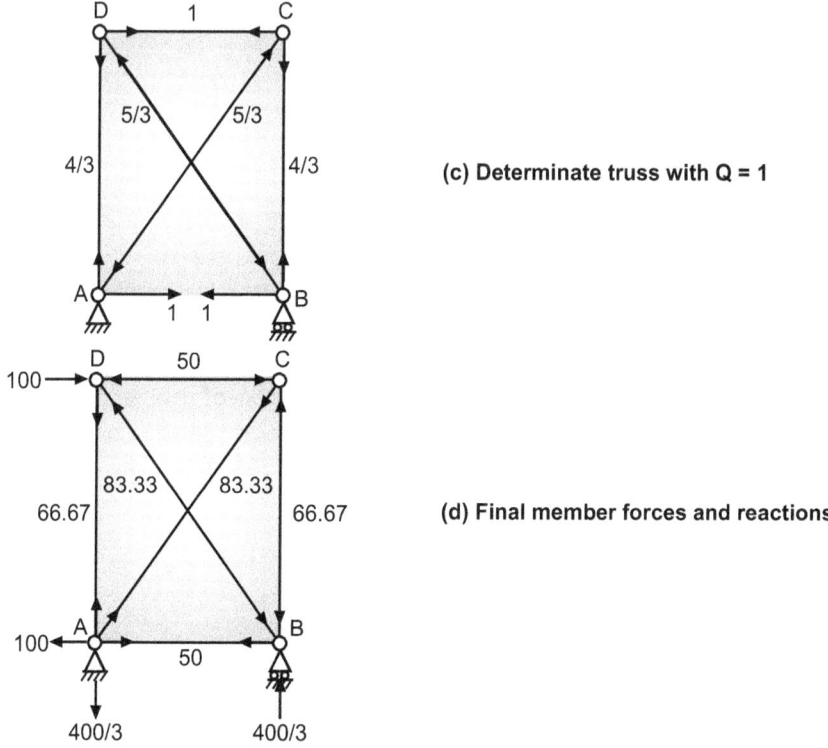

(c) Determinate truss with Q = 1

(d) Final member forces and reactions

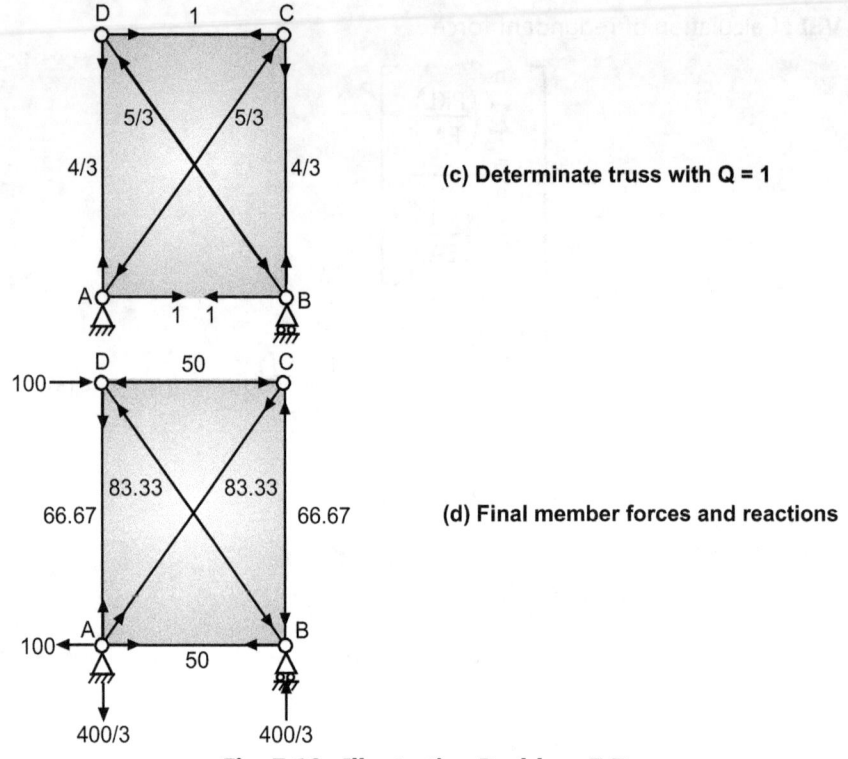

(c) Determinate truss with Q = 1

(d) Final member forces and reactions

Fig. 7.10 : Illustrative Problem 7.7

Step X : Final reaction components at supports (R) :

Using the equation,

$$R = R_p + Q \cdot R_k$$

final reaction components at supports are computed and are as shown in Fig. 7.10 (d).

Problem 7.8 : Analyse the truss supported and loaded as shown in Fig. 7.11 (a). Cross-sectional area of each member in cm² is indicated in brackets. Take E = constant.

Solution : Data :

(i) Truss is supported and loaded as shown in Fig. 7.11 (a). (ii) E = constant.

Objects : (i) Redundant force, (ii) Forces in all the members of truss and

(iii) Reactions at supports.

Concepts and Equations : (i) Principle of superposition, (ii) Analysis of determinate truss, (iii) Compatibility condition and

(iv) $Q = - \left[\dfrac{\sum\limits_{i=1}^{n} \left(\dfrac{PKL}{EA} \right)_i}{\sum\limits_{i=1}^{n} \left(\dfrac{K^2L}{EA} \right)_i} \right]$

Procedure :

Step I : Degree of static indeterminacy (D_{si}) :

(a) Degree of external indeterminacy = $(D_{si})_e = r - 3 = 3 - 3 = 0$

(b) Degree of internal indeterminacy = $(D_{si})_i = m - (2j - 3) = 10 - (2 \times 6 - 3) = 1$

Total degree of static indeterminacy = $D_{si} = (D_{si})_e + (D_{si})_i = 0 + 1 = 1$

Step II : Selection of redundant force (Q) :

Let, $\quad\quad\quad\quad\quad Q$ = Force in member BE (Tensile)

Step III : Basic determinate truss : Member BE is cut and determinate truss is obtained as shown in Fig. 7.11 (b).

Step IV : Superposition : The given indeterminate truss is considered as superposition of (a) basic determinate truss with given loads [Fig. 7.11 (b)] and (b) unknown redundant force 'Q' times the basic determinate truss with unit positive redundant force. [Fig. 7.11 (c)].

Step V : P-analysis of basic determinate truss due to applied loads : Considering static equilibrium of truss all the reaction components (R_p) are found out as shown in Fig. 7.11 (b). Also the forces (P) in all the members of truss are found out and are shown in Fig. 7.11 (b).

Step VI : K-analysis of basic determinate truss : Unit positive force corresponding to 'Q' is applied as shown in Fig. 7.11 (c).

Forces (K) in all the members of truss are found out and are shown in Fig. 7.11 (c). Reaction components (R_k) are zero for this analysis.

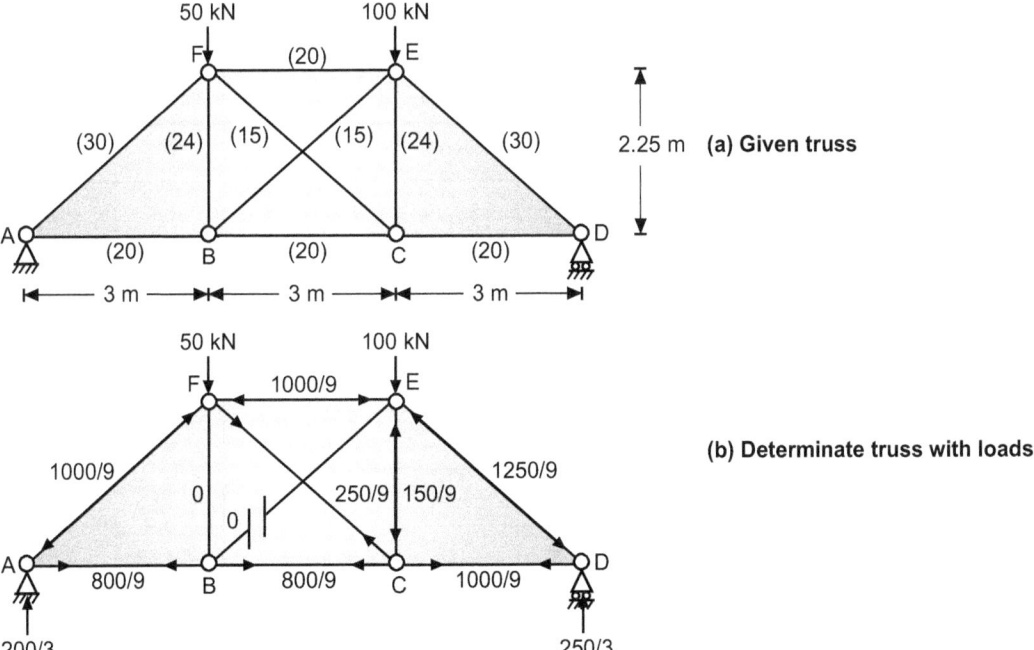

(a) Given truss

(b) Determinate truss with loads

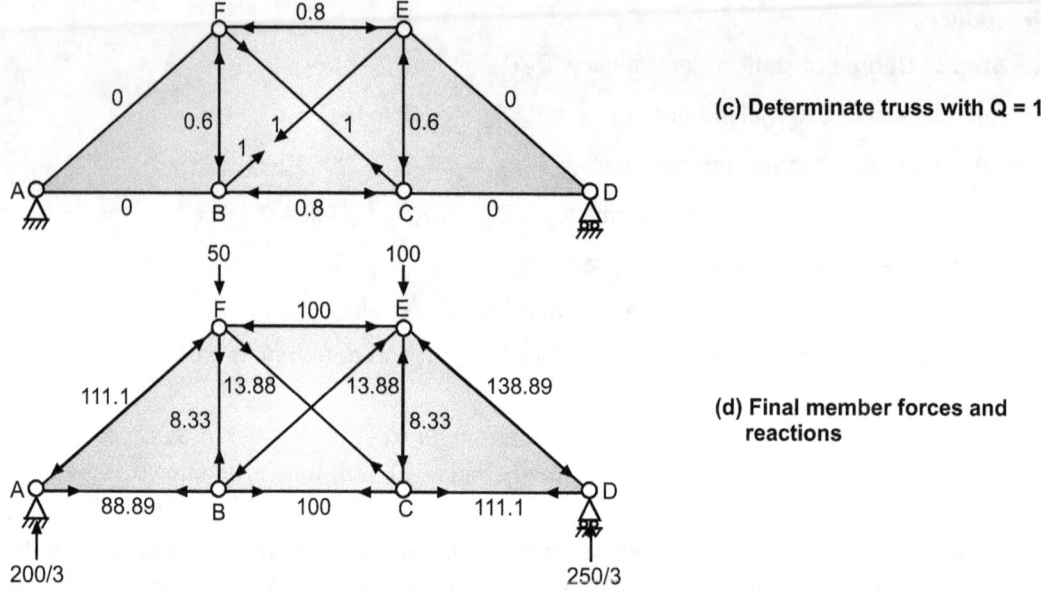

(c) Determinate truss with Q = 1

(d) Final member forces and reactions

Fig. 7.11 : Illustrative Problem 7.8

Step VII : Table for numerical computation :

Sr. no.	Mem.	Length (mm)	Area (mm²)	P (kN)	K	PKL/A	K²L/A	Q (kN)	QK (kN)	P$_f$ = P + QK (kN)
1.	AB	3000	2000	800/9	0	0	0		0	88.89
2.	BC	3000	2000	800/9	−0.8	−106.67	0.96		11.1	100
3.	CD	3000	2000	1000/9	0	0	0		0	111.1
4.	EF	3000	2000	−1000/9	−0.8	133.33	0.96		11.1	−100
5.	BF	2250	2400	0	−0.6	0	0.34	−13.88	8.33	8.33
6.	CE	2250	2400	−150/9	−0.6	9.375	0.34		8.33	−8.33
7.	AF	3750	3000	−1000/9	0	0	0		0	−111.1
8.	DE	3750	3000	−1250/9	0	0	0		0	−138.89
9.	CF	3750	1500	250/9	1	69.44	2.5		−13.88	13.88
10.	BE	3750	1500	0	1	0	2.5		−13.88	−13.88
					Σ =	105.475	7.6			

Step VIII : Calculation of redundant force :

$$Q = -\left[\dfrac{\sum\limits_{i=1}^{n}\left(\dfrac{PKL}{EA}\right)_i}{\sum\limits_{i=1}^{n}\left(\dfrac{K^2L}{EA}\right)_i}\right] = -\left[\dfrac{\sum\left(\dfrac{PKL}{A}\right)}{\sum\left(\dfrac{K^2L}{A}\right)}\right] = -\left(\dfrac{105.475}{7.6}\right)$$

$$= -13.88 \text{ kN} = 13.88 \text{ kN (Compressive)}$$

Step IX : Final forces in all the members of truss (P_f) :

Using the equation,

$$P_f = P + QK$$

final forces in all the members of truss are computed and are as tabulated above and shown in Fig. 7.11 (d).

Step X : Final reaction components at supports (R) :

Using the equation,

$$Q = R_p + Q \cdot R_k$$

final reaction components at supports are computed and are as shown in Fig. 7.11 (d).

7.6 INDETERMINATE TRUSSES WITH LACK OF FIT

The trusses are fabricated with the specific amount of tolerance in the length of members so that the members fit perfectly. But there may be errors in the fabrication, the length of a member of a truss may be slightly more or less than that required for the perfect assembly of members to form the truss. This is called the lack of fit due to the fabrication error.

The fabrication of a determinate truss with lack of fit can accommodate this error and adjust itself without stressing. Whereas in an internally indeterminate truss, a member having fabrication error does not fit in well and the truss does not adjust the discrepancy. The member is to be forced for the right fit and the forces are developed in the members of the truss due to this lack of fit, before the external loading. Therefore, it is necessary to analyse indeterminate trusses for the effect of lack of fit independently. The forces in the members of the truss due to (i) lack of fit and (ii) external loads are then superposed to get the final forces.

Analysis of indeterminate trusses having lack of fit is effectively done by the force method with the following additional concepts :

(i) The member which has lack of fit should be selected as the redundant member.

(ii) The known lack of fit of the redundant member is denoted by D_{QF}.

(iii) The sign convention for D_{QF} is important which is as follows :

D_{QF} is positive if the member is too long.

D_{QF} is negative if the member is too short.

(iv) The equation of the force method is used in the following form

$$D_Q = D_{QF} + F \cdot Q$$

$$0 = D_{QF} + \Sigma \left(\frac{K^2 L}{EA}\right) \cdot Q$$

$$\therefore \quad Q = -\left[\frac{D_{QF}}{\sum_{i=1}^{n} \left(\frac{K^2 L}{EA}\right)_i}\right] \qquad \ldots (7.7)$$

Following problems illustrate the procedure. Note that the numerical values of member properties and material properties are required.

Problem 7.9 : Analyse the truss supported as shown in Fig. 7.12 (a), if member AB is short by 5 mm. Take E = 200 GPa. Cross-sectional area of each member in cm² is indicated in brackets.

Solution : Data :

(i) Truss is supported as shown in Fig. 7.12 (a).

(ii) E = 200 GPa.

Objects :

(i) Redundant force,

(ii) Forces in all the members of truss and

(iii) Reactions at supports.

Concepts and Equations :

(i) Analysis of determinate truss,

(ii) Compatibility condition and

(iii) $Q = -\left[\dfrac{D_{QF}}{\sum_{i=1}^{n} \left(\dfrac{K^2 L}{EA}\right)_i}\right]$

Procedure :

Step I : Degree of static indeterminacy (D_{si}) :

(a) Degree of external indeterminacy = $(D_{si})_e$ = r − 3 = 4 − 3 = 1

(b) Degree of internal indeterminacy = $(D_{si})_i$ = m − (2j − 3) = 6 − (2 × 4 − 3) = 1

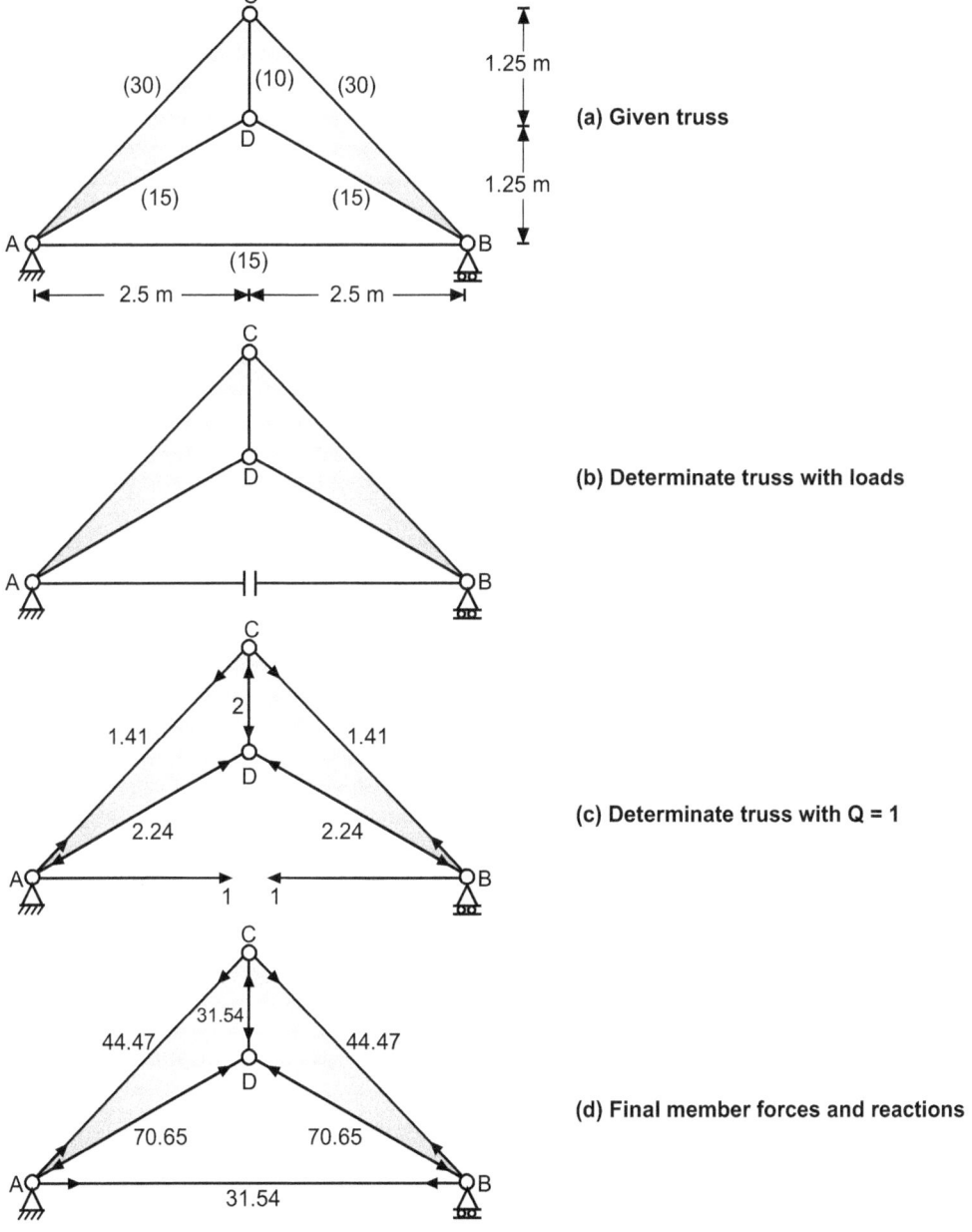

Fig. 7.12 : Illustrative Problem 7.9

Step II : Selection of redundant force (Q) :

Let,   Q = Force in member AB (Tensile)

Step III : Basic determinate truss :

Member AB is cut and determinate truss is obtained as shown in Fig. 7.12 (b).

Step IV : K-analysis of basic determinate truss :

Unit positive force corresponding to 'Q' is applied as shown in Fig. 7.12 (c). Reaction components (R_k) are zero for this analysis. Forces (K) in all the members of truss are found out and are shown in Fig. 7.12 (c).

Step V : Table for numerical computation :

Sr. No.	Member	Length (mm)	Area (mm²)	K	$\frac{K^2 L}{A}$	Q (kN)	$P_f = QK$ (kN)
1.	AD	2795	1500	− 2.24	9.35		− 70.65
2.	BD	2795	1500	− 2.24	9.35		− 70.65
3.	AC	3535	3000	1.41	2.34	31.54	44.47
4.	BC	3535	3000	1.41	2.34		44.47
5.	CD	1250	1000	− 2	5.00		− 63.08
6.	AB	5000	1500	1	3.33		31.54
				Σ =	31.71		

Step VI : Calculation of redundant force :

$$Q = -\left[\frac{D_{QF}}{\sum_{i=1}^{n} \left(\frac{K^2 L}{EA}\right)_i} \right]$$

$$= -\left(\frac{-5}{\frac{37.71}{200}} \right) = 31.54 \text{ kN (Tensile)}$$

Step VII : Final forces in all the members of truss (P_f) :

Using the equation,

$$P_f = QK$$

final forces in all the members of truss are computed and are as tabulated above and shown in Fig. 7.12 (d).

Step VIII : Final reaction components at supports (R) : Reaction components at supports are zero.

Problem 7.10 : Analyse the truss supported as shown in Fig. 7.13 (a), if member AC is long by 7 mm. Take E = 200 GPa and cross-sectional area of each member = 350 mm².

Solution : Data :

(i)   Truss is supported and loaded as shown in Fig. 7.13 (a).

(ii)   E = 200 GPa.

Objects :
(i) Redundant force, (ii) Forces in all the members of truss and
(iii) Reactions at supports.

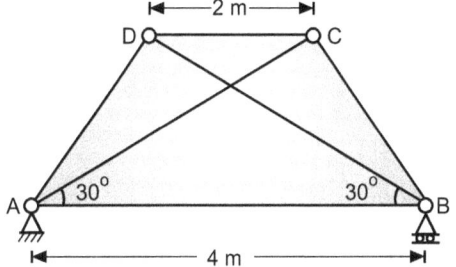

(a) Given truss

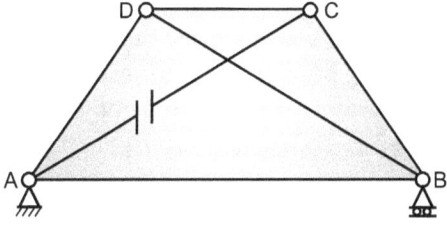

(b) Determinate truss

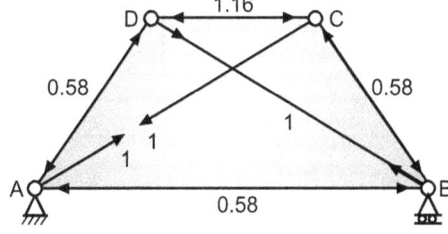

(c) Determinate truss with Q = 1

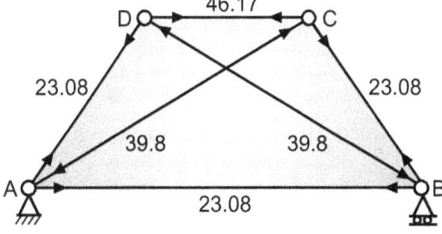

(d) Final member forces and reactions

Fig. 7.13 : Illustrative Problem 7.10

Concepts and Equations :

(i) Analysis of determinate truss,

(ii) Compatibility condition and

(iii) $Q = -\left[\dfrac{D_{QF}}{\sum_{i=1}^{n}\left(\dfrac{K^2 L}{EA}\right)_i}\right]$

Procedure :

Step I : Degree of static indeterminacy (D_{si}) :

(a) Degree of external indeterminacy = $(D_{si})_e = r - 3 = 4 - 3 = 1$

(b) Degree of internal indeterminacy = $(D_{si})_i = m - (2j - 3) = 6 - (2 \times 4 - 3) = 1$

Step II : Selection of redundant force (Q) :

Let,   Q = Force in member AC (Tensile)

Step III : Basic determinate truss :

Member AC is cut and determinate truss is obtained as shown in Fig. 7.13 (b).

Step IV : K-analysis of basic determinate truss : Unit positive force corresponding to 'Q' is applied as shown in Fig. 7.13 (c). Reaction components (R_k) are zero for this analysis. Forces (K) in all the members of truss are found out and are shown in Fig. 7.13 (c).

Step V : Table for numerical computation :

Sr. No.	Member	Length (m)	K	$K^2 L$	Q (kN)	P_f = KQ (kN)
1.	AB	4	− 0.58	1.345		23.08
2.	BC	2	− 0.58	0.673		23.08
3.	CD	2	− 1.16	2.691	− 39.80	46.17
4.	DA	2	− 0.58	0.673		23.08
5.	BD	3.464	1	3.464		− 39.80
6.	AC	3.464	1	3.464		− 39.80
			Σ =	12.31		

Step VI : Calculation of redundant force :

$Q = -\left[\dfrac{D_{QF}}{\sum_{i=1}^{n}\left(\dfrac{K^2 L}{EA}\right)_i}\right] = -\left[\dfrac{7}{\dfrac{12.31 \times 1000}{200 \times 350}}\right]$

    = − 39.80 kN = 39.80 kN (Compressive)

Step VII : Final forces in all the members of truss (P_f) :

Using the equation P_f = QK

final forces in all the members of truss are computed and are as tabulated above and shown in Fig. 7.13 (d).

Step VIII : Final reaction components at supports (R) :

Reaction components at supports are zero.

7.7 TEMPERATURE EFFECTS IN INDETERMINATE TRUSSES

The rise in temperature causes the increase in length of a member and the fall in temperature causes the decrease in length of a member if the member is free to expand or contract. This is called free thermal change in the length and given by (αtL), where α is the coefficient of linear expansion of the material, t is the change in temperature and L is the length of the member. If the free thermal expansion or contraction is prevented, then the stresses are developed. This is in general the effect of temperature.

In this context the following hints will be useful to consider the effects of temperature in trusses.

(i) In a statically determinate structure no internal forces are developed due to temperature changes as the thermal expansions or contractions are not prevented.

(ii) Due to uniform temperature variation in an externally determinate structure, no internal forces are induced.

(iii) Due to non-uniform temperature changes in an externally determinate structure, the internal forces are developed.

(iv) In an externally indeterminate structure there are always temperature effects irrespective of uniform or non-uniform temperature variations.

The forces in members of a truss due to temperature effects are obtained by the force method with the following techniques and for the following common situations.

(A) Externally and internally indeterminate truss subjected to the temperature change in a particular member :

(i) The temperature affected member is selected as the redundant member.

(ii) The force in the redundant member is Q.

(iii) Free thermal change in the redundant member is calculated as (αtL) and denoted by D_{Qt}.

(iv) D_{Qt} is positive if expansion i.e. rise in temperature and D_{Qt} is negative if contraction i.e. fall in temperature.

(v) The usual procedure of the force method is used to find Q and the member forces.

(vi) The basic equation is modified as

$$D_Q = D_{Qt} + F \cdot Q$$

$$\therefore \quad 0 = (\alpha tL) + \Sigma \left(\frac{K^2 L}{EA}\right) \cdot Q$$

$$\therefore \quad Q = -\left[\frac{\alpha tL}{\Sigma \left(\frac{K^2 L}{EA}\right)}\right] \quad \ldots (7.8)$$

(B) Externally indeterminate truss subjected to the uniform temperature change :

(i) The reaction component in the direction of axis of member connecting two supports is selected as the redundant force Q.

(ii) Free thermal expansion / contraction in the complete length of the member connecting the supports is calculated as (αtL) and denoted by D_{Qt}.

It is to be noted that this D_{Qt} corresponds to Q.

(iii) $Q = -\left[\dfrac{(\alpha t L)}{\sum_{i=1}^{n}\left(\dfrac{K^2 L}{EA}\right)_i}\right]$

Following illustrative problems will clarify the procedure in details.

Problem 7.11 : Analyse the truss supported as shown in Fig. 7.14 (a), if member AD is subjected to temperature drop of 30°C. Take E = 200 GPa and coefficient of thermal expansion = α = 1.1 × 10^{-5} /°C, cross-sectional area of each member in cm² is indicated in brackets.

Solution : Data :
(i) Truss is supported and loaded as shown in Fig. 7.14 (a).
(ii) E = 200 GPa. (iii) α = 1.1 × 10^{-5} /°C.

Objects :
(i) Redundant force, (ii) Forces in all the members of truss & (iii) Reactions of supports.

Concepts and Equations :
(i) Analysis of determinate truss, (ii) Compatibility condition and (iii) $Q = -\left[\dfrac{D_{Qt}}{\sum_{i=1}^{n}\left(\dfrac{K^2 L}{EA}\right)_i}\right]$

Procedure :

Step I : Degree of static indeterminacy (D_{si}) :
(a) Degree of external indeterminacy $(D_{si})_e$ = r − 3 = 4 − 3 = 1
(b) Degree of internal indeterminacy $(D_{si})_i$ = m − (2j − 3) = 6 − (2 × 4 − 3) = 1

Step II : Selection of redundant force (Q) :
Let, Q = Force in member AD (Tensile)

Step III : Basic determinate truss :
Member AD is cut and determinate truss is obtained as shown in Fig. 7.14 (b).

Step IV : K-analysis of basic determinate truss : Unit positive force corresponding to 'Q' is applied as shown in Fig. 7.14 (c). Reaction components (R_k) are zero for this analysis, forces (K) in all the members of truss are found out and are shown in Fig. 7.14 (c).

Step V : Table for numerical computations :

Sr. No.	Member	Length (mm)	Area (mm²)	K	$\dfrac{K^2 L}{A}$	Q (kN)	$P_f = QK$ (kN)
1.	AB	4000	2000	1.33	3.56		11.84
2.	BC	3000	1500	1	2		8.90
3.	CD	4000	2000	1.33	3.56	8.90	11.84
4.	AC	5000	2500	− 1.67	5.56		− 14.86
5.	BD	5000	2500	− 1.67	5.56		− 14.86
6.	AD	3000	1500	1	2		8.90
				Σ =	22.24		

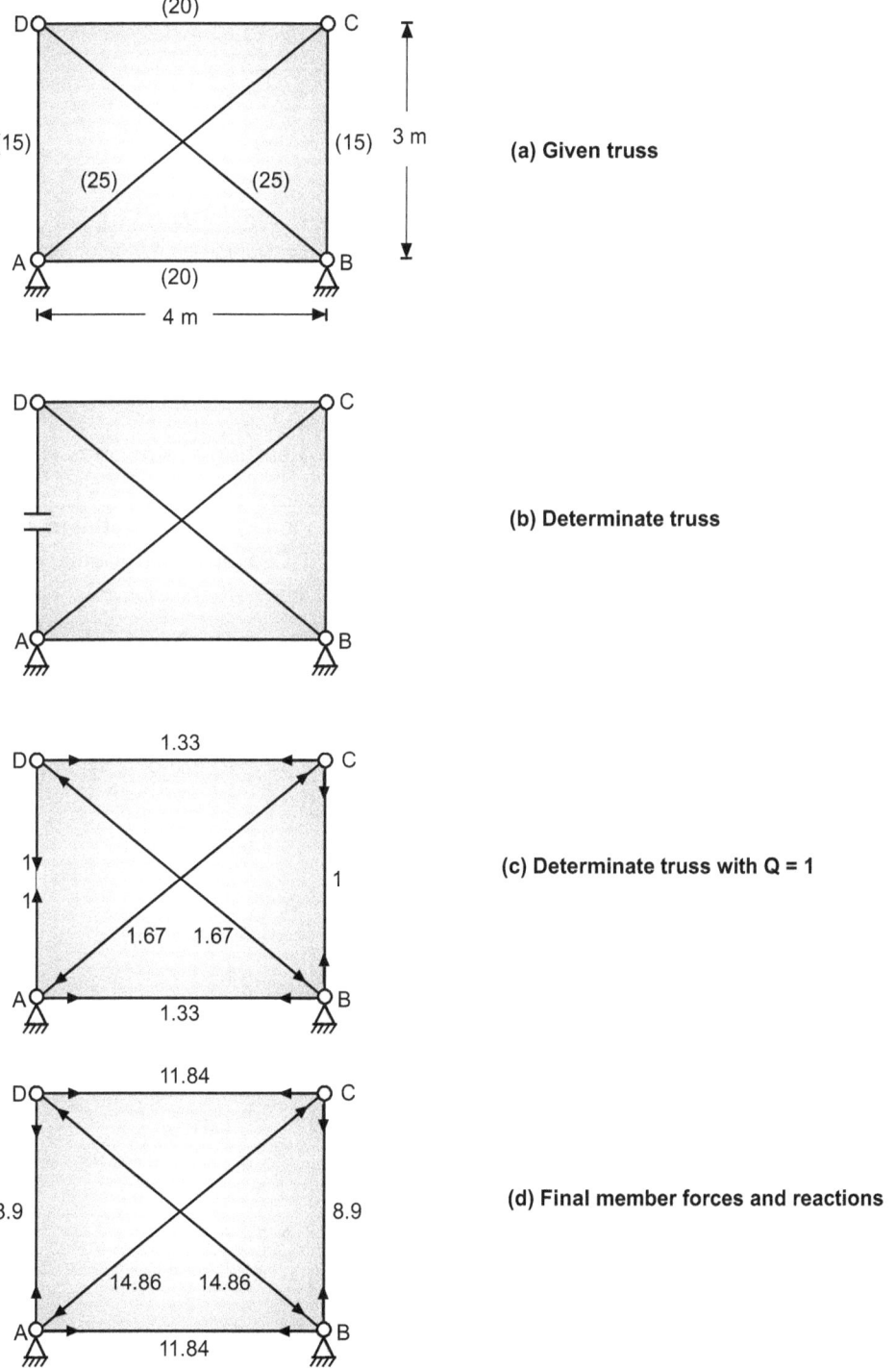

Fig. 7.14 : Illustrative Problem 7.11

Step VI : Calculation of redundant force :

$$Q = -\left[\dfrac{D_{Qt}}{\sum\limits_{i=1}^{n}\left(\dfrac{K^2L}{EA}\right)_i}\right] = -\left[\dfrac{\alpha tL}{\sum K^2L/EA}\right]$$

$$= -\left[\dfrac{-1.1 \times 10^{-5} \times 30 \times 3000}{22.24/200}\right] = 8.90 \text{ kN (Tensile)}$$

Step VII : Final forces in all the members of truss (P_f) :

Using the equation

$$P_f = QK$$

final forces in all the members of truss are computed and are as tabulated above and shown in Fig. 7.14 (d).

Step VIII : Final reaction components at supports (R) : Reaction components at supports are zero.

Problem 7.12 : Analyse the truss supported as shown in Fig. 7.15 (a), if the member AC is subjected to temperature rise of 20°C. Take E = 200 GPa and coefficient of thermal expansion = α = 1.2 × 10^{-5} /°C, cross-sectional area of each member in cm^2 is indicated in brackets.

Solution : Data :
(i) Truss is supported and loaded as shown in Fig. 7.15 (a).
(ii) E = 200 GPa, (iii) α = 1.2 × 10^{-5} / °C.

Objects :
(i) Redundant force,
(ii) Forces in all the members of truss and
(iii) Reactions at supports.

Concepts and Equations :
(i) Analysis of determinate truss,
(ii) Compatibility condition and
(iii) $Q = -\left[\dfrac{D_{Qt}}{\sum\limits_{i=1}^{n}\left(\dfrac{K^2L}{EA}\right)_i}\right]$

Procedure :

Step I : Degree of static indeterminacy (D_{si}) :
(a) Degree of external indeterminacy = $(D_{si})_e$ = r − 3 = 4 − 3 = 1
(b) Degree of internal indeterminacy = $(D_{si})_i$ = m − (2j − 3) = 6 − (2 × 4 − 3) = 1

Step II : Selection of redundant force (Q) :
Let,   Q = Force in member AC (Tensile)

Step III : Basic determinate truss : Member AC is cut and determinate truss is obtained as shown in Fig. 7.15 (b).

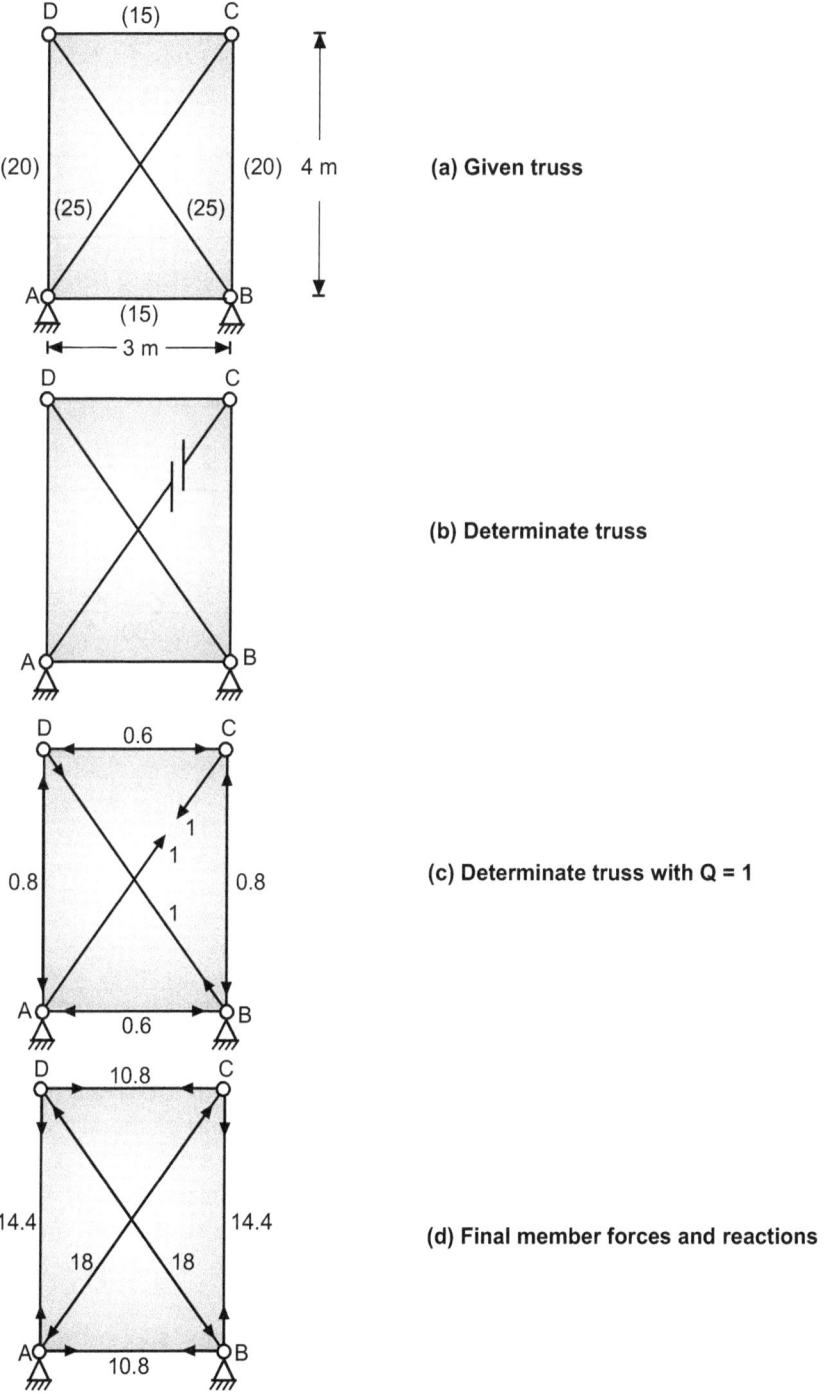

Fig. 7.15 : Illustrative Problem 7.12

Step IV : K-analysis of basic determinate truss : Unit positive force corresponding to 'Q' is applied as shown in Fig. 7.15 (c). Reaction components (R_k) are zero for this analysis. Force (K) in all the members of truss are found out and are shown in Fig. 7.15 (c).

Step V : Table for numerical computation :

Sr. No.	Member	Length (mm)	Area (mm²)	K	$\frac{K^2L}{A}$	Q (kN)	$P_f = QK$ (kN)
1.	AB	3000	1500	– 0.6	0.72		10.8
2.	BC	4000	2000	– 0.8	1.28		14.4
3.	CD	3000	1500	– 0.6	0.72	– 18	10.8
4.	DA	4000	2000	– 0.8	1.28		14.4
5.	BD	5000	2500	1	2		– 18
6.	AC	5000	2500	1	2		– 18
				Σ =	8		

Step VI : Calculation of redundant force :

$$Q = -\left[\frac{D_{Qt}}{\sum_{i=1}^{n}\left(\frac{K^2L}{EA}\right)_i}\right] = -\left[\frac{\alpha t L}{\sum K^2L / EA}\right] = -\left[\frac{1.2 \times 10^{-5} \times 20 \times 3000}{8/200}\right] = -18 \text{ kN}$$

= 18 kN (Compressive)

Step VII : Final forces in all the members of truss (P_f) :

Using the equation, $P_f = QK$

final forces in all the members of truss are computed and are as tabulated above and shown in Fig. 7.15 (d).

Step VIII : Final reaction components at supports (R) :

Reaction components at supports are zero.

7.8 EFFECTS OF YIELDING OF SUPPORT IN INDETERMINATE TRUSSES

The yielding of the support of externally indeterminate truss induces the internal forces in the members of truss. The conventional procedure of the force method is used to analyse the externally indeterminate trusses for the effect of the yielding of the support employing the following particular techniques.

(i) Force corresponding to yielding of support must be selected as the redundant.
(ii) Basic determinate truss is obtained by removing the constraint corresponding to yielding of support. The redundant force is the reaction component corresponding to the yielding.
(iii) The geometrical condition of deformation at the yielding support is that D_Q should be equal to the amount of yielding.
(iv) The basic equation of the force method in the following form is applied to determine the redundant force i.e. the reaction component due to the effect of yielding of support only.

S. E. CIVIL : STRUCTURAL ANALYSIS - I   INDETERMINATE TRUSSES

$$D_Q = F \cdot Q$$

$$\therefore \quad D_Q = \Sigma \left(\frac{K^2 L}{EA}\right) \cdot Q$$

$$\therefore \quad Q = \left[\frac{D_Q}{\sum_{i=1}^{n} \left(\frac{K^2 L}{EA}\right)_i} \right] \quad \quad ...(7.9)$$

where D_Q is the known amount of the yielding of the support i.e. known translation. Generally, it is the settlement of support.

(v) D_Q is considered a positive or negative according to the co-ordinate system i.e. positive in the positive direction of the co-ordinate axes and negative in the negative direction of the co-ordinate axes.

The following problem illustrates the procedure for this case.

Problem 7.13 : Analyse the truss supported as shown in Fig. 7.16 (a), if support B sinks by 3 mm. Take E = 210 GPa and cross-sectional area of each member = 400 mm².

Solution : Data :
(i)   Truss is supported and loaded as shown in Fig. 7.16 (a).
(ii)   E = 210 GPa.

Objects :
(i)   Redundant force, (ii) Forces in all the members of truss and
(iii)   Reactions at supports.

Concepts and Equations :
(i)   Analysis of determinate truss,
(ii)   Compatibility condition and

(iii) $Q = \left[\dfrac{D_Q}{\sum_{i=1}^{n} \left(\dfrac{K^2 L}{EA}\right)_i} \right]$

Procedure :

Step I : Degree of static indeterminacy (D_{si}) :
(a)   Degree of external indeterminacy = $(D_{si})_e$ = r − 3 = 4 − 3 = 1
(b)   Degree of internal indeterminacy = $(D_{si})_i$ = m − (2j − 3) = 9 − (2 × 6 − 3) = 0
     Total degree of static indeterminacy = D_{si} = $(D_{si})_e$ + $(D_{si})_i$ = 1 + 0 = 1

Step II : Selection of redundant force (Q) :
Let,   Q = V_B (↑)

Step III : Basic determinate truss : Roller support at B is removed and determinate truss is obtained as shown in Fig. 7.16 (b).

Step IV : K-analysis of basic determinate truss : Unit positive force corresponding to 'Q' is applied as shown in Fig. 7.16 (c). Reaction components (R_k) and forces (K) in all the members of truss are found out and are shown in Fig. 7.16 (c).

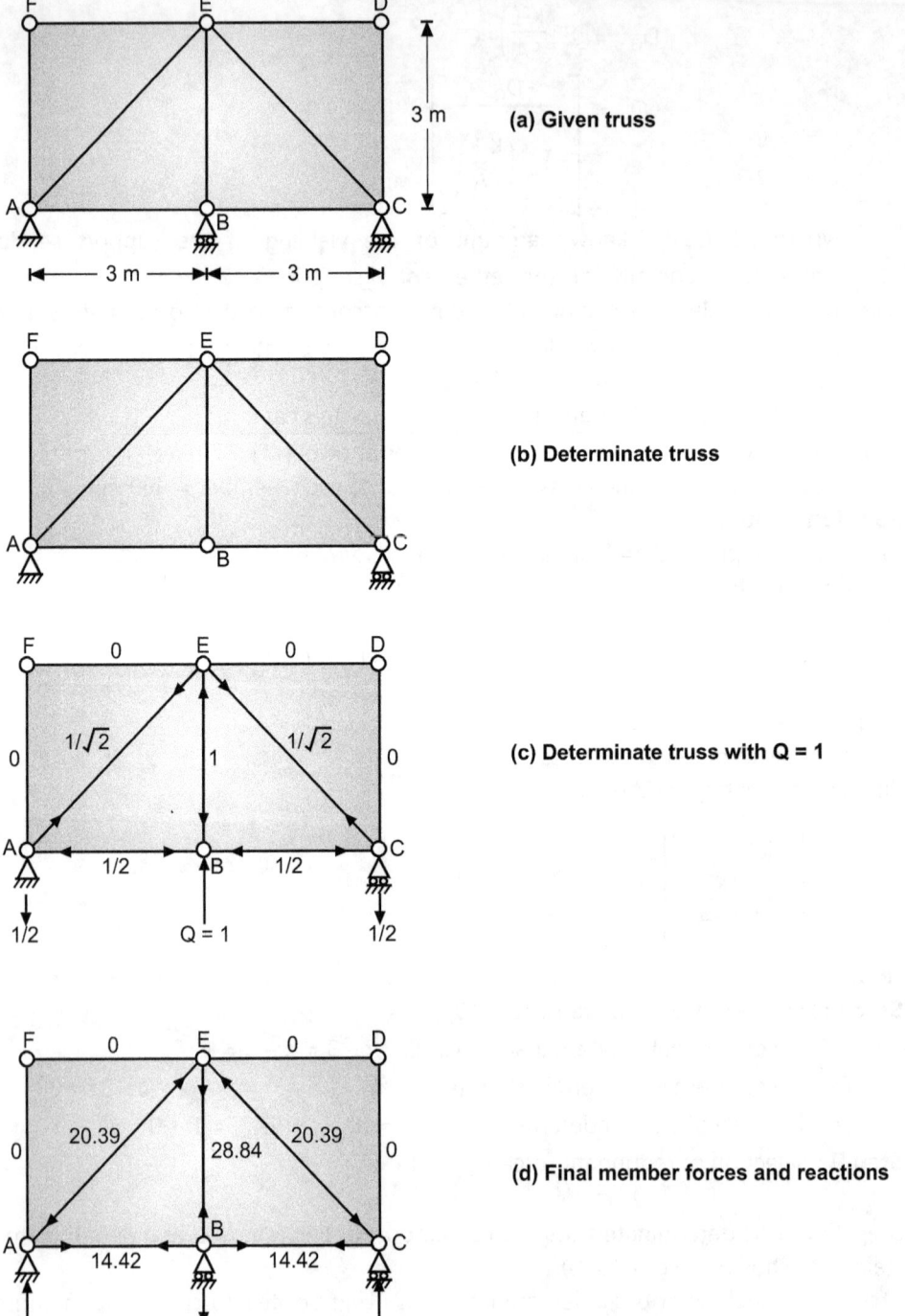

Fig. 7.16 : Illustrative Problem 7.13

Step V : Table for numerical computation :

Sr. No.	Member	Length (m)	K	K²L	Q (kN)	P_f = KQ (kN)
1.	AB	3	− 1/2	0.75		14.42
2.	BC	3	− 1/2	0.75		14.42
3.	CD	3	0	0		0
4.	DE	3	0	0		0
5.	EF	3	0	0	− 28.84	0
6.	FA	3	0	0		0
7.	EB	3	− 1	3		28.84
8.	AE	$3\sqrt{2}$	$1/\sqrt{2}$	$3/\sqrt{2}$		− 20.39
9.	CE	$3\sqrt{2}$	$1/\sqrt{2}$	$3/\sqrt{2}$		− 20.39
				Σ = 8.74		

Step VI : Calculation of redundant force :

$$Q = \left[\dfrac{D_Q}{\sum_{i=1}^{n}\left(\dfrac{K^2 L}{EA}\right)_i}\right] = \left[\dfrac{-3}{8.74 \times 1000 / 210 \times 400}\right] = -28.84 \text{ kN}$$

Step VII : Final forces in all the members of truss (P_f) :

Using the equation

$$P_f = QK$$

final forces in all the members of truss are computed and are as tabulated above and shown in Fig. 7.16 (d).

Step VIII : Final reaction components at supports (R) :

Using the equation

$$R = Q \cdot R_k$$

final reaction components at supports are computed and are as shown in Fig. 7.16 (d).

Problem 7.14 : Analyse the truss supported and loaded as shown in Fig. 7.17 (a). If support B sinks by 3 mm. Take E = 210 GPa and cross-sectional area of each member = 400 mm².

Solution : Data :
(i) Truss is supported and loaded as shown in Fig. 7.17 (a).
(ii) E = 210 GPa

Objects :
(i) Redundant force,
(ii) Forces in all the members of truss and
(iii) Reactions at supports.

Concepts and Equations :
(i) Principle of superposition,

(ii) Analysis of determinate truss,
(iii) Compatibility condition and
(iv) $D_Q = D_{QL} + FQ$

Procedure :

Step I : Degree of static indeterminacy (D_{si}) :

(a) Degree of external indeterminacy = $(D_{si})_e = r - 3 = 4 - 3 = 1$

(b) Degree of internal indeterminacy = $(D_{si})_i = m - (2j - 3) = 9 - (2 \times 6 - 3) = 0$

Total degree of static indeterminacy = $(D_{si})_e + (D_{si})_i = 1 + 0 = 1$

Step II : Selection of redundant force (Q) :

Let, $Q = V_B (\uparrow)$

Step III : Basic determinate truss :

Roller support at B is removed and determinate truss is obtained as shown in Fig. 7.17 (b).

Step IV : Superposition : The given indeterminate truss is considered as superposition of (a) basic determinate truss with given loads [Fig. 7.17 (b)] and (b) unknown redundant force 'Q' times the basic determinate truss with unit positive redundant force (Fig. 7.17 (c)).

Step V : P-analysis of basic determinate truss due to applied loads : Considering static equilibrium of truss all the reaction components (R_p) are found out as shown in Fig. 7.17 (b). Also the forces (P) in all the members of truss are found out and are as shown in Fig. 7.17 (b).

Step VI : K-analysis of basic determinate truss : Unit positive force corresponding to 'Q' is applied as shown in Fig. 7.17 (c). All the reaction components (R_k) and forces (K) in all the members of truss are found out and are as shown in Fig. 7.17 (c).

Step VII : Table for numerical computation :

Sr. No.	Member	Length (m)	P (kN)	K	PKL	K²L	Q (kN)	QK (kN)	$P_f = P + QK$ (kN)
1.	AB	3	47.5	– 1/2	– 71.25	0.75		– 11.93	35.57
2.	BC	3	47.5	– 1/2	– 71.25	0.75		– 11.93	35.57
3.	CD	3	0	0	0	0		0	0
4.	DE	3	0	0	0	0	23.85	0	0
5.	EF	3	– 20	0	0	0		0	– 20
6.	FA	3	0	0	0	0		0	0
7.	EB	3	0	– 1	0	3		– 23.85	– 23.85
8.	AE	$3\sqrt{2}$	$-27.5\sqrt{2}$	$1/\sqrt{2}$	$-82.5\sqrt{2}$	$3/\sqrt{2}$		16.86	– 22.03
9.	CE	$3\sqrt{2}$	$-47.5\sqrt{2}$	$1/\sqrt{2}$	$-142.5\sqrt{2}$	$3/\sqrt{2}$		16.86	– 50.32
				Σ =	– 460.69	8.74			

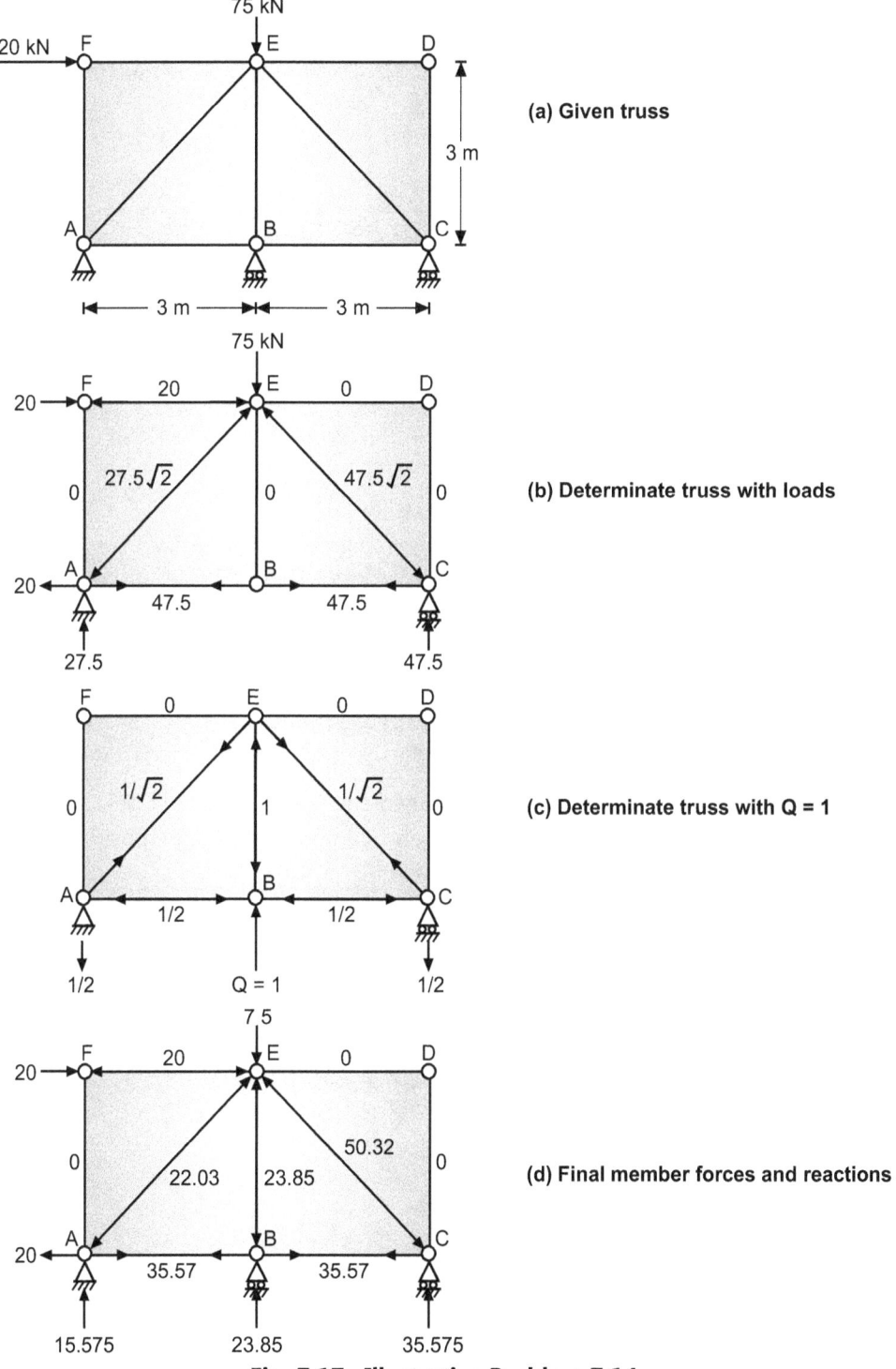

Fig. 7.17 : Illustrative Problem 7.14

Step VIII : Physical requirement of displacement (D_Q) : Vertical translation at B in the given structure = 3 mm (↓) ∴ D_Q = – 3 mm.

Step IX : Calculation of redundant force :
$$D_Q = D_{QL} + FQ$$
where, D_Q = – 3 mm

$$D_{QL} = \sum_{i=1}^{n}\left(\frac{PKL}{EA}\right)_i = \frac{-460.69 \times 1000}{210 \times 400} = -5.48 \text{ mm}$$

$$F = \sum_{i=1}^{n}\left(\frac{K^2L}{EA}\right)_i = \frac{8.74 \times 1000}{210 \times 400} = 0.104 \text{ mm/kN}$$

Substituting in above equation, we get
$$Q = 23.85 \text{ kN } (\uparrow)$$

Step X : Final forces in all the members of truss (P_f) :

Using the equation,
$$P_f = P + QK$$
final forces in all the members of truss are computed and are as tabulated above and shown in Fig. 7.17 (d).

Step XI : Final reaction components at supports (R) :

Using the equation,
$$R = R_p + Q \cdot R_k$$
final reaction components at supports are computed and are as shown in Fig. 7.17 (d).

Note : Similar results of above Problem can also be obtained by superposition of results of Problems 7.1 and 7.13.

Problem 7.15 : The frame shown in Fig. 7.18 is pin jointed to rigid supports A and B and the joints C and D are also pinned. The diagonals AD and BC act independently and all the members are having same cross-sectional area and material. ABC and BCD are equilateral triangles. Initially, there is no load in any of the members which may be assumed weightless. If a load of 5 kN is hung at D, calculate the forces in all the members of the frame.

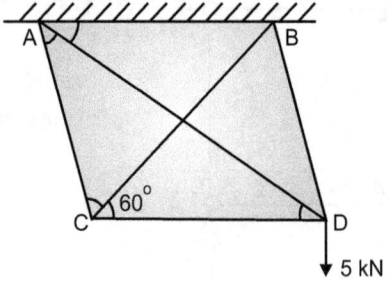

Fig. 7.18

Solution : Internal static indeterminacy = m – 2j = 5 – 2 × 2 = 1.

Redundant : AD.

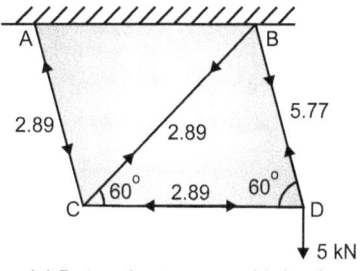
(a) Determinate truss with load

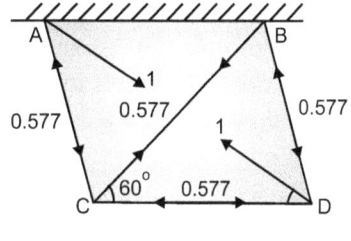
(b) Determinate truss with $\phi = 1$

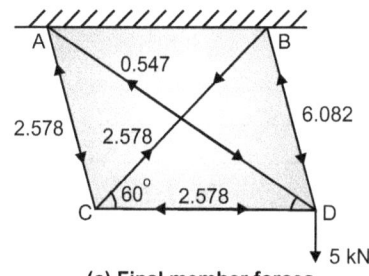
(c) Final member forces

Fig. 7.19

Joint D :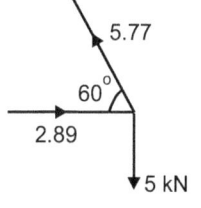

Joint C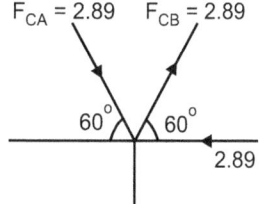

$$\Sigma F_y = 0$$
$$\therefore F_{CA} = F_{CB}$$
$$\Sigma F_x = 0$$
$$+ F_{CA} \cos 60 + F_{CB} \cos 60 - 2.89 = 0$$
$$\therefore F_{CA} = 2.89$$

Member	Length	P	K	PKl	K²L	φ	Qk	Pf = P + QK
AC	L	−2.89	−0.577	1.667/L	0.33L		0.312	−2.578
CD	L	−2.89	−0.577	1.667/L	0.33L		0.312	−2.578
DB	L	5.77	−0.577	−3.33/L	0.33L	−0.547	0.312	6.082
AD	√3 L	0	1	0	√3 L		0	−0.547
BC	L	2.89	0.577	1.667/L	0.33 L		−0.312	2.578
			ΣPKl	1.667/L	ΣK²l = 3.05 L			

EXERCISE

For pin jointed plane trusses in problems 1 to 17, find forces in all the members. Take E = constant. Figures in the bracket indicate cross-sectional areas of members in cm², wherever mentioned. Otherwise A shall be taken constant.

1.

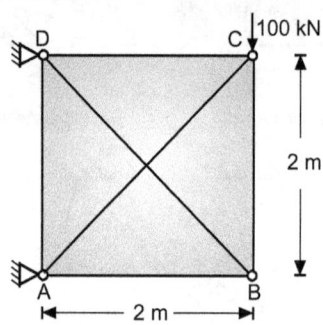

Fig. 7.20

(**Ans.** F_{AB} = – 54.84 kN, F_{BC} = – 54.84 kN, F_{CD} = 45.16 kN, F_{AD} = 45.16 kN, F_{AC} = – 63.87 kN, F_{DB} = 77.55 kN)

2.

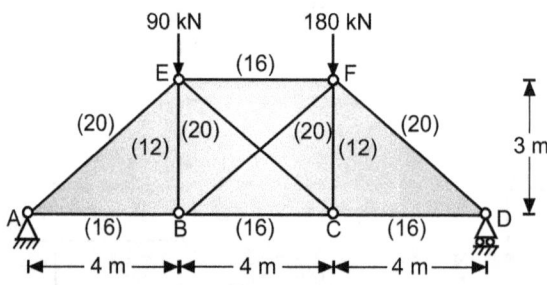

Fig. 7.21

(**Ans.** F_{AE} = – 200 kN, F_{AB} = 160 kN, F_{BC} = 175.65 kN, F_{BE} = 171.74 kN, F_{EF} = – 184.35 kN, F_{EC} = 30.44 kN, F_{CF} = – 18.26 kN, F_{DF} = – 250 kN, F_{DC} = 200 kN, F_{BF} = – 19.56 kN)

3.

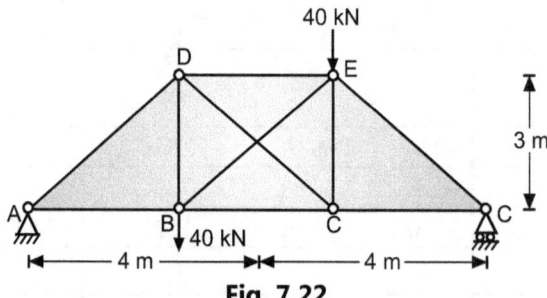

Fig. 7.22

(**Ans.** F_{AB} = 26.6 kN, F_{AD} = – 33.2 kN, F_{BD} = 31.2 kN, F_{DC} = – 18.7 kN, F_{BE} = 14.4 kN, F_{DE} = – 11.6 kN, F_{BC} = 15 kN, F_{EC} = – 48.8 kN)

4.

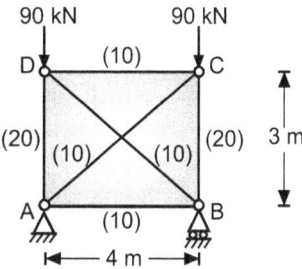

Fig. 7.23

(**Ans.** $F_{AB} = 8$ kN, $F_{DC} = 8$ kN, $F_{AD} = -84$ kN, $F_{BC} = -84$ kN, $F_{AC} = -10$ kN, $F_{BD} = -10$ kN)

5.

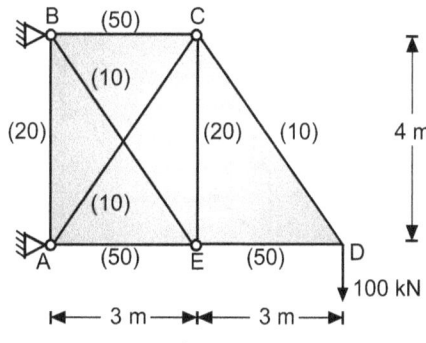

Fig. 7.24

(**Ans.** $F_{AB} = -40.14$ kN, $F_{AE} = -105.11$ kN, $F_{BE} = 50.18$ kN, $F_{BC} = 119.89$ kN, $F_{CE} = -40.14$ kN, $F_{DE} = -75$ kN, $F_{DC} = 125$ kN, $F_{AC} = -74.82$ kN)

6.

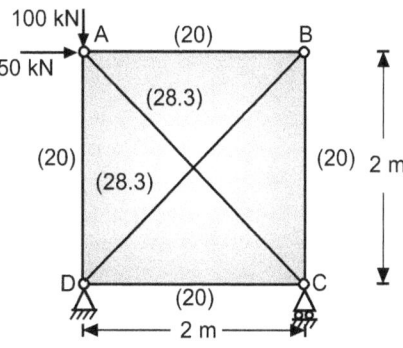

Fig. 7.25

(**Ans.** $F_{AB} = -12.5$ kN, $F_{BC} = 12.5$ kN, $F_{AC} = -53$ kN, $F_{AD} = -62.5$ kN, $F_{DC} = 37.5$ kN, $F_{DB} = 17.68$ kN)

7.

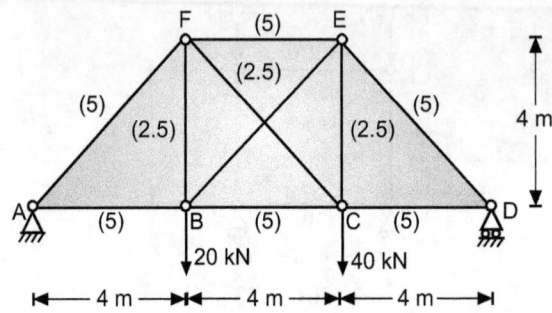

Fig. 7.26

(**Ans.** F_{AB} = 26.67 kN, F_{BC} = 23.06 kN, F_{CD} = 33.33 kN, F_{FE} = – 36.93 kN, F_{AF} = – 37.73 kN, F_{ED} = – 47.06 kN, F_{BF} = 23.06 kN, F_{CE} = 29.73 kN, F_{BE} = 5.08 kN, F_{CF} = 14.5 kN)

8.

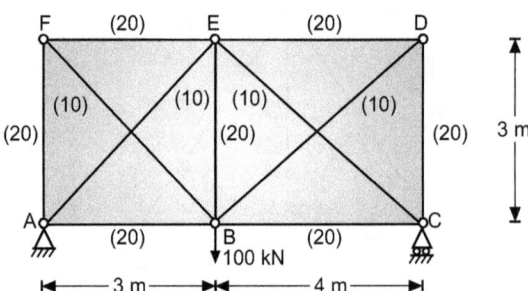

Fig. 7.27

(**Ans.** F_{AB} = 27.2 kN, F_{BC} = 27.2 kN, F_{FE} = – 29.95 kN, F_{ED} = – 30 kN, F_{AF} = 29.95 kN, F_{BE} = 47.55 kN, F_{CD} = – 22.5 kN, F_{AE} = – 38.5 kN, F_{FB} = – 42.3 kN, F_{BD} = – 37.55 kN, F_{EC} = – 33.9 kN)

9.

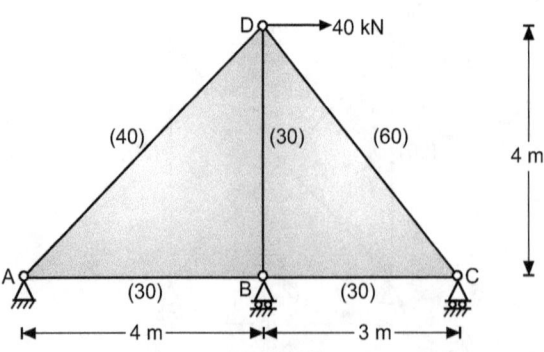

Fig. 7.28

(**Ans.** F_{AB} = 16.12 kN, F_{BC} = 16.12 kN, F_{AD} = 33.77 kN, F_{BD} = – 23.80 kN,

F_{CD} = – 26.87 kN)

10.

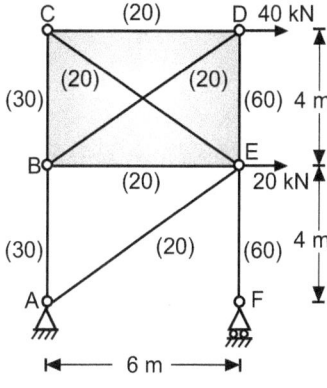

Fig. 7.29

(**Ans.** F_{AB} = 26.67 kN, F_{AE} = 72.11 kN, F_{EF} = – 72.11 kN, F_{BE} = – 40 kN, F_{BC} = 0, F_{BD} = 48.1 kN, F_{CE} = 0, F_{DE} = – 26.67 kN, F_{DC} = 0)

11.

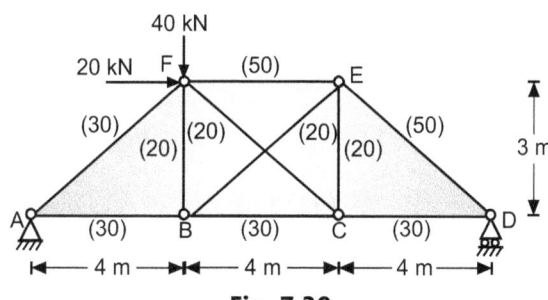

Fig. 7.30

(**Ans.** F_{AB} = 48.89 kN, F_{AF} = – 36.11, F_{BF} = – 10.43 kN, F_{FE} = – 38.35 kN, F_{FC} = – 13.18 kN, F_{BE} = 17.38 kN, F_{BC} = 35 kN, F_{DE} = – 30.55 kN, F_{CE} = 7.91 kN, F_{CD} = 24.44 kN)

12.

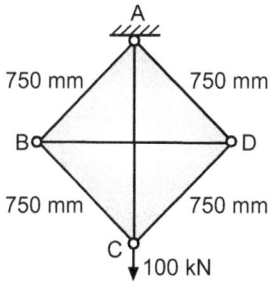

Fig. 7.31

(**Ans.** F_{AB} = 20.72 kN, F_{BC} = 20.72 kN, F_{CD} = 20.72 kN, F_{DA} = 20.72 kN, F_{BD} = – 29.3 kN, F_{AC} = 70.7 kN)

13.

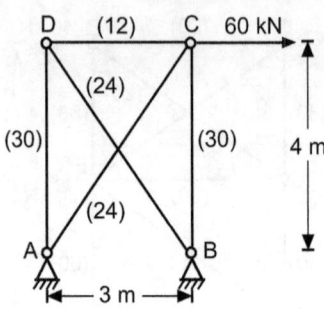

Fig. 7.32

(**Ans.** $F_{AD} = 34.58$ kN, $F_{DC} = 26$ kN, $F_{CB} = -45.42$ kN, $F_{AC} = 56.58$ kN, $F_{BD} = -43.4$ kN)

14.

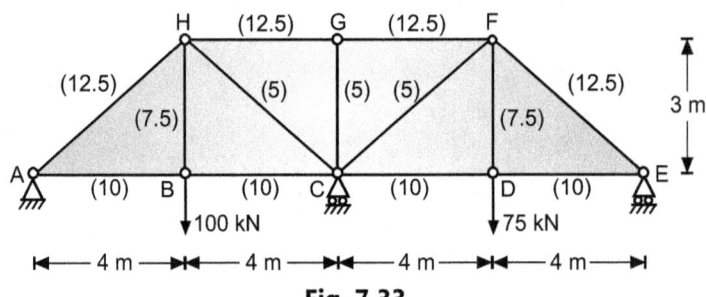

Fig. 7.33

(**Ans.** $F_{AH} = -85.75$ kN, $F_{HG} = -3.92$ kN, $F_{GF} = -3.92$ kN, $F_{FE} = -64.91$ kN, $F_{AB} = 68.625$ kN, $F_{BC} = 68.625$ kN, $F_{CD} = 51.88$ kN, $F_{DE} = 51.88$ kN, $F_{BH} = 100$ kN, $F_{CH} = 80.75$ kN, $F_{CG} = 0$, $F_{CF} = 60.125$ kN, $F_{DF} = 75$ kN)

15.

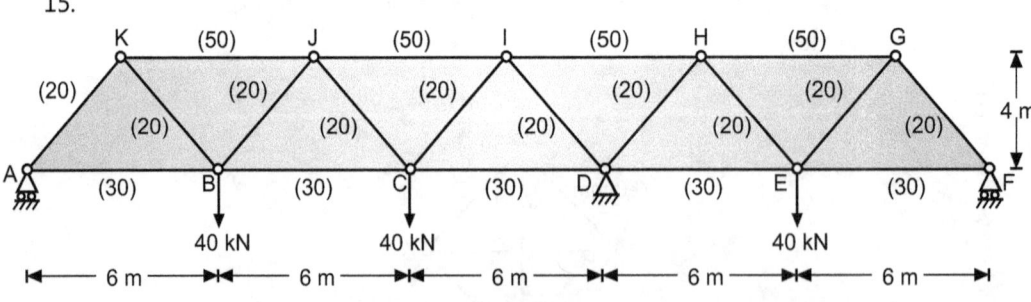

Fig. 7.34

(**Ans.** $F_{AB} = 25.15$ kN, $F_{AK} = -41.92$ kN, $F_{KB} = 41.92$ kN, $F_{KJ} = -50.31$ kN, $F_{BC} = 45.46$ kN, $F_{BJ} = 8.1$ kN, $F_{CJ} = -8.1$ kN, $F_{JI} = -40.62$ kN, $F_{CD} = 5.77$ kN, $F_{CI} = 58.1$ kN, $F_{DI} = -58.1$ kN, $F_{IH} = 29.1$ kN, $F_{DE} = -6.81$ kN, $F_{DH} = -37.11$ kN, $F_{EH} = 37.11$ kN, $F_{HG} = -15.46$ kN, $F_{EF} = 7.73$ kN, $F_{EG} = 12.9$ kN, $F_{FG} = -12.9$ kN)

16.

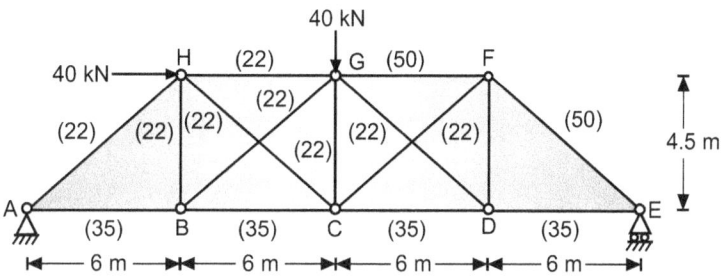

Fig. 7.35

(**Ans.** $F_{AB} = 56.67$ kN, $F_{AH} = -20.83$ kN, $F_{HB} = 10.17$ kN, $F_{HG} = -59.78$ kN,

$F_{HC} = 3.89$ kN, $F_{BG} = -16.95$ kN, $F_{BC} = 70.22$ kN, $F_{GC} = -17.22$ kN,

$F_{DG} = -21$ kN, $F_{GF} = -56.53$ kN, $F_{CD} = 53.47$ kN, $F_{CF} = 24.83$ kN,

$F_{DF} = 12.60$ kN, $F_{EF} = -45.83$ kN, $F_{DE} = 36.67$ kN)

17.

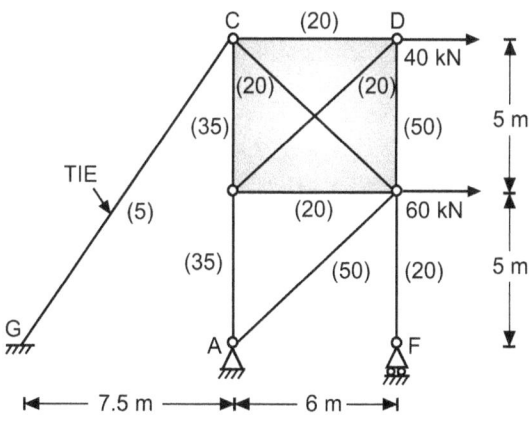

Fig. 7.36

(**Ans.** $F_{AB} = 9.73$ kN, $F_{BC} = -3.18$ kN, $F_{CD} = 24.50$ kN, $F_{CE} = -17.72$ kN,

$F_{BD} = 20.17$ kN, $F_{ED} = -12.91$ kN, $F_{BE} = -15.50$ kN, $F_{EF} = -98.51$ kN,

$F_{AE} = 115.99$ kN, $F_{GC} = 18.16$ kN)

18. A pin jointed rectangular truss is as shown in Fig. 7.37. The member AD is last to be added and is short by 4 mm. Find the forces in all the members when it is forced into position. Take E = 200 GPa. Figures in the bracket indicate cross-sectional areas of members in cm².

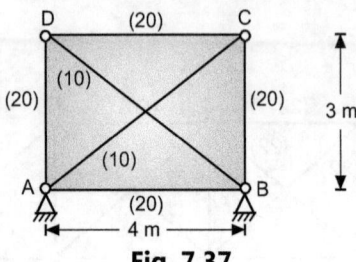

Fig. 7.37

(**Ans.** F_{AB} = 28.04 kN, F_{BC} = 21.08 kN, F_{CD} = 28.04 kN, F_{DA} = 21.08 kN, F_{DB} = – 35.2 kN, F_{AC} = – 35.2 kN)

19. A pin jointed truss is as shown in Fig. 7.38. The member EF is last to be added and is long by 2 mm. Find forces in all the members of truss when it is forced into position. Take E = 200 GPa. Figures in the bracket indicate cross-sectional areas of members in cm².

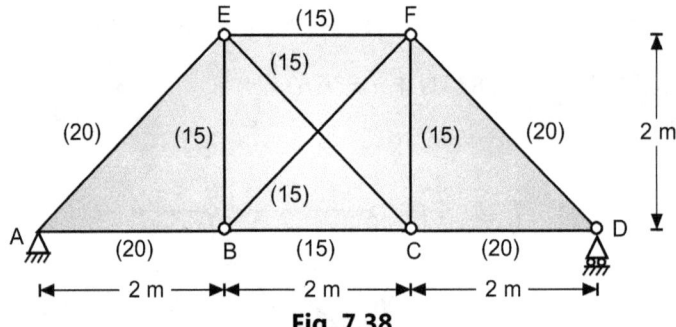

Fig. 7.38

(**Ans.** F_{AE} = 0, F_{AB} = 0, F_{BE} = – 31.1 kN, F_{EF} = – 31.3 kN, F_{EC} = 43.97 kN, F_{BF} = 43.97 kN, F_{BC} = – 31.1 kN, F_{CF} = – 31.1 kN, F_{FD} = 0, F_{CD} = 0)

20. A pin jointed truss is shown in Fig. 7.39. All members has cross-sectional area of 10 cm². If there is a rise of temperature of member BD by 30°C, determine forces due to change in temperature. Coefficient of linear expansion $\alpha = 12 \times 10^{-6}$ per °C and E = 200 GPa.

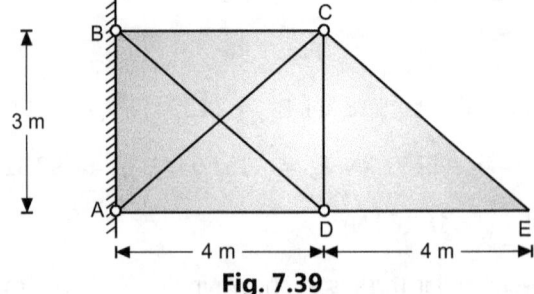

Fig. 7.39

(**Ans.** F_{BC} = 17.77 kN, F_{CD} = 13.33 kN, F_{AD} = 17.77 kN, F_{AC} = – 22.22 kN, F_{BD} = – 22.22 kN, F_{DE} = 0, F_{CE} = 0).

MULTIPLE CHOICE QUESTIONS

1. The truss is shown in Fig. 1. The P-forces are as shown. The vertical deflection of C is

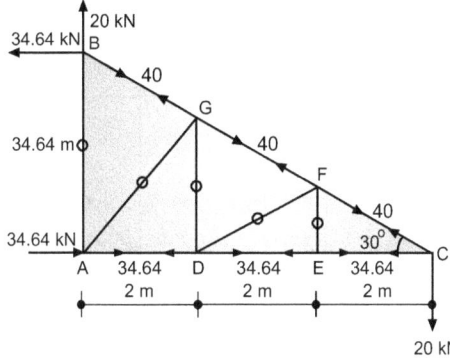

Fig. 1

   (a) 8.28 mm (b) 5.97 mm (c) 2.28 mm (d) 6.77 mm

2. The truss is shown in Fig. 1. The P-forces are as shown. The horizontal deflection of C is

   (a) 0.64 mm (b) 0.52 mm (c) 0.89 mm (d) 0.77 mm

3. The truss is shown in Fig. 2. The P-forces are as shown. Axial rigidity of member is 20000 kN. The vertical deflection of C is

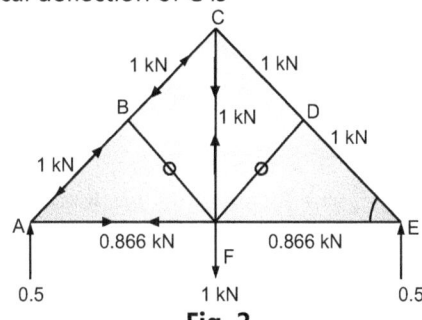

Fig. 2

   (a) 10.16 mm (b) 19.42 mm (c) 34.25 mm (d) 46.77 mm

4. The truss is shown in Fig. 3. The P-forces are as shown. The horizontal deflection of C is

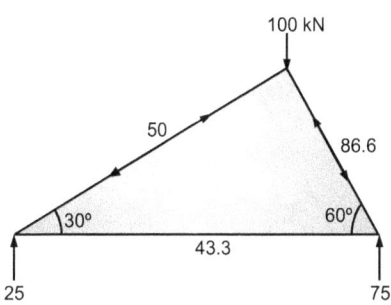

Fig. 3

   (a) 0.4 mm (b) 0.7 mm (c) 0.1 mm (d) 0.5 mm

5. The truss is shown in Fig. 3. The P-forces are as shown. The vertical deflection of C is
   (a) 5.64 mm   (b) 9.52 mm   (c) 7.75 mm   (d) 3.45 mm
6. The truss is shown in Fig. 4. The P-forces are as shown. The vertical deflection of C is

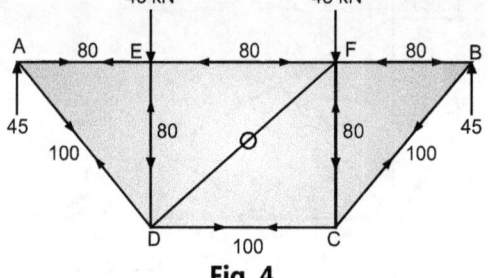

Fig. 4

   (a) 8.29 mm   (b) 6.34 mm   (c) 5.67 mm   (d) 4.30 mm
7. The truss is shown in Fig. 5. The P-forces are as shown. The vertical deflection of C is

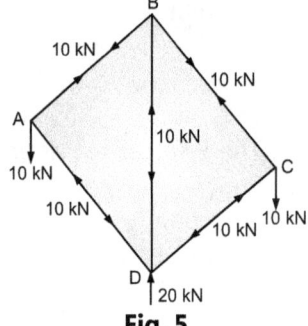

Fig. 5

   (a) 6.97 mm   (b) 7.54 mm   (c) 9.19 mm   (d) 1.75 mm
8. The truss is shown in Fig. 5. The P-forces are as shown. The horizontal deflection of D is
   (a) 0.908 mm   (b) 0.389 mm   (c) 0.117 mm   (d) 0.505 mm
9. The truss is shown in Fig. 6. The P-forces are as shown. The horizontal deflection of C is

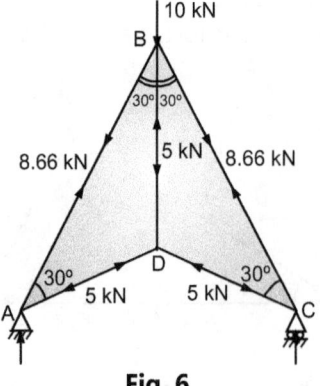

Fig. 6

   (a) 0.24 mm   (b) 0.75 mm   (c) 0.19 mm   (d) 0.57 mm

10. The truss is shown in Fig. 7. The P-forces are as shown. The vertical deflection of C is

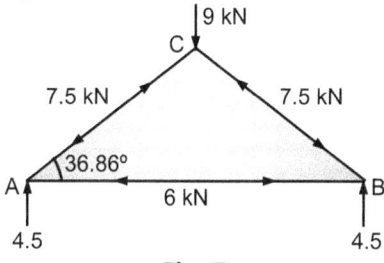

Fig. 7

   (a) 6.97 mm   (b) 2.47 mm   (c) 3.94 mm   (d) 7.34 mm

11. The truss is shown in Fig. 7. The P-forces are as shown. The horizontal deflection of C is

   (a) 7.9 mm   (b) 6.3 mm   (c) 3.9 mm   (d) 1.2 mm

12. The truss is shown in Fig. 8. The P-forces are as shown. The vertical deflection of E is

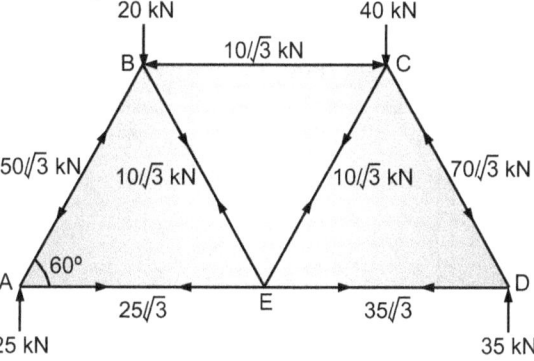

Fig. 8

   (a) 0.3 mm   (b) 0.7 mm   (c) 0.1 mm   (d) 0.5 mm

13. The truss is shown in Fig. 8. The P-forces are as shown. The horizontal deflection of E is

   (a) 0.144 mm   (b) 0.766 mm   (c) 0.333 mm   (d) 0.515 mm

14. The truss is shown in Fig. 9. The P-forces are as shown. The vertical deflection of C is

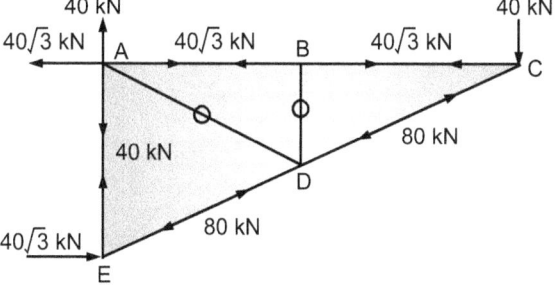

Fig. 9

   (a) 7.415 mm   (b) 3.263 mm   (c) 6.122 mm   (d) 5.566 mm

15. The truss is shown in Fig. 9. The P-forces are as shown. The horizontal deflection of C is
    (a) 0.14 mm   (b) 0.29 mm   (c) 0.33 mm   (d) 0.96 mm
16. The truss is shown in Fig. 10. The P-forces are as shown. The vertical deflection of C is

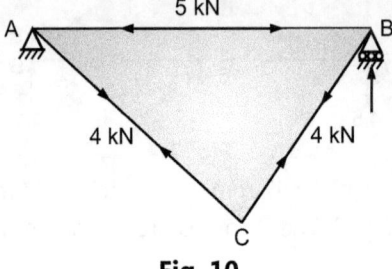

Fig. 10

    (a) 2.45 mm   (b) 7.92 mm   (c) 5.33 mm   (d) 4.56 mm
17. The truss is shown in Fig. 10. The P-forces are as shown. The horizontal deflection of C is
    (a) 0.2 mm   (b) 0.9 mm   (c) 0.8 mm   (d) 0.6 mm
18. The truss is shown in Fig. 11. The P-forces are as shown. Take E = 200GPa, and cross sectional area = 1250 mm^2. The vertical deflection of C is

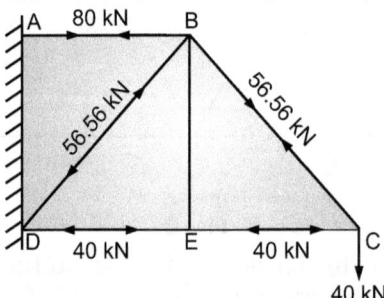

Fig. 11

    (a) 3.2 mm   (b) 4.9 mm   (c) 2.8 mm   (d) 5.6 mm
19. The truss is shown in Fig. 12. The P-forces are as shown. Axial rigidity of truss member is 30000 kN. The horizontal deflection of B is

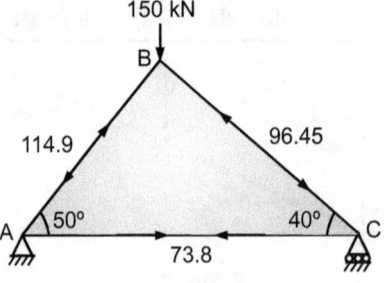

Fig. 12

    (a) 2.65 mm   (b) 5.24 mm   (c) 4.23 mm   (d) 3.11 mm

20. The truss is shown in Fig. 12. The P-forces are as shown. Axial rigidity of truss member is 30000 kN. The vertical deflection of B is
    (a) 11 mm (b) 5 mm (c) 9 mm (d) 14 mm
21. If in a truss, E = 200GPa and vertical deflection is 5.8 mm then summation of (Pkl/A) is
    (a) 200 kN/mm (b) 2000 kN/mm (c) 1200 kN/mm (d) 800 kN/mm
22. If in a truss vertical deflection is 11.54 mm and summation of (Pkl/A) is 923.58 then axial rigidity is
    (a) 40000 kN (b) 400000 kN (c) 80000 kN (d) 35000 kN
23. If in a truss, E = 200GPa and vertical deflection is 2.45 mm then summation of (Pkl/A) is
    (a) 350 kN/mm (b) 256 kN/mm (c) 128 kN/mm (d) 491 kN/mm
24. If in a truss, E = 200GPa and horizontal deflection is 0.8 mm then summation of (Pkl/A) is
    (a) 190 kN/mm (b) 160 kN/mm (c) 120 kN/mm (d) 250 kN/mm
25. If in a truss, E = 200GPa and vertical deflection is 4.9 mm then summation of (PkI/A) is
    (a) 980 kN/mm (b) 256 kN/mm (c) 128 kN/mm (d) 491 kN/mm
26. If in a truss, E = 200GPa and horizontal deflection is 4.67 mm then summation of (PkI/A) is
    (a) 935 kN/mm (b) 875 kN/mm (c) 790 kN/mm (d) 670 kN/mm
27. The truss is shown in Fig. 13. Area of member AB is 1000 mm^2 and E = 200 GPa. For horizontal deflection at C, the value of (Pkl/A) in member is

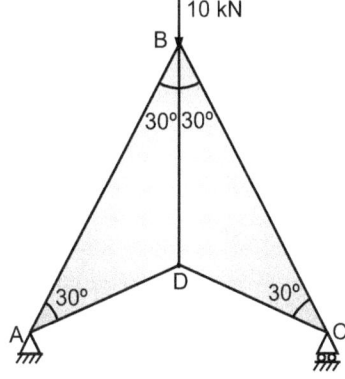

Fig. 13

    (a) 15 kN/mm (b) 8.66 kN/mm (c) 11.25 kN/mm (d) 20 kN/mm
28. The truss is shown in Fig. 13. Area of member CD is 500 mm^2 and E = 200 GPa. For horizontal deflection at C, the value of (Pkl/A) in member is
    (a) 15 kN/mm (b) 8.66 kN/mm (c) 11.25 kN/mm (d) 20 kN/mm

29. The truss is shown in Fig. 14. Area of member AB is 800 mm² and E = 200G Pa. For vertical deflection at E, the value of (Pkl/A) in member is

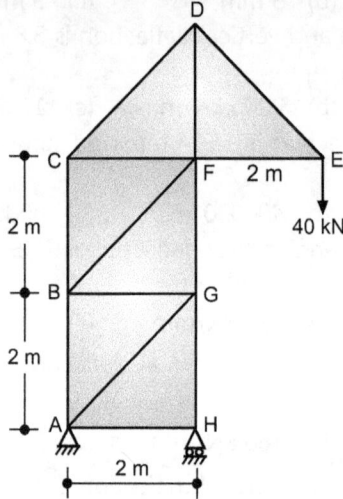

Fig. 14

(a) 40 kN/mm (b) 37.5 kN/mm (c) 115 kN/mm (d) 100 kN/mm

30. The truss is shown in Fig. 14. Area of member BC is 800 mm² and E = 200 GPa. For vertical deflection at E, the value of (Pkl/A) in member is

(a) 40 kN/mm (b) 37.5 kN/mm (c) 115 kN/mm (d) 100 kN/mm

31. The truss is shown in Fig. 14. Area of member CD is 600 mm² and E = 200G Pa. For vertical deflection at E, the value of (Pkl/A) in member is

(a) 400 kN/mm (b) 375 kN/mm (c) 150 kN/mm (d) 100 kN/mm

32. The truss is shown in Fig. 14. Area of member EF is 400 mm² and E = 200 GPa. For vertical deflection at E, the value of (Pkl/A) in member is

(a) 400 kN/mm (b) 175 kN/mm (c) 200 kN/mm (d) 300 kN/mm

33. The truss is shown in Fig. 14. Area of member GH is 800 mm² and E = 200 GPa. For vertical deflection at E, the value of (Pkl/A) in member is

(a) 400 kN/mm (b) 175 kN/mm (c) 200 kN/mm (d) 300 kN/mm

34. The truss is shown in Fig. 14. Area of member GB is 800 mm² and E = 200 GPa. For vertical deflection at E, the value of (Pkl/A) in member is

(a) 40 kN/mm (b) 17.5 kN/mm (c) 20 kN/mm

(d) None of these

35. The truss is shown in Fig. 15. Area of member BC is 500 mm² and E = 200 GPa. For vertical deflection at D, the value of (Pkl/A) in member is

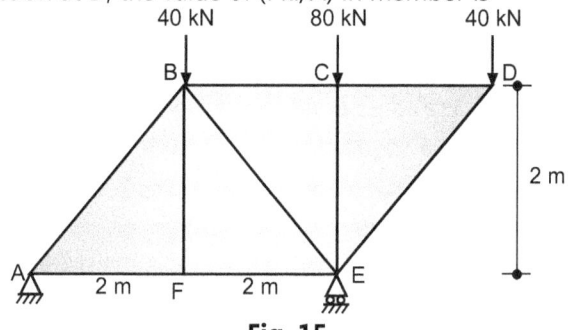

Fig. 15

(a) 140 kN/mm (b) 160 kN/mm (c) 200 kN/mm
(d) None of these

36. The truss is shown in Fig. 15. Area of member BE is 560 mm² and E = 200 GPa. For vertical deflection at D, the value of (Pkl/A) in member is
(a) 183 kN/mm (b) 177 kN/mm (c) 202 kN/mm
(d) None of these

37. The truss is shown in Fig. 15. Area of member BF is 600 mm² and E = 200 GPa. For vertical deflection at E, the value of (Pkl/A) in member is
(a) 46 kN/mm (b) 19 kN/mm (c) 22 kN/mm
(d) None of these

38. The truss is shown in Fig. 15. Area of member ED is 560 mm² and E = 200 GPa. For vertical deflection at D, the value of (Pkl/A) in member is
(a) 404 kN/mm (b) 377 kN/mm (c) 452 kN/mm
(d) None of these-

39. The truss is shown in Fig. 15. Area of member BF is 600 mm² and E = 200 GPa. For vertical deflection at E, the value of (PkI/A) in member is
(a) 46 kN/mm (b) 19 kN/mm (c) 22 kN/mm
(d) None of these

40. The truss is shown in Fig. 16. Area of member AE is 2400 mm² and E = 200 GPa. For vertical deflection at D, the value of (Pkl/A) in member is

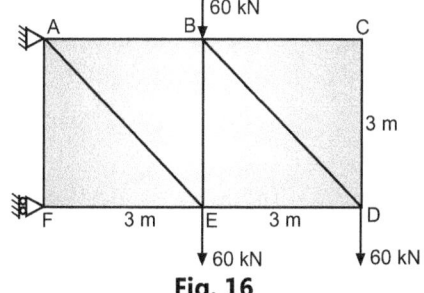

Fig. 16

(a) 617 kN/mm (b) 519 kN/mm (c) 707 kN/mm (d) 678 kN/mm

41. The truss is shown in Fig. 16. Area of member BD is 4800 mm² and E = 200 GPa. For vertical deflection at D, the value of (Pkl/A) in member is
    (a) 297 kN/mm (b) 377 kN/mm (c) 307 kN/mm (d) 278 kN/mm
42. The truss is shown in Fig. 16. Area of member EF is 2400 mm² and E = 200 GPa. For vertical deflection at D, the value of (Pkl/A) in member is
    (a) 700 kN/mm (b) 350 kN/mm (c) 570 kN/mm (d) 675 kN/mm
43. The truss is shown in Fig. 16. Area of member BE is 1200 mm² and E = 200 GPa. For vertical deflection at D, the value of (Pkl/A) in member is
    (a) 700 kN/mm (b) 350 kN/mm (c) 570 kN/mm (d) 675 kN/mm
44. The truss is shown in Fig. 16. Area of member DE is 1200 mm² and E = 200 GPa. For vertical deflection at D, the value of (Pkl/A) in member is
    (a) 700 kN/mm (b) 350 kN/mm (c) 250 kN/mm (d) 200 kN/mm
45. The truss is shown in Fig. 17. Modulus of elasticity of member is 200 GPa. For horizontal deflection at E, the value of Pkl of member AF is

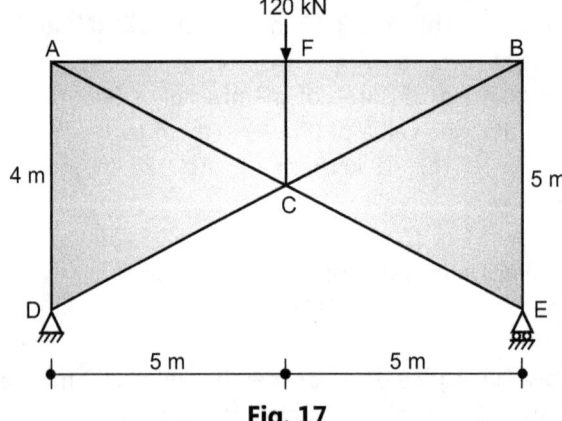

Fig. 17

    (a) 700 kNm (b) 600 kNm (c) 200 kNm (d) 400 kNm
46. The truss is shown in Fig. 17. Modulus of elasticity of member is 200 GPa. For horizontal deflection at E, the value of Pkl of member FB is
    (a) 700 kNm (b) 600 kNm (c) 200 kNm (d) 400 kNm
47. The truss is shown in Fig. 17. Modulus of elasticity of member is 200 GPa. For horizontal deflection at E, the value of Pkl of member AC is
    (a) 838 kNm (b) 745 kNm (c) 812 kNm
    (d) None of these
48. The truss is shown in Fig. 17. Modulus of elasticity of member is 200 GPa. For horizontal deflection at E, the value of Pkl of member AD is
    (a) 310 kNm (b) 260 kNm (c) 150 kNm
    (d) None of these

49. The truss is shown in Fig. 17. Modulus of elasticity of member is 200 GPa. For horizontal deflection at E, the value of Pkl of member FC is

   (a) 310 kNm   (b) 260 kNm   (c) 150 kNm

   (d None of these,

50. The truss is shown in Fig. 17. Modulus of elasticity of member is 200 GPa. For horizontal deflection at E, the value of Pkl of member FC is

   (a) 310 kNm   (b) 260 kNm   (c) 150 kNm

   (d) None of these

51. The truss is shown in Fig. 18. Member HD is considered as redundant and force in member HD is 16.19 kN(C). Force in member AB is

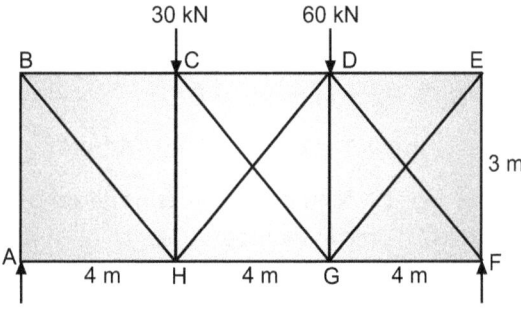

Fig. 18

   (a) 60 kN   (b) 40 kN   (c) 25 kN

   (d) None of these

52. The truss is shown in Fig. 18. Member HD is considered as redundant and force in member HD is 16.19 kN(C). Force in member BC is

   (a) 50 kN   (b) 40.67 kN   (c) 53.33 kN

   (d) None of these

53. The truss is shown in Fig. 18. Member HD is considered as redundant and force in member HD is 16.19 kN(C). Force in member CG is

   (a) 0.90 kN   (b) 4 kN   (c) 2.5 kN   (d) 0.5 kN

54. The truss is shown in Fig. 18. Member HD is considered as redundant and force in member HD is 16.19 kN(C). Force in member DG is

   (a) 65 kN   (b) 45 kN   (c) 35 kN   (d) 50 kN

55. The truss is shown in Fig. 18. Member HD is considered as redundant and force in member HD is 16.19 kN(C). Force in member HG is

   (a) 60 kN   (b) 40 kN   (c) 25 kN   (d) 72 kN

56. The truss is shown in Fig. 19. Member AD is considered as reluctant and force in member AD is 0.54 kN(C). Force in member CB is

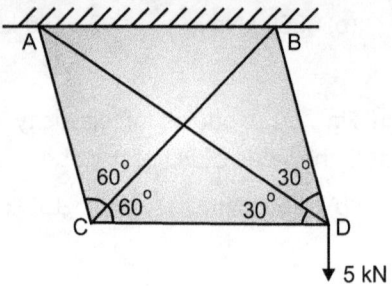

Fig. 19

(a) 2.57 kN (b) 3.13 kN (c) 2.56 kN (d) 1.97 kN

57. The truss is shown in Fig. 19. Member AD is considered as redundant and force in member AD is 0.54 kN(C). Force in member DB is

(a) 4.5 kN (b) 5.1 kN (c) 6.1 kN (d) 3.9 kN

58. The truss is shown in Fig. 19. Member AD is considered as redundant and force in member AD is 0.54 kN(C). Force in member AC is

(a) 2.57 kN (b) 3.13 kN (c) 2.56 kN (d) 1.97 kN

59. The truss is shown in Fig. 20. Member BC is considered as redundant and force in member BC is 3.43 kN(T). Force in member AB is

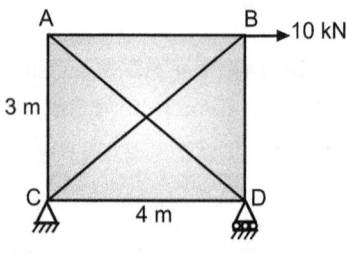

Fig. 20

(a) 2.57 kN (b) 3.13 kN (c) 2.56 kN (d) 1.97 kN

60. The truss is shown in Fig. 20. Member BC is considered as redundant and force in member BC is 3.43 kN(T). Force in member AD is

(a) 2.73 kN (b) 3.43 kN (c) 2.16 kN (d) 1.87 kN

61. The truss is shown in Fig. 20. Member BC is considered as redundant and force in member BC is 3.43 kN(T). Force in member CD is

(a) 2.17 kN (b) 2.83 kN (c) 3.56 kN (d) 4.43 kN

62. The truss is shown in Fig. 20. Member BC is considered as redundant and force in member BC is 3.43 kN(T). Force in member AC is

    (a) 6.72 kN   (b) 7.13 kN   (c) 8.21 kN   (d) 5.97

63. The truss is shown in Fig. 20. Member BC is considered as redundant and force in member BC is 3.43 kN(T). Force in member BD is

    (a) 4.28 kN   (b) 3.32 kN   (c) 5.12 kN   (d) 3.77

64. The frame is shown in Fig. 21. Member AC is considered as redundant and force in member AC is 18N(T). Force in member AB is

    (a) 683N   (b) 887N   (c) 592N   (d) 746N

65. The frame is shown in Fig. 21. Member AC is considered as redundant and force in member AC is 18N(T). Force in member AD is

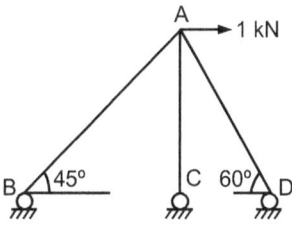

Fig. 21

    (a) 683N   (b) 887N   (c) 592N   (d) 746N

66. The truss is shown in Fig. 22. Member BC is short by 10 mm and (summation $k^2 I/AE$) = 0.864 mm/ kN. Tensile force in member BC is

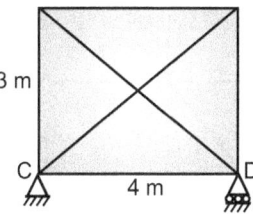

Fig. 22

    (a) 14.8 kN   (b) 11.6 kN   (c) 15.2 kN   (d) 13.77 kN

67. The truss is shown in Fig. 22. Member BC is tensile and short by 10 mm and (summation $k^2 I/AE$) = 0.864 mm/ kN. Force in member AB is

    (a) 9.26 kN   (b) 9.53 kN   (c) 6.94 kN   (d) 11.57 kN

68. The truss is shown in Fig. 22. Member BC is tensile and short by 10 mm and (summation $k^2 l/AE$) = 0.864 mm/ kN. Force in member AC is

    (a) 9.26 kN (b) 9.53 kN (c) 6.94 kN (d) 11.57 kN

69. The truss is shown in Fig. 22. Member BC is tensile and short by 10 mm and (summation $k^2 l/AE$) = 0.864 mm/ kN. Force in member AD is

    (a) 14.8 kN (b) 11.6 kN (c) 15.2 kN (d) 13.77 kN

70. The truss is shown in Fig. 23. Support C is considered as redundant and its value is (– 73.83 kN) i.e. towards left. Force in member AD is

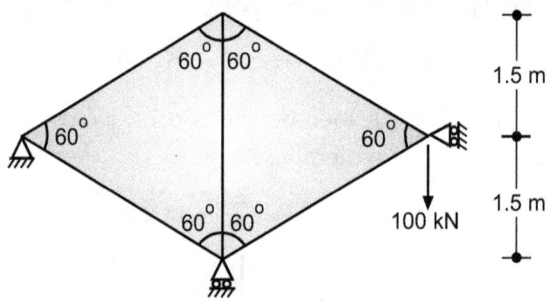

Fig. 23

    (a) 44.8 kN (b) 61.36 kN (c) 55.32 kN (d) 57.18 kN

71. The truss is shown in Fig. 23. Support C is considered as redundant and its value is (–73.83 kN) i.e. towards left. Force in member AB is

    (a) 142.8 kN (b) 163.6 kN (c) 155.2 kN (d) 257.18 kN

72. The truss is shown in Fig. 24. Member BG is redundant and force in member is tensile. Summation of Pkl and $k^2 l$ is 1097 kNm and 9.66m respectively for the truss members. Force in member BG is

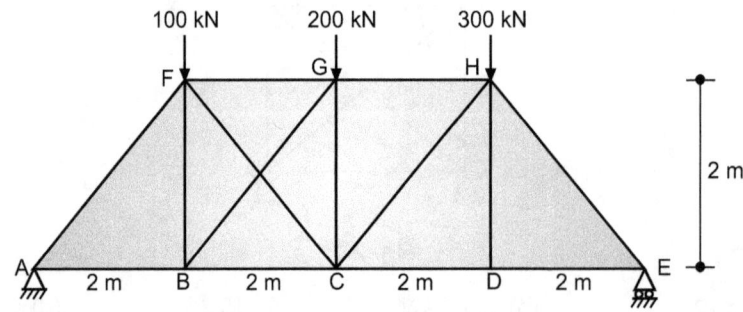

Fig. 24

    (a) 129.2 kN (b) 123.6 kN (c) 115.2 kN (d) 113.6 kN

73. The truss is shown in Fig. 24. Member BG is redundant and Torce in member is tensile. Summation of Pkl and k²l is 1097 kNm and 9.66m respectively for the truss members. Force in member AB is

   (a) 230 kN   (b) 250 kN   (c) 175 kN   (d) 195 kN

74. The truss is shown in Fig. 24. Member BG is redundant and force in member is tensile. Summation of Pkl and k²l is 1097 kNm and 9.66m respectively for the truss members. Force in member BC is

   (a) 159 kN   (b) 178 kN   (c) 169 kN   (d) 136 kN

75. The truss is shown in Fig. 24. Member BG is redundant and force in member is tensile. Summation of Pkl and k²l is 1097 kNm and 9.66m respectively for the truss members. Force in member CD is

   (a) 350 kN   (b) 280 kN   (c) 375 kN   (d) 495 kN

76. The truss is shown in Fig. 24. Member BG is redundant and force in member is tensile. Summation of Pkl and k²I is 1097 kNm and 9.66m respectively for the truss members. Force in member EH is

   (a) 350 kN   (b) 280 kN   (c) 400 kN   (d) 495 kN

77. The truss is shown in Fig. 24. Member BG is redundant and force in member is tensile. Summation of Pkl and k²; is 1097 kNm and 9.66m respectively for the truss members. Force in member HG is

   (a) 350 kN   (b) 280 kN   (c) 400 kN   (d) 495 kN

78. The truss is shown in Fig. 24. Member BG is redundant and force in member is tensile. Summation of Pkl and k²l is 1097 kNm and 9.66m respectively for the truss members. Force in member BG is

   (a) 123 kN   (b) 114 kN   (c) 71 kN   (d) 96 kN

79. The truss is shown in Fig. 24. Member BG is redundant and force in member is tensile. Summation of Pkl and k²l is 1097 kNm and 9.66m respectively for the truss members. Force in member CH is

   (a) 123 kN   (b) 114 kN   (c) 71 kN   (d) 96 kN

80. The truss is shown in Fig. 24. Member BG is redundant and force in member is tensile. Summation of Pkl and k²l is 1097 kNm and 9.66m respectively for the truss members. Force in member CH is

   (a) 326 kN   (b) 194 kN   (c) 271 kN   (d) 296 kN

ANSWERS

1. (c)	2. (b)	3. (a)	4. (d)	5. (c)	6. (b)	7. (d)	8. (b)
9. (a)	10. (c)	11. (d)	12. (b)	13. (a)	14. (b)	15. (d)	16. (a)
17. (c)	18. (c)	19. (b)	20. (d)	21. (a)	22. (c)	23. (d)	24. (b)
25. (a)	26. (a)	27. (c)	28. (b)	29. (d)	30. (d)	31. (b)	32. (c)
33. (a)	34. (d)	35. (b)	36. (c)	37. (d)	38. (a)	39. (d)	40. (c)
41. (b)	42. (a)	43. (b)	44. (d)	45. (b)	46. (b)	47. (a)	48. (c)
49. (d)	50. (d)	51. (a)	52. (c)	53. (d)	54. (d)	55. (b)	56. (a)
57. (c)	58. (a)	59. (a)	60. (b)	61. (d)	62. (c)	63. (a)	64. (b)
65. (d)	66. (b)	67. (a)	68. (c)	69. (b)	70. (d)	71. (a)	72. (d)
73. (b)	74. (c)	75. (a)	76. (d)	77. (c)	78. (b)	79. (c)	80. (a)

❏❏❏

SECTION - II
UNIT IV

Chapter 8
INFLUENCE LINES

8.1 INTRODUCTION

The structures are subjected to dead load or self weight and superimposed loads. Superimposed loads or live loads may be in various forms, for example, static or moving or impact or vibrating and so on. When the structure is subjected to moving type of superimposed loads, the reactions at supports and shear force and bending moments and deflections vary with the varying position of the load system. For working out the critical values of the above mentioned quantities and for deciding the load positions to give these critical values, the graphs of variation of these quantities (for a moving unit load) at a given section, known as *Influence Lines*, are very convenient. Once the influence line or influence line diagram is drawn for a quantity at a particular section, for any load system acting on the member, the calculation of that quantity at the section is very much simplified and work is reduced. The load position so as to give the maximum value of the quantity at the given section, can be readily decided from the influence line for the quantity at the section.

8.2 INFLUENCE LINES FOR SIMPLY SUPPORTED BEAM

In this part, we shall develop the influence lines for reaction, shear force at a section, bending moment at a section, for simply supported beams on both ends.

(a) I.L.D. for Reactions at the Supports : Fig. 8.1 shows CD as a simply supported beam. To draw I.L.D., move unit load throughout the span, so as to draw I.L.D. for reaction at C and D, move the unit load from left support C to the right support D.

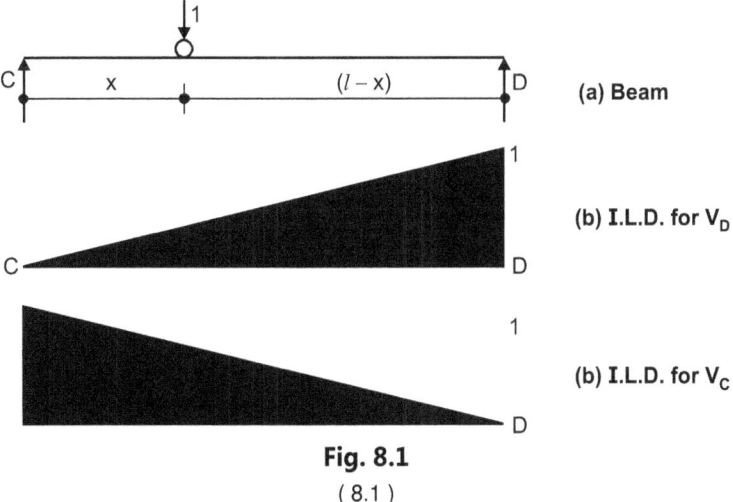

Fig. 8.1

At any instant, the unit load is at a distance x from C.

$$\therefore \quad V_c = \frac{(l-x)}{l} \quad \text{and} \quad V_d = \frac{x}{l}$$

Now, consider unit load is moving from left to right.

I.L.D. for V_d : When unit load is at C, x = 0.

$$\therefore \quad V_d = \frac{0}{l} = 0$$

When unit load is at D, x = l.

$$V_d = \frac{l}{l} = 1$$

Therefore, I.L.D. for V_d is a triangle varying with zero ordinate at C and ordinate as one at D.

I.L.D. for V_c : When unit load is at C, x = 0.

$$V_c = \left(\frac{l-0}{l}\right) = 1$$

When unit load is at D, x = l.

$$V_d = \left(\frac{l-l}{l}\right) = 0$$

Therefore, I.L.D. for V_c is a triangle varying with ordinate as one at C and zero ordinate at D.

Uses of I.L.D. : 1. To determine the reactions for the given system of loads.
    2. To determine the position of load for the maximum reaction.

(1) To determine the reactions for the given system of loads :

Problem 8.1 : A beam CD carries a concentrated load of 30 kN at the centre having span equal to 7.5 m. Find the reactions using I.L.D.

Solution :

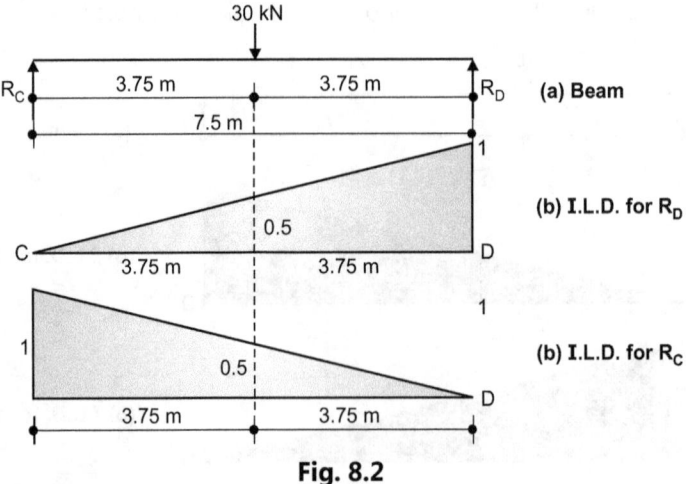

Fig. 8.2

Ordinate at E = 0.5

Reaction at D :

If the unit load is at E, then the reaction at D = 0.5 kN (from I.L.D.)

∴ Due to load 30 kN, reaction at D = Load × Ordinate of I.L.D. = 30 × 0.5 = 15 kN.

Reaction at C :

If the unit load is at E, then the reaction at C = 0.5 kN (from I.L.D.)

∴ Due to load 30 kN at E, reaction at C = Load × Ordinate of I.L.D. = 30 × 0.5 = 15 kN.

Problem 8.2 : A beam CD having span 12 m with concentrated loads as in Fig. 8.3 (a). Find the reactions at C and D using the I.L.D.

Solution :

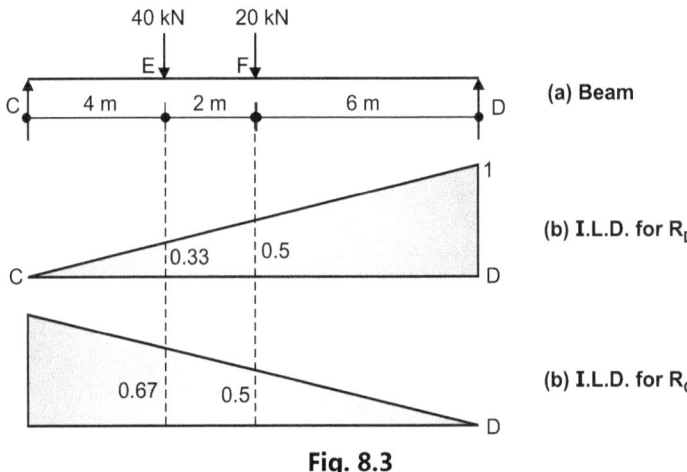

Fig. 8.3

Reaction at D : R_D ⇒

Ordinate of I.L.D. at E = $\frac{1}{12}$ × 4 = 0.33

If unit load is at E, then the reaction R_D = 0.33 kN.

Due to load of 40 kN, reaction at D = Load × Ordinate = 0.33 × 40 = 13.20 kN.

Ordinate of I.L.D. under 20 kN = $\frac{1}{12}$ × 6 = 0.5

If unit load is at F, then reaction at D = 0.5 kN.

Due to load of 20 kN, reaction at F = Load × Ordinate = 0.5 × 20 = 10 kN.

Reaction at C :

Ordinate on I.L.D. under 40 kN = $\frac{1}{12}$ × 8 = 0.67

Due to load of 40 kN, reaction at C = Load × Ordinate = 40 × 0.67 = 26.8 kN.

Ordinate on I.L.D. under 20 kN = $\frac{1}{12}$ × 6 = 0.5

Due to load of 20 kN at F, reaction at C = Load × Ordinate = 20 × 0.5 = 10 kN.

∴ Total reaction at D = 13.20 + 10 = 23.20 kN
Total reaction at C = 26.8 + 10 = 36.8 kN

Problem 8.3 : A simply supported beam with span 10 m is loaded with concentrated loads at 2.5 m, 5.0 m and 7.5 m having values 40 kN, 80 kN and 60 kN respectively. Find the reactions at the supports.

Solution :

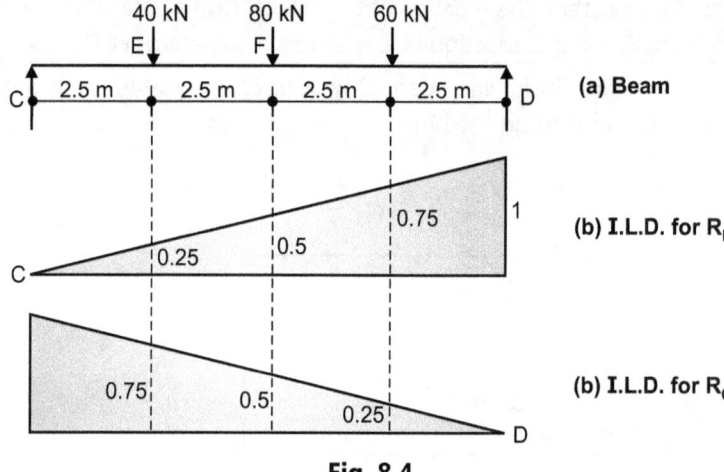

Fig. 8.4

Reaction at D :

Reaction at the support is the product of loads and the respective ordinates of I.L.D.

Ordinates on I.L.D. for R_D at different sections :

$$\text{Ordinate on I.L.D. under 40 kN} = \frac{1}{10} \times 2.5 = 0.25$$

$$\text{under 80 kN} = \frac{1}{10} \times 5 = 0.5$$

$$\text{Ordinate on I.L.D. under 60 kN} = \frac{1}{10} \times 7.5 = 0.75.$$

∴ R_D = Reaction at D = 40 × 0.25 + 80 × 0.5 + 60 × 0.75
= 95 kN

Reaction at C :

Ordinates on I.L.D. for R_C at different sections :

$$\text{Ordinate on I.L.D. under 40 kN} = \frac{1}{10} \times 7.5 = 0.75$$

$$\text{Ordinate on I.L.D. under 80 kN} = \frac{1}{10} \times 5 = 0.5$$

$$\text{Ordinate on I.L.D. under 60 kN} = \frac{1}{10} \times 2.5 = 0.25$$

Similarly, R_C = 40 × 0.75 + 80 × 0.5 + 60 × 0.25
= 85 kN

Problem 8.4 : A beam CD of span 4 m is simply supported at the ends. It is loaded with U.D.L. of 2 m as shown in Fig. 8.5 (a). Find the reactions.

Solution :

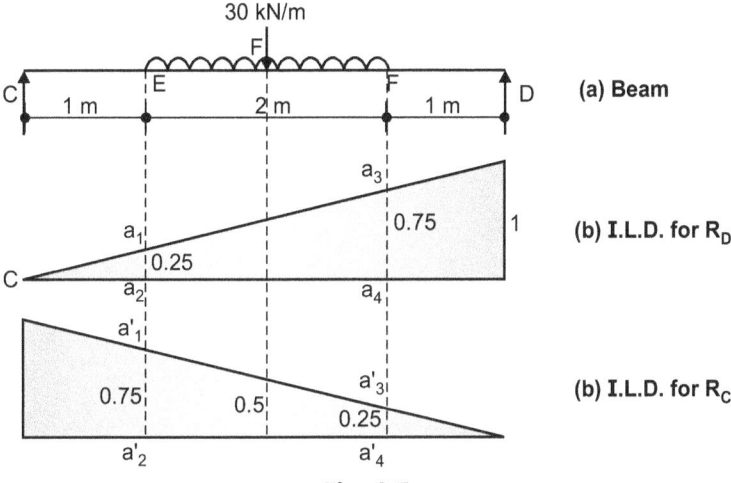

Fig. 8.5

For finding the reactions we take the product of loads and respective ordinates below the load in I.L.D. In case of U.D.L. we have to consider each ordinate under the load that means the area under the uniformly distributed load.

Reaction at D :

Ordinate on I.L.D. at E $= \dfrac{1}{4} \times 1 = 0.25$

Ordinate on I.L.D. at F $= \dfrac{1}{4} \times 3 = 0.75$

∴ Area under the loading = Area of trapezoidal $a_1\ a_2\ a_3\ a_4$

∴ Reaction at D = Load intensity × Area under the load (from I.L.D. for R_D)

$= 30 \times \left(\dfrac{0.75 + 0.25}{2}\right) \times 2 = 30$ kN

Reaction at C :

Ordinate on I.L.D. at E $= \dfrac{1}{4} \times 3 = 0.75$

Ordinate on I.L.D. at F $= \dfrac{1}{4} \times 1 = 0.25$

Reaction at C = Load intensity × Area under load (from I.L.D. for R_C)

= Load intensity × Area of trapezoidal $a'_1\ a'_2\ a'_3\ a'_4$

$= 30 \times \left(\dfrac{0.25 + 0.75}{2}\right) \times 2 = 30$ kN

Problem 8.5 : A beam CD is loaded with U.D.L. of 40 kN/m over the whole span of 8 m. Find the reactions at the supports using I.L.D.
Solution :

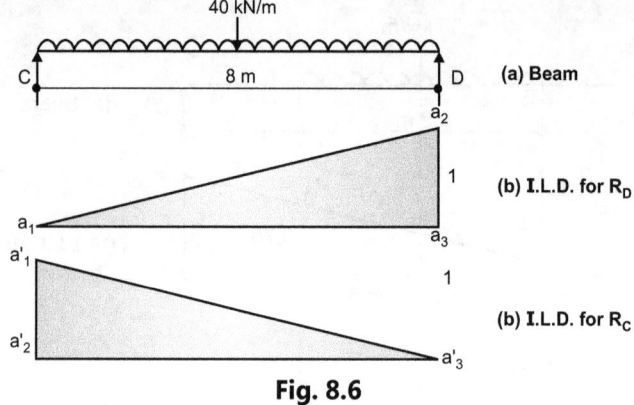

Fig. 8.6

Reaction at D :

∴ Reaction at D = Intensity of loading × Area under the load (from I.L.D. for R_D)

= Intensity of load × Area of $\Delta\ a_1\ a_2\ a_3$ = $40 \times \dfrac{1}{2} \times 1 \times 8$ = 160 kN

(As loading is throughout the span, so we have to consider total area of the I.L.D. diagram.)

Reaction at C : Reaction at C = Intensity of loading
× Area under the load (area from I.L.D. for R_C)

= Intensity of loading × Area of $\Delta\ a'_1\ a'_2\ a'_3$

= $40 \times \dfrac{1}{2} \times 1 \times 8$ = 160 kN

Problem 8.6 : A beam AB of length 9 m is partly loaded with U.D.L. of 20 kN/m upto 3 m from A and a point load of 30 kN is acting at 6 m from A. Find the reactions.
Solution :

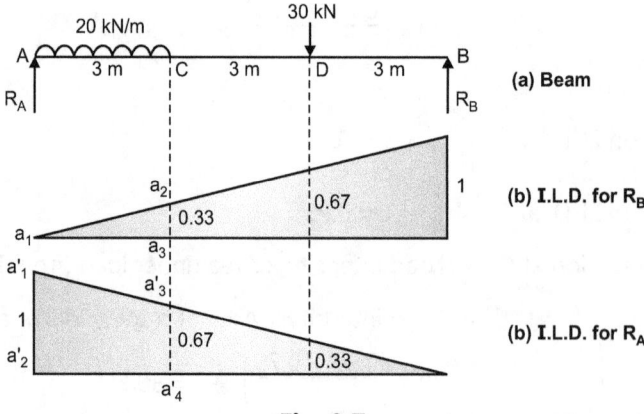

Fig. 8.7

Reaction at B :

$$\text{Ordinate on I.L.D. at C} = \frac{1}{9} \times 3 = 0.33$$

$$\begin{aligned}
\text{Reaction at B} &= \text{Intensity of loading} \times \text{Area under U.D.L.} \\
&= \text{Intensity of loading} \times \text{Area of } \Delta\ a_1 a_2 a_3 \\
&= 20 \times \frac{1}{2} \times 0.33 \times 3 \\
&= 9.999 \text{ kN say } 10 \text{ kN}
\end{aligned}$$

$$\text{Ordinate on I.L.D. at D} = \frac{1}{9} \times 6 = 0.667$$

$$\begin{aligned}
\text{Reaction at B} &= \text{Load} \times \text{Ordinate under the load} \\
&= 30 \times 0.6667 = 20.0 \text{ kN}
\end{aligned}$$

∴ Total reaction at B = Reaction due to U.D.L. + Reaction due to conc. load
$$= 10 + 20 = 30 \text{ kN}$$

Reaction at A :

$$\text{Ordinate on I.L.D. for } R_A \text{ at C} = \frac{1}{9} \times 6 = 0.667$$

$$\begin{aligned}
\text{Reaction at A} &= \text{Intensity of loading} \times \text{Area under the loading} \\
&= \text{Intensity of loading} \times \text{Area of trapezoidal } a_1' a_2' a_3' a_4' \\
&= 20 \times \left(\frac{0.667 + 1}{2}\right) \times 3 \\
&= 50.0 \text{ kN}
\end{aligned}$$

$$\text{Ordinate on I.L.D. for } R_A \text{ at D} = \frac{1}{9} \times 3 = 0.33$$

∴ Reaction at A = Load × Ordinate under the load
$$= 30 \times 0.333 = 10 \text{ kN}$$

∴ Total reaction at A = Reaction due to U.D.L. + Reaction due to conc. load
$$= 50.0 + 10.0 = 60 \text{ kN}$$

(2) To determine the position of load for maximum reaction :

To find the maximum reaction, the ordinate should be as maximum as possible in case of concentrated load. In case of U.D.L., area covered should be as maximum as possible.

Problem 8.7 : A beam CD is loaded with a moving load of 20 kN having span 3 m. Find the position of load for maximum reactions.

Solution :

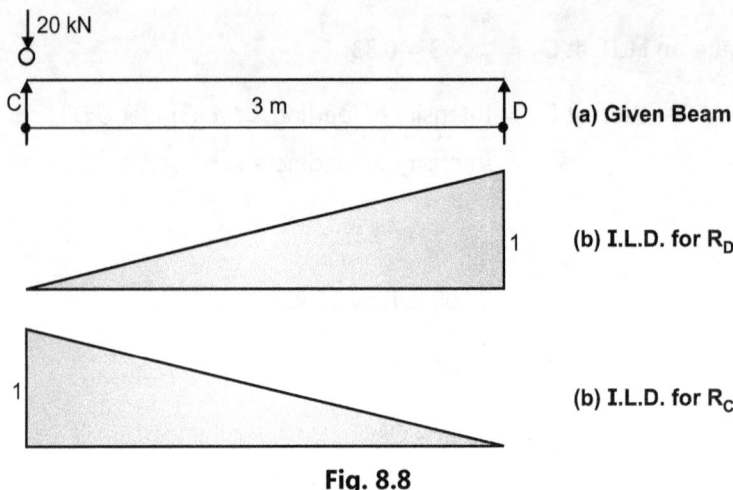

Fig. 8.8

Reaction at support = Load × Ordinate under load

Reaction at D :

For maximum reaction at D, the ordinate under the load should be as maximum. Therefore, maximum ordinate is one at D itself.

Therefore, for maximum reaction at D, 20 kN load should be placed on the support D.

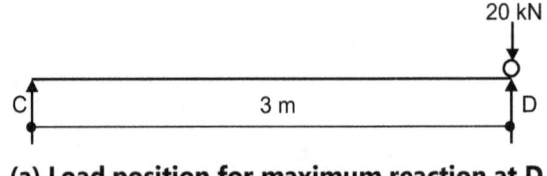

(a) Load position for maximum reaction at D

∴ Maximum reaction at D = 20 × 1 = 20 kN

Reaction at C :

Similarly for maximum reaction at C, we have to place the moving load on C because maximum ordinate on I.L.D. for R_C is at C only.

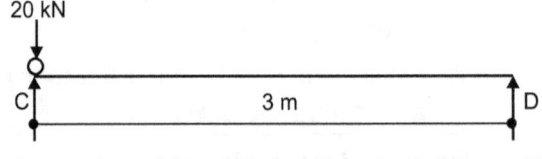

(b) Load position for maximum reaction at C

Fig. 8.9

∴ Reaction at C = Load × Ordinate
= 20 × 1 = 20 kN

Problem 8.8 : A beam AB of 6 m is simply supported at A and B. A distributed live load of 50 kN/m, 2 m long is moving along the girder. Find the position for maximum reaction at A and B of the load.

Solution :

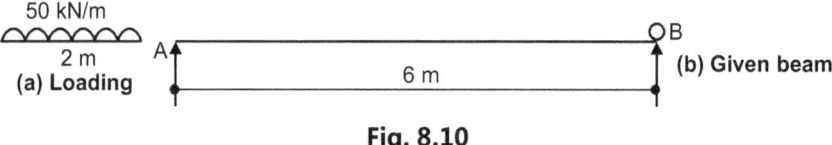

Fig. 8.10

Reaction at B :

For finding maximum reaction due to the moving U.D.L., U.D.L. should be placed so that it can cover maximum area of I.L.D. For maximum reaction at B, if we place U.D.L. in such a way that it ends at B, then it covers maximum area of I.L.D.

Ordinate on I.L.D. for R_B at C = $\frac{1}{6} \times 4 = 0.67$.

∴ Maximum reaction at B = Intensity of loading × Area covered on I.L.D.

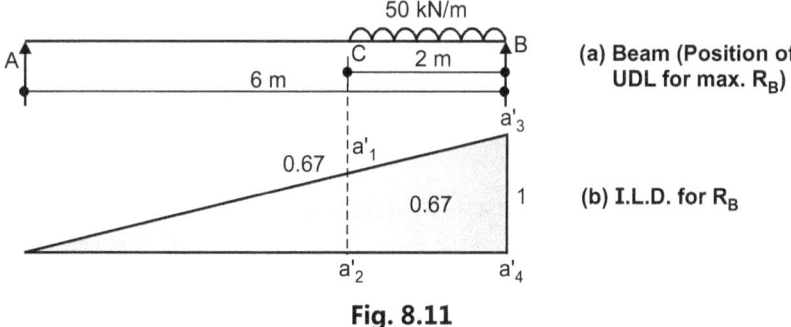

Fig. 8.11

Maximum reaction at B = Load intensity × Area of trapezoidal $a'_1 a'_2 a'_3 a'_4$

∴ Maximum reaction at B = $50 \times \left(\frac{1 + 0.67}{2}\right) \times 2$

= 83.5 kN

Reaction at A :

Similarly for maximum reaction at A, place U.D.L. starting from point A, so that it covers maximum area of the I.L.D. and gives the maximum reaction at A.

Ordinate on I.L.D. for R_A at C' = $\frac{1}{6} \times 4 = 0.67$

∴ Maximum reaction at A = Intensity of loading × Area covered on I.L.D.

∴ Maximum reaction at A = Load intensity × Area of trapezoidal $a_1 a_2 a_3 a_4$

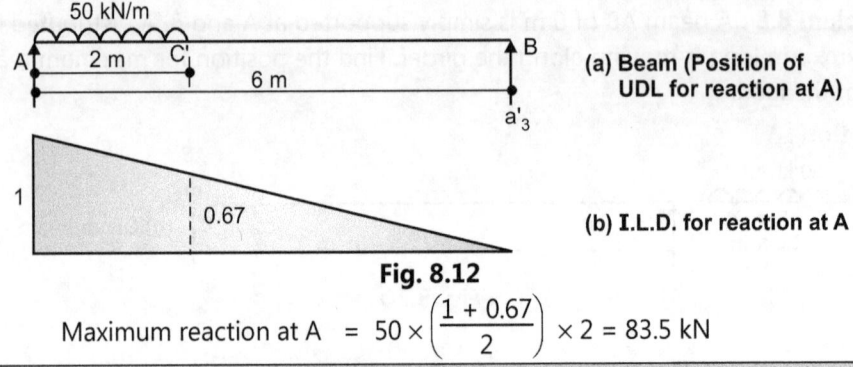

Fig. 8.12

$$\therefore \quad \text{Maximum reaction at A} = 50 \times \left(\frac{1 + 0.67}{2}\right) \times 2 = 83.5 \text{ kN}$$

8.3 INFLUENCE LINE DIAGRAM FOR SHEAR FORCE AT A GIVEN SECTION OF GIRDER

Consider a unit load is moving along the span of a simply supported girder CD. Let E be the section for which I.L.D. for shear force has to be drawn.

Sign convention for shear force :

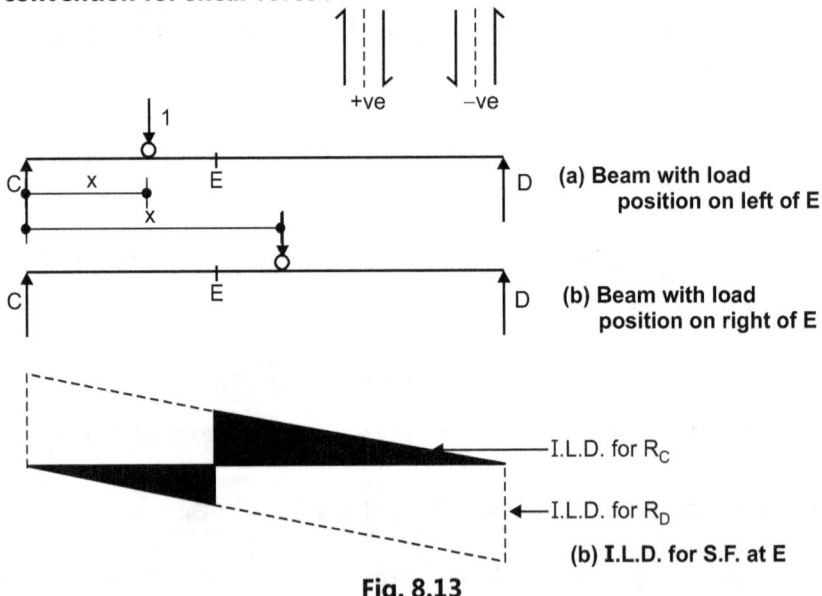

Fig. 8.13

I.L.D. for R_D varies from one at D to zero at C as load is moving along the span. But when the unit load is between the CE, the S.F. at E is $- V_d$. Therefore, part of the I.L.D. for R_D i.e. between C to E is applicable for S.F. at E i.e. S_E.

When the unit load is between E to D, then the S.F. at E is $+ V_c$. Therefore, a part of I.L.D. for V_c is applicable i.e. between E to D.

Thus, part of I.L.D. of V_c and part of I.L.D. of V_d is used for finding the S.F. at a section as shown in Fig. 8.13 (c) for S.F. at E.

(Note : The ordinate should be one at the point or at the section for which I.L.D. for shear has to be drawn.)

I.L.D. for shear force at a section is used for two purposes :
1. To find the S.F. at any section for the given system of loading.
2. To find the maximum S.F. (that may be maximum +ve or maximum –ve) in the structure.

(1) S.F. at any section for the given system of loading :

Problem 8.9 : A simply supported beam CD is loaded as shown in Fig. 8.14 (a). Find the S.F. at 5 m from C by using I.L.D.

Solution :

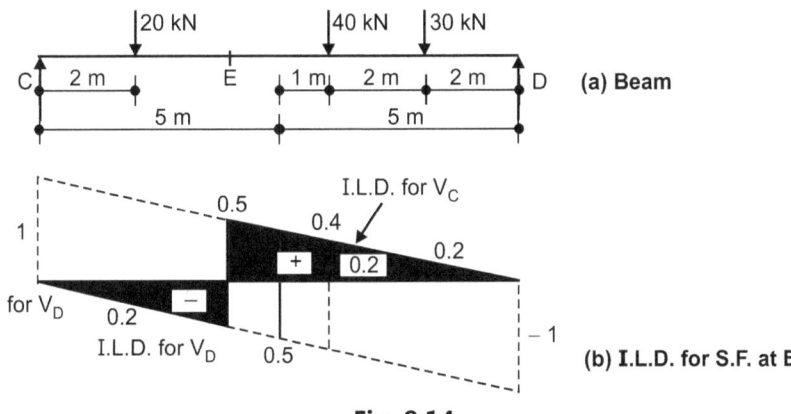

Fig. 8.14

S.F. at E (i.e. 5 m from C) :

Ordinate on I.L.D. under 20 kN = $-\dfrac{1}{10} \times 2 = -0.2$

S.F. at E due to 20 kN = Load × Ordinate
= 20 × –0.2 = – 4 kN
= 4 kN (↓)

Ordinate on I.L.D. under 40 kN = $\dfrac{1}{10} \times 4 = 0.4$

S.F. at E due to 40 kN = Load × Ordinate
= 40 × 0.4 = 16 kN (↑)

Ordinate on I.L.D. under 30 kN = $\dfrac{1}{10} \times 2 = 0.2$

S.F. at E due to 30 kN = Load × Ordinate
= 30 × 0.2 = 6 kN (↑)

∴ S.F. at E
Total S.F. at E (i.e. 5 m from C)
= – 4 + 16 + 6 = 18 kN (↑)

Problem 8.10 : A simply supported beam CD has span 12 m. It is loaded with U.D.L. of 45 kN/m, span 5 m, starts at 3.5 m from C. A concentrated load of 50 kN is acting at 2 m from D. Find the S.F. at 5 m from C.

Solution :

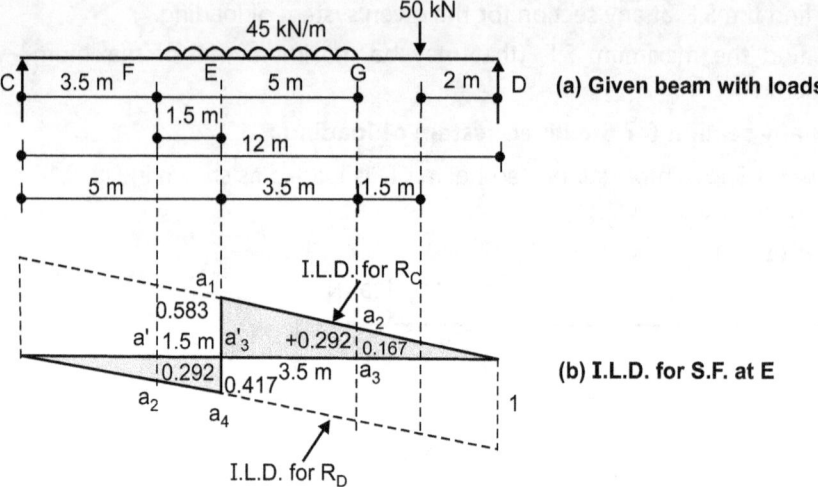

Fig. 8.15

S.F. at E (i.e. 5 m from C) :

Ordinate on I.L.D. at F $= -\dfrac{1}{12} \times 3.5 = -0.292$

Ordinate on I.L.D. at E $= \dfrac{1}{12} \times 5 = 0.417$

Ordinate on I.L.D. at E $= \dfrac{1}{12} \times 7 = 0.583$

Ordinate on I.L.D. at G $= \dfrac{1}{12} \times 3.5 = 0.292$

S.F. at E due to U.D.L. = Intensity of loading × Area covered on I.L.D.

= Intensity of loading × (Area of trapezoidal $a_1\ a_2\ a_3\ a_4$

+ Area of trapezoidal $a_1a_3\ a_2a_3$)

$= 45 \left\{ \left[-\left(\dfrac{0.292 + 0.417}{2}\right) \times 1.5 \right] + \left[\left(\dfrac{0.583 + 0.292}{2}\right) \times 3.5 \right] \right\}$

= 45 [− 0.532 + 1.531] = 44.97 kN

Ordinate on I.L.D. under 50 kN $= \dfrac{1}{12} \times 2 = 0.167$

Due to concentrated load, S.F. at E

= Load × Ordinate on I.L.D.

= 50 × 0.167 = 8.35

∴ Total S.F. at E = 44.97 + 8.35 = 53.32 kN (↑)

(2) Position of moving loads for maximum (+ve or –ve) S.F. at a section :

Problem 8.11 : Two wheel loads of 80 kN and 100 kN are spaced at 3 m. These loads are moving on a girder CD of span 13 m. Any wheel load can lead the other. Find the maximum positive and maximum negative shear force at 5 m from C.

Solution :

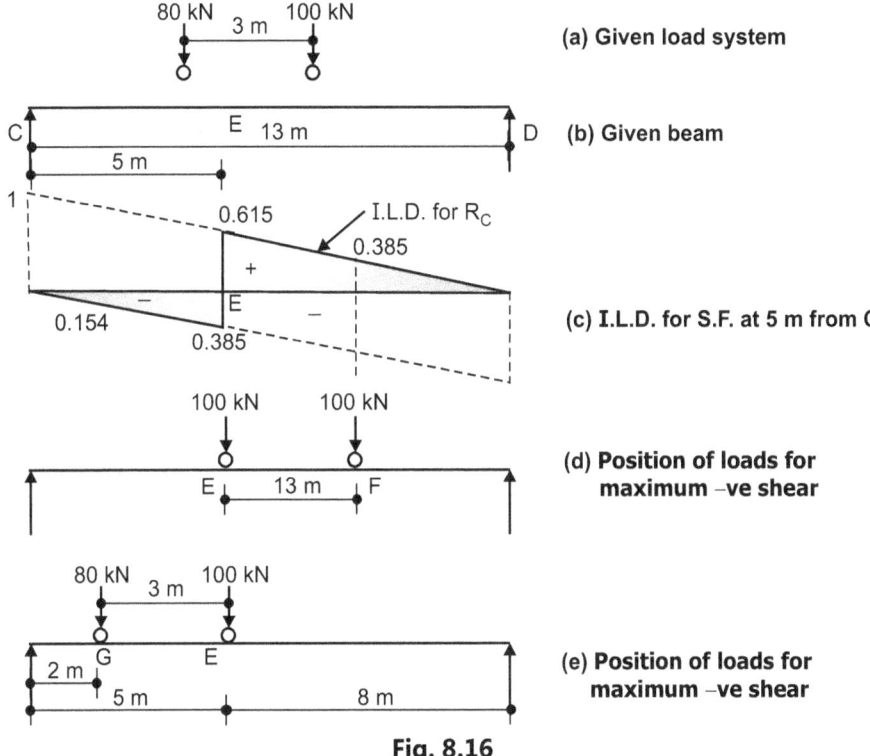

Fig. 8.16

Maximum positive shear :

For finding maximum positive shear at a section, loads should be arranged such that the greater load should be above the maximum ordinate as possible. If possible, all loads should be in the positive portion of the I.L.D.

$$\text{Ordinate on I.L.D. at E} = \frac{1}{13} \times 8 = 0.615$$

$$\text{Ordinate on I.L.D. at E} = -\frac{1}{13} \times 5 = -0.385$$

Ordinate on I.L.D. (at F) under 80 kN

$$= \frac{1}{13} \times 5 = 0.385$$

Load position for maximum +ve shear is as shown in Fig. 8.16 (d).

∴ Maximum +ve shear at E = Load × Respective ordinates
= 100 × 0.615 + 80 × 0.385 = 92.3 kN

Maximum negative shear : (same as above)

The greater load should be above the maximum ordinate of negative portion of I.L.D. All loads should be in negative portion if possible.

Load position for maximum negative S.F. is as shown in Fig. 8.16 (e).

Ordinate on I.L.D. for V_D under 80 kN = $-\frac{1}{13} \times 2 = -0.154$

∴ Maximum –ve S.F. at E = Load × Respective ordinates
= $100 \times 0.385 + 80 \times 0.154$
= 50.82 kN

∴ Maximum +ve shear at E = 92.3 kN
∴ Maximum –ve shear at E = 50.82 kN

Problem 8.12 : For a girder of 20 m long find the maximum S.F. at 7 m from left end if a U.D.L. of 60 kN/m having span 5 m, moves along it.

Solution :

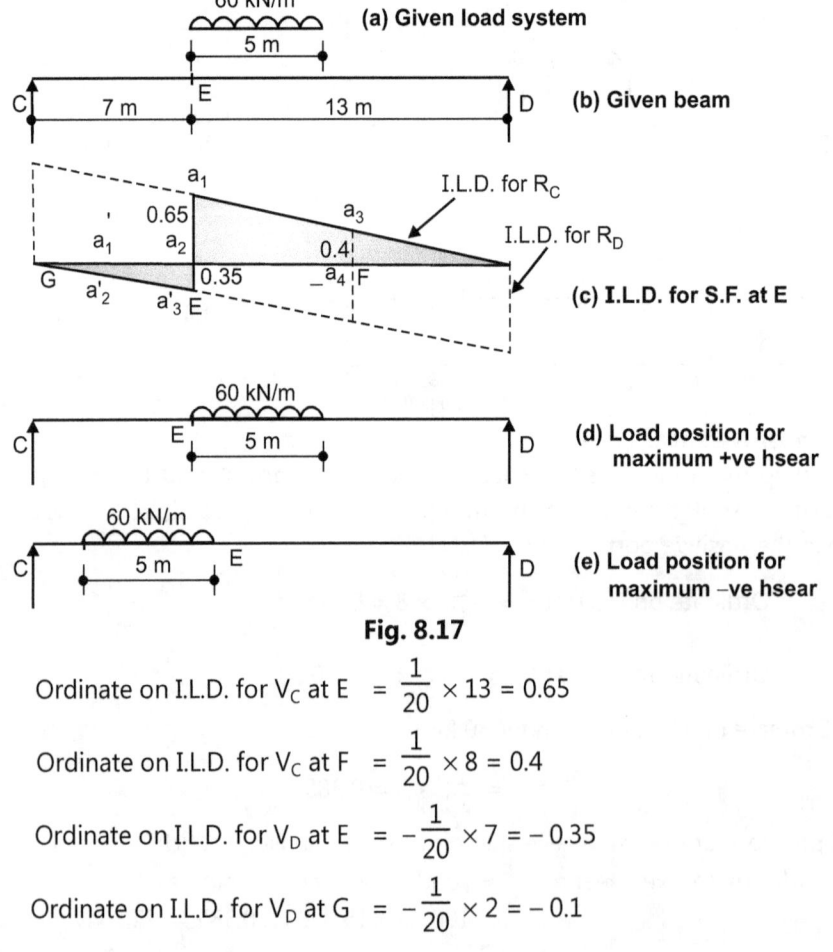

Fig. 8.17

Ordinate on I.L.D. for V_C at E = $\frac{1}{20} \times 13 = 0.65$

Ordinate on I.L.D. for V_C at F = $\frac{1}{20} \times 8 = 0.4$

Ordinate on I.L.D. for V_D at E = $-\frac{1}{20} \times 7 = -0.35$

Ordinate on I.L.D. for V_D at G = $-\frac{1}{20} \times 2 = -0.1$

Maximum Shear :

Load should be placed in such a fashion that it covers maximum area of I.L.D. (value of area should be as greater as possible).

Load position for maximum +ve shear is as shown in Fig. 8.17 (d).

∴ Maximum +ve S.F. at E = Load intensity × Area covered
= Load intensity × Area of trapezoidal $a_1 a_2 a_3 a_4$
= $60 \times \left(\dfrac{0.65 + 0.4}{2}\right) \times 5 = 157.5$ kN

Load position for maximum –ve shear is as shown in Fig. 8.17 (e).

Maximum – ve S.F. at E = Intensity × Area covered
= Load intensity × Area of trapezoidal $a_1' a_2' a_3'$
= $60 \times \left(\dfrac{0.35 + 0.1}{2}\right) 5 = 67.5$ kN

∴ Maximum + ve shear at E = 157.5 kN
Maximum –ve shear at E = 67.5 kN

8.4 INFLUENCE LINE DIAGRAM FOR THE B.M. AT A GIVEN SECTION

Consider a beam CD is simply supported at the ends. Let E be the point or section for which we have to draw I.L.D. for B.M.

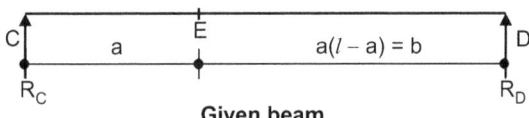

Given beam

Fig. 8.18

As we have to draw I.L.D., move the unit load from left to right.

Portion CE :

When unit load is at a distance x (i.e. $0 > x \leq a$) from C, then the moment at E is given by

$$M_E = R_D \times (l - a)$$

Since $R_D = \dfrac{x}{l}$,

∴ $$M_E = \dfrac{x}{l}(l - a)$$

Thus, this equation is applicable for the portion CE, for any position of unit load.

∴ $M_E = 0$ at $x = 0$

$M_E = \dfrac{a(l-a)}{l}$ at $x = a$

Thus, the B.M. diagram varies from zero at C to $\dfrac{a(l-a)}{l}$ at E.

Portion ED :

When unit load is at a distance x from C (a ≥ x ≤ l), then the moment at E is given by,

$$M_E = R_C \times a$$

Since $R_C = \left(\dfrac{l-x}{l}\right)$,

∴ $\qquad M_E = \left(\dfrac{(l-x)}{l}\right) a$

At E i.e. x = a, $\qquad M_E = \dfrac{a(l-a)}{l}$

At D i.e. x = l, $\qquad M_E = 0$

Thus, the B.M. diagram varies from $\dfrac{a(l-a)}{l}$ at E to zero at C and D when the unit load at E, C and D respectively.

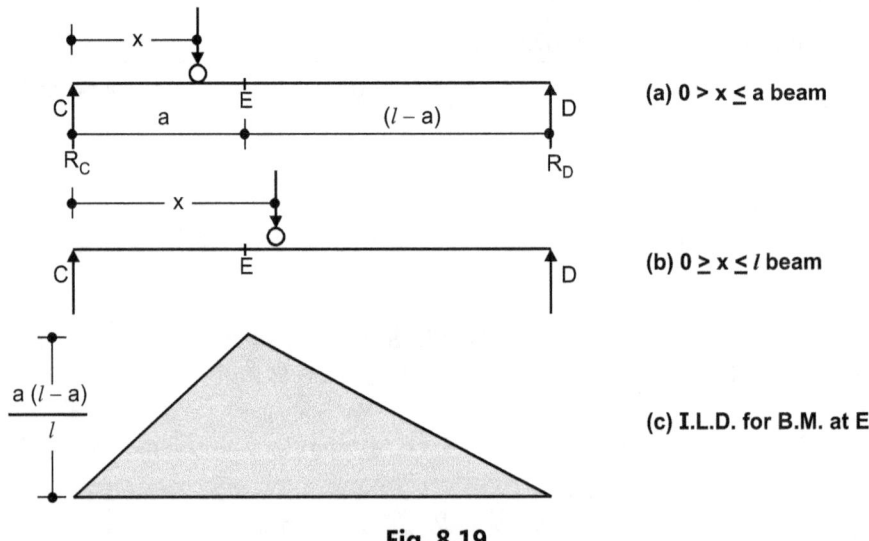

Fig. 8.19

Uses :

1. To find B.M. at any section by the given system of loading.
2. The position of loads to find maximum B.M. in a structure.

(1) To find the B.M. at a section by the given system of loads :

Problem 8.13 : A beam CD is simply supported at C and D with span 8 m. Concentrated loads of 40 kN and 70 kN are acting at 3 m and 6 m from C. Find the B.M. at 5 m from C, using I.L.D.

Solution :

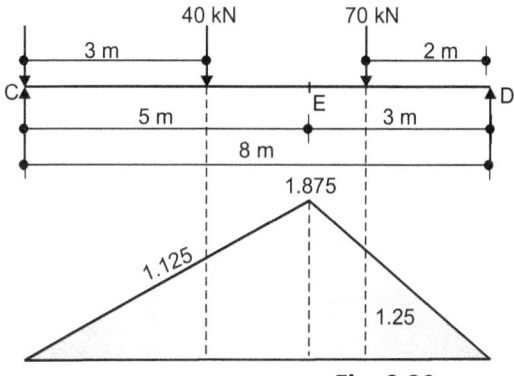

Fig. 8.20

B.M. at E (i.e. 5 m from C) :

As we have to obtain B.M. at 5 m from C, a = 5 m, l = 8 m

So maximum ordinate in I.L.D. at 5 m = $\dfrac{a(l-a)}{l} = \dfrac{5(8-5)}{8} = 1.875$

B.M. at E due to load = Load × Ordinate

Ordinate under 40 kN load = $\dfrac{1.875}{5} \times 3 = 1.125$

B.M. due to 40 kN load = 40 × 1.125 = 45 kN-m

Ordinate under 70 kN load = $\dfrac{1.875 \times 2}{3} = 1.25$

B.M. due to 70 kN = 70 × 1.25 = 87.5 kN-m

∴ B.M. at E = 45 + 87.5 = 132.5 kN-m

Problem 8.14 : A beam CD is loaded with U.D.L. of 35 kN/m over 5 m span starting at 2 m from C. Span of AB is 9 m. Find the B.M. at 5.5 m from C, using I.L.D.

Solution :

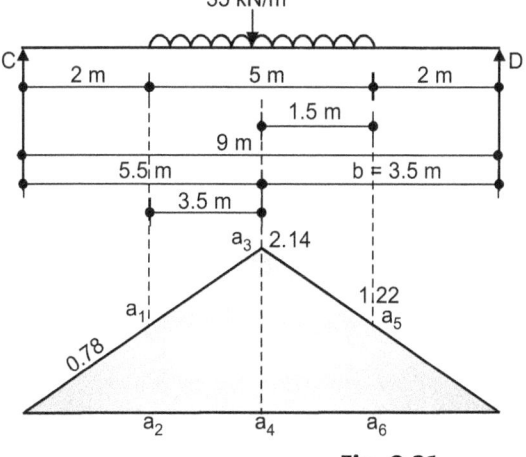

Fig. 8.21

B.M. at E (i.e. 5 m from C) :

As we have to obtain B.M. at 5.5 m from A, so a = 5.5 m, l = 9 m

Thus, maximum ordinate in I.L.D. at 5.5 m from A

$$= \frac{a(l-a)}{l} = \frac{5.5(9-5.5)}{9} = 2.14$$

Ordinate on I.L.D. at point where U.D.L. begins

$$= \frac{2.14}{5.5} \times 2 = 0.78$$

and ordinate on I.L.D. at point where U.D.L. ends

$$= \frac{2.14}{3.5} \times 2 = 1.22$$

$$\begin{aligned}
\text{B.M. at E} &= \text{Load intensity} \times \text{Area covered on I.L.D.} \\
&= \text{Load intensity} \times (\text{Area of trapezoid } a_1a_2a_3a_4 \\
&\qquad + \text{Area of trapezoid } a_3a_4a_5a_6) \\
&= 35 \times \left[\left(\frac{2.14 + 0.78}{2}\right) \times 3.5 + \left(\frac{2.14 + 1.22}{2}\right) \times 1.5 \right] \\
&= 267.12 \text{ kN-m}
\end{aligned}$$

Problem 8.15 : A beam AB is simply supported at A and B having span 12 m. Find the B.M. at 6.5 m from C for the loading system as shown in Fig. 8.22 (a).

Solution : B.M. at E (i.e. 6.5 m from C) :

Ordinate on I.L.D. for B.M. at E :

$$\text{Ordinate at C} = \frac{2.979}{6.5} \times 3 = 1.375$$

$$\text{Ordinate at D} = \frac{2.979}{6.5} \times 6 = 2.75$$

$$\text{Ordinate under 30 kN} = \frac{2.979}{6.5} \times 2 = 0.917$$

$$\text{Ordinate under 45 kN} = \frac{2.979}{5.5} \times 5 = 2.71$$

$$\text{Ordinate under 50 kN} = \frac{2.979}{5.5} \times 4 = 2.167$$

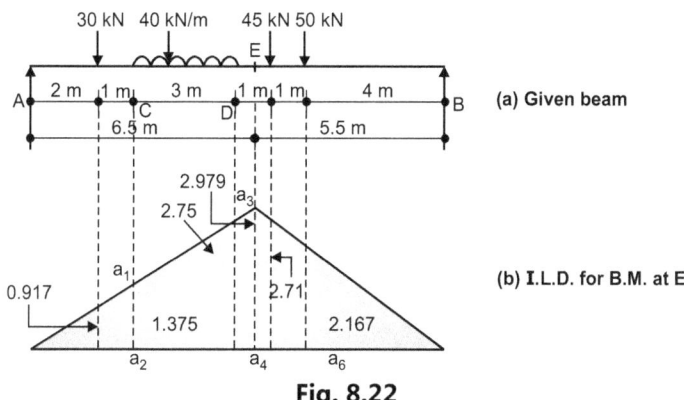

Fig. 8.22

∴ B.M. at E = Load × Ordinate (for conc. loads) + Intensity of load
× Area covered (i.e. trapezoidal area $a_1a_2a_3a_4$)

$$= 30 \times 0.917 + 40 \left(\frac{1.375 + 2.75}{2}\right) \times 3 + 45 \times 2.71 + 50 \times 2.167$$

$$= 27.51 + 247.5 + 121.95 + 108.35 = 505.31 \text{ kN-m}$$

∴ B.M. at E = 505.31 kN-m

(2) To find the position of loads to get the maximum B.M. at the section :

To get the maximum B.M. at a section, concentrated loads should be placed above the maximum ordinate as possible. For maximum B.M., U.D.L. is placed so that it can cover maximum value of the area in I.L.D.

Problem 8.16 : A beam CD is simply supported at the ends. Span of the beam is 12 m. Two wheel loads of 75 kN and 125 kN spaced at 3 m apart move along the beam. Find the maximum B.M. at 4 m from C, if any wheel load can lead other.

Solution :

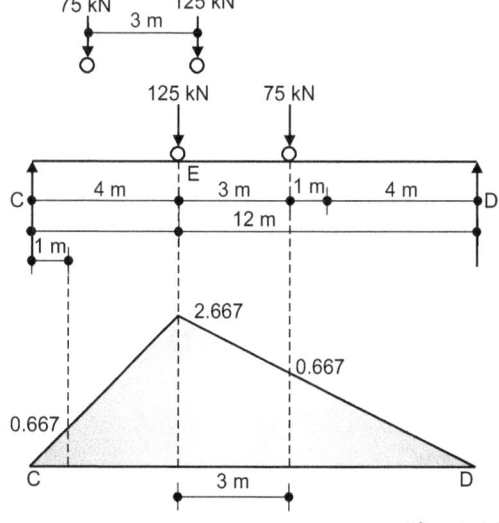

Fig. 8.23

To find the position of the loads, first place the greater load on the maximum ordinate as possible. Then find out the ordinates on both the sides at a distance which is equal to the spacing of loads. Consider maximum of two above.

Max. B.M. at E (i.e. 4 m from C) :

$$a = 4 \text{ m}, \quad l = 12 \text{ m}$$

Ordinates on I.L.D. for B.M. at E $\Rightarrow$

$$\text{Ordinate at E} = \frac{a(l-a)}{l} = \frac{4 \times 8}{12} = 2.667$$

$$\text{Ordinate at F under 75 kN} = \frac{2.667}{8} \times 5 = 1.667$$

$\therefore$ B.M. at E = Loads × Respective ordinates
    = 125 × 2.667 + 75 × 1.667
    = 458.4 kN-m

Problem 8.17 : A uniformly distributed load 5 kN/m, longer than the span, rolls over a beam of 25 m span. Using the influence lines, determine the maximum S.F. and maximum B.M. at a section 10 m from left hand end. **(Dec. 2001)**

Solution :

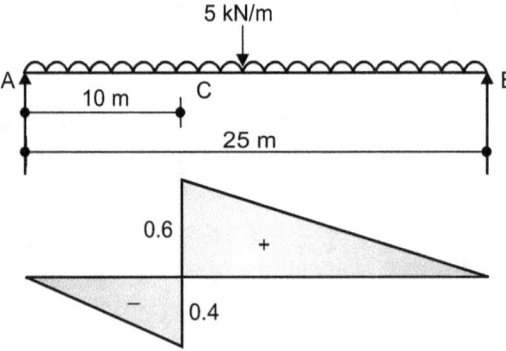

Fig. 8.24 (a)

$\therefore$ S.F. at C = Net area × Intensity = $\left(\frac{1}{2} \times 0.6 \times 15 - \frac{1}{2} \times 0.4 \times 10\right) \times 5$

= (4.5 − 2) × 5 = 12.5 kN (↑)

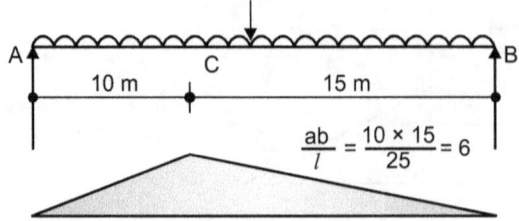

Fig. 8.24 (b)

∴ B.M. at C = Area × Intensity

$$= \frac{1}{2} \times 6 \times 25 \times 5$$

$$= 375 \text{ kN-m}$$

Problem 8.18 : A uniformly distributed load of 5 kN/m intensity, 6 m in length crosses girder of span 40 m from left to right. With the help of influence lines, determine the values of S.F. and B.M. at a point of 12 m from the left end when the head of the load is 16 m from the left support. **(Dec. 2001)**

Solution :

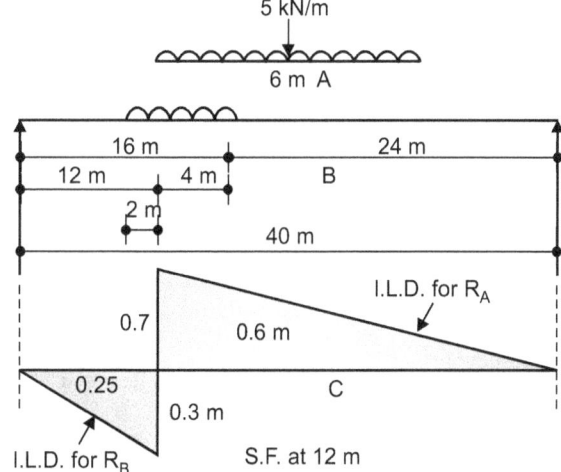

Fig. 8.25

S.F. at 12 m = Area × Load intensity

$$= \left(\frac{0.7 + 0.6}{2}\right) \times 4 \times 5 - \left(\frac{0.25 + 0.3}{2}\right) \times 2 \times 5$$

$$= 13.0 - 2.75 = 10.25 \text{ kN } (\uparrow)$$

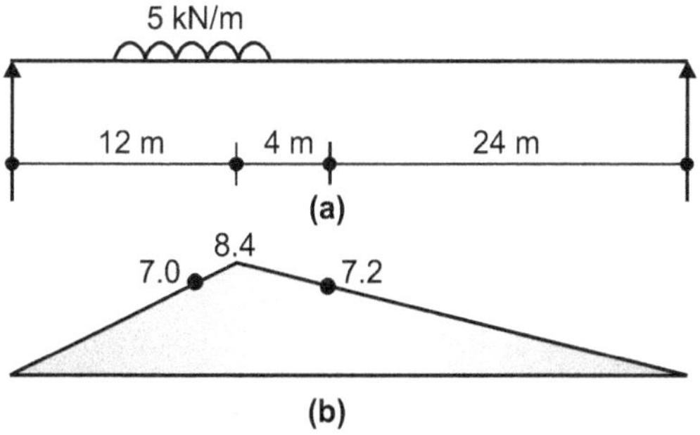

(a)

(b)

Fig. 8.26

$$\text{B.M. at 12 m} = \left(\frac{7+8.4}{2}\right) \times 2 \times 5 + \left(\frac{8.4+7.2}{2}\right) \times 4 \times 5$$

$$= 77 + 156 = 233 \text{ kN-m}$$

8.5 SIMPLY SUPPORTED BEAMS WITH OVERHANG

I.L.D. for beams with overhang :

First draw the I.L.D. for reactions ignoring the overhang. Now extend the influence line drawn to cover the overhanging segments.

I.L.D. for reaction V_d and reaction V_c :

Consider a beam ACDB, simply supported at C and D and overhang as CA and DB. Length between the supports is l. CA = a and DB = b.

First draw the I.L.D. for V_D ignoring the overhang and then produce the influence line for the overhang.

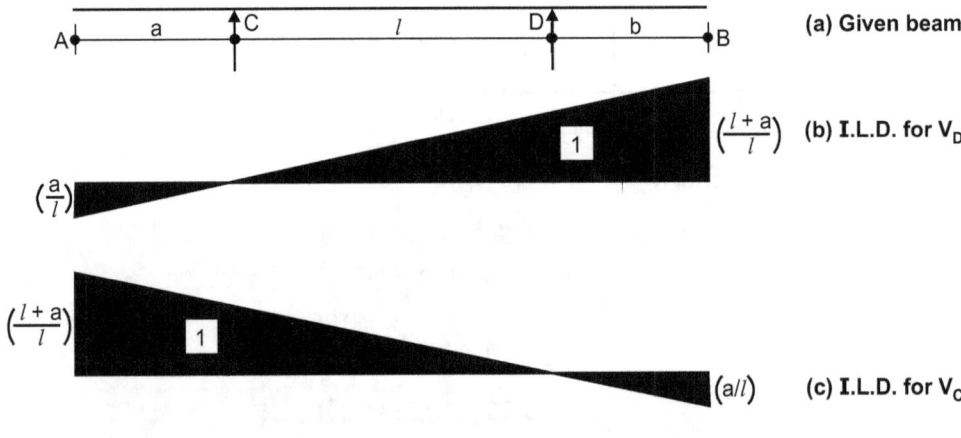

Fig. 8.27

I.L.D. for S.F. at a Section for Overhang Beams :

For drawing the I.L.D. for S.F. at a section, first ignore the overhang portion and draw the I.L.D. for the simply supported beams. Then produce the influence line for the overhang portion.

Consider a beam ACDB simply supported at C and D. Length between the two supports is l. CA = a and DB = b. I.L.D. for S.F. at $l/2$ from any support is as below :

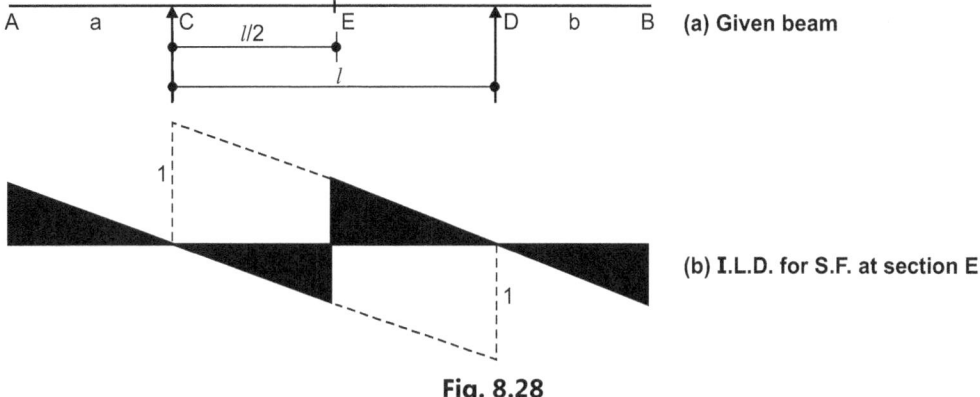

Fig. 8.28

(i.e. at $l/2$ for both the supports)

[Note : First draw the I.L.D for S.F. at E ignoring the overhang portion and then produce influence line for the overhang portion.]

I.L.D. for the B.M. at a Section for Simply Supported Beams with Overhang :

Similar procedure is adopted as that for reactions and S.F. at the section for drawing the I.L.D. at a section for B.M.

First draw the I.L.D. for B.M. at a section ignoring the overhang and then produce the influence line to cover the overhang portion.

Consider a beam ACDB, simply supported at C and D. Length between the supports is l. CA = a and CB = b. I.L.D. for B.M. at a distance $l/2$ from both the supports is as follows :

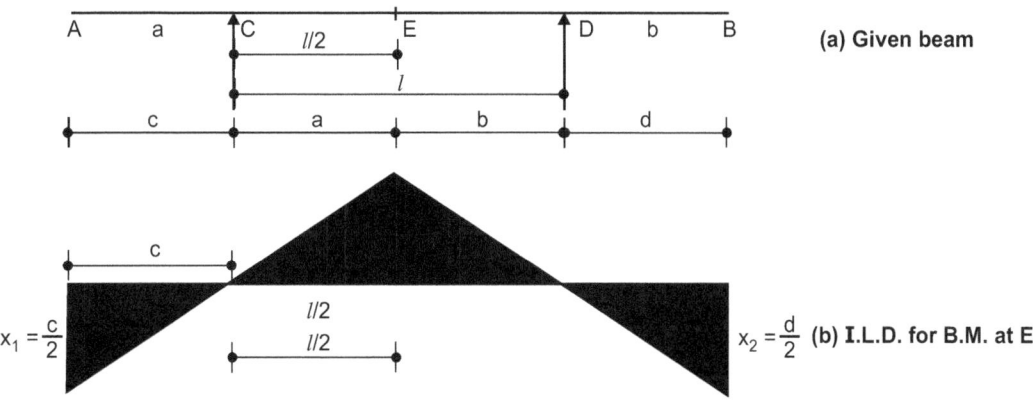

Fig. 8.29

(i.e. E at $l/2$ from both the supports)

From similar triangles, $\dfrac{l/4}{l/2} = \dfrac{x_1}{c}$ $\therefore x_1 = c/2$

Similarly, $\qquad x_2 = \dfrac{d}{2}$

Problem 8.19 : A beam ACDB is of 19 m. It is simply supported at C and D. Length between the supports is 10 m. AC = 5 m and DB = 4 m. A load of 20 kN is acting at A, 30 kN at B. Two concentrated loads of 45 kN and 35 kN are acting at 3 m and 6 m respectively from support C. Find the reactions R_C and R_D, S.F. at 4 m from support C and B.M. at 4 m from support C. (Use I.L.D.)

Solution :

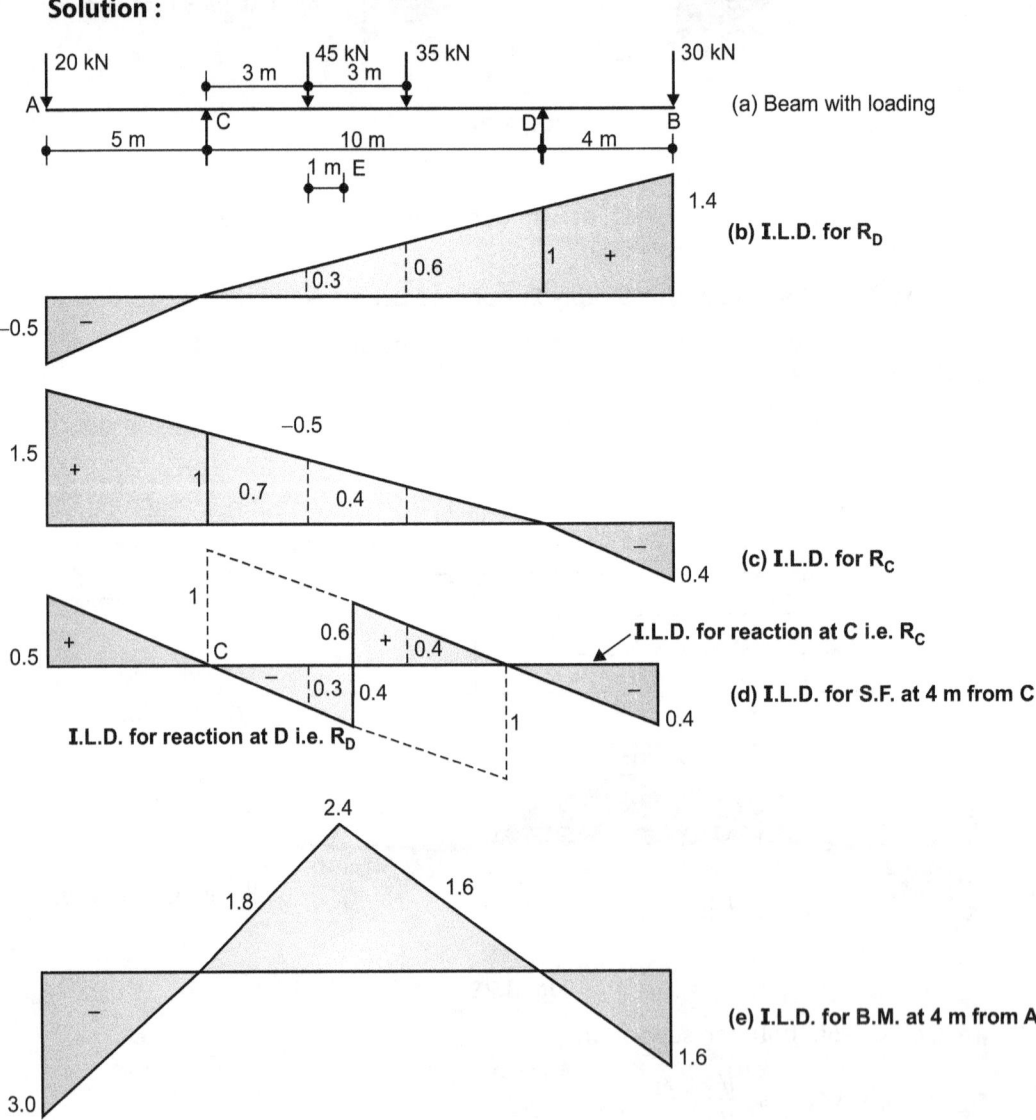

Fig. 8.30

(1) Ordinates at different positions on I.L.D. for R_D :

Ordinate on I.L.D. at point D = 1.0

at point C = 0.0

(Under 20 kN) i.e. at point A = $-\dfrac{1}{10} \times 5 = -0.5$

at point B = $\dfrac{1}{10} \times 14 = 1.4$

Under 45 kN = $\dfrac{1}{10} \times 3 = 0.3$

Under 35 kN = $\dfrac{1}{10} \times 6 = 0.6$

(2) Ordinates at different positions on I.L.D. for R_C :

Ordinate on I.L.D. at point C = 1.0

at point D = 0.0

at point A = $\dfrac{1}{10} \times 15 = 1.5$

at point B = $-\dfrac{1}{10} \times 4 = -0.4$

Under 45 kN = $\dfrac{1}{10} \times 7 = 0.7$

Under 35 kN = $\dfrac{1}{10} \times 4 = 0.4$

(3) Ordinates at different positions on I.L.D. for S.F. at C i.e. at 4 m :

Ordinate on I.L.D. for reaction at C = 1.0

at E = $\dfrac{1}{10} \times 6 = 0.6$

Under 35 kN = $\dfrac{1}{10} \times 4 = 0.4$

at D = 0.0

at B = $-\dfrac{1}{10} \times 4 = -0.4$

Ordinate on I.L.D. for reaction at D = -1.0

at E = $-\dfrac{1}{10} \times 4 = -0.4$

$$\text{Under 45 kN} = -\frac{1}{10} \times 3 = -0.3$$

$$\text{Under 20 kN} = \frac{1}{10} \times 5 = 0.5$$

Reaction at D (R_D) :

$$\text{Reaction at D} = R_D = \text{Loads} \times \text{Respective ordinates}$$
$$= 20 \times (-0.5) + 45 \times 0.3 + 35 \times 0.6 + 30 \times 1.4$$
$$= 66.5 \text{ kN}$$

$\therefore \quad R_D = 66.5 \text{ kN}$

Reaction at C (R_C) :

$$R_C = 20 \times 1.5 + 45 \times 0.7 + 35 \times 0.4 + 30 \times (-0.4)$$
$$= 63.5 \text{ kN}$$

$\therefore \quad R_C = 63.5 \text{ kN}$

S.F. at 4 m from 'C' :

$$S_{4m} = S_E = \text{Loads} \times \text{Respective ordinates}$$
$$= 20 \times (0.5) + 45 \times (-0.3) + 35 \times 0.4 + 30 \times (-0.4)$$
$$= -1.5 \text{ kN}$$

$\therefore \quad S_E = -1.5$
$$= 1.5 \ (\downarrow)$$

B.M. at E (4 m from 'C') :

$$\text{B.M. at E} = \text{Loads} \times \text{Respective ordinates}$$
$$= 20 \times (-3.0) + 45 \times 1.8 + 35 \times 1.6 + 30 \times (-1.6)$$
$$= 29 \text{ kN-m}$$

$\therefore \quad \text{B.M. at E} = 29 \text{ kN-m}$

1. $R_D = 66.5 \text{ kN} (\uparrow)$
2. $R_C = 63.5 \text{ kN} (\uparrow)$
3. $S_E = 1.5 \text{ kN} (\downarrow)$
4. B.M. at E = 29 kN-m

Problem 8.20 : Find the reactions at supports, S.F. at E and moment at E for the beam having load system as shown in Fig. 8.31 (a).

Solution :

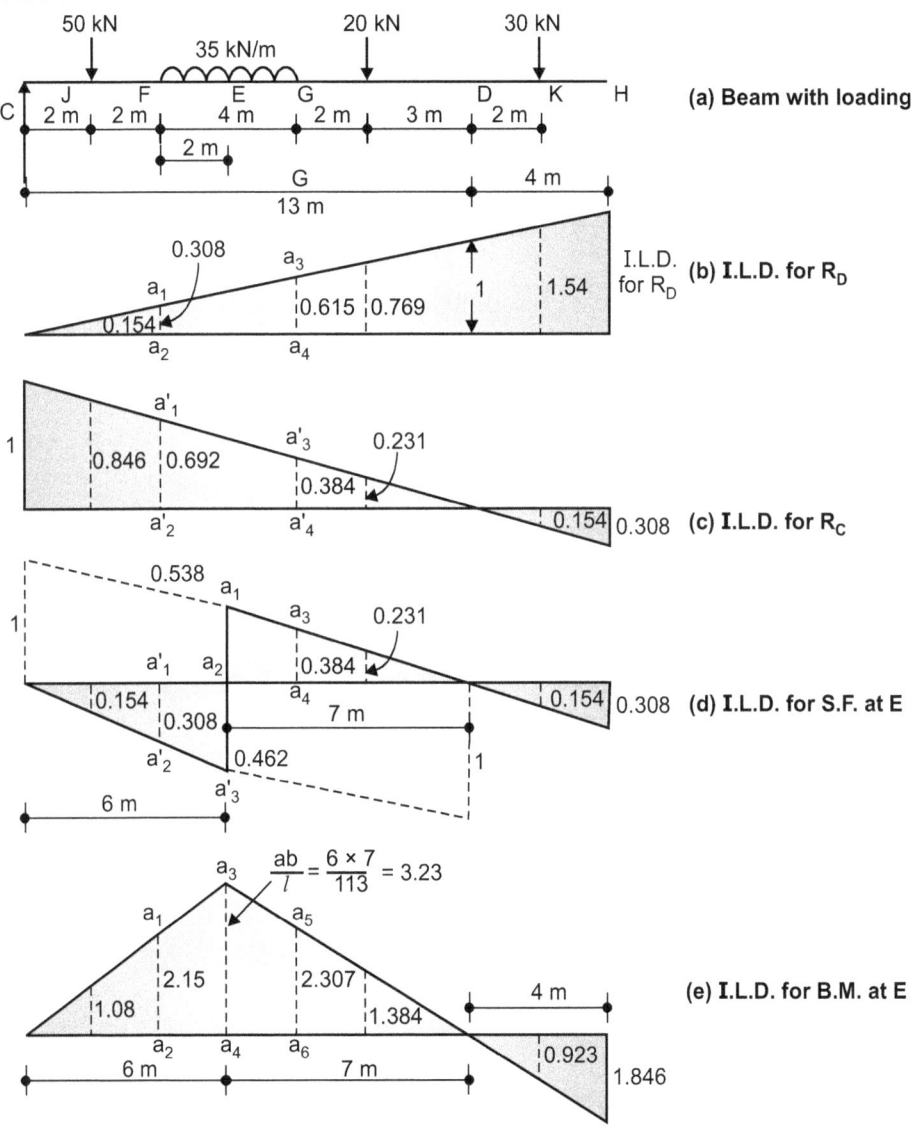

Fig. 8.31

(1) **Ordinates at different positions on I.L.D. for R_D : (Refer Fig. 8.31 (a))**

$$\text{at point D} = 1.0$$

$$\text{at point F} = \frac{1}{13} \times 4 = 0.308$$

$$\text{at point G} = \frac{1}{13} \times 8 = 0.615$$

$$\text{at point H} = \frac{1}{13} \times 17 = 1.307$$

Under 50 kN = $\frac{1}{13} \times 2 = 0.154$, Under 20 kN = $\frac{1}{13} \times 10 = 0.769$

Under 30 kN = $\frac{1}{13} \times 15 = 1.154$

(2) Ordinates at different positions on I.L.D. for R_C : (Refer Fig. 8.31 (c))

at point C = 1.0

at point F = $\frac{1}{13} \times 9 = 0.692$

at point G = $\frac{1}{13} \times 5 = 0.385$

at point H = $-\frac{1}{13} \times 4 = -0.308$

at point D = 0.0

Under 50 kN = $\frac{1}{13} \times 11 = 0.846$

Under 20 kN = $\frac{1}{13} \times 3 = 0.231$

Under 30 kN = $-\frac{1}{13} \times 2 = -0.154$

(3) Ordinates at different positions on I.L.D. for S.F. at E : (Refer Fig. 8.31 (d))

Ordinates on I.L.D. for reaction at C :

at C = 1.0

at E = $\frac{1}{13} \times 7 = 0.538$

at G = $\frac{1}{13} \times 5 = 0.385$

at H = $-\frac{1}{13} \times 4 = -0.308$

Under 20 kN = $\frac{1}{13} \times 3 = 0.231$

Under 30 kN = $-\frac{1}{13} \times 2 = -0.154$

Ordinates on I.L.D. for reaction at D :

at D = -1.0

at E = $-\frac{1}{13} \times 6 = -0.462$

at C = 0.0

at F = $-\frac{1}{13} \times 4 = -0.308$

Under 50 kN = $-\frac{1}{13} \times 2 = -0.154$

(4) Ordinates at different positions on I.L.D. for B.M. at E : (Refer Fig. 8.31 (e))

$$a = 6 \text{ m}, l = 13 \text{ m}$$

$$\text{at E} = \frac{a(l-a)}{l} = \frac{6 \times 7}{13} = 3.23$$

$$\text{at F} = \frac{3.23}{6} \times 4 = 2.15$$

$$\text{at G} = \frac{3.23}{7} \times 5 = 2.307$$

$$\text{at H} = -\frac{3.23}{7} \times 4 = -1.846$$

$$\text{at D} = 0.0$$

$$\text{Under 50 kN} = \frac{3.23}{6} \times 2 = 1.08$$

$$\text{Under 20 kN} = \frac{3.23}{7} \times 3 = 1.384$$

$$\text{Under 30 kN} = -\frac{1.846}{4} \times 2 = -0.923$$

Reaction at D :

Reaction at D = Loads × Resp. ordinates + Intensity of loading × Area covered
(i.e. area of trapezoidal $a_1 a_2 a_3 a_4$)

$$= 50 \times 0.154 + 35 \times \left(\frac{0.308 + 0.615}{2}\right) \times 4 + 20 \times 0.769 + 30 \times 1.154$$

$$= 7.7 + 64.61 + 15.38 + 34.62 = 122.31 \text{ kN}$$

Reaction at C :

Reaction at C = Loads × Resp. ordinates + Intensity of loading × Area covered
(i.e. area of trapezoidal $a_1' a_2' a_3' a_4'$)

$$R_C = 50 \times 0.846 + \left(\frac{0.692 + 0.385}{2}\right) \times 35 \times 4 + 20 \times 0.231 + 30 \times (-0.154)$$

$$= 42.3 + 75.39 + 4.62 - 4.62 = 117.69 \text{ kN}$$

S.F. at E (i.e. 6 m from C) :

S.F. at E = Loads × Resp. ordinates + Intensity of loading × Area covered
(i.e. area of trapezoidal $a_1 a_2 a_3 a_4$ + area of trapezoidal $a_1' a_2' a_3' a_4'$)

$$S_E = 50 \times (-0.154) + 35 \times \left(\frac{-0.308 - 0.46}{2}\right) \times 2$$

$$+ 35 \times \left(\frac{0.538 + 0.384}{2}\right) \times 2 + 20 \times 0.231 + 30 \times (-0.154)$$

$$= -7.7 - 26.88 + 32.27 + 4.62 - 4.62 = -2.31 \text{ kN}$$

$$S_E = 2.31 \text{ kN } (\downarrow)$$

B.M. at E (i.e. 6 m from C):

B.M. at E = Loads × Resp. ordinates + Intensity of loading × Area covered

(i.e. area of trapezoidal $a_1a_2a_3a_4$ + area of trapezoidal $a_3a_4a_5a_6$)

$$\text{B.M. at E} = 50 \times 1.08 + \left(\frac{2.15 + 3.23}{2}\right) \times 35 \times 2$$

$$+ \left(\frac{3.23 + 2.307}{2}\right) \times 35 \times 2 + 20 \times 1.384 + 30 \times (-0.923)$$

$$= 54 + 188.3 + 193.8 + 27.68 - 27.69 = 436.085 \text{ kN-m}$$

∴ R_C = 117.69 kN

R_D = 122.31 kN

S_E = − 2.31 kN = 2.31 kN

B.M. at E = 436.085 kN-m

Problem 8.21 : Two wheel loads of 40 kN and 70 kN spaced at 1 m. Find the position of loads to get maximum +ve shear, maximum −ve shear and maximum +ve B.M. and maximum −ve B.M. for the beam as shown in Fig. 8.32 (b) at section E.

Solution :

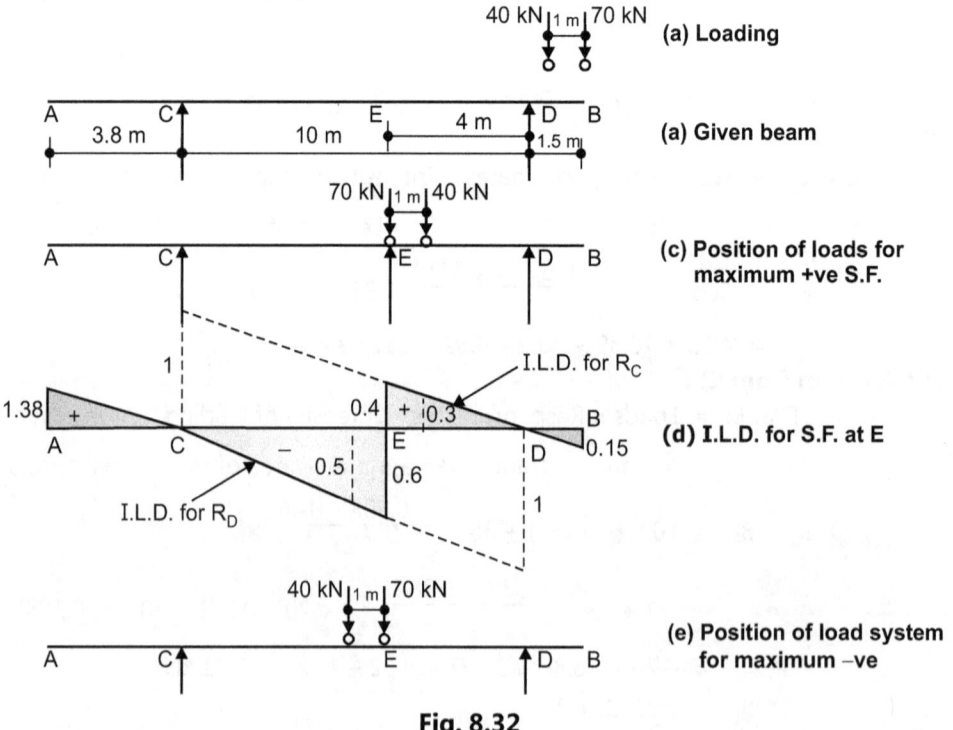

Fig. 8.32

Load position for maximum +ve S.F. and maximum −ve S.F. is as shown in Fig. 8.32 (c) and (e) respectively.

Load position for maximum +ve B.M. and maximum −ve B.M. is as shown in Fig. 8.32 (c) and (e) respectively.

(1) Ordinates at different positions on I.L.D. for S.F. at E :

(a) Position of loads for maximum +ve S.F. :

Ordinates on I.L.D. for reaction at C :

at C = 1.0

at E = $\dfrac{1}{10} \times 4 = 0.4$

(i.e. under 70 kN)

at B = $-\dfrac{1}{10} \times 1.5 = -0.15$

Under 40 kN = $\dfrac{1}{10} \times 3 = 0.3$

(b) Position of loads for maximum −ve S.F. :

Ordinates on I.L.D. for reaction at D

at D = −1.0

at C = 0.0

at A = $\dfrac{1}{10} \times 3.8 = 0.38$

Under 70 kN = $-\dfrac{1}{10} \times 6 = -0.6$

Under 40 kN = $-\dfrac{1}{10} \times 5 = -0.5$

(2) Ordinates at different positions on I.L.D. for B.M. at E : a = 6 m, l = 10 m

at E = $\dfrac{a(l-a)}{l} = \dfrac{6 \times 4}{10} = 2.4$

at D = 0.0

at C = 0.0

at A = $-\dfrac{2.4}{6} \times 3.8 = -1.52$

at B = $-\dfrac{2.4}{4} \times 1.5 = -0.9$

(a) Ordinates for load positions for maximum +ve B.M. :

Ordinate under 70 kN = Ordinate at E = 2.4

Under 40 kN = $\dfrac{2.4}{6} \times 5 = 2.0$

(b) Ordinates for load positions for maximum − ve B.M. :

Ordinate under 70 kN = Ordinate at A = −1.52

Under 40 kN = $-\dfrac{1.52}{3.8} \times 2.8 = -1.12$

Maximum +ve S.F. at E :

Maximum +ve shear force at E = 70 × (0.4) + 40 × (0.3) = 40 kN

Maximum –ve S.F. at E :

Maximum –ve shear force at E = 70 × 0.6 + 40 × 0.5 = 62 kN

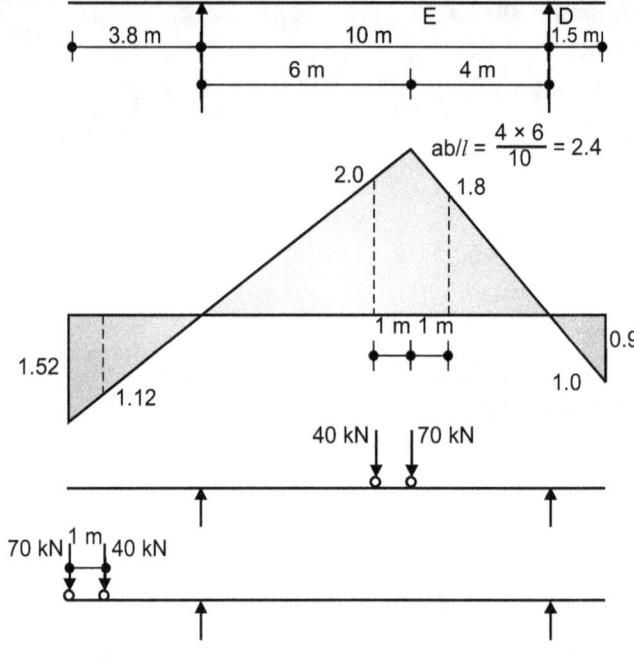

Fig. 8.33

Maximum +ve B.M. at E :

$$\text{Maximum +ve B.M. at E} = 70 \times 2.4 + 40 \times 2.0$$
$$= 248 \text{ kN-m}$$

Maximum –ve B.M. at E :

$$\text{Maximum –ve B.M. at E} = 70 \times (-1.52) + 40 (-1.12)$$
$$= 151.2 \text{ kN-m}$$

Maximum + ve S.F. at E = 40 kN

Maximum – ve S.F. at E = 62 kN

Maximum +ve B.M. at E = 248 kN-m

Maximum – ve B.M. at E = 151.2 kN-m

Problem 8.22 : Find the maximum +ve S.F., maximum –ve S.F., maximum +ve B.M. and maximum –ve B.M. at E. A U.D.L. of 100 kN/m may occupy any position on the girder ACDB. The beam ACDB is as shown in Fig. 8.34 (a).

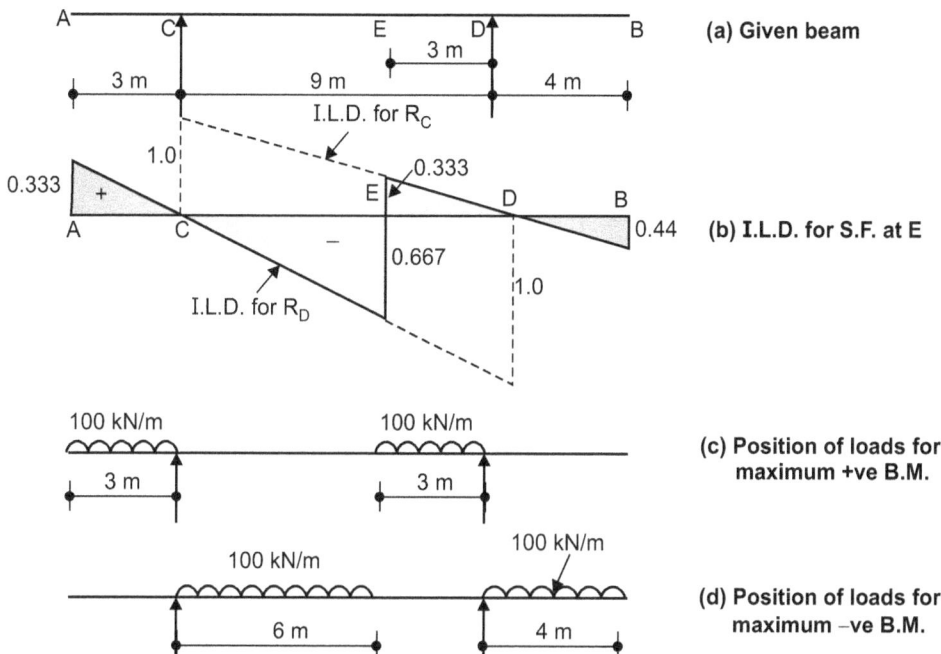

Load position for maximum +ve S.F. and maximum –ve S.F. is as in Fig. 8.34 (c) and (d) resp.

Load position for maximum +ve B.M. and maximum –ve B.M. is as in Fig. 8.35 (c) and (d) resp.

Fig. 8.34

(1) Ordinates at different positions on I.L.D. for S.F. at E :

(a) Ordinates on I.L.D. for reaction at C :

$$\text{at C} = 1.0$$

$$\text{at E} = \frac{1}{9} \times 3 = 0.33$$

$$\text{at D} = 0.0$$

$$\text{at B} = -\frac{1}{9} \times 4 = -0.444$$

(b) Ordinates on I.L.D. for reaction at D :

$$\text{at D} = -1.0$$

$$\text{at C} = 0.0$$

$$\text{at E} = -\frac{1}{9} \times 6 = -0.667$$

$$\text{at A} = \frac{1}{9} \times 3 = 0.33$$

(2) Ordinates at different positions on I.L.D. for B.M. at E :

$$a = 6\text{ m}, \; l = 9\text{ m}$$

$$\text{at E} = \frac{a(l-a)}{l} = \frac{6 \times 3}{9} = 2.0$$

at C = 0.0

at D = 0.0

$$\text{at A} = -\frac{2}{6} \times 3 = -1.0$$

$$\text{at B} = -\frac{2}{3} \times 4 = -2.667$$

Maximum +ve S.F. at E :

$$\therefore \quad \text{Maximum +ve S.F. at E} = \left(\frac{0.333 + 0}{2}\right) \times 3 \times 100 + \left(\frac{0.33 + 0}{2}\right) \times 3 \times 100$$

$$= 99.9 \text{ kN}$$

Maximum –ve S.F. at E :

$$\text{Maximum –ve S.F. at E} = -\left(\frac{1}{2} \times 0.667 \times 6 \times 100 + \frac{1}{2} \times 0.44 \times 4 \times 100\right)$$

$$= -288.1 \text{ kN}$$

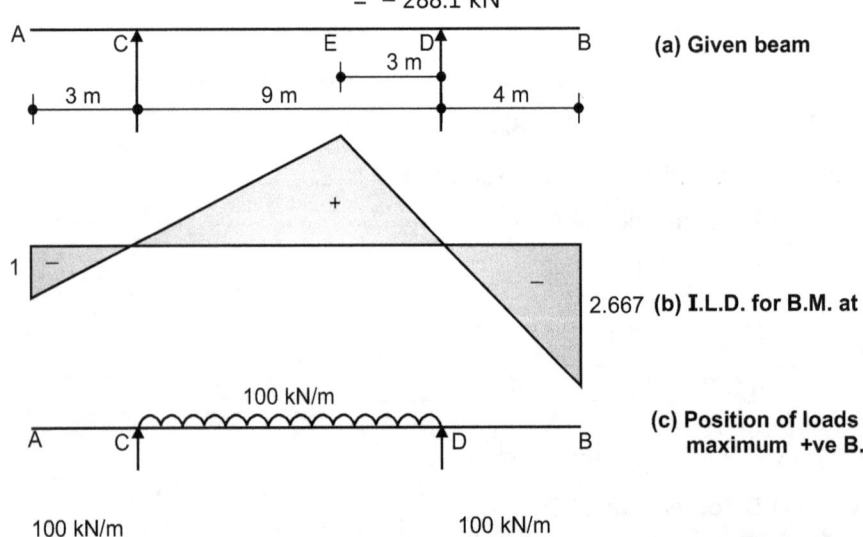

Fig. 8.35

Maximum +ve B.M. at E :

$$\text{Maximum +ve B.M.} = \frac{1}{2} \times 2 \times 100 \times 9 = 900 \text{ kN-m}$$

Maximum −ve B.M. at E :

$$\text{Maximum −ve B.M.} = \frac{1}{2} \times 1 \times 3 \times 100 + \frac{1}{2} \times 4 \times 2.667 \times 100$$

$$= 683.4 \text{ kN-m}$$

∴ Maximum +ve S.F. at E = 99.9 kN

Maximum −ve S.F. at E = 288.1 kN

Maximum +ve B.M. at E = 900 kN-m

Maximum −ve B.M. at E = 683.4 kN-m

EXERCISE

1. Draw I.L.D. for reaction at A, reaction at B, S.F. at a distance x from A and B.M. at a distance x from A as shown in Fig. 8.36.

   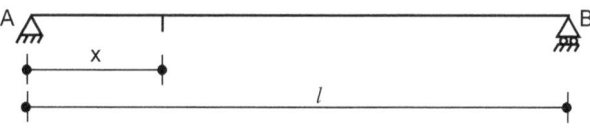

   Fig. 8.36

2. Find the reactions, S.F. and B.M. at a distance 3 m from A. Span AB = 8 m using I.L.D.

   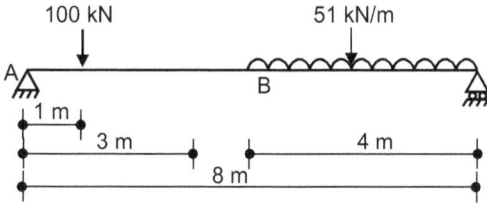

   Fig. 8.37

3. Draw I.L.D. for the reaction at A, B and C. Also draw I.L.D. for S.F. at midpoint of AB and midpoint of BC.

   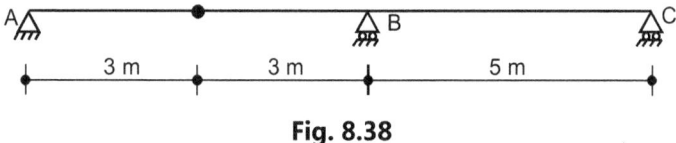

   Fig. 8.38

4. Find the maximum values of the reactions and S.F. for the above problem when U.D.L. of intensity 60 kN/m can take any position on the compound beam.

5. Find the maximum values of the reaction, S.F. and B.M. in problem no. 1 when U.D.L. of intensity 55 kN/m longer than the span traverses on the beam. Also find maximum values of the above when U.D.L. of intensity 50 kN/m traverses on the beam having span 5 m. For this case, x = 8 m and *l* = 16 m.

Chapter 9

INFLUENCE LINE DIAGRAMS FOR PLANE TRUSSES

9.1 INTRODUCTION

Trusses are used in bridges. In bridge, two long trusses are connected by the cross girders. The load is transmitted to the trusses with the help of the cross girders. On each panel points, cross girders are connected through which load is transferred.

If the cross girders are connected to the top panel points, then load is transferred to top panel points and these type of bridge girders are known as deck type bridge girders. If the cross girders are connected to the bottom panel points, then load is transferred through the bottom panel points. These type of bridge girders are known as through type bridge girders.

To draw the influence lines, it is assumed that unit load is acting on the cross girders and unit load is transferred to each main truss. Thus by considering moving unit load acting on the truss and for that influence line has to be drawn.

Different types of trusses are used for the bridges. If I.L.D. for deck type truss has to be drawn, then it is to be considered that the moving unit load is acting on the top panel points.

For through type truss, the unit load is considered to be acting on the bottom panel points only.

As we are considering that force in the truss is only axial (vertical), therefore unit load should act on the panel points only. Thus, moving the unit load on the panel points, we get respective ordinates. Joining of the ordinates gives the I.L.D. for the respective stress element.

While drawing I.L.D., section has to be taken. When unit load is in the left part of the section considered, right part of the truss is solved for equilibrium to calculate force in member.

When unit load is in right part of the truss, left part is solved for equilibrium to calculate force in member.

Sign Convention :

+ ve $\rightarrow$ Compression

− ve $\rightarrow$ Tension.

9.2 I.L.D. FOR DIFFERENT MEMBERS OF N TYPE TRUSS

Fig. 9.1 (b) is N type truss of the through type bridge.

To draw the I.L.D. for the truss, we have to consider that unit load is acting only on the panel points. As truss is through type so that unit load is acting only on the bottom panel points. So moving the unit load on the bottom panel points, we have to calculate the ordinates at respective panel points and joining these ordinates will give you the I.L.D. for the respective members.

9.2.1 I.L.D for Top Chord Members

Take the section 1 - 1 as shown in Fig. 9.1 (a).

When unit load is in left part, consider right part in equilibrium.

Section 1 – 1 cuts the three members. To find the force in u_0u_1 we have to take the moment of all forces @ L_1 because the remaining two members are passing through L_1, so moment of that member forces becomes zero and we can find force in that member easily.

$$\text{Force in member} = P_{u_0u_1} = V_1 \times \frac{l}{h}$$

When unit load is at L_0, $V_1 = 0$ ∴ $P_{u_0u_1} = 0$

When unit load is at L_1, $V_1 = \frac{7}{8}$

$$P_{u_0u_1} = \frac{7}{8}\frac{l}{h}$$

When unit load is at L_2, $V_1 = \frac{6}{8}$

$$P_{u_0u_1} = \frac{6}{8}\frac{l}{h}$$

When unit load is at L_3, $V_1 = \frac{5}{8}$

$$P_{u_0u_1} = \frac{5}{8}\frac{l}{h}$$

When unit load is at L_4, $V_1 = \frac{4}{8}$

$$P_{u_0u_1} = \frac{4}{8}\frac{l}{h}$$

When unit load is at L_5, $V_1 = \frac{3}{8}$

$$P_{u_0u_1} = \frac{3}{8}\frac{l}{h}$$

When unit load is at L_6, $V_1 = \frac{2}{8}$

$$P_{u_0u_1} = \frac{2}{8}\frac{l}{h}$$

When unit load is at L_7, $V_1 = \frac{1}{8}$

$$P_{u_0u_1} = \frac{1}{8}\frac{l}{h}$$

When unit load is at L_8, $P_{u_0u_1} = 0$

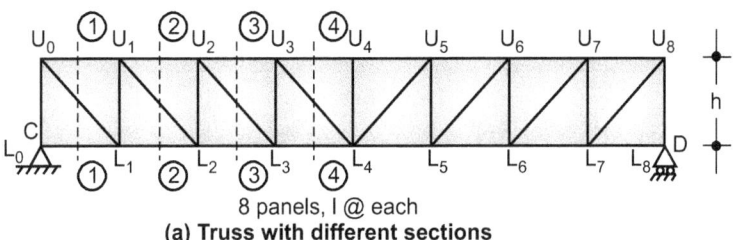

(a) Truss with different sections

I.L.D. for top chords :

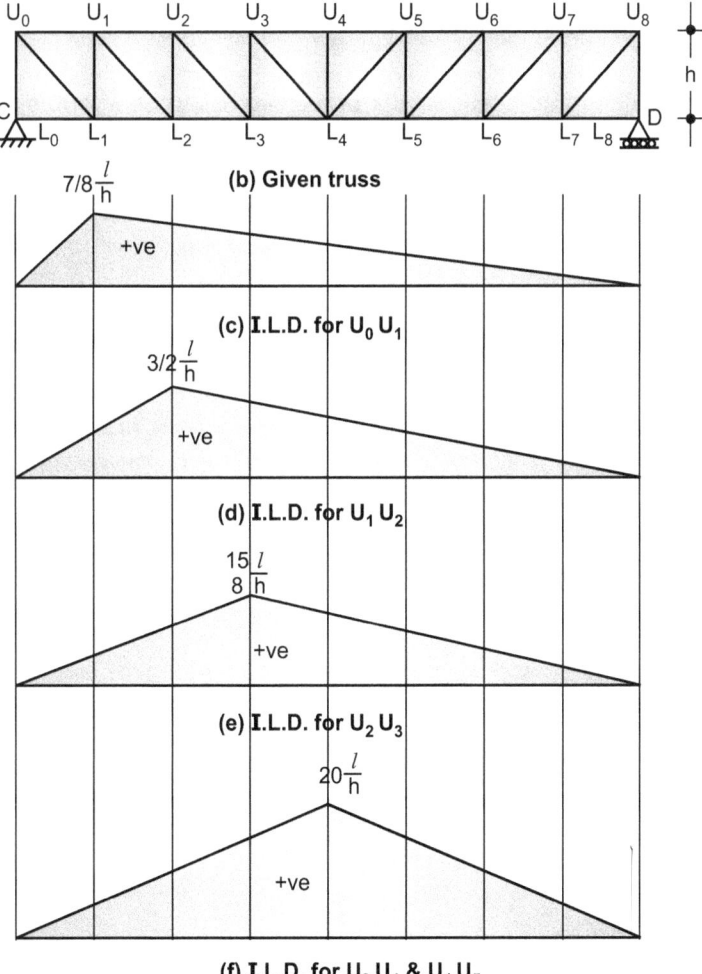

(b) Given truss

(c) I.L.D. for $U_0 U_1$

(d) I.L.D. for $U_1 U_2$

(e) I.L.D. for $U_2 U_3$

(f) I.L.D. for $U_3 U_4$ & $U_4 U_5$

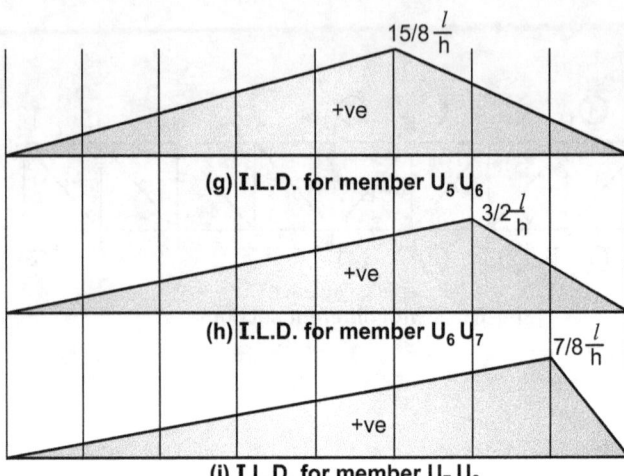

Fig. 9.1

Above figure is drawn by plotting the ordinates at respective points and join them.

For all other top chord members, similar procedure has to be adopted. For $u_1 u_2$, section 2 - 2; for $u_2 u_3$, section 3 - 3; for $u_3 u_4$, section 4 - 4 has to be considered.

9.2.2 I.L.D. for Bottom Chords of N Type Truss

Following truss is N type through bridge truss. To draw the I.L.D for the bottom chords, we have to move unit load through the panel points and calculate the ordinates at respective panel points. Joining of these ordinates give the I.L.D. for the respective members.

I.L.D. for L_0L_1 : There should not be any force in member L_0L_1, though the unit load moves to any panel point. As loads are vertical loads only, so at the joint L_0, no horizontal member or force acts other than L_0L_1. As no other force or member at L_0, so to solve the joint for equilibrium force in member L_0L_1 should be zero.

I.L.D. for L_1L_2 : When unit load is on left part of section, consider right part of the section in equilibrium.

Section 1 – 1 from Fig. 9.2 (a) is considered. Due to this section three members cut. To find the force in member L_1L_2 we have to take moment @ U_1 so the moment of other two member forces becomes zero.

$$P_{L_1L_2} = V_2 \times \frac{l}{h}$$

When unit load is at L_0, $V_2 = 0$

$$P_{L_1L_2} = 0$$

When unit load is at L_1, $V_2 = \frac{7}{8}$

$$P_{L_1L_2} = \frac{7}{8}\frac{l}{h} \text{ (Tensile)}$$

When unit load is on right part, consider left part to be in equilibrium.

$$\therefore \quad P_{L_1L_2} = V_1 \times \frac{l}{h} \text{ (Tensile)}$$

When unit load is at L_2, $V_1 = \frac{6}{8}$

$$P_{L_1L_2} = \frac{6}{8}\frac{l}{h} \text{ (Tensile)}$$

When unit load is at L_3, $V_1 = \dfrac{5}{8}$

$P_{L_1 L_2} = \dfrac{5}{8}\dfrac{l}{h}$

When unit load is at L_4, $V_1 = 4/8$

$P_{L_1 L_2} = \dfrac{4}{8}\dfrac{l}{h}$

When unit load is at L_5, $V_1 = 3/8$

$P_{L_1 L_2} = \dfrac{3}{8}\dfrac{l}{h}$

When unit load is at L_6, $V_1 = 2/8$

$P_{L_1 L_2} = \dfrac{2}{8}\dfrac{l}{h}$

When unit load is at L_7, $V_1 = 1/8$

$P_{L_1 L_2} = \dfrac{1}{8}\dfrac{l}{h}$

When unit load is at L_8, $V_1 = 0$

$P_{L_1 L_2} = 0$

For other bottom chords, sections are shown below. For member $L_2 L_3$ - section 3 - 3, for member $L_3 L_4$ - section 4 – 4 has to be considered.

I.L.D. for bottom chord members :

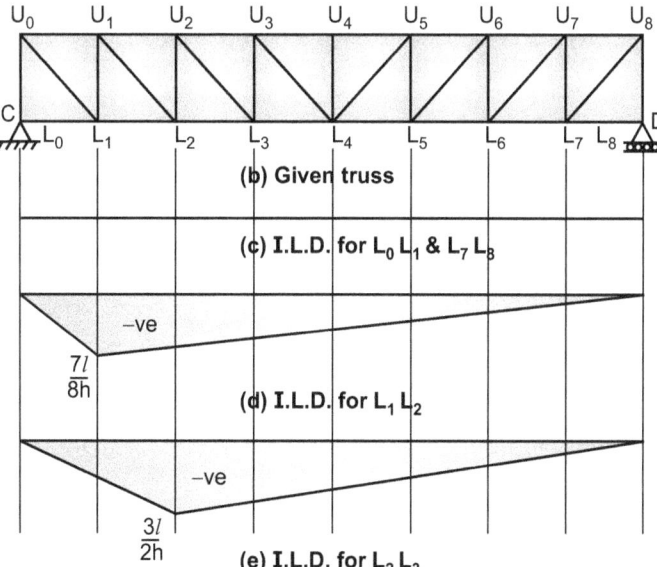

(b) Given truss

(c) I.L.D. for $L_0 L_1$ & $L_7 L_8$

−ve

$\dfrac{7l}{8h}$

(d) I.L.D. for $L_1 L_2$

−ve

$\dfrac{3l}{2h}$

(e) I.L.D. for $L_2 L_3$

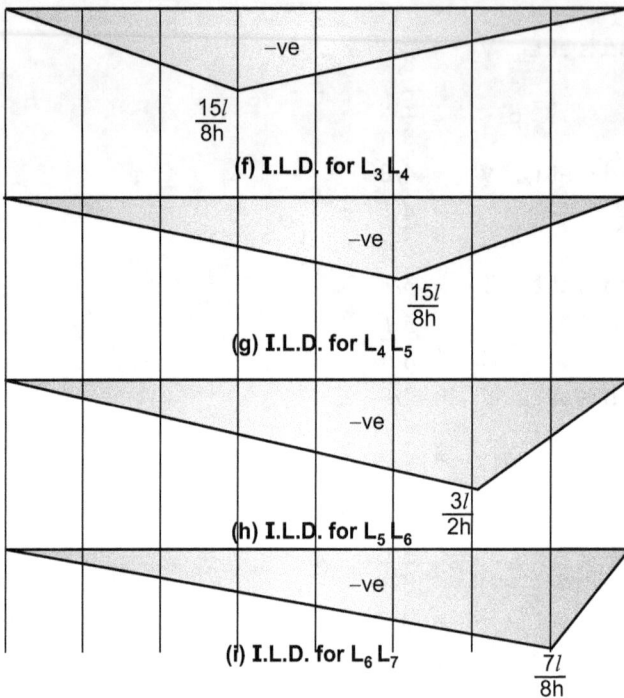

Fig. 9.2

9.2.3 I.L.D. for Vertical Members

Fig. 9.3 (b) is N type through bridge truss.

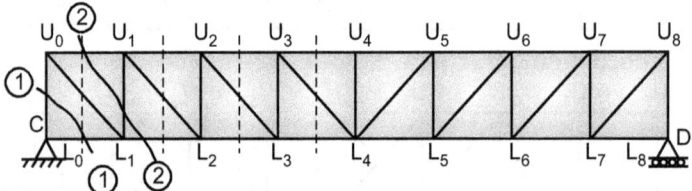

Fig. 9.3 (a) : Truss with diff. sections

I.L.D for vertical member U_0L_0 :

Take the section 1 – 1 as shown in Fig. 9.3 (a) and consider left part of section. Join L_0 as in equilibrium. ∴ $P_{U_0L_0} = V_1$.

When unit load is at L_0, $V_1 = 0$
$$P_{U_0L_0} = 0$$

When unit load is at L_1, $V_1 = 7/8$
$$P_{U_0L_0} = \frac{7}{8} \text{ (Compressive)}$$

When unit load is at L_2, $V_1 = 6/8$
$$P_{U_0L_0} = \frac{6}{8} \text{ (Compressive)}$$

When unit load is at L_3, $V_1 = 5/8$

$$P_{U_0 L_0} = \frac{5}{8} \text{ (Compressive)}$$

When unit load is at L_4, $V_1 = 4/8$

$$P_{U_0 L_0} = \frac{4}{8} \text{ (Compressive)}$$

When unit load is at L_5, $V_1 = 3/8$

$$P_{U_0 L_0} = \frac{3}{8} \text{ (Compressive)}$$

When unit load is at L_6, $V_1 = 2/8$

$$P_{U_0 L_0} = \frac{2}{8} \text{ (Compressive)}$$

When unit load is at L_7, $V_1 = 1/8$

$$P_{U_0 L_0} = \frac{1}{8} \text{ (Compressive)}$$

When unit load is at L_8,

$$P_{U_0 L_0} = 0$$

Calculations for member $U_1 L_1$: Take section 2 – 2 as shown in Fig. 9.3 (a).

For portion upto L_1 i.e. unit load from L_0 to L_1,

$$P_{U_1 L_1} = V_2 \text{ (Tensile)}$$

When unit load is at L_0, $V_2 = 0$

$$P_{U_1 L_1} = 0$$

When unit load is at L_1, $V_2 = 1/8$

$$P_{U_1 L_1} = \frac{1}{8} \text{ (Tensile)}$$

For portion from L_2 to L_8,

$$P_{U_1 L_1} = V_1 \text{ (Compressive)}$$

When unit load is at L_2, $V_1 = 6/8$

$$P_{U_1 L_1} = \frac{6}{8} \text{ (Compressive)}$$

When unit load is at L_3, $V_1 = 5/8$

$$P_{U_1 L_1} = \frac{5}{8} \text{ (Compressive)}$$

When unit load is at L_4, $V_1 = 4/8$

$$P_{U_1 L_1} = \frac{4}{8} \text{ (Compressive)}$$

When unit load is at L_5, $V_1 = 3/8$

$$P_{U_1 L_1} = \frac{3}{8} \text{ (Compressive)}$$

When unit load is at L_6, $V_1 = 2/8$

$$P_{U_1 L_1} = \frac{2}{8} \text{ (Compressive)}$$

When unit load is at L_7, $V_1 = 1/8$

$$P_{U_1 L_1} = \frac{1}{8} \text{ (Compressive)}$$

When unit load is at L_8, $V_1 = 0$

$$P_{U_1 L_1} = 0$$

I.L.D. for vertical members :

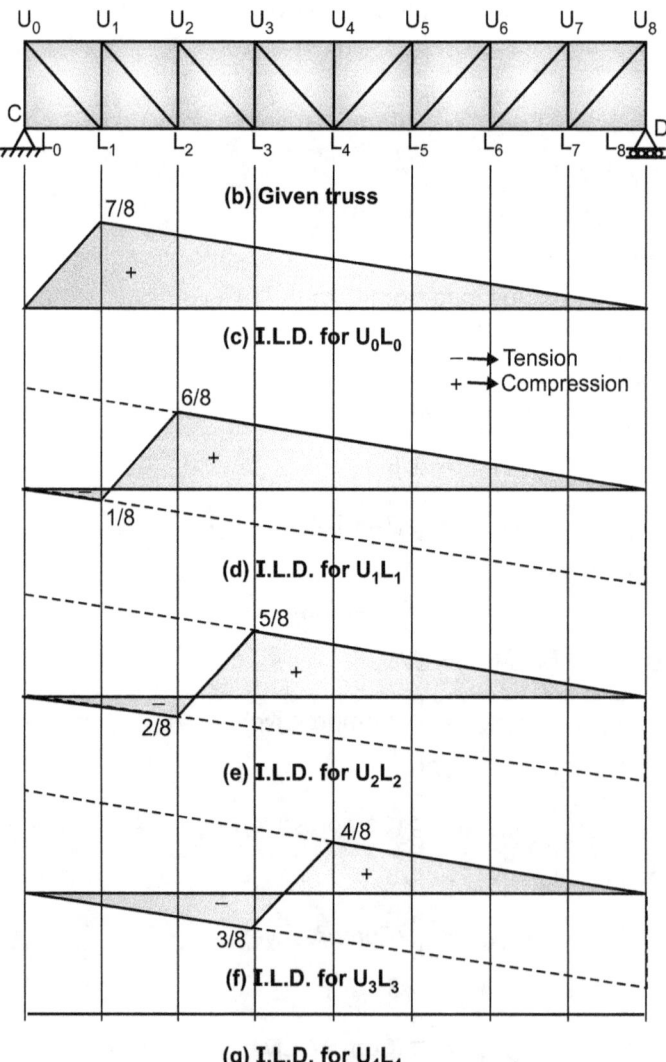

(b) Given truss

(c) I.L.D. for $U_0 L_0$

(d) I.L.D. for $U_1 L_1$

(e) I.L.D. for $U_2 L_2$

(f) I.L.D. for $U_3 L_3$

(g) I.L.D. for $U_4 L_4$

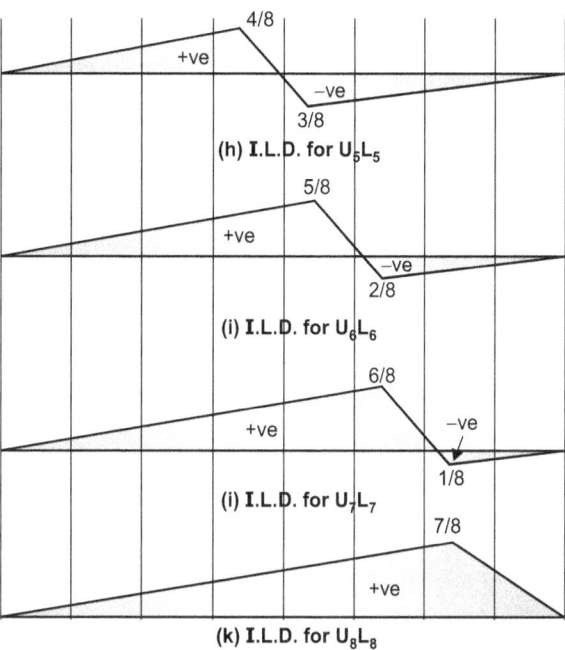

(h) I.L.D. for U_5L_5

(i) I.L.D. for U_6L_6

(j) I.L.D. for U_7L_7

(k) I.L.D. for U_8L_8

Fig. 9.3

9.2.4 I.L.D. for Diagonal Members

Following truss as shown in Fig. 9.4 (b) is N type through bridge truss. To draw the I.L.D. for diagonal members, we have to move the unit load from panel points to panel points and ordinates are calculated for each panel point for that member. Plotting of these ordinates will give the I.L.D. for the respective member.

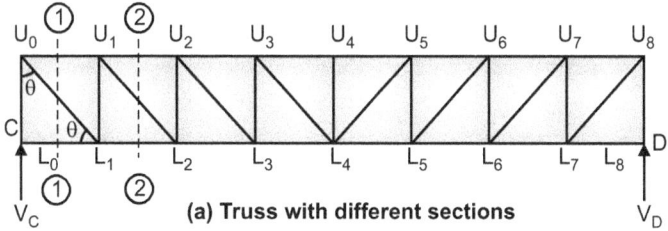

(a) Truss with different sections

I.L.D. for U_0L_1 :

Consider section 1 – 1 as shown in Fig. 9.4 (a).

$$P_{U_0L_1} \sin\theta = \text{Reaction}$$

For unit load on left part, consider equilibrium of right part.

$$P_{U_0L_1} \sin\theta = V_D$$

∴ $\quad P_{U_0L_1} = V_D \operatorname{cosec}\theta$

When unit load is at L_0, $\quad V_D = 0$

∴ $\quad P_{U_0L_1} = 0$

For unit load on right part, consider left part in equilibrium.

For portion L_1 to L_8: $\quad P_{U_0 L_1} \sin\theta = V_C$

$$P_{U_0 L_1} = V_C \operatorname{cosec}\theta \text{ (Tensile)} = 7/8 \operatorname{cosec}\theta \text{ (Tensile)}$$

When unit load is at L_2, $\quad V_C = 6/8$

$$P_{U_0 L_1} = \frac{6}{8} \operatorname{cosec}\theta \text{ (Tensile)}$$

When unit load is at L_3, $\quad V_C = 5/8$

$$P_{U_0 L_1} = \frac{5}{8} \operatorname{cosec}\theta \text{ (Tensile)}$$

When unit load is at L_4, $\quad V_C = 4/8$

$$P_{U_0 L_1} = \frac{4}{8} \operatorname{cosec}\theta \text{ (Tensile)}$$

When unit load is at L_5, $\quad V_C = 3/8$

$$P_{U_0 L_1} = \frac{3}{8} \operatorname{cosec}\theta \text{ (Tensile)}$$

When unit load is at L_6, $\quad V_C = 2/8$

$$P_{U_0 L_1} = \frac{2}{8} \operatorname{cosec}\theta \text{ (Tensile)}$$

When unit load is at L_7, $\quad V_C = 1/8$

$$P_{U_0 L_1} = \frac{1}{8} \operatorname{cosec}\theta \text{ (Tensile)}$$

When unit load is at L_8, $\quad V_C = 0$

$$P_{U_0 L_1} = 0 \text{ (Tensile)}$$

Plotting the ordinates and joining them gives the I.L.D. for $U_0 L_1$.

I.L.D. for $U_1 L_2$: Consider section 2 – 2 as shown in Fig. 9.4 (a).

When unit load is in left part of section, then,

$$P_{U_1 L_2} = V_B \operatorname{cosec}\theta \text{ (Compressive)}$$

When unit load is at L_0, $\quad V_B = 0$

$$P_{U_1 L_2} = 0$$

When unit load is at L_1, $\quad V_B = 1/8$

$$P_{U_1 L_2} = \frac{1}{8} \operatorname{cosec}\theta \text{ (Compressive)}$$

When unit load is in the right part of the section

$$P_{U_1 L_2} = V_A \operatorname{cosec}\theta \text{ (Tensile)}$$

When unit load is at L_2, $\quad V_A = 6/8$

$$P_{U_1 L_2} = \frac{6}{8} \operatorname{cosec}\theta \text{ (Tensile)}$$

When unit load is at L_3, $\quad V_A = 5/8$

$$P_{U_1 L_2} = \frac{5}{8} \operatorname{cosec}\theta \text{ (Tensile)}$$

When unit load is at L_4, $V_A = 4/8$

$P_{U_1 L_2} = \dfrac{4}{8} \operatorname{cosec} \theta$ (Tensile)

When unit load is at L_5, $V_A = 3/8$

$P_{U_1 L_2} = \dfrac{3}{8} \operatorname{cosec} \theta$ (Tensile)

When unit load is at L_6, $V_A = 2/8$

$P_{U_1 L_2} = \dfrac{2}{8} \operatorname{cosec} \theta$ (Tensile)

When unit load is at L_7, $V_A = 1/8$

$P_{U_1 L_2} = \dfrac{1}{8} \operatorname{cosec} \theta$ (Tensile)

When unit load is at L_8, $V_A = 0$

$P_{U_1 L_2} = 0$

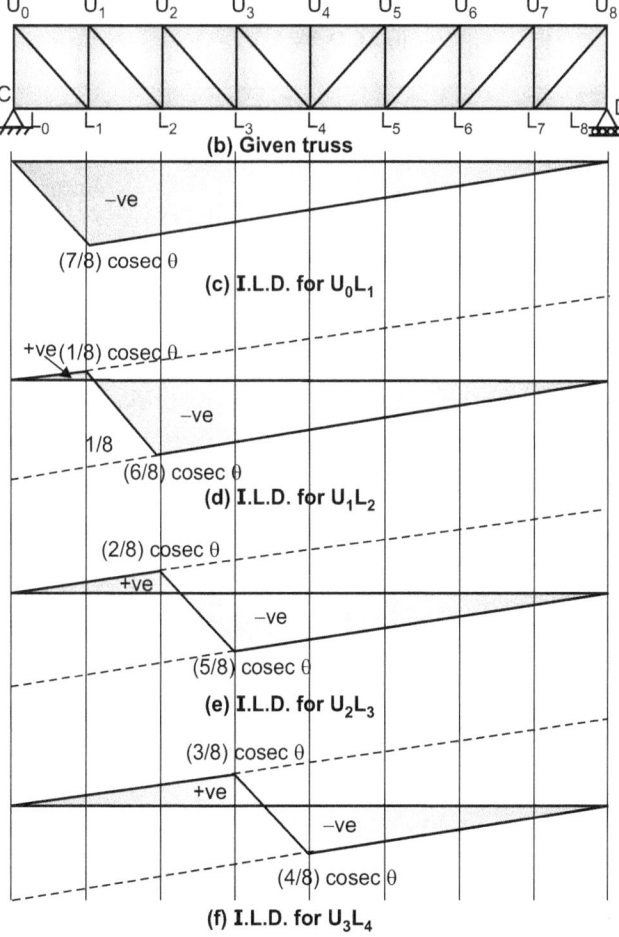

(b) Given truss

(c) I.L.D. for $U_0 L_1$

(d) I.L.D. for $U_1 L_2$

(e) I.L.D. for $U_2 L_3$

(f) I.L.D. for $U_3 L_4$

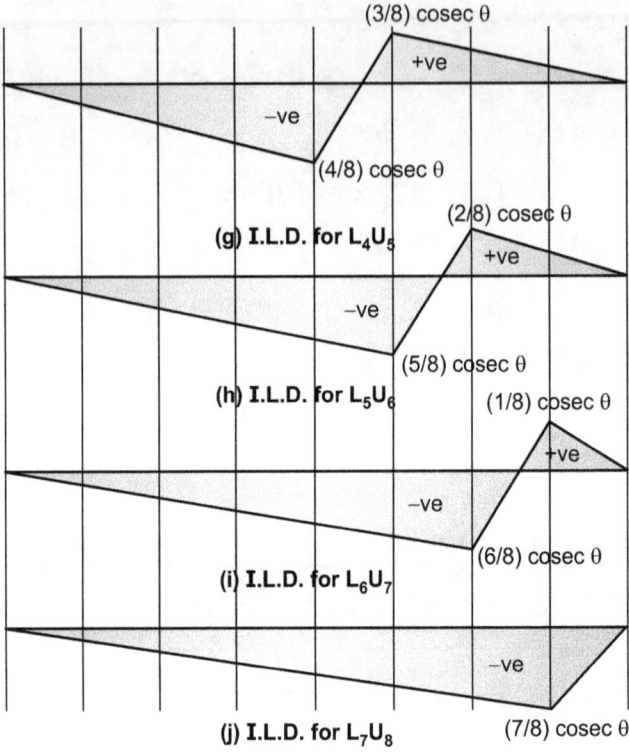

(g) I.L.D. for L_4U_5

(h) I.L.D. for L_5U_6

(i) I.L.D. for L_6U_7

(j) I.L.D. for L_7U_8

Fig. 9.4

9.3 I.L.D. FOR DECK TYPE BRIDGE TRUSS

Difference in through type bridge truss and deck type bridge truss is as follows:

In through type, unit load is moving through the bottom panel points and in case of Deck type unit load is moving through the top panel points. All other points for drawing I.L.D. remains same.

9.3.1 I.L.D. for Top Chord Members of N Type Truss

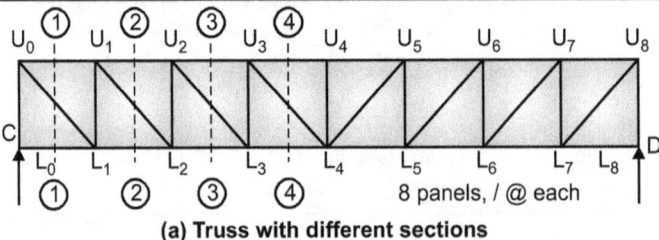

(a) Truss with different sections

Fig. 9.5

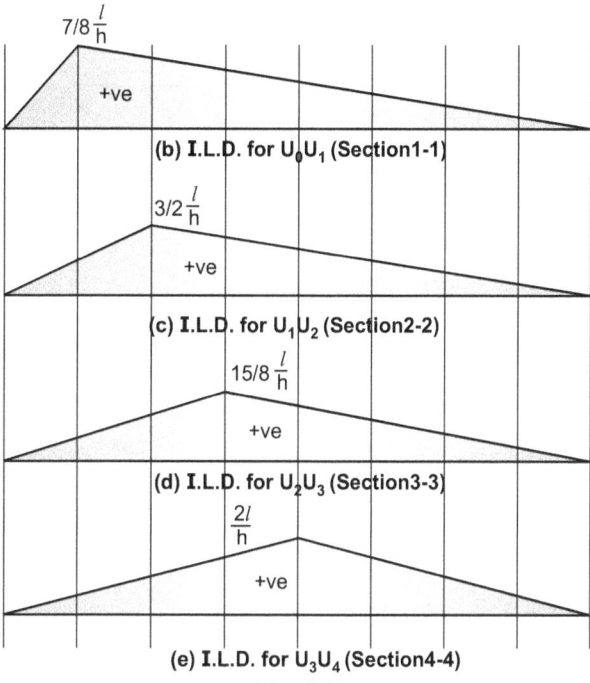

Fig. 9.5

9.3.2 I.L.D. for Bottom Chord Members

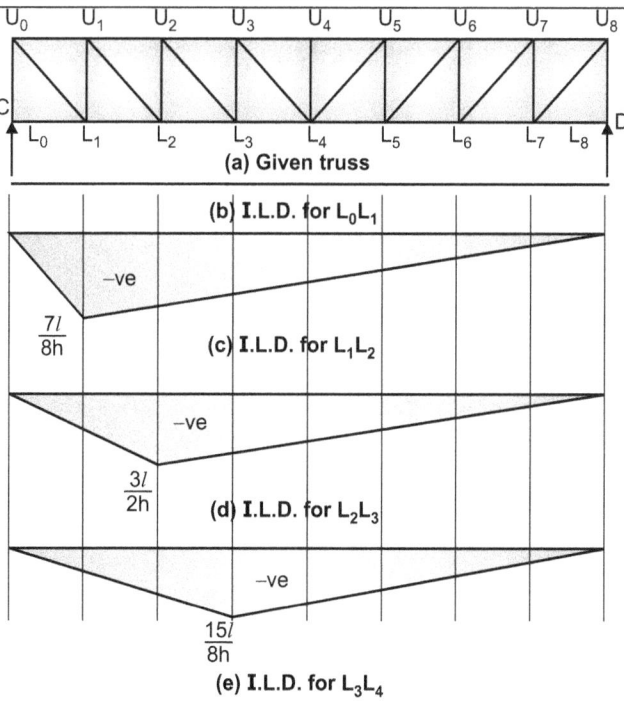

Fig. 9.6

9.3.3 I.L.D. for Vertical Members

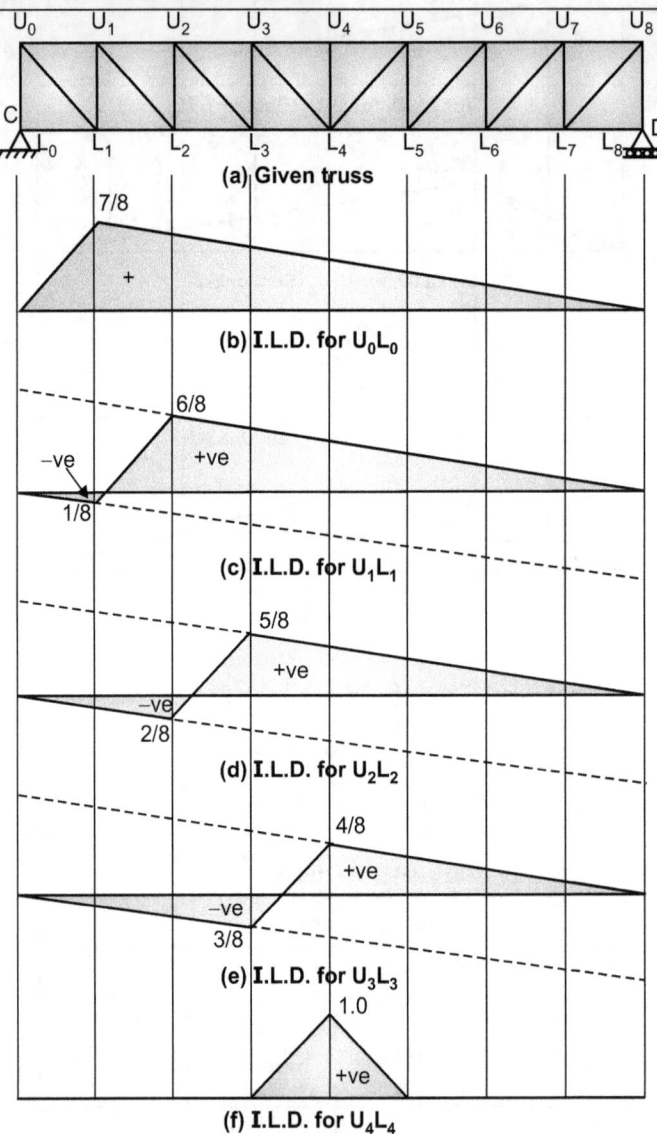

Fig. 9.7

9.3.4 I.L.D. for Diagonal Members

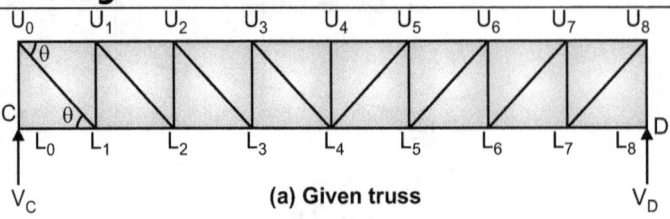

(a) Given truss

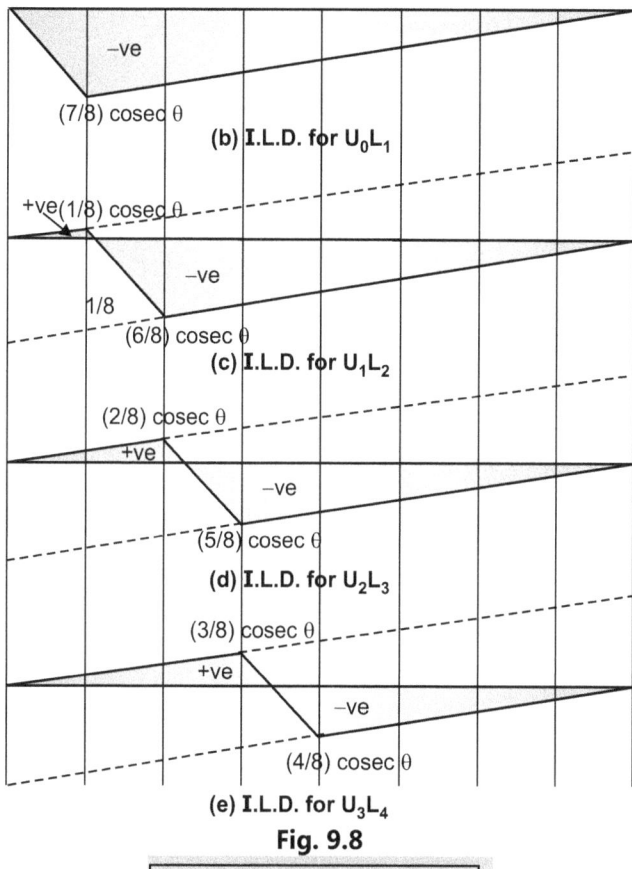

(b) I.L.D. for U_0L_1

(c) I.L.D. for U_1L_2

(d) I.L.D. for U_2L_3

(e) I.L.D. for U_3L_4

Fig. 9.8

SOLVED PROBLEMS

Problem 9.1 : For a truss as shown in Fig. 9.10 (a) draw I.L.D. for forces in members U_1U_2, U_1L_1, L_1L_2, and U_1L_2, if unit load traverse on bottom chord.

If this truss is traversed by U.D.L. of intensity 10 kN/m, longer than span, then, determine the maximum tensile and compressive forces in members stated above. **(P.U. May 2000)**

Solution :

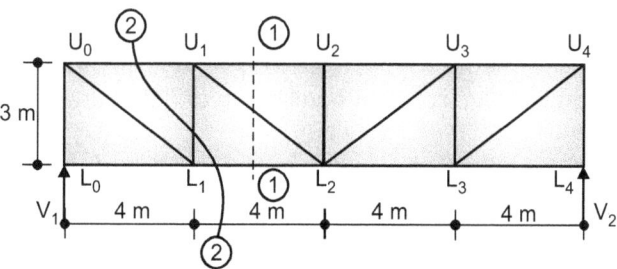

Fig. 9.9 : Truss with different sections

As load traverse through bottom chord, therefore this truss is called as through type bridge truss.

I.L.D. for U_1U_2 (i.e. top chord member):

Consider section 1 – 1 as shown in Fig. 9.9.
Take moment @ L_2. (As members U_1L_2 and L_1L_2 pass through L_2)
When unit load is in left section or part, consider equilibrium of right part.

$$P_{U_1U_2} = V_2 \times \frac{L_2L_4}{h}$$

$\therefore \quad P_{U_1U_2} = V_2 \times \frac{8}{3}$ (Compression)

When unit load is at L_0, $\quad V_2 = 0$
$\qquad P_{U_1U_2} = 0.$

When unit load is at L_1, $\quad V_2 = 1/4$

$$P_{U_1U_2} = V_2 \times \frac{8}{3} = \frac{1}{4} \times \frac{8}{3} = \frac{2}{3} \text{ (Compression)}$$

When unit load is on the right portion, we have to consider equilibrium of left part only. Take moment @ L_2.

$$P_{U_1U_2} = \frac{V_1 \times L_0L_2}{h}$$

$\therefore \quad P_{U_1U_2} = V_1 \times \frac{8}{3}$

When unit load is at L_2, $\quad V_1 = \frac{1}{2}, \quad P_{U_1U_2} = V_1 \cdot \frac{8}{3} = \frac{1}{2} \times \frac{8}{3} = \frac{4}{3}$ (Compression)

When unit load is at L_3, $\quad V_1 = \frac{1}{4}$

$\therefore \quad P_{U_1U_2} = V_1 \cdot \frac{8}{3} = \frac{2}{3}$ (Compression)

When unit load is at L_4, $\quad V_1 = 0$
$\therefore \quad P_{U_1U_2} = 0$

I.L.D. for member U_1U_2 is as shown in Fig. 9.10 (b).

I.L.D. Calculations for L_1L_2 (Bottom chord):

Take section 1 – 1 as shown in Fig. 9.9.
Take moment @ U_1 (As members U_1L_2 and U_1U_2 pass through U_1)
When unit load is on left part, consider equilibrium of right part.

$\therefore \quad P_{L_1L_2} = \frac{V_2 \times L_1L_4}{h} \qquad \therefore P_{L_1L_2} = V_2 \times \frac{12}{3}$

When unit load is at L_0, $\quad V_2 = 0$
$\qquad P_{L_1L_2} = 0$

When unit load is at L_1, $\quad V_2 = \frac{1}{4}, \quad P_{L_1L_2} = \frac{1}{4} \times \frac{12}{3} = 1$

When unit load is in the right part, we have to consider equilibrium of left part.

$\therefore$ $\qquad P_{L_1 L_2} = V_1 \times \dfrac{L_0 L_1}{h}$

When unit load is at L_2, $\quad V_1 = \dfrac{1}{2}$, $P_{L_1 L_2} = \dfrac{1}{2} \times \dfrac{4}{3} = \dfrac{2}{3}$

When unit load is at L_3, $\quad V_1 = \dfrac{1}{4}$

$\therefore \qquad P_{L_1 L_2} = \dfrac{1}{4} \times \dfrac{4}{3} = \dfrac{1}{3}$

At L_4, $\qquad P_{L_1 L_2} = 0$.

I.L.D. for member $L_1 L_2$ is as shown in Fig. 9.10 (c).

I.L.D. Calculations for Vertical Member $U_1 L_1$:

Take section 2 – 2 as shown in Fig. 9.9. $\sum f_y = 0$

When unit load is on left part, consider the right part of the truss in equilibrium.

$\therefore \qquad P_{U_1 L_1} = V_2$ (Tensile)

When unit load is at L_0, $\quad V_2 = 0$

$\qquad P_{U_1 L_1} = 0$

When unit load is at L_1, $\quad V_2 = 1/4$

$\qquad P_{U_1 L_1} = 1/4$ (Tensile)

When unit load is on right part, consider the left part of the truss in equilibrium.

$\therefore \qquad P_{U_1 L_1} = V_1$ (compression)

When unit load is at L_2, $\quad V_1 = \dfrac{2}{4}$

$\therefore \qquad P_{U_1 L_1} = \dfrac{2}{4}$ (Compression)

When unit load is at L_3, $\quad V_3 = \dfrac{1}{4}$ $\therefore P_{U_1 L_1} = \dfrac{1}{4}$ (Compression)

When unit load is at L_4, $\quad V_1 = 0$

$\therefore \qquad P_{U_1 L_1} = 0$

I.L.D. for $U_1 L_1$ is as shown in Fig. 9.10 (a).

I.L.D. Calculations for Diagonal Member $U_1 L_2$:

Consider section 1 – 1 as shown in Fig. 9.9.

When unit load is on left part, consider equilibrium of right part.

$\therefore \qquad P_{U_1 L_2} \sin\theta = V_2$ (Compression)

$\therefore \qquad P_{U_1 L_2} = V_2 \csc\theta = 1.67 V_2$ ($\theta = 36.869$)

When unit load is on L_0, $\quad V_2 = 0$ $\therefore P_{U_1 L_2} = 0$

When unit load is on L_1, $V_2 = 1/4$

$\therefore \qquad P_{U_1 L_2} = \dfrac{1}{4} \csc\theta$

When unit load is on right part, consider equilibrium of left part.

$\therefore \qquad P_{U_1 L_2} = V_1 \operatorname{cosec} \theta$ (Tensile)

When unit load is at L_2, $\quad V_1 = \dfrac{2}{4} = \dfrac{1}{2}$

$\therefore \qquad P_{U_1 L_2} = 1.67\, V_1 = 1.67 \times \dfrac{1}{2} = 0.833$

When unit load is at L_3, $\quad V_1 = 1/4$

$\therefore \qquad P_{U_1 L_2} = 1.67\, V_1 = 0.417$

When unit load is at L_4, $\quad V_1 = 0$

$\therefore \qquad P_{U_1 L_2} = 0.$

I.L.D. for $U_1 L_2$ is as shown in Fig. 9.10 (e).

Plotting ordinates for respective members gives I.L.D. for that member.

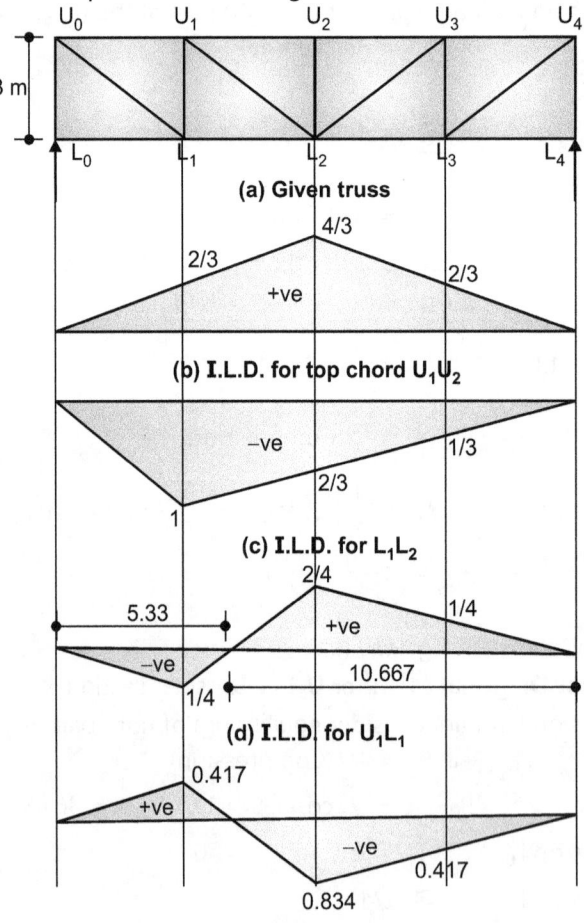

(a) Given truss

(b) I.L.D. for top chord $U_1 U_2$

(c) I.L.D. for $L_1 L_2$

(d) I.L.D. for $U_1 L_1$

(e) I.L.D. for $U_1 L_2$

Fig. 9.10

As the load span is greater than the span of the truss, therefore whole truss is loaded at the bottom chords.

∴ Load in member = Intensity × Area covered on I.L.D.

Member U_1U_2 :

As member is compressive throughout, so no tensile force is developed.

∴ Force in U_1U_2 = Intensity × Area covered

$$= 10 \times \frac{1}{2} \times \frac{4}{3} \times 16 = 106.67 \text{ kN (C)}$$

Maximum compressive force in U_1U_2 = 106.67

Maximum tensile force in U_1U_2 = 0.

Member L_1L_2 :

Moving load acts on any panel point, therefore, force in member is tensile only.

∴ Force in L_1L_2 = Intensity × Area covered

$$= 10 \times \frac{1}{2} \times 1 \times 6 = 80 \text{ kN}$$

Maximum compressive force in L_1L_2 = 0

Maximum tensile force in L_1L_2 = 80 kN.

Member U_1L_1 :

This member is in tension for some part and in compression for some part. Area above base line gives compression area and below base line gives tensile area.

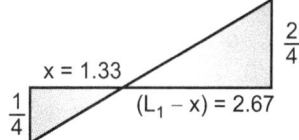

Fig. 9.10 (f)

∴ $\dfrac{x}{1/4} = \dfrac{(4-x)}{2/4}$ ∴ $2x = 4 - x$

∴ $3x = 4$

∴ $x = 1.33$

∴ Maximum compression = Intensity × Compression area

∴ Max. compression = $10 \times \dfrac{1}{2} \times 10.667 \times \dfrac{2}{4}$ = 26.67 kN

Maximum tension = Intensity × Tension area (i.e. –ve area)

$$= 10 \times \frac{1}{2} \times \frac{1}{4} \times 5.33 = 6.66 \text{ kN}$$

Maximum compression = 26.67 kN

Maximum tension = 6.66 kN

Member U_1L_2 :

Maximum compression = Intensity × Compression area

$$= 10 \times \frac{1}{2} \times 0.417 \times 5.33 = 11.11 \text{ kN}$$

Maximum tension = Intensity × Tension area (i.e. –ve area)
$= 10 \times \frac{1}{2} \times 0.834 \times 10.667 = 44.48$ kN

Maximum compression = 11.11 kN
Maximum tension = 44.48 kN

Problem 9.2 : Draw the I.L.D. for members U_3U_4, L_3L_4, U_3L_3, U_4L_4 and U_4L_3 for the truss given in Fig. 9.12 (a) if unit load traverse on the upper chord.

If UDL of intensity 25 kN/m longer than the span of the truss is traversed on the truss, then determine the maximum tensile and compressive forces in members stated above.

Solution :

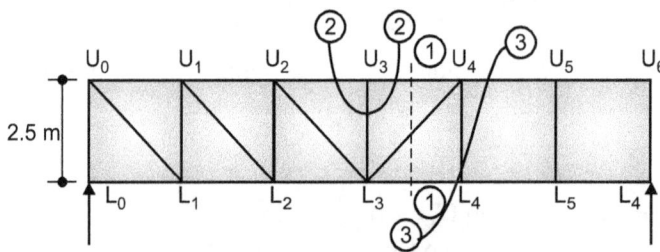

6 panels @ 3m each
russ with different sections
Fig. 9.11

As load is traversing on the upper chord, the bridge truss is deck type bridge truss.

I.L.D. for top chord member U_3U_4 : Consider section 1 – 1 as in Fig. 9.11.

When unit load is on the left part, consider right part in equilibrium.

∴ $\sum M @ L_3 = 0$ (As members U_4L_3 and L_3L_4 pass through L_3)

$$P_{U_3U_4} = \frac{V_2 \times L_3L_6}{h} \text{ (Compression)}$$

When unit load is at U_0, $V_2 = 0$, $P_{U_3U_4} = 0$

When unit load is at U_1, $V_2 = \frac{1}{6}$, $P_{U_3U_4} = \frac{3}{5}$

When unit load is at U_2, $V_2 = \frac{1}{3}$

$$P_{U_3U_4} = \frac{6}{5}$$

When unit load is at U_3, $V_2 = \frac{1}{2}$, $P_{U_3U_4} = \frac{9}{5}$

When unit load is on the right part, consider the left part in equilibrium.

∴ $P_{U_3U_4} = \frac{V_1 \times L_0L_3}{h}$ (Compression)

When unit load is at U_4, $V_1 = \frac{1}{3}$

∴ $P_{U_3U_4} = 6/5$

When unit load is at U_5, $V_1 = \dfrac{1}{6}$

$\therefore \quad P_{U_3 U_4} = \dfrac{3}{5}$

I.L.D. for bottom chord member L_3L_4 : Consider section 1 – 1 as shown in Fig. 9.11.

When unit load is on left part, consider right part in equilibrium.

$$\Sigma M @ U_4 = 0 \quad \text{(As members } U_3U_4 \text{ and } U_4L_3 \text{ pass through } U_4\text{)}$$

$\therefore \qquad P_{L_3 L_4} = \dfrac{V_2 \times L_4 L_6}{h}$ (Tensile)

When unit load is at U_0, $\quad V_2 = 0 \quad \therefore P_{L_3 L_4} = 0$

When unit load is at U_1, $\quad V_2 = \dfrac{1}{6} \quad \therefore P_{L_3 L_4} = \dfrac{2}{5}$

When unit load is at U_2, $\quad V_2 = \dfrac{1}{3}$

$\therefore \qquad P_{L_3 L_4} = \dfrac{4}{5}$

When unit load is at U_3, $\quad V_2 = \dfrac{1}{2}$

$\therefore \qquad P_{L_3 L_4} = \dfrac{6}{5}$

When unit load is on right part, consider right part in equilibrium.

$\therefore \qquad P_{L_3 L_4} = \dfrac{V_1 \times L_0 L_4}{h}$ (Tensile)

When unit load is at U_4, $\quad V_1 = \dfrac{1}{3}$

$\therefore \qquad P_{L_3 L_4} = \dfrac{8}{5}$

When unit load is at U_5, $\quad V_1 = \dfrac{1}{6}$

$\therefore \qquad P_{L_3 L_4} = \dfrac{4}{5}$

I.L.D. for vertical member U_3L_3 : Consider the section 2 – 2 as shown in Fig. 9.11. Therefore in this member, force exists if unit load is on U_3 only.

$\therefore \quad$ Ordinate at all other points is zero and is one at U_3 only.

I.L.D. for vertical member U_4L_4 : Consider section 3 – 3 as shown in Fig. 9.11.

For unit load on left part, consider right part in equilibrium. $\therefore \Sigma F_y = 0$

$\therefore \qquad P_{U_4 L_4} = V_2$ (Compressive)

When unit load is at U_0, $\quad V_2 = 0$

$\therefore \qquad P_{U_4 L_4} = 0$

When unit load is at U_1, $U_2 = \frac{1}{6}$ ∴ $P_{U_4L_4} = \frac{1}{6}$ (Compressive)

When unit load is at U_2, $V_2 = \frac{1}{3}$ ∴ $P_{U_4L_4} = \frac{1}{3}$ (Compressive)

When unit load is at U_3, $V_2 = \frac{1}{2}$

∴ $P_{U_4L_4} = \frac{1}{2}$ (Compressive)

When unit load is on right part, consider left part in equilibrium.

∴ $P_{U_4L_4} = V_1$ (Tensile)

When unit load is at U_4, $V_1 = \frac{1}{3}$

∴ $P_{U_4L_4} = \frac{1}{3}$ (Tensile)

When unit load is at U_5, $V_1 = \frac{1}{6}$

∴ $P_{U_4L_4} = \frac{1}{6}$ (Tensile)

When unit load is at U_6, $V_1 = 0$
∴ $P_{U_4L_4} = 0$

I.L.D. for diagonal member U_4L_3 : Consider section 1 – 1 as shown in Fig. 9.11.
When unit load is on left part, consider equilibrium of right part.

∴ $P_{U_4L_3} \sin\theta = V_2$ (Tensile)

∴ $P_{U_4L_3} = V_2 \csc\theta = 1.562\, V_2$

When unit load is at U_0, $V_2 = 0$
∴ $P_{U_4L_3} = 0$

When unit load is at U_1, $V_2 = \frac{1}{6}$

∴ $P_{U_4L_3} = 0.26$ (Tensile)

When unit load is at U_2, $V_2 = \frac{1}{3}$

∴ $P_{U_4L_3} = 0.52$ (Tensile)

When unit load is at U_3, $V_2 = \frac{1}{2}$

∴ $P_{U_4L_3} = 0.78$ (Tensile)

When unit load is on right part, consider left part in equilibrium.

∴ $P_{U_4L_3} = V_1 \csc\theta$ (Compressive)

When unit load is at U_4, $\quad V_1 = \dfrac{1}{3} \quad \therefore P_{U_4 L_3} = 0.52$

When unit load is at U_5, $\quad V_1 = \dfrac{1}{6}$

$\therefore \qquad P_{U_4 L_3} = 0.26$

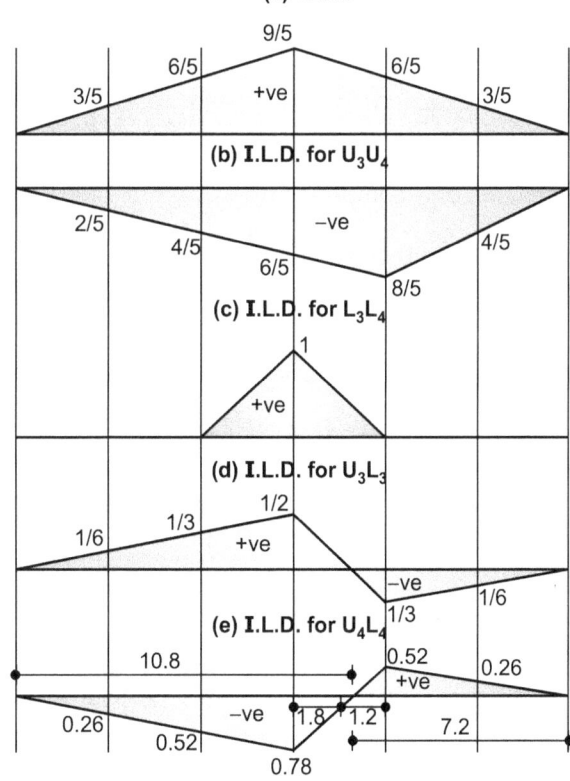

Fig. 9.12

$$\dfrac{1/3}{x} = \dfrac{1/2}{3-x}$$

$$6 - 2x = 3x$$

$\therefore \qquad 5x = 6$

$\therefore \qquad x = \dfrac{6}{5} = 1.2 \text{ m}$

Top chord member U_3U_4 :

Top chord members are always in compression.

$\therefore$ Force in member = Intensity × Area covered

$$= 25 \times \frac{1}{2} \times \frac{9}{5} \times 18 = 405 \text{ kN}$$

$\therefore$ Max. compression in U_3U_4 = 405 kN

Max. tension in U_3U_4 = 0

Bottom chord member L_3L_4 :

Bottom chord members are always in tension.

$\therefore$ Force in member = Intensity × Area covered

$$= 25 \times \frac{1}{2} \times \frac{8}{5} \times 18 = 360 \text{ kN}$$

$\therefore$ Max. compression in L_3L_4 = 0

Max. tension in L_3L_4 = 360 kN

Vertical members U_3L_3 and U_4L_4 :

U_3L_3 : In this member, only compression occurs.

$\therefore$ Max. compression in U_3L_3 = $25 \times \frac{1}{2} \times 1 \times 6 = 75$ kN

Max. tension = 0

For U_4L_4 : This is for part load in tension and for part load in compression.

$\therefore$ Max. compression = Intensity × Area (Compression)

$$= 25 \times \frac{1}{2} \times \frac{1}{2} \times 10.8 = 67.5 \text{ kN}$$

Max. tension = Intensity × Area (Tensile)

$$= 25 \times \frac{1}{2} \times \frac{1}{3} \times 7.2 = 30 \text{ kN}$$

$\therefore$ Max. compression in U_4L_4 = 67.5 kN

Max. tension in U_4L_4 = 30 kN

Force in diagonal member U_4L_3 :

This member is in tension for loading on some part and in compression for some part.

$\therefore$ Max. compression = Intensity × Area (Compressive)

$$= 25 \times \frac{1}{2} \times 7.2 \times 0.52 = 46.8 \text{ kN}$$

Max. tension = Intensity × Area (Tension)

$$= 25 \times \frac{1}{2} \times 10.8 \times 0.78 = 105.3 \text{ kN}$$

Max. compression in U_4L_3 = 46.8 kN

Max. tension in U_4L_3 = 105.3 kN

Problem 9.3 : Construct influence lines for members U_1L_1, U_2L_2, L_1L_2 and U_1L_2 of the truss as shown in Fig. 9.14 (a). Hence, calculate the max. axial force in a member U_1L_1 when a U.D.L. of 30 kN/m and 8 m long crosses the girder on bottom chord. **(Nov. 97)**

Solution :

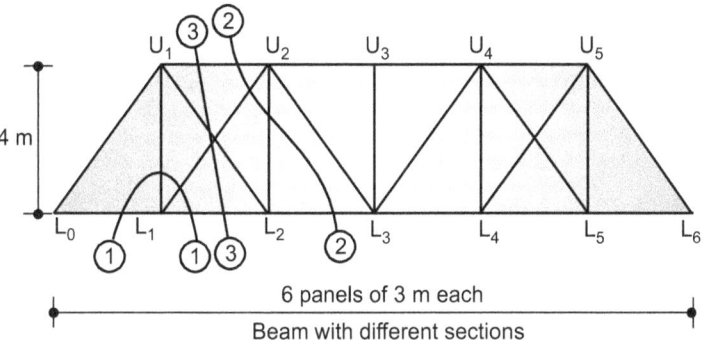

6 panels of 3 m each
Beam with different sections
Fig. 9.13

As the load traverses on the bottom chord, therefore, the bridge truss is through type bridge truss.

1. Calculations for U_1L_1 :

Take section 1 – 1 as shown in Fig. 9.13.

When unit load is at L_0, $\quad P_{U_1L_1} = 0$

at L_1, $P_{U_1L_1} = 1$

Then for any load position, force in the member is zero.

2. Calculations for U_2L_2 :

Take section 2 – 2 as shown in Fig. 9.13.

When unit load is on left part, consider right part in equilibrium ($\Sigma F_y = 0$)

∴ $\quad P_{U_1U_2} = V_2$ (Tensile)

∴ When unit load is at L_0, $\quad P_{U_1U_2} = 0$

at L_1, $P_{U_1U_2} = \dfrac{3}{18}$ (Tensile)

at L_2, $P_{U_1U_2} = \dfrac{6}{18}$ (Tensile)

When unit load is on the right part, consider the equilibrium of left part ($\Sigma F_y = 0$)

∴ $\quad P_{U_1U_2} = V_1$ (Compressive)

When unit load is at L_3, $\quad P_{U_1U_2} = \dfrac{9}{18}$ (Compressive)

at L_4, $P_{U_1U_2} = \dfrac{6}{18}$ (Compressive)

at L_5, $P_{U_1U_2} = \dfrac{3}{18}$ (Compressive)

3. Calculations for L_1L_2:

Take section 3 – 3 as shown in Fig. 9.13.

Consider right part equilibrium when unit load is on the left part. $\sum M @ U_1 = 0$

$$\therefore \quad P_{L_1L_2} = \frac{V_2 \times L_1L_6}{h} \text{ (Tensile)}$$

When unit load is at L_0, $\quad P_{L_1L_2} = 0$

at L_1, $P_{L_1L_2} = 0.625$ (Tensile)

When unit load is on right part, consider equilibrium of left part.

$$\therefore \quad P_{L_1L_2} = V_1 \times \frac{L_0L_1}{h} \text{ (Tensile)}$$

When unit load is at L_2, $\quad P_{L_1L_2} = 0.5$ (Tensile)

at L_3, $P_{L_1L_2} = 0.375$ (Tensile)

at L_4, $P_{L_1L_2} = 0.25$ (Tensile)

at L_5, $P_{L_1L_2} = 0.125$ (Tensile)

at L_6, $P_{L_1L_2} = 0$

4. Calculations for U_1L_2:

Take section 3 – 3 as shown in Fig. 9.13.

Consider equilibrium of right part when unit load is on left part ($\sum F_y = 0$).

$$P_{U_1L_2} = V_2 \operatorname{cosec} \theta \text{ (Compressive)}$$

$$\therefore \quad P_{U_1L_2} = 1.25 V_2$$

When unit load is at L_0, $\quad P_{U_1L_2} = 0$

at L_1, $P_{U_1L_2} = 0.208$ (Compressive)

When unit load is on right part, consider left part in equilibrium ($\sum F_y = 0$).

$$P_{U_1L_2} = V_1 \operatorname{cosec} \theta \text{ (Tensile)}$$

$$\therefore \quad P_{U_1L_2} = 1.25 V_1$$

When unit load is at L_2, $\quad P_{U_1L_2} = 0.833$ (Tensile)

at L_3, $P_{U_1L_2} = 0.625$ (Tensile)

at L_4, $P_{U_1L_2} = 0.417$ (Tensile)

at L_5, $P_{U_1L_2} = 0.208$ (Tensile)

at L_6, $P_{U_1L_2} = 0$

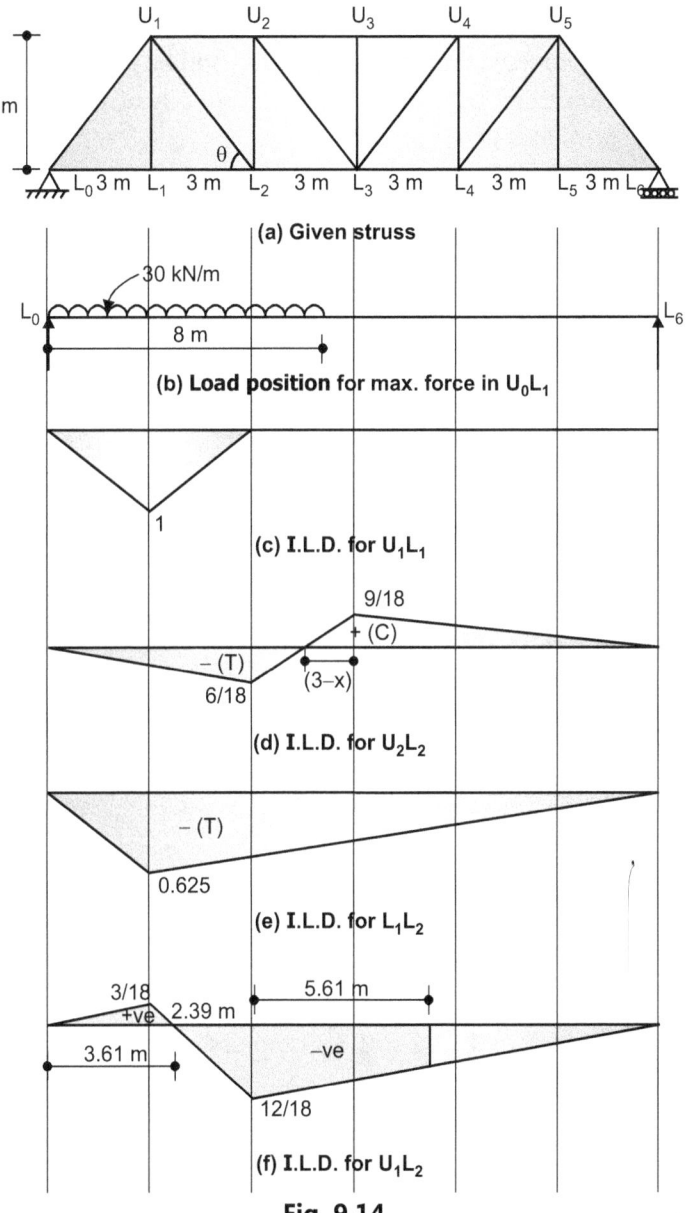

Fig. 9.14

(a) Maximum force in U_1L_1 :

As the I.L.D. for U_1L_1 acts on 6 m and total span of load is 8 m, therefore, we have to put load from left support.

∴   Force in U_1L_1 = Intensity of load × Area covered on I.L.D.

$$= 30 \times \frac{1}{2} \times 1 \times 6 = 90 \text{ kN}$$

∴   Maximum force in U_1L_1 is 90 kN (Tensile)

Problem 9.4 : A pin jointed truss is simply supported at A and B as shown in Fig. 9.15 (a). Draw I.L.D. for force in members U_2U_3, U_2L_3 and L_2L_3. A train of loads travels over the bottom chord of the truss. Determine the force in each of these members when the leading load of the train stands at L_4. **(P. U. Nov. 99)**

Solution :

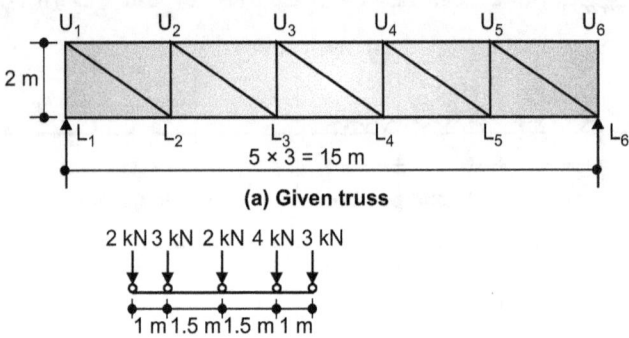

(a) Given truss

(b) Given loading

Fig. 9.15

As load travels over the bottom chord, therefore the truss is through type bridge truss.

1. **Calculations for $U_2 U_3$:**

    Consider section 1 – 1 as shown in Fig. 9.16 (a).
    Consider right part in equilibrium if the unit load is on left part. $\sum M @ L_3 = 0$

    $$P_{U_2U_3} = V_2 \times \frac{L_3L_6}{h} \text{ (Compressive)}$$

    When unit load is at L_1, $P_{U_2U_3} = 0$

    at L_2, $P_{U_2U_3} = 0.9$ (Compressive)

    Now when unit load is on right part after L_2, consider left part in equilibrium.

    $$P_{U_2U_3} = V_1 \times \frac{L_1L_3}{h} \text{ (Compressive)}$$

    When unit load is at L_3, $P_{U_2U_3} = 1.8$ (Compressive)

    at L_4, $P_{U_2U_3} = 1.2$ (Compressive)

    at L_5, $P_{U_2U_3} = 0.6$ (Compressive)

    at L_6, $P_{U_2U_3} = 0$

2. **Calculations for U_2L_3 :**

    Consider section 1 – 1 as shown in Fig. 9.16 (a).
    When unit load is on left part, consider right part in equilibrium ($\sum F_y = 0$)

    $$P_{U_2L_3} = V_2 \cosec \theta \text{ (Compressive)}$$

    When unit load is at L_1, $P_{U_2L_3} = 0$

    at L_2, $P_{U_2L_3} = \frac{3}{15}$ (Compressive)

When unit load is at L_3, i.e. to the right side, therefore consider left part in equilibrium ($\sum F_y = 0$).

$$P_{U_2 L_3} = V_1 \csc \theta \text{ (Tensile)}$$

When unit load is at L_3, $\quad P_{U_2 L_3} = \dfrac{9}{15}$ (Tensile)

$\qquad$ at L_4, $P_{U_2 U_3} = \dfrac{6}{15}$ (Tensile)

$\qquad$ at L_5, $P_{U_2 U_3} = \dfrac{3}{15}$ (Tensile)

3. Calculations for $L_2 L_3$:

Consider section 1 – 1 as shown in Fig. 9.16 (a).

When unit load is on left part, consider right part in equilibrium $\sum M @ U_2 = 0$

$$P_{L_2 L_3} = \dfrac{V_2 \times L_2 L_6}{h} \text{ (Tensile)}$$

When unit load is at L_1, $\quad P_{L_2 L_3} = 0$.

$\qquad$ at L_2, $P_{L_2 L_3} = 1.2$ (Tensile)

When unit load is on right part, consider left part in equilibrium $\sum M @ U_2 = 0$.

$\therefore \qquad P_{L_2 L_3} = V_1 \times \dfrac{L_1 L_2}{h}$

$\qquad$ at L_3, $P_{L_2 L_3} = 0.9$ (Tensile)

$\qquad$ at L_4, $P_{L_2 L_3} = 0.6$ (Tensile)

$\qquad$ at L_5, $P_{L_2 L_3} = 0.3$ (Tensile)

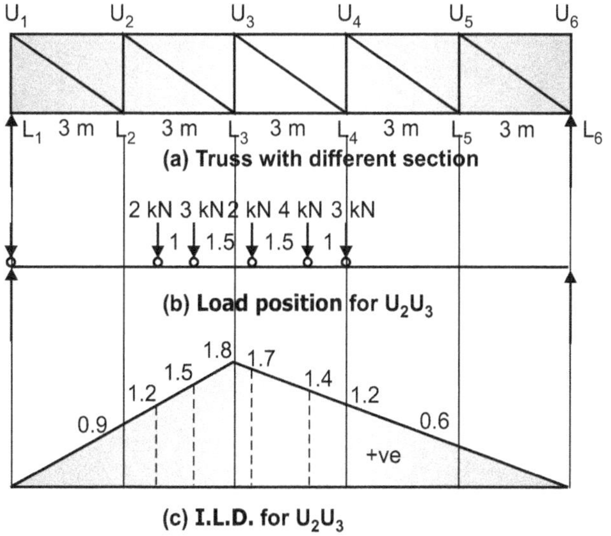

(a) Truss with different section

(b) Load position for $U_2 U_3$

(c) I.L.D. for $U_2 U_3$

Fig. 9.16

∴ Force in U_2U_3 = Load × Respective ordinates

= 2 × 1.2 + 3 × 1.5 + 2 × 1.7 + 4 × 1.4 + 3 × 1.2

= 19.5 kN

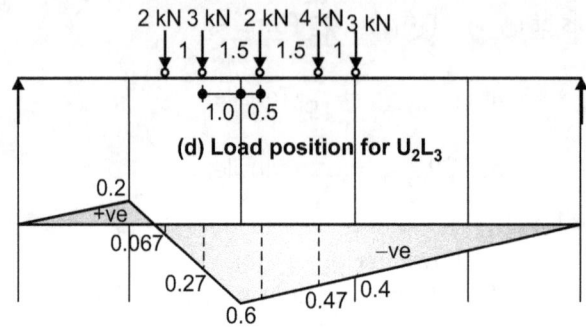

(d) Load position for U_2L_3

(e) I.L.D. for U_2L_3

Fig. 9.16

∴ Force in member = Loads × Respective ordinates

= 2 × 0.067 + 3 × 0.27 + 2 × 0.57 + 4 × 0.47 + 3 × 0.4

= 5.164 kN

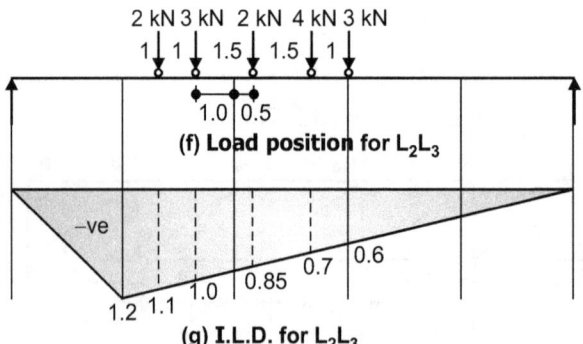

(f) Load position for L_2L_3

(g) I.L.D. for L_2L_3

Fig. 9.16

Force in member $L_2 L_3$ = Loads × Respective ordinates

= 2 × 1.1 + 3 × 1.0 + 2 × 0.85 + 4 × 0.7 + 3 × 0.6

= 11.5 kN

∴ Force in member U_2U_3 = 19.5 kN (Compressive)

Force in member U_2L_3 = 5.16 kN (Tensile)

Force in member L_2L_3 = 11.5 kN (Tensile)

Problem 9.5 : An N type truss girder of 24 m span consists of 8 panels of 3 m each with height of truss 4 m. Draw the I.L.D. for top chord, bottom chord and diagonal members in the second panel. If an .D.L. of 50 kN/m of length 5 m traverses the bottom chord of the girder, calculate the maximum forces in the above mentioned members. **(Nov. 99)**

Solution : As load traverses on bottom chord, therefore through type bridge truss.

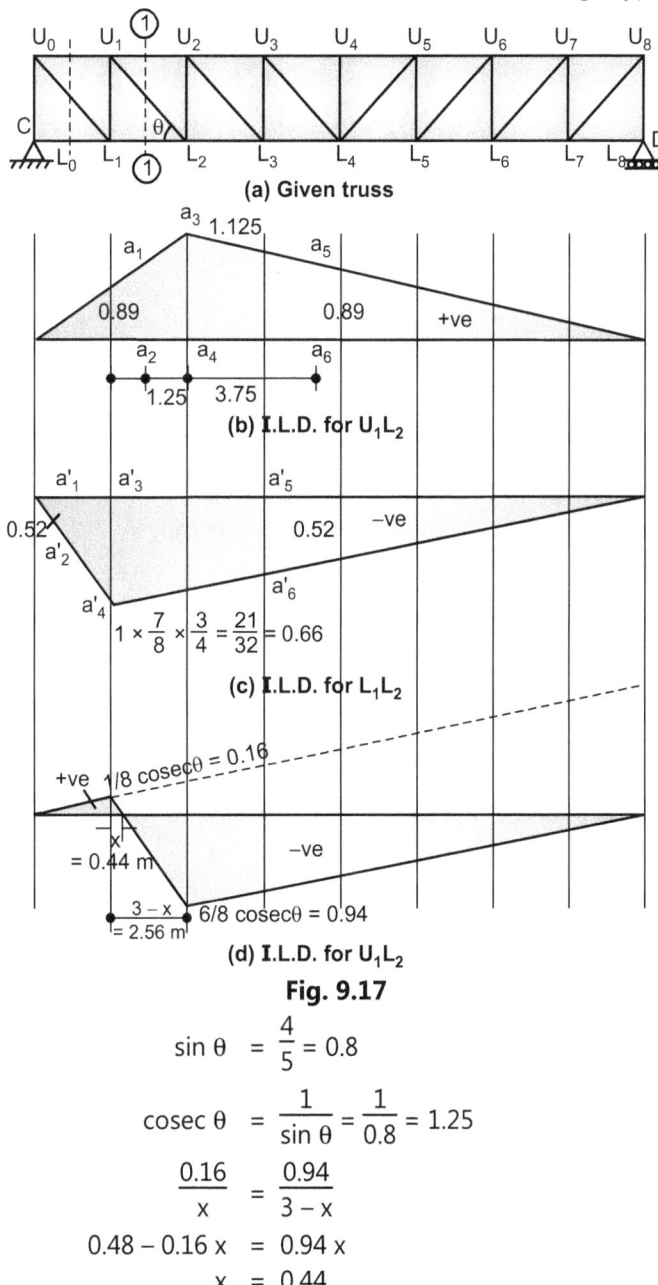

Fig. 9.17

$$\sin \theta = \frac{4}{5} = 0.8$$

$$\csc \theta = \frac{1}{\sin \theta} = \frac{1}{0.8} = 1.25$$

$$\frac{0.16}{x} = \frac{0.94}{3-x}$$

$$0.48 - 0.16 x = 0.94 x$$

∴
∴ $x = 0.44$

I.L.D. for top chord : $U_1 U_2$:

Take section 1 – 1 as shown in Fig. 9.17 (a).

When unit load is on left part, consider equilibrium of right part. Take moment @ $L_2 = 0$.

When unit load is at L_2, $P_{U_1 U_3} = \dfrac{R_B \times L_2 L_8}{h}$ (Compressive)

When unit load is on right part, consider equilibrium of left part M @ $L_2 = 0$.

Or $P_{U_1 U_3} = \dfrac{R_A \times L_0 L_2}{h}$

When unit load is at L_2, $R_B = \dfrac{2}{8}$

$P_{U_1 U_3} = \dfrac{9}{8} = 1.125$

∴ Maximum ordinate is at $L_2 = 1.125$

At L_0 and at L_8, $P_{U_1 U_3} = 0$

∴ I.L.D. is as shown in Fig. 9.17 (b).

∴ This top chord member is always in compression.

U.D.L. is less than the span of the girder. So it is placed in such a manner so that we can get maximum force in the member.

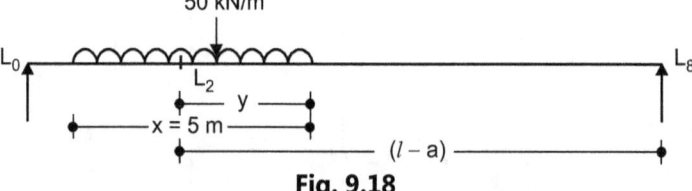

Fig. 9.18

We have a formula for getting maximum area covered in case of maximum B.M. at a given section.

$$y = \dfrac{x(l-a)}{l}$$

where, $(l - a)$ = Distance on right side of L_2 = 18 m
 x = Length or span of U.D.L. = 5 m
 l = Span of girder = 24 m

y is getting i.e. the distance of U.D.L. on right of L_2

$$y = \dfrac{5 \times 18}{24} = 3.75 \text{ m}$$

∴ Ordinate on I.L.D. of $U_1 U_2$ is as shown in Fig. 9.17.

On right side ordinate at 3.75 m from L_2 (i.e. at starting of U.D.L.)

$$= \dfrac{1.125}{18} \times (18 - 3.75) = 0.89$$

Ordinate on left side (i.e. at the end of U.D.L.)

$$= \frac{1.125}{6}(6 - 1.25) = 0.89$$

Area under U.D.L. = Area of trapezoidal $a_1a_2a_3a_4$ + Area of trapezoidal $a_3a_4a_5a_6$

$$= \left(\frac{0.89 + 1.125}{2}\right) \times 3.75 + \left(\frac{0.89 + 1.125}{2}\right) \times 1.25 = 5.04 \text{ m}$$

∴ Force in member U_1U_2 = Area under load × Intensity of load
= 5.04 × 50 = 251.88 kN

Force in L_1L_2 : I.L.D. for L_1L_2 is as shown in Fig. 9.17 (c).

$$y = \frac{x(l - a)}{l}$$

where, x = Length of span of UDL = 5 m
$(l - a)$ = Distance on right of L_1 = 21 m

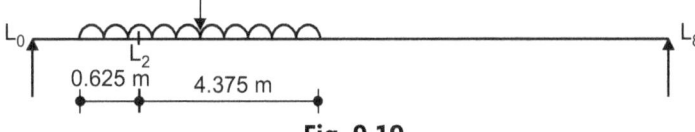

Fig. 9.19

l = Span of girder = 24 m

∴ $y = \frac{5 \times 21}{24} = 4.375 \text{ m}$

Ordinate on I.L.D. of L_1L_2 is as shown in Fig. 9.17 (c).
On right side ordinate at 4.375 m from L_1

$$= \frac{0.66}{21} \times (21 - 4.375) = 0.52$$

Ordinate on left side at 0.625 m from L_1 = $\frac{0.66}{3}(3 - 0.625) = 0.52$

Area covered under U.D.L. = Area of trapezoidal $a'_1 a'_2 a'_3 a'_4$ + Area of trapezoidal $a'_3 a'_4 a'_5 a'_6$

$$= \left(\frac{0.52 + 0.66}{2}\right) \times 0.625 + \left(\frac{0.52 + 0.66}{2}\right) \times 4.375 = 2.95 \text{ m}$$

∴ Maximum tensile force in the member
= Intensity of loading × Area covered under loading
= 50 × 2.95 = 147.5 kN

Force in member U_1L_2 : I.L.D. for U_1L_2 is as shown in Fig. 9.17 (d).
Max. compressive force in U_1L_2 = +ve area under loading × Intensity of loading

+ve area under loading $= \frac{1}{2} \times 0.94 \times 5 = 2.35 \text{ m}$

∴ Maximum compressive force in member
= 2.35 × 50 = 117.5 kN (Compressive)

Maximum tensile force in U_1L_2 = – ve area under loading × Intensity of loading

–ve area under loading = $\frac{1}{2} \times 0.16 \times 3.44 = 0.275$ m

∴ Maximum tensile force in U_1L_2
= 0.275 × 50 = 13.76 kN (Tensile)

Problem 9.6 : Construct influence line diagram for forces in members U_2U_3, U_2L_3 and L_2L_3 of the truss shown in Fig. 9.20 (a).

If uniformly distributed load of 20 kN/m intensity longer than the span traverses the span, calculate the maximum values of force in the members. **(P. U. Dec. 98)**

Solution :

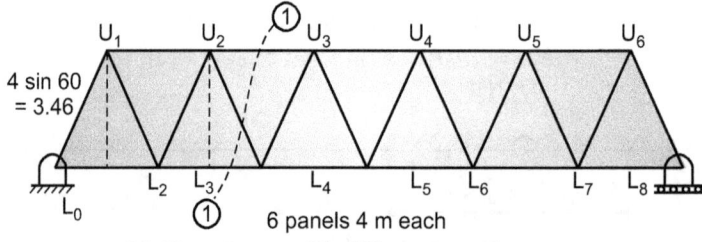

(a) Given truss with different sections

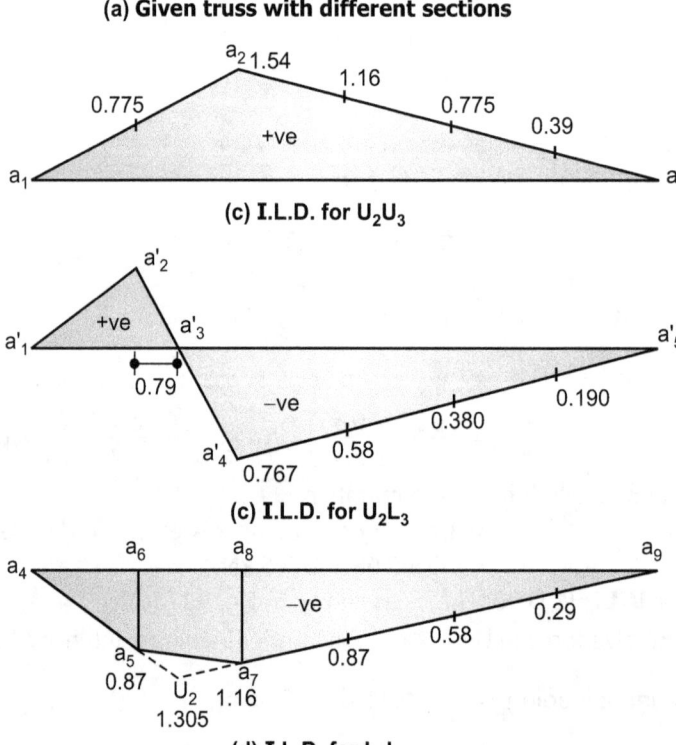

(c) I.L.D. for U_2U_3

(c) I.L.D. for U_2L_3

(d) I.L.D. for L_2L_3

Fig. 9.20

1. **I.L.D. for $U_2 U_3$ (i.e. top chord member):**

   Consider section 1 – 1 as shown in Fig. 9.20 (a).
   When unit load is on left side of section, consider right part equilibrium $\sum M @ L_3 = 0$.
   $$-R_B \times L_3 L_8 + P_{U_2 U_3} \times 3.46 = 0$$

   $\therefore \quad P_{U_2 U_3} = R_B \times \dfrac{16}{3.46} = 4.62 R_B$

   When unit load is at L_1, $\quad R_B = 0$
   $\therefore \quad P_{U_2 U_3} = 0$

   at L_2, $R_B = \dfrac{4}{24}$

   $\therefore \quad P_{U_2 U_3} = 0.770$ (Compressive)

   When unit load is on right side, consider left part $\sum M @ U_2 = 0$.
   $$R_A \times 8 - P_{U_2 U_3} \times 3.46 = 0$$

   $\therefore \quad P_{U_2 U_3} = \dfrac{R_A \times 8}{3.46} = 2.31 R_A$

   When unit load is at L_3, $\quad R_A = \dfrac{2}{3}$

   $\therefore \quad P_{U_2 U_3} = 1.54$ (Compressive)

   at L_4, $R_A = \dfrac{3}{6}$

   $\therefore \quad P_{U_2 U_3} = 1.16$ (Compressive)

   at L_5, $R_A = \dfrac{2}{6}$

   $\therefore \quad P_{U_2 U_3} = 0.77$ (Compressive)

   at L_6, $R_A = \dfrac{1}{6}$

   $\therefore \quad P_{U_2 U_3} = 0.39$ (Compressive)

   Plotting the ordinates we get I.L.D. for member $U_2 U_3$ as shown in Fig. 9.20 (b).

2. **I.L.D. for $U_2 L_3$:**

   Consider same section 1 – 1 as shown in Fig. 9.20 (a).
   When unit load is on left part, consider right part equilibrium ($\sum F_y = 0$).
   $\therefore \quad P_{U_2 L_3} \sin 60 - R_B = 0$

   $P_{U_2 L_3} = \dfrac{R_B}{\sin 60} = 1.15 R_B$ (Compression)

   When unit load is at L_1, $\quad R_B = 0$
   $P_{U_2 L_3} = 0$

at L_2, $R_B = \dfrac{1}{6}$

∴ $P_{U_2 L_3} = 0.192$ (Compressive)

When unit load is on right part, consider left part equilibrium ($\sum F_y = 0$).

$$P_{U_2 L_3} \sin 60 - R_A = 0$$

∴ $P_{U_2 L_3} = \dfrac{R_A}{\sin 60} = 1.15 \, R_A$

When unit load is at L_3, $R_A = \dfrac{4}{6}$

∴ $P_{U_2 L_3} = 0.77$ (Tensile)

at L_4, $R_A = \dfrac{3}{6}$

∴ $P_{U_2 L_3} = 0.58$ (Tensile)

at L_5, $R_A = \dfrac{2}{6}$

∴ $P_{U_2 L_3} = 0.38$ (Tensile)

at L_6, $R_A = \dfrac{1}{6}$

∴ $P_{U_2 L_3} = 0.19$ (Tensile)

at L_7, $P_{U_2 L_3} = 0$

Plotting the ordinates we get I.L.D. for $U_2 U_3$ as shown in Fig. 9.20 (c).

3. **I.L.D. for $L_2 L_3$:**

Take section 1 – 1 as shown in Fig. 9.20 (a).

When unit load is on left of section, consider right part equilibrium $\sum M$ @ $U_2 = 0$.

$$- R_B \times L_3' L_8 + P_{L_2 L_3} \times h = 0$$

∴ $- R_B \times 18 + P_{L_2 L_3} \times 3.46 = 0$

∴ $P_{L_2 L_3} = \dfrac{18}{3.46} R_B = 5.2 \, R_B$

When unit load is at L_1, $R_B = 0$

∴ $P_{L_2 L_3} = 0$

at L_2, $R_B = \dfrac{1}{6}$

∴ $P_{L_2L_3} = 0.87$

When unit load is on right part, consider part equilibrium of left part, equilibrium $\sum M @ U_2 = 0$.

∴ $R_A \times 6 - P_{L_2L_3} \times 3.46 = 0$

∴ $P_{L_2L_3} = \dfrac{6}{3.46} R_A = 1.734 R_A$

at L_3, $R_A = \dfrac{4}{6}$

∴ $P_{L_2L_3} = 1.16$ (Tensile)

at L_4, $R_A = \dfrac{3}{6}$

∴ $P_{L_2L_3} = 0.87$ (Tensile)

at L_5, $R_A = \dfrac{2}{6}$

∴ $P_{L_2L_3} = 0.58$ (Tensile)

at L_6, $R_A = \dfrac{1}{6}$

∴ $P_{L_2L_3} = 0.29$ (Tensile)

at L_7, $P_{L_2L_3} = 0$

Plotting these ordinates gives the I.L.D. for member L_2L_3 as shown in Fig. 9.20 (d).

1. Maximum force in U_2U_3 :

Area under loading = Area of $\Delta\ a_1a_2a_3$

$= \dfrac{1}{2} \times 1.54 \times 24 = 18.48$

∴ Force in member = Intensity of loading $\times$ Area covered

$= 20 \times 18.48$

$= 369.6$ kN (Compressive)

2. Force in U_2L_3 :

(a) Maximum compressive force = Intensity of loading $\times$ +ve area covered under loading

$=$ Intensity of loading $\times$ Area of $\Delta\ a_1'\ a_2'\ a_3'$

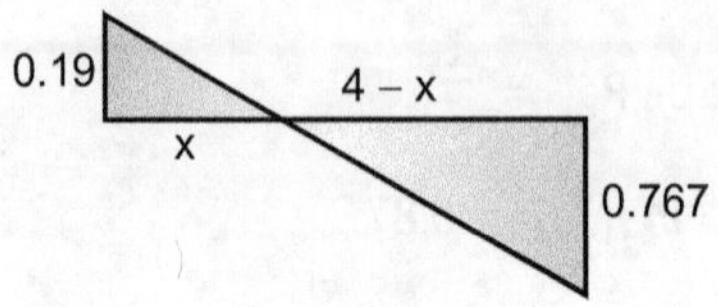

Fig. 9.20 (e)

$$\therefore \quad \frac{x}{0.19} = \frac{4-x}{0.77}$$

$$\therefore \quad x = 0.79$$

$$\therefore \quad \text{+ve area under loading} = \frac{1}{2} \times 0.19 \times 4.79$$

$$= 0.46$$

$$\therefore \text{Maximum compressive force} = 20 \times 0.46$$

$$= 9.2 \text{ kN (Compressive)}$$

(b) Maximum tensile force = Intensity of loading × –ve area covered under loading

$$= \text{Intensity of loading} \times \text{Area of } \Delta\ a_3'\ a_4'\ a_5'$$

$$-\text{ve area covered under loading} = \frac{1}{2} \times 0.767 \times 19.21$$

$$= 7.4$$

$$\therefore \quad \text{Maximum tensile force} = 20 \times 7.4$$

$$= 148 \text{ kN (Tensile)}$$

3. **Maximum tensile force in $L_2 L_3$:**

Maximum tensile force = Intensity of loading × –ve area covered.

= Intensity of loading × (Area of $\Delta\ a_4 a_5 a_6$

+ Area of trapezoidal $a_5 a_6 a_7 a_8$ + Area of $\Delta\ a_7 a_8 a_9$)

$$= 20 \times \left(\frac{1}{2} \times 0.87 \times 4 + \frac{1}{2}(0.87 + 1.16) \times 4 + \frac{1}{2} \times 1.16 \times 16 \right)$$

$$= 20 \times 15.08$$

$$= 301.6 \text{ kN (Tensile)}$$

Problem 9.7 : A Pratt truss of 10 panels of 5 m each and height 6 m is as shown in Fig. 9.21 (a). Draw I.L.D. for forces in members $U_4 U_5$, $U_4 L_5$ and $L_4 L_5$.

Calculate the maximum tensile and/or compressive forces in the above members if a U.D.L. of 57.5 kN/m longer than the span crosses the truss. **(P. U. Dec. 2000)**

Solution :

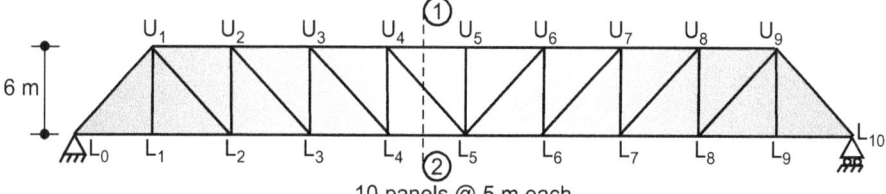

10 panels @ 5 m each
(a) Given truss with different sections

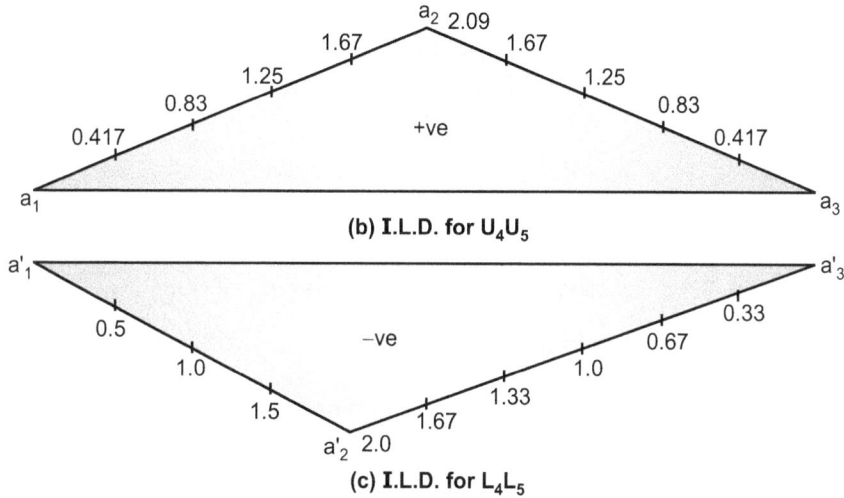

(b) I.L.D. for U_4U_5

(c) I.L.D. for L_4L_5

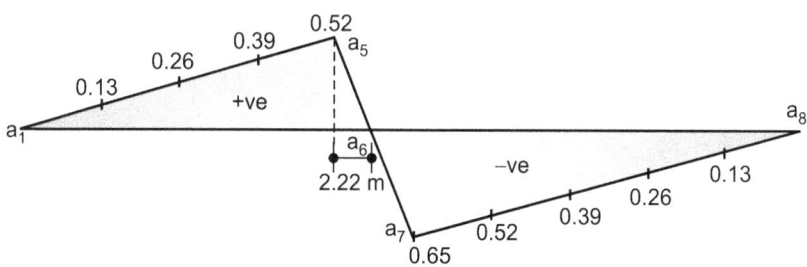

(c) I.L.D. for U_4L_5

Fig. 9.21

1. I.L.D. for U_4U_5 (i.e. top chord member) :

Take section 1 – 1 as shown in Fig. 9.21 (a).

When unit load is on left part of section, consider equilibrium of right part $\sum M$ @ $L_5 = 0$.

$$\therefore \quad -R_B \times 25 + P_{U_4U_5} \times 6 = 0$$

$$\therefore \quad P_{U_4U_5} = \frac{25}{6} R_B = 4.17 R_B$$

When unit load is at L_0, $R_B = 0$

∴ $P_{U_4 U_5} = 0$

at L_1, $R_B = \dfrac{5}{50}$

∴ $P_{U_4 U_5} = 0.417$ (Compressive)

at L_2, $R_B = \dfrac{10}{50}$

∴ $P_{U_4 U_5} = 0.83$ (Compressive)

at L_3, $R_B = \dfrac{15}{50}$

∴ $P_{U_4 U_5} = 1.25$ (Compressive)

at L_4, $R_B = \dfrac{4}{10}$

∴ $P_{U_4 U_5} = 1.67$ (Compressive)

at L_5, $R_B = \dfrac{25}{50}$

∴ $P_{U_4 U_5} = 2.09$ (Compressive)

When unit load is on right part, consider equilibrium of left part $\sum M @ L_5 = 0$.

$R_A \times 25 + P_{U_4 U_5} \times 6 = 0$

∴ $P_{U_4 U_5} = \dfrac{25}{6} R_A = 4.17 R_A$

When unit load is at L_6 = 1.67 (Compressive)

at L_7 = 1.25 (Compressive)

at L_8 = 0.83 (Compressive)

at L_9 = 0.417 (Compressive)

at L_{10} = 0

Plotting the ordinates gives the I.L.D. for member $U_4 U_5$ as shown in Fig. 9.21 (b).

2. **I.L.D. for member $L_4 L_5$:**

   Take section 1 – 1 as shown in Fig. 9.21 (a).

   When unit load is on left part, consider equilibrium of right part $\sum M @ U_4 = 0$.

   ∴ $-R_B \times 30 + P_{L_4 L_5} \times 6 = 0$

   ∴ $P_{L_4 L_5} = 5 R_B$ (Tensile)

   When unit load is at L_0, $R_B = 0$

   ∴ $P_{L_4 L_5} = 0$

at L_1, R_B = 0.1 (Tensile)

$\therefore \quad P_{L_4 L_5}$ = 0.5 (Tensile)

at L_2, R_B = 0.2

$\therefore \quad P_{L_4 L_5}$ = 1.0 (Tensile)

at L_3, R_B = 0.3

$\therefore \quad P_{L_4 L_5}$ = 1.5 (Tensile)

at L_4, R_B = 0.4

$\therefore \quad P_{L_4 L_5}$ = 2.0 (Tensile)

When unit load is on right part of section, consider equilibrium of left part $\sum M$ @ $U_4 = 0$.

$\therefore \quad R_A \times 20 - P_{L_4 L_5} \times 6 = 0$

$\therefore \quad P_{L_4 L_5} = \dfrac{20}{6} \times R_A = 3.33 \, R_A$ (Tensile)

When unit load is at L_5, $\quad R_A$ = 0.5

$\therefore \quad P_{L_4 L_5}$ = 1.667 (Tensile)

at L_6, R_A = 0.4

$\therefore \quad P_{L_4 L_5}$ = 1.33 (Tensile)

at L_7, R_A = 0.3

$\therefore \quad P_{L_4 L_5}$ = 1.0 (Tensile)

at L_8, R_A = 0.2

$\therefore \quad P_{L_4 L_5}$ = 0.67 (Tensile)

at L_9, R_A = 0.1

$\therefore \quad P_{L_4 L_5}$ = 0.33 (Tensile)

Plotting of ordinates gives ILD for $L_4 L_5$ as shown in Fig. 9.21 (c).

3. **I.L.D. for $U_4 L_5$:**

Take section 1 – 1 as shown in Fig. 9.21 (a).

When unit load is on left part, consider equilibrium of right part.

$\therefore \quad P_{U_4 L_5} \times \sin \theta = P_{U_4 L_5} \sin 50.19 = R_B$

$\therefore \quad P_{U_4 L_5} = 1.3 \, R_B$

When unit load is at L_0, $R_B = 0$

$\therefore \quad P_{U_4L_5} = 0$

at L_1, $R_B = 0.1$

$\therefore \quad P_{U_4L_5} = 0.13$ (Compressive)

at L_2, $R_B = 0.2$

$\therefore \quad P_{U_4L_5} = 0.26$ (Compressive)

at L_3, $R_B = 0.3$

$\therefore \quad P_{U_4L_5} = 0.39$ (Compressive)

at L_4, $R_B = 0.4$

$\therefore \quad P_{U_4L_5} = 0.52$ (Compressive)

When unit load is on right part, consider equilibrium of left part.

$\therefore \quad -P_{U_4L_5} \sin\theta + R_A = 0$

$$P_{U_4L_5} = \frac{R_A}{\sin\theta} = 1.15\, R_A$$

When unit load is at L_5, $R_A = 0.5$

$\therefore \quad P_{U_4L_5} = 0.65$ (Tensile)

When unit load is at L_6, $R_A = 0.4$

$\therefore \quad P_{U_4L_5} = 0.52$ (Tensile)

at L_7, $R_A = 0.3$

$\therefore \quad P_{U_4L_5} = 0.39$ (Tensile)

at L_8, $R_A = 0.2$

$\therefore \quad P_{U_4L_5} = 0.26$ (Tensile)

at L_9, $R_A = 0.1$

$\therefore \quad P_{U_4L_5} = 0.13$ (Tensile)

at L_{10}, $R_A = 0$

$\therefore \quad P_{U_4L_5} = 0$

Plotting the ordinates gives the I.L.D. for U_4L_5 as shown in Fig. 9.21 (a)

1. Force in member U_4U_5 :

Compressive force in U_4U_5 = Intensity of loading × Area covered by U.D.L.
= Intensity of loading × Area of Δ $a_1a_2a_3$
= $57.5 \times \frac{1}{2} \times 2.09 \times 50$ = 3004.38 kN (Compressive)

2. Force in member L_4L_5 :

Tensile force in L_4L_5 = Intensity of loading × Area covered by U.D.L.
= Intensity of loading × Area of Δ $a'_1 a'_2 a'_3$
= $57.5 \times \frac{1}{2} \times 2.0 \times 50$ = 2875 kN (T)

3. Force in member U_4L_5 :

Compressive force in U_4L_5 = Intensity of loading × +ve area covered under loading
= Intensity of loading × Area of Δ $a_4a_5a_6$

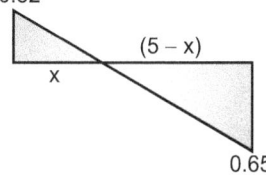

Fig. 9.21 (e)

$$\frac{0.52}{x} = \frac{0.65}{5-x}$$

∴ $x = 2.22$

∴ Maximum compressive force = $57.5 \times \frac{1}{2} \times 0.52 \times 22.22$ = 332.19 kN (Compressive)

Maximum tensile force in U_4L_5 = Intensity of loading × −ve area covered under loading
= Intensity of loading × Area of Δ $a_6a_7a_8$
= $57.5 \times \frac{1}{2} \times 0.65 \times 27.78$ = 519.14 kN (Tensile)

Problem 9.8 : Draw the influence lines for forces in members u_2u_3, u_2l_3 and l_2l_3 of the truss shown in Fig. 9.22. If a line load of 65 kN/m longer than the span traverses the truss, find the maximum value of forces in the members mentioned above.

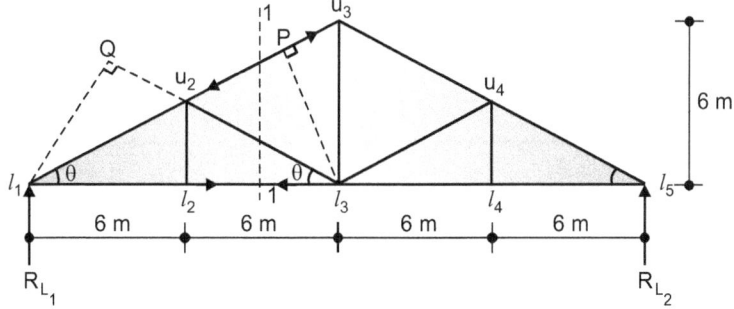

Fig. 9.22

Solution : Pass the section (1) – (1) cutting the required members, as shown in Fig. 9.22.

I.L. for $F_{u_2u_3}$: When unit load traverses from l_1 to l_2, consider equilibrium of right side portion of the truss.

$\Sigma M_{l_3} = 0 + \circlearrowleft$

$$R_{L_5} \times 12 - F_{u_2u_3} \times Pl_3 = 0$$

$$Pl_3 = l_1l_3 \sin \theta = 12 \times \frac{6}{\sqrt{6^2 + 12^2}} = 5.366 \text{ m}$$

$\therefore \qquad F_{u_2u_3} = \frac{1}{5.366} \times R_{L_5} \times 12$

$$= \frac{1}{5.366} \times \text{B.M. at } l_3$$

$\therefore$ I.L. for $F_{u_2u_3}$ from l_1 to l_2 = $\frac{1}{5.366} \times$ I.L. for B.M. at l_3.

I.L. for B.M. at l_3 has ordinate at $l_3 = \frac{12 \times 12}{24} = 6$ and zero at ends.

$\therefore$ Ordinate at l_2 of I.L. for B.M. at $l_3 = \frac{6}{12} \times 6 = 3$.

$\therefore$ Ordinate at l_2 of I.L. for $F_{u_2u_3} = \frac{1}{5.366} \times 3 = 0.559$.

When unit load traverses from l_3 to l_5, consider equilibrium of left side portion of the truss.

$\Sigma M_{L_3} = 0$

$R_{L_1} \times 6 - F_{u_2u_3} \times Pl_3 = 0$ ... $F_{u_2u_3}$ is compressive

$\therefore \qquad F_{u_2u_3} = \frac{1}{5.366} \times R_{L_1} \times 6$

$\therefore$ Ordinate at l_3 of I.L. for $F_{u_2u_3} = \frac{1}{5.366} \times 6 = 1.118$.

When unit load traverse from l_2 to l_3, ordinate of I.L. for $F_{u_2u_3}$ vary linearly from 0.559 at l_2 to 1.118 at l_3 i.e. in the same straight line. I.L for $F_{u_2u_3}$ is shown in Fig. 9.23.

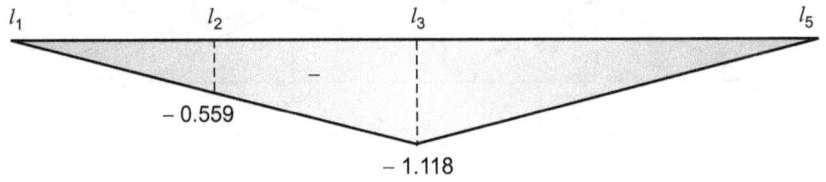

Fig. 9.23

For maximum value of $F_{u_2u_3}$ from the I.L. it is clear that entire span should be load.

∴ Maximum value of $F_{u_2u_3}$ = Area of I.L for $E_{u_2u_3}$ × Intensity of U.D.L.

$$= -\left(\frac{1}{2} \times 24 \times 1.118\right) \times 65$$

$$= -872.158 \text{ kN (Compressive)}$$

I.L. for $F_{u_2l_3}$: Inclination of member u_2l_3 is defined with respect to horizontal by

$\phi = \tan^{-1}\left(\frac{3}{6}\right) = 26.565°$.

∴ Distance l_1Q i.e. arm for $F_{u_2l_3}$ = 12 sin ϕ = 12 sin 26.565

∴ l_1Q = 5.366 m

When unit load traverse from l_1 to l_2, consider equilibrium of right side portion of the truss.

$\sum M_{l_1} = 0 + \circlearrowleft$

∴ $R_{L_5} \times 24 - F_{u_2l_3} \times 5.366 = 0$ ... $F_{u_2l_3}$ is compressive

∴ $F_{u_2u_3} = \frac{24}{5.366} \times R_{L_5} = 4.4726\, R_{L_5}$

∴ I.L. for $F_{u_2u_3}$ between l_1 to l_2 = 4.4726 × I.L. for R_{L_5}

∴ Ordinate of I.L. for $F_{u_2u_3}$ at $l_2 = \frac{4.4726 \times 1}{24} \times 6 = 1.118$

When unit load traverse from l_3 to l_5, consider equilibrium of left side portion of the truss.

Again $\sum M_{L_1} = 0 + \circlearrowleft$

Since R_{L_1} passes through point l_1 and there is no other force acting on the left side portion we get,

$F_{u_2l_3} \times l_1Q = 0$

∴ $F_{u_2l_3} = 0$

∴ From l_3 to l_5, the ordinate of I.L. for $F_{u_2l_3}$ is zero. When unit load travels from l_2 to l_3, the co-ordinate of I.L. for $F_{u_2l_3}$ vary linearly from ordinate 1.118 at l_2 to zero at l_3. The I.L. for $F_{u_2l_3}$ is as shown in Fig. 9.24.

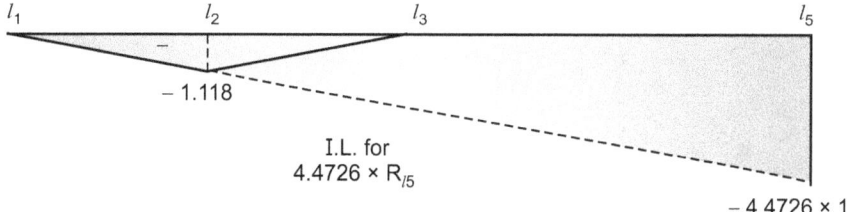

Fig. 9.24 : I.L. for $F_{u_2l_3}$

For maximum value of $F_{u_2 l_3}$ the load should be placed on portion l_1 to l_3.

∴   Maximum value of $F_{u_2 l_3}$ = Area of I.L. for $F_{u_2 l_3}$ × Intensity of U.D.L.

$$= -\left(\frac{1}{2} \times 12 \times 1.118\right) \times 65$$

$$= -436.02 \text{ kN (Compressive)}$$

I.L. for $F_{l_2 l_3}$: When unit load traverse from l_1 to l_2, consider equilibrium of right side portion of the truss.

$\Sigma M_{u_2} = 0 + \circlearrowleft$

$R_{L_5} \times 18 - F_{l_2 l_3} \times 3 = 0$ ... $F_{l_2 l_3}$ is tensile

∴ $F_{l_2 l_3} = \frac{1}{3} \times$ B.M. at u_2

∴   I.L. for $F_{l_2 l_3}$ between l_1 to $l_2 = \frac{1}{3} \times$ I.L. for B.M. at u_2.

Ordinate at u_2 of I.L. for B.M. at u_2 will be $\frac{6 \times 18}{24} = 4.5$.

∴   Ordinate of l_2 of I.L. for B.M. at u_2 = Same as that for u_2 = 4.5.

∴   Ordinate at l_2 of I.L. for $F_{l_2 l_3} = \frac{1}{3} \times 4.5 = 1.5$

When unit load traverse from l_3 to l_5, consider equilibrium of left side portion of the truss.

Again $\Sigma M_{u_2} = 0 + \circlearrowleft$

∴ $R_{L_1} \times 6 - F_{l_2 l_3} \times 3 = 0$ ... $F_{l_2 l_3}$ is tensile.

∴ $F_{l_2 l_3} = \frac{1}{3} \times$ B.M. at u_2

I.L. for $F_{l_2 l_3}$ between l_3 to l_5 = I.L. for B.M. at u_2.

Ordinate of I.L. for $F_{l_2 l_3}$ at l_3 = $\frac{1}{3} \times$ Ordinate at l_3 of I.L. for B.M. at u_2

$$= \frac{1}{3} \times \frac{4.5}{18} \times 12 = 1$$

When unit load traverse between l_2 to l_3, the I.L. for $F_{l_2 l_3}$ vary linearly from value 1.5 at l_2 to value 1.0 at l_3 i.e. in the same straight line. Fig. 9.25 shows the I.L. for $F_{l_2 l_3}$.

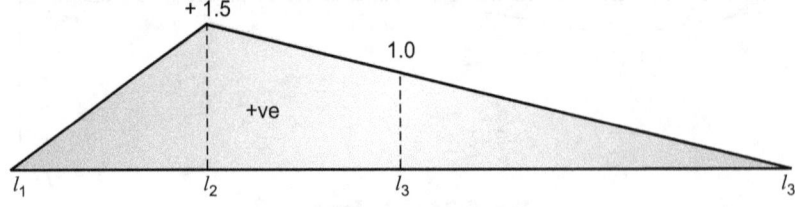

Fig. 9.25 : I.L. for $F_{l_2 l_3}$

For maximum value of $F_{l_2 l_3}$, it is obvious from the I.L. that entire span should be loaded.

∴ Maximum value of $F_{l_2 l_3}$ = Area of I.L. for $F_{l_2 l_3}$ × Intensity of U.D.L.

$$= \left(\frac{1}{2} \times 24 \times 1.5\right) \times 65$$

$$= 1170 \text{ kN}$$

Problem 9.9 : For the through type bridge truss shown in Fig. 9.26, draw influence line diagram for the axial forces in members $U_2 U_3$, $U_2 L_3$ and $L_2 L_3$. Using these diagrams, find the maximum forces induced in the above members when a U.D.L. of 10 kN/m longer than the span passes over.

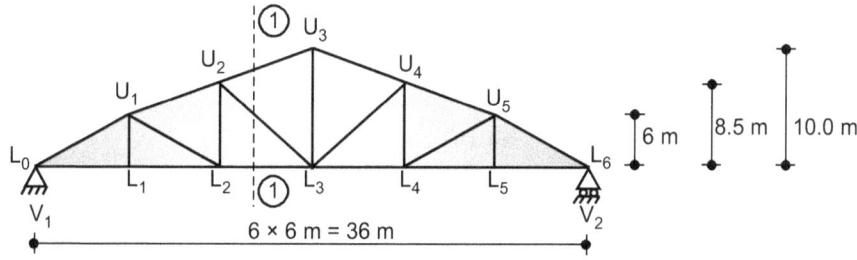

Fig. 9.26

Solution : 1. I.L.D. for $U_2 U_3$: Take section as (1)–(1).

For unit load between $L_0 L_2$, consider right part of the section $\sum M$ @ L_3.

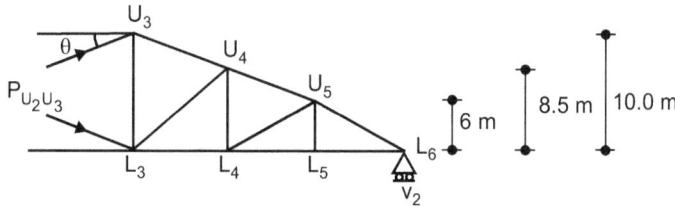

Fig. 9.27

$$\tan \theta = \frac{1.5}{6} \quad \therefore \theta = 14.03$$

$$P_{U_2 U_3} \cos \theta \times 10 = V_2 \times 18$$

$$P_{U_2 U_3} \cos \theta = 1.8 V_2$$

$$P_{U_2 U_3} = \frac{1.8 V_2}{\cos 14.03} = 1.86 V_2$$

When unit load is at L_0, $V_2 = 0$

$$P_{U_2 U_3} = 0$$

When unit load is at L_1, $V_2 = \dfrac{1}{6}$

$P_{U_2U_3} = 0.31$ (Compressive)

When unit load is at L_2, $V_2 = \dfrac{1}{3}$

$P_{U_2U_3} = 0.62$ (Compressive)

When unit load is on right part, consider left part of the section.

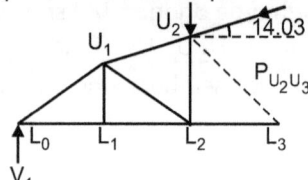

Fig. 9.28

$\sum M @ L_3$

$\therefore \quad P_{U_2U_3} \cos 14.03 \times 8.5 + P_{U_2U_3} \sin 14.03 \times 6 = V_1 \times 18$

$\therefore \quad 9.7\, P_{U_2U_3} = V_1 \times 18$

$P_{U_2U_3} = 1.856\, V_1$

When unit load is at L_3, $V_1 = \dfrac{1}{2}$

$P_{U_2U_3} = 0.93$ (Compressive)

When unit load is at L_4, $V_1 = \dfrac{1}{3}$

$P_{U_2U_3} = 0.62$ (Compressive)

When unit load is at L_5, $V_1 = \dfrac{1}{6}$

$P_{U_2U_3} = 0.31$ (Compressive)

When unit load is at L_6,

$P_{U_2U_3} = 0$

2. **I.L.D. for $L_2 L_3$:**

Take section same as (1)-(1). For unit load between $L_0 L_2$, consider right part of the section.

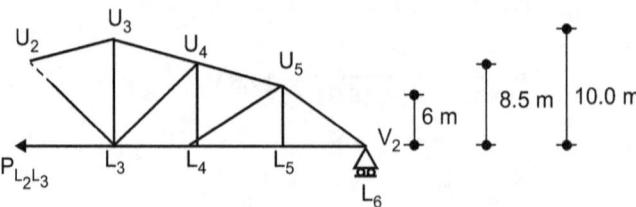

Fig. 9.29

$\Sigma M @ U_2$

$$P_{L_2 L_3} \times 8.5 = V_2 \times 24$$

$\therefore \quad P_{L_2 L_3} = 2.824 V_2$

When unit load is at L_0, $V_2 = 0$

$$P_{L_2 L_3} = 0$$

When unit load is at L_1, $V_2 = \frac{1}{6}$

$$P_{L_2 L_3} = 0.471 \text{ (Tensile)}$$

When unit load is at L_2, $V_2 = \frac{1}{3}$

$$P_{L_2 L_3} = 0.942 \text{ (Tensile)}$$

For unit load between $L_3 L_6$, consider left part of the section.

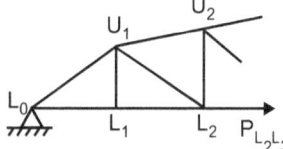

Fig. 9.30

$\Sigma M @ U_2 \quad P_{L_2 L_3} \times 8.5 = V_1 \times 12$

$\therefore \quad P_{L_2 L_3} = 1.412 V_1$

When unit load is at L_3, $V_1 = \frac{1}{2}$

$$P_{L_2 L_3} = 0.706 \text{ (Tensile)}$$

When unit load is at L_4, $V_1 = \frac{1}{3}$

$$P_{L_2 L_3} = 0.471 \text{ (Tensile)}$$

When unit load is at L_5, $V_1 = \frac{1}{6}$

$$P_{L_2 L_3} = 0.236 \text{ (Tensile)}$$

3. **I.L.D. for $U_2 L_3$:**

Consider same section as (1)–(1). When unit load is on left part, consider right part of the section.

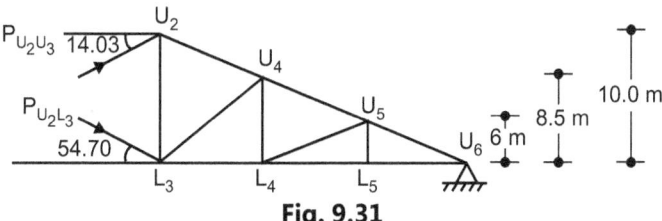

Fig. 9.31

$\Sigma f_y = 0$, $\theta_{U_2 L_3}$ with horizontal = $\tan^{-1} \dfrac{8.5}{6} = 54.78°$

$- P_{U_2 U_3} \sin 14.03 + P_{U_2 L_3} \sin 54.78 - V_2 = 0$

$0.242\, P_{U_2 U_3} - 0.817\, P_{U_2 L_3} + V_2 = 0$

When unit load is at L_0, $V_2 = 0$

$\qquad P_{U_2 U_3} = 0$ (Refer I.L.D. of $P_{U_2 U_3}$ at L_0)

$\therefore \qquad P_{U_2 U_3} = 0$

When unit load is at L_1, $V_2 = \dfrac{1}{6}$

$\qquad P_{U_2 U_3} = 0.31$

$\therefore \quad 0.242 \times 0.31 - 0.817\, P_{U_2 L_3} + \dfrac{1}{6} = 0$

$\therefore \qquad P_{U_2 L_3} = 0.296$ (Compressive)

When unit load is at L_2, $V_2 = \dfrac{1}{3}$

$\qquad P_{U_2 U_3} = 0.62$

$\therefore \qquad P_{U_2 L_3} = 0.592$ (Compressive)

When unit load is on right part, consider left part of the section.

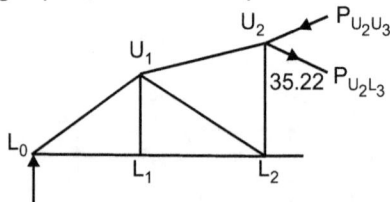

Fig. 9.32

$- P_{U_2 U_3} \sin 14.03 - P_{U_2 L_3} \cos 35.22 + V_1 = 0$

$- 0.242\, P_{U_2 U_3} - 0.817\, P_{U_2 L_3} + V_1 = 0$

When unit load is at L_3, $V_1 = \dfrac{1}{2}$

$\qquad P_{U_2 U_3} = 0.93$

$\therefore \qquad P_{U_2 L_3} = 0.337$ (Tensile)

When unit load is at L_4, $V_1 = \dfrac{1}{3}$

$\qquad P_{U_2 U_3} = 0.62$

$\therefore \qquad P_{U_2 L_3} = 0.224$ (Tensile)

When unit load is at L_5, $V_1 = \dfrac{1}{6}$

$P_{U_2U_3} = 0.31$

$P_{U_2L_3} = 0.112$

When unit load is at L_6, $V_1 = 0$

$P_{U_2U_3} = 0$

$\therefore \quad P_{U_2L_3} = 0$

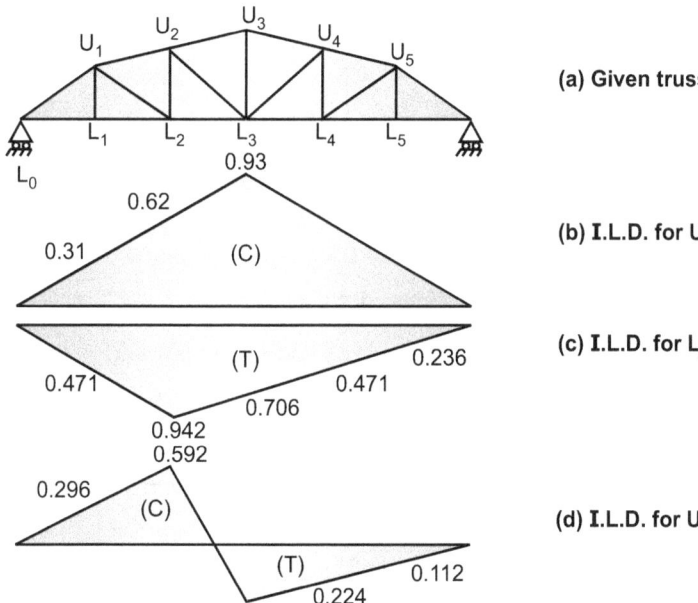

Fig. 9.33

EXERCISE

1. Draw I.L.D. for the members U_1U_2, U_1L_2, L_1L_2 and U_1L_1.

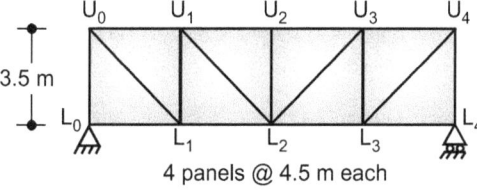

Fig. 9.34

2. Draw I.L.D. for members U_1L_1, U_1U_2 and L_1L_2 when unit load is moving on bottom chord.

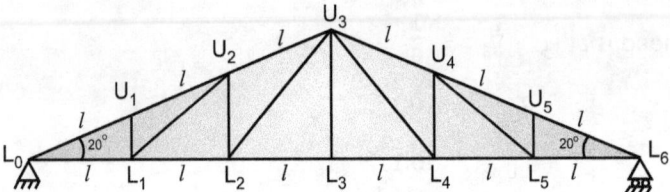

Fig. 9.35

3. Draw I.L.D. for members U_3U_4, U_4L_3 and L_3L_4 and find the maximum compressive and tensile force in the member when U.D.L. of 35 kN/m longer than the span traverse.

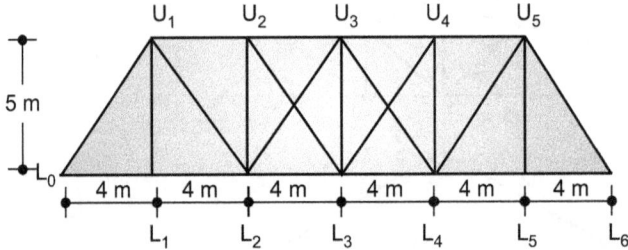

Fig. 9.36

4. Draw I.L.D. for members U_2U_3, U_2L_3, U_3L_3 and L_2L_3 when bridge is deck type bridge. Also find maximum forces in member when U.D.L. of intensity 60 kN/m having span 10 m traverses on it.

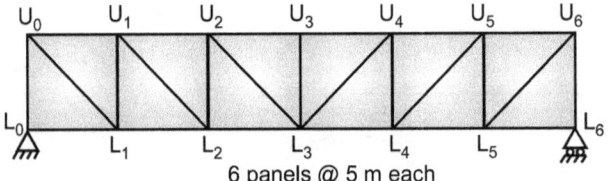

6 panels @ 5 m each

Fig. 9.37

5. Draw I.L.D. for any top chord, bottom chord, vertical and diagonal member for the truss as shown in Fig. 9.38. Also find maximum forces in member when the load system as shown in Fig. 9.38 traverses on it.

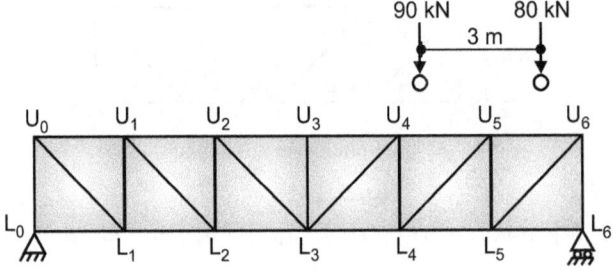

Fig. 9.38

MULTIPLE CHOICE QUESTIONS

1. A beam is as shown in Fig. 1. The reaction at A is

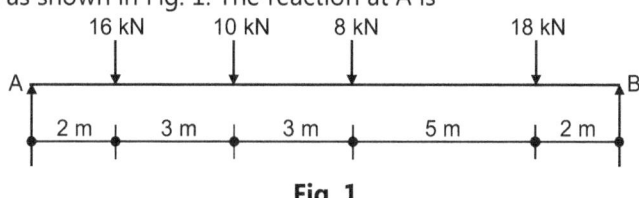

Fig. 1

    (a) 26.67 kN   (b) 27.77 kN   (c) 25.5 kN   (d) 23.33 kN

2. A beam is as shown in Fig. 1. The reaction at B is

    (a) 24.99 kN   (b) 25.33 kN   (c) 52.33 kN   (d) 26.67 kN

3. Determine the shear force at a section 7 m from left hand side of the beam as shown in Fig. 1

    (a) 6.7 kN   (b) 0.67 kN   (c) 1.67 kN   (d) 5.67 kN

4. Find the bending moment at a distance 6 m from L.H.S., A of the beam given in Fig. 1

    (a) 43 kN-m   (b) 81 kN-m   (c) 86 kN-m   (d) 64 kN-m

5. A beam is as shown in Fig. 2. The reaction at A is

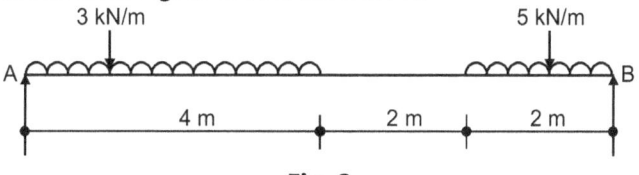

Fig. 2

    (a) 11.45 kN   (b) 12.13 kN   (c) 10.25 kN   (d) 21.55 kN

6. A beam is as shown in Fig. 2. The reaction at B is

    (a) 11.75 kN   (b) 11.45 kN   (c) 12.13 kN   (d) 10.89 kN

7. Determine the shear force at the centre of beam shown in Fig. 2.

    (a) 2.25 kN   (b) 17.5 kN   (c) 1.75 kN   (d) 2.5 kN

8. A beam is as shown in Fig. 3. The reaction at A is

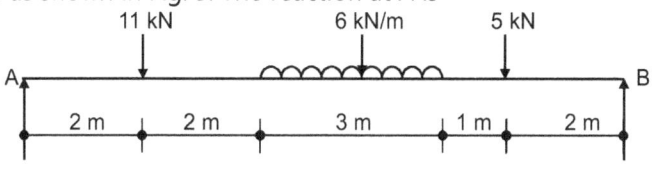

Fig. 3

    (a) 1.79 kN   (b) 17.9 kN   (c) 1.8 kN   (d) 18.9 kN

9. A beam is as shown in Fig. 3. The reaction at B is

    (a) 14.2 kN   (b) 15.5 kN   (c) 16.1 KN   (d) 17.1 kN

10. Determine bending moment at the centre of beam as shown in Fig. 3.
    (a) 53.5 kN-m   (b) 55.5 kN-m   (c) 51 kN-m   (d) 44.5 kN-m
11. A beam is as shown in Fig. 4. The reaction at A is

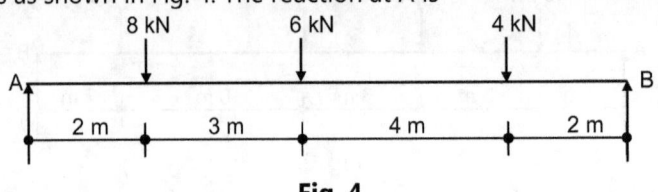

Fig. 4

    (a) 10 kN   (b) 10.45 kN   (c) 11.45 kN   (d) 1.045 kN
12. A beam is as shown in Fig. 4. The reaction at B is
    (a) 13.45 kN   (b) 7.45 kN   (c) 9.5 kN   (d) 11.5 kN
13. A beam is as shown in Fig. 5. The reaction at A is

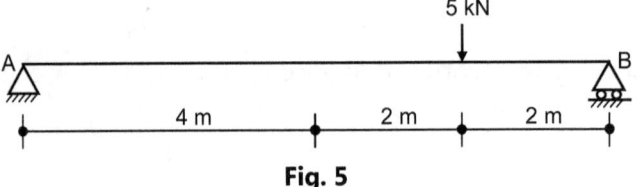

Fig. 5

    (a) 1.25 kN   (b) 3.75 kN   (c) 2.25 kN   (d) 5.25 kN
14. A beam is as shown in Fig. 5. The reaction at B is
    (a) 1.25 kN   (b) 3.75 kN   (c) 2.25 kN   (d) 5.25 kN
15. A beam is as shown in Fig. 6. The reaction at A is

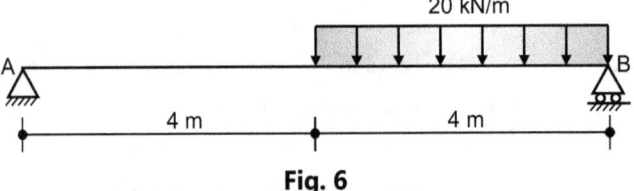

Fig. 6

    (a) 25 kN   (b) 37.5 kN   (c) 25 kN   (d) 20 kN
16. A beam is as shown in Fig. 6. The reaction at B is
    (a) 75 kN   (b) 70 kN   (c) 60 kN   (d) 20 kN
17. A beam is as shown in Fig. 7. The reaction at B is

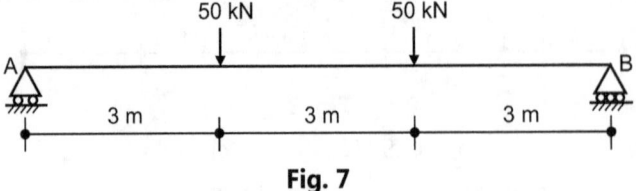

Fig. 7

    (a) 50 kN   (b) 70 kN   (c) 35 kN   (d) 65 kN

18. A beam is as shown in Fig. 7. The reaction at A is
    (a) 35 kN   (b) 65 kN   (c) 50 kN   (d) 25 kN
19. A beam is as shown in Fig. 8. The reaction at A is

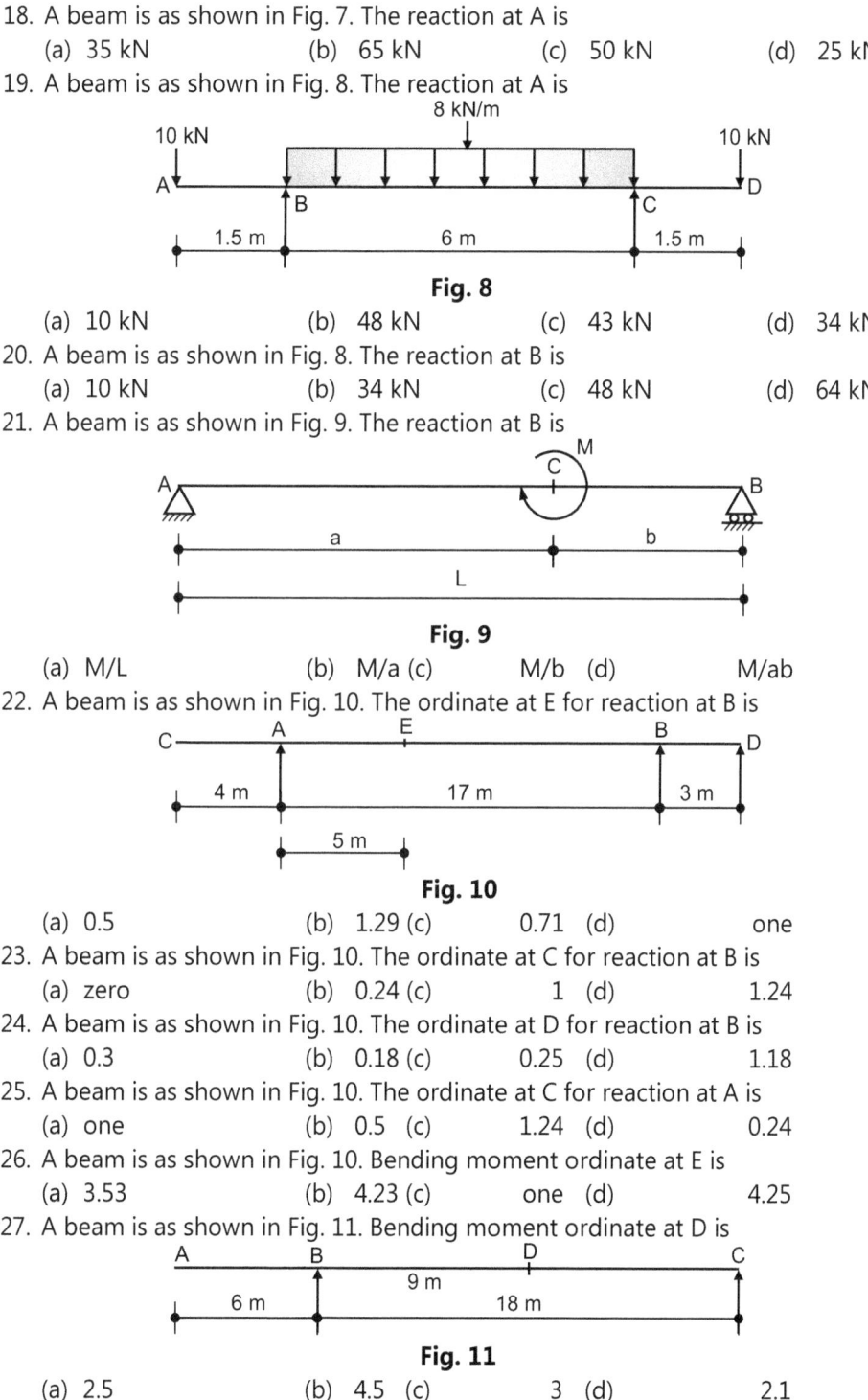

Fig. 8

    (a) 10 kN   (b) 48 kN   (c) 43 kN   (d) 34 kN
20. A beam is as shown in Fig. 8. The reaction at B is
    (a) 10 kN   (b) 34 kN   (c) 48 kN   (d) 64 kN
21. A beam is as shown in Fig. 9. The reaction at B is

Fig. 9

    (a) M/L   (b) M/a   (c) M/b   (d) M/ab
22. A beam is as shown in Fig. 10. The ordinate at E for reaction at B is

Fig. 10

    (a) 0.5   (b) 1.29   (c) 0.71   (d) one
23. A beam is as shown in Fig. 10. The ordinate at C for reaction at B is
    (a) zero   (b) 0.24   (c) 1   (d) 1.24
24. A beam is as shown in Fig. 10. The ordinate at D for reaction at B is
    (a) 0.3   (b) 0.18   (c) 0.25   (d) 1.18
25. A beam is as shown in Fig. 10. The ordinate at C for reaction at A is
    (a) one   (b) 0.5   (c) 1.24   (d) 0.24
26. A beam is as shown in Fig. 10. Bending moment ordinate at E is
    (a) 3.53   (b) 4.23   (c) one   (d) 4.25
27. A beam is as shown in Fig. 11. Bending moment ordinate at D is

Fig. 11

    (a) 2.5   (b) 4.5   (c) 3   (d) 2.1

28. A beam is as shown in Fig. 11. Ordinate at A for I.L.D. of B.M. at D is
   (a) 2.5 (b) 4.5 (c) 2.1 (d) 3
29. A beam is as shown in Fig. 11. Ordinate at D for reaction at B is
   (a) 1.5 (b) 1.67 (c) 0.33 (d) 0.67
30. A beam is as shown in Fig. 11. Ordinate at D for reaction at C is
   (a) 2 (b) 1.5 (c) 1 (d) 0.5
31. A beam is shown in Fig. 12. Reaction at C is

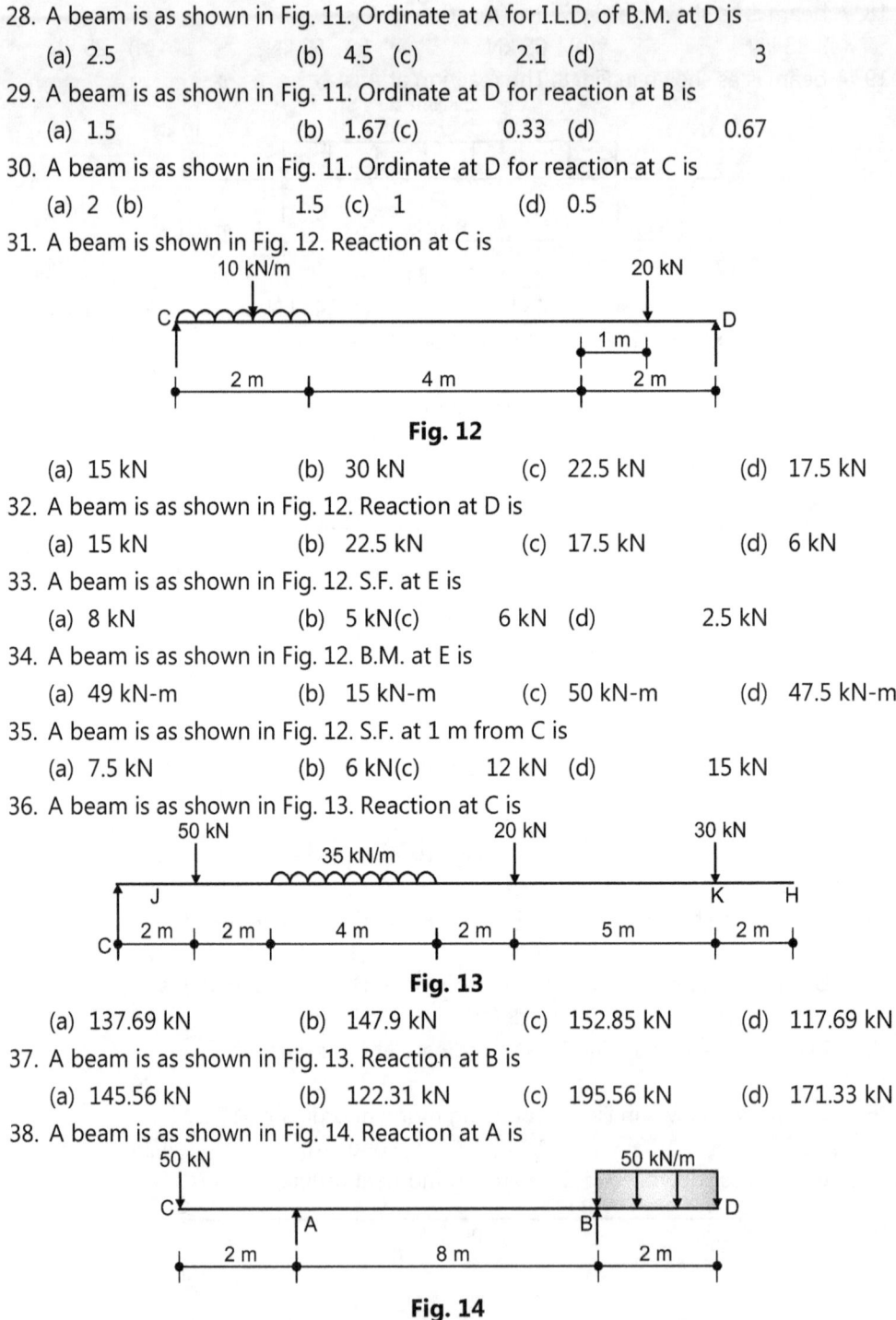

Fig. 12

   (a) 15 kN (b) 30 kN (c) 22.5 kN (d) 17.5 kN
32. A beam is as shown in Fig. 12. Reaction at D is
   (a) 15 kN (b) 22.5 kN (c) 17.5 kN (d) 6 kN
33. A beam is as shown in Fig. 12. S.F. at E is
   (a) 8 kN (b) 5 kN (c) 6 kN (d) 2.5 kN
34. A beam is as shown in Fig. 12. B.M. at E is
   (a) 49 kN-m (b) 15 kN-m (c) 50 kN-m (d) 47.5 kN-m
35. A beam is as shown in Fig. 12. S.F. at 1 m from C is
   (a) 7.5 kN (b) 6 kN (c) 12 kN (d) 15 kN
36. A beam is as shown in Fig. 13. Reaction at C is

Fig. 13

   (a) 137.69 kN (b) 147.9 kN (c) 152.85 kN (d) 117.69 kN
37. A beam is as shown in Fig. 13. Reaction at B is
   (a) 145.56 kN (b) 122.31 kN (c) 195.56 kN (d) 171.33 kN
38. A beam is as shown in Fig. 14. Reaction at A is

Fig. 14

   (a) 5.46 kN (b) 9.12 kN (c) 1.90 kN (d) 3.55 kN

39. A beam is as shown in Fig. 14. Reaction at B is
    (a) 7.56 kN (b) 5.88 kN (c) 2.79 kN (d) 4.04 kN
40. A beam is as shown in Fig. 15. Ordinate of I.L.D. for reaction B at A is

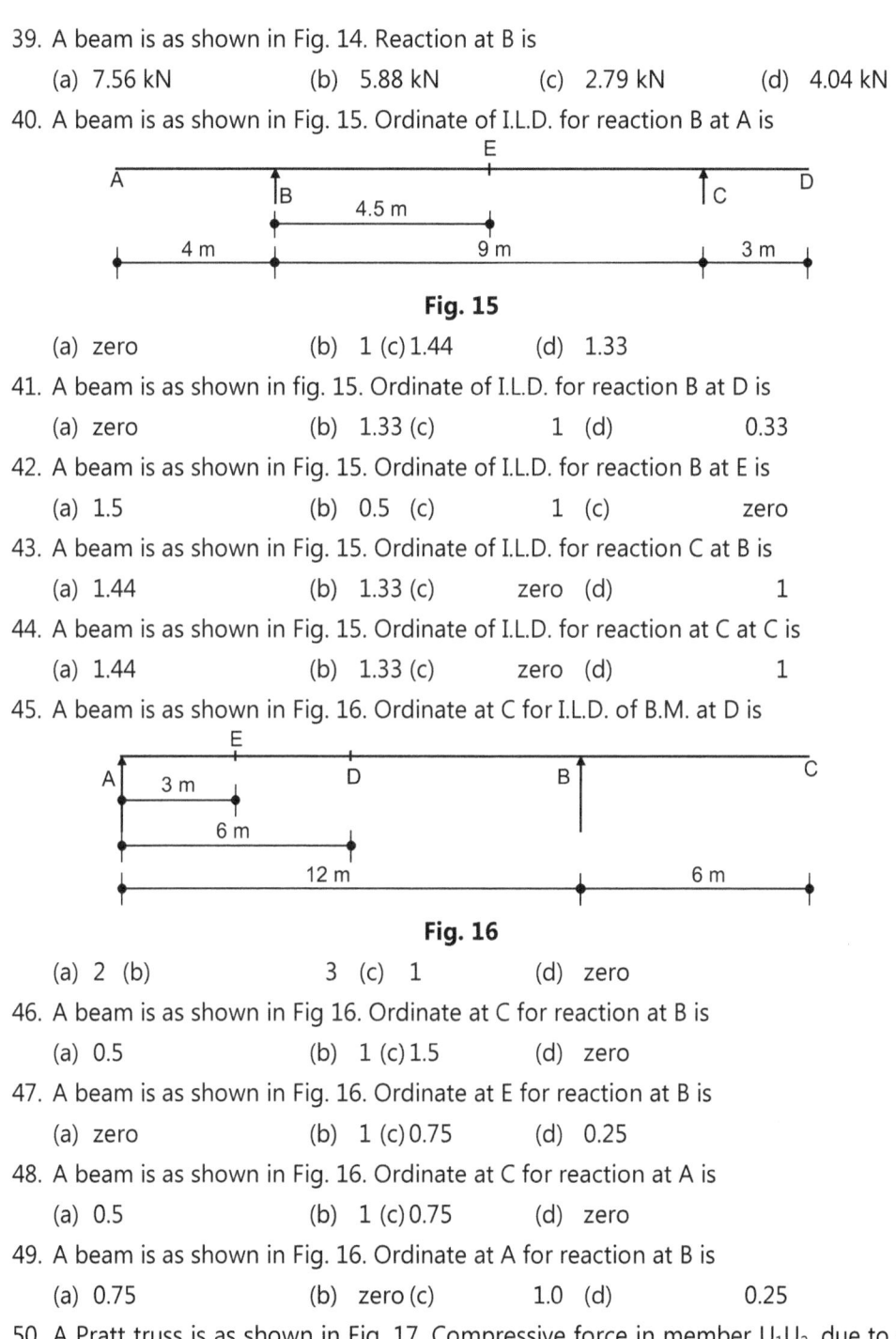

Fig. 15

    (a) zero (b) 1 (c) 1.44 (d) 1.33
41. A beam is as shown in fig. 15. Ordinate of I.L.D. for reaction B at D is
    (a) zero (b) 1.33 (c) 1 (d) 0.33
42. A beam is as shown in Fig. 15. Ordinate of I.L.D. for reaction B at E is
    (a) 1.5 (b) 0.5 (c) 1 (c) zero
43. A beam is as shown in Fig. 15. Ordinate of I.L.D. for reaction C at B is
    (a) 1.44 (b) 1.33 (c) zero (d) 1
44. A beam is as shown in Fig. 15. Ordinate of I.L.D. for reaction at C at C is
    (a) 1.44 (b) 1.33 (c) zero (d) 1
45. A beam is as shown in Fig. 16. Ordinate at C for I.L.D. of B.M. at D is

Fig. 16

    (a) 2 (b) 3 (c) 1 (d) zero
46. A beam is as shown in Fig 16. Ordinate at C for reaction at B is
    (a) 0.5 (b) 1 (c) 1.5 (d) zero
47. A beam is as shown in Fig. 16. Ordinate at E for reaction at B is
    (a) zero (b) 1 (c) 0.75 (d) 0.25
48. A beam is as shown in Fig. 16. Ordinate at C for reaction at A is
    (a) 0.5 (b) 1 (c) 0.75 (d) zero
49. A beam is as shown in Fig. 16. Ordinate at A for reaction at B is
    (a) 0.75 (b) zero (c) 1.0 (d) 0.25
50. A Pratt truss is as shown in Fig. 17. Compressive force in member U_1U_2, due to dead load of 10kN/m covering the entire span and a moving live load of 20 kN/m longer than the span, is

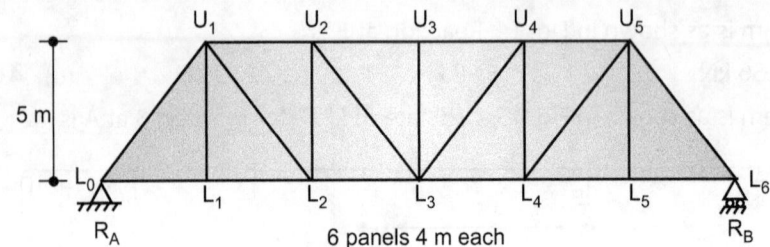

Fig. 17

(a) 385 kN (b) 292 kN (c) 472 kN (d) 192 kN

51. A Pratt truss is as shown in fig.17. Maximum tensile force in member U_1U_2, due to dead load of 10 kN/m covering the entire span and a moving live load of 20 kN/m longer than the span, is
    (a) 38 kN (b) 42 kN (c) 72 kN (d) 12 kN

52. A Pratt truss is as shown in Fig. 17. Maximum compressive force in member U_2L_2, due to dead load of 10 kN/m covering the entire span and a moving live load of 20 kN/m longer than the span, is
    (a) 58 kN (b) 32 kN (c) 92 kN (d) 62 kN

53. A Pratt truss is as shown in Fig. 17. Force in member L_1L_2, due to dead load of 10 kN/m covering the entire span and a moving live load of 20 kN/m longer than the span, is
    (a) 280 kN (b) 240 kN (c) 120 kN (d) 225 kN

54. A Pratt truss is as shown in Fig. 17. Force in member U_1L_1, due to dead load of 10 kN/m covering the entire span and a moving live load of 20 kN/m longer than the span, is
    (a) 80 kN (b) 40 kN (c) 100 kN (d) 60 kN

55. A Pratt truss is as shown in Fig. 17. Force in member L_0U_1, due to dead load of 10 kN/m covering the entire span and a moving live load of 20 kN/m longer than the span is
    (a) 385 kN (b) 292 kN (c) 472 kN (d) 192 kN

56. A Pratt truss is as shown in Fig. 17. Maximum tensile force in member U_1L_2, due to dead load of 10 kN/m covering the entire span and a moving live load of 20 kN/m longer than the span, is
    (a) 280 kN (b) 200 kN (c) 220 kN (d) 240 kN

57. A Pratt truss is as shown in Fig. 17. Minimum tensile force in member U_1L_2, due to dead load of 10 kN/m covering the entire span and a moving live load of 20 kN/m longer than the span, is
    (a) 88 kN (b) 66 kN (c) 98 kN (d) 76 kN

58. A Pratt truss is as shown in Fig. 18. Tensile force in member L_1L_2 due to dead load of 9 kN/m covering the entire span and a moving live load of 17 kN/m longer than the span, is

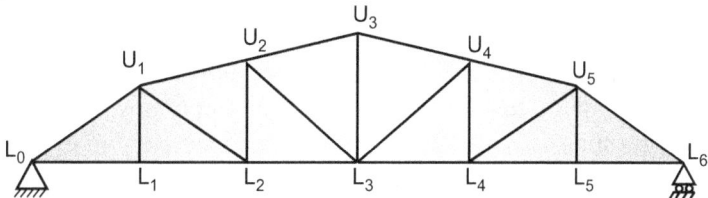

6 panels 4 m each
Fig. 18

(a) 312 kN (b) 232 kN (c) 346 kN (d) 198 kN

59. A Pratt truss is as shown in Fig. 18. Maximum tensile force in member U_2L_2, due to dead load of 9 kN/m covering the entire span and a moving live load of 17 kN/m longer than the span, is
(a) 78 kN (b) 68 kN (c) 88 kN (d) 98 kN

60. A Pratt truss is as shown in Fig. 18. Minimum tensile force in member U_2L_2, due to dead load of 9 kN/m covering the entire span and a moving live load of 17 kN/m longer than the span, is
(a) 15 kN (b) 6 kN (c) 11 kN (d) 8 kN

61. A Pratt truss is as shown in Fig. 18. Force in member U_1U_2, due to dead load of 9 kN/m covering the entire span and a moving live load of 17 kN/m longer than the span, is
(a) 179 kN (b) 321 kN (c) 371 kN (d) 218 kN

62. A Pratt truss is as shown in Fig. 18. Maximum compressive force in member U_1L_2, due to dead load of 9 kN/m covering the entire span and a moving live load of 17 kN/m longer than the span, is
(a) 58 kN (b) 36 kN (c) 49 kN (d) 67 kN

63. A Pratt truss is as shown in Fig. 18. Maximum tensile force in member U_1L_2, due to dead load of 9 kN/m covering the entire span and a moving live load of 17 kN/m longer than the span, is
(a) 25 kN (b) 62 kN (c) 42 kN (d) 56 kN

64. A Warren truss is as shown in Fig. 19. Maximum tensile force in member L_1L_2, due to dead load of 11 kN/m covering the entire span and a moving live load of 18 kN/m longer than the span, is

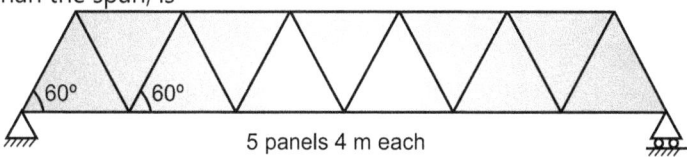

5 panels 4 m each
Fig. 19

(a) 311 kN (b) 335 kN (c) 264 kN (d) 218 kN

65. A Warren truss is as shown in Fig. 19. Maximum compressive force in member U_2U_3, due to dead load of 11 kN/m covering the entire span and a moving live load of 18 kN/m longer than the span, is
    (a) 415 kN (b) 385 kN (c) 300 kN (d) 400 kN

66. A Warren truss is as shown in Fig. 19. Maximum tensile force in member U_2L_2, due to dead load of 11 kN/m covering the entire span and a moving live load of 18 kN/m longer than the span, is
    (a) 159 kN (b) 138 kN (c) 143 kN (d) 184 kN

67. A Warren truss is as shown in Fig. 19. Minimum tensile force in member U_2L_2, due to dead load of 11 kN/m covering the entire span and a moving live load of 18 kN/m longer than the span, is
    (a) 40 kN (b) 56 kN (c) 24 kN (d) 67 kN

68. A Warren truss is as shown in Fig. 19. Maximum compressive force in member U_2L_2, due to dead load of 11 kN/m covering the entire span and a moving live load of 18 kN/m longer than the span, is
    (a) 159 kN (b) 138 kN (c) 143 kN (d) 184 kN

69. A Warren truss is as shown in Fig. 19. Minimum compressive force in member U_2L_2, due to dead load of 11 kN/m covering the entire span and a moving live load of 18 kN/m longer than the span, is
    (a) 40 kN (b) 56 kN (c) 24 kN (d) 67 kN

70. A sloping chord through type truss is as shown in Fig. 20. Compressive force in member U_2U_3, due to dead load of 10 kN/m covering the entire span and a moving live load of 15 kN/m longer than the span, is

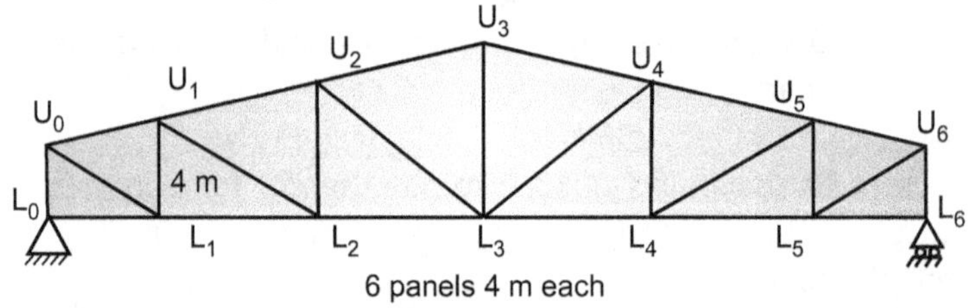

Fig. 20

    (a) 459 kN (b) 338 kN (c) 413 kN (d) 309 kN

71. A sloping chord through type truss is as shown in Fig. 20. Tensile force in member L_1L_2, due to dead load of 10 kN/m covering the entire span and a moving live load of 15 kN/m longer than the span, is
    (a) 350 kN (b) 250 kN (c) 400 kN (d) 300 kN

72. A sloping chord through type truss is as shown in Fig. 20. Compressive force in member U_0L_0, due to dead load of 10 kN/m covering the entire span and a moving live load of 15 kN/m longer than the span, is
    (a) 350 kN (b) 250 kN (c) 400 kN (d) 300 kN

73. A sloping chord through type truss is as shown in Fig. 20. Maximum compressive force in member U_2L_3, due to dead load of 10 kN/m covering the entire span and a moving live load of 15 kN/m longer than the span, is
   (a) 24 kN (b) 55 kN (c) 38 kN (d) 76 kN

74. A sloping chord through type truss is as shown in Fig. 20. Maximum tensile force in member U_2L_3, due to dead load of 10 kN/m covering the entire span and a moving live load of 15 kN/m longer than the span, is
   (a) 45 kN (b) 75 kN (c) 28 kN (d) 37 kN

75. A truss is as shown in Fig. 21. Maximum tensile force in member L_1L_2, due to dead load of 12.5 kN/m covering the entire span and a moving live load of 22.5 kN/m longer than the span, is

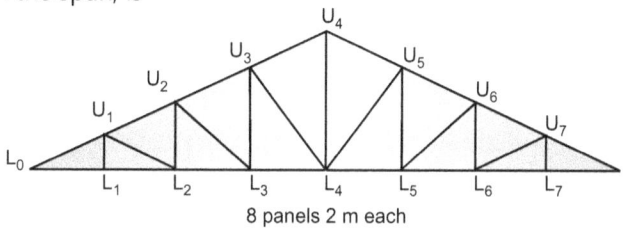

Fig. 21

   (a) 710 kN (b) 750 kN (c) 585 kN (d) 672 kN

76. A truss is as shown in Fig. 21. Maximum compressive force in member U_1L_0, due to dead load of 12.5 kN/m covering the entire span and a moving live load of 22.5 kN/m longer than the span, is
   (a) 718 kN (b) 759 kN (c) 687 kN (d) 772 kN

77. A truss is as shown in Fig. 21. Tensile force in member U_1L_1, due to dead load of 12.5 kN/m covering the entire span and a moving live load of 22.5 kN/m longer than the span, is
   (a) 60 kN (b) 70 kN (c) 35 kN (d) 90 kN

78. A truss is as shown in Fig. 21. Compressive force in member U_1U_2, due to dead load of 12.5 kN/m covering the entire span and a moving live load of 22.5 kN/m longer than the span, is
   (a) 690 kN (b) 590 kN (c) 610 kN (d) 640 kN

79. A truss is as shown in Fig. 22. Force in member U_4L_4, due to dead load of 10.5 kN/m covering the entire span and a moving live load of 21.5 kN/m longer than the span, is

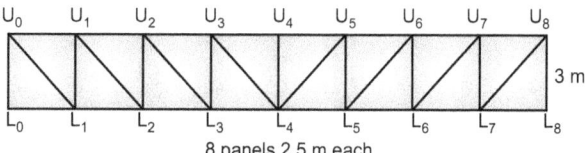

Fig. 22

   (a) Zero (b) 90 kN (c) 61 kN
   (d) None of these

80. A truss is as shown in Fig. 22. Force in member L_0L_1, due to dead load of 10.5 kN/m covering the entire span and a moving live load of 21.5 kN/m longer than the span, is

   (a) 15 kN (b) 90 kN (c) 61 kN
   (d) None of these

81. A truss is as shown in Fig. 22. Compressive force in member L_0L_1, due to dead load of 10.5 kN/m covering the entire span and a moving live load of 21.5 kN/m longer than the span, is

   (a) 399 kN (b) 499 kN (c) 439 kN (d) 469 kN

82. A truss is as shown in Fig. 22. Maximum ordinate of ILD of member U_4U_5 is

   (a) 1 (b) 0.73 (c) 1.67 (d) 1.25

83. A truss is as shown in Fig. 22. Maximum ordinate of ILD of member U_7U_8 is

   (a) 1 (b) 0.73 (c) 1.67 (d) 1.25

84. A truss is as shown in Fig. 22. Maximum ordinate of ILD of member L_7L_8 is

   (a) Zero (b) 1 (c) 1.25
   (d) None of these

85. A truss is as shown in Fig. 22. Maximum ordinate of ILD of member L_5L_6 is

   (a) Zero (b) 1 (c) 1.25
   (d) None of these

86. A truss is as shown in Fig. 22. Maximum tensile force in member U_2L_3, due to dead load of 10.5 kN/m covering the entire span and a moving live load of 21.5 kN/m longer than the span, is

   (a) 211 kN (b) 124 kN (c) 99 kN (d) 176 kN

87. A truss is as shown in Fig. 22. Minimum tensile force in member U_2L_3, due to dead load of 10.5 kN/m covering the entire span and a moving live load of 21.5 kN/m longer than the span, is

   (a) 21 kN (b) 31 kN (c) 57 kN (d) 55 kN

88. A truss is as shown in Fig. 22. Tensile force in member U_3L_3, due to dead load of 10.5 kN/m covering the entire span and a moving live load of 21.5 kN/m longer than the span, is

   (a) 21 kN (b) 31 kN (c) 57 kN (d) 55 kN

89. A truss is as shown in Fig. 22. Compressive force in member U_3L_3, due to dead load of 10.5 kN/m covering the entire span and a moving live load of 21.5 kN/m longer than the span, is

   (a) 29 kN (b) 13 kN (c) 75 kN (d) 45 kN

90. A deck truss is as shown in Fig. 23. Compressive force in member DK, due to dead load of 8 kN/m covering the entire span and a moving live load of 19 kN/m longer than the span, is

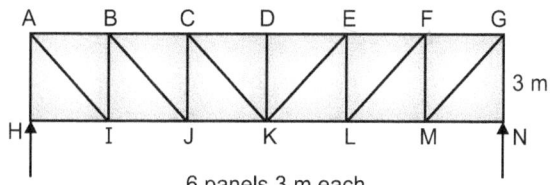

Fig. 23

(a) 129 kN   (b) 108 kN   (c) 78 kN   (d) 99 kN

91. A deck truss is as shown in Fig. 23. Compressive force in member DE, due to dead load of 8 kN/m covering the entire span and a moving live load of 19 kN/m longer than the span, is

(a) 239 kN   (b) 268 kN   (c) 299 kN   (d) 365 kN

92. A deck truss is as shown in Fig. 23. Tensile force in member KL, due to dead load of 8 kN/m covering the entire span and a moving live load of 19 kN/m longer than the span, is

(a) 309 kN   (b) 297 kN   (c) 279 kN   (d) 323 kN

93. A deck truss is as shown in Fig. 23. Minimum compressive force in member CJ, due to dead load of 8 kN/m covering the entire span and a moving live load of 19 kN/m longer than the span, is

(a) 30 kN   (b) 39 kN   (c) 45 kN   (d) 23 kN

94. A deck truss is as shown in Fig. 23. Maximum compressive force in member CJ, due to dead load of 8 kN/m covering the entire span and a moving live load of 19 kN/m longer than the span, is

(a) 79 kN   (b) 148 kN   (c) 127 kN   (d) 93 kN

95. A deck truss is as shown in Fig. 23. Maximum tensile force in member BJ, due to dead load of 8 kN/m covering the entire span and a moving live load of 19 kN/m longer than the span, is

(a) 79 kN   (b) 148 kN   (c) 127 kN   (d) 93 kN

96. A deck truss is as shown in Fig. 23. Minimum tensile force in member BJ, due to dead load of 8 kN/m covering the entire span and a moving live load of 19 kN/m longer than the span, is

(a) 30 kN   (b) 39 kN   (c) 45 kN   (d) 23 kN

97. A deck truss is as shown in Fig. 24. Force in member U_1U_2, due to dead load of 12 kN/m covering the entire span and a moving live load of 17 kN/m longer than the span, is

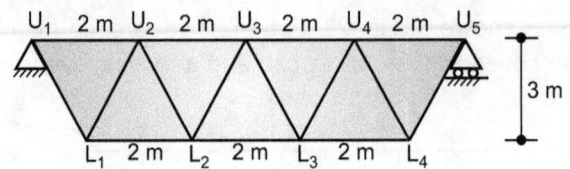

Fig. 24

(a) 32 kN (b) 39 kN (c) 55 kN (d) 29 kN

98. A deck truss is as shown in Fig. 24. Minimum tensile force in member U_2U_3, due to dead load of 12 kN/m covering the entire span and a moving live load of 17 kN/m longer than the span, is

(a) 51 kN (b) 61 kN (c) 58 kN (d) 69 kN

99. A deck truss is as shown in Fig. 24. Minimum tensile force in member L_1L_2, due to dead load of 12 kN/m covering the entire span and a moving live load of 17 kN/m longer than the span, is

(a) 51 kN (b) 61 kN (c) 58 kN (d) 69 kN

100. A deck truss is as shown in Fig. 24. Minimum tensile force in member U_2L_1, due to dead load of 12 kN/m covering the entire span and a moving live load of 17 kN/m longer than the span, is

(a) 92 kN (b) 76 kN (c) 83 kN (d) 109 kN

ANSWERS

1. (a)	2. (b)	3. (b)	4. (c)	5. (c)	6. (a)	7. (c)	8. (b)
9. (c)	10. (a)	11. (b)	12. (b)	13. (a)	14. (b)	15. (d)	16. (c)
17. (a)	18. (c)	19. (d)	20. (b)	21. (a)	22. (c)	23. (d)	24. (b)
25. (d)	26. (a)	27. (b)	28. (d)	29. (b)	30. (d)	31. (d)	32. (b)
33. (d)	34. (d)	35. (a)	36. (d)	37. (b)	38. (a)	39. (d)	40. (c)
41. (d)	42. (b)	43. (c)	44. (d)	45. (b)	46. (c)	47. (d)	48. (a)
49. (b)	50. (a)	51. (d)	52. (c)	53. (b)	54. (c)	55. (a)	56. (d)
57. (b)	58. (c)	59. (a)	60. (d)	61. (c)	62. (c)	63. (a)	64. (b)
65. (d)	66. (c)	67. (a)	68. (c)	69. (a)	70. (d)	71. (b)	72. (b)
73. (c)	74. (a)	75. (d)	76. (a)	77. (b)	78. (c)	79. (a)	80. (d)
81. (b)	82. (c)	83. (b)	84. (a)	85. (c)	86. (d)	87. (b)	88. (a)
89. (c)	90. (b)	91. (d)	92. (d)	93. (a)	94. (c)	95. (c)	96. (a)
97. (d)	98. (b)	99. (b)	100. (a)				

UNIT- V

Chapter 10

THREE-HINGED ARCHES

10.1 INTRODUCTION

An arch is nothing but a curved beam with convexity upwards and for which horizontal movement at support is restrained. An arch is a structural form which serves the same purpose as a beam but have some additional advantages because of the thrust action. When a curved beam has hinges at supports only, we call it as two hinged arch. But when an additional hinge is introduced in the rib of the curved beam usually at the crown, it becomes a three hinged arch. We shall restrict our scope to three hinged arches only.

10.2 THEORETICAL ARCH OR LINE OF THRUST

A flexible cable when subjected to a given load system, tension is developed in its various segments and the shape of the cable will correspond to the funicular polygon for the given load system. If the cable segments are replaced by straight links, pinned together at the load points, tension in each link will be same as in the corresponding segment of the cable.

Fig. 10.1 (a) shows the cable subjected to a load system. If the linkwork is inverted with loads acting downwards, the links are subjected to direct axial thrust only and there is no bending moment and shear force anywhere. Such a linkwork is known as *Linear arch* or *Theoretical arch*.

It is obviously not possible to give an arch its theoretical shape of the funicular polygon, since the moving loads will pass over an arch and it cannot be made to change its shape to suit the varying load positions. The centre line of an arch is normally given a parabolic, circular or elliptic shape.

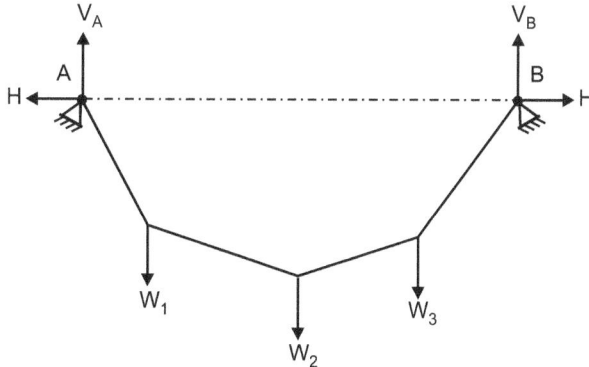

(a) Cable subjected to loads

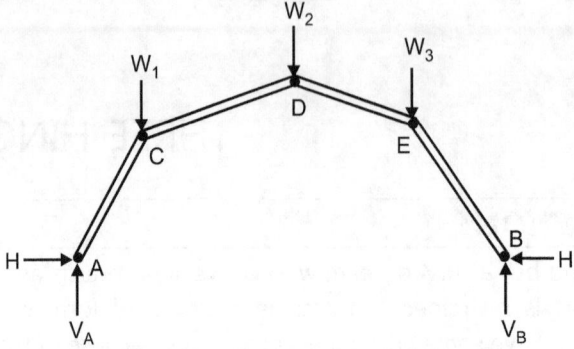

(b) Inverted linkwork as theoretical arch
Fig. 10.1

For an arch of a given shape, the theoretical or linear arch will represent the line of thrust i.e. the actual line of action of the thrust in the respective segments. Any cross-section of the actual arch is subjected to (i) a normal thrust N, (ii) a shear force V, and (iii) a bending moment M.

10.3 EDDY'S THEOREM FOR BENDING MOMENT

The theorem states that, the bending moment at any point of an arch axis is proportional to the vertical intercept between the theoretical arch and the centre line of the actual arch (i.e. arch axis).

Consider an actual arch ACB shown in Fig. 10.2. Let the dotted curve A'C'B' be the theoretical or linear arch for a uniformly distributed load. This dotted curve also represents the line along which the internal thrust acts.

Now take any point P' on the line of thrust A'C'B' and through this point P' draw a vertical line meeting the actual arch ACB at P. We know that the direction of thrust N at the point P' will be along the tangent at this point as shown in Fig. 10.2. Let the direction of the normal thrust be θ with horizontal. This thrust N can be resolved into two components at P', such that

$$N_H = N \cos \theta \text{ and } N_V = N \sin \theta$$

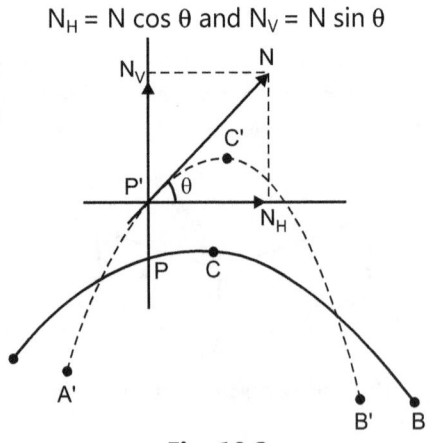

Fig. 10.2

The bending moment of this thrust at the point P on the actual arch

$$= N \cos \theta \times \text{Vertical distance PP'} + N \sin \theta \times 0$$
$$= N \cos \theta \times PP'$$

But $N \cos \theta$ represents the horizontal thrust in the arch and is constant quantity throughout its length, if there are no horizontal loads on the arch. Hence, the bending moment at P is proportional to the vertical distance PP' between the theoretical and actual arch axes.

10.4 THREE HINGED ARCH

A three hinged arch is a curved beam with both end supports hinged and a third hinge in the rib of the beam usually at the highest point i.e. crown.

Consider a three hinged arch ACB as shown in Fig. 10.3.

The supports A and B of arch are called *springings*. The curved line ACB is the axis of the arch. The highest point of the arch is known as crown. The height of the crown from the springings is known as *rise of the arch*.

For a three hinged arch, corresponding to the two hinged supports, we have in all four unknown reaction components as shown in Fig. 10.3. The usual conditions of static equilibrium are three viz. $\Sigma F_x = 0$, $\Sigma F_y = 0$ and $\Sigma M = 0$. In addition, corresponding to the third hinge in the rib, we have the condition that, bending moment at C i.e. $BM_C = 0$ and hence three hinged arch is statically determinate curved beam.

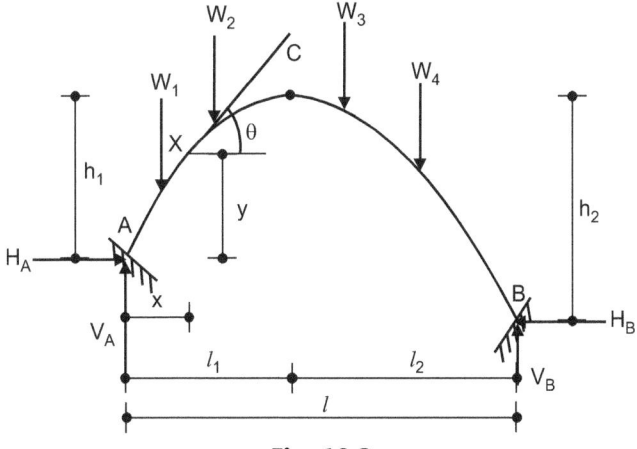

Fig. 10.3

From $\Sigma F_x = 0$, we get

$$H_A = H_B = H \quad \text{... for vertical loads}$$

$\Sigma F_y = 0$ will give $\quad V_A + V_B = \Sigma W$

$\Sigma M_B = 0$ will give

$$V_A l + H(h_2 - h_1) = M_{WB} \quad \text{... (10.1)}$$

where M_{WB} is moment of given loads about B.

Applying the fourth condition i.e. $BM_C = 0$, we get

$$V_A l_1 - H h_1 - M_{WC} = 0$$

$$\therefore \quad V_A l_1 - M_{WC} = H h_1 \qquad \ldots (10.2)$$

where M_{WC} is moment of loads on left portion about C.

Solving equations (10.1) and (10.2) for V_A and H, we get values of V_A and H and then by substituting these values in other equations, we get all the unknown reaction components. For springings at same level, we get V_A and V_B directly just like a horizontal beam of the same span l. To obtain the horizontal thrust H, we apply the condition that bending moment at hinge C = 0.

$$V_A l_1 - M_{WC} - H h = 0$$

where $h_1 = h_2 = h$ is the crown height.

$$\therefore \quad H = \frac{V_A l_1 - M_{WC}}{h}$$

Note here that the numerator is nothing but the bending moment at C for a straight horizontal beam of the same span l.

$$\therefore \quad \text{Horizontal thrust,} \quad H = \frac{\text{Bending moment at crown considering straight beam}}{\text{Rise of crown from springings}}$$

$$H = \frac{\text{Beam bending moment at C}}{\text{Rise}} \qquad \ldots (10.3)$$

At any cross-section of the arch whose co-ordinates are (x, y) [See Fig. 10.3] bending moment will be given by, $\quad BM_x = (\text{Beam bending moment})_x - H \cdot y \qquad \ldots (10.4)$

where beam bending moment is the bending moment at the section considering a straight horizontal beam of same span and loading as that for the arch and $H \cdot y$ is thrust moment.

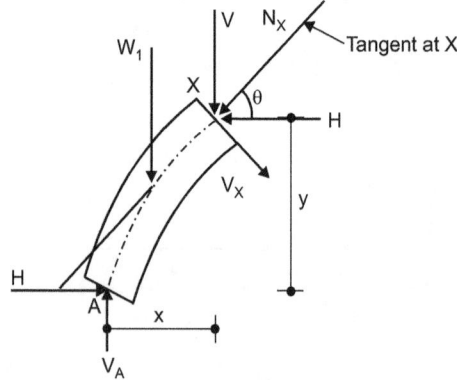

Fig. 10.4

Considering the portion AX, the vertical and horizontal actions on the section (See Fig. 10.4) are

$$V = V_A - W_1$$

i.e. the vertical shear force at the section as for a straight horizontal beam, and H = H, the horizontal thrust of the arch.

Let the tangent at X be making angle θ with horizontal.

Resolving V and H in the direction of normal to the cross-section (i.e. along tangent at X), the normal thrust at the section,

$$N_x = H \cos \theta + V \sin \theta \qquad \ldots (10.5)$$

Resolving V and H in the cross-sectional plane, the shear force at the section,

$$V_x = V \cos \theta - H \sin \theta \qquad \ldots (10.6)$$

(Downward shear on right side is taken +ve).

Thus, equations (10.4), (10.5) and (10.6) give us the straining actions at the section. The resultant thrust on the section will be,

Resultant thrust, $\qquad T_x = \sqrt{V^2 + H^2} = \sqrt{N_x^2 + V_x^2} \qquad \ldots (10.7)$

10.4.1 Three-Hinged Parabolic Arch

A three-hinged arch, whose axis is parabolic, is known as a *three-hinged parabolic arch*.

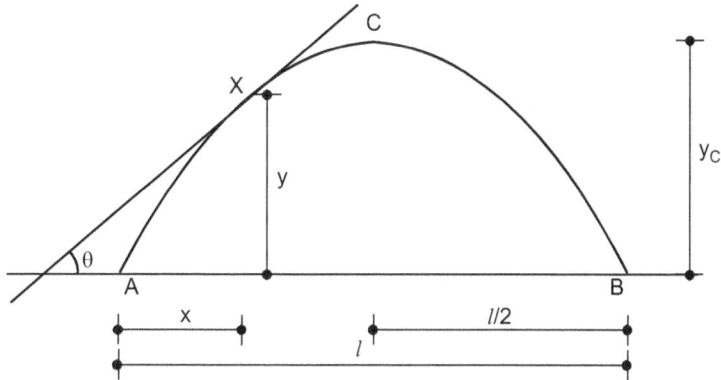

Fig. 10.5

Consider a three-hinged parabolic arch ACB, having hinges at supports A and B and at the crown C as shown in Fig. 10.5. Consider a section X whose co-ordinates are (x, y) from the origin taken at left side hinge A. With origin at A, the equation of the centre line of the parabolic arch is,

$$y = kx(l - x), \text{ where k is a constant.}$$

We have at $x = \dfrac{l}{2}$, $y = y_c$ as rise of the arch

$$\therefore \qquad y_c = k \dfrac{l}{2}\left(l - \dfrac{l}{2}\right)$$

$$\therefore \qquad k = \dfrac{4y_c}{l^2}$$

Substituting this value of k in the equation of the parabola,

$$y = \dfrac{4y_c}{l^2} x (l - x) \qquad \ldots (10.8)$$

This equation is also applicable with origin at B.

The slope of the tangent at section X, as defined by angle θ will be,

$$\left(\frac{dy}{dx}\right)_X = \frac{d}{dx}\left(\frac{4y_c}{l^2}(lx - x^2)\right)$$

∴ $$\frac{dy}{dx} = \tan\theta = \frac{4y_c}{l^2}(l - 2x) \qquad \ldots (10.9)$$

With uniformly distributed load over entire span, the beam moment diagram is a parabola. Thus, the linear arch or theoretical arch for the uniformly distributed load is parabolic. From Eddy's theorem we know that, the bending moment at a section of an arch axis is proportional to the vertical intercept between the theoretical arch and centre line of the actual arch. The actual arch being parabolic and for case of u.d.l. the theoretical arch is also a parabolic one, thus there won't be any intercept between the two. In fact, the theoretical arch and actual arch are identical. Hence, for a parabolic arch subjected to u.d.l. on entire span, there is no bending moment anywhere in the arch. And this is the ideal situation. At any section there will be thrust only.

SOLVED PROBLEMS

Problem 10.1 : A three-hinged parabolic arch of 20 m span and 3 m rise is carrying a point load of 100 kN at a section 7.5 m from the left support. Find the value of horizontal thrust and B.M. at a point 7.5 m from the right support.

Data : As shown in Fig. 10.6 (a).
Required : Horizontal thrust and B.M.
Concept : Equilibrium equations.

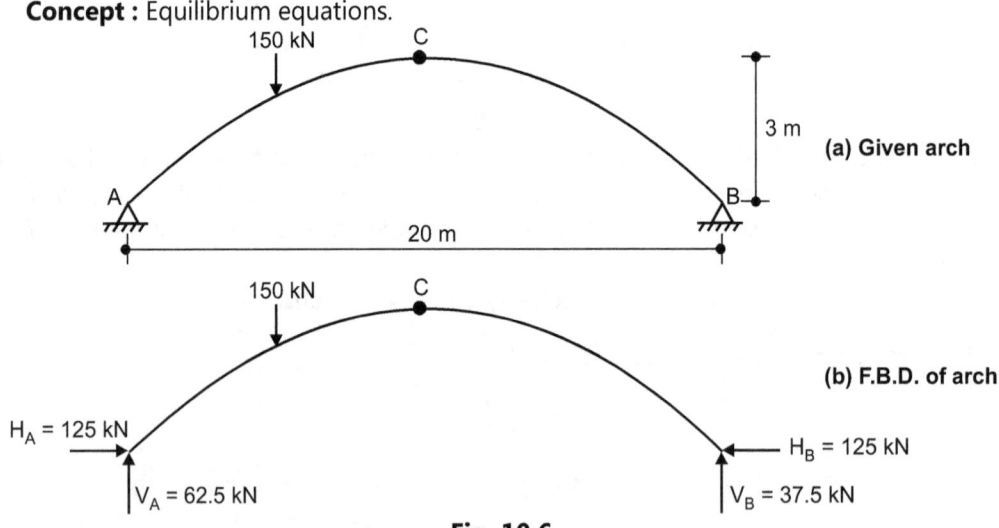

Fig. 10.6

Solution : Step I : Applying equilibrium equation of moment,
Moment @ B = 0
$-V_A \times 20 + 100 \times 13.5 = 0$
∴ $V_A = 62.5$ kN

Step II : Applying equilibrium equation in vertical direction,

$$\Sigma F_y = 0$$
$$V_A + V_B - 100 = 0$$
$$\therefore V_B = 100 - 62.5$$
$$= 37.5 \text{ kN}$$

Step III : Internal hinge is at point 'C'. Applying equilibrium equation of moment on left of hinge C,

$$H_A \times 3 - V_A \times 10 + 100 \times 2.5 = 0$$
$$H_A \times 3 - 62.5 \times 10 + 250 = 0$$
$$\therefore H_A = 125 \text{ kN}$$

Step IV : Applying equilibrium equation in horizontal direction,

$$H_A - H_D = 0$$
$$\therefore H_A = H_D = 125 \text{ kN}$$

Step V : Vertical ordinate at point E. Vertical co-ordinate at point 'E' :

$$y = \frac{4\,hx}{l^2}(l - x)$$

We have, $h = 3$ m, $x = 12.5$ m, $l = 20$ m

$$\therefore y_E = \frac{4 \times 3 \times 12.5\,(20 - 13.5)}{20^2} = 2.81 \text{ m}$$

Step VI : Bending moment at E from right support.

$$B.M._E = V_B \times 7.5 - H_B \times y_E$$
$$= 37.5 \times 7.5 - 125 \times 2.81$$
$$= -70 \text{ kN-m}$$
$$\therefore B.M._E = 70 \text{ kN-m } (\circlearrowright)$$
$$\text{Horizontal thrust} = 125 \text{ kN}$$
$$B.M. \text{ at } E = 70 \text{ kN-m}$$

Step VII : F.B.D. of arch is as shown in Fig. 10.6 (b).

Problem 10.2 : A three-hinged arch is loaded and supported as shown in Fig. 10.7 (a). Determine vertical reaction at supports and horizontal thrust.

Data : A three-hinged arch is supported and loaded as shown in Fig. 10.7 (a).

Required : Horizontal thrust.

Concept : Equilibrium equations.

Solution : Step I : Applying equilibrium equation of moment,

$$\text{Moment @ B} = 0$$
$$-V_A \times 24 + 12 \times 12 \times 18 = 0$$
$$\therefore V_A = 108 \text{ kN}$$

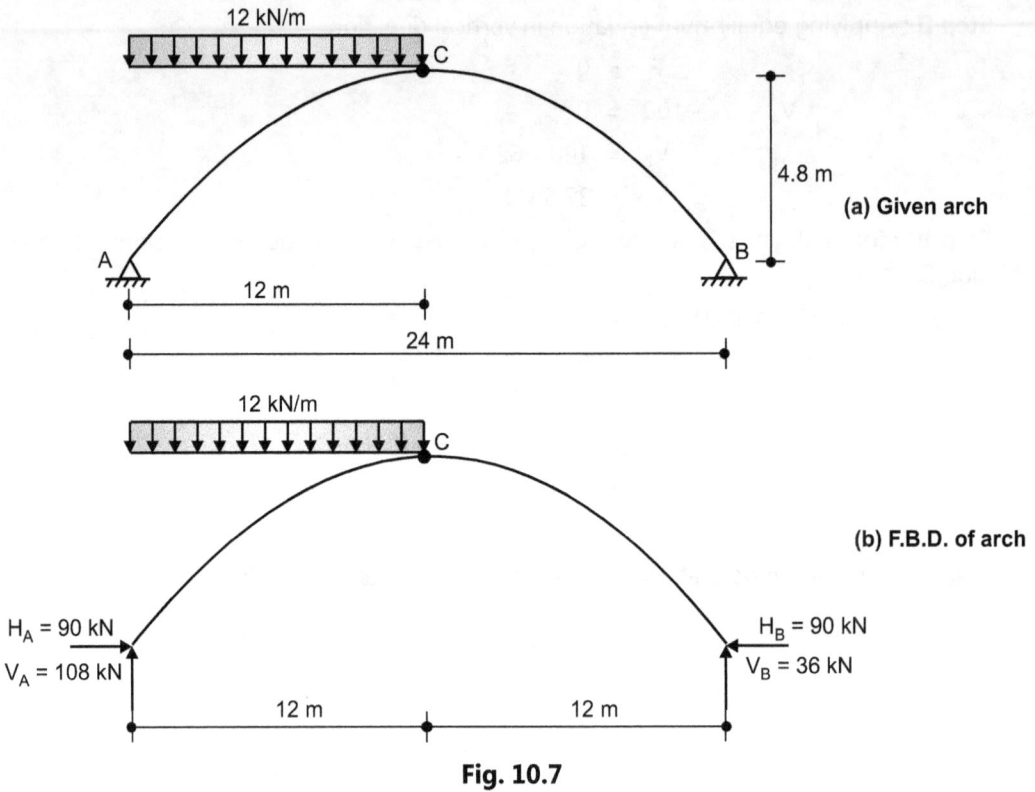

Fig. 10.7

Step II : Applying equilibrium equation of forces in vertical direction,

$$V_A + V_B - 12 \times 12 = 0$$
$$\therefore \quad V_B = 36 \text{ kN}$$

Step III : Considering portion AC and applying equation of moment at internal hinge 'C',

$$\text{Moment @ C} = 0$$
$$-V_A \times 12 + H \times 4.8 + 12 \times 12 \times 6 = 0$$
$$-108 \times 12 + H \times 4.8 + 12 \times 12 \times 6 = 0$$
$$\therefore \quad H = 90 \text{ kN}$$
$$\therefore \quad \text{Horizontal thrust} = 90 \text{ kN}$$

Step IV : F.B.D. of arch is as shown in Fig. 10.7 (b).

Problem 10.3 : A three-hinged parabolic arch is loaded and supported as shown in Fig. 10.8 (a). Determine horizontal thrust and vertical reaction at supports.

Data : As shown in Fig. 10.8 (a).

Required : Horizontal thrust.

Concept : Equilibrium equations.

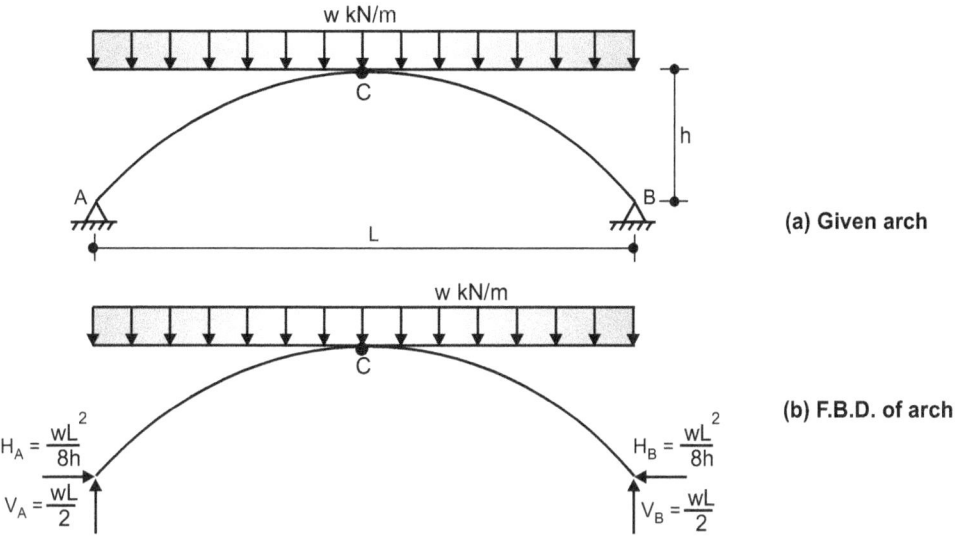

Fig. 10.8

Solution : Step I : Applying equilibrium equation of moment,

$$\text{Moment @ B} = 0$$

$$\therefore -V_A \times L - w \times L \times \frac{L}{2} = 0$$

$$\therefore V_A = \frac{wL}{2}$$

Step II : Applying equilibrium equation in vertical direction,

$$V_A + V_B - wL = 0$$

$$\therefore V_B = \frac{wL}{2}$$

Step III : Considering left part of internal hing, and applying equilibrium equation of moment @ hinge,

$$-V_A \times \frac{L}{2} + w \cdot \frac{L}{2} \cdot \frac{L}{4} + H \times h = 0$$

$$-\frac{wL}{2}\frac{L}{2} + \frac{wL^2}{8} + H \times h = 0$$

$$\therefore H = \frac{wL^2}{8h}$$

$$\therefore \text{Horizontal thrust} = \frac{wL^2}{8h}$$

Step IV : F.B.D. of arch is as shown in Fig. 10.8 (b).

Problem 10.4 : A three-hinged arch is loaded and supported as shown in Fig. 10.9 (a). Support B is at 2.5 m above support A. Determine vertical and horizontal reactions at supports.

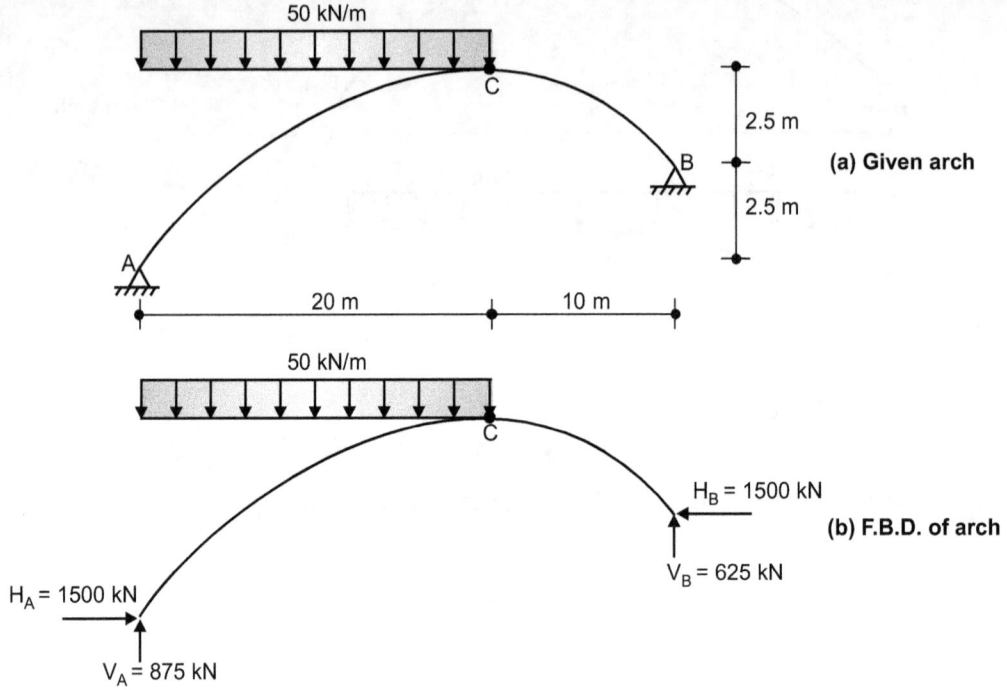

Fig. 10.9

Data : A three-hinged parabolic arch is loaded and supported as shown in Fig. 10.9 (a).
Required : Reactions at supports.
Concept : Equilibrium equations.
Solution : Step I : Applying equilibrium equation of moment on left portion of hinge at 'C',

$$\text{Moment at C} = 0$$
$$-V_A \times 20 + H_A \times 5 + 50 \times 20 \times 10 = 0$$
$$\therefore \qquad V_A = 500 + \frac{H_A}{4} \qquad \ldots (1)$$

Step II : Applying equilibrium equation of moment on right portion of hinge at 'C',

$$\text{Moment @ C} = 0$$
$$-V_B \times 10 + H_B \times 2.5 + 50 \times 10 \times 5 = 0$$
$$\therefore \qquad V_B = 250 + \frac{H_B}{4} \qquad \ldots (2)$$

Step III : Applying equilibrium equation in horizontal direction,

$$H_A - H_B = 0$$
$$\therefore \qquad H_A = H_B = H \qquad \ldots (3)$$

Step IV : Applying equilibrium equation in vertical direction,

$$V_A + V_B - 50 \times 30 = 0$$

Substituting values of V_A, V_B, H_A and H_B from equations (1), (2) and (3),

$$500 + \frac{H}{4} + 250 + \frac{H}{4} - 1500 = 0$$

$$\therefore \quad H = 1500 \text{ kN} \quad \ldots (4)$$

Substituting value of H from equation (4) into equations (1) and (2),

$$\therefore \quad V_A = 500 + \frac{H}{4} = 500 + \frac{1500}{4}$$

$$\therefore \quad V_A = 875 \text{ kN}$$

$$V_B = 250 + \frac{H}{4} = 250 + \frac{1500}{4} = 625 \text{ kN}$$

Step V : F.B.D. of arch is as shown in Fig. 10.9 (b).

Problem 10.5 : A three-hinged parabolic arch is supported and loaded as shown in Fig. 10.10 (a). Determine the reactions at support. Also determine B.M. at D.

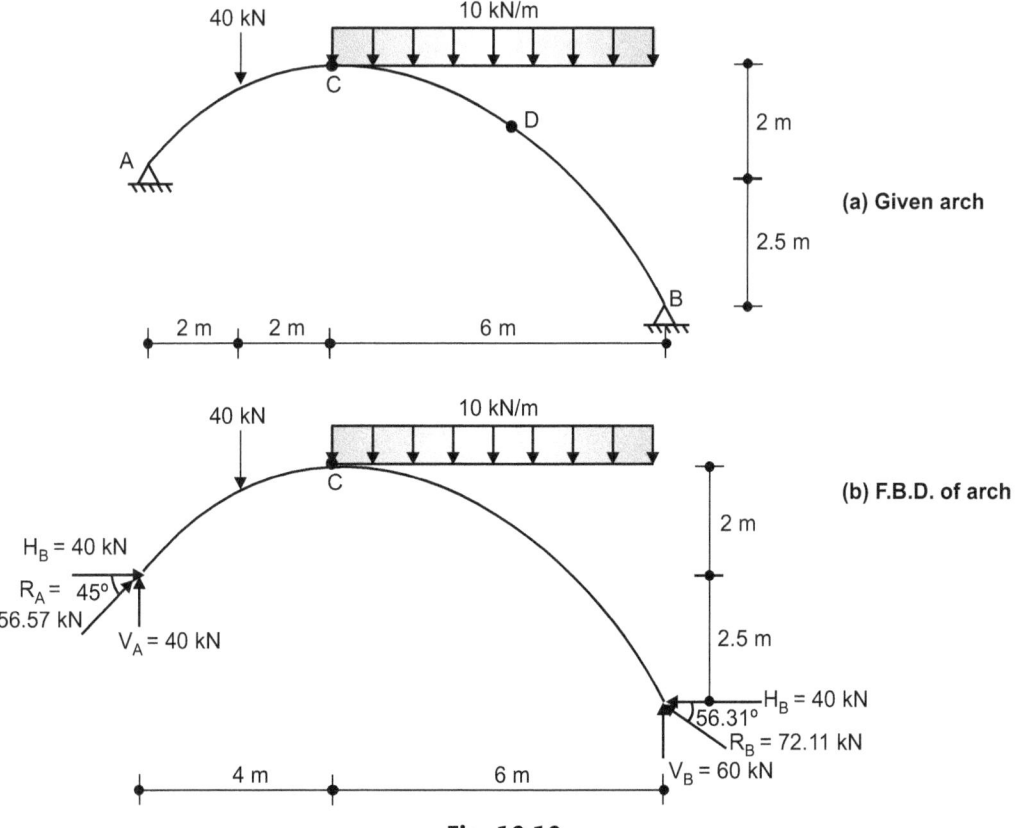

Fig. 10.10

Data : A three-hinged arch is supported and loaded as shown in Fig. 10.10 (a).

Required : Reactions at supports and B.M. at D.

Concept : Equilibrium equations.

Solution : Step I : Applying equilibrium equation of moment on left portion of hinge at 'C',

$$\text{Moment @ C} = 0$$

$$-V_A \times 4 + H_A \times 2 + 40 \times 2 = 0$$

$$\therefore \quad V_A = 20 + \frac{H_A}{2} \quad \ldots (1)$$

Step II : Applying equilibrium equation of moment on right portion of hinge at 'C',

$$V_B \times 6 - H_B \times 4.5 - 10 \times 6 \times 3 = 0$$

$$V_B = 30 + \frac{3}{4} H_B \quad \ldots (2)$$

Step III : Applying equilibrium equation of forces in horizontal direction,

$$H_A - H_B = 0$$

$$H_A = H_B = H \quad \ldots (3)$$

Step IV : Applying equilibrium equation of forces in vertical direction,

$$V_A + V_B - 40 - 10 \times 6 = 0 \quad \ldots (4)$$

Substituting values of V_A, V_B, H_A and H_B in equation (4),

$$20 + \frac{H}{2} + 30 + \frac{3}{4} H - 100 = 0$$

$$\frac{5H}{4} = 50$$

$$\therefore \quad H = 40 \text{ kN}$$

$$\therefore \quad V_A = 20 + \frac{40}{2} = 40 \text{ kN}$$

$$V_B = 30 + \frac{3H}{4} = 30 + \frac{3}{4} \times 40 = 60 \text{ kN}$$

Step V : Reaction at supports :

At support A :

$$R_A = \sqrt{V_A^2 + H^2} = \sqrt{40^2 + 40^2} = 56.57 \text{ kN}$$

$$\theta = \tan^{-1}\left|\frac{V}{H}\right| = \tan^{-1}\left|\frac{40}{40}\right| = 45°$$

At support B :

$$R_B = \sqrt{60^2 + 40^2} = 72.11 \text{ kN}$$

$$\theta = \tan^{-1}\left|\frac{60}{40}\right| = 56.31°$$

Step VI : Bending moment at D. Considering right part of point D,

Vertical ordinate at D, $y = \dfrac{4hx}{L^2}(L-x)$

Above equation is applicable for symmetrical arch. So that, we have to consider symmetrical arch, length of arch is 12 m.

$$\therefore \quad y_D = \dfrac{4 \times 4.5 \times 3}{12^2}(12-3)$$

$\therefore \quad y_D = 10.375$ m

Bending moment at D $= V_B \times 3 - H \times y_D - 10 \times 3 \times 1.5$
$= 60 \times 3 - 40 \times 3.375 - 45$
$= 0$

∴ Bending moment at D is zero.

Step VII : F.B.D. of arch is as shown in Fig. 10.10 (b).

Problem 10.6 : A three-hinged parabolic arch is loaded and supported as shown in Fig. 10.11 (a). Determine normal thrust and radial shear at 4 m from the left support.

Data : A three-hinged arch is loaded and supported as shown in Fig. 10.11 (a).

Required : Normal thrust and radial shear at 4 m from left support.

Concept : Equilibrium equations.

Solution : Step I : Applying equilibrium equation of moment,

Moment @ B $= 0$
$-V_A \times 18 + 10 \times 9 \times 13.5 = 0$

$\therefore \quad V_A = 67.5$ kN ... (i)

Step II : Applying equilibrium equation of force in vertical direction,

$\Sigma F_y = 0$
$V_A + V_B - 10 \times 9 = 0$

$\therefore \quad V_B = 22.5$ kN ... (2)

Step III : Internal hinge is at point C. Applying equilibrium equation of moment for left portion of C about point C.

$-V_A \times 9 + H_A \times 3 + 10 \times 9 \times 4.5 = 0$ ... (3)

Substituting value of V_A from equation (1) into equation (3),

$-67.5 \times 9 + 3H_A + 405 = 0$

$\therefore \quad H_A = 67.5$ kN

Step IV : Applying equilibrium equation of force in horizontal direction,

$\Sigma F_x = 0$

$\therefore \quad H_A - H_B = 0$

$\therefore \quad H_A = H_B = 67.5$ kN

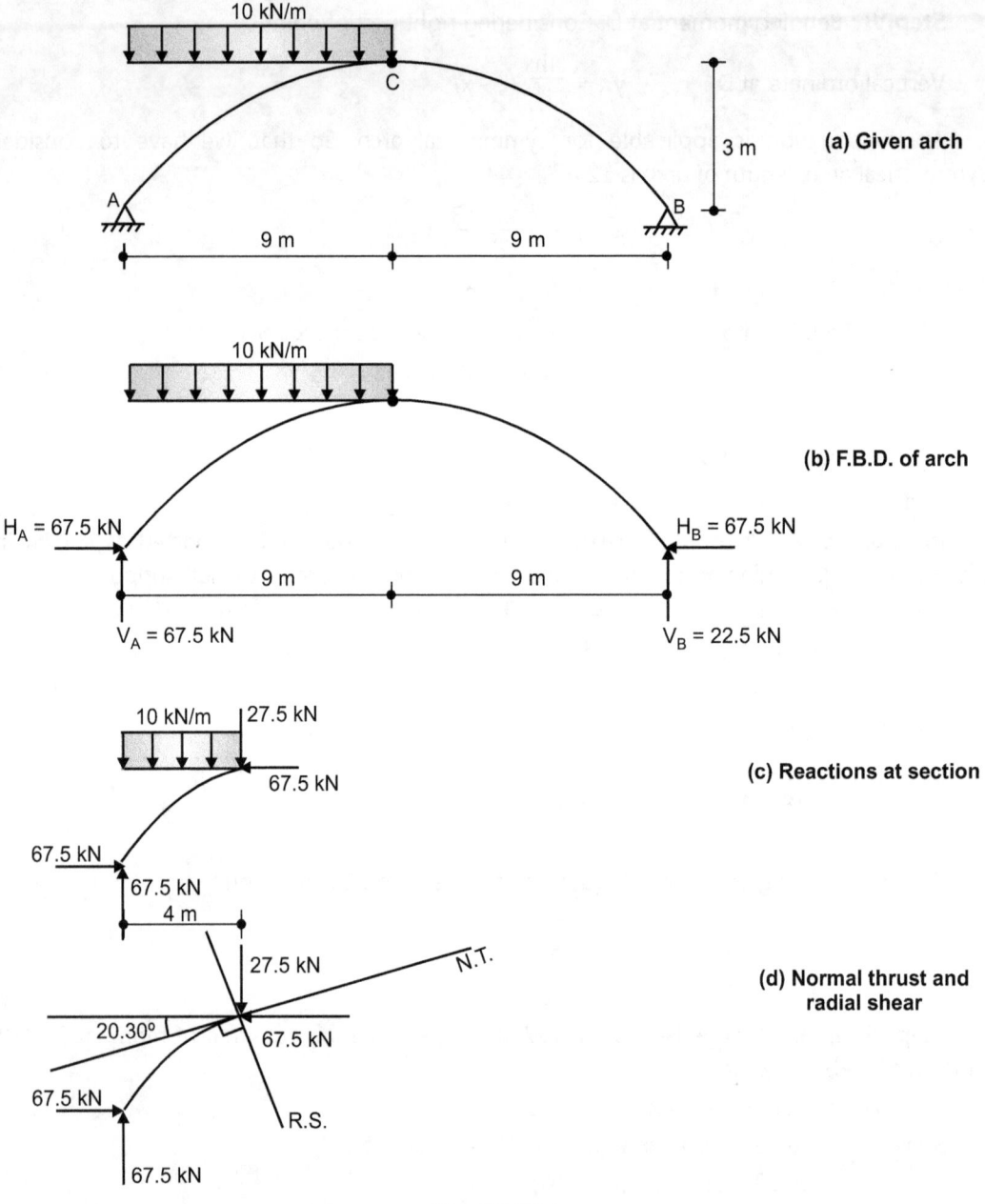

Fig. 10.11

Step V : FBD of arch is as shown in Fig. 10.11 (b).

Step VI : Normal thrust is a force acting along the tangent at the section. Radial force is the force acting perpendicular to the tangent at the section. The angle of tangent is 'θ' at the section.

We have
$$y = \frac{4hx}{L^2}(L-x)$$
$$\frac{dy}{dx} = \frac{4h}{L^2}(L-2x)$$

At x = 4 m, h = 3 m, l = 18 m

$$\tan\theta = \frac{dy}{dx} = \frac{4 \times 3}{18^2}(18 - 2 \times 4)$$

∴ $\tan\theta = 0.37$

∴ $\theta = 20.30°$

Step VII : Considering the part of arch on left of section. Applying equilibrium equation, the reactions at the section are as shown in Fig. 10.11 (c).

Step VIII : Normal thrust and radial shear are as shown in Fig. 10.11 (d).

Step IX : Resolving the forces along tangent at the section,

Normal thrust = V sin θ + H cos θ

= 27.5 sin 20.30 + 67.5 cos 20.30

= 72.84 kN (20.30°)

Step X : Resolving the forces perpendicular to the tangent at the section,

Radial shear = V cos θ – H sin θ

= 27.5 cos 20.30 – 67.5 sin 20.30

= – 2.37 kN

= 2.37 kN (69.70°)

Problem 10.7 : A three-hinged parabolic arch of 20 m span and 4 m central rise, carries a point load of 150 kN at 4 m from left support. Calculate the normal thrust and radial shear under the load. Calculate the maximum positive and negative bending moment.

Data : As shown in Fig. 10.12 (a).

Required : Normal thrust, shear force, positive and negative B.M.

Concept : Equilibrium equations.

Solution : Step I : Applying equilibrium equation of moment,

Moment @ B = 0

$-V_A \times 20 + 150 \times 16 = 0$

∴ $V_A = 120$ kN

Step II : Applying equilibrium equation in vertical direction,

$\Sigma F_y = 0$

$V_A + V_B - 150 = 0$

∴ $V_B = 30$ kN

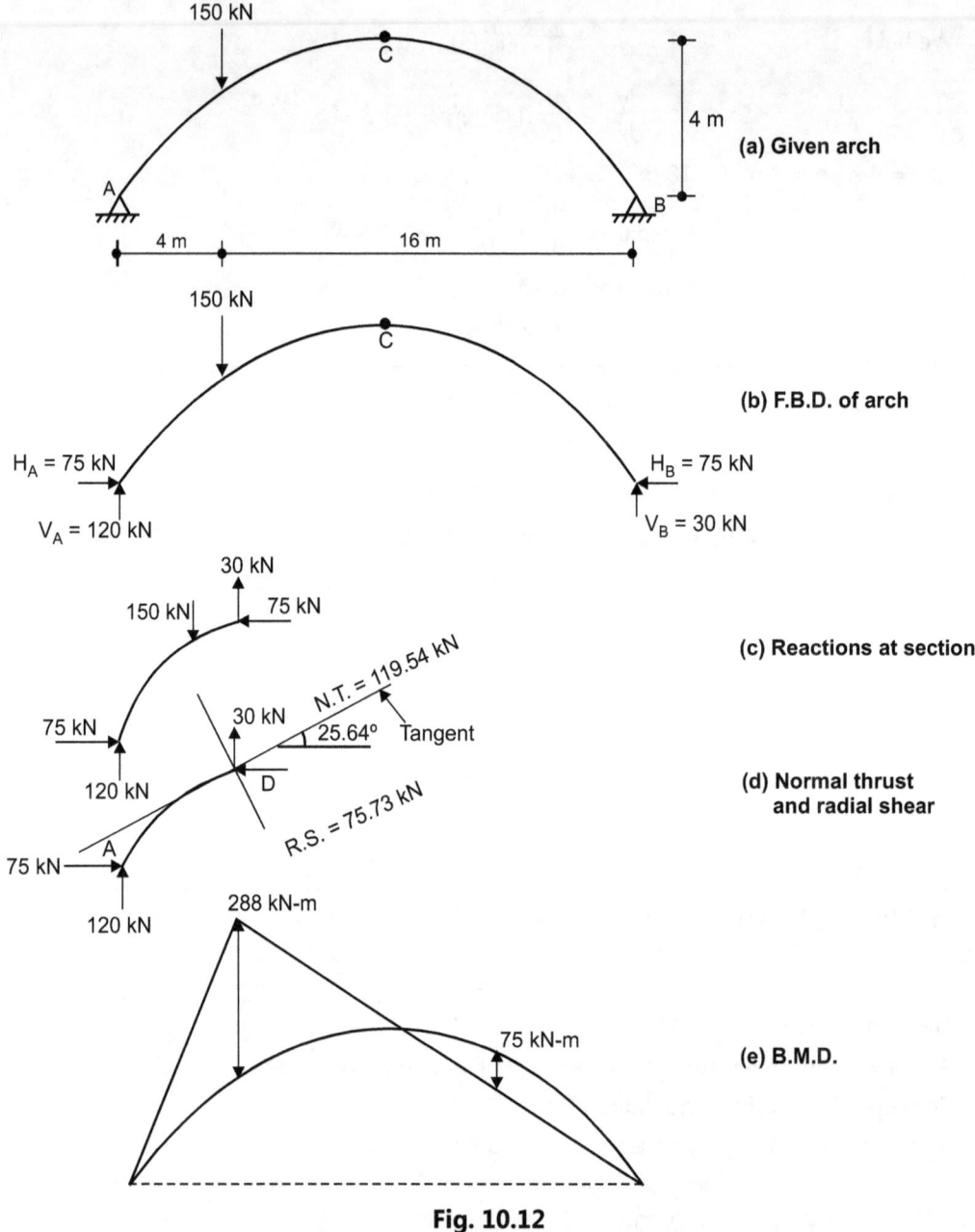

Fig. 10.12

Step III : Internal hinge is at point C. Applying equilibrium equation of moment on left part of hinge C,

$$-V_A \times 10 + H_A \times 4 + 150 \times 6 = 0$$

$$\therefore \quad H_A = 75 \text{ kN}$$

Step IV : Applying equilibrium equation in horizontal direction,

$$\Sigma F_x = 0$$
$$H_A - H_D = 0$$
$$\therefore \quad H_A = H_D = 75 \text{ kN}$$

Step V : F.B.D. of arch is as shown in Fig. 10.12 (b).

Step VI : Normal thrust is a force acting along the tangent at the section. Radial shear force is the force acting perpendicular to the tangent at that section. The angle of tangent is 'θ' at the section.

We have,
$$y = \frac{4hx}{l^2}(l-x)$$

$$\frac{dy}{dx} = \frac{4h}{l^2}(l-2x)$$

At x = 4 m, h = 4 m, l = 20 m.

$$\therefore \quad \tan\theta = \frac{dy}{dx} = \frac{4 \times 4}{20^2}(20 - 2 \times 4)$$

$$\therefore \quad \tan\theta = 0.48$$
$$\therefore \quad \theta = 25.64°$$

Step VII : Considering the part of arch on left of section. Applying equilibrium equation, the reactions at the section are as shown in Fig. 10.12 (c).

Step VIII : Normal thrust and radial shear is as shown in Fig. 10.12 (d).

Step IX : Resolving the forces along normal at the section,

$$\therefore \quad \text{Normal thrust} = V \sin\theta + H \cos\theta$$
$$= 120 \sin 25.64 + 75 \cos 25.64$$
$$= 119.54 \text{ kN}$$

Step X : Resolving the forces perpendicular to the tangent at the section,

$$\therefore \quad \text{Radial shear} = V \cos\theta - H \sin\theta$$
$$= 120 \cos 25.64 - 75 \sin 25.64$$
$$= 75.73 \text{ kN}$$

Step XI : Maximum positive B.M.

Maximum positive B.M. occurs under the load.

$$\therefore \quad \text{Maximum positive B.M.} = V_A \times 4 - H \times y_D$$

Vertical ordinate at D.

$$y_D = \frac{4hx}{l^2}(l-x) = \frac{4 \times 4 \times 4}{20^2}(20-4)$$
$$= 2.56 \text{ m}$$

$$\therefore \quad \text{Maximum positive B.M.} = 120 \times 4 - 75 \times 2.56 = 288 \text{ kN-m}$$

Step XII : Maximum negative B.M.

Maximum negative B.M. occurs in right part of internal hinge i.e. between C to B.

Maximum negative moment = $V_B \times x - H \times y$

$$M = 30 \times x - 75 \times \frac{4 \times h \times x}{l^2}(l-x)$$

For maximum B.M. take derivative w.r.t. x and equal to zero.

$$\therefore \quad \frac{dM}{dx} = 30 - \frac{300 \times 4}{20^2}(20 - 2x)$$

$$0 = 30 - 3(20 - 2x)$$

$$0 = 30 - 60 + 6x$$

$$\therefore \quad x = 5 \text{ m}$$

∴ Maximum negative B.M. occurs at 5 m from right support.

Vertical ordinate at 5 m from right.

$$y_E = \frac{4hx}{l^2}(l-x)$$

$$= \frac{4 \times 4 \times 5}{20^2}(20 - 5) = 3 \text{ m}$$

∴ Maximum negative B.M. = $30 \times 5 - 75 \times 3$

$$= -75 \text{ kN-m}$$

Bending moment diagram is as shown in Fig. 10.12 (e).

Problem 10.8 : A three-hinged parabolic arch has a span of 40 m and a central rise of 8 m. Five wheel loads of 4 kN, 4 kN, 6 kN, 6 kN and 5 kN spaced 2 m, 3 m, 2 m and 3 m in order, cross the arch from left to right, with 4 kN load leading. When leading load is 25 m from left support, determine

(a) Horizontal thrust.

(b) Bending moment, normal thrust and radial shear under the tail load.

Data : The position of load system and arch is as shown in Fig. 10.13 (a).

Required : Horizontal thrust, bending moment, normal thrust and radial shear.

Concept : Equilibrium equations.

Solution : Step I : Applying equilibrium equation of moment,

Moment @ B = 0

$-V_A \times 40 + 4 \times 15 + 4 \times 17 + 6 \times 20 + 6 \times 22 + 5 \times 25 = 0$

$$\therefore \quad V_A = 12.63 \text{ kN}$$

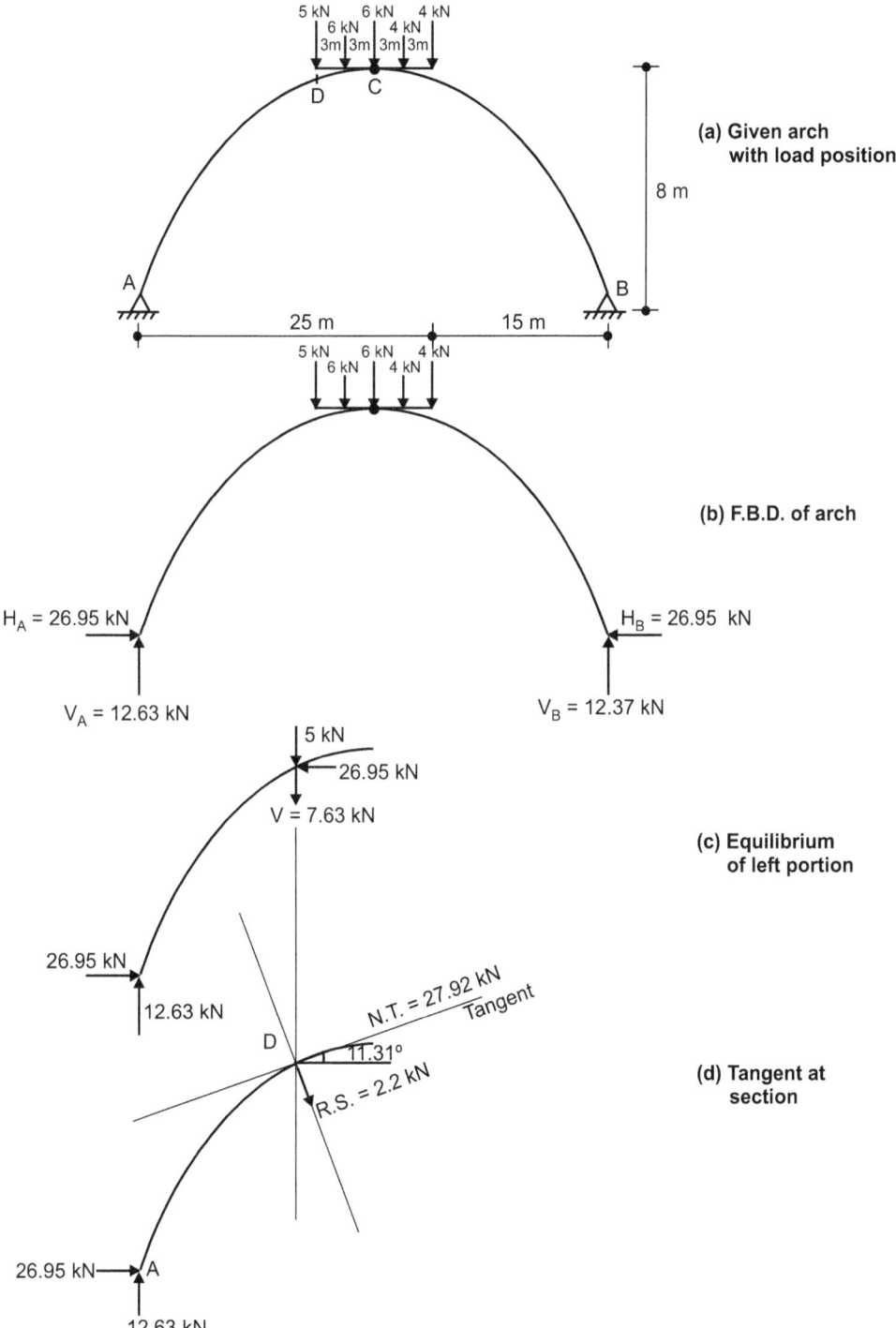

Fig. 10.13

Step II : Applying equilibrium equation of forces in vertical direction,

$$\therefore \quad V_A + V_B - 5 - 6 - 6 - 4 - 4 = 0$$

$$\therefore \quad V_B = 12.37 \text{ kN}$$

Step III : Internal hinge is at 'C'. Applying equilibrium equation of moment of left portion of C about 'C',

$$-V_A \times 20 + H_A \times 8 + 5 \times 5 + 6 \times 2 = 0$$

$$\therefore \quad -12.63 \times 20 + 8 H_A + 25 + 12 = 0$$

$$\therefore \quad H_A = 26.95 \text{ kN}$$

Step IV : Applying equilibrium equation of forces in horizontal direction,

$$\Sigma F_x = 0$$

$$H_A - H_B = 0$$

$$\therefore \quad H_A = H_B = 26.95 \text{ kN}$$

Step V : B.M. at tail end (15 m from LHS).
Vertical ordinate at 15 m.

$$y = \frac{4hx}{l^2}(l-x)$$

$$y = \frac{4 \times 8 \times 15}{40^2}(40-15)$$

$$= 7.5 \text{ m}$$

$$\therefore \quad \text{B.M.} = -V_A \times 15 + H \times 7.5$$

$$= -12.63 \times 15 + 26.95 \times 7.5$$

$$= 12.68 \text{ kN-m } (\circlearrowleft)$$

Step VI : F.B.D. of arch is as shown in Fig. 10.13 (b).

Step VII : Normal thrust is a force acting along tangent at the section. Radial shear is a force acting perpendicular to tangent at that section. The angle of tangent is 'θ' at the section.

$$y = \frac{4hx}{l^2}(1-x)$$

$$\frac{dy}{dx} = \tan\theta = \frac{4h}{l^2}(l-2x)$$

$$\tan\theta = \frac{4 \times 8}{40^2}(40 - 2 \times 15)$$

$$\tan\theta = 0.2$$

$$\therefore \quad \theta = 11.31°$$

Step VIII : Considering part of arch on left of section.
Applying equilibrium equation, the reactions at section are as shown in Fig. 10.13 (c).

Step IX : Normal thrust and radial shear is as shown in Fig. 10.13 (d).

Step X : Resolving forces along tangent.

$$\text{Normal thrust} = V \sin \theta + H \cos \theta$$
$$= 7.63 \sin 11.31 + 26.95 \cos 11.31$$
$$= 27.92 \text{ kN } (\overset{11.31°}{\nearrow})$$

Step XI : Resolving force perpendicular to tangent,

$$\text{Radial shear} = -V \cos \theta + H \sin \theta$$
$$= -7.63 \cos 11.31 + 26.95 \sin 11.31$$
$$= -2.2 \text{ kN}$$
$$= 2.2 \text{ kN } (\overset{78.69°}{\searrow})$$

Problem 10.9 : A three-hinged parabolic arch is loaded and supported as shown in Fig. 10.14 (a). Determine :

(a) Reactions at supports.

(b) Bending moment, normal thrust and radial shear at a distance of 15 m from LHS.

Data : As shown in Fig. 10.14 (a).

Required : Reactions, B.M., normal thrust and radial shear.

Concept : Equilibrium equations.

Solution : Step I : By using property of parabolic arch, l_1 and l_2 is calculated.

$$\therefore \quad \frac{l_1}{\sqrt{h_1}} = \frac{l_2}{\sqrt{h_2}}$$

$l_1 = x$ m, $\therefore l_2 = (30 - x)$ m, $h_1 = 6$ m, $h_2 = 1.5$ m.

$$\therefore \quad \frac{x}{\sqrt{6}} = \frac{30 - x}{\sqrt{1.5}}$$

$$\therefore \quad 1.22 \, x = 2.45 \, (30 - x)$$
$$\therefore \quad x = 20.0 \text{ m}$$
$$\therefore \quad l_2 = 20 \text{ m and } l_2 = 10 \text{ m}$$

Step II : Applying equilibrium equation of moment of left portion of hinge about hinge at 'C',

$$-V_A \times 20 + H_A \times 6 + 20 \times 10 = 0$$

$$\therefore \quad V_A = 10 + \frac{3}{10} H_A \quad \ldots (1)$$

Step III : Applying equilibrium equation of moment of right portion of hinge about hinge at 'C',

$$V_B \times 10 - H_B \times 1.5 = 0$$

$$\therefore \quad V_B = \frac{3}{20} H_B \quad \ldots (2)$$

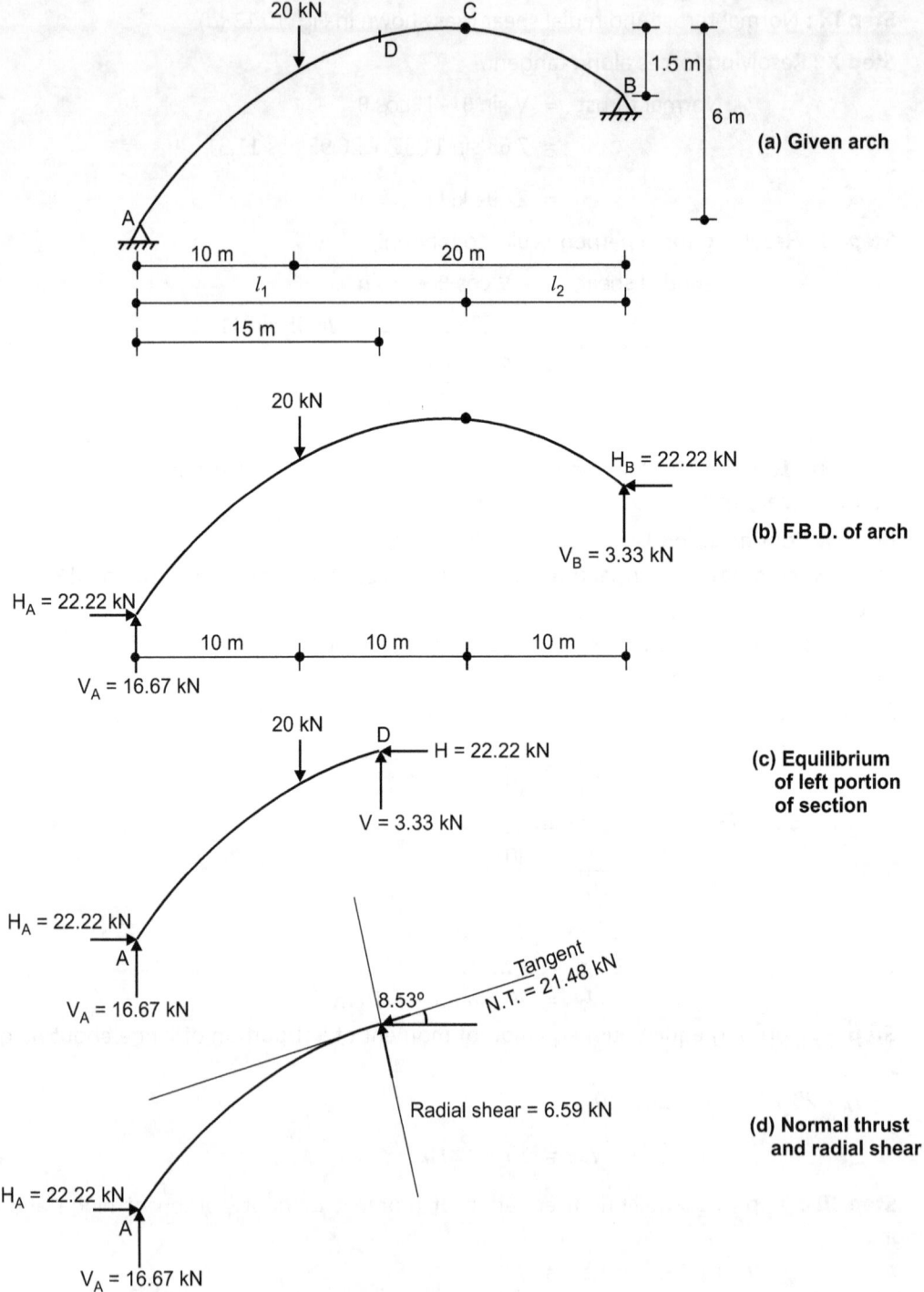

Fig. 10.14

Step IV : Applying equilibrium equation of forces in horizontal direction,

$$\Sigma F_x = 0$$
$$H_A - H_B = 0$$
$$\therefore \quad H_A = H_B = H \quad \ldots (3)$$

Step V : Applying equilibrium equation of forces in vertical direction,

$$\Sigma F_y = 0$$
$$V_A + V_B - 20 = 0 \quad \ldots (4)$$

Substituting values of V_A, V_B, H_A and H_B from equations (1), (2) and (3),

$$10 + \frac{3}{10}H + \frac{3}{20}H - 20 = 0$$

$$\frac{9}{20}H = 10$$

$$\therefore \quad H = 22.22 \text{ kN}$$

$$V_A = 10 + \frac{3}{10}H$$
$$= 10 + \frac{3}{10} \times 22.22 = 16.67 \text{ kN}$$

$$V_B = \frac{3}{20}H = \frac{3}{20} \times 22.22 = 3.33 \text{ kN}$$

Step VI : F.B.D. of arch is as shown in Fig. 10.14 (b).

Step VII : B.M. at 15 m from LHS : Vertical ordinate at 15 m from LHS.

$$\therefore \quad y = \frac{4hx}{L^2}(L - x)$$

To determine the vertical ordinate, we have to consider symmetrical arch, so that length of arch is considered as 40 m.

$$\therefore \quad y_D = \frac{4 \times 6 \times 15}{40^2}(40 - 15) = 5.625 \text{ m}$$

$$\therefore \quad \text{B.M.} = -V_A \times 15 + 20 \times 5 + H \times 5.625$$
$$= -16.67 \times 15 + 100 + 22.22 \times 5.625$$
$$= -25.06 \text{ kN-m}$$
$$= 25.06 \text{ kN-m } (\cup)$$

Step VIII : Normal thrust is a force acting along the tangent at the section. Radial shear is a force acting perpendicular to the tangent at that section. The angle of tangent is 'θ' at the section.

$$y = \frac{4hx}{L^2}(L - x)$$

$$\frac{dy}{dx} = \frac{4h}{L^2}(L - 2x)$$

$$\frac{dy}{dx} = \tan\theta = \frac{4 \times 6}{40^2}(40 - 2 \times 15)$$

$$\tan\theta = 0.15$$

$$\therefore \quad \theta = 8.53°$$

Step IX : Considering the part of arch on left of section. Applying equilibrium equations, the reactions at the section are as shown in Fig. 10.14 (c).

Step X : Normal thrust and radial shear is as shown in Fig. 10.14 (d).

Step XI : Resolving the forces along the tangent at the section,

$$\therefore \quad \text{Normal thrust} = -V \sin\theta + H \cos\theta$$

$$= -3.33 \sin 8.53 + 22.22 \cos 8.53$$

$$= 21.48 \text{ kN } (\overset{8.53°}{\searrow})$$

Step XII : Resolving the forces perpendicular to the tangent at the section,

$$\text{Radial shear} = V \cos\theta + H \sin\theta$$

$$= 3.33 \cos 8.53 + 22.22 \sin 8.53$$

$$= 6.59 \text{ kN } (\overset{81.47°}{\nearrow})$$

Problem 10.10 : A three-hinged semicircular arch has span 20 m and 5 m central rise. It carries a concentrated load of 150 kN at 5 m from left hand support. Determine :

(a) Horizontal thrust,

(b) Vertical reactions,

(c) Bending moment under the load.

Data : As shown in Fig. 10.15 (a).

Required : Horizontal thrust, vertical reactions, maximum bending moment.

Concept : Equilibrium equations.

Solution : Step I : Applying equilibrium equation of moment,

$$\text{Moment @ B} = 0$$

$$\therefore \quad V_A \times 20 + 150 \times 15 = 0$$

$$\therefore \quad V_A = 112.5 \text{ kN}$$

Setp II : Applying equilibrium equation of forces in vertical direction,

$$\Sigma F_y = 0$$

$$V_A + V_B - 150 = 0$$

$$\therefore \quad V_B = 37.5 \text{ kN}$$

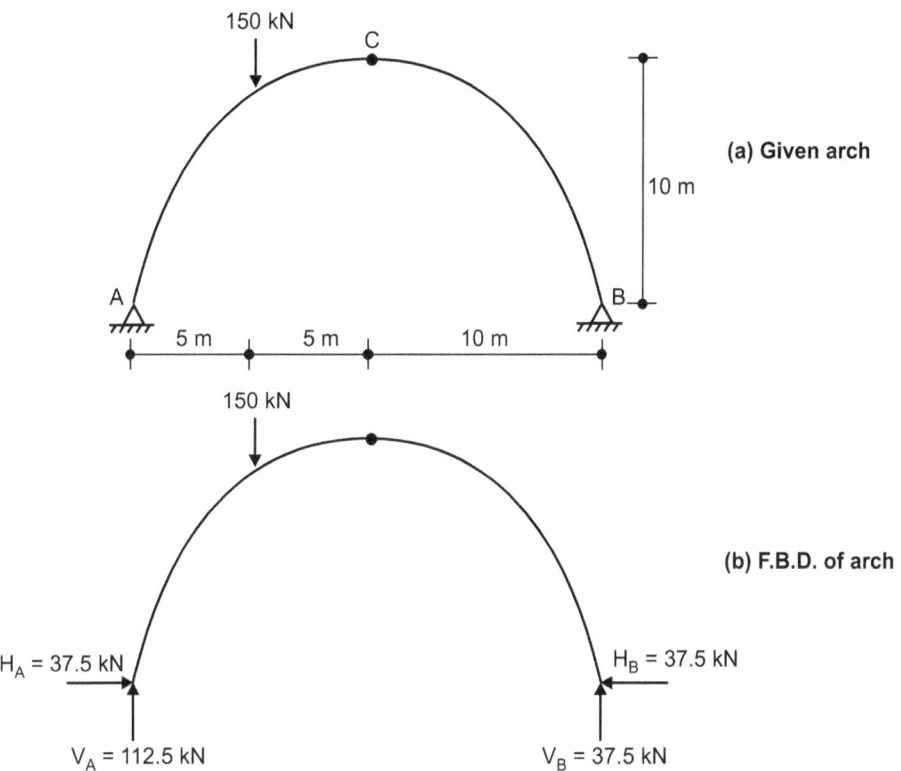

Fig. 10.15

Step III : Internal hinge is at point 'C'. Consider left portion of hinge 'C' and applying equilibrium equation of moment at C,

$$\text{Moment @ C} = 0$$
$$-V_A \times 10 + 150 \times 5 + H_A \times 10 = 0$$
$$\therefore \quad H_A = 37.5 \text{ kN}$$

Step IV : Applying equilibrium equation of force in horizontal direction,

$$H_A - H_B = 0$$
$$\therefore \quad H_A = H_B = 37.5 \text{ kN}$$

Step V : Maximum positive B.M. occurs under the load.
Vertical ordinate under the load,

$$y = \sqrt{R^2 - x^2}$$
$$y = \sqrt{10^2 - 5^2}$$
$$y = 8.66 \text{ m}$$

$$\therefore \quad \text{B.M.} = V_A \times 5 - H \times 8.66 = 112.5 \times 5 - 37.5 \times 8.66$$
$$= 237.75 \text{ kN-m}$$

Step VI : F.B.D. of arch is as shown in Fig. 10.15 (b).

Problem 10.11 : A three-hinged semicircular arch of radius R carries a uniformly distributed load of w per unit run over the whole span. Determine horizontal thrust and maximum bending moment for the arch.

Data : As shown in Fig. 10.16 (a).

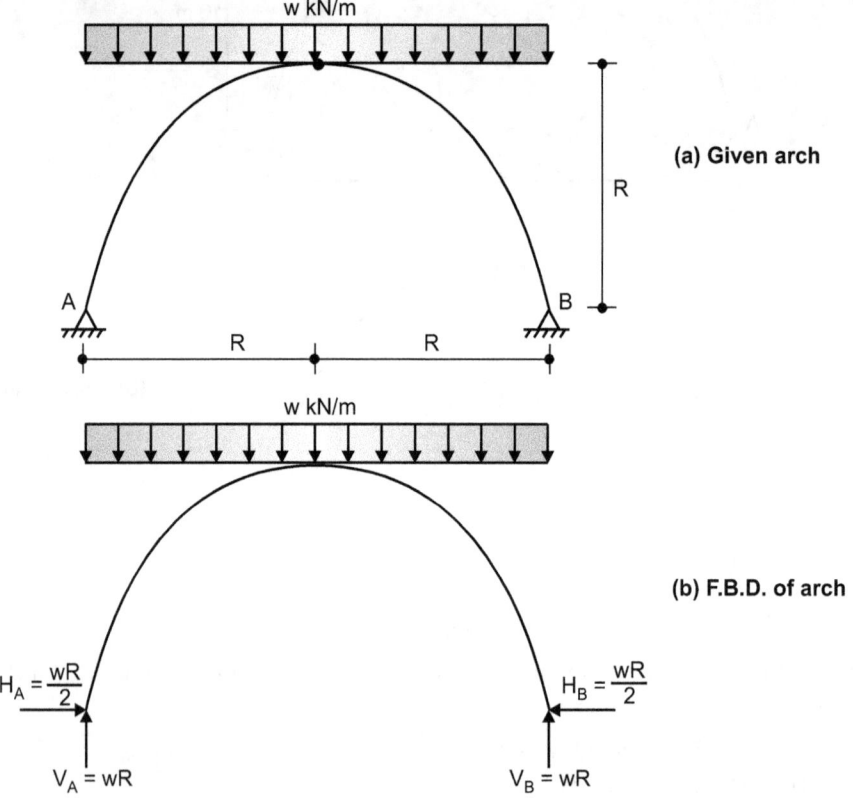

(a) Given arch

(b) F.B.D. of arch

Fig. 10.16

Required : Horizontal thrust and maximum bending moment.

Concept : Equilibrium equations.

Solution : Step I : Applying equilibrium equation of moment,

$$\text{Moment @ B} = 0$$
$$-V_A \times 2R + w\,2R \cdot R = 0$$
$$\therefore \quad V_A = wR$$

Step II : Applying equilibrium equation of forces in vertical direction,

$$\Sigma F_y = 0$$
$$V_A + V_B - w\,2R = 0$$
$$\therefore \quad V_B = wR$$

Step III : Internal hinge is at point 'C', considering left portion of hinge and applying equilibrium equation of moment about 'C',

$$\text{Moment @ C} = 0$$

$$-V_A \times R + H_A \times R + w \cdot R \frac{R}{2} = 0$$

$$\therefore \quad H_A = \frac{wR}{2}$$

Step IV : Applying equilibrium equation of forces in horizontal direction,

$$\Sigma F_x = 0$$
$$H_A - H_B = 0$$
$$\therefore \quad H_A = H_B = \frac{wR}{2}$$

Step V : Bending moment at any section x. (Refer Fig. 10.16).

$$M_x = -w \cdot R \cdot x + \frac{wx^2}{2} + H \cdot y$$

$$= -w \cdot R \cdot R(1-\cos\theta) + \frac{wR}{2}(1-\cos\theta) \cdot R(1-\cos\theta) + \frac{wR}{2} \cdot R\sin\theta$$

$$= -wR^2(1-\cos\theta) + \frac{wR^2}{2}(1-\cos\theta)^2 + \frac{wR^2}{2}\sin\theta$$

$$M_x = -\frac{wR^2}{2}(1-\cos\theta)[2-(1-\cos\theta)] + \frac{wR^2}{2}\sin\theta$$

$$= -\frac{wR^2}{2}(1-\cos\theta)(1+\cos\theta) + \frac{wR^2}{2}\sin\theta$$

$$= -\frac{wR^2}{2}(1-\cos^2\theta) + \frac{wR^2}{2}\sin\theta$$

$$= -\frac{wR^2}{2}\sin^2\theta + \frac{wR^2}{2}\sin\theta$$

$$= \frac{wR^2}{2}[\sin\theta - \sin^2\theta] \qquad \ldots (1)$$

$\sin\theta$ being greater than $\sin^2\theta$ the bending moment at any section is hogging B.M. i.e. positive B.M.

$$\frac{dM_x}{dx} = 0 = \frac{wR^2}{2}[\cos\theta - 2\sin\theta\cos\theta]$$

$$\cos\theta(1-\sin\theta) = 0$$

$$\therefore \quad \cos\theta = 0 \text{ or } (1-2\sin\theta) = 0$$

$$\therefore \quad \theta = 90° \text{ or } \sin\theta = \frac{1}{2} \therefore \theta = 30°$$

Bending moment at θ = 90° is zero at crown, so that maximum B.M. occurs at θ = 30°.

Substituting θ = 30° in equation (1),

∴ Maximum B.M. $= \dfrac{wR^2}{2}(\sin 30 - \sin^2 30)$

$= \dfrac{wR^2}{8}$

Distance of point of maximum B.M.

$= R \cos 30$

$= 0.87 R$ from left and right support

Step VI : F.B.D. of arch is as shown in Fig. 10.16 (b).

EXERCISE

1. Derive the expression for horizontal thrust when half the span of the three-hinged arch is loaded with UDL of intensity w/m run and span of the arch is L.
2. Find the reactions for the three-hinged arch when it is loaded as shown in Fig. 10.17.

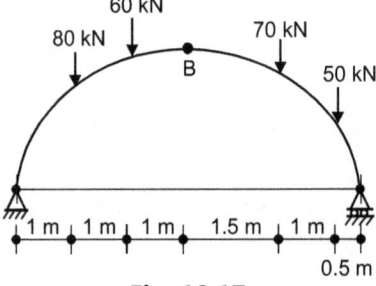

Fig. 10.17

Chapter 11
TWO-HINGED ARCHES

11.1 INTRODUCTION

Two-hinged arch is the arch consisting of two-hinges at the supports only. As there are two supports, there is only one segment BCD as an arch between these supports.

As there are four unknown reactions and only three equilibrium equations, so the structure is indeterminate structure. So equilibrium condition has to be used.

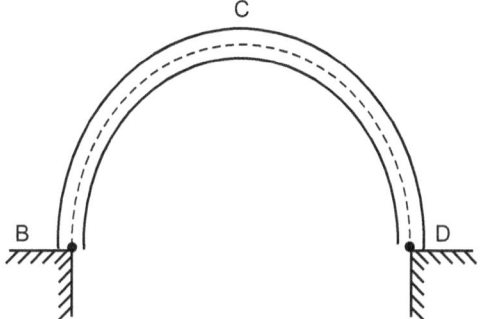

Fig. 11.1 : Given structure

11.2 DERIVATION FOR HORIZONTAL THRUST

Consider the displacement of one hinge with the other hinge as zero, so by applying this condition we can easily find the horizontal thrust.

$$B.M._x = (\text{Beam moment} - H_B \times y)$$
$$M_x = (M - H_B \times y)$$

∴ Total strain energy stored, $S_i = \int \dfrac{M_x^2}{2EI} ds$

By Castigliano's second theorem,

$$\dfrac{\partial S_i}{\partial H_B} = \text{Displacement} = 0 = \dfrac{\partial}{\partial H} \int \dfrac{(M - H_B \times y)^2}{2EI} ds$$

$$= \int \dfrac{2(M - H_B \times y)}{2EI} y \, ds$$

$$0 = \int \dfrac{(M - H_B \times y)}{EI} y \, ds$$

$$H_B = H_D = H$$

$$0 = \int \dfrac{My \, ds}{EI} - \int \dfrac{H \times y^2 \, ds}{EI}$$

(11.1)

$$\therefore \quad H = \int \frac{My\,ds}{EI} \bigg/ \int \frac{y^2\,ds}{EI}$$

If flexural rigidity of the member EI is constant, then,

$$H = \frac{\int My\,ds}{\int y^2\,ds}$$

11.3 HORIZONTAL THRUST FOR CONCENTRATED LOAD AT CROWN

A two-hinged parabolic arch ACB loaded with a concentrated load W at the crown is shown in Fig. 11.2 (a). F.B.D. of arch is as shown in Fig. 11.2 (b)

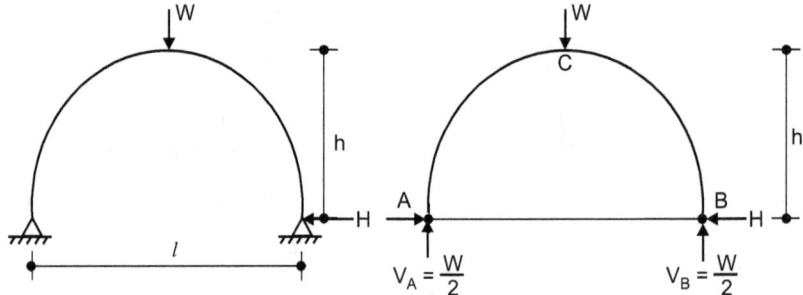

Fig. 11.2

Equation for horizontal thrust for general loading is as follows :

$$H = \frac{\int My\,dx}{\int y^2\,dx}$$

$\int My\,dx:\quad M = \dfrac{W}{2}x$

$\qquad\qquad y = \dfrac{4hx}{l^2}(l-x)$

$$\therefore \quad \int My\,dx = 2\int_0^{l/2} \frac{W}{2} x \times \frac{4hx}{l^2}(l-x)\,dx$$

$$= \frac{4wh}{l^2} \int_0^{l/2} (x^2 l - x^3)\,dx = \frac{4wh}{l^2}\left[\frac{x^3 l}{3} - \frac{x^4}{4}\right]_0^{l/2}$$

$$= \frac{4wh}{l^2}\left[\frac{l^4}{24} - \frac{l^4}{64}\right] = \frac{4wh}{l^2}\left[\frac{5\,l^4}{64 \times 3}\right] = \frac{5}{48} wh\,l^2$$

$$\int y^2\, dx = \int_0^l \left[\frac{4hx}{l^2}(l-x)\right]^2 dx = \int_0^l \frac{16\,h^2 x^2}{l^4}(l-x)^2\, dx$$

$$= \frac{16\,h^2}{l^4} \int_0^l \left[x^2(l^2 - 2lx + x^2)\right] dx$$

$$= \frac{16\,h^2}{l^4}\left[\frac{x^3 l^2}{3} - \frac{2lx^4}{4} + \frac{x^5}{5}\right]_0^l = \frac{16\,h^2}{l^4}\left[\frac{l^5}{3} - \frac{l^5}{2} + \frac{l^5}{5}\right]$$

$$= \frac{16\,h^2}{l^4}\left[\frac{10\,l^5 - 15\,l^5 + 6\,l^5}{30}\right] = \frac{16\,h^2}{l^4}\left[\frac{l^5}{30}\right] = \frac{8\,h^2 l}{15}$$

$$\therefore \quad H = \frac{\int My\, dx}{\int y^2\, dx} = \frac{\dfrac{5}{48} wl^2 h}{\dfrac{8\,h^2 l}{15}}$$

$$= \frac{15 \times 5\, wl}{8 \times 48 \times h} = \frac{25\, wl}{128\, h}$$

$$\therefore \quad H = \frac{25}{128}\frac{wl}{h}$$

11.4 TWO-HINGED PARABOLIC ARCH SUBJECTED TO ANY GENERAL SYSTEM OF LOADS

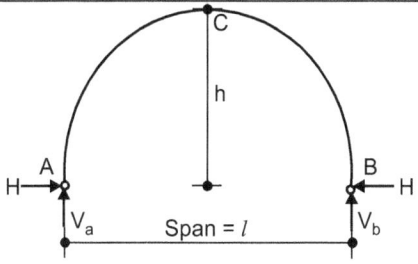

Fig. 11.3

The horizontal thrust is given by

$$H = \frac{\int \dfrac{My\, ds}{EI}}{\int \dfrac{y^2\, ds}{EI}}$$

If the flexural rigidity of the member is same, then the equation becomes

$$H = \frac{\int My \, ds}{\int y^2 \, ds}$$

where,
M is the free bending moment at any section ignoring the moment due to horizontal thrust.

$$y = \frac{4hx}{l^2}(l-x)$$

$$ds^2 = dy^2 + dx^2$$

$$\therefore \quad ds = \left(\sqrt{1 + \left(\frac{dy}{dx}\right)^2}\right) dx$$

$$\frac{dy}{dx} = \frac{4h}{l^2}(l-2x), \text{ put in above equation}$$

$$\therefore \quad ds = \left(\sqrt{1 + \left[\frac{4h}{l^2}(l-2x)\right]^2}\right) dx$$

$$\therefore \quad H = \frac{\int My \, ds}{\int y^2 \, ds}$$

$$= \frac{\int M \times \frac{4hx}{l^2}(l-x) \times \left(\sqrt{1 + \left[\frac{4h}{l^2}(l-2x)\right]^2}\right) dx}{\int \left[\frac{4hx}{l^2}(l-x)\right]^2 \times \left(\sqrt{1 + \left[\frac{4h}{l^2}(l-2x)\right]^2}\right) dx}$$

But the integration of the above part is very difficult, so we have to consider some assumption.

Assume that the moment of inertia is not same throughout. It is considered as

$$I = I_0 \sec \theta$$

I_0 – Constant

θ – Angle of inclination of the tangent to the arch at any point with horizontal.

At crown, $\theta = 0$

$$\therefore \quad I = I_0$$

Thus, I_0 is the M.I. at the crown of the arch.

$$\frac{dy}{dx} = \tan \theta \qquad \qquad \frac{dy}{ds} = \sin \theta$$

$$\frac{dx}{ds} = \cos\theta$$

$$I = I_0 \sec\theta$$

$$H = \frac{\int \frac{My\, ds}{EI}}{\int \frac{y^2\, ds}{EI}} = \frac{\int \frac{My\, dx \sec\theta}{EI_0 \sec\theta}}{\int \frac{y^2\, dx \sec\theta}{EI_0 \sec\theta}}$$

$$= \frac{\int My\, dx}{\int y^2\, dx} \quad \text{(EI is constant for the member)}$$

11.5 TWO-HINGED ARCH LOADED WITH U.D.L.

Case I : Two-hinged parabolic arch loaded with U.D.L. on the whole span.

Derivation for the horizontal thrust :

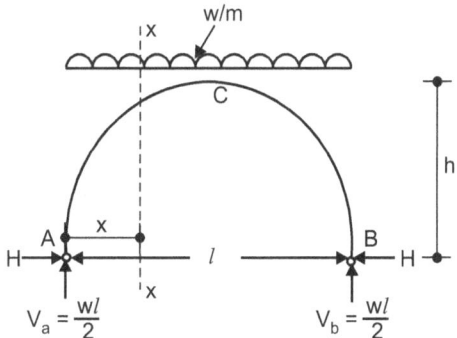

Fig. 11.4

Let ACB be a two-hinged arch as shown in Fig. 11.4. It is loaded with U.D.L. having intensity w/m run. l be the span of the arch.

$$\therefore \quad M_x = \left(V_a \times x - \frac{wx^2}{2}\right) = \frac{wl}{2}x - \frac{wx^2}{2} = \frac{wx}{2}(l-x)$$

$$\therefore \quad H = \frac{\int M_x\, y\, dx}{\int y^2\, dx}$$

$$y = \frac{4hx}{l^2}(l-x)$$

$$\therefore \quad H = \frac{\int_0^l \left(V_a x - \frac{wx^2}{2}\right) \times \frac{4hx}{l^2}(l-x)\,dx}{\int_0^l \left[\frac{4hx}{l^2}(l-x)\right]^2 dx} = \frac{\int_0^l \frac{wx}{2}(l-x) \times \frac{4hx}{l^2}(l-x)\,dx}{\int_0^l \left[\frac{16h^2x^2}{l^4}(l-x)^2\right]dx}$$

$$= \frac{\frac{w}{2} \times \frac{4 \times h}{l^2} \int_0^l [x^2(l-x)^2]\,dx}{\frac{16h^2}{l^4} \int_0^l [x^2(l-x)^2]\,dx}$$

As integration part in numerator and denominator is same, so cancel each other.

$$\therefore \quad H = \frac{wl^2}{8h}$$

Case II : Half span of the two-hinged arch loaded with U.D.L. having intensity w/m run.

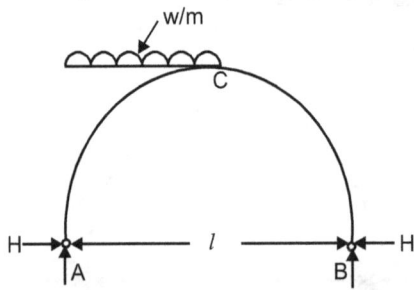

Fig. 11.5 (a) : Left part of C loaded with U.D.L.

Let H be the horizontal thrust, due to loading as shown in Fig. 11.5 (a).

Now apply the U.D.L. of intensity w/m run on right part of the arch.

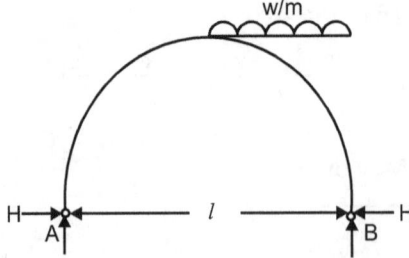

Fig. 11.5 (b) : Right part of C loaded with U.D.L.

Let H be the horizontal thrust due to loading as shown in Fig. 11.5 (b).

Now we apply the U.D.L. of w/m run over the whole span as shown in Fig. 11.5 (c).

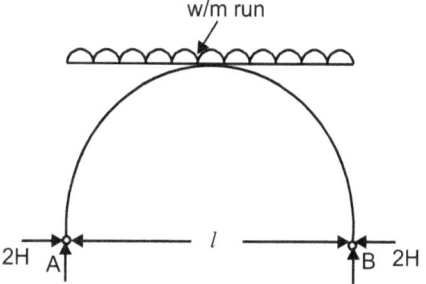

Fig. 11.5 (c) : Whole span loaded with U.D.L.

The horizontal thrust should be 2H due to loading as shown in Fig. 11.5 (c).

But for fully loaded two-hinged arch with w/m run,

$$2H = \frac{wl^2}{8h}$$

Therefore, horizontal thrust for the two-hinged arch loaded with intensity of loading w/m run on half the span is half the horizontal thrust due to fully loaded span of the arch.

$$\therefore \quad H = \frac{wl^2}{16h}$$

Derivation for the horizontal thrust :

A two-hinged parabolic arch of span l and central rise h carries a point load W at a distance 'a' from left hand support.

Assume, $\quad I = I_0 \sec \theta$

Deriving from first principles, show that the horizontal thrust 'H' is given by the expression

$$H = \frac{5}{8} \frac{w}{hl^3} a(l-a)(l^2 + al - a^2)$$

A two-hinged arch is loaded with a load W at 'a' from left support.

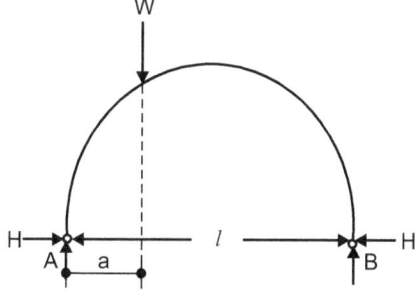

Fig. 11.6 (a)

Let H be the horizontal thrust due to loading as shown in Fig. 11.6 (a).

Now, consider the same load W at distance 'a' from right support.

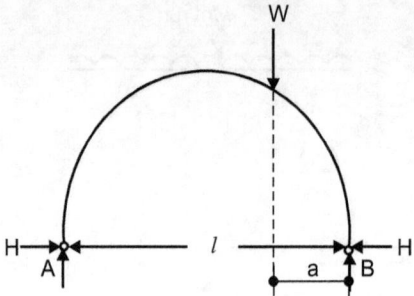

Fig. 11.6 (b)

Let H be the horizontal thrust due to loading as shown in Fig. 11.6 (b).

Now, load the two hinged arch with loads W at distance 'a' from both the supports.

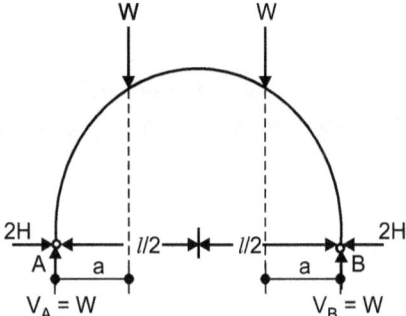

Fig. 11.6 (c)

Horizontal thrust should be 2H due to loading as shown in Fig. 11.6 (c).

$$\therefore \quad 2H = \frac{\int My\, dx}{\int y^2\, dx}$$

$$M = wx \quad \rightarrow \quad 0 < x \leq a$$

$$M = w(x) - w(x-a)$$

$$= wa \quad \rightarrow \quad a < x \leq \frac{l}{2}$$

$$y = \frac{4hx}{l^2}(l-x)$$

$$\int My\, dx = 2\left[\int_0^a wx \times \frac{4hx}{l^2}(l-x)\, dx + \int_a^{l/2} wa \times \frac{4hx}{l^2}(l-x)\, dx\right]$$

$$= 2\left[\frac{4wh}{l^2}\int_0^a x^2(l-x)\,dx + \frac{4wah}{l^2}\int_a^{l/2} x(l-x)\,dx\right]$$

$$= 2\left[\frac{4wh}{l^2}\left[\frac{x^3 l}{3} - \frac{x^4}{4}\right]_0^a + \frac{4\,wah}{l^2}\left[\frac{x^2 l}{2} - \frac{x^3}{3}\right]_a^{l/2}\right]$$

$$= 2\left[\frac{4\,wh}{l^2}\left[\frac{a^3 l}{3} - \frac{a^4}{4}\right] + \frac{4wah}{l^2}\left[\left(\frac{l^3}{8} - \frac{l^3}{24}\right) - \left(\frac{a^2 l}{2} - \frac{a^3}{3}\right)\right]\right]$$

$$= 2\left[\frac{4wha^3}{l^2}\left(\frac{4l - 3a}{12}\right) + \frac{4\,wah}{l^2}\left[\frac{l^3}{12} - a^2\left(\frac{3l-2a}{6}\right)\right]\right]$$

$$= \frac{8\,wha}{l^2}\left[\left[\frac{4\,la^2 - 3a^3}{12}\right] + \left[\frac{l^3}{12} - \frac{3a^2 l}{6} + \frac{2a^3}{6}\right]\right]$$

$$= \frac{8\,wha}{l^2}\left[\frac{a^3 + l^3 - 2a^2 l}{12}\right] = \frac{8wha}{12\,l^2}\left[(l-a)(l^2 + la - a^2)\right]$$

$$\int_0^l y^2\,dx = \int_0^l \left[\frac{4hx}{l^2}(l-x)\right]^2 dx = \int_0^l \frac{16h^2 x^2}{l^4}(l-x)^2\,dx$$

$$= \frac{16h^2}{l^4}\int_0^l x^2(l^2 - 2lx + x^2)\,dx = \frac{16h^2}{l^4}\left[\frac{x^3 l^2}{3} - \frac{2lx^4}{4} + \frac{x^5}{5}\right]_0^l$$

$$= \frac{16h^2}{l^4}\left[\frac{l^5}{3} - \frac{l^5}{2} + \frac{l^5}{5}\right] = 16\,h^2 l\left[\frac{1}{30}\right] = \frac{8h^2 l}{15}$$

$$\therefore\quad 2H = \frac{\int My\,dx}{\int y^2\,dx}$$

$$2H = \frac{\dfrac{8\,wha}{12\,l^2}(l-a)(l^2 + la - a^2)}{\dfrac{8\,h^2 l}{15}}$$

$$\therefore\quad H = \frac{5w}{8hl^3}a(l-a)(l^2 + la - a^2)$$

SOLVED PROBLEMS

Problem 11.1 : A two-hinged arch of span 30 m is loaded with a concentrated load 50 kN situated at 7.5 m from left support. Rise of arch is 6 m. Find the horizontal thrust.

Data : As shown in Fig. 11.7 (a).

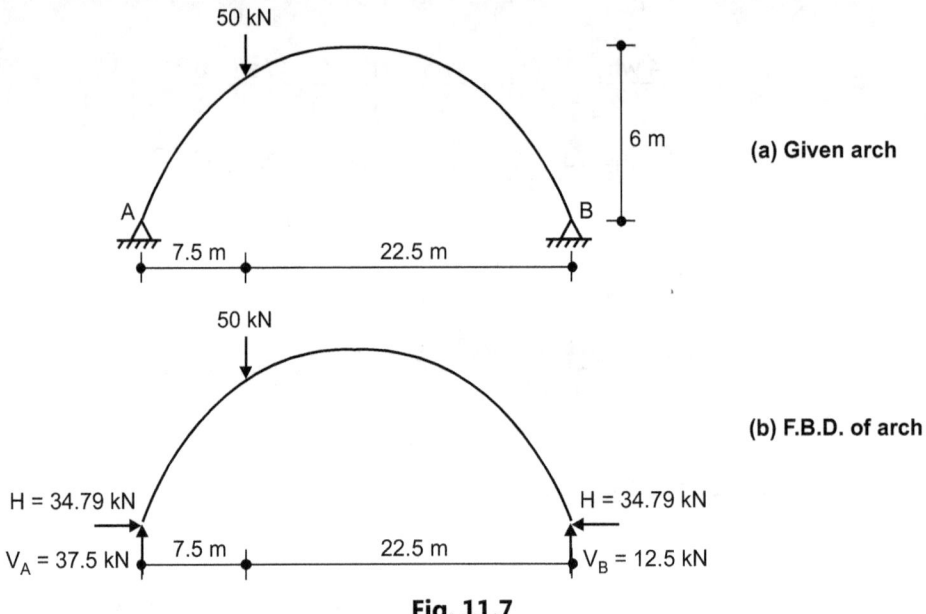

(a) Given arch

(b) F.B.D. of arch

Fig. 11.7

Required : Horizontal thrust.

Concept : Equilibrium equation and Castigliano's second theorem.

Solution : Step I : Applying equilibrium equation of moment,

$$\text{Moment @ B} = 0$$
$$-V_A \times 30 + 50 \times 22.5 = 0$$
$$V_A = 37.5 \text{ kN}$$

Step II : Applying equilibrium equation of forces in vertical direction,

$$\Sigma F_y = 0$$
$$V_A + V_B - 50 = 0$$
$$\therefore \quad V_B = 12.5 \text{ kN}$$

Step III : Using equation of horizontal thrust,

$$H = \frac{\int My \frac{ds}{EI}}{\int y^2 \frac{ds}{EI}} \qquad \ldots (1)$$

$$\int My\frac{ds}{EI} = \int_0^{7.5}(37.5x)\cdot\frac{4hx}{L^2}(L-x)\frac{dx}{EI} + \int_0^{22.5}12.5x\cdot\frac{4hx}{L^2}(L-x)\frac{dx}{EI}$$

$$= \int_0^{7.5}37.5x\cdot\frac{4\times 6\times x}{30^2}(30-x)\frac{dx}{EI} + \int_0^{22.5}12.5x\times\frac{4\times 6\times x}{30^2}(30-x)\frac{dx}{EI}$$

$$= \frac{3427.73}{EI} + \frac{16611.32}{EI} = \frac{20039.05}{EI} \quad \ldots (2)$$

$$\int y^2\frac{ds}{EI} = \int_0^{30}\left[\frac{4hx}{L^2}(L-x)\right]^2\frac{dx}{EI} = \int_0^{30}\frac{16\times 6^2 x^2}{30^4}(30-x)^2\frac{dx}{EI} = \frac{576}{EI} \quad \ldots (3)$$

Substituting values in equation (1),

$$H = \frac{\left(\dfrac{20039.05}{EI}\right)}{\left(\dfrac{576}{EI}\right)} = 34.79 \text{ kN}$$

Horizontal thrust = 34.79 kN

Step IV : FBD of arch is as shown in Fig. 11.7 (b).

Problem 11.2 : A two-hinged arch of span 40 m is loaded in the U.D.L. of intensity 30 kN/m over the whole span. Find horizontal thrust if rise of arch is 8 m.

Data : As shown in Fig. 11.8 (a).

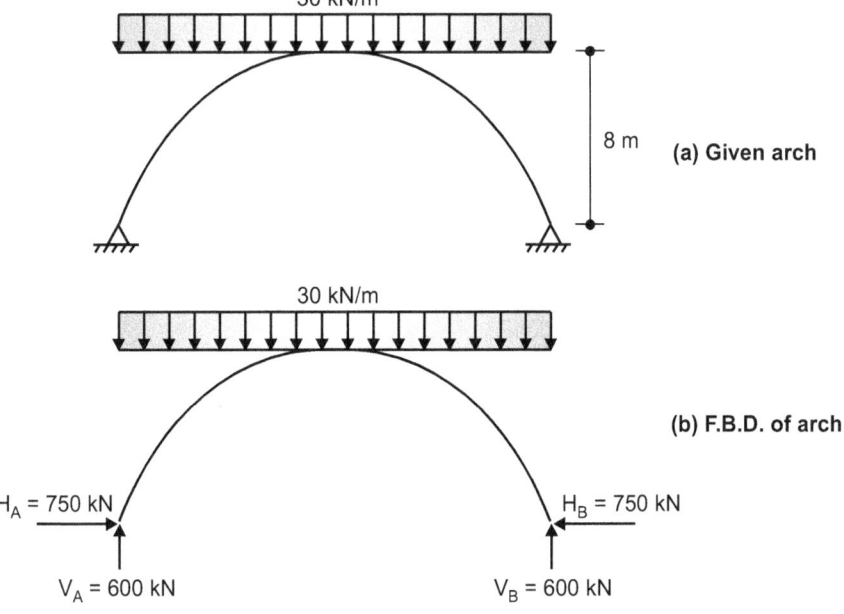

Fig. 11.8

Required : Horizontal thrust.

Concept : Equilibrium equation and Castigliano's second theorem.

Solution : Step I : Applying equilibrium equation of moment.

$$\text{Moment @ B} = 0$$
$$-V_A \times 40 + 30 \times 40 \times 20 = 0$$
$$V_A = 600 \text{ kN}$$

Step II : Applying equilibrium equation of forces in vertical direction,

$$\Sigma F_y = 0$$
$$V_A + V_B - 30 \times 40 = 0$$
$$\therefore \quad V_B = 600 \text{ kN}$$

Step III : Using equation of horizontal thrust,

$$H = \frac{\int My \frac{ds}{EI}}{\int y^2 \frac{ds}{EI}} \qquad \ldots (1)$$

$$\int My \frac{ds}{EI} = 2 \int_0^{20} \left(600x - \frac{30x^2}{2}\right) \cdot \frac{4hx}{L^2}(L-x) \frac{dx}{EI}$$

$$= 2 \int_0^{20} (600x - 15x^2) \cdot \frac{4 \times 8x}{40^2}(40-x) \frac{dx}{EI}$$

$$= \frac{1}{25} \int_0^{20} (600x - 15x^2)(40x - x^2) \frac{dx}{EI}$$

$$= \frac{1024000}{EI} \qquad \ldots (2)$$

$$\int y^2 \frac{ds}{EI} = \int_0^{40} \left[\frac{4hx}{L^2}(L-x)\right]^2 \frac{dx}{EI} = \int_0^{40} \frac{16 \times 8^2 x^2}{40^4}(40-x)^2 \frac{dx}{EI}$$

$$= \frac{1365.33}{EI} \qquad \ldots (3)$$

Substituting values in equation (1),

$$H = \frac{\left(\frac{1024000}{EI}\right)}{\left(\frac{1365.33}{EI}\right)} = 750 \text{ kN}$$

$$\therefore \quad \text{Horizontal thrust} = 750 \text{ kN}$$

Step IV : F.B.D. of arch is as shown in Fig. 11.8 (b).

Problem 11.3 : Prove that for a hinged parabolic arch (wherein $I = I_C \sec \theta$) with usual notation subjected to uniformly distributed load over entire span, there is no bending moment.

Data : As shown in Fig. 11.9 (a).

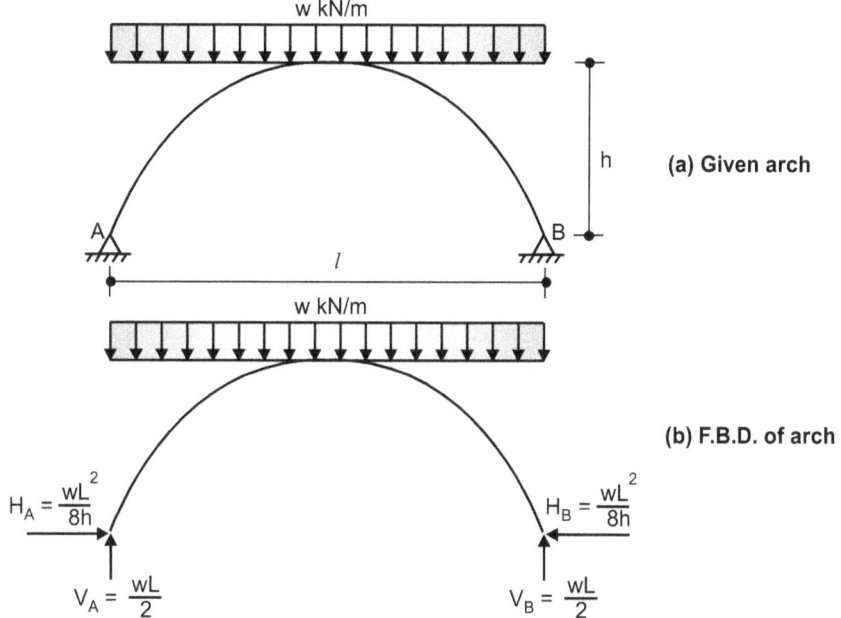

Fig. 11.9

Required : BMD is zero at each point.
Concept : Equilibrium equations and equation of horizontal thrust.
Solution : Step I : Applying equilibrium equation of moment,

Moment @ B = 0

$$-V_B \times L + w \cdot L \cdot \frac{L}{2} = 0$$

$\therefore \qquad V_A = \dfrac{wL}{2}$

Step II : Applying equilibrium equation of forces in vertical direction,

$$\Sigma F_y = 0$$
$$V_A + V_B - w \cdot L = 0$$

$\therefore \qquad V_B = \dfrac{wL}{2}$

Step III : Using equation of horizontal thrust,

$$H = \frac{\int My \frac{ds}{EI}}{\int y^2 \frac{ds}{EI}} \qquad \ldots (1)$$

$$\int My \frac{ds}{EI} = 2 \int_0^{L/2} \left(V_A \cdot x - \frac{wx^2}{2}\right) \cdot \frac{4hx}{L^2}(L-x) \cdot \frac{dx}{EI}$$

$$= 2 \int_0^{L/2} \left(\frac{wL}{2} \cdot x - \frac{wx^2}{2}\right) \cdot \frac{4h \cdot x}{L^2}(L-x) \frac{dx}{EI}$$

$$= 2 \int_0^{L/2} \frac{4h}{L^2}\left(\frac{wL}{2}x^2 - \frac{wx^3}{2}\right)(L-x) \frac{dx}{EI}$$

$$= \frac{8h}{L^2} \int_0^{L/2} \left[\frac{wL^2}{2}x^2 - \frac{wL\,x^3}{2} - \frac{wL}{2}x^3 + \frac{wx^4}{2}\right] \frac{dx}{EI}$$

$$= \frac{8h}{L^2}\left[\frac{wL^2}{2}\frac{x^3}{3} - \frac{2wL\,x^4}{8} + \frac{wx^5}{10}\right]_0^{L/2}$$

$$= \frac{8h}{L^2}\left[\frac{wL^2}{2} \cdot \frac{L^3}{24} - \frac{2wL^5}{128} + \frac{wL^5}{320}\right]$$

$$= \frac{8h}{L^2}(wL^5)\left[\frac{1}{48} - \frac{1}{64} + \frac{1}{320}\right]$$

$$= \frac{8h \cdot wL^3}{120} = \frac{wL^3 h}{15} \qquad \ldots (2)$$

$$\int y^2 \frac{ds}{EI} = 2\int_0^{L/2}\left[\frac{4hx}{L^2 EI}(L-x)\right]^2 = 2\int_0^{L/2}\frac{16h^2 x^2}{L^4 EI}(L^2 - 2Lx + x^2)\frac{dx}{EI}$$

$$= 2\int_0^{L/2} \frac{16h^2}{EI\,L^4}(L^2 x^2 - 2Lx^3) + x^4)\frac{dx}{EI}$$

$$= \frac{32h^2}{L^4}\left[\frac{L^2 x^3}{3} - \frac{2Lx^4}{4} + \frac{x^5}{5}\right]_0^{L/2}$$

$$= \frac{32h^2}{EI\,L^4}\left[\frac{L^5}{24} - \frac{L^5}{32} + \frac{L^5}{160}\right] = \frac{32h^2}{EI\,L^4}\left[\frac{13L^5}{480}\right]$$

$$= \frac{8}{15}h^2 L \qquad \ldots (3)$$

Substituting values in equation (1),

$$\therefore \quad H = \frac{\left[\dfrac{wL^3 h}{15}\right]}{\left[\dfrac{8}{15}h^2 L\right]} = \frac{wL^2}{8h}$$

Step IV : Bending moment at any section,

$$M_x = -V_A \cdot x + w \cdot x \cdot \frac{x}{2} + H \cdot y$$

$$= -\frac{wL}{2}x + \frac{wx^2}{2} + \frac{wL^2}{8h}\left[\frac{4hx}{L^2}(L-x)\right]$$

$$= -\frac{wL}{2}x + \frac{wx^2}{2} + \frac{wx}{2}(L-x)$$

$$= -\frac{wL}{2}x + \frac{wx^2}{2} + \frac{wLx}{2} - \frac{wx^2}{2}$$

$$= 0$$

∴ B.M. at any section is zero.

Step V : F.B.D. of arch is as shown in Fig. 11.9 (b).

Problem 11.4 : A two-hinged parabolic is loaded and supported as shown in Fig. 11.10. Determine horizontal thrust.

Data : As shown in Fig. 11.10 (a).

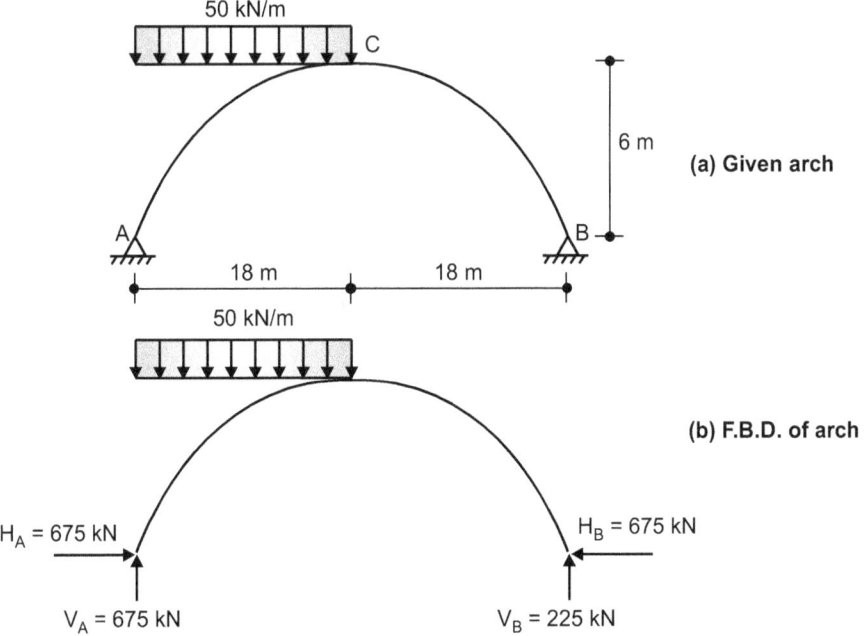

Fig. 11.10

Required : B.M.D.

Concept : Equilibrium equation and Castigliano's second theorem.

Solution : Step I : Applying equilibrium equation of moment,

$$\text{Moment @ B} = 0$$

$$-V_A \times 36 + 50 \times 18 \times 27 = 0$$

$$\therefore \quad V_A = 675 \text{ kN}$$

Step II : Applying equilibrium equation of forces in vertical direction,

$$\Sigma F_y = 0$$

$$V_A + V_B - 50 \times 18 = 0$$

$$\therefore \quad V_B = 225 \text{ kN}$$

Step III : Using equation of horizontal thrust,

$$H = \frac{\int \frac{My\, ds}{EI}}{\int y^2 \frac{ds}{EI}} \qquad \ldots (1)$$

$$\int My \frac{ds}{EI} = \int_0^{18} \left(V_A \cdot x - \frac{50x^2}{2}\right) \cdot \frac{4hx}{l^2}(l-x) \cdot \frac{dx}{EI} + \int_0^{18} V_B \cdot x \cdot \frac{4hx}{l^2}(L-x) \frac{dx}{EI}$$

$$\int_0^{18} (675x - 25x^2) \cdot \frac{4 \times 6 \times x}{36^2}(36-x)\frac{dx}{EI} + \int_0^{18} 225x \cdot \frac{4 \times 6 \times x}{36^2}(36-x)\frac{dx}{EI}$$

$$= \frac{284310}{EI} + \frac{182250}{EI} = \frac{466560}{EI} \qquad \ldots (2)$$

$$\int y^2 \frac{dx}{EI} = \int \left[\frac{4hx}{L^2}(l-x)\right]^2 \frac{dx}{EI} = \int_0^{36} \left[\frac{4 \times 6 \times x}{36^2}(36-x)\right]^2 \frac{dx}{EI} = \frac{691.2}{EI} \qquad \ldots (3)$$

Substituting values in equation (1),

$$\therefore \quad H = \frac{\left[\frac{466560}{EI}\right]}{\left[\frac{691.2}{EI}\right]} = 675 \text{ kN}$$

Step IV : F.B.D. of arch is as shown in Fig. 3.26 (b).

Problem 11.5 : A two-hinged parabolic arch of span 20 m and rise 5 m carries a uniformly distributed load of 30 kN/m over the left half of the span and a concentrated load of 90 kN at the crown. Find horizontal thrust at each support.

Data : As shown in Fig. 11.11 (a).

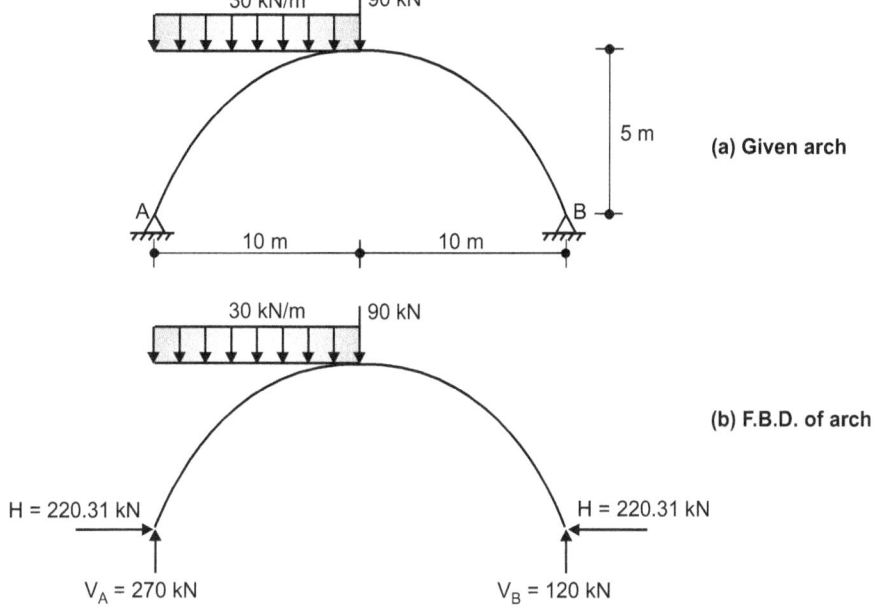

Fig. 11.11

Required : Horizontal thrust.

Concept : Equilibrium equations, Castigliano's second theorem.

Solution : Step I : Applying equilibrium equation of moment,

$$\text{Moment @ B} = 0$$

$$-V_A \times 20 + 30 \times 10 \times 15 + 90 \times 10 = 0$$

$$\therefore \quad V_A = 270 \text{ kN}$$

Step II : Applying equilibrium equation of forces in vertical direction,

$$\Sigma F_y = 0$$

$$V_A + V_B - 30 \times 10 - 90 = 0$$

$$\therefore \quad V_B = 120 \text{ kN}$$

Step III : Using equation of horizontal thrust,

$$H = \frac{\int My \frac{ds}{EI}}{\int y^2 \frac{ds}{EI}} \qquad \ldots (1)$$

$$\int My \frac{ds}{EI} = \int_0^{10} \left(270x - \frac{30x^2}{2}\right) \frac{4hx}{L^2}(L-x) \frac{dx}{EI} + \int_0^{10} 120x \cdot \frac{4hx}{L^2}(L-x) \frac{dx}{EI}$$

$$= \int_0^{10} (270x - 15x^2) \cdot \frac{4 \times 5 \times x}{20^2} (20-x) \frac{dx}{EI}$$

$$+ \int_0^{10} 120x \times \frac{4 \times 5x}{20^2} (20-x) \frac{dx}{EI}$$

$$= \frac{1}{20} \int_0^{10} (270x - 15x^2)(20x - x^2) \frac{dx}{EI} + \int_0^{10} 6x^2 (20-x) \frac{dx}{EI}$$

$$= \frac{33750}{EI} + \frac{25000}{EI} = \frac{58750}{EI}$$

$$\int y^2 \frac{dx}{EI} = \int_0^{20} \left[\frac{4hx}{L^2} (L-x) \right]^2 \frac{dx}{EI} \qquad \ldots (2)$$

$$= \int_0^{20} \frac{16 \times 5^2 \times x^2}{20^4} (20-x)^2 \cdot \frac{dx}{EI} = \frac{266.67}{EI} \qquad \ldots (3)$$

Substituting values in equation (1),

$$H = \frac{\left(\frac{58750}{EI}\right)}{\left(\frac{266.67}{EI}\right)} = 220.31 \text{ kN}$$

Step IV : F.B.D. of arch is as shown in Fig. 11.11 (b).

Problem 11.6 : A two-hinged semi-circular arch of radius R carries a concentrated load W at the crown. Show that the horizontal thrust at each support is $\frac{W}{\pi}$. Assume uniform flexural rigidity.

Data : As shown in Fig. 11.12 (a).

Required : Uniform flexural rigidity.

Concept : Equilibrium equations, Castigliano's second theorem.

Solution : Step I : Applying equilibrium equation of moment,

$$\text{Moment @ B} = 0$$
$$-V_A \times 2R + W \times R = 0$$
$$\therefore \quad V_A = \frac{W}{2}$$

Step II : Applying equilibrium equation of forces in vertical direction,

$$V_A + V_B - W = 0$$
$$\therefore \quad V_B = \frac{W}{2}$$

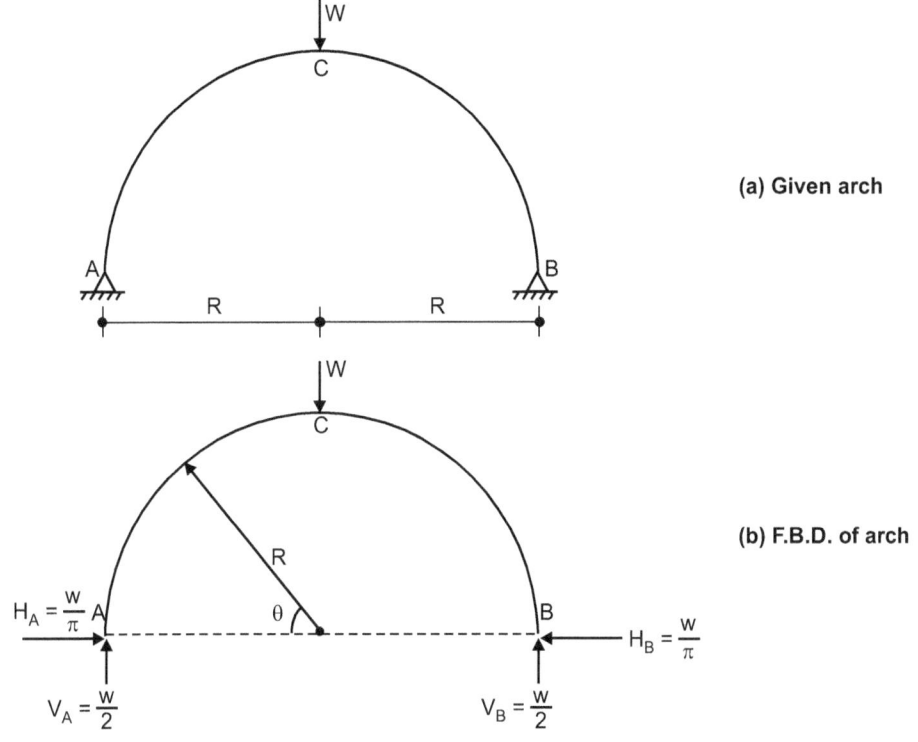

Fig. 11.12

Step III : Using equation of horizontal thrust,

$$H = \frac{\int My \frac{ds}{EI}}{\int y^2 \frac{ds}{EI}} \qquad \ldots (1)$$

$$x = R - R\cos\theta = R(1-\cos\theta), \quad y = R\sin\theta, \quad ds = R\,d\theta$$

$$\int My \frac{ds}{EI} = 2\int_0^{\pi/2} \frac{W}{2} \cdot R(1-\cos\theta) \cdot R\sin\theta \cdot R\,d\theta$$

$$= wR^3 \int_0^{\pi/2} (1-\cos\theta)\cdot \sin\theta\, d\theta$$

Substituting $(1-\cos\theta) = x$

$\therefore \qquad dx = \sin\theta$

$$\int My \frac{ds}{EI} = wR^3 \int_0^{\pi/2} x \cdot dx = wR^3 \left[\frac{x^2}{2}\right]_0^{\pi/2}$$

$$= wR^3 \left[\frac{(1-\cos\theta)^2}{2}\right]_0^{\pi/2} = wR^3\left[\left(\frac{1}{2}\right)^2 - 0\right] = \frac{wR^3}{4} \qquad \ldots (2)$$

$$\int y^2 \frac{ds}{EI} = \int_0^\pi R^2 \sin^2\theta \cdot R\, d\theta$$

Substitute $\sin^2\theta = \dfrac{(1-\cos 2\theta)}{2}$

$$\therefore \int y^2 \frac{ds}{EI} = 2\int_0^{\pi/2} \frac{R^3}{4}(1-\cos 2\theta)^2 \cdot d\theta = \frac{2R^3}{4}[\theta - \sin 2\theta \cdot 2]_0^{\pi/2}$$

$$= \frac{R^3}{2}\left[\frac{\pi}{2} - 0\right] = \frac{\pi R^3}{4} \qquad \ldots (3)$$

Substituting values in equation (1),

$$H = \frac{\left[\dfrac{wR^3}{4}\right]}{\left[\dfrac{\pi R^3}{4}\right]} = \frac{w}{\pi}$$

∴ Horizontal thrust $= \dfrac{w}{\pi}$ kN

Step IV : FBD of arch is as shown in Fig. 11.12 (b).

Problem 11.7 : A parabolic two-hinged arch of span 28 m and a central rise of 4.9 m is subjected in a U.D.L. of 42 kN/m over a length of 8 m as shown in Fig. 11.13. Draw B.M.D. highlighting all the salient features.

$I = I_C \sec\theta$, where symbols carry their usual meaning.

Data : As shown in Fig. 11.13 (a).
Required : B.M.D.
Concept : Equilibrium equations and Castigliano's second theorem.
Solution : Step I : Applying equilibrium equation of moment,

Moment @ B = 0
$-V_A \times 28 + 42 \times 8 \times 24 = 0$
∴ $V_A = 288$ kN

Step II : Applying equilibrium equation of forces in vertical direction,

$V_A + V_B - 42 \times 8 = 0$
∴ $V_B = 48$ kN

Step III : Using equation of horizontal thrust,

$$H = \frac{\int My \dfrac{ds}{EI}}{\int y^2 \dfrac{ds}{EI}} \qquad \ldots (1)$$

$$\int My \frac{ds}{EI} = \int_0^8 \left(288x - 42 \cdot x \cdot \frac{x}{2}\right) \cdot \frac{4hx}{L^2}(L-x)\frac{dx}{EI} + \int_0^{20} 48x \cdot \frac{4hx}{L^2}(L-x)\frac{dx}{EI}$$

$$= \int_0^8 (288x - 21x^2) \times \frac{4 \times 4.9x}{28^2}(28-x)\frac{dx}{EI} + \int_0^{20} 48x \times \frac{4 \times 4.9x}{28^2}(28-x)\frac{dx}{EI}$$

$$= \frac{15421}{EI} + \frac{41600}{EI} = \frac{57021}{EI} \qquad \ldots (2)$$

$$\int y^2 \frac{ds}{EI} = \int_0^{28}\left[\frac{4hx}{L^2}(L-x)\right]^2 \frac{dx}{EI} = \int_0^{28} \frac{4^2 \times 4.9^2 x^2}{28^4}(28-x)^2 \frac{dx}{EI} = \frac{358.55}{EI} \qquad \ldots (3)$$

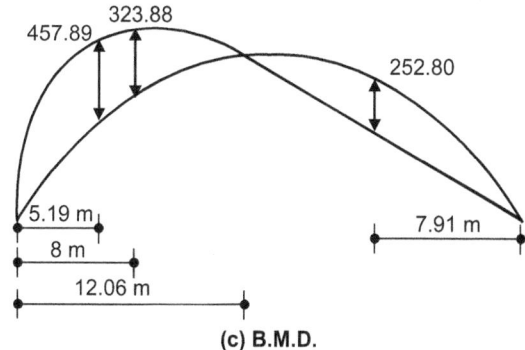

(a) Given arch

(b) F.B.D. of arch

(c) B.M.D.

Fig. 11.13

Substituting in equation (1),

$$H = \frac{\frac{57021}{EI}}{\frac{358.55}{EI}} = 159.03 \text{ kN}$$

Step IV : Maximum bending moment :
1. Maximum hogging bending moment occurs in region A.C.

$$\therefore \quad \text{B.M.} = V_A \times x - 42 \cdot \frac{x^2}{2} - H \times \frac{4hx}{L^2}(L-x)$$

$$= 288x - 21x^2 - 159.03 \times \frac{4 \times 4.9x}{28^2}(28-x) \quad \ldots (4)$$

To get maximum bending moment, take derivative of B.M. w.r.t. x and equate to zero

$$\therefore \quad \frac{dM}{dx} = 0 = 288 - 42x - 3.98(28 - 2x)$$

$$x = 5.19 \text{ m}$$

Substitute in equation (4),

$$\therefore \quad \text{Maximum bending moment} = 288 \times 5.19 - 21 \times (5.19)^2 - 3.98 \times 5.19 (28 - 5.19)$$
$$= 457.89 \text{ kN-m}$$

Maximum hogging moment = 457.89 kN-m

2. B.M. at the end of U.D.L. (at point D),

Substituting x = 8 in equation (4),

$$\text{B.M.} = 288 \times 8 - 42 \times 8 \times 4 - 159.03 \times \frac{4 \times 4.9}{(28)^2} \times 8(28-8) = 323.88 \text{ kN-m}$$

3. Point of contraflexure : Point of contraflexure occurs between D and C.

$$\text{B.M.} = 288x - 42 \times 8 (x - 4) - 159.03 \times \frac{4 \times 4.9 \times x}{(28)^2}(28-x) \quad \ldots (5)$$

Equating B.M. to zero

$$0 = 288x - 336(x - 4) - 3.98(28x - x^2)$$
$$0 = 3.98x^2 - 159.44 + 1344$$

$$\therefore \quad x = 12.06 \text{ m and } x = 28 \text{ m}$$

$\therefore$ B.M. is zero at 12.06 m from left support.

4. Maximum sagging bending moment,

$$\text{B.M.} = V_B \times x - H \times y$$

$$= 48x - \frac{159.03 \times 4 \times 4.9 \times x}{(28)^2}(28-x)$$

$$M = 48x - 3.98x(28-x) \quad \ldots (6)$$

To get maximum B.M. take derivative w.r.t. x.

$$\therefore \quad \frac{dM}{dx} = 0 = 48 - 3.98(28 - 2x)$$

$$\therefore \quad x = 7.97 \text{ m}$$

Substituting in equation (6),

∴   Maximum B.M. $= 48 \times 7.97 - 3.98 \times 7.97 (28 - 7.97)$
                                          $= -252.80$ kN-m

∴ Maximum sagging moment = 252.80 kN-m

Step V : F.B.D. of arch is as shown in Fig. 11.13 (b).

Step VI : B.M.D. is as shown in Fig. 11.13 (c).

Problem 11.8 : A parabolic arch hinged at both ends has a span of 60 m and a rise of 12 m. A concentrated load of 8 kN acts at 15 m from the left hand hinge. The second moment of area varies as the secant of the slope of the rise axis. Calculate the horizontal thrust and the reaction at the hinge. Also calculate the maximum bending moment anywhere on the arch.

Data : As shown in Fig. 11.14 (a).

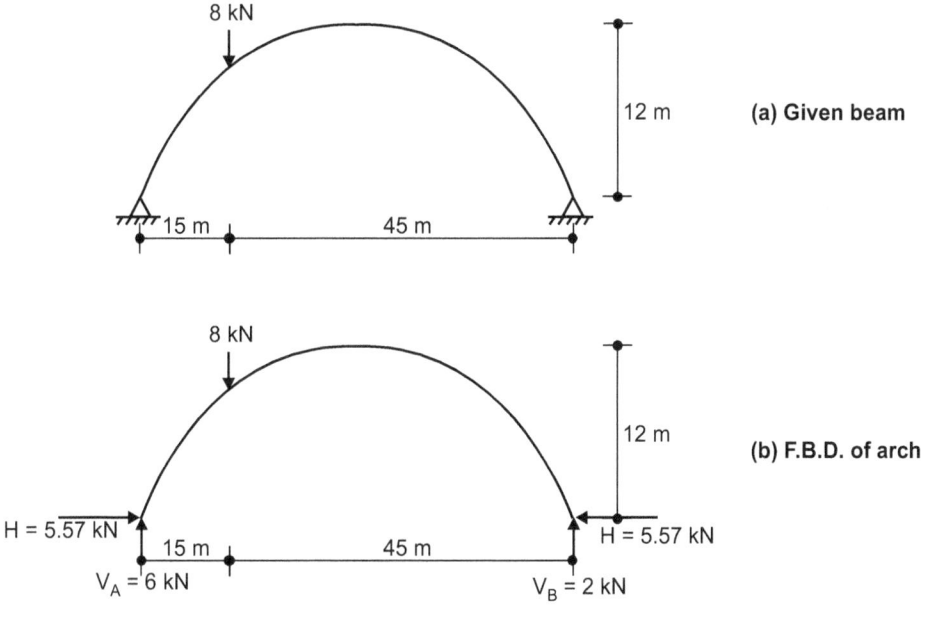

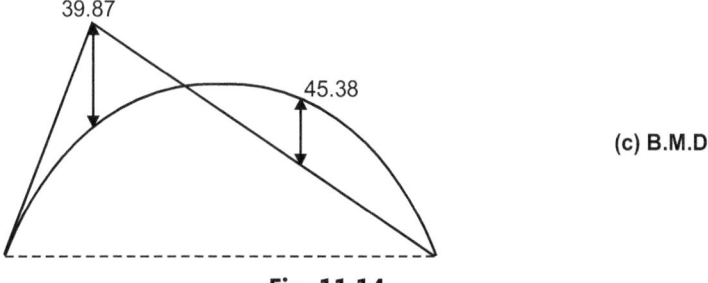

Fig. 11.14

Required : Horizontal thrust, reaction at the hinge and maximum bending moment.
Concept : Equilibrium equations and Castigliano's second theorem.
Solution : Step I : Applying equilibrium equation of moment,

$$\text{Moment @ B} = 0$$
$$-V_A \times 60 + 8 \times 45 = 0$$
$$\therefore \quad V_A = 6 \text{ kN}$$

Step II : Applying equilibrium equation of forces in vertical direction,

$$V_A + V_B - 8 = 0$$
$$\therefore \quad V_B = 2 \text{ kN}$$

Step III : Using equation of horizontal thrust,

$$H = \frac{\int My \frac{ds}{EI}}{\int y^2 \frac{ds}{EI}} \quad \ldots (1)$$

$$\int My \frac{ds}{EI} = \int_0^{15} 6x \cdot \frac{4hx}{L^2}(L-x) \frac{dx}{EI} + \int_0^{45} 2 \cdot x \cdot \frac{4hx}{L^2}(L-x) \frac{dx}{EI}$$

$$= \int_0^{15} 6x \times \frac{4 \times 12x}{60^2}(60-x) \frac{dx}{EI} + \int_0^{45} 2x \times \frac{4 \times 12 \times x}{60^2}(60-x) \frac{dx}{EI}$$

$$= \frac{2}{25} \int_0^{15} x^2 (60-x) \frac{dx}{EI} + \frac{2}{75} \int_0^{45} x^2 (60-x) \frac{dx}{EI}$$

$$= \frac{4387.5}{EI} + \frac{21262.5}{EI} = \frac{25650}{EI} \quad \ldots (2)$$

$$\int y^2 \frac{ds}{EI} = \int_0^{60} \left[\frac{4hx}{L^2}(L-x)\right]^2 \frac{dx}{EI} = \int_0^{60} \frac{4^2 \times 12^2 \times x^2}{60^4}(60-x)^2 \frac{dx}{EI}$$

$$= \frac{1}{5625} \int_0^{60} x^2 (60-x)^2 \frac{dx}{EI} = \frac{4608}{EI} \quad \ldots (3)$$

Substituting values in equation (1),

$$\therefore \quad H = \frac{\frac{25650}{EI}}{\frac{4608}{EI}} = 5.57 \text{ kN}$$

$$\therefore \quad \text{Reaction at A} = \sqrt{V_A^2 + H^2}$$
$$= \sqrt{6^2 + 5.57^2} = 8.19 \text{ kN}$$

$$\theta = \tan^{-1}\left(\frac{V_A}{H}\right) = \tan^{-1}\left(\frac{6}{5.57}\right) = 47.13°$$

∴ R_A = 8.19 kN (∡47.13°)

$$\text{Reaction at B} = \sqrt{V_B^2 + H^2} = \sqrt{2^2 + 5.57^2} = 5.92 \text{ kN}$$

$$\theta = \tan^{-1}\left(\frac{V_B}{H}\right) = \tan^{-1}\left(\frac{2}{5.57}\right) = 19.75°$$

∴ R_B = 5.92 kN (∡19.75°)

Step IV : Maximum bending moment :

(a) Maximum hogging bending moment occurs under the load.

$$B.M._{max} = V_A \times 15 - H \times y_D$$

$$\text{Vertical ordinate at D} = \frac{4hx}{L^2}(L-x) = \frac{4 \times 12 \times 15}{60^2}(60-x) = 9 \text{ m}$$

$$B.M._{max} = 6 \times 15 - 5.57 \times 9 = 39.87 \text{ kN-m}$$

Maximum hogging moment = 39.87 kN-m

(b) Maximum sagging bending moment occurs between CB.

$$B.M._{max} = V_B \times x - H \times y = 2x - 5.57 \times \frac{4hx}{L^2}(L-x)$$

$$= 2x - 5.57 \times \frac{4 \times 12 x}{60^2}(60-x)$$

$$= 2x - \frac{267.36 x}{3600}(60-x) \quad \ldots (4)$$

For maximum bending moment take derivative of B.M. w.r.t. x and equate to zero.

∴ $$\frac{dM}{dx} = 0 = 2 - \frac{267.36}{3600}(60-2x)$$

∴ x = 16.54 m from right support

Substituting x in equation (4),

∴ $$B.M._{max} = 2 \times 4 - \frac{267.36}{3600} \times 16.54 (60 - 16.54)$$

$$= -45.38 \text{ kN-m}$$

∴ Maximum sagging moment = 45.38 kN-m

(c) Point of contraflexure.

$$B.M. = 6x - 5.57 \times \frac{4hx}{L^2}(L-x) - 8(x-15)$$

$$M = 6x - 5.57 \times \frac{4 \times 12x}{60^2}(60-x) - 8(x-15)$$

$$= 6x - \frac{267.36}{60^2}(60x - x^2) - 8x + 120$$

For point of contraflexure, B.M. = 0

$$0 = 6x - \frac{267.36}{60^2}(60x - x^2) - 8x + 120$$

$$2x = -\frac{267.36}{60^2} \times 60x + \frac{267.36}{60^2}x^2 + 120$$

$$0 = -6.46x + \frac{267.36}{60^2}x^2 + 120$$

$$\therefore \quad x = 26.89 \text{ m}$$

Step V : F.B.D. of arch is as shown in Fig. 11.14 (b).

Step VI : B.M.D. is as shown in Fig. 11.14 (c).

Problem 11.9 : A parabolic two-hinged arch has a span of 80 m and a rise of 10 m. A U.D.L. of 2.5 kN/m covers half the span. If $I = I_o \sec \theta$, find out the horizontal thrust at the hinges and the bending moment at 15 m from the left hinge. Also find normal thrust and radial shear at this section.

Data : As shown in Fig. 11.15 (a).

Required : Bending moment, horizontal thrust, normal thrust and radial shear.

Concept : Equilibrium equations and equation of horizontal thrust.

Solution : Step I : Applying equilibrium equation of moment,

$$\text{Moment @ B} = 0$$

$$-V_A \times 80 + 2.5 \times 40 \times 60 = 0$$

$$\therefore \quad V_A = 75 \text{ kN}$$

Step II : Applying equilibrium equation of forces in vertical direction,

$$V_A + V_B - 2.5 \times 40 = 0$$

$$\therefore \quad V_B = 25 \text{ kN}$$

Step III : Using equation of horizontal thrust,

$$H = \frac{\int \frac{My\,ds}{EI}}{\int y^2 \frac{ds}{EI}} \qquad \ldots (1)$$

$$\int My \frac{ds}{EI} = \int_0^{40}\left(75x - \frac{2.5x^2}{2}\right)\frac{4hx}{L^2}(L-x) + \int_0^{40} 2.5x \times \frac{4hx}{L^2}(L-x)\frac{dx}{EI}$$

$$= \int_0^{40}(75x - 1.25x^2) \times \frac{4 \times 10x}{80^2}(80-x)\frac{dx}{EI} + \int_0^{40}\frac{2.5x \times 4 \times 10x}{80^2}(80-x)\frac{dx}{EI}$$

$$= \frac{260000}{EI} + \frac{16666.6}{EI} = \frac{276666.67}{EI} \qquad \ldots (2)$$

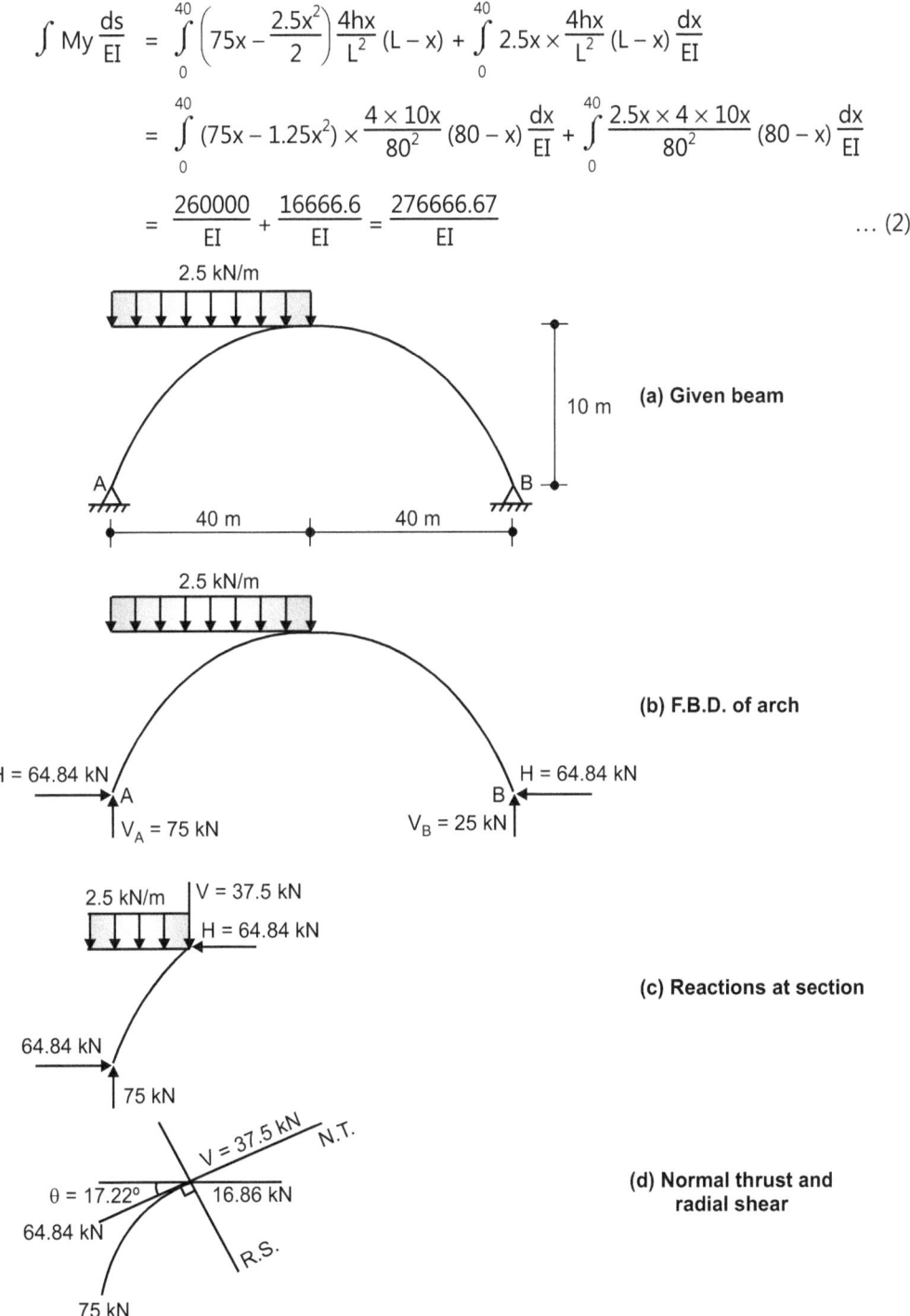

Fig. 11.15

$$\int y^2 \frac{ds}{EI} = \int_0^{80} \left[\frac{4hx}{L^2}(L-x)\right]^2 \frac{dx}{EI} = \int_0^{80} \frac{4^2 \times 10^2 \times x^2}{80^4}(80-x)^2 \frac{dx}{EI}$$

$$= \frac{4266.67}{EI} \quad \ldots (3)$$

Substituting values in equation (1),

$$H = \frac{\left(\frac{276666.67}{EI}\right)}{\left(\frac{4266.67}{EI}\right)} = 64.84 \text{ kN}$$

Step IV : Bending moment at 15 m : Consider the left part of the section.

$$\therefore \quad \text{B.M. at 15 m} = V_A \times 15 - \frac{2.5 \times 15^2}{2} - 64.84 \times \frac{4hx}{L^2}(L-x)$$

$$= 75 \times 15 - \frac{2.5 \times 15^2}{2} - 64.84 \times \frac{4 \times 10 \times 15}{80^2}(80-x)$$

$$= 448.63 \text{ kN-m}$$

Step V : F.B.D. of arch is as shown in Fig. 11.15 (b).

Step VI : Normal thrust is a force acting along the tangent at the section. Radial force is a force acting perpendicular to the tangent at the section. The angle of tangent is 'θ' at the section.

We have, $\quad y = \frac{4hx}{L^2}(L-x)$

$$\frac{dy}{dx} = \tan\theta = \frac{4h}{L^2}(L-2x)$$

At x = 15 m, $\quad \tan\theta = \frac{4 \times 10}{80^2}(80 - 2 \times 15)$

$$\tan\theta = 0.31$$

$$\therefore \quad \theta = 17.22$$

Step VII : Considering part of arch on left section. Applying equilibrium equation, the reactions at the section are as shown in Fig. 11.15 (c).

Step VIII : Normal thrust and radial shear is as shown in Fig. 11.15 (a).

Step IX : Resolving forces along tangent at the section,

Normal thrust $= V \sin\theta + H \cos\theta$

$$= 37.5 \sin 17.22 + 64.84 \cos 17.22$$

$$= 73.04 \text{ kN } (\nearrow \theta = 17.22)$$

Step X : Resolving forces perpendicular to the tangent at section,

Radial shear $= H \cos\theta - V \sin\theta = 64.84 \cos 17.22 - 37.5 \sin 17.22$

$$= 50.83 \text{ kN } (\searrow \theta = 72.78)$$

Problem 11.10 : A two-hinged arch of span 20 m and rise 5 m. It carries two concentrated loads of 50 kN and 100 kN at 4.5 m and 9 m. Find normal thrust and radial shear at 7 m from left support.

Data : As shown in Fig. 11.16 (a).

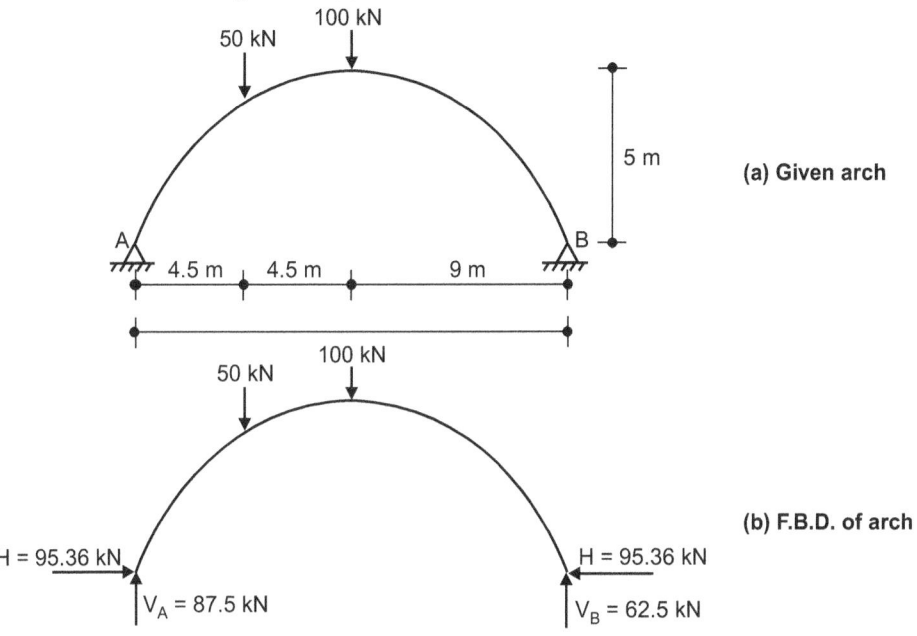

(a) Given arch

(b) F.B.D. of arch

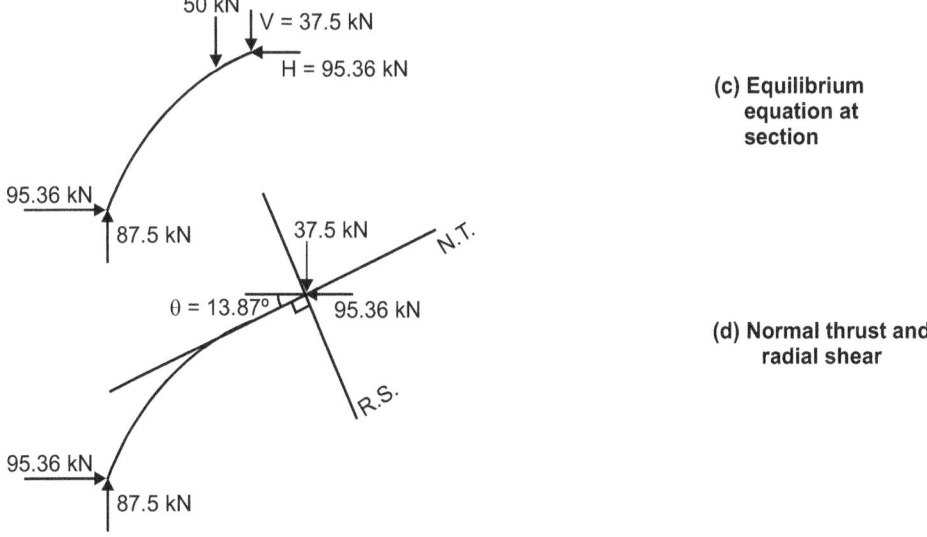

(c) Equilibrium equation at section

(d) Normal thrust and radial shear

Fig. 11.16

Required : Normal thrust and radial shear.

Concept : Equilibrium equations and Castigliano's second theorem.

Solution : Step I : Applying equilibrium equation of moment,

$$\text{Moment @ B} = 0$$

$$-V_A \times 18 + 50 \times 13.5 + 100 \times 9 = 0$$

$$V_A = 87.5 \text{ kN}$$

Step II : Applying equilibrium equation of forces in vertical direction,

$$V_A + V_B + 50 + 100 = 0$$

$$\therefore \quad V_B = 62.5 \text{ kN}$$

Step III : Using equation of horizontal thrust,

$$H = \frac{\int My \frac{ds}{EI}}{\int y^2 \frac{ds}{EI}}$$

$$\int My \frac{ds}{EI} = \int_0^{4.5} 87.5x \cdot \frac{4hx}{L^2}(L-x) \cdot \frac{dx}{EI} + \int_{4.5}^{9} [87.5x - 50(x-4.5)] \frac{4hx}{L^2}(L-x) \frac{dx}{EI}$$

$$+ \int_0^{9} 62.5x \cdot \frac{4hx}{L^2}(L-x) \frac{dx}{EI}$$

$$= \int_0^{4.5} 87.5x \times \frac{4 \times 5 \times x (18-x)}{18^2} \frac{dx}{EI} + \int_{4.5}^{9} [87.5x - 50(x-4.5)]$$

$$\frac{4 \times 5 \times x (18-x)}{18^2} \frac{dx}{EI} + \int_0^{9} 62.5x \times \frac{4 \times 5 \times x}{18^2}(18-x) \frac{dx}{EI}$$

$$= \frac{2399.41}{EI} + \frac{9940.43}{EI} + \frac{10546.88}{EI} = \frac{22886.72}{EI}$$

$$\int y^2 \frac{ds}{EI} = \int_0^{18} \left[\frac{4hx}{L^2}(L-x)\right]^2 \frac{dx}{EI} = \int_0^{18} \left[\frac{4 \times 5 \times x}{18^2}(18-x)\right]^2 \frac{dx}{EI}$$

$$= \frac{240}{EI}$$

$$H = \frac{\int My \frac{ds}{EI}}{\int y^2 \frac{ds}{EI}} = \frac{\left(\frac{22886.72}{EI}\right)}{\left(\frac{240}{EI}\right)} = 95.36 \text{ kN}$$

Step IV : F.B.D. of arch is as shown in Fig. 11.16 (b).

Step V : Normal thrust is a force acting along the tangent at the section. Radial force is a force acting perpendicular to the tangent at the section. The angle of tangent is 'θ' at the section.

We have, $$y = \frac{4hx}{L^2}(L-x)$$

$$\frac{dy}{dx} = \frac{4h}{L^2}(L-2x)$$

∴ $$\tan\theta = \frac{dy}{dx} = 4 \times 5 \frac{(18 - 2 \times 7)}{18^2} = 0.247$$

∴ $$\theta = 13.87°$$

Step VI : Considering part of arch on left of section. Applying equilibrium equation, the reactions at the section are as shown in Fig. 3.32 (c).

Step VII : Normal thrust and radial shear is as shown in Fig. 11.16 (d).

Step VIII : Resolving forces along tangent at the section,

Normal thrust = $V \sin\theta + H \cos\theta = 37.5 \sin 13.87 + 95.36 \cos 13.87$

= 101.57 kN

Step IX : Resolving forces perpendicular to tangent,

∴ Radial shear = $V \cos\theta - H \sin\theta = 37.5 \cos 13.87 - 95.36 \sin 13.87$

= 37.49 kN

Problem 11.11 : A two-hinged parabolic arch is as shown in Fig. 11.17 (a). Find normal thrust and radial shear at 6 m from the left support.

Data : As shown in Fig. 11.17 (a).

Required : Horizontal thrust and radial shear.

Concept : Equilibrium equations and equation of horizontal thrust.

Solution : Step I : Applying equilibrium equation of moment,

Moment @ B = 0

$-V_A \times 20 + 30 \times 10 \times 15 = 0$

∴ $V_A = 225$ kN

Step II : Applying equilibrium equation of forces in vertical direction,

$V_A + V_B - 30 \times 10 = 0$

∴ $V_B = 75$ kN

Step III : Using equation of horizontal thrust,

$$H = \frac{\int My \frac{ds}{EI}}{\int y^2 \frac{ds}{EI}} \qquad \ldots (1)$$

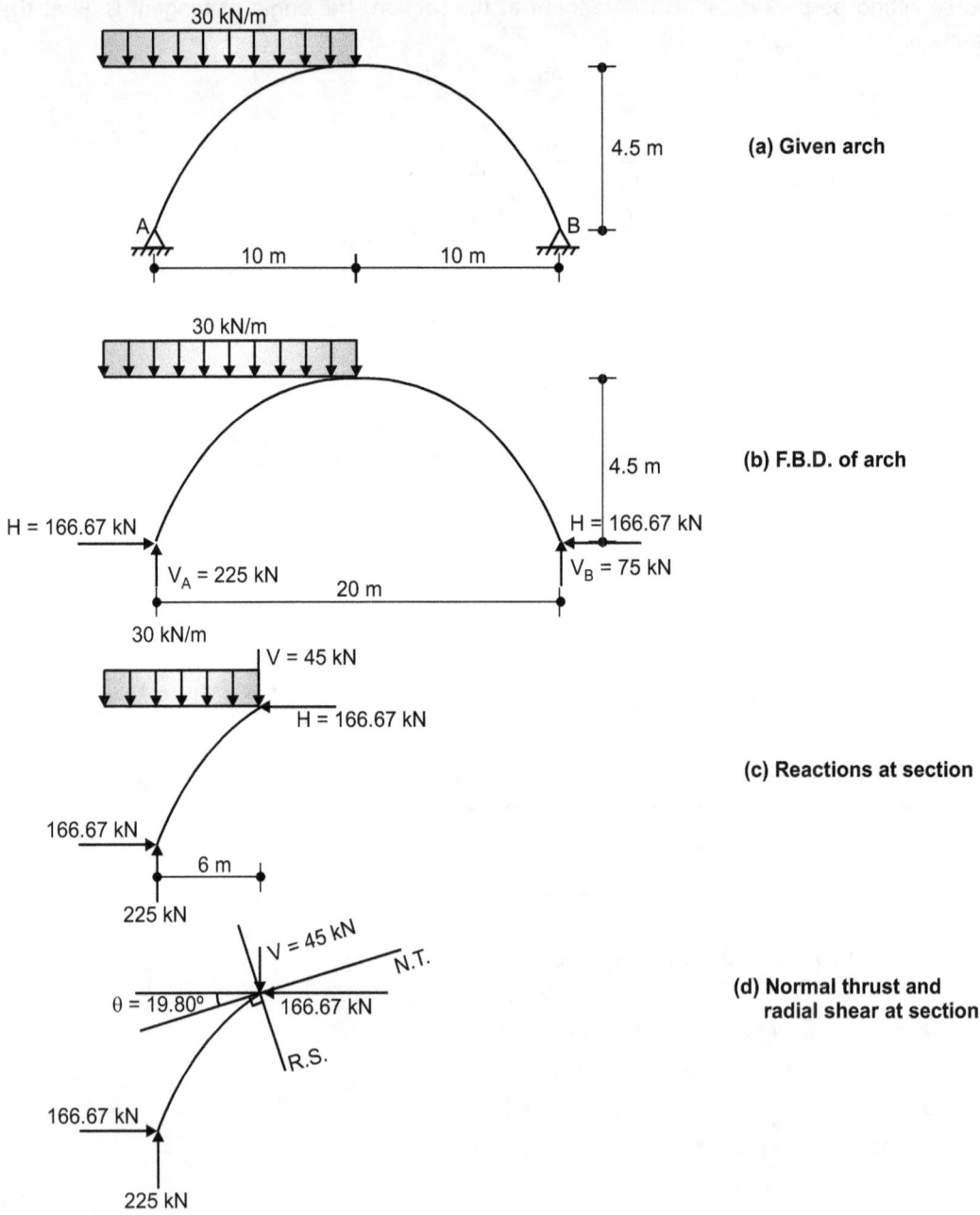

Fig. 11.17

$$\int My \frac{ds}{EI} = \int_0^{10} \left(225x - \frac{30x^2}{2}\right) \frac{4hx}{L^2}(L-x) \frac{dx}{EI} + \int_0^{10} 75x \cdot \frac{4hx}{L^2}(L-x) \frac{dx}{EI}$$

$$= \int_0^{10} (225x - 15x^2) \frac{4 \times 4.5x}{20^2}(20-x) \frac{dx}{EI} + \int_0^{10} 75x \times \frac{4 \times 4.5x}{20^2}(20-x) \frac{dx}{EI}$$

$$= \frac{21937.5}{EI} + \frac{14062.5}{EI} = \frac{36000}{EI} \quad \ldots (2)$$

$$\int y^2 \frac{ds}{EI} = \int_0^{20} \left[\frac{4hx}{L^2}(L-x)\right]^2 \frac{dx}{EI} = \int_0^{20} \frac{4^2 \times 4.5^2 x^2}{20^4}(20-x)^2 \frac{dx}{EI} = \frac{216}{EI} \quad \ldots (3)$$

Substituting values in equation (1),

$$H = \frac{\left(\frac{36000}{EI}\right)}{\left(\frac{216}{EI}\right)} = 166.67 \text{ kN}$$

Step IV : F.B.D. of arch is as shown in Fig. 11.17 (b).

Step V : Normal thrust is a force acting along the tangent at the section. Radial force is a force acting perpendicular to the tangent at the section. The angle of tangent is 'θ' at the section.

We have,
$$y = \frac{4hx}{L^2}(L-x)$$

$$\frac{dy}{dx} = \frac{4h}{L^2}(L-2x)$$

At x = 6 m,
$$\frac{dy}{dx} = \tan\theta = \frac{4 \times 4.5}{20^2}(20 - 2 \times 6)$$

$$\tan\theta = 0.36$$

∴ $$\theta = 19.80°$$

Step VI : Considering the part of arch on left of the section. Applying equilibrium equations, the reactions at the section are as shown in Fig. 11.17 (c).

Step VII : Normal thrust and radial shear are as shown in Fig. 11.17 (d).

Step VIII : Resolving the forces along tangent at the section,

∴ Normal thrust = V sin θ + H cos θ
= 45 sin 19.80 + 166.67 cos 19.80
= 172.06 kN (↗ 19.80°)

Step IX : Resolving the forces perpendicular to the tangent,

Radial shear = H sin θ − V cos θ = 166.67 sin 19.80 − 45 cos 19.80
= 14.12 kN (↘ 70.20°)

EXERCISE

1. Derive the expression for horizontal thrust as

$$H = \int_x \frac{My\,ds}{EI} \Big/ \int \frac{y^2\,ds}{EI}$$

for two-hinged arch.

2. Draw I.L.D. for horizontal thrust when whole arch is loaded with U.D.L. of 50 kN/m. Span of arch is 30 m. Also draw I.L.D. for normal thrust and radial shear at a distance 10 m from support A.

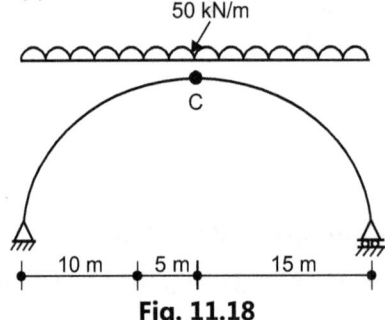

Fig. 11.18

3. Find the horizontal thrust for the two-hinged arch ACB when loaded with U.D.L. of intensity 32 kN/m.

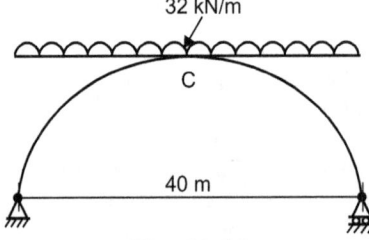

Fig. 11.19

❏❏❏

UNIT - VI

Chapter 12

PLASTIC THEORY

12.1 PRIMARY CONCEPTS OF PLASTIC COLLAPSE

Linear elastic analysis of structures have been discussed in earlier chapters to determine the stresses and deformations under working load. Plastic analysis will be introduced in this chapter to understand the behaviour of steel beams and frames in the plastic range. The aim of the plastic analysis is to assess the load at which a structure fails by the plastic collapse i.e. the development of excessive deflection. The basic concepts of plastic collapse are illustrated by the behaviour of a simply supported steel I-beam carrying a central concentrated load as shown in Fig. 12.1 (a). As the load increases, the central deflection also increases as shown in Fig. 12.1 (b).

Upto the load W_y, the beam is elastic and the extreme fibre stress reaches the yield stress σ_y. The stress distribution over the section at load position is shown in Fig. 12.1 (c). At the load W_y, the central deflection Δ increases very sharply for small increase in the load. As the load is increased further, the beam may fail catastrophically by buckling at the load W_{cr} as shown in Fig. 12.1 (b). But before the load W_{cr}, the collapse of the beam is considered at the load W_u due to excessive deflections. Therefore, the behaviour of the beam is idealized by the indefinite deflection under the constant load W_u as represented by the dotted line in Fig. 12.1 (b). The idealized stress distribution over the cross-section of the beam at W_u is shown in Fig. 12.1 (c). The plastic hinge is said to be formed at the point C as shown in Fig. 12.1 (d) and the structure i.e. beam is transformed into a mechanism as shown in Fig. 12.1 (e). From the above illustration, the plastic behaviour is characterized by the following primary concepts :

(i) **Plasticity :** It is defined as the state of permanent deformation without fracture in a material, caused by the stresses which are greater than the yielding stresses.

When all fibres of the beam section in compression and tension zones reach the yield stress σ_y of the material, the cross-section is said to be in fully plastic state as shown in Fig. 12.1 (c).

(ii) **Plastic hinge :** When the entire cross-section of the beam becomes fully plastic, an infinitely small increase in applied moment would cause large increase in curvature. This effect is known as the *plastic hinge*. The distinct feature of the plastic hinge is that it can undergo indefinite rotation at the constant moment. Plastic hinge is not a section but it is the zone of yielding near the section of full plasticity as shown in Fig. 12.1 (d). However, for the analysis, the plastic hinge is assumed at the section. Plastic hinge is different than a structural hinge. A structural hinge is physical arrangement of frictionless hinge which cannot resist moment. Plastic hinge is a virtual hinge due to effect of stresses, carrying constant moments on either side of the section. Therefore, it is considered as rusty hinge.

(iii) **Plastic moment :** The bending moment required to develop a plastic hinge is termed as the plastic moment and denoted by M_p. It is related to the yield stress of the material and the cross-section of the beam. Thus, it is the property of the section. Plastic moment is given by

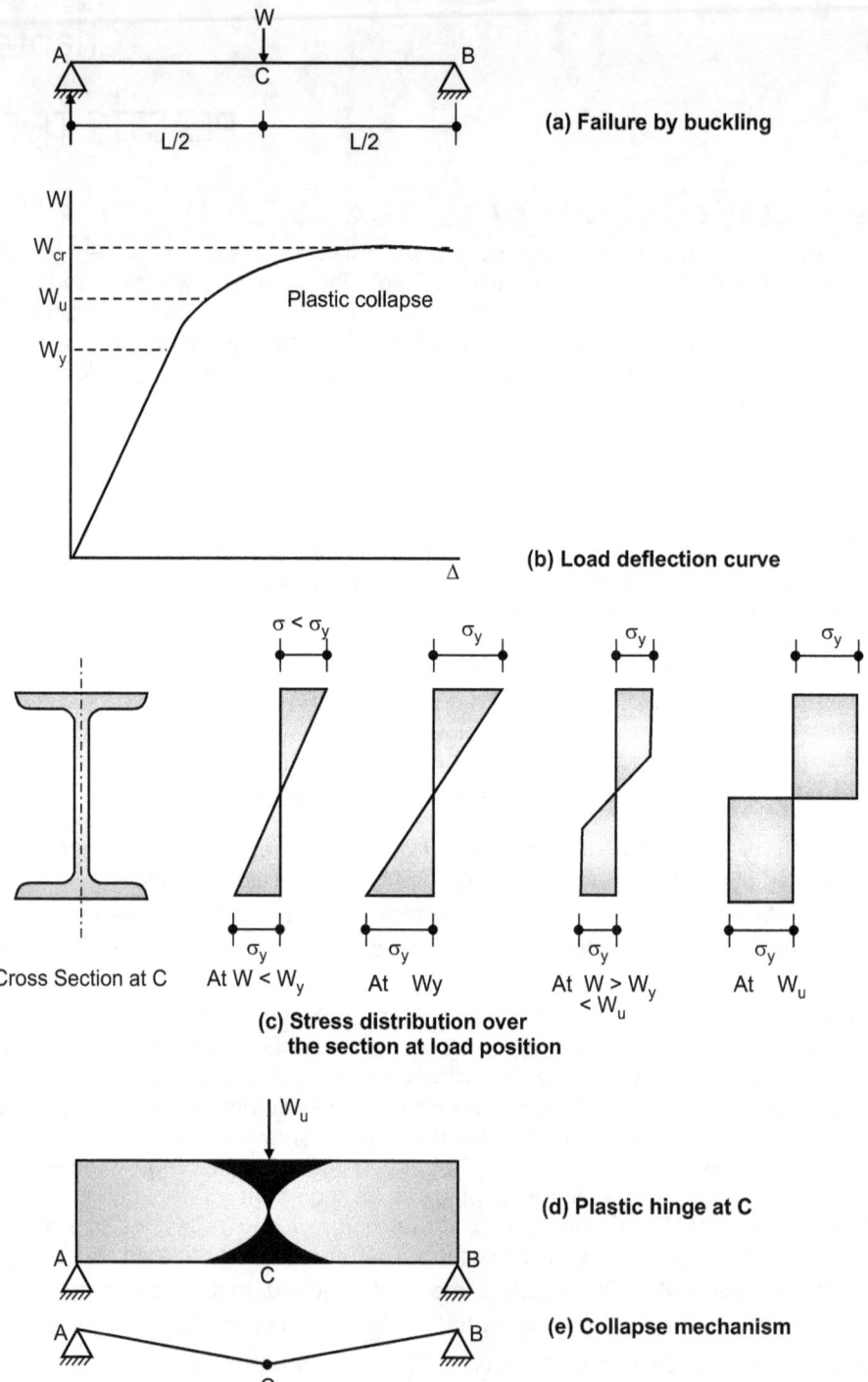

Fig. 12.1 : Elastic - Plastic Behaviour of Beam

$$M_p = \int_{Area} (\sigma_y \cdot dA)\, y$$

(iv) Plastic collapse : It is a condition at which the indefinite deflection occurs at the constant load or a condition in which small increase in load will cause indefinite deformation. Plastic collapse is also termed as collapse mechanism.

(v) Plastic collapse load : The load at which plastic collapse occurs is the plastic collapse load. It is also termed as the ultimate load and denoted by W_u.

(vi) Load factor : The ratio of the collapse load to the working load is called the load factor and it is denoted by λ.

With these primary concepts of plastic collapse, plastic theory is to be developed to analyze the beams and frames to predict the ultimate load.

12.2 ASSUMPTIONS OF PLASTIC THEORY

Plastic analysis, mainly based on plastic theory of bending, is simplified on the following assumptions :

(i) The material is ductile and elastic plastic.
(ii) The stress-strain relation is idealized as bilinear in tension as well as compression as shown in Fig. 12.2. The material follows Hooke's law upto the yield stress σ_y and then yields plastically at constant stress. This means that OA is a straight line having a slope equal to the modulus of elasticity E and AB is horizontal extending without limit.
(iii) Strain hardening is neglected.　(iv) The deformations are small.
(v) Originally plane sections remain plane.
(vi) There are no residual stresses.　(vii) The beam is initially straight.
(viii) The beam is bend by pure bending. The influence of axial force and shear force on the plastic moment is neglected.

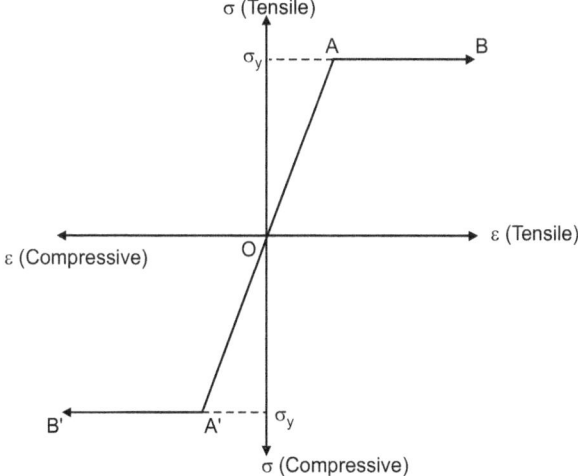

Fig. 12.2 : Idealized stress-strain curve

(ix) The cross-section is symmetrical with respect to an axis which lies in the plane of bending.
(x) The loading is proportional.
(xi) The cross-section has a maximum resisting moment equal to plastic moment.
(xii) The spread of the plastic hinge is neglected and the plastic hinge forms at the critical section.
(xiii) Behaviour is elastic in between plastic hinges.
(xiv) Connections proportioned for full continuity transmit the plastic moment.
(xv) No instability occurs prior to the attainment of the ultimate load.
(xvi) Sufficient number of plastic hinges are formed to transform a structure into a mechanism.

12.3 ELASTIC-PLASTIC BENDING

The rectangular cross-section of breadth b and depth D is subjected to bending moment about an axis parallel to the breadth i.e. neutral axis, as shown in Fig. 12.3. The strain distributions and stress distributions are shown in Fig. 12.3 (a) to (c), as the applied moment is progressively increased. For both the elastic and elastic-plastic ranges, the relations between the extreme fibre stress, the bending moment and the curvature can be easily developed as given below.

It may be noted that the curvature ϕ is the rate of change of slope of the cross-section of the beam i.e. $\phi = \dfrac{d\theta}{ds}$. Following stages are important to investigate.

(i) When the entire section is elastic as shown in Fig. 12.3 (a), the bending stress is given by

$$\sigma = \frac{M}{I} \cdot y \qquad \ldots (12.1)$$

where I is the second moment of area about the neutral axis. The curvature is expressed by

$$\phi = \frac{\varepsilon}{y} = \frac{M}{EI}$$

(ii) When the extreme fibre stresses just equal to the yield stress, the elastic range ends and the bending moment is called the *yield moment*, M_y. Bending stress and yield moment and curvature are related by

$$\sigma_y = \frac{M_y}{I}(D/2)$$

$$\phi_y = \frac{2\varepsilon_y}{D} = \frac{M_y}{EI}$$

$$\therefore \quad M_y = \frac{\sigma_y I}{(D/2)} = \sigma_y \left(\frac{bD^2}{6}\right) = \sigma_y Z_e \qquad \ldots (12.2)$$

where Z_e is the elastic section modulus.

(iii) As the moment is increased beyond M_y, the stress distribution may be partly elastic and partly plastic as shown in Fig. 12.3 (b). It may be noted that the maximum strains will exceed the yield strain ε_y but the maximum stresses remain constant at σ_y. It can be shown that bending moment is obtained by :

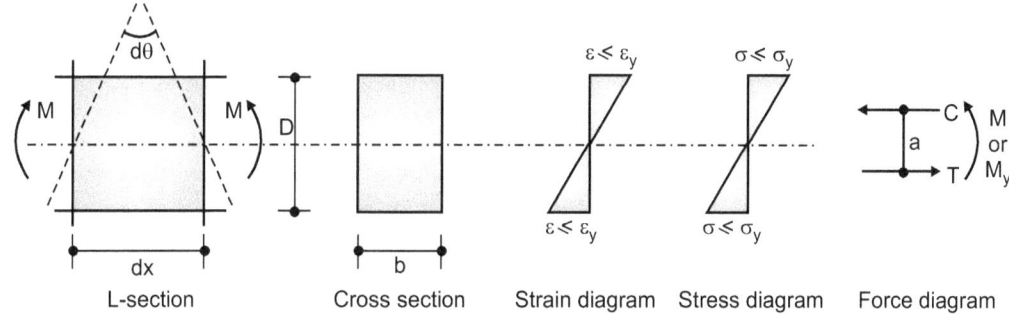

(a) Elastic range

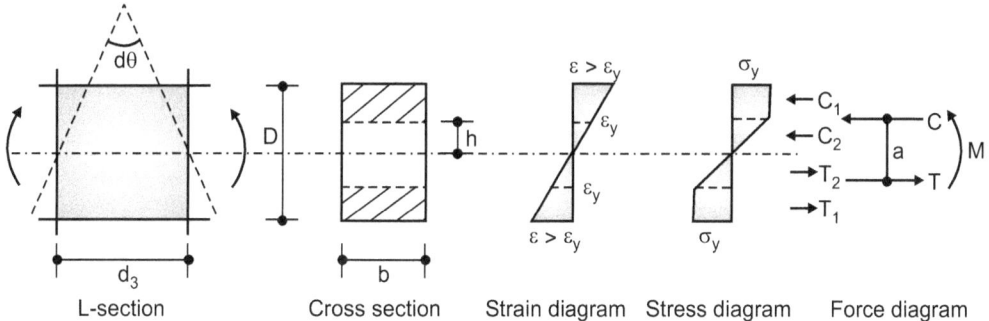

(b) Plastic range

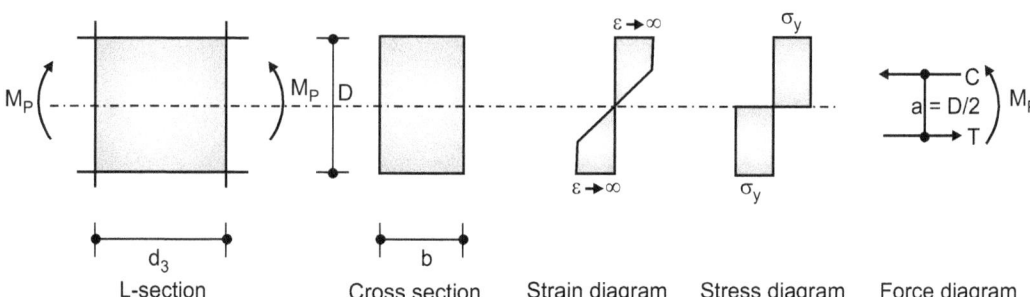

(c) Fully plastic condition

Fig. 12.3 : Elastic-Plastic Bending

$$M = \left(\frac{1}{2}\sigma_y \cdot b \cdot h\right)\left(\frac{4}{3}h\right) + \left[\sigma_y b\left(\frac{D}{2}-h\right)\right]\left(\frac{D}{2}+h\right)$$

$$= \sigma_y b\left[\frac{D^2}{4} - \frac{1}{3}h^2\right] \qquad \ldots (12.3)$$

The corresponding curvature is given by

$$\phi = \frac{\varepsilon_y}{h}$$

(iv) With further increase in M, more fibres become plastic until the whole cross-section is plastic as shown in Fig. 12.3 (c). The bending moment at full plasticity is called the plastic moment, M_p and expressed as :

$$M_p = (\sigma_y)\left(\frac{bD}{2}\right)\left(\frac{D}{2}\right) = (\sigma_y)\left(\frac{bD^2}{4}\right) = \sigma_y Z_p \qquad \ldots (12.4)$$

The quantity $\left(\frac{bD^2}{4}\right)$ is called plastic section modulus and denoted by Z_p.

From above discussions it is interesting to obtain the bending moment - curvature relation in non-dimensional form as follows :

$$\frac{M}{M_y} = \frac{\sigma_y b\left[\frac{D^2}{4} - \frac{1}{3}h^2\right]}{\sigma_y b \frac{D^2}{6}}$$

$$\therefore \quad \frac{M}{M_y} = \frac{\sigma_y b \frac{D^2}{4}}{\sigma_y b \frac{D^2}{6}} - \frac{\sigma_y bh^2/3}{\sigma_y bD^2/6}$$

$$\therefore \quad \frac{M}{M_y} = 1.5 - 2\frac{h^2}{D^2}$$

As $\quad \phi = \frac{\varepsilon_y}{h}$ and $\phi_y = \frac{2\varepsilon_y}{D}$

$$\therefore \quad \frac{M}{M_y} = 1.5 - 2\frac{(1\,\varepsilon_y/\phi)^2}{(2\,\varepsilon_y/\phi_y)^2}$$

$$\therefore \quad \frac{M}{M_y} = 1.5 - 0.5\left(\frac{\phi_y}{\phi}\right)^2 \qquad \ldots (12.5)$$

The moment-curvature relation in non-dimensional form is shown in Fig. 12.4 which gives the following important conclusions.

M tends to a limiting value 1.5 M_y as ϕ becomes very large. Therefore in the limit, when M = 1.5 M_y, ϕ is infinite.

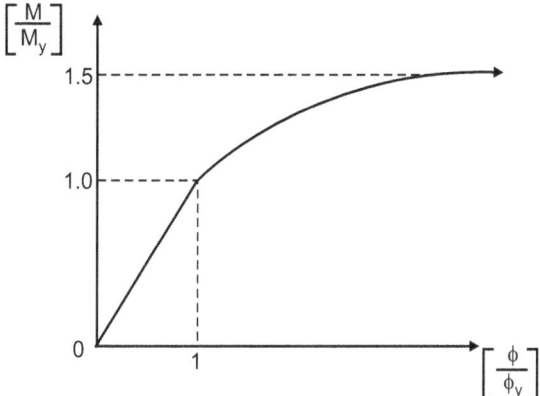

Fig. 12.4 : Non-dimensional moment-curvature relationship for rectangular section

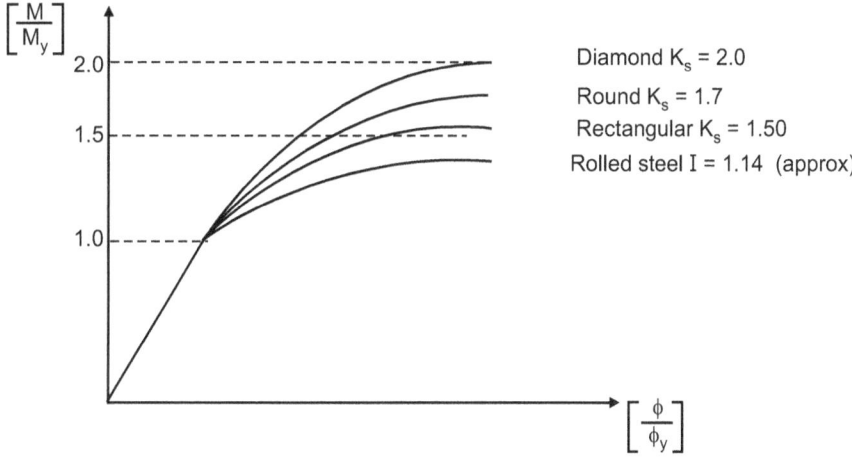

Diamond K_s = 2.0
Round K_s = 1.7
Rectangular K_s = 1.50
Rolled steel I = 1.14 (approx)

(a) Non-dimensional moment-curvature relationship for typical beam sections

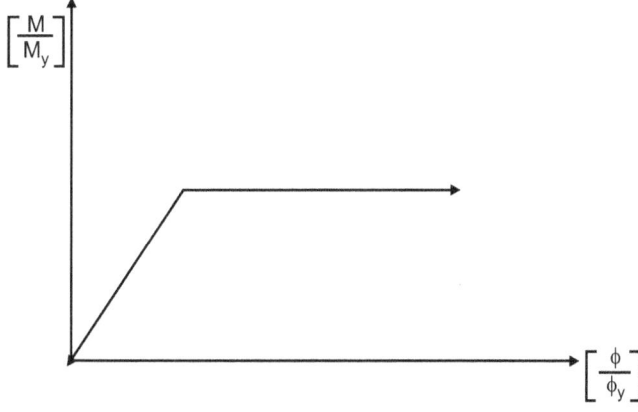

(b) Idealized non-dimensional moment-curvature relationship

Fig. 12.5 : Moment-curvature relationships

This limiting condition corresponds to the fully plastic state of the cross-section and the corresponding bending moment is the plastic moment M_p. Because of infinite curvature, this effect is considered as the formation of the plastic hinge at the section.

12.4 SHAPE FACTOR AND PLASTIC SECTION MODULUS

The ratio of the plastic moment M_p of a section to its yield moment M_y is called the *shape factor* and denoted by K_s.

The shape factor for a rectangular section is :

$$K_s = \frac{M_p}{M_y} = \frac{\sigma_y \, bD^2/4}{\sigma_y \, bD^2/6} = \frac{Z_p}{Z_e} = 1.5$$

The shape factor depends solely on the shape of the cross-section. For the given cross-section, the shape factor can be derived. Shape factors for various cross-sections are as follows :

- Diamond section : 2.0
- Circular section : 1.7
- Rectangular section : 1.5
- Rolled steel beam section: 1.15 (approximately)

At any stage of transverse loading on a beam, the equilibrium specifies that the resultant force on the cross-section must be zero i.e.

$$\int_{Area} (\sigma)(dA) = 0 \qquad \ldots (12.6)$$

Accordingly, in elastic bending, the neutral axis must pass through the centroid of the cross-section.

Under fully plastic condition, the above equilibrium equation becomes

$$\int_{Area} (\sigma_y)(dA) = 0 \qquad \ldots (12.7)$$

If σ_y is same for tension and compression, then

$$\int_{Area} (dA) = 0$$

Therefore in plastic bending, the neutral axis must divide the cross-section into two equal areas. For symmetrical section, plastic neutral axis coincides with the elastic neutral axis, passing through the centroid of the section.

For unsymmetrical section in plastic bending, the position of the neutral axis changes. It means plastic neutral axis does not pass through the centroid but it divides the area into two equal parts as shown in Fig. 12.6 (a). If the yield stress is same in tension and compression, the position of the plastic neutral axis is determined from the condition

$$A_c = A_t = \frac{A}{2}$$

where A is the total area of cross-section of the beam.

A_c is the area of cross-section in compression.

A_t is the area of cross-section in tension.

And the plastic section modulus is computed from the equation

$$Z_p = \frac{A}{2} \cdot \bar{y}_c + \frac{A}{2} \cdot \bar{y}_t \qquad \ldots (12.8)$$

where $\bar{y}_c$ is the distance of the centroid of A_c from plastic neutral axis.

$\bar{y}_t$ is the distance of the centroid of A_t from plastic neutral axis.

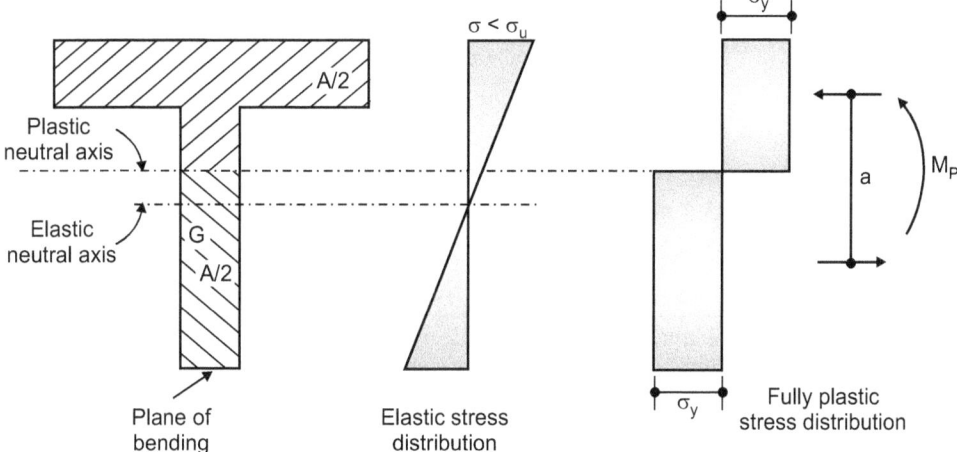

(a) Fully plastic stress distribution and moment for cross-section with $\sigma_{yc} = \sigma_{yt} = \sigma_y$

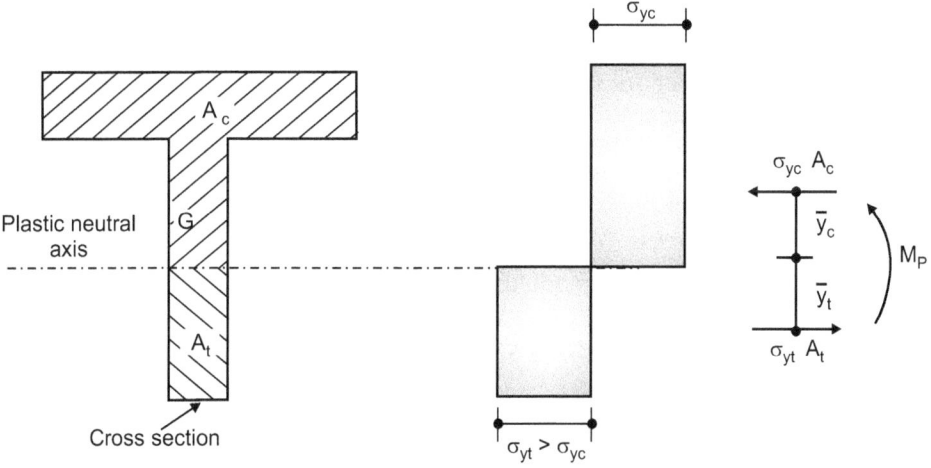

(b) Fully plastic stress distribution and moment for cross-section with $\sigma_{yt} > \sigma_{yc}$

Fig. 12.6 : Plastic moment for unsymmetrical beam section

The plastic moment of a section is the product of the yield stress and the plastic section modulus.

i.e. $\quad M_p = \sigma_y \cdot Z_p = \sigma_y \cdot \frac{1}{2} A \cdot \bar{y}_c + \sigma_y \cdot \frac{1}{2} A \cdot \bar{y}_t$ ... (12.9)

It may be noted that if the yield stress is different in tension and compression, the plastic neutral axis will not divide the cross-section into two equal parts as shown in Fig. 12.6 (b). Therefore, the position of plastic neutral axis, in this case, is obtained from the equation

$$\sigma_{yc} \cdot A_c = \sigma_{yt} \cdot A_t \qquad \ldots (12.10)$$

And the plastic moment of the section is to be obtained carefully by taking moments of forces about the plastic neutral axis, as given by the equation

$$M_p = \sigma_{yc} \cdot A_c \cdot \bar{y}_c + \sigma_{yt} \cdot A_t \cdot \bar{y}_t \qquad \ldots (12.11)$$

The shape factor also measures the ratio of M_p to M_y, therefore, it is reflected in moment curvature curve in the form of transition from M_y to M_p, as shown in Fig. 12.5 (a) for different shapes.

If the shape factor is assumed as one then M_p is equal to M_y and the moment-curvature curve is idealized as bilinear as shown in Fig. 12.5 (b).

12.4.1 Plastic Analysis of Cross-Section

The procedure of plastic analysis of cross-section of a beam is formulated as below :
Data : (i) Cross-section : Shape and size. (ii) Material : Yield stresses, σ_y.
Objects : (i) Shape factor. (ii) Plastic moment.
Concepts and Equations : (i) Theory of plastic bending.
(ii) $K_s = \dfrac{Z_p}{Z_e}$ or $K_s = \dfrac{M_p}{M_y}$ (iii) $M_p = \sigma_y \cdot Z_p$ or $M_p = \sigma_{yc} A_c \bar{y}_c + \sigma_{yt} A_t \bar{y}_t$

Procedure :
(A) For symmetric sections having $\sigma_{yc} = \sigma_{yt}$
Step I : Locate elastic neutral axis.
Step II : Locate plastic neutral axis using $A_c = A_t$.
Step III : Find elastic section modulus (Z_e).

$$Z_e = \frac{I}{Y}$$

Step IV : Find plastic section modulus (Z_p).

$$Z_p = A_c \cdot \bar{y}_c + A_t \cdot \bar{y}_t$$

Step V : Find shape factor (K_s).

$$K_s = \frac{Z_p}{Z_e}$$

(B) (i) For symmetric sections having $\sigma_{yc} \neq \sigma_{yt}$
(ii) For unsymmetric sections having $\sigma_{yc} = \sigma_{yt}$ and
(iii) For unsymmetric sections having $\sigma_{yc} \neq \sigma_{yt}$

Step I : Locate elastic neutral axis.
Step II : Locate plastic neutral axis using $A_c = A_t$.
Step III : Find elastic section modulus (Z_e).

(a) Elastic section modulus with reference to compression side = $Z_{ec} = \dfrac{I}{y_c}$

(b) Elastic section modulus with reference to tension side = $Z_{et} = \dfrac{I}{y_t}$

Step IV : Find yield moment (M_y) :
(a) Yield moment with reference to compression side = $M_{yc} = \sigma_{yc} \cdot Z_{ec}$
(b) Yield moment with reference to tension side = $M_{yt} = \sigma_{yt} \cdot Z_{et}$.
∴ Yield moment = M_y = Least of M_{yc} and M_{yt}

Step V : Find plastic moment (M_p) :

$$M_p = \sigma_{yc}(A_c \cdot \bar{y}_c) + \sigma_{yt}(A_t \cdot \bar{y}_t)$$

Step VI : Find shape factor (K_s) :

$$K_s = \dfrac{M_p}{M_y}$$

SOLVED PROBLEMS

Problem 12.1 : For the cross-section of a beam shown in Fig. 12.7 (a), find the shape factor.

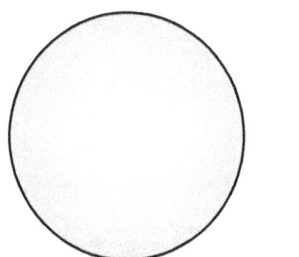  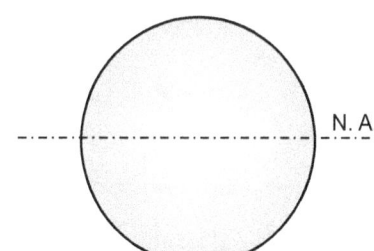

(a) Given cross-section of the beam   (b) Elastic and plastic neutral axis of cross-section

Fig. 12.7 : Illustrative Problem 12.1

Solution : Data : Cross-section of the beam as shown in Fig. 12.7.
Object : Shape factor (K_s).

Concepts and Equations : (i) Theory of plastic bending. (ii) $K_s = \dfrac{Z_p}{Z_e}$

Procedure :

Step I : Elastic neutral axis : Horizontal axis passing through the centroid of cross-section as shown in Fig. 12.7 (b).

Step II : Plastic neutral axis : Horizontal axis passing through the centroid of cross-section as shown in Fig. 12.7 (b).

Step III : Elastic section modulus (Z_e) :

$$I = \frac{\pi}{64}(D)^4$$

$$Z_e = \frac{I}{Y} = \frac{(\pi/64)\,D^4}{D/2} = \frac{\pi}{32}(D)^3$$

Step IV : Plastic section modulus (Z_p) :

Sr. No.	Area in compression	Distance of c.g. of 'A_c' from plastic neutral axis ($\bar{y}_c$)	$A_c \cdot \bar{y}_c$
1.	$\frac{\pi}{8}(D)^2$	$\frac{4D}{6\pi}$	$\frac{D^3}{12}$

Sr. No.	Area in tension (A_t)	Distance of c.g. of 'A_t' from plastic neutral axis ($\bar{y}_t$)	$A_t \cdot \bar{y}_t$
1.	$\frac{\pi}{8}(D)^2$	$\frac{4D}{6\pi}$	$\frac{D^3}{12}$

$$Z_p = A_c \cdot \bar{y}_c + A_t \cdot \bar{y}_t = \frac{D^3}{12} + \frac{D^3}{12} = \frac{D^3}{6}$$

Step V : Shape factor (K_s) :

$$K_s = \frac{Z_p}{Z_e} = \frac{D^3/6}{(\pi/32)\,D^3} = \frac{32}{6\pi} = 1.697$$

Problem 12.2 : For the cross-section of a beam shown in Fig. 12.8 (a), find the shape factor.

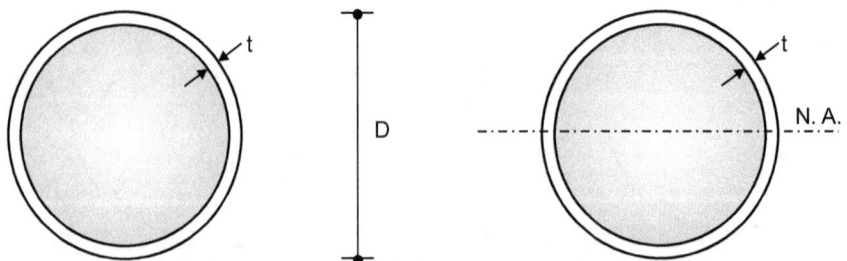

(a) Given cross-section of the beam   **(b)** Elastic and plastic neutral axis of cross-section

Fig. 12.8 : Illustrative Problem 12.2

Solution : Data : Cross-section of the beam as shown in Fig. 12.8 (a).
Object : Shape factor (K_s).
Concepts and Equations :

(i) Theory of plastic bending. (ii) $K_s = \dfrac{Z_p}{Z_e}$.

Procedure :

Step I : Elastic neutral axis : Horizontal axis passing through the centroid of cross-section as shown in Fig. 12.8 (b).

Step II : Plastic neutral axis : Horizontal axis passing through the centroid of cross-section as shown in Fig. 12.8 (b).

Step III : Elastic section modulus (Z_e) :

$$I = \frac{\pi}{64}(D^4 - (D-2t)^4) = \frac{\pi}{64}(D^4 - (D^2 - 4tD + 4t^2)^2) = \frac{\pi D^3 t}{8}$$

(∵ Neglecting terms of t^2 and t^3 as 't' is very small compared to 'D').

$$Z_e = \frac{I}{y} = \frac{\pi D^3 t/8}{D/2} = \frac{\pi D^2 t}{4}$$

Step IV : Plastic section modulus (Z_p) :

Using the result of Problem 12.1.

$$Z_p = \frac{1}{6}(D^3 - (D-2t)^3) = \frac{1}{6}[D^3 - D^3 + 6D^2 t + 12Dt^2 - 8t^3] = D^2 t$$

(∵ Neglecting terms of $t^2 - 8t^3$)

Step V : Shape factor (K_s) :

$$K_s = \frac{Z_p}{Z_e} = \frac{D^2 t}{\pi D^2 t / 4} = 1.274$$

Problem 12.3 : For the cross-section of a beam shown in Fig. 12.9 (a), find the shape factor.

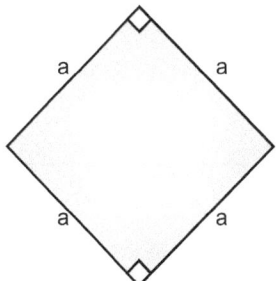
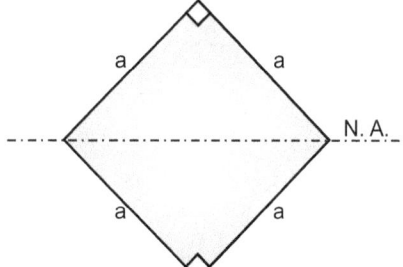

(a) Given cross-section of the beam (b) Elastic and plastic neutral axis of cross-section

Fig. 12.9 : Illustrative Problem 12.3

Solution : Data : Cross-section of the beam as shown in Fig. 12.9.
Object : Shape factor (K_s)
Concepts and Equations :
(i) Theory of plastic bending.
(ii) $K_s = \dfrac{Z_p}{Z_e}$

Procedure :

Step I : Elastic neutral axis : Horizontal axis passing through the centroid of cross-section as shown in Fig. 12.9 (b).

Step II : Plastic neutral axis : Horizontal axis passing through the centroid of cross-section as shown in Fig. 12.9 (b).

Step III : Elastic section modulus (Z_e) :

$$I = 2\left[\frac{1}{12}(\sqrt{2}\,a)\left(\frac{1}{\sqrt{2}}\right)^3\right] = \frac{a^4}{12}$$

$$Z_e = \frac{I}{y} = \frac{a^4/12}{a/\sqrt{2}} = \frac{a^3}{6\sqrt{2}}$$

Step IV : Plastic section modulus (Z_p) :

Sr. No.	Area in compression (A_c) (mm²)	Distance of c.g. of 'A_c' from plastic neutral axis ($\bar{y}_c$) (mm)	$A_c \cdot \bar{y}_c$ (mm³)	Sr. No.	Area in tension (A_t) (mm²)	Distance of c.g. of 'A_t' from plastic neutral axis ($\bar{y}_t$) (mm)	$A_t \cdot \bar{y}_t$ (mm³)
1.	$\frac{1}{2}(\sqrt{2}\,a)\frac{a}{\sqrt{2}}$ $=\frac{a^2}{2}$	$\frac{1}{3}\left(\frac{a}{\sqrt{2}}\right)$ $=\frac{a}{3\sqrt{2}}$	$\frac{a^3}{6\sqrt{2}}$	1.	$\frac{1}{2}(\sqrt{2}\,a)\frac{a}{\sqrt{2}}$ $=\frac{a^2}{2}$	$\frac{1}{3}\left(\frac{a}{\sqrt{(2)}}\right)$ $=\frac{a}{3\sqrt{2}}$	$\frac{a^3}{6\sqrt{(2)}}$

$$Z_p = A_c \cdot \bar{y}_c + A_t \cdot \bar{y}_t = \frac{a^3}{6\sqrt{2}} + \frac{a^3}{6\sqrt{2}} = \frac{a^3}{3\sqrt{2}}$$

Step V : Shape factor (K_s) :

$$K_s = \frac{Z_p}{Z_e} = \frac{a^3/3\sqrt{2}}{a^3/6\sqrt{2}} = 2$$

Problem 12.4 : For the cross-section of a beam shown in Fig. 12.10 (a), find the shape factor.

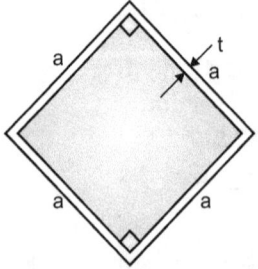 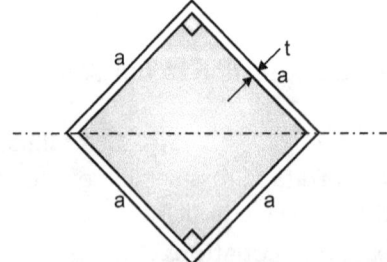

(a) Given cross-section of the beam   (b) Elastic and plastic neutral axis of cross-section
Fig. 12.10 : Illustrative Problem 12.4

Solution : Data : Cross-section of the beam as shown in Fig. 12.10.
Object : Shape factor (K_s).

Concepts and Equations : (i) Theory of plastic bending. (ii) $K_s = \dfrac{Z_p}{Z_e}$

Procedure :

Step I : Elastic neutral axis : Horizontal axis passing through the centroid of cross-section as shown in Fig. 12.10 (b).

Step II : Plastic neutral axis : Horizontal axis passing through the centroid of cross-section as shown in Fig. 12.10 (b).

Step III : Elastic section modulus (Z_e) :

$$I = \frac{1}{12}(a^4 - (a-2t)^4) = \frac{2a^3 t}{3}$$

(∵ Neglecting terms of t^2 and t^3 as 't' is very small as compared to 'a')

$$Z_e = \frac{I}{y} = \frac{2a^3 t/3}{a/\sqrt{2}} = \frac{2\sqrt{2}\, a^2 t}{3}$$

Step IV : Plastic section modulus (Z_p) :

Using the result of example :

$$Z_p = \frac{1}{3\sqrt{2}}(a^3 - (a-2t)^3) = \frac{1}{3\sqrt{2}}[a^3 - (a^3 - 6a^2 t + 12at^2 - 8t^3)]$$

$$= \sqrt{2}\, a^2 t \qquad (\because \text{Neglecting terms of } t^2 \text{ and } t^3)$$

Step V : Shape factor (K_s) :

$$K_s = \frac{Z_p}{Z_e} = \frac{\sqrt{2}\, a^2 t}{2\sqrt{2}\, a^2 t/3} = \frac{3}{2} = 1.5$$

Problem 12.5 : For the cross-section of a beam shown in Fig. 12.11 (a), find the shape factor and plastic moment if permissible yield stress in compression and tension is 250 MPa.

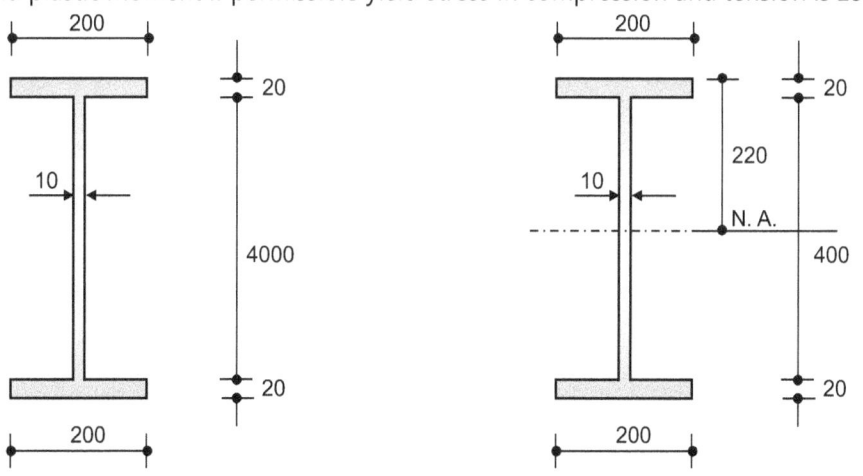

(a) Given cross-section of the beam (b) Elastic and plastic neutral axis of cross-section

Fig. 12.11 : Illustrative Problem 12.5

Solution : Data : (i) Cross-section of the beam as shown in Fig. 12.11.
(ii) Material yield stress : σ_y = 250 MPa.
Objects : (i) Shape factor (K_s).
(ii) Plastic moment (M_p).
Concepts and Equations :
(i) Theory of plastic bending.
(ii) $K_s = \dfrac{Z_p}{Z_e}$
(iii) $M_p = \sigma_y \cdot Z_p$.

Procedure :

Step I : Elastic neutral axis : 220 mm from top (∵ By symmetry) as shown in Fig. 12.11 (b).

Step II : Plastic neutral axis : 220 mm from top (∵ By symmetry) as shown in Fig. 12.11 (b).

Step III : Elastic section modulus (Z_e) :

$$I = \frac{200 \times (440)^3}{12} - \frac{190 \times (400)^3}{12} = 406.4 \times 10^6 \text{ mm}^4$$

$$Z_e = \frac{I}{y} = \frac{406.4 \times 10^6}{220} = 1.847 \times 10^6 \text{ mm}^3$$

Step IV : Plastic section modulus (Z_p) :

Sr. No.	Area in compression (A_c) (mm²)	Distances of c.g. of 'A_c' from plastic neutral axis ($\bar{y}_c$) (mm)	$A_c \cdot \bar{y}_c$ (mm³)	Sr. No.	Area in tension (A_t) (mm²)	Distances of c.g. of 'A_t' from plastic neutral axis ($\bar{y}_t$) (mm)	$A_t \cdot \bar{y}_t$ (mm³)
1.	200 × 20 = 4000	$200 + \dfrac{20}{2} = 210$	840000	1.	200 × 20 = 4000	$200 + \dfrac{20}{2} = 210$	840000
2.	200 × 10 = 2000	$\dfrac{200}{2} = 100$	200000	2.	200 × 10 = 2000	$\dfrac{200}{2} = 100$	200000
		$\Sigma =$	1040000			$\Sigma =$	1040000

$$Z_p = A_c \cdot \bar{y}_c + A_t \cdot \bar{y}_t$$
$$= 1040000 + 1040000 = 2.08 \times 10^6 \text{ mm}^3$$

Step V : Shape factor (K_s) :

$$K_s = \frac{Z_p}{Z_e} = \frac{2.08 \times 10^6}{1.847 \times 10^6} = 1.126$$

Step VI : Plastic moment (M_p) :

$$M_p = \sigma_y \cdot Z_p = (250 \times 2.08 \times 10^6) \times 10^{-6} = 520 \text{ kNm}$$

Problem 12.6 : Cross-section of the beam shown in Fig. 12.12 (a) is subjected to sagging bending moment. Find the shape factor if permissible yield stress in compression and tension is σ_y. Hence, assuming factor of safety = 1.7, find load factor.

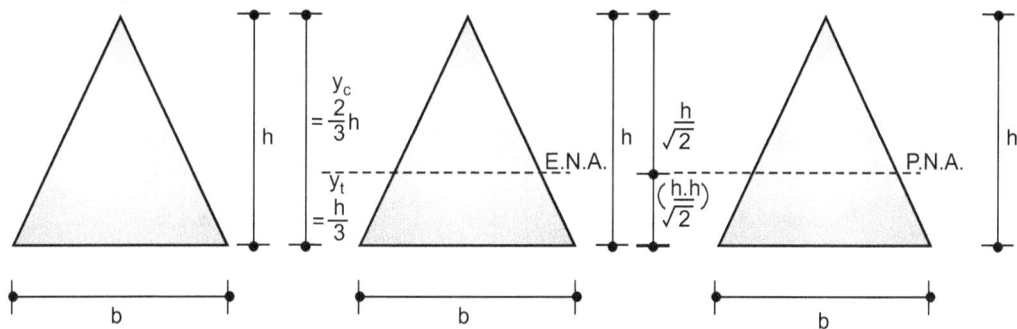

(a) Given cross-section of the beam
(b) Elastic neutral axis of the cross-section
(c) Plastic neutral axis of the cross-section

Fig. 12.12 : Illustrative Problem 12.6

Solution : Data : (i) Cross-section of the beam as shown in Fig. 12.12 (a).
(ii) Material yield stresses : $\sigma_{yc} = \sigma_{yt} = \sigma_y$

Objects : (i) Plastic moment (M_p), (ii) Shape factor (K_s).

Concepts and Equations :

(i) Theory of plastic bending; (ii) Shape factor (K_s); (iii) $K_s = \dfrac{M_p}{M_y}$

Procedure :

Step I : Elastic neutral axis : $2h/3$ from top.

$$\therefore \quad y_c = \left(\dfrac{2}{3}\right)h \text{ and } y_t = h/3 \text{ as shown in Fig. 12.12 (b).}$$

Step II : Plastic neutral axis :

Width of triangle at a distance x_p from top = $b' = \left(\dfrac{b}{h}\right) x_p$

$$A_c = A_t$$

$$\therefore \quad \dfrac{1}{2}\left(\dfrac{b}{h}\right) x_p^2 = \dfrac{b + (b+h) x_p}{2}(h - x_p)$$

$$\therefore \quad 2x_p^2 = h^2 \text{ i.e. } x_p = \dfrac{h}{\sqrt{2}} \text{ from top.}$$

Step III : Elastic section modulus (Z_e) : $I = \dfrac{bh^3}{36}$

(a) Elastic section modulus with reference to compression side = $Z_{ec} = \dfrac{I}{y_c} = \dfrac{bh^3/36}{(2/3)h} = \dfrac{bh^2}{24}$

(b) Elastic section modulus with reference to tension side = $Z_{et} = \dfrac{I}{y_t} = \dfrac{bh^3/36}{h/3} = \dfrac{bh^2}{12}$

Step IV : Yield moment (M_y) :

(a) Yield moment with reference to compression side = $M_{yc} = \sigma_{yc} \cdot Z_{ec} = \sigma_y (bh^2/24)$

(b) Yield moment with reference to tension side = $M_{yt} = \sigma_{yt} \cdot Z_{et} = \sigma_y (bh^2/12)$

∴ Yield moment = M_y = Least of M_{yc} and $M_{yt} = \sigma_y \left(\dfrac{bh^2}{24}\right)$

Step V : Plastic moment (M_p) :

Sr. No.	Area in compression (A_c) (mm²)	Distance of c.g. of 'A_c' from plastic neutral axis ($\bar{y}_c$) (mm)	$A_c \cdot \bar{y}_c$ (mm³)	Sr. No.	Area in tension (A_t) (mm²)	Distance of c.g. of 'A_t' from plastic neutral axis ($\bar{y}_t$) (mm)	$A_t \cdot \bar{y}_t$ (mm³)
1.	$\dfrac{bh}{4}$	$(1/3) h/\sqrt{2}$	$\dfrac{bh^2}{12\sqrt{2}}$	1.	$\dfrac{bh}{4}$	$\left(\dfrac{b' + 2b}{b' + b}\right) \times \left(\dfrac{h - h/\sqrt{2}}{3}\right)$ = 0.15 h	$(0.15) \times \dfrac{bh^2}{4}$

$$M_p = \sigma_{yc} (A_c \cdot \bar{y}_c) + \sigma_{yt} (A_t \cdot \bar{y}_t)$$

$$= \left[\sigma_y \left(\dfrac{bh^2}{12\sqrt{2}}\right) + \sigma_y \left(\dfrac{0.15\, bh^2}{4}\right)\right] = \sigma_y (0.096\, bh^2)$$

Step VI : Shape factor (K_s) : $K_s = \dfrac{M_p}{M_y} = \dfrac{\sigma_y (0.096\, bh^2)}{\sigma_y (bh^2/24)} = 2.31$

Step VII : Load factor :

Load factor = Factor of safety × Shape factor = $K_s \times K_s$ = 1.7 × 2.31 = 3.297

Problem 12.7 : Cross-section of the beam shown in Fig. 12.13 (a) is subjected to sagging bending moment. Find the shape factor if permissible yield stress in compression and tension is 230 MPa and 280 MPa respectively.

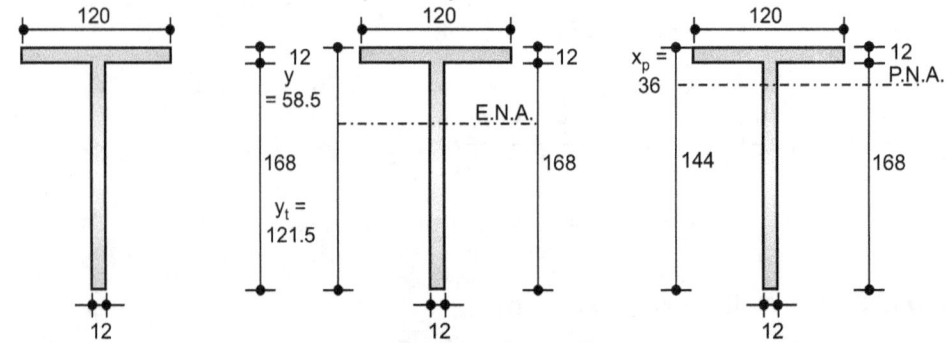

(a) Given cross-section of the beam (b) Elastic neutral axis of the cross-section (c) Plastic neutral axis of the cross-section

Fig. 12.13 : Illustrative Problem 12.7

Solution : Data : (i) Cross-section of the beam : as shown in Fig. 12.13 (a).
(ii) Material yield stresses : σ_{yc} = 230 MPa and σ_{yt} = 280 MPa.

Objects : (i) Plastic moment (M_p).
(ii) Shape factor (K_s).

Concepts and Equations :
(i) Theory of plastic bending
(ii) $M_p = \sigma_{yc} (A_c \cdot \bar{y}_c) + \sigma_{yt} (A_t \cdot \bar{y}_t)$
(iii) $K_s = \dfrac{M_p}{M_y}$

Procedure :

Step I : Elastic neutral axis :
$$x_e = \dfrac{120 \times 12 \times 6 + 168 \times 12 \times (12 + 168/2)}{120 \times 12 + 168 \times 12}$$
= 58.5 mm from top
∴ y_c = 58.5 m and y_t = 121 mm as shown in Fig. 12.13 (b).

Step II : Plastic neutral axis : Assuming that, plastic neutral axis lies in web :
$A_c = A_t$
$(120 \times 12) + (x_p - 12) \times 12 = (180 - x_p) \times 12$
∴ x_p = 36 mm from top (>12 mm o.k.) as shown in Fig. 12.13 (c).

Step III : Elastic section modulus (Z_e) :
$$I = \dfrac{120 \times 12^3}{12} + (120 \times 12)(58.5 - 6)^2 + \dfrac{12 \times 168^3}{12} + (12 \times 168)(12 + 168/2 - 58.5)^2$$
= 11.56 × 10^6 mm^4

(a) Elastic section modulus with reference to compression side = Z_{ec}
$$= \dfrac{I}{y_c} = \dfrac{11.56 \times 10^6}{58.5} = 19.7 \times 10^4 \text{ mm}^3$$

(b) Elastic section modulus with reference to tension side = Z_{et}
$$= \dfrac{I}{y_t} = \dfrac{11.56 \times 10^6}{121.5} = 9.52 \times 10^4 \text{ mm}^3$$

Step IV : Yield moment (M_y) :
(a) Yield moment with reference to compression side = $M_{yc} = \sigma_{yc} \cdot Z_{ec}$
= (230 × 19.7 × 10^4) 10^{-6} = 45.31 kNm
(b) Yield moment with reference to tension side = $M_{yt} = \sigma_{yt} \cdot Z_{et}$
= (280 × 9.52 × 10^5) 10^{-6} = 26.66 kNm
∴ Yield moment = M_y = Least of M_{yc} and M_{yt} = 26.66 kNm

Step V : Plastic moment (M_p) :

Sr. No.	Area in compression (A_c) (mm²)	Distances of c.g. of 'A_c' from plastic neutral axis ($\bar{y}_c$) (mm)	$A_c \cdot \bar{y}_c$ (mm³)	Sr. No.	Area in tension (A_t) (mm²)	Distance of c.g. of 'A_t' from plastic neutral axis ($\bar{y}_t$) (mm)	$A_t \cdot \bar{y}_t$ (mm³)
1.	120 × 12 = 1440	$36 - \dfrac{12}{2} = 30$	43200	1.	144 × 12 = 1728	$\dfrac{144}{2} = 72$	124416
2.	(36 − 12) × 12 = 288	$36 - \dfrac{12}{2} = 12$	3456			Σ =	124416
		Σ =	46656				

$$M_p = \sigma_{yc} (A_c \cdot \bar{y}_c) + \sigma_{yt} (A_t \cdot \bar{y}_t)$$
$$= (230 \times 46656 + 280 \times 124416) \times 10^{-6} \text{ kNm} = 45.567 \text{ kNm}$$

Step VI : Shape factor (K_s) :

$$K_s = \frac{M_p}{M_y} = \frac{45.567}{26.66} = 1.709$$

Problem 12.8 : Cross-section of the beam shown in Fig. 12.14 (a) is subjected to sagging bending moment. Find the shape factor if permissible yield stress in compression and tension is 200 MPa and 250 MPa respectively.

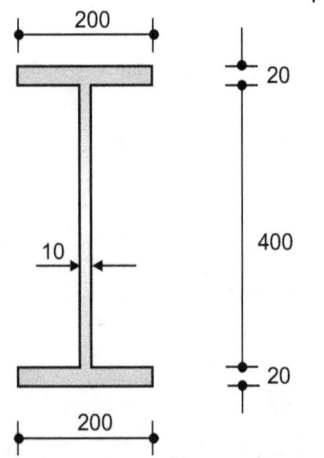
(a) Given cross-section of the beam

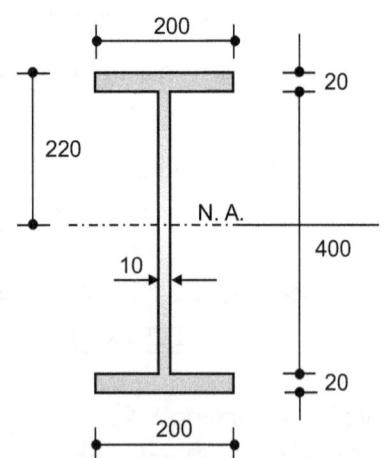
(b) Elastic and plastic neutral axis of cross-section

Fig. 12.14 : Illustrative Problem 12.8

Solution : Data : (i) Cross-section of the beam : as shown in Fig. 12.14 (a).
(ii) Material yield stresses: σ_{yc} = 200 MPa and σ_{yt} = 250 MPa

Objects : (i) Plastic moment (M_p). (ii) Shape factor (K_s).

Concepts and Equations :

(i) Theory of plastic bending. (ii) $M_p = \sigma_{yc}(A_c \cdot \bar{y}_c) + \sigma_{yt}(A_t \cdot \bar{y}_t)$. (iii) $K_s = \dfrac{M_p}{M_y}$

Procedure :

Step I : Elastic neutral axis : 220 mm from top (∵ By symmetry) as shown in Fig. 12.14 (b).

Step II : Plastic neutral axis : 220 mm from top (∵ By symmetry) as shown in Fig. 12.14 (b).

Step III : Elastic section modulus (Z_e) :

$$I = \frac{200 \times (440)^3}{12} - \frac{190 \times (400)^3}{12}$$

$$= 406.4 \times 10^6 \text{ mm}^4$$

(a) Elastic section modulus with reference to compression side = Z_{ec}

$$= \frac{I}{y_c} = \frac{406.4 \times 10^6}{220} = 1.847 \times 10^6 \text{ mm}^3$$

(b) Elastic section modulus with reference to tension side = Z_{et}

$$= \frac{I}{y_t} = \frac{406.4 \times 10^6}{220} = 1.847 \times 10^6 \text{ mm}^3$$

Step IV : Yield moment (M_y) :

(a) Yield moment with reference to compression side = $M_{yc} = \sigma_{yc} \cdot Z_{ec}$

$$= (200 \times 1.847 \times 10^6)\, 10^{-6} = 369.4 \text{ kNm}$$

(b) Yield moment with reference to tension side = $M_{yt} = \sigma_{yt} \cdot Z_{et}$

$$= (250 \times 1.847 \times 10^6)\, 10^{-6} = 461.75 \text{ kNm}$$

Yield moment = M_y = Least of M_{yc} and M_{yt} = 369.4 kNm

Step V : Plastic moment (M_p) :

Sr. No.	Area in compression (A_c) (mm²)	Distances of c.g. of 'A_c' from plastic neutral axis ($\bar{y}_c$) (mm)	$A_c \cdot \bar{y}_c$ (mm³)	Sr. No.	Area in tension (A_t) (mm²)	Distances of c.g. of 'A_t' from plastic neutral axis ($\bar{y}_t$) (mm)	$A_t \cdot \bar{y}_t$ (mm³)
1.	200 × 20 = 4000	$\dfrac{200 + 20}{2}$ = 210	840000	1.	200 × 20 = 4000	$\dfrac{200 + 20}{2}$ = 210	840000
2.	200 × 10 = 2000	$\dfrac{200}{2}$ = 100	200000	2.	200 × 10 = 2000	$\dfrac{200}{2}$ = 100	200000
			Σ = 1040000				Σ = 1040000

$$M_p = \sigma_{yc}(A_c \cdot \bar{y}_c) + \sigma_{yt}(A_t \cdot \bar{y}_t)$$

$$= (200 \times 1040000 + 250 \times 1040000) \times 10^{-6} \text{ kNm}$$

$$= 468 \text{ kNm}$$

Step VI : Shape factor (K_s) :

$$K_s = \frac{M_p}{M_y} = \frac{468}{369.4} = 1.27$$

Problem 12.9 : Cross-section of the beam shown in Fig. 12.15 (a) is subjected to sagging bending moment. Find the shape factor if permissible yield stress in compression and tension is 200 MPa and 240 MPa respectively.

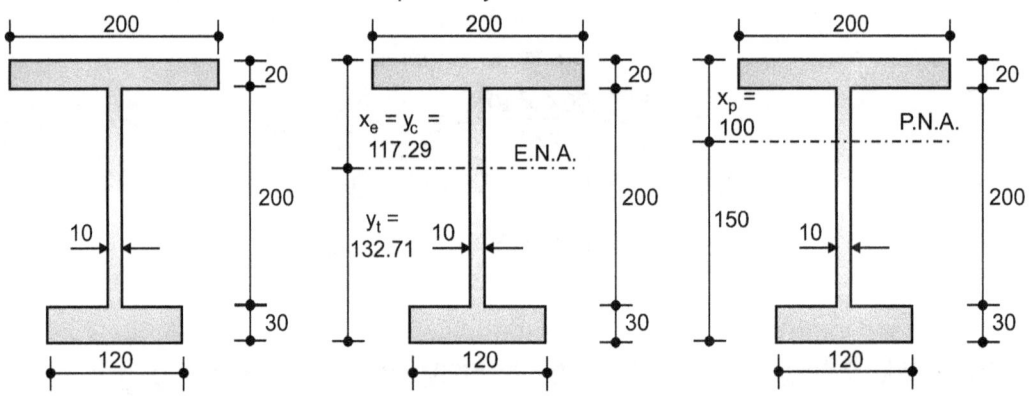

(a) Given cross-section of the beam

(b) Elastic neutral axis of the cross-section

(c) Plastic neutral axis of the cross-section

Fig. 12.15 : Illustrative Problem 12.9

Solution : Data : (i) Cross-section of the beam : as shown in Fig. 12.15 (a).

(ii) Material yield stresses : σ_{yc} = 200 MPa and σ_{yt} = 240 MPa

Objects : (i) Plastic moment (M_p).

(ii) Shape factor (K_s).

Concepts and Equations :

(i) Theory of plastic bending

(ii) $M_p = \sigma_{yc}(A_c \cdot \bar{y}_c) + \sigma_{yt}(A_t \cdot \bar{y}_t)$

(iii) $K_s = \dfrac{M_p}{M_y}$

Procedure :

Step I : Elastic neutral axis :

$$x_e = \frac{200 \times 20 \times (20/2) + 200 \times 10 \times (20 + 200/2) + 120 \times 30 \times (220 + 30/2)}{200 \times 20 + 200 \times 10 + 120 \times 30}$$

= 117.29 mm from top

∴ y_c = 117.29 mm and y_t = 132.71 mm as shown in Fig. 12.15 (b).

Step II : Plastic neutral axis : Assuming that; plastic neutral axis lies in web.

$$A_c = A_t$$

$$200 \times 20 + (x_p - 20) \times 10 = (220 - x_p) \times 10 + 120 \times 30$$

∴ x_p = 100 mm from top (> 20 mm o.k.) as shown in Fig. 12.15 (c).

Step III : Elastic section modulus (Z_e) :

$$I = \frac{200 \times 20^3}{12} + (200 \times 20)(117.29 - 10)^2 + \frac{10 \times 200^3}{12}(120 - 117.29)^2$$

$$+ \frac{120 \times 30^3}{12} + (120 \times 30)(235 - 117.29)^2$$

= 1.03 × 10⁸ mm⁴

(a) Elastic section modulus with reference to compression side = Z_{ec}

$$= \frac{I}{y_c} = \frac{1.03 \times 10^8}{117.29} = 8.78 \times 10^5 \text{ mm}^3$$

(b) Elastic section modulus with reference to tension side = Z_{et}

$$= \frac{I}{y_t} = \frac{1.03 \times 10^8}{132.71} = 7.76 \times 10^5 \text{ mm}^3$$

Step IV : Yield moment (M_y) :

(a) Yield moment with reference to compression side = $M_{yc} = \sigma_{yc} \cdot Z_{ec}$

= (200 × 8.78 × 10⁵) × 10⁻⁶ = 175.6 kNm

(b) Yield moment with reference to tension side = $M_{yt} = \sigma_{yt} \cdot Z_{et}$

= (240 × 7.76 × 10⁵) × 10⁻⁶ = 186.24 kNm

∴ Yield moment = M_y = Least of M_{yc} and M_{yt}

= 175.6 kNm

Step V : Plastic moment (M_p) :

Sr. No.	Area in compression (A_c) (mm²)	Distances of c.g. of 'A_c' from plastic neutral axis ($\bar{y}_c$) (mm)	$A_c \cdot \bar{y}_c$ (mm³)	Sr. No.	Area in tension (A_t) (mm²)	Distances of c.g. of 'A_t' from plastic neutral axis ($\bar{y}_t$) (mm)	$A_t \cdot \bar{y}_t$ (mm³)
1.	200 × 20 = 4000	$\dfrac{100+20}{2} = 210$	360000	1.	(150 – 30) × 10 = 1200	$\dfrac{(150-30)}{2} = 60$	72000
2.	(100 – 20) × 10 = 800	$\dfrac{(100-20)}{2} = 40$	32000	2.	120 × 30 = 3600	$150 - \dfrac{30}{2} = 135$	486000
		Σ =	392000			Σ =	558000

$$M_p = \sigma_{yc}(A_c \cdot \bar{y}_c) + \sigma_{yt}(A_t \cdot \bar{y}_t)$$
$$= (200 \times 392000 + 240 \times 558000) \times 10^{-6} \text{ kNm}$$
$$= 212.32 \text{ kNm}$$

Step VI : Shape factor (K_s) :

$$K_s = \frac{M_p}{M_y} = \frac{212.32}{175.6} = 1.209$$

Chapter 13
PLASTIC ANALYSIS

13.1 INTRODUCTION

The conversion of a structure into the collapse mechanism by the formation of plastic hinges is the key consideration of plastic analysis of structures. For the sake of simplicity it is assumed that a fully plastic hinge is formed at section as soon as the extreme fibre stress reaches the yield stress. In other words, the shape factor of the section is assumed as unity. Plastic hinge is capable of withstanding a constant bending moment equal to the plastic moment of the section, allowing continuous rotation. The load carrying capacity of a structure depends only on the value of the plastic moment and not on the complete moment-curvature relations. An idealized elastic-plastic moment-curvature relation, shown in Fig. 13.1 (a), taking the shape factor as unity, is further simplified to the rigid plastic relation shown in Fig. 13.1 (b). The rigid plastic behaviour neglects the elastic curvature being very small compared with the theoretically infinite curvature after plastic hinge formation.

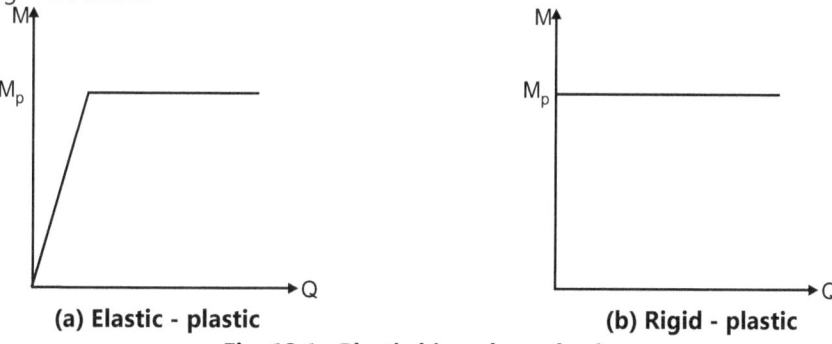

(a) Elastic - plastic (b) Rigid - plastic
Fig. 13.1 : Plastic hinge hypothesis

When a statically indeterminate structure is subjected to steadily increasing loads, the formation of the first plastic hinge does not in general cause plastic collapse. Further increase of the loads can usually be carried and other plastic hinges form successively until finally there are sufficient number of plastic hinges to transform the structure into the mechanism. Further increase in load will cause indefinite deformation, thus the plastic collapse occurs. A mechanism specified by one displacement is called one degree of freedom (DOF). Mechanisms of one DOF are only considered in simple plastic analysis.

In plastic methods of structural analysis, no consideration is given to the sequence of formation of the plastic hinges which cause the collapse mechanism. Therefore, tracing of complete loading history is not required for the purposes of simple plastic analysis. Only the mechanism state of a structure is the main concern. The effects of axial forces and shear forces are neglected and local bucking, lateral bucking and shear failure are all prevented.

13.2 TYPES OF MECHANISMS

The possible hinge locations in a structure may be at the point of (i) fixed support, (ii) interior support, (iii) rigid joint, (iv) concentrated load, (v) internal point. The plastic hinge at end simple, hinged or roller support or at free end is not possible. The potential hinge locations are called *critical sections* or *cardinal sections*.

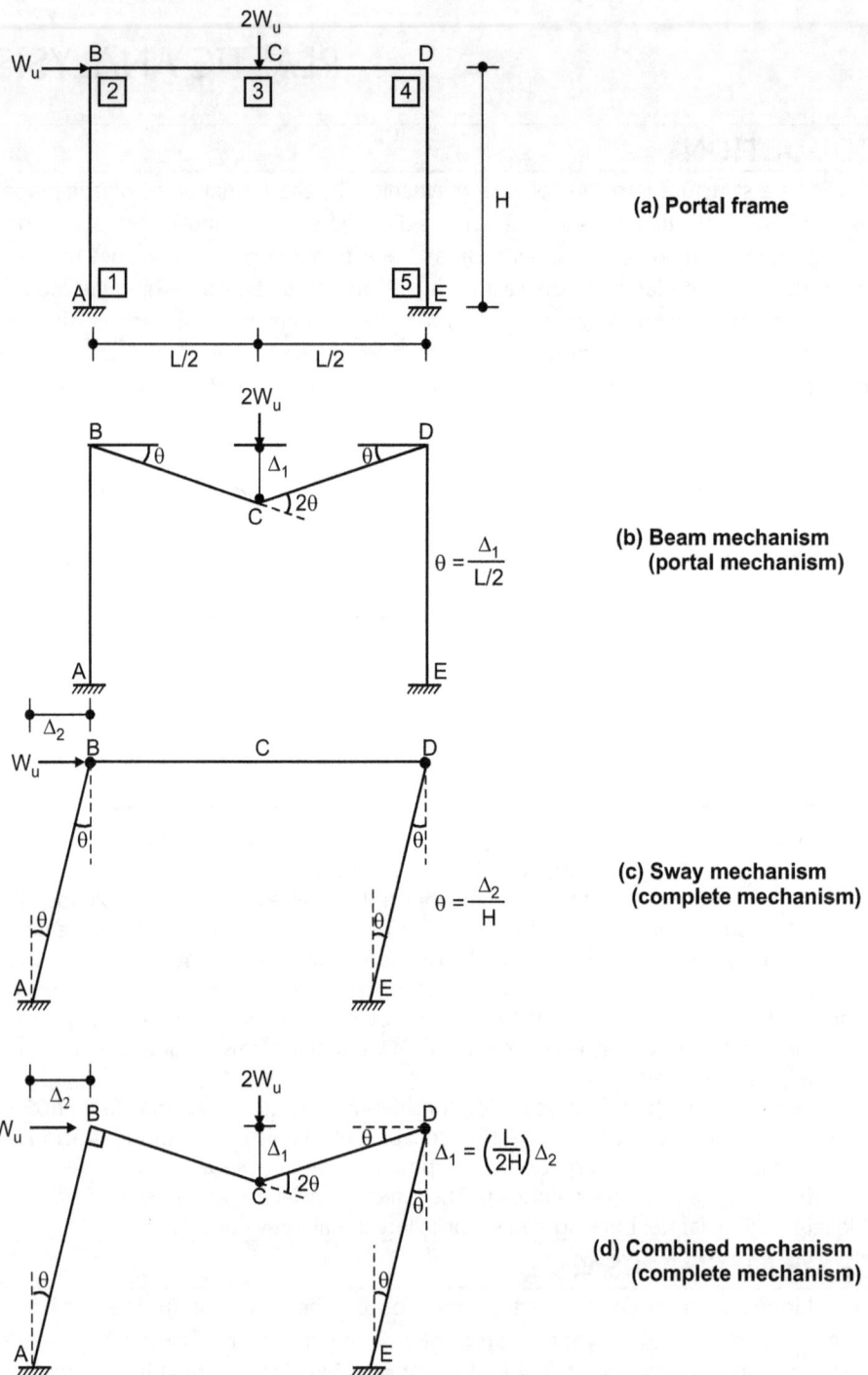

Fig. 13.2 : Types of Mechanisms

At a joint the critical section is considered in the weakest member. The bending moment diagram between two adjacent critical sections is straight lines, therefore plastic hinge cannot occur between critical sections in general.

Singe bay, single storey frame shown in Fig. 13.2 (a) is considered to illustrate the different types of mechanisms. Mechanisms are classified in different ways as given below :

(i) Beam mechanism is shown in Fig. 13.2 (b). A beam mechanism, in general, requires three plastic hinges.

(ii) Sway mechanism is shown in Fig. 13.2 (c). A sway mechanism, in general, requires four plastic hinges.

(iii) Combined mechanism is shown in Fig. 13.2 (d) which is the combination of beam mechanism and sway mechanism.

(iv) Independent mechanism : A mechanism which cannot be obtained from linear combination of the others is called as *independent mechanism*. Any two of three mechanisms i.e. beam, sway and combined can be regarded as the independent mechanism. In general, there will be a number of independent mechanisms which is equal to the number of independent equations of equilibrium. If there are n possible plastic hinge positions and D_{si} is degree of redundancy there will be $(n - D_{si})$ independent mechanisms.

For the frame under consideration there are five critical sections as shown in Fig. 13.2 (a) and three redundancies. i.e. n = 5, D_{si} = 3. Therefore there will be two (5 – 3) independent mechanisms i.e. two out of beam, sway and combined mechanism.

(v) Joint mechanism : A local rotation of the joint as a rigid body is known as joint mechanism or joint rotation. This is illustrated with respect to the portal frame shown in Fig. 13.3 (a) having different plastic moments for the beam and column sections. In such a case, the plastic hinges do not form at the joints but at the adjacent sections in the members.

Therefore, the number of critical sections n will be 7 as shown in Fig. 13.3 (a) and the number of independent mechanisms will be four i.e. 7 – 3 = 4. These mechanisms are beam sway, joint mechanisms of B and D. The combined mechanism is obtained from combination of these mechanisms. The beam mechanism with the plastic hinges in the beam is shown in Fig. 13.3 (b). The sway mechanism with the plastic hinges in the column is shown in Fig. 13.3 (c). The combination of beam and sway mechanisms is shown in Fig. 13.3 (d). The joint rotation at B as a rigid body cancels the two hinges at joint B and the combined mechanism shown in Fig. 13.3 (e) is obtained. The joint rotation at D is shown in Fig. 13.3 (f) and (g) resulting the corresponding mechanisms.

(vi) Complete mechanism : If the degree of redundancy of a structure is D_{si}, then formation of D_{si} number of plastic hinges will make the structure statically determinate and $(D_{si} + 1)$ number of plastic hinges will convert the structure to a mechanism. This type of mechanism with $(D_{si} + 1)$ hinges is termed as the complete collapse mechanism. The complete mechanism is statically determinate as the distribution of bending moments can be obtained by statics.

The sway mechanism and combined mechanism of the frame shown in Fig. 13.3 (c) and (d) contain four plastic hinges and hence considered as the complete collapse mechanisms.

In this context, it may be noted that a given statically determinate structure needs only one plastic hinge for the complete collapse mechanism and indeterminate structure needs more than one as per the degree of static indeterminacy.

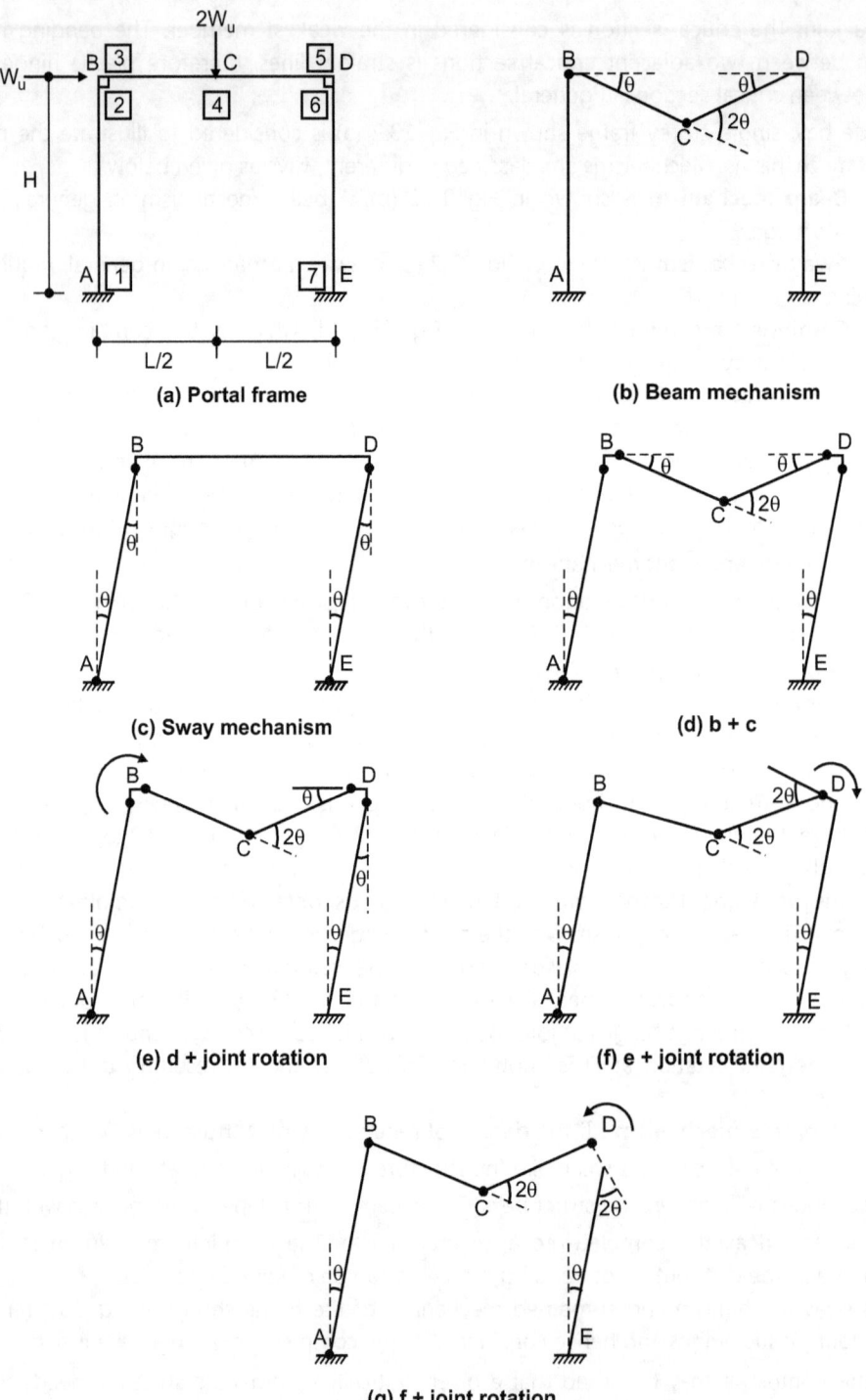

Fig. 13.3 : Types of Mechanisms

When the collapse mechanism is not complete in this sense, it may be either partial or over complete.

(vii) Partial collapse mechanism : A mechanism due to formation of number of plastic hinges less than (D_{si} + 1) is known as *partial collapse mechanism*. In this situation, there is a failure of part of the structure by the mechanism. Remaining part of the structure is intact. However, for the purpose of plastic analysis this is also considered as failure because of indefinite deflection of structure. A partial collapse mechanism is statically indeterminate. Beam mechanism of a portal frame, shown in Fig. 13.3 (b) is the partial collapse mechanism.

(viii) Over complete mechanism : The term over complete mechanism is used when there are two or more mechanisms. The over complete mechanism is specified by two degrees of freedom. The over complete mechanism involves more than (D_{si} + 1) plastic hinges. The over complete mechanism occurs at certain definite values of the ratios of the applied loads when the plastic moments of beam and columns are different. The over complete mechanism represented in Fig. 13.4 as an addition of sway mechanism and combined mechanism.

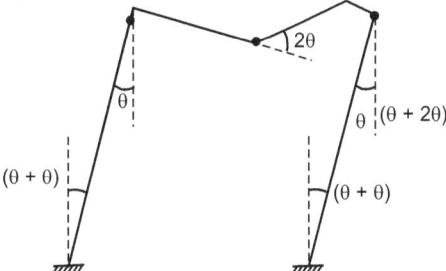

Fig. 13.4 : Over complete Mechanism

13.3 FUNDAMENTAL THEOREMS OF PLASTIC ANALYSIS

A structure in its collapse state should satisfy three conditions :

(i) **The mechanism condition :** It means that the sufficient number of plastic hinges transform the structure into a mechanism. This condition is known as kinematical condition or kinematic admissibility.

(ii) **The equilibrium condition :** It specifies that the bending moment distribution is in equilibrium with the collapse load. This condition is called as statical condition or static admissibility.

(iii) **The yield condition :** It means that the bending moment nowhere exceeds the plastic moment M_p. This condition is termed as safe condition or safety.

These three conditions are necessary and sufficient for the determination of the true collapse load of a structure.

As per the master conditions of plastic collapse, following fundamental theorems are formulated to assess the collapse load.

(i) Uniqueness Theorem :

It states that if a bending moment distribution can be obtained which satisfies the three conditions of mechanism, equilibrium and yield, then the collapse load corresponding to such bending moment distribution will be the true collapse load. The uniqueness theorem does not mean that mechanism itself is unique.

(ii) Lower Bound Theorem :

It states that if a bending moment distribution can be found which satisfies the conditions of equilibrium and yield then the corresponding load must be less than or equal to the true collapse load. As the mechanism condition is not satisfied, the structure will not collapse under the calculated load. The theorem is also known as *static theorem* since the equilibrium condition is fulfilled. The yield condition is ensured therefore the theorem is called as *safe theorem*. The theorem is not much useful and convenient for the plastic analysis of structures.

(iii) Upper Bound Theorem :

It states that the collapse load obtained from any assumed mechanism for a given structure must be either greater than or equal to the true collapse load. It cannot be less than the true collapse load. As the mechanism is assumed, the mechanism condition is satisfied. Therefore, the theorem is also known as *kinematic theorem*. The equilibrium condition is satisfied but the yield condition is not satisfied and hence the theorem is called as *unsafe theorem*. This is also true in a design sense that the plastic moment M_p obtained from an assumed mechanism is smaller than that actually required. The theorem is useful and convenient to process the plastic analysis of structures.

The three theorems of plastic collapse are only valid for rigid - plastic structures.

The three theorems are consolidated in the following format :

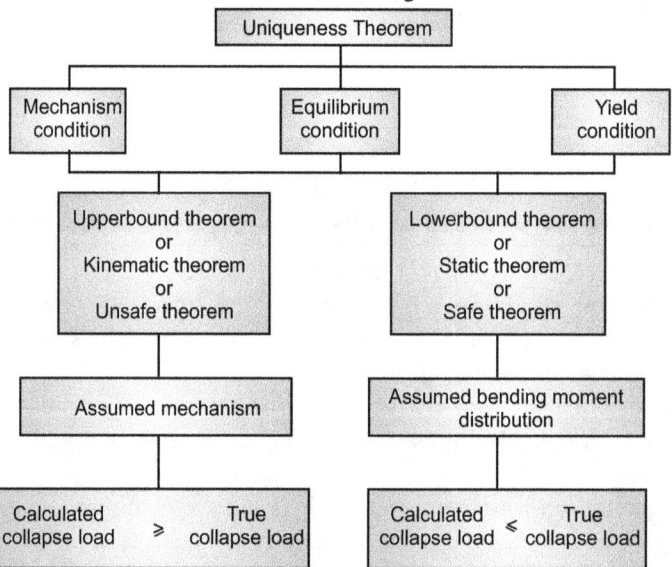

13.4 PLASTIC ANALYSIS OF STRUCTURES

13.4.1 General

The object of plastic analysis is to find the true collapse load of the given structure. There may be number of possible collapse mechanisms for the structure except the simple structure having only one mechanism. To arrive at the true collapse load, plastic analysis must satisfy the conditions of mechanisms, equilibrium and yield. It is difficult to include all three necessary and sufficient conditions in one operation. Therefore, two methods, based on the fundamental theorems of plastic collapse, are formulated as given below.

13.4.2 Mechanism Method

True collapse load of the given structure is obtained from collapse loads of different assumed mechanisms of the structure. The method involves the analysis of the mechanism. The kinematical theorem is the key of the method, therefore it is also known as kinematical method or upper bound method giving the upper values of collapse loads than the true collapse load.

The basic principle of the method is that during the plastic collapse the work done by the external loads is equal to the work absorbed in the plastic hinges. The mechanism is defined by the arbitrary displacement, other displacements are obtained from geometry. Therefore, this principle is expressed in a virtual work equation as

$$\Sigma (P \cdot \Delta) = \Sigma (M_p \cdot \theta) \quad \ldots (13.1)$$

where the loads P and the plastic moments M_p are considered as the equivalent set of forces and the displacements of loads Δ and rotations of plastic moments θ are the compatible set of displacements.

The mechanism method is also called as work method or virtual work method. It may be noted that :

(i) at the collapse mechanism the plastic hinges divide the structure or part of the structure into several rigid members which are assumed to remain straight so that all rotations take place in the plastic hinges,
(ii) the mechanism is specified by one common co-ordinate i.e. single degree of freedom,
(iii) at each plastic hinge the work absorbed must be positive irrespective of the sign of the hinge rotation.

The method consists of the following main steps :

(i) Decide the locations of potential plastic hinges which may be supports, joints, concentrated load points, points of zero shear in portions subjected to distributed loading.
(ii) Identify possible collapse mechanisms formed by the certain plastic hinges.
(iii) Compute the collapse loads associated with each of these possible mechanisms by virtual work equation.
(iv) The true collapse load will be the lowest of the collapse loads obtained in step IV.
(v) A statical check is necessary if there is uncertainty about the number of possible mechanisms.
The collapse bending moment diagram is drawn for the mechanism that gives the lowest collapse load.
If the bending moment ordinate nowhere exceeds the plastic moment M_p of that section, then the uniqueness theorem ensures that this mechanism will give the true collapse load.
(vi) If bending moment somewhere is greater than M_p at that section then the yield condition is not satisfied and the correct mechanism is to be searched.

13.4.3 Equilibrium Method

The collapse load of a given structure is assessed by the assumed bending moment diagram satisfying the conditions of equilibrium and yield i.e. static theorem. Therefore, the method is also known as statical method or lower bound method giving lower values of loads than the collapse load. The general procedure of the method involves the following main steps :

(i) the redundant moments are selected,

(ii) bending moment diagram is constructed by the superposition of the free moment diagram on to the redundant moment diagram in such a way that
(iii) a mechanism is formed.
(iv) the value of the collapse load is then calculated from statics.

The procedure of the equilibrium method is illustrated with respect to the following example of beam.

SOLVED PROBLEM

Problem 13.1 : The beam is supported and loaded with ultimate loads as shown in Fig. 13.5 (a). Find the collapse load. The section of the beam is of constant M_p throughout and $M_p = 32$ kNm.

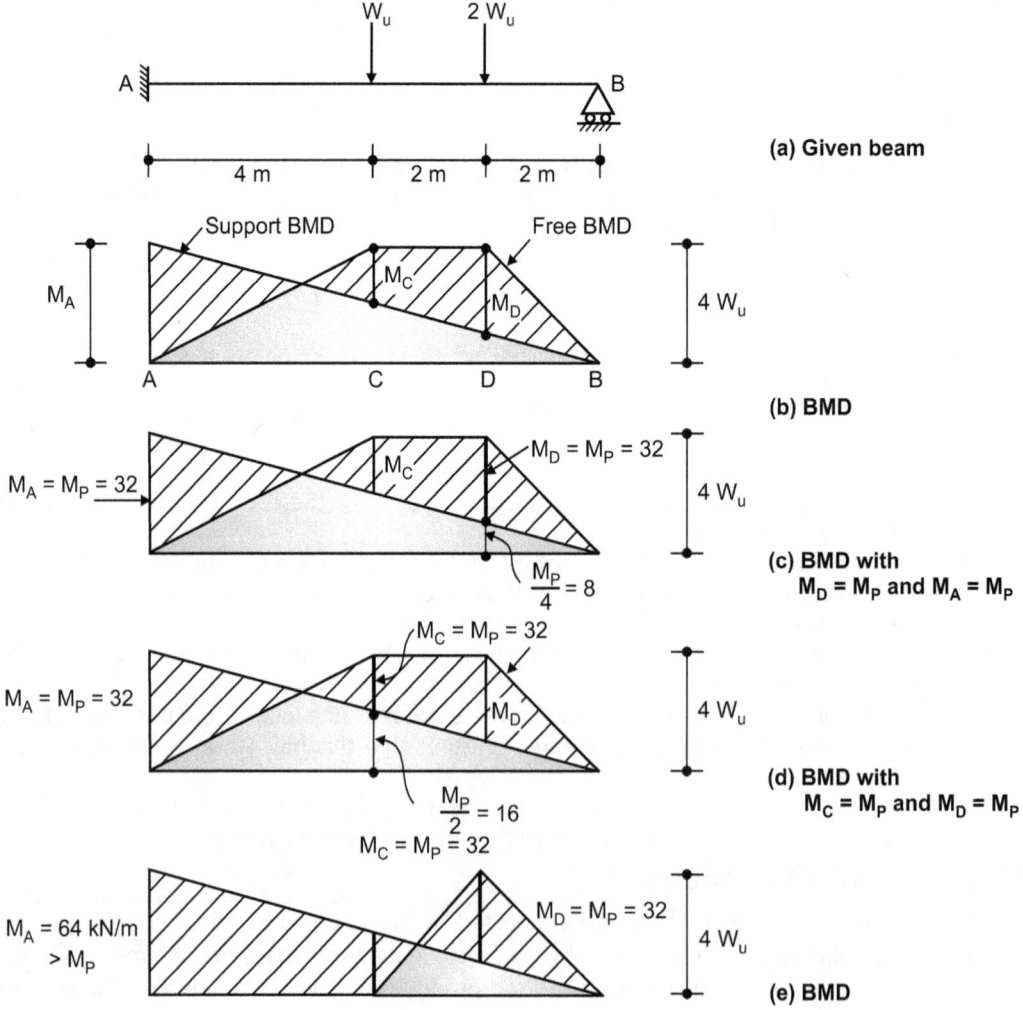

Fig. 13.5 : Equilibrium Method (Illustrative Problem 13.1)

Solution : Data :
(i) Structural configuration dimensions, support conditions.
(ii) Loads - Magnitudes, directions and positions.
(iii) Member properties - Uniform cross-section of the beam with plastic moment M_p = 32 kNm.

Object : Collapse load (or load factor).

Concepts and Equations :
(i) Equilibrium method.
(ii) Bending moment and geometry of bending moment.

Procedure :

Step I : Free bending moment diagram is constructed as shown in Fig. 13.5 (b).

$$R_{Bf} = \frac{12W + 4W}{8} = 2W, R_{Af} = W$$

$$M_{Bf} = 2W \times 2 = 4W, M_{Cf} = 4W$$

Step II : Support bending moment diagram is superposed on free bending moment diagram as shown in Fig. 13.5 (b)

Step III : Two hinges are required for a mechanism.

Step IV : Three possible bending moment distributions for mechanism are considered as shown in Fig. 13.5 (c), (d) and (e).

Step V : Analysis of each possible bending moment distribution :

(i) Bending moment ordinates at A and C are equal to M_p as shown in Fig. 13.5 (c).

From geometry of BMD,

$$M_D = M_p = 32 = 4W_u - 8$$

∴ $4W_u = 40$

∴ $W_u = 10$ kN

(ii) Bending moment ordinates at C and A are equal to M_p = 32 kNm as shown in Fig. 13.5 (d).

$$M_C = M_p = 32 = 4W_u - 16$$

∴ $4W_u = 48$

∴ $W_u = 12$ kN

(iii) Bending moment ordinates at C and D are equal to M_p = 32 as shown in Fig. 13.5 (e).

This is not possible as M_D cannot be equal to M_p due to geometry of B.M.D. In fact, $M_D > M_C$. Also M_A is greater than M_p, therefore, this possibility is neglected.

Step VI : True collapse load : The possible bending moment distributions correspond to the possible mechanisms also.

True collapse load = Lower of 10 kN and 12 kN

∴ $W_u = 10$ kN

13.5 APPLICATION OF PLASTIC ANALYSIS TO STEEL BEAMS

A statically determinate beam has an unique collapse mechanism and therefore very simple to analyze. A statically indeterminate beam e.g. fixed beam, continuous beam may fail by different possible beam mechanisms according to the data of structural configuration, support conditions, loading and plastic moment capacities. However, it is not a difficult task to identify the possible mechanisms in case of beam problems. Once the mechanisms are obtained the ultimate load can be obtained either by equilibrium method or mechanism method.

13.5.1 Equilibrium Method

In particular cases, the equilibrium method is suitable. The bending moment diagram is drawn by superposing the free bending moment diagram on the support (redundant) moment diagram. At the locations of plastic hinges of a mechanism the bending moment ordinates are considered as M_p of known values. And the ultimate or collapse load is found from the geometry of the bending moment diagram. If the bending moment anywhere in the beam exceeds M_p the corresponding mechanism and bending moment distribution are discarded and only the bending moment distribution satisfying the requirements of mechanism and yield are retained and accordingly the true collapse load will be the lowest of the collapse loads obtained. The equilibrium method, in general, is not convenient and therefore not recommended.

13.5.2 Mechanism Method

The possible mechanisms are identified and analyzed by work equation to obtain the collapse load of each mechanism. The true collapse load is the lowest of these values, if no mechanism is skipped and for each mechanism the conditions of equilibrium and yield are satisfied. The method is straight forward if all mechanisms are correctly identified which is possible in the normal situation of the beam problems. Therefore, mechanism method should be preferred.

Distributed loads on a beam :

Beams carrying the concentrated loads are comparatively simple to analyze as the potential plastic hinge locations are explicitly known at the load positions. If the beams are subjected to the distributed loads, the location of the plastic hinge is not known but can be obtained. Therefore, assuming the opposition of plastic hinge, by an unknown distance x the position of plastic hinge 'x' be obtained from the condition that moment is maximum or the shear force is zero at that point. Otherwise the collapse load of the mechanism is expressed in terms of x, using the work equation. As the lowest load is of concern, the concept of minima gives the value of x i.e. $\frac{dW_u}{dx} = 0$.

If M_p is of interest, M_p is expressed as the function of known ultimate load and unknown x, using work equation of the mechanism. And the position of the plastic hinge i.e. x is then obtained by $\frac{dM_p}{dx} = 0$. This additional consideration of location of the plastic hinge in the member under the distributed load will be clarified in the numerical examples.

The work done by the uniformly distributed ultimate load is calculated as the product of rate of loading and the area under the displacement diagram of the loaded part of the beam due to the mechanism. It may be noted again that in a mechanism the beam part remains straight in between the plastic hinges.

SOLVED PROBLEMS

Following Problems illustrate the application of plastic theory to analysis of beams :

Problem 13.2 : The beam is supported and loaded with ultimate load as shown in Fig. 13.6 (a). Find the collapse load and draw B.M.D. at collapse. The section of the beam is of constant M_p throughout.

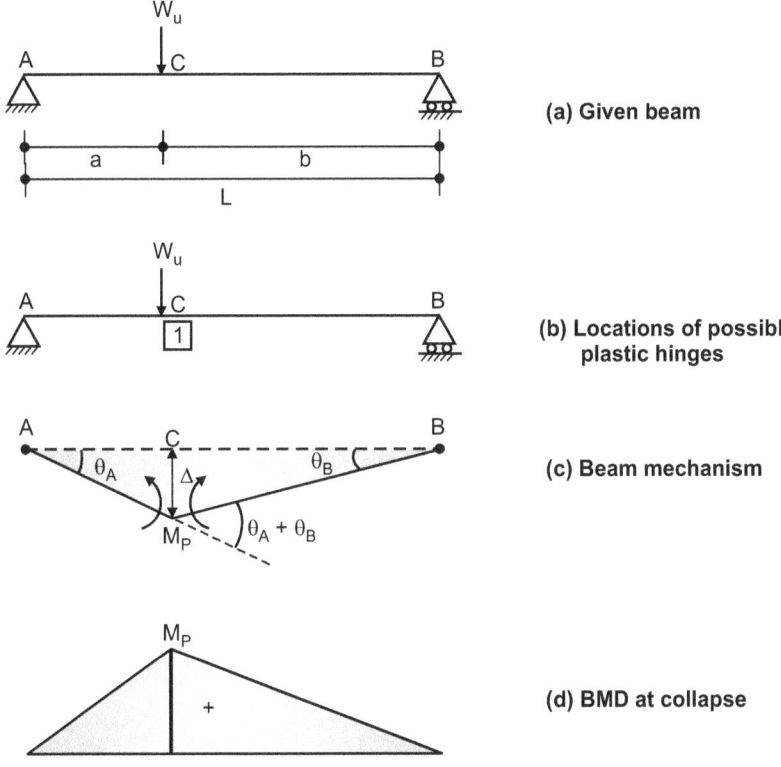

Fig. 13.6 : Illustrative Problem 13.2

Solution :

Data : The beam is supported and loaded as shown in Fig. 13.6 (a).

Object : Collapse load.

Concepts and Equations :

(i) Mechanism method.

(ii) Work equation : External work done (W_e) = Internal work done (W_i).

Procedure :

Step I : Degree of static indeterminacy = D_{si} = 0

Step II : Potential sections for plastic hinges : One location as shown in Fig. 13.6 (b).

Step III : Identification of possible collapse mechanism : Maximum plastic hinges for complete mechanism = $D_{si} + 1 = 0 + 1 = 1$.

Number of independent mechanisms = 1 − 0 = 1

Step IV : Analysis of possible mechanism :

Beam mechanism is as shown in Fig. 13.6 (c).

(a) Kinematics of the mechanism : The rotation of plastic hinge at C = $\theta_A + \theta_B$, where $\theta_A = \dfrac{\Delta}{a}$ and $\theta_B = \dfrac{\Delta}{b}$ as shown in Fig. 13.6 (c).

(b) Virtual work equation and collapse load :

$W_e = W_i$ i.e. $W_u \cdot \Delta = M_p (\theta_A + \theta_B)$

$\therefore \quad W_u \cdot \Delta = M_p \left(\dfrac{\Delta}{a} + \dfrac{\Delta}{b}\right)$

$\therefore \quad$ Collapse load $= W_u = \dfrac{M_p \cdot L}{ab}$

Step V : B.M.D. at collapse as shown in Fig. 13.6 (d).

Note : If point load W_u is acting at centre, then collapse load is given by

$$W_u = \dfrac{4M_p}{L}$$

Problem 13.3 : The beam is supported and loaded with ultimate load as shown in Fig. 13.7 (a). Find the collapse load and draw B.M.D. at collapse. The section of the beam is of constant M_p throughout.

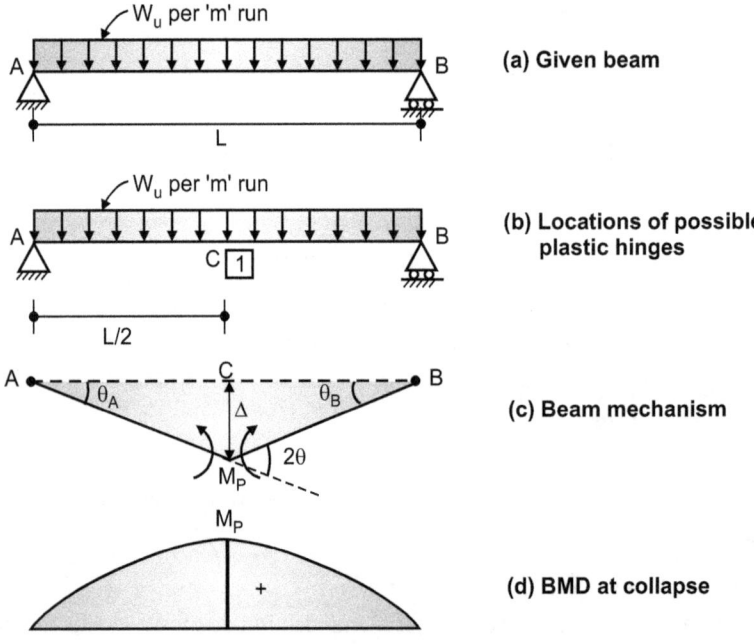

Fig. 13.7 : Illustrative Problem 13.3

Solution :

Data : The beam is supported and loaded as shown in Fig. 13.7 (a).

Object : Collapse load.

Concepts and Equations :

(i) Mechanism method.

(ii) Work equation : External work done (W_e) = Internal work done (W_i).

Procedure :

Step I : Degree of static indeterminacy = D_{si} = 0

Step II : Potential locations for plastic hinges : One location as shown in Fig. 13.7 (b).

Step III : Identification of possible collapse mechanisms : Maximum plastic hinges for complete mechanism = D_{si} + 1 = 0 + 1 = 1

Number of independent mechanisms = 1 – 0 = 1

Step IV : Analysis of possible mechanism : Beam mechanism is as shown in Fig. 13.7 (c).

(a) Kinematics of the mechanism : The rotation of plastic hinge at C = 2θ.

where $\theta = \dfrac{\Delta}{L/2} = \dfrac{2\Delta}{L}$ as shown in Fig. 13.7 (c).

(b) Virtual work equation and collapse load :

$$W_e = W_i \text{ i.e. } W_u \left(\dfrac{1}{2} \times L \times \Delta\right) = M_p (2\theta)$$

$$\therefore \quad W_u \dfrac{1}{2} \cdot \Delta = M_p \cdot 2 \left(\dfrac{2\Delta}{L}\right)$$

$$\therefore \quad \text{Collapse load} = W_u = \dfrac{8M_p}{L}$$

Step V : B.M.D. at collapse as shown in Fig. 13.7 (d).

Problem 13.4 : The beam is supported and loaded with ultimate load as shown in Fig. 13.8 (a). Find the collapse load and draw B.M.D. at collapse. The section of the beam is of constant M_p throughout.

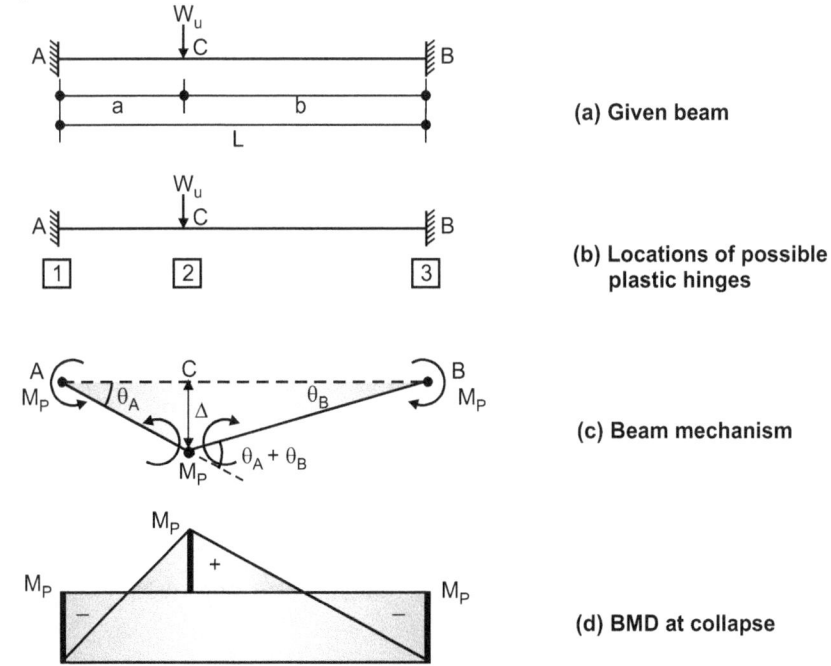

Fig. 13.8 : Illustrative Problem 13.4

Solution :
Data : The beam is supported and loaded as shown in Fig. 13.8 (a).
Object : Collapse load.
Concepts and Equations :
(i) Mechanism method.
(ii) Work equation : External work done (W_e) = Internal work done (W_i).

Procedure :
Step I : Degree of static indeterminacy = D_{si} = 2.
Step II : Potential locations for plastic hinges : Three locations as shown in Fig. 13.8 (b).
Step III : Identification of possible collapse mechanisms :
Maximum plastic hinges for complete mechanism = D_{si} + 1 = 2 + 1 = 3.
Number of independent mechanism = 3 − 2 = 1.
Step IV : Analysis of possible mechanism : Beam mechanism is as shown in Fig. 13.8 (c).
(a) Kinematics of the mechanism :

The rotation of plastic hinge at A = $\theta_A = \dfrac{\Delta}{a}$

The rotation of plastic hinge at B = $\theta_B = \dfrac{\Delta}{b}$

The rotation of plastic hinge at C = $\theta_A + \theta_B = \dfrac{\Delta}{a} + \dfrac{\Delta}{b}$ as shown in Fig. 13.8 (c).

(b) Virtual work equation and collapse load :
$$W_e = W_i \text{ i.e. } W_u \cdot \Delta = M_p (\theta_A) + M_p (\theta_A + \theta_B) + M_p (\theta_B)$$

$$\therefore \quad W_u \cdot \Delta = M_p \left(\dfrac{\Delta}{a}\right) + M_p \left(\dfrac{\Delta}{a} + \dfrac{\Delta}{b}\right) + M_p \left(\dfrac{\Delta}{b}\right)$$

$$\therefore \quad \text{Collapse load} = W_u = \dfrac{2M_p \cdot L}{ab}$$

Step V : B.M.D. at collapse load as shown in Fig. 13.8 (d).
Note : If point load W_u is acting at centre, then collapse load is given by,
$$W_u = \dfrac{8M_p}{L}$$

Problem 13.5 : The beam is supported and loaded with ultimate load as shown in Fig. 13.9 (a). Find the collapse load and draw B.M.D. at collapse. The section of the beam is of constant M_p throughout.

Solution :
Data : The beam is supported and loaded as shown in Fig. 13.9 (a).
Object : Collapse load.
Concepts and Equations :
(i) Mechanism method.
(ii) Work equation : External work done (W_e) = Internal work done (W_i).

Procedure :
Step I : Degree of static indeterminacy = D_{si} = 2

Step II : Potential locations for plastic hinges : Three locations as shown in Fig. 13.9 (b).

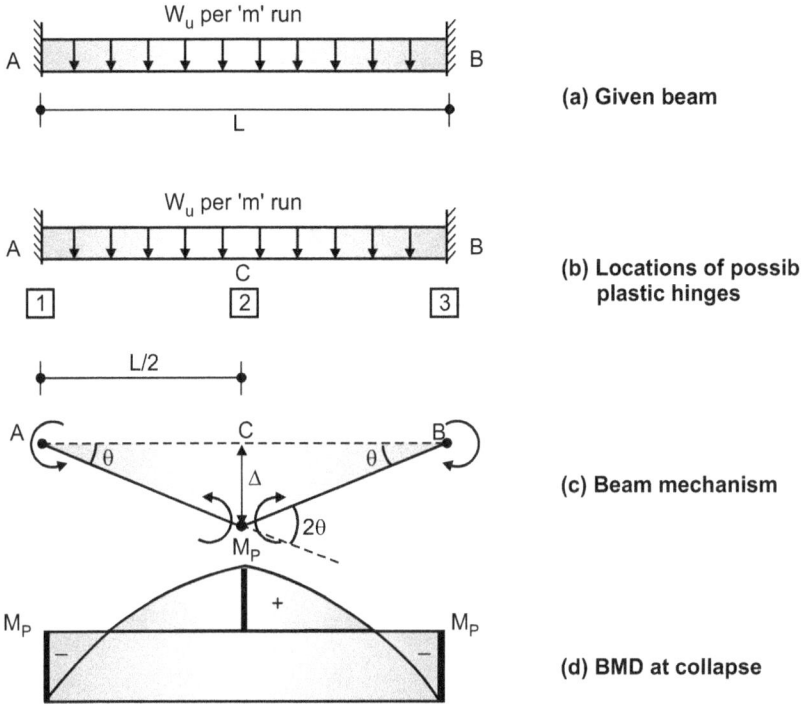

Fig. 13.9 : Illustrative Problem 13.5

Step III : Identification of possible collapse mechanisms :

Maximum plastic hinges for complete mechanism = $D_{si} + 1 = 2 + 1 = 3$

Number of independent mechanism = $3 - 2 = 1$

Step IV : Analysis of possible mechanism :

Beam mechanism is as shown in Fig. 13.9 (c).

(a) Kinematics of the mechanisms :

The rotation of plastic hinge at A = $\theta = \dfrac{\Delta}{L/2} = \dfrac{2\Delta}{L}$

The rotation of plastic hinge at B = $\theta = \dfrac{\Delta}{L/2} = \dfrac{2\Delta}{L}$

The rotation of plastic hinge at B = $2\theta = \dfrac{4\Delta}{L}$ as shown in Fig. 13.9 (c).

(b) Virtual work equation and collapse load :

$W_e = W_i$ i.e. $W_u \left(\dfrac{1}{2} \cdot L \cdot \Delta\right) = M_p (\theta) + M_p (2\theta) + M_p (\theta)$

$$\therefore \qquad W_u \cdot \frac{L}{2} \cdot \Delta = M_p\left(\frac{2\Delta}{L}\right) + M_p\left(\frac{4\Delta}{L}\right) + M_p\left(\frac{2\Delta}{L}\right)$$

$$\therefore \qquad \text{Collapse load} = W_u = \frac{16 M_p}{L^2}$$

Step V : B.M.D. at collapse as shown in Fig. 13.9 (d).

Problem 13.6 : The beam is supported and loaded with ultimate load as shown in Fig. 13.10 (a). Find the collapse load and draw B.M.D. at collapse. The section of the beam is of constant M_p throughout.

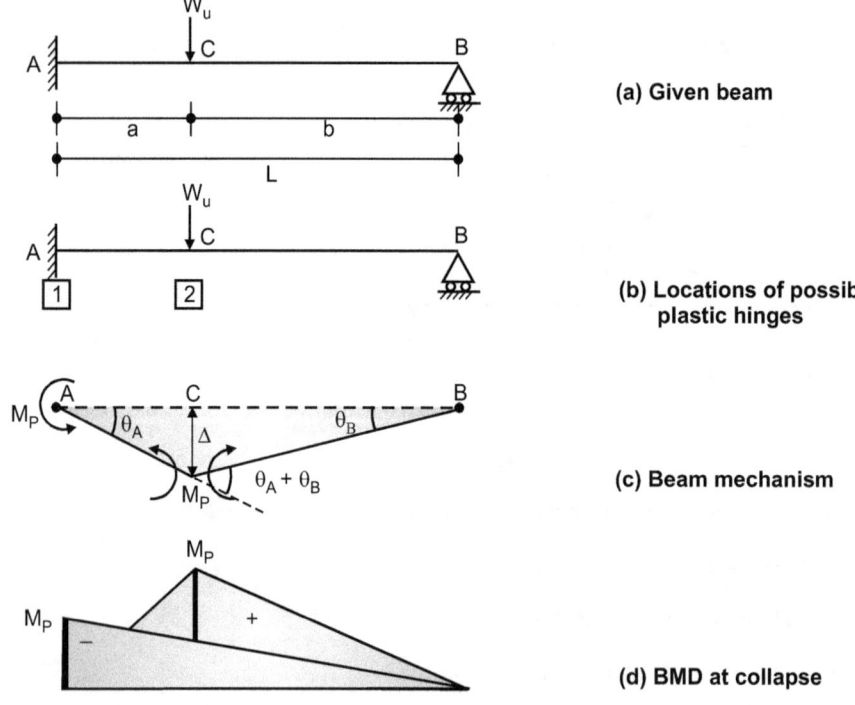

Fig. 13.10 : Illustrative Problem 13.6

Solution : Data : The beam is supported and loaded as shown in Fig. 13.10 (a).
Object : Collapse load.
Concepts and Equations :
(i)   Mechanism method.
(ii) Work equation : External work done (W_e) = Internal work done (W_i).
Procedure :
Step I : Degree of static indeterminacy = D_{si} = 1.
Step II : Potential locations for plastic hinges : Two locations as shown in Fig. 13.10 (b).
Step III : Identification of possible collapse mechanisms :
Maximum plastic hinges for complete mechanism = D_{si} + 1 = 1 + 1 = 2.
Number of independent mechanism = 2 – 1 = 1.

Step IV : Analysis of possible mechanism :
Beam mechanism is as shown in Fig. 13.10 (c).

(a) Kinematics of the mechanism : The rotation of plastic hinge at A = $\theta_A = \dfrac{\Delta}{a}$.

The rotation of plastic hinge at C = $\theta_A + \theta_B = \dfrac{\Delta}{a} + \dfrac{\Delta}{b}$ as shown in Fig. 13.10 (c).

Note that the hinge at B is not a plastic hinge.

(b) Virtual work equation and collapse load :
$W_e = W_i$ i.e. $W_u \Delta = M_p (\theta_A) + M_p (\theta_A + \theta_B)$

∴ $W_u \Delta = M_p \left(\dfrac{\Delta}{a}\right) + M_p \left(\dfrac{\Delta}{a} + \dfrac{\Delta}{b}\right)$

∴ Collapse load = $W_u = \dfrac{M_p (L + b)}{ab}$

Step V : B.M.D. at collapse as shown in Fig. 13.10 (d).

Note : If point load W_u is acting at centre, then collapse load is given by

$$W_u = \dfrac{6 M_p}{L}$$

Problem 13.7 : The beam is supported and loaded with ultimate load as shown in Fig. 13.11 (a). Find the collapse load and draw B.M.D. at collapse. The section of the beam is of constant M_p throughout.

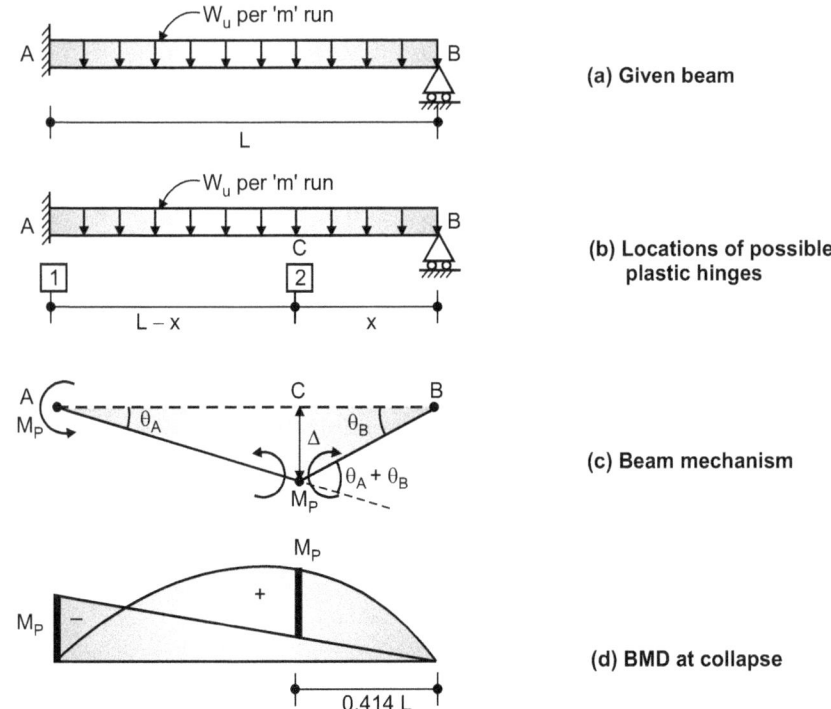

(a) Given beam

(b) Locations of possible plastic hinges

(c) Beam mechanism

(d) BMD at collapse

Fig. 13.11 : Illustrative Problem 13.7

Solution :

Data : The beam is supported and loaded as shown in Fig. 13.11 (a).

Object : Collapse load.

Concepts and Equations :
(i) Mechanism method.
(ii) Work equation : External work done (W_e) = Internal work done (W_i).

Procedure :

Step I : Degree of static indeterminacy = D_{si} = 1.

Step II : Potential locations for plastic hinges : Two locations as shown in Fig. 13.11 (b).
Let x be the distance from B where plastic hinge will be formed.

Step III : Identification of possible collapse mechanisms :
Maximum plastic hinges for complete mechanism = D_{si} + 1 = 1 + 1 = 2.
Number of independent mechanisms = 2 – 1 = 1.

Step IV : Analysis of possible mechanism : Beam mechanism is as shown in Fig. 13.11 (c).
(a) Kinematics of the mechanism : The rotation of plastic hinge at A is

$$\theta_A = \frac{\Delta}{L-x}$$

The rotation of plastic hinge at C is

$$\theta_A + \theta_B = \frac{\Delta}{L-x} + \frac{\Delta}{x} \text{ as shown in Fig. 13.11 (c).}$$

(b) Virtual work equation and collapse load :

$$W_e = W_i$$

$$\therefore \quad W_u \left(\frac{1}{2} L \cdot \Delta\right) = M_p (\theta_A) + M_p (\theta_A + \theta_B)$$

$$\therefore \quad W_u \cdot \frac{L}{2} \cdot \Delta = M_p \left(\frac{\Delta}{L-x}\right) + M_p \left(\frac{\Delta}{L-x} + \frac{\Delta}{x}\right)$$

$$\therefore \quad W_u \cdot \frac{L}{2} = M_p \left[\frac{1}{L-x} + \frac{1}{L-x} + \frac{1}{x}\right]$$

$$\therefore \quad W_u = \frac{2M_p}{L} \left[\frac{L+x}{x(L-x)}\right] \quad \ldots \text{(A)}$$

Theoretically, there are infinite mechanisms. The correct mechanism is the one which needs minimum load. Expression for W_u in terms of unknown distance x is formulated as above and now the load is minimized by differentiation.

∴ Differentiating equation (A) with respect to x and equating to zero,

$$\frac{dW_u}{dx} = \frac{d}{dx}\left[\frac{2M_p}{L}\left(\frac{L+x}{x(L-x)}\right)\right] = 0$$

$$\therefore \quad \frac{dW_u}{dx} = x^2 + 2xL - L^2 = 0 \quad \ldots \text{(B)}$$

Solving the quadratic equation (B), we get

$$x = 0.414 L$$

Substituting the value of x in equation (A), we get

$$W_u = \frac{2M_p}{L}\left[\frac{L + 0.414 L}{0.414 L (L - 0.414 L)}\right]$$

$$W_u = 11.656 \frac{M_p}{L^2}$$

Step V : B.M.D. at collapse : as shown in Fig. 13.11 (d).

Problem 13.8 : The beam is supported and loaded with ultimate load as shown in Fig. 13.12 (a). Assuming beam of constant M_p throughout, compute the ultimate load for different values of 'a'.

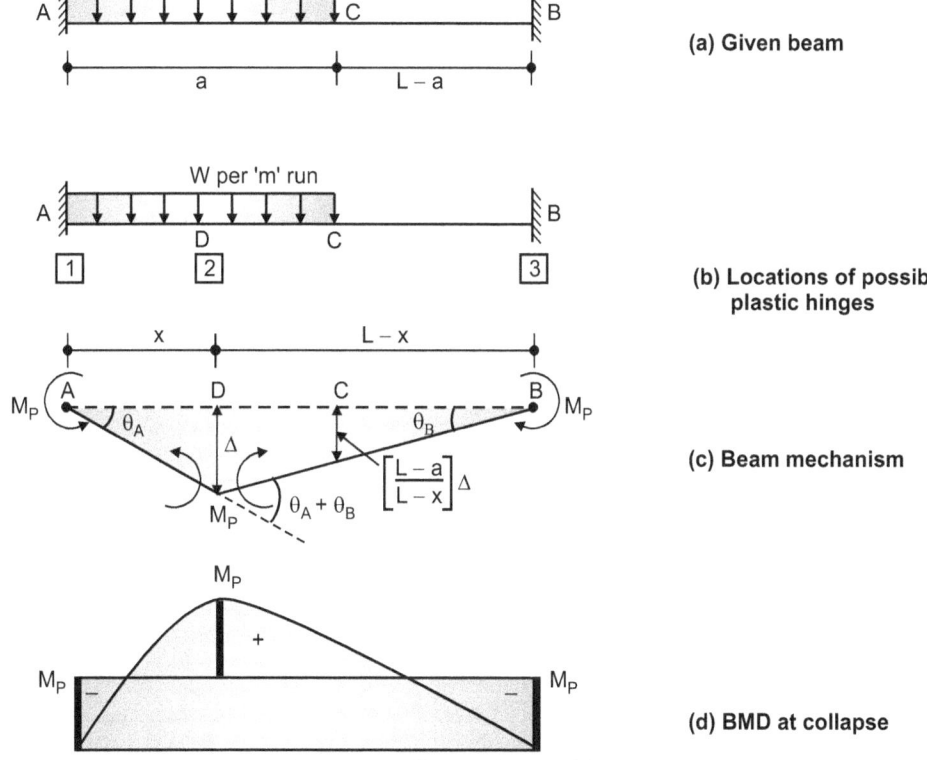

Fig. 13.12 : Illustrative Problem 13.8

Solution :
Data : The beam is supported and loaded as shown in Fig. 13.12 (a).
Object : Collapse load.
Concepts and Equations :
(i) Mechanism method.
(ii) Work equation : External work done (W_e) = Internal work done (W_i).

Procedure :
Step I : Degree of static indeterminacy = D_{si} = 2.
Step II : Potential locations for plastic hinges : Three locations as shown in Fig. 13.12 (b).

Step III : Identification of possible collapse mechanisms :
Maximum plastic hinges for complete mechanism = $D_{si} + 1 = 2 + 1 = 3$
Number of independent mechanism = $3 - 2 = 1$

Step IV : Analysis of possible mechanisms :
Beam mechanism is as shown in Fig. 13.12 (c).

(a) Kinematics of the mechanism :

The rotation of plastic hinge at A = $\theta_A = \dfrac{\Delta}{x}$

The rotation of plastic hinge at B = $\theta_B = \dfrac{\Delta}{L-x}$

The rotation of plastic hinge at D = $\theta_A + \theta_B = \dfrac{\Delta}{x} + \dfrac{\Delta}{L-x}$

(b) Virtual work equation :

$$W_e = W_i \text{ i.e. } W_u\left[\dfrac{1}{2} \times L \times \Delta - \dfrac{1}{2} \times (L-a) \times \left(\dfrac{L-a}{L-x}\right)\Delta\right] = M_p(\theta_A) + M_p(\theta_A + \theta_B) + M_p(\theta_B)$$

$$\therefore \quad \dfrac{W_u}{2} \cdot \Delta\left[L - \dfrac{(L-a)^2}{L-x}\right] = M_p\left(\dfrac{\Delta}{x}\right) + M_p\left(\dfrac{\Delta}{x} + \dfrac{\Delta}{L-x}\right) + M_p\left(\dfrac{\Delta}{L-x}\right)$$

$$\dfrac{W_u}{2}\left[L - \dfrac{(L-a)^2}{L-x}\right] = M_p\left(\dfrac{2L}{x(L-x)}\right)$$

$$W_u = \left[\dfrac{-4L}{a^2 x - 2aLx + Lx^2}\right] M_p$$

For minimum value of W_u, $\dfrac{dw_u}{dx} = 0$

Differentiating equation (A) with respect to x and equating to zero;

$$x = \dfrac{a(2L-a)}{2L}, \text{ substituting in equation (A), we get}$$

$$W_u = \dfrac{16 M_p L^2}{a^2 (2L-a)^2}$$

Step V : Different values of 'a' and corresponding collapse load : as given in Table 13.1.

Table 13.1

a	0.2 L	0.4 L	0.5 L	0.6 L	0.8 L	L
W_u	$123.45 \dfrac{M_p}{L^2}$	$39.06 \dfrac{M_p}{L^2}$	$28.44 \dfrac{M_p}{L^2}$	$22.675 \dfrac{M_p}{L^2}$	$17.36 \dfrac{M_p}{L^2}$	$16 \dfrac{M_p}{L^2}$

Step VI : B.M.D. at collapse : as shown in Fig. 13.12 (d).

Problem 13.9 : The beam is supported and loaded with ultimate loads as shown in Fig. 13.28 (a). Find the plastic moment and draw B.M.D. at collapse. Assume beam of constant M_p throughout.

Solution :

Data : The beam is supported and loaded as shown in Fig. 13.12 (a).

Object : Plastic moment.

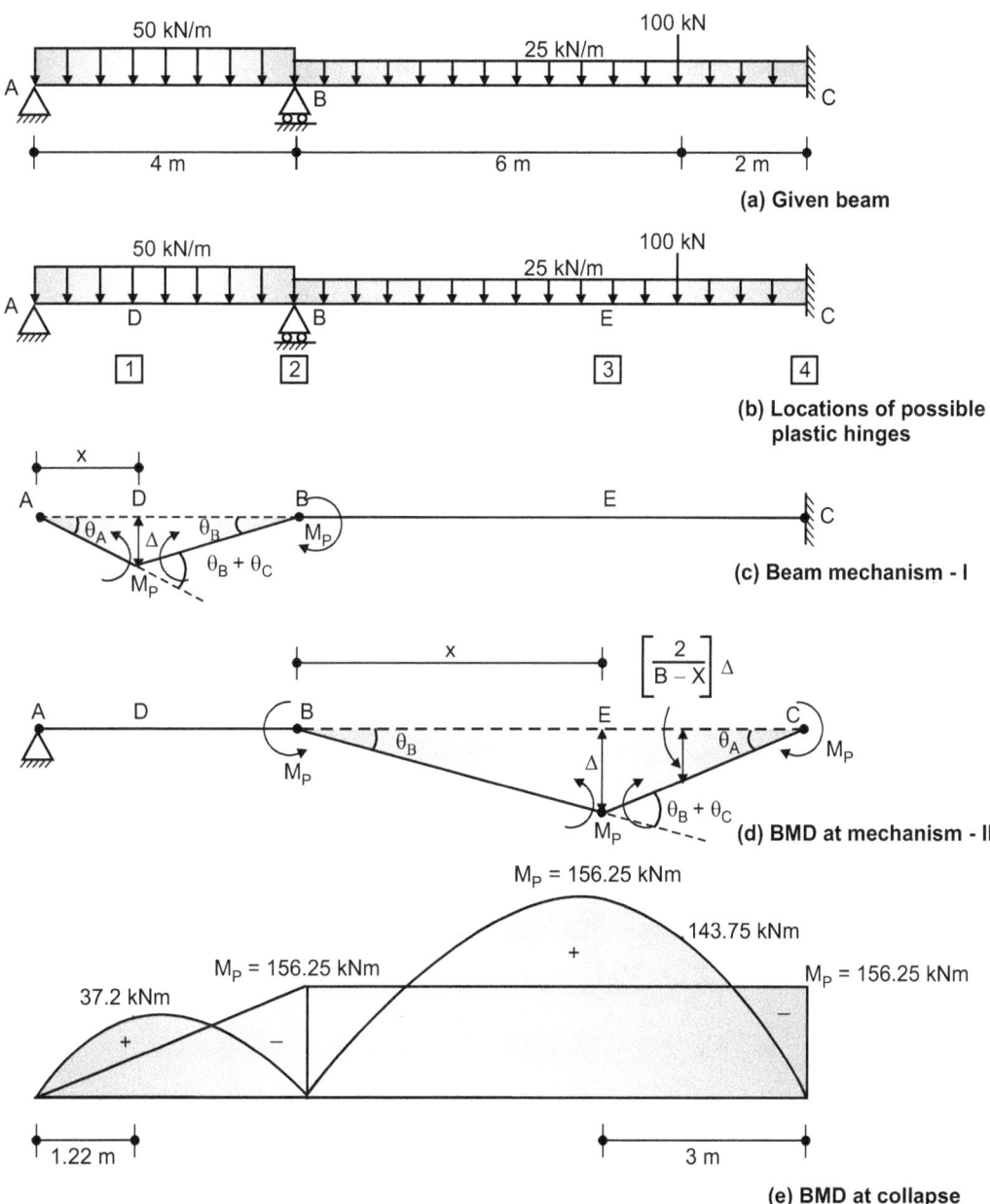

Fig. 13.13 : Illustrative Problem 13.9

Concepts and Equations :
(i) Mechanism method,
(ii) Work equation : External work done (W_e) = Internal work done (W_i).

Procedure :
Step I : Degree of static indeterminacy = D_{si} = 2.

Step II : Potential locations for plastic hinges : Four locations as shown in Fig. 13.13 (b).
Step III : Identification of possible collapse mechanisms :
Maximum plastic hinges for complete mechanism = D_{si} = 1 + 2 = 3.
Number of independent mechanisms = 4 − 2 = 2.
Step IV : Analysis of possible mechanisms : Beam mechanism - I is as shown in Fig. 13.13 (c). This mechanism is similar to that of propped cantilever carrying u.d.l. throughout the span and having constant M_p.

∴ Using the result derived earlier in Problem 13.16,

$$W_u = 11.656 \frac{M_p}{L^2} \text{ i.e. } M_p = \frac{W_u L^2}{11.656} = \frac{50 \times 4^2}{11.656} = 68.63 \text{ kNm.}$$

and $x = 0.414 L = 0.414 \times 4 = 1.656$ m

Beam mechanism - II is as shown in Fig. 13.13 (d).

(a) Kinematics of the mechanism :

The rotation of plastic hinge at B = $\theta_B = \dfrac{\Delta}{x}$

The rotation of plastic hinge at C = $\theta_C = \dfrac{\Delta}{8 - x}$

The rotation of plastic hinge at E = $\theta_B + \theta_C = \dfrac{\Delta}{x} + \dfrac{\Delta}{8 - x}$

(b) Virtual work equation :

$$W_e = W_i \text{ i.e. } 25 \left(\frac{1}{2} \times 8 \times \Delta\right) + 100 \left(\frac{2}{8 - x}\right) \Delta$$

$$= M_p (\theta_B) + M_p (\theta_B + \theta_C) + M_p (\theta_C)$$

∴ $$100 \Delta \left(\frac{200}{8 - x}\right) \Delta = M_p \left(\frac{\Delta}{x}\right) + M_p \left(\frac{\Delta}{x} + \frac{\Delta}{8 - x}\right) + M_p \left(\frac{\Delta}{8 - x}\right)$$

∴ $$100 + \frac{200}{8 - x} = M_p \left(\frac{1}{x} + \frac{1}{x} + \frac{1}{8 - x} + \frac{1}{8 - x}\right)$$

∴ $$M_p = \frac{1000 x - 100 x^2}{16}$$

For maximum value of M_p; $\dfrac{d}{dx}(M_p) = 0$

∴ Differentiating equation (A) with respect to x and equating to zero we get x = 5 m, substituting in equation (A).

M_p = 156.25 kNm

∴ Plastic moment = M_p

= Greatest value of M_p obtained among all above mechanisms

= 156.25 kNm

Step V : B.M.D. at collapse : as shown in Fig. 13.13 (e).

Problem 13.10 : The beam is supported and loaded as shown in Fig. 13.14 (a). Find the plastic moment and draw B.M.D. at collapsed. Assume load factor = 1.8 and beam of constant M_P throughout.

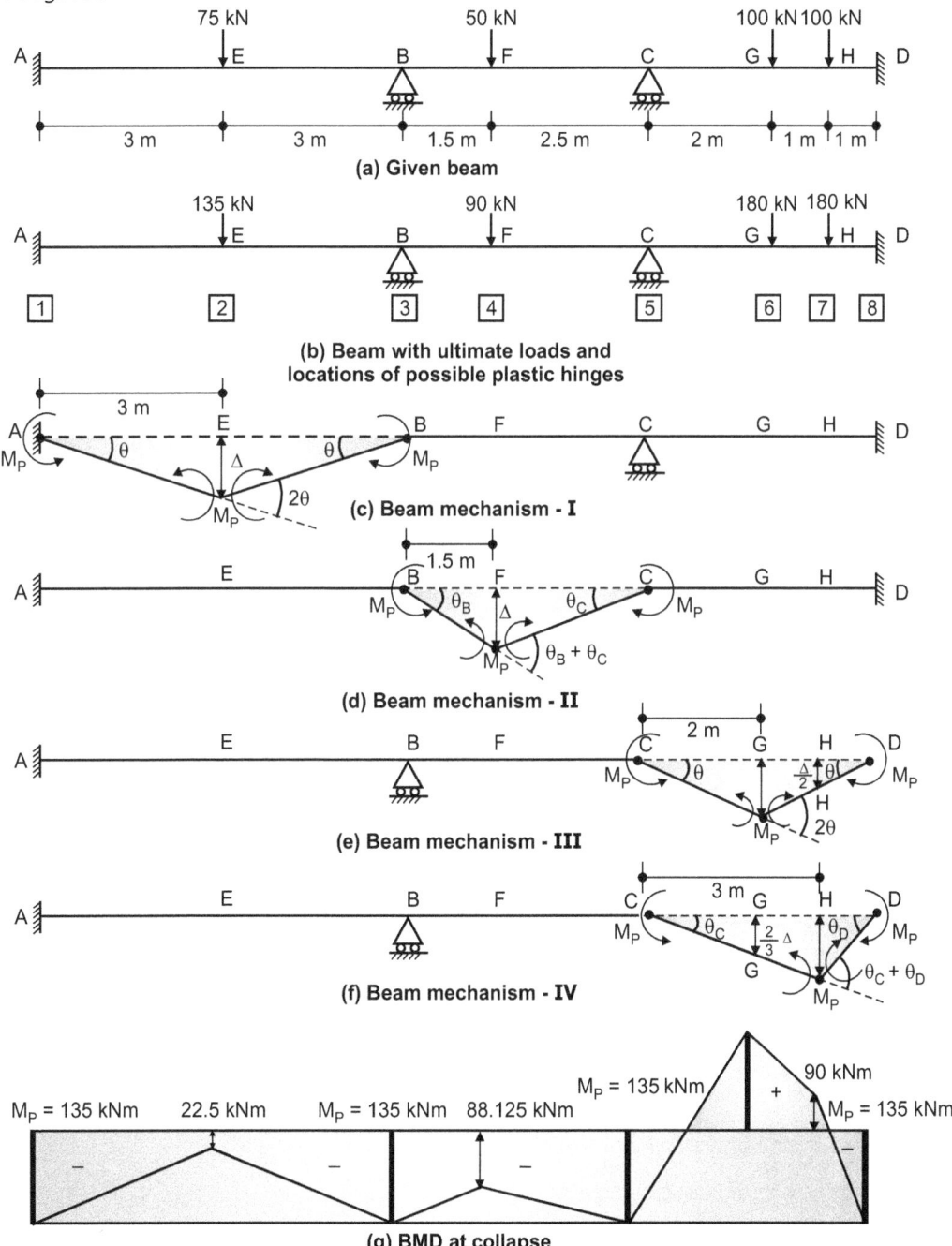

Fig. 13.14 : Illustrative Problem 13.10

Solution :
Data : The beam is supported and loaded as shown in Fig. 13.14 (a).
Object : Plastic moment.
Concepts and Equations : (i) Mechanism method.
(ii) Work equation : External work done (W_e) = Internal work done (W_i).
Procedure :
Step I : Degree of static indeterminacy = D_{si} = 4.
Step II : Potential locations for plastic hinges. Eight locations as shown in Fig. 13.14 (b).
Step III : Identification of possible collapse mechanisms :
Maximum plastic hinges for complete mechanism = D_{si} + 1 = 4 + 1 = 5.
Number of independent mechanisms = 8 − 4 = 4.
Step IV : Analysis of possible mechanisms :
(i) Beam mechanism - I is as shown in Fig. 13.14 (c).
(a) Kinematics of the mechanism :

The rotation of plastic hinge at A = $\theta = \dfrac{\Delta}{3}$

The rotation of plastic hinge at E = $2\theta = \dfrac{2\Delta}{3}$

The rotation of plastic hinge at B = $\theta = \dfrac{\Delta}{3}$

(b) Virtual work equation :
$W_e = W_i$ i.e. $135\,\Delta = M_p(\theta) + M_p(2\theta) + M_p(\theta)$

$\therefore \quad 135\,\Delta = M_p\left(\dfrac{\Delta}{3}\right) + M_p\left(\dfrac{2\Delta}{3}\right) + M_p\left(\dfrac{\Delta}{3}\right)$

$\therefore \quad M_p = 101.25$ kNm

(ii) Beam mechanism - II is as shown in Fig. 13.14 (d).
(a) Kinematics of the mechanism :

The rotation of plastic hinge at B = $\theta_B = \dfrac{\Delta}{1.5}$

The rotation of plastic hinge at C = $\theta_C = \dfrac{\Delta}{2.5}$

The rotation of plastic hinge at F = $\theta_B + \theta_C = \dfrac{\Delta}{1.5} + \dfrac{\Delta}{2.5}$

(b) Virtual work equation :
$W_e = W_i$ i.e. $90\,\Delta = M_p(\theta_B) + M_p(\theta_B + \theta_C) + M_p(\theta_C)$

$\therefore \quad 90\,\Delta = M_p\left(\dfrac{\Delta}{1.5}\right) + M_p\left(\dfrac{\Delta}{1.5} + \dfrac{\Delta}{2.5}\right) + M_p\left(\dfrac{\Delta}{2.5}\right)$

$\therefore \quad M_p = 42.1875$ kNm

(iii) Beam mechanism - III is as shown in Fig. 13.14 (e).
(a) Kinematics of the mechanism :

The rotation of plastic hinge at C = $\theta = \dfrac{\Delta}{2}$

The rotation of plastic hinge at G = $2\theta = \Delta$

The rotation of plastic hinge at D = $\theta = \dfrac{\Delta}{2}$

(b) Virtual work equation :

$$W_e = W_i \text{ i.e. } \quad 180 \cdot \Delta + 180 \cdot \frac{\Delta}{2} = M_p(\theta) + M_p(2\theta) + M_p(\theta)$$

$$\therefore \quad 270\Delta = M_p\left(\frac{\Delta}{2}\right) + M_p(\Delta) + M_p\left(\frac{\Delta}{2}\right)$$

$$\therefore \quad M_p = 135 \text{ kNm}$$

(iv) Beam mechanism - IV is as shown in Fig. 13.14 (f).
(a) Kinematics of the mechanism :

The rotation of plastic hinge at C = $\theta_C = \frac{\Delta}{3}$

The rotation of plastic hinge at D = $\theta_D = \Delta$

The rotation of plastic hinge at H = $\theta_C + \theta_D = \frac{\Delta}{3} + \Delta$

(b) Virtual work equation :

$$W_e = W_i \text{ i.e. } 180 \cdot \Delta + 180 \times \frac{2}{3}\Delta = M_p(\theta_C) + M_p(\theta_C + \theta_D) + M_p(\theta_D)$$

$$\therefore \quad 300\Delta = M_p\left(\frac{\Delta}{3}\right) + M_p\left(\frac{\Delta}{3} + \Delta\right) + M_p(\Delta)$$

$$\therefore \quad M_p = 112.5 \text{ kNm}$$

Plastic moment = M_p
= Greatest value of M_p obtained among all above mechanisms
= 135 kNm

Step V : B.M.D. at collapse : as shown in Fig. 13.14 (g).

Problem 13.11 : The beam is supported and loaded with ultimate loads as shown in Fig. 13.15 (a). Find the plastic moment and draw B.M.D. at collapse. Assuming beam of constant M_p throughout.

Solution : Data : The beam is supported and loaded as shown in Fig. 13.15 (a).
Object : Plastic moment.
Concepts and Equations :
(i) Mechanism method.
(ii) Work equation : External work done (W_e) = Internal work done (W_i).
Procedure :
Step I : Degree of static indeterminacy = D_{si} = 2.
Step II : Potential locations for plastic hinges = Five locations as shown in Fig. 13.15 (b).
Step III : Identification of possible collapse mechanisms :
Maximum plastic hinges for complete mechanism = $D_{si} + 1 = 2 + 1 = 3$.
Number of independent mechanisms = 5 – 2 = 3.
Step IV : Analysis of possible mechanisms :
(i) Beam mechanism - I is as shown in Fig. 13.15 (c).
(a) Kinematics of the mechanism :

The rotation of plastic hinge at A = $\theta = \frac{\Delta}{2}$

The rotation of plastic hinge at E = $2\theta = \Delta$

The rotation of plastic hinge at B = $\theta = \frac{\Delta}{2}$

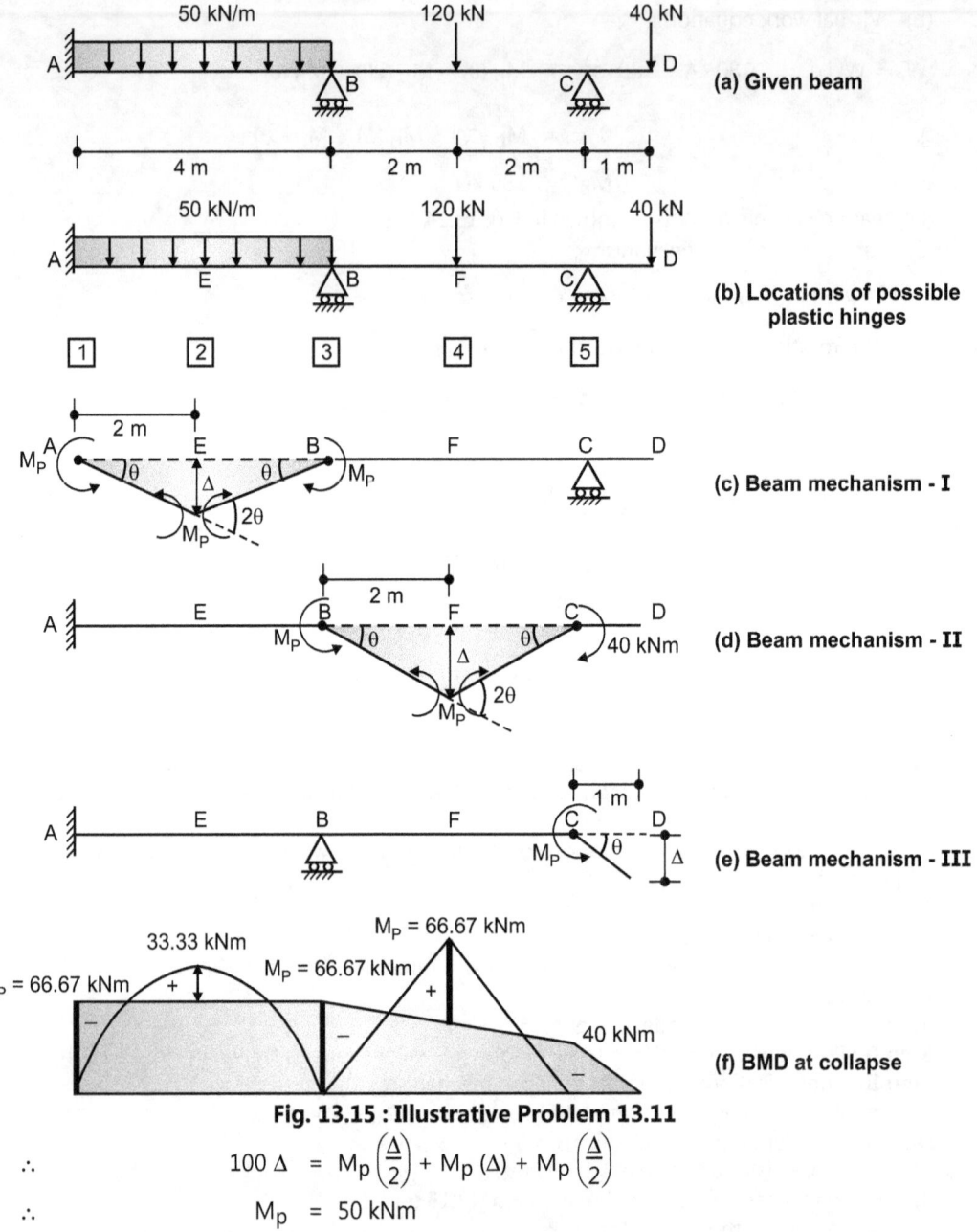

Fig. 13.15 : Illustrative Problem 13.11

$$\therefore \quad 100\,\Delta \;=\; M_p\left(\frac{\Delta}{2}\right) + M_p\,(\Delta) + M_p\left(\frac{\Delta}{2}\right)$$

$$\therefore \quad M_p \;=\; 50 \text{ kNm}$$

(ii) Beam mechanism - II is as shown in Fig. 13.15 (d). Note that at C no plastic hinge is formed for this mechanism.

(a) Kinematics of the mechanism :

The rotation of plastic hinge at B = $\theta = \dfrac{\Delta}{2}$

The rotation of plastic hinge at F = $2\theta = \Delta$

The rotation of plastic hinge at C = $\theta = \dfrac{\Delta}{2}$

(b) Virtual work equation :

$W_e = W_i$ i.e. $\quad 120\,\Delta = M_p(\theta) + M_p(2\theta) + 40(\theta)$

$\qquad\qquad\qquad\qquad = M_p\left(\dfrac{\Delta}{2}\right) + M_p(\Delta) + 40\left(\dfrac{\Delta}{2}\right)$

$\therefore \qquad\qquad M_p = 66.67$ kNm

(iii) Beam mechanism - III is as shown in Fig. 13.15 (e).

(a) Kinematics of the mechanism :

The rotation of plastic hinge at C = $\theta = \Delta$

(b) Virtual work equation :

$W_e = W_i$ i.e. $\quad 40\,\Delta = M_p(\theta) = M_p(\Delta)$

$\therefore \qquad\qquad M_p = 40$ kNm

Plastic moment = M_p

= Greatest value of M_p obtained among all the above mechanisms

= 66.67 kNm

Step V : B.M.D. at collapse as shown in Fig. 13.15 (f).

Problem 13.12 : The beam is supported and loaded with ultimate loads as shown in Fig. 13.16 (a). Find the plastic moment and draw B.M.D. at collapse.

Solution : Data : The beam is supported and loaded as shown in Fig. 13.16 (a).

Object : Plastic moment.

Concepts and Equations :

(i) Mechanism method.

(ii) Work equation : External work done (W_e) = Internal work done (W_i).

Procedure :

Step I : Degree of static indeterminacy = $D_{si} = 2$

Step II : Potential locations for plastic hinges : Five locations as shown in Fig. 13.16 (b).

Step III : Identification of possible collapse mechanisms :

Maximum plastic hinges for complete mechanism = $D_{si} + 1 = 2 + 1 = 3$.

Number of independent mechanisms = $5 - 2 = 3$.

Step IV : Analysis of possible mechanisms :

(i) Beam mechanism - I is as shown in Fig. 13.16 (c). This mechanism is similar to that of propped cantilever carrying u.d.l. throughout the span and having constant M_p.

$\therefore \quad$ Using the result derived earlier in Problem 13.7,

$W_u = 11.656\,\dfrac{M_p}{L^2}$ i.e. $M_p = \dfrac{W_u L^2}{11.656} = \dfrac{100 \times 4^2}{11.656} = 137.27$ kNm

and x = 0.414 L = 0.414 × 4 = 1.656 m

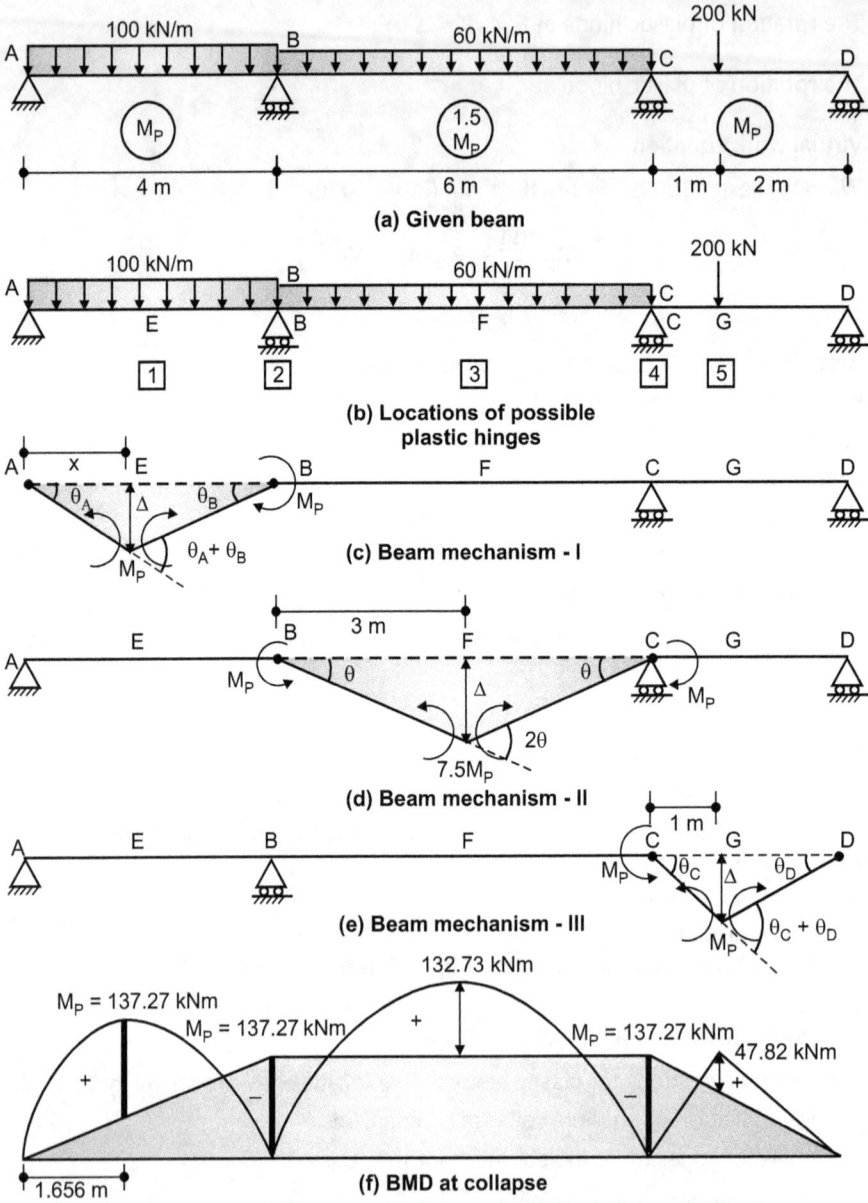

Fig. 13.16 : Illustrative Problem 13.21

(ii) Beam mechanism - II is as shown in Fig. 13.16 (d).

(a) Kinematics of the mechanism :

The rotation of plastic hinge at B = $\theta = \dfrac{\Delta}{3}$

The rotation of plastic hinge at F = $2\theta = \dfrac{2}{3}\Delta$

The rotation of plastic hinge at C = θ = $\frac{\Delta}{3}$

(b) Virtual work equation :

$W_e = W_i$ i.e. $60\left(\frac{1}{2} \times 6 \times \Delta\right) = M_p(\theta) + 1.5 M_p(2\theta) + M_p(\theta)$

∴ $180 \Delta = M_p\left(\frac{\Delta}{3}\right) + 1.5 M_p\left(\frac{2}{3} \cdot \Delta\right) + M_p\left(\frac{\Delta}{3}\right)$

∴ $M_p = 108$ kNm

(iii) Beam mechanism - III is as shown in Fig. 13.16 (e).

(a) Kinematics of the mechanism :

The rotation of plastic hinge at C = $\theta_C = \Delta$

The rotation of plastic hinge at D = $\theta_D = \frac{\Delta}{2}$

The rotation of plastic hinge at G = $\theta_C + \theta_D = \Delta + \frac{\Delta}{2}$

(b) Virtual work equation :

$W_e = W_i$ i.e. $200 \Delta = M_p(\theta_C) + M_p(\theta_C + \theta_D)$

∴ $200 \Delta = M_p(\Delta) + M_p\left(\Delta + \frac{\Delta}{2}\right)$

∴ $M_p = 80$ kNm

Plastic moment = M_p
= Greatest value of M_p obtained among all the above mechanisms
= 137.27 kNm

Step V : B.M.D. at collapse : as shown in Fig. 13.16 (f).

Problem 13.13 : The beam is supported and loaded with ultimate loads as shown in Fig. 13.17 (a). Find the plastic moment and draw B.M.D. at collapse.

Solution :

Data : The beam is supported and loaded as shown in Fig. 13.17 (a).

Object : Plastic moment.

Concepts and Equations :

(i) Mechanism method.
(ii) Work equation : External work done (W_e) = Internal work done (W_i).

Procedure :

Step I : Degree of static indeterminacy = D_{si} = 2

Step II : Potential locations for plastic hinges : Five locations as shown in Fig. 13.17 (b).

Step III : Identification of possible collapse mechanisms :

Maximum plastic hinges for complete mechanism = $D_{si} + 1 = 2 + 1 = 3$.

Number of independent mechanisms = 5 − 2 = 3.

Step IV : Analysis of possible mechanisms :

(i) Beam mechanism - I is as shown in Fig. 13.17 (c).

This mechanism is similar to that of propped cantilever carrying u.d.l. throughout the span and having constant M_p.

∴ Using the result derived earlier in Problem 13.7,

$$W_u = 11.656 \frac{M_p}{L^2} \text{ i.e. } M_p = \frac{W_u L^2}{11.656} = \frac{60 \times 3^2}{11.656} = 46.33 \text{ kNm}$$

and

$$x = 0.414 L = 0.414 \times 3 = 1.242 \text{ m}$$

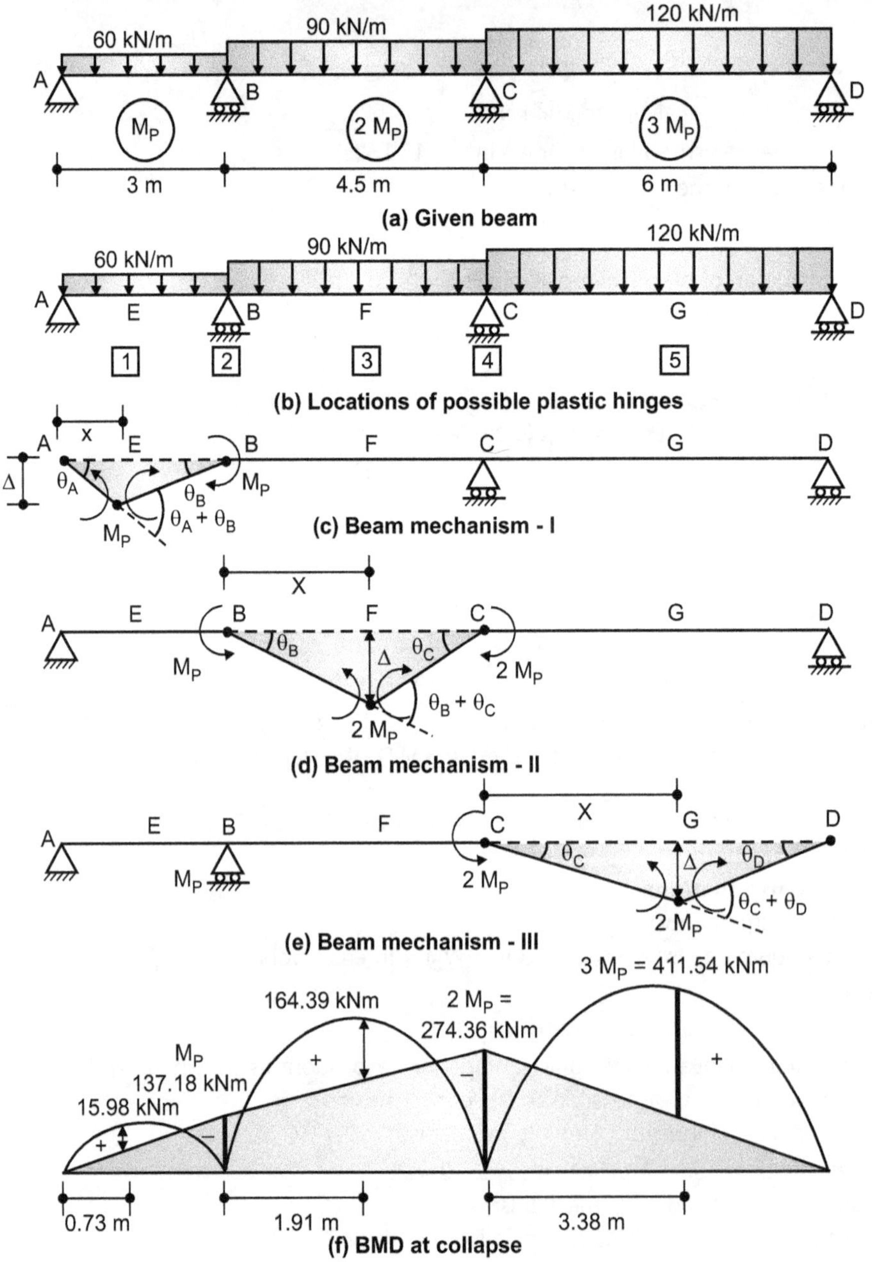

Fig. 13.17 : Illustrative Problem 13.13

(ii) Beam mechanism-II is as shown in Fig. 13.17 (d). Here the moments are different at the ends, hence location of plastic hinge between B and C is not exactly known. Let plastic hinge be formed at a distance x from B.

(a) Kinematics of the mechanism :

The rotation of plastic hinge at B = $\theta_B = \dfrac{\Delta}{x}$

The rotation of plastic hinge at C = $\theta_C = \dfrac{\Delta}{4.5 - x}$

The rotation of plastic hinge at F = $\theta_F = \theta_B + \Delta_C = \dfrac{\Delta}{x} + \dfrac{\Delta}{4.5 - x}$

(b) Virtual work equation :

$$W_e = W_i \text{ i.e. } 90\left(\dfrac{1}{2} \times 4.5 \times \Delta\right) = M_p(\theta_B) + 2M_p(\theta_B + \theta_C) + 2M_p(\theta_C)$$

$$\therefore \quad 202.5\,\Delta = M_p\left(\dfrac{\Delta}{x}\right) + 2M_p\left(\dfrac{\Delta}{x} + \dfrac{\Delta}{4.5-x}\right) + 2M_p\left(\dfrac{\Delta}{4.5-x}\right)$$

$$\therefore \quad 202.5 = \left[\dfrac{13.5 + x}{x\,(4.5 - x)}\right] M_p$$

$$\therefore \quad M_p = 202.5\left[\dfrac{x\,(4.5 - x)}{13.5 + x}\right] \qquad \ldots (A)$$

For maximum value of M_p, $\dfrac{dM_p}{dx} = 0$

∴ Differentiating equation (A) with respect to x and equating to zero, we get

$$x = 2.088$$

Substituting in equation (A), we get

$$M_p = 65.42 \text{ kNm}$$

(iii) Beam mechanism - III is as shown in Fig. 13.17 (e). Here the moments are different at the ends, hence location of plastic hinge between C and D is not exactly known. Let plastic hinge be formed at a distance x from C.

(a) Kinematics of the mechanism :

The rotation of plastic hinge at C = $\theta_C = \dfrac{\Delta}{x}$

The rotation of plastic hinge at $D = \theta_D = \dfrac{\Delta}{6-x}$

The rotation of plastic hinge at $G = \theta_C + \theta_D = \dfrac{\Delta}{x} + \dfrac{\Delta}{6-x}$

(b) Virtual work equation :

$$W_e = W_i \text{ i.e. } 120\left(\dfrac{1}{2} \times 6 \times \Delta\right) = 2M_p(\theta_C) + 3M_p(\theta_C + \theta_D)$$

$\therefore \quad 360\Delta = 2M_p\left(\dfrac{\Delta}{x}\right) + 3M_p\left(\dfrac{\Delta}{x} + \dfrac{\Delta}{6-x}\right)$

$\therefore \quad 360 = \left[\dfrac{30 - 2x}{x(6-x)}\right]M_p$

$\therefore \quad M_p = 360\left[\dfrac{x(6-x)}{30-2x}\right]$ ... (B)

For maximum value of M_p, $\dfrac{dM_p}{dx} = 0$

$\therefore$ Differentiating equation (B) with respect to x and equating to zero, we get

$x = 3.28$ m

Substituting equation (B) with respect to x and equating, we get

$M_p = 137.18$ kNm

Plastic moment $= M_p$

$= $ Greatest value of M_p obtained among all the above mechanisms

$= 137.18$ kNm

Step V : B.M.D. at collapse : as shown in Fig. 13.17 (f).

13.6 APPLICATION OF PLASTIC ANALYSIS TO STEEL FRAMES

There may be number of possible mechanisms like beam, sway and combined, in rectangular frames as the frames are highly indeterminate. Therefore, plastic analysis of frames is more involved process. However, the present work is restricted to single bay single storey rectangular frames. Analysis of such frames is simpler and effectively carried out by the mechanism method after identifying all possible mechanisms correctly. The equilibrium method becomes complicated in case of frames and hence may not be used. Mechanism method is best suited for all types of loads including the distributed loads. The location of plastic hinge in a member subjected to uniform load is found by using the same concepts as explained previously. Work done by u.d.l. also needs attention.

Following problems illustrate the application of mechanism method to the analysis of frames.

SOLVED PROBLEMS

Problem 13.14 : The frame is supported and loaded with ultimate loads as shown in Fig. 13.18 (a). Find the plastic moment. The members of the frame are of constant M_p.

Solution :

Data : The frame is supported and loaded as shown in Fig. 13.18 (a).

Object : Plastic moment.

Concepts and Equations :

(i) Mechanism method.

(ii) Work equation : External work done (W_e) = Internal work done (W_i).

Step I : Degree of static indeterminacy = D_{si} = 3

Step II : Potential locations for plastic hinges : Five locations as shown in Fig. 13.18 (b).

Step III : Identification of possible collapse mechanism : Maximum plastic hinges for complete mechanism = D_{si} + 1 = 3 + 1 = 4

Number of independent mechanisms = 5 – 3 = 2

Combined mechanism is obtained from linear combination of beam and sway mechanism.

Step IV : Analysis of possible mechanisms :

(i) Beam mechanism is as shown in Fig. 13.18 (c).

(a) Kinematics of the mechanism :

The rotation of plastic hinges at B and D = $\theta = \dfrac{2\Delta'}{L}$

The rotation of plastic hinge at C = $2\theta = \dfrac{4\Delta}{L}$

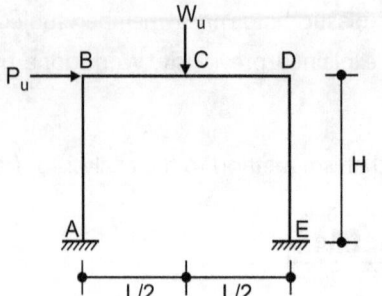

(a) Given frame

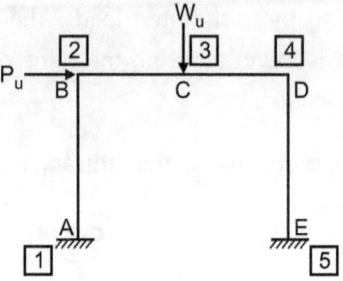

(b) Locations of possible plastic hinges

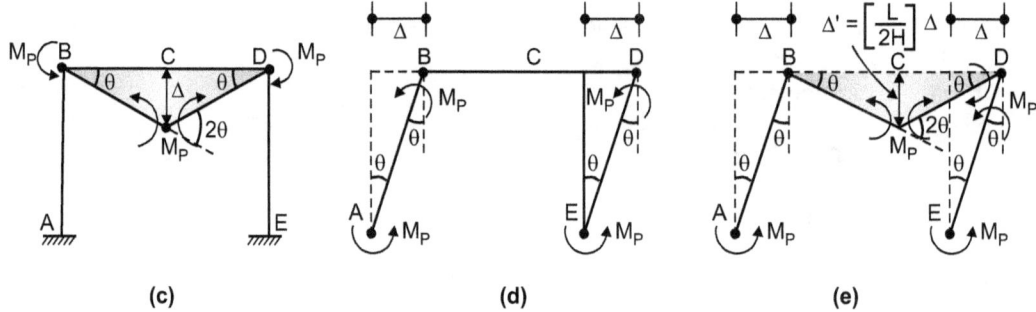

(c)   (d)   (e)

Fig. 13.18 : Illustrative Problem 13.14

(b) Virtual work equation :

$W_e = W_i$ i.e. $W_u \cdot \Delta' = M_p(\theta) + M_p(2\theta) + M_p(\theta)$

∴ $W_u \cdot \Delta' = M_p\left(\dfrac{2\Delta'}{L}\right) + M_p\left(\dfrac{4\Delta'}{L}\right) + M_p\left(\dfrac{2\Delta'}{L}\right)$

∴ $M_p = \dfrac{W_u L}{8}$

(ii) Sway mechanism is as shown in Fig. 13.18 (d).

(a) Kinematics of the mechanism :

The rotation of all plastic hinges = $\theta = \dfrac{\Delta}{H}$

(b) Virtual work equation :

$W_e = W_i$ i.e. $P_u \cdot \Delta = M_p(\theta) + M_p(\theta) + M_p(\theta) + M_p(\theta)$

∴ $P_u \cdot \Delta = 4 M_p (\Delta/H)$

∴ $M_p = \dfrac{P_u \cdot H}{4}$

Combined mechanism is as shown in Fig. 13.18 (e).

(a) Kinematics of the mechanism :

The rotation of plastic hinges at A and E = $\theta = \dfrac{\Delta}{H}$

The rotation of plastic hinges at C and D = $2\theta = \dfrac{2\Delta}{H}$

(b) Virtual work equation :

$W_e = W_i$ i.e. $\quad P_u \cdot \Delta + W_u \Delta' = M_p(\theta) + M_p(2\theta) + M_p(2\theta) + M_p(\theta)$

∴ $\quad P_u \cdot \Delta + W_u \left(\dfrac{L}{2H}\right) \Delta = M_p \left(\dfrac{\Delta}{H}\right) + M_p \left(\dfrac{2\Delta}{H}\right) + M_p \left(\dfrac{2\Delta}{H}\right) + M_p \left(\dfrac{\Delta}{H}\right)$

∴ $\quad P_u + \dfrac{W_u L}{2H} = \dfrac{6 M_p}{H}$

∴ $\quad M_p = \dfrac{P_u \cdot H}{6} + \dfrac{W_u \cdot L}{12}$

∴ Plastic moment = M_p

= Greatest value of M_p obtained among all the above mechanisms

Problem 13.15 : The frame is supported and loaded with ultimate loads as shown in Fig. 13.19 (a). Find the collapse load factor.

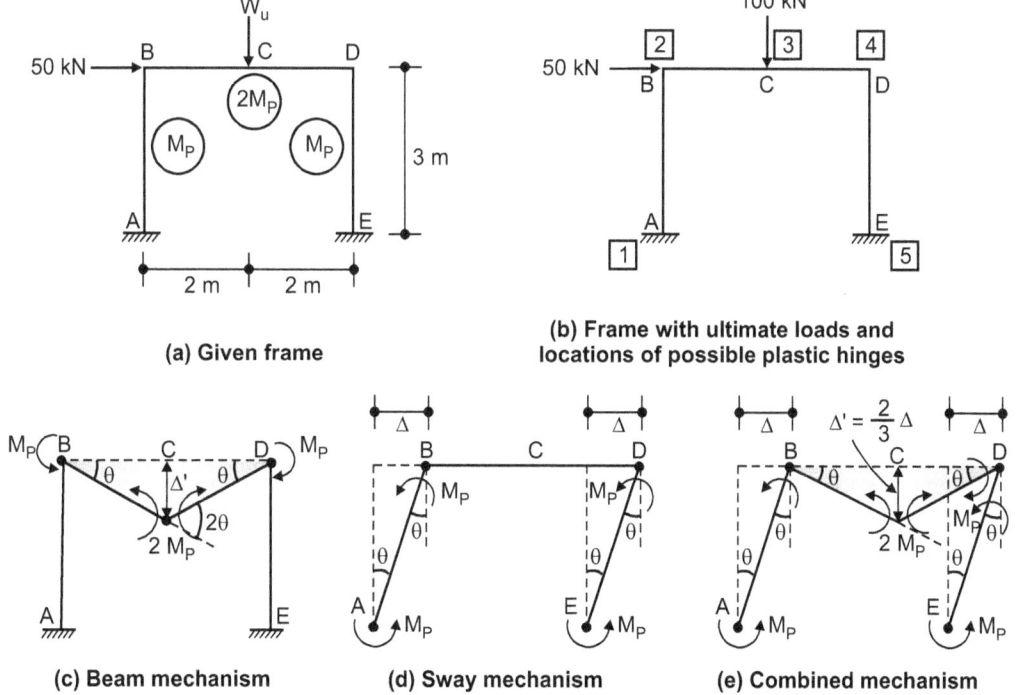

(a) Given frame

(b) Frame with ultimate loads and locations of possible plastic hinges

(c) Beam mechanism   (d) Sway mechanism   (e) Combined mechanism

Fig. 13.19 : Illustrative Problem 13.15

Solution :
Data : The frame is supported and loaded as shown in Fig. 13.19 (a).
Object : Collapse load factor (λ).
Concepts and Equations :
(i) Mechanism method :
(ii) Work equation : External work done (W_e) = Internal work done (W_i).
Procedure :
Step I : Degree of static indeterminacy = D_{si} = 3.
Step II : Potential locations for plastic hinges : Five locations as shown in Fig. 13.19 (b).
Step III : Identification of possible collapse mechanisms :
Maximum plastic hinges for complete mechanism = $D_{si} + 1 = 3 + 1 = 4$.
Number of independent mechanisms = 5 – 3 = 2.
Combined mechanism is obtained from linear combination of beam and sway mechanism.
Step IV : Analysis of possible mechanisms :
(i) Beam mechanism is as shown in Fig. 13.19 (c).
(a) Kinematics of the mechanisms :

The rotation of plastic hinges at B and D = $\theta = \dfrac{\Delta'}{2}$

The rotation of plastic hinge at C = $2\theta = \Delta'$

(b) Virtual work equation :
$W_e = W_i$ i.e. $(100\,\lambda)\,\Delta' = M_p\,(\theta) + 2M_p\,(2\theta) + M_p\,(\theta)$

$\therefore \quad (100\,\lambda)\,\Delta' = M_p\left(\dfrac{\Delta}{2}\right) + 2M_p\,(\Delta') + M_p\left(\dfrac{\Delta'}{2}\right)$

$\therefore \quad \lambda = \dfrac{3M_p}{100}$

Sway mechanism is as shown in Fig. 13.19 (d).
(a) Kinematics of the mechanism :

The rotation of all plastic hinges = $\theta = \dfrac{\Delta}{3}$

(b) Virtual work equation :
$W_e = W_i$ i.e. $(50\,\lambda)\,\Delta = M_p\,(\theta) + M_p\,(\theta) + M_p\,(\theta) + M_p\,(\theta)$

$\therefore \quad (50\,\lambda)\,\Delta = 4M_p\left(\dfrac{\Delta}{3}\right)$

$\therefore \quad \lambda = \dfrac{4M_p}{150}$

Combined mechanism is as shown in Fig. 13.19 (e).

(a) Kinematics of the mechanism : The rotation of plastic hinges at A and E = $\theta = \dfrac{\Delta}{3}$

The rotation of plastic hinges at C and D = $2\theta = \dfrac{2\Delta}{3}$

(b) Virtual work equation :
$W_e = W_i$ i.e. $(50\,\lambda)\,\Delta + (100\,\lambda)\,\Delta' = M_p\,(\theta) + 2M_p\,(2\theta) + M_p\,(2\theta) + M_p\,(\theta)$

∴ $(50\lambda)\Delta + (100\lambda)\frac{2}{3}\Delta = M_p\left(\frac{\Delta}{3}\right) + 2M_p\left(\frac{2\Delta}{3}\right) + M_p\left(\frac{2\Delta}{3}\right) + M_p\left(\frac{\Delta}{3}\right)$

$$\left(\frac{350}{3}\right)\lambda = \frac{8M_p}{3}$$

∴ $\lambda = \frac{8}{350}M_p$

∴ Collapse load factor = Smallest value of λ obtained among all above mechanisms

$$\lambda = \frac{8}{350}M_p$$

Problem 13.16 : The frame is supported and loaded with ultimate loads as shown in Fig. 13.20 (a). Find the plastic moment and draw B.M.D. at collapse.

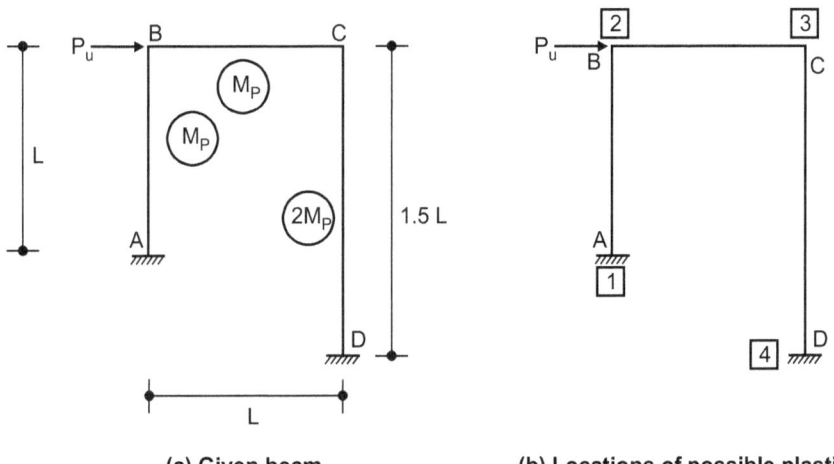

(a) Given beam   (b) Locations of possible plastic hinges

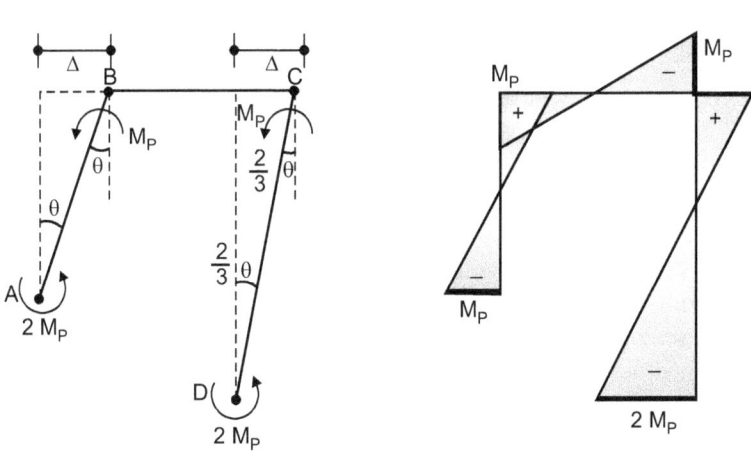

(c) Sway mechanism   (d) BMD at collapse

Fig. 13.20 : Illustrative Problem 13.16

Solution :

Data : The frame is supported and loaded as shown in Fig. 13.20 (a).

Object : Plastic moment.

Concepts and Equations :
(i)   Mechanism method.
(ii) Work equation : External work done (W_e) = Internal work done (W_i).

Procedure :

Step I : Degree of static indeterminacy = D_{si} = 3.

Step II : Potential locations for plastic hinges : Four locations as shown in Fig. 13.20 (b).

Step III : Identification of possible collapse mechanisms :

Maximum plastic hinges for complete mechanism = D_{si} + 1 = 3 + 1 = 4

Number of independent mechanism = 4 − 3 = 1

It should be noted that only sway mechanism is possible.

Step IV : Analysis of possible mechanisms :

Sway mechanism is as shown in Fig. 13.20 (c).

(a) Kinematics of the mechanism :

The rotation of plastic hinges at A and B = $\theta = \dfrac{\Delta}{L}$

The rotation of plastic hinges at C and D = $\dfrac{2}{3}\theta = \left(\dfrac{2}{3}\right)\dfrac{\Delta}{L}$

(b) Virtual work equation :

$W_e = W_i$ i.e. $\quad P_u \cdot \Delta = M_p(\theta) + M_p(\theta) + M_p\left(\dfrac{2}{3}\theta\right) + 2M_p\left(\dfrac{2}{3}\theta\right)$

$\therefore \quad P_u \cdot \Delta = M_p\left(\dfrac{\Delta}{L}\right) + M_p\left(\dfrac{\Delta}{L}\right) + M_p\left(\dfrac{2}{3}\right)\dfrac{\Delta}{L} + 2M_p\left(\dfrac{2}{3}\right)\dfrac{\Delta}{L}$

$\therefore \quad M_p = \dfrac{P_u \cdot L}{4}$

Step V : B.M.D. at collapse : as shown in Fig. 13.20 (d).

Problem 13.17 : The frame is supported and loaded with ultimate loads as shown in Fig. 13.21 (a). Find the plastic moment and draw B.M.D. at collapse.

Solution :

Data : The frame is supported and loaded as shown in Fig. 13.21 (a).

Object : Plastic moment.

Concepts and Equations :
(i)   Mechanism method.
(ii) Work equation : External work done (W_e) = Internal work done (W_i).

Procedure :

Step I : Degree of static indeterminacy = D_{si} = 3.

Step II : Potential locations for plastic hinges : Five locations as shown in Fig. 13.21 (b).

Step III : Identification of possible collapse mechanisms :

Maximum plastic hinges for complete mechanism = $D_{si} + 1 = 3 + 1 = 4$

Number of independent mechanisms = $5 - 3 = 2$.

Combined mechanism is obtained from linear combination of beam and sway mechanism.

Step IV : Analysis of possible mechanisms :

(i) Beam mechanism is as shown in Fig. 13.21 (c).

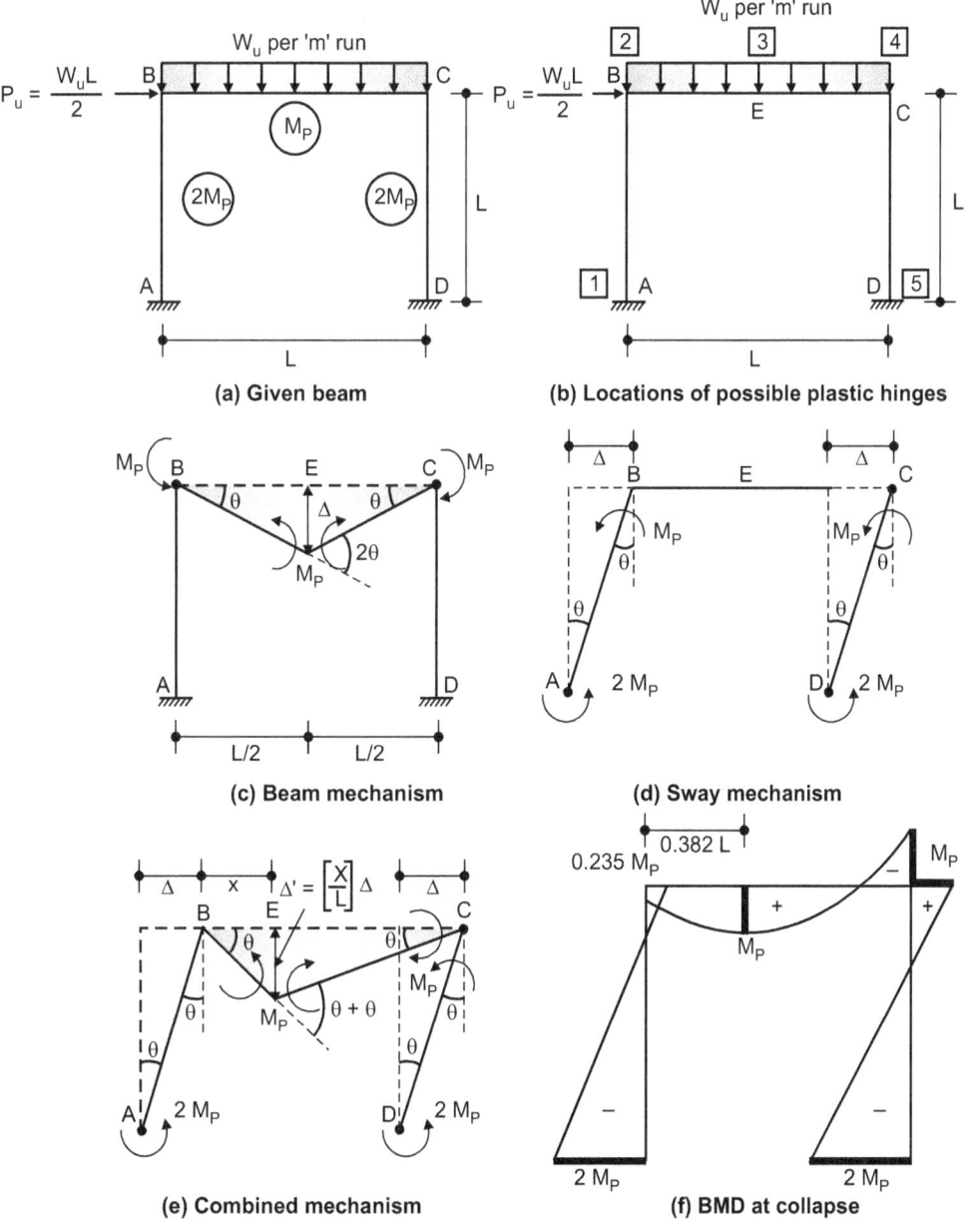

Fig. 13.21 : Illustrative Problem 13.17

(a) Kinematics of the mechanism : The rotation of plastic hinges at B and C = $\theta = \dfrac{2\Delta'}{L}$

The rotation of plastic hinge at E = $2\theta = \dfrac{4\Delta'}{L}$

(b) Virtual work equation :

$W_e = W_i$ i.e. $W_u \left(\dfrac{1}{2} \times L \times \Delta'\right) = M_p(\theta) + M_p(2\theta) + M_p(\theta) + M_p(\theta)$

$\therefore \quad \dfrac{W_u L}{2} \cdot \Delta' = M_p\left(\dfrac{2\Delta'}{L}\right) + M_p\left(\dfrac{4\Delta'}{L}\right) + M_p\left(\dfrac{2\Delta'}{L}\right)$

$\therefore \quad M_p = \dfrac{W_u L^2}{16}$

(ii) Sway mechanism is as shown in Fig. 13.21 (d).

(a) Kinematics of the mechanism :

The rotation of all plastic hinges = $\theta = \dfrac{\Delta}{L}$

(b) Virtual work equation :

$W_e = W_i$ i.e. $P_u \cdot \Delta = 2M_p(\theta) + M_p(\theta) + 2M_p(\theta) + M_p(\theta)$

$\therefore \quad \dfrac{W_u L}{2} \cdot \Delta = 6M_p\left(\dfrac{\Delta}{L}\right)$

$\therefore \quad M_p = \dfrac{W_u L^2}{12}$

(iii) Combined mechanism is as shown in Fig. 13.21 (e).

(a) Kinematics of the mechanism : The rotation of plastic hinges at A and D = $\theta = \dfrac{\Delta}{L}$

The rotation of plastic hinges at C and E = $\theta + \theta' = \dfrac{\Delta}{L} + \dfrac{x \cdot \Delta}{L(L-x)}$

(b) Virtual work equation :

$W_e = W_i$ i.e. $P_u \cdot \Delta + W_u\left(\dfrac{1}{2} \times L \times \Delta'\right) = 2M_p(\theta) + M_p(\theta + \theta') + M_p(\theta + \theta') + 2M_p(\theta)$

$\therefore \; P_u \cdot \Delta + W_u \cdot \dfrac{1}{2} \cdot \left(\dfrac{x}{L}\right)\Delta = 2M_p\left(\dfrac{\Delta}{L}\right) + M_p\left(\dfrac{\Delta}{L} + \dfrac{x\Delta}{L(L-x)}\right) + M_p\left(\dfrac{\Delta}{L} + \dfrac{x\Delta}{L(L-x)}\right) + 2M_p\left(\dfrac{\Delta}{L}\right)$

$\therefore \quad \dfrac{W_u}{2}(L + x) = \left(\dfrac{6}{L} + \dfrac{2x}{L(L-x)}\right)M_p$

$\therefore \quad M_p = \dfrac{W_u}{4}\left(\dfrac{L^3 - x^2 L}{-2x + 3L}\right)$ ... (A)

For maximum value of M_p, $\dfrac{d}{dx}(M_p) = 0$

$\therefore$ Differentiating equation (A) with respect to x, we get

$x = 0.382 L$

Substituting in equation (A), we get

$M_p = \dfrac{W_u L^2}{10.47}$

∴ Plastic moment = M_p
= Greatest value of M_p obtained among all the above mechanisms
= $\dfrac{W_u L^2}{10.47}$

Step V : B.M.D. at collapse : as shown in Fig. 13.21 (f).

Problem 13.18 : The frame is supported and loaded with ultimate loads as shown in Fig. 13.22 (a). Find the plastic moment. The members of the frame are of constant M_p.

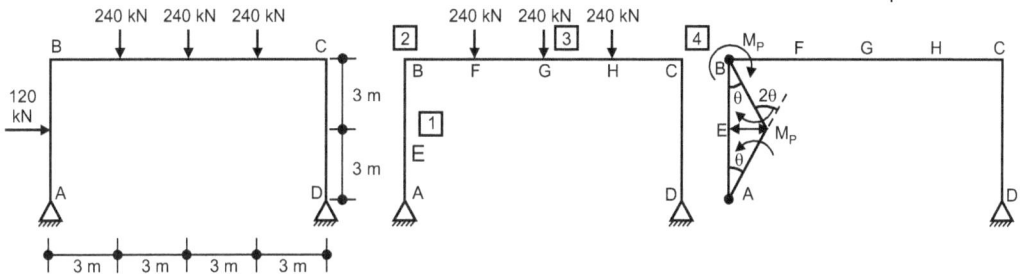

(a) Given beam   (b) Locations of possible plastic hinges   (c) Beam mechanism- I

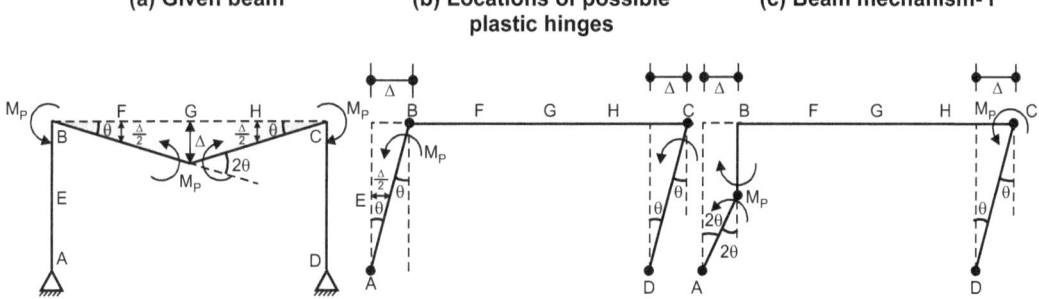

(d) Beam mechanism- II   (e) Sway mechanism   (f) Combined mechanism - I

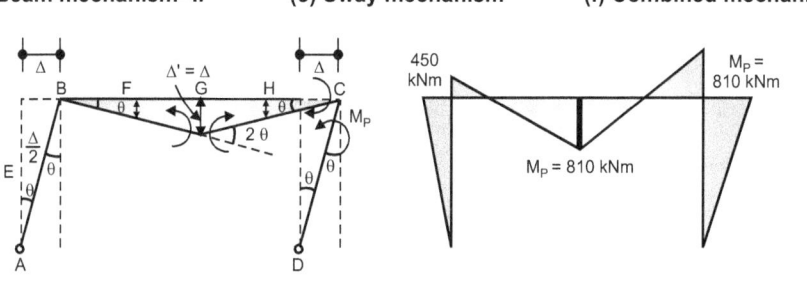

(g) Combined mechanism - II   (h) BMD of collapse

Fig. 13.22 : Illustrative Problem 13.18

Solution :
Data : The frame is supported and loaded as shown in Fig. 13.22 (a).
Object : Plastic moment.

Concepts and Equations :
(i) Mechanism method.
(ii) Work equation : External work done (W_e) = Internal work done (W_i)

Procedure :

Step I : Degree of static indeterminacy = D_{si} = 1.

Step II : Potential locations for plastic hinges : Four locations as shown in Fig. 13.22 (b).

Step III : Identification of possible collapse mechanisms :
Maximum plastic hinges for complete mechanism = D_{si} + 1 = 1 + 1 = 2.
Number of independent mechanisms = 4 – 1 = 3.

Two combined mechanisms are obtained from linear combination of beam and sway mechanism.

Step IV : Analysis of possible mechanisms :

(i) Beam mechanism - I is as shown in Fig. 13.22 (c).

(a) Kinematics of the mechanism :

The rotation of plastic hinge at B = $\theta = \dfrac{\Delta}{3}$

The rotation of plastic hinge at E = $2\theta = \dfrac{2\Delta}{3}$

(b) Virtual work equation :

$W_e = W_i$ i.e. $120 \Delta = M_p (2\theta) + M_p (\theta)$

∴ $120 \Delta = M_p \left(\dfrac{2\Delta}{3}\right) + M_p \left(\dfrac{\Delta}{3}\right)$

∴ $M_p = 120$ kNm

(ii) Beam mechanism - II is as shown in Fig. 13.22 (d).

(a) Kinematics of the mechanism :

The rotation of plastic hinges at B and C = $\theta = \dfrac{\Delta'}{6}$

The rotation of plastic hinge at G = $2\theta = \dfrac{\Delta'}{3}$

(b) Virtual work equation :

$W_e = W_i$ i.e. $240 \cdot \dfrac{\Delta'}{2} + 240 \cdot \Delta' + 240 \cdot \dfrac{\Delta'}{2} = M_p (\theta) + M_p (2\theta) + M_p (\theta)$

∴ $480 \Delta' = M_p \left(\dfrac{\Delta}{6}\right) + M_p \left(\dfrac{\Delta}{3}\right) + M_p \left(\dfrac{\Delta}{6}\right)$

∴ $M_p = 720$ kNm

(iii) Sway mechanism is as shown in Fig. 13.22 (e).

(a) Kinematics of the mechanism : The rotation of all plastic hinges = $\theta = \dfrac{\Delta}{6}$

(b) Virtual work equation :

$W_e = W_i$ i.e. $120 \cdot \dfrac{\Delta}{2} = M_p (\theta) + M_p (\theta)$

$\therefore$ $\qquad 120 \cdot \dfrac{\Delta}{2} = 2M_p \left(\dfrac{\Delta}{6}\right)$

$\therefore$ $\qquad M_p = 180$ kNm

(iv) Combined mechanism - I is as shown in Fig. 13.22 (f).

(a) Kinematics of the mechanism :

The rotation of plastic hinges at A and E = $2\theta = \dfrac{\Delta}{3}$

The rotation of plastic hinge at C = $\theta = \dfrac{\Delta}{6}$

(b) Virtual work equation :

$W_e = W_i$ i.e. $\quad 120\,\Delta = M_p\,(2\theta) + M_p\,(\theta)$

$\therefore \qquad 120\,\Delta = M_p \left(\dfrac{\Delta}{3}\right) + M_p \left(\dfrac{\Delta}{6}\right)$

$\therefore \qquad M_p = 240$ kNm

(v) Combined mechanism - II is as shown in Fig. 13.22 (g).

(a) Kinematics of the mechanism :

The rotation of plastic hinges at G and C = $2\theta = 2\left(\dfrac{\Delta}{6}\right) = \dfrac{\Delta}{3}$

(b) Virtual work equation :

$W_e = W_i$ i.e. $120 \cdot \dfrac{\Delta}{2} + 240 \cdot \dfrac{\Delta}{2} + 240 \cdot \Delta + 240 \cdot \dfrac{\Delta}{2} = M_p\,(2\theta) + M_p\,(2\theta)$

$\therefore \qquad 540 \cdot \Delta = 2M_p \left(\dfrac{\Delta}{3}\right)$

$\therefore \qquad M_p = 810$ kNm

$\therefore$ Plastic moment = M_p

= Greatest value of M_p obtained among all above mechanisms

= 810 kNm

Step V : B.M.D. at collapse : as shown in Fig. 13.22 (h).

13.7 STANDARD RESULTS OF PLASTIC ANALYSIS

Plastic analysis of simple structures like beams and portal frames, presented in the previous article are very much useful for further studies. Therefore, some of the results of standard cases are consolidated and given in Table 13.2 for direct applications to analysis and design problems of beams and frames.

Table 13.2

Sr. no.	Case	Sketch	Mechanism	Ultimate load W_u	Plastic moment M_p
1.	Fixed beam with central point load	W_u at L/2, L/2	(mechanism sketch)	$W_u = \dfrac{8M_p}{L}$	$M_p = \dfrac{W_u L}{8}$
2.	Fixed beam with off centre point load	W_u at a, b	(mechanism sketch)	$W_u = \dfrac{2LM_p}{ab}$	$M_p = \dfrac{W_u b}{2L}$
3.	Fixed beam with uniform load on the whole span	w_u/m over L	(mechanism sketch)	$w_u = \dfrac{16M_p}{L^2}$	$M_p = \dfrac{W_u L^2}{16}$
4.	Fixed beam with uniform load on the whole span	w_u/m, a, b, L, x	(mechanism sketch)	$w_u = \dfrac{16M_p L^2}{a^2(2L-a)^2}$	$M_p = \dfrac{W_u a^2(2L-a)^2}{16L^2}$
5.	Propped cantilever with central point load	W_u at L/2, L/2	(mechanism sketch)	$W_u = \dfrac{6M_p}{L}$	$M_p = \dfrac{W_u L}{6}$
6.	Propped cantilever with off centre point load	W_u at a, b	(mechanism sketch)	$W_u = \dfrac{M_p(L+b)}{ab}$	$M_p = \dfrac{W_u ab}{L+b}$
7.	Propped cantilever with uniform load on whole span	w_u/m over L	(mechanism sketch)	$w_u = \dfrac{11.67\, M_p}{L^2}$	$M_p = \dfrac{W_u L^2}{11.67}$
8.	Single bay single storey portal with central point load on beam and lateral point load	W_u, P_u, M_P, H, L/2, L/2	I, II, III	$W_u = \dfrac{8M_p}{L}$ $P_u = \dfrac{4M_p}{H}$	$M_p = \dfrac{W_u L}{8}$ $M_p = \dfrac{P_u H}{4}$ $M_p = \dfrac{P_u H}{6} + \dfrac{W_u L}{12}$

#	Description	Frame	Mechanism	W_u / P_u	M_p
9.	Single bay single storey portal with uniform load on beam and lateral load (non-uniform section)	P_u, w_u/m, M_p, $2M_p$, $2M_p$, L	(i)	$W_u = \dfrac{16 M_p}{L^2}$	$M_p = \dfrac{W_u L^2}{16}$
			(ii)	$P_u = \dfrac{12 M_p}{L^2}$	$M_p = \dfrac{W_u L^2}{12}$
			(iii)	$W_u = \dfrac{10.47 M_p}{L^2}$	$M_p = \dfrac{W_u L^2}{10.47}$
10.	Single bay single storey portal with hinged bases and with central point load on beam and colateral load (uniform section)	P_u, W_u, M_p, M_p, M_p, H, $L/2$, $L/2$	(i)	$W_u = \dfrac{8 M_p}{L}$	$M_p = \dfrac{W_u L}{8}$
			(ii)	$P_u = \dfrac{2 M_p}{H}$	$M_p = \dfrac{P_u H}{2}$
			(iii)		$M_p = \dfrac{P_u H}{4} + \dfrac{W_u L}{8}$

13.8 PLASTIC DESIGN OF STEEL BEAMS AND FRAMES

There are two usual methods of structural design. The conventional method known as *working stress method* is based on the concept of allowable stress and elastic behaviour. The other method called as 'Ultimate strength method or *ultimate load method*, is based on the concept of inelastic or plastic behaviour and ultimate load. Ultimate strength method is more rational and is being accepted all over. With respect to steel structure this approach is known as *plastic design*. The plastic design procedure differs from the working stress method in three important aspects given below :

(i) Ultimate loads are used instead of working loads. In arriving at the ultimate loads, the dead and live loads are considered separately and each is increased by a different load factor suggested by the code, to account for the most severe loading combinations.

(ii) Knowing the ultimate loads, the forces and moments in members are determined by plastic analysis, as a reverse procedure of obtaining the collapse or ultimate load.

(iii) The members are so proportioned that their ultimate strength exceeds or at least equals, the forces and moments produced by ultimate loads.

(iv) The members are checked for performance under working or service loads. This includes consideration of deflections, fatigue, dynamic response, buckling, local buckling, local yielding and other structural characteristics.

The concepts of plastic design of the members only for flexure are introduced here, although plastic design as a whole needs more explanation. It is interesting to note that plastic design allows to provide the plastic moment of members as we decide. In this context the basic principle of plastic design (ultimate load design) is that load distribution in statically indeterminate structure is based on the load carrying capacity of the members. This is *'the programmatic concept of structural action i.e. when one tells the structure what to do, it will try do it'*.

This concept is introduced and illustrated with the following simple examples of beam and portal.

SOLVED PROBLEMS

Problem 13.19 : Design the uniform section for the continuous beam supported and loaded as shown in Fig. 13.23 (a) if the load factor is 1.7 and yield stress of steel is 250 N/mm².

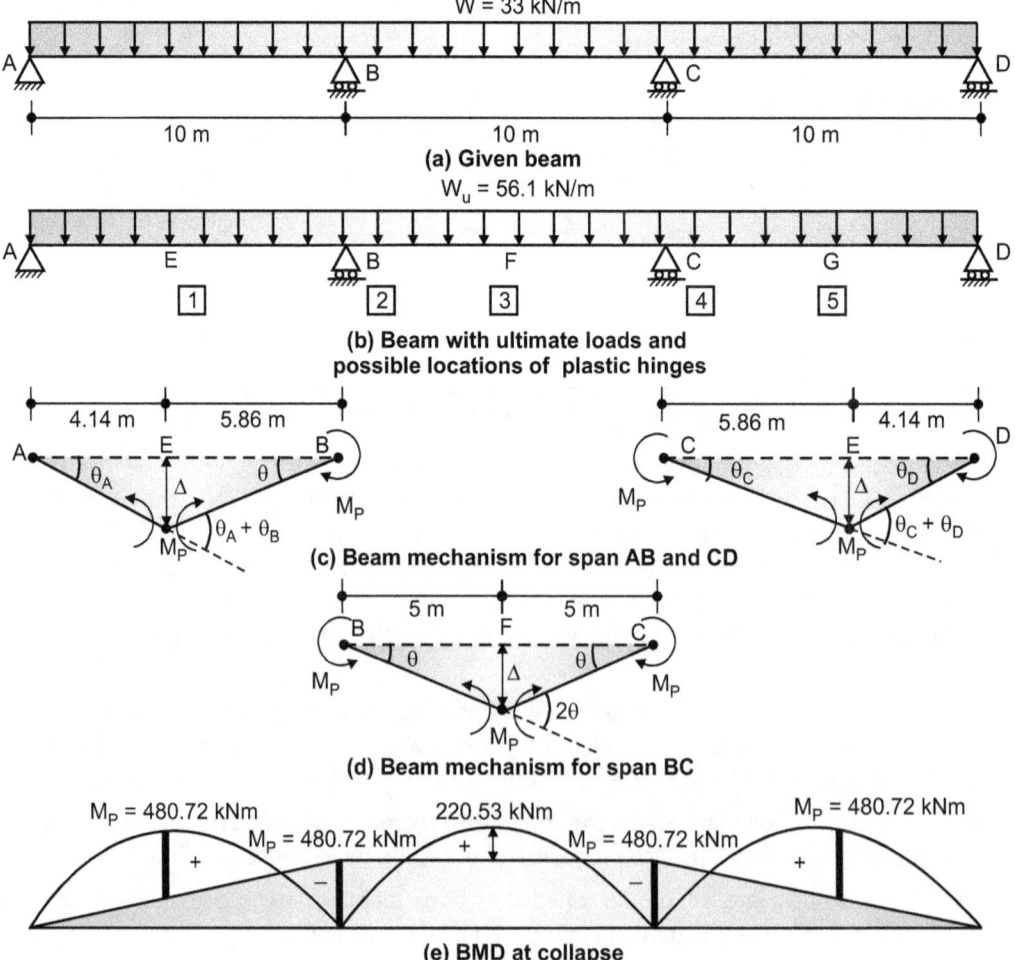

Fig. 13.23 : Illustrative Problem 13.19

Solution : (i) Structural configuration : Dimensions, support conditions as shown in Fig. 13.23 (a). AB = BC = CD = L = 10 m.

(ii) Loads : Uniformly distributed load of 33 kN/m on all spans as shown in Fig. 13.23 (a).

w = 33 kN/m

(iii) Load factor = γ = 1.7

(iv) Yield stress = σ_y = 250 N/mm²

(v) Uniform section.

Object : Design of the beam section for flexure only.

Concepts and Equations :

(i) Plastic method : Mechanism method work equation of a mechanism.

$\Sigma W\Delta = \Sigma M\theta$ or standard results.

(ii) Bending moment distribution - BMD.

(iii) $Z_p = \dfrac{M_p}{\sigma_y}$

Procedure :

Step I : Ultimate load or collapse load.

$W_u = \gamma \times w = 1.7 \times 33 = 56.1$ kN/m

Step II : Plastic analysis :

(i) Degree of static indeterminacy = D_{si} = 2.

(ii) Potential locations for plastic hinges : Five locations as shown in Fig. 13.23 (b).

(iii) Maximum plastic hinges for complete mechanism = D_{si} + 1 = 2 + 1 = 3.

(iv) Analysis of possible mechanisms :

(a) Beam mechanism for span AB and CD is as shown in Fig. 13.23 (c).

Using the standard result from Table 13.2,

$$M_p = \dfrac{W_u L^2}{11.67} = \dfrac{56.1 \times 10^2}{11.67} = 480.72 \text{ kNm}$$

Plastic hinge occurs at E and G i.e. 0.414 (L) = 0.414 × 10 = 4.14 m from A and D respectively.

(b) Beam mechanism for span BC is as shown in Fig. 13.23 (d).

Using the standard result from Table 13.2,

M_p = Greatest value of M_p obtained among all the above mechanisms

= 480.72 kNm

Step III : Checking the yield condition :

BMD at collapse is as shown in Fig. 13.23 (e). It should be noted that no where BM exceeds

M_p = 480.72 kNm

Step IV : Plastic section modulus required

$$Z_p = \dfrac{M_p}{\sigma_y} = \dfrac{480.72 \times 10^6}{250} = 1.922 \times 10^6 \text{ mm}^3$$

Step V : Elastic section modulus. Assuming shape factor 1.15 for I section,

$$K_s = \frac{Z_p}{Z_e} \quad \therefore Z_e = \frac{Z_p}{K_s} = \frac{1.922 \times 10^6}{1.15} = 1.671 \times 10^6 \text{ mm}^3$$

Step VI : Selection of the section corresponding to Z_e, the rolled steel section is selected referring to the steel tables.

ISMB 500 @ 87.14 kg/m giving $Z_{xx} = 1810 \times 10^3$ mm³

It may be noted that as this design is not economical, it can be designed economically as illustrated in the next example.

Problem 13.20 : Design the economical section for the beam using the cover plates wherever necessary for the continuous beam supported and loaded as shown in Fig. 13.24 (a). Assume the load factor 1.7 and yield stress 250 N/mm².

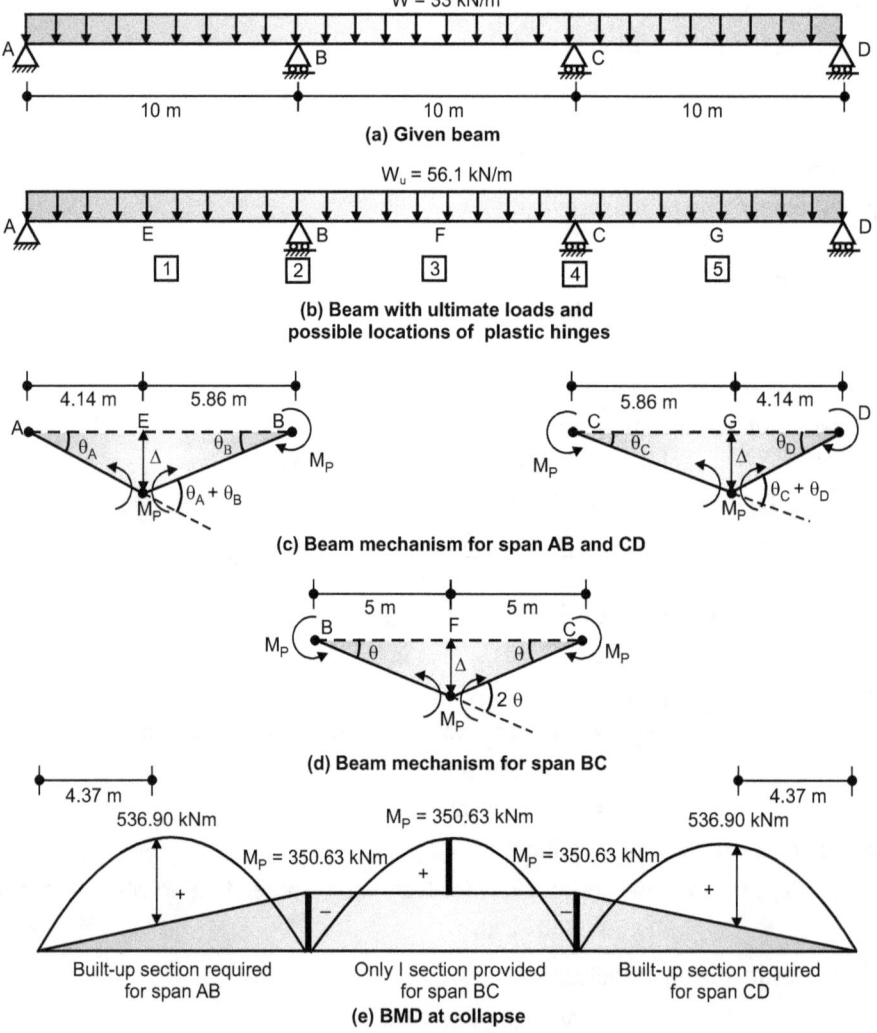

Fig. 13.24 : Illustrative Problem 13.20

Solution : Data : (i) Structural configuration as shown in Fig. 13.24 (a).
$$AB = BC = CD = L = 10 \text{ m}$$
(ii) Loads as shown in Fig. 13.24 (a).
$$w = 33 \text{ kN/m}$$
(iii) Load factor $= \gamma = 1.7$
(iv) Yield stress $= \sigma_y = 250 \text{ N/m}^2$

Object : Design of beam section with cover plates.

Concepts and Equations :
(i) Plastic method : Mechanism method.
(ii) Work equation of a mechanism.
(iii) $Z_p = \dfrac{M_p}{\sigma_y}$
(iv) Bending moment distribution – B.M.D.

Procedure :

Step I : Ultimate load.
$$W_u = \gamma \cdot w = 1.7 \times 33 = 56.1 \text{ kN/m}$$

Step II : Plastic analysis :
(i) Degree of static indeterminacy $= D_{si} = 2$
(ii) Potential locations for plastic hinges : Five locations as shown in Fig. 13.24 (b).
(iii) Maximum plastic hinges for complete mechanism $= D_{si} + 1 = 2 + 1 = 3$.
(iv) Analysis of possible mechanisms :
(a) Beam mechanism for span AB and CD is as shown in Fig. 13.24 (c).
Using the standard result from Table 13.2,
$$M_p = \dfrac{W_u L^2}{11.67} = \dfrac{56.1 \times 10^2}{11.67} = 480.72 \text{ kNm}$$
Plastic hinge occurs at E and G i.e. $0.414 (L) = 0.414 \times 10$
$$= 4.14 \text{ m from A and D respectively}$$
(b) Beam mechanism for span BC is as shown in Fig. 13.24 (d).
Using the standard result from Table 13.2,
$$M_p = \dfrac{W_u L^2}{16} = \dfrac{56.1 \times 10^2}{16} = 350.63 \text{ kNm}$$
B.M.D. at collapse is as shown in Fig. 13.24 (e).

Vertical reaction at A $= \dfrac{-350.63}{10} + \dfrac{56.1 \times 10}{2} = 245.44 \text{ kN } (\uparrow)$

To locate point of zero SF in span AB, from A,
$$245.44 - 56.1 (x) = 0$$
$\therefore \quad x = 4.37 \text{ m}$
$\therefore$ Maximum sagging moment for span AB
$$= 245.44 \times 4.37 - 56.1 \times \dfrac{(4.37)^2}{2}$$
$$= 536.90 \text{ kNm}$$

All above values are same for span CD by symmetry.

Step III : Minimum plastic moment required
$$M_p = 350.63 \text{ kNm as per the requirements of the central span BC}$$

Step IV : Plastic section modulus
$$Z_p = \frac{M_p}{\sigma_y} = \frac{350.63 \times 10^6}{250} = 1.403 \times 10^6 \text{ mm}^2$$

Step V : Elastic section modulus :
Assuming $K_s = 1.15$
$$K_s = \frac{Z_p}{Z_e} \therefore Z_e = \frac{Z_p}{K_s} = \frac{1.403 \times 10^6}{1.15} = 1.220 \times 10^6 \text{ mm}^3$$

Step VI : Selection of section :
From steel table selecting the appropriate section.
ISLB 450 @ 65.26 kg/m giving
$$Z_{xx} = 1.223 \times 10^6 \text{ mm}^4$$

Step VII : Cover plates for end spans AB and CD.
(i) As the section ISLB is selected on the basis of the central span BC, it is not adequate for the end spans AB and CD.
(ii) M_p for end spans = 536.90 kNm
(iii) Z_p required for end spans = $\dfrac{M_p}{\sigma_y} = \dfrac{536.90 \times 10^6}{250} = 2.147 \times 10^6 \text{ mm}^3$

(iv) Z_e for end span = $\dfrac{Z_p}{K_s} = \dfrac{2.147 \times 10^6}{1.15} = 1.867 \times 10^6 \text{ mm}^3$

(v) Additional section modulus required and to be provided by cover plates
$$Z_{e\text{ plates}} = 1.867 \times 10^6 - 1.223 \times 10^6$$
$$= 0.643 \times 10^6 \text{ mm}^2$$

(vi) Area of cover plate one on either side (i.e. top or bottom) of the section
$$Z_{e\text{ plate}} = A_{plate} \times D$$
When D is taken as the depth of the I section provide
$$0.643 \times 10^6 = A_{plate} \times 450$$
$$\therefore A_{plate} = 1431 \text{ mm}^2$$

(vii) Size of the cover plate provided 180 mm × 8 mm one cover plate at top and bottom of ISLB 450.
$\therefore$ Area of plate provided = 180 × 8 = 1440 mm² > 1431 mm² ... O.K.

Step VII : Checking the section for the yield condition.

Accordingly the actual moment of inertia and modulus of section M_p can be calculated and BM distribution can be verified so that no where the bending moment exceeds M_p at that section at collapse at any of the possible mechanism.

Problem 13.21 : Design the uniform section of the beam and columns of the portal frame supported and loaded as shown in Fig. 13.25 (a). If the load factor is 2.0 and the yield stress of steel is 250 N/mm².

PLASTIC ANALYSIS

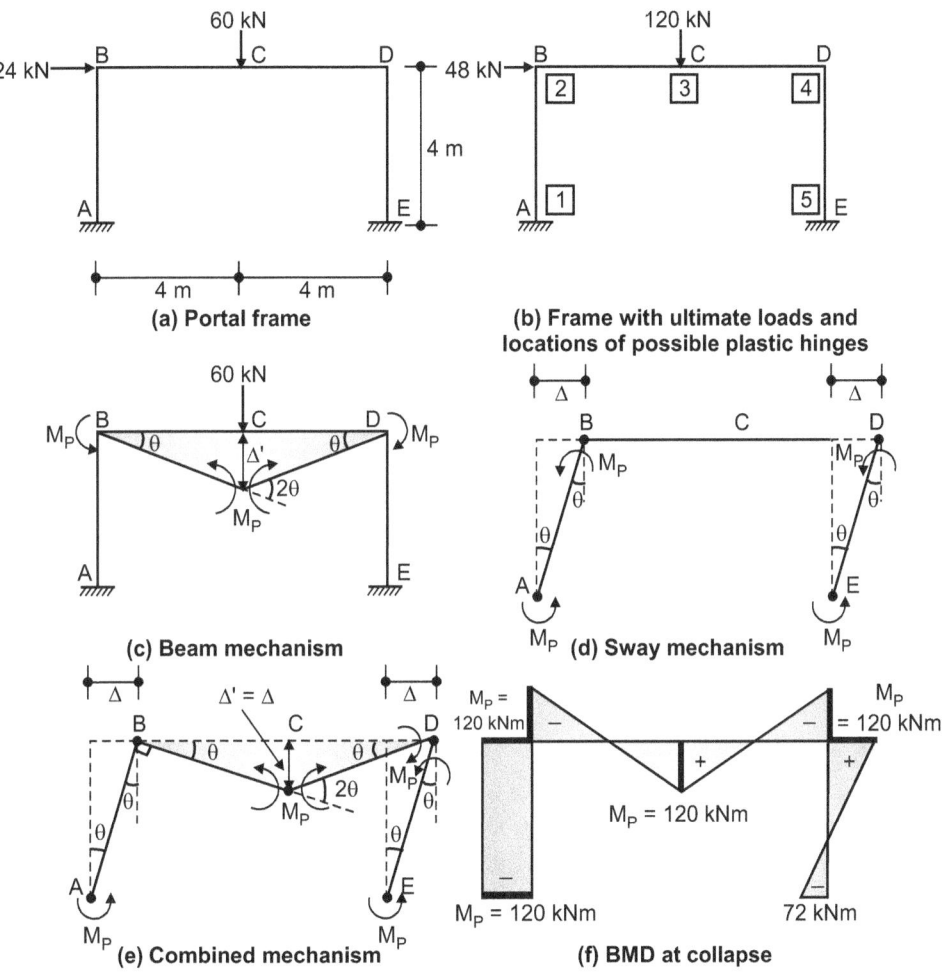

Fig. 13.25 : Illustrative Problem 13.21

Solution : Data : (i) Structural configuration : Dimensions support conditions as shown in Fig. 13.25 (a), L = 8 m, H = 4 m.

(ii) **Loads :** Magnitudes, directions and positions as shown in Fig. 13.25 (a) W = 60 kN, P = 24 kN

(iii) Load factor = γ = 2.0

(iv) Same section for beams and columns.

Object : Design of the section for flexure only.

Concepts and Equations :

(i) Plastic method : Mechanism method. (ii) Work equation of a mechanism. (iii) $Z_p = \dfrac{M_p}{\sigma_y}$

Procedure : Step I : Ultimate load :

Beam load, W_u = 60 × 2 = 120 kN
Lateral load, P_u = 24 × 2 = 48 kN

Step II : Plastic analysis :
(i) Degree of static indeterminacy = D_{si} = 3.
(ii) Positions of plastic hinges as shown in Fig. 13.25 (b).
(iii) Maximum plastic hinges for complete mechanism.
$$D_{si} + 1 = 3 + 1 = 4$$
(iv) Minimum hinges for partial mechanism i.e. beam mechanism = 3.
(v) Possible mechanisms.

(a) Beam mechanism for BD : Three plastic hinges at B, D and midspan of BD i.e. C as shown in Fig. 13.25 (*c). Either by work equation or by using the standard result of this case of mechanism :
$$M_p = \frac{W_u L}{8} = \frac{120 \times 8}{8} = 120 \text{ kNm}$$

(b) Sway mechanism : Four plastic hinges at A, B, D and E as shown in Fig. 13.25 (d). Either by work equation or by using the standard result already derived for this case of mechanism :
$$M_p = \frac{P_u H}{4} = \frac{48 \times 4}{4} = 48 \text{ kNm}$$

(c) Combined mechanism: Four plastic hinges at A, C, D and E as shown in Fig. 13.25 (e).

Either by work equation or by using the standard result already derived for this case of mechanism.
$$M_p = \frac{P_u H}{6} + \frac{W_u L}{12} = \frac{48 \times 4}{6} + \frac{120 \times 8}{12} = 112 \text{ kNm}$$

Step III : Required plastic moment
$$M_p = \text{Largest of 120, 48 and 112} = 120 \text{ kNm}$$

It represents that the beam mechanism governs the design and as the same uniform section is to be used the beam member dominates the design. The design is not economical for the column section.

Step IV : Checking the yield condition B.M.D. at collapse is as shown in Fig. 13.25 (f). No where the bending moment should exceed them M_p = 120 kNm at the collapse under the governing mechanism. Other mechanism will not be possible at the given ultimate load.

∴ M_p required = 120 kNm

Step V : Plastic section modulus required,
$$Z_p = \frac{M_p}{\sigma_y} = \frac{120 \times 10^6}{250} = 0.48 \times 10^6 \text{ mm}^3$$

Step VI : Elastic section modulus :
$$Z_e = \frac{Z_p}{K_s} = \frac{0.48 \times 10^6}{1.15}$$

Section VII : Selection of the section corresponding to Z_e, the rolled steel section is selected referring to the steel tables. ISMB 250 @ 57.37 kg/m giving Z_{xx} = 410 × 10³ mm³.

For economical design the different sections for columns and beams can be selected for which the proportion of M_p of columns and beams is to be decided and accordingly M_p required for columns and beams can be obtained from the plastic analysis. This is not illustrated here considering the limited scope of this topic in this subject of analysis.

EXERCISE

1. Explain and illustrate precisely the following :

   (i) Linear elastic stress-strain curve for structural steels, (ii) Elastic-plastic stress-strain curve for structural steels, (iii) Rigid plastic stress-strain curve for structural steels, (iv) Moment curvature relation, (v) Plastic hinge, (vi) Shape factor, (vii) Plastic mount of resistance, (viii) Collapse mechanism, (ix) Load factor.

   State clearly (i) Upper-bound theorem and (ii) Lower-bound theorem.

   Illustrate the methods of plastic analysis with respect to a simple example.

2. Find the shape factor for the section shown in Fig. 13.26 to 13.29.

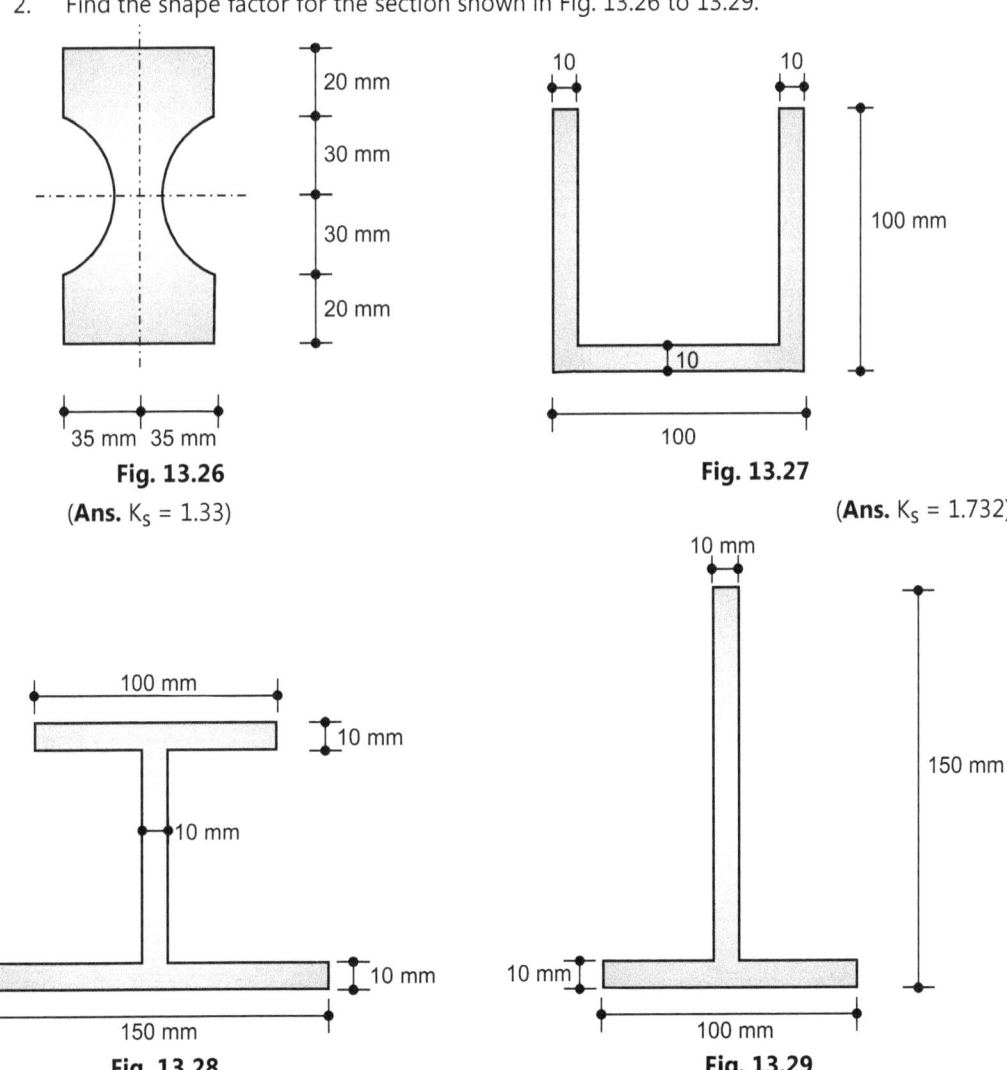

Fig. 13.26
(**Ans.** K_S = 1.33)

Fig. 13.27
(**Ans.** K_S = 1.732)

Fig. 13.28
(**Ans.** K_S = 1.288)

Fig. 13.29
(**Ans.** K_S = 1.833)

3. Determine the plastic section modulus of the section shown in Fig. 13.30.

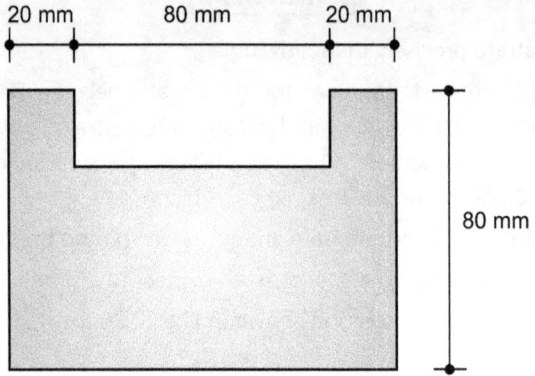

Fig. 13.30

(**Ans.** 10.2×10^4 mm³)

4. Show that the plastic moment capacity M_p of I-section shown in Fig. 13.31 is given by the expression

$$M_p = \frac{27.1 \, D^3}{800} \sigma_y f_y$$

where D is the overall depth of the beam and f_y is the field stress. Also calculate the shape factor.

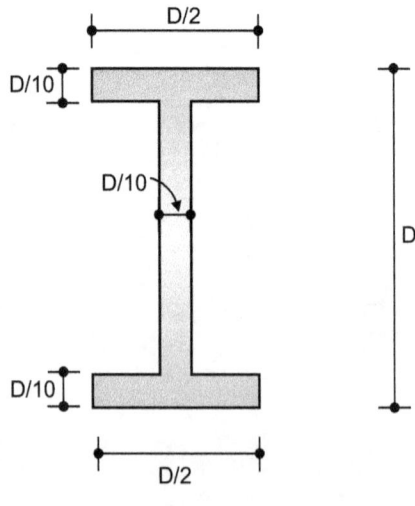

Fig. 13.31

5. A propped cantilever of span 5 m and of uniform plastic moment of resistance 150 kNm is subjected to a load 'W' as shown in Fig. 13.32. If the load W may be applied at any position within the span, determine the minimum value of W that will cause collapse.

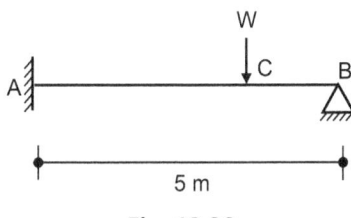

Fig. 13.32

(**Ans.** 174.85 m)

6. A fixed beam of 6 m span has to support a uniformly distributed load of 12 kNm on the left half span. If the plastic moment of the section is 100 kNm, determine the load factor.

   (**Ans.** Load factor = 2).

7. A fixed beam AB of span 6 m and of uniform section is loaded as shown in Fig. 13.33. The load factor is 1.75 and shape factor is 1.15. The yield stress is 250 N/mm². Determine the sectional modulus of the beam. Also locate the positions of the plastic hinges.

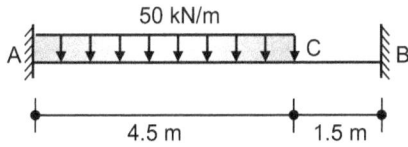

Fig. 13.33

(**Ans.** $Z = 60.1 \times 7 \times 10^3$ mm³)

8. A fixed beam is loaded as shown in Fig. 13.34. Calculate the collapse load for the beam if the plastic moment of resistance of the uniform section of the beam is 30 kNm.

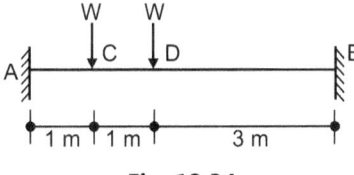

Fig. 13.34

(**Ans.** 40 kN)

9. A steel beam of uniform cross-section is to be designed for the ultimate loads as shown in Fig. 13.35. Estimate the plastic moment of resistance of the beam required.

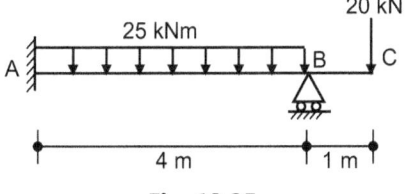

Fig. 13.35

(**Ans.** 26.67 kNm)

10. A beam ABC of uniform moment of resistance M_p is loaded with uniform load w/m throughout the length as shown in Fig. 13.36. Show that the ultimate load is given by the expression $W_u = \dfrac{15.42\ M_p}{L^2}$.

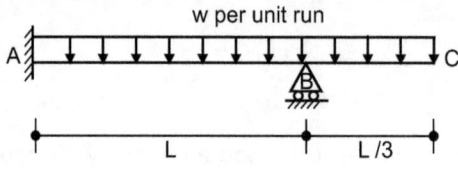

Fig. 13.36

11. A three span continuous beam ABCD is supported and loaded as shown in Fig. 13.37. The beam has uniform cross-section plastic moment of resistance of 80 kNm. Estimate the ultimate load and draw B.M.D. at the collapse.

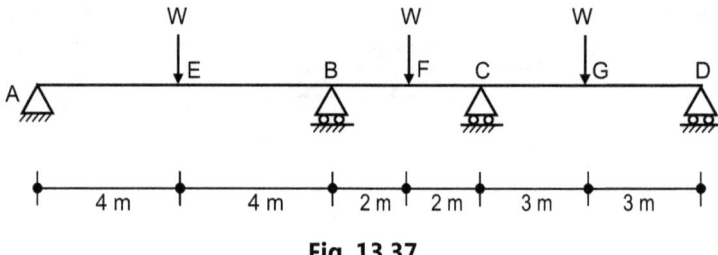

Fig. 13.37

(**Ans.** $W_u = 60$ kN)

12. The ultimate loads on each span of a continuous beam ABCD are shown in Fig. 13.38. Calculate the required values of plastic moments MP_1, MP_2, MP_3 of beam spans AB, BC, CD respectively, if MP_2 is greater uniform MP_1 and MP_3.

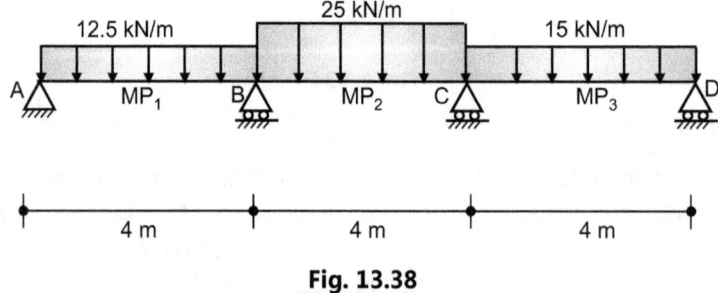

Fig. 13.38

(**Ans.** $MP_1 = 171.48$ kNm, $MP_2 = 309$ kNm, $MP_3 = 205.8$ kNm)

13. A portal frame shown in Fig. 13.39 carries the working loads as shown. The members of the frame are of uniform plastic moment of resistance of 100 kNm. Estimate the load factor.

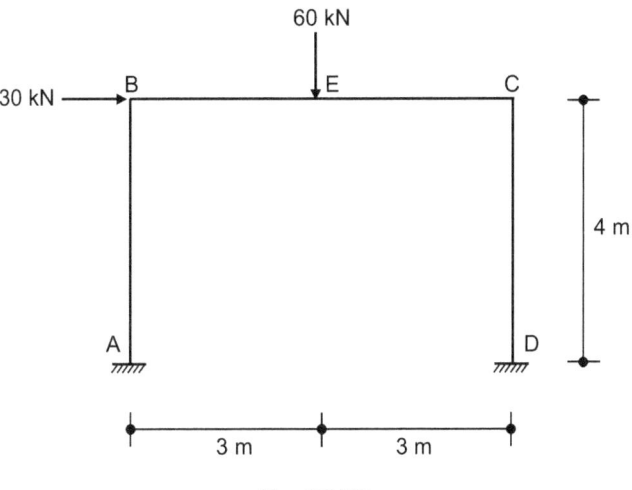

Fig. 13.39

(**Ans.** $\lambda = 2.0$)

14. A portal frame is supported and loaded as shown in Fig. 13.40. If the members of the frame have a constant plastic moment of resistance M_p, show that the collapse load for the frame is given by $W_u = \dfrac{2M_p L}{ab}$.

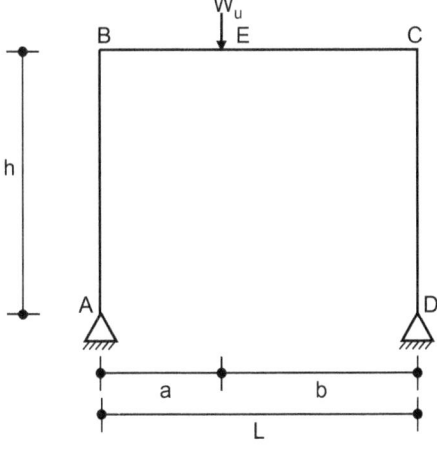

Fig. 13.40

15. A portal frame is supported and loaded as shown in Fig. 13.41. The plastic moment of resistance of the beam section is M_p and that of column sections is $2\,M_p$. Analyse the possible collapse mechanisms shown and determine the ultimate load for the frame.

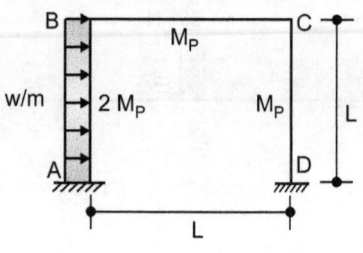

Fig. 13.41

$$\left(\textbf{Ans. } W_u = \frac{12\,M_p}{L^2}\right)$$

16. A portal frame is supported and loaded as shown in Fig. 13.42. The plastic moment of resistance of the section of the column AB and beam BC is 240 kNm, of the column CD is 120 kNm. Estimate the ultimate load for the frame.

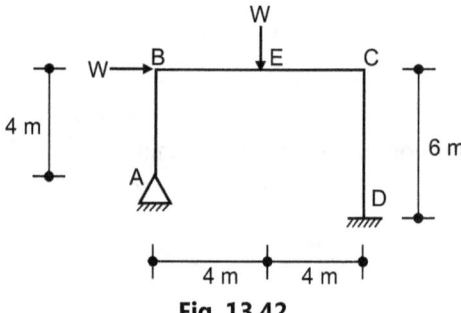

Fig. 13.42

(**Ans.** $W_u = 95$ kN)

17. A portal frame is supported and loaded as shown in Fig. 13.43. The members of the frame have uniform section of plastic moment of resistance of 100 kNm. Find the collapse load factor.

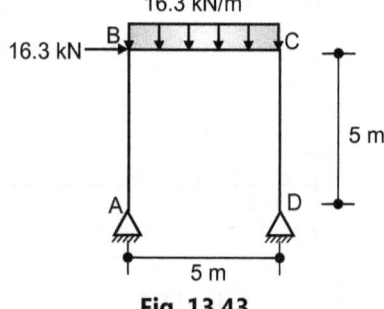

Fig. 13.43

❏❏❏

www.ingramcontent.com/pod-product-compliance
Lightning Source LLC
Chambersburg PA
CBHW080527300426
44111CB00017B/2633